An Anglo-Chinese Vocabulary of the Ningpo Dialect

W. T. Morrison

Alpha Editions

This edition published in 2020

ISBN : 9789354042027

Design and Setting By
Alpha Editions
www.alphaedis.com
email - alphaedis@gmail.com

As per information held with us this book is in Public Domain. This book is a reproduction of an important historical work. Alpha Editions uses the best technology to reproduce historical work in the same manner it was first published to preserve its original nature. Any marks or number seen are left intentionally to preserve its true form.

AN
ANGLO-CHINESE
VOCABULARY
OF THE
NINGPO DIALECT.

BY

REV. W. T. MORRISON.

Formerly Missionary in Ningpo.

REVISED AND ENLARGED.

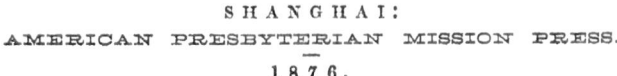

SHANGHAI:
AMERICAN PRESBYTERIAN MISSION PRESS.
1876.

PREFACE.

Many have expressed surprise on their first arrival at Ningpo, that no Dictionary, or suitable text-book of any kind, has ever been prepared, to facilitate the acquisition of the local dialect; and those who have wished to learn it, have been compelled to begin *de novo*, to accumulate, by a toilsome process, a vocabulary, or transcribe one already partially prepared. The present work is an attempt to supply this felt want. The author began immediately on his arrival, nearly sixteen years ago, the collection of a vocabulary for personal use. This in process of time grew to a considerable size, and the idea was suggested of putting it into a more permanent and accessible form. The suggestion was taken up, and has resulted in the present work.

During the earlier period of preparation, Lobschied's and Medhurst's Dictionaries, and Williams' and Edkins' Vocabularies were freely consulted. Every word however has been subsequently examined and re-examined with the help of five different Chinese teachers, and no pains have been spared to secure accuracy as far as possible.

Just before his death, the Rev. Dr. Knowlton reviewed the entire manuscript, and added many Chinese words and phrases.

The original plan was to give the equivalents of the English words in the Romanized System, and also in the Chinese character, adhering as closely as possible to the sound of the colloquial. In carrying out this plan great difficulties were encountered.

It was found that if characters were used to represent the

precise sound of the colloquial word or phrase, the meaning would often be sacrificed: if, on the other hand, such characters were chosen as would fairly express the meaning, the sound must often be disregarded. Again, no two teachers could be found, who would agree, as to the character which should be used to represent certain sounds; for example, in the word *"na-hwun"* which means infant, one teacher would write the *hwun* 歡 to like, another would write *hwun* 喚 to suck, another, *hwó* 花 a flower; and, as many such doubtful cases occur in the dialect, ambiguity and confusion would be the result, were this plan adhered to. The third and greatest difficulty lay in the fact, that there *are no characters* to represent a large number of colloquial *sounds*, as will be seen by the Syllabary following the preface.

No doubt one thoroughly acquainted with the dialect, and with the *reng-li*, could say absolutely that certain words must be expressed by certain characters. This field, interesting as it is, has as yet been quite unexplored in Ningpo, all our books excepting the Church Prayer-book having been written in the Romanized System. It would therefore be presumption on the part of the author, to lay down a system for writing the colloquial in the character; and this work, with the kindred one of "tracing out the laws of gradual corruption," is left for those whose attainments better fit them for the task.

The method of giving the sense in the character, and sacrificing the sound where it could not be avoided, has been finally adopted as affording the most satisfactory solution of the many difficulties, at least so far as the present purpose is concerned. In cases, therefore, where there is no acknowledged character corresponding to the colloquial word, borrowed characters, *i. e.* those having the same sound but not the same meaning, are avoided, and current *reng-li* is given instead. (Borrowed ones may have slipped in, but not intentionally.) The example given above will illustrate this point: the characters, 嫺 歡, 嫺 喚, or

PREFACE. v

媱 花, borrowed to represent the word *na-hwun*, infant, mean respectively *liking* or *sucking milk*, and *milk-flower*, and not *infant*; they are therefore discarded, and the veng-li characters 嬰 孩 *(ing-œ)* which mean infant are used. It is hoped that this plan of writing the characters will make the book more generally useful than it otherwise would have been, and that it may also prove a help to Chinese students wishing to learn English.

In a few cases where no *reng-li* equivalents could be found, Mandarin expressions are used.

Sometimes the colloquial phrase expresses a peculiar, and purely local shade of meaning; in such cases the approximate meaning has been given as nearly as possible in the *veng-li*, or the characters have been omitted.

Instances will no doubt occur, where characters will suggest themselves to the student, which, at first sight, seem to be more appropriate than those used. These however may be just the instances in which the characters have been changed over and over again, and those finally adopted have been the result of repeated examinations. A very simple example is the word *siao-nying*, meaning *child* in the colloquial. It would seem self-evident that 小 人 would be the appropriate characters, but in the *reng-li* these signify a bad or mean man: the characters 小 孩 *(siao-œ)* are therefore substituted.

As a Ningpo teacher might not always know whether certain expressions would be current elsewhere, an experienced Shanghai teacher was employed, who read over the work, and in the presence of, and with the approval of the Ningpo teacher, altered such words and sentences as were unintelligible to him.

The late revisions have produced more changes than were anticipated when the system of attaching small circles to the characters was first adopted, and they might perhaps as well have been omitted; but they are allowed to remain, as they may aid the memory in retaining characters.

PREFACE.

Tone marks have been omitted, not because tones are deemed unimportant, for they certainly should be observed, especially in some cases, as in distinguishing between *shü* 水 water and *shü* 書 book, between *ping* 氷 ice, and *ping* 餅 cake, &c., &c.; but there seemed to be so much uncertainty about the tones of many words, that it was deemed safer to leave the student to learn them from the teacher, rather than from marks. The marks on the accented syllables will aid the learner in pronouncing correctly. Although great pains have been taken to have the accents correctly marked, yet errors will doubtless be found, and difference of opinion will exist as to their proper location in many words.

Teachers differ so greatly, in accent, in their modes of defining, and in their pronunciation, both of the colloquial, and of the character, that there is room for endless criticism, and, moreover, it is not to be expected that the first book of its kind can at all approach perfection. A perfect vocabulary could only result from the combined wisdom and experience of many. If however this little work shall aid any one in acquiring a knowledge of this widely spoken dialect, or if it should incite some one of greater attainments and experience, to make a perfect Ningpo vocabulary, the labor it has cost will not have been in vain.

We here thank heartily those who have encouraged or aided us in any way, and especially the Rev. J. A. Leyenberger, who has assisted in various ways, and who kindly furnishes the Syllabary, which follows the preface, and also a list of Geographical names, which will be found at the end of the volume.

LIST OF SYLLABLES

IN THE

NINGPO DIALECT.

From the following list it will be seen that a large number of the sounds have no character to represent them. From this arises the difficulty of using the Chinese character in the preparation of books in the local dialect, and the consequent necessity of employing some other method. The Roman system is now largely used for this purpose, and thousands of books have been printed in this character, and are in daily use by the people.

Those syllables which cannot properly be represented by Chinese characters, may be subdivided into two classes:—

I. Those which have absolutely no character in the language to express them, as *dza, fœ, gœn, ve.*

II. Those syllables, which may be represented by a character, but their pronunciation has become corrupted, as *kao* for *kyiao, kœn* for *kyin, wœn* for *ngwœn.*

ALPHABETICAL LIST OF SYLLABLES.

1	A		34	Bun	盤	67	Ding	定
2	'A		35	Cih	拙	68	Do	駝
3	Ah	阿	36	C'ih	出	69	Doh	獨
4	'Ah		37	Cing	震	70	Dong	同
5	Ang		38	C'ing	春	71	Dô	
6	'Ang		39	Coh	竹	72	Dôh	跛
7	Ao	奧	40	C'oh	觸	73	Dông	堂
8	'Ao	號	41	Cong	中	74	Dön	團
9	Æ	愛	42	C'ong	沖	75	Du	徒
10	'Æ	害	43	Cô		76	Djih	絕
11	Æn	唵	44	C'ô	扯	77	Djing	
12	'Æn		45	Công	掌	78	Djoh	蜀
13	Ba		46	C'ông	窗	79	Djong	重
14	Bæ	敗	47	Cü	主	80	Djô	搽
15	Bœn	辦	48	C'ü	處	81	Djông	常
16	Bah	白	49	Cün	專	82	Djü	住
17	Bang		50	C'ün	穿	83	Djün	傳
18	Bao	鮑	51	Da	大	84	Dz	慈
19	Be	備	52	Dæ	代	85	Dza	
20	Beh	勃	53	Dæn	但	86	Dzæ	在
21	Beng	盆	54	Dah	達	87	Dzæn	暫
22	Beo	掊	55	Dang	宕	88	Dzah	宅
23	Bi	皮	56	Dao	道	89	Dzang	
24	Biao	瓢	57	De	隊	90	Dzao	曹
25	Bih	闢	58	Deh	特	91	Dzeh	擇
26	Bin	便	59	Den	潭	92	Dzeng	存
27	Bing	平	60	Deng	騰	93	Dzeo	愁
28	Bo	婆	61	Deo	頭	94	Dzi	池
29	Boh	薄	62	Di	地	95	Dzia	
30	Bong	逢	63	Diah	疊	96	Dziah	着
31	Bô	罷	64	Diao	調	97	Dziang	長
32	Bông	旁	65	Dih	敵	98	Dziao	潮
33	Bu	浦	66	Din	田	99	Dzih	直

ALPHABETICAL LIST OF SYLLABLES.

100	Dzin	漸	136	Gen		172	Hah	嚇
101	Dzing	城	137	Geng		173	Hang	
102	Dziu	綢	138	Geo		174	Hao	好
103	Dzoh	族	139	Go		175	He	
104	Dzong	從	140	Gong	共	176	Heh	黑
105	Dzô	茶	141	Gô		177	Hen	漢
106	Dzông	藏	142	Goh		178	Heng	狠
107	Dzu	助	143	Gông		179	Heo	螢
108	E		144	Gwa		180	Ho	火
109	'E		145	Gwæn		181	Hoh	
110	Eh	遏	146	Gwah		182	Hong	烘
111	'Eh	盒	147	Gwang		183	Hô	
112	En	暗	148	Gwe	葵	184	Hôh	霍
113	'En	汗	149	Gweh		185	Hwa	
114	Eng	恩	150	Gweng		186	Hwæn	償
115	'Eng	恒	151	Gwông	狂	187	Hwah	豁
116	Eo	嘔	152	Gwu		188	Hwang	
117	'Eo	後	153	Gyi	其	189	Hwe	灰
118	Fah	法	154	Gyia		190	Hweh	忽
119	Fæ		155	Gyiæn		191	Hweng	昏
120	Fæn	反	156	Gyiah	蹻	192	Hwô	化
121	Feh	弗	157	Gyiang	強	193	Hwông	況
122	Feng	分	158	Gyiao	橋	194	Hwu	呼
123	Feo	否	159	Gyih	極	195	Hwun	歡
124	Fi	非	160	Gyin	健	196	Hyi	喜
125	Foh	福	161	Gying	近	197	Hyiæ	駭
126	Fong	風	162	Gyiu	求	198	Hyiah	譁
127	Fông	方	163	Gyü	具	199	Hyiang	香
128	Fu	富	164	Gyüih	掘	200	Hyiao	孝
129	Ga		165	Gyüing	羣	201	Hyih	歇
130	Gæ	戯	166	Gyün	權	202	Hyin	險
131	Gæn		167	Gyüoh	局	203	Hying	與
132	Gah		168	Gyüong	窮	204	Hyiu	臭
133	Gang		169	Ha		205	Hyü	許
134	Gao		170	Hæ	海	206	Hyüih	血
135	Geh		171	Hæn	寬	207	Hyüing	熏

ALPHABETICAL LIST OF SYLLABLES.

208	Hyün	喧	244	K'eh	刻	280	Kwô	挂
209	Hyüoh	畜	245	Ken	干	281	Kw'ô	誇
210	Hyüong	兄	246	K'en	看	282	Kwông	光
211	Hyüô	蝦	247	Keng	根	283	Kw'ông	曠
212	I	意	248	K'eng	肯	284	Kwu	古
213	Ia		249	Keo	茍	285	Kw'u	苦
214	Iæ	野	250	K'eo	口	286	Kwun	官
215	Iah	約	251	Ko	果	287	Kw'un	寬
216	Iang	央	252	K'o	可	288	Kyi	幾
217	Iao	要	253	Koh	國	289	Ky'i	氣
218	Ih	一	254	K'oh	哭	290	Kyiah	甲
219	In	烟	255	Kong	公	291	Ky'iah	却
220	Ing	因	256	K'ong	孔	292	Kyiang	姜
221	Iu	幽	257	Kô		293	Ky'iang	腔
222	Jæ	惹	258	K'ô		294	Kyiao	教
223	Jih	十	259	Kôh	各	295	Ky'iao	巧
224	Jing	人	260	K'ôh	壳	296	Kyiae	戒
225	Joh	辱	261	Kông	扛	297	Ky'iae	揩
226	Jô		262	K'ông	康	298	Kyih	急
227	Jông		263	Kun		299	Ky'ih	乞
228	Jü	樹	264	K'un		300	Kyin	見
229	Jün	善	265	Kwa		301	Ky'in	謙
230	Ka		266	K'wa		302	Kying	經
231	K'a	卡	267	Kwæ	怪	303	Ky'ing	輕
232	Kah	隔	268	Kw'æ	快	304	Kyiu	救
233	K'ah	客	269	Kwah	括	305	Ky'iu	邱
234	Kang		270	Kwang		306	Kyü	句
235	K'ang		271	Kw'ang		307	Ky'ü	去
236	Kao	高	272	Kwæn	關	308	Kyüih	決
237	K'ao	考	273	Kw'æn		309	Ky'üih	缺
238	Kæ	改	274	Kwe	貴	310	Kyüing	均
239	K'æ	開	275	K'we	虧	311	Ky'üing	窘
240	Kæn		276	Kweh	骨	312	Kyün	捐
241	K'æn	堪	277	Kw'eh	闊	313	Ky'ün	勸
242	Ke		278	Kweng	滾	314	Kyüoh	鞠
243	Keh	割	279	Kw'eng	坤	315	Ky'üoh	曲

ALPHABETICAL LIST OF SYLLABLES.

xi

316	Kyüong	迥	352	Lo		388	Mih		滅
317	Ky'üong	穹	353	Loh	綠	389	Min		面
318	Kyüŏ	嘉	354	Loh		390	Ming		明
319	Kyüŏh	覺	355	Long	龍	391	Miu		膠
320	Ky'üŏh	確	356	Lô		392	Mo		慕
321	Kyüông	降	357	Lô		393	Mo		
322	La		358	Lôh	落	394	Moh		木
323	La		359	Lông	浪	395	Moh		
324	Lah	蠟	360	Lông	亂	396	Mong		蒙
325	Lah		361	Lön	路	397	Mô		馬
326	Lang		362	Lu		398	Mô		
327	Lang		363	Lu		399	Móng		忙
328	Lao	老	364	M		400	Mun		滿
329	Lao		365	M		401	Na		
330	Læ	來	366	Ma		402	Na		
331	Læn	藍	367	Ma		403	Næ		乃
332	Le	雷	368	Mæ	買	404	Næ		
333	Le		369	Mæ	麥	405	Næn		難
334	Leh	勒	370	Mah		406	Nah		捺
335	Len		371	Mah		407	Nao		腦
336	Leng	論	372	Mang		408	Ne		
337	Leo	樓	373	Mang		409	Neh		訥
338	Leo		374	Mao	毛	410	Neh		
339	Li	里	375	Mao	慢	411	Nen		男
340	Li		376	Mæn	美	412	Nen		
341	Liah	畧	377	Mæn	沒	413	Neng		能
342	Liang	良	378	Me		414	Neng		耨
343	Liao	了	379	Me		415	Neo		
344	Lih	力	380	Meh		416	Ng		
345	Lih		381	Men		417	Nga		
346	Liu	連	382	Meng	門	418	Nga		
347	Ling	林	383	Meng		419	Ngæ		呆
348	Ling		384	Meo	謀	420	Ngæn		嚴
349	Liu	流	385	Mi	米	421	Ngah		額
350	Liu		386	Mi	描	422	Ngah		
351	Lo	羅	387	Miao		423	Ngang		

ALPHABETICAL LIST OF SYLLABLES.

424	Ngao	敖	460	Nyiu	鈕	496	Peng	本
425	Ňgao		461	Ňyiu		497	P'eng	烹
426	Ngeh		462	Nyü	愚	498	Peo	褒
427	Ngen	岸	463	Nyüing		499	P'eo	剖
428	Ngeng	硬	464	Nyün	元	500	Pi	比
429	Ngeo	偶	465	Nyüoh	玉	501	P'i	批
430	Ngo	峨	466	Nyüong	濃	502	Piao	表
431	Ngô	我	467	Nyüông		503	P'iao	票
432	Ňgô		468	O	窩	504	Pih	必
433	Ngoh	岳	469	'O	禾	505	P'ih	匹
434	Ňgoh		470	Oh	屋	506	Pin	變
435	Ngông	昂	471	Ong	翁	507	P'in	偏
436	Ngwæn	患	472	'Ong	洪	508	Ping	氷
437	Ngwe	危	473	Ô		509	P'ing	品
438	Ngweh	兀	474	'Ô		510	Po	波
439	Ngwu	吾	475	Ôh	惡	511	P'o	破
440	Ngwun	玩	476	'Ôh	或	512	Poh	北
441	Ni		477	Ông	盎	513	P'oh	撲
442	No	懦	478	'Ông	杭	514	Pong	
443	Noh		479	Pa		515	P'ong	捧
444	Nong	農	480	P'a		516	Pô	把
445	Ňong		481	Pæ	拜	517	P'ô	怕
446	Nô	拿	482	P'æ	派	518	Pông	邦
447	Nông	囊	483	Pæn	班	519	P'ông	
448	Nön	嗳	484	P'æn	攀	520	Pu	補
449	Nu	奴	485	Pah	百	521	P'u	鋪
450	Nyi	泥	486	P'ah	拍	522	Pun	半
451	Nyiah	虐	487	Pang		523	P'un	泮
452	Nyiang	仰	488	P'ang		524	R	耳
453	Nyiæn	念	489	Pao	報	525	S	四
454	Ňyiæn		490	P'ao	拋	526	Sa	
455	Nyiao	堯	491	Pe	貝	527	Sæ	
456	Ňyiao		492	P'e	配	528	Sæn	帥
457	Nyih	溺	493	Peh	不	529	Sah	山
458	Nyin	年	494	P'eh	潑	530	Sang	薩
459	Nying	迎	495	Pen		531	Sao	撒

ALPHABETICAL LIST OF SYLLABLES. xiii

532	Se	雖	568	T'œ	泰	604	T'oh		東
533	Seh	色	569	Tæn	且	605	Tong		通
534	Sen		570	T'æn	嘆	606	T'ong		
535	Seng	生	571	Tah	搭	607	Tôh		
536	Seo	叟	572	T'ah	塔	608	T'ôh		託
537	Shœ	奢	573	Tang	打	609	Tông		當
538	Shih	失	574	T'ang		610	T'ông		湯
539	Shing	舜	575	Tao	刀	611	Tô		朶
540	Shoh	叔	576	T'ao	討	612	T'ô		
541	Shong		577	Te	對	613	Tön		端
542	Shön	選	578	T'e	推	614	T'ön		湍
543	Shô	耍	579	Tch	德	615	Ts		子
544	Shông	春	580	T'ch	脫	616	T's		此
545	Shü	世	581	Ten		617	Tsa		
546	Shün	宣	582	T'en	貪	618	Ts'a		
547	Si	西	583	Teng	等	619	Tsœ		再
548	Sia		584	T'eng	吞	620	Ts'œ		采
549	Siœ	寫	585	Teo	斗	621	Tsæn		贊
550	Siah	削	586	T'eo	偷	622	Ts'æn		產
551	Siang	相	587	Ti	低	623	Tsah		隻
552	Siao	小	588	T'i	體	624	Ts'ah		察
553	Sih	錫	589	Tia		625	Tsang		
554	Sin	先	590	Tiah		626	Ts'ang		
555	Sing	心	591	T'iah	貼	627	Tsao		早
556	Siu	手	592	Tiao	吊	628	Ts'ao		草
557	So	鎖	593	T'iao	挑	629	Tse		追
558	Soh	宿	594	Tih	的	630	Ts'e		翠
559	Song	松	595	T'ih	鐵	631	Tseh		側
560	Sô	所	596	Tin	點	632	Ts'ch		測
561	Sôh	索	597	T'in	添	633	Tsen		
562	Sông	賞	598	Ting	丁	634	Tseng		尊
563	Sön	算	599	T'ing	聽	635	Ts'eng		寸
564	Su	數	600	Tiu	丟	636	Tsco		走
565	Ta		601	To	多	637	Ts'co		湊
566	T'a	他	602	T'o	拖	638	Tsi		祭
567	Tæ	帶	603	Toh	督	639	Ts'i		妻

ALPHABETICAL LIST OF SYLLABLES.

640	Tsia		676	U	烏	712	Wó	話
641	Ts'ia		677	Ü	於	713	Wŏ	蛙
642	Tsiæ	者	678	Üih	攬	714	Wóng	王
643	Ts'iæ	且	679	Üing	慍	715	Wŏng	注
644	Tsiah	霄	680	Un	宛	716	Wu	胡
645	Ts'iah	綽	681	Ŭn	怨	717	Wun	綏
646	Tsiang	將	682	Üô	亞	718	Yi	移
647	Ts'iang	搶	683	Üóh	郁	719	Yia	
648	Tsiao	照	684	Üong	永	720	Yiæ	也
649	Ts'iao	超	685	Vah	伐	721	Yiah	藥
650	Tsih	即	686	Væn	萬	722	Yiang	羊
651	Ts'ih	切	687	Ve		723	Yiao	搖
652	Tsin	翦	688	Vch	佛	724	Yih	亦
653	Ts'in	千	689	Veng	文	725	Yin	現
654	Tsing	進	690	Vco	浮	726	Ying	引
655	Ts'ing	親	691	Vi	維	727	Yiu	有
656	Tsiu	酒	692	Voh	伏	728	Yü	雨
657	Ts'iu	秋	693	Vong	馮	729	Yüih	月
658	Tso	做	694	Vông	房	730	Yüing	云
659	Ts'o	磋	695	Vu	輔	731	Yün	遠
660	Tsoh	捉	696	Wa		732	Yüô	下
661	Ts'oh	促	697	Wă		733	Yüoh	疫
662	Tsong	總	698	Wæ	懷	734	Yüôh	育
663	Ts'ong	聰	699	Wæ̆		735	Yüong	榮
664	Tsó	詐	700	Wæn	還	736	Z	是
665	Ts'ô	岔	701	Wæ̆n	挽	737	Za	
666	Tsóh	足	702	Wah	滑	738	Zæ	
667	Ts'óh	錯	703	Wăh	挖	739	Zæn	
668	Tsông	章	704	Wang		740	Zah	
669	Ts'ông	倉	705	Wăng		741	Zang	
670	Tsön	鑽	706	We		742	Zao	
671	Ts'ön	竄	707	Wĕ	威	743	Ze	隨
672	Tsu	租	708	Weh	活	744	Zch	
673	Ts'u	初	709	Wĕh	頦	745	Zen	鱻
674	Tu	都	710	Weng	魂	746	Zeng	
675	T'u	土	711	Wĕng	溫	747	Zeo	

ALPHABETICAL LIST OF SYLLABLES.

748	Zi	徐	753	Zih	舌	758	Zong	
749	Zia		754	Zin	染	759	Zŏ	
750	Ziah	弱	755	Zing	盛	760	Zŏh	唇
751	Ziang	像	756	Ziu	受	761	Zông	上
752	Ziao	兆	757	Zo		762	Zu	

A comparison of the syllables in the Ningpo Dialect with those of other dialects North and South shows that there is considerable variation in the number. This will be seen from the following table.

Dialects.	Initials.	Finals.	Whole No. of syllables
Canton	23	53	707
Swatow	..	..	674
Amoy or Changchow	15	50	846
Fuchow	15	33	928
Ningpo	30	44	762
Shanghai	33	44	660
Peking	25	43	420

This variation is perhaps partly due to the different methods adopted by foreigners for distinguishing the sounds, and partly perhaps to the fact that two characters which have the same sound in one dialect often have different sounds in another. The great discrepancy between the number of sounds in the Court dialect and those of the more Southern Provinces is somewhat remarkable. But this difference is explained by the fact that in the former the *jih sing* is suppressed, while it is of very frequent occurrence in the latter.

EXPLANATIONS.

1. In many cases, an equivalent for the leading word is found immediately after it in Italics; this is not a definition of the English word, but the translation of the Chinese word or phrase following it.

2. The system for spelling the Ningpo sounds, is that used by common consent for printing all the books in the Ningpo dialect, by whatever mission published.

3. Any foreigner who learns the colloquial, should get the sounds from a native who is acquainted with the Romanized system, as quite new sounds are given to many letters, thus— cing is pronounced *ching*; i, has the sound of the English *e*, *e* of *a*, &c., &c.

4. The classifiers are placed in brackets after nouns.

5. The syllable *veng*, after a word, is a contraction of *veng-li* [wen-li], showing, either that there was no colloquial equivalent, or that while such a sentence might be understood among literary men, it would not be understood by ordinary people.

6. The small circle after a character denotes that the *sounds* of the colloquial, and the character differ; it may be by corruption, or because there being no character for the spoken word, another supposed to have the same meaning is substituted.

7. There are some sounds, in pronouncing which, teachers differ greatly as in saying *sih* or *shih*, *soh* or *shoh*, *siang* or *hyiang*, *cong* or *tsong*, *djöng* or *dzông*, *keh* or *kah*, *heh* or *hah*, &c., &c. These differences are often marked in brackets.

8. As the distinction between the sounds *oh* and *ôh* is thought by many to be unimportant, it has been omitted in this work.

A VOCABULARY

OF THE

NINGPO DIALECT.

A, usually unexpressed; expressed by a numeral followed by its classifier, thus, *a man,* ih-go nying' 一個°人°; — *pen,* ih-ts pih' 一枝筆; — *book,* ih-peng shü' 一本書. For classifiers see The Nyingpo Primer 寗波土° 話° 初° 學°

ABACUS, sön'-bun 算盤 (ih-min); *do you understand the —?* ng sön'-bun hyiao'-teh feh 你° 算盤 曉得否°?

ABANDON, *to* ky'i'-diao 棄了°; tiu'-diao 丢去°, or 丢了°; djih'-diao 絕了°; gwæn'-diao 損°去°

ABANDONED, *infant — by its mother,* na-hwun' be ah-nyiang' tiu'-diao-de 嬰°孩°被阿娘丢去°了°; *left off entirely* (as the use of strong drinks, &c.), üong'-yün ka'-de 永遠戒°了°; *morally —,* vu-sô'-peh-ts 無所不至

ABASE, *to bring low,* ti-loh'-ky'i' 低落去°; *to degrade,* kông'-loh 降°落; — *him,* kông' gyi loh' 降°其落

ABASHED, *to be —,* dzæn-gwe'-vu-di' 慚愧無地; wông-k'ong'-peh-la' 惶恐之°至°

ABATE, *to* kæn'-loh 減°落; kæn-ky'ing' 減°輕; — *the price,* kæn'-loh kô'-din 減°落價°錢°; — *the rigor of punishment,* ying-vah' kæn-ky'ing' 刑罰減°輕

ABATED, *the wind has —* (somewhat), fong iu'-tin 風小°點; *ditto* (entirely), fong sih'-de 風息了°

ABBESS, *Buddhist* tông'- kô-s-t'a 當家°師太°; *Roman Catholic —,* nyü'-siu-dao-tsiang 女修道長

ABBOT, *Buddhist* fông-dziang' 方丈; *Roman Catholic —,* siu-dao'-yün-tsiang 修道院長

ABBREVIATE, *to — strokes in writing,* siao' sia pih' wah 小寫°筆

畫; liao-gying' sia 謬近寫°; p'o'-ti sia' 破體寫°; t'eo-læn' sia 偷懶寫°

ABDICATE, to — the throne, (and hence office), t'e we' 退位; — in favor of another, nyiang we' 讓°位

ABDOMEN, du'-bi 肚皮

ABDUCT, to — (by deception), kwæ'-tæ 拐帶; — by force, ngang-pih'-leh-ky'i 硬°逼得去°

ABED, læ min-zông' li 在°眠床裡

ABET, to aid, pông-dzu' 幫助; — in crime, dzu-dziu'-we-nyiah' 助紂爲虐 (veng); to put one up to, ts'ön'-teh 攛掇; ditto (something bad), t'iao-so' 挑唆

ABETTOR, cü'-so 主唆

ABHOR, to u'-su 惡憎; dislike excessively, k'eh'-ts'eng; in-tseng' 厭憎

ABIDE, to djü 住; deng' 停; kyiu'-deng 久停

ABILITY, dzæ-neng' 才能; du'-dzæ 肚才; dzæ-dzing 才情; peng'-z 本事; vu'-nyih-ts 武藝°子; perfect in mental and moral character, dzæ-djün' teh' be 才全德備; give according to your —, ze lih-liang' dzu-c'ih' 隨力量助出; — tsiao ng'-go lih-liang' do-c'ih' 照你個°力量拕出; ze kô fong hyin', 隨家豐儉

ABJECT, mean or poor, bing-dzin' 貧賤; — in condition (as slaves, &c.), pe-dzin' 身賤

ABJURE, to vah-tsiu' ky'i'-djih 罰咒棄絕; — going, vah-tsiu' feh ky'i' 罰咒弗去°

ABLE, neng-keo' 能殼; we 會; has strength equal to, lih tsoh' 力足; is he — to do it? gyi neng-keo' tso' feh 其能殼做否°? he is —, gyi we tso' 其會做; he is not — to do it, vu lih' neng we' 無力能爲; lih' sô peh gyib' 力所不及; an — man, yin dzæ-dzing-go nying 有才情個°人°

ABOARD, loh-jün'-de 落船了°; zông-jün'-de 上船了°; læ-jün'-li 在°船裡

ABODE, djü-kyü' 住居; djü-oh' 住屋; where is your —? djü-kyü' ah-li' 住居何°處°? where is your honorable —? fu'-zông ah-li' 府上何°處°?

ABOLISH, to fi 廢; fi'-diao 廢了°; — law, fi'-diao lih-fah' 廢了°律法

ABOMINABLE, k'o-'eng' 可恨; k'o-u'-ts-gyih' 可惡之極

ABOMINATE, to 'eng 恨; ün-'eng' 怨恨; 'eng-gyih' 恨極

ABORIGINES, t'u'-jing 土人°; — of the middle and South of China, miao-ts 苗子

ABORTION, siao'-ts'æn 小產; do-t'æ' 墮胎; do sing' 墮娠; to cause —, tang t'æ' 打胎

ABO   5   ABU

ABOUNDS in, ting to' 頂多; fi-væn'-ts to' 非凡之多;— every where, c'ü-c'ü tu yin' 處處都有; mun' di tu z' 滿地都是; the Eastern part — in coal, Tong' pin me-t'æn' ting to' 東邊煤炭頂多

ABOUT, da-iah' 大約; iah'-læ 約來; mao 毛; mao-kwu' 毛估;— thirty li,* da-iah' sæn'-jih li' 大約三十里;— tæn, k'ao jih' nearly, ts'ô'-fch-to' 差弗多; round —, s'-tsiu-we' 四周圍; s'-deh-lön'-ky'ün 四國圍圈; dön-ky'ün' 團圈

* A li is about one third of an English mile.

ABOVE, zông 上; zông-deo' 上頭; te'-zông 對上;— the house, læ oh' te'-zông 在屋對上; over and —, ling-nga' 另外'; yü-wæ' 餘外;— me in rank (one grade), p'ing'-kyih pi ngô' kao' ih-teng 品級比我高一等

ABREAST, bing'-ba 並排°

ABRIDGE, to tsah'-tön 摘短; kæn'-liah 減略

ABROAD, beyond customs' barriers, kwæn nga' 關外°; beyond the frontier, k'eo' nga 口外°; spread —, 'ang-k'æ' 行開; yiang-k'æ' 揚開; po'-yiang'-k'æ 播揚開; comes from —, dzong nga-deo' læ 從外頭來; gone —, c'ih yün'-meng' ky'i'-de 出遠門去了°

ABRUPTLY, deh-jün' 突然

ABSCESS, doh-dzing-kwun' 毒成瘡°

ABSCOND, to dao-tseo' 逃走; tseo'-t'eh 走脫

ABSENT, feh læ'-tong, 弗在°此°; m'-neh læ'-tong 不°在這裏°

ABSENT-MINDED, forgetting what one is doing, vông'-gyi-sô'-yi 忘其所以; sing'-feh-dze-yin' 心不°在焉 (used in reproach).

ABSOLUTE power, gyün-shü' liao-fch-teh' do 權勢極大°

ABSOLVE, to sô 赦°; min 免°; sô'-min 赦°免°;— from sin, sô ze' 赦°罪

ABSORB, to seng'-tsing 沁°進; heng'-tsing.

ABSTAIN, to — for a time, gyi 忌;— entirely, ka 戒°;— from food, gyi zih' 忌食;— voluntarily, zi nyün' ka 自°願戒°; zi kying' zi 自°禁自°;— from wine, ka tsiu' 戒°酒;— from opium, ka a-p'in' 戒°鴉°片

ABSTEMIOUS in food, and drink, ing'-zih yiu-tsih' 飲食有節

ABSTRACT, tsah'-iao 摘要 (ih-go)

ABSTRUSE, sing-ao' 深奧

ABSURD, beyond reason, ü-li'-feh-'ch' 于理弗合; dzing-li'-ts nga' 情理之外°;— talk, hen-wô' 憨話

ABUNDANT, to'-leh-kying' 多得緊; more than is needed, yiu yü' 有餘; plentiful, fu'-tsoh 富足;

— (as trees, or fruit), meo-zing' 茂盛;— crops, or — year, nyin'-koh fong-teng' 年穀豐登; da-joh' z nyin 大熟時年; — crops, wu' koh fong teng' 五穀豐登

ABUSE, to treat badly, long-song'; to injure, 'æ 害; to revile, mô 罵; zoh-mô' 辱罵; to — by diminishing one's due, k'eh'-dæ 刻待; — by soiling (as a book, or one's character), tsao-t'ah' 蹧蹋;— the weak, ky'i-vu' 欺侮

ABUSED, who — this book? keh' peng shti' be jü' tsao-t'ah'-diao-de 這°本書被誰蹧蹋了°?

ABYSS, m-ti'-k'ang 無°底坑; m-ti'-sing-den 無°底深潭; fathomless —, væn-dziang'-sing-den 萬丈深潭

ACADEMY, shü-kwun' 書館; shü-vông 書房

ACCELERATE, to press forward, ts'e 催;— parturition, ts'e-sang' 催生°; to increase speed gradually, dzin'-dzin kw'a'-ky'i-læ 漸漸快°起來; bu-bu kying'-ky'i-læ 步步緊起來; ih-bu' kw'a' ih-bu — 步快°一步; ih-bu' kying' ih-bu — 步緊一步

ACCEDE, to tah-ing' 答應; ing-jing' 應認; yüing 允; i 依;* did not —, feh tah'-ing 弗答應; feh yüing 弗允

* These characters usually denote simply a reply, but here they denote an affirmative reply.

ACCEDED, (he) — to what I wanted, ngô sô iao'-go tah'-ing-de 我所要个°答應了°

ACCENT, sing-ing' djong 聲音重

ACCENT, to sing-ing' bin ky'ing' djong 聲音辨輕重

ACCEPT, to ziu 受; sin 收; ling'-ziu 領受; pray you —, ts'ing ng' teng ngô siu'-sin 請你°與°我收收; I, having accepted, cannot forget your kindness, ngô ziu-ts' ko-sing'-feh-ky'i' 我受了過心不°去°;— your kind invitation, mong ng' zing'-dzing ngô læ ling'-ziu 蒙你°情我來領受

ACCEPTABLE, 'eh-i'-go 合意个°; 'eh-sih'-go 合式个°

ACCESSION to the throne, teng-we' 登位;— to office, jih tsih' 襲職

ACCIDENT, to meet with an — (injury), p'ong-djoh 'æ' 逢°着°害; nyü 'æ' 遇害°; ditto, (ill luck), p'ong-djoh hwe-ky'i 逢°着°晦氣

ACCIDENTALLY, ngeo'-jün 偶然; neo'-ts'eo 偶°湊

ACCOMMODATE, to — one's self to, jing'-dzong 順從; ditto (to circumstances), k'en'-ky'i sang'-dzing 隨°機而°行°

ACCOMMODATING, (of a person), yün-t'ong' 圓通; 'o-t'ong' 和通; — in lending, &c., k'eng t'ong-yüong' 肯通融

ACCOMPANY, to dong-de' ky'i 同隊去°; jü-de' ky'i 聚隊去°; ih-dong' ky'i 一同去°; dô-kô' ky'i 大家去°; 'eo'-leh ky'i 候了去°; — on the way (or escort), be'-leh ky'i 陪了去°; song'-leh ky'i 送了去°.

ACCOMPLICES, dong-tông' 同黨; tso'-tông 佐黨.

ACCOMPLISH, to complete, tso'-dzing 做成; dzing-kong' 成功; wun-kong' 完功; to — nothing, sang deng-dæn'.

ACCORDING to, tsiao 照; dziu 就; agreeably, kyü 據; i 依; 'eo 候; jü 如; 'eh 合; — my idea, tsiao ngô i'-s 照我意思; — to my seeing, tsiao ngô k'en'-læ 照我看來.

ACCOUNT, tsiang 帳; to give in one's — of money entrusted, pao'-siao-diao 報銷了°; ditto, falsely, hyü-pao' 虛報; to reckon up an —, sön-tsiang' 算帳; difficult to — for, næn ka'-shih 難解°說; to enter on —, zông tsiang' 上帳; to draw up an —, k'æ tsiang' 開帳; to settle an —, ka tsiang' 解帳; fu tsiang' 付帳; on — of, we 爲°; ing-r' 因而; on no —, tön'-feh-k'o' 斷弗可; ts'ih'-feh-k'o' 切弗可.

ACCOUNT-BOOK, tsiang'-bu 帳簿.

ACCOUNTABLE, you are —, hyiang ng' z veng' 向你是問; hyiang ng' dziah-lôh' 向你著落; I am not —, feh' z ngô'-go kwæn-dzih' 不°是我个°關涉.

ACCOUNTANT, tsiang'-vông 帳房; kwun-tsiang' cü-kwu 管帳个人°.

ACCUMULATE, to tsih'-jü 積聚; tsih'-hyüoh 積蓄; tsih'-loh 積落.

ACCURATE, without faults, 'ao-vu' ts'o'-c'ü 毫無錯處; bing'-vu ts'o'-ts'oh 並無錯錯; feh-ts'o' 弗錯; minute, ts'-si 仔細.

ACCUSATION, (written), zông-ts' 狀子 (ih-tsiang); to bring in an — (on both sides), dzing-zông' 呈狀.

ACCUSE, to — before an officer, kao'-zông' 告狀; — falsely, bwông'-kao 誣告; he accuses me of stealing, gyi ün ngô t'eo'-go 其屈°我偷个°.

ACCUSER, nyün-kao' 原告; the person accused, be-kao' 被告; your —, kao' ng-go cü'-kwu 告你个°人°.

ACCUSTOMED, to become —, long-kwæn' 弄慣; tso'- kwæn 做慣; tso' jing-joh' 做純熟; — to do, kwæn'-tso-go 慣做个°; can't become — to hearing (it), t'ing'-feh-kwæn' 聽弗慣.

ACHE, t'ong 痛; head —, deo-t'ong' 頭痛; tooth —, ngô-ts' t'ong' 牙°齒痛.

ACHIEVE, to dzing-kong' 成功; with fixed aim, (he) will — his

object, yiu' ts kying'-dzing 有志竟成; — *renown*, kong-ming' dzing-dziu' 功名成就

ACKNOWLEDGE, *to own*, jing 認; *to confess*, tsiao-jing' 招認; — *being in the wrong*, jing ts'o' 認錯; *unwilling to* —, feh k'eng' jing' 弗肯認; *unwilling to* — *a debt*, la tsa' 賴°債°

ACORN, ziang'-ts 橡子 (ih-ko)

ACQUAINTANCE, siang-joh'-go 相熟个°; joh-nying' 熟人°; nying-teh'-go nying' 認得个°人°; *mere* —, p'iao'-miao beng-yiu' 標緲朋友

ACQUAINTED *with*, joh-sih' 熟識; *he is well* — *with the business*, keh'-go z-nyih' gyi ting' joh-sih' 這°个事業其頂熟識; — *with him many years*, teng gyi' to nyin' siang-yü 與其多年相與

ACQUIESCE, *to* i 依; ing-yüing' 應允; *I certainly* — *in your decision*, ng' ding-kwe', ngô vu yiu' feh i' 你定規我無有弗依

ACQUIRE, *to* tsang 掙°; tsang'-tsing 掙°進; dzæn 賺; djün; — *money*, tsang' dong-diu' 掙°銅錢°; — *possessions*, tsang' kô-kyi' 掙°家°計; — *knowledge*, kô cü'-sih 加°知識

ACQUIT, *to* — *him*, ding' gyi, ṁ zẹ' 定其無°罪; shü' gyi, ṁ zẹ' 恕其無°罪

ACRE, (Chinese), meo 畝; m; *an* — *of* (field) *land*, ih meo' din 一畝田

ACROSS, wang 橫°; *lying* — *the road*, wang' lu tong 橫°於路上°

ACT, *to* tso 做; tsoh 作; — *a play*, tso hyi'-veng 做戲文; *to* — *well*, tso nying' hao' 做人°好; — *benevolently*, we jün' 爲善; 'ang jün 行善

ACTIONS, 'ang-we' 行°爲; tsoh'-we 作爲; sô-tsoh'-sô-we' 所作所爲; *bad* —, wa 'ang-ts' 孬行°止; *that is a good action*, keh' z ih-go hao' 'ang-we' 這°是一个°好行°爲

ACTIVE, *fond of action*, hao' dong'-go 好°動个°; — *and intelligent*, weh-p'eh' 活潑; ling-dong 靈動; *quick* (in work), kyih'-tsao 急躁; *strong and* —, mô-lih'.

ACTOR, *stage* hyi'-ts 戲子; pæn-ts 班子

ACTRESS, nyü'-pæn-ts 女班子

ACTUAL, *true*, jih-we' 實爲; *proved by* — *experiment*, væn'-cing-liao 範準了

ACTUALLY, *really*, jih-dzæ' 實在; jih-yi 實係; ky'üoh'-jih 確實

ACUTE, *sharp*, tsin 尖; — *discernment*, (by figure), ngæn'-lih tsin' 眼力尖; — *pain like a knife cutting*, t'ong' ziang tao' c'oh ka 痛像刀轄一°樣°

ADAGE, dzoh-wô' 俗話; *ancient*

—, kwu'-wô 古話; lao'-wô-deo 老話頭 (ih-kyü)

ADAPT, to — one's self to time or place, tsœ' tao ah-li', z ah-li' 做到阿裡是阿裏; ts'' ih-z', pe' ih-z' 此一時彼一時; can — himself to circumstances, neng ky'üih' neng sing' 能屈能伸

ADAPTED to use, hao'-yüong'-go-de 好用个°; — to his use, 'eh-gyi'-go yüong' 合其个° 用

ADD, to kô 加°; t'in 添; tseng 增; ts'eo 湊; kô-ts'eo 加°湊; t'in-ts'eo' 添湊; tseng-ts'eo' 增湊; — coal, kô me-t'æn' ts'eo' 加°煤炭湊

ADDITION (in Arithmetic), kô-fah' 加°法

ADDITIONAL, nga 外°; ling-nga' 另外°; — expense, nga' fi 外°費; nothing —, bih' vu nga kô' 別無外°加°; — pleasure (as a new son), t'in hyi' 添喜

ADDRESS, I wish to — you, ngô iao teng ng kông' 我要與你°講°; how shall I — him? ts'ing-hwu' gyi jü 稱呼其誰°? — a number of people, te cong'-nying kông' ih-fæn 對衆人°講°一番

ADDRESS, he made a good —, gyi fah'-hwe-leh hao' 其發揮得°好; very good —, do fah'-hwe 大°發揮; — (of a letter, place only), di-ming' 地名; di-kyiah'-ing; superscription (on a letter), sing'-min 信面

ADEPT, joh-siu' 熟手; — (in that branch), ting' cün-meng' 頂專門

ADEQUATE, enough, keo 够; tsoh足; is —, keo-de 够了°; do you feel — (to it)? ng 'ôug'-leh-djü' feh 你°降得°住否°? ng hao p'e-fu feh 你°好配副否°?

ADHERE, to nyin-lao' 粘牢; can't make it —, nyin'-feh-lao 粘弗牢; will —, we kao-nyin'-go 會膠粘个°; — (as iron to a magnet), hyih'-lao 吸牢

ADJACENT, siang-gying' 相近; — countries, siang-gying'-go koh' 相近个° 國

ADJOINING, ling 鄰; — country, ling koh' 鄰國; — room, kah'-pih ih-kæn vông' 隔壁一間°房

ADJUDICATE, to try, sing 審; to judge, sing'-p'un 審判; p'un'-tön 判斷

ADJUST, to tsing'-teng 整頓; tsing-li 整理; — these stones, keh'-sing zah-deo' iao tsing'-teng hao 這°些石°頭要整頓好; — matters, tsing-li' z-ken' 整理事幹; — (or put things in order), tsing'-zi 整齊°; — the hair, li deo-fah' 理頭髪

ADMINISTER, to bæn 辦; bæn'-li 辦理; — affairs, bæn'-li z-ken'

ADMIT 辦理事幹; to — medicine to a person, do yiah' peh nying ky'üoh' 拿°藥給°人°吃°; — public affairs, bæn' kong-z' 辦公事

ADMIRAL, se'-s-di-toh 水師提督

ADMIRABLE, gyih-me' 極美; gyih-hao' 極好; gyih-miao' 極妙

ADMIRE, to ky'i'-mo 企慕; cong-æ' 鍾愛; (as rare things), hyi-hen' 希罕; — and long for (or wish to be like), ky'i'-nyiang 企仰; — and desire, nyiang'-vông 仰望

ADMIRED, I have long — his great reputation, ngô hyiang'-læ mo' gyi'-go da ming' 我向來慕其°个°大名

ADMIT læm, peh' gyi tseo'-tsing-læ 俾°其走進來; nyiang' gyi tsing'-læ 讓°其進來

ADMONISH, to —(not to do), ky'ün'-kyiæ 勸解; ky'ün'-sih 勸釋; — (to do) ky'ün'-min 勸勉

ADOPT, to — (as an outsider), ling 領; ming-ling' 螟蛉; — a male relative, (of the same family name), lih-kyi' 立繼; dzing-kyi' 承繼; ko-kyi' 過繼; ditto from love, æ'-kyi 愛繼; — the nearest nephew, ing-kyi' 應繼

ADOPTED child, ling'-ts 領子 (of the same family name), kyi'-ts 繼子; — brother, (of different family name), nyi hyüong-di' 義兄弟; kyi'-pa hyüong-di' 結°拜°兄弟

ADORE, to kying'-kying-djong-djong pa' 敬敬重重拜°

ADORN, to —(as the person), tsông-pæn' 裝扮; tsah'-kwah 紮刮; — (as houses), tsông-sih' 裝飾; (as things), tsông-wông' 裝潢 These four expressions may be used interchangeably, but according to good usage it is better to distinguish them.

ADRIFT, t'eng'-læ-t'eng'-ky'i' 氽來氽去°; t'eng'-k'æ-de 氽開了°

ADROITNESS with the hand, siu'-fah p'ih'-t'eh 手法狠°快°; siu'-fah c'ih-gyi' 手法出奇

ADULATION, vong-dzing 奉承; ts'in-vong' 諂奉; shü'-kwu 世故; ts'eo'-c'ü 湊趣

ADULT, arrived at — age, zông-ting' 上丁; dzing-ting' 成丁; tsiang'-dzing 長成; dzing-nying'-tsiang'-da 成人°長大

ADULT, do-nying' 大°人°; school for adults (of either sex), do shü-vông' 大°書房; — school for males, kying-kwun' shü-vông' 經館書房

ADULTERATE, to ts'æn-'o' 攙和; ts'æn-tsing' 攙進; ts'æn-long' 攙攏; — with water, ts'æn-t'ông' 'o-shü' go 攙湯和水个°

ADULTERER, kæn-fu' 姦夫; yia'-lao-kong 野°老公

ADULTERESS, kæn-vu' 姦婦

ADULTERY, kæn-ying' 姦淫; a case of —, kæn-en' 姦案;

to commit —, væn kæn-ying' 犯姦淫

ADVANCE, to zông-zin' 上前°; price will —, kô'-din iao kyü'-zông-de 價°錢°要貴°上了°; kô'-din iao tsiang'-zông-de 價°錢°要漲上了°; to improve, tsing'-ih 進益; hao'-ky'i-læ 好起來; — wages (before the time), yü-ts' sing-kong' 預支辛工; tsæn kong-din' 趲工錢°; in — of me, pi ngô' zông-zin' 比我上前°

ADVANCED in years, yiu'-sing nyin-kyi' de 有些°年紀了°

ADVANTAGE, profit, bin-i' 便宜°; benefit, ih'-c'ü 益處; hao-c'ü' 好處; to take of — him, tsin gyi'-go zông-fong' 佔其个°上風; take — of another, tsin nying-kô' min-ts' 佔人°家°面子

ADVENTUROUS, fond of going into danger, hwun-hyi' tseo hyin' lu 歡喜走險路

ADVERSARY, dziu-dih' 讎敵; ün-kô' 冤家°; te'-deo 對頭

ADVERSE, feh-jing' 弗順; feh-jing'-kying 弗順境; feh-jing'-liu 弗順溜; — day, nyih-jing' feh-te' 日°辰弗對; — wind, tông-deo' fong 當頭風; (against the wind), teo' fong 對風; tao' fong 倒風;— current, teo'-shü 對水°

ADVERSITY, (as sickness, fires, persecution), tsæ-næn' 災難; — (in business, &c.), z-yüing' feh-hao' 時運弗好; tao-yüing' 倒運; in —, loh-boh'-de 落薄了°; in times of — trust in God, yiu tsæ'-næn z-'eo k'ao'-djoh Jing-ming' 有災難時候靠著神明

ADVERTISE, to kao'-bah 告白°; — in a paper, zông-pao' 上報; teng-pao' 登報; do you — your goods? ng'-go ho' yiu zông-pao'-leh ma 你°个°貨有上報了°嗎°?

ADVERTISEMENT, kao'-bah 告白° (ih-tsiang); — of goods, &c., tsiao-ts' 招紙; to put up an. — (i.e. paste up), t'iah' tsiao-ts' 貼招紙

ADVICE, ky'ün'-hwô 勸化; won't listen to —, feh k'eng t'ing ky'ün 弗肯聽勸; feh ziu ky'ün'-hwô 弗受勸化; I'll give you a piece of —, ngô ky'ün'-hwô ng ih-fæn' 我勸化你°一番; I will take your —, ngô t'ing' ng-go ky'ün' 我聽你°个°勸; ling'-kyiao, ling'-kyiao 領教領教

ADVISE, to ts'-kyiao 指教 (not proper in the first person); — (or tell) a person, kao'-hyiang-nying-dao 教°向人°道; I beg you to — me, ngô ts'ing' ng ts'-kyiao ngô 我請你°指教我; I — you not to go, ngô co ng vong' ky'i' 我叫°你°不用°去°

ADVISER (to one ignorant), hô-tông-ngæn' 蝦°當眼°

ADVOCATE, *mediator*, cong-pao' 中保; *attorney*, dzong-s' 訟師

AFAR, yün'-yün 遠遠; yiao-yün' 遙遠

AFFABLE, ky'in-'o' 謙和; 'o-ky'i' 和氣

AFFAIR, z 事; z-ken' 事幹; z-t'i' 事體; (ih-gyin, ih-ky'i, ih-tsông, ih-tön); *important —*, iao'-z 要事; da-z' 大事; *that's my —* (in anger), dæn'-ming ngô 但憑我

AFFECT, *to influence*, ken' -dong 感動; kyih'-dong 激動; — *to be a scholar*, kô'-s-veng 假斯文; — *to be wise, but thus betray folly*, long-ky'iao'-fæn-cih' 弄巧反拙

AFFECTION *for equals, or inferiors*, æ'-sih 愛惜; — *for superiors*, æ'-kying 愛敬; *having great —*, (or affectionate), æ'-sing djong' 愛心重; ts'ing-gying' 親近; *warm —*, æ'-sing nyih' 愛心熱°; *filial —*, hyiao' sing 孝心

AFFINITY, *natural* t'in sing'siang-lin' 天性相連

AFFIX *to a word*, dang-kyiah'-go z-ngæn' 宕腳个°字眼°

AFFLICT, *to* næn 難; næn-næn'; mo-næn' 磨難; *Heaven afflicts*,

t'in kông tsæ' 天降°災; t'in kông'-loh kw'u'-næn 天降°落苦難

AFFLICTED, *to be —*, ziu næn' 受難; tsao'-djoh tsæ-næn' 遭着°災難; *greatly —*, kw'u'-sah-de 苦煞了°; kw'u ky'üoh'-feh-ko'-de 苦吃°弗過了°

AFFLICTION, wæn'-næn 患難; kw'u'-næn 苦難; tsæ-næn' 災難

AFFORD, *can you — to buy it?* ng yiu lih-liang' hao ma' feh 你°有力量好買°否?*I can — it*, ngô hao' ma 我好買°; ngô dong-din' yiu' 我銅錢°有; *can't — to buy*, ma'-feh-ky'i' 買°弗起; c'ih'-feh-ky'i' 出弗起; *can't —* (such expense), lih-liang' tông-feh-djü' 力量當弗住; ky'üoh'-feh-loh' 吃°弗落

AFFRONT, *to* teh'-ze 得罪; *to a person* (by speaking of what he is jealous of), væn-nying-kô'-go gyi' 犯人°家°个°忌; — *unintentionally*, ngwu'-væn' 誤犯

AFFRONTED, kwa'-tih - de 怪°的了°

AFLOAT *on the sea*, læ hæ'-li p'iao-dông' 在°海裡飄蕩; *floating*, vu'-tih 浮°的

AFOOT, *come* bu-'ang' læ 步行°來; tseo'-leh læ 走得°來

AFRAID, p'ô'-go 怕个°; læ-tih p'ô' 正°在°怕; *don't be —*, hao-vong p'ô' 不°用°怕; feh-dzæwu 弗°礙°事°; *nothing to be — of*, ts'-wô lao'-hwu 紙畫老虎 *lit.*, only a pictured tiger.

AFTER, 'eo 後; 'eo-deo 後頭; 'eo-læ 後來; yi 'eo 以後; — *ages*, 'eo'-shü 後世; — (you) *have finished* (you) *can go*, wun-kong-ts, bao ky'i' 完工了°好° 去°; *after this* (or that), dzong-ts"-ts-'eo' 從此之後; — *this time*, dzong-kying'-yi-'eo' 從今 以後; ky'i-kô'; — *a month*, ih-yüih'-ts' 'eo' 一月之後; *come* — (me), (*i. e.* subsequently), ze-'eo' læ 隨後來; — *all*, kyin-kying 究竟; kyiu'-kyiu - kwe-nyün' 九九歸原

AFTER-BIRTH, pao 胞; pao - i' 胞衣

AFTERNOON, 'ô'-pun-nyih 下°半 日°; tsiu'-ko-'eo' 晝過後; wu'-'eo 午後; 'ô'-wu 下午

AGAIN, tsæ 再; yi 又°; djong 重; *do* (it) —, tsæ' tso 再做; *say* (it) —, tsæ' wô 再話; *over and over* —, tsæ'-sæn-tsæ-s' 再三再 四; ih'-r-tsæ', tsæ-r-sæn' 一而 再再而三

AGAINST *me*, teng ngô' tsoh-te' 與° 我作對; *leaning or resting* —, gæ 戤; gæ'-djoh 戤著; k'ao'-djoh 靠著; *leaning* — *the wall*, gæ'-leh ziang' 戤於°墻; *ditto*, (as a picture), ziang-li hyih-tih; *touch* or *strike* —, bang 掽; bang-djoh 掽°著°; *brush* or *rub*

—, ts'ah 擦; ts'ah'-djoh 擦着'; *the varnish is tender*, (*i. e.* fresh) *must not rub* — (it), ts'ih neng-neng'-tih feh k'o ts'ah'-djoh 漆 嫩嫩的弗可擦着'; — *reason*, feh-'eh' ü-li' 弗合于理; ü-li' feh-vu' 于理弗符; — *the wind*, teo' fong 對風

AGAR-AGAR, hæ'-ts'æ 海菜; zih-hwô'-ts'ao' 石花草

AGE, nyin-kyi' 年紀; *what is your —?* (ordinary address), to-siao' nyin - kyi' 多少年紀? (more respectful), kwe'-kang 貴 庚? tseng-kang' 尊庚? ng to-siao' kwe'-kang 你°多少貴庚°? *respectfully ask your lofty —?* ts'ing' meng kao ziu' 請問' 高壽? *what is his —* (of a *child*)? kyi shü' 幾歲°?

AGE, shü 世; *an —* (generation), shü'-dæ 世代; *through endless ages*, tao shü'-shü-dæ'-dæ 到世 世代代

AGED, lao 老; nyin-lao'- de 年 老了°; *an — person*, nyin-lao'-go 年老个°; lao'-nyin nying 老年人°; lao'-dzing nying 老 成人°

AGENT, kying-siu' 經手; tông-siu' 當手; kwun-tsiang' 管帳; *to act as an — in selling another's goods*, kyi'-ma 寄賣

AGGRANDIZEMENT, *country's* —, koh'-kô hying-wông' 國家興旺;

only cares for self —, tsih' iao zi' hao' 只要自°好

AGGRAVATE, *to* kô djong 加°重 long-leh yüih-fah' djong' 弄得 越發重; *to provoke anger*, pih-leh sang ky'i' 逼得°生°氣

AGGREGATE, *the sum total*, tsong'-su 總數; gong 共; t'ong'-gong 統共; gong-kyi' 共計

AGGRESSOR, sin dong'-siu-go 先動手个; sin 'ô'-siu-læ tang'-go 先下°手來打个°

AGHAST, hah'-sah 嚇煞; *stupefied with fear*, hah'-ngæ-de 嚇呆了°; hah'-su-de 嚇酥了°; hah'-hweng-de 嚇惛了°

AGITATE, *to* dong 動; tang'-dong 打動; c'oh'-dong 觸動; yiao-dong' 搖動; — *the water*, kao'-dong shü' 攪°動水

AGITATED *by fear, &c.*, sing' ling-ling'-dong 心慄慄動; — *by wind*, be fong' yiao-dong' 被風搖動

AGO, *how long* —? kyi nyin' zin 幾年前°? *twenty years* —, nyiæn nyin' zin 廿年前°; *not long* —, feh kyiu' 弗久; feh yün' 弗遠; *long* —, nyin-dæ' yün' 年代遠; dziang-kyiu'-de 長久了°

AGREE, *to* — *well together*, 'eh-deo' 合頭; te 對; vu 符; siang-nyi' 相宜; 'eh-nyi' 合宜; teo-deo' 鬭頭; dô-kô'

siang-te' 大°家°相對; deo-kyi' 投機 (used of persons only); *to correspond*, te'-kying 對經; *can't* —, p'ing'-feh-long' 抨弗攏; 'eh-feh-long' 合弗攏; *the two reckonings* —, liang'-p'in tsiang, te'-go 兩篇帳對个°; — *together to buy*, iah'-ding iao ma' 約定要買°; — *upon a day*, iah'-ding nyih-ts' 約定日°子; *two parties* —, liang' siang dzing-nyün' 兩相情願

AGREEABLE *to*, 'eh-nyi' 合宜; 'eh-sih' 合式; *being in the sun is* —, sa' læ nyih-deo-li 'eh-nyi'-go 曬在°日°頭裏合宜个°; — *person*, nying 'o-ky'i'-go 人°和氣个°

AGREEMENT, iah 約 (ih-go); *written* — (in trade), nyi-tæn' 議單; nyi-kyü' 議據; *to make an* —, iah'-hao 約好; iah'-jih 約實; wô-hao' 話好; *to make a written* —, lih iah' 立約; sia nyi-tæn' 寫議單

AGRICULTURE, nong-z' 農事 (veng); cong-din' z-ken' 種田事幹

AGROUND, *to run* —, koh 擱; koh-ts'in' 擱淺; *ditto, on sand*, ts'in sô' 淺沙; *ditto, on the mud*, ts'in du' 淺塗

AGUE, *fever and* —, nyiah-dzih' 瘧疾; ma-za'-bing 買柴病;

fah-'en-nyih' 發寒熱; *tertian* —, s'-nyih-bing' 四日°病; s'-nyih-liang'-deo-pæn' 四日°兩頭班

AHEAD, læ zin-deo' 在°前°頭; — *of me*, pi ngô' zông-zin' 比我上前°

AID, *to* pông-dzu' 幫助; vu'-dzu 扶助; siang-pông 相幫; pông-ts'eng' 幫襯; — *with strength* (*i. e.* in labor), dzu lih' 助力; pông lib' 幫力; —*with money*, dzu dzæ' 助財; — *the government with money*, dzu hyiang' 助餉; *ditto, with militia*, dzu üong' 助勇

AIM, *take good* —, k'ô-ding' cing'-deo tang' 擎定準頭打; miao-deo' k'ô-leh cing' 苗頭擎°得準; — *high* (in life), ts'-hyiang iao lih'-leh kao' 志向要立得°高; *his* — *is to excel*, gyi'-go ts'-hyiang du-zông'-tsing 其°个°志向圖上進

AIR, ky'i 氣; *wind*, fong 風; *the* — *we breathe*, yiang-ky'i' 陽氣; seng-ky'i' 生氣; *in the* —, k'ong' li 空裡; pun'-k'ong cong 半空中; *birds fly in the* —, tiao' yün-k'ong'-li fi' 鳥°在懸空裏飛

AIR, *to* t'eo-t'eo ky'i' 透透氣; t'ong-t'ong fong' 通通風; — *the room*, vông'-ts peh gyi t'eo-t'eo ky'i' 房子俾°其透透氣; — *clothes in the sun*, i-zông' sa'-sa gyi 衣裳曬°曬°; *ditto in the shade*, i-zông' lông-lông' gyi 衣裳晾晾; — *or cool it*, liang' ih-liang' 涼一涼

AIR-PUMP, hyih-ky'i'-c'ih-go kô-sang' 吸氣出个°傢生°

AIRS, *to put on* —, tsông-mo' tsoh-yiang' 粧模作樣

ALACRITY, *to do with* —, kao-hying' tso 高興做; dzing-nyün' tso 情願做

ALARM, *in a state of* —, hah'-sah-de 嚇煞了°; *must not* — *him*, m-nao' peh gyi ziu-kying' 弗°可°俾°其°受驚; m-nao' peh gyi ky'ih-hoh' 弗°可°俾°其°吃°嚇°

ALARMED, ky'ih-hoh'-de 吃°嚇°了°; *he seemed greatly* —, gyi yiu kying-hwông' siang'-mao 其有驚慌相貌

ALARMING *intelligence*, kying-wông'-go sing'-sih 驚惶个°信息; hyüong-veng' 凶聞

ALAS! 'æ 唉°! 'a'-yia 哎喲°!

ALBUMEN *in an egg*, dæn-bah' 蛋白°; — *in hens' eggs*, kyi-ts' ts'ing' 雞子青

ALCOHOL, *Chinese* siao-tsiu' 燒酒; *pure ditto*, tsing-tih'-siao 眞滴燒

ALIKE, ih-yiang' 一樣; ih-sih' 一式; ih-seh' ih-yiang' 一色一樣; t'ih'-seh-vu-r' 貼色無

二；— in most things, da dong' siao' yi 大同小異
ALIVE, weh'-go 活个°；— or dead? weh'-go si'-go 活个°死个°？ is he still —? gyi wa dzæ shü' feh 其還°在°世否°？ wa kæ-tong' feh 還°在否°？ he is still —, wa dzæ' 還°在
ALL, long'-tsong 攏總; tu 都; ih'-gong 一共; ih-kæ' 一概; ih'-t'ong 一統; t'ong'-gong 統共; tu-kyi' 都計; — men (or everybody), cong'-nying 衆人°; take out — the things, tong-si' long'-tsong do-c'ih' 東西攏總扡出; tong-si' ih'-kæ do-c'ih' 東西一概扡出; — the way, ih-lu' 一路
ALLAY, to untie, ka 解°; — pain, ka t'ong' 解痛; to check, ts 止; — thirst, ts k'eh' 止渴; — anger, sih ky'i' 息氣
ALLEGE, to wô-leh kyih'-jih 話得°碻實; to — as an excuse, ziæ'-k'eo wô 藉口話; tsia' tso yin-nyü' 借°做言語; — a false reason, t'oh kwu' 托故
ALLEGORY, nyü'-i 寓意; do-dön'-go pi'-fông 大°段个°比方
ALLEVIATE, to — his burden, ky'ing' gyi-go tæn'-deo 輕其°个°擔頭; to — pain, t'ong' ka-ka-bo' 少°解痛勢; pain will be alleviated, t'ong' we siao-tin' 痛會少點; t'ong' we ky'üih'-tin 痛會缺點

ALLEY, an —, ih-da-long' 一堘°俐°
ALLIANCE, to form a family —, ding-ts'ing' 定親; to form an — between countries, lih-ming-iah' 立盟約
ALLOT, to — to each his share, tsiao'-kwn kyüing-feng' 照股均分; — equally, bing-feng' 平分; kyüing-feng' 均分
ALLOW, to cing 准; byü 許; ing-jing 應認; I do not — him to go, ngô feh cing' gyi ky'i' 我弗准其去; feh byü' gyi ky'i' 弗許其去°; — him to do, cing' gyi tso 准其做
ALLOWABLE, proper, tsoh'-hying 作興; k'o'-yi 可以; not —, feh hyü'-go 弗許个°
ALLOY, to ts'æn-kô' 攙假°; ts'æn-'o' 攙和
ALLUDE, to — to, di-gyih' 提及; di-ky'i' 提起; to whom do you —? ng' sô di-gyih'-go z jü' 你所提及个°是誰°？
ALLURE, to yiu 誘; ying'-yiu 引誘; hong-yiu 哄誘; — him to gamble, yiu gyi tu' 誘其賭
ALLUREMENT, bait, nyü-deo' 餌頭; ditto (for birds), me-deo' 媒頭; these are both used figuratively, in speaking of persons; thus, by what — was (he) caught? be soh-go nyü-deo' zông keo-go 被甚°麼°餌°頭上鈎个°; be soh'-go me-deo'

tsing-long'-go 被甚°麼°媒頭進籠个°

ALLUSION, to make an unpleasant —, kông ing-wô' 講°陰°話; k'ao-toh' 拷聲°; toh lang-djü' 射°冷°鎚°

ALLY, te'-siu 對手; lin-siu' 連手 (ih-go)

ALMANAC, lih-jih' 曆°日; t'ong-shü' 通書; wông-lih' 皇曆; Foh-kien —, Kyin'-lih 建曆 (ih-peng)

ALMIGHTY, vu-sô'-peh-neng' 無所不能; djün-neng' 全能; yiang-yiang' neng-keo' 樣樣能殼

ALMOND, 'ang'-nying 杏°仁°; bitter —, kw'u' 'ang-nying 苦杏仁° (ih-lih)

ALMOST, ts'ô'-feh-to' 差弗多; shü'-kyi-wu 庶幾乎; kyi-kyi'-wu 幾幾乎; ts'ô-feh-læ'-ky'i 差弗來去°; ts'ô-fông'-feh-to 差仿弗多; siang-ky'ü'-peh yün' 相去不遠

ALMS, to give —, pu'-s dong-din' 佈施°銅錢°; sô dzin' 砂錢; to give — to people, tsiu-tsi' nying-kó' 賙濟人°家

ALMS-GIVER, s'-cü 施主; a great —, do s'-cü 大°施主

ALOES, lu-we' 蘆薈

ALOFT, læ zông-deo' 在°上頭; on the mast, læ we-ken' teng 在°桅杆上°

ALONE, doh-zi' 獨自°; doh-ih' 獨—; he is there —, gyi doh-zi'

læ-kæn' 其°獨自°在°彼°; person — in the world, kwu-sing'-nying 孤身人°; tæn-sing'-nying 單身人°

ALONG with, ih-dong' 一同; dong-de' 同隊; come — with me, teng ngô' ih-dong' ky'i 與°我一同去°; teng ngô' jü-de' ky'i 與°我聚隊去°

ALOUD, kao-sing' 高聲; hyiang'-liang 響亮; in ordinary tones, ze-k'eo' 隨口; to read or study —, doh 讀; ze-k'eo' doh 隨口讀; to cry —, k'oh 哭; ditto, (as an infant) kyiao 叫

ALPACA, yü'-sô 羽紗; figured —, hwô yü'-sô 花羽紗

ALPHABET, letters of the —, z-meo' 字母

ALREADY, yi'-kying 巳經

ALSO, yi 又°; yia 也°; wa-yiu' 還°有; there is — another teacher, yi yiu' ih-we sin-sang' 又有一位先生°; wa-yiu' ih-we 還°有一位; you can come —, ng yia' hao læ 你°也°好來

ALTAR, tsi'-dæn 祭壇

ALTER, to kæ 改; kæ'-ko 改過; kæ'-wun 改換; keng-kæ' 更改; kæ'-pin 改變; should — one character, ih'-go z' iao kæ' 一个°字要改; — this garment, by making smaller, keh' gyin i-zòng' iao kæ'-siao' 這件

衣裳要改小; cannot —, kæ'-feh-læ 改弗来

ALTERCATE, to tsang-zao' 相爭°

ALTERNATE, to — with another in performing, ling'-leh tso' 輪°了°做; diao-læ'-wun-ky'i tso' 調來換去°做; ling-kæ'-ling-ky'i tso' 輪°來輪°去°做; diao-læ'-diao-ky'i tso' 調來調去°做

ALTERNATE, on — days, kah' nyih 隔日°; kæn' nyih 間°日°

ALTERNATE, to act as an —, tso dæ-siu' 做代手

ALTERNATIVE, to choose one of two alternatives (i. e. difficulties), liang'-næn-ts cong kæn ih'-yiang 兩難之中揀°一樣; no —, 並 tang'-sön 無°打算; 並 fah'-ts 無°法子; vu lu' k'o tseo' 無路可走; vu kyi' k'o s' 無計可施

ALTHOUGH, se-tsih' 雖卽; se-jün' 雖然

ALTOGETHER, ih'-kæ 一槪; ih-zi' 一齊'; ih-tsong' 一總; 'o'-jün 全°然; jih-feng' 十分; — bad, ih'-kæ wa' 一槪孬°; — wrong, 'o'-jün feh-te' 全°然不對; — unable, væn'-væn peh-neng' 萬萬不能

ALUM, ming-væn' 明攀; bah-væn' 白°攀

ALWAYS, z-djông' 時常; peh'-djông 不常; djông-djông' 常常; me'-djông 每常; dziang-

t'ong' 長通; coh'-kwun; — been so, lao'-lao z-ka 回°回°如°此°; lao' kwe-kyü 老規矩

AM is often understood; I — going, (in parting), ngô ky'i'-de 我去°了°; I — here, ngô' læ-tong' 我在°此°; læ-tong' 在°此°; I — writing, ngô' læ-tih sia' 我現在°寫°

AMALGUM, to apply a pewter —, dông sih 盪錫; zông sih 上錫

AMANUENSIS, dæ-sia'-go-nying 代寫°个°人°; dæ-pih' 代筆; dæ-shü' 代書; copyist, ts'ao-sia'-go-nying 抄寫°个°人°

AMASS, to te-tsih' 堆積; te-tsih'-jü-sæn' 堆積如山

AMAZED, hyi-gyi'-sah-de 希奇煞了°; afraid, kying-hyiæ'-de 驚駭了°

AMAZING, wonderful, hyi-gyi' 希奇; gyi-tsæ' 奇哉; c'ih-gyi' 出奇

AMBASSADOR, ky'ing-ts'a' 欽差°

AMBER, hwu'-p'ah 琥珀; false —, mih-lah'-p'ah 蜜蠟珀; — beads, hwu'-p'ah cü 琥珀珠

AMBIGUOUS, weh-dong' 活動; obscure, en'-dong-dong 暗洞洞; — words, weh-dong'-go shih-wô' 活動个°說話; words having double meaning, sông-kwæn' shih-wô' 雙關說話

AMBITIOUS, to be — of fame, du ming' 圖名; — of gain, du li'

圖利;— *of false fame*, du hyü ming' 圖虛名

AMEN, üô'-meng 亞孟 (the English word transferred); *so be it*, dzing-sing'-sô-nyün' 誠心所願

AMEND, *to reform*, kæ-oh'-dzong-jün' 改惡從善; kæ'-ko-tso nying' 改過做人°

AMETHYST, læn-pao'-zah 藍寶石°

AMIABLE, sing'-dzing 'o-nyün' 性情和順

AMICABLE, 'o-moh' 和睦; siang-æ' 相愛

AMID, cong-nyiang' 中央°

AMISS, ts'o 錯; dzæn 綻; *to speak* —, kông' ts'o 講°錯; kông' dzæn 講°綻

AMMUNITION, hô'-yiah-dæn-ts' 火藥彈子

AMNESTY, eng-sô' 恩赦°; eng-tsiao' 恩詔; — *from the emperor*, wông-eng'-da-sô' 皇恩大赦°

AMONG *them*, dzæ-ne' 在內; dzæ-gyi-cong' 在其中; dzæ-dziang' 在塲; *he also was — them*, gyi yia' dzæ-ne' 其也°在內; *ne is also pronounced* nen.

AMOUNT, ih-gong' 一共; t'ong'-gong 統共; tsong'-gong 總共; gong'-kyi 共計; tsong'-kyih 總揭; tsong'-su 總數; *what is the —?* ih-gong' to-siao' 一共多少?

AMPLE, *abundant*, ts'iah'-ts'iah yiu'-yü 綽綽有餘

AMPUTATE, *to* tsæn-dön'; kah'-dön 割斷; *to saw off*, ka'-loh 鋸°落

AMULET, bih-zia'-go vu' 眸邪°个°符; wu-sing' vu 護身符; *a silver lock hung about the neck of delicate children to prevent death*, 'ông'-so 項鎖. See CHARM.

AMUSE, *to — one's self*, hyi'-hyi 嬉戲; *ditto (by walking about, &c.)*, bah-siang' 白相; *ditto (by drinking, &c.)*, tsoh-tsoh-loh' 作作樂; — *him (i. e. a child, primarily by deceiving)*, hong-hong' gyi 哄哄其; *to divert one's mind*, sæn sing' 散心

AMUSED, *pleased*, k'æ-sing'-tih-de 開心的了°

ANALYSIS, *chemical* hwô'-yüoh 化學

ANALYZE, *to* feng-ts'ing' 分清; — *a subject*, p'o' di 破題; — *chemically*, feng-k'æ' peng'-tsih 分開本質; — (*as an essay*), me moh' feng-ts'ing' 眉目分清; — *logically*, kyiu' gyi peng'-nyün 究其本原

ANARCHY, liao-lön' z-t'i' 繚亂事體; *a time of —*, lön' feng'-feng z-shü 亂紛紛時世

ANATOMY, *science of the human body*, djün-t'i'-sing-leng' 全體新論; *bones, joints and internal*

organs, kweh'-tsih-dzông-fu' 骨節臟腑
ANCESTORS, tsu'-tsong 祖宗; tsu'-sin 祖先; tsu'-zông 祖上
ANCHOR, mao 錨 (ih-meng); to cast —, p'ao mao' 拋錨; to drag —, yiu mao' 拽錨; to weigh —, ky'i mao' 起錨
ANCHORAGE, p'ao mao'-go-di'-fông 拋錨个°地方
ANCIENT, kwu 古; — times, kwu-z-tsih' 古時節; men of — times, kwu-z-tsin' nying 古時節°人°; tông-ts'u'-ts nying 當初之人°
AND, teng 與°; lin 連; you — I, ng' teng ngô' 你與°我
ANECDOTE, kwu'-z 故事; tin 典; tell an —, kông ih'-go kwu'-z 講°一個°故事; tell an amusing —, kông ih'- go siao'-wô 講°一個°笑話
ANGEL, t'in-s' 天使; jing-s' 神使; t'in-jing' 天神
ANGER, ô'-wông; ông; ky'i 氣; nu 怒; to excite —, kyih nu' 激怒; excite him to —, long' gyi ô'-wông 弄其動°怒°; kyih gyi nu' 激其怒; appease —, sih nu' 息怒; ditto by confessing, making a feast, &c., siao-siao ky'i' 消消氣; nursing one's — (i. e. belly-full of —), ih-du'-ts-ky'i 一肚之氣; eyes standing out with —, nu'-ngæn'-deh-tsin' 怒眼°凸皆

ANGLE, an ih-koh' 一角°; acute —, tsin koh' 尖角°; obtuse —, dzia koh' 斜°角°; right —, dzih koh' 直角°
ANGRY, ông'-de; fah-ông'-de; væn-ông'-de; fah-nao'-de 發惱了°; ô'-wông-de; sang-ky'i'-de 生°氣了°; fah-nu'-de 發怒了°; dong-nu'-de 動怒了°; læ-tih sang-ky'i' 正在°生°氣; very —, long-do' fah-ông'; ky'i'-sah 氣煞; to grow suddenly — and rude, fæn'-loh min-k'ong' 變°面孔; ziang ts'a'-nying-lin'-ka 像差°人°个°臉; — and cross, fông-tiao'-de 放刁了°; læ-tih s-sing 正在°使性
ANIMAL, cong-sang' 畜生°; quadrupeds, tseo'-siu 走獸; (horse, cow, ass) sang-k'eo' 牲口; wild —, yia'-siu 野°獸; — food, hweng 'ô'-væn 葷下飯; hweng-sing' 葷腥; to eat — food, ky'üoh hweng' 吃°葷; commence eating — food after abstaining, k'æ hweng' 開葷
ANIMATE, to — him, long' gyi weh-ky'i'-læ 弄其活起來; s'-teh gyi sing nyih' 使得其心熱°
ANISE, star we-hyiang' 茴香; pah koh' 八角°
ANKLE, kyiah'-tsang 脚脖°; kyiah'-bu-lu-den' 脚滿蘆頭°; — joint, kyiah'-gao 脚胲°

ANNALS, koh'-s 國史; *historical compilations*, kông-kæn' 綱鑑; — *of the dynasties*, lih-dæ s'-kyi 歷代史記

ANNEX, *to* djoh-zông' 績上; pu'-zông 補上; djoh-pu' 績補; djoh-tseng' 績增

ANNIHILATE, *to* mih-wun' 滅完; mih ken-zing' 滅乾淨; siao-mih'-wun 消滅完

ANNOUNCE, *to* pao 報; cü-we' 知會; — *it*, pao' ih-sing 報一聲; *to inform*, t'ong-cü' 通知; t'ong-pao' 通報

ANNOY, *to* væn-nao' 煩惱; tsi-tsco' 嘈䏲°; lo'-so 囉唆

ANNOYED, feh næ'-væn 弗耐煩; væn-nao'-go 煩惱个°; *excessively* —, væn-nao'-sah-de 煩惱煞了

ANNUALLY, nyin-nyin' 年年; me'-nyin 每年; djoh-nyin' 逐年; lih-nyin' 歷年

ANNUL, *to* fi 廢; fi'-diao 廢了°

ANOINT, *to* fu-yiu' 傅油; djô-yiu' 搽油; fi-dzông' 非常

ANOMALOUS, gyi-c'ih'-kwn-kwa 奇出古怪°

ANONYMOUS, feh-c'ih'-ming-go 弗出名个°; — *defamatory placard*, m-deo'- pông 無°頭榜; vu-ming'-kyih'-t'iah 無名揭帖°

ANOTHER, bih'-go 別个°; ling-nga' ih-go 另外°一个°; —

man, bih' nying 別人°; *have* —, wa-yiu' ih'-go 還°有一个°; ling-yiu' ih-go 另有一个°; *come again* — *day*, kæ' nyih tsæ' læ 改日°再來; *love one* —, pe'-ts' siang-æ' 彼此相愛; dô-kó' siang-æ' 大°家相愛

ANSWER, *to* ing 應; ing'-tah 應答; tah'-ing' 答應; — (*more at length*), we-tah' 回答; tah, also pron. teh; — *back* (*as when reproved*), ing-cü' 應嘴; *will it* — *or not?* hao'-s-teh feh 好使得否°? *will it* — (*your*) *idea or purpose?* 'ch-i' feh 合意否°

ANSWER, *question and*—, ih-meng' ih-tah' 一問°一答; *verbal* —, we-ing' 回音; *written* —, we-sing' 回信

ANT, wun-hwun' 螻蟻° (ih-go)

ANTAGONIST, te'-dih 對敵; — *in a game*, dih-sin' 敵手

ANTENNÆ, *of insects*, djong-su' 蟲鬚

ANTICIPATE *pleasure*, siang hying' 想興頭; *not as I anticipated*, peh c'ih' ngô sô liao'-go 不出我所料个°; *did not* —, liao-feh-tao' 料弗到; — *difficulty*, yü-sin' liao' yiu næn-c'ü' 預先料有難處; *you* — *my wishes*, ng sin' teh'-djoh ngô' sing-i' 你先得着°我心意; — *his wishes*, ts'æ-djoh' gyi sing-siang' 猜着°其心想; — *and hardly*

ANTIDOTE, (medicine), ka-doh'-go yiah 解°毒个°藥; — *for all poisons*, ka-pah'-doh 解°百°毒

ANTIPATHY, *to have an* —, gyi 忌; *I have a great* — *to spiders*, kyih-cü' ting væn ngô' gyi' go 蜡蛛頂犯我忌个°

ANTIQUARY, *one versed in antiquities*, poh-kwu'-go cü'-kwu 博古个°人; *one fond of antiquities*, æ kwu tong'-go nying 愛古董个°人

ANTIQUES, kwu'-ky'i 古器; kwu'-tong-wæn'-ky'i' 古董玩°器; kwu'-ho 古貨

ANTIQUITY, *times of* —, zông-kwu' z-'eo 上古時候; *of great* —, t'a' kwu 太°古

ANTITHESIS, te'-kyü 對句

ANVIL, t'ih-tsing-den' 鐵椹'頭'; t'ih'-teng'-deo 鐵磴頭

ANXIOUS, *to be* —, tæn-sing-z' 擔心事; iu-li' 憂慮; fông'-sing-feh-loh' 放心弗落; kwô'-nyiæn 罣念; kyi'-kwô 記罣; *I am* — *about him*, ngô' dæ gyi iu-li' 我代其憂慮; *don't be too* —, peh pih ko' li 不必過慮; *tired of waiting*, sing'-tsiao 心焦

ANY, *have you* — *?* ng yiu' feh 你°有否? *not* —, m̄'-teh 沒有°; *has* — *one been here?* yiu soh'-go nying læ-ko' 有甚°麼°人°來過?

ANYTHING, soh'-go or soh'-si 甚°麼°; *do you want* — *?* ng iao soh'-si 你°要甚°麼? (better to say to a stranger), soh'-go z-ken, or soh' ken 甚°麼°事幹? 'o-ken' 何幹? *I do not want* —, ngô feh iao' soh'-si 我弗耍甚°麼°

APART, zi kwun' zi 自°管自°; koh' zi feng-k'æ' 各自°分開; li-k'æ'-liao 離開了; *sit* —, zi kwun' zi zo' 自°管自°坐; *place (them) a little* —, fông'-leh k'æ'-tin 放得°開點; *to pull* —, te'-k'æ 扤開; *ditto with the fingers*, p'ah'-k'æ 擘開

APATHETIC, moh 木; moh-hying-hying'

APE, See MONKEY.

APEX, ting-den' 頂頭; nao'-tsin 腦尖

APIECE, *how many cash* — *?* kyi'-go dong-din ih'-go 幾個°銅錢°一个°? *three cash* —, sæn'-go dong-din ih'-go 三个°銅錢°一个°; *give them a dollar* —, me' nying coh gyi ih-kw'e' fæn-ping' 每人°給°其一塊番餅; kyin' nying peh gyi ih-kw'e' fæn-ping' 見人°給°其°一塊番餅

APOLOGIZE, *to* be feh-z' 賠弗是; be li' 賠禮; shü ze' 請罪; shü ih-go ze' 請°一个°罪

APOLOGY, *to make an* —, beih'-go feh-z' 賠一个°弗是; be ih-go li' 賠一个°禮
APOSTASY, be-kyiao' 背°教
APOSTATE, be-kyiao'-go nying 背°教个°人°
APOSTLE, s'-du 使徒
APOTHECARY, yiab-tin'-kwun 藥店夥; k'æ-yiab-tin'-go 開藥店个
APPARATUS, ky'i'-gyü 器具; *philosophical* —, keh-veh'-go ky'i'-gyü 格物个°器具
APPARENT, hyin'-jün 顯然; hyin'-r-yi-kyin' 顯而易見; hyin'-kyin 顯見
APPARENTLY *is so*, siang-mao z'-ka 榀貌如°此°; —, *but not really*, z-z'-r-fi' 似是而非
APPARITION, *to see a ghost*, kyin kyü' 見鬼°; *any strange sight*, gyi-ying'-kwæ'-ziang 奇形怪狀°; iao-kwa' 妖怪°; tsing-kwa' 精怪°
APPEAL *to a superior*, wông-zông' su' 往上訴; — *to any one to remove an accusation*, gyiu sing shih' 求伸雪; gyiu sing ün' 求伸冤
APPEAR, *to be manifest*, yin-c'ih'-læ 現出來; hyin'-yin 顯現; *very like a man*, tsing'-ziang ih-go nying' 正像一个°人°; *this appears larger*, p'e-mo' ziang keh ih'-go do' 胚模像這°一

個°大°; — (*as a deity*), hyin-sing' 顯聖
APPEARANCE, siang'-mao 榀貌; p'e-mo' 胚模; kwông-kying' 光景; *wears a suspicious* —, ying-tsih' k'o nyi' 形跡可疑; *miserably poor* — (*used of persons*), pe-pe' go siang'-mao 卑卑个° 榀貌; *has the* — (or *appears to be*), dzing-ying' 情形; *fearful* —, ying-shü' 形勢
APPEASE, *to* — *anger*, sih nu' 息怒; *ditto by owning one's fault, &c.*, siao ky'i' 消氣
APPEND, *to attach* (as by a string), kyih 結; kyih'-zông 結上; — *at the end*, dzoh 續; dzoh-zông' 續上; *to add to*, pu-ts'eo' 補湊
APPENDIX (to a book), pu-yi' 補遺; dzoh-tsæ'-go shih-wô' 續載个°說話; — *to a writing*, tsæ'-p'i 再批
APPERTAIN, *to* — *to*, joh-ü' 屬于; dzæ'-ü 在于
APPETITE, (good or bad) we-k'eo' 胃口; — (great or small) zih-liang' 食量; *good* —, k'æ-we' 開胃; *no* —, we-k'eo' feh k'æ' 胃口弗開
APPLAUD, *to* — *with a cheer*, heh-ts'æ' 喝采; *to praise*, ts'ing-tsen' 稱讚; peo-tsiang' 襃奬
APPLE, *a large* —, bing-ko' 蘋果; *small yellow* — *with red tinge*, hwô-'ong' 花紅. There is no generic term for apples.

APPLICABLE, 'eh-djoh' 合着°; siang-vu' 相符;— to everybody, koh-nying siang-vu' 各人°相符; not — to him, ü gyi' feh vu' 與其弗符; teng gyi' feh 'eh 與°其弗合

APPLICATION, export c'ih' k'eo pao'-tæn 出口報單; import —, tsing' k'eo pao'-tæn 進口報單

APPLY, to have recourse to, deo 投; — to the customs, pao kwæn' 報關;—to the local constable, deo di-pao' ky'i' 投地保去°; to the clergyman, deo-tao kyiao'-s di'-fông 投到敎師地方°; — the mind, cün-r'-cü'-ts 專而致°之; cün-sing' 專心

APPOINT, to ming 命; to settle upon, ding 定; who was appointed to go? ming jü' ky'i 命誰°去°? ding jü' ky'i 定誰°去°? —(to each his duties), feng-p'a' 分派°; — a day, ding ih-go nyih-ts' 定一个°日°子°; ditto (in the future), ding ih-go gyi' 定一个° 期

APPOINTED, time not yet —, vi'-ding gyi' 未定期; who was — to go? ming jü' ky'i 命誰°去°? I was — to come, ngô z vong-ming'-r-læ'-go 我是奉命而來个°;— by an officer, vong' kwun'-go ming 奉官个°命; vong-hyin'-go 奉憲个°;— by the emperor, vong-ts'-go 奉旨个°

APPOINTMENT, ming 命; who receives that —? jü' ziu keh-go ming' ni 誰°受這个°命呢? a good —, hao' ts'a-s' 好差°使

APPOSITE, 'eh-shing'-go 合榫个°; siang-'eh'-go 相合个°

APPRECIATE, to k'en'-tao 看到; k'en'-tao-kô 看到家°; do not — (it), k'en'-feh-tao-kô 看弗到家°; — fully, k'en'-t'ong-t'eo' 看通透; ts'ih'-ti k'en 徹底看

APPREHEND, to seize, k'ô 拿°; gying 擒; to understand, ming-bah' 明白°; hyiao'-teh 曉得; tong 懂

APPRENTICE, du-di' 徒弟 (ih-go); to be an —, deo s-vu' 投師父; to — him, peh gyi tso du-di' ky'i 俾°其做徒弟去°; peh gyi 'oh du-di'.

APPROACH, to gying'-long 近攏; — (as a person), tseo'-long-læ 走攏來; gying-sing' 近身; he fears to —, gyi p'ô' gying'-long 其怕近攏; the time approaches, z-'eo' gying'-long læ-de 時候近攏來了°

APPROBATION, cong'-i 中意; jü i' 如意; has my —, jü ngô'-go i' 如我个°意; 'eh ngô' sing-i' 合我心意

APPROPRIATE, to — to one's self, and deny it, la-meh' 賴°沒; ky'üoh'-meh 吃°沒

APRICOT, 'ang'-ts 杏子 (ih-go).
APRON, (Chinese) man's —, yü-pu' 圍布; ditto (like a skirt), yü-gyüing' 圍裙; tsoh'-gyüing 作裙; (Chinese) woman's large —, yü-sing-pu'-læn' 圍身布襴.
APT to learn, ih-kao' ziu we' 敩就會; — to get angry, yüong-yi' sang-ky'i' 容易生氣.
AQUEDUCT, tsih'-shü-kwun 接水管.
ARBITRARY, z-yi'-we-z' 自以爲是.
ARBOR, liang-bang' 涼棚; grape —, ts'-bu-dao bang' 紫葡萄棚 (ih-go).
ARBUTUS, tree-strawberry, yiang-me' 楊梅.
ARCH, gwæn-dong' 環洞.
ARCHED window, gwæn-dong' ts'ông 環洞牕; — bridge, gwæn-dong' gyiao 環洞橋.
ARCHER, kong-tsin'-siu 弓箭手.
ARCHERY, kong-tsin'-gyi-nyi' 弓箭技藝.
ARCHITECT, head mechanic, ziang-deo' 匠頭; tsoh'-deo 作頭. The Chinese here have no architect proper.
ARCHIVES, the place for the —, koh'-s-kwun 國史館; the records as just written, jih-loh' 實錄; ditto when revised, kông-kæn'-li tsæ-loh'-go.
ARDENT, nyih-sing' 熱心.

ARDUOUS, sing-k'wu' 辛苦; lao-loh' 勞碌; dziah-lih' 着力.
ARE is generally unexpressed; where — you? ng' læ ah-li' 你在何處? we — here, ah-lah ke-tong' 我等在此; — there any? yiu' m-teh 有沒有?
AREA, di-dziang' 地塲; what is the — of China? Cong-koh' di-dziang' yiu dza do' 中國地方有怎樣大?
ARGUE, to dispute, bin'-leng 辨論; to reason, nyi-leng' 議論.
ARID, dry, ken-sao' 乾燥; parched with the sun, sa'-sao-de 曬燥了.
ARISE, to bó-ky'i' 爬起; ky'i'-læ 起來.
ARISTOCRACY, hyiang-sing 鄉紳; sing-kying' 紳矜.
ARITHMETIC, sön'-yüoh 算學; rules of —, sön'-fah 算法.
ARM, siu'-kwang 臂膀 (ih-tsah).
ARMLET, glass liao siu'-gyüoh 料手鐲.
ARM-PIT, kah'-ts-'ô 胳下.
ARMOR, kw'e-kah' 盔甲.
ARMORY, kyüing-gyüoh' 軍局 (ih-zo).
ARMS, (clubs and spears, but not cannon), ky'i'-yiæ 器械.
ARMY, soldiers, ping-mô' 兵馬; to raise an —, ky'i-ping' 起兵; fah-ping' 發兵.
AROMATIC taste, lah-ho-ho' mi'-dao 辣呵呵味道.
AROUND, tsiu-we' 周圍; dön

ky'ün' 團圖; *walk once* —, tsiu-we' tseo ih'-cün 周圍走一轉; *all* —, s'-dön-lön'-ky'ün (or s' dch, &c.), 四圍繞圍; *walk* —, d ön-ky'ün' tseo-tæn'-cün 團圓走轉

AROUSE, *to awaken*, long su'-sing 弄蘇醒; eo diao'-kao' 叫覺°; — *by reminding of duty*, di-sing' 提醒

ARRAIGN, *to* — *a person*, ta nying' læ sing'-meng 帶人°來審問°; di nying' læ 提人°來

ARRANGE, *to* tsing 整; pa 擺°; tsing'-teng 整頓; *to* — *properly*, pa' tön-tsing' 擺°端正; — *in succession*, tsiao ts'^v-jü tsing'-tsing hao 照次序整整好; — *regularly*, tsing tæn'-zi 整齊°; — *tastefully* (as household articles), pa'-leh teh-fah' 擺得得法; — (things that have been displaced), siu-jih'-ko* 收拾過; — *affairs*, z-ken' en-ba' hao 事幹安排好; — *in battle array*, pa dzing-shü' 擺°陣勢

* This also means to gather up and take away, as dishes after eating.

ARREST, *to seize*, k'ô 拿°; k'ô'-djoh 拿着°; *to stop*, ts'-djü 止住; *to bring a warrant for* —, ying ba' k'ô nying' 行牌°拿°人°

ARRIVE, *to* tao 到; *when did you* —? ng' kyi'-z tao'-go 你°幾時到个°?

ARROGANT, ngæn'-ka-do' 眼界°大°; zi-tseng'-zi-do' 自尊自°大°; k'en'-nying'-feh-ky'i' 看人°弗起

ARROW, tsin 箭 (ih-ts)

ARROW-ROOT, *native* ngeo'-feng 藕粉

ARSENAL *for storage*, kyüing-kong'-tsong'-gyüoh 軍工總局;— *for manufacture*, cü'-dzao-gyüoh' 製造局

ARSENIC, p'i-sông' 砒礵; sing'-zah 信石°

ART, *the* fah'-ts 法子; fông-fah' 方法; *the* — *of bread-making*, tso mun-deo' go fah'-ts 做饅頭个°法子

ARTS, gyi-nyi' 技藝; siu'-nyi 手藝; *the six Chinese* —, loh nyi' 六藝; *viz*, *etiquette*, li 禮; *music*, yüoh 樂; *archery*, ziæ 射; *trades*, nyü 御; *literature*, shü 書; *mathematics*, su 數; *the hundred* —, pah'-kong-gyi-nyi' 百°工技藝

ARTERIES, hyüih'-mah-kwun 血脈管; — *and veins*, hyüih'-kwun 血管; we byüih'-kwun 迴血管

ARTFUL, diao-bi' ; kæn-tsô' 奸°詐; kwe'-kyi to'-tön 詭計多端

ARTICLE, *a clause*, or *rule*, ih-diao' 一條; ih-kw'un 一款; ih-'ông 一項; *an* — (of goods) ih-gyin' 一件; ih-yiang 一樣;

the articles *a* or *an* are expressed by classifiers, thus, *a teacher*, ih-we' sin-sang' 一位先生°; *an ox*, ih-deo' yüong-ngeo' 一隻°雄牛°.
ARTICULATION, *distinct* k'eo'-ts' ts'ing-t'ong' 口齒清通.
ARTIFICE, *trick*, tsô'-kyi 詐計.
ARTIFICIAL, *made by man*, nying tso'-c'ih-læ-go 人°做出來个°.
ARTILLERY, *cannon*, do-p'ao' 大礮; — *men*, p'ao'-sin 礮手.
ARTISAN, s-vu' 司務; s-vu' ziang-nying 司務匠人°; ziang° 匠.
ARTIST, *one who paints pictures*, tæn-ts'ing' sin'-sang 丹青先生°.
ARTLESS, ve'-tsông-kô'-go 弗°會°裝假° 个°; *true*, tsing-dzing'-jib-i' 真情實意.
AS, *for example*, *like*, or *as if*, hao'-ziang 好像; tsing'-ziang 正像; — *you say*, tsiao ng' sô wô' 照你°所話; — *you please*, ze ng' 隨你°; ze ng' bin' 隨你°便; ze-bin' ng 隨便你°; — *much as you please*, ze ng' to-siao' 隨你°多少; — *I walked along*, ngô tseo'-ko z-'eo' 我走過時候; — *good — you*, ziang ng' ka kwun hao' 像你°這般好; *do just — I tell you*, ngô wô dza tso', ng dza tso' 我話怎°做你°怎°做; ngô wô, ih'-z-ih', wô, nyi'-z-nyi' 我話一是一話二°是二°; — *before*, dzing-gyiu' 仍舊; i-

gyiu' 依舊; dzing-voh' 仍復; — *usual*, tsiao' djông 照常; tsiao wông'-z 照往時; tsiao 'æn-tsao'-ts; *a ball — large — an egg*, ziang kyi-dæn', ka kwun do ih-dön' 像鷄蛋一樣大°一團.
ASAFŒTIDA, a'-we 阿°魏.
ASCEND, *to* sing-zông 升上; — *by walking*, tseo'-zông 走上.
ASCERTAIN, *to — by inquiry*, meng dziah'-jih 問°着實; tang'-t'ing ming-bah' 打聽明白°; *to know certainly*, hyiao'-teh dziah'-jih 曉得着實.
ASCRIBE, *to* kwe-ü' 歸于; kwe-peh' 歸與°; — *glory to God*, kwe yüong-wô' ü Jing-ming' 歸榮華于神明; — *merit to another*, kwe kong' ü nying' 歸功于人°; — *blame to him*, kwe zo' ü gyi' 歸罪于其.
ASHAMED, wông-k'ong' 惶恐; dzæn-gwe' 慚愧; *slightly —*, feh-'hao'-i'-s 弗好意思; næn we'-dzing 難爲情; wông-gwe' 惶愧; bao'-ky'in 抱歉; weh'-la-siang; weh'-la-tsi-tsi; *are you not — ?* ng yiu feh-hao'-i'-s ma 你°有弗好意思麽°? *you ought to be — of it*, keh' z ng' kæ wông-k'ong'-go 這是你°該惶恐个°; (I) *am — to see you*, kyin ng-go min' feh kæ' 見你°个°面弗來; te' ng feh djü' 對你°弗住; *to feel*

—, kyüoh'-teh dzæn-gwe'-siang 覺得慚愧相; p'ô' wông-k'ong' 怕惶恐; — *of his appearance* (a scholar), 'en-sön'-siang 寒酸相

ASHES, hwe 灰; coal —, me-t'æn' hwe 煤炭灰; wood —, za hwe' 柴灰

ASHORE, læ-ngen-zông' 在°岸上; zông-ngen'-de 上岸了°

ASK, to meng 問°; — *and see*, meng-meng'-k'en 問°問°看;—*indirectly*, t'en'-meng-kyi'-k'en' 探探看; — *a question*, meng ih'-sing 問°一聲; — *a favor*, k'eng' ih-go dzing' 懇一个°情; t'ao' ih-go kwông' 叨一个°光;—*for a cup of water*, t'ao' ih-pe' shü' 討一杯水°;—*about*, bun-meng' 盤問°; — *your pardon*, ts'ing ng' nyün-liang' ngô 請你°原諒我; *to invite*, ts'ing 請; — *of whom?* hyiang' jü' meng 向°誰°問°? — *of me*, dziao ngô' meng 向°我問°; — *a girl in marriage* (in behalf of one's son or one's ward), gyiu ts'ing' 求親

ASKEW, dzin.

ASLANT, ts'ia or zia 斜°

ASLEEP, kw'eng'-joh-tih 睡熟的; *foot —*, kyiah mô-tseh'-long' 脚麻了°

ASPARAGUS, long-shü'-ts'æ 龍鬚°菜 (Mandarin); in Ningpo it is called *foreign bamboo*, nga-koh' shing 外°國筍

ASPECT, siang'-mao 相貌; ying-yüong' 形容

ASPERITY *of manner*, oh'-cü-ngæn-siang' 惡嘴眼相; — *of tone*, k'eo'-ky'i zah-ngang' 口氣石硬°; p'eng-deo' 噴頭

ASPIRE, to siang' kao-zông'-ky'i 想高上去°; *can't — to union with*, kao-p'æn'-feh-læ 高攀弗來 (polite).

ASS, *an* ih-p'ih li'-ts' 一匹驢子

ASSAIL, to — (in words), tô'-mô 唾罵; — *Confucianism*, tô'-mô jü-kyiao' 唾罵儒敎; *to strike*, dong'-siu tang' 動手打

ASSASSIN, ts''-k'ah 刺客

ASSASSINATE, to 'ang-ts' 行°刺; en'-di sah nying' 暗地殺人°

ASSAULT, *to make the first —*, sin long' 先弄; sin dong' siu 先動手

ASSEMBLE, *to* jü'-long 聚攏; jü'-jih 聚集; we-long' 會攏

ASSENT, *to* ing-yüing' 應允; tseng 遵; *I — to your proposition*, ngô' tseng ng'-go ming' 我遵你°个°命; tseng ming' 遵命

ASSERT, *to* ih-k'eo ngao'-ding 一口鹸°定; gyin-k'eo' kyih'-jih 箝口硈實; — *that one's self is in the right*, tsang zi' yiu' li 爭自°有理; — (one's) *rights*, tsang yin' veng 爭有分

ASSESS, *to fix customs' tax*, ding se' 定稅; *estimate ditto*, kwu se' 佔稅

ASSEVERATE, *to testify with an oath,* vah-tsiu', tso bing-kyü' 罰咒做憑據
ASSIDUITY, *with* gying-lih' 勤力; *to work with* —, cün-kong'-gyi-z' 專攻其事
ASSIGN, *to—duties, or employments,* feng-p'a' 'ông-tông' 分派行當; p'a sang-weh' 派生活; — *a day,* 'æn'-ding nyih-ts' 限定日子
ASSIMILATE, *to cause them to resemble,* s'-teh gyi-siang-ziang' 使得其相像; *dispositions gradually* —, sing'-dzing dzin'-'eh 性情漸合
ASSIST, *to* pông-dzu' 幫助; pông-ts'eng' 幫襯; vu'-dzu 輔助; siang-pông 相幫; — *in managing affairs,* pông-bæn' 幫辦; — *her to her chair,* tông' gyi zông gyiao' 撐其上橋; — *him into the boat,* vu gyi' zông jün' 扶其上船
ASSISTANT, pông-bæn'-go 幫辦个
ASSOCIATE, dong-de' 同隊; de-ho' 隊夥; *friend,* beng-yiu' 朋友; — *in business,* dong-z' 同事; — *in school,* dong ts'ông' 同䆫
ASSOCIATE, *to* dong-bun' 同伴; — *in business,* gao-siu' 交手; — (*as friends,*) kyih'-kyiao 結交; ts'eo-de' 湊隊; *I was associated with him three years,* ngô' teng gyi dong-bun' sæn nyin' 我

與其同伴三年; — *with the good, forsake the evil,* ts'ing' kyüing-ts', yün siao'-nying 親君子遠小人
ASSOCIATION *for relief of widows,* kwu-sông' we' 孤孀會; — *for giving coffins and medicine,* sô-zæ', s-yiah'-go we' 捨材施藥个會; — *for giving food,* cing'-tsi we' 賑濟會
ASSORT, *to* yiang-tang'-yiang feng' k'æ' 樣樣分開; ih-le' ih-le' feng-k'æ' 一類一類分開
ASSUAGE, *to* ka 解; — *sorrow,* ka iu' 解憂; ka meng' 解悶 — *pain,* ka t'ông' 解痛
ASSUME *the liberty of doing,* jün'-cün 擅專; *to* — *another's power, or place,* dæ-công' gyün-ping' 代掌權柄; dæ-we'-jing-z' 代為人事; dæ-we-liao-li' 代為料理 (công is also pron. tsông).
ASSURANCE, *excess of boldness,* 'eo' ô-lin 厚丫臉; tæ' ô-lin' 默丫臉; si'-bi-la-lin' 死皮賴臉
ASSURE, *to* — *confidently,* kyih'-kyih'-jih-jih' wô' 硈硈實實話; sah'-jib wô' 煞實話
ASSUREDLY, pih'-ding 必定; pih'-jün 必然
ASTHMA, hao-bing' 痞病
ASTONISH, *to* kying-hyiæ' 驚駭; *astonished to see* (it), ih k'en'-kyin ziu hyi-gyi'-sah-de 一看見就希奇煞了

ASTONISHING *progress* (in study), ka kw'a'-leh zông tao hyi-gyi'-go 習°學°得°快°倒希奇个°

ASTRAY, *gone* tseo' ts'o 走錯; mi-lu'-de 迷路了°; tseo ts'o' lu-de 走跌路了°

ASTRIDE, gyi-mô'-zo 騎馬坐°; *ought not to sit — the chair*, ü-ts feh k'o' gyi-mô'-zo 椅°子弗可騎馬坐

ASTRINGENT *medicine*, siu-lin'-go yiah' 收斂个°藥; ts-dza' yiah' 止瀉°藥

ASTROLOGER, ba pah'-z cü'-kwu 排°八字个°人°; k'en ng'-sing sin'-sang 看五星先生°; sön'-ming sin'-sang 算命先生°

ASTRONOMER, t'in-veng'-z 天文士; *imperial —*, ky'ing-t'in'-kæn' 欽天監°

ASTRONOMY, t'in-veng' 天文

ASUNDER, dön'-k'æ-de 斷開了°; *broken — (or in two)*, te' ao-dön-de 對拗斷了°

ASYLUM, *foundling* yüoh-ing'-dông 育嬰堂; *— for the aged (really for beggars)*, kwu-lao'-yün 孤老院

AT, læ or dzæ 在°; *— home*, læ oh'-li 在°家°裡; *— this place*, læ-tong' 在°此°; *— that place*, læ-kæn' 在°彼°; *— Peking*, dzæ Poh'-kying 在北京; *— first*, ky'i-ts'u' 起初; *arrived — the same time*, tsæn'-zi tseo'-tao 一齊°走到; bing'-zi tao'

並齊°到; *— this (or that) time*, keh'-go z-'eo' (or læ keh'-go z-'eo') 這°個°時候

ATHEIST, feh siang'-sing yiu Jing-ming'-go nying 弗相信有神明个°人°; *the — needs only to hear the thunder, "feh sing' Jing-ming', dæn t'ing' le sing'"* 弗信神明但聽雷聲

ATLAS, di-du'-shü 地圖書 (ih-ts'ah)

ATMOSPHERE, t'in-ky'i' 天氣; t'in-kong'-ts-ky'i' 天空之氣

ATOMS, *to divide into —*, feng' tao dzih-si'-si 分到極°細細

ATONE, *to — for sin*, joh ze' 贖罪; cü'-joh z' 取贖罪

ATROCIOUS, *cruel*, hyüong-oh' 兇惡; *— crime*, ze do oh'-gyih 罪大惡極

ATTACH, *to* lin 連; lin-long' 連攏; sang-long' 生°攏; *to append*, kyih 結

ATTACHED (as a friend, &c.), lin-long'-liao 連攏了°; kao-nyin'-go 膠°粘个°; ts'ih-t'iah-go 切貼个°; t'iah'-sing-go 貼°身个°

ATTACK, *to* kong-tang' 攻打; tang 打; *to make the first — (by striking)*, sin dong'-siu tang' 先動手打

ATTAIN, *to — one's object*, jü nyün' teh'-djoh 如願得著; ts'ing' sing jü i' 稱心如意; *— a good position (in any thing)*, tao-leh hao'-go di-bu' 到得°好个°地步; — the (Chinese) degree of A. B., jih 'oh' 入學°; tsing siu'-dzæ 進秀才; — the (Chinese) degree of A. M., cong kyü' nying 中舉人°; teng pông' 登榜; the last is used for any high literary rank after cong kyü.

ATTEMPT, to try, s'-s-k'eu 試試看; make a trial or —, s-ih'-s 試一試; tso'-tso-k'eu 做做看

ATTEND, to heed, yüong-sing' 用心; liu-sing' 留心; tông-sing' 當心; —, to one's duties, kwu'-djoh peng'-veng 顧著°本分; siu-veng' 守分; tso-veng-ne'-ts-z' 做分內之事; en-veng-siu-kyi' 安分守己°; — the sick, voh'-z bing-nying' 服事病人°; tông-dzih' bing-nying' 當值病人°; — a funeral, song-sông' ky'i 送喪去°; — another's call, t'ing s'-hwun 聽使喚

ATTENTION, to pay — to what is said, liu-sing' t'ing' 留心聽; yüong-sing' 用心; to pay no — to the person addressing (i. e. turn the nose to the wall), bih' ts'ong' dziao ziang'.

ATTENTIVE, we yüong-sing' 會用心; k'eng liu-sing' 肯留心; —(to business), pô-dziang' 巴亟

ATTRACT, to hyih'-ying 噏引

ATTRACTION, hyih'-lih 噏力; hyih'-gying 噏勁

ATTRACTIVE, yiu hyih'-gying 有噏勁; strongly —, do yiu hyih'-gying 大°有噏°勁°; hyih'-gying dza hao' 噏勁甚°好 (used of persons only in a bad sense).

AUCTION, to sell goods by —, ma kyiao'-ho 賣°叫貨

AUDIENCE, large ju t'ing'-go nying to' 聚聽个人°多

AUNT, paternal kwu-mô' 姑母°; maternal —, yi-mô' 姨母°

AUSPICIOUS, kyih'-li 吉利; — day, nyih-ts' kyih'-li 日°子吉利; — omen, kyih' ziao 吉兆

AUSTERE, strict, nyin-lah' 嚴辣

AUTHENTIC, k'ao'-leh-jih-go 靠得°實个°

AUTHOR of a book, cü shü', lih shih' go nying 著書立説个°人°; — of a false report, ky'i yiao-yin'cü-kwu 起謠言个°人°

AUTHORITY, gyün-ping' 權柄; unjust use of —, gyün-shü' 權勢; to have official — for doing, kwun cing' li 'ang' 官准吏行°; to use —, or threats in oppressing another, yi shü', ky'i nying' 以勢欺人°; tang-pô'-shü, long nying -kô 打霸勢弄人°家

AUTHORIZE, to ming 命; — officially, we 委; kao-dae' gyün-ping' 交°代權柄

AUTHORIZED by a magistrate, vong hyin' we' go 奉憲委个°; has a certificate, yiu tsih'-tsiao 有執照

AUTUMN, Ts‘iu-t'iu' 秋天
AUXILIARY, pông-dzu'-go 帮助个°;— troops, kyiu'-ping 救兵
AVAIL., to ts‘ing 趁;— one's self of the convenience, ts‘ing bin' 趁便;— myself of your going, to send a letter, ts‘ing ng'-go bin', ta ih-fong sing' ky‘i' 趁你°个便帶°一封信去°;— one's self of an opportunity, ts‘ing kyi-we' 趁機會;— of this opportunity, ts‘ing'-ts‘ kyi-we' 趁此機會
AVARICIOUS, t‘en-dzæ'-go 貪財个°; extremely —, iao din', feh iao ming' 要錢°弗要命
AVENGE, to pao-dziu' 報讐;— a brother's injury, pao hyüong-di'-go dziu' 報兄弟个°讐; sing-ün' 伸寃
AVENUE, do-lu' 大°路; kwun-dông'-do-lu' 官塘大°路; — within an inclosure, üong'-dao 甬道
AVERAGE, t‘ong-ts‘ô' 通扯;— price, t‘ong-ts‘ô' ‘ông'-dzing 通扯行情
AVERSION, have an — to, in 厭 tseng 憎; u 惡°; in'-tseng 厭憎; I have an — to him (on seeing), ngô ih-kyin' ziu tseng' gyi 我一見就°憎其
AVOID, to bi 避; bi-ko' 避過;— danger, bi hyin' 避險; to hide from, to'-bi 躱避;— one's creditors, to'-bi tsa'-cü 躱避債主

AWAIT, to teng'-‘eo 等候; teng'-dæ 等待;— that day, teng'-dæ keh'-go nyih-ts' 等待這°個°日°子
AWAKE, to su-sing 蘇醒; diao-kao' 調覺°; sing 醒
AWAKENED by great noise, do sing'-hyiang kying su'-sing-go 大°聲響驚蘇醒个°
AWARD, to ding 定; tön 斷; p‘un 判; ding-ding'-k‘en 定定看
AWARDING just rewards or punishments, yiu-sông' yiu-vah'-go 有賞有罰个°; yiu en'-fông 有安放
AWARE, to know, teh'-cü 得知; hyiao'-teh 曉得; I was not — (of it) beforehand, ngô yü'-sin feh teh'-cü 我預先弗得知
AWAY, went — yesterday, zô-nyih' ky‘i'-de 昨°日°去°了°; take —, do-ko' 拕過; to throw —, k‘ang'-diao 抛°了°; tiu-diao' 丟去° or 丟了°; ô-diao 搋°了°; ditto (as liquids), tao'-diao 倒了°; go —, tsco'-k‘æ 走開; tsco'-ko 走過
AWE, filled with —, kying' we' 敬畏
AWFUL, k‘o we'-go 可畏个°
AWKWARD, ao'-siu-ao'-kyiah; ngang-ky‘iang'-dao-bih 作°事硬°強°; stiff hands and feet, ngang-siu'-ngang-kyiah' 硬手硬脚

Awl, tsön-ts or cün'-ts 鑽子 (ih-me)
Awning, to put up an —, ts'ang tsiang'-bong 撐°帳篷; ditto over a court, (for some special occasion), mun-t'in-tsiang 幔天帳
Awry, hwa 歪; dzin 斜°; all —, hwa-cü'-p'ih'-kyiah 歪嘴僻脚
Ax, Axe, fu'-deo 斧頭 (ih-pô)
Axiom, z-jün'-ts-li' 自然之理
Axle, leng-gyüoh' 輪軸; leng-bun'-sing-ts' 輪盤心子
Azure, t'in-læn'-seh 天藍色

B

Babble, senseless talk, lön-shih'-diao-bin' 亂說刁辯; wu-yin'-lön-dao' 胡言亂道
Baboon, keo-deo-weh-seng' 狗頭猢°猻
Baby, na-hwun' 嬰°孩° (ih-go)
Babyish, na-hwun i'-tsi-ka 像°嬰°孩°樣°式°
Bachelor, kw'ông'-fu 曠夫 not common, but used in the Four Books; very young —, siao'-kwun-nying 小官人°; kwông-kweng' 光棍 (a term of reproach implying a bad character.)
Back, the pe'-tsih 背脊; to carry on the —, pe 背; behind one's —, pe'-'eo 背後
Back, come cün-læ' 轉來; kyü'-læ 歸°來; walk —, tao'-tseo-cün-læ' 倒走轉來; when will (he) come —? kyi'-z kyü'-læ' 幾時歸°來?

Back-bite, to — a person, pe'-'eo kông nying 背後講°人°
Back-bone, tsih'-kweh 脊骨
Back-court, 'eo-ming-dông'; 'eo-kyin-t'in' 後天井°
Back-door, 'eo'-meng 後門
Back-stitch, to keo 勾
Backward, to walk —, tao'-t'eng'-bu tseo' 倒退°步走; to fall —, nyiang' t'in tih'-tao 仰天跌倒; ditto, (as in studies), t'e'-loh 退落; walk — and forward, tseo'-læ, tseo'-ky'i 走來走去°
Backward, averse to undertake, p'ô' zông-siu' 怕上手; late in developing wisdom (as a child), ts'ong-ming' k'æ-leh dzi' 聰明開得°遲; dull, dzi-deng' 遲鈍
Bacon, salted pork, 'æn cü'-nyüoh 鹹°豬肉°; ditto smoked, in'-cü-nyüoh' 醺猪肉°
Bad, wa 孬°; feh-hao' 弗好; tæ 歹; thoroughly — disposition, 'ô'-liu p'e'-ts 下°流胚子; 'ô'-tsoh p'e'-ts 下°作胚子; — name, wa ming'-sing 孬°名聲; very — name, ts'iu' ming'-sing 醜名聲
Badge, 'ao 號; kyi'-'ao 記號; distinguishing —, pin-'ao' 編號
Baffled, tang'-sön feh-t'ong' 打算弗通; tang'-sön-feh-c'ih' 打算弗出
Bag, dæ 袋; leather —, bi-dæ' 皮袋 (ih-tsah)

BAGGAGE, 'ang-li' 行°李; (a load, ih-tæn; half a load, ih-deo.)
BAIL, to give written security for, gyü pao'-zông 具保狀
BAIT, tiao'-ng-nyü' 釣魚°餌°
BAKE, to p'ang 烹°;—in hot ashes, or coals, we 煨
BAKER, bread-maker, mun-deo' s-vu' 饅頭司務
BALANCE, t'in-bing' 天平; kw'u'-bing 庫平; dzao-bing' 曹平 &c., (ih-kô); the several kinds have different names according to the number of ounces to the lb.
BALANCE, to — exactly, ih'-z-bing dæn' 一字平坦°; ih-weh-liang'-bing 一畫兩平; to — accounts, kyih tsiang' 揭帳
BALD-HEADED, kwông deo' 光頭; bald on the crown, t'ah ting' 禿頂
BALE, a ih-pao' 一包; a — of cotton, ih-pao min-hwô' 一包棉花; to do up a —, tang kw'eng' 打綑; tang pao' 打包
BALL, gyiu 毬; roll a —, le gyiu' 擂毬 (ih-go)
BALLAD, ky'üoh'-ts 曲子; siao'-ky'üoh 小曲; siao'-diao 小調 (ih-tsah)
BALLAST, to take in —, tang ts'ao', stone —, ts'ao'-zah 壓°舟°石°; for —, ah-ts'ông' yüong 壓艙用
BALLOON, ky'i'-gyiu 氣毬
BALUSTRADE, ken-ken' 欄杆;—

for stairs, vu-siu' 扶手; one or more horizontal bars, lu-t'æ'-tông 扶°梯檔
BAMBOO, coh 竹; (ih-keng, ih-kwang, ih-ts; with a root, ih-cü);— grove, coh' ling 竹林;—for eating, shing 筍;— canes, coh' ken 竹竿; to whip with a —, tang pæn'-ts 打板子; the sacred —, t'in coh' 沃竹
BANANA, ts'ing-kyiao' 青蕉; hyiang-kyiao' 香蕉
BAND, a tape or strip, ih-keng ta' 一根帶°;— of drawers, or skirt, iao 腰; a — of men, ih-de nying 一隊人°; a — of soldiers, ih-ts' ping-mô' 一支兵馬; a — of musicians, ih-pæn' c'ü-tông 一班°吹°手°
BANDAGE, to dzin 纏;—the feet, dzin kyiah' 纏脚; ko kyiah' 裹脚
BANDAGES, foot kyiah'-sô 裹°脚°布°, used by Chinese females.
BANDITTI, dzeh-fi 賊匪; gyiaug-dao' 強盜; local —, t'u'-fi 土匪 (ih-tông, ih-pæn)
BANG, to — with a stick, &c., k'ao 拷;— against, bang-djoh' 撞著°
BANGING noise, bang-bang'-hyiang 嘭嘭響; dang-dang'-hyiang 宕宕響
BANISH, to (1,000 to 2000 li) veng-liu' 問流;— (a few hundred li), veng-du' 問徒;— (be-

yond the frontier for life, or for posterity), ts'ong-kyüing' 充軍

BANK of earth, na-nyi dông' 泥塘; — of stone, kao-k'en' 高礅; mound, kao-te' 高堆; river —, kông-ngen' 江°岸; kông-dông 江°塘; — for money, nying-'ao' 銀號;— bill, nying-p'iao' 銀票

BANQUET, tsiu'-zih 酒席; tsiu'-yin 酒筵; do-tsiu'; to go to a —, fu zih' 赴席; to partake of a —, zo zih' 坐席; to prepare a —, shih zih' 設°席; bæn do-tsiu'.

BANTER, to hyi'-hyiah 戲謔; he banters me, gyi' teng ngô hyi'-hyiah 其與°我戲謔

BAPTISM (by sprinkling), si'-li 洗禮; — (by immersion), tsing'-li 浸禮; to receive —, ling si'-li 領洗禮; ziu tsing'-li 受浸禮

BAPTIZE, to —, 'ang si'-li 行°洗禮; 'ang tsing'-li 行°浸禮

BAR, cross wang-tông' 橫°檔; ditto for a door, meng-shün' 門閂; secret —, kyü-shün'; en-shün' 暗閂; upright —, dzih-tông' 直檔; ditto for door, teng'-shün 直閂; sand —, sô-t'æn' 沙灘

BAR the door, shün meng' 閂門; shut the door and — it, kwæn meng', loh shün' 關門落閂

BARB, hook with a —, tao'-tsah-keo' 倒紮鈎; barbed spear, keo-lin'-ts'iang 鈎鐮鎗

BARBARIAN, mæn-nying' 蠻人°; yia'-nying 野°人°; outside —, fæn-nying' 番人°; yi-nying' 夷人°; friendly —, joh-fæn' 熟番: strange, and hence unfriendly —, sang-fæn' 生°番

BARBAROUS, cruel, yi-hyüong'-væn-oh' 行兇作°惡

BARBER who shaves heads, t'i-deo'-s-vu' 薙頭司務

BARE, c'ih 出; kwông 光; — arms, siu'-kwang c'ih'-liao.

BARE-FACED, shameless, tæ-liu' 歹臉; 'eo' min-bi' 厚面皮

BARE-FOOTED, c'ih-kyiah' 出脚

BARE-HEADED, c'ih-deo' 出頭

BARELY, tsih 只; tæn-tsih' 單只; — enough to use, tsih' keo yüong' 只殼用

BARGAIN, to argue the price, leng'-liang kô'-din 論量價°錢°; kông 'ông-dzing' 講°行情

BARGAIN, to agree upon a — (after arguing), kông'-k'æ 講°開; picked up a good —, ts'eh'-læ-go ky'iao'-cong 撮來个°巧幷; hoped to gain, but lost by the —, iao' bin-i, shü bin-i' 要便宜°輸便宜°

BARK of a tree, jü bi' 樹皮

BARKS, the dog —, keo kyiao' 狗叫

BARLEY, mi'-jing 米仁; — (as a medicine), i-yi'-jing 薏苡仁
BAROMETER, fong-yü'-piao 風雨表 (ih-go)
BARRACKS, ying-vông' 營房
BARREL, dong 桶; *flour* —, min-feng-dong' 麵粉桶; — (*i. e.* a drum-shaped tub), hwô-kwu-dong' 花鼓桶; *four barreled revolver*, s'-meng-deo siu'-ts'iang 四門頭手鎗
BARREN *land*, peh' mao-ts di' 不毛之地; — *womb*, zah t'æ' 石°胎
BARRICADE, dza-sah' 寨柵; — *of earth*, nyi-dzing' 泥城; — *of stakes*, sah'-lah 柵欄°
BARRICADE, *to* coh dza-sah' 築寨柵; coh nyi-dzing' 築泥城 (coh or tsoh)
BARRIER, *customs*' kwæn-k'eo' 關口; k'a'-ts sah'-lah 卡子柵欄'
BARTER, *to* ho'-diao-ho' 貨調貨; yi-ho'-yih ho' 以貨易貨; kao-yih' 交°易
BASE, *of low birth*, pe-zin' 卑賤°; 'ô'-zin 下°賤°; — *morally*, 'ô'-liu 下°流; 'ô'-tsoh 下°作
BASE, *bottom*, *or stand*, zo-ts' 座°子; bun-ts' 盤子
BASHFUL, p'ô-siu' 怕羞; p'ô-wông-k'ong' 怕惶恐
BASIN, beng 盆; tseng 甑; bun 盤; *wash* — (face), min-beng' 面盆; min-dong' 面桶; *bread*

—, mun-deo' bun 饅頭盤 (ih-tsah)
BASKET (with a handle), læn 籃; *clothes* —, lo 籮; *fruit* —, bu 籓; *charcoal* —, leo 簍; — *for washing rice*, dao-lo' 淘籮; sao-kyi' 筲箕; *provision* —, ho'-zih-læn' 火食籃; *work* —, tsia-k'ong-læn' 織°筐°籃 (ih-tsah)
BASTARD, yia'-cong 野°種; zeh-cong' 雜種; (foreign and Chinese), c'ün-cong' 串種
BASTE, *to* ting 釘; *first* — (it), sin ting'-ih-ting 線釘一釘; — *coarsely*, dziang-tsing' ting 長針釘
BAT, pin-foh' 蝙蝠; *bat's dung*, yia-ming'-sò 夜°明沙 (Med.)
BATH, *to take a* —, gyiang ih-go nyüoh' 洗°一個°浴°
BATHE, *to* gyiang nyüoh' 洗°浴°
BATHING-TUB, gyiang'-nyüoh-dong 洗°浴°桶
BATTER, *to* k'eh'-bang 磕撞; — *and spoil*, k'eh'-bang-diao 磕撞壞°
BATTERED *by the weather*, (*i. e.* rain and sun), yü tang', nyih sa', wæ'-de 雨打日°曬壞了°
BATTERY *for mounted cannon*, p'ao'-dæ 礮臺
BATTLE, *to fight a* —, tang ih' dzing 打一陣; *field of* —, tsin'-dziang 戰塲

BATTLE-AXE, yüih-fu' 鉞斧
BATTLEMENT, embrasure, p'ao'-meng 礮門
BAWL, to ying-ky'i'-ka-kyiao' 喧譁之°聲
BAY, hæ-wen' 海灣 (ih go);— horse, ts'ih' mô 赤馬
BAYONET, heo mi-pô' 鼉尾°巴
BE, to — at home, læ oh'-li 在°家°裏; let it — there, peh gyi kæ-kæn' 俾其在°彼°; — (in the imperative), iao 要; yüong 用; — careful, iao kwu'-djoh 要顧着°; yüong kwu'-djoh 用顧着°
BEACH, sea hæ pin-yin' 海邊沿
BEACON in the sea, hæ'-li-go piao-deo' 海裡个°標頭; light-tower, liang-t'ah' 亮塔; mound from which smoke rises to warn of danger, in-teng' 烟墩
BEADS, officers' dziao-cü' 朝珠; Buddhist rosary, su'-cü 數珠; aromatic —, hyiang-cü' 香珠; common —, siao-liao-cü' 燒料珠 (i. e. burned material); ngô'-cü 瓦°珠; a string of —, ih-c'ün cü' 一串珠
BEAK, bird's tiao cü-gyin' 鳥°嘴箝
BEAM, an important —, 'ang-diao' 桁條; the central — in the roof, tong'-liang 棟樑; — under the floor, koh'-sah 閣柵
BEAN, deo 荳 (ih-hh); the full number of beans in a pod, ih-kyih' 一莢
BEAN-CURD, deo-vu' 荳腐; tsiang'-deo-vu' 醬荳腐
BEAN-POD, deo-kyih'-k'oh' 荳莢壳
BEAR, to — on the shoulders, pe 背; to sustain, tông 當; tæn-tông' 擔當; dzing-tông' 承當; can — (it), tông-leh'-djü 當得°住; hao' dzing-tông' 好承當; ky'üoh'-leh-lôh 吃得°落; 'ông-leh'-djü 降得°住; can't — it, tông-feh-djü 當弗住; ky'üoh'-feh-lôh 吃弗落; I'll — the blame, tsah'-vah ngô', dzing-tông 責罰我承當; — fruit, kyih ko'-ts 結果子; sang ko'-ts 生°果子; kyih ko' 結果; the last is also used in speaking of persons, thus, nying kyih'-ko'-de 人°結果了°, means that the man has come to his end: if he has friends and money, he has come to a good end, hao'-kyih-ko' 好結果; has come to a bad end, m-kyih'-ko 無結果; — a child, sang na-hwun' 生°嬰°孩°; — the loss, be-din' ken-z' 賠錢°幹事; — in mind, liu dzæ sing'-li 留在心裏;— on one's heart (as something at a distance), kyi'-kwô 記罣; ought to — patiently, ing-kæ' jing'-næ 應該忍耐;

ing-kæ' 'en-jing' 應該合忍; can't — patiently, jing'-næ-feh-djü' 忍耐弗住; neh'-feh-djü' 納弗住; — with (or be indulgent to), kw'un yüong' 寬容; ought not to — with, yüong'-feh-teh'-go 容弗得个°; — witness, tso te'-tsing 做對証

BEARD, ngô.su' 髭鬚.

BEARER, burden kyiah'-pæn 脚班; kyiah'-fu 脚夫; t'iao-fu' 挑夫; kyiah'-tæn 脚擔; sedan —, gyiao-fu' 轎夫; — of a letter, song-sing'-go 送信个°; ta-sing'-go 帶信个°

BEAST, cong-sang' 畜生; wild —, yia'-siu 野°獸; — (a term of reproach), ky'üoh'-sang.

BEASTLY conduct, cong-sang' 'ang-we' 畜生°行°爲; gying-siu' 'ang-we' 禽獸行°爲

BEAT, to tang 打; k'ao 敲°; djü; — rice, tang dao' 打稻; gwæn dao' 摜稻; — (as the pulse), t'iao 跳; — a drum, k'ao kwu' 敲°鼓; — cotton, dæn min-hwô' 彈棉花; — clothes (in washing), djü i-zông 搗衣裳; — the back, djü pe' 敲°背; — down the price, tang'-loh kô-diæ 打落價°錢°; — time, ah pæn' 拍°板; — the breast (meaning, I'll be responsible), tah hyüong' 拍°胸

BEAUTIFUL, hao'-k'en 好看; —

(lit., pleasing), teh-nying'-sih 得°人°惜; zi-tsing'; very —, me'-mao 美貌; piao-cü' 標緻

BEAUTIFY, to tsông-sih' 妝飾; tsah'-kwah 紥刮; tsông-pæn' 妝扮; tang-pæn' 打扮 (the latter used of the person only.)

BEAVER-SKIN, (or otter-skin), t'ah' bi 獺皮

BECALMED, no wind, fong-ky'i', tu 朆-neh 風氣都沒°有°; ship is —, fong 朆-neh, jün dong'-feh-dong' 風沒°有°船動弗動

BECAUSE, ing-we' 因爲; we'-leh 爲了°; we'-tih-z 爲的是

BECOME, to tso 做; dzing 成; pin 變; fah 發; to — a king, tso wông-ti' 做皇帝; — a good man, dzing ih-go hao' nying' 成一个° 好人°; caterpillar becomes a butterfly, djong' pin'-hwô wu-diah' 蛊變化蝴蝶; — rich, fah' dzæ 發財; — angry, fah ông'; what will — (of it) in the end? dza kyih'-gyüoh 怎結局? dza kyih'-sah 怎°結煞?

BECOMING to him, (garments), 'eh gyi'-go sing-dzæ' 合其个° 身材; that dress is — to you, keh' gyiæ i-zông, teng ng' siang-nyi' 這°件衣裳與°你°相宜

BED, or BEDSTEAD, min-zông' 眠床° (ih-tsiang); want to go to

—, iao min-zông'-li ky'i-de 耍眠床°裡去°了°
BED-BUG, ts'iu'-djong 臭°蟲
BED-CURTAINS, tsiang'-ts 帳子
BEDDING, p'u-kæ' 鋪蓋
BED-FELLOW, p'ing-zông-go 摒床°个°; dong zông'-go nying 同床°个°人°; p'ing-p'u'-go 摒鋪个°
BED-ROOM, my ngô'-go vông 我个°房; sleeping-room, ngo-vông' 臥房; kw'eng'-vông 睡房, rarely used.
BED-TIME, kw'eng'-go z-'eo' 睡个°時候; en-cü' z-'eo 安置時候
BEE, fong-ts' 蜂子; honey —, mih-fong' 蜜蜂 (ih-go)
BEE-HIVE, (tub-shaped), fong-dong' 蜂桶 (ih-tsah)
BEEF, ngeo-nyüoh' 牛°肉°; a roast of —, lo'-s, the English word.
BEEF-STEAK, (beef to be fried), t'ah'-go ngeo-nyüoh' 燗个°牛°肉°; the best is from the parts called, pah'-z-kweh 八字骨, ô-bang-kweh yin', (low), and sæn-koh-lông 三角°廊
BEER, bitter wine, kw'u'-tsiu 苦酒; bi'-tsiu, the English word combined.
BEES-WAX, mih-lah' 蜜蠟; yellow —, wông-lah' 黃蠟
BEET, 'ong-ts'æ'-deo 紅菜頭
BEFALL, to ling-djoh' 臨°着
BEFITTING, 'eh-nyi' 合宜; nyi 宜

BEFORE, some time —, zin-deo' 前°頭; dzong-zin' 從前°; in front, læ zin-deo' 在°前°頭; læ min-zin' 在°面前°; — the flood, 'ong-shü' yi-zin' 洪水°以前°; — and behind, ziu 'eo' 前°後; — the door, læ meng zin' 在°門前°; came — me, sin'-jü rgô' læ'-go 先我來个°; as —, dzing-gyiu' 仍舊; i-gyiu' 依舊; tsiao-gyin' 照舊; — one's eyes, læ ngæn min-zin' 在眼°面前

* This expression implies also time near, whether just past, or just coming, and also a very short distance; thus: —if a person died a few days since, ngæn'-min-zin si'-go 眼面前死°个°

BEFOREHAND, yü'-sin 預先; tsao'-tsao 早早; tsao'-sin 早先; to prepare —, yü'-sin be-bæn' hao 預先備辦好
BEFRIEND, to tsiao'-ing 照應
BEG, to t'ao 討; — for, gyiu-ky'ih 求乞; to entreat, gyiu-k'eng' 求懇; — food (i.e. rice), t'ao væn' 討飯; iao væn' 要飯; ditto (politely) tsia liang' 借°粮; — mercy, or favor (for another on the ground of greater respectability), t'ao dzing' 叨情; ma min-k'ong' 賣°面孔; — you to excuse me, gyiu ng nyün-liang'-ngô 求你°原諒我; — your pardon, teh' ze 得罪 (lit., I have sinned against you); — (as a Buddhist priest (or nun) for the

BEG 40 BEL

monastery), hwô-yün' 化緣; ts'ao hwô' 抄化

BEGGAR, t'ao-væn'-go 討飯个°; ky'ih'-kæ 乞丐; *professional male* —, kao'-hwô-ts 叫化子°; *looks like a* —, t'ao'-væn-siang 討飯相

BEGIN, *to* k'æ-siu' 開手; ts'u-k'æ'-siu 初開手; ky'i'-siu 起首; dong-siu' 動手; tso-ky'i-deo' 做起頭; ts'u-ky'i'-deo 初起頭; k'æ-kô'; k'æ-dæ'; k'æ-deo-meng' 開頭; *beginning to learn*, 'oh ky'i-deo' 學°起頭; *ditto books*, zông-'oh' 上學°; — *a journey*, dong-sing' 動身; *ditto by boat*, k'æ-jün' 開船; — *a long journey*, ky'i-dzing' 起程; — *a large work* (as building a house), dong-kong' 動工; hying-kong' 興工

BEGINNER, *one inexperienced*, nga-'ông' 外行; *raw hand*, sang-siu' 生手; *one doing a thing for the first time*, bao-z' tsʻo'-go 暴時做个°

BEGINNING, ky'i-deo' 起頭; ky'i'-ts'u 起初; bao-z' 暴時; *in the* —, toh'-fah-ts-deo 元始; *ditto of the world*, k'æ-bih'-go z-'eo 開闢个°時候; k'æ-t'in'-p'ih-di z-'eo' 開天闢°地時候

BEGONE! ky'i 去°! tseo'-k'æ 走開! tseo'-ko 走過!

BEGRUDGE *him the possession of*, pô-feh-neng'-keo gyi ǎ'-teh 巴

弗能穀其沒°有°;— *giving*, feh-sô'-teh, dzæ-c'ih' 弗捨°得助出

BEHALF, *on account of*, we'-leh 爲了°; *I speak in* — *of my younger brother*, ngô we'-leh ah-di kông'-go 我爲了°阿弟講个°; *for him*, dæ gyi' 代其; t'i' gyi 替其

BEHAVES *well*, sih'-sih-ka-go.

BEHAVIOR, 'ang-we' 行°爲; 'ang-i'-dong-zing' 行意動靜; 'ang-ts'-kyü'- dong 行°止舉動; *childish* —, siao'-nying i'-tsi 小孩°意致°

BEHEAD, *to* sah-deo' 殺頭; tsæn-deo' 斬頭; c'ü kyüih' 取決; — *him*, sah-gyi-deo' 殺其頭

BEHIND, 'eo'-pe 後背; — *time* ko-z'-de 過時了°; — *the times*, be-z'-de 背°時了°; — *one's back*, pe'-'eo 背後

BEHIND-HAND *with one's work*, sang-weh' deh-loh'-de 生°活疊落了°; sang-weh te'-ky'i-læ-de 生°活堆去°來了°; sang-weh' tin-ky'i'-tong-de 生°活丟去了°

BEHOLD! ts'ia'-k'en 且°看! nô!

BELCH, *to* — (from the stomach), tang-eh' 打呃; — (as a volcano), p'eng 噴

BELFRY, cong-leo' 鐘樓 (ih-zo)

BELIEVE, *to* siang-sing' 相信; — *entirely*, toh'-jih siang-sing' 篤

實相信; an exclamation, as much as to say *don't believe it*, 'æ 唉°! yi 咦! expressing both disbelief and surprise, yiu-ka'-t'in-wô'.

BELIEVER, siang-sing'-go cü'-kwu 相信个人°

BELL, *large* cong 鐘 (ih-kô); *small* —, ling 鈴 (ih-go)

BELL-CLAPPER, cong-zih' 鐘舌 (ih-go)

BELLOWS, ky'in-fong'-go tong-si' 牽風个東西; *Chinese* —, fong-siang' 風箱 (ih-bu); *to blow the* —, ky'in fong-siang' 牽風箱

BELLY, dn'-bi 肚皮; — *ache*, du'-bi t'ong' 肚皮痛

BELONGS, joh-ü' 屬于; dzæ-ü' 在于

BELOVED, ts'ing-æ'-go 親愛个°; dzih-din'-go 值錢个° (primarily worth money).

BELOW, 'ô-deo' 下頭; ti-'ô' 底下°

BELT, ta 帶°; — *for the waist*, iao-ta' 腰帶° (ih-keng)

BEMOAN, to ta'-k'oh-ta-kyiao' 帶哭帶叫; æ-dziang' kw'u'-nao k'oh 哀腸苦腦哭

BENCH, teng 凳; pæn'-teng 板凳; *low* —, a'-teng 矮凳 (ih-keng, ih-kwang)

BEND, to ao'-cün 拗轉; ao'-wæn 拗彎; — (as a bow), pæn-k'æ' 扳開; — *forward*, eo'-tao 俯

BENEATH, ti-'ô' 底下°; — *the table*, coh'-teng ti-'ô' 桌凳底下°

BENEDICTION, coh-foh'-go shih-wô' 祝福个°說話

BENEFACTOR, eng-nying' 恩人°

BENEFICIAL, yiu ih'-c'ü 有益處; — *to him*, yiu ih' ü gyi' 有益於其

BENEFIT, ih'-c'ü 益處; hao-c'ü' 好處; *favor*, eng-we' 恩惠; *no* —, vn ih' 無益; *not only no* — *but on the contrary, injury*, fi-dæn' vu ih', fæn'-cün yiu 'æ' 非但無益反轉有害

BENEVOLENT, hao'-we-jün'-z 好爲善事; — *heart*, jing-æ'-go sing 仁愛个°心

BENT, wæn'-go 彎个°; — *and crooked*, wæn-ky'üoh'-go 彎曲个°

BENUMBED, moh'-de 木了°; *hands* —, siu moh'-de 手木了°

BEQUEATH, *to* yi-loh' 遺落; gao-loh'; — *property*, yi'-loh ts'æn-nyih 遺落產業

BERATE, *to* joh or zoh 辱; zoh-mô' 辱罵; *to* — *people*, joh-nying'-mô'-tao 辱人°罵倒

BEREAVED *of one's husband*, vi-vông'-jing 未亡人; ming-neh'-de 命沒°有了°; — *of one's wife*, dön-yin' 斷弦; shih-ngeo' 失偶; — *of a son*, sông-ting' 喪丁; — *of a brother*, siu'-tsoh sông-diao'-de 手足傷壞°了°

BESEECH, to gyiu-k'eng' 求懇; gyiu 求;— *earnestly*, ts'ih'-sing gyiu' 切心求; kw'u'-kw'u gyiu' 苦求

BESIDE, *at the side of*, læ bông-pin' 在°旁邊; tseh'-pin 側邊;— (himself) *with anger*, ky'i' hweng-de 氣悟了°

BESIDES, ling-nga' 另外°; djü-ts'-ts'nga' 除此之外°; *moreover*, ping'-ts'ia 弁且

BESIEGE, to we-kw'eng' 圍困; dön-dön' we-djü' 團團圍住

BESMEAR, to lön-du' 亂塗; lön-dzö' 亂搽; tsao 遭;— *the wall with mud*, ziang'-li, lön-du' na-nyi' 牆裡亂塗爛°泥

BESMEARED, *face — with molasses*, dông-lu' du-leh mun' min-k'ong 糖滷塗得滿面孔;— *the hands*, tsao'-leh mun' siu 塗°得°滿手

BESPEAK, to ding-hao' 定好; wô-hao' 話好; t'ao'-hao 討好°; *is the chair bespoken?* gyiao-ts t'ao'-hao ma 轎子討好麼°?

BEST, *the* ting'-hao 頂好; gyih-bao' 極好; ting'-zông-teng' 頂上等; kyü-tsé' 居最; tsé'-hao 最好; *the very —*, tsæ'-m-tsæ-hao' 再無°再好; *like this the best*, tsé' hwun-hyi keh'-go 最歡喜這°个°

BESTIR *one's self*, zi kyih' zi 自激自°

BESTOW, *to* s'-peh 賜給; sông'-s 賞賜;— *happiness*, sông'-s foh'-ky'i 賞賜福氣

BET, *to* tu-tong-dao' 賭東道

BETEL-NUT, ping-lông' 檳榔

BETRAY *treacherously*, ma'-long 賣弄;— *one's master for honor*, ma-cü' gyiu yüong 賣主求榮;— (as a secret), c'ih k'eo' 出口; lu fong' 露風; *Judas betrayed* (*i.e.* sold) *Jesus*, Yin-da' ma-Yiæ-su'-diao 猶大賣°耶穌了°

BETROTH, *to —* (a daughter), hyü-c'ih' 許出; he'-peh, or hyü'-peh 許與°;— (a son), ding-ts'ing' 定親

BETROTHAL *papers*, shü-ts' 禮書; *to exchange ditto*, 'ô-ding' 下°定; ko-shü' 傳紅'; 'ang-p'ing' 行°聘; 'ô-p'ing' 下°聘

BETTER, *a little* hao-tin' 好點; cün-cü'-tin 精°緻點; *still —*, keng'-kô hao' 更加°好; yüih-fah' hao 越發好; veng-nga'-hao 分外°好; kah'-nga hao 格外°好;— *than that*, hao-jü' keh'-go 好如這个°; pi keh'-go hao 比這个°好; ko'-jü keh'-go 過如這个°;— *that I should go*, feh jü ngô' ky'i' hao' 弗如我去°好; *the quicker, the —*, yüih kw'a' yüih hao' 越快越好;— *die*, tao'-feh-jü si', hao' 到弗如死好;

ting —, læ-tih hao'-ky'i-læ 正°在°好起來
BETTER, *to make* —, tso cün-cü'-tin 做精°致點; long hao-tin' 弄好點
BETWEEN, *sit* —, *us*, zo' læ ah'-lah cong-nyiang' 坐在°我等中央; *a go* — (in marriage), me-nying' 媒人°; *ditto* (in business), cong-nying' 中人°
BEWAIL, *to* 'ao-li'-da-k'oh' 號啕°大哭
BEWARE, *be on your guard*, bông-be' 防備; *be careful*, tông-sing' 當心; *keep away from*, yün'-bi 遠避
BEWILDER, *to* mi 迷; mi-djü 迷住
BEWILDERED, hweng-mi'-de 惛迷了°
BEWITCH, *to* yüong zia-fah' yiu-'oh' 用邪°法誘惑
BEWITCHED, ziu mi'-tih-de 受迷了°
BEYOND, yi-nga' 以外°; ts-nga' 之外°; — *the bridge*, gyiao keh' ngen' 橋那°岸; — (over) *the river*, tê' kông 對江°; *on that side*, keh'-pun-pin 那°半邊; — *my calculations*, c'ih ngô i'-siang ts-nga' 出我意想之外°; *to live* — *one's means*, vông'-yüong dong-din' 妄用銅錢°
BIAS, *to cut* —, ts'ia' zæ 斜°裁; *to cut satin on the* —, zia'-diao dön'-ts 斜°條緞子

BIASSED, *prejudiced*, sang-wang-sing'-de 生°橫°心了°
BIB, *an infant's* —, 'ô-bô-teo' 下°吧兜; — *used when eating*, ky'üoh-væn-pe-tæn' 吃飯背單; væn-tæn' 飯單; zih-tæn' 食單
BIBLE, Sing'-shü 聖書; Sing'-kying 聖經
BICKER, *to* k'eo'-kyüoh 口角; siang-tsang' 相爭°
BICKERING, *endless* to-k'eo'-to-zih' 多口多舌
BID *him go*, wô-hyiang'-gyi-dao', hao ky'i' 告訴°其好去°; — *him come in*, eo gyi tsing' læ 叫°其進來; — *adieu*, bih'-ih-bih' 別一別
BIER, kwun-zæ'kô'-ts 棺材°架°子
BIG, *do* 大°; *to grow* —, do-ky'i'-læ 大°起來; *to talk* — (boast), kông do-wô' 講大°話
BIGOTED, tsih'-ih feh t'ong' 執一弗通; tsih'-ih-feh-sing' 執一弗信; tsih'-mi-peh-ngwu' 執迷不悟
BILE, kw'u'-tæn 苦膽
BILGE-WATER, jün-ing'.
BILL *for silver*, nying p'iao' 銀票; — *for cash*, dzin-p'iao' 錢票; — *of sale*, fah'-p'iao' 發票; *to make out a* —, k'æ fah'-p'iao 開發票; — *of lading*, pao'-ho-tæn 報貨單
BILL *of a bird*, tiao cü-gyin' 鳥°嘴箝

BILLET, *note*, bin-z' 便字; z-den' 字條。
BILLION, jih væn'-væn 十萬萬
BILLOW, do lông' 大°浪 (ih)
BIN, *rice* mi' gyü 米櫃°; *coal* —, me-t'æn' gyü 煤炭櫃°
BIND, *to* pông 綁; kw'eng 綑; kw'eng-pông 綑綁; dzin 縛;— *that man*, keh-go nying kw'eng'-pông gyi 這°个°人°綑綁其;— *the feet*, dzin kyiah' 纏腳;— *the head*, pao deo' 包頭;— *the edge*, pin-yin', kweng ih'-da 邊沿綑一堆;— *books*, ting shü' 釘書; *bound firmly*, bo-djü'-liao 縛°住了; *to* — *as an apprentice*, zông kwæn-shü' 上關書
BINDING *of a book*, shü-min' 書面;— *is bad and must be renewed*, shü-min' wa', iao wun'-ko 書面孬°要換過
BIOGRAPHY, 'ang-jih' 行°術 (ih-peng)
BIRD, *a* ih-tsah tiao' 一隻鳥
BIRD-CAGE, tiao-long' 鳥°籠 (ih-tsah)
BIRD'S-NEST, k'o 窠; *edible* —, in'-o 燕窩 (ih-go)
BIRD-LIME, nyin-tiao'-go kao' 黏鳥°个膠°
BIRTH, *the time of* —, sang-c'ih-læ' z-'eo' 生°出來時候; *give* — *to a son*, sang ih-go ng-ts' 生°一个兒°子; *of low* —, zin-t'æ' 賤°胎; *of high* —, kwo'-ts 賞子

BIRTH-DAY, sang-nyih' 生°日°
BIRTH-PLACE, nyün-zih' 原籍; keng-sang'-t'u-yiang' 根生°土養; c'ih'-sing-ts-di' 出身之地
BISCUIT, siao'-ping 小餅; siao' mun-deo' 小饅頭
BISHOP, kyin-toh' 監督
BIT, *a little* —, ih-tin' 一點; ih-ngæn'; *a piece*, ih-kw'e' 一塊
BITCH, keo-nyiang' 母°狗°
BITE, *to* ngao 皎; *take a* —, ngao ih-k'eo' 皎°一口; *ditto* (as an animal), dzæn ih-k'eo'; *pepper bites the mouth*, wu-tsiao' lah cü'-pô 胡椒辣嘴吧
BITS *of a bridle*, mô'-ziah'-ts 馬嚼子;— *of broken crockery*, un mi-fu' 磁屑°
BITTER, kw'u 苦; *very* —, zah kw'u' 雜苦
BITUMEN, lih-ts'ing' 瀝青
BLACK, heh 黑, u 烏 both used of paint, hair, &c.; ts'ing 青, yün-seh' 元°色, both used of cloth, garments, thread, and silk; — *cotton cloth*, ts'ing pu' 青布;— *and blue* (as a bruise), u-ts'ing' 烏青;— *man*, heh' nying 黑人°; — *eyes*, ngæn'-cü u' 眼°珠烏
BLACKING, *shoe* shih-'a'-go-me' 刷鞋°个°煤; *stove* —, shih-ho'-lu-me' 刷火爐煤
BLACKEN, *to* long heh' 弄黑; tsao heh' 遭黑;— (*i. e. polish*) *the stove*, ho'-lu ts'ah' gyi yiu kwông' 火爐擦其有光;— *one's*

character, ao-tsao' shü p'eh' 壓精水°澱; 'en hyüih' p'eng nying' 含血噴人°.

BLACKSMITH, t'ih'-s-vu 鐵司務; t'ih'-ziang 鐵匠°.

BLADDER, *man's* bông-kwông', or bông-hwông 膀胱; *hog's* —, cü shü'-p'ao 猪尿°脬°.

BLADE, *a — of grass*, ih-keng ts'ao' 一根草; *knife* —, tao-sing' 刀身 (rare); *edge of* —, tao-k'eo' 刀口; *shoulder* —, væn-ts'iao' kweh 飯鍫骨.

BLAMABLE, kæ tsah'-vah 該責罰; yiu ts'o'-c'ü 有錯°處; *he is* —, kwe-gyiu' ü gyi' 歸咎于其.

BLAME, *to* s-we'; tsah 責; tsah'-be 責備; tsah'-vah 責罰; — *mentally*, kwa 怪°; — *unjustly*, ts'oh'-kwa 錯怪; *can — me*, kwe gyiu' ü ngô' 歸咎于我; *need not — me*, moh kwa' ngô 莫怪°我; — *another, when guilty one's self*, t'e-t'oh' 推托.

BLAMELESS, vu k'o tsah'-go 無可責个; vu-tsah'-c'ü 無責處; 並 ts'o'-c'ü 無錯°處; *entirely* —, 'ao vu' ts'o'-c'ü 毫無錯°處.

BLAND, weng-'o' 溫和; no-jün' 懦善.

BLANK, k'ong 空; bah 白°; — *book*, k'ong bu'-ts 空簿子.

BLANKET, nyüong-bi' 羢被°; nyüong-t'æn' 羢毯 (ih-diao).

BLASPHEME, *to* sih'-doh 褻瀆.

BLAST, *a* ih-dzing fong' 一陣風.

BLAZE, ho'-yin 火焰; yin-deo' 焰頭.

BLAZE, *to — up*, ho'-yin ts'ong-zông' 火焰冲上; — *abroad*, koh'-c'ü djün-yiang' 各處傳揚.

BLEACH, *to* p'iao'-bah 漂白°.

BLEATING, yiang'-kyiao 羊叫; 羋 咩°.

BLEED, *to* c'ih-hyüih' 出血; *to — a person*, teng nying' fông hyüih' 與°人°放血; — *by lancing quickly*, t'iao hyüih' c'ih 挑血出.

BLED *to death*, hyüih' liu-sah'-de 血流死了°.

BLEMISH, pæn-pô' 瘢疤; pæn-tin' 瘢點; —(in the flesh, or in one's character), yüô-tin' 瑕玷; *fault*, mao-bing' 毛病.

BLEND, *to mix*, 'o-long' 和攏; 'o-tæn'-long 和打°攏; c'ün'-long 串攏; — *thoroughly*, c'ün'-leh diao-yüing' 串得°調匀; *to unite*, siang-lin' 相連; p'ing-long' 拚攏.

BLESS, *to* coh-foh' 祝福; — *God*, coh'-zia Jing-ming' 祝謝 神明; — (as priests do), ts'æn'-nyiæn 懺念.

BLESSEDNESS, *happiness*, foh'-ky'i 福氣; foh'-veng 福分.

BLESSING, *to ask a — upon*, coh'-tsæn 祝讚.

BLIGHT *from wet*, læn 爛

BLIGHTED *harvest*, kæn nyin-dzing' 減°年成; nyin-dzing' wa' 年成孬°; — *hopes*, sing-hwé-i'-læn 心灰意懶

BLIND, hah-ngæn' 瞎眼; — *person*, hah'-ts 瞎子; sông-ngæn' moh-pih' 雙眼°摸壁; kwu'-moh 瞽目; — *in one eye*, doh-ngæn' 獨眼°; *blinded and deceived*, ziu mong pi'-de 受蒙蔽了°

BLIND, *to* mun 瞞; ming-mun'-en'-p'in 明瞞暗騙; mun-sæn'-en'-s 瞞三掩°四; *blinded by love*, be æ'-sing tsô-pi'-de 被愛心遮°蔽了°

BLINDS, *window* k'æn'-meng 板窗°; *venetian* —, fæn-ts'ông 翻窗; pah'-yih-ts'ông 百葉窗; *bamboo* —, coh lin'-ts 竹簾子; *let down ditto*, lin'-ts 'ô'-loh 簾子下°落

BLINDFOLD, *to* pao ngæn'-tsing 包眼°睛

BLIND-MAN'S-BUFF, moh-en'-ts 摸暗子

BLINK, *to wink*, ngæn'-tsing sah'-sah 眼睛眨眨

BLINKING *eyes (i.e. half shut)*, to-sah-ngæn' 多睡眼°; ziang hô-c'ü-ngæn' ka 像瞌眵眼°个°

BLISTER, p'ao 皰; *to raise a* —, ky'i p'ao' 起皰; — *plaster*, ky'i p'ao' kao-yiah' 起皰膏藥

BLITHE, p'ao'-c'ing; kw'a'-weh 快°活

BLOAT, *to* fah-hyü' 發虛; fah-cong' 發腫

BLOCK *of wood*, ih-kw'é' moh-deo' 一塊木頭; *chopping* —, tsing-deo' 椹頭; *hatter's* —, mao-kw'é' 帽盔; — *for printing*, ing'-pæn 印板; *child's blocks* siao-jü-den' 小樹頭°

BLOCKADE, *to* — *a river*, fong kông 封港; — *a port*, fong hæ'-k'eo 封海口

BLOCKHEAD, ngæ-moh'-deo 呆木頭; ngæ-nying' 呆人°

BLOOD, byüih 血; *to shed* —, liu hyüih' 流血

BLOOD-RELATION, ts'ing-kweh'-hyüih 親骨血

BLOOD-SHOT *eyes*, ngæn'-tsing 'ong' 眼°睛紅

BLOOD-THIRSTY, sah'-sing djong' 殺性重

BLOOD-VESSELS, hyüih'-kwun 血管; — *and tendons*, mah-loh' 脈絡

BLOSSOM, hwô 花 (ih-tô)

BLOSSOM, *to* k'æ-hwô' 開花

BLOT, *spot*, tsih'-le 跡累; *ink-spot*, moh-tsih' 墨跡 (ih-go)

BLOT, *to* tang moh-tsih' 打墨跡; — *out*, du-diao' 塗了°

BLOTCH, 'ong-pæn' 紅斑; cü-sô'-pæn 硃砂斑 (ih-tin)

BLOTTER (for daily accounts),

liu-shü' bu 流水°簿; *paper* —, seng-moh'-go ts 沁墨个°紙
BLOW, *to give a* —, tang ih' kyi 打一記; *give thirty blows* (with a bamboo). tang sæn'-jih pæn' 打三十板; *a — with the fist*, ih-gyün' 一拳
BLOW, *to* c'ü 吹°; — *the trumpet*, c'ü 'ao-dong' 吹°號筒; *the wind blows on me*, fong c'ü'-djoh ngô' 風吹°着°我; — *the nose*, hying bih-deo' 掀鼻°頭; — *out the candle*, c'ü' lah-coh' u 吹°熄°蠟燭; — *hard*, 'eo-ky'i'-lih c'ü' 侯氣力吹°; — *down*, c'ü-tao' 吹°倒; — *away*, c'ü-ky'i' 吹°去°; — *up with gunpowder*, yüong ho'-yiah hong-diao' 用火藥轟壞°
BLUDGEON, do-deo'-kweng 大°頭棍
BLUE, kæn 藍; *light* —, yüih-bah' 月白°; *very dark* —, sing-læn' 深藍; ts'ing-læn' 清藍; ih-p'ing-læn' 一品藍; *Prussian* —, yiang-ts'ing' 洋青; — *vitriol*, tæn'-væn 胆礬
BLUFF *language* (or manner), pæn'-pæn-go k'eo'-ky'i 板板个°口氣
BLUNDER, *to* ts'o'-shih 錯°失; long-ts'o' 弄錯
BLUNDERING, ts'o'-shih to 錯°失多
BLUNT (as an edge), deng 鈍; — *in manner*, dzih-sing 直心;

— *in manner, or language*, sing-k'eo'-kw'a 心直°口快°; *very — language*, toh'-fong-deo shih-wô' 篤鋒頭說話
BLURRED (as print), mo-wu'-de 模糊了°; — (as writing), moh-tsih' k'a-k'æ' 墨跡揩開; — *eyes*, ngæn'-tsing hwô'-de 眼°睛花了°
BLUSH, *to* 'ong-ky'i'-læ 紅起來; — *easily* (thin skin), min-bi boh' 面皮薄
BLUSTER, *to talk noisily*. hæ-we'-gyi-dæn' 海外奇談
BOAR, p'oh-cü'; *wild hog*, yia-cü' 野猪
BOARD, *a* ih-kw'e pæn' 一塊板; *chess* —, gyi-bun' 棋盤
BOARDS, *the six* —, loh bu' 六部 *viz* : —
Board of Civil Office, li-bu' 吏部
„ *of Revenue*, wu'-bu 戶部
„ *of Rites*, li-bu' 禮部
„ *of War*, ping-bu' 兵部
„ *of Punishments*, ying-bu' 刑部
„ *of Works*, kong-bu' 工部
BOARD, *to* kyi'-deng 寄庼; *to take one's meals*, kyi'-væn 寄飯; kyi-zih' 寄食; — *money*, væn-din' 飯錢°
BOAST, *to* p'u-tsiang' 鋪張; ts'ing-neng' 稱能; ts'ing-hyüing' 稱䚒; *to make an empty* —, c'ô-dæn' 詫誕; p'u-kying'; kw'ô-k'eo' 誇口; kông do-wô' 講°大°

話; kông kw'eh'-wô 講閒話
BOASTING, always — of one's good deeds, kwæn'-iao-zông cü 慣要發°誚°; zông'-cü-zông-teh'.
BOAT, jün 船; t'ing 艇; sæn-pæn' 杉舨 (ih-tsah); passenger —, 'ông-jün' 航船; ferry —, du-jün' 渡船; foot-paddle —, kyiah-wô-jün' 腳划船
BOAT-LOAD, a ih-zæ' 一 蟻
BOATMAN, head lao-da' 老大; assistant —, jün'-li-ho'-kyi 船裡夥計
BODY, kyi'-sing; sing-t'i' 身體; the whole —, weng'-sing 渾身; 'en kyi'-sing 遍°身°體°
BODILY, kyi'-sing-go 身°體°上°; — energies, tsing-jing' 精神
BODY-GUARD, of the emperor, z-we' 侍衛; — of officials, ming-tsông' 民壯
BOG, wu-nyi'-di 汙°泥地; læn-din' 爛田
BOIL, ts'ông 瘡 (ih-go); — caused by heat, nyih-cih' 熱°癤; nyih-cih-len' 熱°癤癏
BOIL, to ts 煮°; zah 煠; kweng 滾; — some water, shü teng'-teng kweng 水°燉燉滾; — the milk, na kweng-kweng' gyi 嬭°要°燉°滾; — sugar, tsin dông 煎糖; — the egg soft, kyi-dæn' iao ts'-leh dông-wông'-go 雞蛋要煮°得蕩黃°个°; — tender, ts nen' 煮頓

BOILER, Chinese 'oh 鑊 (ih-k'eo); tin —, mô'-k'eo-t'ih ko' 馬口鐵鍋
BOILING water, kweng' shü 滾水°; k'æ shü' 開水°; — hot (i. e. bubbling), dah-dah' kweng 沓沓滾
BOISTEROUS, hæ-we'-gyi-dæn' 海外°奇談
BOLD, not afraid, tæn'-ts do' 膽子大°; presumptuous, tæn'-ts do yia'-ky'i' 膽子大°野氣; not bashful, feh-p'ô'-wông-k'ong' 弗怕惶恐; 'eo-min'-bi 厚面皮; — bad woman, p'eh'-vu 潑婦
BOLDLY, fông'-tæn 放膽; to speak —, k'æn-kæn'-r-dæu' 侃侃而談
BOLT of a door, meng-shün' 門閂
BOLT the door, shün meng' 閂門
BOND for house, or money lent, pih'-kyü 筆據; customs' —, pao'-tæn 保單; deed, veng-ky'i' 文契
BONDS, in —, or bound in chains, be lin-diao' so'-djü-liao 被鏈鎖條住了°
BONE, kweh'-deo 骨頭 (ih-keng)
BONNET, a hat, ih-ting mao-ts' 一頂帽子; man's — for protection from wind, fong-teo' 風兜; old woman's ditto, yü-deo'-mao 圍°頭帽
BONZE, 'o-zông' 和尚

BOOK, shü 書 (ih-peng, ih-bu, ih-ts'ah); *religous* —, kying 經
BOOK-BINDER, ting-shü'-go-nying 釘書个人°
BOOK-CASE, shü-djü' 書廚; *an open* —, shü-kô' 書架°
BOOK-KEEPER, kwun'-tsiang sin'-sang 管帳先生°
BOOK-SELLER, shü-k'ah' 書客; shü-fông'-tin'-kwun' 書坊主人
BOOK-STORE, shü-fông'-tin 書坊店
BOOR, *countryman*, hyiang-'ô'-nying 鄉下°人°
BOORISH, ts'u-mæn' 粗蠻
BOOTS, hyü 鞾; *rain* —, yü'-hyü' 雨鞾; ting-hyü' 釘鞾 (*a pair*, ih sông)
BOOTY, *stolen* tsông 贓; zeh-tsông' 賊贓; zeh-t'eo-ho' 賊偷貨; *arms taken in war*, deh-læ'-ky'i'-yiæ 奪來个°器械; *plunder*, lo'-læ-go tong-si' 擄來个°東西
BORAX, bang-sô' 硼砂; yüih-zah' 月石°
BORDER, *margin*, pin-yin' 邊沿; *boundary*, kao-ka' 交界°;—(*of a field*), ts'-ka 址界°;—(*of a country*), we-ka'-go di-fông' 爲界°个°地方;—*of a garment*, i-zông' ken-den' 衣裳°衿頭°
BORE, *to* tsön, *or* cün 鑽;—*a hole*, tsön ngæn'-ts 鑽眼°子

BORN, *when was the baby* —? na-hwun' ky'i'-z sang-go 嬰°孩°幾°時生个°?
BORN AGAIN, *to be* dao'-sing tsæ sang'-c'ih-læ 道心再生出°來; *leave the old for the new*, ky'i'-gyiu' wun-sing' 棄舊換新; *begin again to live*, ih'-li-tsnying'; dzong-sin'-tso-nying' 重新°做人°; *as if to cast skin, and change bones*, ziang t'eh'-bi-wun-kweh'-ka 像脫皮換骨个°
BORROW, *to* tsia 借°; *borrowed money*, tsia'-kw'un 借°欵; tsia'-'ông 借°項
BOSOM, gwa 懷°; hyüong-kwun'-deo 胸膛°頭; *put in the* —, k'ông læ gwa'-li 囥在°懷裡
BOTANY, *the science of* —, hwô-moh'-gyüong-li-go 'oh-veng' 花木窮理个°學°問; *a Chinese work on* —, Gyüing-fông'-pu 羣芳譜
BOTCH-WORK, sang-weh' liao-ts'ao' 生°活潦草; sang-weh' liao-piao' 生°活潦表; sang-weh' ts'u-ts'ao' 生°活粗糙; feh ziang' sang-weh' 弗像生°活
BOTH, liang-go tu' 兩个°都; 'o-liang'-go; liang-'ô' 兩下°; liang-dzao' 兩造; pe'-ts' 彼此;—*are good*, liang'-k'o 兩可; *they are* —*there*, liang-go tu' læ'-kæn 兩个°都在°

彼°; are you — well? ng-lah 'o-liang-go tu hao' yia' 你等°兩个°都好唷°?

BOTHER, to ts'ao 嘈; lo'-so 囉唆; do not — me, m-nao ts'ao ngô' 弗°可°嘈我

BOTTLE, glass po-li' bing' 玻璃瓶 (ih-go); put into a —, tsi læ po-li' bing'-li 歯在°玻璃瓶裡

BOTTOM, ti 底

BOTTOMLESS, m-ti'-go 無°底个°

BOUGH, ô-ts' 極°枝 (ih kwang, ih-p'ing, ih-tiao)

BOUND, limit, 'æn'-cü 限°制; without —, m-'æn'-liang-go 無°限°量个°

BOUND, tied, bo-djü'-liao 縛°住了; kw'eng'-djü-liao 綑住了

BOUND, to set limits, lih 'æn' 立限°; — (as a state), kông siang-gyü'-go di'-fông 講°相距个°地方

BOUND, to — upward, t'iao'-ky'i-læ 跳起來; tsæu-ky'i-læ 躜起來; to — back, p'ong-cün-læ 撞°轉來; tao'-p'ong-cün' 倒撞°轉

BOUNDARY, feng-ka'-go di'-fông 分界°个°地方; frontier, kao-ka' 交°界°; landmark, ts'-ka 址界°.

BOUNDLESS, m-'æn'-cü 無°限°制; — ocean, hæ' m-pin' m-ngen'-go 海無°邊無°岸个°;

— love, æ'-sih m-gyüong'-dzing-go 愛惜無°窮盡个°

BOUNTIFUL, free in giving, c'ih'-siu do' 出手大°; — (as God, or as the emperor), kwông'-s-eng-we' 廣賜恩惠; — feast, tsiu'-zih fong-fu' 酒席豐盛°

BOUNTY, 'co'-s 厚賜; — (of a superior), sông'-s 賞賜; imperial —, wông-eng' 皇恩°

BOW, to make a — (with hands together), tsoh-ih' 作揖; a low — (in the same way), tang-kong' 打拱; — (bending one knee), tang ts'in-ts' 打蹲子; tang siao'-gyü 打小跪°; — and touch head, k'eh-deo' 磕頭; ditto and worship, k'eh'-deo li'-pa 磕頭禮拜°

BOW, kong 弓 (ih tsiang); to shoot with a —, zih 射; to shoot a bird with a —, zih' ih-tsah tiao' 射一隻鳥°

BOWELS, du'-dziang 肚腸; du'-bi 肚皮

BOW-KNOT, bu-kwu'-kyih 勢°鶻結; weh kyih' 活結; tie a —, tang bu-kwu'-kyih 打勢°鶻結

BOWL, un 碗 (ih tsah); finger —, gyiang'-siu-un 洗°手碗

BOWL-MENDER, ting-un'-go 釘碗个°

BOW-MAN, kong-tsin'-siu 弓箭手

BOW-STRING, kong-yin' 弓弦

BOW-WINDOW, pun'-yüih-ts'ông' 半月牕

BOX, siang-ts' 箱子 (ih-tsah); small —, 'eh-ts' 盒子 (ih-go).
BOX, to — with the fists, tang gyün-deo' 打拳頭; — the ear, tang r'-kwông 打耳光; — the cheek tang pô-công 打巴掌; — the mouth, tang teo-cü' 打兜嘴; to inclose in a box, tsông kæ siang-ts' li 裝在°箱子裡.
BOX-WOOD tree, wông-nyiang' jü' 黃楊°樹.
BOY, ẅæn孩°; u-ẅæn'; nen-ẅæn' 男孩°; siao-ẅæn' 小孩°; — (from ten to sixteen), dong-ts' 童子; a waiting — is called, ah-siao' 阿小; a — (serving in a school), shü-dong' 書僮.
BRACE (as in houses), ts'ang-djü' 撐柱; — (as in furniture), ts'ang-tông' 撐檔; — resting on the ground, tsiu'-djü 斈柱.
BRACE, to — by adding a piece, s' ih-go t'iah'-boh 使一个°貼°枕°; t'iah' ih-kw'e 貼°一塊.
BRACELET, siu'-gyüoh 手鐲 (one, ih-tsah; a pair, ih-te, ih-sông; a set, ih-fu).
BRACKET for supporting a shelf, ts'ang 撐 (ih-go).
BRACKETS, to inclose in —, keo-tsing' 勾進.
BRACKISH water, 'æn shü' 鹹°水°.
BRAG, to ts'ing-neng' 稱能; empty boast, kw'ô-k'eo' 誇口. See BOAST.
BRAID, silk s-bin' 絲辮; dotted

—, cü-zing' 珠繩; gold —, kying-bin' 金辮; to make —, tang bin' 打辮.
BRAID, to tang-bin' 打辮; gao-long' 絞攏; — the hair, tang bin'-ts 打辮子; — baskets, tang læn' 打籃; gao læn' 絞籃.
BRAIN, nao'-si 腦髓.
BRAN, wheat fu-bi' 麩皮; mah-bi' 麥皮; rice —, si'-k'ông 細糠; — flour, t'ong' feng 粗°粉. See UNBOLTED.
BRANCH of a tree, ô-ts' 椏°枝 (ih-kwang, ih-p'ang); — of a river, or family, ts-p'a' 支派°.
BRANCH, to feng ts-p'a' 分支派°.
BRAND, ho'-za-deo 火柴頭 (ih-kwang).
BRAND, to — (as criminals), ts'-z' 刺字; ts'ih-z' 刺字; — with a hot iron, tang ho'-ing 打火印; tang ho'-lao-ing' 打火烙°印; —(a priest, or devotee), fu kyiæ' 付戒; to receive such a —, ziu kyiæ', or ziu ka' 受戒.
BRANDISH, to yüih-læ' yüih-ky'i' 甩°來甩°去°.
BRANDY, nga'-koh siao-tsiu' 外°國燒酒; beh-kæn'-di, (the English word.)
BRASIER, dong-s'-vu 銅司務; dong-ziang' 銅匠°; traveling —, siao'-lu-s-vu' 小爐司務.
BRASS, dong 銅.
BRAVADO, yiao-vu' yiang-ẅe'-go kông'-shih 耀武揚威个°講°.

式°; c'ô-dæn'-go shih-wô 發°翻°个°說話. See BOAST.

BRAVE, üong'-ken 勇敢; *having great courage*, yiu tæn'-liang 有膽量; yiu ken-tæn' 有肝膽; *a — person*, ih-diao hao'-hen 一條好漢

BRAWL, *to* ts'ao'-nao 嘈鬧; tsang-zao' 爭°嘈°

BRAWNY, tsah'-ngang 實硬

BRAYING, *the — of an ass*, li-ts' kyiao' 驢子叫

BRAZEN, dong'-tso-go 銅做个°; *— faced* (thick), 'eo'-ô-lin-go 厚丫°臉个

BRAZIER, *a pan for coals with perforated cover*, ho'-ts'ong 火燼 See BRASIER.

BREACH, *to make a — in a wall*, ts'ah ziang-dong' 拆墻洞; *come in through the —*, ziang-dong'-li tsön-tsing'-læ 墻洞裏鑽進來; *there is a — of friendship between us*, ngô' teng gyi' djih-kyiao' 我與其絕交; *a — of morality*, sông fong-hwô' 傷風化; *— of promise*, shih-sing' 失信; shih-iah' 失約; *— of marriage contract*, t'e-hweng' 退婚; *ditto on the woman's part*, la-ts'ing' 賴°親

BREAD, mun-deo' 饅頭; *a slice of —*, ih-p'in' mun-deo' 一片饅頭

BREADTH, kw'eh 闊; *what is the — of that?* keh' yiu to'-siao kw'eh' 這°有多少闊!—*in cloth* (a little wider than common), foh'-meng kw'eh' 幅門闊; *a — of cloth*, ih-foh pu' 一幅布; *less a hair's —*, (lit. an eye-brow hair), ts'ô ih ni-mao' 差一眉°毛; *a hand —*, siu'-kwông ka kw'eh' 手掌°一°樣闊

BREAK, *to — in small pieces* (as cups, tiles, &c.), k'ao-wu' 敲°爛°; *— in pieces*, k'ao-se' 敲°碎; *— apart*, p'ah'-k'æ 擘開; *— (as a stick or pencil)*, dön ao'-dön 拗斷; *— by striking*, tang'-se 打碎; *ditto (as a stick)*, tang'-dön 打斷; *— by a blow*, k'ao-sông' 敲°傷; *— one's word*, shih-sing' 失信; sông-iah' 爽約; *— land*, k'æ-k'eng' cong-din' 開墾種田

BREAKFAST, t'in nyiang'-væn 天°亮°飯; tsao'-væn 早飯

BREAST, hyüong-kwun'-deo 胸懷°; *the breasts*, na 嬭°; *woman's —*, na-bu 嬭°袋° (one, ih-tsah)

BREAST-BONE, hyüong-dông'-kweh 胸膛骨

BREAST-PLATE, wu-sing'-kying 護心鏡

BREATH, ky'i 氣; k'eo'-ky'i 口氣; *offensive —*, k'eo'-ky'i ts'iu' 口氣臭°; *can't draw one's —*, ih' ky'i feh cün' 噎氣弗轉; *there is not a — of air*, ih tin' fong tu m̄'-neh 一點風都沒°有°; a 一, ih hwu' 一呼'; out of 一, ky'i'-kying 氣緊; pant for 一, t'eo ky'i' 嗒°氣'; 一 has stopped, ky'i dön'-de 氣斷了°.

BREATHE, to hwu-hyih' 呼吸; hwun'-tsing hwun-c'ih' 喚進喚出; to 一upon one's hands, ky'i' hô læ siu'-li 氣呵°在°手裡; so warm can't 一, ka nyih', ky'i' t'eo'-feh-cün' 這樣熱°氣透弗轉.

BRED, well kao'-hyüing-hao' 敎°訓好; understands politeness (said of a child), sih li'-sing 識理性; ill 一, feh sih li'-sing 弗識理性; m̄ kao'-hyüing-go 無°敎°訓个°.

BREECHES, kw'u 袴 (ih-diao).

BREED, to 一 children, sang ng'-bu nön' 生°兒°哺囡; to 一 cattle, yiang ngeo' 養牛°; to 一 lice, sang seh' 生虱.

BREEZE, gentle 'o fong' 和風; there is a little 一, vi-vi' yiu tin fong' 微微有點風; steady, favorable 一, ih-dzih' jing-fong' 一直順風.

BRETHREN, hyüong-di' 兄弟; di'-hyüong 弟兄.

BREVITY, with 一 and clearness, kyin'-r-ming' 簡而明.

BREW, to 一 wine, tso tsiu' 做酒 zao tsiu' 造°酒; nyiang tsiu' 釀酒 (veng); brewing mischief, læ-

tih hying 'o' de' 正°在°與禍了°.

BRIBE, hwe'-lu 賄賂; to take a 一, ziu hwe' 受賄.

BRICK, cün-deo' 磚頭 (ih-kw'e); bricks and tiles, ngô'-yiao-ho 瓦°窰貨.

BRICK-KILN, yiao 窰; siao yiao' 燒窰 (ih-go).

BRICK-LAYER, mason, nyi-shü'-s-vu' 泥刷°司務.

BRIDAL-DRESS, kong-tsông' 宮粧; 一 (for the second day), hwô-ao' 花襖; head-dress and robe, vong-kwun', yün-ling 鳳冠圓領; bridal outfit, kô'-tsông 嫁°粧.

BRIDE, sing-læ'-sing-vu' 新來新婦; sing-nyiang'-ts 新娘子; sing-kwu'-nyiang 新姑娘. The latter is used by the song'-nyiang-ts. See BRIDES-MAID.

BRIDE-CHAMBER, dong-vông' 洞房.

BRIDEGROOM, sing-lông' 新郎; siao'-kwun-nying 小官人°.

BRIDES-MAID. The Chinese have none, but instead, have attendants called, ze-kô'-a-m 隨嫁°阿°姆°, and song'-nyiang-ts 送娘.

BRIDGE, gyiao 橋; river 一, kông-gyiao 江°橋 (ih-keng, ih-diao); floating 一, veo-gyiao' 浮橋; 一 of the nose, bih-deo liang' 鼻°樑.

BRIDLE. the reins, mô' kyiang-zing 馬韁繩°; the head gear, mô'-

long-deo 馬籠頭; *the bits*, mô'-ziah-ts' 馬嚼子; mô'-k'eo-t'ih 馬口鐵
BRIDLE, *to* t'ao long-deo' 套籠頭; *saddled and bridled*, mô' p'è'-hao-de 馬配好了°
BRIEF, kyin'-kyin-kyih-kyih' 簡簡潔潔; ling'-kying; kyin'-bin 簡便
BRIER, *thorn bush*, ts'ʻ-jü 有° 刺 个樹
BRIGADE *of troops*, ih-de'ping-mô' 一隊兵馬; ih-ts' ping-mô' 一支兵馬
BRIGHT, kwông-liang' 光亮; ming-liang' 明亮; *polish it* —, ts'ah'gyi liang' 擦其亮; *dazzling* —, shih'-kwah liang' 雪光°亮; — *weather*, t'in' ts'ing-kwông'-kyiao-kyih' 天清光皎潔; væn'-li-vu-yüing' 萬里無雲
BRIGHTEN, *to rub bright*, mo kwông' 磨光; ts'ah' kwông 擦光; *to illumine*, tsiao'-djoh 照著°; ing'-djoh 映著°; — *one's intelligence*, ts'ong-ming' k'æ-c'ih'-læ 聰明開出來; *the sky brightens*, t'in lông'-ky'i-læ-de 天朗起來了°; — *up*, (as an idol, when his eyes are uncovered, or humorously, when a dirty face is washed), k'æ kwông' 開光
BRILLIANT (as coloring), kwông-ts'æ' 光彩; —(as light), kwông-yiao' 光耀

BRIM, k'eo 口; pin 邊; *cup's* —, pe-ts' k'eo 杯子口; *jar's* —, kông pin' 江邊
BRIMFUL, mi-mun' 平°滿; 'eo-yin' 候沿
BRIMSTONE, liu-wông' 硫磺
BRINE, 'æn-lu' 鹹滷; lu'-djü; yin-lu' 蓝滷
BRING, *to* do'-læ 拏°來; ta'-læ 帶°來; the latter has the idea of bringing, at the same time with something else, thus, — *the eggs and also the sugar*, kyi-dæn' do-læ', dông' hao ta'-læ 鷄蛋拏°來糖好帶°來; — *back* (something borrowed), ta-læ wæn' 帶°來還; — *trouble on one's self*, zi c'ü' gyi 'o 自°取其禍; zi zing' gyi kw'u' 自°尋°其苦
BRING FORTH *a child*, sang na-hwun' 產嬰°孩;—*fruit*, kyih ko'-ts 結果子; sang ko'-ts 生果子
BRING — (it) *up*, do-zông'-læ 拏°上來;—*up a child*, yiang siao' nying do' 養小孩大°; *ditto, to have every thing it likes*, yiang' kyiao 養嬌
BRINK, pin-yin' 邊沿; ts'ing'-pin 趁邊; *just on the* —, ts'ing'-pin-dziah-ngen' 趁邊着岸; — *of a river*, kông pin-yin' 江°邊沿
BRINY, 'æn-go 鹹°个°
BRISK, kyih'-tsao 急躁;— *beer*,

tsiu c'ong'-leh kyih' 酒冲得急; c'ong is also pron. ts'ong.

BRISTLES, *pig's* —, cü-tsong' 豬鬃

BRITTLE, ts'e'-ts'e; ts'e 脆

BROAD, kw'eh 闊; kwông'-kw'eh 廣闊; *make it broader*, tso gyi kw'eh'-tin 做其闊點

BROAD-CLOTH, do-nyi' 大呢; *fine* —, siao'-nyi 小呢; to'-lo-nyi' 哆囉呢

BROCADE *silk*, hwô-dziu' 花綢;— *satin*, mo-peng'-dön 摹本緞

BROGUE, t'u'-ing 土音; *cannot speak three words without his* —, sæn kyü' feh li peng'-ky'iang 三句弗離本腔

BROIL, *to* tsih 炙; hong 烘; koh 㷊; *cut* (it) *in pieces and* — (it), ts'ih'-leh p'in tang' p'in, tsih'-ih-tsih' 切得片打片炙一炙

BROKER, ma-siu' 買手; *money* —, t'æn-sin'-sang 聽行情先生

BROKER'S-SHOP, (exchange), dzin-tin' 錢店

BRONZE, *old* kwu'-dong 古銅;— *color*, kwu'-dong seh 古銅色

BROOD *of chickens*, ih-k'o' siao kyi' 一窩小鷄

BROOD, *to* — *on eggs*, bu dæn' 菢蛋; u dæn'; *brooding over* (as sorrow), ts'ih-sing'-de 切心了

BROOK, ky'i-k'ang' 溪坑 (ih-diao, ih-da).

BROOM, sao'-tsiu 掃帚; *small* —, *or brush*, shih'-tsiu 刷帚 (ih-pô)

BROTH, t'ông 湯; *mutton* —, yiang-nyüoh t'ông 羊肉湯

BROTHEL, c'ông-kô 娼家; meng-k'æn' 門檻; dông-ming' 堂名; — *boat* (at Hangchow), kông-sæn-jün' 江山船; c'ông is also pron. ts'ông.

BROTHER, *elder* ah-ko' 阿哥; ah-kön'; *younger* —, ah-di' 阿弟

BROTHER-IN-LAW, *elder sister's husband*, tsi'-fu 姊夫; *younger sister's husband*, me-fu' 妹夫

BROTHERLY, jü-hyüong'-ziah-di' 如兄若弟

BROTHERS, hyüong-di' 弟兄

BROW, nao'-k'oh 腦壳; *the sides of the* —, ngah-koh' 額角; *to knit the brows*, zeo mi-deo' 縐眉頭

BROW-BEAT, *to* we'-pih 威逼

BROWSE, *to* k'eng jü'-ô-ts' 齦樹椏枝

BROWN *color*, tsong-seh' 棕色; *reddish* —, 'ong-tsong' 紅棕; *the color of wet* — *sugar*, ts'-dông seh 紫糖色; *fry it* (yellow), t'ah gyi wông' 爛其黃; *fry it very* —, t'ah gyi ts'-dông seh 爛其紫糖色

BRUISE, sông-'eng' 傷痕; — (where the blood is collected), ü'-byüih 瘀血; *black and blue*

—, u-ts'ing' 烏青;— (on fruit, or the mark of a — on flesh), sông-pô' 傷疤

BRUISE, to sông 傷; seng 損; long sông-seng 弄傷損; to — by falling, tih'-sông 跌傷; — by something falling upon, ah'-sông 壓傷; — by striking against, bang-sông 撞傷; — by shutting between, gah-sông 夾傷; — by beating, tang'-sông 打傷; to — (as drugs), sông-se', or song-se' 舂碎

BRUSH, shih'-tsin 刷帚 (ih-pô)

BRUSH, to shih 刷; to — teeth, shih ngô-ts' 刷牙齒

BRUTALLY, to treat a person —, oh'-sing-oh'-fi dæ nying' 惡心惡肺待人

BUBBLES, p'ao 泡; froth, beh 浡; to blow —, c'ü p'ao' 吹泡

BUBBLE, to — up, ky'i beh' 起浡

BUCK, yüong-loh' 雄鹿

BUCKET, shü'-dong 水桶 (ih-tsah; a pair, ih-tæn)

BUCKWHEAT, gyiao-mah' 蕎麥 (a grain, ih-lih)

BUD, leaf ngô 芽; ngô-den' 芽頭; flower —, nyü 蕊; hwô-nyü 花蕊

BUD, to —, ts'iu ngô' 抽芽; pao ngô' 苞芽; fah ngô' 發芽

BUDGET, a bag of something, ih-dæ veh-gyin' 一袋物件; a bundle in a cloth, pao-voh' 包袱

BUDDHA, veh 佛

BUDDHISM, veh-kyiao' 佛教; sih'-kyiao 釋教

BUDDHIST, veh-kyiao'-li-go nying' 佛教裡个人; veh-meng-di'-ts 佛門弟子

BUDDHIST-PRIEST, 'o-zông' 和尚; I, an humble —, sô-mi' 沙彌

BUFF color, dæn' wông 淡黃

BUFFALO, shü'-ngeo 水牛 (ih-deo)

BUG, djong 蟲; bed —, ts'iu'-djong 臭蟲 (ih-go)

BUGBEAR, kwa'-ky'i tong'-si 怪氣東西

BUGLE, nga'-koh 'ao-teo' 外國號斗

BUILD, to ky'i 起; zao 造; tang 打; — a house, ky'i ih-tsing oh' 起一進屋; — a boat, zao ih tsah-jün' 造一隻船; — a wall, tang ih-dao ziang' 打一道墻

BUILDER, ky'i'-zao-go s-vu' 起造个司務

BUILDING, oh 屋; oh'-yü 屋宇

BULB, deo 頭; onion —, ts'ong-deo' 葱頭; taro —, nyü-na'-deo 芋艿頭

The Chinese do not distinguish bulbous roots.

BULGING, protruding, deh-c'ih'-liao 凸出了

BULKY, do-gyin'-deo 大件頭

BULL, yüong ngeo' 雄牛 (ih-deo)

BULLET, leaden k'æn-dæn' 鉛彈
BULLION, veng-nying' 紋銀
BULLOCK, siao' yüong-ngeo' 小雄牛° (ih-deo)
BULLY, to bluster or swagger, hah'-sæn-wô'-shü 嚇山話水°
BULRUSH, lu-ken' 蘆竿; lamp-wick —, teng ts'ao' 燈草; matting —, zih-ts'ao' 席草
BULWARKS, city walls, dzing-ziang' 城牆; earthen rampart, nyi-dzing' 泥城; the sides of a ship, 'en-dông' 旱塘; ken'-dông 趕塘; a fortification, p'ao'-dæ 礮臺
BUMP, bang-sông' 挬°傷 (ih-t'ah)
BUMP, to k'eh'-bang 磕撞°; k'eh'-djoh 磕著°
BUNCH, a handful, ih-pô 一把; a — of grass, ih-pô ts'ao 一把草; a — of flowers, ih-nyiah hwô' 一捻花; a — of grapes, ih-gyiu' ts'-bn-dao 一毬紫葡萄; a — of keys, ih-c'ün yiah-z' 一串鑰匙
BUNDLE, a —, ih pao' 一包
BUNGLE, to c'uh-ho'; tso' feh loh'-dzih 做弗落直; tso' feh lin'-ky'in 做弗順°手; tso' feh ding'-tông 做弗定當
BUOY, mao-ing' 錨映; vu-dong' 浮°筒 (ih-go)
BUOYANT, floating, kying-veo' 輕浮; buoyant spirits, t'in-sing 'o-loh' 天性和樂

BURDEN, tæn'-ts 擔子; tæn'-deo 擔頭; heavy —, djong' tæn 重擔; a — for one man to carry with a bamboo, ih-tæn' 一擔; a — for two men to carry between them, ih kông' 一扛; a — carried on the back, ih-kyin' 一肩
BURDENSOME, næn tông' 難當
BUREAU, a chest of drawers, ih-tsiang gyü-coh' 一張櫃桌
BURGLAR who breaks into houses, ts'ah ziang-dong' go zeh' 拆牆洞个°賊°
BURIAL matters, en-tsông' z-t'i' 安葬事體; — place, en-tsông'-go di-fông' 安葬个°地方; — ground, veng-di' 墳地; public ditto, nyi-cong'-di 義塚地; nyi-sæn' 義°山
BURN, ho t'ông'-sông 火燙傷
BURN, to siao 燒; me mæ'; dziah 煠; tin 點; — paper (for the dead), siao ts' 燒紙; — mock-money, siao sih'-boh 燒錫箔; — down (as a house), me-diao' dziab-diao' 煠壞°; — incense, tin hyiang' 點香; siao hyiang' 燒香; this oil will not —, keh'-go yiu, tin'-feh-dziah'-go 這°个°油點弗煠°个°; — a corpse, ho'-tsông 火葬; — the filth off a ship's bottom, dæn jün' 燂船; face burns like fire, min-k'ong nyih', ziang ho'

siao' ka 面孔熱°像火燒个°. BURNED to death, dziah-sah'-de 燆死°了°. BURNING, smell of something —, iu-ho'-ky'i 烟火氣; — hot (as with fever), ho'-nyih 火熱°; fah-siao' 發燒. BURNISH, to mo-kwông' 磨光. BURROW, di-dong' 地洞. BURROW, to kong di-dong' 打°地洞; rabbits —, t'u' we kong di-dong' 兎會打°地洞. BURST, to — (with a noise), pao'-k'æ 爆開; to crack open, kwah'-k'æ 豁開; the cannon —, do-p'ao tsô'-k'æ-de 大° 礮㪔開了°; p'ao tsô'-de 礮㪔了°; — out laughing, fah-siao' 發燒. BURY, to en-tsông' 安葬. BUSH, siao'-jü 小樹 (ih-cü) BUSHEL, sæn teo' 三斗; three teo equal 30 quarts. BUSHY tail, mi'-pô bong-song 尾°巴°蓬鬆; — beard, ngô'-su nyüong 牙°鬚°濃. BUSINESS, z-ken' 事幹; z-t'i' 事體; what is your honorable —? ng yiu' soh-go kwe'-z 你°有甚麼°貴事? ditto occupation? ng soh'-go kwe-'ông' go 你°甚麼°貴行个°? to mind one's own —, en-veng'-siu-kyi' 安㕦守己°; what — is it of yours? ng kwun' gyi tso soh' 你°管其做甚°麼°? one's appropriate —, ne-'ông' 內行; it is not

your —, feh' z ng' veng-ne'-ts-z' 弗是你°分內之事; talks constantly of his own —, sæn kyü' feh li peng ky'iang 三句弗離本腔; — hours, bæn tsing'-vu z-'eo' 辦正務時候. BUSTLE, nao-nyih' 鬧熱°; — and noise, nao-nyih'-bang-sang. BUSTLING, nyih-nao' 熱°鬧; — hospitality, dæ nying-k'ah' nyih-zah' 待客人°熱°心°. BUSY, employed, yiu z-ken' 有事幹; — and hurried, môngmông'-loh-loh' 忙忙碌碌; harvesting is a — time, keh dao' mông' z-'eo' 割稻忙時候. BUT, dæn'-z 但是; only, tæn-tsih' 單只; tsih'-z 只是; we were all there — you, djü-liao ng' ah'-lah tu læ'-kæn 除了°你°我°等都在彼°; — for you, ky'ü-leh ng' 虧°得你°; ziah feh'-z ng' 若弗是你°. BUTCHER, du-fu' 屠夫; — of hogs, sah-cü-du' 殺猪屠; the seller of meat, tsing-deo'-s-vu' 椹頭司務; to open a butcher's shop, k'æ du-wu' 開屠戶. BUTCHER, to sah 殺; — people, sah'-loh pah'-sing 殺戮百姓. BUTLER, one who looks after things generally, kwun-z'-go 管事个°; toh-djü' 督廚. BUTT, to gyüih 觙; tiao'; ts'oh'; — end of a stick, bông'-go do

deo' 大°頭棒 (deo or den.)
BUTTER, na-yiu'媚°油; beh-t'ah', transferred from the English.
BUTTERFLY, wu-diah' 蝴蝶 (ih-tsah)
BUTTOCKS, p'i'-kwu 屁股
BUTTON, nyiu'-ts 鈕子 (ih-lih); cap —, ting'-ts 頂子; common cap —, mao tih'-ts 帽結°子
BUTTON, to nyiu'-long 鈕攏; — it, nyiu-ih'-nyiu 鈕一鈕; k'eo'-ih-k'eo' 扣一扣
BUTTON-HOLE, nyiu'-p'æn 鈕襻
BUY, to ma'-tsing 買°進; ma 買°; ma-læ' 買°來°; to — and sell, ma'-ma 買°賣°; to — rice, dih mi' 糴米; — wine, tang tsiu' 買酒; — oil, iao yiu' 買°油; — cloth, ts'ô pu' 買°布
BUYER, ma'-cü 買°主
BUZZING, z-z'-hyiang; 'ong-'ong'-hyiang 洪洪響; the — of mosquitoes, meng-djong' hyiang' 蚊°蟲響; du-du'-hyiang.
BY that road, dzong keh'-da lu 從這°條路; injured — him, be gyi 'æ' 被其害; close —, gying 近; — no means, bing'-fi 並非; — all means, ts'in-væn' 千萬; — what means? yüong soh'-go fông-fah' 用甚°麼方法? — day, nyih-li' 日°裡; — night, yia-li' 夜°裏; — himself (there), doh-zi' kæ'-kæn 獨自°在°彼; — chance, neo'-ts'eo 偶湊; ngeo'-jün 偶

然; sell — the pound, leng kying' ma 論勱買°; to say — heart, be 背°; come one — one, ih'-go ih'-go læ' 一个一个來; — and —, ko'-leh ih-zông' 過了°一息°; — and — will come, deng' ih-zông' ziu læ'; to pass —, tseo'-ko 走過
BY-PATH, tseh'-lu 側路
BY-STANDER, bông-nying' 旁人°; disgraceful for bystanders (i. e. others) to see, bông-kwun'-peh-yüö' 旁覷不雅

C

CABAL, kyih-tông' 結黨; kæn tông' 奸黨
CABBAGE, (native) yellow wông-yia'-ts'æ 黃矮菜; Shantung —, Sæn-tong' ts'æ 山東菜
CABIN in a vessel, jün'-li-go k'ah'-ts'ông 船裡个°客艙; straw hut, ts'ao'-oh 草屋; ts'ao'-ts'iang 草廠; ts'ao'-sô 草厫
CABINET minister, tsæ'-siang 宰相; siang'-koh 相國; address-ed as koh'-lao 閣老 and da yüoh-z 大學士
CABLE, ts'ih 大°繩°; bamboo —, mih-ts'ih' 篾竹繩°; palm husk —, tsong ts'ih' 棕篾°繩°
CACKLE, to tô-ts'; hens — after laying eggs, kyi-nyiang' pao ts' 雞娘報子
CAGE, long 籠; bird —, tiao-long' 鳥籠; — for criminals,

moh-long' 木籠 (ih-tsah)
CAJOLE, to yi vong'-dzing yi hong'-p'in 叉°奉承叉°哄騙
CAKE, kao 糕; flat —, ping 餅 (ih-go); — shop, dzô-zih' tin 茶食店; kao-ping' tin 糕餅店; sponge —, dæn-kao' 蛋糕
CALAMITY, 'o'-se 禍崇; tsæ-næn' 災難; — changed to blessing, cün-'o' we-foh' 轉禍爲福
CALCINE, to tön-hwe' 煅灰; — gypsum, tön zah-kao' 煅石膏
CALCULATE, to sön 算; sön-tsiang' 算帳; you — correctly, ng sön feh ts'o' 你°算弗錯; — destinies, sön ming' 算命
CALDRON, do 'oh' 大°鑊
CALENDAR (printed sheet), lih-jih-tæn 曆日單; tsin-li'-tæn 瞻禮單; li'-pa-tæn 禮拜單 (ih-tsiang)
CALF, siao'-ngeo 小牛°; very young —, siao-ang' 犢 (ih-deo); — of the leg, kyiah-nyiang-du'
CALIBER, size of the bore, p'ao'-meng ts'ah'-ts'eng 礮門尺°寸; weight of the ball, dæn'-ts to'-siao djong' 彈子多少重
CALICO, white bah-yiang-pu' 白洋布; printed —, hwô-yiang'-pu 花洋布
CALK, to seh leo-dong' 塞漏洞; — a boat, dzang jün'.
CALL, to eo; hwun 喚; kyiao 叫°; — loudly, hyiang'-hyiang eo 響響叫°; — to mind, ts'eng'-ky'i-læ

忖起來; siang'-ky'i-læ 想起來; cannot — to mind, ts'eng'-feh-c'ih' 忖弗出; by what name are you called ? ng' kyiao-leh soh'-go ming'-z 你叫甚°麼°名字? ng co soh-go ming'-z? to call out, eo-tæn'-ky'i 叫°起; hyiang-tæn'-ky'i 響起; — the cat, mæn hwun'-leh-læ 猫°呼°得來; — on him to pray, ts'ing gyi' tso tao'-kao 請其做禱告; — upon (visit), mông-mông' 望'望°
CALLIGRAPHY, hao-pih'-fah 好筆法
CALLING, occupation, z-nyih' 事業; 'ông-nyih' 行業; 'ông-tông' 行當; (polite), kwe'-'ông 貴行; trade, siu'-nyi 手藝
CALLOW bird, c'ih-k'o'-go tiao° 出䈿个鳥°; as yet no feathers, wa 还'-neh c'ih mao' 還沒°有°出毛
CALM weather, dzing kwông' kyiao kyih' 晴光皎潔; — wind and wave, bing fong' zing lông' 平風靜浪; — mind, sing' ts'ing-zing' 心淸靜; sing en-tæn' 心安耽
CALM, to — the mind, en sing' 安心; — his anger, ah gyi-go ho 壓其个火
CALMLY, en-tæn' 安耽; en-en'-zing-zing' 安安靜靜
CALUMNIATE, to pông'-hwe 謗毀; tsing dzæn-yin' 進讒言

CALUMNY, dz'en-yin' 讒言
CALVE, to sang siao-aung' 生°犢°
CAMBRIC, zông yiang'-sô 上洋紗; light blue —, kying-læn' si-pu' 京藍細布; coh'-pu 竹布
CAMEL, loh-do' 駱駝 (ih-tsah)
CAMELLIA, dzô-hwô' 茶花
CAMLET, yü'-dön 羽緞; imitation —, yü'-dziu 羽綢
CAMOMILE, dried — flowers, ken-kyüih' hwô 甘菊花
CAMP, ying-za' 營寨°
CAMPHOR, tsông-nao' 樟腦; ping p'in' 冰片; — tree, tsông-jü 樟樹
CAMP-CHAIR, mô'-ü 馬椅°; mô'-tsah-ü 馬紮椅°; leather bottomed (native) —, bi-mô'-ü 皮馬椅° (ih-pô)
CAN, oil yiu-kwun' 油罐 (ih-go)
CAN, neng-keo' 能彀; we 會; — (implying permission, or fitness) hao'-s-teh 好使得; k'o'-s-teh 可使得; k'o'-yi 可以; — but, feh'-teh-feh 弗得弗; — do (it), tso'-leh-læ 做得來; — not do (it), tso'-feh-læ 做弗來
CANAL, 'o 河; 'o-kông 河港 small —, siao 'o' 小河; siao' 'o-kông' 小河港; branch — (soon terminating), zao 漕; the Grand —, Yüing 'o' 運河; kông 江° a river, and kông 港 a canal, differ in tone, the form-

er being bing-sing, the latter zông-sing. Tides rise in the former, not in the latter.
CANARY-BIRD, z-zing'-tiao 時辰°鳥°
CANCEL, to blot out, du-diao' 塗壞°; to cross out (as figures), djü-diao' 除去°; keo-siao' 勾銷
CANDID, dzih-sông' 直爽
CANDIDATE (for the lowest literary rank), dong-sang' 童生°; veng-dong' 文童; — to be chosen, 'eo-shün' 候選; — for office, 'eo-pu' 候補 also used in ordinary matters.
CANDIED fruits, dông-ko' 糖菓; honeyed fruits, mih-tsin' 蜜餞; — or honeyed jujubes, (often called dates), mih-tsao' 蜜棗; — oranges, kyüih'-ping 橘餅
CANDLE, lah-coh' 蠟燭 (ih-ts); foreign —, yiang-coh' 洋燭; marriage —, hwô-coh' 花燭; blow out the —, lah-coh' c'ü u' 蠟燭吹°熄°
CANDLESTICK, coh'-dæ 燭臺; lah-coh-dæ' 蠟燭臺° (ih-tsah)
CANDOR, with dzing'-jih-vu-ky'i-go 誠實無欺个°
CANDY, dông 糖; some of the best Ningpo candies are, cowhide —, ngeo-bi'-dông 牛°皮糖; black seed slices, hah-kyiao-ts'ih' 黑澆切; lotus-thread —, ngeo'-s-dông' 藕絲糖; rice —, tong'-

mi-dông' 涷米糖; *peanut* —, hwô-seng dông' 花生糖 &c.

CANE, *rattan*, bah-deng' 白籐; — *seated chair*, deng-min' ü'-ts 籐面椅°子

CANE, bông 棒; kwa'-dziang 拐°杖; æ'-dziang 捘°杖 (ih-keng)

CANGUE, do-kô' 大°枷° (ih-min); *to wear the* —, pe do-kô' 背°大°枷°

CANISTER, *tea* dzô-yih'-kwun 茶葉罐

CANNIBAL, ky'üoh nying'-go nying 吃人°个人°

CANNON, do-p'ao' 大°礮 (ih-meng)

CANNON-BALL, do-dæn'-ts 大°彈子

CANNONADE, *to* yüong p'ao' tang 用礮打

CANNOT, feh neng'-keo 弗能彀; s'-feh-teh 使弗得; ve, or feh we 弗會°; — *go*, ky'i'-feh-læ 去°弗來; *must not go*, ky'i'-feh-teh 去°弗得; — *on any account*, væn-feh-k'o' 萬弗可; ts'ih'-feh-k'o' 切弗可; tön'-wu-feh-k'o' 斷乎弗可; — *part with* (or regret to part with), feh-só'-teh 弗捨°得; — *spare*, siao'-feh-teh 少弗得; hyih'-feh-læ' 歇弗來; — *reach* (it), liao'-feh-djoh' 撩弗着°; — *see* (it), k'en'-feh-kyin' 看弗見; — *believe* (it), siang-sing'-feh-læ' 相信弗來; — *find* (it), zing'-feh-djoh' 尋弗着°.

CANON, *church rule*, kyiao' kwe 敎規

CANONIZE, *to declare a deceased person to be a saint*, si-ts' ts'ing-gyi' z sing'-nying 死之稱其是聖人°.

CANOPY (carried before an officer), wông-lo'-sæn 黃羅傘; — *presented for merit*, væn-ming'-sæn 萬民傘

CANTANKEROUS, kæn-ka' 尲尬

CANTHARIDES, pæn-mao' 斑螯

CANTO, *a division*, ih-p'in' s' 一篇詩; *a book*, ih-peng s' 一本詩; ih-kyün s' 一卷詩

CANVASS, *to examine*, dzô-ts'ah 查察; k'ao'-kyiu 考究; — (for votes, pupils &c.), kyiu 糾; kyiu-long' 糾攏; *sail-cloth*, fong'-bong pu 風篷布; sô-pu' 紗布

CAP, siao'-mao 小帽; bin-mao' 便帽; *small silk* —, un'-mao 䙅帽; si-kwô-bi' 西瓜皮 (ih-ting); *to put on the* —, ta' mao-ts' 戴°帽子; *take off the* —, tsoh' mao-ts' 除帽子

CAPABLE *of doing*, hao'-tso 好做; ky'üoh'-leh-loh-go 吃°得落个°

CAPABILITY, vu-nyih'-ts 武藝; neng-ken 能幹; *mental* —, dzæ-neng' 才能

CAPACIOUS, kw'un-do' 寬大°; kw'un-ts'iah' 寬綽

CAPACITY, *mental* ts-tsih′ 資質; dzæ 才; *he has a — for something great,* (*i.e.* the main beam), gyi z tong′-liang-ts dzæ′ 其是棟梁之才; *small —,* mah-sin′-ts dzæ 藐綫之才

CAPE (of land), we′-koh 匯角°; hæ′-koh 海角°; — (worn by an officer), p'i-kyin′ 披肩; *lady's* —, yün p'i′-i 圓披衣

CAPER, *to* t'iao′-t'iao 跳跳; t'iao-t'iao, peng′-peng 跳跳奔奔

CAPITAL, *chief,* ting′ do 頂大°; — *crime,* si′ze 死罪; — *scheme,* miao kyi′ 妙計

CAPITAL (of a country), kying-dzing′ 京城; kying-tu′ 京都 (ih-zo); *stock in trade,* peng′-din 本錢°; *to lose —,* zih peng′ 折°本

CAPITULATE, *to* deo-'ông 投降

CAPON, sin′-kyi 騸雞 (ih-tsah)

CAPRICIOUS, 'oh-z°-'oh-pin′ 或是或變; *very —,* kwu-kwa′-deo 古怪°頭

CAPSTAN *for an anchor,* ts'ô mao′-go bun′ 車錨个°盤; — (on land), ts'ô-dong′ 車筒

CAPTAIN, *chief,* cü 主; — *of a boat,* jün′-cü 船主; *military —,* yiu-kyih′ 遊擊; — *of a hundred men,* pah′-tsong 百總

CAPTIOUS, wang p'i-bing, jü′ p'i-bing 橫批評豎批評; zing′-z ts'ao′-nao 尋°事譟鬧

CAPTIVATED, *I am — by it,* ngô′ be gyi′ ts'ih-sing′-de 我被其切心了°

CAPTIVE, lo-ky'i′-go nying′ 擄去°个°人°; — *soldier,* gying′-ky'i-go ping 擒去°个°兵

CAPTIVE, *to take —,* lo′-ky'i 擄去°; *ditto* (as a soldier), gying′-leh-ky'i 擒得°去

CAPTURE, *to* k'ô′-djoh 掔°着°; cô-djoh′ 擄着°

CARCASS, p'oh′-s 仆屍; — *of a man,* s-sin′ 屍首; si′-s 死屍; — *of a horse,* si-mô′ 死°馬; — *of a cow,* tao′-ngeo 死°牛

CARD, t'iah′-ts 帖子; — (simply containing one's name), p'in-ts 片子; — *of invitation,* ts'ing′-t'iah 請帖; *visiting —,* pa′-t'iah 拜帖; — *of thanks,* zia′-t'iah 謝帖; *send a —,* do ih-go t'iah′-ts ky'i′ 掔°一个° 帖子去

CARD-CASE, pa′-t'iah-'eh′ 拜°帖盒°; *card-bag* (Chinese), p'in′-ts-dæ 片子袋

CARDAMOM-SEEDS, deo-k'eo′ 豆蔻; bah-k'eo′ 白蔻; sô-jing′ 砂仁

CARDS, ts-wu-bæn′ 紙糊牌°; *to play —,* c'ô-bæn′ 圖°牌°

CARE, *anxiety,* lao-sing′ 勞心; iu-li′ 憂慮; s-li′ 思慮

CARE, *to — for,* kwu′-djoh 顧着°; tsiao′-kwu 照顧; k'en′-kwu 看顧; *take —,* siao′-sing 小心;

tso-gyi' 留心; tông-sing 常心; dzæ-sing 在心
CAREFUL, kying'-jing-go 謹慎个; siao'-sing-go 小心个; — (about little things), ts'-si 仔細; to be — of (as things), yüong ts'-tsih 要°小°心°; æ'-sih 愛惜
CARELESS, hweh'-liah 忽略; feh siao'-sing 弗小心; feh kwn'-djoh 弗顧着°; — (in omitting), shih-kyin'-tin 失檢點; to treat precious things in a — way, bao'-din-t'in-veh' 暴珍天物
CARGO, jün'-li-go ho'-veh 船裡个°貨物; jün-ho' 船貨; to discharge —, ky'i ho' 起貨; zông ho' 上貨
CARICATURE, to draw a — ridiculing a person, sia ih-go du' tsao-siao nying' 寫°一个圖嘲笑人°
CARMINE, foreign yiang-'ong' 洋紅; — (for the face, &c.) in-tsi' 胭脂°
CARNAGE, sah'-loh 殺戮; promiscuous —, lön-sah' 亂殺
CARNAL, joh-ü nyüoh-sing 屬于肉身; depraved, zia 邪°; — desires, nyüoh-sing' s-yüoh° 肉身私慾
CARNELIAN, mô'-nao 瑪瑙
CAROUSE, to nao-tsiu' 鬧熱°酒興°
CARP, a fish, li'-ng 鯉魚° (ih-kwang)

CARP, to — at, hah' mao-üu 瞎埋°怨
CARPENTER, moh-s-vu' 木司務; moh-ziang'-s-vu 木匠°司務 (ih-go)
CARPET, mao-t'æn' 毛毯; tsin-t'æn' 氍毹; t'æn'-ts 毯子
CARRIAGE, ts'ô-ts' 車子; mô'-tsô-ts' 馬車子; four-wheeled —, s'-leng-ts'ô 四輪車 (ih-zo, ih-dzing)
CARRIER, burden t'iao-fu' 挑夫; kyiah'-pæn 脚班; letter —, sing'-pæn 信班; tseo-sing'-go 走信个°
CARRION, ts'iu'-nyüoh 臭°肉°; læn-nyüoh' 爛肉
CARROT, 'ong lo-boh' 紅蘿蔔
CARRY, to — on the head, deo-li ting' 頭頂; — on the shoulders or back, pe 負; — by a pole, (one man) t'iao 挑; — (by two men), dæ 擡; kông 扛; — by a handle or chain, (as a basket, teapot, &c.), ky'ih 挈; — in the hand, do 拏°; — away, do'-leh-ky'i' 拏°得去°; — a child, siao-nying' bao-leh tseo'-tseo 小孩抱得°走走; only willing to be carried, lin-siu'-sang 連手生'; — in the bosom, gwa'-li ts'ô'-leh-ky'i 懷°裏扠°得去°; — a letter, ta sing' 帶°信; — an umbrella, ta sæn' 帶°傘; do sæn' 拏°傘; — an open ditto, tæ sæn' 戴傘; — on the arm (as a dress), siu-li gwæn' 手裏

摜;— *on the arm* (by a handle), siu-li t'ao' 手裏套;— *under the arm*, leh-ts' 'ô gyih 胛°子下°辮;— *on the arm* (as strings of cash), gyiao 撟

CART, liang'-leng-ts'ô' 兩輪車 (ih dzing, ih-zo)

CARTILAGE, ts'e'-kweh 脆骨

CARTRIDGE, p'e'-hao-liao ho'-yiah-pao' 配好了火藥包

CARVE, to — (ornamentally), tiao-k'eh' 雕刻; tiao-hwô' 雕花; — *meat*, ts'ih nyüoh' 切肉°

CARVER (in wood), tiao-hwô'-s-vu 雕花司務

CARVING *knife*, ts'ih-nyüoh'-go tao' 切肉个°刀

CASE, t'ao 套; *pillow* —, tsing'-deo-t'ao' 枕頭套; 'eh 盒; *watch* —, piao'-'eh 表匣°; *card* —, pa'-t'iah-'en' 拜帖盒°; k'oh-ts' 壳子; *spectacle* —, ngen-kying k'oh'-ts 眼°鏡壳子; dæ 袋; *fan* —, sin'-ts-dæ 扇子袋

CASE *at law*, en'-gyin 案件; *circumstances of a* —, dzing-tsih' 情節; dzing-yiu' 情由; *difficult ditto*, ky'üoh'-tsih 曲折; *state of affairs*, kwông-kying' 光景

CASH, *a* —, ih-go dong-din' 一个°銅錢°; *a string of* —, ih-c'ün' dong-din' 一串銅錢°

CASK, dong 桶; *a wine* —, ih-tsah tsiu'-dong 一隻酒桶

CASKET *for head, and other ornaments*, deo-min-siang' 飾箱

CAST, *to* (as metals), cü 鑄

CAST, *to throw down*, gwæn-diao' 摜去°;— *young*, do-t'æ' 墮胎; — *the skin* (as a snake), t'eng k'oh' 脫°壳;— *off* (as a bad son), p'i'-t'æn-diao 吒°嘆了°;— *away*, t'ih'-c'ih 剔出; tiu-diao' 丢去°;— *down in mind*, iu-üoh' 憂鬱

CASTANETS, (bones), ts'oh'-pæn 作°樂°的°綿板

CASTER, ts'ih'-sing-kô' 七星架°

CASTOR-OIL, pi-mô'-yiu 蓖麻油

CASUALLY, ngeo'-ts'eo 偶湊; ngeo'-jün 偶然

CASUALTY, wang-'o' 橫°禍; fi-læ'-ts 'o 飛來之禍; t'in-li tih'-loh-læ'-go 'o' 天降之°禍

CASTRATE, *to* mô;— *an animal*, kyih 羯; in 閹

CAT, mæn 貓°(ih-tsah); *let the* — *out of the bag*, shih'-wô kông'-leh c'ih-kyiah'-de 說話講°得出脚了°

CATALOGUE *of books*, shü-moh' 書目;— *of names*, ming-moh' 名目;— *of goods*, ho'-tæn 貨單

CATARACT, boh-pu' 瀑布; *waterfall*, kwô'-loh-shü;— *in the eye*, zông-tsông 上瘴

CATARRH, *influenza*, sông-fong 傷風; *chronic* —, nao'-liu 腦漏

CATCH, to k'ô 擎°; — a thief, k'ô' zeh 擎°賊°; — fish, k'ô ng' 捕魚°; — (as water), zing 盛°; — (as something thrown), tsih 接; — cold, sông fong' 傷風; — a disease, teh bing' 得病; ditto by infection, bing yin-læ' 病來延

CATECHISM, veng-teh' 問答 (ih-peng)

CATERPILLAR, hairy mao-djong' 毛蟲; — found on vegetables, ts'æ' djong 菜蟲

CATHEDRAL, cü'-kyiao-dông' 主教堂; bishop's —, kyin-toh'-dông' 監督堂

CATHOLIC, kong-gong'-go 公共个°; a Roman Catholic, T'in-cü'-kyiao-nying' 天主教人°

CATTLE, a herd of —, ih-dziao ngeo' 一羣°牛°; beasts of burden, sang-k'eo' 牲°口

CATTY, a ih-kying' 一斤; sell by the —, leng kying' ma 論斤買°

CAUGHT, k'ô'-djoh-de 擎°着°了°; tsih-djoh-de 接着°了°; — in the wrong, and have nothing to say, loh-gah'-de; — in the rain, nyü-djoh yü' de 遇着°雨了°

CAUSE, yün-kwu' 緣故; ing-deo' 因頭; keng-yiu' 根由; yün-yiu' 緣由; dzing-yiu' 情由; dzing-tsih' 情節; sô-yi-jün' 所以然; beginning, ky'i-ing' 起因; what is the — of it? sob-go yün-kwu 甚°麽°緣故?

dza sô-yi-jün' 怎°樣°所以然? without —, vu-yün-vu-kwu' 無緣無故; to gain a — (before a magistrate), ying kwan'-s 赢官司

CAUSE me sorrow, lin-le' ngô iu-meng' 連累我憂悶; ta'-li ngô iu-meng' 帶累我憂悶; s' teh ngô iu-meng' 使得我憂悶; — one to feel uncomfortable, cü'-s-teh nying' feh en'-tæn 致使得人°弗安耽

CAUTERIZE with hot iron, t'ông 燙; — with burning herbs, &c., kyiu 灸°

CAUTION, to use —, tso-gyi' 留心°; — lest he forget, di-sing' 提醒; exhort, ky'ün 勸

CAUTIOUS, kwu-zin' kwu-'eo' 顧前°顧後; circumspect, ts'-si 仔細

CAVALRY, mô'-ping 馬兵

CAVE, dong 洞; sæn-dong 山洞; sæn-ngæn'-dong 山巖洞

CAVIL, to p'i-poh' 批駁; p'i-siah' 批削

CAVITY, k'ong 孔; dong 洞; ky'iao 窈; the seven cavities, (ears, nose, mouth, eyes), ts'ih' ky'iao 七窈

CEASE, to hyih 歇; ts 止; deng 停°; — from, hyih'-loh 歇落

CEASELESS, feh-hyih' 弗歇; feh-ts' 弗止; feh-deng' 弗停°; ih-zông' feh teh k'ong' 一息弗得空

CEDAR, pah'-jü 柏樹
CEILING of boards, t'in-hwó'-pæn 天花板; ting'-kab-pæn 頂隔板; — of lath and plaster, nyi-t'in'-mun 泥天壗; nyi ting'-kah'-pæn 泥頂隔板; want a —, iao mun'-ih-mun 要壗一壗
CELEBRATE, to — one's birthday, tso sang' 做生°; what are you celebrating? ng yiu soh'-go hyi'-ky'ing z-ken' 你有甚麼喜慶事幹?
CELEBRATED, veng-ming'-go 聞名个°; c'ih-ming'-go 出名个°; — physician, ming i' 名醫; — scholar, ming jü' 名儒; — shop, yiu ming-sing'-go tin' 有名聲个°店
CELL in a prison, nying-vông' 人房; — for literary condidates, 'ao-ts' 號子
CELLAR, di-ing'-ts 地管子; di-yüih' 地穴; di-kao' 地窖
CEMENT, lime, zah-hwe' 石°灰; glue, kao 膠°; varnish and flour —, sang ts'ih' min-feng' 生漆麵粉
CEMETERY, veng-t'æn' 墳灘
CENSER, hyiang-lu' 香爐; swinging —, di-lu' 提爐; tiao'-lu 吊爐
CENSOR, nyü-s' 御史
CENSORIOUS, kwæn'-we p'i-bing' 慣會批評
CENSURABLE, kæ tsah'-be 該責備; yiu ts'o'-c'ü 有錯處

CENSURE, he received a great deal of —, gyi ziu nying-kô' hyü'-to tsah'-be 其受人°家°許多責備
CENSUS, a-wu'-ts'ah 門°牌册: to take the —, zao a-wu'-ts'ah 造°門°牌册; — tables, nying-ting'-ts'ah 人°丁册
CENTER, or CENTRE, the cong-nyiang' 中央°; tông-cong' 當中; — of a circle, yün-ky'ün' cong-sing' 圓圈中心
CENTIPEDE, meng-kong' 蜈蚣° (ih-kwang); — bite, meng-kong' ngao' 蜈蚣°鮫; meng kong' ting' 蜈蚣叮
CENTRAL forces, cong-nyiang'-go lih-dao' 中央°个°力道; — road, cong lu' 中路
CENTUPLE, kô ih-pah' be 加°一百°倍
CENTURION, pah'-tsong 百°總
CENTURY, ih-pah' nyin 一百°年
CEREMONIOUS, to-li'-go 多禮个°; do not be so —, feh pih' kyü li' 弗必拘禮
CEREMONY, li 禮; li'-mao 禮貌; li'-tsih 禮節
CERTAIN, ih-ding' 一定; ding-jih' 定實; a — person, mo' nying 某人°; a — day, mo' nyih 某日°
CERTAINLY, pih'-ding 必定; pih'-kying 畢竟; tön'-jün 斷然; kyüih'-ding 決定; jih-dzæ' 實在; — not, ih-ding' peh-yih' 一定不易

CERTIFICATE, *recommendation*, tsin'-shü 薦書; tsiao'-we 照會; *proof*, bing-kyü' 憑據; — *for money*, bing-tæn 憑單; *customs' general* —, tsong'-tæn 總單

CERTIFY, *to* lih bing-kyü' 立憑據

CESSATION *of work*, deng kong' 停°工; hyih kong' 歇工

CHAFE, *to rub*, soh'-soh 搎搎; no'-no 挪挪; *to rub off the skin*, bi' ts'ah'-t'ah 皮擦脱; bi' ts'ah'-sông 皮擦傷

CHAFED *in mind*, sing'-li ts'iao'-soh-soh'-go-de 中°心°如°刺°

CHAFF (of rice), k'ông 糠; long'-k'ông 礱糠; *pounded* —, si'-k'ông 細糠; *the inner hull of wheat*, fu-bi' 麩皮; mah-bi' 麥皮

CHAFFER, *to* leng-liang' kô'-din 論量價°錢°

CHAFING-DISH (containing coals for keeping tea warm), nön'-lu 煖爐; — (for vegetables) nön'-ko 煖鍋; *steam heater for food*, t'ông bo'-ts 湯婆子; nön'-un 煖碗

CHAGRIN, *to feel* —, ao'-nao 懊惱

CHAIN, lin-diao' 鏈條 (ih-fu)

CHAIR, ü-ts 椅°子 (ih-pô); *arm* —, ü'-ts yiu k'ao'-siu-go 椅°子有靠手个°; *folding* —, tsih'-diah-ü' 摺疊椅°; *camp* —, mô'-tseh-ü' 馬扎椅°; *sedan* —, gyiao-ts' 轎子 (ih-ting);

tilt the —, gyiao-ts' sing-ky'i'-læ 轎子升起來; *set it (the chair) down level*, fông gyi bing' 放其平

CHAIR-BEARER, gyiao-fu' 轎夫 (ih-ming); gyiao-pæn' 轎班; gyiao-nying' 轎人°

CHALK, bah-t'u' 白°土

CHALLENGE, *to* t'ao tsin' 討戰; *to reject a* —, min'-tsin 免戰

CHAMBER, *bed* ngo-vông' 臥房; vông-kæn' 房間°; kw'eng-kæn' 寢°室°; *a lady's* —, ne-vông' 內房; *officer's* —, zông-vông' 上房; — *pot*, shü-bing' 尿瓶; yia-wu' 夜°壺; bin-wu' 便壺; *wooden ditto*, yia-dong' 夜°桶

CHAMBER-MAID, a-m' 阿°姆°; ah-sao' 阿嫂; *female slave*, ô-deo' 丫頭

CHAMOIS, ling-yiang 羚羊

CHAMOMILE. See CAMOMILE.

CHAMP, *to chew*, ziah 嚼

CHANCE, *by* vu-i'-cong 無意中; neo'-ts'eo 偶湊; ih'-feh-læ'-kwu 一弗來顧; *met by* —, ngeo'-jün p'ông'-djoh-de 偶°然逢着°了°; *seize the best* —, tsin bin-i' 佔便宜°; tsin siang-ing'; *seize the first* —, tsin zông-fong' 佔上風; tsin min-ts' 佔面子

CHANCELLOR, *literary* 'oh'-dæ 學°臺; — (of the Imperial Academy), da tsong'-dzæ 大總裁; (styled) tsong-s' 宗師

CHANDLER. *tallow* lah-coh'-s-vu 蠟燭司務

CHANGE, *to* keng-kæ' 更改; pin 變; pin'-wun' 變換; pin'-yih 變易; — *for the worse*, pin'-diao 變壞°; — *color*, pin seh' 變色; pin'-wun ngæn-seh' 換顏°色; — *in appearance*, pin yiang' 變樣; — *disposition*, sing'-dzing keng-pin' 性情更變; sing'-dzing pin'-hwô 性情變化; — *one's dress*, wun i-zông' 換衣裝; — *often*, cün-pin' 轉變; — *a dollar*, de fæn-ping' 倒番餅; — *one's mind*, sing cün-diao' 心轉調; *to exchange*, wun 換; diao 調; diao-wun' 調換; *cannot be changed* (altered), keng-kæ'-feh-læ 更改弗來; kæ'-ko-feh-læ 改過弗來; *changed in heart, or mind* (generally for the worse), sing' weh'-de 心活了°; sing' weh-dong'-de 心活動了°; sing pin'-de 心變了°

CHANGEABLE, hyih'-hyih yiu kyi-pin' 時時有機變; fæn'-foh-vu-djông 反覆無常 (djông or dzông); — (as weather, or clouds), ts'in-pin'-væn'-hwô 千變萬化

CHANGER, *money* dzin-tin'-kwun 錢店中°人°

CHANNEL, shü'-lu 水°路; shü'-dao 水°道; *to dig a* —, k'æ 'o-dao' 開河道

CHANT, *to* — *religious books*, (as Buddhists do), nyiæn kying' 念經; dzong kying' 誦經; — *and worship*, pa ts'æn' 拜°懺

CHAOTIC, weng'-deng 混沌

CHAP, *to* — (as the hands), c'ing-ts'ah' 皴坼; k'æ-kyüing' 開皯

CHAPEL, li-pa-dông' 禮拜°堂 (ih-go)

CHAPTER, *a* ih-tsông' 一章; ih-p'in' 一篇

CHAR, *to* tön 煅; siao 燒; *this wood is charred*, keh'-go za tön' tso t'æn'-de 這°个°柴煅做炭了°

CHARACTER, *letter*, z 字; z-ngæn' 字眼° (ih-go); *understands characters*, sih'-teh z' 識得字; *a person's* —, p'ing'-'ang' 品行; nying-p'ing' 人°品; p'ing'-kah 品格; ming-tsih' 名節; *his* — *is worthless*, gyi-go p'ing'-'ang feh ky'i'-djong 其个°品行弗器重; *lose one's* —, shih ming-tsih' 失名節

CHARCOAL, t'æn 炭; *soft wood* —, fu-t'æn' 麩炭; *hard wood* —, bah-t'æn 白°炭

CHARGE, *expense*, fi'-yüong 費用; *I will bear the* —, keh z ngô dzing-dzih'-go 這°是我承值个°; *he gave it in my* —, gyi kao-dæ' peh ngô' 其交代與°我; *a* — *to be borne*, po'-tih go tseh'-zing 背的个°責任; t'iao-tih-go tæn'-deo 挑的°个°擔頭

CHARGE, *to command*, feng-fu' 吩附; — *repeatedly*, ting-coh' 叮囑; *to entrust*, t'oh 託; kao-dæ° 交代 &c.; *to put in — of another* (as papers of office &c.), kao-bun' 交盤°; — *on account*, zông tsiang' 上帳; — *him with a fault*, wô ze' kwe'-ü gyi' 話罪歸于其; — *falsely*, ün-wông' 冤枉; ün-ky'üih' 冤屈; 'en hyüih' p'eng nying' 含血噴人°; — *the fault to me*, kwe gyiu ü ngô 歸咎于我; — *with a fault* (in one's hearing, but not to his face), k'ao-toh'; — *a price*, t'ao kô'-din 討價° 錢°; *to attack*, ts'ong-fong' 衝鋒

CHARITABLE, yiu jing-æ'-sing 有仁愛心; yiu dz-pe'-sing 有慈悲心; yiu ts'eh-ing'-ts-sing 有惻隱之心; *very —*, kwông' tso hao'-z 廣做好事

CHARITABLY, *deal — with him*, dæ gyi kw'un-shü' 待其寬恕

CHARITY, jing-æ' 仁愛; *to give —*, tsiu-tsi' nying-kô 賙濟人° 家°; 'ang hao'-z 行°好事; pu'-s nying-kô' 佈施人°家°

CHARM, (paper with characters), vu 符 (ih-dao); — *for the body*, wu-sing'-vu 護身符; — (for the wrist), dao-weh' 桃核; — (for the neck of children), 'ông'-so 項鎖; — (for the bed), ts'ông-bu-'en' 菖蒲孩°; dong-din'-pao'-kyin 銅錢° 寶劍; — (over the door), pao'-en-ts 保安紙; — (in the ancestral hall), cing'-dzeh-vu 鎮宅符; — (for protecting house furniture and utensils, pasted on at the New Year), ts'ing-long'-ts 青龍紙

CHARM, *to — away bad influences*, bih zia' 辟邪°; — *away disease* (by incantation), c'ih'-kying'djü-bing' 出經治病; *ditto* (by incantation, and written characters), yüong vu-tsiu'djü bing' 用符咒治病; *to captivate*, mi-weng' 迷魂

CHARMED (as by a spell), jih-mi-weng'-dzing-de 入迷魂陣了°

CHARMING *person*, gyih-me'-go nying 極美个°人°; — *music*, hyih weng-ling' go yüoh' 攝魂靈个°樂

CHART, *marine* dziu-hæ'-du 籌海圖 (ih-tsiang)

CHARTER, *to — a vessel*, tsu jün' 租船; shü' jün 賃°船

CHASE, *the* tang-liah' 打獵

CHASE, *to* tse-ken' 追趕; ken'-zông-ky'i 趕上去°

CHASM, di' lih-k'æ'-go di'-fông 地裂開个°地方 (ih-da)

CHASTE, ts'ing'-kyih' 清潔; tsing-kyih' 貞潔, said of women; tsing-tsih' 貞節, used when a single or widowed woman remains chaste.

CHASTISE, to punish, tsah'-vah 責罰; tang 打;— severely, djong' tsah'-vah 重責罰; ying-vah' 刑罰 is used for legal punishment but not often in school, or in the family.

CHASTITY (of men), sin-nyi' 守義;— (of maidens), siu-tsing' 守貞;— (of women), siu-tsih' 守節

CHAT, to dæn'-dæn 談談; jü-jü' 叙叙; kông-kông 講°講°; idle talk, 'æn wô' 閒°話; siao' wô 笑話

CHATTLES, kô-s'-jih-veh' 家°私什物; kô-yüong'-jih-veh' 家°用什物

CHATTER, to ts'ih'- ts'ih - ts'oh-ts'oh kông 說°話 嘈雜講°; kông in' wô 講 燕話; teeth —, ngô'-ts' siang-tang' 牙°齒相打

CHEAP, zin 賤°; bin-i' 便宜°; (cheaper than it ought to be), ky'iao 巧; ky'ing-ky'iao' 輕巧; — (the proper price) siang-ing' 相應; feh-kyü' 弗貴°; can you sell cheaper? ng' kô'-din hao weh-dong'-tin feh 你°價°錢好活動點否°?

CHEAPEN, to kæn kô' 減°價°

CHEAT, one who gets by pretence, kwa'-ts 拐°子; one who pretends to be what he is not, pæn kô'-nying 扮假°人°

CHEAT, to ky'i 欺; p'in 騙; hong 哄; ky'i-p'in' 欺騙; hong-p'in 哄騙; can — men, cannot — God, nying' k'o ky'i', Jing, feh-k'o' ky'i 人°可欺神弗可欺; to — by asking more than one pays (in buying for another), loh dong-din' 落銅錢°; every trade has its cheating, pah' 'ong pah' bi 百°行百°弊; to get something on false pretences, kwa'-p'in 拐°騙; to get money ditto, p'in dong-din' 騙銅錢°; he can't — me, gyi' kwa ngô', kwa'-feh-ky'i' 其拐我拐弗去°.

CHECK, order for money, nying-p'iao' 銀票

CHECK, to stop, or hinder, tön'-djü 擋住; lah-djü' 拉住; tsu'-djü 阻住; — by comparing, te'-ko 對過;— disease, djü bing 治病;— diarrhœa, ts dza' 止瀉

CHECKED, disease is —, bing ts'ô'-loh-lœ'-de 病漸差了°; bing-shü' ky'ing-k'o'-de 病勢輕可了°; bing song'-de 病鬆了°

CHEEK, cü'-bu 嘴輔° (ih-min); the right —, jing-pin' cü'-bu 順邊嘴輔°

CHEEK-BONES, gyün-kweh' 頰骨; high —, gyün'-kweh kao' 頰骨高

CHEER, entertainment, tsiu'-zih 酒席; — him up, kw'un gyi'-go sing' 寬其个°心; k'æ gyi' go sing' 開其个°心; to encourage, min'-li 勉勵;— by *striking hands and feet*, siu vu tsoh-dao-go ts'ing-tsæn' 手舞足蹈个° 稱讚

CHEERFUL, ken-sing'-go 甘心个°; *always* —, djông-djông' hyi'-siao-yin-k'æ' 常常喜笑顏開

CHEERFULLY, *do* ken-sing'dzing-nyün tso' 甘心情願做; dziung-nyün' do-c'ih' 情願拿°出; *give* —, byi' dzu 喜助; loh dzu' 樂助

CHEERLESS, c'ü-hyiang 無°趣向; *narrow and — place*, di-fông' 'ah-'ah-tsah-tsah feh sông'-kw'a 地方狹窄弗爽快°

CHEESE, ngeo-na' ping 牛°嬭°餅; jü' ping 乳餅

CHEMISE, t'i-li sæn' 襯°裡衫 (ih-gyin)

CHERISH, *hold as dear*, ziang pao'-pe ka tông-sing' 像寶貝个°當心; — *resentment*, ün'-'eng sing'-li dzeng'-tih 怨恨心裡存的; ün'-ky'i feh sæn' 怨氣弗散; ün'-ky'i k'eo-li 'en'-tih 怨氣口裏含的

CHERRY, ang-dao' 櫻桃; ang-cü' 櫻珠 (ih-go); — *color*, nyi'-'ong seh 二°紅色

CHESS, ziang'-gyi 象棋; — *board*, gyi-bun' 棋盤; — *men*, gyi-ts' 棋子; — *pawns*, ping-tseh' 兵卒; *to play* —, tsiah gyi' 著棋

CHEST, siang-ts' 箱子 (ih-tsah); — *of tea*, ih-siang dzô-yih' 一箱茶葉; *the breast*, hyüong-kwun'-deo 胸管°頭

CHESTNUT, lih-ts' 栗子 (ih-go); — *tree*, lih-ts' jü 栗子樹 (ih-cü)

CHEW, *to* ziah 嚼

CHICKEN, kyi 雞; siao-kyi' 小雞 (ih-tsah)

CHICKEN-POX, shü'-deo 水°痘

CHIDE, *to* tsah 責; tsah'-be 責備; — *in a severe tone*, heng ch°

CHIEF, *the first*, di-ih-go 第一个°; *the head*, deo 頭; deo-nao' 頭腦; *of — importance*, deo iao-kying' 第一要緊; — *of an army*, nyün-sæ' 元帥; tsiang-kyüing' deo-moh' 將軍頭目

CHIEFLY, di-ih' 第一; *more than half*, ih-do-pun' 一大半; — *indebted to you*, di-ih' to-dzing' ng 第一多承你°

CHILBLAIN, tong'-tsoh 凍瘡 (ih-go); *to have chilblains*, sang tong'-tsoh 生°凍瘡

CHILD, siao-nying 小孩°; *an infant*, na-hwun' 嬰°孩°; *with* —, yiu sing-yüing' 有身孕; *to bear children*, sang na-hwun' 生°嬰°孩°

CHILD-BED, *in* zông zo'-dong 上坐°桶; ling-beng' 臨盆

CHILDHOOD, siao-læ'-z-'eo' 小來時候; iu'-nyin 幼年; siao-nyin-z-tsi' 少年時節

CHILDLESS, m'-teh ng-nô' 沒°有°兒°女°; m'-teh sang-loh'

CHI 73 CHO

沒°有°生°落; vu-'eo 無後 CHILDREN, ng-nö' 兒°女°; ng-ts nön'; *little boys*, siao-wæn' 小兒°

CHILL, *in a* —, 'en seo-seo 寒凍凍

CHILLY, lang'-ts'ing-ts'ing 冷°清清; *very* —, 'en-gying'-gying 寒噤噤; — *from fear*, hah-leh kyiah' siu ping-lang' 嚇得°脚手冰冷°

CHIMNEY, in-ts'ong' 烟囱 (ih-dao); *lamp* —, teng-tsæn in-dong' 燈盞烟囱 (ih-kwun)

CHIN, 'ô'-bô 下吧°

CHINA, Cong-koh 中國; Da-ts'ing'-koh 大清國; Cong-wô' 中華; — *proper*, Jih-pah' sang 十八省

CHINA-ASTER, kyüh'-hwô 菊°花

CHINA-WARE, dz-ky'i' 磁器; *fine* —, si' dz-ky'i' 細磁器

CHINESE, *native of China*, Cong-koh nying' 中國人°; Hen'-nying 漢人°; — *language*, Cong-koh' wô' 中國話; — *character*, Hen' z 漢字

CHINK, hwah'-lih-vong 豁裂縫 (ih-da); *very small* —, hwah'-u; — *of dollars*, yiang-dzin' sing-byiang' 洋錢聲響

CHIPS, moh-fi' 木屑°

CHIP, *to* — *wood*, siah jü 削樹

CHIRP, *to* — (*as a sparrow*), kyiao 叫; *noisy chirping* (*as of magpies*), ts'ao 吵

CHISEL, zoh 鑿 (ih-kwun)

CHIT-CHAT, 'æn-wô' 閒話; k'ong'-deo-wô 空頭話

CHOICE, *selected*, kæn'-shün-go 揀選個°; t'iao'-shün-go 挑選個°; — *goods*, zông-teng'-go ho'-veh 上等個°貨物; — *friend*, zông-teng'-go beng-yiu' 上等個°朋友; *I have no* —, vu sô' kæn'-dzeh 無所揀°擇

CHOIR *of singers*, ih-pæn we ts'ông'-go cü'-kwn 一班會唱個°人°

CHOKE, *to* — *with something in the throat*, gang wu-long' 哽喉嚨; — *to death*, gang'-sah 哽煞; *to* — *to death with the hand*, k'ah'-sah 搭煞

CHOLERA, *vomiting and purging*, hoh'-lön' t'u-sia 霍亂吐瀉°; *spasms in the limbs*, kyiah-kying'-tiao 脚筋吊

CHOLERIC *temperament*, sing'-kah ts'ao' 性格躁°; sing'-dzing bao-ts'ao' 性情暴躁°; sing'-ts kyih' 性子急; *temperament like thunder*, sing-ts ziang le ka-go 性子如°雷

CHOOSE, *to* t'iao 挑; kæn 揀°; shün 選; kæn'-shün 揀°選; kæn'-dzeh 揀°擇; *whichever you* —, ze ng' kæn 隨你°揀°

CHOP, *to* p'ih 劈; *to* — *wood*, p'ih za' 劈柴; — *meat fine*, nyüoh tsæn-se' 肉°切碎; *a mark*, z-'ao' 字號; *mutton* —, yiang ba'-kweh 羊排°骨

CHOPPING-BOARD, tsing-pæn' 椹板
CHOPPING-KNIFE, boh-tao' 厨刀 (ih-pô)
CHOP-STICKS, kw'æn 筷° (a pair ih-sông)
CHORD *of a musical instrument,* yin-sin' 絃線 (ih-keng)
CHORISTER, *choir-leader,* ling-deo' ts'ông'-go 領頭唱个°
CHOWDER, ng-kang' 魚°羹°
CHRIST, Kyi-toh' 基督
CHRISTIAN, siang-sing Yiæ-su'-go nying 相信耶穌个°人°; *disciple of Jesus,* Yiæ-su' meng-du' 耶穌門徒; Kyi-toh'-du 基督徒
CHRISTIANITY, Yiæ-su' kyiao 耶穌教
CHRONICLES, s'-kyi 史記; kông-kæn' 綱鑑°; — (in the Bible), Lih-dæ-ts' liah 歷代志畧
CHRONOLOGY, pin-nyin'-kyi'-loh 編年紀錄
CHRYSALIS, kyin 繭; — *of a silk-worm,* zen-kyin' 蠶繭
CHURCH, *body of christians,* kyiao'-we 教會; kong-we' 公會; kyiao'-meng 教門; *place of worship,* li-pa-dông' 禮拜°堂; — *member,* kyiao'-yiu 教友; dzæ-kyiao'-go 在教个°
CHURLISH, *rude,* ts'u-lu' 粗鹵; *niggardly,* pi'-si 鄙細; pi'-seh 鄙嗇

CICATRICE, CICATRIX, pô 疤; — *of a wound,* sông-pô' 傷疤
CIDER, bing-ko'-tsiu 平菓酒
CINDERS, siao-dzing'-go me' 燒剩个°煤; *pick out the —,* siao-dzing'-go me', kæn'-c'ih 燒剩个°煤揀°出
CINNABAR, cü-sö' 硃砂
CINNAMON, nyüoh-kwe' 肉°桂; kwe'-bi 桂皮; *the best —,* zông-yiao' kwe 上猺桂;—*tree,* kwe'-jü 桂樹
CIPHER, *to* sön 算; the word ling 零, a fragment, is used to denote parts of tens, parts of hundreds, &c.; thus 108 is read, ih-pah ling pah 一百°零八; 1050 is read, ih ts'in ling ng-jih 一千零五°十
CIRCLE, yün-ky'ün' 圓圈 (ih-go); *draw a —,* wô ih-go ky'ün' 畫一个°圈; *center of a —,* yün-ky'ün'-go cong-sing' 圓圈个°中心
CIRCLING, dön-ky'ün' yü-tæn'-cün 團圈圍°轉
CIRCULAR, *official* tsiao'-we 照會; *business —,* cü-tæn' 知單; *send round a —,* feng cü-tæn' 分知單
CIRCULATE, *to* — (as air &c.) yüing-dong' 運動; — (as a person), tseo'-dong 走動; 'ang-dong' 行°動; — (as the blood), cün'-dong 轉動;—(as a report), yiang-k'æ' 揚開

CIRCUMCISION, tsiu-keh'-li 周割禮
CIRCUMFERENCE, tsiu-we' 周圍; what is the — of the earth? di-gyiu tsiu-we' yiu to-siao' li 地球周圍有多少里?
CIRCUMJACENT, tsiu'-we-siang-gying' 周圍相近
CIRCUMLOCUTION, wæn-wæn'-ky'üoh-ky'üoh-go kông' 彎彎曲曲個°講°
CIRCUMSCRIBED by difficult circumstances, be kying'-hwông dzin-djü'-liao 被境況纏住了; the space is —, dæn-dziang' be di-gyüoh' 'æn'-sah-liao 壇場被地局限°煞了
CIRCUMSPECT, ts'-si 仔細; siao'-sing-go 小心個°
CIRCUMSTANCES, kwông-kying' 光景; dzing-ying' 情形; kying'-hwông 境況; judging from — (as of a country), k'en'-k'en ying-shü' 看看形勢; accommodate one's self to —, ze-kyi' ing'-pin 隨機應變; to act according to —, tso z-ken', k'en'-ky'i sang'-dzing 做事幹看起生°情; kyin-kyi'-r-ying' 見機而行; yielding to — I let you go, ngô dzong-gyün', peh ng ky'i' 我從權俾°你°去°; in reduced —, gyüong'-de 窮了°
CIRCUMVENT, to — plans, p'o fah' 破法
CITE, to call, djün-tsing'-læ 傳進來; — from a book, shü'-li ying'-læ 書裡引來
CITIZEN, dzing-li'-nying 城裡人°
CITRON, large (citrus medica), hyiang-lön' 香橼; Buddha's hand, veh-siu' 佛手
CITY, dzing-ts' or zing-ts' 城子; (ih-zo); — wall, dzing-ziang' 城牆; — moat, dzing-dzi' 城池
CIVIL, polite, yiu li' 有禮; yiu li'-mao 有禮貌; yiu li'-tsih 有禮節; — and military, veng vu' 文武
CIVILITY, li 禮; li'-mao 禮貌; li'-tsih 禮節
CLAIM, I — your promise, ng sô ing-hyü, ngô iao-de 你°所應許, 我要了°; — one's money, t'ao doung-din' kyü-læ 討銅錢°歸來; have a right to —, yiu meng-veng' hao t'ao' 有名°分好討
CLAIMANT, t'ao'-cü 討主
CLAM, yün-keh' 圓蛤 (ih-go)
CLAMBER, to bô-zông 爬上; weh'-zông 挖上; hyih'-zông; — up (a rope or pole), jing-zông'-ky'i 循上去°
CLAMOR, to nao 鬧; ts'ao'-nao 吵鬧
CLAMOROUS, nao-nyih'-go 鬧熱°個°; nao-nao'-nyih-nyih-go ts'ao' 鬧鬧熱°熱°個°吵
CLAN, dzoh 族; dzoh-veng' 族分 (ih, and ih-go); belonging to the —, dzoh cong' 族中; all of a

family, zi-kô'-nying 自°家°人°; *of the same* —, dong-dzoh'-go 同族个°; dong-sing' go 同姓个°; *of the same family name but of a different* —, dong sing' feh we dzoh 同姓不°宗

CLANDESTINE, s-'ô' 私下°; kyü-tao-ih-koh; t'eo-bun' 偷瞞°; en'-me 暗昧

CLANDESTINELY, ing'-dzông 隱藏

CLANK (of a chain), lông-lông'-hyiang 鋃鋃響

CLAP, *to* kwah 摑; — *on the face*, kwah' ih-kwông 摑一掌°; — *the table, &c.*(as if angry), kwah'-coh tang-teng' 摑桌打凳

CLAP *of thunder*, p'ih'-le 霹靂° (ih-go)

CLARIFY, *to* di-ts'ing' 提清; — *it by settling*, ting' gyi-ts'ing 淀°其清; — *by skimming*, keh' ken-zing' 格乾淨°; — *by straining*, li' ken-zing' 濾乾淨°

CLASH, *to* k'eh'-k'eh-bang-bang' 磕磕撞°撞°; — *in opinion*, i'-s ts'o-p'ing' 意思差摒; i'-s gah-tang'.

CLASP, *n.* k'eo 扣; tah'-k'eo 搭扣

CLASS, *sort*, le 類 (ih); *a* — *of pupils*, ih-pæn' 'oh-sang'-ts 一班學°生°子; — (*in society*), teng 等; kyih 級

CLASSICS, *Chinese* kying-shü' 經書; s'-shü ng'-kying 四書五°經

CLASSIFY, *to* feng le' 分類; feng 'ao-sü' 分號數

CLAW, tsao 爪; kyiah'-tsao 脚爪

CLAY, na-nyi' 坭; *potter's* —, wông na-nyi' 黃坭

CLEAN, ken-zing' 乾淨°; kyih'-zing 潔淨°; ts'ing-kyih' 清潔; — *as snow*, kying'-ken-shih-zing' 鏡乾雪淨°

CLEAN, *to* long ken'-zing 弄°乾淨°; — *by washing*, gyiang' ken-zing 洗°乾淨°; — *up* (as *a place, &c.*), tsiu-tsoh'.

CLEAR, ming 明; *very* — (as water, glass, &c.), kwang'-ts'ing 洸清; pih'-po'-s-ts'ing' 碧波四清; — (as ideas), ling'-ts'ing 靈清; — *weather*, t'in zing' 天晴°; — *profit*, zing dong'-din 淨°錢; — *from blame*, 'ao'-vu yüô-tin' 毫無瑕玷; pih'-po'-s ts'ing' 碧波四清

CLEAR, *the weather will* —, t'in we k'æ' 天會開; — *up* (by explanation), kông' ming-bah' 講明白°; — *the way*, nyiang lu' 讓路; *ditto by calling* (before an officer), heh dao' 喝道; — *one's self*, feng ka' 分解°

CLEARLY, ming-tông'-tông 分°明; ts'ing-t'ong' 清通; t'eo' ming-bah'-go 透明白°个°

CLEARNESS *of vision*, ngæn'-kwông tsin' 眼°光尖; ngæn'-ho tsin' 眼°火尖; ngæn'-tsing liang' 眼°睛亮

CLE 77 CLO

CLEAVE, to p'ih-劈; p'ih'-k'æ 劈開
CLEAVER for wood, za-tao' 柴°刀; ken-tao' 鋸°刀 (ih-pô)
CLEFT, vong-dao' 縫道; crack, hweh'-lih-vong 轄裂縫; hweh'-u 轄裂° (ih-da)
CLEMENCY, to treat with —, kw'un-shü' dæ 寬恕待; kw'un-dæ' 寬待; treat a person with —, dæ nying kw'un' 待人°寬
CLEPSYDRA, dong-wu-tih'-leo 銅壺滴漏
CLERGYMAN, kyiao'-s 敎°師 (ih-we)
CLERK, writer, dæ-shü' 代書; dæ-pih' 代筆; — (in a store), ho'-kyi 夥計; — (in a ya-men) shü-bæn' 書辦
CLEVER, ling-ky'iao' 靈巧; ling-li' 伶俐; hwæn 儇°
CLEVERLY done (as work), si'-ky'iao 細巧
CLIFF, zah-pih' 石°壁; ts'iao'-pih 峭壁
CLIMATE, shü'-t'u 水°土; fong-ky'i' 風氣; is the — good or bad? shü'-t'u hao' wa 水土好孬°? unfavorable —, shü'-t'u feh voh' 水°土弗服; fong-ky'i' feh-te' 風氣弗對
CLIMB, to bô 扒; byih; weh 挖; — a tree, byih jü' 挖°樹; — the wall, bô ziang' 扒牆; — a hill, weh sæn' 挖山; — a rope, jing zing' 循繩

CLINCH, to hold fast, nyiah lao' 捻牢; — a nail, ting-cü' cün-kyiah' 釘銖轉脚; — (as a matter), k'ao-ting'-cün-kyiah' 拷釘轉脚
CLING, to byih'-lao 噲牢; la-lao' feh fông' 拉°牢弗放; — to his mother, byih-kying ah-nyiang' di'-fông 不°離°其°母°
CLIP off a little (with scizzors), tsin'-tin-diao 剪點去°; zæ-tin'-diao 裁點去°
CLIPPINGS of cloth, se-pu-den' 碎布頭; pu-tsin'-se 布剪碎
CLOCK, z-ming'-cong 自鳴鐘 (ih-kô); what o'clock is it? kyi tin'-cong 幾點鐘? one o'clock, ih tin'-cong 一點鐘
CLOCK and watch maker, cong-piao'-s-vu 鐘表司務
CLOD, a ih-kw'e na-nyi' 一塊坭
CLOG, to choke up, seh'-sah 塞煞; seh'-djü 塞住
CLOGGED, shoes — with mud, 'a, na-nyi' dong-mun'-de 鞋俸°坭遭°滿了°
CLOGS, moh-gyih' 木屐; jü-'a' 樹鞋°; hyiang-'a' 響鞋° (a pair, ih-sông)
CLOISTER, Buddhist z 寺; en 菴°; Taoist —, kwun 觀; nunnery, nyi-kwu' en 尼姑菴
CLOSE of life, lao'-mæn z-'eo 老邁時候; sông yü væn'-kying 桑榆晚景 (veng); sunset

of life, nyih-deo' loh-sæn' z-'eo 日°頭落山時候。
CLOSE *the door,* kwæn meng' 關門; — *all the doors and windows,* kwæn-meng'-dông-wu 關門閉戶; — *the eyes,* ngæn'-tsing pi'-long 眼°睛閉攏; *ditto,* (when sleepy), ngæn'-tsing mi-long' 眼°睛眯攏; — *the mouth,* cü'-pô pi'-long 嘴吧閉攏; — *a letter,* fong sing' bao 封信好; — *a book,* shü' siu-long' 書收攏; — *in* (as with brick), diah-sah' 疊煞; ts-sah'; seh-sah' 塞煞; mun-sah' 堘煞; — (as a wound), sang-long' 生°攏; — (as a boil), siu-k'eo' 收口。
CLOSE (in texture), si'-kyih 細潔; kyih'-jih 硈實; *niggardly,* pi'-seh 鄙嗇; ky'i'-liang siao' 氣量小; liang tseh' 量窄; lin'-kyin 連寠; gyih-li'-li; — *weather,* t'in-ky'i seh'-meng 天氣塞悶; — *by,* siang-gying' 相近; — *to,* t'iah'-gying 貼近。
CLOSET, djü 廚; — *in the wall,* pih'-djü 壁廚 (ih-k'eo); *small —* (in a corner, under stairs, &c.), beh-keh-long' 鵓鴿籠; *secret* —, kah-ziang' 夾°牆; *water —*, siao'-bin vông-ts' 小便房子; mao-k'ang' 毛°坑°。
CLOT, *to* nying-long' 凝攏。
CLOTH, pu 布 (used alone, only for cotton cloth); *good native cotton —*, du'-pu 杜布; *linen —*, mô-pu' 麻布; keh'-pu 葛布; coh'-pu 竹布; *nankeen,* ts'-hwô-pu' 紫花布; *bleached foreign —*, bah-yiang'-pu 白洋布; *grass —*, 'ô-pu' 夏布; *twilled cotton —*, zia-veng' pu 斜°紋布; *oiled —*, yiu-pu' 油布; *broad —*, nyi 呢; *woolen —* (flannel, &c.), nyüong-pu' 絨布。
CLOTHES, i-zông' 衣裳°; i-voh' 衣服。
CLOTHES, *he — me,* gyi peh ngô' c'ün-tsiah' 其給°我穿著°; ngô i-zông' z gyi' kwun'-go 我衣裳°是其管个°; ngô c'ün-djoh' gyi-go 我穿著°其个°。
CLOUD, yüing 雲; *red —*, 'ong ngô' 紅霞°; — *of dust,* hwe, bang-bang'-yiang 灰飛°揚了°。
CLOUDLESS, væn-li'-vu-yüing' 萬里無雲。
CLOUDY *weather,* zông-yüing t'in' 上雲天; ing t'in' 陰天; ing-a' t'in 陰靉°天。
CLOVES, ting-hyiang' 丁香。
CLOWN (in a play), siao-hwô-lin' 小花臉; (a) *rustic,* hyiang-'ô'-nying 鄉下°人°。
CLOWNISH, *like a clown,* ziang siao-hwô-lin' ka 像小花臉; *coarse,* ts'u-lu' 粗鹵; ts'u-ts'ao' 粗糙。
CLOYED, *to be* ky'üoh'-bi-de 吃°疲了°; ky'üoh'-in'-de 吃°厭了°; ky'üoh'-leh in'-tsao-tsao 吃°得°厭遭遭。

CLUB, kweng'-ts 棍子 (ih-keng)
CLUB together and hire a boat, tah jün' 搭船; to — together for eating, p'ing ho'-zih 摒火食; — together to live, p'ing-deng' 摒庤; — together to buy, p'ing ma' 摒買°
CLUE, deo-jü' 頭緒; can't find the — (to the idea), moh-feh-djoh' deo-jü' 摸弗着°頭緒; to trace out a —, jing deng' 攀°籐; have the —, yiu tsông-tsing' 有眰証; no — to the thief, zeh' ṃ-ing' ṃ-tsong'-de 賊無°影無°踪了°
CLUMSY, dön-ky'iao-go 不°入°竅个°
CLUSTER, ih-gyiu 一毬; ih-p'ang'.
CLUTCH, to c'ô 撮°
COAGULATE, to nying-long' 凝攏; kyih'-long 結攏; tong 凍
COAL, me-t'æn' 煤炭 (a piece, ih-kw'e)
COALESCE, to 'eh-long' 合攏; will not —, 'eh-feh-long' 合弗攏
COAL-MINE, me-t'æn' yüih 煤炭穴; me sæn' 煤山
COAL-SCUTTLE, me-t'æn' dong 煤炭桶
COARSE, ts'u 粗
COAST, hæ'-pin 海邊; all along the —, yin hæ' ih-tæ' 沿海一帶
COAST, to sail along the —, yin-hæ'-pin s' 沿海邊駛

COAT, long — to be worn with a girdle, bao-ts' 袍子; zông-mun', (a country term); long —, kah'-ao 袂襖; do-sæn' 大°衫; short jacket, mô'-kwô 馬䙅; foreign overcoat, do-i' 大°衣
COAT (of paint or white-wash), ih-du' 一塗; one —, tæn-du' 單塗; two coats of varnish, sông-du ts'ih 雙°塗漆; first —; deo-ih' du 頭一塗
COAX, to nyün' cü'-du 軟制度; yüong nyün'-kong 用軟工
COB, corn loh-koh sing' 稑穀心
COBWEB, bong-dzing' 塵塵; spider's —, kyih'-cü' mông' 蛣蛛網; kyih'-cü' lön-mông' 蛣蛛亂網°
COCHINEAL, ngô-læn'-mi 呀嚂米
COCK, yüong-kyi' 雄雞; kong-kyi' 公雞 (ih-tsah)
COCKSCOMB, kyi-kwun' 雞冠; — (a flower), kyi-kwun'-hwô' 雞冠花
COCK-CROWING, kyi-di'-go z-'eo' 雞啼个°時候
COCKLE, hen-ts' 蚶子
COCKROACH, ts'ông-lông' 蝻蟰 (ih-go)
COCOA-NUT, gyia-biao' 茄瓢 (ih-go)
COCOON, kyin 繭; — of silk-worms, zen-kyin' 蠶繭
CODE of laws, lih-li' 律例
CO-EQUAL, bing-teng' 平等; bing'-kyin 並肩; dong-po' 同輩

COERCE, to ah'-cü 壓°制; iah-cü' 挾制; ah'-shü 壓°勢
CO-ETERNAL, üong-yün dong-dzæ' 永遠同在
COFFEE, kô-fi 喫°啡, transferred from the English.
COFFEE-POT, kô-fi wu' 喫°啡壺
COFFER, nying-siang' 銀箱; yiang-siang' 洋箱; — for cash, dzin-gyü' 錢櫃°
COFFIN, kwun-zæ' 棺材°; kwun-moh' 棺木 (ih-k'eo); — containing the corpse, (i.e. the spirit coffin) ling-gyiu' 靈柩; to place in the —, jih-lin' 入殮; jih-moh' 入木; loh lin' 落殮; to see the body placed in the —, song-lin' 送殮
COFFIN-MAKER, kwun-zæ'-s-vu' 棺材°司務; keh'-zæ-s-vu' 合材°司務
COG of a wheel, leng-bun-ts' 輪盤齒 (ih-go)
COGENT, yiu gying-dao' 有勁道; — arguments, sô kông' dzing-li'-go 所講°情理個
CO-HEIR, to be dong ziu ts'æn-nyih 同受產業
COHERE, to kao-nyin' 膠°粘; nyin-long' 黏攏
COIL, a — of iron wire, ih-bun t'ih-s 一盤鐵絲; a — of rope, ih-dön zing' 一團繩
COIN, cash, dong-din 銅錢; dollars, yiang-dzin' 洋錢°

COIN, to — cash, cü dong-din' 鑄銅錢°
COIR, tsong-li' 棕櫚
COLANDER, tin sieve, mô'-k'eo-t'ih' s' 馬口鐵篩
COLD, lang 冷°; icy —, ping-lang' 冰冷°; to grow —, lang'-ky'i-læ 冷°氣來; to catch —, sông fong' 傷風; very — (as food, or a person), ping-kweh'-s-lang' 冰骨四冷°; seng'-kweh-deo 沁骨頭; to feel —, kyüoh'-teh lang' 覺得冷°; teh'-cü lang' 得知冷°
COLDLY, lang'-dæn 冷°淡; dæn-boh' 淡薄; he treated me —, gyi dæ ngô lang'-dæn 其待我冷°淡
COLIC, sô-ky'i' 痧氣; severe —, kao'-dziang-sô 絞°腸痧
COLLAPSE, in —, t'eh-nyün'-de 脫元了°; to — (as a vessel), ih'-long 凹攏; to shrivel, pih'-long 㽹攏
COLLAR, ling 領 (ih-keng)
COLLATE, to compare critically, ts'æn-k'ao' 參考
COLLECT, to — (as persons), jü'-long 聚攏; jü'-jih-long 聚集攏; siu'-jih-long 收拾攏; tsing'-long-læ 整攏來; to — from various places, seo-lo' 搜羅; — (as money), teo 兜; — voluntary small contributions, teo veng-ts' 兜分°子; — large contributions, siu kyün-'ông' 收捐項;

— revenue, siu-se' 收稅; to make up a sum of money, kyün-long' dong-din' 捐攏銅錢°.
COLLECTOR of land taxes, siu-zin-liang'-nying 收錢°糧人°; du-ts'a' 嗝差; liang-ts'a' 糧差; — of customs, siu-se' go-nying 收稅个°人°.
COLLEGE, shü-yün' 書院 (ih-go).
COLLIER. gyüih-me-t'æn'-go-nying 掘煤炭个°人°; k'æ-me-t'æn'-go-nying 開煤炭个°人°; charcoal maker, siao-t'æn'-nying 燒炭人°.
COLLIDE, to te'-deo-p'ong'; dô-kô bang' 大°家°撞; dô-kô dzông' 大°家°撞.
COLLOCATION (of words), lin-p'ing-go fah'-ts 連摒个°法子.
COLLUDE, to dô-kô' tang'-sön hong'-p'in 大°家°打算哄騙.
COLONEL, ts'æn-tsiang' 叅將; fu'-tsiang 副將.
COLONIZE, to form a new settlement, sing hying' ih-go mô'-deo 新興一个°碼頭.
COLOR, ngæn-seh' 顏色; neutral —, ts'in' seh 淺色; bright —, ts'e' seh 翠色; to lose —, shih seh' 失色; to change —, pin seh' 變色; faded —, ngæn-seh t'e'-diao-de 顏°色退掉了°; of the same —, ping seh' 拚色; of nearly the same —, (when they ought to be alike or quite different), deh seh' 套色.

COLOR, to nyin seh' 染色; to — red, nyin 'ông' 染紅.
COLUMN, djü'-ts 柱子 (ih-keng); — of characters, ih-da z' 一排字; ih-'ông' z 一行字; — of smoke, ih-kwu in' 一股烟 large ditto, ih-bong in' 一縷烟.
COMB, coarse s 梳°; fine —, bi-kyi' 篦箕 (ih-kwun); honey —, fong-k'o 蜂窩°.
COMB, to — the hair, s' deo-fah' 梳°頭髮; — and arrange ditto, s' deo' 梳°頭.
COMBAT, to siang-tang' 相打; — (as an army), tang-tsiang' 打仗°; — (as people among themselves), tang-nying-dzing' 打人°陣.
COMBINE, to 'eh-long' 合攏; combined strength, dong-sing' yiah-lih' 同心協力.
COME, to læ 來; coming, læ'-de 來了°; has —, læ-ko'-de 來過了°; came yesterday, zô-nyih'-ts læ'-go 昨°日°子來个°; I will — immediately, ngô ziu læ' 我就°來; — back the same day, tông'-nyih cün'-we 當日轉回; when did you — (up)? ng kyi'-z zông-læ' 你°幾時上來? — down (as Christ), kông'-loh 降落; — apart, t'ah'-k'æ 脫°開; — to such an end, ka' kyih-ko' 這°樣°結果; coming events, tsiang-læ'-go z-ken' 將來个°事幹.

COMET, sao'-tsin-sing' 掃帚星; we'-sing 彗星 (ih-lih)

COMFORT, to ky'ün'-ka 勸解; ka-meng' 解悶; sæn-sing 散心; en-we' 安慰; *he comforted me*, ngô ky'ü-leh gyi ky'ün'-ka 我 蔚 了 其 勸 解.

COMFORTABLE, shih'-i 適意; ziu'-yüong 受用; sông'-kw'a 爽快; hao'-ko; *this chair is very* — (*to sit in*), zo'-læ keh' pô ü'-ts ting ziu'-yüong 坐在 這把椅子頂受用; *in* — *circumstances*, weng-pao' 溫飽

COMFORTABLY *dressed*, c'ün'-leh pao'-nön 穿得飽煖

COMFORTLESS, 'ao-vu'c'ü'-hyiang 毫無趣向

COMICAL, hao fah-siao' 好發笑; ying nying' siao 引人笑

COMMAND, feng-fu' 吩咐; *an officer's* —, ling 令; 'ao-ling' 號令; *to issue a* —, c'ih 'ao-ling' 出號令

COMMAND, *to* feng-fu 吩咐

COMMANDER, *military—of a province*, di-toh' 提督; *naval* —, se'-s di-toh' 水師提督

COMMANDMENT, kyiæ 誡; *the ten commandments*, jih-diao kyiæ' 十條誡

COMMEMORATE, *to* kyi'-nyiæn 記念

COMMENCE, *to* zông sin' 上手; —*for the first time*, k'æ-sin' 開手. See BEGIN.

COMMEND *to your care*, t'oh ng kwun 託你管; — *him*, ngao' gyi hao' 贊其好; *to recommend*, kyü'-tsin 舉薦; *to praise*, ts'ing-tsæn' 稱讚; pao'-kyü 保舉

COMMENDATION, ts'ing-tsæn' 稱讚; *I am not worthy of that* —, keh'-go ts'ing-tsæn' ngô tông'-feh-ky'i' 這个稱讚我當弗起

COMMENT, *to* kông-ka' 講解; cü'-ka 註解

COMMENTARY, cü'-ka 註解; *fine print* —, si'-cü 細註 (ih-peng)

COMMENTATOR, cü cü-ka go nying 註註解个人

COMMERCE, kao-yih' 交易; ma'-ma 買賣; t'ong-sông' 通商

COMMISERATE, *to* k'o'-lin 可憐; æ-lin' 哀憐

COMMISSARY, yüing-liang'-kwun 運糧官 (generally the officer who has the care of the rice tribute).

COMMISSON, *officer's* bu'-tsiao 部照; —*for a special service*, we-ba 委牌; *a factor's percentage*, yüong-din' 用錢

COMMISSION, *to* we 委; —*him to manage*, we gyi bæn' 委其辦

COMMISSONER, we'-yün 委員; — *of customs*, se'-vu-s 稅務司; *salt* —, yin-yüing'-s 鹽運司

COMMIT, to t'oh 託; t'oh'-fu 託付; kao-dæ' 交代; to — to an inferior, fu'-t'oh 付託; I — this child to your care, keh-go siao-nying' ngô t'oh ng kwu'-djoh 這个小孩我託你顧着; — sin, væn ze' 犯罪; has committed sin, zo-ze'-liao 坐罪了; — to prison, loh lao-kæn' 落牢監; siu kæn' 守監 or 收監.

COMMITTEE, we'-bæn 委辦; deh-p'a' cü-kwn 特派个人.

COMMODIOUS, convenient, yiang-yiang' bin-tông' 樣樣便當; large, kw'un-ts'iah' 寬綽.

COMMON, ordinary, bing-dzông' 平常; bing-su' 平素; — (every day) use, bing-jih' yüong' 平日用; dzoh-nyih yüong' 逐日用; — clothes, bin-i' 便衣; bin-voh' 便服; — saying, dzoh'-wô' 俗話; too —, t'eh dzoh' 過於俗; — people, bing-deo' pah'-sing 平頭百姓; in — use, t'ong-yüong'-go 通用个; — custom, dzông-kwe' 常規; dzoh-li' 俗例; easy to be bought (or obtained), yüong-yi' ma 容易買; sang'-lih ma 省力買; to eat in —, p'ing ky'üoh 摒吃; to live in —, p'ing deng' 摒定.

COMMONLY so, da-kæ' z-ka 大概如此; bing-dzông' z-ka 平常如此.

COMMON-PLACE, feh c'ih'-seh 弗出色; feh hyi'-gyi 弗希奇.

COMMOTION, nao-nyih' 鬧熱; disturbance, ts'ao'-nao 吵鬧; why is this —? dza-we' ka nao-nyih' 如何這鬧熱? to cause a —, cü'-s-teh nao-nao' nyih-nyih' 致使得鬧鬧熱熱.

COMMUNE, to dæn-sing' 談心; fi'-fu-ts dæn' 肺腑之談; to partake of the Lord's Supper, ky'üoh sing'-væn-ts'æn 吃聖晚餐.

COMMUNICATE, he communicated it to me, z gyi' wô-hyiang'-ngô-dao-go 是其話向我道个; — news, pao sing'-sih 報信息; t'ong-fong'-pao-sing' 通風報信; t'ong-cü' sing'-sih 通知信息 (generally something secret, or improper); — disease, bing-yin-ko' 病延過.

COMMUNICATION, læ-læ'-ky'i-ky'i 來來去去; constant —, wông-læ-peh-djih' 往來不絕; verbal —, k'eo'-sing 口信 (ih-go); written —, shü-tsah' 書札 (ih-fong); official —, veng-shü' 文書; — from a foreign power, &c., tsiao'-we 照會 (ih-koh).

COMMUNION, the Lord's Supper, sing'-væn-ts'æn 聖晚餐; Cü' væn-ts'æn 主晚餐; — of saints, sing'-du siang-t'ong' 聖徒相通.

COMMUTE, to — a greater punishment for a less, kô ze'-ming 加°罪名;— a less punishment for a greater, kæn ying-vah' 減°刑罰
COMPACT, closely united, kyih'-jih 硈實;— (as the body), kyih'-kweng;— (as cloth), kyih'-tsoh 硈足;— (as a house), kying'-ts'eo 緊簇
COMPACT, a contract which is torn in two, and given to each party, 'eh-dong' 合同
COMPANION, de-ho' 隊夥; ts'eo-de' 湊隊; dong-de' cü-kwu 同隊个人; tso-de'-go nying 做隊个°人°; idle companions, sæn-beng' s-yiu' 三朋四友
COMPANY of soldiers, ih-de ping' 一隊兵; corporation, kong-s' 公司; fond of —, hwun-hyi' nying-k'ah' 歡喜客°人°; fond of idle —, hwun-hyi' sæn-beng'-s-yiu' 歡喜三朋四友
COMPARABLE, k'o'-pi 可比
COMPARE, to pi 比; pi'-kyiao 比較; pi'-pi-k'en' 比比看; — (as writings or numbers), te'-te-k'en' 對對看; te'-ko 對過
COMPARED, cannot be —, pi-feh-læ-go 比弗來个°
COMPARISON, pi'-yü 比喻; pi'-fông 比方; pi'-jü 比如; to draw a —, yüong pi'-fông pi-ih'-pi 用比方比一比; no —, ing'-tsong pi'-feh-læ 影踪

比弗來; m-kao' hao pi' 沒°有°好比
COMPASS, to environ, we-tæn'-cün 圍打°轉;— with or about, yü-cün' 圍°轉; nyiao-tæn'-cün 繞°打°轉
COMPASS, the Mariner's ts'-nen-tsing 指南針; hyiang'-bun 向盤;— used (by sorcerers) in selecting spots of ground, keh'-hyiang-bun 格向盤
COMPASSION, æ-lin'-sing 哀憐心; feel —, kyüoh'-teh yiu æ-lin'-sing 覺'得有哀憐心; to excite one's —, ken'-dong nying-go dz-pe'-sing 感動人°个°慈悲心
COMPEL, to pih'-leb 逼勒; ky'iang'-cü 強°制; ngang-iao' 硬要; ngang-k'ô' 硬拿°
COMPELLED, to be ngang-ts'-ts.
COMPENDIUM, ts'eh'-iao 撮要; tsah'-iao 摘要 (ih-peng);— of history, kông-kæn' ts'eh'-iao 綱鑑°撮要
COMPENSATE, to pao'-tah 報答; we-wæn' 回還; to make a return for some favor, pao-teh' 報德; pu'-pao 補報; this compensates for my loss (in money), keh' hao ti'-dzông ngô'-go su' 這°好抵償我个°數;— for your trouble, dziu-pao' ng-go lao-kw'u' 酬°報你°个°勞苦
COMPENSATION, I expected no —, ngô feh siang'-vông yiu we-wæn'

我弗想望有回還; *thank money*, zia-din' 謝°錢°; *reward money*, sông'-din 賞錢°; *a slight extra* — (*i.e. tea money or wine money*), dzö'-din 茶錢°; tsiu'-din 酒錢°; *have given him a — for his trouble*, dziu'-gyi-lao'-ko-de 巳°酬其勞

COMPETE, *to* bih 奔°; bih-gyiao'; tsang zông'-loh 爭°上落; — *for honor and wealth*, tseng-ming'-deh-li' 爭名奔利; tsang ming-sing' 爭°名聲; — *in trade*, bih sang-i' 奔生°意°; *able to — with*, k'o'-yi te'-dih 可以對敵; bing'-kyin-go 並肩个°

COMPETENT, *having ability*, yiu dzæ-'oh' 有才學°; yiu du'-dzæ 有肚才; — *to do* (a certain thing), nô-siu'-go 挐手个°; — *for*, k'o'-yi tæn-tông' 可以擔當; 'eh-yüong'-go 合用个°

COMPETITOR, ts'iang ing-yüong'-go nying 爭°英雄个°人°

COMPILE, *to* we'-jih-long 棠集攏

COMPILER, we'-jih-go nying' 棠集个°人°

COMPLACENT, *satisfied*, teh'-i-yiang'-yiang 得意揚揚

COMPLAIN *of trouble*, su kw'u' 訴苦; su t'ong'-kw'u 訴痛苦; — *of grievances*, su üu' 訴寃; — *of one's difficulties*, kông zi'-go mæn-c'u' 講自°个°難處;

— *of others behind their back*, pe' 'eo kông ko'-tön 背後講°過短; *to find fault with*, mao-üu' 埋°怨; s-we'.

COMPLEMENT, *full* ngah'-ts tsoh'-de 額子足了°; ngah'-ts mun'-de 額子滿了°; su'-moh zi-de 數目齊°了°; — *not full*, su' feh tsoh' 數弗足

COMPLETE, *not wanting*, djün-be' 全備; jih-djün' 十全; jih-tsoh' 十足; *finished*, wun-djün' 完°dzing-dziu' 成就; dzing-kong' 成功; — *happiness*, djün foh' 全福

COMPLETE, *to* tso'-dzing 做成; tso' wun-djün' 做完全; *to — arrangements*, bæn'-leh t'o'-tông 辦得妥當

COMPLETELY, jih-feng 十分; djün-djün' 全°全; — *consumed by fire*, ho' dziah-kwông'-de 火燒光了°; — *chilled*, weng'-sing tu lang'-de 渾身都冷°了°

COMPLEX, se'-væn 碎煩

COMPLEXION, min-seh' 面色; ky'i'-seh 氣色

COMPLIANT, yün-weh' 圓活; ze-væn' tao-væn' 隨意°而行°

COMPLICATED, *involved*, lin-lin'-ky'in-ky'in 連連率率; — *and intricate*, tsi-li'-tsæo-leo' 嚌哩喞嘍; — *affair*, dzin-ziao'-go z-t'i' 櫃繞个°事體

COMPLIMENT, *praise*, ts'ing-tsæn

稱讚; *to fish for a —*, t'ao nying-kô' vong'-dzing 討人°家°奉承; la-s' t'iao læ teng'-bun-li; *empty —*, veo-veng' shih-wô' 浮文說話; k'eh'-t'ao shih-wô' 客°套說話

COMPLIMENTS, *present my — to him*, dæ ngô' ts'ing-ts'ing gyi en' 代我請請其安

COMPLY, *to* i 依; *I will — with (your wishes)*, ngô' we i'ng 我會依你°; tseng-kyiao' 遵教

COMPOSE, *to* cü 著; cü'-tsoh 著作; *— a book*, cü shü' 著書; *— and collect*, cü-jih' 著述; *— an essay*, tso veng-tsông' 做文章; *— verse*, tso s' 做詩

COMPOSED (in mind), sing-ding' 心定; ding-ding'-sing-sing'; sing t'ih'-ding 心貼定; sing' feh-dong' 心弗動; *perfectly —*, sing-seh'-feh-dong' 聲色弗動

COMPOSED *of two or three things*, liang'-sæn-yiang' keh'-long tso-go 兩三樣合攏做个°; *— of more than one article*, feh ts' ih-yiang' tsô'-c'ih-go 弗止一樣做出个°

COMPOSITION, *essay*, veng-tsông' 文章

COMPOUND, kah'-dzeh-go 夾°雜个°

COMPRADORE, kông'-bah-bo 岡勃佗', *transferred from the English*; *one who buys provisions for*, ma'-bæn 買°辦; *one who buys goods*, ma'-ho sin-sang 買°貨先生°

COMPREHEND, *to* ming-bah' 明白; tong 懂; hyiao'-teh 曉得

COMPREHENSIVE, yiu hyü'-to pao-kweh'-tih 有許多包括的

COMPRESS, *to* ah 壓°; *— on both sides*, keh kyih'-jih 夾°硈實

COMPROMISE, *to* tsiah'-wu-gyi cong' 酌乎其中; liang'-tsia 兩借°; liang'-pin tseo-tæn'-long 兩邊走攏

COMPULSION, *by* min'-ky'iang 勉強

COMPUTE, *to* sön 算; p'a 派°; p'a'-p'a-k'en' 派°派°看

COMRADE, de-bo' 隊夥; dong-de'-nying 同隊人°; *comrades (in amusement)*, sæn-beng'-s-yiu' 三朋四友

CONCAVE, t'en-tsing' liao-go 凹°進了个°

CONCEAL, *to* k'ông 囥; *— and deceive*, mun 瞞; *— from another*, mun-sæn'-en-s' 瞞三掩四; *I can't from — you*, mun-ng'-feh-teh-shih' 瞞你°弗得說; *— one's name*, nyih-ming' nyih-sing' 匿名匿姓

CONCEDE, *to grant*, cing 准; *to yield*, nyiang 讓°

CONCEIT, *a foolish —*, ts'eng'-kong veo-r' peh-jih' 心°思°浮而不實; ts'eng'-deo hyü'-go

想°頭虛个°; ts'eng'-kong, neng-shih' peh-neng-ying' 心°思°能說不能°行

CONCEITED, zi sön' dzæ'-'óng 自°算在行;—(in talking), iao ts'ing-neng 要稱能

CONCEIVABLE, ts'eng'-leh-tao'-go 忖得°到个°

CONCEIVE, to — (in the womb) ziu-yüing 受孕; ziu-t'æ 受胎; — an idea, ky'i-i' 起意; ky'i-kyin' 起見;— a purpose, fah sing' 發心

CONCENTRATE, to kwe-cong' 歸宗;— the mind, ih-sing c'ong' ih-yüoh' 一身充一役; sing kwe-long' 心歸攏

CONCEPTION, idea, i'-s 意思; i'-kyin 意見

CONCERN, siang-ken' 相干; what — is it of mine? teng ngô soh'-go siang-ken' 與°我甚°麼°相干? ü ngô 'o-ken' 于我何干? yü ngô 'o-dzih' 與我何涉?

CONCERN, to belong to, joh'-ü 屬°于; ü 于; yü 與; kwæn 關; it does not—me, yü ngô'vu dzih' 與我無涉; feh kwæn'-djoh ngô' z-ken 弗關着我事幹; it does — me, yü ngô' yiu kao-kwæn' 與我有交°關; ü ngô yiu' kwæn-yi' 于我有干係; do not — yourself, hao-vong' fi-sing° 弗°用°費心

CONCERNED for, dziah-kyih' 着急; tæn-iu' 擔憂

CONCERT, in p'e' hao-liao-go 配好了个°; siang-p'e'-go 相配个°

CONCERT, to dô-kô' tang'-sön 大°家°打算

CONCILIATE, to —(by kindness), teng gyi' 'o-hao' 與其和好; to render friendly, s'-teh gyi 'o-moh' 使其和睦

CONCILIATING, act in a — manner and he will be conciliated, yüong nyün'-kong pa'-pu, peh gyi pa'-pu-tao'-de 用軟功擺°佈俉°其擺°佈倒了°

CONCISE, kyin'-kyih 簡潔; tön'-kyih 短潔; ts'ing-ts'u' 清楚; ling'-kying 靈緊;— in speaking tsin'-sao.

CONCH, ngô-lo' 牙°螺

CONCLUDE, to wun 完; liao 了; wun-kyih' 完結;— the business, wun z' 完事; liao z' 了事

CONCLUSION, kyih'-sah 結煞; — of a discourse, kyih kyü' 結句; kwæn-meng' shih-wô' 關門說話

CONCLUSIVE, words are —, shih-wô' kông'-leh loh-shing' 說話講°得°落榫

CONCORD, in 'o-moh' 和睦; kông'-leh-læ 講°得°來;— in sounds, sing - ing' tsæn'-zi 聲音齊°集°; dong-sing' siang-ing' 同聲相應

CONCOURSE, *a crowd of people,* ih-dœ'-dziao nying' 一大°輩°人; *a great many,* vu-ts'in'-dæn'-go 無千大萬个°.

CONCUBINE, ah-yi' 阿姨; siao lao-nyüing' 小老婆°; *styled,* p'in-vông' 偏房; tseh'-shih 側室; jü'-fu-nying' 如夫人°; — *paid by the month,* pao lao'-nyüing 包老婆°.

CONCUPISCENCE, yüoh-sing' 慾心; s-yüoh'-sing 私欲心.

CONCUR, *I* — *with him,* ngô teng' gyi dong-i' 我與°其同意; ngô teng' gyi tso' i-s, 我與°其同°意思; ngô yia' ka i'-s 我也°這°意思.

CONCUSSION, *severe* tsing-tsing'-dong li-'æ' 振動利害.

CONDEMN, *to* ding zœ' 定罪; — *him to death,* ding' gyi si'-zœ 定其死°罪; — *the boat as bad,* ding keh' tsah jün wa' 定這°隻船孬°.

CONDENSE, *to* long kyih'-jih 弄硈實; — *by pressure,* ah kyih'-jih 壓硈實; — *by pressure of the hand,* ky'ing kyih'-jih 揿硈實; — *by pressure of the feet,* dah kyih'-jih 踏硈寔.

CONDESCEND, *to* kyiông'-ling 降臨; kông'-loh di-we' 降落地位; — *to buy of,* s'-kwu 賜顧; 'ô'-kwu 下°顧; — *to help in trouble,* kwông'-kwu 光顧.

CONDIGN, kœ ziu' 該受.

CONDIMENTS, liao-li' 料理; pông-dco' 幫頭; *wine as a condiment,* liao-tsiu' 料酒.

CONDITION (*whether as officer, teacher, or trades-man, &c.*), di-we' 地位; — (*arrived at*), di-bu' 地步; — (*whether sick or poor, rich or well, &c.*), kying'-di 境地; kying'-hwông 境況.

CONDITION, *I make one* —, ngô' lih ih-go 'æn' 我立一个°限°; *must not violate* (*i. e. step over*) *the* —, feh-k'o' ko' 'æn' 弗可過限°.

CONDOLE, *to* — *with,* dô-kô' t'æn'-sih 大°家°嘆息.

CONDUCT, tsoh'-we 作爲; 'ang-i'-dong-zing 行°意動靜; kyü'-ts 'ang-dong' 舉止行°動; sô-tsoh'-sô-we' 所作所爲; 'ang-we' 行°爲; *very bad* —, 'ô'-tsoh 'ang-we' 下°作行°爲; 'ô'-lin 'ang-we' 下°流行°爲.

CONDUCT, *to* ying'-dao 引導; ta'-ling 帶°領; ling 領.

CONDUCTOR, ying'-dao cü'-kwu 引導个°人°; ling-lu'-go nying' 領路个°人°.

CONE, yün ti' tsin dco' 圓底尖頭.

CONFECTIONERY, *sugared things* (*as fruits*), mih-tsiu' 蜜餞. See CANDY.

CONFEDERATE, *adj.* c'ün'-'eh-liao 串合了°; t'ong-dong'-liao 通同了°.

CONFER, to — (office), fong 封; — (favors), s 賜; sông 賞

CONFER, to consult, siang-liang' 商量; siang-sông' 相商

CONFERENCE, to hold a —, ih-fæn we-nyi' 一番會議; to meet for —, jü'-we siang-nyi' 聚會相議

CONFESS, to jing 認; tsiao-jing' 招認; — something wrong, jing ts'o' 認錯; nying shü' 認㲀

CONFIDANT, n. sing-foh' 心腹

CONFIDE, to instruct, t'oh-sing' 托信; can — in him, gyi t'oh'-sing-leh-ko' 其托信得°過; gyi k'ao'-leh-djü'-go 其靠得°住个°; to believe, siang-sing' 相信

CONFIDENT, certain, yiu'-su 有數; vu nyi' 無疑; self —, zi siang'-sing zi' 自°相信自°

CONFIDENTLY, jih-z'-jih-loh' 實是實落

CONFIDENTIAL, hao'-t'oh-siang-sing' 好托相信; t'oh'-sing-leh-ko 托信得°過; secret, kyi-mih' 機密

CONFINE, to restrict, iah'-soh 約束; tsu'-djü 阻住; — by a guard, kwun'-ah 管押°

CONFINED, close, meng-ky'i' 悶氣; — or narrow quarters, bun-djün'-feh cün'-go di-fông' 盤旋弗轉个°地方

CONFINEMENT, time of — (wo-man's), tso-sang'-m z-'eo' 做產°母°時候; ditto, arrived, ling-ts'æn' 臨產

CONFIRM, to — as true, ding-jih' 定實; — by proof, ying'-tsing 引証; to establish, kyin-kwu' 堅固

CONFIRMATION, the rite of —, kyin-sing'-li 堅信禮

CONFISCATE, to ts'ong kong' 充公; jih kwun' 入官

CONFLAGRATION, ho'-tsong do'-leh-kying' 火鐘大°得°緊; ho'-tsæ 火災

CONFLICT, to gyih-gah' 紏葛°; dzih-kah'-dæo 交戰; to fight, kao-tsin' 交戰; tang-tsiang' 打仗°

CONFORM to the pattern, tsiao yiang' tso 照樣做; obey, i-dzong' 依從

CONFOUNDED, confused, wu-li'-wu-du' 霧裏糊塗; perplexed mong'-tong 懵懂 (mong or mông)

CONFRONT, to — with criticism, tông-min' poh' 當面駁; — with threats, tông-min' heng'-hô.

CONFUCIUS, K'ong'-fu-ts 孔夫子

CONFUSE, to lön 亂; weng'-lön 混亂; — his mind, lön' gyi'-go sing' 亂其个°心

CONFUSED, wu-li'-wu-du' 霧°裏糊塗; m-dæo'-m-jü 無°頭無°緒; — in mind, sing lön' 心亂; — or in confusion, ô-koh-

lön'-kying; very —, lön-ts'ih-pah-tsao' 亂七八遭.
CONFUTE, to poh'-tao 駁倒.
CONFUTED, utterly —, poh'-leh k'æ-k'eo' feh læ° 駁得°開口弗來°; li ky'üih' dz gyüong' 理屈辭窮 (veng.)
CONGEE, coh or tsoh 粥; hyi-væn' 稀飯; — boiled very smooth and nice, tsoh' ts-leh dziu-lin' 粥炎°得°綢綫.
CONGENIAL, yiu yün-veng' 有緣分; sing-i' siang-dong' 心意相同.
CONGESTION of the heart, hyüih' jü'-long læ sing'-li 血聚攏在°心裏.
CONGRATULATE, to 'o-'o' 賀賀; (I) — you, dao ng'-go hyi' 道你°个°喜; kong-hyi' kong-hyi' 恭喜恭喜; 'o ng'-go hyi' 賀你°个°喜.
CONGREGATION, jü'-long-go nying' 聚攏个°人°.
CONGRESS of the U. S., Da-mé nyi-tsing'-we 大美議政會.
CONJECTURE, to surmise, ts'æ-doh' 猜度°; — rightly (guess), ts'æ-djoh' 猜著°.
CONJOINTLY, dong-pông' 同幇; dô-kô' 大°家°.
CONJUGAL love, fu-ts'i' dzing-veng' 夫妻情分; — duties, fu-ts'i' meng-veng' 夫妻名分.
CONJURER, pin hyi'-fah-go nying 變戲法个°人°; one who con-jures by spirits, yüong vu-jih' go nying 用巫術个°人°.
CONNECT, to lin-long' 連攏; lin-p'ing' 連拼.
CONNECTED, lin-long'-liao 連攏了; siang-lin'-liao 相連了; (as ideas), kwun'-c'ün 貫串; can or ought to be —, siang-lin' 相連.
CONNECTION, one's own family — of the same name, kô-kyün' 家°眷; — having a different family name, ts'ing-kyün' 親眷.
CONNIVE, intentionally fail to see ngæn'-k'æ-ngren'-pi 眼°開眼°閉; tsông-leh m-neh k'en'-kyin 粧得°沒°有°看見.
CONQUER, to tang'-ying 打贏; teh-sing' 得勝; — self, k'eh kyi' 克己 (veng.)
CONQUERED, tang'-ba-de 打敗°了°; shü-de' 輸了°.
CONQUEROR, teh-sing' cü'-kwu 得勝个°人°.
CONQUEST, obtained by —, tang'-ying teh-læ'-go 打贏得來个°.
CONSANGUINEOUS, tih'-ts'ing-go 嫡親个°; ts'ing-kweh'-hyüih 親骨血.
CONSCIENCE liang-sing 良心; t'in-liang' 天良; t'in-li'-liang-sing' 天理良心; z'-fi-ts sing 是非之心; — smitten, kw'e sing'-z 愧心事; — not darkened, liang-sing' peh-mé 良心不昧.
CONSCIENTIOUS, yiu' liang-sing'

go 有眞心个°;— *in conduct,* tsiao liang-sing' tso' nying 照眞心做人°。

CONSCIENTIOUSLY, 'eh-djoh t'in-li' 合着°天理 (djoh or dzoh).

CONSCIOUS *of pain,* kyüoh'-teh t'ong'-go 覺得痛个°; *faculties clear* (as a sick person), seh'-deo ts'ing; ts'ing-t'ong 清通

CONSECRATE, *to* tseng-ky'i' 尊起; — (as first fruits &c. to the Emperor), tsing-kong' 進貢; *the rite of consecrating ditto, to parents,* zông-sing-go li' 當°新个°禮

CONSECRATED (as food), zing'-go 淨°个°

CONSECUTIVE, lin-ky'in'-go 連牽个°; *come on ten — days,* lin-ky'in' læ jih nyih' 連來十日°; *three — years,* deh-lin' sæn nyin' 疊°連三年

CONSENT, *to* ing-yüing' 應允; ing-jing' 應認

CONSEQUENCES, kwæn-yi' 關係; kyiao-kwæn' 交關; *bad —,* kwæn-ngæ' 關碍; *if you do not believe, what will be the — ?* ng feh siang'-sing, yiu soh'-go kwæn-yi' 你°弗相信有甚麼°關係？

CONSEQUENTIAL, teng-p'ing'-go siang'-mao 敦品个°相貌

CONSIDER, *to* tsing-tsiah' 斟酌; — *carefully,* ts-si tsing-tsiah' 仔細斟酌; *take time to —,* mæn-mæn' tsing-tsiah' 慢慢斟酌

CONSIDERABLE, feh-ky'üih' 弗缺; feh-siao' 弗少; *to* 多

CONSIDERATE, t'i'-t'iah-go 體貼个°; yiu ts'eh-ing'-ts sing' 有惻隱之心

CONSIGN *to his hands,* t'oh' læ gyi'-go siu-li' 托在°其个°手裏; — *for sale,* t'oh'-ma' 托買'

CONSIST *in,* dzæ-ü' 在于; (Chinese say) *Life consists in wealth,* "Dzæ, yü ming' siang'-lin" 財與命相連

CONSISTENCY, *no* feh-dzing t'i'-t'ong 弗成體統

CONSISTENTLY, *to act —,* yin-ying' siang-vu' 言行相符

CONSOLATION, en-we' 安慰

CONSOLE, *to* en-we' 安慰; kw'un-sing' 寬心

CONSPICUOUS, t'iao'-c'ih-liao 挑出了; t'eo'-c'ih-liao 透出了; t'iao'-yiang-go 挑樣个°; yün-ling'-ling pa'-c'ih-liao 懸空擺出

CONSPIRACY, kæn-tông' 奸黨; *to form a —,* kyih tông' 結黨

CONSPIRE, *to* c'ün'-dong 串同; t'ong-dong'-tsoh-bi' 通同作弊; — *and swear together not to give up,* ky'üoh hyiang-hwe' tsiu 吃香灰酒

CONSTABLE, di-pao' 地保; politely called, t'a'-se 太°歲

CONSTANT, *steadfast,* sing-kyin' 心堅; *always the same,* nyih-nyih' jü-ts'° 日°日°如此

CONSTANTLY, *always*, z-djông' 時常; djông-djông' 常常; — *so*, djông-djông' jü-ts' 常常如此 (djông or dzông.)

CONSTELLATIONS, *the twenty eight* —, r-jih-pah siu' 二十八宿

CONSTERNATION, *in* kying-hwông-de 驚慌了

CONSTIPATION, do-ka' feh t'ong' 大解弗通

CONSTITUTE, *to form*, hying 興; *to establish*, lih 立; shih'-lih 設立; — *by appointment*, fông 放

CONSTITUTION, ti'-ts 底子; peng'ti-ts 本底子; nyün-ky'i' 元氣; *strong* —, ti-ts tsah'-cü 底子圍硬

CONSTRAIN, *to impel*, ts'e-pih' 催逼; — (him) *to stay*, gyiang' liu 强留; ngang liu' 硬留

CONSTRAINED *to stay*, feh'-teh-feh deng' 弗得弗停; *in a* — (*contracted*) *position*, gyüoh-ts'oh' 侷促

CONSTRUCT, *to* ky'i 起; zao 造; tang 打; tsoh 築; — *a house*, zao oh' 造屋; ky'i oh' 起屋; — *a bridge*, zao gyiao' 造橋; tsoh gyiao' 築橋; — *a boat*, tang jün' 造船; — *a wall*, tang ziang'; tsoh ziang' 築墙

CONSTRUE, *to explain*, ka'-shih 解說; *to translate*, fœn-yih' 繙譯

CONSUL, ling'-z-kwun 領事官; *British* —, Da-Ing' ling'-z-kwun 大英領事官; *vice* —, fu'-ling-z 副領事

CONSULATE, ling'-z fu 領事府

CONSULT, *to* siang-liang' 商量; siang-sông' 相商; sông-nyi' 商議; — *carefully*, tsing-tsiah' 斟酌

CONSUME *by fire*, me-diao' 煤壞; siao-diao' 燒壞; — *entirely*, hwô-u-yiu' 化為烏有; — *by extravagance*, hwô'-fi-diao 化費了; — *by decomposition*, hwô'-diao 化壞 (also used for the former).

CONSUMMATE, *to* dzing 成; dzing-djün' 成全; dzing-dziu' 成就

CONSUMPTION, (*disease*), ziah-bing 弱病; lao-ky'ih'-bing 癆怯病

CONSUMPTIVE, yiu ziah-bing'-go ti'-ts læ'-tih 有弱病个底子

CONTACT, *to come in* — *with*, bang-djoh' 撞着; ts'ah'-djoh 擦着

CONTAGIOUS, iao-yin'-go 要延个

CONTAIN, *to* tsi 齎; tsông 裝; — (*as a boat*), tsœ 載; *how much oil will it* —? yiu to-siao yiu' hao tsi 有多少油好齎?

CONTAMINATE, *to* ta'-diao 帶壞; ta'-loh 帶落

CONTEMN, *to* k'en-ky'ing' 看輕; — *him as worthless*, k'en gyi z ts'œn'-deo 看其是偃憸

CONTEMPLATE, *to* ngwu 悟; si-si'-go ts'eng' 細細个忖

CONTEMPLATION, (Buddhist)

ngwu-jün' 悟禪; (Taoist) —, ngwu-dao' 悟道

CONTEMPORARY, dong z-'eo' 同時候; tso z-'eo'.

CONTEMPT, I treat him with —, ngô' k'en gyi ky'ing' 我看其輕; ngô k'en-gyi-feh-ky'i' 我看其弗起; ngô k'en'-feh-zông-ngæn' 我看弗上眼; ngô ky'ing-mæn' gyi 我輕慢其; he is treated with —, gyi peh nying-kô' k'en-ky'ing'-liao 其被人°家°看輕了

CONTEMPTIBLE, feh-jih'-nying-ngæn' 弗入人°眼; ky'ing 輕; — conduct, ky'ing-zin' 'ang-we 輕賤°行°為

CONTEND, to — (in words), siang-tsang' 相爭°; — (in fight), siang-tang' 相打

CONTENTED, cü-tsoh' 知足; tsoh'-sing 足心; zi-cü'-veng-liang 自°知分量

CONTENTIOUS, hwun-hyi' tsang-leng' 歡喜爭°論; p'ô t'a'-bing 怕太°平

CONTENTS (of a book), moh-loh 目錄

CONTEST, to tsang 爭°; to emulate, pi'-sæ 比賽

CONTEXT, zông-'ô-veng' 上下文

CONTIGUOUS, t'iah'-gying 貼近; vu-gying' 附近

CONTINENT, n. da-tsiu' 大州; adj. we tsih-yüoh' 會節欲

CONTINUALLY, z-djông' 時常; djông-djông' 常常 (djông or dzông); dziang-t'ong'.

CONTINUE, to feh-hyih' 弗歇; feh-dön' 弗斷; — here, dzing-gyin' læ'-tih 仍舊在°此°

CONTINUOUS, lin-lin' 連連; tsih'-lin 接連; ih'-lin 一連; a month's — rain, yü lin-lin' loh ih-ko'-yüih 雨連連落一個月

CONTORT, to — (as mouth, or limbs), ky'in-long' 牽攏; ky'in-cün' 牽轉

CONTRABAND goods, kying' ho 禁貨; — traffic, væn kying'-go sang-i' 犯禁个°生°意

CONTRACT, nyi-tæn' 議單; iah約; — for work, dzing-læn'-p'iao 承攬票; — for marriage, shü-ts' 書子

CONTRACT, to shorten, soh 縮; siu 收; soh'-long 縮攏; ih'-tsah'; — the brows, tseo'-mi-deo' 皺眉頭; — a habit, jih-kwæn' 習慣; — a habit of drinking or smoking, ky'üoh' nyin 吃°癮

CONTRACTED mind, ky'i'-liang 'ah-tsah' 氣量狹°窄; du'-liang siao' 度量小; — place, di-fông' gyüoh-ts'oh' 地方侷促

CONTRADICT, to ing-cü' 違言; — one's self, zin-yin' feh-te 'eo' nyü 前°言弗對後語; — one's own testimony, fæn-kong' 翻供

CONTRADICTORY, teo'-deo-feh-long'-go 對°頭 弗 攏 个°; 'eh-shing'-feh-long'-go 合榫 弗 攏 个°; ts'o-gen'; feh-tě'; feh-vu' 弗符; feh-'eh'-deo 弗 合頭

CONTRARY ideas, i'-s siang-fæn' 意思相反;—in disposition, ao'-ky'iang 拗腔; ao'-diao-peh-hying' 拗調不馴°; kwæ'-p'ih 乖僻;—wind, teo' fong 鬭風

CONTRAST in quality, hao' wa ts'ô-yün 好孬°差遠;—in size, do siao' ts'ô-yün 大小差遠;—in height, dziang a' da' feh siang'-dong 長矮大弗相同; heightened by —, pi'-ih-pi keng'-kô hao'-de 比一比更加好了; worse by —, ih-pi'-kyin keng'-kô feh-z'-de — 比肩更加弗是了°

CONTRIBUTE, to kyün 捐; kyün-dzu' 捐助;—for idolatry, teo veng-ts' 兜分子; like to —, hyi' dzu 喜助; loh dzu 樂助

CONTRIBUTIONS, kyün-'ông' 捐項; kyün-kw'œn' 捐款

CONTRITE heart, sing sông' 心傷; t'ong'-hwe-ts sing' 痛悔之心

CONTRIVANCE, ingenious ky'iao'-miao tong'-si 巧妙東西

CONTRIVE, to shih'-siang-c'ih-læ 設°想出來; tang'-mo-c'ih-læ' 打摹出來;— a scheme (for injuring &c), shih kyi-meo' 設°機謀

CONTROL, to kwun'-soh 管束;—one's self, zi iah'-soh zi 自°約束自°; under his —, læ gyi siu'-'ô 在°其手下°

CONTROVERSY, fond of —, hwun-hyi' bin'-leng 歡喜辯論

CONTUMACIOUS, ngwu-nyih' 忤逆;—(son), ngwu-nyih'-peh-hyiao' 忤逆不孝;—son and brother, peh-hyiao'-peh-di 不孝不弟

CONTUMELY, jôh or zoh 辱; tsao-t'ah' 蹧蹋; to bear —, ziu-zoh' 受辱; to treat with —, ying-zoh' 刑辱

CONTUSION, sông 傷; severe — (by beating), tang'-sông li-'æ' 打傷利害

CONVALESCENT, læ-tih hao'-ky'i-læ 現°今°好起來

CONVENE, to jü 聚; jü'-long 聚攏

CONVENIENCE, suit your —, zo-ng'-bin' 隨你°便; zo-bin' ng 隨便你°; dzong-ng'-bin' 從你°便

CONVENIENT, bin 便; bin-tông 便當; while — (do something else), jing-bin' 順便; jing-sin' 順手;—(i. e. without going out of the way), jing-da' 順䠔

CONVENT, Buddhist en 菴; dông 堂; z 寺; yün 院; Taoist —, kwun 觀; Roman Catholic —, siu'-dao-yün' 修道院

CONVERSANT with, joh-sih' 熟

識; *perfectly* —, joh-t'eo'-liao 熟透了

CONVERSE, *to* dæn'-dæn 談談; jü-jü' 叙叙; — *of what is in the heart*, dæn-sing' 談心

CONVERSION, *the time of* —, kæ'-ko z-'eo' 改過時候

CONVERT, we-sing'-liao-go nying' 回心个°人°

CONVERT, *to change*, kæ 改; wun 換; pin'-yih 變易; *to* — *a man*, cih'-cün nying-go ling-sing' 挈轉人°个°靈性; pin'-wun nying'-go ky'i'-tsih 變換人°个°氣質

CONVEX, deh-c'ih' liao-go 凸出了个°

CONVEY *thither* (as letters, presents &c.), kyi'-læ 寄來; ta'-læ 帶°來; — *there*, kyi'-ky'i 寄去°; ta'-ky'i 帶°去°; — (as goods), yüing-læ' 運來; yüing-ky'i' 運去°; — *there* (as people), peh gyi ts'ing'-leh-ky'i 與°其趁了去°

CONVICT, *n.* væn'-nying 犯人°

CONVICTED *of sin*, kyüoh'-teh zi'-go ze' 覺得自个°罪; — *deeply*, c'oh'-sing næn-ko' 猎°心難過

CONVINCE, *to* k'æ-dao' 開導 k'æ-t'ong' 開通; — *him of sin*, peh gyi zi kyüoh'-teh yin ze' 俾°其自°覺得有罪; —*him of error*, tsing'-ming gyi-go ts'o' 證明其个°錯

CONVINCED *by argument*, bin'-leng voh'-de 辯論服了; *I am* —, ngô' voh-cü'-de 我服制了°

CONVOKE, ts'ing jü'-long 請聚攏; eo-long' 叫°攏; co-zi' 叫°齊

CONVOY, *to* wu-song' 護送

CONVULSED *with laughter*, siao-leh weng'-sing dong'-feh-gyi 笑得渾身動弗及°

CONVULSIONS, kying-fong'-bing 驚瘋病

CONVULSIVELY, *crying* weh-djông'-weh-tin' k'oh' 活撞活頗哭

COOK, long-væn'-go 弄飯个°; djü-deo' 廚頭; djü-kong' 廚工; — *in a ya-mun*, djü-ts' 廚子; *head* —, da-s'-vu 大司務; *under* —, 'o'-tsao 下°竈

COOK, *to* long væn' 弄飯; *to boil*, ts 煮°; — (*i. e. boil*) *well*, ts joh' 煮熟; *to bake*, p'ang 烹°; *to steam*, hen 燉; *to fry* (as meat), t'ah 煠; — (as doughnuts), zah 煠°; *to simmer*, teng 燉; *to roast* (as coffee or chestnuts), ts'ao 炒; *to broil*, tsih 炙; koh 烤°

COOL, lang'-ing 冷°陰; ing'-liang 陰涼; — *water*, ing'-liang-go shü' 陰涼个°水°; — *weather*, t'in' ing'-liang 天陰涼; — (*breezy*), fong-liang' 風涼; *seek a* — *place*, zing fong-liang' 尋風涼; — *it*, long gyi lang' 弄

其 冷°; *let it* —, peh gyi lang' 佛 其 冷°; lang-lang' gyi 冷° 冷° 其; lang kæn'; *wait till it cools,* teng gyi lang'-de 等 其 冷° 了°。

COOLLY, *to treat a person —*, lang'-dæn nying-kô' 冷° 待° 人° 家°。

COOLY, *or* COOLIE, siao'-kong 小 工; c'ih-ts'u'-go nying 出 粗 个° 人°; — *for burdens*, kyiah-pæn' 脚 班。

COOP, *chicken* kyi-long' 雞 籠; — (for day use, with no bottom), kyi-tsao' 雞 罩; *to shut in a* —, kwæn'-tsing long'-li 關 進 籠 裡。

COOPERATE, *to* keh'-tso 合° 做; p'ing-tso' 拼 做。

COPARTNER, p'ing ho'-kyi 拼 夥 計。

COPIOUS, to 多; hyü'-to 許 多; — *rain*, dzing-deo' yü 陣 頭 雨; do yü 大° 雨。

COPPER, ts'-dong 紫 銅; 'ong-dong' 紅 銅 (a sheet, ih-p'in; a bar, ih-diao)。

COPPERAS, loh-væn 綠 礬。

COPPER-SMITH, *brazier*, dong-s'-vu 銅 司 務。

COPY, deng 謄; ts'ao 抄; — *neatly*, deng-ts'ing' 謄 清。

COPYING-PRESS, ing'-shü-kô 印 書 架°。

CORAL, sæn-wu' 珊 瑚。

CORD, zing 繩; soh 索; *strong* —, kyih'-jih-go or tsah'-cü-go zing' 砝° 實° 个° 繩°; *to make* —, tang zing' 打 繩。

CORDIAL (to guests), nyih-zah'; *warm-hearted*, nyih-sing 熱 心。

CORD-MAKER, zing-soh'-s-vu' 繩° 索 司 務。

CORE, sing 心。

CORK, seh'-deo 屑 頭 (ih-go)。

CORK, *to — a bottle*, seh bing-k'eo' 屑 瓶 口。

CORK-SCREW, k'æ seh'-deo jün-ts' 開 屑 頭 旋 子; cün'-ts 鑽 子。

CORN, *Indian* loh-koh' 稑 穀; pao'-r-mi 保 兒 米; — *meal*, (Indian meal), loh-koh' feng 稑 穀 粉。

CORN (on the foot), kyi-ngæn' 雞 眼°; kyiah'-tsi 脚 䠺; *to dig out a* —, t'ih kyi-ngæn 剔 雞 眼°。

CORNELIAN, mô'-nao 碼 碯。

CORNER, koh 角°; koh-loh-den' 角° 落 頭°; *turn a* —, cün-wæn' 轉 彎; *lonely* — (or place), wæn' koh 彎 角°。

CORPOREAL, nyüoh-sing'-go 肉° 身 个°。

CORPS, *a — of soldiers*, ih-de ping' 一 隊 兵; ih-ts ping' 一 支 兵。

CORPSE, s-siu' 屍 首; p'oh'-s 仆 屍; s-yia' 屍 骸° (term of reproach)。

CORPULENT, vi-p'ông' 肥 胖; — *from disease*, fah hyü' 發 虛; fah cong' 發 腫。

CORRECT, *not wrong*, feh-ts'o' 弗

錯°; feh-dzæn' 弗綻; *perfectly* —, 'ao'-feh-ts'o' 毫弗錯; ih-ngæn'-fsh-ts'o' 一點弗錯; *upright*, tsing'-dzih 正直; tön-fòng' 端方; *proper*, kwe-kyü' 規矩

CORRECT, *to* — (mistakes), kæ'-hao 改好; kæ-tsing 改正; *to reprove*, tsah'-vah 責罰

CORRESPOND, *to* — (by letters), yiu shü-sing' læ-wòng' 有書信來往

CORRESPONDS, te'-go 對个°; siang-te'-go 相對个°; siang'-'eh'-go 相合个°; — *in size*, m-dô'-siao 無°大°小°

CORROBORATE, *to* s'-teh hao k'ao-jih' 使得好靠實

CORRODE, *to* siu'-wun 銹完; me-læn' 霉爛

CORRUPT, *to* wæ-diao' 壞了°; *to — customs* (and hence morals), wæ-diao' fong-djoh' 壞了°風俗

CORRUPT, *become — in morals*, jih-'ô' 習下°; *rotten*, læn-wu' 爛腐°; *stinking*, ts'iu 臭°

CORRUPTIBLE, iao wæ-diao'-go 要壞了°个°

COSMETICS, siu yüong-mao'-go tong'-si 修容貌个°東西

COST, *price*, kô'-din 價°錢°; kô'-sæn; — *of living* (is) *high*, kyiao'-yüong do' 繳用大°

COSTIVE, do-ka' sao'-kyih 大°解°燥結

COSTLY, kô'-din kyü' 價°錢°貴°

COSTUME, *fashionable* z-sih'-go i-zông' 時式个衣裳°; *to wear Chinese* —, Cong'-koh tang'-pæn 中國打扮

COT, *my humble* —, sô-'ô' 舍°下°; sô'-pin 舍°邊; — *bed*, doh-ze' min-zông' 獨睡眠床

COTTAGE, *hut*, sô 厙°; *straw* —, ts'ao'-oh 草屋; mao-ts'ao'-oh 茅草屋 (ih-tsing)

COTTON, min-hwô' 棉花; — *cloth*, pu 布; *good native ditto*, du'-pu 土°布; — *thread*, min-sô' 棉紗; *to beat* — (light), tang min-hwô' 打棉花

COTTON-GIN, kao-hwô-ts'o' 絞°花車

COUCH, c'ing-teng' 春凳; t'ah-zông' 榻床°

COUGH, *has a* —, yiu ts'iang'-bing.

COUGH, *to* ts'iang; k'eh'-seo 咳嗽; seo 嗽

COULD, neng-keo' 能殼; k'o'-yi 可以; — *not stop*, feh neng'-keo ts' 弗能殼止; hyih'-feh-læ 歇弗來

COUNCIL, *to hold a* —, kong-nyi' 公議; *to convene a* —, jü kong-nyi' 聚公議

COUNCIL-CHAMBER, kong-sô' 公所

COUNSEL, *to* lih cü'-i 立主意; c'ih cü'-i 出主意; ky'ün 勸; — *together*, dô-kô' siang-liang' 大°家°商量; *he keeps his* own —, gyi'-go cü'-i feh k'eng peh nying-kô hyiao'-teh-go 其个°主意弗肯與人°家曉得个°

COUNSELOR, lih cü'-i-go nying 立主意个°人°; *officer's* —, mo-yiu' 慕°友; styled, s-yia' 師爺°

COUNT, *to* su 數; — *and see*, su'-su-k'en 數數看; *esteem*, sön 算; — *no disgrace, but honor*, yi-joh', we-yüong' 以辱爲榮 (veng)

COUNTENANCE, min-yüong' 面容; yüong-mao' 容貌; min-k'ong' 面孔; *looked me out of* —, k'en'-leh ngô wông-k'ong'-siang 看得°我惶恐相; *to keep one's* —, tsông lao'-ky'i 粧老氣; *can't keep his* —, lao-ky'i tsông'-feh-læ' 老氣粧弗來

COUNTER, *against*, fæn'-hyiang 反向; tsoh-teo' 作對

COUNTER *in a shop*, gyü-deo' 櫃°頭 (ih-k'eo)

COUNTERACT, *to make good*, hwô-hao' 化好; *to make evil*, pin-wa'° 變孬°; hwô'-diao 化壞°

COUNTERFEIT, *to* kô'-mao 假°冒; ngwe-zao' 僞造°

COUNTERFEIT *dollar*, kô' fæn-ping' 假°番餅; kô' yiang-dzin 假°洋錢

COUNTERMAND, *to* — *an order*, diao cü'-i 調主意; *to* — *an*

official order, wun 'ao-ling' 換號令

COUNTERPANE, *thin cover to be added*, t'in-kæ-bi' 添蓋被°

COUNTLESS, su'-feh-pin 數弗遍; vu-su'-go 無數个°

COUNTRY, koh 國; *a tract of* —, di-fông' 地方; (rural) —, hyiang-'ô' 鄉下°; *foreign* —, nga-koh' 外°國; *your honorable* —, kwe-koh' 貴國

COUNTRYMAN, hyiang-'ô'-nying 鄉下°人°

COUNTY, *a* ih-fu' 一府

COUPLE, *to* kwe-long' ih-te' 歸攏一堆; *to join*, lin-long' 連攏; *to match*, p'e'-long 配攏

COUPLE, *a* ih-te' 一對; *a pair* ih-sông' 一雙; *a married* —, liang'-fu-ts'i' 兩夫妻

COURAGE, tæn'-liang 膽量; üong'-ken 勇敢; tæn'-ts 膽子; ken-tæn' 肝膽; *great* —, tæn'-liang do' 膽量大°; tæn'-ts-p'eh' 膽子潑

COURAGEOUS, yiu' tæn'-liang 有膽量

COURSE, *road*, lu 路; (ship's) —, hyiang'-dao 向導 (ih-da); — *hitherto* (of action), seng-bing 生平; *the short* —, liao-gying' lu 嘹近路; *what is the best — to take?* 'ah-li' ih da lu hao' 何°處一埭路好? *of — it is so*, z-jün' z-ka' 自然如°此°; *adopt a* —, yüong' ih-go fông-fah' 用一个°方法

COURSES, (catamenia), yüih-kying' 月經; yüih-kô' 月家°
COURT (of a Chinese house), ming-dông' 明堂; small ditto, t'in-tsing' 天井; place where the Emperor receives his —, kying-lön'-din 金鑾殿; to go to —, zông-dziao' 上朝
COURT officers, da-dzing' 大臣; — dress, dziao-i' 朝衣
COURT, to — favor, t'ao-hao' 討好; to flatter, vong'-dzing 奉承; shü'-kwu 世故; — some one's daughter by a middle-man, teng ling-æ' tso me' 與°令愛作°媒
COURTEOUS, yiu li'-lu 有禮路; ky'in-'o' 謙和
COURTESY, li 禮; li'-ky'i 禮體°; he was invited by — (or out of respect), we-leh tseng-kying' gyi ts'ing' gyi læ-go 爲了°尊敬其請其來个°; treat him with —, long-djong' gyi 隆重其
COURTIER, bun-kô'-go 伴駕°个°; z-dzing' 侍臣
COUSIN, male —, by father's brother, dông-hyüong'-di 堂兄弟, sons of father's and mother's sisters, and mother's brother's sons, piao'-hyüong-di 表兄弟; female —, dông-tsi'-me 堂姐妹; piao'-tsi-me 表姐妹
COVENANT, iah 約; to make a —, lih iah' 立約; ding iah' 定約
COVER, kæ 盖 (ih-go); take off the —, kæ' hyiao-ko' 盖拐過; —

(as for books, umbrellas, &c.), t'ao 套; — for letters, sing'-fong 信封; sing'-k'oh 信壳
COVER, to kæ 盖; to screen (as from wind, &c.), tsô 遮; tsô-kæ' 遮°盖; tsô-in' 遮掩; — (as with a basket), tsao 罩
COVERLET, kæ-min'-go bi 盖面个°被°; wadded —, min-bi' 棉被
COVERTLY, mih-mih'-go 密密个°
COVET, to t'en 貪; sang t'en-sing' 生°貪心
COVETOUS, yiu t'en-sing' 有貪心
COW, ngeo 牛°; yellow —, wông-ngeo' 黃牛°; water buffalo, shü'-ngeo 水°牛° (ih-deo)
Cow him, long'-leh gyi' dong'-dæn-feh-læ' 弄得°其動彈弗來
COW-BEZOAR, ngeo-wông' 牛黃
COW-DUNG, ngeo-feng' 牛°糞; ngeo-o' 牛°屎
COW-SHED, ngeo-gyin' 牛°檻
COWARD, 无 tæn'-ky'i-go nying' 無°膽氣个°人°; 无 tæn'-liang-go nying 無°膽量个°人°
COXCOMB, æ p'iao-yih'-go nying 愛飄逸个°人°; dissolute —, hwô-hwô' kong-ts 花花公子; — (a flower), kyi-kwun'-hwô 雞冠花
COY, iu'-siu 幽羞; p'ô iu'-siu 怕幽羞
COZY room, (i. e. a room for quiet enjoyment), en-loh'-kong 安樂宮
CRAB, ha 蟹°

CRAB-APPLE, hæ'-dông-ko 海棠菓
CRACK, hwah 豁; hwah'-u 豁縫°; hwah'-lih-vong' 豁裂縫; a seam (as between boards), vong縫 (ih-da)
CRACK, to hwah 豁; k'æ hwah'-lih 開豁裂; —from heat, pao'-hwah 爆豁
CRACKED, k'æ hwah' de 開豁了°; — apart, hwah'-k'æ de 豁開了°
CRACKERS, fire p'ao'-dziang 礮仗; pah'-ts-p'ao 百子礮
CRADLE, basket yiao-læn' 搖籃
CRAFTY, kæn-tiao' 奸刁; diao-bi'.
CRAM, to seh'-pao 屭飽; seh'-mun 屭滿
CRAMP of muscles, kying' geo-long' 筋拘°攣
CRANIUM, kw'u-lu'-deo 骷髏頭
CRAPE, wu-tseo' 湖綢; thin — (or gauze), sô 紗
CRASH (as of wall falling), tao'-t'ah sing-hyiang' 倒塌聲響; — (as of dishes falling), tao'-fæn sing-hyiang' 倒翻聲響
CRAVAT, ling'-ta 領帶 (ih-diao, ih-keng)
CRAVE, to beseech, gyiu-k'eng' 求懇; to desire, siang 想; — food &c. (as one destitute), fah-zao' 發糟°; zao-ky'i'-ka 糟起
CRAVING (at a particular time, as for opium), nyin-deo' 癮°頭
CRAWL, to bô 爬

CRAZY, tin'-de 癲了°; veng-tin' 文癲; — person, tin-ts' 癲子; tin-nying' 癲人°; fiercely —, fah-gwông' 發狂; vu'-tin 武癲
CREAK, ing'-ang 月月; the doors —, meng' ing'-ang læ-tih hyiang' 門月月響; — (as a boat-scull), u'-cih-ga'; — (as a chair), kyi'-ka; — (as a wheel), ka-ka-hyiang'.
CREAM, na'-yiu 嬭°油; na'-bi 嬭°皮
CREASE, üih'-u 攬印°; tsih'-u 摺印°; fold it in the old —, tsiao lao' u tsib 照老印摺; tsiao nyün u' tsih' 照原印°摺; wrinkle, tseo'-u 皺印°
CREASE, must not — (it), m-nao' üih'-diao 弗°可°攬壞°
CREATE, to zao 造°; zao'-c'ih-læ 造°出來; zao-hwô 造°化
CREATION, the time of —, k'æ-t'in'-p'ih-di z-'eo' 開天闢°地時候; the things created, t'in-di'-væn'-veh 天地萬物
CREATOR, the zao'-hwô Cü'-tsæ 造°化主宰; zao væn-veh'-go Cü'-tsæ 造°萬物个°主宰
CREATURES, seng-ling' 生靈; yiu byüih'-ky'i-go tong-si' 凡°有血氣者°
CREDENCE, to give —, siang-sing' 相信; can't give —, siang-sing'-feh-læ 相信弗來
CREDENTIALS, tsih'-tsiao 執照; bing-kyü' 憑據

CRE 101 CRO

CREDIBLE, z'-joh k'o-sing' 似屬可信
CREDIT, his — is good, gyi-go bats' hao' 其个°牌°子好; to his —(praise), hao ngao gyi'; bought on —, sô-læ'-go 賒來个°
CREDITABLE performance, ming kong' 名工; iao ngao-ngao' gyi.
CREDITOR, t'ao'-cü 討主; tsa'-cü 債°主
CREDULOUS, ky'ing-yi' siang-sing' 輕易相信; ih-t'ing' ziu siang-sing' 一聽就°相信
CREED, apostles s-du' sing'-kying 使徒信經
CREEK, siao-ts'ô-kông' 小㲼港; siao-kông' 小港 (ih-da)
CREEP, to bô 爬
CREST of a cock, kwun'-deo 冠頭
CREW, sailors, shü'-siu 水°手
CREVICE, vong 縫; hwah'-vong 豁縫 (ih-da)
CRICKET, ting-s-ts' 蟋蟀°; yiu-tih-ling' 油的蛉 (ih-tsah)
CRIME, djong'-ze 重罪; to commit a —, væn djong' ze 犯重罪
CRIMINAL, væn'-nying 犯人°;
  In the 4th month, persons called *væn-nying* walk in idolatrous processions, dressed in red. These persons had vowed when sick, that if restored, they would be publicly regarded as *criminals*, or *væn-nying*, as they supposed the sickness was a punishment for some crime.
CRIMSON, ts'-'ong 紫紅
CRINGE, to pe-kong-ky'üih'-tsih 卑躬屈節; — (as a beggar), li-di'-'ô-pe'.

CRIPPLE, væn dzæn'-dzih'-liao-go nying' 犯殘疾个°人° See LAME.
CRISIS, kwæn 關; kwæn-deo' 關頭; — is past, kwæn' ko'-de 關過了
CRISP (as cakes), su 酥; — (as pears), song-ts'e' 鬆脆
CRITERION, cing'-tseh 準則
CRITIC, p'i-bing'-go cü'-kwu 批評个°人°; zing leo-dong'-go nying' 尋漏洞个°人°
CROAK, frogs keh'-pô we kyiao' 蛤蚆會叫
CROAKING, always (said of a person), zeo-shü-bu-kwu' ka 愁°水°鵁°鴣; zing' kyiao zing', yü kyiao' yü 晴°叫晴°雨叫雨
CROCKERY, porcelain, dz-ky'i' 磁器; earthen-ware, ngô'-ho 瓦°貨
CROCODILE, ngoh-ng' 鱷魚°
CROOKED, wæn 彎; having many turns, wæn-ky'üoh' go 彎曲个°; — and twisted, wæn-nyiao' 彎繞°
CROP (of a fowl), teng 膆; an abundant —, nyin-dzing' da-joh' 年成大熟; spring — bad, c'ing'-hwô wa' 春花孬°; poor — (i.e. 80 parts out of 100), pah'-tsih nyin-se' 八折年歲; scant —, kæn nyin-dzing' 減°年成
CROP, to bite off, ngao'-ky'i 齩去°
CROSS, jih-z'-kô 十字架°; died on the —, si' læ jih-z'-kô zông' 死°在°十字架°上

CROSS, *adj.* kwu'-kwa-deo 古怪頭; kwu-tiao'-deo 孤刁頭; feh-'o'-ky'i 弗和氣; tiao-djü-kwu'-seh 膠柱鼓瑟; *to put on a —look,* fæn cü'-lin 反嘴臉
CROSS, *to* ko 過; tseo'-ko 走過; *— the ferry,* ko du' 過渡; *— the feet* (or legs), gao kyiah' 交脚; *to lay across,* wang fông' 橫放; *must not — him,* feh-k'o ao'-ky'iang gyi 弗可拗強其
CROSS-BAR, wang-shün' 橫閂 (ih-keng)
CROSS-BEAM, wang-tông' 橫檔 (ih-keng)
CROSS-EXAMINE, *to* fæn'-foh bun-meng' 反覆盤問; tao'-meng jing-meng' 倒問順問; bun-kyih' 盤詰
CROSS-EYED, zia'-bah-ngæn 斜白眼
CROUCH, *to* gwu 躭; *— in hiding,* gwu-leh iu' 躭得幽
CROUP, 'eo'-fong 喉風
CROW, lao'-ô' 老鴉 (ih-tsah)
CROW, *to —* (as a cock), di 啼; *to — over,* ts'ing-üong 稱勇; *you need not —,* ng hao-vong ying üong'-shü-ts 你弗用行勢
CROW-BAR, gyiao-kweng' 橇棍 (ih-keng)
CROWD, *a* ih-dziao'nying 一羣人
CROWD, *to* üong'-tsi 擁擠; a-tsi' 挨擠; *— together for a bad purpose,* jü'-jih-nying'-cong 聚集人衆

CROWDED, a-lih'-bah-lang'; *closely —,* a-kyin'-ts'ah'-pe 挨肩擦背; a-tsi'-feh-k'æ' 挨擠弗開
CROWN, bing-t'in'-kwun 平天冠; *—* (worn by a bride, or the wife of a kyü-nying &c.), vong-kwun' 鳳冠; *— of the head,* deo-ti'-sing 頭頂心
CRUCIFIX, jih-z'-kô 十字架; (Shanghai) kwu-ziang 苦像; *wear a —,* ta' jih-z'-kô 帶十字架
CRUCIFY, *to* ting læ jih-z'-kô zông 釘在十字架上
CRUDE, sang 生; feh-joh 弗熟; *— ideas,* i'-s feb dziu'-lin 意思弗綢練
CRUEL, k'eh 刻; k'eh'-doh 刻毒; *very —,* koh-ken' 樊乾; *savage,* hyüong-oh' 兇惡; *— disposition,* sing-s' k'eh' 心思刻; *— oppression,* bao-nyiah' 暴虐
CRUISE, *to — on the rivers,* jing-kông' 巡港; *— on the ocean,* jing-yiang' 巡洋
CRULLERS, fæn-kyih' 麵反結; *to boil —,* zah fæn-kyih' 煠反結
CRUMBS, se 碎; *— of bread,* mun-deo' se 饅頭碎; *to drop —,* lông-zih' 狼藉
CRUMBLE, long-se' 弄碎; *will —,* iao se' 要碎; *— in the hand,* nyiah-se' 捏碎
CRUMPLE, *to* dön-long' 搏攏; lön-dön' 亂搏

CRUSH, to — (as something soft), ah'-pih 壓爩; — (as something hard), ah'-se 壓碎; ah'-wu 壓腐°; — to death, ah'-sah 壓殺°; to subdue, ah'-voh 壓服

CRUST of bread, mun-deo'-bi' 饅頭皮

CRUTCH, lông-t'ông' 榔檔° (ih-go); to use crutches, s lông-t'ông' 使榔檔°

CRY, to — (as a baby), kyiao 叫; — and lament, k'oh 哭; di-di' k'oh-k'oh' 啼啼哭哭; ready to — (sour nose), sön-bih' 酸鼻; to — out suddenly si' ih-sing; — out loudly, wæ-wæ'-hyiang 營°營°響

CRYSTAL, shü'-tsing or sc'-tsing 水°晶

CUB of a bear, siao-yüong' 小熊 (ih-tsah)

CUBE, loh-min'-cün-fông' 六面轉方

CUBEBS, dzing-gyia' 澄茄

CUBIT, (Chinese, from elbow to knuckles), ih-tsin' 一肘

CUCUMBER, wông-kwô' 黃瓜 (ih-keng)

CUD, chew the —, cün ziao' 轉噍°

CUDGEL, kweng'-ts 棍子; to beat with a —, tang kweng'-ts 打棍子; — for beating clothes, lin-djü' 練槌° (ih-go)

CUE, bin'-ts 辮子; fah bin' 髮辮 (ih-kwang)

CUFF, give him a —, kwah' gyi ih-kwông' 摑°其一光; sin' gyi ih-kwông' 搧其一光

CUFF, to kwah 摑°; — the cheek, kwah pô-công' 摑°巴掌

CUFF, ziu-t'ao' 袖套; hoof shaped — attached to the sleeve, mô'-di-ziu' 馬蹄袖; a sleeve with — turned back, fæn-ziu' 翻袖; tsao'-ziu 罩袖

CULINARY utensils, long-væn' kô-sang' 弄飯家°貨°

CULL, to pick, tsah 摘; tsah'-c'ih-læ' 摘出來; to choose, kæn 揀°

CULLENDER. See COLANDER.

CULPABLE, k'o-kwa' 可怪°

CULPRIT, yiu-ko'-væn-cü'-kwu 有過犯个°人°; criminal, væn'-nying 犯人°

CULTIVATE, to plough land, kang din' 耕田; to sow, cong din' 種田; — the fields, cong'-din' da-di' 種田藔°地; kang-cong'-din-di' 耕°種田地; — flowers, tsæ-cong hwô' 栽種花; — virtue, siu tch' 修德; cultivated land, joh di' 熟地

CUMBERED with heavy things, be djong' sô le' 被重所累

CUMBROUS, t'o le'-go 拖累个°; — to a person, le nying' go 累人°个°

CUNNING, knowing, kwæ'-ky'iao 乖巧; deceitful, diao-bi'; kæn-tsô' 奸詐; very —, kæn-tiao' 奸刁; slippery, weh-t'eng'-weh-kweng' 活氽活滾

CUP, pe-ts' 杯子; large —, cong
   盅; tea —, dzô-pe' 茶杯 (ih-tsah)
CUPBOARD for dishes, un'-tsæn-
   djü' 碗盞廚; — for provisions,
   ka-djü' 食°廚 (ih-k'eo)
CUPIDITY, t'en-du'-sing 貪圖心;
   great —, t'en-du'-sing djong 貪
   圖心重
CURABLE, hao-i' 好醫; i'-leh-læ'
   醫得°來
CURB for a horse, mô'-lah-k'eo' 馬
   勒口
CURB, to restrain, iah'-soh 約束;
   to subdue, ah'-cü 壓制; — the
   passions, k'eh'-djü s-yüoh' 克治
   私慾
CURD, milk nying-long'-liao-go na'
   凝攏了個嬭°; bean —, deo-
   vu' 豆腐
CURDLE, to nying-long' 凝攏
CURE, to i 醫; i-hao' 醫好; —
   disease, i bing' 醫病; — meat
   with salt, yin nyüoh' 鹽肉°
CURIOSITY, has great —, iao Ieo-
   Ieo'-weh-weh' 要鐐鐐挖挖;
   desire to find out matters, tang'-
   t'ing siao-sih' 打聽消息; desire
   to see, iao k'en'-k'en-siang' 要看
   看; curiosities, hwô-seh' tong'-si
   花色東西; antique ditto, kwu'-
   tong wæn'-ky'i 古董玩°器
CURIOUS, hwun-hyi' tang'-t'ing
   歡喜打聽; hwun-hyi' t'eo-
   k'en' 歡喜偷看; artfully con-
   structed, hyi-gyi' kwu'-kwa 希
   奇古怪°

CURL, to kyün'-long 捲攏; to
   — the hair, kyün fah' 捲髮
CURLY hair, s-ts' fah' 獅子髮
CURRENCY, money in circulation,
   t'ong-yüong'-go nying-dzin' 通
   用個銀錢; t'ong-'ang' dong-
   din' 通行°銅錢°
CURRENT price, da-kæ' kô'-din 大
   概價°錢°; in — use, t'ong
   yüong' 通用; — expenses, kying-
   fi' 經費; s'-fi 使費; kyiao-
   yüong' 繳用; dao-yiao'; — rate,
   'ông-dzing 行情
CURRENT, the — is strong, shü'-go
   læ-long' gyin' 水個來龍健
CURRY-POWDER, kyiang-wông'-
   feng 姜黃粉
CURRY-COMB, mô'-bao 馬刨
   (ih-pô)
CURSE, to tsiu'-mô 咒罵; tsiu'-
   cü 咒咀
CURSORILY, liao-piao' 聊表; da-
   liah' 大略; veo-min' 浮面
CURTAIL, to siu-bo' 收縛°; siu-
   soh'-long 收縮攏; — expenses,
   fi'-yüong siu-soh'-tin 費用收
   縮點; fi'-yüong gyin'-sang 費
   用儉省°; — (one's) life, ziu-
   shü' kæn-tön' 壽歲減°短;
   kæn ziu' 減°壽
CURTAIN for a bed, tsiang'-ts 帳
   子; — for a door, meng-lin' 門
   簾; window —, ts'ông-lin' 窗
   簾; bamboo —, lin-ts' 簾子
CURVE, to wæn 彎; curving in
   and out, wæn-nyiao' 彎橈;

curving, like the moon or a bow, yüih-kong' shih 月宮式°

CUSHION, din-tsʻ 墊子; *pin —,* tsing-tsʻah' 針插 (ih-go)

CUSTODY, *to take into —,* kʻóʻ-djoh 攀°著°; *to be in —,* kwunʻ-ah 管押°

CUSTOM, *usage,* kwe-kyü' 規矩; *— of a country,* fong-djoh' 風俗; *— of a place,* hyiang-fong' or hyiang-fông 鄉風; tʻu-fong 土風; *it is the —,* lao'-lao z-kaʻ 每°每°如此°; *it is his —,* gyi kwænʻ-djông z-kaʻ 其慣常如此°; *give him your —,* ʻôʻ-kwu gyi 下°顧其

CUSTOM-HOUSE, seʻ-kwæn 稅關; *to slip the —,* tʻeo-ko kwæn' 偷過關

CUSTOMARY, tsiao laoʻ-li 照老例; *— presents,* tsiao djôngʻ-kwe, song-liʻ 照常規送禮; *— walk,* tsiaoʻ djông' tseo-tseo' 照常走走

CUSTOMERS, *our* ahʻ-lah cüʻ-kwu 我°等°主顧; *old —,* lao' cüʻ-kwu 老主顧

CUSTOMS, *Commissioner of —,* seʻ-vuʻ-s 稅務司; *Inspector of —,* cong' seʻ-vu-s 總稅務司; *customs' duty,* seʻ-din 稅錢°; *avoid paying ditto,* tʻeo seʻ 偷稅

CUSTOM-STATION, kyün-gyüoh' 捐局; kʻa-ts 卡子

CUT, *n.* (with a knife), tao-sông'

刀傷 (ih-da); — *in books,* wô-du' 畫圖 (ih-go)

CUT, *to — with a knife,* kah' 割; tsæn 斬; *— a gash,* kah'-kʻæ 割開; *— asunder,* kah'-dön 割斷; tsænʻ-dön 斬斷; *— grain,* kah dao' 割稻; *— or carve meat,* tsʻih nyüoh' 切肉°; *— in slices,* tsʻih-pʻin' 切片; *— a slice of bread,* tsʻih' ih-pʻin' mun-deo' 切一片饅頭; *— with a scizzors,* tsin 剪; *— the hair,* tsin deo-fah' 剪頭髮; *— or trim ditto,* tæn deo-fah'; *to — out garments,* zæ i-zông' 裁衣裳; *— or trim off, a little,* zæ-tinʻ-diao 裁°點去°; *— a pattern,* zæ yiang-tsʻ 裁樣子; *to — off the head,* tsæn deo' 斬頭; *— down a tree,* tsoh jü' 剧樹; *— off branches,* tsænʻ-diao ô-tsʻ 斷了°椏枝; *— in pieces* (as a pig, &c.), ih-tao ihʻ-tao, tön-tænʻ-kʻæ 一刀一刀斷開; tönʻ-leh tao-tangʻ-tao 斷得刀打刀; *— off an arm,* siuʻ-kwang tsænʻ-loh' 手骨°斬落; *— one's own throat,* zi-veng' 自°刎; *— another's throat,* kah wu-long' 割喉嚨; *— a capon,* sin kyi' 騸雞; *— glass,* zæ poʻ-li' 裁°玻璃; *to engrvae,* tiao-kʻeh' 雕刻; *— wages,* kæn kong-din' 減工錢°; *— friendship,* djih kyiao' 絕交; *— off communication,* dönʻ-djih læ-wông 斷絕

來往;— *off relationship between parent and child*, dön-dzing' djih-yi' 斷情絕義;— *across by a shorter way*, liao-gying' lu tseo 蹺近路走;— *teeth*, c'ih ngô-ts' 出牙°齒;— *or give a blow* (with a stick), k'ao' ih-kyi 拷一記;— *or give a blow* (with a sword), tsæn' ih-kyin 斬一劍;— *or give a blow* (with a whip), tang-ih'-pin 打一鞭

CUTANEOUS, læ bi-fu' li 在°皮膚裏;— *diseases*, bi-fu'-go bing' 皮膚个°病

CUTCH, r'-dzô 兒茶

CUTLASS, *a curved knife worn at the side*, iao-tao' 腰刀

CUTLER, tang-tao'-s-vu' 打刀司務

CUTLERY, fong-kw'a'-go kô-sang' 鋒快°个°器皿°

CUTLET, *a cut of meat*, ih-p'in nyüoh' 一片肉°

CUTTING-BOARD *for meat*, tsing-pæn' 椹板; *cutting-block*, tsing-deo' 椹頭

CUTTLE-FISH, moh-ng' 墨魚°; u-zeh' 烏鯽°; *dried* —, ming-fu' 螟蜅 (ih-go);— *bone*, u-zeh'-kweh 烏鯽°骨

CYCLE, (sixty years), kyiah'-ts 甲子; hwô-kyiah'-ts 花甲子; *years of a* —, nyin-kang' 年庚

CYCLOPEDIA, poh-veh'-go-shü' 博物个°書

CYLINDER, dziang-yün-t'i' 長圓體; ngô-dong'-shih 瓦°筒式°

CYMBALS, dzô-beh' or ts'ô-beh'; *large* —, do beh' 大°鈸; *smaller* —, ts'ih'-ts 小°鈸; *very small* —, gen-ts'ön'.

D

DAB, *to throw dirt upon*, na-nyi' kwang'-djoh 泥潑°蒼°

DABBLE *in water*, long shü' 弄水°

DAGGER, ts'-tao' 刺刀; *two edged* —, sông-min' kyin 雙面劍 (ih-pô)

DAGUERREOTYPE, tsiao'-siang 照相

DAILY, nyih-nyih' 日°日°; me-nyih' 每日°; djoh-nyih' 逐日°; nyih-dzoh' 日°逐;— *food*, nyih-nyih'-go ky'üoh'-zih 日°日°个°吃°食

DAINTY *as to food*, ky'üoh'-zih k'ao'-kyiu 吃°食考°究; ky'üoh'-zih kæn-ka' 吃°食尷°尬°; *a* —, ts'ing-c'ü'-go tong'-si 清泚个°東西

DALLY, *to* (the sexes), nen-nyü' o-kyin'-tah-pe' 男女和°肩搭背

DAM *for water*, ky'i 閘°;— *with mud slide for boats*, pô 礗; *in* 堰

DAM, *to* — *up water*, kwæn-djü' shü 關住水°

DAMAGE, *pay the* —, long-diao'-de be-wæn' 弄壞了°賠還

DAMAGE, *to* — *by bruising* (as

DAM 107 DAR

fruit), ts‘ah'-sông 擦傷; *to spoil*, i'-diao; long-diao' 弄壞°; wæ-diao' 壞了°

DAMAGED, *torn or broken*, yiu p‘o'-dzæn-go 有破綻个°; *spotted (by water, &c.*), yiu tsih'-tsoh-go 有汁泥个°; *goods — by water*, shü'-tsih ho' 水°汁貨

DAMASK, dön-pu' 緞布

DAMN, *condemn him to eternal punishment*, ding' peh gyi ziu üong'-kw‘u ying-vah' 定俾其°受永苦刑罰

DAMNED, *to be —*, vah-loh' di-nyüoh' 罰落地獄; üong' zo di-nyüoh' 永坐°地獄

DAMNED, *the* ziu üong'-kw‘u-go nying 受永苦个°人

DAMP, dziao-sih' 潮濕; yiu sih'-ky‘i 有濕氣; *very —*, sih'-ky‘i djong' 濕氣重; *to become —*, wæn dziao' 還潮; cün dziao' 轉潮; fæn-dziao' 翻潮

DAMPEN *it*, long gyi' nyüing-tsiu'-go.

DAMSEL, do-kwu'-nyiang 大°姑娘; kwe'-nyü 閨女

DANCE, *to* t‘iao-vu' 跳舞

DANDLE, *to — on the knee*, kyiah' teo-teo' 脚抖抖; *— in the hand*, siu song-song' 手聳聳

DANDRUFF, kw‘u'- k‘oh - in' 頭變°歷

DANDY, p‘iao-yih' nying 飄逸人°; *an officer's son highly dressed*

but not of good character, hwô-hwô'-kong'-ts 花花公子

DANGER, ngwe-hyin' 危險; *to get into —*, tsao'-djoh ngwe-hyin' 遭著°危險; *in —*, ngwe-hyin' li-hyiang' 危險裡向; *rush into — in spite of remonstrance &c.*, weh'-leh feh-næ'-væn 活得°弗耐煩

DANGEROUS, hyin'-hyin 險險; ngwe'-go 危个°; hyin'-loh 險霍; hyin'-dao-dao 險逃逃; yin-'æ' 有害; *— to life*, sing'-ming kao-kwæn' 性命交°關; *— to sit there*, keh'-deo zo, yiu fong-ho' 那°邊坐°有風火; keh'-deo zo, yiu ken-yi' 那°邊坐°有干係°

DANGLE, *to* dang 宕; dang-dang'-dong 宕宕動

DAPPLED, pæn-poh'-go 斑駁个°

DARE, *to* ken 敢; *— not do*, feh ken tso' 弗敢做

DARING, mao do'-tæn-go 冒大°膽个°; *— person*, mao do'-tæn go nying 冒大°瞻个°人

DARK, en 暗; heh'-en 黑暗; en'-lih-boh-long'; en'-c‘ih-c‘ih' 暗睫睫; en'-dong-dong 暗瞳瞳; *nearly —*, t‘in'kw‘a en'-de 天快°暗了°; *very —*, moh-ts‘eh'-di-en' 墨漆地暗; *afraid of the —*, p‘o en'-go 怕暗个°; *— color*, sing seh' 深色; *— blue*, sing læn' 深藍

DARKEN, *to — slightly*, tsô-ing'

遮°陰; — *completely*, tsô-en'
遮°晤.

DARLING, *dearly loved*, ting' dzih-din'-go 頂值錢°个°; — *child*, nön-nön' (used for both sexes).

DARN, *to* kang 耕°; — *in ball-stitch*, c'ün 穿; *to mend by imitating the texture of the stuff*, tsih' pu 緻補; — *stockings*, kang mah' 耕°襪 (pu mah' 補襪 which is often used, is incorrect, as it means to mend with a patch); — *slightly*, kang' liang tsing' 耕°兩針.

DART *carried in the sleeve*, ziu-tsin' 袖箭.

DART, *to forth*, zah-c'ih'-læ.

DASH, *to* — *against*, ts'ong-dzông' 衝撞; dzông-djoh' 撞着°; *waves* — *up*, lông p'eh-zông-læ' 浪潑上來; — *down*, ts'ong-loh' 衝落; *ditto, by knocking against*, dzông-tao' 撞倒.

DATE, *time*, z-'eo' 時候; *what month?* kyi yüih'-li 幾月裡? soh'-go yüih-veng' 甚°麼°月份? *at what date? i. e. in what dynasty?* læ soh'-go dziao-dæ' 在°甚°麼°朝代? *year of the reign*, nyin-'ao' 年號; *year of the cycle*, nyin-kang' 年庚.

The date of the year is reckoned by dynasties, reigns, and cycles. The cycle is only used for present time.

DATE, *jujube*, tsao'-ts 棗子; *honeyed and dried* —, mih-tsao'

蜜棗; *black* —, heh-tsao' 黑棗; *red* —, 'ong-tsao' 紅棗.

DAUB, *to* lön-du' 亂塗; lön-dzô' 亂搽.

DAUGHTER, nön 女°; *how many daughters have you?* ng' yiu kyi'-we ling-æ' 你°有幾位令愛? kyi-we' ts'in-kying' 幾位千金? *I have three daughters*, ngô' yiu sæn'-go siao-nyü' 我有三个°小女.

DAUGHTER-IN-LAW, sing-vu' 媳婦; *oldest son's wife*, do sing-vu' 大°媳°婦; *second son's wife* (when there are more), nyi-vông' sing-vu' 二°房媳°婦; (if there are only two sons), *the second* —, siao' sing-vu' 小°媳°婦.

DAUNTED, *nothing* 'ao-vu' gyü-dæn' 毫無懼憚.

DAUNTLESS, tæn-da'-jü-t'in' 膽大如天.

DAWN, u-long'-song z-'eo' 烏曚曉°時候; t'in'-kw'a-liang' 天快亮; t'in'-bah-c'ong'-ky'i 天白赠起; tong-fông'-diao-bah' 東方曉°白.

DAY, *a* ih-nyih' 一日°; *a day's work*, ih-kong' 一工; *a day's wages*, ih-kong' kong-din' 一工工錢°; *the first* — *of the month*, ts'u-ih' 初一; *1st and 15th of the month*, soh' vông 朔望; *what* — *of the month is this?* kying'-tsiao z ts'u-kyi' 今朝是初幾? kyih-mih' z ts'u-kyi' 今

DAY 109 DEA

日°是初幾? the 15th, jih-ng' 十五'; yüih-pun' 月半; every —, me'-nyih 每日°; nyih-nyih' 日°日°; — and night, nyih yia' 日°夜; all —, tsing nyih' 竟日°; dziang nyih' 長日°; half a —, pun' nyih 半日°; every other —, kæn' nyih 間日°; lucky —, hao' nyih-ts 好日°子; unlucky —, nyih-ts' wa' 日°子孬; the same —, tông nyih 當日°; — before yesterday, zin nyih' 前日°; — after tomorrow, 'eo nyih' 後日°; whatever — you please, ze ng' 'ah-li ih nyih' 隨你那裡一日°; how many days? kyi nyih' 幾日°? to-siao' nyih'-ts 多少日°子? ten days, jih nyih' 十日°.

DAY-BOOK, liu-shü'-bu 流水簿

DAY-BREAK, t'in liang' z-'eo' 天亮時候; nyih-deo' fông-kwông' z-'eo' 日頭放光時候

DAY-LIGHT, nyih-deo'-kwông' 日頭光; nyih-kwông' 日°光; t'a'-yiang-kwông' 太陽光

DAY-TIME, in the —, nyih-li' 日°裡; nyih-cong-deo' 日°中頭; ts'ing-t'in'-bah-nyih 青天白日°

DAZZLING light, kwông'ziang tsing c'oh' ka 光如針戳; kwông' li-'æ' 光利害; my eyes are dazzled, or overpowered by the light, ngô ngren'-kwông teo'-feh-djü' 我眼°光兜弗住; dih-feh-ko' 敵弗過

DEAD, si'-de 死了°; ko'-de 過了°; vông-ko'-de 亡過了°; m-neh'-de 沒°有°了°; ky'ü'-shü-de 去世了°; just —, ky'i dön'-de 氣斷了°; — tree, jü ô'-de 樹殭了°; jü kw'u'-de 樹枯了°; jü si'-de 樹死°了°; — body, s-siu' 屍首; p'oh'-s 仆屍; si'-s 死°屍; — cow, tao' ngeo 倒牛°; — fish, veng-ng' 文魚°; — (as a backslider in religion), dao'-sing si'-liao 道心死°了°; the place of the —, ing-s' 陰司; ing-kæn' 陰間°

DEADLY, iao sah-nying'-go 要殺人°个°; — poison, iao yiah-sah'-go 要藥殺个°

DEADNESS, ziang si'-liao ka'-go 像死°了°个°; coldness, lang' sing 冷°心

DEAF, long-bang' 聾聵; ng'-tô long' 耳朵聾; born —, sang-dzing long-bang' 生°成聾聵; — and dumb person, ô'-ts 啞子

DEAFEN, you — me with your noise, ngô ng'-tô be ng ts'ao'-long-de 我耳°朵被你譟聾了°

DEAFNESS, affected —, or — in one ear, tsia'-mi-long' 借米聾; pretended —, tsông kô' ng-to long' 裝假°耳°朵聾

DEAL, a great —, hyü'-to 許多; I cause you a — of trouble, tao

DEA 110 DEB

iao ng' ziu hyü'-to lao-loh' 倒要你受許多勞碌; to lao' 多勞; fi sing' 費心

DEAL *out to them,* feng-feng' peh gyi-lah' 分分給伊等; — *honestly,* kong-dao' dæ nying' 公道待人°; — *impartially,* m̀ p'in'-sing dæ nying' 無偏心待人°

DEALER *in cotton,* tso min-hwo' sang-i' go 做棉花生意个°

DEAR, *costly,* kyü 貴°; kô'-din kyü' 價°錢貴°; *how —,* dza kyü' 甚貴°; — *child,* dzih-diu'-go siao-nying' 值錢°个小孩°; sing-deo' nyüoh 心頭肉°; weh-pao' 活寶

In writing letters the address "Dear friend" is unknown; Mr. 'Ong Siao' Hyiang writing to Mr. Wòng, in lieu of "Dear Mr. Wòng" writes, "Wòng Sin'-Sang s-zih'" 王先生史席 or "veng kyi'" 文几, and signs himself 'Ong Siao'-Hyiang; to an official's name he adds, "dæ-'ô'" 臺下, and signs "O. S. H. teng'-siu," 頓首 *i. e.* bow low; to a friend's name he adds "koh'-'ô'" 閣下; a pupil signs by adding "yin-di'" 賢弟 (masc.) or "nyü-di'" 女弟 (fem.), to his or her name; if writing to an equal or inferior add, "jü-min'" 如面 or "jü-ngwu'" 如晤; a gentleman writing to a lady addresses her as "s-meo'" 師母 "or tsòng-tsz'" 粧次; a youth to father's, mother's or teacher's name adds, "tseng-zin'" 尊前

DEARLY *loved,* ts'ing-æ'-go 親愛个°; *ditto* (of a superior), ting æ'-kying-go 頂愛敬个°; *ditto* (of an equal or inferior), ting æ'-sih-go 頂愛惜个°

DEARLY *bought,* ma' kyü-de 買°貴°了°; ma' ky'üoh-kw'e'-de 買吃°虧了°

DEARTH, siu-kah' feh-zông 收割弗上; *great —,* ts'-lih vu-siu' 子粒無收; *a year of —,* hwông-nyin' 荒年; *a year of scarcity* (of vegetables or fruit), siao' nyin 小年

DEATH, si 死°; — *of the emperor,* kô peng' 駕崩; *the day of one's —,* si' gyi 死期; *the time of —,* ky'ü-shü' z-'eo' 去世時候; ling-cong' z-'eo' 臨終時候; ling-si' z-'eo 臨死時候; *natural —,* jün' cong 善終; bing kwu' 病故; — *by violence,* oh' si 惡死°; wang si' 橫死°; *how old were you at your mother's —?* ng' to-siao nyin-kyi' sông meo'-go 你多少年紀喪母个°? *the time of your father's —,* sông vu' z-'eo' 喪父時候

DEATHLESS, ve' si-go 勿°會°死个°

DEATH-LIKE, ziang si'-yiang ka 像死°一樣; *to put on a — appearance,* tsông si'-yiang 裝死°樣

DEATH-WARRANT, sah nying'-go tsiao'-shü 殺人°个詔書

DEBAR, *to shut out,* kwæn-c'ih' 關出; *not to allow,* feh cing' 弗准

DEBASED, to be jih-'ô' 習下°; jih-'ô'-liu 習下°流
DEBATE to bin'-leng 辯論
DEBAUCHEE, tsiu-seh'-ts-du' 酒色之徒
DEBILITATED in body, sing-t'i' boh-ziah'-de 身體簿弱了°; peng'-z wa'-de 本事孬°了°
DEBILITY, ṁ-lih' 無°力; t'eh-nyün' 脱元; bi'-t'ah-lông'-t'ông.
DEBT, tsa 債°; to owe a —, ky'in tsa' 欠債; to be in —, pe tsa' 背債; tsa'-veo 債負; vi wun' wei' 未完; heavily in —, kw'e-k'ong' 虧空; to pay off — (by borrowing), din kw'e'-k'ong 墊虧空
DEBTOR, ky'in'-cü 欠主
DECALOGUE, jih-diao kyiæ' 十條誡
DECAMP, to move a camp, pun-ying-dza' 搬營寨; bah-ying' 拔營
DECAPITATE, to sah-deo' 殺頭; tsæn-deo' 斬頭
DECAY, to sæ-ba' 衰敗°; to rot, læn-wu' 爛腐°; decayed tree, jü læn'-de 樹爛了°; decayed leaves, læn-yih' 爛葉
DECEITFUL, kæn-tsô'-go 奸°詐个°; wily, kwe'-kyi to-tön' 詭計多端
DECEIVE, to p'in 騙; hong 哄; ky'i 欺; hong'-p'in 哄騙; ky'i-p'in' 欺騙; kwa'-p'in 拐°騙; to — by concealing, mun-p'in' 瞞騙; cannot — him, p'in'-gyi-feh-læ' 騙其弗來

DECENCY, becoming behavior, lin'-c'ü 廉耻; no —, lin'-c'ü ṁ-neh'-de 廉耻沒°有°了°; he has no sense of —, gyi lin'-c'ü tu feh æ-go 其廉耻都勿愛个°
DECIDE, to ding-kwe' 定規; ding-jih' 定實; kyüih'-ding 決定; hard to —, kyüih-tön'-feh-loh 決斷弗落
DECISION, I leave it to your —, iao ng' ding-kwe' 要你°定規; peh ng' tso cü' 俾你°作°主; firm —, cü'-i k'ô'-ding-de 主意孥°定了°; a person of —, kyüih'-lih-go nying 決裂个°人°; of no —, ṁ-nô'-neh'-go 無°孥捻个°
DECK of a ship, ts'ông 艙; ts'ông-min' 艙面
DECK, to adorn, tsông-sih' 裝飾; tsông-pæn' 裝扮; tsah'-kwah 紮刮; — (as a bad woman), tô'-pæn 朶扮
DECLAIM, to rant, kao-dæn' kw'eh-leng' 高談闊論
DECLARE, to kao'-su 告訴; wô 話; to proclaim, djün-yiang' 傳揚; — to every one, vong nying' kao'-su 逢人°告訴; to — war, tang tsin'-shü 打戰書
DECLINE, to refuse, dz 辭; t'e-dz' 推辭; foh 覆; we-foh' 回覆; — to see visitors, dz k'ah'-kæh 辭客; — an invitation, foh

ts'ing 覆請; dz ts'ing' 辭請;
— *ond return*, pih'-wæn 璧還;
ditto with thanks, dz-zia' 辭謝°;
to go down, hyiang 'ô' 向下°;
the price has declined, kô-din
soh'-de 價°錢°縮了°; 'ông'-
dzing t'eng-de 行°情余了°;
the sun is declining, nyih-deo'
tang-ts'ia' 日°頭打斜°; —
years, nyin'-kyi lao'-mæn-de 年
紀老邁了°

DECORATE, *to* tsông-sih' 粧飾;
— (*as living things*), tsông-pæn'
粧扮

DECORUM, li'-cü 禮制; *to observe*
—, sin li'-cü 守禮制; *to
violate the rules of* —, be li' 悖
禮 See DECENCY.

DECOY, *to entice*, ying'-yiu 引誘;
— *to a trap*, p'in' gyüoh 騙°局

DECOY *bird*, me-deo' 媒頭 (ih-
tsah)

DECREASE, *to* ky'üih'-long-ky'i'
缺攏去°; kæn'-loh-ky'i 減°
落去°; — *in size*, siao'-long-
ky'i 小攏去°

DECREE, *emperor's* ts'-i 旨意;
zông-yü' 上諭; tsiao'-shü 詔
書; *official's* —, 'ao-ling' 號令

DECREE, *to* c'ih-ling' 出令; c'ih
'ao-ling' 出號令; — (*as the
emperor*), ts'-i pæn'-loh-læ 旨
意頒落來; *to fix* or *appoint*,
shih'-lih 設°立

DECREPIT, *forgetful and making
mistakes*, lao'-mah-long'-cong 老
邁°龍鍾; *old, weak, and useless*,
lao'-ziah vu-yüong 老弱無
用; oh'-tsoh 齷齪

DECRY, *to cry down as worthless*,
wô' 丠-yüong'-go 話無°用个°;
to censure and cut down, p'i-siah'
批削; — *a person*, kông nying
wa' 講°人°孬°

DEDICATE, *to* — (as a child), hyin
獻; vong'-hyin 奉獻; — *to
God's service*, vong'-z Jing-ming'
yüong-go 奉事神明用个°;
tseng-ky'i' peh Jing-ming' 奪
起°與°神明

DEDUCE, *to infer*, ying' gyi kwe-
nyün' 引其歸原; kyiu'-kyiu-
kwe-nyün' 九九歸原; t'e-leng'
推論; t'e-tæn'-k'æ kong' 推打
開講°

DEDUCT, *to* djü 除; djü-loh' 除
落; k'eo'-djü 扣除

DEED, *an action*, ih-tön' 'ang-we' 一
端行°為; ih-tsông' z-t'i' 一椿
事體; *his deeds*, gyi sô tso'-go
z-t'i' 其所做°个事體; —
of merit, hao'-z 好事 hao' z-ken'
好事幹; *writing*, ky'i 契;
ky'i'-kyü 契據; — *for land*,
di-ky'i' 地契; — *for a house*,
oh'-ky'i 屋契 (ih tsiang)

DEEM, *to* ts'eng-ts'eng' 忖忖; yi-
we' 以為; dao-z' 道是

DEEP, sing 深; —*well*, tsing sing'
井深; — *color*, sing-seh' 深色

DEEPEN, *to* — (as a hole), k'æ-leh

sing'-tin 開得°深點;— color (by dyeing), nyin sing'-tin 染°深點

DEER, loh 鹿;— sinews, loh-kying' 鹿筋; deer's horns, loh' koh 鹿角°

DEFACE, to tsao-t'ah' nga-min' 蹧蹋外面

DEFALCATION, See EMBEZZLE.

DEFAME, to pông'-hwe 謗毀; hwe'-pông 毀謗

DEFAULTER, one who fails to appear in court, feh-tao-en'cü'-kwu 弗到案个人°; one who fails to account for money, pao-siao'-feh-c'ih'-go cü'-kwu 報銷弗出个°人°

DEFEAT, to conquer, ying 贏; tang'-ying 打贏;— his plan, ba' gyi sô meo-we'-go 敗其所謀為个°

DEFEATED, ba'-de 敗了°;—(in fight), tang'-ba-de 打敗°了°; tang'-ba-tsiang'-de 打敗°仗了°; tang'-shü-de 打輸了

DEFECT, fault, mao-bing' 毛病; deformity, dzæn-dzih' 殘疾; to have ditto, væn dzæn-dzih 犯殘疾; blemish or scar, pæn-pô' 瘢疤;— in weaving cotton, t'iao'-sô 挑紗; ditto in silk, t'iao'-s 挑絲; p'o'-dzæn 破綻; many defects, tsih'-ky'üih-pah'-ky'üih 七缺八缺

DEFECTIVE, dzæn-ky'üih'-peh-djün' 殘缺不全

DEFEND, to protect, pao'-wu 保護; to prepare for resistance, bông-tu' 防堵; to be on guard, kying'-siu 謹守; to vindicate, feng-p'eo' 分剖

DEFENDANT, (Law) be'-kao 被告

DEFER, to nga 挨°; ah 壓°;— till to-morrow, nga' tao ming-tsiao' 挨°到明朝;— the day, tsæn nyih-ts' 攛日°子; kæ gyi' 改期

DEFER, to t'e-peh' 推與°; t'e-nyiang' 推讓°;— to your opinion, t'e'-peh ng' ding-kwe' 推與°你定規

DEFERENTIAL, kyü-soh' 拘束; kyü'-kyü-jün 拘拘然

DEFICIENCY in numbers, ky'üih'-su 缺數; there is a —, yiu ky'üih'-tih 有缺的; make up the —, ky'üih-su iao pu'-tsoh 缺數要補足

DEFICIENT, ky'in 欠; ts'ô 差; ky'üih 缺; not enough, feh keo' 弗彀

DEFILE in the hills, sæn-vong' 山縫 (ih-da)

DEFILE, to long'-leh lah-t'ah' 弄得°邋遢; long-leh lah-lih'-lah-t'ah' 弄得°邋裡邋遢; long'-leh nyi-sing'-peh-la' 弄得°泥腥不賴; long-leh ao-lih'-peh-tsao' 弄°得垔裡百糟

DEFINE, to — limits, ding 'æn'-cü 定限°制; to explain, ka'-sbih 解°說

DEFINITE words, shih-wô' ling-ts'ing' 說話靈清; words not sufficiently —, shih-wô' ky'in feng-ts'ing' 說話欠分清; shih-wô' feh-loh'-dzih 說話弗落直; shih-wô' yiu zông'-loh 說話有上落
DEFINITION, ka'-shih 解說
DEFORMED, dzæn-dzih' 殘疾; to become —, væn dzæn-dzih' 犯殘疾
DEFRAUD, to — of, ky'üoh'-meh 吃°沒; ziah-meh' 嚼沒; t'eng-ky'üoh' 吞吃°
DEFRAY, to c'ih 出; t'ing 聽; — the expense, c'ih fi'-yüong 出費用
DEFY, to provoke war, kyih'-dong nying tang-tsiang 激動人°打仗°; to challenge, t'ao-tsin' 討戰
DEGENERATE, to wa-loh'-ky'i 孬落去°; sæ-ba'-loh-ky'i' 衰敗落去°; t'e-pæn'-loh-ky'i' 推板落去°; tao'-tsiang-i-soh' 倒漲又°縮
DEGRADE, to ky'ih'-loh 挈落; kông'-loh 降°落; — to a lower office, kah-tsih' 革職; kông-kyih' 降°級; to take away the button, tsah ting'-ta 摘頂戴°
DEGREE, grade, teng'-kyih 等級; the highest literary —, di-ih' kah 第一甲°; called, zông-nyün' 狀元; the 1st — (i. e. lowest), siu'-dzæ 秀才; to obtain the — of siu-dzæ, jih 'oh' 入學; tsing 'oh' 進學; the 2nd —, kyü'-

nying 舉人°; the 3rd —, tsing'-z 進士; has he a literary —? gyi' yiu sing-kying' feh 其有紳衿否°? what —? soh'-go sing-kying' 甚°麼°紳衿? he has the — of siu-dzæ, gyi z dzæ-dziang' 其是在庠; to obtain the higher degrees, cong 中
DEGREE, (Geom.), one —, ih-du' 一度
DEGREES, by dzin'-dzin 漸漸; mæn-mæn' 慢慢
DEIFY, to —(when done by the emperor), fong bu-sah' 封菩薩; ts'ih'-fong 勅封; — him, tseng gyi' we bu-sah' 尊其爲菩薩
DEIFICATION (when done by the emperor), fong bu-sah'-go ngæn-deo' 封菩薩个°銜頭; — to a higher grade, tse-fong' 追封; kô-fong' 加°封
DEJECTED in appearance, we-t'ah'-t'ah 痿塌塌; — in mind, sing-hwe'-i'-læn 心灰意懶
DELAY, to tæn-koh' 耽擱; to ask for —, iah 約; ditto in paying debt, iah-tsa' 約債°
DELEGATE, dæ-li'-go nying' 代理个°人°; to send as a —, we 委
DELEGATE, to — authority, kao'-c'ih gyün-ping' 交出權柄; to receive delegated authority, dæ tsông' gyün-ping' 代掌權柄
DELIBERATE, to tsing-tsiah' 斟酌; nyi' 議; kong-nyi' 公議; siang-nyi' 相議

DELIBERATIVE *body*, we'-nyi 會議 (ih-go)
DELICATE, *fine*, si 細;— (as workmanship), si'-ky'iao 細巧; *tender*, neng 嫩;— *and pretty* (as a child), neng-æ'-æ 嫩藹藹;— *food*, ts'ing-c'ü ky'üoh'-zih 清泚吃°食
DELICIOUS, sông'-k'eo 爽口
DELIGHT, *to — him*, peh gyi kao-hying' 俾其高興
DELIGHTED, kao-hying' 高興; *perfectly —*, kw'a'-weh'-sah-de 快°活煞了°; hwun-t'in'-hyi-di' 歡天喜地
DELINEATE, *to — by description*, kông'-tin ying-tsih' 講°點形跡; kông'-tin ing'-tsong 講點形踪 (tsong or cong)
DELIRIOUS, nyih-hweng'-de 熱昏了°;— *talk*, nyih-wô' 熱話
DELIVER, *to save*, kyiu 救;— *out of trouble*, kyiu'-kw'u kyiu-næn' 救苦救難;— *in his extremity*, kyiu' gyi kyih' 救其急; *to set free*, sih'-fông 釋放; — (as a letter), kao-dæ'-c'ih 交°代出;— *to him*, kao-dæ' peh gyi 交°代給°其;— *at the door*, song'-zông meng 送上門; *have you delivered the message?* keh' ky'i z-t'i ng yiu wô-ko' ma 這°件事體你°有話過麼'?— *by a midwife*, siu-sang' 收生°; tsih-sang' 接生°

DELUDE, *to cheat*, ky'i-p'in' 欺騙; tah shih'-gyiao 搭雪橋;— *by false promises*, ko'-gyiao, bah-gyiao' 過橋拔橋; *why do you — me?* ng dza'-we peh ngô' pe moh-sao' 你甚°麼°俾°我背木稍?
DELUDED, *to be —*, pe moh-sao' 背木稍; pe bô' 背耙
DELUSION, moh-sao' 木稍; *laboring under a —*, pe moh-sao' de 背木稍了°
DELUGE, 'ong-shü 洪水°; *the —* 'ong-shü-fæn-tsiang' 洪水泛漲
DEMAND, *in great —*, 'ông-ts'iao' 昂°俏
DEMAND, *to* t'ao 討; iao 要; *he demands too much*, gyi t'ao t'eh' to 其討太°多;— *forcibly*, ngang-iao' 硬要;— *pertinaciously*, ts'in-gyiu', væn-gyiu' 千求萬求
DEMANDED, *grant a little, more will be —*, teh'-bu tsing'-bu 得步進步
DEMOLISH, *to* ts'ah'-hwe 拆毀
DEMON, oh'-kyü 惡鬼° (ih-go)
DEMONIAC, *one possessed by a demon*, jih-mo'-go nying 入魔个°人°
DEMONSTRATE *to you*, peh ng k'ao-jih' 俾°你°靠實;— *step by step*, gyin'-tang-gyin k'ao-jih' 件件靠實;— (as a calculation), pih'-tang-pih k'ao-jih' 筆筆靠實

DEMURE, pæn'-pæn go 板板个° — countenance, lao'-lin 老臉
DEN of thieves, zeh k'o' 賊窠; tiger's —, lao'-hwu k'o' 老虎窠; hwu'-yüih 虎穴; lao'-hwu dong' 老虎洞
DENOTE, to yiu i'-s 有意思; the character ho, denotes riches, ho' z yiu dzæ-veh'-go ka'-shih 貨字有財物个° 解° 說; to indicate, ts'-tin 指點
DENOUNCE, to stigmatize, p'i-siah' 批削; — one really bad, c'ih gyi'-go ts'iu' 出其个° 醜
DENSE foliage, jü-yih mih-kying' 樹葉密緊; jü-yih' mih-mih'-zeng-zeng 樹葉密密層° 層°; — crowd, nying' mih-kying' 人° 密緊; nying' a-tsi'-feh-k'æ 人° 挨° 擠弗開; — fog, vu-lu nyüong' 霧露濃; — population, nying-in' væn-to' 人° 烟繁多
DENT, a ih-go den' 一个° 潭
DENT, to c'oh-den' 斫潭; c'oh-dong' 斫洞
DENY, to — the truth of, wô feh-z'-ka 話弗是如°此°; to refuse to grant, feh-cing' 弗准; feh-ing'-hyü 弗應許; to disown, feh-tsiao'-jing 弗招認; feh-jing', or feh-nying' 弗認; to — one's-self, ky'i'-diao zi'-go s-sing 棄了°自个° 私心
DEPART, to li-k'æ' 離開; bih-k'æ' 別開; — far away, yün'-k'æ 遠開; — on a journey, c'ih-

meng'-ky'i 出門去°; — this life, ky'ü-shü' 去世
DEPARTMENT, sphere of duties, peng'-veng 本分; en-veng'-siu-kyi' 安分守己; — of a prefect, fu 府
DEPEND, to — on, k'ao-djoh 靠着°; i-k'ao 依靠; — on one's parents, k'ao'-djoh do-nying'-go foh'-ky'i 靠著° 大° 人° 个° 福氣; what has he to — upon? gyi' yiu soh'-si hao k'ao' 其有甚° 麼好靠? no relatives to — upon, loh-ts'ing' vu'-k'ao 六親無靠; a person, &c., upon whom to —, k'ao-sæn 靠山; the man can be depended upon, nying k'ao-leh-djü-go 人° 靠得住个°; he cannot be depended upon, k'ao gyi'-feh-jih 靠其弗住
DEPENDENCE, without vu-i'-vu-k'ao 無依無靠; — (but not firm), gæ-deo' 戲頭
DEPICT, to — by drawing, sia' ih-go du' 寫一个° 圖; — in language, kông' ying-kying' 講° 影景
DEPLORABLE, zing-we'-k'o'-sih 甚為可惜
DEPLORE, to pe-t'æn' 悲嘆
DEPOPULATED, nying' siu'-jih-wun'-de 人° 收拾完了°
DEPORTMENT, kyü-ts'-'ang-dong' 舉止行°動; 'ang-i'-dong-zing' 行°意動靜

DEPOSE, to — a king, fi'-diao wông-ti' 廢了皇帝;—from office, kah tsih' 革職

DEPOSIT, to lay down, fông'-loh 放落;—money in the bank, nying-ts' dzeng læ dzin-tin'li 銀子存在°錢°店裡; the money deposited, dzeng-'ông' 存項; dzeng-kw'un' 存欵

DEPOT, building for public use, gyüoh 局;—for arms, kyüing-ky'i'-gyüoh 軍器局; open place for storage, ts'iang 廠;—for coal, me-t'æn' ts'iang 煤炭廠; freight —, ko'-dông-'ông' 過塘行°

DEPRAVE, to piu'-diao 變壞°; wæ-diao' 壞了°;—the mind, wæ nying' sing-jih' 壞人°心術

DEPRAVED, thoroughly 'o'-tsoh p'e' 下°作胚; 'o'-liu p'e' 下°流胚

DEPRECIATE, to — others, kông bih' nying feh-tao'-kô 講°別人°弗到家°;—one's own merits or abilities (often used in a false sense), ky'in-hyü' 謙虛; do not —yourself, hao-vong' ky'in-hyü' 弗°用°謙虛

DEPREDATE, to plunder, ts'iang'-deh 搶奪; ts'iang'-kyih 搶刦

DEPRESS, to lower by pressure, ah'-loh 壓°落

DEPRESSED in spirits, 無 sing'-siang 無°心想; we-we'-ze-ze' 痿痿痺痺

DEPRIVE, to take away, do'-leh-ky'i' 拕°得°去°; ditto by force, deh'-leh-ky'i 奪得°去°;—of that, over which we have some control, siu'-leh-ky'i' 收得°去°;—of privilege, ih-tsông me'-z siu-tsing' 一椿美事收進; God has deprived me of my son, Jing-ming' pô ngô ng-ts' siu-leh-ky'i' 神明把我兒子收得°去°

DEPTH, sing 深; what is the — of this well? keh' k'eo tsing' to-siao sing' 這口井多少深?

DEPUTE, to we 委

DEPUTY, we'-yün 委員 (ih-we)

DERANGE, to put out of order, kao'-lön 攪°亂

DERANGED, insane, fah-tin' 發癲; fah-gwông' 發狂; fah-c'ü' 發癡

DERIDE, to sông-ky'üoh' 傷曲; tsao-siao' 嘲笑; kông dæn'-wô 講°談話

DERIVATION, peng' ti-ts 本底子; that is of foreign —, keh peng' ti-ts, z nga-koh' læ-go 這°本底子是外°國來个°

DERIVED, whence is it —? keh'-go ky'i-ts'u' dzong 'o'-r læ' 這°个起初從何而來? it was — from China, peng'-læ z Cong-koh' c'ih'-go 本來是中國出个°

DEROGATORY to one's rank or character, t'eh-p'ing' 脫品; shih'-kw'un' 失欵

DESCEND, to loh'-ky'i 下°去°; loh'-læ 下°來; kông'-loh 降°下°; — *a hill*, tseo'-loh sæn' 走下°山; — *from heaven*, 'ô'-kông' 下°降°; *Jesus descended from heaven*, Yiæ-su' 'ô-kông'-de 耶穌下°降了°; — (as an estate), yi-loh'-læ 遺下°來

DESCENDANT, 'eo'-dæ 後代; ts'-seng 子孫

DESCENT, loh'-ky'i 落去°; *the — was dangerous*, keh-go loh'-ky'i ngwe-hyin'-go 這°个°落去°危險个°; *of honorable —*, kong-ts' kong-seng' 公子公孫; *direct —*, tih'-p'a 嫡派°

DESCRIBE, to ying-yüong' 形容; — *a balloon for me*, ky'i'-gyiu yiang-shih', hao ying-yüong' peh ngô t'ing' 氣球樣式好形容俾°我聽; *cannot — it*, wô' feh siang-ziang-go 話弗相像个°

DESERT, *sandy* sô-di' 沙地; — *place*, peh'-mao-ts-di' 不毛之地; *wilderness*, kw'ông-iæ 曠野 (ih-t'ah)

DESERT, *what is deserved*, ing-kæ' ziu 應該受

DESERT, to ky'i'-diao 棄了°

DESERTER *from the army*, dao-ping' 逃兵; — *from a ship*, jün'-li dao-zông'-go 船裡逃上个°

DESERVE, to ing-tông' ziu 應當受; li' sô tông-jün'-go 理所當然个°; *he deserves the reward*, keh-go sông'-pao, gyi' ing-tông' ziu 這°个°賞報其應當受

DESIGN, to tang'-tsiang 打將; i'-s iao 意思要; *he designs to build a house*, gyi tang'-tsiang ky'i ih-tsing oh' 其打將起一進屋

DESIGN, i'-s 意思; dzeng-sing' 存心; *my — is to give it to a friend*, ngô i-'s, song-peh beng-yiu' 我意思送給°朋友

DESIGNEDLY, yiu'-i 有意; kwu'-i 故意; deb-i' 特意; deh-we' 特為

DESIRABLE, *very* meo-ts'-peh-teh' 謀之不得 (primarily too good to be obtained).

DESIRE, to sing'-siang 心想; iao'-siang 要想 (more intense than the former); — *earnestly*, hyüih'-sing siang' 血心想

DESIRE, sing-siang' 心想; sing-nyün' 心願; *his desires are too great*, gyi-go sing-siang' mang' 其个°心想猛°; *have long had that —*, kyiu' yiu-ts' sing' 久有此心

DESIST, to stop, hyih 歇; — *from*, hyih-siu' 歇手; fông-siu' 放手

DESK, *writing-case*, s'-pao-'eh' 四寶盒; *writing-table*, s'-pao-coh' 四寶桌

DESOLATE, ts'i-liang' 悽涼; vu-liao' vu-liao' 無聊無聊; ziang-kwu-tiao'-ka 像孤烏°樣°式°

DES 119 DET

DESOLATE, to long'-leh ling'-ling'-loh-loh' 弄得零零落落
DESPAIR, vu-k'o-vông' 無可望; in utter —, djih' vu-k'o-vông' 絕無可望
DESPERADO, vông-ming'-ts-du' 亡命之徒; fi'-du 匪徒; vu-la' 無賴; local —, dziu-di'-oh'-kweng 就地惡棍
DESPERATE, I grew —, ngô oh'-c'ih-de 我惡出了
DESPERATION, driven to —, pih'-leh zông-t'in'-vu-lu', jih-di'-vu-meng' 逼得上天無路入地無門; in —, deo-tseo ṃ-lu' 投走無路
DESPICABLE, feh-jih'-ngæn 弗入眼; — employment, pe-zin' 'ông-tông' 卑賤行當; t'ao'-væn 'ông-tông' 討飯行當
DESPISE, to ky'ing-mæn' 輕慢; k'en-ky'ing' 看輕; ts'iao-feh-ky'i' 瞧弗起; every one despises him, ko'-ko nying' k'en'-gyi-ky'ing' 個個人看其輕
DESPONDENT, sing hwe' i'-læn 心灰意懶; desire weaker than before, ts'-hyiang ziah'-de 志向弱了; sing-i' dæn'-de 心意淡了
DESPOTIC, bao-nyiah'-go 暴虐個; — power, gyün-shü' byüong' 權勢兇
DESSERT, tin'-sing or tia'-sing 點心, properly a light relish taken to sustain, but not to satisfy.

DESTINED by the will of Heaven to become great, t'in-i' s-jün' hyiang-wông 天意使然興旺; — by fate to decay, ming-kæ'-jü-ts' sæ-ba' 命該如此衰敗
DESTINY, end, kyih'-gyüoh 結局; fate, ming-yüing' 命運; yüing-dao' 運道
DESTITUTE of friends, kyü-moh'-vu-ts'ing' 舉目無親; ṃ-beng-yiu' 無朋友; — of clothing and food, vu-i, vu-zih' 無衣無食
DESTROY, to siao-hwô'-diao 銷化壞; siao-hwe'-diao 銷毀了; — utterly, tsao-t'ah' ken-zing' 蹧蹋乾淨; — (by fire or otherwise), hwe' ken-zing' 毀乾淨; — by tearing down, ts'ah'-hwe 拆毀; — (as living creatures), mih-diao' 滅壞; — life, sah seng', 'æ ming' 殺生害命
DETACH, to separate, feng-k'æ' 分開; to disunite, ts'ah'-k'æ 拆開, ts'ah'-loh 拆落; to — a body of soldiers, feng-fah' ih-ts ping' 分發一枝兵; feng-p'a ih-de ping' 分派一隊兵
DETAIN, to liu 留; liu-djü' 留住; liu-loh' 留落; — forcibly, ngang-liu' 硬留; it rains and Heaven detains the guest, "yü loh, T'in' liu k'ah'" 雨落天留客
DETECT, to k'en'-c'ih 看出; k'en'-p'o 看破; — errors, k'en'-c'ih

DET 120 DEV

ts'o'-c'ü 看出錯°處; *the thief was detected*, zeh' p'o-en'-de 賊°破案了°

DETER, *to* tsu'-tông 阻當; læn-tsu' 攔阻; tsu'-djü 阻住; — *one from doing*, tsn'-tông nying feh tso' 阻當人°弗做

DETERMINATION, cü'-i 主意; *he has* —, gyi yiu' cü'-i 其有主意; gyi cü'-i kyüih'-tön 其主意決斷°; *firm* —, lao cü'-i 牢主意; cü'-i k'o'-ding-de 主意擎°定了°

DETERMINE, *to* ding-kwe' 定規; ding cü'-i 定主意; kyüih'-ding 決定

DETERMINED, *to be* —, k'o'-ding cü'-i 拿°定主意; — *to do*, công-dzing' nyiah-ding'-de 章程捻定了°

DETEST, *to* 'eng 恨; k'o-u' 可惡; *I* — *him*, ngô ün'-wu gyi' de 我怨乎其°了°

DETESTABLE, *perfectly* k'o-u'-ts-gyih' 可惡之極; 'eng-gyih'-de 恨極了°

DETHRONE, *to* — *a king*, ts'in' wông-we' 遷皇位; deh wông-we' 奪皇位

DETRACT, *to* — *from a man's good character*, hwe nying'-ts jün' 毀人°之善 See DEPRECIATE.

DETRIMENT, 'æ 害; *no* —, m-kao' soh-go 'æ' 沒°有°甚麼害; m-'æ'-c'ü' 無害處

DEVASTATION *by soldiers*, ping-hwông' 兵荒; — *by drought*, 'en'-hwông 旱荒; — *by water*, shü'-hwông 水°荒

DEVELOP, *to* k'æ-k'æ' 開開; — *one's intellect*, nying'-go ts'ong-ming' k'æ-c'ih'-læ 人°个°聰明開出來; ts'ong-ming' k'ön-k'æ' 聰明孔°開 (sometimes used of grown people in ridicule); — *ideas*, i'-s t'æn-tæn'-k'æ 意思攤攤開

DEVIATE, *to* tseo'-ts'ô 走差; ts'ô'-k'æ 叉開

DEVIATION, *a slight* — *at first, may amount at last, to a thousand li*, "tseo'-ts'ô 'ao-li, t'e'-pæn ts'in-li" 差以°毫釐謬以°千里

DEVICE, *simple* fông-fah' 方法; *ingenious* —, kyi-kwah' 機括; *crafty* —, kyi-meo' 機謀; kyi'-kao 計較°

DEVIL, *evil spirit*, kyü 鬼°; mo-kyü' 魔鬼°; oh'-kyü 惡鬼°; *the* —, Mo-kwe' 魔鬼; *possessed with a* —, jih-mo'-go 入魔个°; *under a devil's influence*, ziu kyü-mi' 受鬼°迷; *been stroked by a* — (and therefore bad), kyü' lo-deo'-de 鬼°攞頭了°; kyü' kwah'-de 鬼°摑了°; the last two used in reviling.

DEVIOUS, *crooked*, wæn-ky'üoh'-go 彎曲个°

DEVISE, *to* tang'-mo 打摹; — *a way*, tang'-sön ih-go fông-fah'

DEV 121 DIE

打算一个°方法; zao' fông-fah' 造°方法; shih fah' 設°法; — *a scheme*, shih kyi' 設°計; *ready in devising*, pin' t'ong 變通

DEVOLVE, *to transfer*, sia' peh 卸與°; *my duties — upon him*, ngô meng-veng' sia peh gyi' tso' 我名°分°卸°與°其做; — *the responsibility on some one else*, sia kyin-ts' 卸肩°子; *this devolves on me*, keh' kwo ngô' tso' 這歸我做

DEVOTE, *to* tseng-ky'i' 尊起; liu-ky'i 留起; — *to God*, tseng-ky'i' peh Jing-ming' 尊起與°神明; — *six hours a day to study*, ih-nyih' li-hyiang' loh tin'-cong kong-fu' tseng-ky'i' doh shü' 一日°裏向六點鐘工夫尊起讀書

DEVOUR, *to swallow without chewing*, t'eng ky'üoh 吞吃°; *to eat rapidly*, ziah-loh' sön'-tsiang' 嚼落算帳; — *a book*, 'o peng' t'eng-loh'-ky'i 和本吞落去°

DEVOUT, gyin-sing' 虔心

DEW, lu-shü' 露水°; *drops of* —, tin' tang tin lu-shü' 點點露水°

DEXTROUS, siu weh-p'eh' 手活潑

DIABOLICAL *arts*, iao-fah' 妖法; *great skill in ditto*, iao-jih' li-'æ' 妖術利害

DIAGRAM, du'-go da-liab' 圖个°大略; du'-go da-tsih'-moh 圖

个°大節目; *to draw a* —, tang' ih-go du' 打一个°圖

DIAL, *sun* jih-kwe' 日晷; — *plate of a clock*, cong min-ts 鐘面子 (cong or tsong)

DIALECT, *local* t'u'-wô 土話; hyiang-dæn' 鄉談; *the Ningpo* —, Nying-po' wô' 寧波話

DIAMETER, cong-sin' 中線

DIAMOND, kying-kông'-cün 金剛鑽 (cün or tsön) (ih-lih)

DIAPHRAGM, keh'-moh 膈膜 (veng.)

DIARRHEA, dza-bing' 瀉病; du-foh sia' 肚腹瀉; *chronic* —, lao' dza-bing' 老瀉°病

DIARY, jih-kyi'-loh 日記錄

DICE, seh'-ts 色子; deo-ts' 骰子; *to throw* —, dzih seh'-ts 擲色子; — *box*, seh'-ts 'eh' 色子盒

DICTATE, *to* k'eo-djün 口傳; *to write as dictated*, i k'eo' dæ shü' 依口代書; *write as fast as dictated*, kông' dza kw'a, sia' dza kw'a 講°怎°快寫°怎°快

DICTIONARY, *alphabetical* z-meo di-kông 字母提綱; z-nyü' we-ka' 字語彙解°; — *arranged according to the radicals*, z-tin' 典; z-we' 字彙

DIE, *to* si 死; ky'ü-shü' 去世; ling-cong' 臨終; do-kao'kw'eng'-joh 大°覺睡熟 (coarse); — *young*, iao ziu' 夭壽; tön' ming 短命; — *a natural death*, jün

cong 善終 (cong or tsong);
— *from disease*, bing kwu' 病故;— *an unnatural death*, wang si' 橫死°; oh' si 惡死;— *by starvation*, ngo-sah' 餓殺;— *satisfied*, ngæn'-tsing pi-leh-ky'i' 眼睛閉得°去° (*lit.* with eyes shut.)

DIET, *to eat sparingly,* ky'üoh' leh si' 吃得°細; tsih ing'-zih 節飲食; siao shü' ky'üoh' tin 少些°吃點: *to avoid a certain kind of food*, gyi zih' 忌食; gyi cü' 忌嘴; *to live on a vegetable* — (as the Buddhists do), ky'üoh ts'æ' 吃°菜; kyüoh su' 吃°素

DIFFER, *to* yiu feng-pih' 有分別; — *greatly,* do' yiu feng-pih' 大°有分別; *differs much,* ts'ô hyü'-to 差許多; long-do' koh'-yiang 弄大°各樣; da' feh siang'-dong 大不°相同; kao-ti' peh-ih' 高低不一; (it) *differs very little,* ts'ô yiu'-'æn 差有限°; ts'ô feh to' 差弗多; shü'-vi koh'-yiang 些微各樣

DIFFERENCE, feng-pih' 分別; *what is the —?* yiu soh'-go feng-pih' 有甚°麽分別? yiu soh'-go koh'-yiang 有甚°麽各樣? *what is the — in length?* dziang tön' ts'ô' to-siao' 長短差多少?

DIFFERENT, koh'-yiang 各樣; feh z ih-yiang' 弗是一樣; *the two are —,* liang' k'æ-dæ' 兩開蓋;— *kinds,* koh'-seh

koh-'ao' 各色各樣; *entirely* —, 'o'-jün koh-yiang' 和然各樣; — *from the rest,* dzah-ngah' 雜°碎

DIFFICULT, næn 難; keh'-tah 絀°葛°; feh yüong'-yi 弗容易; *very —,* væn næn' 萬難

DIFFICULTIES, næn 難; næn-c'ü' 難處

DIFFIDENT, yiu hyü-hyih'- bing 有虛怯°病; we fah-neng'-go 會發嫩个°

DIFFUSE, *to spread abroad,* yiang-k'æ' 揚開

DIFFUSE *in style,* væn 繁; væn-zeh' 繁雜; veo-veng' to' 浮文多

DIG, *to* gyüih 掘; dao 掏

DIGEST, *to — food,* zih' siao-hwô' 食消化

DIGESTION, *bad* bi-we' wa' 脾胃孬°

DIGNIFIED, yiu we-nyi' go 有威儀个°

DIGNITY, we-nyi' 威儀; *great* —, we-nyi' djong' 威嚴重; *assumed —,* kw'un'-shih do' 款式°大°; kô'-ts do' 架°子大°

DIGRESS, *to — in speaking,* ling-nga' di-ky'i ih-yiang' z-t'i' 零外°提起一樣事體

DIGRESSION, i-nga'-ts z 意外°之事

DIKE, *a bank to prevent inundation,* dông 塘

DILAPIDATED, fong-tao'-ba-loh'

go 風倒敗°落个°; tong-t'æn' si-tao'-go 東坍西倒个°
DILATE, to — (as the eye), fông'-k'æ-læ 放開來
DILATORY, nga-nga' ts'i-ts'i; in'-in tsiang-tsiang'; mæn-t'ang'-t'ang 慢遲°遲°; dang宕°; wun-deng'-deng 綏鈍鈍
DILIGENT, pô-kyih' 把急; zông'-kying 上緊; gying-lih' 勤力
DILLY-DALLY, to yiu-dang' 遊宕'
DILUTE, to 'o'-leh dæn' 和得°淡; to thin, 'o'-leh boh' 和得°薄
DIM, indistinct, feh ts'ing'-t'ong 弗清通; eyesight — (naturally), ngæn'-kwông deng' 眼°光鈍; ditto from age &c., ngæn-tsing hwô'-de 眼°睛花了°; — lamp, teng-tsæn' en' 燈盞暗; ngæn'-kwông sæn'-de 眼°光散了°
DIME, ih koh' 一角°
DIMENSIONS, what are its —? yiu to-siao' do' 有多少大°? yiu dza-kwun' do 有怎樣°大°?
DIMINISH, to kæn 減°; kæn'-loh 減°落; ky'üih 缺; siao 少; cannot —, kæn' feh-teh 減°弗得; — in size, siao'-long ky'i' 小攏去°; — in number, ky'üih'-long-ky'i' 缺攏去°; ky'üih'-feh-læ, feh-ky'üih' 缺弗來弗缺; — expens's, fi'-yüong kæn'-tin-diao 費用減°點去°
DIMITY, liu'-diao-pu 柳條布
DIMPLE, tsiu-den' 酒潭
DIN of voices, zæng-zæng'-hyiang

屑°屑°響;— of hammers, &c., ding-ding'-dang-dang hyiang'.
DINE, to ky'üoh da-ts'æ' 吃°大菜; ky'üoh tsiu'-ko-væn' 吃°酒過飯; ky'üoh cong-væn' 吃°中飯; ky'üoh tsiu'-væn 吃°酒飯
DINGY color, hweng' seh 昏色; — from age, in-t'ang'-t'ang; without polish, deng kwông' 鈍光
DINING-ROOM ky'üoh-væn-kæn' 吃°飯間°; da-ts'æ-vông' 大菜房
DINNER, væn 飯; da-ts'æ' 大菜; noon meal, tsiu'-væn 酒飯; tsiu'-ko-væn 酒過飯
DIP, to — up water, iao' shü' læ' 舀水°來; — water with the hands, p'ong shü' 捧水°; — in water, or immerse, shü'-li tsing' ih-tsing' 水裡浸一浸;— the pen in ink, pih' w̄eng moh' 筆搵墨; — and wet, w̄eng-w̄eng sih' 搵搵濕
DIPLOMA, certificate, tsiao 照; scholar's —, veng'-bing' 文憑; priest's —, du-diah 度牒° (ih-tsiang)
DIPPER, shü'-zôh 水°瓢; wooden —, ao'-teo 拗斗; 'oh-bin' 鑊瓢
DIRECT, to manage, kwun'-li 管理; liao-li' 料理; coh'-fu 囑附; to tell or give orders, wô' 話; — (a traveller), ts'-ying 指引

DIRECT, dzih 直;— *road*, dzih lu' 直路

DIRECTION, *in what —? *'ah-li' ih-hyiang' 何°處°一向 or 阿裡一向? *in that —*, keh' ih-hyiang' 那°一向; *I do not understand his directions*, sô coh'-fu ngô' feh tong' 所嚼附我弗懂; *give him the — or address*, ming-moh', wô-hyiang'-gyi-dao' 名目話向其道;— *of a letter*, di-kyiah'-ing 地脚音

DIRECTLY, ziu 就°; *I will come —*, ngô' ziu læ' 我就來

DIRECTOR *of affairs*, cong'- kwun 總管; cong'-li 總理 (cong or tsong)

DIRGE, pe-sông'-go ko' 悲傷个°歌; *lamentation*, æ-ko' 哀歌

DIRTY, ao-tsao' 聖糟; lah-t'ah' 邋遢; ao-lih'-peh-tsao' 聖裏°百糟; seh'-dch 塞達; nyi-sing' 泥腥; lah-lih'-lah-t'ah' 邋裏°邋遢; t'i-t'a' 渧汰;— *sweepings*, leh-seh' 垃圾°

DIRTY, *to long* ao'-tsao 弄聖糟, &c.

DISABLED, vu-neng'-we 無能爲;— *intellectually*, tsing-jing' fi'-diao-de 精神廢掉了°

DISADVANTAGE, ky'üoh'- kw'e 吃°虧; *bought at a —*, ma' ky'üoh-kw'e' 買°吃°虧; ma' shü-de 買°輸了°; *working at a*—, ka' tso, feh teh'-fah 如°此°做弗得法

DISADVANTAGEOUS, le'-ze-go 累墜个°; feh-bin'-i 弗便宜°

DISAGREE, *to* feh-deo'-kyi 弗投機;— *in opinion*, (*lit.* wrongly joined), i'-s ts'o-p'ing' 意思差拼; *unsuited*, feh-te' 弗對; feh teo'-deo 弗對°頭; feh 'eh-shing' 弗合榫

DISAGREEABLE, næn-tông' 難當; in'-ky'i 厭氣; *no pleasure*, m-c'ü' 無°趣; *very* —, m-c'ü'-ts-gyih' 無°趣之極;— *weather*, t'in-kô' m-c'ü' 天家°無°趣;— *person*, tseng nying' 憎人°; teh'-nying-væn-tseng' 得人°犯憎; min-moh' k'o-tseng' 面目可憎;— *ways*, i'-tsi tseng 意致°憎;— *to do*, næn-hyi'; næn we'-dzing 難爲情

DISAPPEAR, *to —suddenly*, hweh'-jün feh-kyin' 忽然弗見

DISAPPOINTED, *to be* i'-s shih'-loh 意思失落; shih-vông' 失望; *I was — in my expectations*, ngô sô vông' shih'-loh-de 我所望失落了°

DISAPPROVE, *to* feh yüoh'-i 弗欲意

DISARM, *to* kyüing-ky'i' siu-jih'-ko 軍器收拾過

DISARRANGE, *to* kao'-lön 攪亂; dao-lön' 掏亂;— *so, one can*-

not do anything, ts'ao'-lön dæn-dziang' 譟亂壇場

DISASTER, fi-læ'-ts 'o' 飛來之禍; *a* —, ih-go 'o' 一個°禍; ih-ky'i' hyüong z'-t'i 一起凶事體

DISASTROUS, hyüong 凶; li-'æ' 利害

DISBAND, *to* —(troops),ts'ih'-we 撤回;—(school), sæn-kwun' 散館

DISBELIEVES *everything*, pah'-feh-siang'-sing 百弗相信

DISBURSE, *to* do-c'ih' 拕出

DISCARD, *to* tiu-ky'i' 丟去°; *has been discarded*, tsoh'-ko-de 作過了°, koh'-ko-de 擱過了°

DISCERN *clearly by the eye*, k'en'-ts'ing-t'ong' 看清通; — *between true and false*, bin'-pih tsing-kô' 辨別°真假°

DISCERNMENT, ngæn'-lih 眼°力°, kyi-ling' 機靈; liu-liang' 流亮; *great* —, ngæn'-lih hao' 眼°力好

DISCHARGE, *to* — (as firearms), fông 放; *to let out*, fông'-c'ih' 放出; — (as a prisoner), fah-fông' 發放; — *a debt*, tsa' t'eh-c'ih' 債脫出; — *one's duty*, dzing peng'-veng 盡本分°, pô meng-veng 把名°分°; — *cargo*, ky'i ho' 起貨

DISCIPLE, *learner*, meng-du' 門徒; 'oh-sang-ts' 學°生°子; di'-ts 弟子; meng-seng' 門生

DISCIPLINE *to* — (as a church member), tsiao kyiao'-kwe tsah'-vah 照教規責罰

DISCLAIM, *to* feh-jing' 弗認; feh tsih'-jing 弗接認

DISCLOSE, *to expose to view*, lu-c'ih' 露出; *to leak out*, sih'-leo 洩漏; — *a secret*, tseo'-leo fong-sing' 走漏風聲; sih'-leo kyi-kwæn' 洩漏機關; lu-fong' 露風

DISCOLOR, *to* ngæn-seh' fæn'-diao 顏°色翻壞°; tseo ngæn-seh' 走顏°色; pin seh' 變色

DISCOMFORT, *in* feh ziu'-yüong 弗受用; feh shih'-i 弗適°意

DISCOMMODE, *to* le 累; — *a person*, le nying' feh bin 累人°弗便; ta'-li nying' feh bin' 帶累°人°弗便

DISCONCERT, *to* long-lön' 弄亂; ih-z-li', m-cü'-i 一時裡無°主意

DISCONCERTED, sing-hwông' i-lön' 心慌意亂

DISCONNECTED, feh-lin'-p'ing 弗連摒

DISCONSOLATE, en'-tah-feh-læ' 安搭弗來; vu-k'o' en-we' 無可安慰

DISCONTENTED, feh-mun'-i 弗滿意; pah'-feh-hwun'-hyi 百弗歡喜

DISCONTINUE, *to* hyih'-loh 歇落; ts 止

DISCORD, *variance*, feh tsih'-yiah 弗浹洽; — *in sound*, yüing' feh-'eh' 韻弗合

DISCOUNT on price of goods, k'eo'-deo 扣頭; tsih'-deo 折頭; two out of every hundred, kyiu'-pah k'eo 九八扣; kyiu'-pah tsih 九八折; ten out of every hundred, kyiu' k'eo 九扣; kyiu tsih 九折

DISCOURAGE, to long'-leh gyi-sing' lang' 弄得°其心冷°; to break his inclination to do, tang-dön'-gyi-go hying'-cü 打斷其个°與致; discouraged, ts'-hyiang tih'-tao-de 志向跌倒了°

DISCOURTEOUS, m li'-sing 無禮性; — behavior, ang-we', m li'-sing 行°爲無°禮性

DISCOVER, to find, zing-c'ih'-læ 尋°出來; zing-djoh' 尋着°(djoh or dzoh); — a plot, kyi-meo' k'en'-p'o 機謀看破

DISCREET, yiu kyin'-sih 有見識; prudent, kwu-zin' kwu-'eo' 顧前°顧後

DISCRIMINATE, to feng-bin'ts'ing-t'ong' 分辨清通; feng-ts'ing' dao-bah' 分青道白

DISCUSS, to leng 論; — a subject, leng' ih ky'i' z-t'i' 論一起事體

DISDAIN, to miao'-z 藐視; k'en'-feh-zông-ngæn' 看弗上眼°

DISDAINFUL, k'en'-nying'-feh-zông-ngæn' 看人°弗上眼°

DISEASE, bing 病; bing-tsing' 病症 (ih-dziang); to have a disease, sang bing' 生°病; yiu t'ong'-yiang 有痛癢

DISENGAGED from business, m-kao' z-ken' 沒°有°事幹; at present —, keh'-zông k'ong'-go 這°時空个°

DISENTANGLE, to ka'-k'æ 解°開; ka'-sæn 解°散

DISFIGURE, to siang'-mao kæ'-diao 相貌改壞°; — the face, kæ siang' 改相

DISGORGE, to t'u'-c'ih' 吐出

DISGRACE, to tao-me' 倒楣; — him, peh' gyi tao-me' 俾°其倒楣; tao'-gyi-me' 倒其楣; disgraced, tao-leh-me'-de 倒得°楣了°; you not only — yourself but the church, ng feh tæn'-tsih zi tao'-me yia peh kong-we'-li tao-me' 你弗單只自°倒楣也°俾°公會裡倒楣; — by berating, siu'-joh 羞辱; disgraced by ditto, zin-joh' 受辱 (joh or zoh)

DISGRACEFUL affair, tao-me' z-ken' 倒楣事幹

DISGUISE, to tsông-pæn' 粧扮; to go in —, zi' tsông-pæn'-leh-ky'i' 自°粧扮得去°; the king dressed in the — of a subject, wông-ti' kæ'-wun i-zông' tsông-pæn' pah'-sing 皇帝改換衣裳粧扮百姓

DISGUSTING, zô'-in 惹°厭; in'-u 厭惡°; væn'-in 犯厭

DISH, beng-ts' 盆子 (ih-tsah); dishes, un'-tsæn-diah-ts' 碗盞碟°子

DIS   127   DIS

DISH, to — up, beng-ts' tsi'-læ 盆子盛來

DISHONEST, feh-lao'-jih 弗老實; feh-dzing'-jih 弗誠實; kæn-tsô' 奸詐; veo-r'-peh-jib' 浮而不實; feh-cong-'eo' 弗忠厚 (cong or tsong); nails too long (i. e. will take a little), ts'-k'ah hying' 指甲與

DISHONOR, to — a person, 'æ nying' m-t'i'-min 害人°無°體面; disgrace a person, tao-nying'-me' 倒人°楣

DISHONORABLE business, m-min-moh' z-t'i' 無°面目事體

DISINCLINED, kæn'-teh 懶得; — to do, kæn'-teh tso' 懶得做

DISINHERITED, ts'æn'-nyih m-veng, ken'-c'ih-de 產業無分°趕出了°

DISINTERESTED, yiah-ky'i' 俠氣; — nyi-ky'i' djong' 義氣重

DISLIKE, to feh hwun'-hyi 弗歡喜; feh cong'-i 弗中意

DISLOCATE, to — a joint, gao'-kwu t'eh-yüih' 胶股脫穴

DISLODGE, to drive out, ken'-c'ih 趕出; — (as a miscreant), ky'ü-djoh' 驅逐

DISLOYAL to the government, feh-voh' wông-hwô' 弗服王化

DISMAL, m-c'ü'-go 無°趣個°; ing'-seh-seh 陰煞煞; dark, en'-c'ih-c'ih 暗黔黔

DISMASTED, we-kæn' sông-diao'-de 桅°杆傷壞°了°

DISMAY, filled with — , mun'-sing gyü-dæn' 滿心懼憚

DISMISS, to — , (as servants), tang-fah-ky'i' 打發去°; — him, hyih' gyi 歇其; — (as a congregation), peb gyi sæn'-k'æ 俾其散開; — (officially), fah'-sæn 發散; — school, fông-'oh' 放學°; sæn-kwun' 散舘; — (as a teacher), we-foh' 回覆

DISMISSAL, I request a — , ngô ts'ing' ng, cing' ngô t'e-dz' 我請你准我推辭; (an officer) requests — , ts'ing k'æ-ky'üih' 請開缺

DISMOUNT, to — from a horse, loh mô' 落馬; t'iao'-loh mô' 跳落馬

DISOBEDIENT, feh-k'eng'-t'ing' wô 弗肯聽話; feh ziu kao'-hyüing 弗受敎°訓; — son, peh'-hyiao ng-ts' 不孝兒°子; — and perverse son, wu-nyih'-go ng-ts' 忤逆個°兒°子

DISOBEY, to we-be' 違背; feh i'-jing 弗依順; we-nyih' 違逆

DISOBLIGING, feh cing' min-dzing 弗准面情; very — , 'ao' feh cing'-dzing 毫弗准情

DISORDERLY, lön· ts'ih'-pah-tsao' 亂七八遭; tossed about east and west, tong-gwæn', si-gwæn' 東摃西摃°; — and noisy as children, djông 瞳; — and quarrelsome, seng-z' ts'ông-'o' 生事鬧禍

DISOWN, to feh-jing' 勿認; feh tsih'-jing 弗接認;— for fear of consequences, feh tsiao-deo' 弗招頭

DISPARAGE, to u'-tsông 污葬;— him, kông gyi ti 講其低

DISPASSIONATE, ding-ding'-diah-diah' 定定奪°奪°

DISPEL, to hwô'-diao 化去°; ka'-k'æ 解°開; sæn'-k'æ 散開;— doubt, nyi-sing' hwô'-diao 疑心化去°; ka nyi' 解°疑;— sorrow, sæn-sæn meng' 散散悶; ka-ka meng' 解°解°悶

DISPENSARY, s'-yiah-gyüoh 施藥局

DISPENSE, to feng-peh' 分給°

DISPENSED, can be — with, k'o'-yi feh-yüong'-go 可以弗用个°; hao-hyih'-go 好歇个°; hao-sang'-go 好省°个°

DISPERSE, to tseo'-sæn 走散; sæn'-k'æ 散開

DISPLACE, to fông' ts'o 放差°; en dzæn' 安賺;— repeatedly, lön-fông 亂放

DISPLAY, to spread out, pa'-k'æ 擺開; t'æn-k'æ' 攤開; to exhibit, hyin'-c'ih 顯出; he displays ability in speaking, gyi hyin'-c'ih k'eo'-dzæ hao' 其顯出口才好;— dress, sæ' voh-seh' 賽服色;— wealth, sæ fu' 賽富;— one's beauty, sæ mao' 賽貌;— the feet, sæ kyiah' 賽脚; empty —, do-ba'-dziang 大°排°塲; p'u-p'a' 鋪派°

DISPLEASE, to long-leh feh hwun'-hyi 弄得°弗歡喜;— me, peh ngô feh hwun'-hyi 俾°我弗歡喜; long' ngô feh yüoh'-i 弄我弗欲意

DISPOSE, to set in order, also to — of, en-ba' 安排°; en-teng' 安頓; how will you — of that unexpected gain? keh'-pih nga-kw'a', dza en'-teng 這°筆外°快°怎°安頓?

DISPOSED, I feel — to give it to him, ngô i'-s z iao peh gyi' 我意思是要給°其

DISPOSITION, sing'-kah 性格; sing'-dzing 性情; sing-dziang' 心腸; hasty —, sing'-kah kyih' 性格急; sing'-dzing bao-ts'ao' 性情暴躁; cross —, sing-ts'ao' 性躁; perverse —, sing'-kah kwæ'-p'ih 性格乖僻; bad — (also bad habit pertinaciously adhered to), wa bi'-ky'i 孬°脾氣; make a good — of it, iao tsing'-kying yüong' 要正經用

DISPROPORTIONED, feh siang'-p'e 弗相配

DISPROVE, to prove to be false, feng-ming' z kô'-go 分明是假°个°

DISPUTE, to bin'-leng 辯論;— angrily, tsang-leng' 爭論

DISQUIETED, feh en'-tæn 弗安

軌；— (as a country), feh t'a'-bing 弗太°平
DISREGARD, to peh-yi'-we-i' 不以爲意; pay no attention, feh liu'-sing 弗留心; ko'-r-peh-liu' 過而不留; — life, feh kwu sing'-ming 弗顧性命
DISREPUTABLE, m-ó'-lin-go 無°了臉个°; ti-vi' 低微; — person, feh ts'ing'-bah-go nying 弗淸白个°人; feh loh-dzih-go nying 弗落直个°人°
DISRESPECT, to treat with —, mao-væn' 冒犯; c'oh'-væn 觸犯; ditto purposely, c'ong-dzong' 衝撞; c'ong-væn' 衝犯
DISRESPECTFUL, feh-kong'-kying 弗恭敬
DISSATISFIED, feh-cü'-tsoh 弗知足; feh-tsoh' 弗足; sing'-li feh-jü'-i 心裡弗如意; I am — with him, gyi feh-'eh' ngô-go i' 其弗合我个°意; gyi feh-jü' ngô-go i' 其弗如我个°意
DISSECT, to — at a Chinese inquest, siah'-kweh-nying' 削骨驗
DISSEMBLE, to pretend to be honest, tsông lao'-jih 妝老實; kô lao'-jih 假老實; — well, tsông'-leh ziang' 妝得°像; pæn'-leh ziang' 扮得°像
DISSEMINATE, to po-yiang'-k'æ 播揚開
DISSENT, to feh-'eh' 弗合; — from the crowd, feh-'eh' jing-

dzing' 弗合人情; — from one's superiors, feh-'eh' zông-i' 弗合上意
DISSERTATION, a ih-p'in leng' 一篇論
DISSEVER, to feng-k'æ' 分開; ts'ah'-k'æ 拆開; — with a knife, tsæn-k'æ' 斬開
DISSIMILAR, feh siang'-ziang, 弗相像; very —, da' feh-siang'-dong 大弗相同
DISSIPATE sadness, ka-ka meng' 解解°悶; sæn-sæn sing' 散散心
DISSOLUTE, fông'-dông 放蕩
DISSOLVE, to melt, yiang 烊; sah 煞; hwô 化; yiang-diao' 烊了°; — in water, shü'-li 'o-k'æ' 水°裡和開; shü'-li yiang-k'æ 水°裡烊開; — (i. e. cut), friendship, djih kyiao' 絶交; — partnership, feng tsiang' 分帳; feng siu' 分手
DISSUADE, to exhort and caution, ky'ün'-kyiæ 勸戒; exhort him to stop, ky'ün'-sih gyi byih' 勸息其歇
DISTANCE, yün 遠; li-yün' 離遠; what is the — apart? to-siao' yün 多少遠? the — is about five li, da-iah' ng' li yün' 大約五°里遠
DISTANTLY connected (as relatives or ideas), su-yün' 疏遠
DISTASTE, m i'-c'ü 無°意趣
DISTEND, to — with wind, fah-

p'ông', or fah-p'oh' 發膀; to bloat, fah-tsiang' 發脹

DISTILL, to tsing 蒸; tsing'-ky'i-læ 蒸起來

DISTINCT, separate, feh siang'-lin 弗相連; different, koh'-bih 各別; clear, ts'ing-t'ong 清通 — articulation, k'eo'-ing ts'ing-t'ong 口音清通; k'eo'-ing ts'ing-k'oh' 口音清確°

DISTINCTLY, to see —, k'en' ts'ing-tong' 看清通

DISTINGUISH, to bin'-pih 辯別°; feng-pih' 分別°; I can't — it, therefore it must be hard to discern, ngô bin'-feh-c'ih'-læ, sô'-yi da-kæ næn feng-bin' 我辯弗出來所以大概難分辯

DISTINGUISHED, yiu ming-vông' 有名望; ming-vông' do' 名望大°

DISTORT, to ao'-hwa 拗歪

DISTORTED, hwa 歪; — mouth, hwa-cü' 歪嘴

DISTRACT, to — the mind, feng sing' 分心

DISTRACTED mind, sing-mông'-feh-ding' 心忙弗定; sing-lön' 心亂; almost — (crazed), weng-feh'-jih-mo' 魂弗入墓

DISTRESS, kw'u'-ts'u 苦楚; kw'u'-næn 苦難; suffering, kw'u'-t'ong 苦痛; in —, læ-tih kyüoh'-kw'u'-ts'u 來的吃苦楚; læ'-tih ziu kw'u'-t'ong 來的受苦痛

DISTRESSED (in appearance), zeo-mi' tang-pah'-kyih 愁°眉°打百結; in mind, sing-li kw'u' 心裡苦; iu-üih' 憂鬱°; iu-iu'-üoh-üoh' 憂憂鬱°鬱°

DISTRIBUTE, to feng-p'a' 分派°; — impartially, kong-bing' feng' 公平分; kyüing feng' 均分; — books, feng shü' 分書; — type, wæn z' 還字

DISTRICT, yün 縣; region, di-fông 地方; — magistrate, cü-yün' 知縣; — examinations, yün-k'ao' 縣考; god of a small —, t'u'-di-bu'-sah 土地菩薩

DISTRUST to nyi-'oh' 疑惑; ts'æ-nyi' 猜疑

DISTURB to kying'-dong 驚動

DISTURBANCE, nao-z' 鬧事; to get up a —, ts-z' 滋事

DISTURBED in mind, sing'-li-yiao-yiao'-peh-ih' 心裡搖搖不一; — in sleep, kw'eng'-feh-en'-jün 睡°弗安然

DISUSE, not to use, feh-yüong' 弗用; fallen into disuse, dziang-kyiu' feh-tsoh' 長久弗作

DITCH, wu-nyi-den' 污泥潭; yiang-keo-den' 陽溝潭; to dig a —, dao keo' 掏溝

DITTY, t'æn-wông' 攤黃; ky'üoh'-ts' 曲子; siao'-diao 小調 (ih-tsah)

DIVE, to sah-kong' 殺攻; sah-kong'-loh-ky'i' 殺攻落去°

DIVER, sah-kong'-go nying 殺攻個°人。
DIVERGE, to — gradually, dzin'-dzin-ts'ô'-k'æ-ky'i' 漸漸义開去°
DIVERS, several, kyi-go' 幾個°; hao-kyi'-go 好幾個°。
DIVERSE, different, koh-yiang' 各樣; several kinds, hao-kyi'-yiang 好幾樣
DIVERSION, for —, siao-ky'in'-yüong-go 消遣用個°
DIVERSITY, koh 各;— in opinion, koh'-nying yiu koh-i'-s 各人°有各意思; koh'-tsih-ih-kyin' 各執一見; but little —, sao-we-zông'-loh 稍爲上落; sao'-yiu-feh-dong' 稍有弗同;— in kind, koh-dzong-gyi-le' 各從其類;— in color and pattern, koh'-seh koh-yiang' 各色各樣
DIVERT, to — the mind, sæn-sæn-sing' 散散心; siao-siao-ky'in' 消消遣; siao-siao-'æn' 消消閒。
DIVEST of clothing, kw'un i' 寬衣; i-zông' t'eh'-loh 衣裳脫落
DIVIDE, to feng 分; feng-k'æ' 分開;— by cutting, ts'ih'-k'æ 切開; ditto (as a fish. melon &c.), p'o-'k'æ 破開; — in halves, te'-feng-k'æ' 對分開; te'-ts'ih-k'æ' 對切開;— in three parts, feng' tso sæn kwu' 分做三股; — equally, tsiao' kwu kyüing-feng' 照股均分;— by a partition, lah-k'æ'; kah-k'æ 隔開
DIVIDED mind, ih sing' ts'ong liang yüoh' 一心充兩用
DIVIDEND, kæ-feng' 該分
DIVINATION, ky'i-k'o' sön-ming' 起課算命
DIVINE, to — (with three cash), poh-k'o' 卜課; ky'i-k'o' 起課; to settle doubt, kyüih nyi' 決疑; — (with lettered bamboos), ts'iu-ts'in' 抽籤:— with a motto, on paper, ts'eh z' 測字; ditto before an idol, gyiu ts'in' 求籤; meng ts'in-s' 問°籤詩;— with a bird, gyin bæn' 箝牌; to tell fortunes, sön ming' 算命; p'i ming-ts' 批命帋
DIVINE, belonging to God, kwe'-ü Jing-ming' 歸于神明; proceeding from God, dzæ'-ü Jing-ming' ka læ' 在于神明而°來; to become —, dzing Jing' 成神
DIVINE, a clergyman, kyiao'-s 敎師; Roman Catholic —, jing-vu' 神父; a theologian, cü'-ka sing'-shü-go sin-sang' 註解聖書个°先生°
DIVINER, ky'i'-k'o sin'-sang 起課先生°;— of places, fong-shü' sin'-sang 風水°先生°; fortune teller, sön'-ming sin'-sang 算命先生°
DIVINITY, the essence of God, Jing t'i' 神體; a —, ih'-we Jing-

ming′ 一位神明; ih-we′ bu-sah′ 一位菩薩; *treatise on* —, Jing-dao′ cong-leng′ 神道總論

DIVISION, *Math.* feng-fah′ 分法
DIVISOR, feng-su′ 分數
DIVORCE, *to* li′-diao lao′-nyüing 離了老女°; *a writing of* —, li-shü′ 離書
DIVULGE, *to* lu-fong′ 露風; sih′-leo 洩漏;— *a secret*, tseo′-leo fong-sing′ 走漏風信
DIZZINESS, deo-yüing′ 頭暈; deo′ yüing-yüing′-dong 頭暈暈動
DO, *to* tso 做; tsoh 作; 'ang 行°; we 為; *when will you* — *it*, ng kyi′-z we tso 你°幾時會做; *cannot* — (it), tso′-feh-læ 做弗來; — *not*, feh-k'o′ or m-nao′ 弗可; hao-vong′ 弗用°; feh iao′ 弗要; *to* — *evil many times*, tsoh-oh′ to-tön′ 作惡多端; — *good deeds* (or give alms), 'ang jün′ 行°善; tso hao′-z 做好事; *whatever we* —, sô-tsoh′ sô-we′ 所作所為; *will this* — *or not?* keh′ hao′-s-teh feh 這好使得否°? *it will* —, hao′-s-teh go 好使得个°; *How do you* —? ng′ hao′ feh 你°好否°? ng′ hao′ yiæ 你°好也°? *I* — *not know*, ngô′ feh hyiao′-teh 我弗曉得
DOCILE, t'iah′-voh 貼°服
DOCK, *open space for making and repairing vessels*, jün-ts'iang′ 船廠;— *occupied by one vessel*, jün-'ong′; *in* — *for repairs*, jün-ts'iang′-li læ-tih siu′ 船廠裡來的修

DOCTOR, i-sang′ 醫生°; 'ang-i′ sin′-sang 行°醫先生°
DOCTRINE, dao′-li 道理; — *of religion*, kyiao′-cong dao′-li 教中道理
DOCUMENT, veng-ky'i′ 文契;— *for presentation to the emperor*, tseo′-tsông 奏章
DODGE, *to* to′-sin 躱閃 (not an equivalent).
DOE, ts'-loh′ 雌鹿 (ih-tsah)
DOG, keo 狗; wun-kyi′ 黃°犬° (ih-tsah)
DOG-KENNEL, keo-k'o′ or keo-k'un′ 狗窠
DOGGED *looks*, min-k'ong′ heh′-pong 面孔黑奔°; min vu hyi-seh 面無喜色
DOINGS, tsoh′-we 作為
DOLEFUL, *lonely and miserable* (as persons or places), dzih-moh′ 寂寞; kwu-ts'i′ 孤悽; — *sound* (of living creatures), ts'i-ts'æn′-go sing-ing′ 悽慘个聲音; pe-æ′-go sing-ing′ 悲哀个聲音
DOLL, 'en 孩° (ih-go)
DOLLAR, fæn-ping′ 番餅; yiang-dzin′ 洋錢 (ih-kw'e); *quarter of a* —, liang′-koh-pun′ 兩角°半; *ditto, the coin*, s-k'æ′ 四開; *half a* —, pun′-kw'e 半塊; *ditto, the coin*, te′-k'æ 對開

DOL　　　　　　133　　　　　　DOU

DOLT, ngæ-nying' 呆人°; ngæ-moh'-deo 呆木頭
DOMESTIC *affairs*, kô-vu' z 家°務事; — *use*, kô yüong' 家°用; — *produce*, c'ih'-ts'æn 出產; *the six — animals*, loh-hyüoh' 六畜; sang-k'eo' 牲°口; — or *native cloth*, du'-pu 土°布
DOMESTIC, *servant*, yüong-nying' 傭人°; *male slave*, kô-nying' 家°人° (ih-go)
DOMINION, *jurisdiction*, kæ-kwun' 該管; *the British —*, Da-Ing' kæ-kwun' 大英該管
DOMINEERING, do-yiang' 大°樣
DOMINOES, *bone* bæn 牌°; kweh-ba' 骨牌° (a set, ih fu); *to play —*, c'ô bæn' 扯°牌°
DONE, *finished*, tso'-wun-de 做完了°; tso'-ko-tih-de 做過的了°; dzing-kong-de 成功了°; *well cooked*, joh 熟; *insufficiently —*, ky'in joh' 欠熟; *can't be —*, tso'-feh-læ 做弗來; long'-feh-læ' 弄弗來; dong'-siu-feh-læ' 動手弗來; 'o'-siu-feh-læ' 下°手弗來
DONKEY, li-ts' 驢子 (ih-p'ih)
DONOR, s'-cü 施主; — (of charity), sô'-cü 捨°主
DOOM, *to condemn*, ding zœ' 定罪; — *to eternal punishment*, ding ziu üong'-kw'u ying-vah' 定受永苦刑罰
DOOR, meng 門 (ih-deo, ih-sin); *at the —*, meng-k'eo-den' 門口

頭°; *front —*, zin-meng 前°門; *back' —*, 'eo'-meng 後門; *shut the —*, kwæn meng' 關門; *open the —*, k'æ meng' 開門; *lock the —*, so meng' 鎖門; *next —*, kah'-pih meng' 隔壁門
DOOR-KEEPER, kwun-meng'-go nying 管門个°人°; *an old —*, kwun-meng lao-den' 管門老頭°
DOOR-SILL, di-voh' 地栿
DORMITORY, vông-kæn 房間°; kw'eng'-kæn 睡°間°; ngo-vông' 臥房
DOSE, *a* ih-voh' 一服; *how many doses shall I take?* ngô' kæ ky'üoh' kyi voh' 我該吃°幾服?
DOT, *a* ih-tin' 一點
DOTAGE, (in his) —, mong'-tong-de 懞懂了°; gyi lao'-be-de 其老背了°(used in reproach).
DOTE, *to — upon*, ziang weh-pao' ka æ' 像活寶介°愛; æ'-jü tsông'-zông ming-cü' 愛如掌上明珠
DOUBLE, sông 雙; — *thread*, sông-keng' sin 雙根線; — *minded*, sæn-sing' liang-i 三心兩意; — *entendre* sông-kwæn' shih-wô' 雙關說話; — *price*, sông-be' kô-din 雙倍價°錢°; liang-be kyü 兩倍貴°; kô-be to' 加°倍多
DOUBLE, *to* kô' ih-be' 加°一倍

— money at interest, te'-peng te-li' 對本對利; — up (as paper), te üih'-cün 對欝轉; te tsih'-long 對摺攏; — in trade, te dzæn din' 對賺錢°; 'eh-ts din' 合子錢°

DOUBT, to nyi-sing' 疑心; ts'æ-nyi' 猜疑; nyi-'oh' 疑惑; in —, nyi-'oh'-peh-kyüih 疑惑不决

DOUBTFUL, it is m-su' 無°數; — (and uncertain), weh-lih' weh-deh', 活立活踢°; iao'-bông feh-ding' 要防弗定; yün-shü' 懸勢; yün-shü'-dang-tsiang 懸勢歪將

DOUBTLESS, ih-ding' 一定; vu-nyi' 無疑

DOUGH, sang min'-feng 生°麵粉; light (as —), song'-de 鬆了°; fah-t'eo'-de 發透了°

DOVE, pæn-kyiu' 斑鳩 (ih-tsah)

DOVETAIL, to ô - ts'iah'- mi'- pô shing'-deo (magpie-tail) 鴉鵲尾°巴榫頭

DOWAGER, the empress —, wông-t'a'-'eo 皇太后

DOWN, 'ô 下°; loh 落; walk —, tseo'-loh-læ 走落來; take it —, 'ô-loh'ky'i 下°落去°; put (it) —, fông'-loh 放落; en-loh'-ky'i 安落去°; sit —, zo-tæn'-loh, 坐打°落; lie —, kw'eng'-tao 睡倒; ditto, kw'eng'-loh-ky'i 睡落去°; lie — a while, le ih'-zông;

placed upside —, fæn'-hyiang fông'-tih-de 反向放的°了°; please sit —, ts'ing zo' 請坐°

DOWN, soft feathers, nyüong mao' 絨毛

DOWNCAST, w̃e-deo-t'ah-nao' 痿頭場腦; w̃e-w̃e'-ze-ze' 痿痿瘁°瘁°; pih'-pih-sih-sih.

DOWNHILL, to walk tseo'-loh sæn 走落山

DOWNRIGHT, plainly, ming-ming'-tông-tông' 明明當當; — falsehood, ming-ming' z kô'-wô 明明是假°話

DOWRY of money, lands, houses &c. (which a woman brings at marriage), ze-kô' 隨嫁; ze-lin'-din 隨奩錢°; furniture and clothing, tsông-lin' 粧奩; furniture, kô'-tsông 嫁粧; bedding, p'u-dzing' 鋪陳; — (which the husband gives to the wife's father), p'ing'-kying 聘金

DOXOLOGY, dzong-tsæn'-ko 頌讚歌

DOZE, to hwô-ky'i' 花起; tang-k'eh'-c'ong 打瞌睡; gyün-ky'i' 倦起; to have a —, hwô' ih-hwô 化一化; just ready to sleep, kw'eng'-joh kw'a 睡°熟快; just ready to wake, tsiang diao-kao' 將調覺°

DOZEN, a jih-nyi' 十二

DRAFT, rough ts'ao'-kao 草稿 (ih-go); — of exchange, we-p'iao' 匯票 See DRAUGHT.

DRA 135 DRA

DRAG, to Ia; ky'in 縴; te 自; t'o 拖; t'a; — (as a boat), te'-ky'in or ts'ô-ky'in' 自縴; — a net, t'a mông' 拖網; — on the ground (as a dress), t'o di 拖地; — one into difficulty, t'o-nying'-loh-shü 拖入°落水°

DRAGGLE, to t'o ao'-tsao 拖墾糟; — in the mud, t'o'-djoh na-nyi' 拖着爛泥; — and wet, t'o sih' 拖濕

DRAGON, long 龍 (ih-keng, ih-kwang); dragon's blood, hyüih-gyih' 血竭

DRAGON-FLY, ts'ing-ding' 蜻蜓 (ih-tsah)

DRAIN, covered —, ing-keo' 陰溝; open —, yiang-keo' 陽溝

DRAIN, to — off water, keo 溝

DRAKE, yüong-æn' 雄鴨° (ih-tsah)

DRAMA (in verse), hyi'-ky'üoh 戲曲; — for the stage, byi'-peng 戲本

DRAUGHT, a swallow of water, ih-k'eo shü' 一口水; a — of fish, ih-mông ng' 一網魚°; — of wind, pih'-fong 壁風; leo-fong' 漏風; do not let a — blow (on you), feh-k'o' pih'-fong c'ü 弗可壁風吹°; — of a ship, jün ky'üoh-shü' sing-ts'in' 船吃°水深淺; make a — of soldiers, ts'iu ping' 抽兵; bah ping' 扱兵

DRAUGHTS, game of we-gyi' 圍棋; to play —, tsiah we-gyi' 着圍棋

DRAW, to pull, te 自; Ia; t'o 拖; — up the curtain, meng-lin' te'-zông-ky'i 門簾自上去°; — water, tang shü' 打水°; — near, tseo'-long-læ 走攏來; gying'-long-læ 近攏來; — out, bah-c'ih' 扱出; tsoh'-c'ih 斷出; — out nails, bah ting-cü' 扱釘銖; — out teeth, tsoh'-loh ngô-ts'' 斷落牙°齒; — a picture, sia wô' 寫°畫; miao-wô' 描畫; tang du' 打圖; — from nature, i pih' sia 意筆寫°; — by looking at a pattern, ing'-ko-læ 印過來; deo-ko'-læ 投過來; t'eh'-ko-læ 搨過來; — from a pattern through paper, ing'-leh sia' 印得°寫°; — a likeness, sia ziang' 寫°像; sia' 'ang-loh' 寫°行樂; — lots (by long and short slips), ts'iu' dziang-tön 抽長短; ditto (by bits of paper rolled up), ts'ah' ts-meh-deu' 撮紙抹頭°; — customers, Ia ma'-cü 拉°買主; I wish to — your custom, ngô' iao nyiang'-p'æn ng 我要佝攀你°; — the hands into the sleeves, siu soh'-tsing-ky'i 手縮進去°

DRAWBACK, customs' dzeng p'iao' 存票

DRAW-BRIDGE, (to draw up) tiao'-gyiao 弔橋; movable bridge, weh-gyiao' 活橋 (ih-diao)

DRAWER, ts'in-teo' 抽斗 (ih-tsah); pull out a —, ts'iu-teo yi-c'ih'-læ 抽斗移出來; push in the —, ts'iu-teo yi-tsing'-ky'i 抽斗移進去°

DRAWERS, kw'u 褲; inner —, t'i'-li kw'u 替裡褲 (ih-diao, ih-iao)

DRAWING, du 圖; sia-go du' 寫°个° 圖 (ih-go); wô 畫 (ih-tsiang, if mounted, ih-foh); to make a —, tang ih-go du' 打一个° 圖; miao ih-go du' 描一个° 圖; sia ih-go du' 寫一个° 圖

DRAWING-PENCIL, miao-hwô'-pih 描花筆 (ih-ts)

DRAWL, to kông'-leh, ga-ngô'-ga-teh.

DREAD, p'ô 怕; gyü-dæn' 懼憚; full of —, ky'ih'-hyin-ky'ih-hoh' 吃險吃霍

DREADFUL, p'ô'p'ô-go 怕怕个°

DREAM, mong 夢 (also pron. mông); lön-mong' 亂夢

DREAM, to tso mong 做夢; never dreamed of it, mong'-li siang'-feh-tao'-go 夢裡想弗到个°

DREARY, m-hying'-cü 無°興致

DREDGE river mud, nyin' 'o-nyi' 捻河泥; — with flour, sen'-tin miu-feng' 霰點麩粉

DREGS, tsô 渣; sediment, kyiah 脚; — strained from wine, tsao 糟

DRENCH, to soak, seng'-t'eo 沁°透; heng'-t'eo.

DRENCHED with rain, li'-nga tu' seng'-t'eo 裡外°都沁°透; wu-dah-dah'-go-de 腐°沓沓了°

DRESS, clothing, i-zông' 衣裳; every day —, ts'u-c'ün' i-zông' 粗穿衣裳; ze-dzông' i-zông' 隨常衣裳; visiting —, c'ih-k'ah' i-zông' 出客衣裳; si'-c'ün i-zông' 細穿衣裳; very particular as to —, c'ün i-zông' ting k'ao'-kyiu 穿衣裳頂考究; careless in — (dirty), c'ün'-leh lah-t'ah' 穿得邋遢; dirty and ragged (in —), lô-tsô.

DRESS, to put on clothes, c'ün i-zông' 穿衣裳; — a child, teng siao-nying' c'ün i-zông' 搭°小人°穿衣裳; well dressed, c'ün'-leh, bin k'ah-ky'i-go 穿°得便客氣个°; poorly dressed, c'ün'-leh pe-pe'-go 穿°得卑卑个°

DRESSING-GLASS, tsiah-i-kying' 著衣鏡 (ih-min)

DRIBBLE, to fall in drops, tin'-tang-tin ti'-loh 點打點滴落; to slaver, liu zæn'-dzô-shü' 流涎沫水

DRIED, ken 乾; — in the sun, sa'-ken-de 曬°乾了°; — fruits, ken ko'-ts 乾果子; — apples, bing-ko ken' 苹果乾; — grapes, bu-dao ken' 葡萄乾; fæn-dao' 番萄; — peaches, dao-fu' 桃鋪; — persimmons, z'-ping 柿餅; — fish, ng-siang 魚°鯗

DRIFT, to be driven with the current, ze shü' t'eng-læ t'eng-ky'i' 隨水氽來氽去°; boat drifting for bad purposes, t'eng-kông-jün' 氽江° 船

DRILL, to — a hole, cün dong' 鑽洞 (cün or tsön);— a small hole, tsön ngæn'-ts 鑽眼°子;— as troops, ts'ao-lin' 操練; going to —, loh ts'ao' ky'i 落操去°

DRINK, to ky'üoh 吃°; hah 呷; he wants to drink a little water, gyi iao ky'üoh' ih-tin shü' 其要吃°一點水°;— (as horses), ing 飲

DRINK, fondness for —, t'en tsiu' 貪酒

DRIP, to ti'-loh-læ 滴落來

DRIPPING-PAN, baking-pan, p'ang-bun' 烹°盤

DRIVE, to — cows, ken ngeo' 趕牛°;— him out, ken' gyi c'ih' 趕其出;— out mosquitoes, tæn' meng-djong' 撣°蚊°虫;— a nail, k'ao' ih-me' ting-cü' 拷一枚釘鉄;— against, djông-djoh' 撞着

DRIVING rain, zia-fong'yü 斜°風雨

DRIZZLE, to loh-yü'-mao-s' 落雨毛絲; it drizzles, læ-tih loh-yü-mao-s' 來的落雨毛絲

DROLL, hao fah-siao' go 好發笑个°

DROMEDARY, doh-fong-do' 獨峰駝 (ih-deo)

DRONE, the male bee, yüong-fong' 雄蜂 (ih-tsah)

DROOL, to — (as an infant), c'ih zæn'-dzô-shü' 出涎沫°水°

DROOP, to — (as a flower), dang-loh' 荏落;— the head forward, deo' eo-tæn'-tao 頭傴°打°倒;— the head on one side, deo gwæn-tao'.

DROP, a ih tin' 一點; a — of water, ih tin shü 一點水

DROP, to fall in drops, ti'-loh' 滴落; to fall, tih'-loh 跌落; let it drop, peh gyi tih'-loh 俾°其跌落;— (as ripe fruit), t'eng'-loh 脫落;— by spoonfuls, ih diao-kang' ih diao-kang' tao'-tih 一調羹°一調羹°倒的

DROPSY, shü'-kwu bing' 水°臌病; kwu'-tsiang bing' 臌脹病

DROSS, vu'-tong-go tsô' 浮°當°个°渣

DROVE, ih-dziao' 一羣; ih-de' 一隊; a — of cattle, ih-dziao ngeo' 一羣牛

DROUGHT, 'en 旱; t'in 'en' 天旱; Summer —, 'en-ô' 旱夏°; Winter —, 'en tong' 旱冬

DROWN, to tsing'-sah 浸殺;— one's self, deo-shü' si' 投水死°;— one's-self in the canal, deo 'o' si' 投河死°

DROWSY, hweng-gyün' 昏倦; gyün-ky'i' 倦起

DRUDGE, to tso kw'u'-kong 做苦工

DRUGGIST, yiah-tin'-kwun 藥店官

DRUGS, yiah-dzæ' 藥材

DRUG-SHOP, (large) yiah-dzæ 'ông' 藥材行°; (small) —, yiah-tin' 藥店

DRUM, kwu 鼓; *large* —, do kwu' 大°鼓; *small* —, teo' kwu 斗鼓; — *bulging in the middle*, hwô kwu' 花鼓 (ih-go)

DRUMMER, kwu-siu' 鼓手 (ih-ming)

DRUM-STICK, kwu-djü' 鼓槌° (ih-tsah)

DRUNK, tsiu' ky'üoh-tse 酒吃°醉

DRUNKARD, tsiu'-kyü 酒鬼°; tse'-hen 醉漢 (ih-go)

DRY, sao 燥; ken 乾; — *as powder*, feng'-sao 粉燥; — *ground*, sao' di 燥地; — *wood*, ken za' 乾柴; sao' za 燥柴; *the canals are* —, 'o-ken' shü-sao' 河乾水°燥

DRY, to — *in the sun*, sa 曬°; — *by the fire*, hong 烘; *ditto something slightly damp*, be 焙; — *in the open air*, lông 朗

DUCK, æn 鴨; *wild* —; yia'-æn 野°鴨°; shü'-æn 水°鴨 (ih-tsah); *duck's eggs*, ah'-dæn °鴨蛋; — *meat*, ah' nyüoh 鴨肉°

DUCTILE, nying 韌

DUE, *how much is* — *you?* ng' yiu to-siao' tsiang læ nying deo' 你

有多少帳在°何°處°? what is required, veng' sô ing-teh'-go 分°所應得个; *what is proper*, li' sô tông-jün' 理所當然; *arrived in time*, tsiao z-eo' tao'-liao 照時候到了°

DUEL, liang'-'ô siang-tang' 兩下°相打

DULL, meng-meng'-hweng-hweng' 悶悶昏昏; — *color*, hweng' seh 昏色; — *of hearing* (primarily, affected deafness), tsia'-mi-long' 借米聾

DULY, *at the time*, tsiao z-'eo' 照時候; cing' z-k'eh 準時刻; 'æn' z-k'eh 限°時刻; *letter — received*, sing, cing'-z-k'eh siu-tao'-de 信準時刻收到了°; — *prepared*, yü-be' ding-tông' 預備定當

DUMB, ô' k'eo vu-yin' 啞°口無言; — *and staring*, moh-ding'-k'eo'-ngæ 目定口呆; *speechless*, vé kông 弗°會講; *a deaf and dumb person*, ô'-ts 啞子

DUN *color*, t'ih' seh 鐵色; — *for money*, dong-din' t'ao'-leh lo-so, or dong-din' t'ao-leh tsi-tseo' 銅錢°討得°囉唆

DUNCE, *one of no capacity*, c'ing'-dzæ 蠢才; nyü-c'ü'-peh-dzin'-go nying 愚痴不智°个°人°

DUNG, o 屎; feng 糞; *manure*, bi; liao 料

DUNGEON, lao-kæn' 牢監°

DUPE, *to* keo-ying' 勾引; *his* —,

gyi'-go zih' 其个°食; ziu gyi'-go nyü' 受其个°愚

DURABLE, næ-kyiu' 耐久; kying-yüong' 經用; — (as clothing), kying-c'ün' 經穿

DURING three years, sæn nyin' li-hyiang' 三年裡向; — the time I was in Shanghai, ngô' læ Zông-hæ' z-'eo 我在°上海時候

DUSK, wông-hweng' 黃昏 corruptly called wun-hwun-den'; sah-en' 雲°暗

DUST, hwe-dzing' 灰塵; thick —, hwe-dzing'-bang-bong' 灰塵髱髱

DUST, to — by wiping, k'a hwe-dzing' 揩°灰塵; — by whipping, tæn hwe-dzing' 撣灰塵

DUST-BRUSH, feather mao-shih'-tsiu 毛刷帚 (ih-kwun)

DUST-CLOTH, k'a-hwe'-pu 揩°灰布 (ih-kw'e)

DUST-PAN, peng-teo' 畚斗 (ih-tsab)

DUTCH, 'O-læn'-koh-go 荷蘭國个°; — man, 'O-læn nying' 荷蘭人°

DUTIFUL, hyiao'-jing 孝順; — son, hyiao'-ts 孝子

DUTY, meng-veng' 名°分°; one's own —, peng-veng 本分°; Customs' —, se'-din 稅錢°; — memo, zông-se'-tæn 上稅單; wun-se'-tæn 完稅單; — proof, siu-se'-tæn 收稅單

DWARF, a'-ts 矮°子

DWARF, to — by bending branches, bun-jü' 蟠樹

DWELL, to djü 住; deng 庉; — alone, ih-go nying' zi' deng 一个°人°自°庉

DWELLING, where is your honorable —? ng fu'-zông ah-li' 你°府上何°處°? my humble —, bi-sô' 敝舍°; — house, djü-dzeh' 住宅; — place, deng-sing'-ts-c'ü' 庉身之處; djü-kyü' 住居; ditto of the family, djü-kô' 住家

DWINDLE, to grow less by degrees, dzin'-dzin siao'-long-ky'i 漸漸小攏去°

DYE, to nyin 染°; — by dipping, ̆wch 搵°; — cotton cloth, nyin pu' 染°布; — red, nyin 'ong' 染°紅; — by brushing, shih' nyin 刷染°

DYER, nyin'-s-vu 染°司務

DYE-STUFF, ngæn-liao' 顏°料

DYING, tsiang dön-ky'i' 將斷氣; kw'a ling-cong'-de 快°臨終了°; — words, yi-yin' 遺言; — commands, yi-ming' 遺命

DYNASTY, dziao-dæ' 朝代; the present —, peng-dziao 本朝; the beginning of ditto, peng-dziao k'æ-koh' 本朝開國

DYSENTERY, 'ong-li' 紅痢; hyüih'-li 血痢

DYSPEPSIA, ky'üoh'-zih feh hwô 吃°食弗化; we-kô ̆wa' 胃家孬°

E

EACH, koh 各; me 每; — *by himself* or *itself*, koh'-nying kwun zi' 各人管自°; *they love — other*, gyi-lah' dô-kô' siang-æ' 伊等°大°家°相愛; gyi-lah pe'-ts' siang-æ' 伊等°彼此相愛; — *end*, liang' deo 兩頭; *ditto (of many ends)*, me' ih-go deo' 每一个°頭; — *person has one*, koh' nying yiu ih'-go 各人°有一个°; — *man*, ko'-ko nying 個個人°; koh' nying 各人°; — *kind*, me' yiang 每樣; koh' yiang 各樣; *take three of — kind*, koh' yiang do' sæn-go 各樣拿三个°; me' yiang do sæn' go 每樣拿°三个°; *one to —*, ih'-go kah'-ky'i; *a dollar to — man*, koh nying' ih-kw'e fæn-ping' 各人°一塊番餅

EAGER, ts'ih'-sing 切心; — *expectation*, ts'ih'-sing siang'-vông 切心想望; hyüih'-sing siang'-vông 血心想望

EAR, ng'-tô 耳朵 (tô or to); *deaf —*, ng'-tô long' 耳°朵聾; *ringing in the ears*, ng'-tô 'ong-'ong'-hyiang 耳°朵鬨鬨響; — *ache*, ng'-tô t'ong' 耳°朵痛; *in at the right — out at the left (i. e. inattentive)*, jing-tsah' ng'-tô tsing' tsia'-tsah ng'-to c'ih' 右°隻°耳°朵進左°隻耳°朵出°; — *brush*, siao-sih'-ts 消息

子; — *pick*, leo' ng-tô w̃æn' 鑢耳°朵彎; — *ring*, gwænts' 環°子; — *wax*, ng'-tô ö' 耳°蒙°; *to bore the ear*, c'ün' ng'-tô ngæn' 穿耳°朵眼°; *an — of corn*, ih-ts' loh-koh' 一枝稞穀; ih-be' loh-koh' 一穗°稞穀

EARLY, tsao 早; — *in the day*, ts'ing-tsao' 清早; — *in the morning*, tsao' t'in-liang 早天亮; — *and late*, or *morning and night*, tsao'-æn 早晏°; *come —*, tsao'-læ 早來

EARN, *to* dzæn 賺; — *money*, dzæn' dong-din' 賺銅錢°

EARNEST, nyih-sing' 熱心; hyüih'-sing 血心; ih'-sing ih'-i 一心一意; cün-sing' cü-ts' 專心致志; *in —*, nying'-tsing' 認真; *make an — effort*, nying' ih'-k'eo ky'i' 忍一口氣; — *at one work*, cün-kong'-gyi-z' 專攻其事

EARTH, *the* di-gyiu' 地球; *the ground*, di-yiang' 地陽; *earth*, na-nyi' 坭; nyi-t'u' 泥土

EARTHEN-WARE, ngô'-ho 瓦貨

EARTH-QUAKE, di-cing' 地震; t'in-yiao' di-dong' 天搖地動

EARTH-WORM, ts'oh'-zin, c'ih-zin, or c'oh-zin, 曲蟮; di-zen' 地蠶

EASE, *at* en-tæn' 安然; hao 好; *no care*, m-sing' m-z' 無°心無°事; *to do with —*, tso

leh ky'ing-fæn' 做得°輕泛
EASE, can you — me a little ? ng' hao' peh ngô kw'un-s'-tin feh 你°好俾°我寬舒點否°!
EASILY, yüong-yi' 容易°; sang'-lih 省°力
EAST, tong 東; — side, tong-pin' 東邊; — wind, tong fong' 東風; — gate, tong meng' 東門
EASTWARD, hyiang-tong' 向東; dziao-tong' 朝東
EASY, yüong-yi' 容易°; sang'-lih 省°力; not hard, feh næn' 弗難; light, ky'ing-yi' 輕易°; in — circumstances, Weng-pao'-go 温飽個°; keo' ky'üoh, keo' yüong' 彀吃彀用; — in treating others, no-jün' 懦善; — in manners, ts'ong-yüong' 從容; z-dzæ' 自在
EAT, to ky'üoh 吃°; p'in 騙; — rice or a meal, ky'üoh væn' 吃°飯; — enough, ky'üoh pao 吃°飽; — only vegetables (as the Buddhists do), ky'üoh ts'æ' 吃°菜; can't — it, ky'üoh'-feh-læ' 吃°弗來; don't like to —, ga' k'eo; — (as insects do), cü 蛀; have eaten, ky'üoh'-ko'-de 吃°過了°; p'in'-ko'-de 騙過了°
EATABLE, k'o-yi ky'üoh' 可以吃°
EATABLES, ky'üoh'-zih 吃°食
EATING-HOUSE, tsiu'-kwun-tin' 酒館店; small —, væn-tin' 飯店

EAVES, yin-deo' 簷頭; — of the house, oh'-yin-deo' 屋簷頭
EAVES-DROPPER, one who listens at the partition, ih-pih t'ing' 隔°壁聽 (ih-go)
EBB-TIDE, t'e'-dziao 退潮; loh-shü' 落水
EBONY, u-moh' 烏木
ECCENTRIC person, kwæ-p'ih'-go nying 乖僻個°人°; c'ih'-wu-gyi-le'-go nying 出乎其類個°人°
ECHO, ing'-ky'i-go sing-hyiang' 應起個°聲響
ECLIPSE of the sun, wu-jih' 糊日; jih-zih' 日蝕; — of the moon, wu-yüih' 糊月; yüih-zih' 月蝕
ECLIPSE, wông-dao' 黃道
ECONOMIZE, to tso-nying-kô' 做人°家°; gyin'-iah 儉約
ECONOMICAL, saving, gyin'-sang 儉省; kyin'-sang 儉省°; keh; keh-sön' 合算
ECSTATIC, hwun-hyi' ko-deo' 歡喜過頭; ko'-ü hwun-hyi' 過於歡喜
EDDY, bun-shü' 盤水; jün-shü' 旋水 (ih-go)
EDGE, bông-pin' 旁邊; pin-yin' 邊沿; — of a knife, tao-fong' 刀鋒; tao-k'eo' 刀口; has lost its —, fong-deo' tih'-loh-de 鋒頭跌落了°
EDGE, to — up, yi-long'-ky'i 移攏去°; yi-long'-læ 移攏來
EDGEWISE, can't get a word in

—, ih-kyü' tu ts'æn'-feh-tsing 一句都申°弗進; ts'ah' yin feh zông' 插言弗上.

EDGING, kwe'-ts 桂子; siang-diao' 鑲條

EDICT, kao'-z 告示; *imperial* —, zông-yü' 上諭; sing'-ts 聖旨; wông-rông 皇榜; tsiao'-shü 詔書; *the Sacred* —, Sing'-yü Kwông'-hyüing 聖諭廣訓

EDIFY, *to* — *him*, peh gyi tsing-ih' 俾其進益

EDIT, *to* ting'-tsing 訂正

EDITION, *the first* — (printed), di-ih'-ts'ing'-c'ih-go shü' 第一次印出个°書; *the first* — (cut on blocks), ts'u k'eh'-c'ih-go shü' 初刻出个°書

EDITOR, ting'-tsing-go cü'-kwu 訂正个°主顧

EDUCATE *him*, dzing-dziu'gyi-go dzæ-'oh' 成就其个°才學°

EDUCATION, *good* 'oh-jih' hao' 學°術好; dzæ-'oh' kwông' 才學°廣; *a person of* —, yiu 'oh-veng' go nying' 有學°問个°人

EEL, nun 鰻; *field* —, wông-zin 黃鱔; nyi-ts'iu' 泥鰍; jün'-yü 鱔魚 (ih-keng)

EFFACE, *to blot out*, du-diao' 塗壞; —(*from the mind*), mo-wu' 模糊

EFFECT, *with what* —? yiu soh'-go pin'-dong 有甚°麼變動? yiu soh'-go seng-seh' 有甚°麼

生色? *no* —, vu-tsi'-ü-z' 無濟于事; feh-c'ih'-seh 弗出色; *to have a good* — (as medicine), yiu yiao-nyiæn' 有效驗; yiu ing'-'ao 有應效°; yiu ing'-nyiæn' 有應驗; *the* — *of drought*, t'in 'en'-go yün-kwu 天旱个°緣故; *cause and* —, ing-ko' 因果; *to see no* — *from one's instructions*, sô kao' feh kyin yiao' 所敎°弗見效; *bad* — *of misconduct* (regarded as supernatural), ing-tsih' 陰隲

EFFECTED, *he has* — *a great deal*, gyi sô tsoh'-we yiu hyü'-to seng-seh' 其所作爲有許多生色; gyi sô tsoh-we yiu hyü'-to z-ken' 其所作爲有許多事幹

EFFEMINATE, *womanish*, siao-nyiang'-deo ying 形°如小娘; nyü'-siang-go 像°女相

EFFERVESCE, *to* p'u-c'ih'-læ; p'eng-c'ih'-læ 噴出來

EFFICACIOUS, ling-ing'-go 靈應个°; — *medicine*, ling-tæn'-miao-yiah' 靈丹妙藥; — *deity*, ling-ing' bu-sab' 靈應菩薩

EFFICACY, gying-dao' 劼道; lih-dao' 力道; *has* —, yiu ling-ing' 有靈應; *owing to the* — *of the medicine*, ky'ü'-leh yiah'-go gying'-dao 虧得°藥个°劼道; — *of prayer*, tao-kao'-go lih-dao' 禱告个°力道

EFFICIENT (as a person), vu yiu' feh tao-kô' 無有弗到家; vu yiu' feh dzing-kong 無有弗成功

EFFIGY, image, ngeo'-ziang 偶像°; straw man, ts'ao'-kao' nying 草絞人°

EFFORT, to make an —, c'ih lih' 出力; yüong lih' 用力; make a great —, do' c'ih' lih 大°出力; 'eo-ky'i'-lih 盡氣力; make a strenuous mental —, fah-veng' yüong-kong 發憤用功; united —, dong-sing' yiah-lih' 同心協力; dô-kô' c'ih-lih' 大°家出力

EFFRONTERY, tæ ô'-lin 厚°臉; 'eo-bi' ô'-lin 厚皮丫臉; what —! ô'-lin tæ'-leh wô'-feh-læ' 丫臉獃得話弗來!

EGG, dæn 蛋; hen's —, kyi-dæn' 雞蛋; duck's —, ah'-dæn 鴨蛋 (ih go)

EGG-PLANT, gyiæn 茄°

EIGHT, pah 八; — times, pah' tsao, &c. 八次°

EIGHTEEN, jih-pah' 十八

EIGHTH, di-pah' 第八

EIGHTY, pah'-jih 八十

EITHER and or are expressed by 'oh-tsia' 或者° or wa-z' 還是 used twice, thus : — great or small, 'oh-tsia' do, 'oh-tsia' siao' 或者°大或者°小; — to-day or tomorrow, wa-z kyih-mih wa-z ming-tsiao 還是今°日° 還°是明朝; I would not choose —, ngô ih'-go tu kæn-feh-cong' 我一个°都揀弗中 (cong or tsong); — one, feh-leng' ah-li ih'-go 弗論阿裡一个°; ze-bin' 'ah-li ih'-go 隨便何°處°一个°

EJECT, to ken'-c'ih 趕出; (when done by an officer) ky'ü-djuh' 驅逐

ELABORATE, adj. si'-cü 細致 dzing-si' 誠細

ELAPSE, to ko 過; five years have elapsed, ko'-leh ng'-nyin de 過得°五°年了°

ELASTIC, springy, neng-soh' neng-sing', 能縮能伸; neng-sing' neng-geo'; — tape or band, kying'-kw'un ta' 緊寬帶°

ELATED, teh'-i yiang'-yiang 得°意揚揚

ELBOW, siu-tsang-cü-den' 手腕°

ELDER, do-jü' 大°如; — brother, ah-ko' 阿哥; — sister, ah-tsi' 阿姊

ELDER, an tsiang'-lao 長老

ELDERLY, kw'a lao'-de 快°老了°; bin-lao-kwun'.

ELDEST son, do ng'-ts 大°兒°子; tsiang'-ts 長子; — daughter, do-nön' 大°囡; tsiang'-nyü 長女

ELECT, to kæn'-shün 揀°選; t'iao'-shün 挑選; God's —,

Jing-ming′ sô kæn′- shün-go nying′ 神明所揀選个°人°

ELECTRIC, *to receive an — shock*, din-ky'i′ jih-sing′, fah-kying′- de 電氣入身發驚了°

ELECTRICAL *machine*, fah-din′- ky'i-go ky'i′-ming 發電氣个°器皿

ELECTRICITY, din′-ky'i 電氣

ELEGANT, wô-li′ 華麗; me-li′ 美麗; — *colors*, ngwen-seh′ yin-li′ 顏色豔麗

ELEGY, Wæn′-dz 輓詞 (ih-p'in)

ELEMENT, *the first principle*, nyün ti′-ts 原底子; peng′-tsih 本質; *the five* (Chinese) *elements*, ng′-ying 五°行; *air is the — we live in*, ky'i′ z ah-lah weh-ming′ go nyün-peng′ 氣是我°等°活命个°原本

ELEPHANT, ziang 象; *white —* bah-ziang′ 白象; *gray —*, hwe-ziang′ 灰象 (ih-deo)

ELEPHANTIASIS, do-kyiah-fong′ 大°脚瘋

ELEVATE, *to exalt*, di-zông′-ky'i 提上去°; kao-kyü′ 高舉; kyü′-zông 舉上; sing-zông′ 升上; dæ-ky'ih′-zông 擡挈上; *to — the hand*, siu′ di-tæn′-ky'i 手提打°起; *to —* (something in the hand), di-kao′ 提高; di-zông′-ky'i 提上去°; *— the head*, dæ deo′ 擡頭

ELEVEN, jih-ih′ 十一; *— o'clock*, jih-ih′ tin-cong 十一點鐘

ELEVENTH, *the* di jih-ih′ 第十一; *the — month*, jih-ih′ yüih 十一月

ELICIT *to* ying′-c'ih-læ 引出來; *— his ideas*, ying gyi-go i-s′ c'ih′-læ 引其个°意思出來

ELLIPTICALLY, *to speak* ky'ih′-long kông′ 挈攏講; soh′-long kông′ 縮攏講

ELM, yü-jü′ 榆樹 (ih-cü)

ELOPE, *to* s-peng′ 私奔; s-dao′ 私逃; *the girl has eloped*, nyiang′-ts keng nying′ tseo′-de 娘子跟人°走了°

ELOQUENT, *having the power of moving the feelings*, we dong nying′-go dzing′ 會動人°个°情; *having the power of expression*, k'eo-neng′-zih-bin′ 口能舌辯; yiu k'eo′-dzæ 有口才

ELOQUENTLY, *to speak* kông′-lch k'eng′-ts'ih 講得°懇切

ELSE, ling-nga′ 另外°; i′-nga 意外°; bih 別; *have you something —?* ling-nga′ yiu′ feb 另外°有否°? *excluding that, is there anything —?* djü keh′-go ts-nga′ wa-yiu′ ma 除這个°之外還°有嗎°? *somebody —*, bih′ nying 別人°; *nobody — knows*, m′-teh bih-nying hyiao′-teh 沒°有別人°曉得; *I was laughing at something —*, sô siao′, ngô yiu bih′ i 所笑我有別意

ELSEWHERE, bih-c'ü' 別處; bih' t'ah di'-fông 別塌地方

ELUCIDATE, to kông'-ka ts'ing-t'ong' 講解清通

ELUDE, to yüong kyi'-ts'ah to'-bi 用計策躲避

EMACIATED, kweh'-seo jü-za' 骨瘦如柴°

EMANCIPATE, to sih'-fông 釋放

EMBALM, to hyiang-liao' jih-s'-foh'-cong 香料實尸腹中 (veng)

EMBANKMENT on a river bank, kông-dông' 江°塘; — by the sea, hæ'-dông 海塘; earth-work, to 操

EMBARGO, kying c'ih'-k'eo 禁出口

EMBARK, to loh jün' 落船; zông jün' 上船

EMBARRASS, to involve in perplexity, lin-le' 連累; ky'in-le' 牽累; greatly perplexed, le-sah'-de 累殺了°

EMBARRASSED through fear, gyü hyih'-de 懼懾了°; — in speaking, kông-shih gyüoh-gyüoh'-ts'oh-ts'oh' 講式侷侷促促; — in funds, siu'-deo kyih'-kyü 手頭拮据; greatly ditto, ky'üing-peh' 窘廹

EMBASSADOR, ky'ing-ts'a 欽差; the persons attending an —, ze-yün' 隨員

EMBELLISH, to tsông-sih' 裝飾 tsah'-kweh hao' 紮刮好

EMBERS, smoldering fire, iu-iu' go ho' 悠悠个°火

EMBEZZLE, to s-'ô' liao-yüong' 私下°撩用; — money entrusted for others, liao-yüong' kong-'ông' nying'-ts 撩用公行銀子; — the emperor's money, liao-yüong hyiang'-nying 撩用餉銀

EMBLEM, piao'-'ao 表號; — of justice, piao'-'ao en'-dzông kong-bing'-go i'-s 表號暗藏公平个°意思

EMBOLDENS me, fông' ngô-go tæn' 放我个°胆

EMBRACE, to — in the arms, o-tæn'-long; o'-leh bao'; — an opportunity, ts'ing'-kyi-we' 趁機會; dzing' kyi-we' 乘機會; embraced within, pao'-kwah dzæ-ne' (ne or nen) 包括在內; pao-kwah'-tsing 包括進

EMBROIDER, to siu hwô' 綉花; tso' hwô' 做花; tso pang-ts' 做繃子

EMBROIDERY, a piece of —, siu' hwô p'in'-ts 綉花片子; — shop, kwu'-siu-tin' 顧綉店; siu'-hwô-tin' 綉花店

EMBROIL, to be-le' 被累; le'-tsing-dzæ-ne' 累進在內

EMBRYO, dzing-yüing' 成孕°

EMERGE, to ts'ön-c'ih'-læ 竄出來; — suddenly, ts'ön-ky'i'-læ 竄起來

EMERGENCY, kying'-kyih z-ken' 緊急事幹; prepare for an

—, bông-be′ wun′-kyib 防備緩急; be-bæn′ iao′-kying iao′-mæn 備辦要緊要慢

EMETIC, t‘u′ yiah 吐藥

EMIGRATE to a foreign country, ts‘in-kyü′ nga-koh′ 遷居外國

EMINENT, kao-tsiah′ 高霄; kao-kwe′ 高貴;— in scholarship, kao-dzæ′ 高才;— official, kao-kwun′-hyin′-tsiah 高官顯霄

EMIT, to fah′-c‘ih 發出; to — light (as a lamp), fah liang′ 發亮; — light (as the sun or fire), fah-kwông′ 發光;— sparks, pao′-c‘ih ho′-sing læ 爆出火星來

EMOLUMENTS of office, (unlawful), siu-læ′-go fi′ 收來个費; the regular salary of officials, fong′-loh 俸祿; what is given outside of salary to prevent squeezing, yiang′-lin 養廉

EMOTIONS, the seven ts‘ih′ dzing 七情; viz., pleasure, hyi 喜; anger, nu 怒; grief, æ 哀; joy, loh 樂; love, æ 愛; hatred, u 惡; desire, yüoh 欲; to excite the —, dong dzing 動情

EMPEROR, wông-ti′ 皇帝; wông-zông′ 皇上; the present —, tông-kying′ wông-zông′ 當今皇上; the present — (is styled), Kwông-jü′ wông-ti′ 光緒皇帝; the deceased —, sin-wông′ 先皇

EMPHASIZE in reading, sing-ing′ doh-leh djong′ 聲音讀得重

EMPHATICALLY, kông′-leh sah′-pô 講得煞覇; kông′-leh kyih′-jih 講得硈實

EMPIRE, the Chinese —, Cong-koh′ 中國; T‘in-‘ô′ 天下°; Da-ts‘ing′-koh 大清國; Da-dông′-koh 大唐國

EMPLOY, to yüong 用;— means, yüong fông-fah′ 用方法;— one's time, yüong kong′ 用工; I — my time in study, ngô yüong kong′ doh shü′ 我用工讀書

EMPLOYMENT, any thing which engages one's time, z-ken′ 事幹; z-t‘i′ 事體; business, ‘ông-tông′ 行當; occupation, z-nyih′ 事業; ‘ông-nyih′ 行業; in steady —, tang-dziang′ 打常°; dziang-nyin′-go 長年个°;— for a short time, ts‘eh-tön′ 撮短; tön-kong′ 短工

EMPORIUM, commercial sea-port, mô′-deo 馬頭; market-town, cing′-deo 鎮頭

EMPOWER, to kao′-fu gyün-ping′ 交付權柄

EMPRESS, the wông-‘eo′ 皇后; — dowager, wông-t‘a′-‘eo 皇太后

EMPTY, k‘ong 空; hyü 虛;— place, k‘ong di′-fông 空地方; — talk, k‘ong′-deo-shih-wô 空頭說話; hyü-wô′ 虛話 now means deceitful talk;— or meaningless characters, hyü z'-ngæn 虛字眼°

EMPTY, to tao'-c'ih 倒出; tao'-diao 倒去°; — entirely, tao'-k'ong 倒空; tao' ken-zing' 倒乾净°

EMULATE, to ts'iang' zông-zin' 搶上前°; — him, ken'-gyi-zông, ih-yiang' 赶其上一樣; — another's skill or strength, pi'-sæ 比賽

ENABLE, to dzu-lih' 助力; pông-lih' 帮力; he enabled me to do it, gyi' dzu ngô'-go lih' hao tso' 其助我个°力好做

ENACT, to — law, lih' ih-diao fah' 立一條法; — laws, shih'-lih lih-fah' 設°立律法

ENAMORED, ts'ih'-sing-go siang-s 切心个°相思; ts'ih-sing-go ky'i'-mo 切心个°企慕; — till sick, sang siang-s'-bing 生相思病

ENCAMP, to tsah-ying' 箚°營; tsah-ying dza' 劄°營寨

ENCAMPMENT (of an army), ying-bun' 營盤; ying-dza' 營寨

ENCHANT, to hold by a spell, mi-weng' 迷魂; bewitch by giving something, 'ô-kwu' 下°蠱

ENCHANTED, jih mi-weng'-dzing 入迷魂陣

ENCHANTER, one who enchants by sorcery, yüong'-zia-fah'-go 用邪°法个°; — (a priest), yiu-fông'-seng 遊方僧

ENCIRCLE, to we-cün' 圍轉; we-kw'eng' 圍困; we-djü' 圍住

ENCOMIUM, peo-tsiang' shih-wô' 褒獎說話

ENCOMPASS, to dön-ky'ün' we-djü' 團圈圍住; dön-ky'ün' kw'eng'-djü 團圈困住

ENCOUNTER, the two armies had an —, liang' pin tang' ih-we' ko'-de 兩邊打一回過了°

ENCOUNTER, to nyü-djoh' 遇着°; p'ong'-djoh 逢着°

ENCOURAGE, to min'-li 勉勵; — him, tsông' gyi-go tæn' 壯其个°膽

ENCROACH, to dzin'-dzin tsin' 漸漸佔; bu-bu' tsin-tsing' 步步佔進; sea encroaches on the land, hæ' iao t'eng di' 海要吞地

ENCUMBERED, burdened, t'o-t'o'-ts'i-ts'i 拖拖累累; bound, dzin'-ziao-de 纏繞了°

END, deo' 頭 (ih); both ends, liang' deo 兩頭; turn the other —, diao deo' 調頭; from one — to the other, dzong-deo' ts-vi' 從頭至尾; the conclusion, kyih'-sah 結煞; from the beginning to the —, dzong ky'i-deo tao kyih'-sah 從起頭到結煞; ditto carefully, i-deo'-ngeng'-tsih 依頭痕°節; what will the — be? dza kyih'-sah ni 怎°結煞呢? come to a bad — (death), Wa min' ngæn 歪°眼; Wa kyih'-gyüoh 歪結

局; m kyih'-gyüoh 無° 結局
ENDANGER, to fông' læ ngwe-hyin' di'-fông 放在° 危險地方; — one's life, pô' sing'-ming fông' læ ngwe-hyin di-fông 把性命放在°危險地方; sing'-ming do'-leh yiang-hyi'-hyi 性命拿°得°羊戲戲
ENDEAVOR, to dzing sing-lih' 盡心力; I endeavored but did not succeed, ngô sing-lih'-dzing'-ko-de, dæn'-z tsô'-feh-tao 我心力盡過了°但是做弗到
ENDLESS, m̂ gyüong'-dzing 無°窮盡; m̂ dzing'-gyi 無°盡期; —quarrelling, nao-nao'peh-hyin' 嘈鬧不休
ENDOW with a dower, be kô'-tsông 備嫁°粧
ENDURANCE, beyond 'en-yüong'-feh-djü'-de 含容弗住了°
ENDURE, to a 挨; — a day at a time, ih-nyih' a' ih-nyih' 一日°挨一日°; can't — it (living so), a'-feh-ko'-ky'i 挨弗過去°; ditto (can't get along with), ah-feh-ko'-ky'i 壓° 弗過去°; yüong'-feh-ko'-ky'i 容弗過去°; tông'-feh-djü 當弗住 ditto (i.e. can't be patient), neh'-feh-djü' 納弗住; næ'-feh-djü' 耐弗住; — patiently, jing'-næ ziu 忍耐受; — suffering, ziu-kw'u' 受苦; ditto patiently, we nying t'ong' 會忍°痛; — patiently (as reproach), jing'-

ky'i t'eng-sing' 忍氣吞聲; — pain, ngao-t'ong' 熬痛; — without complaint, 'en yüong 含容; — silently, neh'-leh sing-deo' ho 納得°心頭火
ENDURING, lasting, næ-kyiu' 耐久; iu-kyiu' 悠久; dziang-kyin' 長久
ENDWISE, on end, dzih-teng' 直竪°; place —, teng'-ky'i-fông' 竪起放
ENEMY, ün-kô' 寃家°; te'-deo 對頭; dziu-nying' 讐人°; military —, dziu-dih' 讐敵; the opposing army, dib-ping' 敵兵
ENERGY, force, lih 力; to work with —, dzing'-lih tsô' 盡力做; do with whole heart, and strength, dzing'-sing gyih-lih tsô' or dzing-sing-dzing-lih tso 盡心竭力做; to rouse one's energies, teng'-ky'i tsing'-jing 頓起精神
ENERVATE, to s'-teh nyün'-ziah' 使得軟°弱; s-teh t'eh-lih' 使得脫力
ENFEEBLED, tsing'-lih sæ'-de 精力衰了°; mentally —, tsing'-jing sæ'-de 精神衰了°
ENFORCE, to — obedience, pih'-leh i-dzong' 逼勒依從; — his obedience, ngang-k'ô' gyi i-dzong' 硬拿°其依從
ENGAGE, to ding-jih' 定實; wô-hao' 話好; iah'-hao 約好; to promise, ing-dzing' 應承; I have already engaged another

man, ih-go nying' ngô yi'-kying ding-jih'-de 一个°人°我已經定實了; — three workmen, ding sæn'-go kong-nying' 定三个工人°; — a boat, t'ao' ih-tsah jün' 討一隻船; the boat is engaged, jün t'ao'-loh-de 船討落了°; I am engaged at present, keh-zông'-li ngô yiu z-ken' 這°時°程我有事幹

ENGINE, steam —, ky'i'-kyi 氣機; long-deo' 龍頭

ENGINE-ROOM, long-deo-kæn' 龍頭間; t'ih-ts'ông' 鐵倉

ENGLISHMAN, Da-Ing' nying 大英人°; Ing-kyih'-li nying' 英吉利人°; English cloth, Da-Ing c'ih'-go pu° 大英出个°布

ENGRAVE, to — on metals, zen 鏨; k'eh 刻; — on stone, wood, precious stones, metals, zoh (or joh) 鏨; k'eh 刻; tiao 雕; — characters, k'eh z 刻字; — an image, tiao ngeo'-ziang 雕偶像°; — on the heart, k'eh læ sing'-li 刻在°心程; k'eh-kweh' ming-sing' 刻骨銘心

ENGRAVER on metals, zen'-hwô-s-vu' 鏨花司務; — on wood, tiao-hwô'-s-vu' 雕花司務; tiao-k'eh'-ziang 雕刻匠°; — of characters, k'eh-z'-s-vu' 刻字司務; — on stone, hwô-ts'ao'-zah-s-vu' 花草石司務

ENGROSS, this engrosses my time, ngô'-go kong-fu' tsih p'e'-fu keh'-go yüong-dziang' 我个°工夫只配副這°用場; — one's attention, ih-sing' ts'ong-ih-yüoh' 一身充一役 (ts'ong or c'ong); ih-dzing tsi'-lu 一程躋路

ENIGMA, me-ts' 謎子; — on a lantern, teng-me' 燈謎

ENJOIN, to coh'-fu 囑附; ting-coh' 叮囑

ENJOY, to hyiang 享; — the happiness of old age, hyiang lao'-foh 享老福; to take satisfaction in, ziu'-yüong 受用; I — wearing this hat, keh' ting mao'-ts ta'-leh ngô ziu'-yüong 這°頂帽子戴°得我受用; I enjoyed the meeting to-day very much, kyih-mih' li'-pa ngô ting' ziu-yüong' 今°日°禮拜°我頂受用

ENJOYMENT, kw'a'-loh 快°樂; — in absence of care, kw'a'-weh 快°活

ENLARGE, to tso-leh do'-tin' 做得°大°點; — upon, kông'-leh dziang'-si' 講得詳細; t'e-k'æ' kông 推開講; — one's experience, kwông-kyin'-veng 廣見聞

ENLIGHTEN, to fah'-ming 發明; to — the mind, k'æ-sing 開心; k'æ-ky'iao' 開竅; p'o-nyü' 破愚

ENMITY, dziu-hyih or dziu-ky'ih 仇隙; ün'-ky'i 寃氣

ENNOBLE, to hyiang-zông'-ky'i 向上去°
ENORMOUS, ko'-ü do' 過於大°; enormously wicked, ôh'-gyih 惡極; ôh' tao pin' 惡到邊
ENOUGH, keo 够; tsoh 足; is it —? keo'-de feh 够了否°? exactly —, tsing'-keo 儘°够; ditto (hence definite), k'eo-feng'-k'eo-sü' 扣分扣數; — and some over, fu'-sbü 富庶; nông-sbü'; yiu-yü' 有餘
ENQUIRE, to ask, meng 問°; go in and —, tseo'-tsing meng ih'-sing 走進問°一聲
ENRAGE, to kyih'-leh nu' fah'-ts'ong-kwun' 激得°怒髮冲冠 lit., so that the hair will rise and lift the hat from the head; nu'-ky'i ts'ong-t'in' 怒氣冲天
ENRICH, to become rich, fah dzæ' 發財; — one's self at others' expense, seng-jing'-li-kyi' 損人利己; ditto by foul means, meo-t'eng' nying-kô' 謀吞人°家; — land, üong din' 壅田
ENROLL, to — as soldiers' and candidates' names, zông ts'ah-ts 上冊子
ENSIGN, gyi-'ao' 旗號
ENSLAVE, to tông nu-boh' yüong 當奴僕用; ts'ong nu' 充奴
ENSNARE, to — a person, hong nying' zông tông' 哄人°上當; long-loh nying 籠絡人°; hong nying' zông keo' 哄人°上鈎;

yiu' nying loh ky'ün-t'ao' 誘人°落圈套
ENSUE, to keng'-leh-læ 跟得°來; ze'-leh-læ 隨得°來; bad things certainly will —, ze'-'eo tsong yiu ẅa-z' 隨後終有孬事
ENSURE, to s'-teh ih-ding' 使得一定; to guaranty, pao-hao' 包好; — a cure, pao-i' 包醫; — deliverance from trouble, pao' c'ih deo' 包出頭
ENTANGLE, to dzin-long' tang-kyih' 纏攏打結; foot entangled in a thread, kyiah' sin dzin'-tih 脚線纏的; kyiah sin pang'-tih 脚線繃的
ENTER, to tseo'-tsing 走進;— the church, jih kyiao' 入敎;— on life favorably, tang gyin-kw'eng' 打乾坤; ting'-t'in-lib-di' 頂天立地;— the priesthood, c'ih-kô' 出家°;— the army, deo-kyüing' 投軍; deo-ts'ong' 投充;— on the book, zông bu'-ts 上簿子; teng bu'-ts 登簿子;— a name (of person or ship), kwô 'ao' 掛號
ENTERPRISE, new undertaking, sing-hying' z-ken' 新興事幹; to start an —, tang'-ih-fæn' gyin-kw'eng' 打一翻乾坤
ENTERPRISING, we sing hying' z-ken' go 會新興事幹个°; yiu cü-üong' 有智勇; be-bun' nying-k'ah 陪伴客人°

ENT　　　　151　　　　ENV

ENTERTAIN *guests*, be-bun'nying-k'ah 陪伴客人°; *to receive, we* 會; tsih'-dæ 接待; — *well (i. e. in talking)*, dæ k'ah' dæn-t'u' hao 待客談吐好; — *hospitably*, kw'un-dæ' nying-k'ah' 欵待客人°

ENTERTAINMENT, *feast*, tsiu'-zih 酒席

ENTHRONE *him*, t'e gyi' teng-we' 推其登位

ENTHUSIASTIC, ky'i hyüih'-sing 起血心

ENTICE, *to* ying'-yiu 引誘

ENTIRE, *perfect*, djün-be' 全備; *it is* — (*i. e. all here*), long'-tsong kæ'-tih 攏總在°; *an — orange*, tsing-ko' kyüih'-ts 正個橘子; *an — chicken*, tsing'-tsah kyi' 全隻雞

ENTIRELY, djün-jün' 全然; 'o-jün' 和然; — *forgotten*, djün-jün' mông-kyi'-de 全然忘記了

ENTITLED, ing-kæ'-go 應該个°; — *to receive*, li'-tông ziu' 理當受; ing-tông' teh-go 應當得个°

ENTOMOLOGY, k'ao'-kyiu djong-dzi' 'oh-veng 考究虫豸學問

ENTRAILS, du'-dziang 肚腸

ENTRANCE, tseo'-tsing-go lu' 走進个°路 — *of the river*, kông-k'eo' 江°口; — *and exit*, c'ih-jih'-ts lu' 出入之路

ENTRAP, *he wishes to — you*, gyi iao ng' zông-tông' 其要你°上當

ENTRAPPED, zông-tông'-de 上當了°; loh-ky'ün'-t'ao'-de 落圈套了°

ENTREAT, *to* gyiu-k'eng' 求懇 gyiu-ky'ih' 求乞

ENTRUST, *to* kao-dæ' 交°代; —*to*, t'oh'-fu 託付; — *to an inferior*, fu'-t'oh 付託; — *an important matter*, djong'-t'oh 重託

ENTRY, *a narrow hall*, long-dông' 俰°堂; *central hall*, cong-kæn' 中間°

ENTWINE, *to* dzin'-ziao 纏繞

ENUMERATE, *to count*, su'-su-k'en' 數數看; kyin'-kyin-k'en' 校檢看

ENVELOP or ENVELOPE *for a letter*, sing'-k'oh 信壳; sing'-fong 信封; fong-dong' 封筒; sing'-t'ao 信套

ENVELOP, *to wrap*, pao 包; *to encase*, t'ao'-tsing 套進

ENVIABLE, *he is* —, peh nying' ky'i'-gyi-feh-ko' 俾°人°氣其弗過

ENVIOUS, sang dzib-tu'-sing 生°嫉妬心; teh-teh-dong; ky'i'-feh-ko' 氣弗過

ENVOY, koh-s' 國使; ts'a-kwun' 差官 (ih-we)

ENVY *n.* tu'-gyi-sing 妬忌心

ENVY, *to* ky'i'-feh-ko 氣弗過;

EPI   152   ERA

I — him, ngô ky'i'-gyi-feh-ko' 我氣其弗過
EPIDEMIC, z-tsing' 時症; z-yüoh'-bing 時疫病; Weng-bing' 瘟病
EPISCOPAL *church*, Kyin-toh'-kong'-we 監督公會
EPISTLE, shü-sing' 書信; sing'-tsah 信札; *Paul's —* , Pao'-lo shü-sing' 保羅書信
EPITAPH, veng'-li-go pe-kyi' 墳裡个° 碑記
EPOCH, siang-kah'-go z-'eo' 相隔个° 時候
EQUAL, or *about — in age*, dong-nyin' siang-shü' 同年相歲°; *— in age and rank*, bing'-teng 並等; bing'-kyin 並肩; dong-pe' 同輩; *— in size*, ih-yiang' do' 一樣大°; *ditto* (as potatoes, apples &c.), diao-yüing' 調勻; *— parts*, kyüing-yüing' 均勻; *— value*, tso' kô'-din 同° 價錢°; *— days and nights*, tsiu'-yia bing 晝夜°平; *— weight*, ih-yiang djong' 一樣重; *I am not — to it*, ngô lih' sô feh-gyih' 我力所弗及; *you are not — to him*, ng feh gyih'-jü gyi' 你弗及其; *you are — to him*, ng sæ'-ko-jü gyi 你° 賽過如其; *make them —* (in size), tso'-leh diao-yüing' 做得° 調勻
EQUALLY, *divide them —* , kyüing-feng' 均分; feng'-leh diao-yüing' 分得° 調勻

EQUANIMITY, sing-seh'-feh-dong' 聲色弗動; *with perfect —* , c'ü'-ts t'æ'-jün 處之泰然
EQUATOR, ts'ih-dao' 赤道
EQUILIBRIUM, bing-ts'ing' 平稱; t'in-bing' 天平
EQINOX, *vernal —* , c'ing-feng' 春分; *autumnal —* , ts'iu-feng' 秋分
EQUIPPED, *fully* (arms prepared), kyüing-tsông' zi-be'-liao 軍裝齊備了
EQUITABLE, kong-dao' 公道; kong-bing' 公平
EQUIVALENT, *adj.* te'-diao 對調; *— expressions*, liang'-kyü shih'-wô i'-s siang-dong' 兩句說話意思相同; *to return an —* (as for a present received), wæn li' 還禮
EQUIVOCAL, 'en'-wu-dao'go 含糊道个°; *borrow the shadow of excuse* or *reason*, tsia'-ing go 借°因个°
EQUIVOCATE, *to* ing-yiang'-gæ' 陰陽戲; kông'-leh 'en-weng'-go 講得°含混个°; kông tsia'-ing-go shih-wô' 講°借°因'个°說話; kông 'en-wu-dao'-go shih-wô' 講°含糊道个°說話; *— in answering*, (*lit.* lean upon the question), gæ ing' 戤因
ERA, nyin-'ao' 年號 (nyin, the year of the reign, 'ao, the year of the cycle); *the Christian —* , Yiæ-su kyüông-shü' 耶穌降世

ERADICATE, to lin keng' bah-ky'i' 運根拔去°

ERASE, to — with a pen, du-diao' 塗壞°; — with a knife, ts'æn'-diao 鏟壞°

ERE, zin 前°; — he comes, gyi, vi-læ'-ts-zin' 其未來之前°; — long, peh kyiu' 不久

ERECT, to jü 堅; jü'-ky'i 堅起; — a house, jü oh' 堅屋; — a shed of matting or branches, tah bang' 搭棚; — a stage, tah dæ' 搭臺

ERECT, dzih 直; pih'-dzih 筆直; standing —, pih'-dzih lih'-tong 筆直立當; sit —, 'pih'-t'ing zo' 筆挺坐°

ERMINE skin, nying-c'ü'-bi 銀鼠皮

ERR, to wander from the right way, tseo ts'ô' lu 走义路; tseo' ts'o 走錯; — in judgment, ts'o'-cü'-i 錯主意; kyin'-sih dzæn 見識赚

ERRAND, an ih yiang ts'a-s' 一樣差使; I want you to do an —, ngô yiu ih-yiang ts'a-s' iao ng tso' 我有一樣差使要你°做

ERRAND-BOY, ts'a-dong'-go nying 差動个°人; ts'a-dong'-kyi-go 差動計个°; ts'a-s' 差使; t'ing-ts'a-go nying 聽差个°人

ERRATA, ngo-z' 訛字; ts'o' z 錯字

ERRATIC, ying-tsong'-vu-ding' 行踪無定

ERRONEOUS, ts'o 錯; yi-tön' 異端; zia 邪°; — doctrine, yi-tön'-go dao'-li 異端个°道理

ERROR, ts'o'-c'ü 錯處; ko'-shih 過失; ko'-tön 過端; sih'-tsiah 失著°

ERUPTION on the skin, le 累; a volcano in —, ho'-sæn læ-tih p'eng'-c'ih-læ 火山現°在°嘣出來

ESCAPE, to dao-tseo' 逃走; already escaped, dao-t'eh' de 逃脫了°; to — punishment, bi-ko ying-vah' 避過刑罰

ESCORT, to (as a mark of attention), song 送; be 陪; to protect on a journey, wu-song' 護送

ESOPHAGUS, zih-kwun 食管

ESPECIAL, di-ih' 第一; deo-ih' 頭一; of — importance di-ih' iao'-kying 第一要緊; you will pay — attention, ng iao di-ih' liu-sing' 你°要第一留心

ESPOUSE, to affiance, ding-ts'ing' 定親; to wed, tso ts'ing' 做親

ESSAY, a literary —, ih-p'in leng' 一篇論; a moral —, ky'ün' shü-veng 勸世文

ESSAY, to try, s'-s-k'en' 試試看; to make a trial of, s'-ih-s 試一試;

ESSENCE, *constituent qualities of any thing*, sing'-tsih 性質; — (as of beef), tsih'-shü 汁水°; — *of ginger*, kyiang-tsih' 薑汁; *fragrant* —, hyiang-tsih' 香汁 vulgarly called hyiang-shü' 香水°

ESSENTIAL, *cannot be dispensed with*, ky'üih'-feh-læ-go 缺弗來个°; hyih'-feh-læ-go 歇弗來个°; siao'-feh-teh-go 少弗得个°

ESTABLISH, *to* kyin-kwu' 堅固; *to make him or it stable*, peh' gyi lih lao' 俾° 其立定; *to institute*, shih'-lih 設立; kyin'-lih 建立

ESTATE, *condition*, di'-we 地位; *houses and lands*, ts'æn'-nyih 產業; *shops &c.*, kyi-nyih' 基業

ESTEEM, *to* k'en'-djong 看重; ky'i'-djong 器重

ESTEEMED, *he is to be* —, gyi dziah-djong'-go 其著重个°

ESTIMATE, *to* kwu-kwu'-k'en 估估看; — *the price*, kwu kô'-din 估價°錢°; — *present value*, z-dzih' kwu-kô' 時值估價°

ESTRANGE, *to become estranged*, sang su'-ky'i-læ 生°疏起來; — *entirely*, su 疏; — *(another)* li-kyin' 離間

ETERNAL, *without end*, üong'-yün 永遠; üong'-kwu ts'in-ts'iu' 永古千秋; vu gyüong'-dzing

無窮盡; *without beginning or end*, vu-s'-vu-cong' (cong or tsong) 無始無終; — *life*, üong-yün'weh-ming' 永遠活命; *ditto* (in the Taoist sense), dziang-seng' peh'-lao 長生不老

ETHICS, leng-djông'-ts dao' 倫常之道

ETIQUETTE, li 禮; *the rules of* —, li'-fah 禮法; *to observe ditto*, siu li'-fah 守禮法; *book on* —, li'-kyi shü 禮記書

ETYMOLOGY, *work on* —, shih'-veng 說文 (ih-ts'ah, ih-bu)

EULOGY, *a* ih-p'in' ts'ing-tsæn'-go veng' 一篇稱讚个°文

EUNUCH, t'a-kæn' 太監°; — *from birth*, dong-ts'-lao 童子老

EUPHONY, diao -'o' sing-ing'-go 調和聲°音个°

EVACUATE *the city*, t''e'-c'ih dzing' 退出城

EVADE, *to* to 躲; bi 避; to'-ko 躲過; bi'-ko 避過; — *difficulties*, to næn 躲難; — *the payment of debt*, to tsa' 躲債°; — *by putting upon another*, t'e-we 推諉; — *consequences*, sia ken-yi' 卸°干係

EVANGELICAL *doctrine*, foh'-ing tsing dao' 福音眞道

EVAPORATE, *to pass off in vapor*, ky'i sæn'-k'æ siu-zông 氣散開收上; c'ih-ky'i' 出氣; — *by the sun*, sa' sao 曬°燥; — *by the fire*, hong sao' 烘燥

EVA　　　　　155　　　　　EVE

EVASIVE *answer*, 'en-weng' we-teh' 含混回答

EVEN, *level*, bing 平; bing-dzih' 平直; — *numbers*, sông-su' 雙數; — *tempered*, sing-bing' ky'i-'o 心平氣和; 'o-bing' sing-kah 和平性格; *now we are* —, næn'-kæn hao tang bing-ts'ih 現°在°好打平尺; ah'-lah ts'ô bing-kyiao'-de, 我°等°扯平交了°

EVEN *you were there*, ng tao' yia we læ'-kæn 你°倒也°爲在°彼°; *he* — *would not wash his hands*, lin siu tu feh - k'eng gyiang' 連手都弗肯洗°; — *if you whip him he does not fear*, ziu-z tang' gyi yia feh p'ô' 就是打其也°弗怕

EVENING, yia-deo' 夜°頭; yia-tao' 夜°到; yia-mæn-den' 夜°晚°頭; *toward* —, yia-kw'a 夜°快°; *come this* —, *after you have eaten supper*, kyih-mih' yia'-tao yia'-væn ky'üoh'-ko læ 今°日°夜°到夜°飯吃°過來

EVENLY, bing 平; *regularly*, zi ch'i 齊°; zi-jih' 齊°集; *smoothly* (as paint), yüing 匀; yüing-zing' 匀淨; *rub it on* —, k'a'-leh diao-yüing 揩°得°調匀

EVENT, z-ken' 事°幹; z-t'i' 事°體; *joyful* —, hyi'-z 喜事; *a joyful* — *happened to us to day*, kyih-mih' ah-lah teh'-djoh ih-yiang' hyi'-z 今°日°我°等°得°

着°一樣喜事; kyih-mih' ah-lah k'æ-sing hwô' 今°日°我°等°開心花; *mournful* —, sông-sing'-go z-ken' 傷心个°事°幹; *future* —, vi-kæ'z or mi-kæ'z 未來事; *at all events, you will come*, se-tsih' z-ka' dæn-z ng' iao læ' 雖只如°此°, 但是你要來

EVENTFUL, *that was an* — *year*, keh ih-nyin' do-siao' z-t'i' væn'-leh-kying 這°一年大°小事°體繁得°緊

EVER, *always*, peh'-djông 不常; dziang-t'ong' 長通; *have you* — *met him?* dzong-zin'yiu we-djoh'-gyi-ko' ma 從前°有會着°其過嗎°? — *since that*, dzong-ts'yi-læ 從此以來; z-ts' ts-'eo' 自此之後; *for* — *and* —, tao shü'-shü dæ'-dæ 到世世代代

EVERGREEN *trees*, feh we kw'u'-go jü' 弗會枯个°樹

EVERLASTING, üong'-yün 永遠; m gyüong'-dzing 無窮盡; — *fire*, üong'-feh-u'-go hô' 永弗熄°个°火

EVERY, me 每; koh 各; — *day*, me' nyih 每日°; nyih-nyih' 日日°; — *one takes care of himself*, koh' nying kwun zi' 各人°管自°; — *body*, cong' nying 衆人°; — *body says*, da-tsong' wô' 大°衆話; ko'-ko nying 個個人; *goods of* — *kind*, pah'-yiang hŏ'-veh 百樣貨物; — one has his own idea, koh' yiu koh' i 各有各意

EVERY-WHERE, koh'-c'ü 各處; tao'-c'ü 到處; c'ü'-c'ü 處處; koh-tao'-c'ü 各到處; koh-tao'-koh-c'ü 各到各處; 'en'-tao-c'ü; kon'-koh-loh-loh' 角°角°落落 (lit. in every co ner.); I have looked — and cannot find it, ngô koh'-c'ü zing', on zing'-feh-d'jh' 我各處尋°都尋°弗著°

EVIDENCE, conclusive proof, tsing'-kyü 証據; bing-kyü' 憑據, jih-bing' jih-kyü 實憑實據; testimony, te'-tsing 對証; ocular —, kyin'-tsing 見証; — in a case, k'eo'-kong 口供

EVIDENT, have proof, yiu'-bing yiu-kyü' 有憑有據; cicarly to be seen, hyin'-kyin 顯見; ming-tông'-tông hao k'en'-kyin 明當當好看見

EVIL, oh 惡; to do —, troh oh' 作惡; forsake —, oh' z-ken' ky'i'-diao 惡事幹棄了°; forsake the —, fol'ow the good, kæ-oh'-dzong-jün' 改惡從善; I certainly love no —inter's against you, ngô bing'-m-neh' oh'-i dæ ng' 我並無°惡意待你°; — spirit, oh' kyü 惡鬼; mo-kwe' 魔鬼 (ih-go); Mo kwe in the Bible stands for The Evil Ol.e; return — for —, yi-oh' pao-oh 以惡報惡; yiu'-dziu pao-dziu' 有讎報讎; return — for good, yi-oh' pao-teh' 以惡報德; eng-tsiang' dziu-pao' 恩將讎報; return good for —, yi-teh' pao-oh' 以德報惡; — star, hyüong sing' 凶星; carry — reports, pun-teo' z'-fi 搬兜是非; pun-cü' 搬嘴

EWE, ts'i'-yiang 雌羊 (ih' tsah)

EWER, miu-shü-bing 面水瓶

EXACT, accurate, cing 准; my clock is very —, ngô̂ go cong' ting cing 我个鐘頂准; precise, en'-pæn-ts 按板子

EXACTLY, k'eo'-k'eo 扣扣; tsing 真; — right, ih-ngæn'-feh-ts'o' 一點°弗錯; 'ao-li'-feh-ts'o' 毫厘弗錯; 'ao'-feh-t'e'-pen 毫弗推班; do not agree, shü-vi' ts'o'-ih-ngæn' 些微差°一點°; sao-we' feh-te' 稍爲弗對; corresp nds —, 'eo-feng'-'eo-su' 候分候數; feng-ngæn'-feng-shing 分眼分樁; ky'iah'-k'eo; — suits my taste (as food), keh-go' mi-dao te ngô zih-sing ky'iah-k'eo 這个味°道對我食性个°; — wh it I wanted, sih'-vong ngô-go i' 適逢我个意

EXAGGERATE, to kông-ko-deo' 講過頭; hah'-sæn-wô'-shü 嚇山話水°

EXAGGERATED talk; vu-ky'i'-deng-deng shih-wô' 霧氣騰

膁說話;— boasting, c'ô'-kæn sbih-kw'ch' 扯誕說闊

EXALT làm, tseng gyi' zông' 發其上; dæ-gɔi' kao 擡其高; — above merit, dae leh pun' t'iõ kao' 擡得°半天高

EXAMINE, to dzô-ts'ah' 查察; t'i'-ts'ah 體察; nying 贐; — one's-self, zi dzô'-ts'ah zi' 自°查察自°; — for a degree, k'ao'-s 考試; — pupils, k'ao' 'oh-sang-ts' 考學°生°子; — into the nature of things, keh veh' 格物; poh veh' 博物; — (as an offender), keng-dzô' 跟查; bun-dzô' 盤查; — by asking questions, bun-kyih' 盤詰

EXAMINATION hall (for examining siu-dzæ), ts'ah-yün' 察院; ditto (for examining kyü-nying). kong'-yün 貢院

EXAMINER, customs' nyin'-ho-siu 驗貨手

EXAMPLE, pông'-yiang 榜樣; piao'-yiang 表樣; set a good —, lih' ih-go hao' pông'-yiang 立一个°好榜樣; will follow your —, we keng' ng-go pông'-yiang 會跟你个°榜樣; we k'en' ng-go yiang' 會看你°个°樣; give me an —, yüong ih-go pi'-fông peh ngô t'ing' 用一个°比方俾°我聽; examples in phrases, kyü-nyü'-deo 句語頭

EXASPERATE, to — làm, kyih' gyi-go nu' 激其个°怒; ts'oh'-gyi-go nu' (ts'oh or c'oh) 觸其个°怒; ts'oh'-væn gyi-go ô'-wông.

EXCAVATE, to gyüih-c'ih'-læ 掘出來; dao ih-go den' 掏一个°潭

EXCEED, to ko 過; to — the appointed time, nyih-ts' kc-deo' 日°子過頭; ko gyi' 過期; to be greater than, ko'-jü 過如; do-jü' 大°如; no love exceeds a mother's, æ'-sih-siung do'-jü ah-nyiang m'-teh-gɔ 愛惜心大°如阿娘沒°有°个°; — the bounds of propriety, yüih-c'ih'-kwe-kyü' 越出規矩

EXCEL, to ken' zông-zin' 趕上前; tseo' zông-zin' 走上前°; strive to —, ts'iang'-ts'iang zông-zin' 蹌蹌上前°; I cannot — làm, ngô feh neng'-keo ken' gyi zông-zin' 我弗能彀趕其上前°

EXCELLENCY, his or your —, da-jing' 大人; his —, Mr. Way, We' Da-jing' 衛大人

EXCELLENT, yin 賢; yiu-teh' 賢德; — man, kyüing s' 君子; nying liang-jün' 人°良善; thoroughly — man, yi.-liang' fông'-tsing 賢良方正; — flavor, mi-dao' gyih-miao' 味°道極妙; — plan, miao fah' 妙法; — idea, miao i' 妙意; — penman's p, miao pih' 妙筆; — woman, nyü'-nying sang'-leh miao′ 女人°生°得°妙; nyü′-nying sang′-leh kyüô′ 女人°生°得°佳 (in the Chinese sense of excellence, i.e. dutiful affable and intelligent).

EXCEPT, unless, jü-ziah′ 如若

EXCEPT, EXCEPTING, djü-c'ih 除出; djü′ 除, with ts-nga′ 之外°; all were there — him, djü gyi ts-nga′ tu læ′-kæn 除其之外°都在彼°

EXCEPTIONS, with few —, væn cong-ts ih′ 萬中之一; ts'in-cong′ siao-yiu′-go 千中少有个°

EXCESS, surplus, to-deo′ 多頭; good to —, ko′-ü hao′ 過于好; eat, drink, or do anything to —, ko liang 過量; ko-du′ 過度; ko veng 過分

EXCESSIVE, EXCESSIVELY, the heat is excessive, or it is excessively hot, nyih ko-deo′ 熱過頭; — stupid, ko′-ü beng′ 過于笨; — angry, ông tao gyih-deo′ 怒到極頭; jih-feng′ ô-wông.

EXCHANGE, to diao-wun′ 調換; te′-diao 對調; — for good and all, diao-jih′ 調實; diao-k'æ′ 調開; — this for a better pen, diao ih-ts′ hao-tin′-go pih′ 調一枝好點个°筆; wun′ ih-ts′ hao-tin′-go 換一枝好點个°

EXCITABLE, yüong-yi′ fah′-dong 容易發動

EXCITE, to dong 動; kyih 激

kyih′-dong 激動; tang′-dong 打動; ts'e-dong′ 催動; — him to anger, or to fight, yüong gyi′-go kyih′-kong 用其个°激工; — to discord, t'iao-so′ 挑唆; — to action, kyih′-li 激勵; — to gratitude, ken′-kyih 感激

EXCLAIM, to cry out, byiang′-ky'i-læ 響起來; eo-ky'i′-læ 喊°起來

EXCLUDE, to djü-c'ih′ 除出; djü-ky'i′ 除去°

EXCLUDING, djü 除; ts-nga′ 之外°; — this, djü-ts'′ ts-nga′ 除此之外°

EXCLUSIVE, not wishing to associate with others, gah-de′-feh-long′ 湊°隊弗攏; kao-p'ing′-feh-long 交°摒弗攏

EXCOMMUNICATE, to ken′-c'ih kong-we′ 趕出公會; ken-c'ih kyiao′ 趕出教

EXCORIATE, to rub off the skin, bi ts'ah′-ky'i 皮擦去°; bi mo-ky'i′ 皮磨去°

EXCREMENT, bi 屎; liao 料; feng 糞; — of birds, tiao-o′ 鳥°屎°

EXCRUCIATING pain, kw'u′-t'ong 苦痛

EXCUSABLE, very dzing′ yiu k'o nyün′ 情有可原

EXCUSE, to use or borrow as an —, tsia ing-deo′ 借°因頭

EXCUSE, to regard with indulgence, kw'un-shü′ 寬恕; 1

beg you to — me, ts'ing' ng kw'un-shü' ngô 請你°寬恕我; ditto for some inadvertency, teh'-ze 得罪; shih-kwu' 失顧; —(as for a fault, or for absence), nyün-liang' 原諒; — me, for not accompanying you (as to the gate), kw'un-shü' ngô feh song' ng 寬恕我弗送你°; ditto to a greater distance (as to the boat), shü ngô' feh yün'-song ng 恕我弗遠送你° — me from doing, min' ngô tso' 免我做; cannot —, min'-feh-læ 免勿來; to feel for and —, t'i'-liang 體諒; — another's fault, pao yüong' 包容

EXECRABLE, k'o'-u-go 可惡°个°

EXECRATE, to abhor, 'eng-gyih' 恨極; to curse, tsiu'-mô 咒罵

EXECUTE, to tso 做; — orders, t'ing feng-fu' 聽吩附; tsiao feng-fu' 照吩附 (tso may be either expressed, or understood); — for a crime, sah'-ze 殺罪; four criminals are to be executed (by beheading), s'-go væn'-nying iao sah-deo' 四个°犯人°要殺頭

EXECUTION ground, sah'-dziang 殺塲; fah'-dziang 法塲 (ih t'ah)

EXECUTIONER, 'ong-gyi'-siu 紅旗手; kwe'-ts-siu 刽子手 (ih-go)

EXECUTOR, ziu coh'-t'oh go nying 受囑託个°人°

EXEMPLARY, hao tso piao'-yiang 好做表樣; tsing'-p'a-go 正派个°

EXEMPLIFY, to piao'-ming 表明

EXEMPT, to min 免; — from soldier's duty, min' tông-ping' 免當兵

EXEMPTION certificate (customs'), min' se-tæn 免稅單

EXERCISE the body, 'ang-dong' sing'-t'i 行°動身體

EXERT, to c'ih 出; — strength c'ih-lih' 出力; — skill, c'ih siu'-dön 出手段; — one's self, zi' zông'-kying 自°上緊; — one's self greatly, nu' lih 努力; — one's self when weak, ts'ang 撐; ditto (still more), ngang ts'ang' 硬撐; — to the utmost si' ts'ang 死°撐

EXHALATION, vapor, ky'i 氣; noxious —, we'-ky'i 穢氣; tsông ky'i' 瘴氣; poisonous —, doh ky'i' 毒氣; offensive —, ts'iu' ky'i 臭°氣; dzoh ky'i' 濁氣; hurtful — from the earth, t'u' ky'i 土氣

EXHALE from the ground, di-yiang' ky'i' c'ih 地下°氣出; the flowers — their fragrance, hwô t'u'-c'ih hyiang-ky'i' 花吐出香氣

EXHAUST, to use up, yüong-wun' 用完; — the strength, ky'i-lih

yüong-wun' 氣力用完; t'eh lih' 脫力; *exhausted by walking*, ky'i'-lih tseo'-wun-de 氣力走完了°.

EXHIBIT, *to show*, lu-c'ih' 露出; hyin'-c'ih 顯出; *exhibits a bad disposition*, lu'-c'ih ẅa sing'-kah' 露出孬°性格; *he exhibits great patience*, hyin'-c'ih gyi-go jing'-næ feh' siao 顯出其个°忍耐弗少; — *goods*, pa'-k'æ ho'-veh 擺開貨物; — *choice things in temples*, pa-tsi' 擺祭.

EXHILARATE, *to* dzn hying' 助興; *he is exhilarated with wine*, gyi hying'-cü z tsiu' dzu' go 其興致是酒助个°; — *with opium*, a-p'in' di tsing-jing' 鴉片提精神.

EXHORT, *to* ky'ün 勸; — *earnestly*, sah'-k'eo ky'ün' 用°力°勸; kô gying-dao' ky'ün 加勸道勸.

EXILE, *one exiled for breaking the laws*, kyüing-væn' 軍犯.

EXILE, *to* bæn ts'ong-kyüing' 辦充軍 See BANISH.

EXIST *always*, djông-djông' yiu' 常常有.

EXISTENT, *self* z-jün'-r-jün yiu'-go 自然而然有个°.

EXONERATED, *to be* — *from blame*, ze'-ming t'eh'-diao-de 罪名脫了°.

EXORBITANT, do hyü'-deo 大°虛價°; — *charges*, t'ao' kô, hah'- sæn wô-shü' 討價°嚇山話水°.

EXORBITANTLY *dear*, t'æ kyü' 太貴°; kyü ko-deo' 貴過頭; kah'-nga kyü 格外°貴°; t'ao' kô mông-bah-yiang-yiang 討價°漫°白洋洋.

EXORCISE, *to* — *by the Taoist divinity*, vong Nyüoh-wông-da'-ti ts'-i djü zia' 奉玉皇大帝旨意除邪°.

EXOTIC *plants*, nga-koh' læ-go hwô'-moh 外°國來个°花木.

EXPAND, *to* — (as rice in boiling, seeds, &c.) *or to dilate upon*, hwô'-k'æ 化開; — (as a bird its wings), tô'-k'æ 撐°開; gwah'-k'æ; — (as flowers, leaves, &c.) fông'-k'æ 放開; — *the mind*, k'æ sing ky'iao' 開心竅; k'æ ky'iao'-meng 開竅門; — (as water in freezing), kao-k'æ' 膠°開; tsiang 脹; tsiang'-k'æ 脹開.

EXPANSE, *a great* mang-yiang'-yiang 漫°洋洋; *the firmament*, ky'üong-ts'ông' 穹蒼.

EXPECT, *to* siang'-pih 想必; *suppose*, liao 料; *think*, siang 想; ts'eng 忖; *I* — *guests*, ngô siang'-pih nying-k'ah' læ 我想必客人°來; *I* — *him*, ngô liao-tao' gyi læ 我料到其來; ngô peng'-i zin-deo' siang læ' 我本意前°頭想來; *could not be expected*, i'-siang-feh-tao' 意想弗到; *constantly expecting*,

læ-tih yün'-vông 在°此°懸望
EXPECTORATE, to t'u dæn' 吐痰
EXPEDIENT, fitting, ü li' siang-nyi' 于禮和宜; profitable, yiu ih' 有益; yiu bin-i' 有便宜°
EXPEDIENT, an ih-go fah'-ts 一个°法子; ih-go fông-fah' 一个°方法
EXPEDITE, to do quickly, ken'-kying tso' 趕緊做; kw'a'-soh tso' 快°快°做
EXPEL, to ken'-c'ih 趕出; kah'-diao 革去; — by bad means, p'ih-c'ih' 撇出
EXPEND, to use, yüong 用; — much time and strength, yüong kong-fu' teng sing-lih' feh siao' 用工夫等心力弗少
EXPENDITURE, k'æ-siao' 開銷; yüong-dziang' 用場
EXPENSE, yüong'-du 用度; great —, yüong'-du-do' 用度大°; extra —, to fi' 多費
EXPENSES, 'æn-fi' 開°費; profitless — (as money given to officials), fi'-yüong 費用; — (of any establishment), kyiao'-yüong 繳°用; k'æ-kyiao' 開繳; family —, kô-yüong' 家°用; kô'-li-go kyiao'-yüong 家°裡个°繳°用 — that may be cut down, dao-yiao'; what are your daily —? ng' nyih-nyih' iao to-siao' k'æ-kyiao' 你°日°日°要多少開繳? travelling —,

bun-fi' 盤費; bun-jün' 盤纏°
EXPERIENCE, to pass through, yüih-lih' 閱歷; kying-lih' 經歷; has experienced (as hardships), kying-fong' kying-lông' ko-de 經風經浪過了°; sông'-shih ah'-ko de 霜雪壓過了°
EXPERIENCE, of large —, veng-kwô'-cü to' 聞寡知多; kyin'-kwông-sih-da' 見廣識大; tell one's —, kông tsong-dziang' 講裹腸; kông tsong-ky'üoh' 講裹曲 (ih-fæn)
EXPERIENCED man, nying lao'-lin' 人°老練; yüih'-lih-ko'-go nying' 閱歷過个°人°; nying kyiu-lin'-dzing kông' 人°久練成鋼; — hand, joh siu' 熟手
EXPERIMENT, to tsoh'-mo 琢磨; tsoh'-mo-ky'i-k'en' 且琢磨看
EXPERT, jih-kwæn' 習慣; very —, jih-kwæn' dzing z-jün' 習慣成自然; nô siu'-hyi 鐢手戲; — and then inventive, joh-neng' seng ky'iao' 熟能生巧
EXPIATE, to — sin, joh ze' 贖罪
EXPIRATION of a time, z-'eo' wun'-de 時候完了°; gyi-deo' mun'-de 期頭滿了°; nyih-ts' mun'-de 日°子滿了°
EXPLAIN, to ka'-shih 解說; — clearly, ka'-shih ming-bah' 解°說明白; can you — it to me? ng hao ka'-shih peh ngô t'ing' feh 你°好解°說俾°我聽否°?

EXPLANATION, verbal kông'-ka 講°解°; written —, cü'-ka 註解°; I cannot understand his —, gyi'-go kông'-ka ngô t'ing'-leh feh ts'ing-ts'u' 其个°講°解° 我聽得°弗清楚

EXPLETIVE, hyü'-z-ngæn 虛字眼°; — for rounding a sentence, cün'-tsih-go z-ngæn' 轉折个°字眼°.

EXPLICIT, ts'ing-t'ong' 清通; ming-bah' 明白; nothing hidden, 'o-bun' t'oh'-c'ih 和盤托出

EXPLODE, to pao'-k'æ 爆開

EXPLOIT, fi-dzông'-ts z' 非常之事

EXPLORE, to dzô-k'ao' 查考; — a region, dzô-k'ao' di-fông'-go dzing-ying' 查考地方个°情形

EXPORT, to ho tsông-c'ih-ky'i' 貨裝出去°.

EXPORTS, c'ih'-k'eo ho'-veh 出口貨物

EXPOSE, to lu-c'ih' 露出; c'ih-lu'-lu 出露露°; — the face, min-k'ong' c'ih-lu'-lu 面孔出露露°; — the person, c'ih'-sing-lu'-t'i 出身露體; — one's self to public gaze (in reproach), c'ih'-kwa-lu-ts'iu' 出乖°露醜; — his shame, c'ih' gyi-go ts'iu' 出其个° 醜; — one's faults, shü' pu'-læn-kæn 數°布襴裪; — (another's secrets), toh'-p'o 挑°破; the countryman exposes his ignorance of the rules of so-ciety, hyiang-'ô'-nying iao ky'in t'u 鄉下°人°顯°出°土氣°

EXPOSTULATE, to c'ih'-lih ky'ün' 出力勸; kw'u'-kw'u ky'ün' 苦苦勸

EXPOUND, to (in speaking), kông'-ka 講°解°; — (in writing), cü'-ka 註解°

EXPRESS, to — in words, kông'-c'ih-læ 講°出來; cannot —, kông'-feh'-c'ih'-læ 講°弗出來; cannot — adequately, kông'-feh-tao' 講°弗到

EXPRESS, to — oil, tsô-yiu' 榨油

EXPRESS, footman, ta-kyih'-sing-go 帶急信个°; — who runs by stages (formerly horseman), ts'in-li'-mô 千里馬

EXPRESSION, an ih-kyü' shih-wô' 一句說話; a phrase, ih-kyü', kyü-nyü'-deo 一句句語頭; familiar —, dzoh-wô' 俗話; forced —, min'-ky'iang shih-wô' 勉强說話

EXPRESSIVE countenance, min-k'ong' weh-siang' 面孔活相

EXPRESSLY, on purpose, deh-we' 特爲; deh-i' 特意; kwu'-i 故意; plainly, ming-ming' 明明

EXPUNGE, to (as an idea), sæn-kæ' 刪改; — with a pin, du-diao' 塗壞°; wipe out, k'a'-diao 揩壞°.

EXQUISITE, beautiful, me'-li 美麗; delicate, si'-cü 細緻; — workmanship, si'-ky'iao' sang-weh' 細巧生°活

EXTEMPORIZE, to ze-k'eo kông'-c'ih 隨口講°出; ze-i' kông'-c'ih 隨意講°出; kông'-c'ih sön'-tsiang 講°出算帳; *extemporizes well*, c'ih-k'eo'-dzing-tsông' 出口成章

EXTEND, to — (as reports, rivers), t'ong-k'æ' 通開; — (as disease, fire, customs), yin-k'æ' 延開; — (as liquids spilt), seng'-k'æ 沁開; — *to every part*, tsiu-tao' 周到; — *the hand*, sing siu' 伸手; — *the arm*, siu' sing-dzih 手伸直; — (lie) *at full length*, dzih kw'eng' 直睡°

EXTENSIVE, kwông'-kw'eh 廣闊; *the ruin caused by the flood is* —, tsao'-djoh shü'-tsæ di'-fông kwông'-kw'eh-leh-kying' 遭著水°災地方廣闊得緊; — *learning*, 'oh-veng poh' 學°問博

EXTENT, *what is the — of his learning?* gyi-go dzæ-'oh' yiu kyi feng' 其个°才學°有幾分? *what is the — of the flood?* do-shü' tsao'-djoh to'-siao di'-fông 大°水°遭著多少地方?

EXTENUATE, to — (as a fault), kæn ky'ing' 減輕; *will* —, hao ky'ing-k'o' 好輕可

EXTERIOR, *the outside*, nga-deo' 外°頭; nga-pin' 外°邊; *the outer surface*, nga min' 外°面

EXTERMINATE, to djih-diao' 絕壞°; — *utterly*, mih-wun' 滅完; tsæn-ts'ao' djü-keng' 斬草除根

EXTERNAL *appearance*, nga-kwông' min 外°光面; nga meng'-min 外°門面

EXTINCT, *volcano is* —, ho'-sæn si'-de 火山死了°; *some species of animals are* —, yiu kyi le' cong-sang' djih-cong'-de 有幾類畜°牲°絕種了°

EXTINGUISH *fire*, mih ho' 滅火; — *the lamp*, teng-tsæn' long gyi u' 燈盞弄其熄°; — *a fire*, kyiu ho' 救火; *hopes are extinguished*, siang'-vông ziang ho' p'eh-u'-de 想望像火澄熄°了

EXTIRPATE, to djih-wun' 絕完 lin keng' bah-diao' 連根拔去°

EXTOL, to dzong'-tsæn 頌讚

EXTORT, to *force*, pih'-leh 逼勒; — *a confession from him*, pih-leh gyi' tsiao-jing' 逼勒其招°認; — *money*, leh-soh dong-din' 勒索銅錢°; — soh-tsô dong-din' 索詐銅錢°

EXTRACT, to bah-diao' 拔去°; bah-c'ih' 拔出; bah-loh' 拔落 tsoh'-diao 劇壞; — *essence* (by soaking), tsih'-shü tsing'-c'ih 汁水°浸出

EXTRAORDINARY, kah-nga' 格外°; fi-dzông' 非常; fi-væn' 非凡

EXTRAVAGANT, to be — *in using*, lông'-yüong 浪用; lông'-fi 浪費; *to be wasteful*, hwô'-fi 花費

EXTREME, gyih-deo' 極頭; *bad*

in the —, ẅa' tao gyih-deo' 尋 到 極 頭; to be in — poverty, gyüong-gyih'-de 窮 極 了°
EXTREMITY, at the — of the road, (also used fig.), tao zing'-deo 到 盡 頭; in —, vu lu' k'o tseo' 無 路 可 走
EXTRICATE, to t'eh'-c'ih 脫 出; t'eng'-c'ih; di-bah' 提 拔; — from difficulty, kyiu næn' 救 難; he extricated me from difficulty, (or owing to him I was &c.), ky'ü'-leh gyi' keh-go næn-deo' ngô t'eh'-c'ih-de 虧°得°其這° 个° 難 頭 我 脫 出 了°
EXUBERANT spirits, hyi'- ky'i yiang-yiang' 喜 氣 揚 揚; ditto in talking, hyi'-siao yin-k'æ' 喜 笑 言 開
EXULTANT, hwun-t'in'-hyi-di' 歡 天 喜 地; hwun-hyi' jü-yü' teh-sô' 歡 喜 如 魚 得 水; — triumph of soldiers, k'ao' teh-sing' kwu 敲° 得 勝 鼓
EYE, ngæn'-tsing 眼° 睛 (ih-tsah); ngæn'-moh 眼° 目; needle's —, tsing-ngæn' 針 眼°; see with one —, doh ngæn' k'en 獨 眼° 看
EYES, bright ngæn'-tsing liang' 眼° 睛 亮; both —, sông-ngæn' 雙 眼°; see with one's own —, ts'ing ngæn' k'en' 親 眼° 看; before one's —, læ ngæn'-zin 在° 眼° 前°; — open, ngæn'-tsing k'æ'-tih 眼° 睛 開 的; — shut, ngæn'-tsing pi'-tih 眼° 睛 閉 的

EYE, to — closely, ngæn'-tsing ts'ing'-ting k'en' 眼° 睛 瞪 盯 看
EYE-BALL, ngæn'-u cü' 眼° 烏 珠; ngæn'-cü 眼° 珠
EYE-BROWS, mi-mao' 眉° 毛; the forehead just above the —, medeo' 眉 頭
EYE-LASHES, ngæn'-seh mao' 眼° 睫° 毛
EYE-LIDS, ngæn'-p'ao-bi' 眼° 泡 皮
EYE-SERVANT, yiu min-zin' pe-'eo'-go nying 有 面 前° 背 後 个° 人°
EYE-SIGHT, ngæn'-kwông 眼° 光; ngæn'-lih 眼° 力; ngæn'-fah 眼° 法
EYE-WITNESS, ts'ing ngæn' k'en'-kyin-go nying 親 眼° 看 見 个° 人°; was an —, ts'ing-ngæn'-moh-tu' ko-de 親 眼° 目 睹 過 了°

F

FABLE, yü-yin' 喻 言 (ih-go); Æsop's Fables, I-sô-bô'-go yü-yin' 伊 沙 婆 个° 喻 言
FABRICATE, to devise falsely, nyiah-zao'-c'ih-læ 揑 造° 出 來; zi' tso yin-nyü' 自° 做 言 語
FABULOUS, hwông - dæn - peh - kying' 荒 誕 不 經; — ages, miao'-môeng z-shü' 渺 茫 時 世
FACE, min-k'ông' 面 孔 (ih-fu); ô'- lin 丫 臉 (in a bad sense); no shame, m-ô'-lin 無° 臉° 恥°;

— *to face*, te' min 對面; *to open the — by pulling hairs* (as for a Chinese bride), k'æ min' 開面; *surface*, min-teng' 面子°.

FACE, *to — the south*, dziao nen' 朝南; *in what direction does this house —?* keh tsing oh' hyiang'-dao dziao soh'-go 這° 進屋向道朝甚°麼°? *to turn the — away*, min-k'ong' nyin-cün' bih-hyiang' 面孔側°轉別向.

FACETIOUS, we byiah'-yin 會諧言.

FACILITATE, *to* s'-teh yüong-yi' 使得容易; s'-teh sang'-lih 使得省力.

FACILITIES, bin-tông' 便當; *many —*, hyü'-to bin-tông' 許多便當; yiang-yiang' bin-tông' 樣樣便當.

FACILITY, *he does it with great —*, gyi-go siu'-shü weh-p'eh' 其个°手勢活潑; gyi-go siu'-shü jing-dzeh' 其个°手勢潤澤.

FACING, hyiang'-djoh 向著; — *outward*, dziao nga' 朝外°.

FACT, *it is a —*, keh' z jih-z' 這°是實事; *the facts*, jih-dzing' 實情; jih-tsih' 實節.

FACTION *having injurious designs*, nyih tông' 逆黨; *that —*, keh' ih tông kyih'-long 這°一黨結攏.

FACTOR, tsóng-k'ah' 莊客.

FACTORY, *manufactory*, do coh'-dziang 大°作塲; — *where factors do business*, siao' z-'ao' 小字號; *The Foreign Factories at Canton*, jih-sæn 'ông 十三行.

FACULTY, *mental ability*, dzæ-neng' 才能; — *of speech*, neng shih' neng wô' 能說能話.

FADE, *to —* (by exposure or age), ngæn-seh in' 顏°色蔫; — (by washing &c.), ngæn-seh t'e'-diao 顏°色退了°.

FAG-END *of a web of cloth*, kyi-deo' 機頭; — *of cotton cloth*, kyi-deo' pu 機頭布.

FAGGED *out*, kw'eng'-vah-de 困乏了°.

FAGOT, *a bundle of brush with the leaves*, yih-za' 葉柴°; nyün'-za 軟°柴° (ih-pô).

FAIL, *to be insufficient*, ky'in 欠; *to grow less by degrees*, dzin'-dzin ky'üih'-long-ky'i' 漸漸缺攏去°; *strength is failing*, lih-ky'i' læ-tih sæ' 力氣將衰; *you have failed in your duty*, ng'-go meng-veng' ky'in tsiu'-tao 你°个°名°分°欠周到; *to — in doing a thing*, z-ken shih'-ngwu 事幹失悞; *the firm has failed*, 'ông tao'-de 行倒了°; 'ông tao'-diao-de 行倒壞了°.

FAIL, *I will come without —*, cing'-ding-feh-ngwu' ngô læ'-gyi; ngô ih-ding læ 我一定來.

FAILING, mao-bing' 毛病; oh'-mao-bing 惡毛病.

FAILURE, feh' tao'-kô 弗到家°; shih'-ngwu 失悞; — *in answering* (expectations), feh mun'-i 弗滿意

FAIN, *would — do it*, pô-feh-neng'-keo tso' 巴弗能彀做

FAINT *from weariness*, ky'i' feh tsih' 氣弗接; t'eh-lih' 脫力; — *and fall*, yüing'-tao 暈倒; *about to —*, hweng-dzing-dzing' 昏沉沉; *to — away*, fah yüing' 發暈; ao'-ky'i 暈°去°

FAINT *sound*, sing-hyiang' ing-ing'-dong 聲響隱隱動; — *color*, ngæn-seh dæn' 顏色淡; ts'in' seh 淺色

FAINT-HEARTED, m̄-tæn'-ky'i-go 無°膽氣个°; gyü-ky'ih' 懼怯

FAIR, *clear* (as water), ts'ing 清; — *weather*, t'in-zing 天晴; — *complexion*, bi-fu bah-t'oh' 皮膚白; — *wind*, jing fong' 順風; — *price*, kô'-din bing-dzih' 價°錢°平直; — *dealing*, dzih-ky'i' 直氣; dzih sông' 直爽; *beautiful*, me'-mao 美貌; — *outside, defective within*, nga yin yü', r ne' peh tsoh' 外°有餘而內不足 (veng.)

FAIR, *market*, z'-nyih 市日°; *the* — (held in Ningpo when the chancellor comes), di-'oh'-da 考°市°

FAITH, siang-sing'-go sing 相信个°心; *the virtue of —*, sing'-tch 信德; — *in Christ*, siang-sing' Kyi-toh-go sing 相信基督个°心°

FAITHFUL, cong-sing'-go 忠信个°; — *to one's word*, yin-ying' siang-vu' 言行相符; — *words, displeasing to the ear, but beneficial*, "cong-yin' nyih r' li' ü ying'" 忠言逆耳利於行 (veng.)

FAITHLESS, *unbelieving*, feh siang'-sing-go 弗相信个°; — *to promises*, k'eo'-z, sing-fi' 口是心非; m̄ sing'-iah 無°信約

FALL, *to — over*, tih'-tao 跌倒; — *from a higher place*, tih'-loh 跌落; — *behind*, loh 'eo' 落後; — *from a horse*, tih'-loh mô' 跌落馬; — *to pieces, or come apart*, t'ah'-k'æ 塌開; t'ah loh 塌落; — (as a house), t'æn'-loh 坍落; t'æn-tao' 坍倒; — *entirely*, t'æn-t'ah' 坍塌; tao'-t'ah 倒塌; *ready to — from rot*, me'-de 霉了°; — (as hair, teeth, fruit, &c.), t'eng'-loh 脫°落; — (as flowers), zia 謝°; *the tide is falling*, dziao-shü' t'e'-de 潮水退了°; dziao-shü' læ-tih t'e'-loh 潮水現°在°退落; — *into sin*, 'æn'-loh ze'-li 陷°落罪裡; *lest you — into a bad habit*, k'ong'-p'ô ng wa-yiang' 'oh-kwæn' 恐怕你孥°樣學°慣; — *in love with*, ngæn'-tsing k'en'-leh tih'-loh, 眼°睛看得°跌落

FALLACIOUS words, hyü-sih'-ts dz' 虛飾之詞; tsông-sih'-c'ih-læ-go shih-wô' 裝飾出來个°說話

FALLIBLE, we ts'o' 會錯

FALLOW, pale yellow, dæn wông' 淡黃; uncultivated land, hwông din' 荒田

FALSE, kô 假°; hyü 虛; vu 誣; ngwe 僞; feh-kwe-jih' 弗歸實; to bear — witness, kô'-tso te'-tsing 假°做對証; vông'-tsing 妄証;— much, true little, hyü to' jih siao' 虛多實少°;— doctrines, zia dao'-li 邪°道理;— reputation, yiu-ming'-vu-jih' 有名無實;— report, ngo djün' 訛傳

FALSEHOOD, hwông'-wô 謊話; hyü-wô' 虛話; tell a —, kông hwông'-wô 講°謊話; kông hyü-wô' 講°虛話; shih hwông' 說謊

FALTERING accents, ňg-ňg'-nga-nga-go shih-wô' 唔唔噯噯°个°說話;— steps, kyiah'-bu c'ong'-c'ong-dong; kyiah'-bu k'ô'-feh-wěng' 脚步拿°弗穩

FAME, ming-vông' 名望; ambitious for —, t'en ming' 貪名; (person) of great —, yiu do ming-vông' 有大°名望

FAMED places, yiu'-ming'-go di'-fông 有名个°地方; far —, ming-yiang'-s-hæ 名揚四海

FAMILIAR with, joh 熟;— with the classics, kying-shü' joh-go' 經書熟个°;— friend, siang-hao' beng-yiu' 相好朋友;— expression, jing-joh'-go shih-wô' 順熟个°說話

FAMILY, kô 家°; a — or the head of a —, ih-veng nying-kô' 一分人°家°; one's immediate —, oh'-li 家°裡; oh'-li-go nying' 家°裡个°人°; kô-kyün' 家°眷; kô-siao' 家°小; the Li —, Li-kô' 李家°; whole —, 'eh kô' 合家°; all of the same — name, 'eh dzoh 合族; zi-kô-nying 自°家°人°; — name, sing 姓; have you a —? tseng-fu' yiu jü 尊府有誰°? yiu kô-siao' m̀'-teh 有家°小沒°有°? is your — well? ng-lah fu'-zông tu hao' feh 你府上都好否°? (familiarly) ne'-kyün hao' feh 內眷好否°? did your — come with you? ng'-go pao'-kyün dong-læ' feh 你个°寶眷同來否°? a rich —, fu'-kô 富家°; ing-wu' 殷戶; poor —, gyüong nying'-kô 窮人°家°; ruined —, ky'ing'-kô dông-ts'æn' 傾家°蕩產; he is a disgrace to his —, gyi' tao ih-kô'-go mư' 其倒一家°个°楣; all under heaven are one —, t'in-'ô' ih-kô' 天下一家°; how many families? kyi veng' nying'-kô

幾爻人°家°? to-siao′ in-tsao′ 多少烟竈? — *worship*, 'eh-kô′ li-pa 合家°禮拜°.

FAMINE, *year of* —, hwông-nyin′ 荒年; *seven years of* —, ts'ib′ nyin do-hwông-nyin 七年大荒年.

FAMISH, *to* ngo-sah′ 餓殺

FAMOUS, c'ib-ming′-go 出名个°; — *even to the capital*, ming′-cing ti′-tu 名震帝都

FAN, sin′-ts 扇子 (ib-pô); *feather* —, (*i. e.* of hawk feathers), ing-mao′ sin 鷹毛扇; *white folding* —, bah-pæn′ sin 白紙°扇; *black ditto*, yiu-ts′ sin 油紙扇; *round silk* —, yüih-kong′ sin 月宮扇; *palm-leaf* —, pô-tsiao′ sin 芭蕉扇; *close the* —, sin′-ts hao siu-long 扇子好收攏; *open the* —, sin′-ts t'æn-t'æn′-k'æ 扇子攤攤開

FAN, *to* tang sin′ 打扇; — *one's self*, zi sin-sin 自°扇扇

FANCY, *to imagine*, i'-ngwu 意悟; *I have a — for that child*, keh′-go siao-nying′ ngô cong′-i gyi 這°个°小人°我中意其

FANG, *tusk*, liao-ngô′ 撩牙°

FANNING-MILL, sin-koh′-mi fong-siang 扇穀米風箱

FAR, yün 遠; *how — is it from here to your place?* dông-deo tao ng-lah keh′-deo to-siao yün′ 這°邊°到你那°邊°多少遠? *not very* —, feh-da′ li-yün′ 弗

大離遠; *gone — away*, li-yün′ k'æ-de 離遠開了°; *as — as heaven from earth*, t'in-ts'ô′-di-yün′ 天差地遠; — *better*, hao hyü′-to 好許多

FAR-SIGHTED, ngæn′-kwông yün′ 眼°光遠

FARCE, *all a* — (*i. e.* making a great show with nothing to back it), k'ong′-k'oh kô′-ts 空売架°子; *ditto* (as in work), mun sang′-nying-ngæn′ 瞞生°人°眼

FARE, *to — well at table*, ing′-zih hao′ 飲食好; *ditto*, (as a guest), kong-ing′ hao 供應好; *price of passage*, bun-jün′ 盤纏; *bill of* —, ts'æ′-moh 菜目

FARE-WELL, siao-be′ 少陪 (said only by the person going); *to bid farewell*, bih′-ib-bih 別一別; *ditto* (formally before going on a journey), dz-'ang′ 辭行°; *to accompany and bid* —, song-'ang′ 送行°; *to give a — dinner to one going*, tsin-'ang′ 餞行

FARINACEOUS *food*, feng′-zih 粉食; *wheat food*, mah-zih′ 麥食

FARM, din-tsông′ 田庄; *the Wông family* —, Wông-kô′ tsông 王家°庄

FARMER, din′-wu 佃戶; cong-din-tsông′-go nying′ 種田庄个°人°; *the owner of a farm*, tsông-cü′ 庄主; *farmer's hired assistants*, tsông-k'ah′ 庄客; kong-nying′ 工人

FARRIER, *horse doctor*, i-mô'-go sin'-sang 醫馬个°先生°
FARTHER, *more remote*, yün-tin- 遠點; *go a little* —, ko-ky'i tin 過去°點; *put (it) farther in*, tsæ tsing'-tin 再進點; *still* —, keng-kô yün' 更加°遠; *take no — notice of it*, vong to' ky'i ts'æ' gyi 不°要°多睬其°; *have you anything — to say?* wa-yiu' shih-wô' m̈-teh 還°有說話嗎°?
FARTHEST, ting-yün' 頂遠; *the — shop*, ting yün' keh-bæn tin' 頂遠這°爿店
FASCINATED *by him*, weh-ling' ziang læ gyi siu'-li ka 魂靈像在°其手裡
FASCINATING, we hyih-weng-go 會攝魂个°
FASHION, *style*, kw'un'-shih 欸式; *new* —, sing shih' 新式°; z shih' 時式°; *old* —, lao' shih 老式°; gyiu kw'un' 舊款; *out of* —, ko-z'-de 過時了°; *extremely out of* —, be-z' 背時
FASHIONABLE, z-dao' 時道'; da-tsoh' 大作; z-kw'un' 時欸°; z-shih 時式°; *not* —, feh-tsoh'-de' 弗作了°; feh-z'-de 弗時了°
FAST, *firm*, lao-k'ao' 牢靠' tsah'-cü; — *asleep*, kw'eng sah'-kao 睡°煞覺
FAST, *quickly*, kw'a'-kw'a 快°快°; soh'-soh 速速; 'ao-sao'; — *fellow*, fông'-dông 放蕩

FAST, *to keep a church* —, siu tsa' 守齋°; *a great* —, do tsa' 大°齋°
FAST, *to* kying-zih' 禁食; — *from meat (as the Buddhists do)*, ky'üoh ts'æ' 吃°菜
FASTEN, *to make firm*, long lao-k'ao' 弄牢靠; — *with a nail*, ting' lao 釘牢; — *the door*, meng kwæn-leh lao 門關得°牢; — *by tying*, bo lao' 縛牢; pông' lao 綁牢; — *a boat with a stake*, jün' tsông lao 船樁牢
FAT, công 壯 (công or tsông); p'ông 膀; — *and hearty (as a child)*, mi-p'ông-deo° 肥膀頭°
FAT, *pork* cü-yiu' 猪油; *beef* —, ngeo-yiu' 牛油
FATAL *to life*, sing'-ming c'ih-t'eh' 性命出脫; — *disease*, si'-tsing 死症
FATE, ming 命; su 數; T'in-ming' 天命; T'in-su' 天數; T'in-i' 天意; *dreadful* —, kyih'-su 劫數; *as — would have it*, ming' kæ jü-ts'' 命該如此
FATHER, ah-tia' 阿爹' ah-pah' 阿伯; tia'-tia 爹爹; *how is your* —? vu'-lao hao' feh 父老好否°? *my — is well*, kô'-vu hao'-go 家父好个°; (*very respectful*) *your* —, tseng-da'-jing 尊大人; ling-tseng' 令尊; — *and mother*, vu'-meo 父母; *deceased* —, sin-vu' 先父; sin-kyüing' 先君; *Hea-*

venly —, T'in-vu' 天父; — in the Catholic church, jing-vu' 神父

FATHERS, the we-tsu' 會祖; ancient bishops, kwu kyiu-toh' 古監督.

FATHER-IN-LAW on the husband's side, kong-kong' 公公; ah-kong'; 阿公; — on the wife's side, dziang'-nying 丈人; nguh-vu' 岳父

FATHERLESS, m̄-tia'-go 無爹个

FATHERLY man, yiu-ts'-wu vu'-lao 猶之乎父老

FATHOM, to sound, tang sing-ts'in' 打深淺; tang shü'-deo 打水頭

FATIGUED, dziah-lih' 着力; — and sleepy, bi-gyün' 疲倦; extremely —, kw'eng'-gyih-liao 困極了

FATIGUING work, dziah-lih' sang-weh' 着力生活

FATTEN, to —(as animals), yiang côngʻ (côngʻ or tsông) 養壯; — a goose in close confinement, zeo ngo' 囚鵝

FATTY, yiu-nyi' 油膩; yin'-go 油个

FAULT, mao-bing' 毛病 (ih-go); moral —, ts'o'-c'ü 錯處; ko'-shih 過失; suffer for one's own —, zi' tsoh nyih' 自作孽; it is not my —, feh'-z ngô'-go mao'-bing 弗是我个毛病; feh' z ngô'-go ts'o' 弗是我个錯; good, but has faults, me' cong'-peh-tsoh' 美中不足; to find —, mao-ün' 埋怨; zing leo-dong' 尋漏洞; — finding, leh-leh'-gah-gah; kæn-ka' 尷尬; give him a duck's egg without a crack, he will find a hole in it, "m̄-vong ah-'ts iao zing dong'" 無縫鴨子要尋洞

FAULTLESS, m̄ mao'-bing-go 無毛病个; m̄ p'i'-bing go 無批評个

FAVOR (to an inferior), eng-we' 恩惠; eng-s' 恩賜; eng-tin' 恩典; to regard with — (as a superior an inferior), eng-c'ong'-dæ 恩待; to ask a —, t'ao we' 叨惠; k'eng dzing' 懇情; gyiu fông-bin' 求方便; beg you to grant a —, gyiu ng' s eng' 求你賜恩 (s eng can only be said of a superior); t'ao kwông' 叨光; k'eng ng'-go dzing' 懇你个情

FAVORITE, teh-c'ong'-go 得寵个; c'ong-æ'-go 寵愛个; sô æ'-go 所愛个; teh-i'-go 得意个

FAWN, to (as a dog, or as a workman making a great ado, about heaviness of work &c., for the sake of being coaxed), iao jing-mao'-lo 要順毛擢

FEAR, to p'ô 怕; p'ô'-gyü 怕懼; wě'-gyü 畏懼; — God, p'ô'-gyü Jing-ming' 怕懼神明;

— *the consequences*, p'ô ken-yi' 怕干係; p'ô tæn ao-tsao' 怕担噪糟; *do not* —, hao-vong p'ô 不°用°怕; *nothing to* —, feh-dzæ'-wu 弗礙事°; feh-fông'-teh 弗妨得; *for — that*, k'ong'-p'ô 恐怕

FEARFUL, *afraid*, p'ô 怕; *inspiring fear* (as a place, &c.), p'ô'-p'ô 怕怕; p'ô'-shü-shü 怕哦哦

FEARING *imaginary things*, sing hyü' 心虛

FEARLESS, feh p'ô' 弗怕; — *of death*, feh p'ô' si 弗怕死°

FEASIBLE, tso'-leh-læ' go 做得°來个°

FEAST, tsiu'-zih 酒席; tsiu'-yin 酒筵; *to make a —*, bæn tsiu' 辦酒; *to go to a —*, fu zih' ky'i 赴席去°; *wedding —*, hao'-nyih tsiu' 好日°酒

FEAT, gyi-z' 奇事 (ih-ky'i); gyi-c'ih'-kwu-le' z-t'i' 奇出古類事體

FEATHER, mao 毛 (ih-keng); *plumage*, mao-yü' 毛羽; *fabric made of feathers*, yü'-mao 羽毛; *how beautiful his feathers are*, gyi' go mao-yü sang'-leh dza hao'-k'en 其个°毛羽生°得甚°好看; — *bed*, mao-nyüoh'-ts 毛褥°子; — *pillow*, (i. e. of goose feathers) ngo-mao-tsing' 鵝毛枕; — *brush*, mao shih'-tsiu 毛刷篲 (ih-kwun)

FEATURES, kweh'-kah 骨格; *regular* —, kweh'-kah loh-dzih' 骨格落直; *coarse* —, kweh'-kah ts'u-lu' 骨格粗魯; *fine* —, ng'-kwun sin'-li 五°官秀麗; *beautiful* — (in a Chinese sense), me-ts'ing'-moh-siu' 眉清目秀

FEE, FEES, (given to doctors and others), zia-din' 謝°錢°; *to pay* —, song' zia-din' 送謝°錢°; *pen money* (given to teachers), pih'-ts 筆資; *small tribes* (given to officers), fi'-din 費錢°; *entrance* —, k'æ-meng'-fi 開門費; meng-pao' 門包; — (given to boatmen, servants &c., for extra services). dzô-din' 茶錢°; tsiu'-din 酒錢°

FEEBLE, pih'-t'ah-t'ah 癟楂°楂°; — *constitution*, ti'-ts tæn-boh' 底子單薄

FEED, *to* ü 飼; *have you fed the baby?* na-hwun ü' ko ma 嬰孩°飼過嗎°? —, We 喂 (generally used for animals); *to supply with food* (as masters to workmen), cong væn' 供°飯; *ditto* (polite), kong-ing 供應

FEEL, *to* moh 摸; — *and see*, moh-moh'-k'en 摸摸看; — *the heat*, teh'-cü nyih' 得知熱°; p'ô nyih' 怕熱°; — *the cold*, teh'-cü lang' 得知冷; p'ô lang' 怕冷°; — *happy*, kyüoh'-teh hwun-hyi'-siang 覺得歡喜相; kaobying' 高興; — tired, teh'-cü dziah-lih' 得知着力; — compassion, fah dz-pô' sing 發慈悲心; — angry, fah ông' 發怒; — the pulse, tah mah' 切°脈; k'en mah' 看脈; — one's way and then try, s'-t'en 試探; — for and excuse, t'i'-liang 體諒

FEELING, dzing 情; great —, dzing 'eo' 情厚; dzing djong' 情重; no fellow —, m̂-dzing m̂-nyi' 無°情無°義°; to move men's feelings, tang'-dong nying-go dzing' 打動人°个°情; tender —, nyün' sing-dziang' 軟心腸; to hurt the —, sông dzing' 傷情

FEIGN, to tsông 裝; tsông kô' 裝假°; — sickness, tsông bing' 裝病

FELL, tih-tao'-ko 跌倒過; — (as a person), tih-ko' 跌過; to — a seam, nyiao' ih-da vong' 縫一埭縫; nyiao' ih-da wông-zin'-kweh 縫一埭黃鱔°骨; to — timber, tsoh jü' 斬樹

FELL design, oh kyi'-kao 惡計

FELLOW companion, de-ho' 隊夥 dong-de' 同隊; dong-bun' 同伴; class —, dong-ts'ông' 同窗; dong-nyiu' 同硯°; brave —, hao'-hen 好漢; noble —, da-dziang'-fu 大丈夫; generous —, k'ông'-k'æ dziang'-fu 慷慨丈夫; wicked —, vu-la' 無賴

FELLOW, has a — feeling, yiu-dzing'-yiu-nyi' 有情有義°

FELLOWSHIP, to have — with, siang-kyiao' 相交; kyiao-t'ong' 交通

FELON, malefactor, djong'-væn 重犯; iao'-væn 要犯

FELONY, crime punishable with death, si'-ze 死罪; crime punishable with banishment, ts'ong-ze' 充罪

FELT, tsin 氈; — hat, tsin mao' 氈帽; — carpet, tsin t'æn' 氈毯

FEMALE, nyü 女; — sex, nyü'-liu-ts-pe' 女流之輩; — slave, ô-deo' 丫頭

FEMININE, nyü'-nying go 女人°个°; — employment, nyü'-kong-sang-weh' 女工生°活; womanish, ziang nyü'-nying ka' 像°女人°

FENCE, bamboo ts'iang-pô' 籬°笆; wooden railing, læn-ken' 闌干; very high —, lu-dzing 木°柵

FENCE, to make a bamboo —, tang ts'iang-pô' 打籬°笆; — with the sword, vu-tao' 舞刀; hyi-tao' 戲刀

FENCING-MASTER, kao tao'-fah-go kao'-s 敎刀法个°敎師

FERMENT, to — as dough, fah kao 發酵; fah-ky'i-læ 發起來; — (as fruit and vegetables), fæn 泛

FEROCIOUS, hyüong-mang' 兇猛°

FERRIAGE, du-jün'-din 渡船錢°
FERRY, du 渡; — boat, du-jün' 渡船; — man, du-jün' lao'-da 渡船老大
FERTILE soil, liang din' 良田; me'-di 美地
FERTILIZE, to tsæ-be' 栽培; üong 壅
FERULE, kao'-fông 戒°方 (ih-kw'e)
FERVENT in heart, nyih-sing' 熱°心; ts'ih'-sing 切心
FERVENTLY, hyüih'-sing 血心; very —, ky'i hyüih'-sing 起血心
FERVID, hot, ho'-nyih 火熱°
FESTER, to generate pus, sang nong' 生°膿; tsoh nong' 作膿
FESTIVAL, tsih'-k'eng 節跟°
FETCH, to do-læ' 拿°來; — (when coming), ta'-læ 帶°來; — (as a chair), teh'-leh-læ 撥得°來
FETID, ts'iu 臭°; — breath, k'eo'-ky'i ts'iu' 口氣臭°
FETTER, chain for the feet, kyiah'-liao 脚鐐 (a pair, ih fu).
FETTER, to (both hands and feet), zông liao-k'ao' 上鐐栲; fettered, (restrained), ñyin-kyiah' pæn-sin' 黏脚扳手; kyih'-kyü 拮据
FETUS, t'æ-yüing' 胎孕; small —, dzing-yüing' 成孕
FEUD, in a state of —, kyih ün-dziu' liao 結冤讐了
FEVER, nyih-bing' 熱°病; has

—, læ-tih fah nyih 正°在°發熱° — is rising, læ-tih nyih-ky'i'-læ 來的熱°起來; — is going down, nyih læ-tih t'e'-ky'i-læ 熱°正°在°退起來; — is broken, nyih ts'-de 熱°止了°; nyih t'e' ken zing' de 熱°退乾净了°; intermittent —, dziao-nyih' bing 潮熱°病
FEVER AND AGUE, nyiah-dzih' bing 瘧疾病; ma-za' bing 買柴病
FEVERISH, kyi'-sing nyih'-go 身°體°熱°個°; very —, kyi'-sing ho'-nyih-go 身°體°火熱°個°
FEW, kyi'-go 幾個°; yiu'-'æn 有限°; m to'-siao 無°多少°; a —, m-kyi' go 無°幾個°; feh to' 弗多; two, three, or four, liang 兩; I will come after a — days, ko' kyi nyih ngô læ'-gyi 過幾日°我來
FIB, kô'-wô 假話; hwông-wô 謊話
FIBERS, FIBRES, (as in turnips &c)., kying 經; — (in orange peel), loh 絡; slender rootlets, su 鬚; — in meat, t'iah'-nyüoh-go si' kying 貼°肉°個°細°筋°
FICKLE, fæn-foh'-feh-ding 反覆弗定; yiao-yiao' peh-jih' 搖搖不實
FICTION, books of siao' shü 小書; 'æn shü 閒書; siao' shih 小說
FICTITIOUS, kô'-zao-go 假造°個°; hwông-dông' 荒唐

FIDDLE, *two stringed* wu-gying' 胡琴; *four stringed* —, bi-bô' 琵琶; — *with three strings or more*, yin-ts' 絃子; *to play (the* —) *with a bow*, ga; *ditto with the fingers*, dœu 彈; *to tune a* —, diao yin' 調絃

FIDDLE-BOW, yin-kong' 絃弓 (ih-go)

FIDDLE-STRING, yin-sin' 絃線 (ih-keng)

FIDELITY, cong-sing' 忠心

FIELD, din 田 (ih-ky'in); *battle* —, tsin'-dziang 戰場 (ih-go)

FIERCE, mang 猛°; — *aspect*, ying-shü üong'-mang 形勢勇猛°; — *as a tiger*, ziang mang' hwu ka 像猛°虎; — *wind*, mang' fong 猛°風; *fiercely angry*, fah' nu ziang mang'-tsiang ka 發怒像猛°將

FIFTEEN, jih-ng' 十五°; *the fifteenth*, di jih-ng' 第十五°

FIFTH, di ng' 第五°; — *month*, — *day*, ng' yüih ts'u ng' 五月初五°

FIFTIETH, di ng'-jih 第五°十

FIFTY ng'-jih 五°十; — *years old*, ng'-jih shü'-de 五°十歲°了°

FIG, vu-hwô'-ko 無花果 (ih-go); *dried figs*, vu-hwô'-ko ken' 無花果乾

FIGHT, *to* (as two or more persons), siang-tang' 相打; — (a hundred or more, as clans), tang nying dzing' 打人°陣; — (as

soldiers), tang-tsiang' 打°仗; kao-tsin' 交戰; *to* — *determinedly*, hytüih'-tsin 血戰; *they are having a* —, gyi-lah' læ'-tih tang siang-tang' 伊等°現°在° 相打

FIGHTER, tang'-siu 打手 (ih-go)

FIGURATIVE *expression*, pi'-fông shih-wô' 比方說話; tsia' yüong tso pi'-fông go 借用做比方个°

FIGURE, *an image*, ngeo'-ziang 偶像; ying-ziang' 形像 (ih-go), (of men and animals, as toys), 'en 孩°; *he has a fine* —, gyi i-kô' hao 其衣架°好; *figures* 1,2,3, &c., mô'-ts 碼子; *by* — *of speech*, weh yüong' 活用; *without ditto*, jih yüong' 實用; — *on cloth*, hwô-deo' 花頭; *woven* —, tsih'-c'ih-go hwô-deo' 織出个°花頭

FIGURED (as cloth), yiu hwô-deo' 有花頭; — *calico's*, ing'-hwô yiang'-pu 印花洋布

FILE, ts'o 銼 (ih-pô)

FILIAL, hyiao'-jing 孝順; — *son*, hyiao'-ts 孝子

FILINGS, *iron* t'ih'-sô 鐵沙

FILL, *to* tsi 齎; — *full*, tsi' mun 齎滿; — *a hole* (as in a wall), seh' mun 塞滿; — *a hole* (as in the earth) din mun' 填滿; *to* — *a boat*, jün' tsông-mun' 船裝滿

FILM, *a* ih-zeng i 一層翳;

FIL 175 FIN

a — *has grown over the eye*, ngæn'-tsing zông-tsông-de' 眼睛上瘴了°.

FILTER, li-shü'-bing 濾水°瓶 sô-leo'-kông 沙漏缸° (ih-go)

FILTER, *to* li 濾; *filtered water*, li-shü' 濾水°.

FILTH, ao-tsao' 坒糟; *so much* —, ka' hyü-to ao-tsao' 這°許多坒糟; *sweepings*, leh-seh' 拉圾; *to remove* —, bô leh-seh' 扒拉圾°; wnn leh-seh' 換拉圾°. Countrymen come in and remove filth, giving a few cash or a coarse broom in exchange, hence wnn.

FILTHY, ao-tsao' 坒糟; lah-t'ah' 邋遢; nyi-sing' 坭腥; — *language*, ao-tsao' shih-wô' 坒糟說話.

FIN, ts' 翅; *all the lower fins*, wô shü' 牙°鬣; *the thick dorsal fins*, gyi-ts'iang' 鬐鎗; *shark's fins are used for food, and are called* yü-ts" 魚翅.

FINAL, kyih'-sah 結煞; tah'-leh-meh 末結煞; — *decision*, tao kyih'-sah ding-kwe'-hao 到結煞定規好.

FINALLY, tao'-ti 到底; cong-ü' 終於; kwe-keng' 歸根; ts'ih'-ti 徹底; kyiu'-kying 究竟.

FINANCE, *the tribute*, zin-liang' 錢糧; *customs' revenue*, kwæn-se' 關稅; *governor of* — (in each province), pu'-tsing-s' 布政使; væn-dæ' 藩臺.

FIND *by seeking*, zing-djoh' 尋°著; zing-c'üh'-læ 尋出來; *I have found out your idea*, ng'-go i'-s ngô zing-djoh'-de 你个°意思我尋著了°; *I cannot* — *h'm*, ngô zing-gyi'-feh-djoh' 我尋其弗著°; *to find one's self* (in food), pao væn' 包飯; *to* — *time*, sang' koug-fu' 省°工夫; *ditto, by stealing from other duties*, t'eo-kong'-bah-fu' 偷工夫; *to* — *fault with*, mao-ün' 埋°怨 See FAULT-FINDING.

FINE, *to pay a* —, do'-c'ih vah-kw'un' 拿°出罰欵.

FINE, *not coarse*, si 細; — (as meal), t'i'-t'i 夷-t'i'; *very* — (good), gyih dao'-di 極道地; *beautiful*, miao 妙; *very ditto*, gyih miao' 極妙; — (as workmanship, ornaments, a garden, &c.) tsing-cü' 精緻.

FINE, *to* vah nying-ts' 罰銀子; vah dong-din' 罰銅錢°.

FINELY, si'-si 細細; tsing cü' 精緻; — *written*, sia'-leh tsing-cü' 寫°得精緻; — *executed picture*, du si'-ky'iao 圖細巧.

FINERY *wanting in taste*, ziang pô'-hyi ka'; *wearing fantastic* —, c'ün ziang' tso hwô-kwu'-hyi i-zông 穿像做花鼓戲衣裳°.

FINGER, ts'-deo 指頭 (ih-meh); ts'-meh den' 指拇頭°*the middle* —, cong-ts' 中指; *little* —,

siao' meh-ts'-deo 小拇指頭
FINGER-BOWL, gyiang'-siu-un' 洗°手碗 (ih-tsah)
FINGER-RING, ka'-ts 戒°指 (ih-go).
FINISH, to tso-wun' 做完; tso'-dzing 做成; tso' loh-œ° 做落臺; add to any active verb the particles, hao 好, wun 完; thus: when will you — writing? ng kyi'-z we sia-wun 你°幾時會寫°完? kyi-z sia'-hao 幾時寫°好? to — work, dzing kong' 成功; liao kong' 了功; wun kong' 完功
FINISHED, it is —, hao'-de 好了°; tso-hao'-de 做好了°; wun-kong'-de 完功了°; well finished, tao-kô' 到家; ts'-yi dzing'-yi 至矣盡矣
FINITE, yiu 'œu'-cü 有限°制
FIR tree, sœn-jü' 杉樹; — wood, sœn moh' 杉木
FIRE, ho 火; hot or fierce —, ho mang' 火猛; ho-wông' 火旺; god of —, ho'-jing bu'-sah 火神菩薩; to make a —, sang ho' 生°火; to set — to (as a house), fông ho' 放火; on — (as house, boat, or goods), ho dziah' 火燼; there was a — last night, zô-yia' yiu ho-tsong' 昨°夜°有火鐘; take —, ky'i-ho' 起火; how did it take —? dza ky'i'-ho 怎°起火? to put out — with water, p'eh ho u' 潑火熄°; ditto (as a

house on —), kyiu-ho' 救火; to — a cannon, fông p'ao' 放砲; to — tea, ts'ao dzô-yih' 炒茶葉
FIRE-ARMS, ho'-ky'i 火器
FIRE-BRAND, za-deo'-ho 柴°頭火
FIRE-CRACKERS, p'ao'-dziang 爆竹°
FIRE-ENGINE, shü'-long 水°龍; foreign —, yiang shü'-long 洋水°龍
FIRE-FLY, ho-ing-den' 螢火 (ih-go)
FIRE-MAN, kyiu'-ho-ping 救火兵 (ih-go)
FIRE-PAN, brass — for warming feet, ho-'ts'ong 脚°爐; earthen —, ngô ho-ts'ong' 瓦°火熄
FIRE-SHIP, yüong ho-kong-jün' 用火攻船 (ih-tsah)
FIRE-WOOD, za-bœn' 柴片; brushwood, nyün za' 軟柴°; yih za' 葉柴°
FIRE-WORKS, hwô-p'ao' 'eh-ts' 花砲盒子
Each kind of — has its distinctive name.
FIRKIN, siao' hwô-kwu dong' 小花鼓桶 (ih-go)
FIRM, lao-k'ao' 牢靠; kyih'-jih 硈實; cloth — in texture, pu kyih'-jih 布硈實; — purpose, cü'-i ding-jih 主意定實;— footed, kyiah'-dah jih-di' 脚踏實地
FIRM, 'ông-kô' 行家°; what is the name of your —? ng pao' 'ao kyiao'-leh soh-go' tsino-ba' 你

寶號叫甚°麼°招牌°﹗ng pao 'ông kyiao-leh soh-go z -'ao' 你°寶行叫得°甚°麼°字號﹖
FIRMAMENT, ky'üong-ts'ông 穹蒼
FIRMLY, lao 牢; place —, fông'-leh lao' 放得°牢; stands —, lih-leh' lao' 立得°牢
FIRST, the —, di-ih' 第一; deo-ih' 頭一; the — one, deo-ih'-go 頭一个°; — ancestor, s'-tsu 始祖; bih-tsu' 鼻祖; — class, di-ih' pæn 第一班; — in a class, deo-ih'-ming 頭一名; — crop, di-ih' kyü 第一舉; — crop of rice, tsao' dao 早稻; ditto of tea, deo dzô' 頭茶; koh yü'-zin dzô' 穀雨前茶; — story, di-ih' zeng 第一層; —, of only two stories, leo-'ô' 樓下°; — fruits, sin kyih'-loh-go ko'-ts 先結落个°果子; — head, di-ih' zeng 第一層; — importance, deo-ih' iao'-kying 頭一要緊; sin iao'-kying 先要緊; — month, tsing yüh' 正月; the — of the month, ts'u-ih' 初一; — born, deo sang' 頭生°; — born son, tsiang'-ts 長子; the 1st, 2nd, and 3rd sons (corresponding with the first, second, and third months of each season of the year), mang 孟°; dzong 仲; kyi 季; — set the table, then scald the tea, sin' pa coh'-teng 'eo' p'ao dzô' 先擺

桌橙後泡茶; the — or important move in chess, di-ih' tsiah 第一著°
FIRSTLY, di-ih' zeng 第一層; di-ih' dön 第一段; di-ih' tön 第一端; di-ih' diao' 第一條; di-ih' kw'un' 第一欵; di-ih' 'ông 第一行; di-ih' yiang 第一樣
FISH, ng 魚° (ih-kwang); fresh —, sing-sin' ng 新鮮魚°; fresh water —, dæn' shü ng 淡水°魚°; 'o li'-go ng' 河裏个°魚°; salt water —, 'æn shü' ng 鹹水°魚°; hæ-li'-go ng' 海裡个°魚°; — slightly salted and dried, dæn'-siang 淡鯗; (dried but not opened), ng-ken' 魚°乾; very salt, 'æn-siang' 鹹鯗; ng-k'ao 魚烤; — spawn or roe, ng-ts' 魚子; very young ditto, ng-iang' 魚秧
FISH, to k'ô ng' 捕魚°; — with a hook, tiao ng' 釣魚°; — with a net, pæn ng' 扳魚; — in the sea, k'ô yiang'-sang 洋°內°捕魚°; to — for praise, kwu ming' tiao yü 沽名釣譽
FISHERMAN, k'ô-ng'-go nying 捕魚°个°人°; yü-ong' 漁翁; fish-woman, yü-bo' 漁婆
FISH-GLUE, ng-kao' 魚膠°
FISH-HOOK, tiao'-ng-keo' 釣魚°鈎 (ih-me)
FISH-MARKET, ma ng' z'-k'eo 買魚°市口

FISHING-ROD, tiao'-ng-ken' 釣魚竿 (ih-kwang)
FISHY taste, ng'-go mi'-dao 魚个味道; — smell, ng sing-ky'i' 魚腥氣; sing-ngæn' ky'i.
FISSURE, hwah'-lib-vong 豁裂縫 (ih-da); a crack in rock, zah-kah u' 石楞
FIST, gyün-deo' 拳頭; to give a blow with the —, k'ao' ih-gyün 拷一拳
FIT, a — of ague, ih-pæn' ma-za'-bing 一班買柴病; a — of anger, ih-dziang ky'i' 一塲氣 to have a convulsion, fah-kyüih' 發厥; — (with crying like a lamb), yiang-tin' bing 羊癲病 —(with crying like a pig), cü-tin' bing 猪癲病; by fits and starts, pæn-zông pæn-loh' 班上班落
FIT suitable, siang-nyi' 相宜; siang-te' 相對; siang-vu' 相符; not —, feh siang'-nyi 弗相宜; 'eh'-feh-long' 合弗攏
FIT, to — to, p'e 配; fitted to (as a handle to a pen), p'e'-long liao 配攏了; this dress fits well, keh gyin i-zông sing-kô' siang-p'e' 這件衣裳身架相配; does not —, feh tah'-te 弗搭對; to — up a house, oh' tsông-sih' hao 屋裝飾好
FITLY spoken, shih-wô 'eh-shing'-go 説話合榫个; shih-wô' feng-ngæn' feng-shing 説話分眼分寸

FIVE, ng 五; the — planets, ng' sing 五星; — elements, ng' ying 五行; — tastes (sweet, sour, bitter, pungent, salt), wu' vi 五味; — virtues, wu' djông 五常; —relations, wu' leng 五倫
FIVE-FOLD, ng'-be 五倍
FIX, to fasten (in the ground, on the floor, &c.) tsông lao' 椿牢; settle upon, ding-jib' 定實; ding-kyin' 定見; — a time, ding z-'eo' 定時候; — a day, 'æn'-ding nyih-ts' 限定日子; to — the mind upon, in hearing, cün-sing' t'ing' 專心聽; — in the mind, lao kyi' dzæ sing' 牢記在心
FIXED determination, lih-ding' cü'-i 立定主意; — by fate, ming cü'-ding 命注定; ming sang-dzing' 命生成; eyes — upon, ngæn'-tsing ts'ing'-ting k'en' 眼睛瞪盯看; —price, ding-kô' weh-ih' 定價劃一; peh r' kyüô 不二價; — purpose, ih-ding' i'-s 一定意思; not yet — or determined, vi ding' 未定; wa m̃'-neh ding-kwe' 還沒有定規
FIZZLE, to — out, fông c'ü-c'ü.'
FLABBY, (as flesh), c'ô'-c'ô-dong (c'ô or ts'ô).
FLAG, to (on the road), tang kyiah'-kweh-nyün' 脚跛; — in doing anything, (by figure), ziang tang kyiah'-kweh-nyün ka' 像

FLA 179 FLE

脚°跛°樣°式°; *indisposed to work*, læn'-teh tso 懶得°做

FLAG, gyi 旗 (ih-sin, ih-min); — *or board asking quarter*, min'-tsin ba 勉戰牌°; — *of surrender*, 'ông-gyi 降旗; — *ship*, ta-ling jün' 帶°令船; — *staff*, gyi ken' 旗杆 (ih-ts); — *stone*, zah-pæn' 石°版 (ih-kw'e); *to lay ditto*, p'u zah-pæn' 鋪石°版

FLAGRANT *crime*, ze'-oh t'ao-t'in' 罪惡滔天; ze'-da oh-gyih' 罪大惡極

FLAIL (used for beating the sesame seeds, &c.), lin-Wæn' kô 連環°枷 (ih-go)

FLAKE, *small — of snow*, shih-hwô' 雪花; *large — of snow*, shih'-p'in 雪片

FLAKE, *to — off*, k'oh'-ky'i 掣°起

FLAME, yin-deo' 焰頭 (ih-bong)

FLANKS *of an animal*, iao-hyih' 腰脅; — *of an army*, tso-yiu'-kyüing 左右軍

FLANNEL, nyüong pu' 絨布

FLAP, *to* gwah; — *back and forth* gwah-læ' gwah-ky'i'

FLARE, *to — up as flame*, ho'-kwông dzih-ts'ông' 火光直冲; — *into a passion*, ho'-ky'i dzih-ts'ông' 火氣直冲

FLASH, *to* fah'-c'ih liang-kwông' 發出亮光; *to* — (as lightning), tang hoh-sin 發電光

FLAT, pin 扁; *to press —*, ky'ing pin; *level*, bing 平

FLAT-IRON, loh-t'ih' 烙鐵 (ih-go)

FLATTEN, *to* tso pin' 做扁; long-pin' 弄扁; ah'-pin 壓°扁

FLATTER, *to* vong'-dzing 奉承; shü'-kwu 世故; peo-tsiang' 褒獎 (*lit.* over-praise); — *those higher than one's self*, nyi kao-deo'-pih 戴°高°帽°子; *thanks, you flatter me*, dzing-peo', dzing peo' 承褒承褒

FLATTERER, vong'-dzing-tsing' 奉承精; vong'-dzing-tong' 奉承慣 (ih-go)

FLATTERY, vong'-dzing-go shih-wô' 奉承个°說話

FLATULENCE, ky'i' feh yüing'-dong' 氣弗運動; ky'i üoh'-tih 氣鬱的; *to relieve —*, li ky'i' 利氣; yüing ky'i 運氣

FLAVOR, hyiang 香; ky'i'-mi 氣味°; *taste*, mi-dao' 味°道; *has the — of ginger*, yiu sang-kyiang'-go ky'i'-mi 有生°薑个°氣味°; *add —* (as to cake &c.), kô-hyiang'-ts'eo 加香湊

FLAW (as in glass), pæn-tin' 斑點; — (in cloth), p'o'-dzæn 破綻

FLAX, mô 麻; dzi'-mô 苧°麻; — *seed*, mô-ts' 麻子

FLAY, *to* poh bi' 剝皮

FLEA, tsao 蚤; t'iao'-tsao 跳蚤; pæn'-tsao 板蚤 (ih-go)

FLEA-BITE, tsac-ting' 蚤叮;

FLE 180 FLO

lice and flea-bites many, hence, annoying, uncomfortable, seh-ting' tsao-ngao' 虱叮蚤鮫

FLEDGED, yiah-sao-kwu' ngang' 翼°翅°股硬; not yet —, yiah-sao'-kwu' wa m̄-neh ngang' 翼°翅°股還°沒°有°硬

FLEE, to run away, peng'-tseo 奔走; dao-tseo' 逃走; to — from trouble, dao næn' 逃難°; — from calamity, bi 'o'-se 避禍祟

FLEECE, ta'-bi yiang'-mao 帶皮°羊毛

FLEECE, to cut off the —, tsin yiang mao' 剪羊毛; to — the people, poh'-siah pah'-sing 剝削百姓

FLEET a — of fishing boats, ih-pông k'ô-ng-jün' 一幫捕魚°船; a — of war ships, ih-dé' tsin'-jün 一隊戰船

FLEET, as if flying, ziang fi' ka kw'a' 如°飛之°快°

FLEETING, time is —, or light and shadow fly like arrows, kwông'-ing jü tsin' 光陰如箭; — and deceitful pleasures, ngæn'-zin-hwô' 眼°前花

FLESH, nyüoh 肉°; the body nyüoh-sing' 肉°身;

FLESHY, vi-p'ông' 肥膵; công or tsông 壯; how — you are, ng sing'-t'i dza vi-p'ông 你°身體甚°肥膵°; — person, công'-p'ông-ts 壯膵°子 (disrespectful).

FLEXIBLE, hao-ao'-go 好拗个°; ao'-leh-cün'-go 拗得°轉个°

FLIGHT, a — of stairs, ih-bu lu-t'æ' 一步扶°梯°; a few steps, kah'-bu-kæn' 階°梯°間°

FLIMSY writing, veo-boh'-go veng-li' 浮薄个°文理; veng-li ts'in'-boh 文理°淺薄; — pretext, ming-ming'-go ziæ-tön' 明明个°借端; — cloth hyi-pu' 稀布

FLINCH, to p'ô-t'ong' p'ô-yiang' 怕痛怕癢; without flinching, nying t'ong' 忍°痛

FLING, to throw, tiu 丟; — with force, k'ang; ang; gwæn 摜; — away, k'ang-diao; ang-diao; tiu'-diao 丟去°

FLINT, ho'-zah 火石° (ih-kw'e)

FLIPPANT style of talking, tih'-tih-tah-tah lön-kông' lön-wô' 的的搭搭亂講°亂話

FLIRT, n. hong'-nying-tsing' 哄八°精

FLOAT, to vu 浮°; floating on the water, læ shü' min-teng' vu'-tih 在°水°面上°浮°的

FLOATING-BRIDGE, or bridge of boats, veo-gyiao' 浮橋

FLOCK, ih-dziao' 一羣°; ih-dé' 一隊; ib-dzing' 一陣; — of sheep, ih-dziao-yiang' 一羣°羊

FLOCK, to — together, dzing-gyüing' kyih-dé' 成羣結隊

FLOG, to — with a ratan, tang deng-diao' 打籐條; — with

FLO 181 FLU

a lash, tang pin-ts' 打鞭子
FLOOD, do shü' 大水°; *the Flood*, 'Ong-shü' 洪水°; *to* — , fah do-shü' 發大水°; tso do-shü' ; — *tide*, tsiang'-dziao 漲潮
FLOODING, (menstrual), hyüih'-pong 血崩°
FLOOR, di-pæn' 地板 (properly the lower —); *upper* —, leo-pæn' 樓板
FLOOR, *to* bih di-pæn' 鋪°地板
FLORA, hwô-ts‘ao' 花草; ts‘ao'-moh 草木
FLORID *style* (of writing), veng-li' hwô-p‘ao' 文理時° 新°
FLORIST, k‘ao'-kyiu hwô'-go nying 考究花个° 人°
FLOSS-SILK, sæn'-sin 散線 (a thread, ih-keng)
FLOUNCE, *to* — *about*, pin-dong' pin-t‘iao' 徧動徧跳; weh-djông' weh-tin' 活撞活頓
FLOUR, feng 粉; *wheat* — , min-feng' 麵粉; mah-feng' 麥粉; *rice* — , mi'-feng 米粉; *the best or first sifted* — , deo-s' feng 頭篩粉
FLOURISH, *to* hying-wông' 興旺; — (as trade), hying-long' 興隆; — *luxuriantly* (as foliage), meo-zing' 茂盛; — *a sword*, vu kyin' 舞劍; yüih kyin' 試° 劍
FLOW, *to* liu 流; — *down*, liu-loh 流落; — *through*, liu-t‘ong 流通; *the tears flowed down*,

ngæn-li'-shü liu'-loh-læ'-de 眼° 淚水° 流落來了°
FLOWER, hwô 花 (ih-tô); *a cluster of flowers*, ih-gyiu hwô' 一毬 花; *a bunch of* —, ih-nyiah hwô' 一捻花; *to pick* —, tsah hwô' 摘花; ao hwô' 拗花
FLOWER, *to* k‘æ hwô' 開花
FLOWER-GARDEN, hwô-yün' 花 園
FLOWER-POT, hwô-beng' 花盆 (ih-go)
FLOWER-VASE, hwô-bing' 花瓶 (ih-go)
FLOWERY-KINGDOM (*i.e.* China), Cong-wô'-koh 中華國
FLUCTUATE, *to* 'oh-zông' 'oh-loh' 或上或落; zông-zông'-loh-loh 上上落落
FLUENT, jing-liu' 順流; — *in speech*, we-kông'-we-wô' 會講° 會話; jing-k‘eo' t‘eng'-c‘ih 順 口衆° 出; — *in replies*, ing'-te jü-liu' 應對如流; pah'-læ-pah-tah.
FLUID, *whatever will flow*, we liu'-go tong-si' 會流个° 東西
FLUKE *of an anchor*, mao-ts‘' 錨 齒 (ih-go)
FLUSH, *to blush*, 'ong-ky‘i'-læ 紅 起來; fah 'ong' 發紅; — *in money*, dong-din' tsiang-tsong' 銅 錢° 有° 餘°
FLUSHED (with wine), min-k‘ong' zông lin' 酒醉面° 孔°; — (with anger or shame), 'ong'-min' ts‘ih-

kying' 紅面赤筋; 一 (with heat), 'ong-min' da-tsiang 紅面大將

FLURRIED, hwông-mông' 慌忙; læ-loh'-feh-gyi'; hwông-kyih' hwông-mông' 慌急慌忙

FLUTE, dih-ts' 笛子 (ih-kwun); to play or blow the —, c'ü dih-ts' 吹°笛子

FLUTED like the lobes of an orange, kyüih'-ts-kæn' yiang'-shih 橘子瓣°樣式

FLUTING-IRON, t'ông i-zông' ho'-gyin 燙衣裳'火箝 (ih-pô)

FLUTTER, to — without flying, gwah'-kyi gwah'-kyi gwah'-feh-kao'; heart all in a —, sing bih-bih'-t'iao 心闢闢跳°; sing-hyü'-deh-tsin 心虛肉°顫

FLY, to fi 飛; to — about, fi'-læ fi-ky'i' 飛來飛去°; — swiftly, fi-p'ao' 飛跑°; — loose (as dress), gen-gen'-dong.

FLY, the house —, ts'ông-ing' 蒼蠅 (ih-tsah); the dragon —, ts'ing-ding' 蜻蜓

FLY-POISON, ts'ông-ing'-go doh-yiah' 蒼蠅个°毒藥

FLY-SPECK, ts'ông-ing' o 蒼蠅屎°

FLYING-FISH, 'ong-nyiang-ng', (a species found at Ningpo).

FOAL of a horse, siao' mô 小馬; — of an ass, siao' li-ts' 小驢子

FOAM, bah-meh' 白沫; to —, ky'i bah-meh' 起白沫; — at the mouth, nyin-zæn kao'-c'ih 黏涎°攪出; c'ü beh' 吹°沫°

FOCUS, hyüoh-kwông'-go di'-fông 蓄光个°地方; jü-kwông'-go-di'-fông 聚光个°地方

FODDER, ts'ao'-liao 草料; to cattle, ü ngeo' 餓°牛

FOE, dziu-nying' 讐人°; te'-deo 對頭; ün-kô' 冤家°; a fighting —, dziu-dih' 讐敵

FOG, vu-lu' 霧露; dense —, vu-lu djong 霧露重; vu-lu nyüong' 霧露濃

FOGGY (as an explanation), vu-ky'i'-deng'-deng 霧氣騰騰

FOIBLE, bing 病; every man has a —, ko'-ko nying yiu ih-go bing' 個個人°有一個病; old —, lao' mao'-bing 老毛病; lao' bi-ky'i 老牌氣

FOIL his plans, p'o gyi' go kyi-kwæn' 破其个°機關

FOIL, leaf, yih-ts' 葉子; thin —, boh 箔; gold —, kying yih' 金葉; kying boh' 金箔

FOLD, sheep yiang-gyin' 羊樵 (ih-kæn); crease made in folding, tsih'-u 摺痕; u 痕°; a plait, ih kæn 一間°

FOLD, to tsih 摺; — together, tsih-tæn'-long 摺打攏; — (as a hem, paper &c.), üih 攦; fold it properly, tsih' gyi hao 摺其好; — the arms, gao siu' 交°手; — the hands, nyiah-siu' 捻手; ten —, jih be' 十倍

FOLIAGE, yih 葉; *luxuriant* —, yih meo-meo'-zing-zing 葉茂茂盛盛

FOLLOW, *to* keng 跟; keng-leh' 跟得°; keng-djoh' 跟着°; — *me,* keng-ngô' læ 跟我來; — *him* (*i. e.* his example), keng-leh' gyi tso' 跟得°其做; keng-leh' gyi 'oh' 跟得°其學; k'en gyi yiang' 看其樣; — *immediately,* ze kyiah'-'eo-keng' læ 隨脚後跟來; — *after a little,* ze-'eo' læ 隨後來; — *the pattern,* i yiang' wô weh-lu' 依樣畫胡°蘆; *hence it follows,* sô'-yi yiu' 所以有; keh'-lah yiu' 故°此有; *as follows,* ziu-z' 就°是

FOLLOWER, *one who follows to wait upon,* keng-ze' 跟隨; keng-pæn' 跟班; — *of a doctrine,* meng-du' 門徒

FOLLY, kyin'-sih nyü' 見識愚; nyü-kyin' 愚見

FOND, *to be fond of,* dzih-din' 值錢° (said of those below us in age, or of things); *very fond of* (as food), ting' hwun-byi ky'üoh' 頂歡喜吃; tse' æ ky'üoh' 最愛吃°; *weakly — and over-indulgent,* nyih-æ' peh-ming' 溺愛不明; — *of study,* hwun'-hyi doh shü' 歡喜讀書; hao doh' 好讀; *partially —,* p'in æ' 偏愛; — *of wine,* t'en tsiu' 貪酒; — *of lust,* t'en sch' 貪色; —

of moving about (*i. e.* unsettled), æ-dong'-go 愛動个°

FONT, *baptismal* — (small), 'ang si'-li-go bun'; 行°洗禮个盤; *ditto* (large), 'ang si'-li go kông' 行°洗禮个°缸

FONT, *a — of type,* ih-fu' k'æn-z' 一副鉛字

FOOD, ky'üoh'-zih 吃°食; *grain, beans, &c.,* liang-zih' 糧食; k'eo'-liang 口糧; *all — eaten with rice,* 'ô-væn' 下°飯; ts'æ'-su 菜蔬; — *for a journey,* ho'-zih 火食; ken-liang' 乾糧; lu-ts'æ' 路菜; *wheaten —,* mah zib' 麥食; *nourishing —,* pu' zih 補食; *excellent —,* zông-p'ing' ts'æ'-su 上品菜蔬; *we have only the plainest —,* ah'-lah, tsih' yiu ts'u dzô, dæn' væn 我°等°只有粗茶淡飯; *rich —,* yiu-ky'i' 'ô-væn 葷°腥'下°飯; *to prepare —,* long væn' 弄飯

FOOL, do-vu'; hen-deo' 憨頭; nyü-c'ü' mong'-tong-go 愚痴懵懂个°; *are you trying to act the —?* ng soh' fah-do hen'-leh ma 你°甚°麼°發大°憨嗎°?

FOOL *him,* peh gyi t'æn-ts'ong'佴°其受°佴°; teng gyi na-'o' 與°其嬉°戲° (polite); — *and injure him,* teng gyi oh' c'ü'-siao 與°其惡取笑; *fooled by me,* zông ngô-go ts'oh'-deo 受°我个°騙

FOOLISH, hen 憨; ngæ 呆;— *affair*, hen' z'-t'i 憨事體;— *words*, c'ing'-c'ing shih-wô' 蠢蠢說話; *like a fool*, do'-vu lin'-ky'i; *ditto* (more severe), ziang fah-c'ü' ka 像發痴;— *hopes*, c'ü-sing vông'-siang 痴心妄想

FOOT, kyiah 脚; *bound —*, dzin-ko'-liao kyiah' 纏過了脚; *— asleep*, kyiah' mô-tsah'-de 脚麻了°; the Chinese divide the feet of animals into *claw-footed*, kyiah-tsao 脚爪, and *palm-footed*, (*i. e.* those that walk on the palms, as bears, and monkeys); kyiah'-tsông 脚掌; *duck's —*, ah' kyiah pæn' 鴨脚版; *infantry*, bu'-ping 步兵; *a Chinese —* (of ten inches), ih ts'ah' 一尺°; *buy by the —*, leng ts'ah'-deo ma' 論尺頭買°; *go on —*, bu-'ang' 步行°; 'ang'-leh ky'i' 行得去°; *— of a mountain*, sæn kyiah' 山脚

FOOT-BALL hao t'ih'-go gyiu' 好踢个°毬; *to kick a —*, t'ih gyiu' 踢毬

FOOT-PATH siao' lu 小路;— *between the fields*, din-zing'-lu 田塍°路;— *across the fields*, din'-li-go liao-lu' 田裡个°蹞路; liao-din'-koh 蹞田角°

FOOT-PRINT kyiah'-ing 脚印

FOOT-RULE ts'ih 尺 (ih-kwun); *tailor's —*, zæ-ts'ih' 裁°尺;

carpenter's —, lu'-pæn-ts'ih' 魯班尺

FOOT-STOOL, dah'-kyiah-teng' 踏脚櫈 (ih-go); koh'-kyiah-teng' 擱脚櫈 (ih-keng); *native — of plaited straw*, bu-dön 蒲團

FOOT-STEPS, kyiah'-tsih 脚跡; kyiah'-u 脚印°; *follow in my —*, bu-bu' ing ngô'-go kyiah'-tsih 步步印我个°脚跡

FOOT-STOVE, ho'-ts'ong 脚°爐

FOP, p'iao-yih'-nying 飄逸人°; *an officer's son highly dressed but not of good character*, hwô-hwô-kong'-ts 花花公子

FOPPISH, æ-p'iao-yih'-go 愛飄逸个°

FOR, *instead of*, t'i 替; dæ 代; dæ-teng' 代等; *on account of*, we-leh' 為;— *what reason?* we-leh soh'-go yün-kwu' 為甚麼°緣故?— *what?* we-leh soh'-si 為甚°麼°?— *cash*, we'-tih-z' dong-din' 為的是銅錢°; *as — me*, ziah'-z ngô' ni 若是我呢°; kông'-tao ngô' 講到我; ts-ü ngô' 至於我; *there is no occasion — it*, (to a person asking), keh-z hao-vong' 這是不°用°; keh' z peh-pih' 這°是不必; *ditto* (to one doing), keh' z vu-we' 這°是無為; *— what price was it sold?* soh'-go kô'-din ma-c'ih'-go 甚°麼°價°錢°買出个°? *large — (his) age*, kw'e-we' 傀偉; do-dao' 大°道; buy — me, ng' teng ngô' ma' 你°與°我買°; — holding tea, hao tsi dzô' 好齒茶; good — fever, hao t'e nyih' go 好退熱°个°; we' djü dziao-nyih' 會治潮熱°; — example, pi'-fông 比方; — three hours, sæn tin'-cong kong-fu' 三點鐘工夫; good — nothing, m̂'-kao yüong-dziang' 無°用場; to go — good, ky'i'-ts feh læ'-de 去°之弗來了°; ih-ky'ü' feh we' 一去弗回; pray — grace, gyiu eng-we' 求恩惠; — ever, üong'-yün 永遠; — as much as, kyi'-kying 旣經; exchange what is of no use to me but useful to him — vice versa, kying-djü'wun nyüoh-ta' 金鎚換玉帶°.

FORBEAR, to cease, hyih 歇; deng loh' 停°落; to bear with, jing'-næ 忍耐.

FORBID, to kying 禁; kying'-djü 禁住; — him to do it, kying' gyi feh tso' 禁其弗做; to do what is forbidden, væn kying' 犯禁.

FORCE, lih 力; owing to the — of truth, ky'ü'-leh dao-li'-go lih' 全°虧°道理个°力; to use —, yüong gyiang' 用强; — of momentum, læ-shü' 來勢; has — of character, yiu kying-liang' 有勁°兩; strength and prowess, kông-gyiang' 剛强; by —, min'-ky'iang 勉强; forces (troops, &c.), ping-mô' 兵馬; nying-mô' 人°馬.

FORCE, to pih 逼; ngang-k'ô' 硬拿°; ngang iao' 硬要; — to do something bad or disgraceful, pih' zông liang-sæn' 逼上梁山; — him to write, pih' gyi sia' 逼其寫°; to beg with — or — one to give, gyiang' t'ao 强討.

FORCED to do, w̌a-feh-læ tso 獄°弗來做.

FORD, to liao 膠; — a stream, liao ky'i-k'ang' 膠溪坑.

FORE, before, either in position, or in time, zin 前°; — before in time, sin 先.

FOREARM, n. 'ô' siu-kwang' 臂°; siao' siu-kwang.

FORE-ARM, to bông-be' kyüing-ky'i' 防備軍器.

FOREBODE, to — evil, bông 'o'-se 防禍祟; bông 'eo'-læ w̌a 防後來孬°.

FORE-CAST, to yü-sin' liao-leh-tao' 預先料得°到; to contrive beforehand, sin tang'-sön 先打算; able to — the future, yiu sin-kyin' ts-ming' 有先見之明.

FORE-FATHERS, tsu'-tsong 祖宗; tsu'-sin 祖先; sin-tsu' 先祖.

FORE-FOOT, zin kyiah' 前°脚; fore-hoof, zin di' 前°蹄.

FORE-GO, to — a pleasure, ky'i-diao ih-ky'i hwun-hyi' z-t'i' 棄了°一椿°歡喜事體; 一

FOR 186 FOR

for another, nyiang' peh bih' nying 讓°給°別人°

FORE-GOING, *the* (what is written), zông-veng' 上文

FORE-GROUND, bu'-we gying' 步位近

FOREHEAD, nao'-k'oh 腦壳; *the middle of the* —, nao'-meng 腦門; *the corners of the* —, ngah-koh' 頟角; *high* —, t'in-ding kao' 天庭高

FOREIGN, nga-koh' 外°國; yiang' 洋; — *goods*, nga-koh' ho' 外°國貨; yiang ho' 洋貨

FOREIGNER, nga'-koh-nying 外°國人°; si-pin-nying' 西邊人°; 'ong-mao-nying' 紅毛人° (vulgar); *foreign woman*, nga'-koh nyü'-nying 外°國女人°; 'ong'-mao lao'-nyüing 紅毛老女° (vulgar)

FORE-KNOW, *to* yü'-sin hyiao'-teh 預先曉得; sin-cü' 先知

FOREMOST, ting' zin-deo' 頂前頭; dzih-dzih' zin-deo' 極極前°頭

FORENOON, zông-pun'-nyih 上半日°

FORE-ORDAIN, *to* yü'-sin cü'-ding 預先注定; yü'-sin ding-kwe' 預先定規

FORE-RUNNER, sin-fong' 先鋒

FORE-SEE, *to* yü'-sin k'en'-kyin 預先看見

FORE-SIGHT, sin-kyin' ts-dzæ' 先見之才

FORE-SHADOWING, yü'-sin-go ing'-ts 預先个°影子

FOREST, dzong-ling' 叢林 (ih-c'ü)

FORE-STALL, *to take beforehand*, sin tsin'-leh ky'i' 先佔得去°; —, *and do one's self*, tsin'-leh zi' tso' 佔得自°做

FORE-TASTE, *have a* — *of heavenly bliss*, T'in-zông'-go foh'-ky'i sin yiu' ih-ngæn' zông-djoh'-de 天上个°福氣先有一點°嘗著°了; *only a small* — *of misery* (or happiness), sæn pah' kying sang-kyiang' wa tsih'-leh zông'-djoh lah ngô-deo' 三百°勑生°薑還°只得嘗°著°辣芽°頭

FORE-TELL, *to* yü'-sin kông' 預先講; *foretold*, yü'-sin wô-ko'-de 預先話過了°

FORETHOUGHT, sin liao-tao' 先料到; *owing to his* —, ky'ü-leh gyi' sin liao-tao' 虧°得°其先料到

FOREVER, üong'-yün 永遠;

FORE-WARN, *to* yü'-sin kying'-kyiæ 預先警戒

FORFEIT *something good on account of wrong doing*, hao' z-t'i we-leh ts'o', shih'-diao 好事體會錯失°了°; — *one's life for another's*, ih ming', ti' ih ming' 一命抵一命; din ming' 抵命

FORGE, *to* — *iron*, tang t'ih' 打鐵

FORGE *for iron,* tang-t'ih'-go lu-ts' 打鐵个°爐子
FORGE, to — *a name,* mao ming' 冒名；— *cash,* s- cü' dong-din' 私鑄銅錢；— *a name to obtain money,* mao ming' p'in dzæ-veh' 冒名騙財物；— *a seal,* zao kô' ing 造°假°印
FORGERY, *the crime of —*, ngwe-zao'-go ze'-ming 僞造个°罪名
FORGET, *to* mông-kyi' 忘記；— *favors,* mông-kyi' hao-c'ü' 忘記好處
FORGETFUL, m kyi'-sing 無°記性; *very —,* ao- vu' kyi'-sing 毫無記性; cün-ü' mông-kyi' 專于忘°記; jün-vông' 善忘；— *of favors,* vông-eng' veo-nyi' 忘恩負義; kwu-veo' 辜負
FORGIVE, *to* nyiao-sô' 饒赦; sô'-diao* 赦了; nyiao 饒° min 免; k'un-shü 寬恕; nyiao-shü 饒恕；— (as slight offences), nyün-liang' 原諒; *I have forgiven him,* ngô' nyiao'-leh gyi de 我饒°得°其了°

* Nyiao-sô, and sô-diao, can only be used in speaking of God's or an officer's forgiveness. The other words, may be used more commonly.

FORK, ts'ô 叉; *silver —,* nying-ts'ô' 銀叉 (ih-pô); — *in a road,* ts'ô-lu 叉路; *the place where it forks,* s'-ts'ô lu-k'eo' 四叉路口
FORLORN, kw'u 苦; *destitute,* kwu-gyüong' 孤窮; *miserable,* kwu-ts'i' 孤悽; — *and destitute*

person, kw'u'-nao-ts' 苦惱子
FORM, *appearance,* mo-yiang' 模樣; siang'-mao 相貌; *what — had it?* dza' mo yiang' 怎°模樣? *shape,* yiang-shih' 樣式; — (of man) sing-dzæ 身材; jing-dzæ 人材
FORM, *to — from clay,* su 塑; — *in the hand* (as dough), nyiah 揑; — *by piling upon* (as snow or mud), te 堆; — *an idol,* su bu-sah' 塑菩薩; — *a rabbit,* nyiah' ih-tsah t'u' 揑一隻兔; — *a snow priest,* te shih'-'o-zông' 堆雪和尚; — *with a mould,* su'-ts ing'-c'ih-læ 模°子澆°出來; — *a plan,* tso'-c'ih ih-go fah'-ts 做出一个°法子; — *a plot,* shih kyi-meo' 設計謀
FORMAL, *having the form without the substance,* yiu'-ming vu-jih' 有名無實; nga' yiu-yü', r ne' peh-tsoh' 外°有餘而內不足; *ceremonious,* to-li'-go 多禮个°; k'ah'-ky'i 客氣
FORMALITY, hyü-veng' 虛文; veo-veng 浮文
FORMER *chapter,* zông-tsông' 上章; — *occasion,* zin-deo' ih we' 前頭一回; — *times,* zông-dæ'-go z-'eo' 上代个°時候; — *ages,* zông-kwu' z-shü' 上古時世; — *life,* (before transmigration), zin-seng' 前生; zin-s' 前°世°

FORMERLY, yi-zin' 以前°; dzong zin' 從前°; zin-deo' 前°頭

FORMIDABLE, fi-dong' siao-k'o' 非同小可; fi-dong' r-hyi' 非同兒戲

FORMLESS, m'-neh siang'-mao 沒°有°相貌; vu-ying' vu-ziang' 無形無象°

FORMULA, rule, kwe-tseh' 規則; kwe-diao' 規條; medical prescription, fông-ts' 方子 (ih-go)

FORNICATION, kæn-ying' 姦淫; biao 嫖

FORNICATOR, kæn-fu' 姦°夫; biao-k'ah' 嫖客 (ih-go)

FORSAKE, to ky'i'-diao 棄了°; tiu-diao' 丟去°; to leave, li-k'æ' 離開

FORSWEAR, to deny upon oath, vah-tsiu' m'-teh 罰咒沒°有°

FORT, p'ao'-dæ 礮臺 (ih-zo); to guard a —, siu p'ao'-dæ 守礮臺

FORTH, c'ih 出; to go —, c'ih'-ky'i 出去°

FORTHWITH, lih-k'eh' 立刻; tsih-k'eh' 即刻; mô'-zông 馬上; ziu 就°; ze-siu' 隨手

FORTIFY, to prepare for danger, bông nyü' 防虞°; — with soldiers, bông tu 防堵; — with embankments, tsoh nyi-dzing' 築坭城; to build forts, tsoh p'ao'-dæ 築礮臺

FORTIFIED, small — place, we 衛

FORTNIGHT, jih-s' nyih 十四日°; half month, pun'-ko-yüih' pa 半個月; two weeks, liang' li'-pa 兩禮拜°

FORTUNATE, hao zao'-hwô 好造°化; hao yüing-ky'i 好運氣; kyih-li'-go 吉利个°; yüing'-dao hao 運道好; yiu foh'-ky'i 有福氣; — in coming just when wanted, ts'eo'-ky'iao 湊巧

FORTUNATELY, ying hyi'-teh 幸喜得; ky'ü'-leh 虧°得°; — I did not bring him, ying-hyi'-teh ngô feh ta' gyi læ' 幸喜得吾°弗帶°其來

FORTUNE, yüing-ky'i' 運氣; yüing-dao' 運道; z-yüing' 時運; good —, yüing-ky'i hao' 運氣好; great good —, foh'-veng do' 福分°大°; bad —, boh ming' 薄命; to enjoy good —, avoid (the place of) misfortune, "c'ü-kyih,' bi-hyüong'" 趨吉避凶; to make one's —, fah-dzæ' 發財; to seek one's —, gyiu dzæ' 求財; depending on a wife's —, k'ao' lao'-nyüing-go foh'-ky'i 靠妻°个°福氣; to spend a —, ba kô' 敗°家°

FORTUNES, to tell sön-ming 算命; p'i ming' 批命; ditto, by drawing slips of paper, gyin bæn' 籤牌°; ditto with a book, k'en-hwô kông 看花缸; k'en' liang-deo' gyin 看兩頭籤

FORTUNE-TELLER, sön'-ming sin'-sang 算命先生°; gyin-bæn'-go 籤牌°个°

FORTY, s'-jih 四十; *the fortieth*, di s'-jih 第四十

FORWARD, *to the front*, hyiang zin' 向前°; zông zin' 上前°; ẅông zin' 往前°; *to bend* —, eo-tæn'-tao 僂°僂°

FORWARD, *advanced* (as a child), liu'-liang li-lông'; *putting one's self* —, iao ts'ing-neng' 要稱能; *violating propriety*, feh jing' kwe-kyü' 不循規矩

FORWARD, *to* — (as letters), cün ta' 轉帶°; cün' kao'-dæ 轉交°代

FOSSIL *dug out of the earth*, di-yiang' gyüih-c'ih'-læ-go 地裏°掘出來个°

FOSSILS, kyiang-zah' 殭石°

FOSTER, *to feed*, ü 餘; *to bring up*, yiang 養

FOSTER-FATHER, kyi'-pa ah-tia' 寄拜°阿爹°; nyi-vu' 義°父

FOSTER-MOTHER, kyi'-pa ah-nyiang' 寄拜°阿娘; yiang'-nyiang 養娘

FOUL *air*, djoh-ky'i' 濁氣; — *breath*, k'eo'-ky'i ts'iu' 口氣臭°; *to use* — *means*, ẅang tc'.

FOUND, *to establish*, shih'-lih 設立; — *upon what basis?* k'ao'-djoh soh'-go ti'-ts 靠着°甚°麼°底子?

FOUND, *to* — *a bell*, cü' ih-k'eo cong' 鑄一口鐘

FOUND, *tried and* — *guilty*, p'un'-tön-ko', ze ding-jih'-de 判斷過罪定實了°; *three dollars and* —, kong-væn'-ts-nga sæn kw'e' fæn-ping' 供°飯之外三塊番餅

FOUNDATION *of a house*, di'-kyi 地基;— *of a wall*, ziang kyiah' 墻脚; *lasis*, ti'-ts 底子; — *to go upon*, keng-kyiah' 根脚

FOUNDER *of a sect*, kyiao' deo 教頭; — *in brass*, cü' dong-s-vu' 鑄銅司務; *to fill with water and sink*, dzing-meh' 沉沒; dzing-loh' 沉落

FOUNDLING-ASYLUM, yiang'-yüoh-dông 養育堂; yüoh-ing'-dông 育嬰堂

FOUNTAIN, *source*, nyün-deo' 源頭; *spring*, weh-shü-den' 活水°潭; *foreign* —, si-yiang shü'-fah 西洋水°法

FOUR, s 四; *the* — *points of the compass*, s' hyiang 四向; s' fông 四方; — *seasons*, s' kyi 四季; s' z 四時; — *Books*, S' Shü 四書; *the fourth*, di s' 第四

FOUR-CORNERED, s'-koh'-go 四角°个°

FOUR-FOOTED, s' kyiah 四脚

FOUR-FOLD, s' be 四倍

FOUR-SIDED, s' pin 四邊

FOUR-SCORE, pah'-jih 八十

FOURTEEN, jih-s' 十四; *the fourteenth*, di jih-s' 第十四

FOWL, *the domestic* —, kô kyi' 家°雞 (ih-tsah); *flying creatures*, fi-gying' 飛禽

Fox, wu-li' 狐狸 (ih-tsah);— skin, wu-bi' 狐皮

Fraction, se'-su 碎數; a — over, ling-deo' 零頭; one hundred and a — over, ih-pah ling tin' 一百°零點

Fracture, to ao'-dön 拗斷; fractured bone, kweh'-deo dön'-de 骨頭斷了°

Fragile, feh kying-liu' 弗經練; yüong-yi' se'-go 容易碎个°

Fragments, se'-k'we-deo' 碎塊頭; bits, ling-se' 零碎

Fragrant, hyiang 香; very — p'eng'-hyiang 噴香; to throw off fragrance, t'u hyiang-ky'i' 吐香氣

Frail, hyiah'-hyiah 瘦°弱°;— constitution, ti'-ts hyiah' 底子弱°

Frame for anything to rest or hang upon, kô'-ts 架°子; — to be hung on the wall, kwô'-kying 掛鏡 (ih-go)

Frame, to zao 造°;— laws, zao lih-fah' 造律法; to — a picture, p'e' ih-go kw'ông'-ts' 配一个°框子 (generally square).

Frank, straight forward, dzih-sông' 直爽; honest, lao'-jih 老實

Frankly, tsiao-dzih' 照直; speak —, lao-jih wô 老實話 tell me —, tsiao dzih' wô-hyiang'-ngô-dao 照直話向我道

Frankincense, jü'-hyiang 乳香

Frantically throwing arms about, dzông 撞; crying —, weh-dzông' weh-tin k'oh' 活撞活顛哭

Fraternal love, hyüong-æ'-di-kying' 兄愛弟敬

Fraud, bi'-tön 弊端; tsô'-kyi 詐計; kæn-kyi' 奸計; to use —, tsoh bi'-tön 作弊端 yüong tsô'-kyi 用詐計

Fraudulently obtained, tsoh-bi' læ'-go 作弊來个°; obtained by gross deception, kwa'-p'in læ'-go 拐°騙來个°

Freakish, sing-siang' moh-feh-ding' 心想摸弗定; ze-wæn' tao'-wæn 隨彎到彎

Freckle, n. kyiah'-tsi-pæn' 霜痣斑

Free to do as one pleases, zi hao' tso cü'-i 自°好做主意; to set free, sih'-fông 釋放; too — and irreverent in speaking, ky'ing-cü' boh-zih' 輕嘴薄舌; — schools, yi'-'oh or nyi'-'oh 義學°; without charge, bah 白°; to cross the ferry —, bah' ko-du' 白過渡; to eat rice —, ky'üoh bah væn' 吃°白飯; — from anxiety, kw'un-sing' 寬心;— from customs' duty, min se' 免稅; — in spending money, kw'un-siu' 寬手; song-siu' 鬆手

Free, to — from all obstacles, yiu fông-'æ'-go tu djü-diao' 有妨害个°都除去°

FREELY, without fear, fông'-tæn 放膽; willingly, dzing-nyün' 情願; nyün-i' 願意

FREEZE, to kyih ping' 結氷°;— to death, tong'-sah 凍死°;— the canals, kao kông' 膠°港

FREIGHT, lading of ship, jün'-li go ho'-veh 船裡个° 貨物; secret — (for avoiding customs), s-ho' 私貨;— paid for transportation, shü'-kyiah 水°脚

FREQUENTLY, le'-ts' 屢次; le'-djông 屢常

FRESH, sing-sin' 新鮮;— fish, sing-sin' ng' 新鮮魚°; not salt, dæn 淡; colors — and bright, ngæn-seh' sin-ming' 顏°色鮮明

FRESHEN it, (as salt fish), ts'iu'-gyi dæn' 浸°其淡

FRESHET, do shü 大°水°; to have a —, fah do-shü' 發大°水°

FRET, gæn; to — one, tsi-tseo' 嘈°嘈°; long gyi sing-væn'-tsi-tsao' 弄其心煩嘈°嘈; — one's self, zi-t'æn'-zi 自°嘆自°; p'i-dziang' p'i-tön' 批長批短

FRETFUL, gæn-gæn'tao-tao, used especially of old people.

FRETTED (by something), ông-beh'-tsi-tsao.

FRICTION, feh wah' 發滑; ts'iao'-ts'iao 糙°糙°; a great deal of —, ting-ts'iao' 頂糙°

FRIDAY, li-pa-ng' 禮拜°五°

FRIEND, beng-yiu' 朋友; siang-hao' 相好; siang-kyiao 相交; intimate —, cü-kyi' beng-yiu' 知己朋友; moh-nyih' beng-yiu' 莫逆朋友; ts'ih'-t'iah beng-yiu' 切貼朋友;— in trouble, wæn'-næn beng-yiu' 患難朋友; very good friends, ting kông'-leh-læ beng-yiu' 頂講°得°來°朋友; nyi-ky'i' beng-yiu' 義°氣朋友

FRIENDLESS, m̄-beng'-yiu 無°朋友; kwu sing' 孤身

FRIENDLY, 'o-moh'-go 和睦个°; ts'ing-æ'-go 親愛个°; kông'-leh-læ'-go 講°得°來个°;— (after a quarrel), 'o-de' 和了°

FRIENDSHIP, kyiao-dzing' 交情 a — exists, yiu kyiao-dzing' læ-tih 有交情个°; to break —, djih kyiao' 絕交

FRIGHTEN, to — one, long nying' ky'ih-hoh' 弄人°吃嚇;— away, hah'-t'e 嚇°退; to — one greatly (lit., to death), long nying' hah'-sah-de 弄人°嚇°殺了

FRIGHTENED, ky'ih-hoh'-de 吃嚇°了°; ky'ih-kying'-tih-de 吃驚的了°; ziu-kying'-de 受驚了°

FRIGHTFUL appearance, p'ô'-p'ô-go siang'-mao 怕怕个° 相貌; — place, hyiu'-hoh-go di'-fông 可°懼°的地方;— noise, sing-hyiang' ky'ih-hoh'-go 聲響吃嚇°个°

FRINGE, su-deo' 鬚頭;— around a mandarin's hat, ing-ts' 纓子

FRI　　　　　　192　　　　　　FRU

FRISK, *to jump about*, t'iao-læ' t'iao-ky'i' 跳來跳去°.

FRITTER, *n.* yiu-zah'-dön 油煤糰 (ih-go).

FRIVOLOUS, ky'ing-veo' 輕浮.

FRO, *go to and* —, læ-læ' ky'i-ky'i 來來去°去°; læ-wông 來往.

FROG, din-kyi' 田雞 (ih tsah); *green* —, ts'ing-wô 青蛙.

FROLIC, do hyi' 大°戲; do na'-'o 大°嬉戲; *rough play*, mæn tô' hyi'-deo.

FROM, dzong 從; *hinder him* — *coming*, tsu' gyi feh læ' 阻其弗來; — *Ningpo to Shanghai*, dzong Nying-po' tao Zông-hæ' 從寧波到上海.

FRONT, min-zin' 面前°; *in* — *of the house*, læ oh' min-zin' 在°屋面前°; — *door* (or *gate*), zin meng' 前°門; *do* meng' 大°門; ziang meng' 牆°門; deo meng' 頭門; — *room*, zin vông' 前°房.

FRONTIER, pin-kyiang' 邊疆; kao-ka' 交°界°; *go to the* —, tao pin-kyiang' ky'i 到邊疆去°; *within the* —, kying' ne 境內; *beyond the* —, kying' nga 境外°.

FROST, *white* sông 霜.

FROST-BITTEN, tong'-loh-de 凍落了°; ziang ngao'-loh-de 像°鹼落了°.

FROSTY *weather*, t'in' loh sông' 天落霜.

FROTH, beh 浡

FROWARD, gyüih-gyiang' 倔強; gyiang'-deo gyüih-nao' 強頭倔腦; *contrary*, 'ang-deo'-tsoh'-kying.

FROWN, *to* tseo mi-deo' 縐眉°頭; — *from uneasiness or displeasure*, zeo mi-deo' 愁眉°頭.

FROZEN, kyih-ping'-de 結氷了°; *spoiled by freezing*, ping-diao'-de 氷壞了°; — *to death*, tong'-sah-de 凍死°了°.

FRUGAL, tso nying-kô' 做人°家°; tsih'-gyin 節儉.

FRUIT, ko'-ts 菓子; *dried* —, ken ko' 乾菓; *kying ko'* 京菓; *to bear* —, kyih ko'-ts 結菓子; *first* — *of the season*, z-sing' ko 時新菓; zông sing'-ko 上新菓.

FRUITFUL, kyib'-leh meo-zing' 結得茂盛; sang'-leh to' 生得多; — *tree*, to sang-ko'-ts-go jü 多生果°子个樹; *this year is a* — *one*, kying nyin ko'-ts do nyin' 今年菓子熟年.

FRUITLESS, feh kyib'-ko-go 弗結菓个; *labor proved* —, kong-fu' loh-k'ong'-de 工夫落空了°; — (*i. e.* useless) *labor*, ngô-go siang'-vông p'o'-ba-diao-de 我个°想望破敗°了°; — *attempt*, bah-bah' s' 白°白°試.

FRUSTRATE, *my hopes are frustrated*, ngô sô' siang'-vông-go loh-k'ong'-de 我所想望个°落空了°.

FRY, to t'ah 爛; — cakes, t'ah ping' 爛餅; — meat, t'ah nyüoh' 爛肉°; — fish, tsin ng' 煎魚°; — by boiling in fat, zah 煤 (also boiling in water, in certain ways); — it brown, t'ah gyi wông' 爛其黃

FRYING-PAN, t'ah'-bun 爛盤; the native —, ngao-bun' 熬盆° (ih-go)

FUEL, fire-wood, za 柴°; good for —, tông za' siao 當柴°燒; dried grass, or — in general, za-ts'ao' 柴°草

FUGITIVE, one flying from trouble, dao-næn'-go nying' 逃難个°人°; escaped criminal, dao-væn' 逃犯

FULFILL, he will — his promises, gyi sô ing-hyü' we dzing-kong'-go 其所應許會成功个°; — a contract, jü iah' 如約; to be —, yiu ing'-nyiæn 有應驗; yiu yiao-nyiæn' 有效驗

FULL, mun 滿; mun'-tsoh 滿足; filled —, tsi-mun'-liao 齒滿了; the — time, z-'eo mun'-de 時候滿了°; z-'eo mun'-tsoh-de 時候滿足了°; face — of joy, mun'-min hwun-hyi' 滿面歡喜; to give a — account of, zing'-yin kông'-c'ih-læ' 盡°言講°出來; — grown, dziang-tsoh' 長°足; — moon, yüih-liang' yün-mun' 月亮圓滿; measure of iniquity —, oh'-kwun

mun-ying' 惡貫滿盈; — to the brim, bing k'eo' 平口; — of flies, ts'ông-ing' heh'-kyih-kao 蒼蠅甚°多°; — allowance, ngah-ts' mun'-de 額子滿了°; — number, su'-moh tsoh' 數目足

FULLER'S-EARTH, wông na-nyi' 黃坭

FULLY, jih-feng' 十分; jih-tsoh' 十足; djün-be' 全備; — prepared, jih-feng' be-hao' de 十分備好了°

FUME, vapor, ky'i 氣; fumes of opium, a'-p'in ky'i' 鴉片氣; — of tobacco, in ky'i' 烟氣

FUMIGATE, to hyüing-in' 熏烟; — with perfume, hyüing-hyiang' 熏香

FUN, to have —, hyi'-hyi 嬉戲; byi'-hyiah 戲謔; to play, na-'o'; only in — (with you), tæn-tsih' teng ng byi'-hyi 單只搭°你° 嬉戲

FUNCTION, kong-yüong' 功用 (veng.)

FUND, capital, peng'-din 本錢°; public fund, koh-t'ông' 國帑; t'ông'-nying 帑銀

FUNDAMENTAL, yiu keng-kyi' 有根基; — principles, ziang-kyiah' 墻°脚

FUNERAL, taking out the coffin, c'ih zæ' 出材°; c'ih sông' 出喪; to have a —, 'ang sông-li' 行°喪禮; c'ih ping' 出殯;

c'ih gyiu' 出柩;— ceremonies, sông-z' 喪事; to go through ditto, bæn sông-z' 辦喪事; to attend a —, song sông' 送喪; song zæ' 送材; — expenses, ping'-tsông-ts fi' 殯葬之費

FUNNEL, leo'-teo 漏斗; jün-ts' 旋子 (ih-go)

FUNNY, laughable, hao'-fah siao' 好發笑; we ying'-nying siao' 會引人°笑

FUR on the body, mao 毛; the skin with — bi-ts' 皮子; — robe, bi bao'-ts 皮袍子; sable —, ts'-tiao-bi 紫貂皮; ditto speckled, (hairs white-tipped), ts-mô'-tiao-bi' 芝麻貂皮; ermine —, nying-c'ü'-bi 銀鼠皮; squirrel —, hwe-tsih'-bi 灰脊皮; ditto (with the bellies), hwe-c'ü' bi 灰鼠皮; rabbit —, zih-c'ü'-bi 碩鼠皮; seal skin, hæ'-lo-bi 海騾皮; beaver or otter skin, t'ah'-bi 獺皮; Astrakhan (black lamb-skin), heh' ts-kao 黑紫羔; white lamb-skin, kao-bi' 羔皮; nyi-mao 二°毛; black and white ditto, hwô-kao' 花羔; unyeaned lamb-skin, koh-cong'-yiang-bi' 各種羊皮; hwe'-koh-cong-bi 灰各種皮; white ditto, cü-r-bi 珠兒皮; fox-skin, wu-bi' 狐皮

FURIOUS, dong-da'-nu'-de 動大°怒了°; hyüong mang' 兇猛

FURIOUSLY, quarrel —, pe ming' zao 亡°命嘈; pe ming' tang' 亡°命打; beat —, heng'-sing-go tang 狠心个°打

FURL, to — the sails, siu bong' 收篷; to pull down the sail, loh bong' 落篷; ditto partly, mô bong; tsô bong 遮°篷

FURLOUGH, to ask a —, kao kô' 告假°; to grant a —, cing' kao-kô' 准告假°

FURNACE, portable earthen —, fong-lu' 風爐; ngô' fong-lo' 瓦'風爐°; native kitchen range, tsao 灶

FURNISH, to prepare, be-bæn' 備辦; — a house, be-bæn' kô-sang' jih-veh' 備辦物°件°— his rice, kong gyi-go væn 供其个°飯

FURROW left by a plow, li gông-s'; — (in the face), veng lu' 紋路; furrowed, tang kæn'-de 打襇了°

FURTHER, a little —, yün-tin' 遠點

FURTHER, to —the business, nyüoh-dzing' gyi-z' 玉成其事 See FARTHER.

FURTHERMORE, ping'-ts'ia 拜且°; wa-yiu' 還°有

FURY, gwông-t'in' gwông-di'-go ô-wông 狂天狂地个°怒°

FURY, virago, p'eh'-vu 潑婦

FUSE, to yiang 煬

FUSIBLE, yiang'-leh k'æ'-go 煬得°開个°

FUSSY, so'-so-se-se' 瑣瑣碎碎 tsi-tsi'-tseo-tseo 嘈嘈嘲嘲
FUTILE, k'ong'-deo go 空頭个 m̄-yüong'-go 無用个; vu-ih 無益
FUTURE, tsiang-læ' 將來; the uncertain —, mi-læ' 未來; 'eo'-læ 後來; — event, tsiang-læ'-go z-ken' 將來个事幹; — misery, 'eo'-læ'-go kw'u'-næn 後來个苦難; the — life, 'ô'-si 下世; to provide for the —, bông'-be tsiang-læ'-go yüong-dziang' 防備將來个用場
FUZZY, yiu nyüong-deo' 有絨頭

G

GABBLING noise (as of many talking), zeo-ky'i' ka sing-hyiang'; zeng-zeng' hyiang; ditto, as of geese, ziang ngo kyiao ka sing-hyiang' 像鵝叫聲响
GADDING about, dziah nying kô' 走人家; ditto, like a cat yiu-hyi'-lông-dông', dziah'-kô-mao ka.
GAG, to — with a stick, ts'ang mih-dæn'-kong 撐篾彈弓; — by stuffing the mouth, seh cü'-pô 塞嘴巴
GAIN, profit, li-sih' 利息; hwô-li' 花利; dzæn'-deo 賺頭; good —, hao dzæn'-deo 好賺頭; hao li'-sih 好利息
GAIN, to get, teh'-djoh 得着; — profit, teh li' 得利; — advantage, teh'-djoh ih'-c'ü 得着益處; — (in play), ying 贏; — a victory, teh-sing' 得勝; — bodily strength, diao-yiang sing-t'i' 調養身體; ditto, by rest, tsiang yiang' 將養; gaining upon him, pi' gyi we zông' 比其會上; læ-tih ken'-gyi-zông zin' 正在趕其上前
GAINSAY, to p'i-poh' 批駁; pæn-poh' 翻駁
GAIT, tseo'-siang 走相
GALA-DAY, k'æ-sing', tsoh-loh'-go nyih-ts' 開心作樂个日子
GALE, do fong' 大風; mang' fong 猛風; gwông fong' 狂風; bao' fong 暴風
GALL, kw'u'-tæn 苦膽; hence courage, tæn'-ts 膽子
GALL-NUTS, be-ts' 梧子; — and copperas, be-ts', loh-væn' 梧子綠礬
GALLOP, to — or run, p'ao 跑; — a horse, p'ao mô' 跑馬
GALLOWS, frame for hanging criminals, tiao væn'-nying-go kô'-ts 弔犯人个架子
GAMBIER, ping-lông'-kao 檳榔膏
GAMBLE, to tu 賭; tu'-poh 賭博; hyi-tu' 戲賭; — with cash by the character pao, tang-pao' 打寶
GAMBLER, tu'-k'ah 賭客; tu'-p'e 賭胚; tu'-kweng 賭棍;

GAM 196 GAT

tu'-zeh 賭賊°; *to arrest gamblers,* k'ô tu 拏°賭
GAMBLING *stall,* tu-t'æn' 賭攤; — *house,* tu'-dziang 賭塲; tu'-gyüoh 賭局; — *tools,* tu'-gyü 賭具
GAMBOGE, deng-wông' 謄黃
GAME, *play,* hyi-shih' 嬉耍°; *play a* — *with dice,* dzih seh'-ts 擲骰°子; *to play a* — *of cards,* ts'ô ts'-wu-bæn' 扯紙糊牌; *play a* — *of chess,* tsiah' ih-bun gyi' 養°一盤棋; *to catch* —, tang-liah' 打癲; *lost the* — (*in gambling*), tu' shü-de 賭輸了°; *to make* — *of one,* hyi'-long nying' 戲弄人°
GANDER, yüong-ngo' 雄鵝
GANG, *a* ih-pông' 一幫; ih-tông' 一黨; *a* — *of robbers,* ih-pông gyiang-dao' 一幫強盜; *the rest of the* —, yü-tông' 餘黨
GANGRENE *has set in,* læn'-leh li-'æ' 爛得°利害
GAP, k'eo 口; — *in the mountains,* sæn ao' 山坳; *to mend or stop a* —, pu ky'üih' 補缺; seh dong' 塞洞; dong mun-seh' 洞墁塞
GAPE, *to* tang hô-hen' 打呵°欠
GARBAGE, ka'-dong-leh-seh' 界°洞垃圾
GARDEN, *vegetable* di-yün' 地園; ts'æ'-yün 菜園 (ih-ky'iu'); *flower*—, hwô-yün' 花園; — *bed,* ling 疄 (ih); — *path,*

siao' lu 小路; di-gông' (ih-da)
GARDENER *for vegetables,* cong-ts'æ'-go nying 種菜个°人°; — *for flowers,* cong-hwô'-go nying 種花个°人°
GARGLE, *to* — *the mouth,* dông k'eo' 盪口; — *the throat,* dông wu-long' 盪喉°嚨
GARLIC, da-sön 大蒜; — *bulbs,* da-sön'-deo 大蒜頭
GARMENT, i-zông' 衣裳; i-voh' 衣服 (a —, ih-gyin; a suit, ih-t'ao); *to wear only one* —, c'ün tæn gyin' i-zông' 穿單件衣裳°; *cotton* — *of a single thickness,* tæn-boh'-tæn 單薄
GARRISON, siu'-ping 守兵; — *of a city,* siu-dzing'-go ping 守城个°兵
GARRULOUS, to-djün-z'-go 多言°
GARTER, mah-ta' 襪°帶° (ih-tsah; a pair, ih-fu)
GAS, ky'i 氣; *coal* —, me-t'æn ky'i 煤炭氣
GASH, sông-k'eo' 傷口; keh'-sông 割傷 (ih-go)
GASP, *to* — *for breath,* ky'i t'eo'-feh-cün' 氣透弗轉; ih'-ky'i feh-cün' 噎氣弗轉
GATE, meng' 門 (ih-deo, ih-sin); *gate in two leaves,* sông-sin' meng 雙扇門; — *shutting off a street,* sah'-lah-meng 柵欄門; *to keep the city gates,* siu dzing-meng' 守城門
GATHER, *to* — *up or together,* siu-

jih-long' 收拾攏; — *in* (as crops), siu-tsing' 收進; siu hwô-li' 收花利; — *flowers*, tsah hwô' 摘花, ts'æ hwô' 採花; — (*in sewing*), ts'oh'-long 撮攏

GATHERS, *to push up the* —, ts'iu-long' 抽攏; *the* —, ts'oh-tih-go kæn' 撮的个°襉

GAUDY, hwô-seh' 花色; hwô-p'ao'.

GAUGE, tseh'-moh 準則°(ih-go)
GAUZE, sô 紗

GAY, *free from care and anxiety*, kw'a'-weh 快活°; — *in laughing, and talking*, hyi'-siao yin-k'æ' 喜笑顏開; — *colors*, yin'-li ngæn-seh' 艷麗顏°色

GAYLY *dressed*, c'ün'-leh-hyin' 穿得°顯

GAZE, *to* ts'ing'-ting k'en' 青盯看

GAZETTE, sing-veng'-pao 新聞報; *Peking* —, Kying-pao' 京報

GELATINE, (native), yiang-ts'æ' 洋菜; *fish-glue*, ng-kao' 魚°膠'

GEM, pao'-zah 寶石°

GENDER, feng nen-nyü' 分男女; — *of brutes*, feng ts'-yüong' 分雌雄; *of the male* —, yüong' ih-le' 雄一類; *of the female* —, ts'' ih-le' 雌一類

GENEALOGY, pu'-yi 譜系; *book of* —, kô-pu' 家°譜 (ih-peng)

GENERAL *term or designation*, tsong'-ming 總名; t'ong-ts'ing' 通稱; *in* — *use*, t'ong-yüong' 通用; t'ong-'ang' 通行°; — (opposed to particular), weng'-kweng 渾混; — *way of doing*, da-kæ' tso'-fah 大概做法

GENERAL *of an army*, tsiang-kyüing' 將軍

GENERALLY, da-kæ' 大概; da-tu' 大都; da-væn' 大凡; da-ti' 大抵; da-be' 大備; *in the main*, da-liah' 大略

GENERATE, *to* sang 生°

GENERATION, dæ 代; *former* —, zông dæ' 上代; *future* —, 'ô' dæ 下°代; *preceding generations*, lih dæ' 歷代; *the present* —, yin-dzæ' keh dæ' 現在一°代; peng'-dæ 本代; *from* — *to* —, tao shü'-shü-dæ-dæ 到世世代代

GENEROUS, ky'i'-kæ 氣概; da-kw'æ' 大快; du'-liang do' 度量大°; *very* —, 'ao-yiah' 豪俠; — *treatment*, 'eo'-dæ 厚待

GENESIS, *the book of* —, Ts'ông'-shü-kyi' 創世記

GENIAL *in manner*, 'o-ky'i 和氣; *lovable*, k'o-æ-go 可愛个°; — *as the Winter's sun* (used in speaking of a favorite teacher, &c.), ziang tong-t'in' nyih-deo ka' ko'-ko nying æ-'go 像°冬天日°頭個個人°愛个°; — *as* (sitting in) *the breezes of spring*, ziang zo-læ c'ing-fong li'-deo ka 像°坐在°春風裏頭

GENIUS, t'in-veng kao' 天分高;

a —, dzæ-ts' 才子; *a boy* —, jing-dong' 神童

GENTEEL, yüô'-cü 雅致; veng-yüô' 文雅; — *dress*, i-zông' veng-zing 衣裳文靜

GENTLE, no-jün' 懦善; lao'-jih 老實; — *disposition*, sing'-kah no-jün' 性格懦善

GENTLEMAN, veng-nying' 文人°; sin-sang' 先生 or 師; *old* —, lao' sin'-sang 老先生°; *act like a* —, iao tso veng-yüô'-go nying 要做文雅个°人°; iao jih-zông' feh iao' jih-'ô' 要習上弗要習下°

GENTLEMEN! cü-we' sin'-sang 諸位先生°! lih-we' sin'-sang 列位先生°!

GENTLY, *lightly*, ky'ing-fæn' 輕泛; *slowly*, wun'-fæn 緩泛; *speak* —, kông ky'ing-yin' si'-nyü 講°輕言細語; *speak more* —, kông ky'ing-sang'-tin 講°輕省°點

GENTRY, *Chinese* sing-kying' 紳衿; hyiang-sing' 鄉紳; sing-kying'-tông 紳衿黨 (used in reproach); — *who oppress others*, p'ô'-hyü-tông' 破靴黨

GENUINE, tsing 真; — *goods*, tsing ho' 真貨; *not* —, kô 假

GENUS, *class*, le 類 (ih)

GEOGRAPHY, di-gyiu'-go 'oh-veng' 地球个°學°問; *book on* —, di-yü'-ts 地輿志

GEOMANCER, fong-shü' sin'-sang 風水°先生°; we-k'en-fong-shü'-go 會看風水°个°; loh-z' sin-sang 六事先生°

GEOMANCY, *the theory of* —, di-li' 地理; fong-shü' 風水°; *book on* —, di-li' shü 地理書; loh-z' shü 六事書

GERM *of a leaf*, ngô-den' 芽°頭°; — *of flowers*, nyü 蕊°; 'en-nyü' 含蕊°

GERMINATE, *to* pao ngô' 苞芽°; ts'iu ngô' 抽芽°; pao ngô-den' 苞芽°頭°

GESTICULATE, *to* tsông siu'-shü 裝手勢; — (more earnestly), tsông kyü'-ts 裝舉止

GET, *to receive*, teh'-djob 得着°; tsih'-ziu 接受; *ditto* (as a package, &c.), do tao' siu 拿°到手; teh-tao' siu 得到手; *to take*, do 拏°; — *it for me*, teng ngô' ky'i do' 替我去°拿°; — *nothing by it*, ih' vu sô teh' 一無所得; *I can't* — *in*, ngô tseo'-feh-tsing' 我走弗進°; *How did the news* — *abroad?* keh sing'-sih dza-djün-k'æ'-go 這°信息怎°傳開个°? *It begins to* — *dark*, t'in en'-long-læ-de 天暗攏來了°; — *up*, bô-ky'i'-læ 爬起來; — *rich*, fab-dzæ' 發財; — *out of* or *rid of*, t'eh'-c'ih 脫出; — *ready* (beforehand) yü-be'-hao 預備好; be-bæn'-hao 備辦好; *go* — (yourself) *ready*, ky'i tsông-hao' 去°裝好; *can't*

— *over it* (*i. e.* keep thinking of it), ko'-sing-feh-ky'i 過°意°弗去°; — *down*, tseo'-loh-ky'i 走落去°; — *angry*, fah ông' 發怒'

GHASTLY, *like a ghost*, kyü'-siang 鬼°相; *death-like*, si'-siang 死°相

GHOST, *spirit*, ling 靈; *Holy Spirit*, Sing-Ling 聖靈; — *of the departed*, kyü 鬼°; *feeding the hungry ghosts*, fông yin-k'eo' 放焰口

GIANT, yi-yiang'-dziang-go nying' 異樣長个°人°; c'ih-kah'-dziang-go nying' 出格長个°人°

GIDDY, *dizzy*, deo-yüing' 頭暈; *to fall from giddiness*, yüing-tao' 暈倒

GIFT, song-go tong'-si 送个東西; *that is a* —, keh'-z song'-læ-go 這°是送來个°; *this is a* — *from my father*, keh-go tong'-si z ah-tia' peh ngô'-go 這个°東西是阿爹給°我个°; *to attend an officer, or literary man who is leaving, with gifts*, tang pô'-shü 打覇勢; *gifts of ceremony*, li 禮; li'-veh 禮物; *to give ditto*, song'-li 送禮; *to give gifts of congratulation*, song 'o'-li 送賀禮

GIFTED, ts-tsih'-hao' 資質好

GIGANTIC, *cannot tell how large*, wô'-feh-læ'-do' 話弗來大°

feh-tsiao dza do' 了°弗°得°大°

GIGGLE, *to* keh'-keh-siao 哈°哈°笑

GILD, *to* du kying' 鍍金; *to* — *by plunging*, seng'-kying 沁金; — *with gold leaf*, t'iah kying' 貼°金; pao kying' 包金

GILLS, *fish* ng-sæ' 魚°鰓

GILT-EDGED, kying-pin'-go 金邊个°

GIMLET, jün-tsön'-ts 旋°鑽子

GINGER, *fresh* sang-kyiang' 生°薑; *dried* —, ken-kyiang' 乾薑; *preserved* —, dông-kyiang' 糖薑; *powdered* —, kyiang-feng' 薑粉

GINGER-BREAD, sang-kyiang' kao 生°薑糕

GINGHAM, gyi-bun'-hwô-go-pu' 棋盤花个°布

GINSENG, jing-seng 人參; *foreign* —, yiang-seng' 洋參

GIRDLE, kyiao'-sing-ta 繳身帶°; — *with clasp*, k'eo'-ta 扣帶°; *bride's* —, koh'-ta 角°帶°; *to put on the* —, kyi kyiao'-sing-ta 繫繳身帶°

GIRL, nyiang-ts' 小°姐°; kwn-nyiang' 姑娘; *slave* —, ô-deo' 了°頭; s'-nyü 使女

GIRLISH, ziang nyiang-ts' ka 像小°姐°; ziang nyiang-ts-den'ka.

GIRTH, *horse's* mô'-du-ta 馬肚帶° (ih-keng, ih-diao)

GIVE, *to* peh 給°, 與°, 俾°; — (*to an inferior*), s 賜; s'-peh 賜給°;

—(to any one), s 施; to present, song'-peh 送 給°; — in charge, kao-dæ 交° 代°; — leave, hyü 許; cing 准; — him an answer, peh gyi we-ing' 給° 其 回音; — him trouble, peh gyi keh'-tah 俾 其 疙瘩; peh gyi we-næn' 俾° 其 爲 難; — a daughter in marriage, kô nön' 嫁° 囡; — vent to anger, c'ih ky'i' 出氣; — place to another, nyiang 讓°; nyiang-peh 讓° 與°; — up one's life, pe ming 亡° 命; sô'-c'ih sing'-ming 捨° 出 性° 命; p'ing ming' 拚命; — to the poor, s'-peh gyüong-nying' 施°給° 窮 人°; tsiu-tsi' nying-kô' 賙 濟 人° 家°; — coffins, sô-s' kwun-moh' 捨 施 棺 木; — up (resistance), voh 服; shü'-voh 輸 服; won't — in at all, ting'-cing 訂 準; — up a thing undertaken, t'e siu' 推 辭'; — up (or lose heart), sing si'-de 心 死° 了°.

GIVER, s'-cü 施 主; c'ih-din s'-cü 出 錢° 施 主; eng-cü 恩 主, the last so called by the receiver.

GIZZARD, cing 肫; cing-tsòng' 肫 掌

GLAD, hwun-hyi' 歡 喜; very —, fi-væn' hwun-hyi' 非 凡 歡 喜; feh'-tsiao dza hwun-hyi' 了° 弗° 得° 歡° 喜

GLADDEN, to — him, peh' gyi hwun-hyi' 俾° 其° 歡 喜; ying' gyi k'æ-sing' 引 其 開 心

GLANCE, a ih-k'en' 一 看; see at a —, ih-moh' liao-jün' 一 目 了 然

GLANCE to — off, ts'ia' ts'ah'-ko 斜° 擦 過; I have glanced over this book, keh' bu shü ngô k'en-k'en ko'-de 這° 部 書 我 看 過 了°

GLANDULAR swelling, heng-weh'; dæn-weh' 痰 核°

GLARE of light, kwông li-'æ' 光 利 害; — of lightning, din-kwông' 電 光; — from water, shü teo'-kwông 水° 鬭 光; glaring eyes, ngæn-tsing-kwông liu'-liu 眼° 睛 光 睜° 睜°

GLASS, po-li' 玻 璃; a pane of —, ih-kw'e' 一 塊; ih-p'in 一 片; to put in a pane of —, p'e ih-kw'e' po li' 配 一 塊 玻 璃; lest the — be broken, k'ong'-p'ô po-li' iao k'ao-se' 恐 怕 玻 璃 要 敲 碎; — beads, liao'-cü 料 珠; po-li' cü 玻 璃 珠; — bottle, po-li' bing 玻 璃 瓶; — ware, po-li' kô'-sang 玻 璃 物° 件°; po-li' ho 玻 璃 貨; — maker, siao po-li' s-vu 燒 玻 璃 司 務

GLAZING (for pottery, &c.), yiu-shü' 油 水°; to put on —, zông' yiu-shü' 上 油 水°

GLEAM, a — of light, ih-sin' liang-kwông' 一 線 亮 光; — of hope, ih-ngæn-ngæn' c'ih-lu' 點° 點° 出 路

GLIB *of tongue*, cü-jing'-bi-boh' 嘴唇皮薄
GLIDE, *to — along*, liu-ko'-ky'i 溜過去°; wah-ko'-ky'i 滑過去°; *— prettily*, ts'ô-ts'ô' tseo dza hao'.
GLIMPSE, *catch a — of*, tsiao-min k'en-kyin 照面看
GLISTEN, *to* t'eo-kwông' 透光; fah-kwông' 發光
GLITTERING, shih'-liang 雪亮; shih'-kwah-liang 雪括亮
GLOBE, gyiu 球; *terrestrial —*, di-gyiu' 地球; *celestial —*, t'in-gyiu' 天球; — (*or shade*) *of a lamp*, teng-tsao 燈罩 (ih-go)
GLOOMY, kwu-ts'i' 孤悽; *— and morose*, ziang meng-dong' lao-hwu' ka 像°悶洞老虎
GLORIFY, *to praise*, ts'ing-tsæn' 稱讚; *— God*, kwe yüong-wô' peh Jing-ming' 歸榮華與°神明
GLORIOUS, kwông-wô'-go 光華個°; yiu yüong-wô' 有榮華; yiu yüong-kwông' 有榮光 (veng.)
GLORY, yüong-wô' 榮華; kwông-ts'æ' 光彩; *to appropriate the — which belongs to another*, tsin bih'-nying-go kwông' 佔別人°個° 光
GLORY, *to — in*, ts'ing hyüing' 稱勳 See BOAST.
GLOSS, *to — over an affair*, tsông-sih' ih-yiang z-ken' 裝飾一樣事幹
GLOSSY, ts-jing' yiu kwông' 滋潤有光; ky'i liang-deo' 起亮頭; *not —*, m̄ kwông'-go 無°光個°
GLOVE, siu'-t'ao 手套 (*a pair*, ih-fu, ih-sông)
GLOWING *charcoal*, siao'-'ong'-go t'æn'-ho 燒紅個°炭火; *— heart*, sing ziang ho-döü' ka nyih 心像°火團熱°; *face — with pleasure*, hwun-hyi-teh 'ong-kwông' mun-min 歡喜得°紅光滿面
GLUE, kao 膠; wông'-kao 洼膠; *Canton —*, Kwông'-kao 廣膠; *fish —*, ng-kao 魚膠°; *cow-skin —*, ngeo-bi'-kao 牛°皮膠°
GLUTTONOUS, t'en-cü'-go 貪嘴個°; t'en-zih'-go 貪食個°; t'en-ky'üoh'-go 貪吃°個°
GNASH *the teeth*, ngao ngô' 齩牙°; ts'ih' ts' 切齒
GNAW, *to* k'eng 齦; *— a board*, k'eng pæn' 齦板
GO, *to* ky'i 去°; *come and —*, læ-wong 來往; læ-læ'-ky'i-ky'i 來來去°去°; *— up*, tseo'-zông-ky'i 走上去°; *— out*, tseo'-c'ih-ky'i' 走出去°; *— on a journey*, c'ih-meng' 出門; *— by or over*, tseo'-ko-ky'i 走過去°; *cannot —*, ky'i'-feh-læ 去°弗來; *— aboard*, loh jün' 落船; zông jün' 上船; *— on shore*, zông-ngen' 上岸; *— astray*, mi-lu 迷路; *the sun goes down*, nyih-deo' loh-sæn' 日頭

落山; — *out* (as fire), u-long'-ky'i 漸°漸°熄了°; — *away to avoid the heat*, bi shü' ky'i 避暑去°; — *your own way then*, dæn'-ming ng' 但憑°你°

GOAD, *to force*, pih 逼; *to excite*, kyih 激; *to urge*, ts'e-ts'e bih' 催促°

GOAT, sæn-yiang 山羊 (ih-tsah)

GO-BETWEEN, *mediator*, 'o-z'-nying 和事人°; — (*in marriage*), me-nying' 媒人°; — (*in buying*), cong-nying' 中人°; cong-nyiang'-nying 中央人°

GOD, Jing-ming' 神明; T'in-cü' 天主; Zông-ti' 上帝; *an idol*, bu-sah' 菩薩; *gods of wood and clay*, nyi-su'-moh-tiao 泥塑木雕; — *of the Buddhists*, Sih'-kyüô-meo'-nyi-veh' 釋迦牟尼佛; — *of War*, Kwæn-ti'-bu-sah 關帝菩薩; — *of the Taoists*, Nyüoh-wông'-da'-ti 玉皇大帝; *founder of the Taoist sect*, T'æ'-zông-lao-kyüing 太上老君; — *of Wealth*, Dzæ-jing'-bu-sah' 財神菩薩; — *of the City*, Dzing-wông'-bu-sah' 城隍菩薩; — *who judges departed spirits*, Nyin-lo'-da-wông' 閻羅大王; *gods — of the Earth* (over districts), T'u'-di bu-sah' 土地菩薩; *of the Kitchen*, Tsao'-kyüing bu-sah' 竈君菩薩; *the Ursa Major* (worshipped by scholars),

Veng-ts'ông'-ti'-kyüing 文昌帝君; — *of thunder and lightning*, Le-tsu'-bu-sah' 雷祖菩薩; Le-kong' 雷公; Le-bo' 雷婆

GODDESS *of Mercy*, Kwun-ing' 觀音; Kwun-shü'-ing-bu-sah' 觀世音菩薩; *Queen of Heaven* (worshipped by sailors), Nyiang-nyiang'-bu-sah' 娘娘菩薩; T'in-'eo'-nyiang'-nyiang 天后娘娘; — *that bestows children*, Song'-ts-nyiang'-nyiang 送子娘娘

GODLY (*lit.* devoted) *person*, gyin-dzing'-go nying 虔誠个°人°

GO-DOWN, dzæn'-vông 棧房

GOING, *the price is — down*, kô'-din læ-tih loh' 價°錢°正在°落; kô'-din læ-tih tih' 價°錢°正°在°跌; *where are you —?* ng'-tao ah-li-ky'i' 你°到何°處°去°?— *home*, kyü oh'-li ky'i 歸家去°; *fire is gone out*, ho' u-de' 火熄°了°

GOITRE, weh-seng-dæ' 猢°猻袋

GOLD, kying-ts' 金子; *pure —*, ts'ih'-kying 赤金; *light colored —*, dæn-kying 淡金; — *dust*, kying-sô' 金沙; — *fish*, kying-ng' 金魚; — *leaf*, kying yih'-ts 金葉子; — *foil*, kying-boh' 金箔

GOLDEN, kying-ts'-tso'-go 金子做个°

GONG, dong-lo' 銅鑼 (ih-min); *to strike the —* k'ao lo' 敲鑼;

strike the — for an alarm, k'ao lön-lo' 敲°亂鑼°

GOOD, hao 好; very —, ting hao' 頂好; very — man, kyüing-ts'-nying 君子人°; ting'-hao nying' 頂好人°; jün nying' 善人°; liang-jün'-nying' 良善人°;— medicine, hao'-yiah 好藥; liang-yiah' 良藥; not so — as, feh gyih'-jü 弗如;— for nothing, fi'-veh 廢物 (chiefly used of persons);— bye, (person going says), siao-be' 少陪; ditto (person staying says), mæn-mæn' ky'i 慢慢去°; are you in — health? ng hao' feh' 你°好否°? ditto (generally to an elderly person), ng gyin' feh 你°健否°? is the child in — health? siao nying' hwæn' feh 小孩好°否°? — night (to one going to bed), ts'ing en-cü' 請安置; in — order, zi-zi'-tsing-tsing 齊°齊°整整; I promise in — faith, ngô' sò wô' we tso-tao' 我所話會做到;— natured, &c., sing'-kah hao' 性格好;— penmanship, pih'-fah hao' 筆法好; da pih' 大筆; much — will come of it, we sang hyü'-to hao'-c'ü 會生°許多好處

GOODNESS, virtue, hao' teh'-ky'i 好德氣; thank you for your great —, to-dzing' ng-go da teh' 多承你°个°大德

GOODS, ho 貨; ho'-veh 貨物;

household —, kô-sang' jih-veh' 家°中°物°件°.

GOOSE, ngo 鵝 (ih-tsah); wild —, t'in ngo' 天鵝; ngang ngo' 雁鵝; — quill, ngo-mao-kwun' 鵝毛管

GORE, clotted blood, nying-long'-liao-go hyüih' 凝攏个°血; — in a garment, toh-koh' 摒角° (ih-go)

GORGEOUS, wô-wô'-li-li 華華麗麗

GORMANDIZER, dzæn-lao'-go nying 貪°饞个°人°.

GOSLING, siao-ngo' 小鵝 (ih-tsah)

GOSPEL, Foh'-ing 福音; preach the —, djün Foh'-ing 傳福音

GOSSIP, to pun shih-wô' 搬說話

GOSSIP, idle 'æn-yin' 'æn-nyü' 閒°言閒°語

GOURD, wu-biao' 瓠瓢 (ih-go); the bottle —, wu-lu' or weh-lu' 葫蘆

GOVERN, to kwun'-li 管理; djü治; công'-kwun 掌管;— China, kwun'-djü Cong-koh' 管治中國; — the family, djü kô 治家°; công'-kwun kô-vu' z 掌管家°務事

GOVERNMENT of a country, koh-tsing' 國政; — of affairs, koh'-kô tsing'-z 國家°政事

GOVERNOR of a province, fu'-dæ 撫臺; — of two or more provinces, tsong'-toh 總督;— of two or more fu cities, dao'-dæ 道臺; of one fu, or department, cü-fu'

知府; — *of a district or county,* cü-yün' 知 縣°

GOWN, *a Chinaman's long* — (worn girded), dziang-sæn' 長 衫; do-sæn' 大°衫; *ditto,* (worn ungirded), bao-ts' 袍 子; *China-woman's* —, ao 襖; do-ao' 大°襖; — *worn over another* —, nga-t'ao' 外°套

GRACE, *favor,* eng-we' 恩 惠; eng-tin' 恩 典; eng-c'ong' 恩 寵; eng-s' 恩 賜; *to say* —, zia-zia' Jing-ming' 謝°謝°神明

GRACEFUL, *easy in motion,* kyü'-ts yuô'-cü 舉 止 雅 致

GRACIOUS (as a superior), ky'in-ziang' 謙 讓; *will grant favor,* we s-eng' go 會 賜 恩 个°; *merciful,* dz-pe'-go 慈 悲 个°

GRADE, teng'-kyih 等 級; *a* —, ih-teng' 一 等; ih-kyih' 一 級

GRADUALLY, dzin'-dzin 漸 漸; *step by step,* ih-bu' ih-bu' 一 步 一 步; — *improving,* dzin'-dzin tsing-ih' 漸 漸 進 益; *ditto in health,* or *trade,* dzin'-dzin hao'-ky'i-læ 漸 漸 好 起 來

GRADUATE, *to mark by degrees,* feng du'-su' 分 度 數

GRADUATE, *first literary* —, (i.e. lowest), siu'-dzæ 秀 才; — *of the second degree,* kyü'-nying 舉 人; — *of the third degree,* tsing'-z 進 士; — *of the fourth degree,* 'en-ling' 翰 林; *to become a* — *of the 1st degree,* tsing 'oh' 進 學; *ditto of the 2nd degree,* cong kyü'-nying 中 舉 人; *ditto of the 3rd degree,* cong tsing'-z 中 進 士; *ditto of the 4th degree,* tin' 'en'-ling 點 翰 林; *the highest of the graduates,* zông nyün' 狀 元

GRAFT, *to* — *a tree,* tsih jü' 接 樹

GRAIN, *five kinds of* —, ng' koh 五°穀°; *viz.,* rice, dao 稻, *fine millet,* soh 黍, *coarse millet,* lu-tsi 稷° (including several varieties), *wheat,* mah 麥 (also including barley and buckwheat), *and beans,* deo 荳°

GRAIN, *texture,* lin 絡; veng 紋; *with the* —, dzih liu' 直 絡; *across the* —, wang liu' 橫 絡; wang veng' 橫°紋

GRAIN, *to* — (in painting, &c.), tso hwô-veng' 做 花 紋

GRAMMAR, veng-yüoh' or veng-'oh' 文 學

GRANARY, ts'ông 倉; — *for rice,* koh' ts'ông 穀 倉; *two granaries,* liang kæn ts'ông' 兩 間°倉

GRAND, *high and large,* kao-do' 高 大°; — (as an officer's train, or a body of soldiers), we-fong' 威 風; — *idea,* i'-s kwông'-kw'eh 意 思 廣 闊; — (as many buildings, or a city), væn-wô' 繁 華

GRANDDAUGHTER, *son's daughter,* seng-nyü' 孫 女; nön-su' 囡° 孫°; *daughter's daughter,* nga-sang-nön' 外°孫°囡°; *ditto's daughter,* yün' nga-sang-nön' 玄 外°孫°囡°

GRANDFATHER on father's side, yia'-yia 爺爺°; tsu'-vu 祖父; deceased —, sin-tsu' 先祖; your ditto, tseng-tsu' 尊祖; ditto (in answer), kô-tsu' 家°祖; mother's father, nga-kong' 外°公; wæ tsu'-vu 外祖父; great — on father's side, t'a'-kong 太°公; tseng-tsu' 曾祖; great great —, kao tsu' 高祖; great — on mother's side, t'a' nga-kong 太°外°公; wæ tseng' tsu 外曾祖; grandfather's older brother, pah'-kong 伯°公; grandfather's older brother's wife pah'-bo 伯°婆 grandfather's younger brother, soh'-kong 叔公; grandfather's younger brother's wife, soh'-bo 叔婆

GRANDMOTHER on father's side, nyiang'-nyiang 娘娘; tsu'-meo 祖母; deceased ditto, sin tsu'-meo 先祖母;—, on mother's side, nga-bo' 外°婆; wæ tsu'-meo 外祖母; deceased ditto, sin wæ-tsu' 先外祖; great — on father's side, t'a'-bo 太°婆; tseng tsu'-meo 曾祖母; ditto on mother's side, t'a'-nga-bo 太°外°婆

GRANDSON, son's son, seng-ts' 孫子; daughter's son, nga-sang' 外°甥; grandson's son, tseng-seng' 曾孫; grandson's grandson, yün-seng' 玄孫

GRANITE, greenish ts'ing zah' 石青°

GRANT, to cing 准; to bestow,

s'-peh 賜給; to allow, ing-hyü' 應許; ing-dzing' 應承;—this once, but never again, 'eo'-peh we-li' 後不爲例

GRAPES, purple bu-dao' 葡萄; ts'-bu-dao 紫葡萄; white —, se'-tsing bu-dao' 水晶葡萄

GRAPHICALLY, weh-siang' 活相;—described, kông'-leh weh-siang' 講得活相

GRAPPLE, to — with hooks, keo-djü' 鉤住; to hold fast, tsah' djü 紮°住

GRASP, to — in the hand, nyiah 捻; to clutch, cô 抓;—firmly, cô lao' 抓°牢 (cô or tsô)

GRASS, ts'ao 草; green —, ts'ing-ts'ao' 青草; to cut, — kah ts'ao' 割草

GRASS-CLOTH, 'ô-pu' 夏°布; (a piece, ih-p'ih)

GRASS-HOPPER, koh'-mang 蟲蜢°; keh'-mang 蚱°蜢°(ih-tsah)

GRATE (in a stove, or furnace), hô'-lu tsah'-li 火爐柵°

GRATE, to —, bao 刨;—nutmeg, bao nyüoh-ko' 刨肉°果;—(i. e. grind) the teeth, mo ngô-ts' 磨牙°齒;—upon the senses, seng'-nying-go 塞°心

GRATEFUL, yiu peng'-sing 有本心; yiu jing-sing' 有仁心; I am — to you (for great favor), ngô ken' ng-go eng' 我感你個°恩; he is —, gyi'-yiu peng'-sing 其有本心; he is — to me, gyi' ken ngô'-go eng' 其感我個°恩

GRATIFIED, hwun-hyi' 歡喜; highly —, sing'-li to'-siao kw'a'-loh 心裡多少快樂

GRATIFY, to — one's desire, dzong sing' sô-yüoh' 從心所欲; seeking to — another's wishes, t'i'-sing t'iah-i'-go 體心貼意個°

GRATITUDE, peng'-sing 本心; ken-eng'-go-sing 感恩個°心; jing-sing 仁心

GRATUITOUSLY, give —, bah-song' 白°送; to eat rice —, bah ky'üoh'-væn 白°吃飯

GRAVE, tomb, veng 墳; veng-mo' 墳墓 (ih-yüih, or ih-ts); to go to the —, worship, and add earth, zông-veng' 上墳; to make a mound over a —, ling-veng' 淋墳; — clothes, ziu-i' 壽衣; ko'-lao-i' 故老衣; lang'-i 冷衣; — stone, (upright) veng'-li-go pe' 墳裡個°碑; veng'-li-go pe-ba' 墳裡個°碑牌°; ditto, (laid lengthwise in the side of the mound), læn-t'u' 攔土; — yard, veng-di' 墳地

GRAVE, lao'-lao 老老; — countenance, min-k'ong' lao'-pæn-pæn 面孔老板板; lao'-lin 老臉; weighty, djong'-jih 重實

GRAVEL, zah-sô' 石°沙; — in the bladder, sô-ling' 沙淋

GRAVELY, lao-lao'-ky'i-ky'i 老氣; — assured me, lao'-ky'i-vu-

dih' teng ngô kông' 老氣無敵與°我講°

GRAVITATION, attraction of —, siang-hyih'-ts-shü 相吸之勢

GRAVITY, tendency to the earth's centre, di-gyiu hyih'-lih 地球吸力

GRAVY, tsih'-shü 汁水; lu 滷; tsih'-lu 汁滷; — tureen, tsih'-shü kwun' 汁水罏

GRAY, hwe-seh' 灰色; (slightly) — haired, deo'-fah hwô-bah'-de 頭髮花白'了°; becoming —, læ'-tih bah-ky'i'-læ 漸°漸°白起來

GRAZE, to rub against, ts'ah'-djoh 擦著°; to eat grass, ky'üoh ts'ao' 吃°草

GRAZIER, yiang ngeo'-go cü'-kwu 養牛個°主顧

GREASE, yiu 油; yiu-nyi' 油膩

GREASE, to dzô yiu' 搭油; ts'ah yiu' 擦油; — the hair, yiu' fu deo-fah' 油傅頭髮

GREASY, yiu yiu-nyi' 有油膩; too — (fat), t'eh' yiu-nyi' 甚°油膩; t'eh yiu' 甚°油

GREAT, do 大; very —, do-leh'-kying 大°得緊; a — many, hyü'-to 許多; — while, hyü'-to kong-fu' 許多工夫; of — advantage, do' yiu' ib'-c'ü 大有益處; of — extent (as the sea), mang-yiang'-yiang 漫洋洋

GREATER than, do-jü' 大°如; — than that, pi gyi' do 比其

GREATEST, the ting'do 頂大°
GREATLY, do-nyiang' 大°樣°; long-do' 弄大°;— mistaken, do-nyiang' ts'eng' ts'o 大°樣°忖錯
大°; still —, keng'-kô do' 更加大°; yü-kô' do 愈加大°; the — part, ih do pun' 一大°半
GREEDY, t'en to' 貪多;—in eating t'en ky'üoh' 貪吃°; dzæn-lao' 貪饞; lao-zao'; wants more than he can chew, "t'en to', ziah'-feh-se'" 貪多嚼弗碎
GREEN, loh 綠; pih'-loh 碧綠; bluish —, shü'-loh 水°綠; pea —, kyiu'-ngô-seh 韭芽°色; greenish lemon color, mih-seh' 蜜色
GREET, to môug-môug' 望°望°; 'co-'co' 候候; to wish peace, ts'ing-en' 請安; to congratulate, 'o-'o' 賀賀; I — (you), kong-hyi' kong-hyi' 恭喜恭喜
GRIEF, pe-sông 悲傷; great —, t'ong'-sông 痛傷; sorrow, iu-meng' 憂悶
GRIEVANCE, wrong, we'-ky'üoh 委屈°; tell one's —, su-ün' 訴冤
GRIEVE me, cü'-s ngô tæn iu-meng' 致使我擔憂悶; long'-leh ngô sing' næn-ko' 弄得°我心難過
GRIEVOUS, heavy, djong 重; afflictive, kw'u 苦; severe, li-'æ' 利害
GRIM, p'ô'-siang 怕相

GRIMACE, to make crooked mouths, tsông hwa-cü' 裝歪°嘴°; li-leh ngô'-ts siao' 齜得°牙°齒°笑; li-ngô'-bô-ts' siao' 齜牙齜齒笑
GRIN, to draw up the lips, showing the teeth, c'ih'-jing lu-ts' 出唇露齒 (not necessarily laughing.)
GRIND, to mo 磨; — to powder, mo-feng' 磨粉; — in a mortar, nyin 研: ditto to powder, nyin-meh' 研末
GRIND-STONE, mo-tao'-zah 磨刀石°
GRIPES, du'-dziang kao'-long 肚腸絞°攏
GRISTLE, deng-kying' 輭骨°; ts'e'-kweh 脆骨 (veng.)
GRIT, the coarse part of meal, feng'-deo 粉頭; sand, sô-nyi' 沙泥
GRITTY, containing sand, yiu sô'-go 有沙个°
GROAN, to üô-üô'-hyiang 呀°呀°響; — loudly, yüô-yüô'-si; groaning with pain, t'ong'-teh üô-üô'-hyiang 痛得°呀°呀°響
GROCERY, zah-ho'-tin 雜°貨店 (where wax, alum, thread, ratan, dye-stuffs, &c., are sold); nen-poh' zah-ho'-tin 南北雜貨店 (where sugar, fruits, nuts, &c., are sold).
GROIN, kah'-kyiah-vong' 夾°脚縫
GROOVE, a ih-da zao' 一埭°漕
GROPE, to moh-læ' moh-ky'i' 摸來摸去°;— in the dark, en'-moh 暗摸

GROSS, *coarse and large*, ts'u-do' 粗大°;— *and vulgar*, yiu-ky'iang'-weh-diao' 油腔滑調;— *language*, yiu-wô' 油話; *in the* —, *or good and bad together*, lin-deo'-ta-kyiah' 連頭帶°脚;— *weight*, lin-bi' 連皮; mao'-kying-liang 毛勍兩; *buy in the* — *or large quantity*, teng'-tông ma' 薆當買°; *price when bought in the* —, t'ong bun' 'ông-dzing' 通盤行情

GROUND, di-yiang 地; *basis*, keng-kyiah' 根脚

GROUND-FLOOR, di-pæn' 地板

GROUNDLESS, m̄-keng'-kyiah 無根脚; m̄-ing'-ts'ong 無影踪

GROUND-NUT, *pea-nut*, hwô-seng' 花生

GROUND-RENT, di tsu'-din 地租錢°

GROUP, de 隊; *in a* —, dzing-de' 成隊; *in groups*, de-tang'-de 隊打隊

GROVE, ling 林; jü-ling' 樹林; *one tree cannot become a* — (*i. e. one alone cannot do the work of many*), "doh-moh' feh-dzing'-ling" 獨木弗成林

GROW, *to* do-ky'i'-læ 大°起來; *to multiply*, to-ky'i'-læ 多起來; hying'-ky'i'-læ 興起來;— *less* (*as a pencil by use*, &c.), siao mo-long'-ky'i 銷磨攏去°; *to* — *cold*, dzin'-dzin lang'-ky'i-læ 漸漸冷°起來; — *into a habit*

dzin'-dzin tso'-kwæn 漸漸做慣; *it grew so*, sang-dzing' z-ka'-go 生°成如°此°; t'in-jün' z-ka'-go 天然如°此°

GROWL, *to* wu-wu'-hyiang 唎唎響

GROWN, *full* dziang-tsoh'; tsoh; tsiang-tsoh' 長足; do-tsoh' 大°足

GRUDGE, *to* (*as money*), feh-sô'-teh' 弗捨°得; *a* —, *or to lay up a* —, kyiæ'-i 介意; *don't lay up a* — *against me*, hao-vong' kyiæ'-i ü ngô 弗"用°介意於我

GRUEL, *meal* boh-go feng'-wu 薄個°粉糊; *rice* —, boh-coh' 薄粥; ing'-t'ông 飲湯; *make rice* —, lin boh-coh'.

GRUFF *in manner*, oh'-cü-ngæn-siang 惡嘴眼相; *to speak gruffly*, wu-long' hyiang-liang kông 喉°嚨響亮講°; yi-li' wæ-læ' kông'; *to reprove gruffly*, heng-hô.

GRUM *looking*, lang'-lin-go 冷臉個°; lao'-pæn-pæn 老板板; *very* —, heng'-hwu-hwu; — *in face and answer*, lang-min' lang-teh' 冷°面冷°答

GRUMBLE, *to* ün 怨;— *to one's self*, zi gæn' zi 自°憾自°; *at heaven and earth*, ün'-t'in 'eng-di' 怨天恨地;— *like a discontented spirit*, ün-wông' kyü'-kyiao 冤枉鬼°叫

GRUNT, to ng-ng'-hyiang 哽哽響; — as a pig, nyü-nyü'-hyiang 嗯°嗯°響

GUARANTEE, pao-p'iao' 保票; pledge, ti'-deo 抵頭; tông'-deo 當頭; ah'-deo 押°頭

GUARANTEE, to pao 保; — success in a lawsuit, pao' tang'-kwun-s 包打官司

GUARD, to pao'-wu 保護

GUARD, to be on one's —, kying'-bông 謹防; tso-gyi' 留°心°; kwu'-djoh 顧着°

GUARD, military pao'-wu-go ping' 保護个°兵; imperial body —, z'-we 侍衛

GUARDIAN, kæ-kwun'-go nying 該管个°人°; — of a child, pao'-nying 保人°; dæ-vu'-meo 代父母

GUESS, to ts'æ 猜; ts'æ-ts'æ'-k'en 猜猜看; to — the meaning, a i'-nyi 猜意義; to estimate, kwu 估; — a riddle, ts'æ mets' 猜謎°子; — one's thoughts, liao sing-s' 料心思; guessed rightly, ts'æ-djoh'-de 猜着°了°; can't —, ts'æ-feh-c'ih' 猜弗出

GUEST, nying-k'ah' 客°人°; to receive (meet) a —, we nying-k'ah' 會客人°; to entertain a —, be k'ah' 陪客; to accompany a —, song k'ah' 送客; belonging to a —, k'ah'-pin-go k'ah'-vông 客房.
客邊个°; — room or parlor,

Guest in the veng-li is k'ah-nying; therefore we transpose the characters wherever nying-k'ah occurs.

GUIDE, ling-lu'-go nying 領路个°人°

GUIDE, to ling 領; lead the way, ling lu' 領路; ying'-dao lu' 引導路; to — the pen (for another), pô pih' 把筆

GUILD, pông 幫; Fuh-kien —, Kyin'-pông 建幫; Canton —, Kwông'-pông 廣幫

GUILE, kæn-tsô' 奸°詐; full of —, jing'-z kæn-tsô' 純°是奸°詐

GUILELESS, dzih-kwah' 直鵠; m̄ tsô'-sing 無°詐心

GUILT, ze 罪; ze'-ming 罪名; to expiate —, ti ze' 抵罪; ti'-siao ze' 抵銷罪

GUILTLESS, m̄ ze' 無°罪; m̄ ze'-ming 無°罪名

GUILTY, yiu ze' 有罪; yiu' ze'-ming 有罪名; — of death, yiu si'-ze 有死°罪

GUISE, man in the — of a woman, nen-tsông'-nyü'-pæn 男裝女扮

GUITAR, four stringed —, bi-bô' 琵琶; three stringed —, yin-ts' 絃子

GULF, ao 澳; wæn 灣

GULL, sea kông-mæn' 朋°鷗°

GULL, to deceive, ky'i-p'in' 欺騙; kwa'-p'in 拐騙

GULP down, t'eng-loh'-ky'i 吞落去°; to — up, t'u'-c'ih 吐出

GUM, jü-kao' 樹膠°;— benjamin, en-sih'-hyiang 安息香
GUMS, ngô-nyüoh 牙°肉°
GUN, ts'iang 鎗; nyiao'-ts'iang 鳥鎗 (ih-kwun); to fire a —, fông nyiao'-ts'iang 放鳥鎗
GUN-BOAT, p'ao'-jün 礮船
GUNNER, ts'iang-siu' 鎗手; cannonier, p'ao'-siu 礮手
GUN-POWDER, ho'-yiah 火藥; to mix —, keh ho'-yiah 合火藥
GUNSHOT, within kong-bu'-li 弓步裡; beyond —, kong-bu'-nga 弓步外°; (these terms are principally used in archery).
GUN-SMITH, cü-ts'iang'-go 鑄鎗个°; a repairer of guns, siu-ts'iang' s-vu' 修鎗司務
GURGLING noise, goh-loh-loh' hyiang' 穀轆轆°響; — in the throat, hao'-ti-dæn zông' sing-hyiang' 喉°嚨痰上聲響
GUSH, to — out, üong'-c'ih 湧出; piao-c'ih' 滾出; pao'-c'ih 爆出; tears — out, ngæn-li pao'-c'ih-læ 眼淚爆出來
GUST, a — of wind, ih-zi fong'; ih-dzing fong' 一陣風
GUSTO, he told it with —, gyi-zi' kông-leh yiu mi-dao' 其自°講°得°有味°道
GUTS, dziang 腸; du'-dziang 肚腸
GUTTER for conveying water, shü'-liu 水°溜; drain, keo 溝
GUTTURAL sound, 'eo-ing' 喉音
GYPSUM, zah-kao' 石°膏

H

HABIT, in the — of smoking, kwæn iao ky'üoh'-in 慣°要吃°烟; — becomes second nature, jih-kyiu' dzing t'in-sing 習久成天性; jih-kwæn' dzing z-jün' 習慣°成自然; it is hard to break up an old —, tso'-kwæn-liao næn kæ' 做慣°了難改; careless habits, wa yiang'-væn 孬°樣式°; bad —, wa bi'-ky'i 孬°脾氣
HABITABLE, hao-djü'-go 好住个°; not —, djü'-feh-læ 住弗來
HABITUAL, it is — with him to do so, gyi su'-djông z-ka' tso'-fah 其素常如°此做法; gyi kwæn' z-ka 其慣°如°此
HABITATION, dwelling house, djü-kyü' 住居; djü-oh' 住屋
HACK, to cut irregularly (with a knife), lön kah' 亂割; ditto (with a knife, or axe), lön tsæn' 亂斬
HAG, m yiang'-væn-go lao-t'a-bo' 無°樣式°个°老太°婆
HAGGARD, t'eh-ying' 脫形
HAGGLE, to — with scizzors, tsin'-leh ky'üih-tsing'-ky'üih-c'ih' 剪得缺進缺出; — with a knife, ts'ih'-leh mao-mao'-ts'ao-ts'ao 切得毛毛草草; — about price, leng-liang kô'-din 論量價°錢°; — (about anything), leng'-kying kwu'-liang 論勍估兩

HAI 211 HAL

HAIL, boh-ts' 雹°子; to —, loh boh-ts' 落雹°子

HAIL, to call, eo 叫°; call loudly, eo-leh hyiang' 叫°得°響; when hailing a stranger, say teacher, sin-sang' 先生°; if elderly say older brother, ah-ko' 阿哥; or uncle, ah-song' 阿叔°; if a mechanic, s-vu' 司務

HAIR on animals, mao 毛; on the human body, 'en-mao' 汗毛; — on the head, deo-fah' 頭髮 (ih-keng)

HAIR-BRUSH, deo-fah' shih'-tsiu 頭髮刷箒; native — (for mucilage), ming'-ts 抿子 (ih-kwun)

HAIR-BREADTH, not the difference of a —, 'ao-vu koh-yiang' 毫無各樣; s-'ao feh-ts'o' 絲毫弗錯; within a — (i. e. eyebrow hair) of being killed, ts'ô-ih min-mao iao sah'-diao-de 差一眉°毛要殺了°

HAIRY (as a person), ng-'mao to 五°毛多

HALE, k'ông-gyin' 康健; kyiah'-ky'ing-siu'-gyin 脚輕手健; sing-tsông' lih-gyin' 身壯力健 only used of young people.

HALF, pun 半; exactly —, te'-pun 對半; p'ih-pun'-pin 劈半邊; — an hour, pun' tin-cong 半點鐘; a dollar and a —, ih-kw'e'-pun 一塊半; — brother, koh'-meo hyüong-di' 各母兄弟; this —, dông'-pun-pin 這°半邊; that —, keh'-pun-pin 那°半邊; — cooked, sang-hwe-boh-loh' 生°灰泊落; pun'-sang-li-joh 半生°裡熟 (also used for a lesson half learned); — done, pun' tso-hao' 半做好; — moon, pun'-pin yüih-liang 半邊月亮; on — pay (soldiers), ky'üoh pun'-feng zin-liang' 吃°半分錢°粮; ditto (officials), ziu pun'-fong 受半俸

HALL, central room, cong-kæn' 中間°; an entrance room, tsing'-c'ih-kæn 進出間°; the principal room in a Chinese house, dông-zin' 堂前°; ancestral —, z-dông' 祠堂; — of assembly, kong-sô' 公所; we'-kwun 會舘; — of audience (emperor's), din 殿 kying-lön'-din 金鑾殿; — of examination (for kyü-nying), kong'-yün 貢院; ditto (for siu-dzæ), ts'ah'-yün 察院; k'ao'-bang 考柵°; — of learning, 'oh-dông 學°堂

HALLOO there, 'e 唉; to shout, wæ-wæ eo-hyiang 高°聲°叫°響

HALLOW, to reverence, tseng-kying' 尊敬; set it apart as holy, tseng-ky'i gyi tso sing'-jün-go 尊敬其做聖善个°

HALO over the head, deo-zông' 'ao-kwông' 頭上毫光; — of wisdom, we'-kwông 慧光; — around

HAL 212 HAN

the moon, yüih-yüing 月暈
HALT, to stop a while, dzæn-z' deng-loh' 曹時停°落; halt! lih-loh' 立落!
HALT, lame, kwa'-kyiah 拐°脚
HALTER for a horse, mô'-long-deo 馬韁頭
HALVE, to te'-feng-k'æ 對分開
HALVES, two liang'-kô-sang'; liang'-pun-pin' 兩半邊
HAM (salted and dried), ho'-t'e 火腿; salted —, yin t'e 醃腿; — in man, kyiah'-ao 脚㘭
HAMLET, a ih-ts'eng 一村
HAMMER, lông-deo' 榔頭; iron —, t'ih djü' 鐵鎚; t'ih' lông-deo 鐵榔頭 (ih-kwun); — handle, lông-deo' ping 榔頭柄
HAMMER, to — iron, tang t'ih' 打鐵; — clothes, djü i-zông' 搗°衣裳°; — a nail, k'ao ting-cü' 敲°釘銖
HAMMOCK, hanging cot, tiao'-zông 吊床°
HAMSTRING, the tendon above the heel, (which the Chinese cut in lieu of the hamstring), kyiah'-kying 脚筋; 'eo'-ts'in-kying 脚跟筋; to cut ditto, kyiah'-kying fông'-dön 脚筋放斷
HAND, siu 手 (ih-tsah); both hands, liang-tsah siu 兩隻手; sông siu' 雙手; give him a — (i. e. help), vu gyi' ih-pô' 扶其一

把; to stretch forth the —, sing siu' 伸手; to shake the —, la siu' 攔手; draw the — into the sleeve, soh siu' 縮手; geo siu'; to come to —, tsih tao' siu 接到手; to carry in both hands, p'ong p'ong°; to join both hands, 'eh-công 合掌; ditto in salutation, kong siu' 拱手; the right —, jing' siu 順手; jing-tsah' siu; the left —, tsia' siu 左°手; an experienced —, joh-siu' 熟手; a raw —, sang-siu' 生°手
HAND, to di 遞; — up, di-zông' 遞上; — to her chair, tông gyi zông gyiao' 扶其上轎; — over, kao-fu' 交付; kao'-dæ 交°代; — down (as tradition), djün-loh'-læ 傳落來
HAND-BASIN (i. e. face-basin), min-dong' 面桶; min-beng' 面盆
HAND-BELL, ling 鈴 (ih-tsah); to ring a —, loh ling' 搖鈴; yiao ling' 搖鈴
HAND-BREADTH, a ih siu'-min kw'eh' 一手面闊
HAND-CUFF, siu'-k'ao 手栲 (a pair, ih-fu)
HANDFUL, a ih-pô' 一把; ih muu'-siu 一滿手
HANDIWORK, siu'-dön 手段
HANDKERCHIEF, kyün-p'æn' 絹帕°; silk — (carried by Chinese women for ornament), siu'-p'ao 手帕°

HANDLE, *straight* ping 柄; *rounded* — or *bale*, gwæn 鐶° (ih-go); there are a few exceptions thus, *a tea-pot* — (at the side) is either, dzô-wu' ping 茶壺柄 or dzô-wu' gwæn 茶壺鐶°; and a *cup* — is, pe-ts ping 杯子柄; ng'-tô-bi 耳°朶皮 is used, but not properly.

HANDLE, *to* long 弄; *to touch*, moh 摸; *to take in the hand, do* læ siu-li 拏°在°手裡; *to move*, dong 動; *must not* —, m̃-nao' long 弗°可°弄; m̃-nao' dong 弗°可°動

HANDSOME (used of persons, pictures, &c.), me'-li 美麗; ts'ing siu' 清秀; *pretty*, hao'-k'en 好看; *very* — *woman*, me' nyü 美女; — (as dress, places, &c.), wô-li' 華麗; yin-li' 艶麗; — (as work), tsing-cü' 精緻; — *as Si-s* (a beauty of antiquity), ziang Si-s ka me'-mao 像°西施美貌

HANDWRITING, pih'-tsih 筆跡; z'-tsih 字跡

HANDY, ling-long' t'ih-t'eo' 玲瓏剔透; *convenient*, bin-tông' 便當

HANG, *to* tiao 弔; — *against* (as against the wall), kwô 掛; *hang* (it) *up*, kwô'-kwô hao' 掛掛好; *to — one's self*, zông-tiao' 上弔; yün-liang' 懸樑; — *a person*, tiao nying sah' 弔人°死; —

to dry (properly, in the shade), lông 晾

HANK, ih-kao' 一絞°; ih-siao 一綃; — *of silk*, ih-kao s-sin' 一絞°絲線; — *of linen thread*, ih-siao-sin' 一綃線

HANKER, *to* — *after*, ts'ih'-sing-go siang' 切心个°想; sah'-k'eo siang'.

HAPPEN, *when will it* —? kyi-z' yiu' 幾時有? *when did it* —? læ kyi-z' 在°幾時? *just happened so*, p'ong'-læ we'-su 遇°著°算°數; *when walking I happened to have water thrown upon my head*, ngô tseo'-go z-'eo yiu shü', teo'-deo tao'-loh-læ 我走時候有水°兜頭倒落來; *happened so once* (to be bad), ngeo' ih-we ts' 偶一爲之; *there happened* (chanced) *to be*, neo'-ts'eo yiu' 偶°湊有; *happened to be right* (or wrong) *for once*, ts'in tsiao gyi vong 千朝奇逢

HAPPILY, *fortunately*, ying-hyi'-teh —, 幸係°得; ky'ü-leh' 虧°得°; ying-r' 幸而

HAPPINESS, foh'-ky'i 福氣; *peace is* —, bing-en' ziu z foh' 平安就°是福; *had the* — *to meet* (him), yiu ying' yü-djoh-de' 有幸遇著°了°; *you have great* —, ng hao' foh'-ky'i 你°好福氣

HAPPY, k'æ-sing' 開心; yiu foh'-ky'i 有福氣; hao'-foh-ky'i 好福氣; kw'a'-weh 快°活; —

man, yiu foh'-ky'i-go nying' 有福氣个人°; foh'-nying 福人°; *I am very* —, ngô sing'-li kw'a'-loh-go 我心裡快樂个°; ngô ting' k'æ-sing' 我頂開心; — *face*, 'o-yin'-yüih-seh' 和顏悅色

HARASS, *to* tsoh-næn' 作難; *harassed*, sing-væn'-tsi-tsao 心煩嘈°嘈; væn-meng' 煩悶; *greatly harassed*, ng'-mô-loh-deo'-cün 五°馬六頭鑽

HARBOR, k'eo 口; hæ'-k'eo 海口; kông-k'eo' 港口; *enter the* —, tsing k'eo' 進口

HARBORING *resentment*, yiu ün'-ky'i dzeng'-tih 有怨氣存的; ün'-ky'i feh-sæn' 怨氣弗散; — *feelings of dislike*, yiu 'eng'-sing kyi'-tih 有恨心記的

HARBOR-MASTER, li'-jün-t'ing' 理船廳

HARD, ngang 硬°; *difficult*, næn 難; — *to do*, næn-tso' 難做; — *water*, sang-shü' 生°水°; shü sing'-dao ngang 水°性道硬°; *egg boiled — as a stone*, dæn ts'-leh zah-ngang'-de 蛋煮得石°硬了°; — *work*, sang-weh' keh-tah 生°活疙瘩; *ditto* (heavy), djong'-deo sang-weh' 重頭生°活; *study —*, yüong kw'u'-kong doh-shü 用苦功讀書; — *to get on with*, (*i. e.* won't bear crossing), næn

ts'ah-ts'o 難作伴°; — *to say or believe*, næn-dao' 難道

HARD-HEARTED, ngang-sing'-go 硬°心个°; sing-dziang-ngang' 心腸硬°

HARDEN, *to become hard* (as the heart, vegetables, &c.), pin-ngang' 變硬°; *will* — (as jelly, &c.), we-ngang' 會硬°; *to grow hard*, ngang-ky'i'-læ 硬°起夾

HARDLY *enough*, sao-we ts'ô'-tin 稍為差點; *I had* — *seated myself when he came*, ngô wa tsih'-leh zo'-loh gyi' ziu læ'-de 我還只坐°落其就°來了°

HARDSHIP, siao'-kw'u 小苦; *great* —, næn-deo' 難頭; *to suffer* —, ky'üoh siao'-kw'u 吃小苦; *suffer great* —, ziu-næn' 受難

HARDWARE, *ironware*, t'ih'-ho 鐵貨; *iron utensils*, t'ih'-ky'i 鐵器

HARDY, kying-kweh'-hao 筋骨好; *firmly knit*, tsah'-cü 堅°固°; *can endure it*, tsah'-cü kying'-leh ky'i 堅°固°經得°起

HARE-LIP, ky'üih-cü' 缺嘴

HARK! t'ing'-tong 聽在°此°!

HARLOT, piao'-ts 婊子; gyi-nyü' 妓女; c'ông-vu' 娼婦 (c'ông or ts'ông)

HARM, *to injure*, 'æ 害; long-song' 弄唆°; *damage*, sông 傷; *I will not* — *you*, ngô feh we' long-song' ng 我弗會弄唆°

你°; no —, feh-dzæ'-wu 不礙°事°; feh-ngæ' 弗碍; feh-fông'-teh 弗妨得
HARMLESS, feh-'æ-nying'-go 弗害人°个°; feh-ngæ'-go 弗碍个°
HARMONIOUS, agreeing in feeling, 'o-moh' 和睦; kông'-leh-læ 講°得°來; dong-sing-'eh-i' 同心合意
HARMONIZE, to —difficulties, diao-'o' 調和; long gy'i 'o-moh' 弄其和睦
HARMONY of the Gospels, Foh'-ing 'eh-ts'æn' 福音合叅
HARNESS to a carriage, tsông mô-ts'ô 裝馬車°; t'ao' ts'ô-ts' 套車°子
HARP, seven stringed —, gying 琴; to play the —, dæn gying' 彈琴
HARROW, loh-din'-bô' 落田鈀 (ih-min)
HARSH to the touch, ts'ao 糙; — voice, ngang-sing' ngang-ky'i' 硬°聲硬°氣; — treatment, dæ nying k'eh'-li 待人°刻薄°
HARTSHORN, deer's horn, loh koh' 鹿角°
HARVEST, to siu kah' 収割; the time of —, siu-kah'-go z-'eo 収割个°時候; harvested not a grain, ts' lih vu siu' 子粒無収
HARVEST, the crops, nyin-dzing' 年成
HASH, to — meat, nyüoh tsæn-se' 肉°切°碎

HASP, meng-gying' 門襻 (ih-go)
HASTE, in —, kw'a 快°; kw'a'-soh 快°速; 'ao-sao; what's your — (flurry)? ng ky'i soh'-go mông'-deo 你°起甚°麽°忙頭? make —, kw'a'-tin 快°點; soh'-tin 速點; do quickly, tso-leh kw'a' 做得°快°; why are you in such —? dza-we ka' læ-feh-gyi' 何°爲°如°此°來弗及°?
HASTEN, to — one's self, zi ken'-kying 自°趕緊; — him, ts'e' gyi kw'a' 催其快°
HASTY, kyih 急; ts'ao 躁; precipitate, kyih-ts'ao' 急躁; — disposition, sing'-kah kyih' 性格急; — way of doing things, deo-gyih'-goh-loh'; — tempered and severe, bao-ts'ao' 暴躁; — and stubborn, ao-pih 靿°拗
HAT, mao-ts' 帽子 (ih-ting); straw —, ts'ao' mao' 草帽; bu-mao' 蒲帽; liang mao' 凉帽; felt —, tsin mao' 氈帽; to put on a —, ta mao' 戴帽; to take off the —, tsoh' mao-ts' 除°帽子; mao'-ts tsoh'-loh 帽子除落
HATCH, to — eggs, dæn bu-c'ih' 蛋菢出; ditto (by heat), dæn' hong-c'ih' 蛋烘出
HATCHET, fu'-deo 斧頭 (ih-pô.)
HATE, to u'-su 惡; k'eh'-ts'eng'; to detest, in-tseng' 厭憎

HATEFUL k'o-u'-go 可惡个°; k'eh'-ts'eng-go.

HATRED, to feel —, kyi 'eng-sing 記恨心; dzeng u'-su-go-sing' 存惡个°心; ill-will, ün'-ky'i 怨氣

HAUGHTINESS is hard to endure, jing-ky'i' næn-tông 神氣難當

HAUGHTY, to put on — airs, pa kô'-ts 擺°架°子; pa-p'ing' 擺°品

HAUL, to t'o 拖; — a great net, t'a do mông' 拖°大°綱°

HAUNCH of mutton, yiang t'e' 羊腿

HAUNTED house, ing-oh' 陰屋

HAVE, yiu 有; — you heard the news? keh'-go sing-sih ng yiu t'ing'-meng-ko' ma 這°个°信息你°有聽聞°過麽? — you any sugar? dông yiu' ma 糖有麽°? (I) — some, yiu 有; — you been to Peking? Poh'-kying ng yiu tao'-ko ma 北京你°有到過麽?

HAVOC, to commit — among, tsao-iang' 遭殃

HAWK, lao-ing' 老鷹

HAY or straw, ken-ts'ao' 乾草; hay-stack, ts'ao'-bong 草逢

HAZARD, danger, hyin 險; ngwe-hyin' 危險

HAZARD, to mao-hyin' 冒險; — one's life, p'un-ming' 拚命; p'un-sô' sing-ming 拚捨°性命

HAZARDOUS, hyin'-go 險个°;

hyin'-dao-dao 險逃逃; hyin'-teng-teng 險等等; hyin'-ling-ling 險懍懍

HAZE, yüing-in' 雲烟; in-vu' 烟霧

HE, gyi 其; — says, gyi wô' 其話; it is —, z gyi' 是其

HEAD, deo 頭; to hang the —, deo t'ang-loh' 頭垂°落; to raise the —, deo-dæ-ky'i' 頭抬起; leader, ling-deo' 領頭; deo-siu'; deo-nao' 頭腦; deo-moh' 頭目; to knock — in worship, k'eh-deo' 磕頭; — of a bed, zông-deo' 床°頭

HEAD, or division, zeng-ts'ı' 層°次; tön 端; dön 段; the first —, di-ih'-zeng 第一層°

HEAD, to — (as an expedition), we-deo' 為頭; — a boat to the north, jün-deo' hyiang-poh' 船頭向北

HEAD-ACHE, deo'-t'ong 頭痛

HEAD-BAND, pao-deo' 包頭 (also a turban)

HEADLONG way of doing, deo-gyih'-goh-loh; acting without thought, mông'-c'ong 懵衝; mông'-djông 懵撞

HEAD-STRONG disposition, gyiang-deo'-gyüih-nao' 强頭倔腦; ang-sing'; cih'-sing 拙性; 'eo-zi' sing'-kah 逞°自°性格

HEAD-WIND, teo'-fong 對風

HEAD-WORKMAN, tsoh'-deo 作頭; ziang'-deo 匠°頭

HEAL, to i 醫; i-hao' 醫好;
— *disease*, i-bing' 醫病; *ditto,
by using sorcery*, yüong fah'-jih
i-bing' 用法術醫病

HEALTH, *in good* —, hao 好;
gyin 健; (as an elderly person)
k'ông-gyin' 康健; *to injure
the* —, sông tsing-jing 傷精
神; *restored to original* —, voh-
nyün' de 復元了°

HEALTHY *constitution*, ti'-ts tsah'-
cü 底子堅°固°; ti'-ts kyih'-
jih 底子砝實; peng'-ling-hao'
本領好; *well*, sông'-kw'a
爽快°; — *look*, ky'i'-seh-hao
氣色好

HEAP, *a* ih-te' 一堆; *large* — *of
earth, bricks, &c.*, kao-sæn-te' 高
山堆

HEAP, *to* — *up*, te-tsih' 堆積;
to pile in a —, diah-long' ih-te'
疊攏一堆

HEAR, *to* t'ing'-meng 聽聞°;
t'ing'-kyin 聽見; *cannot* —,
t'ing'-feh-c'ih' 聽弗出; —
attentively, si'-t'ing 細聽; liu-
sing'-t'ing 留心聽; *distressing
to* —, t'ing'-ts peh-jing' 聽之
不忍; *pretend not to* —, *or pretend to be deaf and dumb*, tsông'-
long tsoh-ô' 裝聾作啞°; —
suddenly, or the first time, p'ih-
deo t'ing-meng 忽°然聽聞°;
how did he —? gyi' dza t'ing'-
meng-go 其怎°聽聞个°?

HEARING, *hard of* ng'-tô moh'

耳°聾°; r'-be 耳°背°; (politely
called), ng'-tô feh-bin' 耳°朵
弗便; *pretending to be ditto*,
tsông'-leh m'-neh t'ing'-meng
裝得°沒°有°聽聞°; tsông kô'
ng-tô' long 裝假°耳°朵聾

HEARKEN, *to* tseh'-leh ng-tô t'ing'
側耳°朵聽; si'-r-kong-t'ing'
洗耳恭聽

HEARSAY, fong-sing' 風信; *can't
rely on mere* —, fong-sing'-k'ao-
feh-jih' 風信靠弗實

HEARSE, (native) zæ-hyin' 材°櫃

HEART, sing 心; *to search one's*
—, dzô-ts'ah' zi'-go sing 查
察自°个°心; *to gain a per-
son's* —, teh nying sing' 得
人°心; *palpitation of the* —,
sing' bih-bih'-t'iao 心怦怦跳;
— *is broken in pieces*, sing'-li
se'-sah-de 心裡碎煞了°;
heart-rending cries, kyiao-leh se'-
se-dong' 叫得°碎碎動

HEARTH, ho-lu teo' 火爐斗

HEARTILY, dzing-sing' 誠心;
with all the heart, djün-fu' sing-
dziang' 全副心腸

HEARTLESS, m̄-sing'-go 無°心
个°; *without feeling*, m̄-dzing'
m̄-nyi' 無°情無°義

HEARTY, *cordial*, nyih-sing-deo'
熱°心頭; — (as food), næ-
kyi' go 耐飢个°; *fat and* —
(as a young person), tsah'-công
囝壯

HEAT, nyih-ky'i' 熱°氣; — *of*

HEA 218 HEE

the body, kyi'-sing'-go nyih-ky'i' 身°體°个°熱°氣 HEAT, *to* — (as metals), tsih' nyih 炙熱°; — *by the fire,* hong-nyih' 烘熱°; — (as food), nyih'-nyih 熱熱°; long-nyih' 弄熱°; — *in flame,* ho dæn'-dæn 火燖燖 HEATHEN, *idolater,* pa bu-sah' nying 拜菩薩人°; pa ngeo'-ziang-go 拜偶像个°; *one out of the church,* nga-kyiao' nying 外°教人°; *one bound by custom,* shü'-dzoh zông' nying 世俗上人°; *unenlightened people,* mong'-tong nying 懵懂人°; HEAVE, *to* — *a sigh,* t'æn ky'i' 嘆氣; *the breast heaves,* hyüong-kwun'-deo byih'-kyi, hyih'-kyi læ-tih dong 胸膛°頭膈膈動 HEAVEN, *the expanse of* —, t'in 天; ky'üong-ts'ông 穹蒼; *the place of happiness,* T'in-dông 天堂; T'in-zông' 天上; *to go to* —, T'in-dông' ky'i 天堂去°; *returned to* — (commonly said of one dead), kwe-t'in'-de 歸天了°; *Heaven's eye is near,* "T'in ngæn gying'" 天眼近 HEAVENLY, T'in'-li-go 天裡个°; — *bliss,* T'in-dông-go foh'-ky'i 天堂个°福氣 HEAVY, djong 重; — *burden,* djong' tæn 重擔; *how* — *is it?* yiu to'-siao djong' 有多少重? — *hands and feet* (said of one

who does things noisily, not gently), djong'-siu-djong'-kyiah 重手重脚 HEAVILY, *to sleep* —, kw'eng sah'-kao 睡°熟° HEDGE, pô 笆; li-pô' 籬笆; *bamboo* —, coh' pô 竹笆; *a lamb caught in a* — (*i.e.* in inextricable difficulty), ta koh yiang' tsing pô-dong' 戴°角°羊進笆洞 HEDGED, *way* — *up,* vu lu' k'o tseo' 無路可走; *completely* — *in,* djih lu'-dzing 絕路程; we-kw'eng'-sah-de 圍困煞了° HEDGE-HOG, 'ao-cü' 豪豬 HEED, *to take care,* kying'-jing 謹慎; kwu'-djoh 顧着°; siao'-sing 小心; *to hear and believe,* t'ing sing 聽信 *do not* — *him,* (as a child playing, &c.) vong kwun' gyi 不用°管其; *ditto,* (as one reviling, &c.) hao-vong' ts'æ gyi' 不°用°睬其 HEEDLESS feh tông-sing-go 弗當心个°; bah-mông'-kwông 白茫光; — *sport* (as holding a child in a dangerous place), mæn-tô hyi'-deo 粗°蠻°戲嬉°; mæn-tô'-tô. HEEDLESSLY, yia'-long-sæn-ts'in 野°弄三千; *to do* —, ts'ao'-ts'ao liao z' 草草了事; tso z-ken' feh læ i' li 做事幹弗在°意裏 HEEL *of the foot,* kyiah 'eo-keng'

脚後跟; — *of the shoe,* 'a-'eo-keng' 鞋°後跟

HEIFER, siao ts'°-ngeo' 小雌牛° (ih-deo)

HEIGHT, *what is the — of that mountain?* keh' zo sæn yiu to-siao kao' 這°座山有多少高?

HEIR, *of the same family name,* dzing-kyi'-go nying 承繼个°人°; tsih-dæ'-go nying 接代个°人°; *one who inherits,* ziu-ts'æn'-nyih-go nying 受產業个°人°

HEIRLESS, *no posterity,* vu-'eo 無後; *the succession is broken,* dön-cong'-de 斷種了°; djih-dæ'-de 絕代了°; djih-dz'-de 絕嗣了°

HELL, di-nyüoh' 地獄; *to fall into or go to —,* loh di-nyüoh' 落地獄; *the sufferings of —,* di-nyüoh'-li-go kw'u'-ts'u 地獄裡个°苦楚

HELM, *the* do 舵; do'-ngô 舵枒°; *to take the —,* pô do' 把舵; k'eh do'-ngô 搭舵枒°; *ditto (if a small —)* pô sao' 把梢

HELMSMAN, do'-kong 舵工; lao'-da 老大

HELP, *to* pông-dzn' 幫助; pông-ts'eng' 幫襯; vu-dzu' 扶助; pông-vu' 幫扶; *to — one another,* dô-k'ô' siang-pông' 大家°相幫; *come and — me,* læ pông' ngô ih-pông 來幫我一幫; teng ngô' tso te'-siu 與°我做對手; *I will — you into the boat,* ngô tông' ng loh jün' 我扶°你°下°船; *— with money, &c.* (in time of bereavement), tiao hao 弔孝°; tiao-sông' 弔喪; *there is no — for it,* m̄-shih'-fah 無°設法; m̄-fah' 無°法; peh-teh'-yi 不得巳; wa'-feh-læ 歇弗來; vu-k'o'-næ-'o 無可奈何; *cannot — doing it,* feh-neng feh-tso 弗能弗傲; feh'-teh feh-tso' 弗得弗做

HELPER, pông-siu' 幫手; te'-siu 對手

HELPLESS, kyü'-dong-feh-læ 舉動弗來; dong'-dæn-feh-læ 動彈弗來; vu-lih'-neng-wè 無力能爲

HELTER-SKELTER, lön-ts'ih'-pah-tsao' 亂七八遭; *to come in —,* lön tseo'-tsing-læ 亂走進來

HELVE, fu'-deo ping 斧頭柄

HEM, *to* nyiao bin' 繞緶; *to turn down a —,* üih bin' 擸緶

HEMISPHERE, pun'-gyiu 半球; *the eastern —,* tong pun'-gyiu 東半球

HEMORRHAGE, hyüih-tsing 血症; *— from the womb,* hyüih'-pong 血崩°

HEMP, mô 麻; dzi'-mô 苎麻; *hempen cloth,* mô pu' 麻布; *— twine,* mô zing' 麻繩

HEN, kyi-nyiang' 母°雞°; *— coop,* kyi-long' 雞籠; *— basket,* kyi-tsao' 雞罩

HENCE, *from this time,* yi-'eo' 以後; ts'-'eo' 此後; dz-'eo' 嗣後; dzong-ts'' yi-'eo' 從此以後; *three years —,* sæn nyin' yi-'eo' 三年以後; ts'-'eo sæn nyin' 此後三年; *therefore,* sô-yi' 所以; keh-lah 故°

HENCEFORTH, or HENCEFORWARD, dzong-kying'-yi-'eo' 從今以後

HER, gyi 其; (*pos.*) gyi-go 其个°

HERALD, *proclaimer,* pao'-z-nying 報事人°

HERBS, ts'ao 草; *medicinal —,* yiah-ts'ao' 藥草

HERD, ih-de' 一隊; ih-dziao' 一群; *a — of cattle,* ih-de ngeo' 一隊牛°

HERDSMAN, k'en-ngeo'-go 看牛个°; k'en-yiang-go 看羊个°; *boy —,* moh-dong' 牧童

HERE, dông-deo 這裡°; ts'-di 此地; *to be —,* læ-tong' 在°; *have been — three years,* læ ts'-di sæn nyin' de 在°此地三年了°; *bring it —,* do tao dông-deo læ' 拿°到這°裡°來; *I am —,* ngô læ-tong' 我在°; *— it is,* dông-deo læ-tong' 在°這°裡

HEREAFTER, tsiang-læ' 將來; 'eo'-læ 後來; 'eo'-deo 後頭

HEREDITARY *nobility,* shü-jih' 世襲; ing'-kwun 蔭官; — (as a trade or profession), shü-djün-go 世傳个°; — (as property, or disease), zông-dæ' yi'-loh-læ'-go 上代遺落來个°

HERESY, zia dao'-li 邪°道理; yi-tön' 異端

HERETIC, zia-kyiao' nying 邪°教人°; yi-kyiao' nying 異教人°

HERMIT, zo-mao-bong'-go 坐°茅篷个°; *— who sits in a confined place and is fed by others,* zo-kwæn' 坐°關

HERO, ing-yüong 英雄; 'ao-gyih' 豪傑; da-dziang'-fu 大丈夫; *strive to be a —,* tsang ing-yüong' 爭°英雄

HEROINE, nyü'-cong 'ao-gyih' 女中豪傑; nyü'-cong dziang'-fu 女中丈夫

HESITATE, *to — in deciding,* yiu yü' peh' kyüih 猶豫不決; *— in speaking,* ňg-ňg'-ňga-ňga kông 唔°唔°呀°呀°講°; *ditto, as if holding a walnut in the mouth,* ziang 'en wu-dao kông' ka 如°含胡桃講°

HESITATING (in speaking), t'eng-t'eng-t'u-t'u 吞吞吐吐; ih-kyü tsing' ih-kyü c'ih' 一句進一句出

HEW, *to — trees,* tsæn jü' 斬樹; *— stone,* k'æ zah-deo' 開石頭; *— down a tree,* jü tsoh'-loh 樹斬落; jü tsoh'-diao 樹斬壞°

HIBERNATE, *to* iu-ko tong' 躱過冬

HICCOUGH, *to* tang-eh' 打呃; tang-ih' 打噎

HIDE, dzông-nyih' 藏匿; to — one's self, iu 幽;— the head, dzông deo' 藏頭;— the face, tsô min-k'ong' 遮面孔;— sin, tsô-in' ze' 遮°掩罪; tsô-kœ' ze' 遮蓋罪; he is hidden, gyi' iu'-kœn.

HIDE, skin, bi 皮; ox —, ngeo-bi' 牛°皮; cow — candy, ngeo-bi' dông' 牛°皮糖

HIDEOUS appearance, siang'-mao ts'iu'-leo-peh-k'œn 相貌憔陋不堪, p'o'-p'ô siang'-mao 可怕相貌;— sound, seng'-ngô sah-nying'-go sing-hyiang'.

HIGH, kao 高; as — as heaven, ziang-t'in' ka-kao' 像天个樣高; a — price invites the distant trader (to sell his goods), kô' kao tsiao yün'-k'ah 價°高招遠客;— rank tsiah'-we kao 爵位高;— officer, tsih-veng-do' 職分°大°;— wind, mang'-fong 猛°風

HIGH-HANDED, pô'-dao 霸道; gyiang-wang'-pô-dao' 强橫霸道; pô'-shü 霸勢

HIGH-MINDED (principles), p'ing'-kah kao 品格高

HIGH-PRIEST, tsi'-s-tsiang 祭司長°; tsi'-s-deo' 祭司頭

HIGH-SPIRITED, ts'-hyiang-kao' 志向高; 'ao'-ky'i 豪氣 (not equivalents.)

HIGH-WATER or tide, dziao-tsiang' tsoh-de 潮漲足了°; bing-dziao' 平潮

HIGH-WAY, kwun-lu' 官路; do-lu' 大°路; kwun-dông'-do-lu' 官塘大°路

HILL, a small —, ih-diao-ling' 一條嶺; a larger —, ih-zo-sœn' 一座°山; climb the hills, bô-sœn' wah-ling 爬山跨°嶺

HILLOCK, ling 嶺 (ih-diao); a grave —, veng-ling 墳陵

HILL-PATH, sœn-lu' 山路

HILL-SIDE, sœn-pin' 山邊

HILL-TOP, sœn-ting-den' 山頂

HILLY ground, sœn-di' 山地; it is all —, tu' z sœn 都是山

HILT, pao'-kyin-ping' 寶劍柄

HIMSELF, zi 自°; he — gave (it) to me, gyi-zi' peh'-ngô 其自°給°我

HIND feet, 'eo'-kyiah 後脚

HINDER, to lah-djü' 攔住; lœn-tsu' 攔阻; tsu'-tông 阻擋; tsu'-djü 阻住; hindered by him, be' gyi lah-djü'-liao 被其攔°住了 what's to — ? 'o-fông'-ni 何妨呢?

HINDRANCE, fông-ngœ' 妨碍; tsu'-kah 阻隔; tsu'-kah-sing 阻隔星; without —, vu-tsu' vu-ngœ' 無°阻無°碍; 'ao'-vu tsu'-kah 毫無阻隔

HINDMOST, meh-'eo' 末後; ting-'eo' 頂後

HINGES, yiao-bi'; yiao-p'œn' 搖襻; to take a door off the —, meng-t'ch'-loh 門脫落

HIP, do-t'e' 大°腿; — joint, do-t'e' gao-kwu 大°腿骨交°股; t'e'-kweh kyiao-tsih' 腿骨交節

HIRE, to kwu 僱; to rent, tsu 租; shü 賃; — a boat, t'ao-jün' 討船

HIRE, wages, kong-din' 工錢°; rent, tsu'-din 租錢°; boat —, jün-din' 船錢°

HIRED, I have — a man, ngô ih-go nying' kwu-hao'-tong-de 我一个°人°僱好了°; one — for a length of time, dziang-kong 長工; tang-dziang'-go; one — for a short time, tön'-kong 短工; ts'eh-tön'-go.

HIS, gyi'-go 其个°; that book is —, keh'-peng shü' z gyi'-go 這本書是其个°

HISTORIAN, kyi-z'-go cü'-kwu 紀事个°人°; compiler of history, siu-s'-go cü'-kwu 修史个°人°

HISTORY, s 史; official records, kông-kæn' 綱鑑°; — of China (in several hundred vols.), Nyiæn s'-s 廿四史; Natural — of China, Da-ts'ing' ih-t'ong'-ts 大清一統志; origin and — (as of a house, &c.), læ-lih' 來歷

HIT, to — against, bang-djoh' 撞°着°; to — (as a mark), tang-djoh' 打着°; for fear a brick may — you, k'ong'-p'ô cün-deo' k'ao'-djoh ng 恐怕磚頭敲着°你; — a target, tang pô'-ts 打靶子; ditto with an arrow, zih-djoh pô'-ts 射着°靶子

HITHER, dông'-byiang 這°向; to run — and thither, peng'-læ-peng-ky'i' 奔來奔去°

HITHERTO, hyiang'-læ, 向來; ih'-hyiang 一向; dzong-læ' 從來

HIVE, bee-tub, fong-dong' 蜂桶 (ih-go)

HIVE, bees fong-ts' dao'-c'ih dong 蜂子逃出桶; to — the bees, fong-ts' siu-tsing 蜂子收進

HOAR-FROST, sông 霜

HOARD, to — up money, k'ông' ngæ' dong-din' 囥呆銅錢°; k'ông si' dong-din' 囥死°銅錢°

HOARSE, sô wu'-long 嗓喉嚨°; so — unable to speak, wu-long ô' 喉°嚨啞

HOARY hair, deo-fah bah'-de 頭髮白了°; black and white mixed, hwô-bah' 花白°; — head-ed man, bah-deo-ong' 白°頭翁

HOAX, to — a person, coh ih-go moh-sao' peh nying pe' 給一个°木梢俾°人°背; he was hoaxed, gyi pe-moh-sao'-de 其背木梢了°; gyi pe-bô'-liao 其背靶了

HOBBLE, to kwa-kyi' kwa-kyi'tseo 跛走

HOBBY, that is his —, keh z gyi p'in-æ'-ts-sing 這°是其偏愛之心

HOD, *a mason's bamboo* —, t'u'-kyi 土箕 (ih-tsah); *coal* —, me-t'æn' dong 煤炭桶

HOE, z-deo' 鋤頭 (ih-pô); *to cut weeds with a* —, siah ts'ao' 削草

HOG, nyi-cü' 泥猪; *wild* —, yia' cü 野猪 (ih-tsah)

HOIST, *to* ts'ô-zông' 扯上; *to* — *a flag*, gyi ts'ô-zông' 旗扯上; — *a sail*, ts'ô bong' 扯篷; bah bong' 拔篷

HOLD, *to* — *in the hand*, do 拿; nyiah 捻; — *it tight*, do-leh lao 拿得牢; — *it still*, ding-ding' go do'-tong 拿定當; dong'-feh-dong do'-tong 拿定其弗動; — *in both hands*, p'ong 捧; — *in the arms*, bao 抱; — (*or clutch*) lim fast, cô gyi lao' 攏其牢; *let go one's* —, fông siu' 放手; — *loosely*, kw'un siu' nyiah'-tih 寬手捻的; song siu' nyiah'-tih 鬆手捻的; — *a pen*, k'ô pih 揢筆; — *on the arm*, gyiao-tih 撟的; — *under the arm*, gah'-tih 擖的; gyih'-tih 挾的; — *on to something*, p'æn' 扳; *can't* — *up* (no strength), ts'ang'-feh-djü 撐弗住; — *up the hand*, siu di-ky'i' 手提起; — *out the hand*, sing siu' 伸手; — *one in suspense*, long'-leh gyi tiao'-dang 使其弗着落; — *in the mouth*, 'en' læ k'eo'-li 含在口裡; — *up the*

dress, i-zông ky'ih-tæn'-ky'i 衣裳挈起; *how much water will (it)* —? hao tsi to-siao' shü 好盛多少水?

HOLD, *ship's* —, jün'-li-go ho'-ts'ông 船裡个貨艙

HOLE, dong-ngæn' 洞眼; dong' 洞 (ih-go); — *in a wall*, ziang dong' 牆洞; *to dig a* — *in the ground*, gyüih ih-go den' 掘一个潭

HOLIDAY, *day free from labor*, fông-kô' nyih-ts' 放假日子; *day free from study*, fông-'oh' nyih-ts' 放學日子; *how many holidays have you?* ng fông' kyi nyih' kô' 你放幾日假?

HOLINESS, sing'-jün teh'-ky'i 聖善德氣

HOLLOW, k'ong 空; k'ong-k'oh'-go 空壳个; k'ong-sing' 空心; *a* — *place*, den 潭; ao 墺; zao 漕; t'en-tsing'-go di-fông 凹進个地方; — *in an ink stone*, nyin-ngô den' 硯潭; nyin-ngô zao' 硯漕; — *of the hand*, siu-sing-den' 手心潭

HOLLOW, *to* — *out*, leo c'ih' 鏤出; — *slightly*, seo or siu 剡

HOLLY-HOCK ziang'-vi-hwô 薔薇花

HOLY, sing 聖; sing'-jün 聖善; — *Bible*, Sing'-shü 聖書; — *Spirit*, Sing'-Ling 聖靈; *the*

— Place, Sing'-sô 聖所; the — of Holies, Ts'-sing-sô 至聖所; God is —, Jing-ming' z sing'-jün-go 神明是聖善个°.

HOME, oh'-li 家°裡; oh'-lô; kô-byiang' 家°鄉; own —, zi oh'-li 自°家°裡; go —, tao oh'-li ky'i'; 到家°裏去°; at home or familiar with (because native to), ne kô' gyün-deo° 內家°拳頭; peng'-tsoh-ho' 本作貨

HOMELESS, m̄-oh-go 無°屋个°; m̄-neh deng-sing'-ts-c'ü' 沒°有°庇身之處; the — who find shelter anywhere, (as beggars, thieves, &c.) deng liang-ding'-go 住°凉°亭个°; kw'eng fi-leo'-go 睡°城°樓个°; tao miao-koh-go'.

HOMELY, not pretty, næn-k'en'-go 難看个°; w̄a-k'en'-go 孬看个°; sang-leh w̄a-k'en' 生°得孬看; very —, ts'iu'-leo 醜陋

HOME-MADE, kô-tsoh'-go 家°作个°; home-woven, peng'-kyi 本機

HOME-SICKNESS, kyi'-teh kô-byiang'-bing 思°鄉病

HONE, mo-tao'-zah 磨刀石 (ih-kw'e)

HONEST, upright and straight forward, dzing-jih' 誠實; ih'-z-ih' nyi'-z-nyi' 一是一二°是二°; — man, web-ih'-nying 劃一人°; teng-'eo'-nying 敦厚人°; cong-'eo'-nying 忠厚人°; 'eo'-dao-nying 厚道人°; — and often simple, lao'-jih 老實; — (won't steal), siu'-kyiah-w̄eng'-djong 手脚穩重; — in trade, lao'-siao-vu-ky'i' 老小無欺

HONESTLY, speak jih-we'-kông 實爲講; kông lao'-jih wô' 講°老實話

HONEY, mih-dông' 蜜糖; honeyed fruit, mih-tsin'-ko 蜜餞果; — poison (i.e. what seems good, but injures), mih-tsin'-p'i-sông' 蜜餞砒霜

HONEY-COMB, mih-fong'-k'o' 蜜蜂窠

HONEY-SUCKLE, kying-nying'-hwô 金銀花

HONG, 'ông 行; foreign —, yiang-'ông' 洋行 (ih-bæn)

HONOR, to respect, k'en'-djong 看重; kying'-djong 敬重; tseng-djong' 尊重; kwe'-djong 貴重; t'e-tseng' 推尊; — parents, kying'-djong vu'-meo 敬重父母; hyiao'-jing tia-nyiang' 孝順爹°娘; reflect — upon parents, tsang-do'-nying'-go ky'i' 爭°大°人°个°氣; tsang-fong ngao-ky'i' 傲氣; you — me, ng'-peh ngô t'i'-min 你°俾我體面; ng'-peh ngô lin'-zông yiu kwông-ts'æ' 你°俾°我臉上有光彩

HONOR, esteem it an —, sön' z yüong-kwông' 算是榮光

HONORABLE, dziah-djong'-go 鄭重個°; *worthy of honor*, kœ-tông' kying'- djong-go 該當敬重個°; *what is your — name?* tseng-sing' 尊姓? kwe-sing' 貴姓? *what is your — country?* kwe-koh' 貴國? *what is your — occupation?* ng-soh'-go kwe-'ông 你°甚°麼°貴行?

HOOD (worn by men), fong-teo' 風兜; — (worn by old women), kwun-ing'-teo 觀音兜 (ih-ting)

HOOF, di-ts' 蹄子 (ih-tsah)

HOOK, keo-ts' 鈎子 (ih-tsah)

HOOK, *to* keo 鈎; — *up*, keo-ky'i'-læ 鈎起來

HOOKED *nose*, ing-cü' bih-deo' 鷹嘴鼻頭°

HOOP, ky'iu 箍°; *tub* —, dong'-ky'iu 桶箍°

HOOP, *to* tang-ky'iu 打箍°

HOOPING-COUGH, lu'-z-k'eh 鷺鷥咳

HOP *on one foot*, doh-kyiah'-t'iao' 獨脚跳

HOPE, *to* siang'-vông 想望; — *he will prosper*, ts'- vông gyi hying-wông' 指望其興旺; — *in vain*, du-jün' siang'-vông 徒然想望

HOPE, siang'-deo 想頭; vông'-deo 望頭; *no* —, m̄-siang'-deo 無°想頭; *there is* —, yiu-sô-vông'-go 有所望個°; *have great* — (*of him or it*), da-yiu' sô-vông' 大有所望; *no* — *of*

the man, nying djih - vông'-de 人°絕望了°; *no — of news*, sing'-sih djih-vông'-de 信息絕望了°; *beyond one's hopes*, hyi'-c'ih-vông-wæ' 喜出望外; *foolish baseless* —, c'ü-sing' vông-siang 癡心妄想

HOPEFUL, *promising*, yiu ts'-vông 有指望; *he is very* —, gyi vông-deo' læ-leh ts'ih' 其望頭來得°切

HOPELESS, m̄ siang'-vông go 無°想望個°; sing sah'-de 心死了°; — *disease, and hence any thing* —, si'-tsing 死°症

HOPES, *his* — *are excited*, gyi siang'-vông bô-ky'i'-tih-de 其想望扒起了°; gyi vông-deo' dong'-de 其望頭動了°; *excite one's* —, ying'-dong nying'-go siang'- vông 引動人°個想望

HORIZON, *the sensible* —, t'in-pin' 天邊

HORIZONTAL, wang 橫; *on a level*, bing 平

HORN, koh 角° (ih-tsah); *two horns*, liang-tsah koh' 兩隻角°; — *for blowing*, so'-na; *shoe* —, 'a-liu' 鞋跛° (ih-go).

HORNED, yiu-koh'-go 有角°個°; *hornless*, m̄-koh'-go 無°角°個°

HORNY *skin on the hands*, sin'-bi ky'i-kyin'-de 手皮起皺°了°

HORRIBLE, iao hah'-sah nying' go 要嚇殺人°個°

HORRID, p'ô-p'ô 可°怕;—to look at (i. e. distresses one), se'-se-dong-go 心°上°不°安°; se'-ky'i-siang.

HORRIFIED, sing-hyü'-dah-tsin' 心虛肉°顫; mô-tseh'-tseh-go.

HORSE, mô 馬 (ih-p'ih); a swift or express —, ts'in-li'-mô 千里馬 to mount a —, zông-mô 上馬; to dismount from a —, loh mô' 落馬; to ride a —, gyi mô'-騎馬; a saw —, moh-mô' 木馬; clothes —, i-kô' 衣架; towel —, siu'-kying-kô' 手巾架°.

HORSE-BACK, on læ mô'-zông 在°馬上.

HORSE-HAIR (from the tail), mô'-mi 馬尾° (ih-keng).

HORSE-RACE, do-p'ao'-mô 大°跑馬.

HORSE-SHOE, t'ih'-ts'ao-'a 鉄草鞋; mô'-di-t'ao 馬蹄套;—of silver, nyün-pao' 元寶 (ih-tsah).

HORSE-WHIP, mô' pin-ts 馬鞭子 (ih-go).

HOSE, mah 襪 (ih-sông); water pipe, sbü'-kwun 水°管 (ih-diao).

HOSPITABLE, æ-k'ah'-go 愛客个°; hwun-hyi' liu nying-k'ah' 歡喜留客人°.

HOSPITABLY, to entertain —, dæ k'ah ing-gying' 待客慇懃; ts-nying' dæ-k'ah hao' 支賓°待客好.

HOSPITAL, i-gyüoh' 醫局 (ih-go).

HOST, or HOSTESS, tong-dao'-cü 東道主; tsih-k'ah'-go 接客个°; landlord, or head of the house, cü'-nying-kô' 主人°家°; tong-kô' 東家; the Heavenly —, T'in-ping'-T'in-tsiang' 天兵天將; army, ping-mô' 兵馬; the whole —, djün-kyüing' 全軍; the — in the Catholic church, sing'-t'i 聖體.

HOSTAGE, pledge, tông-deo' 當頭; ah'-deo 押°頭; detain him as a —, liu' gyi tso tông'-deo 留其做當頭.

HOSTILE, kyih-dziu'-liao-go 結讐了; the two parties are —, liang'-'ô tso ün-kô' 兩下做寃家°.

HOSTILITY, to provoke —, tsiao ün' 招怨; in a state of —, kyih-ün-dziu'-go 結寃讐个°.

HOSTLER, mô'-fu 馬夫 (ih-go).

HOT, ting nyih' 頂熱°;—(lit. warmer than warm), pi nyih' wa nyih' 熱上°加°熱°;—as fire, ho'-nyih 火熱°; sun pouring down like fire, nyih-deo' ziang ho' ka p'eh'-loh læ 日°頭如°火逼°落來°;—(as weather, or fever), ho'-siao-ho-lah' 火燒火辣;—(boiling) water, kweng' shü 滚水°; boiling —, fah' kweng 發滚; dah-dah' kweng 沓沓滚; very — sun, nyih-deo' dah-dah' kweng. — tempered, ho-ky'i' do 火氣大°; sing'-kah ziang ho' ka 性

性格如火°; mao-ts'ao' ho' sing 茅草火星

HOTEL, k'ah'-nyü 客寓; k'ah'-dzæn 客棧; inn, 'ô-c'ü' 厦處

HOUR, ih tin'-cong 一點鐘; the Chinese —, pun' z-zing 半時辰°; half an —, pun' tin-cong 半點鐘; a quarter of an —, ih k'eh' 一刻; an — and a half, ih tin pun' 一點半; an — ago, ih tin'-cong zin-deo' 一點鐘前°頭; an — hence, deng' ih tin'-cong 停一點鐘; deng sæn' djü væn' z 停三餐°飯時

HOUR-GLASS, sô-leo' 沙漏 (ih-go)

HOUR-HAND, ts'-z tsing 指時針; the short hand, tön' tsing 短針 (ih-me)

HOURLY, me' ih tin'-cong 每一點鐘

HOUSE, oh 屋; vông-ts' 房子; oh'-lô; (ih-tsing, ih·t'eo); our — is bad, ah'-lah oh'-lô wa' 我們°房子不好°; houses joined together, lin-p'ing' keh'-djü'-go oh 連拼合°柱个屋; your lofty —, or mansion? fu'-zông 府上? tseng-fu' 尊府? kwe' fu 貴府? in reply say, our humble —, shæ'-kyin 舍間; sô'-kyin; sô-t'ô' 舍°下; sô'-pin 舍°邊; bi-sô' 敝舍°; ice —, ping-ts'iang' 冰廠 (ih-go)

HOUSE-BREAKER who forces doors, gyiao-meng'-go zeh' 撬門个°賊°; — who breaks through the wall, ts'ah-dong'-go zeh' 拆壁°个°賊°

HOUSEHOLD, persons of the —, oh'-li-go nying' 家°裡个人°; (ah-lah oh'-li-nying, without the particle go, is my wife); the whole —, 'o-kô' 和家°; 'eh-kô' 合家°; every —, veng-veng' nying-kô' 每份人°家°; a'-kô a'-wu 挨°家°挨°戶; kô-kô' wu-wu 家家°戶戶; — goods, kô-ho'-jih-veh' 家貨什物

HOUSE-RENT, vông tsu'-din 房租錢°; oh' tsu-din' 屋租錢°; vông din' 房錢°

HOVEL, mud na-nyi' oh 泥屋; straw —, ts'ao' oh 草屋; oh ziang p'o'-yiao ka' 屋像破窑

HOVERING about, dön-dön'-ky'ün-ky'ün læ-tih fi' 團團圈圈來的飛

HOW, in what manner? dza-go' 怎樣°? or 怎°个°? — many? kyi'-go 幾个°? ditto (or — much)? to-siao' 多少? — can I know? ngô' dza hyiao'-teh ni 我怎°曉得呢? — far is it (from one to the other)? li-yün' to-siao' lu' 離遠多少路? ditto, from here there? dzong dông'-deo tao keh'-deo dza kwun yün' 從這裡°到那°裡°怎°樣遠? — long have you been here? ng' læ-leh' to-siao' kong'-fu 你°來了°多少工夫? — *long* (by measure)? dza kwun dziang' 怎°樣°長? — *are you?* ng hao' feh 你°好否°? bao' yia 好呀°? — *old are you?* ng to-siao' nyin'-kyi 你°多少年紀? (politely) *ditto?* kwe'-kang 貴庚? *ditto* (to an old person)? kao-ziu' 高壽? ng da ziu' to-siao' 你°大壽多少? *ditto* (to a child), kyi shü' 幾歲°? *ditto* (to a young woman)? ng to-siao' ts'ing-c'ing' 你°多少青春?

HOWEVER, *although it be so*, se-tsib' z-ka' 雖則°如°此°

HOWL, *when dogs* — *it is a bad sign*, keo' læ-tih k'oh' z peh-kyih'-ts ziao' 狗哭是不吉之兆

HUBBUB, *what is all this* — *?* soh' z-ken', ka nao-nyih'-bang-sang' 何°事°如°此°鬧°熱°

HUDDLE, *to* — *together*, üong'-tsi-long' 擁擠攏; tsi-tæn'-long 擠攏; *sit huddled*, a'-tsi zo' 挨擠坐°

HUFF, *in a* — *of anger*, ho'-ky'i dzih c'ong' 火氣直冲 (c'ong or ts'ong).

HUFFY (from vanity), iao 'ang' piao-gying' 要行°彪勁

HUG, *to* o-long' 抱°攏; o-tæn'-long.

HUGE, do-leh c'ih-gyi' 大°得°出奇; *unusually large*, fi-dzông' do

非常大°; kah'-nga do' 格外°大°

HULL, *the outer* — *of rice*, lohg-k'ông' 礱糠; *the inner* —, si'-k'ông 細糠; *the* — *of a ship*, jün-sing' 船身

HULL, *to take off the outer* — *of paddy*, long koh' 礱穀; *ditto the inner* —, sông mi' 舂米; ts'ah-mi' 䉆米; *to take off both hulls* (usually by a buffallo-mill), nyin koh' 碾穀

HUMILIATE, *to* — *by taunts*, siah-lin' 削臉

HUMMING (of insects), 'ong-'ong'-hyiang 閧閧響

HUMAN, nying'-go 人个°; — *body*, sing-t'i' 身體; — *relations*, jing-leng' 人倫; *what is the length of* — *life?* jing-seng' dzœ shü' neng yiu kyi nyin' 人生在世能有幾年? *the seven* — *affections*, ts'ih dzing' 七情 (veng.)

HUMANE, sing-dz'-go 心慈个°

HUMBLE, ky'in-hyü' 謙虛 (has often a sense of false humility); ky'in-seng' 謙遜; ti-sing'-siao-i 低心小意; *in my* — *opinion*, tsiao ngô' nyü kyin' 照我愚見; *of* — *origin*, c'ih'-sing-ti' 出身低; *my* — *surname*, bi-sing' 敝姓; (I) *your* — (stupid) *brother*, nyü-di' 愚弟

HUMBLE, *to* — *by placing in a lower position*, p'ing'-kyih kông'-

loh-ky'i' 品級降°下°; kông-kyih' 降°級; — *yourself*, zi' pe-vi' 自卑微; *to bring down*, ah'-cü 壓°制

HUMBLY, ti-sing'-siao-i'-go 低心小意个°

HUMILITY, ti-sing-siao-i' 低心小意; ky'in-hyü-go-sing 謙虛个°心; ky'in-seng'-go-sing 謙遜个°心

HUMOR, *in good* —, hwun-hwun'-hyi-hyi 歡歡喜喜; *in bad* —, læ-tih-fah sing'-kah 正在°發性格; *to put him in good* —, peh gyi hwun-hyi' 俾其歡喜

HUMP, *camel's* do-fong' 駝峰

HUMP-BACKED, do-pe'-go 駝背个°

HUNDRED, ih-pah' 一百°; *a — thousand*, ih-pah'-ts'in 一百°千; jih-væn' 十萬; *a — strokes, a — hits* (i. e. sure to hit right), pah'-fah pah'-cong 百°發百°卅 (cong or tsong)

HUNGER, *having* du-kyi' 肚飢; du-pih' 肚饟; *dying with* —, kw'a-ngo-sah'-de 快餓死了°; *to long for*, hyüih'-sing siang' 血心想

HUNT, *to* — *after a thing*, ts'-si-zing' 仔細尋; *ditto, for a long time*, zing'-leh k'o-lin' 尋得可憐; — *it up* (as in a book), dzô-gyi-djoh' 查其着°; *to — wild animals*, tang-liah' 打獵

HUNTER, liah-wu' 獵戶; tang-liah'-go 打獵个°

HURL, *to* — *at*, k'ang'-ko-ky'i 摜°過去°; ang'-ko-ky'i 擲°過去°

HURRICANE, fong-shü' 風水; fong-pao' 風纂; *to blow a* —, tso-fong-shü' 做風水°; tang-pao' 打颮

HURRIED, *and flurried*, hwông-mông' 慌忙; hwông-hwông'-tsiang-tsiang' 慌慌張張; — *in work*, mông-mông'-loh-loh 忙忙碌碌

HURRIEDLY, kyih'-mông 急忙; læ-loh'-feh-gyi' 忙°碌弗及°

HURRY, *in a* —, læ-feh-gyi' 來弗及°; *need not be in a* —, hao-vong' ka læ-feh-gyi' 不°用°如此°來弗及°; *do not* —, feh-iao'-mông' 弗要忙

HURT, *or wound*, sông 傷

HURT, *to bruise*, sông 傷; long-t'ong' 弄痛; long-sông' 弄傷; *to injure*, 'œ' 害; sông-'œ' 傷害; — *by a cut*, k'ch'-sông 磕傷; — *by a fall*, tih'-sông 跌傷; — *by a blow*, tang'-sông 打傷; *will not — you*, feh-wô 'œ' ng' 弗會害你°; *to — one's self*, zi-'œ'-zi 自害自°; *take care and not — him*, kwu'-djoh long gyi t'ong' 顧着°弄其痛; *he — my feelings*, gyi sông' ngô'-go dzing 其傷我个°情

HURTFUL, yiu-'œ'-go 有害个°; wo-'œ'-go 爲害个°

HUSBAND, nen-nyüing 男子°; tông-kô'-nying 當°家°人°; dziang'-fu 丈夫; lao'-kong 老公 (disrespectful); *in what business is your —?* ng'-go nen' tso soh'-go sang-i' 你°个°丈夫°做甚°麼°生°意? *my —,* ah'-lah tông-kô'-nying 我°們°當家人°; gyi'-lah-go ah-tia' 彼等°个°阿爹 (*i. e.* the children's father); *husband's father,* kong-kong 公公; yia'-yia 爺°爺°; *husband's mother,* nyiang'-nyiang 娘娘; *husband's elder brother,* ah-pang 阿伯°; *husband's younger brother,* ah-song' 阿叔°; *ah-pang's wife,* a'-m̂' 阿姆°; *ah-song's wife,* ah-sing' 阿嬸; *husband's older sister,* kwu-mô' 姑母°; *husband's younger sister,* siao' kwu' 小姑; *father's sister's — and husband's sister's —,* kwu-dziang' 姑丈; *elder sister's —,* tsi'-fu 姊夫; *younger sister's —,* me-fu' 妹夫; *mother's sister's —,* and *wife's sister's —,* yi-dziang' 姨丈

HUSBAND, *should — your strength,* yin' lih, feh k'o yüong dzing' 有力弗可用盡; ng-go ky'i'-lih iao tsiang-yiang' 你°个°氣力要長養

HUSBANDMAN, cong'-din-nying 種田人°

HUSH, *to —* (as a child's crying, or an affair), en gyi'-go cü'-pô pi'

按閉°其嘴巴;— (in the imperative), m̂-nao' hyiang 弗°可°響;— *up privately,* s-'ô kæ ming-bah' 私下°遮醜°

HUSK *of paddy,* long-k'ông' 礱糠;— *of corn,* loh-koh' bi 稑穀皮

HUT, siao' oh 小屋 (ih-kæn); *straw —,* ts'ao' oh 草屋; ts'ao' sô 草舍°

HYMN, tsæn'-me-s 讚美詩 (ih-siu)

HYPOCRITE, kô-hao-nying' 假好人°; veh-k'eo'-dzô-sing' 佛口蛇心

HYSTERICS, dæn-mi', sing-ky'iao' 痰迷心竅, (also suddenly gone on a frolic, &c.).

I.

I, ngô 我;— *myself,* ngô-zi' 我自°; *it is —,* z ngô 是我;— *your inferior,* væn-pe' 晚輩;— *your pupil,* (in addressing a superior), væn'-sang 晚生; *ditto* (in addressing one's teacher), meng-sang' 門生°; meng-jing' 門人°;— *your humble brother,* nyü-di' 愚弟;— *your humble sister,* nyü-me' 愚妹

ICE, ping 氷; *a piece of —,* ih-kw'e-ping' 一塊氷; *cold as —,* ziang-ping' ka lang 像氷个°冷°

ICE-CREAM, ping-p'oh'-ting (the English word pudding is transferred)

ICE-HOUSE, ping-ts'iang 氷廠
ICE-JELLY, ping-zih'-hwô (native) 氷石花
ICHTHYOLOGY, se'-dzoh-go 'oh-veng' 水°族學°問
ICICLE, ding-dông' 氷°柱° (ih-keng)
IDEA, i'-s 意思; according to my —, tsiao-ngô'-go i'-s 照我个意思
IDENTICAL, the — person, nyün-gyiu z Leh-go-nying 原舊是這个人°; the — place, dzing'-jün z keh-ten' 仍然是此°處°
IDIOM, kyü'-fah 句法; lin-p'ing-go kyü-fah' 連搦个°句法
IDIOT, m-ling'-sing-go 無°靈性个°; deo-si'-nying 頭世人°; ngæ-ts' 呆子; do'-veh-ling'-sing (in reproach).
IDLE, not industrious, feh-gying'-lih 弗勤力; lazy, læn'-do 懶惰; fond of being —, yiu-siu' hao-'æn' 遊手好閒°
IDLE, to — away time, kong-fu' k'ong'-ko 工夫空°過; to — when not watched, t'eo-læn' 偷懶
IDLER, k'ong-deo-nying' 空頭人°; k'ong'-'æn-nying 空閒人°; dang-k'ah' 宕客
IDOL, image, ngeo'-ziang 偶像; bu-sah' 菩薩; idols of clay, and wood, nyi-su'-moh-tiao' 泥塑木雕
IDOL-PROCESSION, we 會; to form

or have an —, nying-we' 迎會; 'ang-we' 行°會
IDOLATER, pa-ngeo'-ziang-go 拜°偶像个°; pa-bu-sah'-go nying 拜°菩薩个°人°
IDOLATRY, pa-bu-sah'-go z-t'i' 拜°菩薩个°事體
IF, ziah-z' 若是; t'eo'-p'ô; t'ông'-jün 倘然; t'ông'-ziah 倘若; kyüô'-s 假使; jü-ko' 如果;— not so, feo'-tseh 否則; — not, ziah-feh-z' 若弗是;— it be so, t'ông'-jün z-ka' 倘然如°此°; as —, hao'-ziang 好像
IGNITE, to set on fire, ying-dziah' 引燵; tin'-leh-dziah' 點得°燵; fah-ho' 發火; when ignited, ho'-sang-dziah'-de 火生燵了°
IGNOBLE (in birth, or station), zin 賤°; pe-zin' 卑賤°; 'ô'-zin 下°賤°; ti-vi' 低微; of — birth, c'ih'-sing zin'-go 出身賤°个°; — actions, 'ô'-tsoh 'ang-we' 下°作行°為
IGNOMINIOUS, disgraceful, tao-me'-go 倒°楣个°
IGNOMINY, consigned to — 10,000 years, yi ts 'a' væn nyin' 遺臭°萬年
IGNORAMUS, bah-du'-bi 白°肚皮; ts'ao'-pao 草包; one who has never tasted ink, m'-neh ky'üoh-moh-shü' ko 全°無°墨水°; a pretender to knowledge, c'ong dzæ'-'ông nying 充在行

人°; kô'-tsoh ts'ong'-ming 假作聰明

IGNORANT, *not knowing*, feh hyiao'-teh-go 弗曉得个°; feh ming'-bah-go 弗明白个°; — *of rules of propriety, &c.*, feh-sih shü'-vu 弗識世務; — (*i. e. stupid*) *people*, nyü pah'-sing 愚百°姓; nyü ming' 愚民

IGNORE, *to* — *one's own words*, zih-yin' 食言

ILL, *sick*, yiu bing' 有病; *slightly* —, feh sông'-kw'a 弗爽快°; feh shih'-i 弗適°意; næn-ko' 難過; *must not think* — *of*, (or *take ill*), feh k'o kyin kwa' 弗可見怪°; — *arranged*, pa' feh-hao 擺弗好; — *gotten*, keo-ts'ia' teh'-djoh-go 苟°且°得着个°; — *natured*, tiao-cün'-deo-go 刁尖°頭个°; kæn-ka' 尷尬°; — *will*, du'-bing 肚病; ün 怨; ün'-ky'i 怨氣; *treat me* —, dæ ngô Wa' 待我孬°; *ditto* (*if a guest*), dæ ngô boh' 待我薄

ILLEGAL, væn-fah'-go 犯法个°; we-li', væn-fah'-go 違理犯法个°

ILLEGIBLE, doh-feh-loh'-ky'i 讀弗下°去°

ILLEGITIMATE *trade*, væn'-kying-go sang-i' 犯禁个°生°意; — *birth*, t'eo sang' 偷生

ILLIBERAL, ky'i'-liang 'ah-tsah' 器量狹°窄; du'-liang tsah' 肚量窄

ILLIMITABLE, m̄ 'æn'-cü 無限°制; m̄-pin'-m̄-ngen' 無°邊無°岸

ILLITERATE, feh sih'-z 弗識字

ILLNESS, bing 病; *severe* —, djong' bing 重病; *recovered from* —, bing hao'-de 病好了°; bing' djün-yü'-de 病全愈了°

ILLUMINATE, *to* tsiao'-leh ming-liang' 照得°明亮; kwông' tsiao'-djoh 光照着°

ILLUSTRATE, *to* — *by example*, yüong pi'-yü, kông' ming-bah' 用比喻講°明白°; — *by pictures*, yüong du-wô' peh nying hyiao'-teh 用圖畫俾°人曉得

ILLUSTRIOUS, ming'-sing do' 名聲大°; — *for virtue*, teh'-ky'i kao' 德氣高

IMAGE, ziang 像; ngeo'-ziang 偶像; *small* — (generally a toy), 'en 偶孩°

IMAGINE, *to* i'-siang 意想; — (as something incorrect, or fantastic), du'-djün 杜撰; du'-dzao 杜造; — *something false*, zia-ho'-ky'i.

IMAGINATION, *the power of* —, ts'eh'-doh-ts-dzæ' 測度之才; *it is all his own* —, zi kyin' yiu kyü 自°見有鬼°

IMBECILE, ngæ 呆; — *from age*, lao'-moh-long'-c'ong 老邁°龍鍾 (c'ong or ts'ong),

IMBECILE, *n*. ngæ-moh'-deo 呆木頭

IMBEDDED, *buried in*, u'-tsông-tih; — *in mud*, na-nyi-li u'-tsông-tih 賊在泥中°; *sunk*, 'æn-tsing'-tih 陷°進的
IMBITTER, *to* long'-leh kw'u'-go 弄得°苦°个°; *he imbitters my life*, ngô bing-seng' ky'üoh gyi'-go kw'u' 我平生吃°其个°苦°
IMITATE, *to* — (a person), k'en'-yiang' 'oh-yiang 看樣學°樣; k'en-nying' 'oh-yiang' 看人學°樣; — (as work), tsiao' yiang tso' 照樣做; — *others*, nying k'en' nying yiang' 人°看人°樣
IMITATIVE, we 'oh yiang' 會學°樣
IMMATERIAL, vu' ying-t'i' go 無形體个°; m' ying-tsih' go 無形跡个°; — *to me*, ü ngô' vu dzih' 與我無涉
IMMATURE, m'-neh do-tsoh' 沒°有°大°足; m'-neh tsiang'-dzing 沒°有°長成
IMMEASURABLE, liang-feh-læ'-go 量弗來个°; m'-'æn'-go 無限°个°
IMMEDIATELY, ziu 就°; ih'-z-li 一時裏; tsih'-k'eh 即刻; lih-k'eh' 立刻; mô'-zông 馬上
IMMEMORIAL, *from time*—, dzong-kwu'-yi-læ 從古以來
IMMENSE, *very large*, ting'-do' 頂大°; do'-leh-kying 大°得°緊; — *quantity*, to'-feh-ko', yi-to' 多而又°多

IMMERSE, *to* — *in water*, tsing' læ shü'-li' 浸在°水°裡
IMMERSION, *baptism by* —, tsing'-li 浸禮
IMMINENT, *near*, ling-gying' 臨近; *in* — *danger*, ngwe' dzæ tæn' zih 危在旦夕; ngwe-hyin' ling-gying-de' 危險臨近了°; (more intense) ngwe kyih'-de 危急了°
IMMODERATE, t'eh' ko-veng' 太°過分
IMMODEST, feh-p'ô-siu' 弗怕羞; feh-kwu' lin-c'ü' 弗顧廉恥; — *picture*, c'ing kong 春宮 (ih-foh)
IMMOLATE, *to sacrifice animals*, yüong sang-k'eo' tso tsi'-li 用牲口做祭禮; — *a man, in vengeance*, dziu-nying' sah'-ts tsi' 讐人°殺了°祭
IMMORAL, *inconsistent with rectitude*, feh-tön'-tsing 弗端正; feh-tsing'-kying 弗正經
IMMORTAL, ve'-si-go 不°會°死°个°; üong'-weh-go 永活个°; — (in the Buddhist sense) dziang-seng'-peh-lao 長生不老
IMMORTALIZE, *to* liu-fông'-pah-shü' 流芳百°世
IMMOVABLE, dong'-feh-læ'-go 動弗來个°; yi'-feh-dong'-go 移弗動个°
IMMURED *in a prison*, kwæn' læ lao-kæn'-li 關在°牢監裡;

— *in a convent,* loh ing'-siu-yün-li 落隱修院裡
IMMUTABLE, üong' feh-keng-kæ'-go 永弗更改个°; kæ'-pin-feh-læ'-go 改變弗來个°
IMPAIR, *to — wæ-diao'* 壞了°; *— the health (i. e. body),* wæ-diao' sing-t'i' 壞了°身體; *bodily energies still unimpaired,* tsing-jing' wa feh sæ' 精神還弗衰; *impaired fortune,* ts'æn'-nyih ky'üih'-long'-ky'i'-de 產業漸°缺了°
IMPART, *to — instruction,* kao'-hyüing 敎°訓; *willing to — to others,* k'eng' peh nying-kó' 肯給°人°家; *to — the secret (of making),* djün pi'-kyüih 傳秘訣
IMPARTIAL, m-p'in-sing' 無偏心; *just,* kong-dao' 公道; kong-bing 公平; *— man,* ping'-kong vu-s'-go nying 秉公無私个°人°
IMPARTIALLY, bing-yüing 平允; *treat men —*, kong-dao' dæ nying 公道待人°
IMPASSABLE, tseo'-feh-ko'-ky'i 走弗過去°
IMPATIENT, feh-næ'-væn 弗耐煩; feh-jing'-næ 弗忍耐
IMPEACH *him,* fông' gyi-go shü' 放其个°水°; *— an inferior in office,* ts'æn'-tseo' 叅奏
IMPEACHMENT, *written* tseo'-tsông 奏章
IMPEDE, *to* gah-tang'; *impeded (by many things, as baskets, &c.),* t'o-t'o'-ts'i-ts'i 拖拖㧱°㧱°
IMPEDIMENT, gah-tang'; *obstruction,* fông-ngæ' 妨碍; *an — in his speech,* kông shih'-wô bun'-zih-keng-go 講°說話拌°舌根个°
IMPENDING *evil, or woe,* 'o'-se læ deo-zông' 禍祟在°頭上; 'o'-tsiang ling-deo' 禍將臨頭
IMPENETRABLE, tsing'-feh-læ 進弗來; *— to the eye (also used figuratively),* k'en-feh-t'eo' 看弗透
IMPENITENT, feh-zing' hwe'-kæ-go 弗會悔改个°; *obdurate,* t'ih'-tang sing-dziang' 鐵打心腸
IMPERATIVE, pih' ky'iao-leh (or ky'iah-leh) 必須°; vu pih'-ts 務必
IMPERCEPTIBLE *to the eye,* k'en'-feh-c'ih-go 看弗出个°; *— to the touch,* moh'-feh-c'ih'-go 摸弗出个°
IMPERFECT, *not perfect,* feh-djün' 弗全°; dzæn-ky'üih'-go 殘缺个°; *faulty,* yiu mao-bing' 有毛病; t'e-pæn' 推扳; *deficient,* yiu ky'üih' 有缺; feh wun'-djün 弗完全
IMPERIAL, wông-ti'-go 皇帝个° *—(immediate) family,* wông-kô' 皇家°; *—family or tribe,* tsong-shih' 宗室; *— commands,* zông-yü' 上諭; sing'-ts 聖旨; wông-ming' 皇命; *— proclamation,*

wông-pông' 皇榜；— *guards*, z-we' 侍衞；— *palace*, wông-kong' 皇宮；— *censor*, kyin'-ts'ah nyü'-s 監察御史

IMPERIOUS, c'ih'-k'eo-do - yiang' 出口大°樣；c'ih' yin peh seng' 出言不遜

IMPERTINENT, *not knowing what is proper*, feh sih' siang-t'i' 弗識禮°體；*not caring for ditto*, s'-vu gyi-dæn' 肆無忌憚；*thrusting one's self into conversation when not wanted*, iao ts'ah-cü'-go 要插嘴个°；— *fellow (i. e. monkey)*, to-cü' weh-seng' 多嘴猢猻

IMPERTURBABLE *in mind*, sing t'ih'-ding 心鐵定；— *face*, min-k'ong' t'ih'-pæn 面孔鐵板

IMPERVIOUS *to water*, shü seng'-feh-tsing 水°沁弗進；ve'-heng-shü 弗曾°沁水°; feh-ky'üoh'-shü 弗吃°水°；— *to air*, feh-t'ong-ky'i'-go 弗通氣个°

IMPETUOUS, *as the moth rushing into flame*, ziang deo-ho'-ts'ông-ing' ka 像投火蒼蠅；— *torrent*, shü kyih' 水°急

IMPIOUS, miao-z Jing-ming'-go 藐視神明个°

IMPLACABLE, seng-s'-feh-'o' 至°死不°和

IMPLANT *love in the heart*, jing-æ'-go keng-deo' cong læ sing li-hyiang 仁愛个°根頭種在°心裡向

IMPLEMENTS, kô-sang'; ky'i'-ming 器皿；— *of all kinds*, siu'-yüong-kô-sang' 家°用°物°件°

IMPLICATED, lin-liao'-go 連了个°; c'ün'-t'ong-liao-go 串通了个°

IMPLICIT, *to place — confidence in*, ky'üoh'-jih siang-sing' 確實相信；*to give — obedience*, pah'-i-pah'-jing 百°依百°順

IMPLORE, *to* gyiu-k'eng' 求懇

IMPLIED, kwæn'-djoh-tih 關着°的°; *contained within*, pao-tsing'-tih 包進的°; 'en'-tih 含的°; ko'-tsing-tih 裹進的°; *hidden*, k'ông'-tih 囥的°

IMPOLITE, m̅-li'-ky'i 無°禮體；m̅-kwe'-kyü 無°規矩

IMPORT, *meaning*, ka'-shih 解說；i-s' 意思

IMPORT *duties*, tsing'-k'eo se' 進口稅；*imported goods*, tsing'-k'eo ho' 進口貨

IMPORT, *to — goods*, ho' tsông-tsing'-læ 貨裝進來

IMPORTANT, iao'-kying 要緊；*weighty*, djong 重; *not —*, m̅-iao'-teh-kying 無要緊；— *doctrine*, do-dön'-dao-li 大°段道理

IMPORTUNATE, t'ao'-ko-yi-t'ao' 討過叉°討；iao'-zông-kô-iao' 要上加要

IMPORTUNATELY, sah'-k'eo t'ao着° 實°討；ts'ih'-sing gyiu' 切心求；— *and persistently*, o'-nyi-bi'-ts'i t'ao'.

IMPOSE, to — a customs' tax, k'æ ih-'ông sɛ' 開一項稅;—(as a burden), djong'-t'oh 重托; he is imposing on you, læ-tih hong' ng zông gyi'-go tông' 正°在°哄你上其个°當

IMPOSSIBLE to do, tso'-feh-læ 做弗來; long'-feh-læ 弄弗來; quite —, tsing-tsing' tso'-feh læ 眞眞做弗來;—to find a seat, zo'-we ih-ngæn' tu zing'-feh-c'ih 坐位一點°都尋°弗出

IMPOSTOR, kô'-nying 假人°; one who assumes a false name, mao-ming-go cü'-kwu 冒名个人°; one who by deception runs off with a child, or property, kwa'-ts 拐子; an —, ziang kwa'-ts ka 像拐°子

IMPOTENT, weak, nyün'-ziah 輭弱; m̃-lih 無°力;—tao-yiang' 倒陽;—from excess, tsing'-lih-hao'-zing 精力耗盡°

IMPRACTICABLE, tso'-feh-læ 做弗來; long'-feh-læ 弄弗來

IMPRECATE, to tsiu'-mô 呪罵

IMPRECATIONS, mouth full of —, bah-k'eo' tsiu'-cü 滿口呪咀; oh'-k'eo tsiu'-cü 惡口呪咀

IMPREGNABLE, tang'-feh-tsing' 打弗進

IMPREGNATED, to become — (as animals), ziu tsing' 受精;—eggs, ko-shü'-liao-go dæn' 過勢了个°蛋; tang-shü'-liao-go dæn' 打勢過了个°蛋; infused into, as in water, ky'i'-mi-jih-ko' 氣味°入過;—with salt, yiu 'æn'-ky'i jih-tsing' 有鹹°氣入進

IMPRESS of a hand, siu'-go ying-tsih' 手个°形跡; siu'-ing 手印

IMPRESS, to engrave on the heart, k'eh' læ sing'-li 刻在°心裡; to — a messenger, k'ô ts'a-s' 捉差; to — carriers, k'ô fu-ts' 捉°脚°夫

IMPRESSED, to be — on the mind, ts'ih'-ts'ih-dzæ-sing' 切切在心; he — me favorably the first time, ts'u we'-djoh gyi, ngô cong'-i go 初會著°其我中意个°

IMPRESSION, the first — in printing, ts'u ing' 初印; a bad —, ing'-leh mo-wu' 印得°模糊; take an — of a writing on stone, k'ao pe' 拷碑

IMPRINT, to ing 印; tang-ing' 打印

IMPRISON, loh' lao-kæn'-li 落牢監°裡; kwæn'-leh kæn'-li 關在°監裏; ky'ih'-loh lao-kæn-li 挈°落牢監°裡

IMPROBABLE, vi-pih' 未必; næn yiu' 難有; cannot be believed, feh' tsoh sing 弗足信; næn siang'-sing 難相信

IMPROPER, not suitable, feh tsoh-bying 弗作與; fi sô nyi' 非所宜;—(as to make noise in prayers, or walk in with muddy feet), væn gyi' 犯忌

IMPROPRIETY, *where is the* — ? yiu' 'o feh k'o' 有何不°可?
IMPROVE, *to* tsing-ih' 進益; *to grow better,* hao'-ky'i-læ 好起來; — *the opportunity,* ts'ing-kyi-we' 趁機會; — *this opportunity,* ts'ing' ts' kyi'-we 乘°此机會; — *the time,* æ'-sih kwông-ing' 愛惜光陰
IMPROVED *in looks,* min-seh' hao'-jü zin-deo' 面色好如前°
IMPROVIDENT, feh-liu-zin' c'ü-'eo' 弗留前°處後; *the — are always poor,* sön'-kyi feh-tao' ih-si'-gyüong' 算計弗到一世°窮
IMPRUDENT, feh-kwu' zin'eo' 弗顧前°後; — *with regard to health,* feh-pao'-yiang 弗保養
IMPUDENT, m̄-gyi-dæn' 無°忌憚; — *(in reply),* ing-cü' 應嘴
IMPUGN, *to* — *one's motives,* k'eh'-liao gyi 刻薄°料其
IMPULSE, *to give him an* —, ts'e-dong' gyi-go hying'-deo 催動其个°興頭; dzu' gyi-go hying' 助其个°興; *ditto (like giving a push),* yiu-ts-wu' t'e'-ih-pô 猶之乎提°一把; *he acts from* —, gyi'-go tsoh'-we hyüih-ky'i' s-jün' 其个°作爲血氣使然
IMPUNITY, *with (without detection),* feh-p'o-en 弗破案; *to steal with* —, tso-zeh' feh-p'o-en 做賊°弗破案; *can do with*

—, *because free from accustomed restraints,* "T'in kao' wông-ti yün'" 天高皇帝遠
IMPURE, *unclean,* feh-ken-zing' 弗乾淨; feh-kyih'-zing 弗潔淨; feh-ts'ing-kyih' 弗清潔; — *thoughts,* nyiæn-deo' feh kyih'-zing 念頭弗潔淨; sing-zia' 心邪°; — *water,* shü' dzoh' 水°濁
IMPUTE, *to ascribe to,* kwe-peh' 歸給°; — *to us,* sön'-tao ah'-lah ming-'ô' 算到我°等°名下°
IN, læ 在°; dzæ'-li 在裡; ü 於; *he is* — *China,* gyi' læ Cong-koh' 其在°中國; — *the room,* vông'-li 房裡; — *my hand,* læ-ngô' siu'-li 在°我手裡; *come* —, tseo'-tsing-læ 走進來; *go* —, tseo'-tsing-ky'i' 走進去°; *not* — *man,* feh dzæ-ü nying' 弗在於人°; — *this manner,* z-ka' yiang'-shih 如°此樣式; — *order,* a-ts''-jü 挨次序; i-ts''-jü 依次序; tsiao-ts''-jü 照次序; — *order to know,* s'-teh hao hyiao'-teh 使得好曉得; vu-fi' iao hyiao'-teh 無非要曉得; *small* — *comparison with that,* pi'-gyi-siao' 比其小
INACCESSIBLE, tseo'-feh-tao'-go 走弗到个°
INACCURATE, *has mistakes,* yiu-ts'o' 有錯°; yiu-dzæn; — *characters,* ngo z' 訛字

INACTIVE, ngæ 呆; ngæ-teng'-teng 呆等等; ngæ-teh'-poh-loh; ngæ-c'ing'-c'ing 呆蠢蠢

INADEQUATE, feh-tsoh' 弗足

INADMISSIBLE, *cannot be received*, ziu'-feh-læ 受弗來; *cannot be listened to*, t'ing'-feh-læ 聽弗來; *cannot be allowed*, ing-hyü'-feh-læ 應許弗來

INADVERTENTLY, feh-læ'-kwu 弗來顧; ih'-feh-læ'-kwu 一弗來顧

INANIMATE, feh-weh-dong' 弗活動; ngæ 呆

INAPPLICABLE, ʻeh-feh-læ' 合弗來; *sometimes applicable, sometimes* —, yiu ʻeh'-go di'-fông, yiu' feh-ʻeh'-go di'-fông 有合个°地方, 有弗合个°地方

INAPPROACHABLE, gying'-feh-long-go 近弗攏个°

INAPPROPRIATE, feh-siang'-nyi 弗相宜; feh-ʻeh'-li' 弗合理; feh-te' 弗對

INARTICULATE *sounds*, sing-ing' feh-tsʻing' 聲音弗清

INATTENTIVE, feh-liu-sing' 弗留心; feh-kwæn'-sing 弗關心; feh-tông-sing 弗當心; feh-yüong'-sing 弗用心; sing' feh læ'-tih 心弗在°

INAUDIBLE, tʻing'-feh-cʻih'-go 聽弗出个°; tʻing'-feh-kyin'-go 聽弗着°个°; *cannot distinguish*, bin'-feh-læ'-go 辨弗來个°

INAUGURATION *of an officer*, zông zing' 上任, (also used for the commencement of anything).

INAUSPICIOUS, feh-kyih'-li 弗吉利

INBORN, sang-dzing'-go 生°成个°

INCAPABLE *of filling the position, or of doing a certain thing*, dzæ' peh sing zing' 才不勝任

INCAPACITATED *by sickness*, be bing' ʻæ'-leh feh-neng'-keo 被病害得°弗能彀; — *by old age*, be nyin-kyi' sô tsu', feh-neng'-keo 被年紀所阻弗能彀

INCAPACITY, m̄-dzæ'-dzing 無°才情; m̄-peng'-z 無°本事

INCARCERATE, *to* siu'-tsing kæn'-li 收進監裏

INCARNATE, dzing'-leh nyüoh-sing' 成得肉°身; dzing-we' nyüoh-sing' 成爲肉°身

INCAUTIOUS, feh-tso-gyi' 弗留°意

INCENDIARY, fông-hʻo'-go nying 放火个°人°

INCENSE, hyiang 香; — *sticks*, bông'-hyiang 棒香; *ditto for determining night-watches*, ding-kang'-hyiang 定更°香; *to burn* —, tin hyiang' 點香; siao hyiang' 燒香; — *pot*, hyiang-lo', or hyiang-lu 香爐

INCENSE, *to* — *one*, kyih' gyi-go ô'-wông 激其个°怒; ying' gyi'-go ô'-wông 引其个°怒

INCENSED, fah ông'-de 發怒了°; ô'-wông fah-tsoh'-de 怒發作了°; greatly —, ky'i gyih'-de 氣極了°

INCENTIVE, siang'-deo 想頭

INCESSANT, feh hyih' 弗歇; feh ts' 弗止;— talking, kông'-feh-hyih' 講弗歇;— flowing of blood, hyüih'-c'ih feh-ts' 血出弗止

INCEST, lön-leng' 亂倫

INCH, ts'eng 寸; not an — wide, feh tao' ih ts'eng kw'eh' 弗到一寸闊

INCIDENT, a pleasing —, ih tsông hyi z 一椿°喜事

INCIPIENCY, ky'i-ing' z-'eo 起因時候; ky'i-ing' fah-koh' 起因發覺°

INCIPIENT stages of disease, bing' ts'u-fah-go z-'eo 病初發個°時候

INCISORS, the two middle —, meng-zin'-ngô 門前°牙°

INCITE, to kyih 激; ying 引; tang'-dong 打動; to encourage, min'-li 勉勵;— good (or evil) feelings, ken'-kyih 感激

INCLEMENT, severe, nyin; very cold weather, ping-lang' t'in-kô' 極冷天; t'in' keh-ti'-ti lang' 天割剌°剌°冷°

INCLINATION, sing-siang' 心想; ts'-hyiang 志向; to follow one's own —, i zi'-go sing-siang' tso' 依自°個°心想做; he has an — for study, gyi'-go ts'-hyiang iao doh-shü' 其個°志向要讀書

INCLINE, to lean to one side, tang-pin' 打邊;— outward (as a wall), tang-pin' ts'ia-c'ih nga' 打邊°斜出外°;— my heart to goodness, s'-teh ngô-go sing' hyiang'-djoh jün' 使得我個°心向著°善;— the ear to hear, tseh'-leh ng'-tô t'ing 側得°耳°朶聽

INCLOSE, to (as with a fence), we-djü' 圍住; yü-cün' 圍轉;— (as in a letter), fong'-tsing 封進;— in an envelope, t'ao sing'-fong 套信封;— in an extra wrapper, kô fong' 加°封;— in a paper, yüong ts' pao'-ih-pao 用紙包一包

INCLOSURE. The Chinese speak of an inclosure, as that which lies within the wall, or fence; thus, the city is that which lies within the wall, dzing-li' 城裏; the space within a bamboo fence, ts'iang-pô' li-hyiang' 牆笆裏向

INCLUDED within, dzæ-ne' or dzæ-nen 在內; ditto as ideas, pao-kweh'-tih 包括的; pao-'en'-tih 包含的; is this —? keh'-go dzæ-ne' feh 這°個°在內否! not —, feh dzæ'-ne 弗在內

INCOHERENT words, (i. e. words without strength), slih-wô' t'eh-ky'i' go 說話脫氣个°; shih'-wô t'eh-tsih'-go 說話脫節个°

INCOMBUSTIBLE, siao-feh-diao'-go 燒弗壞°个°

INCOME, tsing'-shü 進水°; tsing-nyih' 進業; tsing'-tsiang 進賬; *expenditure exceeds —*, sô-jih' peh-fu' sô-c'ih' 所入不敷所出

INCOMMODE, *do not — yourself to do it*, teng ng feh-bin', bao-vong' tso 與°你°弗便不°用°做

INCOMPARABLE, *transcendent*, pi'-tsong-feh-dong'-go 比眾弗同个°; *cannot be compared with*, pi'-feh-teh'-go 比弗得个°; m̄-kao' pi-deo' 無°比頭

INCOMPETENT, *unequal to a task*, tæn-tông'-feh-djü 擔當弗住; *— as a frog to steady a table leg*, "din-kyi' seh coh'-kyiah si ts'ang'" 田雞扶桌腳死°撐

INCOMPLETE, *not complete*, feh dzing'-kong 弗成功; feh zi'-jih 弗齊°集; *not perfect*, feh djün'-be 弗全備; *unfinished*, feh wun'-djün 弗完全; feh tsiu'-djün 弗周全

INCOMPREHENSIBLE, sih'-feh-t'eo' 識弗°透; moh'-feh-djoh' 摸弗着°; ts'æ'-feh-c'ih' 猜弗出

INCONCEIVABLE, siang'-feh-tao'-go 想弗到个°; ts'eng'-feh-c'ih'-go 忖弗出个°

INCONGRUOUS, feh-siang'-p'e 弗相配; fi-sô-nyi' 非所宜

INCONSIDERATE, feh-li'-we' 弗理會; mông-kyi' li'-we 忘°記理會

INCONSISTENT *talk*, shih-wô' zin-'eo' feh-vu' 說話前後弗符; *words — with one's heart*, k'eo'-z sing-fi 口是心非

INCONSOLABLE, feh-zin' en-we' go 弗受安慰个°; feh-k'eng' t'ing ky'ün' 弗肯聽勸

INCONSTANT, fæn'-foh-feh-ding'-go 反覆弗定个°; fæn'-foh-vu-djông' 反覆無常

INCONTINENT, fông'-cong-s-yüoh'-go 放縱私欲个°

INCONTROVERTIBLE, pæn-poh'-feh-tao'-go 駁弗倒个°

INCONVENIENT, feh-bin'-tông 弗便當; feh-bin' 弗便

INCORPOREAL, vu-ying'-vu-ziang' 無形無像

INCORRECT, *has mistakes*, yiu-t'so' 有錯°; yiu-dzæn'; *the characters are —*, z feh-tön'-tsing 字弗端正

INCORRIGIBLE, vu-fah'-k'o-djü' 無法可治; tsih'-mi-peh-hwô' 執迷不化; — (*as a child*), mæn-bi' 蠻疲; — (*used in reproach*), zah-bi' 賊°疲; bi-gyih'-de 疲極了

INCORRUPTIBLE, ve'-wæ'-diao-go 弗°會°壞个°

INCREASE, *to* hying-wông' 興旺;

INCREDIBLE, siang-sing'-feh-læ' 相信弗來; feh-tsoh-sing' 弗足信

to add to, kô-ts'eo' 加°湊; to grow, do-ky'i'-læ 大°起來;
— his courage, tsông'-gyi-go-tæn' 壯其个°膽; tsiang'-gyi-go-tæn' 長其个°膽

INCREDULOUS, pah'-feh-siang'-sing 百°弗相信

INCULCATE virtue, cong-teh'-ky'i 種德氣; instruct often, le'-djông hyüing'-kyiao 屢常訓敎

INCUMBENT, it is — on me to do, kwe-ngô'-tso' 歸我做

INCUR, væn 犯; væn'-djoh 犯着°; — his anger, væn'-gyi-go ô'-wông 犯其个°怒

INCURABLE, i'-feh-læ'-go 醫弗來个°; m̄-i'-deo 無°醫頭

INDEBTED, I am — to him, ngô'-ky'in' gyi tsa' 我欠其債°; ditto, for kindness, ngô dzing' gyi-go dzing' 我承其个°情; ditto, for great kindness, ngô ky'in' gyi eng-diu nyi'-tsa 我欠其恩錢°義債

INDECENT, fông'-p'eh-la'-sa 放°潑糊°褻; filthy, ao-tsao' 墺糟

INDECISION, m̄-cü'-i 無°主意; m̄-kyüih'-tön 無°決斷; hyüong'-vu-dzing-kyin' 胸無成見

INDEED, ko'-jün 果然; jih-dzæ' 實在; is it — so? ko'-jün z-ka'-feh 果然如°此°否°?

INDEFATIGABLE, dziang-kyiu' feh-gyün' 長久弗倦; tso'-feh-pih'-go 做弗彄个

INDEFINITE, weng-teng'-teng 混滾; feh-feng'-ts'ing 弗分清; the time is —, vu-ding' gyi 無定°期

INDELIBLE, that will not fade, t'e'-feh-diao'-go 褪弗壞个°; that cannot be rubbed out, k'a'-feh-ky'i' 揩弗去

INDELICATE, m̄-t'i'-t'ong 無°體統; shih-t'i'-t'ong 失體統; — language, fi-li'-ts-yin' 非禮之言

INDENTURE, kwæn-shü' 關書; to draw up an —, lih-kwæn-shü' 立關書

INDEPENDENT, sing-kao' ky'i-ngao' 心高氣傲; — and free, zi-yiu'-zi-dzæ' 自°由自°在; following one's own will, 'eo-zi'-go cü'-i 倏自°个°主意

INDEX, table of contents, moh-loh' 目錄

INDIA-RUBBER, k'a-ts'-kao 揩°紙膠°

INDIAN-CORN, loh-koh' 稑穀; pao'-r-mi 保兒米; — meal, loh-koh'-feng 稑穀粉

INDIAN-INK, moh 墨

INDICATES, points, ts'-tin 指點; shows, (or can readily see), k'o kyin'-tch 可見得

INDICT, to kao-zông' 告狀

INDICTMENT, zông-ts' 狀紙 (ih-tsiang)

INDIFFERENCE, to hear with —, t'ing'-ts dæn'-jün 聽之淡然; he took it with —, gyi ziu'-ts dæn'-jün 其受之淡然; dæn'-dæn sing-s t'ing' 不大°用°心聽; a matter of — (to me), feh-leng' 弗論; treat one with —, dæ nying' lang'-dæn 待人°冷淡

INDIFFERENT, not very good, wa hao' 還°好; wa k'o'-yi 還°可以; yia hao' 也°好; p'o-hao' 頗好

INDIGESTION, not digesting, feh siao'-hwô 弗消化; feh hwô' 弗化

INDIGNANT, to be — at, ky'i'-veng 氣忿; I am — at him, ngô teng' gyi dong ky'i'-veng 我爲°其動氣忿; too — to endure it, ky'i'-veng-feh-ko' 氣忿弗過

INDIGNITY, to treat with —, tsao-t'ah' 蹧蹋; ditto (with greater —), sih'-doh 褻瀆; ditto (with greatest —), ling-joh' 凌辱

INDIGO, native din'-ts'ing 靛青; t'u'-din 土靛; foreign—, yiang-læn' 洋藍

INDIRECT, feh-tsiao-dzih' 弗照直; wæn-ky'üoh' 灣曲: — answer, feh-tsiao-dzih' we-teh' 弗照直回答

INDISCREET, kyin'-sih feh tao-kô' 見識弗到家°

INDISCRIMINATELY, feh-leng' 弗論; peh-kyü' 不拘; good or bad —, feh-leng' hao' feh-leng' wa' 弗論好弗論孬°

INDISPENSABLE, siao'-feh-teh' 少弗得; hyih'-feh-læ' 歇弗來

INDISPOSED, not well, yin' tin feh sông-kw'a 有點弗爽快°; — to talk, læn'-teh kông 懶得講; — to work, læn'-teh tso sang-weh' 懶得做生°活

INDISPUTABLE, poh'-feh-læ' 駁弗來; m poh'-deo 無°駁頭; m-kao wô-deo' 無°話頭

INDISSOLUBLE, yiang-feh-k'æ'-go 煬弗開个°; the — bonds of wedlock, kyih'-fah fu'-ts'i' ts'ah'-feh-sæn' 結髮夫妻拆弗散

INDISTINCT, feh ts'ing'-t'ong 弗清通; feh ts'ing'-ts'u 弗清楚; feh ts'ing'-k'oh 弗清確; — as characters, or things in the distance, ing'-ing-dong 隱隱動; u-ing'-ing 黑°隱隱

INDISTINGUISHABLE, weng-weng'-deng-deng 混沌; feng'-feh-c'ih-go 分弗出个°; — by sight, k'en'-feh-c'ih-go 看弗出个°

INDITE, to — verses, di s' 題詩

INDIVISIBLE, feng-feh-k'æ'-go 分弗開个°; feng'-feh-læ'-go 分弗來个°

INDOLENT, t'en-læn'-go 貪懶个°; sang læn'-wông-bing; likes to lie down, t'en-min' læn-do' 貪眠懶惰

INDORSE, to tæn-kyin' 擔肩; dæ-kyin' 擔肩
INDUCE, to cü'-du 制度;— him to stay, cü'-du gyi deng tong 制度其°庇在°此°; kw'un-liu gyi k 留他°;— customers to come, tsiao ma'-cü læ 招買°主來
INDUCEMENT, that is an — to me, keh z ngô t'en-du' go 這°是我貪圖个°; there is no — for me to go, ngô ky'i' m̄-kao' soh-go t'en-du' 我去°沒°有°甚°麼°貪圖
INDULGE, to gratify his wishes, jü gyi'-go sing' 如其个°心; i' gyi-go sing-siang' 依其个°心想; to — (where there should be restraint), yüong-tsong' 容縱; — the passions, fông'-tsong s-yüoh' 放縱私慾
INDULGENT, very yüong-iang' 容養;— and foolish fondness, nyih-æ'-peh-ming' 溺愛不明
INDUSTRIOUS, gying-lih' 勤力
INEBRIATE, n. tse'-hen 醉漢
INEFFECTUAL, feh-tsi'-ü-z' 弗濟于事;— (as medicine), feh-kyin yiao' 弗見效; in vain, bah-lih'-lih' 空°勞°; du-jün' 徒然
INEFFICACIOUS, m̄-ing'-'ao 無°應效°;— (as an idol, or medicine), feh ling'-ing 弗靈應
INEFFICIENT, habitually slack, tso' z-ken' feh-tao-ko' 做事幹弗到家°; pun-lu'-feh-kyih'-go 半途°而°廢°

INEQUALITY in surface, kao-kao'-ti-ti 高高低低; ky'i-ky'i-ky'iao-ky'iao 蹊蹊蹺蹺
INESTIMABLE, vu-kô'-ts-pao 無價°之寶
INEVITABLE, peh-min'-go 不免个°; cannot be escaped, min'-feh-ko 免弗過
INEXCUSABLE, nyün-liang'-feh-læ 原諒弗來
INEXHAUSTIBLE, vu-gyüong'-go 無窮个°; yüong'-feh-wun'-go 用弗完个°
INEXORABLE, m̄-wæn'-we-go 無°挽回个°; — (person), tsih-ih' feh-k'eng' 執一弗肯; feh-cing' dzing; — in carrying out law, tsih-fah' feh-liu dzing' 執法弗留情
INEXPERIENCED, m̄'-neh yüih-lih'-ko 沒°有°閱歷過°; sang-sn'-go 生°疏个°; — in the ways of the world, feh-sih shü'-lu 弗識世路
INEXPERT, feh jing'-joh 弗純熟
INEXPLICABLE, i'-s ka'-shih-feh-c'ih' 意思解°說弗出
INEXPRESSIBLE, kông'-feh-c'ih'-go 講°弗出个°; wô'-feh-læ'-go 話弗來个°
INEXTRICABLE tangle, kyih', ka'-feh-c'ih' 結解弗出;— difficulty, ka'-feh-k'æ'-go keh'-tah 解弗開个°疙瘩
INFALLIBLE, ve-ts'o' 弗°會°錯;

the — (the emperor), sing'-zông 聖上

INFAMY, ts'iu' ming'-sing 醜名聲; eternal —, yi-ts'iu'-væn-nyin' 遺臭°萬年

INFANT, na-hwun' 嬰°孩° (ih-go); ing-r 嬰兒 the veng-li for a male infant.

INFANTICIDE, long-sah' na-hwun' 弄殺嬰°孩°; custom of killing girls, nyih nyü' fong-djoh 溺女風俗

INFANTRY, bu'-ping 步兵

INFATUATED, jih-mi-weng'-dzing-de 入迷魂陣了°; hweng'-tih'-de 惛的了°

INFECT, to — the air, yiang'-ky'i long'-leh doh'-go 陽氣弄得°毒个°; to bring disease, long-c'ih' bing læ 弄出病來; whole body is infected, weng'-sing yiu ts'iu'-ky'i 渾身有臭°氣; bad influences will —, jih-ky'i' iao jih-ko' 習氣要染°

INFECTION, I took the —, ngô bing' be ts'iu'-ky'i jih-tsing'-go 我病被臭°氣入進个°; ngô bing' z heh' ts'iu'-ky'i sang'-go 我病是嗃°臭°氣生°个°

INFECTIOUS, disease is —, bing' iao-yin'-go 病要延个°

INFER, to t'e-k'æ'-ky'i 推開去'; I — that it was you who took it, ngô t'e-leng'-k'æ-ky'i z ng' do'-go 我推論開去°是你°拿个°; from one truth to — the second, veng ih' cü r' 問一知二 (veng.)

INFERENCE, t'e-leng'-k'æ-go i'-s 推論開个°意思; draw a wrong —, t'e-leng' ts'ô' 推論錯°; i'-ziang bông'-pih 倚墻傍壁

INFERIOR in quality, t'e-pæn' tin 推扳點; wa' tin 孬點; ts'ô' tin 差點; the lowest grade, mah teng' 末等; 'ô' teng 下°等; — in age, siao ih'-pe 小一輩; 'ô' ih'-pe 下°一輩; under another's jurisdiction, (as officers, or servants), 'ô'-joh 下°屬; — in learning, 'oh-veng'-ts'in' 學°問淺; — to him, pi-gyi'-ti 比其低

INFESTED, the seas are — with robbers, yiang-wu' dao'-hyin to 洋湖盜險多

INFIDEL, disbeliever in the Scriptures, feh-siang'-sing Sing'-shü-go-nying' 弗相信聖書个°人°

INFINITE, m̄-tæn'-cü 無°限°制; m̄'-tæn'-liang 無°限°量

INFIRM, enfeebled, ky'i'-hyüih sæ'-de 氣血衰了°

INFLAME, to — (as a desire), dong-ho' 動火; — the passions, ying'-dong yüoh-ho' 引動慾火; to grow hot, and painful, ziang-bo' dziah-c'ih' ka 像火燎°出°

INFLAMED eyes, nyih-ngæn' 熱°眼; ho'-ngæn 火眼

INFLATE, *to blow up*, c'ü-p'ông' 吹°脹°
INFLEXIBLE, *that will not bend*, ao'-feb-cün'-go 拗弗轉个°; — *in purpose*, cü'-i m̄-wæn'-we-go 主意無°挽回个°
INFLICT, *to — punishment*, tsah'-vah 責罰; *ditto (by an officer)*, dong ying-vah' 動刑罰; — *a fine*, vah-nying-ts' 罰銀子
INFLUENCE, *yield to his —*, tsiao-gyi'-go dong'-zing tso' 照其个°動靜做; k'en gyi siu'-tsang-cü-den' 看其手法°; *use the — of an official*, i'-kwun t'oh-shü' 倚官托勢; *trusts to foreign —*, gæ nga'-koh shü' 靠°外國勢; *to ward off evil —*, bih-zia 辟°邪°
INFLUENCE, *to* ken'-dong 感動; ken'-hwô 感化; — *for good*, ying'-dao 引導; — *(generally for evil)*, ying'-yiu 引誘; *easily influenced*, ng-tô nyün' 耳°朵軟
INFLUENTIAL, hyüing'-hyiang 熏香
INFLUENZA, shü'-sông-fong' 水°傷風
INFORM, *to* t'ong-cü' 通知; t'ong-pao' 通報; kao'-su 告訴; cü-we' 知會; — *friends of a death*, pao fu'-ing 報訃音; pao si'-sing 報死°信
INFORMANT, t'ong-pao'-go cü-kwu 通報个°人°; t'ong-fong'-pao-sing'-go-nying 通風報信个°人°
INFORMER, *one who informs for selfish ends, &c.*, liu'-long-ky'ing'.
INFREQUENT *times*, m̄-to-siao we-su' 無°多少回數; m̄-kyi'-we 無°幾回; yiu'-tsao'-su 有遭數
INFRINGEMENT *of law*, væn-kying' 犯禁; — *of rules*, væn-kwe' væn-kying' 犯規犯禁
INFURIATED, nu'-fah-ts'ong'-kwun 怒髮冲冠 (ts'ong or c'ong).
INFUSE, *to extract qualities by steeping*, tsing' gyi tsih'-shü c'ih' 浸其汁水°出
INGENIOUS, yiu zao'-tsoh-ts dzæ' 有造°作之才; yiu kyi-ky'iao'-go 有機巧个°; — *contrivance*, ling-ky'iao'-go kô-sang' 靈巧个°器皿°
INGENUOUS, dzih-sông' 直爽
INGOT *of sycee*, veng-nying' 紋銀; nyün-pao' 元寶
INGRAFT, *to — a tree*, tsih-jü' 接樹
INGRATITUDE, SEE UNGRATEFUL.
INGREDIENT, *mix together three ingredients*, sæn-yiang' liao-tsoh' p'e-tæn-long 三樣料作配攏; — *(in a medical prescription)*, ih-vi' 一味
INHABITANTS, *how many —?* to-siao'-nying deng'-tih 多少人°庶的? to-siao' ting-k'eo' 多

少丁口? to-siao' nying'-ting 多少人°丁?
INHABITED, *this house is* —, keh' tsing oh' yiu nying' deng'-tih 這°進屋有人°底的
INHALE, *to — the air*, ky'i hwun'-tsing 氣噢進; byih'-tsing 噏進
INHERIT, *to — property*, tsih'-ziu ts'æn'-nyih 接受產業; — *an office* (trade, &c.), jih tsih' 襲職
INHERITANCE, yi-loh'-læ-go ts'æn'-nyih 遺下來个產業; yi-loh'-læ-go kô-kyi' 遺下來个°家°計
INHOSPITABLE, *afraid of entertaining*, p'ô tsih k'ah' 怕接客; *to treat guests badly*, ky'ing-boh' dæ nying'-k'ah 輕薄待客人°
INHUMAN, oh'-doh 惡毒; — *disposition*, doh-sing' 毒心; sing ziang za-lông' ka 心像豺狼' lông'-sing keo'-fi 狼心狗肺
INIMITABLE, 'oh'-feh-siang-ziang'-go 學°弗相像个°; 'oh'-feh-læ-go 學°弗來个°
INIQUITY, ze 罪; ze-oh' 罪惡; oh'-nyih 惡孽
INJECT, *to — water*, shü' zih-tsing'-ky'i 水°射進去°
INJUDICIOUS, *acting without thought*, *or intelligence*, hwông-dông' 荒唐; mông-bah' 茫白°; *an — act*, ih-dziu'-ts-kyin' — 籌之見

INJURE, *to* 'æ 害; sông-'æ 傷害; *to treat wrongfully*, kw'e-dæ' 虧待; *ditto* (in a greater degree), long-song 弄唆°; *to treat unjustly*, we'-ky'üoh 委曲; — *secretly*, s' ing-sön' 使陰算; en' tsiu-coh' 暗弄°; — *reputation*, sông-'æ' ming-vông 傷害名望; wæ-diao' ming'-sing 壞了°名聲; — *the health*, tsao-t'ah' tsing-jing' 蹧蹋精神
INJURIOUS, *very* ting we-'æ'-go 頂會害个°
INK, moh-shü' 墨水°; *a stick of* —, ih-ding moh' 一錠墨; *carmine* —, in-tsi' shü 胭脂°水°; ts-pin' shü 脂邊水°; *vermilion* —, nying-cü' 銀硃
INKSTAND, moh-kwun' 墨罐 (ih-go)
INKSTONE, nyin-ngô' 硯瓦° (ih-kw'e).
INLAID, k'æn'-siang-go 嵌鑲个°; — *table*, k'æn-siang-go yün-coh 嵌鑲个°圓桌
INLAND, *the inner land*, ne-di' 內地 (ne or nen); *gone* —, tao ne-di' ky'i-de 到內地去了°; — *rivers*, li'-kông 裡港; li'-'o 裡河; — *trade*, ne-di' sang-i' 內地生°意
INMATES, *persons within*, li'-deo nying 裡頭人°; *how many — are living here?* li'-deo to-siao' nying deng'-tih 裡頭多少人°底的?

INN, 'ô-c'ü' 厦°處; k'ah'-nyü 客寓; *rice and lodging shop*, væntin' 飯店 (ih-go)
INNER, li-deo' 裏頭; li-hyiang' 裏向;— *room for women*, nevông 內房 (nen or ne)
INNKEEPER, tin'-cü 店主; (master) lang'-z; tong-kô' 東家°
INNOCENT, feh ing'-kæ kyin-kwa'-go 弗應該見怪个°; — *people*, ts'ing-bah' liang-ming' 清白°良民 (also not ignoble as to birth, or employment); *no distinction between — and guilty*, dzao'-bah feh-feng 皂白弗分
INNOCUOUS, ve'-'æ-go 弗°會°害个°; m̃-'æ-c'ü'-go 無°害處个°
INNUMERABLE, su'-feh-pin'-go 數弗遍个°; sön'- feh-læ'-go 算弗來个°
INOCULATE, *to — with small pox*, cong deo-ts' 種痘子; 'ô miao' 下°苗
INODOROUS, m̃ ky'ï'-mi-go 無°氣味°个°; *no fragrance*, m̃ hyiang-ky'ï'-go 無°香氣个°
INOPPORTUNE, feh-ts'eo'-ky'iao' 弗凑巧
INORDINATE *to excess*, ko-veng' 過分; ko-deo' 過頭; — *appetite*, zih-liang' do ko-deo' 食量甚大°
INQUEST, *to hold an —*, nyin s' 驗屍
INQUIRE, *to ask*, meng 問°; — *into*, bun-meng' 盤問; tang-

t'ing 打聽; dzô-meng' 查問°; — (as an officer, into the state of the people), ts'ah'-fông 察訪
INQUIRER, *religious* bun-meng' dao'-li-go nying' 盤問°道理个°人; k'ao'-kyiu dao'-li cü'-kwu 考究道理个°人°
INQUISITIVE, dzô-dzô'-k'ao-k'ao-go 查查考考个°; *prying*, to-bo'-go 多啵°言°个°; bo-bo'-tah-tah; *excessively —*, ïeo'-zing kweh'-si 問入°骨髓
INSANE, tin 癲; *has become —*, tin-de' 癲了°; *raving*, fah-gwông' 發狂
INSATIABLE, m̃-ti'-ts-go 無°底止个°; — *avarice*, t'en-sing' m̃-ti'-ts 貪心無°底止; t'en-sing' feh tsoh 貪心弗足
INSCRIPTION, sia'-tih-go kyi' 寫°的个°記; — *of praise*, ming-yin' 銘言; *a board, or stone with an —*, pin 匾; ba-pin' 牌°匾; *ditto (over one's door or in a garden)*, pin-ngah' 匾額; *a wide scroll with an —*, z-wô' 字畫; *a pair of narrow ditto*, z-te' 字對
INSCRUTABLE, *cannot be searched into*, dzô-feh-c'ih' 查弗出; *cannot be thought out, or measured*, ts'eh'-doh-feh-læ' 測度弗來
INSECTS, djong 蟲; *flying —*, fi-djong' 飛蟲
INSECURE, feh-weng'-tông 弗穩當

INSENSIBLE, moh-dzih'-dzih 木直直; — *from cold,* tong'-moh-de 凍木了°; *not knowing, or feeling,* feh-kyüoh'-teh 弗覺得; — (*like one dead*), jing'-z feh-cü' 人事弗知

INSEPARABLE, *cannot be divided,* feng'-feh-k'æ' 分弗開; — (*as friends*), li-sing'-feh-læ 離身弗來

INSERT, *to* en-tsing'-ky'i 安進去; — *a character,* k'æn' ih-go z ts'eo' 嵌一个°字湊; pu'-tsing ih-go z' 補進一个°字

INSIDE, li-hyiang' 裡向; li'-deo 裡頭; *the inner surface,* li'-min 裡面

INSIDIOUS, weh-long'-weh-yin' 活龍活現; *crafty,* diao-bi'; *treacherous,* kæn-weh' 奸°猾

INSIGNIA *carried before a Chinese officer,* tsih'-z 執事

INSIGNIFICANT (*as a person, or words*), vu-yüong-vu-joh'-go 無榮無辱个

INSINCERE, feh-dzing'-jih 弗誠實

INSINUATE, *to* — *by remote allusion,* en'-di-li ts'-tin 暗地裡指點

INSIPID, m̄-mi'-dao 無°味°道; dæn 淡 (*generally wanting salt.*)

INSIST, *will not stop,* feh k'eng'-hyih 弗肯歇; *must have,* ih-ding' iao' 一定要; — *upon the full price,* kô'-din ngao'-ding feh-k'eng ky'üih' 價°錢°礙°定弗肯缺

INSNARE, *to* — (as an animal), gyiang-djoh' 擒著°; *wishes to* — *you,* iao ng loh' gyi-go 'æn' 要°你°落其°个°陷°; iao ng loh' gyi-go ky'üin'-t'ao' 要°你°落其°个°圈°套°

INSOLENT, *to treat in an* — *manner,* c'ong-væn' 衝犯; c'ong-djông' 衝撞; — *language,* s'-vu-gyi-dæn'-go shih-wô' 肆無忌憚个°說話

INSOLUBLE, yiang'-feh-k'æ'-go 煬弗開个°

INSPECT, *to* k'en 看; *to go about to* —, jing 巡; jing-dzô' 巡查; — *troops,* k'en-ts'ao' 看操

INSPECTION, *come on a tour of* —, jing-dzô' læ-go 巡查來个°

INSPECTOR-GENERAL OF CUSTOMS, tsong'-se-vu-s 總稅務司

INSPIRE, *to* — *others,* ta'-zông bih'-nying 帶上別人°; *inspired by him* (*i. e. warmed*), sing peh gyi ta'-nyih-de 心被°其帶°熱了°; — *by Heaven,* T'in meh-ky'i'-go 天默啟个°; — *by the Holy Ghost,* be Sing'-ling ken-dong' 被聖靈感動

INSTALL, *to* — *a person as pastor,* lih mo'-nying tso moh-s' 立某人°做牧師

INSTALLMENTS, *to pay by* —, bah-wæn' 拔還; bah-fu' 拔付

INSTANCE, for pi'-fông 比方; pi'-jü 比如; kyüô'-jü 假如
INSTANT, an ih-sah'-z, or ih'-seh-z 一霎時; in an —, tsih'-k'eh' 即刻; on the tenth —, ts'u-jih' keh-nyih' 初十日°
INSTANTLY, ih-sah'-z 一霎時; tsih'-k'eh' 即刻; lib-k'eh' 立刻
INSTEAD OF, t'i' 替; dæ 代; — me, t'i' ngô 替我; one who works — another, t'i'-kong 替工
INSTEP, kyiah'-min 脚面; kyiah'-pe 脚背
INSTIGATE, to — to evil, t'iao-so' 挑唆
INSTILL, to instruct by little and little, yüong-yin-yiang'-go kong'-fu kao'-hyüing 用涵養个°工夫敎°訓
INSTINCT, t'in-sing' 天性; t'in-sang'-dzing-go cü'-kyüoh 天生°成个°知覺
INSTITUTE, to found, lih 立; shih'-lih 設立; — an asylum, lih' ih-go gyüoh' 立一个°局
INSTITUTION of learning, shü-yün' 書院
INSTRUCT, to kao 敎°; kao'-hyüing 敎°訓
INSTRUCTION, primary (i. e. what is first learned), ts'u-ts'u'-'oh 初學
INSTRUCTOR, sin-sang' 先生°; kao'-shü sin'-sang 敎°書先生°
INSTRUMENTS, kô-sang' 家°生°;

ky'i'-ming 器皿; surgical —, nga-k'o' kô'-sang 外°科所°用°之°物; musical —, tsoh-yüoh'-go ky'i'-ming 作樂个°器皿
INSTRUMENTAL, he was — in bringing it about, dzong gyi' seng-kwô' k'æ-ky'i' 從其生化開去°; dzong gyi' seng-fah'-c'ih-læ' 從其生發出來
INSUBORDINATE, feh-k'eng'-voh 弗肯服; — (as subjects of the emperor), feh-voh' wông-hwô' 弗服王化; — (as soldiers), feh-voh' kyüing-ling' 弗服軍令; — (as pupils), feh-voh' kyiao'-hwô 弗服敎化
INSUFFERABLE, cannot be endured with patience, jing'-næ-feh-djü' 忍耐弗住; detestable, peh-k'æn 不堪
INSUFFICIENT, feh-keo' 弗够; feh-tsoh' 弗足; ky'in-to'.
INSUFFICIENTLY, ky'in 欠; — thick, ky'in 'eo' 欠厚
INSULT, you — me, ng siah ngô'-go lin' 你°削我个°臉; to treat with abuse, tsao-t'ah' 蹧蹋; siu'-joh 羞辱; — (a woman), u-zoh' 污辱
INSUPERABLE difficulties, næn-c'ü' kying-lih'-feh-læ 難處經歷弗來
INSUPPORTABLE, tông'-feh-djü' 當弗住; tông'-feh-ky'i' 當弗去°; — pain, t'ong' ngao'-feh-djü' 痛熬弗住

INSURANCE *money,* pao-hyin'-go nying-ts' 保險个° 銀子

INSURMOUNTABLE, See INSUPERABLE.

INSURRECTION, *in a state of* —, lön 亂; tsoh-lön' 作亂; *in rebellion,* fæn 反; dzao-fæn' 造反; *to plot* —, meo-fæn' 謀反

INSUSCEPTIBLE *of impression* (heart), sing dong'-feh-læ 心動弗來

INTANGIBLE, moh-feh-djoh'-go 摸弗着°个°; cô-feh-djoh'-go 擔弗着°个°

INTEGRITY, *a man of* —, tsing'-dzih-go nying 正直个°人°

INTELLECT, ling-sing' 靈性; *fine* —, jing z' ling-sing' 純是靈性; *scanty* —, ling-sing' ky'üih' 靈性缺; — *or capacity,* ts-tsih' 資質

INTELLIGENCE, *great natural* —, t'in-ts'ong'-t'in-ming' 天聰天明

INTELLIGENT, (naturally) ts'-tsih-ling' 資質靈; *knowing,* ts'ih'-t'ong-pah-dah' 七通八達; ts'ong-ming' 聰明; — *and clever,* ts'ong-ming' ling-li' 聰明伶利; ling-ky'iao' 靈巧

INTELLIGIBLE, hao' ming-bah'-go 好明白°个°

INTEMPERATE, *he is* — *in the use of liquors,* gyi' ky'üoh tsiu' ko-liang'-go 其吃°酒過量个°

INTEND, cü'-sing 主心; ding-kyin' 定見; *what do you* — *to do?* ng ding-kyin' tso soh'-si ni 你°定見做甚°麼°呢°? ng cü'-sing tso soh'-go z-ken' 你°主心做甚°麼°事幹?

INTENSE *in the extreme,* tao gyih-deo' 到°極頭; tao-toh'; — *cold,* lang tao-toh' 極冷°; — *admiration,* (and sometimes longing), dza ih'-cong ky'i'-mo 極°企慕

INTENTION, i'-s 意思; *no such* —, 'ao-vu' keh'-go i'-s 毫無這°个°意思; *fixed* —, lih-ding' cü'-i 立定主意; kyüih-i' 决意

INTENTIONAL, deh-i' 特意; kwu'-i 故意; deh-we' 特為

INTENT UPON } ih-dzing-tsi'-lu
INTENTLY,   } 專°務°; tsih'-kwu 只顧

INTER, *to* en-tsông' 安葬

INTERCALARY *month,* yüing-yüih' 閏月

INTERCEDE *for,* dæ gyiu' 代求; cün' gyiu 轉求; *Christ intercedes for our pardon,* Kyi-toh' dæ teng' ah-lah t'a-nyiao' 基督代我°等°討饒°

INTERCEPT, *to* — (as persons, or letters), pun'-lu yi-shih 半路遺失

INTERCESSOR, dæ-k'eng'-gyiu'-go nying 代懇求个°人°; cün'-gyiu-go nying 轉求个°人°

INT 251 INT

INTERCHANGE (of courtesies, &c.) yiu-læ'-yiu-ky'i' 有來有去°; — of goods, yi-ho'-yih-ho' 以貨易貨; diao ho' 調貨

INTERCOURSE, læ-wông 來往; the two countries have a great deal of —, keh' liang koh læ-wông' to' 這°兩國來往多

INTEREST, for your —, ng' do yiu ih'-c'ü 你°大°有益處°; ng' do yiu li'-sih 你°大°有利息; I have an — in it, ü ngô' yiu kyiao-kwæn' 於我有交關; takes — in (as a servant in his work, &c.), tso z-ken' kwæn-sing'-go 做事幹關心个°; — (on money), li'-din 利錢°; li'-sib 利息; to pay —, fu-li' 付利

INTEREST, to — a person, t'iao-dong' nying-go sing' 挑動人°个°心

INTERESTED, yiu c'ü'-hyiang 有趣向; yiu mi-dao' 有味°道°; yiu i'-c'ü 有意趣; — by him, be' gyi t'iao-dong'-de 被其挑動了°

INTERESTING child, siao nying' we ying nying' hwun-hyi' 小囝°會引人°歡喜; that was an — discourse, keh p'in kông'-ka tao c'ih-seh'-go 這°篇講°解°到出色个°

INTERFERE, will it — with you (i. e. your plans)? ü ng' yiu ngæ' feh 於°你°有碍否°?; it will not —, peh-fông' 不妨; (you) need not —, hao-vong' kwun'-tsiang 弗用°管賬

INTERIOR, the inside, li'-deo 裡頭; li-hyiang' 裡向; — of a country, koh tông'-cong 國之°中

INTERLOPER, one who has forced himself in, ts'ông'-tsing-go-nying 闖進个°人°; one who has no right, m̄-veng'-go nying 無°分个°人°

INTERMARRY, to liang'-ô kyih-ts'ing' 兩下°結親

INTERMINABLY, m̄-dzing'-gyi 無°盡期

INTERMISSION, time of cessation, hyih'-go z-'eo 歇个°時候; noon —, hyih tsiu' 歇晝; — (of fever), t'e z-'eo' 退時候; feh-fah'-go z-'eo' 弗發个°時侯

INTERMITTENT hyih'-hyih-deng'-deng 歇歇停停°; — in doing, t'ch'-t'ch-ga-ga tso' 做°; — fever, dziao-nyih'-bing 塞°熱°病

INTERNAL, li'-deo 裡頭; li-hyiang' 裡向; ne 內; — disease, nen bing' 內病 (nen or ne)

INTERPOLATE, to pu'-zông 補上; djoh-ts'eo' 續湊; — a passage, pu'-zông ih-tsih' 補上一節

INTERPOSE, to — obstacles, tsu'-tông 阻擋; — between parties at variance, ky'ün'-ka 勸解°

INTERPRET, to (usually a native dialect) djün wó' 傳話; — (a

foreign language), tso t'ong-z' 做 通 事; *to translate,* fæn-yih' 繙 譯; *to explain,* ka'-shih 解° 說

INTERPRETER (usually of a dialect), djün-wô'-go 傳 話 个°; *ditto to an officer,* dzih-dông-vông'-go 值 堂 个°; — *of a foreign language,* t'ong-z' 通 事; — *of dreams,* ziang-mong'-go nying 詳 夢 个 人°

INTERROGATE, *to examine by questions,* meng 問°; dzô-meng' 查 問°

INTERROGATION, *signs of* — *in the colloquial are,* m? ma 嗎°? ni 呢? yia 呀°? feh 否°? *have you any?* yiu m̄ 有 沒° 有? yiu ma 有 嗎°? *how is it?* dza'-go ni 怎° 樣° 呢? dza-go yia' 甚° 麼° 呀°?

INTERRUPT, *to* gah-tang'; *to break off,* tang'-dön 阻° 隔°; — *work,* tang'-dön kong-fu' 工 夫 被° 阻°

INTERRUPTION, *without* m̄'-neh hyih'-loh 沒° 有° 歇 落

INTERSECT, *to divide in parts,* feng-tæn'-k'æ 分 開; — *at right angles,* jih-z' feng-k'æ 十 字 分 開; — *by a cross line,* wang sin' feng-k'æ 橫° 線 分 開

INTERSECTION, *the point of* —, ts'ô'-k'æ-go di'-fông 义 開 个° 地 方

INTERSTICES, li-vong' 離 縫

INTERTWINE, *to* liang'-tô gao-long' 兩 下° 絞 攏; liang'-tô dzin-long' 兩 下° 纏 攏

INTERVAL *in space,* kah'-k'æ 隔 開; li-yün' 離 遠; *an — of three feet,* kah-k'æ sæn-ts'ah' 隔 開 三 尺°; *an — of a year,* teo-deo' ih-nyin' 週° 年; *an — of two years,* kah' liang-nyin 隔 兩 年

INTERVIEW, *to have an* — (i. e. mutual view), we-kyin' 會 見; *to confer with,* kyin'-min kông' 見 面 講

INTESTINES, du'-dziang 肚 腸

INTIMATE, cü-kyi' 知 己; moh-nyih' 莫 逆; ts'ih'-t'iah 切 貼°; ts'ing-mih' 親 密

INTIMIDATE, *to* hah 嚇; — *him,* hah' gyü 嚇 其; long gyi p'ô'-gyü 弄 其 怕 懼

INTO, læ 在°; li 裡°; tsing 進; li'-deo 裡 頭; li-hyiang' 裡 向; *pour — a bowl,* sia' læ un'-li 樹° 在° 碗 裡; *take* (it) — *the house,* do-tsing' oh'-li 拿° 進 屋 裡

INTOLERABLE, *that cannot be borne,* tông'-feh-djü' 擋 弗 住

INTOLERABLY *bad,* wa-r'-vu-tông' 孬 而 無 當

INTOLERANT, feh-k'eng' yüong-nying'-go 弗 肯 容 人° 个°

INTOXICATE, *to* tse 醉; *wine will — people,* tsiu' we tse nying' 酒 會 醉 人°

INTOXICATED, tsiu-tse'-tih-de 酒 醉 的 了°

INTRACTABLE, gyüih-gyiang' 個強

INTREAT, See ENTREAT.

INTRENCHMENT, camp, ying-bun' 營盤; earth-work, nyi-dzing' 泥城; to make an —, tah' ying-bun' 搭營盤

INTREPID, üong 勇; üong'-tsiang 勇將

INTRICATE, ao'-gao 坳境°; yiu ky'üoh'-tsih 有曲折; having many windings, wæn-nyiao'to' 彎繞多

INTRIGUES, kæn-kyi' 奸計; tsô'-kyi 詐計

INTRODUCE, to — them, ts'-ying gyi ts'ing-hwu' 指引其稱呼; — me, ts'-hyiang-ngô-dao' 指向我道; to begin to speak, k'æ-k'eo' 開口; — a subject, di-ky'i' ih-yiang' z-ken' 提起一樣事幹

INTRODUCTION, a letter of —, t'oh-shü' 託書; — to a book, siao'-ying 小引 (veng); væn-li' 凡例 (veng); ditto (generally not written by the author), jü-veng' 序文; — to a discourse, tsong-mao' 總冒

INTRUDE, to ts'ah-tsing', 插進; gah-tsing'; cün-tsing' 鑽進; c'ông'-tsing 闖進 (also pron. ts'ông'-tsing); — remarks, ts'ah-cü' 插嘴; ts'ah-yin' 插言

INTRUSIVE, we ts'ah-tsing' 會插進

INTRUST, to t'oh 託; t'oh'-fu 託付; kao-dæ' 交°代°; I — this business to you, keh'-yiang z-ken' ngô t'oh'-fu ng' de 這°樣事幹我託付你°了°

INTUITIVE, seng-r'-cü-ts' 生而知之 (veng.)

INUNDATE, to tso do'-shü'; fah-shü' 發水°

INUNDATION, there is an —, yiu' do-shü' 有大°水°; great — (like the Flood) ziang 'Ong-shü'-fæn-tsiang' ka 像洪水°氾漲

INURED to hardships, kw'u kwæn'-liao 苦慣了

INVADE, to — another's borders, væn-ka' 犯界°; to — a place with hostile intentions, ts'ing-tsin' di-fông' 侵佔地方

INVALID, sick person, yiu-bing'-go-nying 有病个°人°

INVALIDATE his will, fi-diao gyi-go yi-coh' 廢了°其个°遺囑 (coh or tsoh)

INVALUABLE, vu-kô'-ts-pao 無價°之寶; ts'in-kying'-næn-ma' 千金難買°

INVEIGLE, to keo'-leh 勾勒; ying'-yiu 引誘; ying'-zô 引惹

INVENT, to shih'-siang-c'ih-læ 設想出來; tang'-mo-c'ih-læ 打摹出來; — a new pattern, zao' sing yiang'-shih 造°新樣式°

INVENTOR, shih-siang'-c'ih-læ' cü'-kwu 設想出來个°人°; ky'i-deo' zao'-go cü'-kwu 起頭造°个°人°

INVERT, to fæn-hyiang' 反向;
— it, foh'-ts 覆之
INVERTED, tao'-toh-go 頂°倒个°;
leave it —, fæn'-hyiang en'-tih
反向安的; — (when it
ought not to be), tao'-hyiang-go
倒向个°; foh'-ken-go 覆蓋
个°
INVEST, to — with the ostrich-
plumed hat, sông' ta'-ling-mao'
賞°戴翎枝°; — a city, we-
kw'eng'-dzing-ts' 圍困城子;
— safely (as money), fông'-leh
t'o'-tông-go 放得妥當个°
INVESTIGATE, to— (as belief, &c.),
k'ao'-kyiu 考究; dzô-k'ao' 查
考; — (as business), tse-kyiu'
追究; — with rigor, nyin-kyiu'
嚴究; nyin-dzô' 嚴查
INVESTMENT, good hao c'ih'-sih
好出息
INVETERATE, kwu'-tsih feh-hwô'
固執弗化; deep-rooted, keng-
sing'-ti'-kwu 根深底固; —
disease, bing' we dzin-sing' 病
會纏身
INVIDIOUS, making an — distinction, feng'-c'ih bin'-pih-læ 分別
出來; exciting envy, long'-leh
yiu tu'-gyi-sing 弄得°有妒
忌心
INVIGORATE, to — the body, diao-
yiang' sing-t'i' 調養身體; —
by rest, tsiang-yiang' 長養
INVIGORATING, yiang-jing'-go 養
神个°; — medicine, pu'-yiah
補藥; it is — there, keh'-deo we
k'ông-gyin' 那°裏°會康健
INVINCIBLE, tang' - feh-ying'-go
打弗贏个°; ying'-feh-læ'-go
贏弗來个°; — foe, vu-dih'-
siu 無敵手
INVISIBLE, k'en'-feh-kyin'-go 看
弗見个°
INVITATION, I accepted his —,
ngô ing-hyü' gyi sô ts'ing' 我
應許其所請; card of —,
ts'ing'-t'iah' 請帖 (ih-go)
INVITE, to ts'ing 請; siang-ts'ing'
相請; siang-iao' 相邀; — with
formality (as a man to be a
pastor, &c.), p'ing'-ts'ing 聘請
INVOICE, ho'-tæn 貨單 (ih-tsiang)
INVOKE, to gyiu-kyiao' or gyiu-
kao' 求敎
INVOLUNTARY, feh-yiu' zi'-go cü'-
i 弗由自个°主意; tso-gyi'-
feh-læ 做意°弗來
INVOLVE, to ta'-li 帶累°; ky'in-
le' 牽累; lin-le' 連累; — in
evil consequences, ta'-li yiu kwæng-
ngæ' 帶累有關碍; — one
in trouble by dying on his hands,
&c., du-vu' 誣詐
INWARD, seated within, li-deo' læ-
tih 在裏頭; toward the inside,
hyiang-li' 向裏; dziao-li' 朝裏
INWARDS, the dzông-fu' 臟腑;
ng-dzông'-loh-fu' 五°臟六腑;
disease has gone to the —, bing'-
jih kao-hwông' 病入膏肓
IOTA, an ih-tin' 一點

IRKSOME, in'-væn 厭煩; in'-ky'i 厭藥
IRON, t'ih 鐵; — wire, t'ih'-s 鐵絲; — filings, t'ih'-sô 鐵沙
IRON heated by charcoal within, ing'-teo 熨°斗; — heated on coals, loh-t'ih' 烙鐵 (ih kwun); to heat (or light) the first—, sang ing'-teo 生°熨°斗; to heat the second, we loh-t'ih' 煨烙鐵; fluting — (or pincers), t'ông'-gyin 燙箝
IRON, to — clothes, t'ông i-zông' 燙衣裳°
IRON-CLAD, t'ih'-kah ping-jün' 鐵甲°兵艚 (ih-'ao)
IRONICAL words, gyiao wô' 搭°橋話; words the opposite of what one means, diao-deo' wô 調頭話; fæn wô' 翻話
IRRATIONAL, without knowledge, m̄-cü'-sih-go 無°知識个°; without intelligence, m̄ ling'-sing-go 無°靈性个°
IRRECLAIMABLE, siu'-feh-kyü-læ 收弗歸°來; — (as a person), siu-liu'-feh-læ' 收留弗來
IRRECONCILABLE, 'o-feh-long' 和弗攏
IRRECOVERABLE, that cannot be restored, wæn-nyün'-feh-læ' 還原弗來
IRREGULAR, not uniform, feh zi'-jih 弗齊集; ts'æn-ts'æn'-ts'-ts' 参参差差; not straight, dzin'-mô-liu; hwa-ts'ia' 歪斜;

— (in doing), feh en'-pæn 弗按板; zông-zông'-loh-loh' 上上落落
IRRELEVANT, feh siang-tc' 弗相對; ts'o-gen'-go; feh 'eh vong' 弗合縫; very —, do'-feh-te' 大°弗對; da' feh-vu' 大弗符
IRREMEDIABLE, m̄-yiah' k'o-i' 無°藥可醫; liao'-feh-teh'-go 了弗得个°
IRREPARABLE, that cannot be repaired, siu-li'-feh-læ' 修理弗來; that cannot be made up, m̄-siu'-dziang 無°收塲
IRREPROACHABLE, m̄-p'i'-bing-go-hao' 無°批評个°好
IRRESISTIBLE, feh-ueng' feh-pa'-voh 弗能弗拜°服; — (as power), kæn-tsu'-feh-djü 攔阻弗住; tsu-tông'-feh-djü 阻擋弗住; irresistibly charmed, voh-lah'-go 拜°服个°
IRRESOLUTE, yiao-yiao'-'oh-'oh 搖搖惑惑; cü'-i feh-ding' 主意弗定; sing-feh-kyin' 心弗堅
IRRESPONSIBLE, he is —, feh kwc' gyi-go sing-zông' 弗歸其个°身上
IRRETRIEVABLE, voh-feh-cün' 復弗轉; voh-nyün'-feh-læ 復原弗來
IRREVERENT, feh kong'-kying 弗恭敬
IRREVOCABLE law, tsih-fah'-jü-sæn' 執法如山; — word

(*i. e.* a word once spoken four horses cannot bring it back), ih-yin' kyi-c'ih' s'-mô-næn-tse' 一言既出駟馬難追

IRRIGATE, to kyiao shü' 澆水°; — *by chain pump*, ts'ô shü' 車水°

IRRITABLE, næn ts'ah'-ts'o-go 難擦挫个°; *very* —, ziang yiang-lah'-mao' ka 像剌°毛蟲°; — *from inflamed liver*, ken-ho' t'eh wông' 肝火太°旺

IRRITATE, *to provoke him*, pih' gyi sang-ky'i' 逼其生氣; c'oh' gyi nu' 觸其怒; — (as a sore spot), væn nyün-pô' 犯原疤; — *extremely*, sông-bi' dong'-kweh 傷皮動骨

IRRITATING *words*, c'oh'-sing-c'oh-ti' shih-wô' 獦心獦肺說話

Is, z 是; yiu 有; — *it good?* keh' z hao' feh 這°是好否°? — *there any?* yiu' m 有沒有°?

ISINGLASS (made from fish-bellies), yü-tu' 魚肚°; — (made from sea-weed), yiang-ts'æ' 洋菜

ISLAND, hæ'-tao 海島; hæ'-sæn 海山 (ih-zo)

ISOLATED (as a person), kwu-sing' 孤身; — (as a house), kwu-ts'ing' lang-loh' 孤清冷落; yün-ling'-ling 懸零零

ISSUE, *result*, kyih'-gyüoh 結局; *what was the* —? dza kyih'-gyüoh 怎°結局? dza kyih-

en' 怎°結案? dza liao-z' 怎°了事?

ISSUE, to — *forth as water*, liu c'ih' 流出; *to* — *forth secretly*, liu-c'ih'-ky'i; *to* — *a proclamation*, c'ih kao'-z 出告示; — *a warrant*, c'ih ba' 出牌

ISTHMUS, in-'eo' 咽喉; t'u'-iao 土腰

IT (generally unexpressed), gyi 其; *bring* — *here*, do' gyi læ' 拿°其來; — *snows*, loh-shih'-de 落雪了°; — *rains*, loh-yü'-de 落雨了°

ITCH, *the* keh'-lao 疥°瘡°

ITCH, *to* yiang 癢

ITEM, *an* —, ih diao' 一條; ih kw'un' 一欵; ih-yiang' 一樣; *an* — *of news*, ih'-go sing-veng' 一个°新聞; — *by* —, yiang-tang'-yiang 一°樣一°樣

ITINERATE *for preaching*, ih-c'ü' ih-c'ü' djün kyiao' 一處一處傳敎

ITSELF, zi 自°; *will move of* —, zi' we dong' 自°會動; *by* —, doh zi' 獨自°

IVORY, ziang-ngô' 象牙°; — *ware*, ziang-ngô' tong'-si 象牙°東西

J

JABBER, *to* kyih'-lih-kwah'-lah kông'; kông in'-wô 講°燕話

JACKET, mô'-kwô 馬褂 (primarily, a riding jacket)

JADED, tso'-vah-liao 做乏了;

vah-lih′-de 乏力了°;— horse, mô tseo′-vah-liao-go 馬走乏了°

JADE-STONE, fi′-ts'e 翡翠; pure green, or serpentine—, pih′-nyüoh 碧玉

JAGGED, ky'üih-tsing′-ky'üih-c'ih′ 缺進缺出;— like a saw, ziang ken′-ts' ka′ 像鋸°齒

JAIL, lao-kæn′ 牢監°

JAILER, lao-deo′ 牢頭; kying′-ts 禁子; an official —, s-nyüoh′-s 司獄°使

JAM of people, nying te-sæn′-tsib-hæ′-go 人°堆山積海个°; ziang diah′-nying-sæn′-ka go 像疊人°山个°

JAM, preserved fruit, ko′-ts tsiang′ 果子醬

JAM, to crowd closely, a-tsi′-feh-k'æ 挨擠弗開;— (as one's finger), gah-sông′ 軋傷

JAR, large water —, shü′-kông 水°缸 (ih-k'eo); small-mouthed —, bing 瓶; bang 甏; wine —, tsiu′-dzing 壜° (ih-tsah)

JAR, to shake, tsing′-tsing-dong 怔怔動;— against, bih-djoh′ 蹩了°一蹳°

JASMINE, (Jasminum Sambac), meh-li′-hwô 茉莉花

JAUNDICE, wông-tæn′-bing 黃疸病; to have the —, sang′ wông-tæn′-bing 生°黃疸病

JAUNT, to take a journey, c'ih-meng′ ky'i 出門去°; to go for pleasure, ky'i hyi′-hyi 去°嬉戲

JAVELIN, ts'iang 鎗 (ih-ts)

JAW, the upper —, zông-bæn′-ngô-zông′ 上爿牙°床; the lower —, 'ô′-bæn-ngô-zông 下爿牙°床

JAW-BONE, 'ô′-bô-kweh′ 下吧骨

JEALOUS, yiu ts'u′-i 有醋意; ky'i′-feh-ko′ 氣弗過; dzih-tu′ 嫉妒; ngæn′-k'ong-ts'in′ 眼孔淺; tu′-gyi 妒忌; hwah-ts'u′-bing 搳醋瓶 (only used of women in ridicule)

JEAN, twilled foreign cloth, zia′-veng yiang-pu′ 斜°紋洋布

JEER, to tsao-siao′ 嘲笑

JEHOVAH, Yiæ-'o′-wô 耶和華

JELLY, very stiff —, kao 膏

JELLIFY, to nying-long 凝攏; kyih′-long 結攏; tang-tong 結凍

JERK, to yih 易; to — away, yih-ko′-ky'i 易過去°; — open, wah′-k'æ 用°扚開

JEST, to kông siao′-wô 講°笑話; kông hyiah′-wô 講°譇話

JESUS, Yiæ-su′ 耶穌; Jesus Christ, Yiæ-su Kyi-toh′ 耶穌基督

JET of water from a pipe, kwun′-ts piao-c'ih′-go shü′ 管子潑出个°水

JET, to spout, piao-c'ih′ 潑出; — (as gas) tsön-c'ih′ 鑽出

JETTY, dao′-deo 街頭; ferry —, du′-deo 渡頭;— for washing, &c., bu-deo′ 埠頭

JEW, Yiu-t'a′-nying 猶太°人°

JEWELS (in general), tsing-cü′pao′-pe 珍珠寶貝

JEWELER, *one who sells jewels*, cü-pao′ k‘ah′-nying 珠寶客人°; *one who cuts precious stones*, nyüoh-ky‘i′ s-vu′ 玉器司務

JINGLING, ting-ting′ tông-tông′ 丁丁璫璫; sing′-sing-sang′-sang.

JOB, *a piece of work*, ih′-go sang-i′ 一个° 生°意; ih-yiang′ sang-weh′ 一樣生°活

JOCOSE, *given to jesting*, ting′-we hyi′-hyiah-go 頂會戲謔个°

JOG, *to — his elbow, or hand*, dzoh gyi-go siu′ 觸°其个°手; *— one's memory*, di-sing′ 提醒; di-deo′ 提頭; ky‘ih′-gyi lin′-ts 掣其令°子

JOGGLE, *to* dong 動; yiao-dong′ 搖°動

JOIN, *to — in doing*, ‘eh-long′-tso 合攏做; dong-tso′ 同做; *— together* (as pieces), p‘ing-long′ 摒攏; tsih′-long 接攏; sang-long′ 生°攏; — (as words or ideas), lin-long′ 連攏; *can be joined*, siang-lin′ 相連; *— successively* (as links), tsih′-lin 接連; — (as premises), t‘iah′-lin 貼連

JOINT, *junction*, gao-kwu′ 鉸°股 *incorrectly called*, yüih-dông 穴堂; *the space between joints*, tsih 節; *out of —*, gao-kwu′ t‘eh-yüih′-de 鉸°股脫穴了°

JOINT-PARTNER, p‘ing-ho′-kyi 摒夥計

JOKE (at some one's expense), hyiah′-yin 謔言; hyi′-hyiah-go shih-wô′ 戲謔个°說話

JOKE, *to* kông-siao′-wô 講笑話

JOKER, kông-siao′-wô-go-nying′ 講°笑話个°人°

JOLLY, hyi′-siao-yin′-k‘æ 喜笑顏開

JOLTING *in a carriage*, zo ts‘ô-ts′, gyih-lih′-goh-loh 坐°車子栗°六°顛°籤°

JOSTLE, *to* a 挨; — *through* (i. e. in), a-tsing′-ky‘i 挨進去°

JOSS-STICKS, bông′-hyiang 棒香 SEE INCENSE.

JOT, *a* ih-tin′ 一點; ih-weh′ 一畫

JOURNAL, *private* jih-kyi′-bu 日記簿; jih-kyi′-loh 日記錄; *day-book*, ts‘ao′-bu 草簿; *the* —, ts‘ing-bu′ 清簿

JOURNEY, *to go on a* —, c‘ih-meng′ ky‘i 出門去°; *go on a long* —, c‘ih yün′-meng 出遠門; *to start on a* —, dong-sing′ 動身; ky‘i-sing′ 起身; *ditto on a long* —, ky‘i dzing′ 起程; *to — by land*, ky‘i ‘en′ ky‘i 起旱去°; loh lu′ ky‘i 陸路去°; *— by water*, shü′-lu ky‘i′ 水°路去°; *— rapidly on foot*, p‘ao-lu′ or bao-lu′ 跑路

JOURNEYMAN, sæn-kong′ 散工; *one hired for a job*, tön′-pông ho′-kyi 短幫夥計

JOY, *to have* —, yiu do hwun'-hyi 有大°歡喜; hwun-hyi'-feh-sah' 歡喜弗煞

JOYOUS, kw'a'-weh 快°活; — *news*, kyüô ing' 佳音; hao' ing 好音

JOYLESS, 'ao-vu' hying'-cü 毫無興致

JUDGE *of a district*, cü-yün' 知縣; — *of a province*, en'-ts'ah-s 按察司

JUDGE, *to* — (a case), sing'-p'un 審判; tön'-hao 斷好; tön'-ding 斷定; *to pass sentence*, p'un'-tön 判斷, — *between* (as compositions, men, &c.), zæ-deh' 裁奪; ding-leng' 定論; — *from circumstances*, gwe'-doh 揣度; *come see and* — (said of an officer), loh-k'en' tön'-hao 查勘而°斷好

JUDGMENT, *he has good* —, gyi'-go kyüih'-tön kao ming' 其个°決斷高明; gyi ming' kyüih'-go 其明決个°; gyi-go kyin'-sih feng-ming' 其个見識分明

JUDGMENT, *the— day*, sing'-p'un nyih'-ts 審判日°子

JUDICIOUS *counsel* (*i. e. safe*), sô ky'ün' t'o'-tông-go 所勸妥當个°

JUGGLE, *to* pin hyi'-fah 變戲法

JUGGLER, tso-hyi'-fah-go nying' 做戲法个°人°

JUICE, tsib 汁; tsih'-shü 汁水

JUICY, yiu tsih' go 有汁个°

JUMBLE, *to* dao-lön' 搗亂; tang-weng' 打混; *jumbled* (good and bad together), weng'-dzeh 混雜

JUMP, *to* t'iao 跳; — *about*, t'iao-t'iao' 跳跳; — *down*, t'iao'-loh-læ' 跳下°來; — *up and down* (in play, anger, &c.), t'eo-ky'i-læ 趒起來; — *up*, t'iao'-zông-ky'i' 跳上去°; — *over*, t'iao'-ko-ky'i 跳過去°

JUNCTURE, *critical point*, iao'-kying kwæn'-deo 要緊關頭; ky'ih'-kying z-'eo' 吃緊時候

JUNIOR *members*, nyin-ky'ing' cü-kwu 年輕个°人°; *I your* — (*i. e.* inferior), væn'-pe 晚輩
    Mr. Wông Junior may be styled Wông Sin-sang, and Mr. Wông Senior, T'a Sin-sang or Lao Sin-sang; Siao Wông Sin-sang for the Junior, which is often used, is disrespectful.

JURISDICTION, kæ-kwun' 該管; *official* —, joh-yün' 屬員; *under his* —, z gyi' kæ-kwun' go 是其該管个°; læ gyi siu'-'ô 在°其手下°

JUST, kong-bing' 公平; kong-dao' 公道; — *price*, kong-bing' kô'-din 公平價°錢°

JUST *as*, *or* — *at the time*, k'eo'-k'eo', kông-kông' 剛剛; ts'ing'-mi-mao'; 'eo-mi'-mao; — *at that time*, sih'-vong gyi-z' 適逢其時; *has come* — *at the right time*, ky'iah'-hao læ-de 恰好來了°;

— *as I was coming it rained*, k'eo'-k'eo ngô læ', loh-yü'-de 恰°恰° 我來落雨了°;— *as you treat me I'll treat you*, ng dza læ', ngô dza ky'i' 你怎°來我怎°去°; *when so anxious to have it right,— the opposite*, p'in-p'in' feh-te' 偏偏弗對;— *like*, tsing'-ziang 正像; k'eo'-k'eo ih-yiang° 貼°準°一樣°;— *now*, dzæ°-s 繞始; dzæ-fông' 繞方; fông'-dzæ 方繞; kông-kông 剛剛;— *what I want*, k'eo-k'eo 'eh'-djoh ngô'-go yüong 正°好° 合着° 我个° 用

JUSTLY, *to treat men*—, dæ nying' kong-dao' 待人°公道; *to receive*—, ing-tông' ziu 應當受

JUSTIFY, *to treat as just, though guilty*, sön tsing'-dzih 算正直

JUT OUT, *to* deh-c'ih' 凸出

JUVENILE *pupils*, din-kyi' 'ob-sang' 小°學°生°; *ditto* (*boys*), mong-dong 蒙童; *to teach ditto*, en din-kyi' 訓蒙;— *sports*, siao nying' hyi'-deo 小孩°嬉戲°

K

KALEIDOSCOPE, væn-hwô-dong' 萬花筒 (ih-go)

KALENDAR, See CALENDAR.

KEEL *of a ship*, jün'-go long-sing' 船个° 龍身

KEEN, *sharp*, kw'a 快°; fong-li'

鋒利;— *eyes*, ngæn'-tsing tsin-li' 眼睛尖利; *ditto* (in a bad sense), lao-ing' ngæn 老鷹眼°;— *blast*, fong' ziang tao kah' 風像刀割°

KEEP, *to* siu 守; pao'-sin 保守;— *the sabbath*, siu li'-pa-nyih' 守禮拜日°;— *watch at night*, siu yia' 守夜°;— *shop*, kwun tin' 管店;— *a secret*, siao'-ho-shih-wô' ve' lu-fong' 私°話 弗會°露風; cü'-pô kying'-jing 嘴巴謹慎;— *back something, which one is unwilling to tell*, 'en-hyüoh' 合蓄;— *off the wind*, tsô fong' 遮風;— *in memory*, kyi'-nyiæn 記念;— *must — away from*, yüong li-k'æ' 要°離開; *keeping house*, læ-tih tông-kô 正在°當家;— *accounts*, zông-tsiang' 上賬; kwun tsiang'; *will —* (or *last well*), kying-k'ông'; næ'-kyiu-go 耐久个°; *will not —*, feh næ'-kyiu 弗耐久;— *order*, ah'-djü 壓服°;— *the rules*, siu kwe' 守規

KEEPER, *gate* kwun-meng'-go 管門个°; *prison —*, kwun-lao-kæn'-go 管牢監个°

KEEPSAKE, *I give you this for a*—, kch'-go peh ng, tso piao'-kyi 這°个°給°你°做表記

KENNEL, keo-k'o' 狗窠 (lit. dog's nest)

KERNEL (of a fruit stone), jing or nying 仁;— *of a nut*, nyüoh

肉°; peach —, dao-jing' 桃仁; apricot —, 'ang'-nying 杏仁; walnut —, wu-dao' nyüoh 胡桃肉°; a — of rice, ih-lih' mi' 一粒米

KEROSENE, ho'-yiu 火油; me-yiu' 煤油

KETTLE, iron t'ih'-kwun 鐵罏 (ih-go); tea —, dzô-wu' 茶壼 (ih-pô)

KEY, yiah-z' 鑰匙 (ih-kwun)

KEY-HOLE, yiah-z'-ngæn 鑰匙眼° (ih-go)

KICK, to t'ih 踢; — one another, t'ih-læ'-t'ih-ky'i' 踢來踢去°; gave me a —, t'ih'-ngô ih-kyiah' ko 踢我一脚過; — a shuttle-cock, t'ih in'-ts 踢燕子

KID, siao' sæn-yiang' 小山羊 (ih-tsah)

KIDNAP, to kwæ'-tæ 拐°帶; to take anything by false means, kwa 拐°

KIDNAPPER, kwa'-ts 拐°子

KIDNEYS, iao-ts' 腰子

KILL, to sah 殺; — by striking, &c., tang'-sah 打殺; — one's self, zi-zing'-si 自尋°死; — one's self with a knife, zi-veng' 自刎

KILN, yiao 窰; brick —, cün-yiao' 磚窰; — for tiles, ngô'-yiao 瓦窰

KIMBO, arms a —, siu' iao'-li t'oh'-tih 手腰裡托的; siu' t'oh-iao' 手托腰

KIND, a sort, ih-yiang' 一樣; ih-'ao' 一號; ih-cong' 一種; ten different kinds, jih-yiang'-sang 十樣生°; many kinds, hyü'-to yiang'-su 許多樣數; a class (of things), ih-le' 一類

KIND, sing hao' 心好; sing-din'-hao' 心田好; sing-jih'-hao 心術好; has — feelings, yiu-dzing'-yiu-nyi' 有情有義°; very —, djong-nyi'-go 重義°个°; dzing-djong' 情重

KINDLE, to — a fire, sang-ho' 生°火; — up (from a little), ho'-sang-dziah' 火生°燆; — one's anger, sing'-ho tin'-dziah 心火點燆; sing'-ho ying'-dziah 心火引燆

KINDLINGS, ying-ho-za' 引火柴; to split —, p'ih'-ying-ho-za' 劈引火柴°

KINDNESS, dzing 情; nyi-ky'i' 義氣; thank you for your —, dzing ng' hao-c'ü' 承你好處; dzing ng' me'-i 承你美意; owing to your —, t'oh'-ng-go-foh' 托你°个°福; mong-ng' dæ-æ' 蒙你°擡愛; I appreciate your —, ngô kyin ng'-go-dzing' 我見你°个°情

KINDRED, near ts'ing-dzoh 親族; distant —, yün-dzoh 遠族; relations in general, ts'ing-kyün' 親眷

KING, wông 王; kyüing-wông 君王; the emperor, wông-ti' 皇帝; — or prince, wông-yia'

王爺; *the — of kings,* væn-wông'-ts-wông 萬王之王
KINGDOM, koh 國; *— of Great Britain,* Da-Ing'-koh 大英國; *the animal and vegetable kingdoms* dong-dzih-ts veh 動植之物 (veng.)
KINGLY *robes,* dziao-voh' 朝服; long-bao' 龍袍; nyü-i 御衣
KISS, *to* ts'ing-cü 親嘴; *to smell the lips,* hyüong-cü 齅嘴; hyiang'-cü 向嘴
KITCHEN, tsao'-keng 竈下°; djü'vông 廚房; djü-'ô 廚下°
KITE, yiao-ts' 鷂紙 (ih-ting); *to fly a —,* fông-yiao-ts' 放鷂紙; *— whistle,* yiao-mang' 鷂鞭
KITTEN, siao-mæn' 小貓 (ih-tsah)
KNACK, *has* we diao-du' 會調度; we diao-deo' toh-koh'; we w̌eh-tang 會挖打
KNAVE, vu-la' 無賴°; di-kweng' 地棍; *great, —,* do-vu'-la 大°無賴°; di'-deo-oh'-kweng 地頭惡棍
KNEAD, *to — dough,* nyüoh-feng' 搇°粉; *— thoroughly,* nyüoh-leh t'ong-t'eo' 搇°得通透
KNEE kyiah'-k'o-deo 腳髁頭 or 膝° (ih-tsah) *to bend one —,* tang-ts'in-ts' 打䠆子
KNEEL, *to* gyü'-loh 跪°落; gyü'-tao 跪°倒; *— on one knee,* tang-siao'-gyü 打小跪°

KNIFE, tao 刀; *pocket —,* siao'-tao-ts' 小刀子; *paper —,* lih-ts'-tao 裁°紙刀; *chopping —,* boh-tao' ; djü-tao' 厨刀; *— for splitting wood,* za-tao' 柴°刀; ke-tao' 鈎°刀 (ih-pô)
KNIT, *to — stockings,* kyih-mah' 結襪; *to — the brows,* zeo-mi-deo' 皺°眉頭; zeo-mi-pah'-kyih 愁眉°百°結
KNOB *of a door,* meng-cih'; *— of a — drawer,* cih'-siu.
KNOCK, *to* tao 搯; *to — at a door,* tao-meng' 搯門; *to strike,* or *pound,* k'ao 拷; *— against,* bang-djoh 撞°著°; gah-djoh' 軋著°; djông-djoh' 撞著°; *— down,* bang-tao' 撞°倒; *ditto from a high place,* bang-loh' 撞°落; *— (a person) down* bang*-tih' 撞°跌; tang'-tao-di '打倒地; *— intentionally,* kwu-i' bang 故意撞°; *— head on the ground, &c.,* k'eh-deo' 磕頭
* Bang, *means to knock unintentionally.*
KNOCK, *give a —,* bang-ih'-kyi 撞°一記; bang-ih'-bang 撞°一撞°; *give another —* (at a door), tsæ tao'-ih-kyi 再搯一記
KNOCKER, k'ao-meng'-go tong'-si 敲門个°東西
KNOLL, te 堆 (ih-go)
KNOT, kyih 結; *hard —,* si' kyih 死°結; *to tie in a —,* tang-kyih' 打結; *— in wood,* jü-tsang' 樹樁; tsang-cü' 樁°棕

KNOTTY, kyih'-deo hyü'-to 結頭許多;— (as wood), yiu tsang-cü' to 有撐梂多

KNOW, to hyiao'-teh 曉得; sih'-teh 識得; nying'-teh 認°得; teh'-cü 得知; I do not —, ngô feh hyiao'-teh 我弗曉得; do you — me? ng' nying'-teh ngô'-feh 你°認°得我否? ng min-jing ngô feh 你面善°我否? he is gone, did you — it? gyi ky'i'-de, ng teh'-cü feh 其去了你°得知否°! — one's self that it is wrong, zi' cü m̀ li' 自°知無°理

KNOWINGLY to do wrong, ming-cü'-kwn'-væn 明知故犯; sih'-fah væn'-fah 設法犯法

KNOWLEDGE, cü'-sih 知識; his — is extensive, gyi-go cü'-sih to 其个°知識多; gyi' kyin'-kwông-sih-da' 其見廣識大; to extend one's —, kwông-kyin'-veng, to cü'-sih 廣見聞多知識

KNUCKLES, siu'-ts-tsih 手指節

KORAN, T'in-kying' 天經

L

LABEL, ts'in-deo' 籤頭; — on goods, tsiao-deo'-ts 招頭紙; ts'in-ts'in-deo' 簽籤頭

LABEL, to — by pasting, t'iah ts'in-deo' 貼°籤頭; t'iah tsiao-deo'-ts 貼招頭紙; to — by placing a slip, kyih' ts'in-deo' 揭籤頭

LABOR, hard work, kw'u' sang-weh' 苦生°活; djong'-næn sang-weh' 重難生°活; toil, lao-loh' 勞碌; lao-kw'u' 勞苦; sing-kw'u' 辛苦; with great — (as when unneccessary, or not accomplishing much), dziah'-kying tô'-lih; nu'-kying-bah-hæn'; to be in —, zông-zo'-dong 上坐°桶; ling-beng' 臨盆 (veng.)

LABOR, to yüong kong' 傭工; tso kw'u'-kong 做苦工; to work, tso sang-weh' 做生°活; — so that perspiration flows, 'en-bô'-yü-ling tso' 汗爬雨淋做; to begin —, zông kong' 上工; to leave off —, hyih kong' 歇工; loh kong' 落工; hyih tsoh' 歇作; to finish —, wun kong' 完工; dzing kong' 成工 liao kong' 了工; — in vain, lao-r'-vu-kong' 勞而無功; bah-bah' lao-loh' 白°白°勞碌; — (as a student), 'ô kw'u'-kong' 下°苦功; yüong kw'u'-kong' 用苦功

LABORED, or forced construction, kông'-fah ky'ih'-lih go 講°法吃力个°

LABORER, kong-nying' 工人°; tso-kong'-go 做工个°; tso-sang-weh'-go 做生°活个°; permanent —, dziang-kong' 長工; dziang-yüong'-go 長用个°; temporary —, tön'-kong 短工; ts'ah-tön'-go 拆短个°

LAB 264 LAM

LABORIOUS, *toilsome*, kw'u 苦; sing-kw'u' 辛苦; lao-kw'u' 勞苦; lao-loh' 勞碌

LABYRINTH, *place where one may lose his way*, iao mi-lu'-go di'-fông 要迷路个°地方; *labyrinthine roads*, lu-kying' ṁ-deo'-jü-go 路徑無°頭緒个°

LACE, cü-lo' 珠羅;— *edging*, cü-lo'-bin 珠羅辮; *any bordering to be tacked on*, kwe'-ts 桂子; *gold* —, kying kwe'-ts 金桂子

LACE, *to* — *with a string*, zing, c'ün-tæn'-ko 繩穿打°過

LACERATE, *to* — *the flesh* (as *with a knife*), bi-nyüoh' lih-k'æ' 皮肉°裂開; bi-nyüoh' kah'-k'æ 皮肉°割開

LACK, LACKING, ky'in; ky'üih 缺; siao 少; ky'üih'-siao 缺少;— *a little* ts'o'-tin 差點

LACKER or LACQUER, yiang-ts'ih' 洋漆;— *ware*, yiang-ts'ih'-go tong-si 洋漆个°東西; *inlaid* — *ware*, yiang-ts'ih', k'æn' lo-din'-go tong-si 洋漆嵌螺鈿个°東西

LAD, dong-ts' 童子; siao'-kwun-nying 小官人°; *a large* —, cong-nying' 中人°; siao 'eo-sang' 小後生

LADDER, t'æ-ts' 梯°子; lu-t'æ' 扶°梯° (ih-bu)

LADLE, zoh 瓢; *soup* —, t'ông diao-kang' 湯調羹° (ih-go)

LADY, dông-k'ah' 堂客; nyü'-dông-k'ah' 女堂客; fu-nying'* 夫人°; *the wife of a teacher, or gentleman*, s-meo' 師母; *an old* —, lao'-bo-bo 老婆婆; *ditto (in an officer's family)*, lao-t'a'-t'a 老太°太°; *ditto (in a teacher's family)*, t'a'-s-meo' 太°師母; *where a gentleman is styled*, lao'-yia 老爺, *the gentleman's wife may be styled*, na'-na 嬭嬭; *young* —, do-kwu'-nyiang 大°姑娘

* This term answers for any lady, but properly belongs only to ladies of the 1st and 2nd rank.

LAG, *to* — *behind*, loh-'eo' 落後;— *purposely*, t'eng'-loh 'eo' 退°落後

LAIR *of a wild beast*, yia'-siu k'o' 野°獸窠

LAKE, wu 湖 (ih-go); *red paint*, in-tsi' 胭脂

LAMB, siao-yiang' 小羊;— *skin with curled wool*, kao-bi' 羔皮; *native ditto*, t'u'-kao 土羔

LAME, *slightly* tin'-kyiah 蹎腳; *weak in the feet*, nyün'-kyiah 軟腳; *very* —, kwa'-kyiah 拐腳; *limping*, zeh-kyiah'-go 蹌腳个° *one foot, or both turned out*, dzin'-kyiah 斜°腳;— *from crooked feet*, p'ih'-kyiah 僻腳; *flinging out the feet in walking*, hwang'-kyiah 甩°腳

LAMENT, *to* kông'-leh pe-pe'-ts'ih-ts'ih 講得°悲悲切切;

t'ong'-k'oh 痛哭; di-k'oh' 啼哭; — *with a loud noise,* 'ao-li'-da-k'oh' 號啕大哭
LAMENTABLE, k'o'-sih 可惜; k'o'-lin 可憐; k'o'-lin-siang 可憐相; — *death,* si'-leh k'o-sông' 死得可傷
LAMP, teng-tsæn' 燈盞 (ih-kwun); *light the* —, tin teng' 點燈; — *light,* teng-kwông' 燈光; *by* — *light,* teng-kwông' 'ô 燈光下; — *black,* teng-me' 燈煤; — *chimney,* teng-t'ao' 燈套; — *shade,* ing-kwông 映光; — *wick,* teng-sing' 燈心; *ditto of pith,* teng-ts'ao' 燈草
LANCET (for discharging matter), lang'-tao or lang-ten' 冷刀; *surgeon's* —, nga-k'o' siao'-tao 外科小刀
LAND, di 地; *cultivated* —, din 田; *uncultivated* —, sang-di' 生地; *a piece of* —, ih-kw'e-di' 一塊地; ih-tseh'-di 一則地; *an acre of* —, ih-meo-din' 一畝田; *dry* —, sao'-di 燥地; *to travel by* —, 'en'-lu ka-tseo' 旱路而走
LAND, to zông-ngen' 上岸; — *goods,* ky'i-ho' zông-ngen' 起貨上岸
LAND-OWNER, nyih-cü' 業主
LAND-TAX, zin-liang' 錢糧; *to pay the* —, deo-zin-liang' 完錢糧
LANDING-PLACE, bu'-deo 埠頭

LANDLORD *of a lodging house, &c.,* tiu'-cü 店主; *one who lets houses, &c.,* vông-tong 房東; oh cü'-nying-kô 屋主人家; vông' cü'-nying-kô 房主人家
LANDMARK, *stone* ts'-ka-zah 址界石
LANDSCAPE, kying'-cü 景致; *fine* —, hao kying'-cü 好景致
LANE, siao'-lu 小路; *long* 衖; 'ông 巷 (ih-da); — *that has no outlet,* toh-sah-long' 不通之衖; si long' 死衖
LANGUAGE, wô 話; shih-wô' 說話; *the English* —, Da-Ing'-wô 大英話; *strong or emphatic* —, djong'-deo shih-wô' 重頭說話; *bad* —, Wa-wô' 孬話; Wa-shih-wô' 孬說話
LANGUID, nyün'-yiang-yiang 軟洋洋; nyün'-bi-bi 軟疲疲
LANTERN, teng-long' 籠橙 (ih-kwun)
LAP, *sit on the* — (lit., *on the knees*), kyiah'-k'o-deo zông zo' 腳髁頭上坐; *in the* —, kyiah'-k'o-deo teo'-tih 腳髁頭兜的; *gathered in the* —, teo-tih 兜的
LAP, *to* — *the edge over,* deh-zông' 疊上; *one edge lapping over another,* pin-yin dzông'-zông'-tih 邊沿撞上的
LAP, *to* — *up water,* shü t'ah'-t'ah-ky'üoh' 水嚃嚃吃

LAPIDARY, nyüoh-ky'ï'-s-vu' 玉器司務

LARD, cü-yiu' 猪油

LARGE, do 大°; how —? dza-kwun'-do 怎°樣°大°? — number of people, hyü'-to nying 許多人°; nying' to 人°多; largest, ting'-do 頂大°; tsæ'-m̄-tsæ-do 再無°再大°; gyih-do' 極大°; — (as if bloated), p'ông 膨; p'oh'-do; very —, do-leh'-kying 大°得°緊; — for one's age, sang-leh dziang-do' 生°得°長大°; kw'e-we' 傀偉; — hearted, sing-di'-k'æ-kw'eh' 心地開闊

LARK, pah-ling' 百°鴒

LARYNX, ky'ï'-kwun-k'eo 氣管口

LASCIVIOUS, t'en-seh'-go 貪色個°

LASH, a whip, pin-ts' 鞭子; to beat with the —, tang pin-ts' 打鞭子

LASSITUDE, he suffers from —, gyi kyüoh-teh nyün-yiang'-yiang 其覺°得軟洋洋; gyi teh'-cü nyün-ky'ï ka.

LAST, kyih'-sah 結煞; meh 末; teh-leh-meh; to the very degree, tao-pin' de 到邊了°; — night, zô-yia' 昨°夜°; zô-nyih' yia'-tao 昨°日°夜°到; — year, gyiu nyin' 舊年; zông-nyin' 上年; year before —, zin nyin' 前°年; — month, zin-ko' yüeh 前°個月; zông

yüih' 上月; — day of the year, nyiæn-kyiu'-yia 廿九夜°; the — but one, kyih'-sah yi-zông'ih'-go 結煞以上一个°; ditto (sometimes in a bad sense), 'ô' shü zông di nyi' 下°數°上第二°; the — day of the world, shü'-kæn-zông meh'-go nyih'-ts 世界°上末个°日°子

LAST, to — well, kying-yüong' 經用; næ-kyiu' 耐久; ditto in wear, ziu-c'ün' 受穿; how long will it —? to-siao' kong-fu' hao yüong' 多少工夫好用?

LAST, shoe-maker's —, 'a hyün'-deo 鞋楦頭; stretch on a —, hyün 楦

LASTING, durable, dziang-kyiu' 長久; næ-kyiu' 耐久; iu-kyiu' 悠久

LASTINGS, yü'-ling 羽綾

LASTLY, tsong-kyiu' 終究; kyih'-sah 結煞; finally, tao'-ti 到底

LATE dzi 遲; æn 晏°; past the time, z-'eo' ko-deo' 時候巳過; the — emperor, sin-wông' 先皇; — father, sin-vu' 先父

LATELY, gying'-læ 近來; keh'-liang-nyih 這°兩日°

LATENT, hyüoh'-tih 蓄的; — heat, nyih-ky'ï' hyüoh'-tih 熱°氣蓄的

LATH, pih-ts'' 壁刺; — and plaster (properly ceiling), nyi-t'in-mun' 泥天璊

LATHE, ts'ô 車

LATHER, soap bi-zao' beh 肥°皂°浮

LATIN, the — language, Lah-ting' wô 辣丁話; Lo-mó' wô 羅馬話

LATITUDE, lines of — , we'-sin 緯線

LATTER, 'eo'-deo-go 後頭个°; 'eo'-læ-go 後來个°

LATTERLY gying'-læ 近來; gying'-z 近時

LAUDABLE, k'o-yi ts'ing-tsæn' 可°以°稱讚

LAUGH, to siao 笑; — aloud, keh'-keh-siao 哈°哈°笑; da-siao' 大笑; to — (when amused), fah-siao' 發笑; need not — at me, hao-vong' siao' ngô 弗°用°笑我; to make a person — , ying' nying siao' 引人°笑; — derisively, lang-siao 冷°笑

LAUGHING-STOCK, kyin'-siao-da-fông' 見笑大方

LATER, a little — , dzi'-tin 遲點; afterward, 'eo'-deo 後頭; the latest, ting 'eo'-deo-go 頂後頭个°; ting kyih'-sah 頂著°末; a year — , ko' ih nyin 過一年; the latest fashion, sing' c'ih-læ'-go z-dao' 新出來个°時道; djün-z'-go 全時个°

LAUGHABLE, hao-siao'-go 好笑个°; hao-fah-siao'-go 好發笑个°

LAUGHTER, kah-kah-siao 哈°哈°笑: ga-ga-siao; ha-ha-siao'.

LAUNCH, to — a ship, sing-jün loh-shü 新船落水°

LAVISH, ky'i-p'ah' do' 氣魄大°; kw'un siu' 寬手; yüong'-leh m-tsih'-cü-go 用無°節制; — in giving, c'ih-sin'-do 出手大°

LAW of the country, fah 法; lih-fah' 律法; lih-li' 律例; wông-fah' 王法; koh-fah' 國法; to break the — , væn fah' 犯法; international — , væn-koh' kong-fah 萬國公法; to go to — , tang kwun-s' 打官司; ky'üoh kwun-s' 吃°官司

LAWFUL, tsiao lih-fah' 照律法

LAWLESS, wang-ying'-peh-fah' 橫行不法 vu-fah'-vu-t'in' 無法無天

LAWN, (grass) bing-bing'-go ts'ao'-di 貼°平个°草地

LAWSUIT, kwun-s' 官司; dzong z' 訟事 (ih-ky'i); to have a — , tang kwun-s' 打官司; the — is settled, kyih-en'-de 結案了°

LAWYER, dzong s' 訟師; (in reproach) tang-tao'-go 打刀个°; writer of indictments, sia-zông-ts'-go 寫°狀紙个°

LAX, song 鬆; kw'un 寬; — in principle, dao'-li k'en-leh ky'ing-song 道理看得°輕鬆

LAXATIVE medicine, sia'-yiah or dza-yiah' 瀉藥

LAY, to — down, fông'-loh 放落; en-loh' 安落; — or spread a cloth, bricks &c., p'u 鋪; — the *table-cloth*, p'u coh'-pu 鋪桌布； — *the foundation* (native), ding sông-bun' 定礤盤； — *upon another* (as blame, &c.), t'e-t'oh' peh bih'-nying 推托與°別人°； — *by*, liu-ky'i' 留起； *ditto money for a purpose*, dzeng-ky'i' dong-din' 存起銅錢； — *up money*, tsih'-loh dong-din' 積聚°銅錢°

LAY, *to* — *eggs*, sang-dæn' 生蛋

LAYERS, *in* ih-zeng' ih-zeng' 層°一層°； zeng-tang'-zeng 層夾°層°

LAZY, kæn'-do 懶惰； — *and fond of ease*, t'en-kæn'-go 貪懶个°

LEAD, k'æn 鉛； *a sheet of* —, ih p'in k'æn' 一片鉛

LEAD-PENCIL, k'æn-pih' 鉛筆

LEAD, *red* 'ong tæn' 紅丹； *white* —, bah-tæn 白丹； k'æn-feng' 鉛粉

LEAD, *to take the* —, tang zin' 打前°； we-deo' 爲頭

LEAD, *to* ling 領； ying 引； ying'-dao 引道； ta'-ling 帶°領； — *by the hand*, siu ling'-leh-ky'i 攜手°而去°； — *the way*, ling lu' 領路； ying lu' 引路； — *me*, ying'-dao ngô 引導我； ta'-ling ngô 帶°領我； — *by the hand, or by a string*, ky'in-leh tseo' 牽了°走； *one who leads another into mischief*, sông-mông' 喪門°

LEADER, deo 頭； we-deo'-go 爲頭个°； deo-siu'; deo-nao' 頭腦； *to be a* —, tso deo' 做

頭； — *of an army*, tsiang-kyüing' 將軍； nyün-sæ' 元帥

LEAF, *a* — (*of plants*), ih-bæn yih' 一瓣°葉； — (*of a door*), ih-sin meng' 一扇門； — (*of a book*), ih yih' 一頁

LEAFLESS *trees*, kwông jü' 光樹

LEAGUE, iah 約 (ih-go)； *to make a* —, lih iah' 立約

LEAK, *to* leo 漏； *the water leaked out*, shü' leo-c'ih'-de 水°漏出了°； *to* — *out* (as news), sih'-leo 洩漏

LEAN, *to depend upon*, i'-k'ao 倚靠； k'ao-djoh' 靠著°； — *on for support*, gæ-djoh' 戤著°； — *the arm on the table*, siu k'ao'-leh coh'-teng 手靠在°桌上°； — *the head on the hand*, deo siu t'oh'-tih, 手托頭； siu t'oh sæ' 手托顋； — *against the wall*, gæ-djoh ziang 戤著°牆； — *forward*, eo'-tao 俯°； — *backward*, nyiang'-ky'i 仰起

LEAN, *thin*, seo 瘦； — *meat*, tsing nyüoh' 精肉°

LEAP, *to* t'iao 跳； — *down*, t'iao'-loh-læ 跳落來； — *over a wall*, t'iao'-ko ziang' 跳過牆

LEARN, *to* 'oh 學°； — *by practice*, 'oh-jih' 學°習； *has learned*, 'oh-we'-de 學°會了°； — *easily*, ih-kao' ziu we' 一教°就會； *commencing to* —, ky'i-deo' 'oh 起頭學°； k'æ-deo'-meng 'oh'； — *thoroughly*, 'oh'-tao tsing-t'ong' 學°到精通

LEARNED, poh'-yüoh-go 博學個°; a — person, poh'-lao 博士°

LEARNER, 'oh-jih'-go nying 學習個°人

LEARNING, 'oh-veng' 學°問; dzæ-'oh' 才學°; profound —, 'oh-veng' sing 學°問深

LEASE, n. tsu-ky'i 租契

LEASE, to — for a term of years, dziang-tsu' 長租; dziang-shü' 長賃°; — and refund the money at the expiration of the lease, tin 典

LEAST, ting' siao 頂少; gyih' siao 極少; at the very —, ts' siao 至少; ting ky'üih' 頂缺; not in the — afraid, ih-ngæn' tu feh p'ó' 一點°都弗怕; 'ao-vu' p'ó'-gyü 毫無怕懼

LEATHER, bi 皮; joh bi 熟皮; — shoes, bi 'a' 皮鞋; — dresser, siao-bi'-s-vu 硝皮司務; made of —, bi' tso-go 皮做個°; tough as —, ziang bi' ka nying 像皮個°朝; — articles, bi-go kô-sang 皮個°器°皿°

LEATHERY, tough, nying-bi'-tiao-tsi 靱疲习挛° (also used for a child which clings to one, and cannot be pulled off, &c.)

LEAVE, ask meng, k'o feh k'o' 問°可弗可; meng, cing' feh cing' 問°准弗准; t'ao k'eo' ky'i 討口氣; — of absence, meng k'o' hyih' feh 問°可歇否°; meng hyih kong' 問°歇工; to grant —, ing-hyü' 應詐; cing'准 (when granted by a superior).

LEAVE, to depart from, li-k'æ' 離開; bih-k'æ 別開; I — it to you, kwe ng' tso cü 歸你°做主; — it for supper, dzing-ky'i' tao yia' ky'üoh' 剩起到夜°吃°; — it here, liu'-tong 留在°此°; nothing left, m̀-neh dzing' 沒°有°剩; — out, or omit, ts'o'-loh 錯落; — me to be killed by the robbers, 'eo ngô', peh gyiang-dao' tang-sah 任°我俾°強盜打殺; cannot —, li-sing'-feh-k'æ' 離身弗開; to take — of, dz 'ang' 辭行'; come to take — of you, læ dz ng'-go 'ang' 來辭你°的°行°

LEAVEN, kao'-shü 酵°水°; to raise with —, fah-kao' 發酵°

LEAVINGS, dzing-loh'-go ling-sé' 剩落個°零碎; — of food, dzing-kang'-dzing-væn' 剩羹剩飯

LECTURE, to — from a moral book, kông jün'-shü 講善書

LEDGER, tsong'-ts'ing-bu 總清簿

LEE, 'ô'-fong 下°風

LEECH, mô'-wòng 螞蝗 (ih-keng)

LEEK, kyiu-ts'æ' 韭菜

LEER, to ts'ia-leh ngæn'-tsing-k'en' 斜°視°

LEES, kyiah 腳

LEFT hand, tsia'-siu 左°手; — side, tsia'-siu-pin 左°手邊; steer to the —, pæn.

LEFT, *a little* —, dzing-leh yiu'-'en 剩得°有限°; —, *or forgotten*, ts'o'-loh-de 錯°落了°; shih'-loh-de 失落了°

LEFT-HANDED, tsia'-siu zông-ziu' 左°手上前°; — *in holding chopsticks*, tsia'-siu k'o'-kw'æn 左°手拿°筷

LEG, kyiah'-kwang 腿 (ih-tsah); — *is broken*, kyiah'-kw'ang döu'-de 腳骨°斷了°

LEGACY, kô-ts'æn' 家產; — *to an adopted son*, ko'-kyi kô-ts'æn' 承°繼°產°業

LEGAL, tsiao lih-fah' 照律法

LEGEND, kwu'-tin 古典

LEGERDEMAIN, pin hyi'-fah 變戲法

LEGGIN (*worn by Chinese women*), ngô-dong' 瓦筩, *worsted* —, nyüong ngô-dong 海°絨瓦°筩 (*a pair*, ih-sông)

LEGIBLE, k'en'-leh-c'ih-go 看得°出°個°

LEGISLATE, *to* zao lih-fah' 造°律°法; ding lih-fah' 定律法

LEGITIMATE, 'eh-li'-go 合理個°; — *child*, ts'ing-sang' 親生°

LEISURE, k'ong 空, *nothing to do*, k'ong'-'æn vu-z' 空閒°無事

LEISURELY, *slowly*, mæn-mæn' 慢慢; wun'-wun 緩緩; mæn-t'eng'-t'eng; wun-t'ang'-t'ang 緩宕°宕°

LEMON, nying-mong 檸檬 (*Cantonese name*); — *color*, dæn-hyiang-seh 沉°香色; *greenish* — *color*, mih-seh' 蜜色; *brownish* — *color*, hyiang'-seh 香色

LEND, *to* tsia'-peh 借給°; *will you* — *me your pen?* ng'-go pih k'o tsia' peh ngô feh 你個°筆可借給°我否°?

LENDER, *money* fông dong-din'-go 放銅錢°個°

LENGTH, *what is its* —? to-siao dziang' 多少長? dza kwun' dziang 怎°樣°長°? *days and nights of equal* —, nyih-yia' ih-yiang dziang' 日夜一樣長; tsiu-yia bing' 晝夜°平

LENGTHEN, *to* — *by piecing*, tsih-dziang' 接長; — *the time*, z-'eo t'o-dziang' 時候拖長; *to grow longer*, dziang-ky'i'-læ 長起來

LENIENT, kw'un-shü' 寬恕

LENIENTLY, *to treat* —, kw'un-dæ' 寬待; *hard to treat* —, dzing-li' næn-yüong' 情理難容

LEOPARD, pao 豹 (ih-tsah)

LEPROSY, da-mô'-fong 大麻瘋; fah'-la-bing 發癩°病

LEPER, sang-da-mô'-fong-go 生°大麻瘋

LESS *in size*, siao-tin' 小點; — *in quantity*, siao-tin' 少點; ky'üih'-tin 缺點; *a little* —, siao ih'-ngæn 少一點; *still* —, keng'-kô siao 更加°少; — *than twenty*, feh tao nyiæn' 弗到廿; *can you take* —? ng yiu ky'üih'-deo feh

你有讓°頭否°? *how much — can you take?* yiu to-siao' hao ky'üih' 有多少好讓°? *in — than an hour*, feh tao' ih tin'-cong 弗到一點鐘; kw'a' ih tin'-cong 快一點鐘; *to grow —*, siao-long'-ky'i 少攏去°.

LESSEN, *to* kæn 減; kæn-siao' 減°少; kæn-loh' 減落.

LESSON, *or task*, kong-k'o' 功課; ih-tsông-shü' 一章書; *show me your —*, ng' shü-li kong-k'o' fæn' peh ngô k'en' 你°書裏功課翻與°我看; *to recite a —* (by rote), be-shü' 背書; *ditto by answering*, ing'-tah 應答.

LEST, k'ong'-p'ô 恐怕; zông-k'ong'-p'ô 尚恐怕; vi-k'ong'-p'ô 惟恐怕.

LET, peh 任°, or 俾°; — *him go*, peh gyi ky'i' 任°其去°; — *him alone*, ze' gyi læ-kæn' 任°其在°彼°; — *go* (as a bird), fông' 放; — *in*, fông'-tsing 放進; — *down* (as a curtain), fông'-loh 放落; — *a house*, tsu-c'ih' 租出; — *to*, tsu-peh' 租與°; — *out what one wishes to keep secret*, dzi-kyi' bun-deo', p'i'-kwn c'ih nga-deo' 雞雞盤頭屁股出外°頭; dzông-deo' lu-vi' 藏頭露尾.

LETTER *of the alphabet*, z-meo' 字母; *Roman letters*, Lo-mô' z 羅馬字.

LETTER, sing 信 (ih-fong); *to direct a —*, sia sing'-min 寫°信面; *to send a —*, ta ih-fong sing' 帶°一封信.

LETTUCE, sang-ts'æ' 生°菜.

LEVEE, *to go to the emperor's —*, zông-dziao' 上朝; *the emperor has a daily —*, wông-ti' nyih-nyih' zo-dziao' 皇帝日°日°坐°朝.

LEVEL, bing-bing' 平平; bing-dzih' 平直; — *road*, bing lu' 平路; *to lay or spread —*, p'u bing' 鋪平; *beat —*, tang-leh bing' 打得°平; tang bing-ts'ih; *to make — by putting something under*, din 墊.

LEVER, gyiao'-kweng 撟棍 (ih keng); *to raise by a —*, gyiao 撟.

LEVITY *in behavior*, ky'ing-veo' 'ang-we' 輕浮行°爲; — *and coarseness in behavior*, ky'ing-p'iao' 'ang-we 輕飄行°爲; — *in words*, ky'ing-boh' shih-wô' 輕薄說話.

LEVY, *to — taxes, or contributions*, lih kyün-kw'un' 立捐欵; — *troops*, tsiao ping' 招兵.

LEWD, t'en-ying'-go 貪淫個°; — *fellow*, ying-fu' 淫夫; — *woman*, ying-vu 淫婦.

LEXICON (arranged according to the radicals), z-we' 字彙; z-tin' 字典. SEE DICTIONARY.

LIABLE *to punishemnt*, li'-tông'-voh-ying' 理當服刑; ze'-ming pe'-tih 負罪; zo-ze'-go 坐罪个°.

LIAR, shih-hwông'-go nying 說謊个人; kông-hwông'-wô-go 講謊話个。

LIBEL, (anonymous) m̆-deo'-pông 無頭榜; vu-ming'-kyih-t‛iah' 無名揭帖

LIBERAL, do du'-liang 大度量; kw‛un-‛ong' du-liang 寬宏度量; ‛ao-yiah' 豪俠; — reward, djong'-sông 重賞; djong'-zia 重謝

LIBERALLY, to treat —, kw‛un dæ' 寬待; ‛eo' dæ 厚待

LIBERATE, to sih'-fông 釋放; fông'-c‛ih 放出

LIBERTINE, debauchee, seh-kwe 色鬼; ying-fu 淫夫; wild, rude fellow, fông'-dông-go-nying 游蕩个人。

LIBERTY, at — to follow one's inclinations, dzong-sing' sô-yüoh' 從心所欲; zi' tso-cü'-i 自做主意; zi-yiu'-zi-dzæ' 自由自在; at — to think, or do as one pleases, z-cü'-ts-gyün 自主之權; at — to suit your convenience, dzong ng'-go bin' 從你个便; ze ng'-go bin' 任你个便; you are taking liberties with my things, ngô-go tong'-si ng-zi tso-cü·i' 我个東西你自做主意; taking liberties with others' things, jün'-cün-go 擅專个; take — with one of another sex, &c., peh-nen-peh-nyü 不男不女; take — (as of

coming into women's apartments, &c.), nen kah vu nyü 男女混雜。

LIBRARIAN, kying-kwun'-shü-zih'-go 經管書籍个。

LIBRARY (large), shü-koh' 書閣; shü-leo' 書樓

LICENSE, tsiao 照; tsih'-tsiao 執照; t‛iah 帖; to take out a —, ling tsiao' 領照; ling-t‛iah' 領帖; to grant a —, kyih tsiao' 給照

LICENSE, to — a preacher, fông cing-s' 放准試

LICENTIOUS, tsong'-fông-yüoh-ho' 縱放慾火; shing-tsong'-s-yüoh' 狗縱私慾; ying-yüoh-vu-du 淫慾無度; — books, ying shü' 淫書; — plays, ying hyi' 淫戲; — songs, ying dz' 淫詞

LICHEES, fresh sin li'-tsi 鮮荔子; dried —, ken li'-tsi 乾荔子

LICK, to t‛in 餂, or 舔

LICORICE-ROOT, ken ts‛ao' 甘草

LID, kæ 該 (ih-go); eye —, ngæn-p‛ao-bi' 眼臕皮

LIE, n. hwông'-wô 謊話; kô'-wô 假話; hyü-wô' 虛話 (ih-kyü)

LIE, to kông hwông'-wô 講謊話; shih-hwông' 說謊

LIE, to kw‛eng 睡; — down, kw‛eng'-loh 睡落; — on the back, nyiang' t‛in kw‛eng 仰睡; — on the face, foh'-ken-kw'eng 覆睡°；— *on the side*, tseh'-leng-kw'eng 側睡°；— *curled up*, geo-leh kw'eng'; (it) *lies on the table*, læ coh'-teng en'-tih; læ coh'-teng fòng'-tih. 放在°桌°上°。

LIFE, seng-ming' 生命；weh-ming' 活命；ming 命；sing'-ming 性命；*save* —, kyiu ming' 救命；*to risk* —, p'un ming' 拚命；*a litter, or hard* —, kw'u' ming 苦命；*happy* —, hao ming' 好命；— *before we came into this world*, zin-si' 前°世°; zin-seng' 前°生; *the present* —, kying'-si 今世°; kying-seng' 今生; *the future* —, 'o'-si 下°世°; læ-seng' 來生; *to lose one's* —, sing'-ming c'ih'-t'eh' 性命休矣；*one's whole* —, ih-sang-ih'-si 一生一世°; bing-seng 平生; we-nying'-dzæ-shü 為人°在世°; ih-si'-we-nying 一世°為人°; *cong-sing'* 終身; *one's — until now*, seng-bing' 生平; ih'-byiang tso'-nying 一向做人°; *eternal* —, üong'-seng 永生; dziang-seng' 長生; üong'-yün weh-ming' 永遠活命; *to be restored to* —, si'-ky'i wæn-weng' 死°去°還魂; *has seen much of* —, shü'-min tu kyin'-ko 經°歷°世°事°; *short* —, tön'-ming 短命; iao-zin' 天壽; *long* —, dziang-ming' 長命; dziang-seng' 長

生; dziang-ziu' 長壽; dziang-ming'-pah'-shü 長命百°歲° (*complimentary*); *full of* — (*i.e.* *always moving*), feh-teh-hyih-go 弗得歇個

LIFELESS, ve'-weh-de 弗°活了°; n-sing'-ming 無°性命；(as if glad of it) teo'-ti si'-le 實°在°死°了°

LIFETIME, weh'-tong-go z-'eo' 活在°的°時候；dzæ'-shü we-nying' 在世為人°

LIFT, *to* — (*with both hands*), teh 摂；— *up*, teh-tæn'-ky'i 摂起；— (*one or more persons*), ts'iah 擦；*cannot* — *it*, do'-feh-dong' 拿°弗動；ts'iah'-feh-dong' 擦弗動；— (*two or more persons*), kông 搯；— *with string, or lever*, kông 扛；dæ 擡；— *up*, ts'iah-tæn'-ky'i 擦起；— *and take away*, ts'iah'-leh-ky'i.

LIGATURE *for binding blood vessels*, tsah hyüih'-mah-go pu' 縶血脈個°布

LIGHT, kwông 光; liang-kwông 亮光; *sun* —, nyih-kwông 日°光; *dim* —, liang'-kwông u-teng'-teng 亮光唔°洞°洞°; *how* — *it is!* dza-liang' 甚°亮! *insufficiently* —, kwông ky'in liang 亮°光不足°; *bring a* —, do-liang'-læ 携燈°來

LIGHT (*in color*), dæn 淡; *a little lighter*, dæn-tin' 淡點; *not heavy*, ky'ing 輕; ky'ing-k'o'

輕可;— wind, ky'ing-fong' 輕風; vi-fong' 微風; eat a — meal, ih-djü' siao ky'üoh' tin — 餐°少吃°點; — matter, ky'ing-k'o' z-t'i' 輕可事體; — work, ky'ing-k'o' sang-weh' 輕可生°活; — bread, mun-deo' ky'ing-song' 饅頭輕鬆

LIGHT, to — a candle, tin lah-coh' 點蠟燭; — a lamp, tin teng' 點燈; light a —, tin liang' 點亮; will not —, tin'-feh-dziah'-go 點弗燶个°; — (as a cigar), tin-ho' 點火; — the fire, sang-ho' 生°火; I will — you (in going), ngô-tsiao'-leh ng ky'i' 我照了°你去°

LIGHTED, well tsiao'-leh shih'-liang 照得°甚°亮; brightly — (lamps or candles), teng-coh'-hwe-wông' 燈燭輝煌; eye — upon, ngæn'-tsing kwæn-djoh'-go 眼睛看°過; bird — upon a tree, tiao' jü-li ding-ko' 此鳥°曾集於樹°

LIGHTEN, to make it light, peh gyi ky'ing' 俾其輕; to — (as lightning), fah-sin' 發閃; long-kwông' sin-din' 龍光閃電

LIGHT-FINGERED person, siao-ts'eh-ts'eh' 小撮撮; ts'eh'-lao 扒°手°

LIGHT-FOOTED, kyiah'-deo ky'ing-fæn' 脚步輕泛

LIGHT-HEADED, thoughtless, ky'ing 輕; feh-djong'-jih 弗重實;

— (as when on a high place), yiao-ling'-ling 頭°搖懍懍; — (as in delirium), hweng-tih'-de 惛了°

LIGHT-HEARTED, kw'un-sing' 寬心; m̄-sing'-m̄-z 無°心無°事

LIGHT-HOUSE, liang-t'ah' 亮塔; teng-t'ah 燈塔 (ih-zo)

LIGHTLY, ky'ing 輕; ky'ing-kw'un' or ky'iing-kun.

LIGHTNING, sin'-din 閃電

LIKE, ziang 像; siang-ziang 相像; siang-dong' 相同; fông-feh' 仿彿; somewhat —, tao'-ziang 倒像; exactly —, ih-yiang' 一樣; tsing'-ziang 正像; ih-seh'-ih-yiang' 一色一樣; seems —, or seems as if, oh'-ziang; hao-ziang 好°像; — (as a picture to a person), weh'-t'eh-ko'; just — (his) father, tsing'-ziang ah-tia' 正像阿爹°; teng ah-tia tso su'-ts (inelegant).

LIKE, to hwun-hyi' 歡喜; cong'-i 中意; as you —, ze ng' 任°你°; choose which you —, ze ng' hwun-hyi kæn ih'-yiang 任°你歡喜揀一樣; what I —, ngô sô sing-miao'-go 我所合°意°个°; just what one likes, jü-sing' ziang-i' 如心像意; I — him, ngô cong'-i' gyi 我中意其; gyi cong ngô'-go i' 其中我个°意

LIKELY, liang-pih 諒必; bông-tao' 防到; jih-r-kyiu' 十而

九; jih'-yiu-kyiu' 十有其°九; very —, kyiu'-feng kyiu'-li 九分九釐

LIKENESS, there is a slight —, yiu tin' siang-ziang' 有點相像; portrait, siao'-tsiao 小照; 'ang-loh' 行樂圖; byi'-yüong 喜容; to draw a —, sia siao'-tsiao 寫小照; to photograph a —, ing siao'-tsiao 映小照; — taken in old age, ziu-yüong 壽容; — hung in the ancestral-hall after death, ziang 像

LIKEWISE, also, yia 也°; in like manner, yia' z-ka 也°是如°此°

LILAC (called in Peking), ting-hyiang'-hwô 丁香花; — color, 'o-hwô' seh 荷花色; shih-ts'ing' 雪青

LILY, golden kying-tsing'-hwô 金針花 (when dried, it is often used for food); wild pink —, tsông-lông'-hwô 蟑螂花

LIMB, the four limbs, s'-ts 四肢; four limbs and one hundred members, s'-ts-pah'-t'i 四肢百°體; — of a tree, ô-ts' 丫枝; cut off a —, ô-ts' tsoh'-diao 丫枝斷去°; limbs spread out, p'ah'-kyiah dô'-siu'.

LIMBER, nyün 軟; mi-nyün' 綿°軟; bamboo when heated becomes —, coh ho'-li dæn-dæn we mi-nyün' 以°竹°燻°之°爲°軟

LIME, stone zah-hwe' 石°灰; the best — comes from Fu-yiang and is called Fu-yiang' hwe 富陽灰; shell —, koh'-hwe 壳灰; unslaked —, sang zah'-hwe' 生°石°灰; slaked —, joh hwe' 熟灰; to mix —, c'ün hwe' 串灰; to pound —, sông hwe' 舂灰

LIME-KILN, hwe-yiao' 灰窰 (ih-go)

LIMIT, 'æn'-cü 限°制; boundary, ka'-'æn 界°限°; no —, m̃ 'æn'-cü 無°限°制; to settle the —, ding ka'-'æn 定界°限°; to pass the —, ko-'æn' 過限°; has a —, yiu' 'æn 有限°

LIMIT, to — the time, 'æn' nyih-ts' 限°日°子; I — you to a dollar, ngô teng ng 'æn'-ding ih-kw'e' fæn-ping' 我與°你°限°定一塊番餅

LIMP, wanting stiffness, nyün'-joh 軟熟

LIMP, to kwa-kyi'-kwa-kyi tseo' 跛°走; ih-kwa', ih-dih' 一拐°一敧; — slightly, zeh-kyiah'-go tseo.

LIMPID, kwang'-ts'ing 光°清; pih'-ts'ing 碧清

LIGHTNING, sin'-din 閃電; a flash of —, sin'-din ih-sin 閃電一閃; sheet —, long'-sæn lông 閃°; that house was struck by — (lit. thunder), keh' tsing oh' le tang'-diao-de 這°進屋雷打壞了°; killed by —, (i. e. a thunder-bolt), p'ih'-lih tang'-sah

霹靂打殺; T'in-lc' tang'-sah
天雷打殺; T'in-li' tang'-sah
天理打殺
LINE, sin 線; straight —, dzih-sin' 直線 (ih-da); to divide by cross —, tang wang kah' 打橫°格; to divide by straight —, tang dzih kah' 打直格; curved —, ẇæn-ying'-go sin 彎形个°線; crooked ink —, ẇæn-ẇæn'-ky'üoh-ky'üoh'-go moh-sin' 彎曲个°墨線; the spaces enclosed by cross lines, kah'-ts 格子; draw a —, weh ih-da sin' 畫一埭線; carpenter's ink —, moh-sin' 墨線; tailor's powder —, feng'-sin 粉線
LINE, to fit a lining, p'e li'-ts 配裡子; p'e-keh'-li.
LINED garments, kah'-i 袷衣; unlined ditto, tæn-i' 單衣
LINEAGE, race, ts-p'a' 支派°; of the — of David, Da-bih' dzoh'-li keh p'a' 大闢族裡這'派
LINEN, coh'-pu 竹布; hempen cloth, mô-pu' 麻布; grass cloth, 'ô-pu' 夏布; hemp, or — thread, mô-sin' 麻線
LINGER, to delay, tæn-koh' 耽擱; to loiter, yiu-lu' 遊路; deng-deng'-tah-tah 或行°或止°
LINGERING, fond of — (as a visitor), deng ih-zông z' ih-zông 停一息°是一息°; — (as disease) in-dzi' 淹滯
LINGUIST, one who speaks several languages, we tang loh'-koh-hyiang'-dæn 會說°六國鄉談
LINING, keh'-li; li'-ts 裡子
LINK, lin-ŵæn-ky'ün 連環°圈 (ih-go)
LINK, to lin-long' 連攏; can be linked, hao siang-lin' 好相連
LINSEED, (hemp seed) wu'-mô'-ts 胡麻子
LION, s-ts' 獅子 (ih-tsah)
LIP, the upper —, zông'-bæn-cü'-jing 上爿嘴唇; the lower —, 'ô'-bæn-cü'-jing 下爿嘴唇; lips, cü'-pô 嘴巴
LIP-SERVICE, yiu' k'eo' vu sing' 有口無心
LIQUID, we liu'-go tong'-si 會流个°東西
LIQUOR, tsih 汁; distilled (Chinese) —, siao'-tsiu' 燒酒; strong ditto, tih'-siao 元'燒酒
LIQUORICE, SEE LICORICE.
LISP, to kông-leh ngao'-zih-keng-go 講°得'鉸舌根个°
LIST, a — (of articles, prices, &c.), ih-p'in tsiang' 一片帳; ib-p'in' ts'ing-tsiang' 一片清帳; — of names, ming-moh' 名目; ditto (on a sheet), kyi'-ming-tæn' 記名單; — (of baggage, &c.), ky'i'-mô-tæn' 起馬單; — of places on a journey, lu-dzing'-tæn 路程單; — of characters, tsah'-c'ih-go' z 摘出个°字; — of goods, ho'-tæn 貨單 (ih-p'in, or ih-tsiang).

LISTEN, to t'ing 聽; must —, yüong t'ing' 要聽; — attentively, tông-sing' t'ing' 當心聽; — secretly, t'eo-bun' t'ing' 私下聽

LISTLESS, feh liu'-sing 弗留心; læn'-tch t'ing' 懶得聽

LITERALLY, to translate —, tsiao nyün ti'-ts fæn-yih' 照原底子繙譯

LITERARY man, yiu-'oh-veng'-go nying 有學問个人; veng-moh'-go-nying 文墨个人; — chancellor, 'oh-dæ' 學臺; the — dialect, veng-wô' 文話; veng-li' 文理; — composition, veng-tsông' 文章; — reputation, veng-ming' 文名, — title, kong-ming' 功名; the god who presides over — men, Veng-ts'ông'-ti'-kyüing 文昌帝君; inferior ditto, Kw'e-sing' bu-sah' 魁星

LITERATI, doh-shü-nying' 讀書人; Confucianists, jü-kô' 儒家

LITHOGRAPH, to t'ah shü 搨書; lithographic plates, zah-deo' k'eh-go t'ah'-shü-pæn 石刻搨書版

LITIGATE, to tang kwun-s' 打官司

LITIGIOUS, jün'-ü hying-dzong' 善于興訟; hao-dzong' 好訟

LITTER of pigs, ih-k'o' siao'-cü 一窩小豬

LITTLE, siao 小; — child, siao-nying' 小孩; — matter, siao-z-ken' 小事幹; siao'-i-s 小意思; a —, ih-ngæn'; ih-ngæn'-ngæn; ih-tin' 一點; ih-tin-tin' 一點點; ih-ti' 一滴; ih-ti'-ti 一滴滴; yiu'-æn 有限; very —, kyìn'-liang' 見量; a — more, to'-tin 多點; to'-ih-ngæn; a very — more, sao'-we to'-tin 稍為多點; siao-shü' to'-tin 少些多點; liah-liah' to'-tin 略略多點; shü-vi' to'-tin 些微多點; add a —, kô ih-tin' ts'eo' 加一點湊, &c. &c.; a — longer, dziang'-tin 長點; a — better, hao-tin' 好點; differs but — (or is about right), ts'ô-feh-to' 差弗多; zông'-loh vu-kyi' 上落無幾; siang-ky'i' ying-kwun' 相去仿佛 (kwun or kun)

LITURGY, p'a'-ding-go kyiao'-kwe 派定个教規

LIVE, to dwell, djü 住; deng 瘝; where do you —? ng'-djü le 'ah-li' 你住在何處? ng djü-kyü' soh-go di-fông 你居甚麼地方? (polite) ng fu'-zông djü-'ah-li' 你府上住何處? to be alive, weh 活; to spend one's days, ko nyih-ts' 過日子; du-nyih' 度日; du kwông-ing' 度光陰; only enough to — on, tsih'-keo wu-k'eo' 只彀餬口; dziang-ming'-pah-shü 長命百歲°;— long, ziu-shü dziang' 壽歲長; wants to 一, iao sing'-ming 要性命; to — by pen and ink, yi pih-moh' du kwông-ing 以筆墨度光陰;— according to one's means (lit. knows where to stop), sih'-k'o'-r-ts 適可而止

LIVELIHOOD, du nyih' 度日°; du kwông-ing' 度光陰; how do you make a —? ng yi soh-si du kwông-ing 你°以甚麽度光陰? ng soh'-go du-nyih' 你°甚麽度日°? ng k'ao soh'-si du nyih' 你°靠甚麽度日°?

LIVELONG, the — day, ih-nyih' tao-yia' 一日°到夜°; tsing-nyih' 儘日°; dziang-nyih' 長日°

LIVELY in motion, weh-dong' 活動; weh-loh' 活絡;— in talking, kông'-leh weh-loh' 講得°活絡

LIVER, ken 肝; beef—, ngeo-ken' 牛°肝

LIVERY, 'ao'-i 號衣

LIVID, ts'ing-heh' 青黑;— bruise, u-ts'ing' 烏青

LIVING things, weh'-go tong-si 活個°東西; weh-veh' 活物; while —, weh'-tong z-'eo' 活在°時候; dzæ-shü' we-nying' 在世爲人°

LIVING, how do you make a —? ng dza du nyih 你°怎度日°? ng tso soh-go sang-i 你°作何°

生°意? ditto (to a gentleman) ng-kwun-di' læ ah-li' 你°就°館°在°何°處°?

LIZARD, in'-deo-dzô' 蠑蚑蛇°; s'-kyiah-dzô' 四腳蛇°

LOAD for a man, ih-tæn' 一擔;— for two men, ih-kông' 一扛; boat—, ih-zæ' 一臟; ih-jün' 一船; having a — on the mind, læ'-tih tæn'-sing-z' 正在°擔心事

LOAD, to tsæ 載; ts'ông 裝; kwun 管; — a boat, jün' tsông ho' 船裝貨;— a cannon, tsông p'ao' 裝礮

LOAD-STONE, hyih'-t'ih-zah' 噏鐵石°; dz-zah' 磁石°

LOAF, a — of bread, ih-go mun-deo' 一個饅頭

LOAFER, yiu-dang'-go-nying 游宕個°人°; yiu-hyi'-lông-dông-go nying' 遊戲浪蕩個°人°

LOAM, yiu-liâ'-go na-nyi' 有力個°坭

LOAN, to tsia-peh' 借°給°; to — a large sum, fông nying-bun' 放銀盤

LOATH or LOTH (to give up), feh-sô'-teh 弗捨°得;— to go, feh-dzing'-nyün ky'i' 弗情願去°

LOATHE, to tseng 憎; tseng-sah' 憎極; I — the thing, k'eh'-go tong-si ngô tse k'o-u'-go 這個°東西我最可惡個°

LOBSTER, great crab, long-hô' 龍蝦 (ih-tsah)

LOCAL, *peculiar to one place*, ih-t'ah di'-fông yiu'-go 一處地方有个°; ih-c'ü' yiu-go 一處有个°; — *products*, t'u'-ts'æn 土產; — *custom*, hyiang-fông; hyiang-fong' 鄉風; t'u'-fong 土風; t'u'-dzoh 土俗; — *banditti*, t'u-fi' 土匪; — *customs differ*, hyiang-fong c'ü'-c'ü bih 鄉風處處別

LOCK *of a door*, so 鎖 (ih-kwun); *canal — with gates*, ky'i 開; — *with inclined plane*, pô 壩; — *of hair*, ih-lu' deo-fah' 一縷頭髮

LOCK, *to* so 鎖; so'-loh 落鎖; — *a door*, so-meng' 鎖門; meng so'-loh 門落鎖; — (as with padlock) zông-so' 上鎖

LOCKED-JAW, ngô' kwæn-kying'-pi 牙°關緊閉

LOCUST, wông-djong' 蝗蟲 (ih-tsah)

LODGE *in a field*, sô 厙

LODGE, *to* deng 庉; *dwell for a time*, dzæn'-deng 暫庉; — *for the night*, soh-yia' 宿夜°; hyih-yia' 歇夜

LODGING-PLACE, deng-sing'-ts-c'ü' 庉身之處; *lodging-shop*, soh'-yia-tin 宿夜°店

LOFT, *a low* —, koh'-teng 上°擱; *house has a* —, oh' yiu koh-teng'-go 屋有上°擱个°

LOFTY, kao-kao' 高高; — *and large*, kao-do' 高大°

LOG *of wood*, moh-deo' 木頭 (ih-dön)

LOGICAL, yiu diao-li'-go 有條理个°; jing-jü'-go 循序个°

LOGWOOD, su-moh' 蘇木

LOINS, *the upper part*, iao-hyih' 腰脅; iao-bo' 腰間°; *at the hips*, do t'e' pin 大°腿邊

LOITER, *to* yiu-dang' 遊宕; *to — on the way*, yiu-lu' 遊路

LOLL, *to — about*, t'en-min' kæn-do 貪眠懶惰; — *the tongue*, zih-deo' t'a-c'ih' 舌頭伸°出

LONELY, lang'-loh 冷落; dzih-moh' 寂寞

LONG, dziang 長; *four feet —*, s' ts'ah dziang 四尺長; *not long enough*, ky'in dziang 弗°殼長; *a — time*, dziang-kyiu' 長久; dziang-yün' 長遠; *how — shall I wait?* ngô iao' teng' to-siao' kong-fu' 我要等多少工夫? — *period of years*, nyin-yün' jih-kyiu' 年遠日久; *how — ago did the Rebels come?* dzong Dziang-mao' læ', tao jü-kying' to-siao' z-'eo' 從長毛來到如今多少時候?

LONG, *to — constantly*, k'eh'-k'eh-neng'-neng siang'-vông 時°時°刻刻想望; — *ardently*, ts'ih'-sing siang' 切心想; yün-vông' 懸望; — *for something superior*, or *above one*, ky'i'-mo 企慕; *I — to see my mother*, ngô ky'i'-mo kyin ah-nyiang' 我企慕

見毋, (ky'i-mo cannot be used in the sentence, my mother longs to see me); — *for* (as for food), siang 想; s-ts'eng' ziang k'eo-k'eh' ka 思忖渾 如口渦

LONG-SUFFERING, næ'-leh dziang-kyiu' 耐得長久; *lenient*, kw'un-shü' 寬恕

LONGER, *a little* —, dziang'-tin 長點; *still* —, keng'-kô dziang' 更加 長; *want it* —, wa-iao dziang 還要長; *to wait a little* —, tsæ' teng-leh dziang' ih-zông 再等得長一息

LONGEVITY, dziang-ziu' 長壽; ziu-shü' dziang 壽歲長

LONGITUDE, *lines of* —, kying-sin' 經線

LOOK or LOOKS, siang'-mao 相貌; shü'-sch 水色; ts-seh' 姿色; *has an honest* —, min-yüong' k'en'-læ dzing-jih'-go 面容看來誠實个

LOOK, *to* k'en 看; siang 相; *take a* —, k'en'-ih-k'en' 看一看; k'en'-k'en-siang 看看相; môong-môong'-k'en 望望看; — *around*, dön-ky'ün' k'en 周圍看; — *up*, dziao zông' k'en 朝上看; dæ-ky'i' k'en 抬起看; — *down*, k'en-'ô' 看下; hyiang-'ô' k'en' 向下看; *stoop and* —, co'-tao k'en' 僵倒看; — *back*, nyin-cün' k'en' 回轉看; we-deo' k'en' 回頭看; — *down upon, or have contempt for*, k'en'-feh-zông-ngæn' 看弗上眼; — *askance*, zia'-k'en 斜看; tseh'-k'en 側看; — *for, or find*, zing 尋; — *for it*, zing-zing' k'en 尋尋看; dzô-dzô' k'en 查查看; *I have looked every where*, ngô tao'-c'ü' zing-pin' ko 我到處尋遍過; — *for, or expect* p'æn'-vông 盼望; — *carefully*, ts'-si k'en' 仔細看; — *after, or take care of*, kwun 管; *you* — *after things here*, ng' kwun-tong' 你管在此; *this dress looks well*, keh' gyin i-zông siang'-mao tao hao'-go 這件衣裳樣式倒好个

LOOKING, *she is fine* —, gyi'-go shü'-sch sang-leh hao' 其个水色生得好

LOOKER *on*, bông-pin' k'en'-go cü'-kwu 旁邊看个人; bông-kwun'-tsiæ 旁觀者

LOOKING-GLASS, kying'-ts 鏡子 (ih-min)

LOOKOUT, *on the* —, læ'-tih tsiao'-liao 正在瞧瞭; *platform for observing enemies*, liao-dæ' 瞭臺; — *on city wall*, fi-leo' 飛樓; *turret*, vông-leo' 望樓; — *for cool air*, jü'-fong-ding 聚風亭

LOOM, kyi 機; — *for cotton cloth* pu'-kyi 布機 (ih-tsiang)

LOOP, p'æn' 襻; — *for a button*, nyiu'-p'æn 鈕襻

LOOP-HOLE *for cannon*, p'ao'

dong-ngæn' 砲洞眼°; *find a — for escape,* zing leo-dong', hao zah-c'ih 尋漏洞好逃°出

LOOSE, *not tight,* song 鬆; kw'un 寬; *unfastened,* sæn-de 散了°.

LOOSEN, to fông song'-tin 放鬆點; — *(bound) feet,* fông kyiah' 放脚.

LOOSENESS *of bowels,* du'-li lœ-tih dzæ' 腹°中°作°瀉°.

LOP, *to — off an ear,* siah'-loh ng'-to 削落耳°朶; — *a branch,* tsoh-diao ô-ts' 斫去°了枝.

LOQUACIOUS, shih-wô' to' 說話多; to-kông'-to-wô' 多講多話; to-cü'-tah-zih' 多嘴搭舌; — *(because thin-lipped),* cü'-jing-bi-boh' 嘴唇皮薄.

LOQUAT, bi-bô' 枇杷.

LORD, cü' 主; — *of Heaven,* T'in-Cü' 天主; *Lord's Supper,* Cü-go væn'-ts'æn 主个晚餐.

LORD, *to — over,* we-deo', we-nao' 爲頭爲腦.

LOSE, *to* shih'-diao 失了°; tiu-diao' 丟去°; — *one's life,* shih'-diao sing'-ming 失了性命, sông sing'-ming 喪性命; sing'-ming c'ih'-t'eh 性命休°矣; — *heart,** læn-t'æn' sing-deo ky'i' 可°歎°可°氣°; — *(opposed to win),* shü'-diao 輸了°; — *courage,* tæn 'en' 膽寒.

* It should be observed that, shih sing' 失心 means to lose one's mind, and not one's heart; shih'-loh 失落 means also to leave behind, or forget.

tæn ky'iah' 膽怯°; — *interest (in),* sing' lang' 心冷°; sing-s' dæn'-dæn 心思淡然; sing ga'; — *flavor,* c'ih ky'i' 出氣; — *savor,* tseo mi' 走味; *to suffer loss,* ky'üoh'-kw'e 吃虧, ky'ih'-kw'e; ky'ih-ky'ü'; — *capital, or — in trade,* zih-peng 折本; kw'e-peng 虧本; kw'e-zih' 虧折°; *how much did you —! ng'* zih to-siao' peng 你°折多少本?

LOST, shih'-diao-de 失了°; *(as a ship),* tso'-diao-de 做壞°了°; *in trade,* sô tseo', tsong'-go 不符總个°; sô zih', diao'-go 蝕出个°; — *to shame,* sông' lin-c'ü' 傷廉耻; fæ'-gyi ô-lin' 弗要°臉; — *time,* kong-fu shih'-loh-de 工夫失落了°; — *appetite,* we-k'eo' t'e-pæn'-de 胃口不佳了°; — *memory,* kyi'-sing t'e-pæn'-de 記性差了°; *missing,* feh-kyin'-de 弗見了°; — *the way,* mi-lu'-de 迷路了°.

LOT, *a — of land,* ih-kw'e-di' 一塊地; *the whole — (of things),* ih'-kwu-nao-r 一槪.

LOTS, *to draw — (bamboo splints),* ts'iu-ts'in' 抽籤; *ditto (bits of paper),* ts'eh-ts'-meh-den' 拈°鬮; *to cast — with dice,* dzih-seh'-ts 擲骰°子.

LOTUS, 'o-hwô' 荷花; lin-hwô' 蓮花; — *seeds,* lin-ts' 蓮子; — *roots,* ngeo 藕.

LOUD, hyiang 響; *speaks*—, kông-leh-hyiang' 講°得°響; — *voice*, sing-ing'-do' 聲音大°; sing-ing'-djong 聲音重; wu-long'-do' 喉°嚨大°; *a little louder*, hyiang-tin' 響點

LOUNGER, *idler*, k'ong'-æn-nying' 空閒人°. SEE LOAFER, LOLL.

LOUSE, seh 虱; *the nid of a*—, seh-ts' 虱子; kyi'-ts 蟣子; *to kill lice*, k'eh seh' 剋虱; *to kill lice by biting*, ngao seh' 鮫虱

LOUSY, seh' sang'-leh-to' 虱生°得°多; seh sang'-leh kao-kao-dong'.

LOVE *of wine*, t'en-tsiu' 貪酒; — *of wealth*, t'en-dzæ' 貪財; — *of lust*, t'en-seh' 貪色; — *of eating*, t'en-ky'üoh' 貪吃; t'en-zih' 貪食

LOVE, *to* æ'-sih 愛惜; — *greatly*, c'ong'-æ 寵愛; *to* — *a superior*, æ'-kying 愛敬; — *an inferior* (*as a child*), dzih-din' 值錢°; — *one another*, dô-kô'-siang-æ' 大°家°相愛; — *and pity*, æ-lin' 愛憐; *he is much loved*, gyi teh-c'ong'-go 其得寵個°; — *and treat partially*, p'in-æ' 偏愛; — *blindly*, nyih-æ' 溺愛

LOVELY, k'o-æ' 可愛; *me* 美; — *woman*, me'-nyü 美女

LOW, *not high*, ti 低; — *coast lands*, du 渡; t'æn 灘; — *land*, di'-shü ti' 地勢低; — *voice*, sing-ing' ti 聲音低;

sing-ing' ky'ing' 聲音輕; wu-long iu' 喉°嚨細°; — *birth*, c'ih-sing' ti-vi' 出身低微; — *tide*, dziao t'e'-zing 潮退盡; dziao loh-ken' 潮落乾; *vulgar*, ts'u-c'ing' 粗蠢; — *in price*, kô'-din ti' 價°錢°低; — (*i. e. poor*) *diet*, ky'üoh'-zih dæn'-boh 吃°食淡薄; ts'u-ts'æ' dæn-væn' 麤菜淡飯

LOWER, *to* — *one's self*, zi-ky'ing', zi-zin' 自°輕自°賤°

LOWER, *a little* —, ti'-tin 低點; — *side*, 'ô'-min 下°面; — *classes*, mæn pah'-sing 頑°民°; siao pah'-sing 小百°姓

LOWEST, ting-'ô'-deo-go 頂下°頭個°; — *class or rank*, meh-teng'-go sing-veng' 末等個°身分; ting 'ô' pe 頂下°輩

LOWLY, *mean*, ti-vi' 低微, pe-vi' 卑微; *humble*, ky'in-hyü' 謙虛

LOW-SPIRITED, sing-hwe i'-læn 心灰意懶

LOYAL, cong-sing 忠心; — *officer*, cong-dzing' 忠臣

LUBRICATE *it*, long gyi wah' 弄其滑

LUCID, ming-ts'ih' 明澈; ming-liang' 明亮

LUCK, zao'-hwô 造°化°; yüing'-ky'i 運氣; yüing'-dao 運道; z-yüing 時運; *good* —, hao yüing'-ky'i 好運氣; hao zao'-hwô 好°得°意°; *when in good*

—, 'ang yüing' z-'eo 行運時候; bad —, zao-hwô w̃a' 勿得°意°; tao-yüing' 倒運; yüing'-dao feh-te' 運道弗通; that was your good — (no right to expect), keh z ng'-go ngah'-koh kao' 這° 是 你 个° 額 角 高; iao-ying' 僥° 倖

LUCKY, yiu zao'-hwô 有造化; yiu ying' 有 幸; — omen, hao ts'æ'-deo 好兆°頭; — day, hao nyih-ts' 好日子; — star, kyih' sing 吉星

LUCRABAN SEED, da-fong-ts' 大楓子

LUCRATIVE, hao fah-dzæ' 好發財

LUDICROUS, hao fah'-siao'-go 好發笑个°

LUG, to dzing'-lih do' 盡力拿'; to drag with all one's strength, 'eo-ky'i'-lih t'o' 儘°氣力拖

LUGGAGE, 'ang-li' 行李; how many pieces of —? kyi gyin' 'ang-li' 幾件行°李?

LUKEWARM, feh-lang'-feh-nyih' 弗冷°弗熱°; nyih-w̃eng-w̃eng' 熱溫溫; w̃eng'-t'eng 溫 和°

LULL, the wind lulls, fong' iu-loh'-ky'i 風聲°漸°靜°; wind lulled, fong sih'-de 風息了°

LUMBER, old things, hyiu'-gyiu tong-si 朽舊東西; wood, moh-deo' 木頭

LUMP, gyi-ts'-kw'e 棋子塊; a ball, ih-dön' 一團; a piece, ih-kw'e' 一塊; to buy in the —, (not in powder), weh-leng' ma 囫圇買°

LUMP, to form lumps, dzing-kw'e' 成塊;— together, tang t'ong-bun' 打通盤; to — the prices, t'ong-ts'ô' kô'-din 通扯價°錢°

LUNAR month, yüih-veng tsiao yüih-liang'ding'-go 月孖°照月亮定个°

LUNATIC, tin-ts' 癲子; fong-tin'-go 瘋癲个°

LUNCH, tin'-sing, or tia'-sing 點心

LUNG-NGAN, kwe'-yün 桂圓; yün ngæn' 圓眼°

LUNGS, fi 肺

LURE, to entice, ying-yiu' 引誘; to tempt, mi-'oh' 迷惑;— away, kwa'-tæ 拐°帶; kwa'-p'in 拐°騙

LURK, to tong-iu'-si-iu' 東避°西避°; tong-tsiang'-si-w̃ông' 東賑西望°

LUSCIOUS, ken-din' 蜜° 甜

LUST, desire for possession, s-yüoh' 私欲; concupiscence, yüoh-ho' 慾火

LUSTING, yüoh-ho' læ-tih dong' 慾火勁; yüoh-ho' fah'-dong 慾火發動

LUSTFUL, t'en-seh' 貪色; extremely —, hao'-seh-ko-du' 好色過度; — person, hao'-seh-ts-du' 好色之徒

LUSTER or LUSTRE, kwông 光

LUSTY fellow, hao'-hen-ts 好漢

LUXURIANT, meo-zing' 茂盛
LUXURIOUS, shiæ-wô', or sô wæ 奢華
LYE, kæn'-shü' 碱水°

M

MACE, *the coat of nutmegs*, nyüoh-ko' bi 玉菓皮; *a tenth of a Chinese ounce*, ih-din' 一錢°
MACERATE, *to — in water*, shü'-li tsing-t'eo' 水裏浸透
MACHINATION, tsô'-kyi 詐計
MACHINE, kyi-ky'i' 機器
MACKEREL, ts'ing-tsön' 青䱒; *horse —*, mô'-kao-ng 馬鮫°魚°; *very coarse ditto*, hwô-lin-djü' 花鏈鎚°
MAD, vu'-tin 武癲; gwông 狂; fong-tin' 瘋癲; *— dog*, fong wun-kyi' 瘋黄°犬°; tin keo' 癲狗; *— with evil desire*, hwô-tin' 花癲; *to become —*, fah tin' 發癲; fah gwông' 發狂
MADAM, (to a lady of rank), na'-na 奶°奶°; t'a'-t'a 太°太°; (to the wife of teacher), s-meo' 師母
MADE *of wood*, jü' tso-go 樹做个°; *well —*, sang-weh' tso-leh hao' 生°活做得°好
MADEIRA-NUT, or *English walnut*, wu-dao' 胡桃
MADMAN, vu'-tin-ts 武癲子
MADNESS, tin-bing' 癲病; *to feign —*, tsông tin' 裝癲
MAGAZINE, *powder* ho'-yiah gyüoh' 火藥局

MAGENTA, (a color), ngô-læn-'ong' 一°品紅
MAGGOTS, *to breed —*, c'ih djong' 出蟲; sang djong' 生°蟲
MAGIC, fah'-jih 法術
MAGICIAN, yiu fah'-jih go jih-z' 有法術个人°; yiu fah'-lih-go cü'-kwu 有法力个人°
MAGIC-LANTERN, ing'-wô-kying' 映畫鏡 (ih-go)
MAGISTRATE, kwun 官; kwun-fu' 官府; styled, lao'-yia 老爺°; *magistrate's office*, or *residence*, ngô-meng' 衙門; *magistrate's hall*, kong-dông' 公堂; do-dông' 大°堂
MAGNANIMOUS, 'ao-yiah' 豪俠; k'ông'-k'æ 慷慨
MAGNET, hyih'-t'ih-zah 吸鐵石°
MAGNIFICENT, wô-li' 華麗
MAGNIFYING-GLASS, hyin'-vi-kying' 顯微鏡; the same word is used for microscope.
MAGNOLIA, *purple* moh-pih'-hwô 木筆花; *white —*, nyüoh-dông'-hwô 玉堂花
MAGPIE, ô-ts'iah' 鴉鵲 (ih-tsah); *— robin*, hyi'-ts'iah 喜鵲
MAHOMETAN, See MOHAMMEDAN.
MAID, MAIDEN, *girl*, nyiang-ts' 娘子; *miss*, do-kwu'-nyiang 大°姑娘; *old —*, lao do-kwu'-nyiang 老大°姑娘; *slave*, ô-deo' 丫頭; s'-nyü 使女
MAIDENLY, *modest*, iu'-siu 幽靜°; p'ô wông-k'ong' 怕惶恐

MAIL-BAG, sing'-dæ 信袋；— boat, sing-pæn-jün' 信船；— carrier, tseo-sing'-go-nying 走信个°人°; official ditto, tseo-veng-shü'-go-nying' 走文書个°人°。

MAIMED, dzæn-dzih'-go 殘疾个°; to become —, væn dzæn-dzih' 犯殘疾。

MAIN, the — reason, do yün-kwu' 大°緣故; — idea, tsing'-i 正意; da i' 大意; good in the —, da kwe'-mo hao' 大規模好。

MAINTAIN, to hold, siu 守; to keep, pao'-siu 保守; can — it, siu'-leh-djü 守得°住; to support, yiang 養; cong 種; cong-yiang' 種養 (commonly pron. tsong-yiang); — one's family, cong-kô' yiang-kyün' 養家°活口°。

MAJESTY, his wông-zông 皇上; sing-zông' 聖上; cü'-ts 主子; his, or your —, væn'-se 萬歲; his — the present Emperor, tông' kying' wông-zông 當今皇上。

MAJOR (in the army), ts'æn-tsiang' 參將; siu'-be 守備。

MAJOR-GENERAL, tsong'-ping 總兵; cing'-dæ 鎮臺; di-toh' 提督。

MAJORITY, ih-do'-pun' 一大°半; eight parts (out of ten), pah'-feng 八分。

MAJORITY, to reach one's —, zông ting' 上丁; already attained —, dzing-ting' 成丁。

MAKE, to tso 做; to build, zao 造; — clothes, tso i-zông' 做衣裳; — a tower, zao t'ah' 造塔; — a road, k'æ lu' 開路; — it better, long' gyi hao'-tin 弄其好點; to cause, long 弄; s'-teh 使得; cü'-s-teh 致使得; peh 俾°; — him afraid, long' gyi p'ô' 弄其怕; s'-teh gyi p'ô' 使得其怕; — a bill, or account, k'æ tsiang' 開帳; — a bed, p'u' min-zông' 鋪眠床°; — it good, t'ing'-djông 聽償; pu'-wæn 補還; — up (the difference), din 墊; — a league, lih-iah' 立約; — or compel him to do, ah' gyi tso' 押°其做; kwun' gyi tso' 管其做; p'in-sang' iao gyi tso' 偏要其做; — believe, tsông kô' 裝假; — believe cry, tsông kô' kyiao 裝假哭; — peace, ka 'o' 解和; — up one's mind, cü'-i kyüih'-tön 主意決斷; it makes no difference, m̄-kao'; ditto which, feh-leng' 弗論; — (form) an association, hying we' 興會; — rules, lih' fah-tseh' 立法則; lih' kwe-kyü' 立規矩。

MAKER, tso'-go cü'-kwu 做个°人°; flower —, hwô'-s-vu 花司務; God, Hwô'-kong 化工。

MALARIA, doh-ky'i' 毒氣; vu-doh'-ts-ky'i 腐毒之氣。

MALAYS, Mo-lu'-nying 嘆嘈人°。

MALE, nen 男; — child, siao'-

wæn' 小兒°; u-wæn'; — *of animals*, yüong 雄
MALEDICTION, tsiu'-mô 咒罵
MALEFACTOR, væn'-nying 犯人°; ze'-væn 罪犯
MALEVOLENT, oh'-doh 惡毒; *likes others to have trouble*, hwun'-hyi bih'-nying ky'üoh'-kw'u 歡喜別人°吃°苦
MALICIOUS, *injuring without cause*, vu-kwu' 'æ'-nying 無故害人°; — *accusation*, vu-kao' 誣告
MALIGN, *to* pông'-hwe 謗毀
MALIGNANT, hyüong-hyüong'-go 凶个°人; *very* —, hyüong sah'-sah 兇煞; — *disease*, hyüong-bing 凶病
MALLEABLE, hao' tang boh'-go 好打薄个°
MALLET, moh-djü' 木鎚; *heavy* —, lông-deo-djü' 榔頭鎚; jü'-lông-deo' 樹榔頭 (ih-go)
MALTREAT, *to* long-song' 弄唆°; tsiu-tsoh' 收拾; — *greatly*, tsao-t'ah' 蹧蹋
MAMMALIA, ky'üoh-na' keh' ih-le' 吃°嬭這°一類
MAN, nying 人°; *every* —, ko'-ko-nying 個個人°; *all men*, cong'-nying 衆人°; — *of propriety or influence*, do-nying'-do-mô' 大°丈°夫°
MAN OF WAR, ping-jün' 兵船; p'ao'-jün 礮船; tsin'-jün 戰船 (ih-tsah)

MANACLE, *to* ting siu'-k'ao 釘手栲; k'ao siu'-k'ao 栲手栲
MANACLES, siu'-k'ao 手栲 (ih-fu)
MANAGE, *to* bæn 辦; kwun 管; liao-li' 料理; diao-du' 調度; — *affairs*, bæn-z' 辦事; *manages well*, diao-du'-leh hao' 調度得°好; *I can* — *it*, ngô'-hao liao-li' 我好料理; — *a family*, djü kô' 治家; kwun' kô' 管家°
MANAGEMENT, *has good* —, yiu hao en'-fòng 有好安頓°
MANAGER, we-deo' 爲頭; — (of larger affairs), tong'-z 董事; siu'-z 首事
MANCHU, Mun'-tsiu nying' 滿洲人°; — *language*, Mun'-tsiu wô' 滿洲話; — *characters*, Mun'-tsiu z' 滿洲字
MANDARIN, kwun 官; kwun-fu' 官府; kwun-yün' 官員 (ih-we); — *dialect*, kwun'-wô' 官話; — *ducks*, ün'-iang 鴛鴦
MANDATE, *imperial* —, wông'-ming' 皇命; zông-yü' 上諭; sing'-ts 聖旨
MANE *of a horse*, mô'-tsong-mao' 馬鬃毛
MANFULLY, *bravely*, üong'-ken 勇敢; kông-iiong' 剛勇
MANGER, *horse's* mô'-zao 馬槽
MANGY *dog*, fah-la'-keo 癩癩狗
MANGLED, keh'-wu-de 割爛°了°; ng'-hwô pao'-lih-de 五°花爆裂了° .

MANHOOD, arrived at —, zông' ting'-de 上丁了°; dzing-nying'-tsiang-da'-de 成人°長大了°; ditto (in reproach), ts'ih'-dziang'-pah-do' 七長八大°

MANIAC, vu'-tin-ts 武癲子

MANIFEST, ship's jün-cü' pao'-tæn 船主報單; ho'-tæn 貨單

MANIFEST, to hyin 顯; lu 露; piao 表; hyin'-c'ih-læ 顯出來; lu'-c'ih-læ' 露出來

MANIFESTLY, ming-tông'-tông 分°明; hyin'-jün 顯然; hyin'-kyin 顯見

MANIFESTO, imperial wông-pông' 皇榜; official —, kao'-z 告示

MANIFOLD varieties, or changes, ts'in-pin'-væn'-hwô 千變萬化; many forms, to'-leh-kying'-go yiang-shih 多°得緊个°樣式

MANKIND, nying' ih-le' 人°一類; all —, 'en'-t'in-'ô nying' 合°天下°人°

MANLY, ziang hao-hen' ka 像好漢

MANNER, fashion, t'æ'-du 態度; t'i'-t'æ 體態; yiang 樣; in like —, ih-yiang'-go 一樣个°; do it in this —, ka' siang-mao tso' 如°此°做; his — is pleasing, gyi'-go t'æ'-du hao' 其个°態度好; his — of speaking is good, gyi'-go dæn-t'u' hao' 其个°談吐好; — of expressing one's self, kông'-fah 講法; has no manners, m̄-li'-ky'i 無°禮體°

MANNERS, or customs, fong-djoh' 風俗; hyiang-fông' 鄉風°

MANSION, fu'-zông 府上; fu'-di 府第; tseng-fu' 尊府

MANTEL or MANTLE-PIECE, ho'-lu-teng; ho'-lu zông-go koh'-kyi 火爐上个°擱几

MANUFACTORY, tsoh'-dziang 作塲; fông 坊; silk —, kyi-fông 機坊; powder —, ho'-yiah-gyüoh' 火藥局

MANUFACTURE, to cü'-zao 製造

MANURE, bi 肥; feng 糞; liao 料; exchange money for —, wun bi' 換糞; — cakes, k'ông'-sô 坑沙

MANURE, to — land, üong din' 蓬田; to water with —, kyiao bi' 澆糞°

MANUSCRIPT, rough draft, ts'ao'-kao 草稿; the improved —, ts'ing'-kao 清稿

MANY, hyü'-to 許多; yiu'-ho; to 多; zing'-kyi; to-siao'; very —, to-to' 多多; ting-to 頂多; to-to'-ih-jün 多多益善; how — men? to-siao' nying' ni? 多少人°呢; not —, m̄-to-siao 無°多少; feh-to' 弗多; hao-kyi'-go 好幾个°; — times, hyü'-to' tsao'-su 許多回°數; too —, t'eh' to 太°多; — thanks, to zia' 多謝; so —, keb-tang; ka-sing'.

MAP, di-li'-du 地理圖 (ih-go, or if for hang-ing, ih-foh); — of the world, di-gyiu'-du' 地球圖

MAPLE, fong-jü 楓樹 (ih-cü)
MAR, to damage, seng'-sông 損傷; her beauty is marred by the blemish, gyi'-go me'-mao be yüö'-tin ta'-loh 其个°美貌被瑕玷滅°色°; gyi'-go me'-mao be yüö'-tin sô 'æ' 其个°美貌被瑕玷所害
MARBLE, Da-li'-zah 大理石°; T'a'-wu-zah 太湖石°; yüing-zah' 雲石°
MARBLED paper, yüing-zah'-tsin 雲石°箋
MARCHING, tired with —, (or walking), tseo'-vah-liao 走乏了
MARE, ts'-mô' 雌馬 (ih-p'ih)
MARGIN, pin 邊; pin-yin' 邊沿; — of a river, kông' pin-yin' 江°邊沿; — of a leaf, pin-da' 邊; upper — ditto, zông'-kah 上格; t'in-deo'; lower ditto, 'ô'-kah 下格; ti'-kah 底格
MARK, or sign of something, kyi'-nying 記認; kyi'-'ao 記號; trace, or the — of a sore, 'eng-tsih' 痕跡; trace, u 痕; finger —, ts'-tsih u 指跡痕; — of folding, tsih'-u 摺痕; üih'-u 攙痕; ink — (spot), moh-tsih' 墨跡; one's private —, hwô-iah' 花押; hwô-z' 花字; receive the — of a Buddhist priest, ziu ka' 受戒; marks of having been moved, ying-tsih' hao'-ziang dong'-ko-liao 形跡好像動過了

MARK, to make a — as a sign, tso' kyi'-nying 做記認; tso' kyi'-'ao 做記號; to make or leave a mark (or spot), tang tsih' 遭°跡; — perpendicularly (as an incorrect character), dzih 直; — with a hot iron, t'ông kyi'-'ao 燙記號; — with attention, and remember, sing'-li tang' ih-go kyih', kyi'-tih 牢°牢°切記
MARKET, z'-min-zông' 市面上; z'-k'eo 市口; country —, z'-cing 市鎮; — day, z'-nyih 市日°; to come into —(as fruit), zông-z' 上市; have cherries come into —? ang-dao' zông'-leh ma 櫻桃出°了嗎? to go to —, c'ih z' ky'i 出市去°; ditto early in the morning, c'ih tsao' z ky'i' 出早市去°; — price, z'-kô 市價°; — street, ka z' 街市; no — (for it), z' zông m̄ siao-dziang' 市上無°銷塲
MARKETABLE, yiu siao-dziang' 有銷塲; siao'-leh-diao'-go 銷得°去°个°
MARKET-MAN, (the seller), 'ông-fæn' 行販; (the buyer), ma'-bæn 買°辦
MARKING-LINE, carpenter's ink —, moh-sin' 墨線; tailor's powder —, feng'-sin 粉線
MARRIAGE, tso-ts'ing' 做親; dzing-ts'ing' 成親; hao'-nyih 好日°; to consult about a —,

MAR 289 MAS

nyi-ts'ing' 議親; — *contract*, hweng-shü' 婚書; shü-ts' 禮書°; — *dower from the father*, tsông-lin' 粧奩; kô'-tsông 嫁°粧; kô'-ts 嫁奩°;—, *from the bridegroom*, or *his father*, p'ing'-li 聘禮

MARRIED, hao'-nyih-ko'-de 完°姻°過了°; *not yet* —, feh-zing' hao'-nyih-ko 弗曾完姻°; (said of the man), feh-zing' c'ü-ts'ing 弗曾娶親; (said of the woman), feh-zing' ko'-meng' 弗曾過門; vi-dzeng' c'ih-kô' 未曾出嫁°

MARROW, kweh'-si 骨髓

MARRY, to — *a wife*, c'ü-ts'ing' 娶親; t'ao-ts'ing' 迎°親; c'ü lao'-nyüing 娶妻°; dæ lao'-nyüing 撐新°人°;— *a husband*, c'ih-kô' 出嫁°; c'ih-koh' 出閣; tso sing-vu' 做新婦;— *a second wife*, dzoh c'ü' 續娶;— *a second husband*, tsæ' tsiao 再醮

MART, *busy* mô'-deo 馬頭

MARTIAL, vu 武; — *appearance*, vu' siang 武相; — *law*, kyüing fah' 軍法

MARTYR *for one's religion*, we dao'-li cü-ming'-go 爲道理致命个°

MARVELOUS, gyi-kwa' 奇怪°; hyi-gyi' 希奇

MASCULINE, yüong 雄; — *gender*, yüong' ih-lø' 雄一類

MASH, to sông-wu' 舂腐°, nyin'-se 研碎; *to crush*, ah'-wu 壓腐°

MASK, yia'-wu-lin'; *to wear a* —, ta kyü'-lin 帶°鬼°臉

MASON, nyi-shü'-s-vu' 泥水司務; nyi-ziang' 泥匠; *stone* —, zah'-s-vu' 石司務; zah-ziang' 石°匠

MASS, *a lump*, ih-dön' 一團; *to say* —, tso' mi'-sah 做彌撒; *the masses*, cong' pah'-sing 衆百°姓

MASSACRE, *to* sah'-loh 殺戮; — *all in a city*, du-dzing' 屠城; — *a village*, mih ts'eng' 滅村°

MASSIVE, yi-do' yi-djong' 叉°大叉°重

MAST, we 桅; we-ken' 桅杆 (ih-ts)

MASTER *of a house*, cü'-nying-kô' 主人°家°; tông-kô' 當家°; — *workman*, tsoh'-deo 作頭; — *of a shop* (hired), pô'-dæ sin'-sang 當°手°先生°; *ditto who has the capital*, lang'-z; tong-kô' 東家°; *teacher*, sin-sang' 先生°; (politely styled) lao'-fu-ts 老夫子; (native) — *of Arts*, kyü'-nying 舉人°

MASTERS, *he who* — *great difficulties*, *will become a great man*, ziu'-teh kw'u' cong kw'u', fông-we jing-zông'-jing 受得苦中苦方爲人上人

MASTERY, *strive for* —, pih-gying' 比劧

MASTICATE, to ziah 嚼

MAT, zih 蓆; zib-ts' 蓆子 (ih-diao); *rattan table* —, deng-din' 籐墊; — *made from palmetto fibres*, tsong-tsin' 棕荐; *foot* —, t'ô-kyiah'-go din'-ts 刷鞋泥°的°墊子; — *awning*, liang'-bang' 涼棚; — *shed*, bong-ts' 蓬子

MATCH, *lucifer* — z-læ'-ho 自來火; — *box*, z-læ'-ho 'eh-ts' 自°來火盒子; — *paper*, ho'-ts 火紙

MATCH, *a happy — is made in Heaven*, T'in-s' liang-yün' 天賜良緣

MATCH, *to* p'e 配; p'e'-long 配攏; p'e'-dzing 配成; p'e'-zông 配上; — *colors*, p'e'-long ping'-seh 配攏拼色; — *this color*, p'e'keh'-go ngæn-seh' 配這°個°顏°色; *the two are well matched*, liang'-go p'e'-dzing' ih-te' 兩個°配成一對

MATE, *companion*, bun 伴; dong-bun' 同伴; *first — on a ship*, da-fu' 大副; *second* —, nyi-fu' 二°副; *school* —, dong-ts'ông' 同窓; *lost her* — (the pair parted), ts'ah te'-de 拆對了°

MATERIALS, liao-tsoh' 料作; tsoh'-liao 作料

MATERNAL *love*, ah-nyiang'-go dz-sing' 母之°慈心; ah-nyiang-go æ'-sing' 母之°愛心; — *uncle*, nyiang-gyiu' 娘舅; gyiu'-gyiu

舅舅; — *grandfather*, nga-kong' 外°公; *grandmother*, nga-bo' 外°婆

MATHEMATICIAN, *the imperial — and astronomer*, ky'ing-t'in'-kæn 欽天監°

MATHEMATICS, sön'-yüoh or sön'-'oh 算學

MATTER, *the essence of* —, tsih 質; *properties of* —, væn-veh'-go sing'-tsih 萬物個°性質; *what's the* —? sah'-go z-ken' 甚°麼°事幹? *trifling* —, siao' z 小°事; *pus*, nong 膿; ao-tsao' 墺糟

MATTING, di-zih' 地蓆; — *in the long piece*, do-bæn'-deo, tsing-kw'e' zih 一°大°爿°正塊之°席; *a roll of* — (large), ih-dön' zih; ih-kw'eng' zih 一捆蓆; *coarse — for wrapping*, bu-pao' 蒲包

MATURE *in knowledge*, cü'-sih joh' 知識熟; — *fruit*, ko'-ts joh' 菓子熟; *that child is very* —, keh'-go siao nying' yiu do nying' t'i'-liao 這個小孩°有大°人°體統°

MATURITY, *arrived at years of* —, do-tsoh'-de 大°足了°; dziang-tsoh'-de 長足了°

MAXIM, keh'-yin 格言

MAY *do it*, k'o-yi tso' 可以做; hao' tso 好做; bao'-s-teh 好使得; — *be so*, 'oh-tsia' z-ka' 或者°如°此°

ME, ngô 我; *he told* —, gyi' wô-hyiang-ngô'-ko'-de 其向我話過了°; gyi teng' ngô' wô-ko'-de 其與°我話過了°

MEAL, a ih-djü' 一筯; ih-ts'æn' 一餐; ih-teng' 一頓; — of rice, ih-djü væn' 一筯飯

MEAL, feng 粉; corn, loh-koh' feng 稑穀粉; wheat flour, min-feng' 麪粉

MEAN about little things, si'-si se-se' 細細碎碎; low, ti-vi' 低微; pe-zin' 卑賤; 'ô'-zin 下°賤°; stingy, sing'-jih pi'-si 心術鄙細; — action, 'ô'-tsoh 'ang-we' 下°作行°為; — spirit-ed, ky'i'-liang 'ah-tsah' 氣量狹窄; k'æn-kyiang'.

MEAN, to intend, siang 想; what do you — to do? ng' siang tso soh'-si 你°想做甚°麼°? what do you —? ng' yiu soh'-go i'-s 你°有甚°麼°意思?

MEANING, i'-s 意思; ka'-shih 解說; saying one thing, — another, k'eo' feh te' sing 口弗對心; yiu' k'eo m̄ sing' 有口無°心

MEANLY, to treat a person —, boh-dæ' nying-kô' 薄待人°家°

MEANS to an end, fông-fah' 方法; fah'-ts 法子; no — of attaining, m̄'-neh fah'-ts hao teh'-djoh 沒有°法子好得著; by no —, bing'-fi 並非; bing'-feh-z 並弗是; by all —, vu-pih'-ts 務必

MEAN-TIME, in the —, ts'ing wông' feh tsih-gao' z-'eo' 青黃不°接°時候

MEASLES, ts'u'-ts 痄子; sick with the —, c'ih' ts'u'-ts 出痄子

MEASURE, to — in feet and inch-es, liang ts'ah'-ts'eng 量尺寸; — and see, liang-liang'-k'en 量量看; — in pints, liang sing-teo' 量升斗

MEASURE and compare length, in 賬; — and see, in'-in k'en' 賬賬看; — by the foot, &c., liang 量; — by the eye, kwu'-kwu-k'en' 估估看; — land, or boats, dziang'-liang 丈量; — the per-son*, liang sing-kô' 量身架

* The Chinese do not measure the person except in the case of criminals.

MEASURE, quart — (nearly), ih-sing' 一升; 10 quarts, ih-teo' 一斗; 10 teo, ih-zah' 一石; do according to the — of your ability, liang-lih' r-ying' 量力而行 (veng.)

MEASURING, the art, or way of —, liang-fah' 量法

MEAT, nyüoh* 肉; lean —, tsing-nyüoh' 精肉°

* Nyüoh used alone signifies pork.

MECHANIC, s-vu' 司務

MEDDLE, to — with other people's affairs, kwun 'æn-tsiang' 管閒°帳; need not — with my af-fairs, hao-vong' kwun ngô'-go 'æn-tsiang' 不°用管我个°

MED 292 MEM

開帳; — in conversation, ts'ah-cü' 謠嘴; ts'ah-yiu' 謠言
MEDDLESOME in affairs, to-kwun' 'æn-tsiang 多管閒帳; to-z'-go 多事个°; — in touching, ts'ih'-siu pah-kyiah' 七手八腳; — in answering when not wanted, ts'ih-tah' pah-tah' 七嗒八嗒
MEDIATE, to ts'ah-ky'ün' 謠勸
MEDIATOR, Cong-pao' 中保; to act as a — in making peace, tso 'o-z' nying 做和事人°
MEDICINE, yiah 藥; to take —, ky'üoh yiah' 吃藥; feel the effect of —, teh' yiah lih' 得藥力; the study of — (healing), i-yüoh' 醫學
MEDITATE, to think quietly, zing-zing'-go ts'eng' 靜靜个°忖; secretly — doing, en'-di shih-siang' 暗地設°想
MEDIUM, observe a due —, tsiah'-wu-gyi-cong 酌乎其中
MEDLEY of things, tong-si' se'-zeh 東西碎雜; zeh'-keh-leng'-teng tong-si' 雜件°東西
MEEK, weng-ziu' 溫柔; weng-'o' 溫和
MEET, to p'ong'-djoh 逢°着°; nyü-djoh' 過着°; we-djoh' 會着°; — accidentally, ngeo'-jün p'ong'-djoh 偶然逢°着°; — suddenly, or for the first time, p'ih-min k'en-kyin 劈面看見; — (again) tomorrow, ming-tsiao' we' 明朝會; to go to —,

nying-tsih' 迎接; failed to —, we'-fch-kyin' 會弗見; to assemble, jü'-long 聚攏; kwe-long' 歸攏; to befall one, tsao-djoh' 遭着°; ling-djoh' 臨着°; — with an accident, tsao'-djoh hwe'-ky'i 遭着°晦氣
MELANCHOLY, iu-üoh' 憂鬱; meng-meng'-peh-loh' 悶悶不樂
MELLOW, nen-joh' 軟°熟
MELODY, ing-yüing' diao-'o' 音韻調和; — of instruments, ing-yüoh' diao-'o' 音樂調和
MELON, kwô 瓜; water — seeds, kwô-ts' 瓜子
MELT, to sah; yiang-k'æ' 煬開; hwô'-k'æ 化開; — silver, sah nying'-ts 煬°銀子
MEMBERS of the body, ts-t'i' 肢體; all the ditto, s'-ts-pah'-t'i' 四肢百°體; church —, kyiao'-yiu 教友
MEMOIR, 'ang-jih' 行述; brief —, djün 傳; the — of Confucius, K'ong'-fu-ts-go 'ang-jih' 孔夫子个°行述
MEMORABLE, üong' feh mông-kyi' 永弗忘°記; ts'ih'-kyi-dzæ-sing 切記在心
MEMORANDUM-BOOK, dzeng-kyi'-bu 存記簿
MEMORIAL (to officials), dzing-dz' 呈詞; ping'-tæn 稟單; — from higher officers, to the emperor, tseo'-tsông 奏章; peng'-tsông 本章

MEMORY, kyi'-sing 記性; excellent — (see, then remember), ko'-moh-peh-vông' 過目不忘

MENCIUS, Mang'-fu-ts 孟夫子

MEND, to ts'eh'-dzæn 攝綻; siu-pu' 修補; to patch, pu 補;— (darn), kang 耕°; to repair, siu 修; siu-li' 修理;— stockings, kang mah' 耕襪; ditto by patching, pu mah';— bowls, &c. (with nails), ting un' 釘碗; If we do not — the little holes, the big holes will cry out bitterly, "siao dong' feh pu', do dong kyiao kw'u" 忽° 小害°大°;— by stitching together, vong-tæn'-long 縫攏

MENSES, yüih-kying' 月經; yüih-kô' 月°家°; to have —(at first), kyi-sing cün 身體'轉; suppression of —, yüih-kying' ding-tsih' 月經停積

MENTAL ability, dzæ-neng' 才能; dzæ-'oh' 才學°;— effort, lao-sing' 勞心; to use ditto, yüong sing-kyi' 用心機

MENTION, to di-ky'i' 提起; need not — names, feh pih'- di-ky'i' ming-deo' 弗必提起名頭

MERCENARY, tsih-ts'eng' dong-din' 只忖銅錢; li'-sing djong' 利心重

MERCHANDIZE, ho'-veh 貨物; foreign —, yiang ho' 洋貨

MERCHANT, sông 商; sông-kô' 商家; traveling —, k'ah'-sông 客商; k'ah'-nying 客人;

silk —, s-sông'-kô 絲商; he is a traveling —, gyi tso k'ah we sông 其出°門°爲商

MERCIFUL, dz-pe'-go 慈悲个°; nyün'-sing-dziang'-go 軟心腸个°

MERCILESS, sing oh' 心惡; sing-heng' 心狠; vu dz-sing' go 無慈心个°

MERCURY, shü'-nying 水°銀

MERCY, dz-pe' 慈悲; the goddess of —, Kwun-ing' bu-sah' 觀音菩薩

MERELY, tæn-tsih' 單只; peh-ko' 不過; tæn-z' 單是; tsih'-z 只是; kwông'-z 光是

MERIDIAN, (noon), cong-wu'-sin 中午線;— of longitude, kying-sin' 經線

MERIT, kong-teh' 功德; kong-lao' 功勞; reputation on account of —, kong-ming' 功名

MERIT, to ing-kæ' teh'-djoh 應該得若°; merits reward, li kæ ts'ing-sông' 理該請賞

MERITED, ing-teh'-go 應得个°

MERRY, p'ao'-c'ing 不°勝歡°喜°; kw'a-weh siao-yiao' 快活逍遙

MESHES, ngæn'-ts 眼洞°; small —, ngæn'-ts mih-kying' 眼洞°密緊; large —, ngæn'-ts hyi 眼洞°稀

MESSAGE, verbal k'eo'-sing 口信; want you to take a —, iao ng' ta ih-go k'eo'-sing 要你°

帶°一个° 口信; take a — for me, teng ngô' djün ih-kyü wô' 替°我傳一句話
MESSENGER, ts'a-s' 差使; — with letters, di-sing'-go-nying 遞信个°人°
METALS, ng'-kying keh-le' 五°金這°一°類
METAMORPHOSIS, pin'-hwô 變化; — of insects, hwô'-seng 化生
METAPHOR, tsia'-yüong-go pi'-fông 借°用个°比方
METEMPSYCHOSIS, loh-dao' 六道; (one kind of) —, deo' t'æ 投胎; the six kinds of —, loh'-dao leng-we' 六道輪迴
METEOR, yi-sing' 移星; fi-sing' 飛星; liu-sing' 流星
METHOD, fông-fah' 方法; fah'-ts 法子; fah'-tseh 法則; excellent —, miao' fah 妙法
METHODICAL, en'-bu-dziu-pæn' 按部就班; — in time, or order, en'-pæn-ts 按班子
METROPOLIS, the capital, tu-dzing' 都城; kying-tu' 京都; kying-dzing 京城
MEW, to ñyiao.
MIASMA, ẅeng-ky'i' 瘟氣; tsông'-ky'i 瘴氣
MICA, foliated ts'in'-zeng-ts' 千層紙
MICROSCOPE, hyin'-vi-kying 顯微鏡 (ih-go, ih-kô)
MIDDAY, tông tsiu'-ko 當晝;

tsing'-wu-z 正午時; just at —, jih-tông' cong wu' 日當中午
MIDDLE, cong-nyiang' 中央°; tông-cong' 當中; tông-cong-nyiang' 當中央°; — of any thing, cong-sing' 中心; in the — of them, ne cong' 內中; — aged, cong-nyin' 中年; — man, cong-nying' 中人°; ditto in planning a marriage, me-nying' 媒人°
MIDDLING, cong-teng' 中等; tsiah'-cong 酌中; pun'-cong-tsiah 半中; cong-bing' 中平; bing-teng' 平等
MIDNIGHT, pun'-yia-ko 半夜°過
MIDWIFE, siu-sang'-bo 收生°婆; tsih-sang'-go 接生'个°; (styled) lao'-nyiang 老娘; nga-bo'.
MIGHT, power, gyün-ping' 權柄; — of body, lih-ky'i' 力氣; gying-dao' 勁道
MIGRATE, to tao bih' c'ü ky'i 到別處去; birds — to the south, tiao fi-ko nen' 鳥飛過南
MILD, ẅeng-'o' 溫和; — disposition, sing'-dzing ẅeng-'o' 性情溫和; sing-ky'i' 'o-bing' 性氣和平; næ-sing'-næ-siang' 耐心耐想; — weather, t'in 'o-nön' 天和暖
MILDEW, to fæn 翻; fah 發; fah-me' 發霉; time for —, tso me' z-'eo' 做霉時候; to spoil with —, me'-diao 霉壞; rot with —, me'-læn 霉爛

MILDEWED, fah'-c'ih-de 發出了°; fah-pæn'-de 發斑了°; fah-pæn-tin'-de 發斑點了°
MILE (Chinese, about one third of an English —), ih li' 一里
MILITARY officers, vu'-kwun 武官; — art, vu' nyi 武藝
MILITIA, hyiang-yüong' 鄉勇
MILK, na 嬭 or 奶; yellow cow's —, wông-ngeo na 黃牛嬭; buffalo's —, shü'-ngeo na 水牛°嬭; deer's —, jü'-loh 乳酪
MILK, to dziu-na' 抔嬭; te-na' 滴嬭
MILKMAN, ma-ngeo-na'-nying 賣牛°嬭人°
MILKY-WAY, t'in-'o' 天河
MILL, stone mo 磨; wooden — for hulling grain, long 礱 (ih-djü'); buffalo ditto, nyin'-ts 碾子 (ih-go); flour —, and room, lo-mo'-fông 羅磨坊
MILLET, (generic name) kao-liang' 膏梁 fine yellow —, soh 粟; siao'-mi 小米; red —, lu-tsi' 穄穄
MILLION, a ih-pah' væn 一百°萬; ih-ziao 一兆; ten millions, ts'in væn' 千萬
MIMIC, to k'en-yiang'-'oh-yiang' 看樣學°樣; mimics well, 'oh-leh ziang' 學°得°像; tsông-leh ziang' 甓得°像
MINCE, to hash fine, tsæn se' 切°碎; minced meat, tsæn-leh se'-se-

go nyüoh' 切°得°細°碎个°肉°
MIND, the intellect, sing-kyi' 心機; fine —, sing-kyi' ling-ky'iao' 心機靈巧; — or heart, sing 心; sing-di' 心地; — made up, cü'-i ding'-de 主意定了°; out of one's —, shih-sing'-de 失心了°; sing wu'-de 心糊了°; engraven on the —, sing'-li k'eh'-tih 心裡刻的; — confused, sing lön' 心亂; wu-li'-wu-du' 霧裡糊塗; to put him in —, di-gyi deo' 提其頭; to keep in —, fông' læ sing zông' 放在°心上; dze sing' 在心
MIND, to obey, t'ing'-dzong 聽從; t'ing 聽; i 依; i-dzong' 依從; do not — it, k'o-yi feh pih' dze i' 可以弗必在意; to attend to, tông-sing' 當心; liu-sing' 留心; yüong sing' 用心; dziah' læ i'-li 著意; — your own business, siu ng'-go peng'-veng 守你°个°本分; ditto, in a good sense, en-veng'-siu-kyi' 安分守己
MINE, ngô'-go 我个°; that book is —, keh'-peng shü z ngô'-go 這本書是我个°
MINE, gold kying sæn' 金山; coal —, me-k'ang' 煤坑; me-yiao' 煤密; me-sæn' 煤山
MINER in coal, k'æ me-t'æn'-go nying' 開煤礦°个人°; —for gold, dao-kying-sô'-go 淘金沙个°

MINERALOGY, kying-zah'-go 'oh-veng' 金石个學問; kying-zih' ts-yüoh' 金石之學 (veng.)
MINGLE, to 'o-tæn'-long 和攏; to blend, diao-'o' 調和
MINISTER of state, da-dzing' 大臣; prime —, tsœ'-siang 宰相; cong-dông' 中堂; — of religion, kyiao'-s 教師
MINISTER, to serve, voh-z' 服事; to wait upon, tông-dzih' 當值; — to one's wants, tsiao'-ing 照應; tsiao'-kwun 照管; tsiao'-kwu 照顧
MINOR, under age, nyin-ky'ing'-go 年輕个; nyin-siao'-go 年少个; nyin-iu'-go 年幼个
MINSTREL, dæn-ts'ông'-go nying 彈唱个人
MINT (for cash), cü'-dzin-gyüob 鑄錢局; peppermint, bo-ho' 薄荷
MINUTE (in time), ih feng' 一分; — hand, dziang-tsing' 長針; minutes of a meeting, tsông-dzing' 章程;
MINUTE, si'-si 細細; dzih-si'-si 極細; mi-mi kwun' do ziang hwe' ka 細如灰
MINUTELY, ts'-si 仔細; dziang-si' 詳細; to investigate —, ts'-si dzô-ts'ah' 仔細查察
MIRACLE, jing-tsih' 神跡; ling-tsih' 靈跡; to work a —, 'ang jing-tsih' 行神跡
MIRE, wu na-nyi' 糊坭; wu-nyi-tsiang' 糊坭漿

MIRROR, kying'-ts 鏡子; large —, tsiah'-i-kying 著衣鏡 (ih-min)
MIRTH, hyi'-siao-yin-k'æ' 喜笑顏開; noisy —, ho-lo'-da-siao' 呵呵大笑
MISANTHROPIC, u'-su cong'-nying-go 惡衆人个
MISAPPREHEND, to li'-we-ts'o' 理會錯; — (in hearing), t'ing ts'o' 聽錯
MISBEHAVE, to feh-siu-veng' 弗守分; feh-en-veng' 弗安分; — one's self, feh en-veng' siu-kyi' 弗安分守己
MISCALCULATE, to sön'-ts'o 算錯; iah'-ts'o 約錯
MISCALL, to eo-ts'o' 叫錯; eo-dzæn 叫綻
MISCARRIAGE, siao'-ts'æn 小產; do-loh' 墮產
MISCELLANEOUS, koh-seh' koh-yiang 各色各樣; zeh'-keh leng'-teng 雜件; zeh-leng-kwu'-teng 零星什物; — articles, zeh-gyih' tong-si 雜件東西; small ditto, se'-gyin tong'-si 碎件東西
MISCHIEF, to do — to things, sông-'æ' tong-si' 傷害東西; to make — (or great trouble), tsiao-'o' 招禍; jô 'o' 惹禍; seng-z'-ts'ông-'o' 生事閙禍; tattling is sure to make —, pun-teo shih'-wô pih' to z'-fi 搬說話必多是非
MISCHIEVOUS, nyih-siu', nyih-

kyiah' 開°手開°脚; *will do harm,* iao ts'ông 'o' go 要鬧禍个°; — *disposition,* ts'ông 'o' p'e 鬧禍胚; — *like a monkey,* ziang weh-seng' ka 像猢猻樣°式°

MISCONDUCT, peh-tön' 'ang-we 不端行爲; 'ang-we' feh loh'-dzih 行爲弗直

MISCOUNT, *to* su-ts'o' 數錯; su-dzæn' 數綻

MISER, k'en'-dzæ-nu' 看財奴

MISERABLE, kw'u'-leh k'o'-lin 苦得°可憐

MISERLY, pi'-si-go 鄙細个°

MISERY, kw'u'-næn 苦難; wæn'-næn 患難; tsæ-næn' 災難; 'o'-næn 禍難

MISFORTUNE, feh kyih'-li z-ken' 弗吉利事幹; feh jing'-liu z'-t'i 弗順溜事體; *to meet with a* —, p'ong'-djoh hwe'-ky'i z-ken' 逢°着°晦氣事幹

MISGIVINGS, ts'æ-nyi' 猜疑; *have a* —, yiu ts'æ-nyi' sing 有猜疑心

MISGOVERN, *to* kwun'-li feh hao' 管理弗好; — (as an official), djü-li' pah'-sing ky'in' hao 治理百姓弗°好

MISINTERPRET, *to* ziang'-diao 詳掉°

MISJUDGE, *to* liao-ts'o' 料錯; k'en-ts'o' 看錯; *I misjudged him,* ngô ts'o', liao-gyi-feh-tao' 我錯料其弗到

MISLAY, *to place wrongly,* fông'-ts'o 放錯; fông'-dzæn 放綻;

to forget or *not know where laid,* feh'-tsiao en' le 'ah-li' 弗知°安在°何°處°

MISLEAD, *to* ta'-li-ts'o' 帶累錯; *he misled me,* gyi ta'-li ngô ts'o' 其帶°累我錯; gyi 'æ'-ngô-ts'o' 其害我錯

MISMANAGE, *to* diao-du' feh hao' 調度弗好; bæn-li' feh-hao' 辦理弗好

MISPLACE, *to* fông'-ts'o 放錯; en-ts'o' 安錯

MISREPRESENT, *to* lön-shih'-tiao-pi' 亂說刁疲°; wu-yin'-lön-dao' 胡言亂道

MISS, kwu-nyiang' 姑娘; *an officer's daughter,* siao'-tsia 小姐

MISS, *to* — *in throwing,* tiu feh-djoh' 丟弗着°; —*in firing, &c.,* tang'-feh-djoh 打弗着°; — *by omitting,* ts'o'-loh 錯落; — *an opportunity,* ts'o'-ko kyi-we' 錯過機會

MISSING, feh-kyin'-de 弗見了°; m-dziah'-loh 無°着°落

MISSPEND, *to* yüong-ts'o' 用錯; *to squander money,* lông'-fi 浪費; — *time,* ts'o'-ko kwông-ing' 錯過光陰

MIST, vi-vi'-si'-yü 微微細雨; yü'-mao-s' 雨絲; — *is falling,* læ-tih loh yü'-mao-s' 正在°下°雨絲

MISTAKE, ts'o 錯; ts'o'-c'ü 錯處; dzæn 綻; *has many mistakes,* ts'o'-c'ü to-leh-kying' 錯

處多得°緊; ts'ih'-dzæn pah-dzæn' 七綻八綻; ts'ih'-ts'o pah'-ts'o 七錯八錯

MISTAKE, to ts'o'-ts'oh 錯錯°; siang'-ts'o 想錯 (See Wrong); k'en'-ts'o 看錯; — in recognizing a person, nying-ts'o' 認°錯; — in speaking, kông'-ts'o 講°錯

MISTER, or MR., (to teachers, and generally to all but artizans), Sin-sang' 先生°; (to officers), lao'-yia 老爺°; (to mechanics), s-vu' 司務

MISTRESS, or MRS., (to a teacher's wife), s-meo' 師母; (to an officer's wife), na'-na 奶奶; (to an officer's mother), t'a'-t'a 太°太°; — of a house, nyü tong'-kô 女東家; tong-kô' 東家°; lang-z-bo'; Mrs Wông, Wông-s-meo' 王師母; Wông'-kô-sao 王家°嫂

MISTRUST, to sing'-li nyi-'oh' 心裡疑惑; half trust, half —, pun'-sing pun-nyi' 半信半疑

MISUNDERSTAND, to i'-s feh-tong' 意思弗懂; to hear wrong, t'ing'-ts'o 聽錯

MISUSE, to dæ-wa' 待孬°; k'eh'-boh dæ 刻薄待; 'æ 害

MITIGATE, to kæn-ky'ing' 減°輕

MIX, to 'o-long' 和攏; 'o-tæn-long'; c'ün'-long 攛攏; — (as medicines), keh'-long 合°攏; — smoothly, 'o-leh diao-yüing' 和得°調勻; diao-'o' 調和

MIXED, jumbled, kah'-dzeh 夾°雜; — as men and women sitting together, weng'-dzeh 混雜; — confusedly, zeh-ts'ih' zeh-pah' 雜七雜八

MOAT, city 'ao-'o' 濠河; dzing-'o' 城河; wall and —, dzing-dzi' 城池

MOB, to nao-z' 鬧事; the —, yia'-ky'i pah'-sing 野°民°; the expedients of a — are numberless, mæn'-fah sæn'-ts'in 蠻法三千

MOCK, to tsao-siao' 嘲笑; c'ü'-siao 取笑

MOCK elephant, tsông-bah-ziang' 裝扮°白°象

MODEL, form, or mold, mo-ts' 模子; mo-yiang' 模樣; pattern, yiang'-ts 樣子

MODEL, to form after a —, tsiao mo'-ts tso' 照模子做; — in clay, su 塑

MODERATE, is yiu tsih'-cü 有節制; be —, yüong-tsih'-cü 用節制; not too much, nor too little, feh-to' feh-siao' 弗多弗少

MODERATE, to restrain, ah'-djü 壓住; tsu'-djü 阻住; — the fire, ho' long-leh iu'-tin 火弄得°幽點

MODERATION, siu-lin' 收斂; tsih'-cü 節制; prudence, kying-wo' 經緯; person of —, nying yiu tsih-cü 人°有節制; fond of —, æ siu-lin-go 愛

收歛个°; *having no —* , 弗-tsih'-cü-go 無°節制个°; 弗-kying-we'-go 無°經緯个°.

MODERN *style*, z-shih' 時式°; z-kw'un' 時款; *— times*, tông kying' z-shü 當今時世; *— times are not equal to the ancient*, kying-næn'- kæn peh-jü kwu-z-tsin' 今不如古

MODEST, yiu lin-c'ü' 有廉耻; iao lin-c'ü' 要廉耻; min-bi boh' 面皮薄; *— (as a girl)*, p'ô iu'-siu 怕羞

MODULATE, *to — the voice*, sing-ing' p'e'-teh diao-yüing' 聲音配搭調勻

MOHAMMEDAN, We-ts' 回子 (ih-go) *not respectful*.

MOHAMMEDANISM, We-we'-kyiao 回回敎

MOIST, dziao 潮; dziao-sih' 潮濕; *just — enough, as fresh food, &c.*, ts-jing' 滋潤; *to become —* , fæn dziao' 汎潮; wæn dziao' 還潮

MOISTEN, *to* long-long' sib 弄弄濕; peh gyi ts-jing' 俾°其滋潤; *to be moistened by rain*, ling-sih' 淋濕

MOISTURE, dziao-sih' 潮濕; sih'-ky'i 濕氣; *much —* , dziao-sih' to' 潮濕多

MOLASSES, dông-lu' 糖滷

MOLD, MOULD, *soft earth*, hao' nyi-nyüoh' 好坭; *thick skinny — (from damp)*, bah-fu' 白°殕; pæn-mao' 斑毛; *spoiled from —* , me-læn'-de 霉爛了°

MOLD, MOULD, mo'-ts 模子; mo'-yiang 模樣; su'-ts 塑子

MOLD, MOULD, *to* fah'-c'ih 發出; *— (with hairs)*, fah-pæn-mao' 發斑毛; fah hwô' 發花; *to — a vessel*, dzing ky'i' 成器; *— (as clay)*, nyiah 揑; su'-c'ih-læ 塑出來; *to cast*, cü'-c'ih-læ 鑄出來; kyiao-c'ih'-læ 澆出來

MOLDER, MOULDER, *to —away, (as wood, stone, &c.)*, dzin'-dzin siao-mo' 漸漸消磨; *— (as dead bodies, &c.)*, dzin'-dzin siao-hwô' 漸漸消化

MOLDY, MOULDY, fah'- c'ih-de 發出了°; fah-bah-fu'-de 發白°殕了°; fah-pæn-mao'-de 發斑毛了°

MOLEST, *to* næn-we' 難爲

MOLT, MOULT, *to* t'eng mao' 褪毛; wun-mao' 換毛

MOMENT, *a* ih-hyih' kong-fu' 一歇工夫; ih-sin' kong-fu' 一線工夫; ih-tin' kong-fu' 一點工夫; *wait a —* , teng' ih-hyih' 等一歇

MONARCH, kyüing-wông' 君王; wông-ti' 皇帝

MONARCHY, kyüing-cü'-ts koh' 君主之國

MONASTERY, *Buddhist* z 寺; en 菴; *Taoist —* , kwun 觀

MONDAY, li-pa-ih' 禮拜°一; *(according to the Roman Catholics)*, tsin-li-nyi' 瞻禮二°

MONEY, *silver*, nying-ts' 銀子; nying-dzin' 銀錢; *cash*, dong-din' 銅錢°; *dollars*, fæn-ping' 番餅; *travelling* —, bun-jün' 盤纏°

MONEY-BOX, dzin-dong' 錢筒; dzin-teo' 錢斗

MONEY-CHANGER, dzin-tin'-kwun 錢店主°人°; *ditto's shop*, dzin-tin' 錢店; *ditto small*, yin-de'-tin 現兌店

MONEY-LENDER, fông-nying-bun'-go 放銀盤利°; fông-dong-din'-go 放銅錢°个°; fông-tsa'-go 放債°个°

MONGOLIAN, Mong-kwu'-nying' 蒙古人°; Dah-ts' 韃子

MONK, *Buddhist* seng-kô' 僧家'; 'o-zông 和尚; *Taoist* —, dao'-z 道士; dao'-kô 道家°; siu-dao'-z 修道士; *Roman Catholic monks* are styled, siang'-kong 相公

MONKEY, weh-seng' 猢°猻; 'eo 猴

MONOPOLIZE, *to* — (in trade), deng'-tsih 囤積

MONOPOLY, *to have a* — *of*, doh-kwæn', doh-sah' 獨關獨塞

MONSOON, *S. W.* si-nen' fong 西南風; *N. E.* — tong-poh' fong 東北風

MONSTER, (departing from the usual type), gyi-ying'-kwæ-ziang' 奇形怪°狀°

MONSTROUS, *large*, c'ih'-kah do 出格大°

MONTH, *a* ih-ko yüih' 一個月; *the first day of the* —, ts'u-ih' 初一; *the beginning of the* —, yüih-ts'u' 月初; *the middle of the* —, yüih-pun' 月半; yüih-pun-keng' 月半跟; yüih-cong' 月中; *the end of the* —, yüih-ti' 月底

MONTHLY, yüih-yüih' 月月; me'-yüih 每月

MONUMENT, pe 碑; *slab*, pe-ba' 碑牌; — *of antiquity*, kwu'-tsih 古蹟

MOOD, *temper*, sing'-dzing 性情; *in pleasant* — (*time*), hwun-hyi' z-'eo' 歡喜時候

MOON, yüih-liang 月亮; *new* —, ngo-me' yüih 蛾眉月; *full* —, yüih-liang' dön-yün' 月亮團圓; yüih-liang' tsing'-dön-yün' 月亮正團圓

MOONLIGHT, yüih-kwông' 月光

MOOR, *to* — *a boat*, boh jün' 泊°船

MOPE, *to* kæn'-we-jing-z' 懶爲人事

MORAL, *agreeing with the right*, tsing'-kying 正經; tön-tsing' 端正; tsing'-p'a 正派°; *the* — (*of a tale*), ih-go yüong-dziang' 一個用塲; *the Chinese* — *law*, ng'-dzông 五°常 viz. love, justice, politeness, knowledge, and truth.

MORAL essays, ky'ün'-shü-veng' 勸世文; jün-shü' 善書
MORALITY, to exhort to —, ky'ün nying' we jün' 勸人爲善; to practise —, 'ang jün' 行°善
MORE, to 多; a little —, to' tin 多點; to' ih-ngæn 多一點; liah-liah' to'-tin 略略多點; sao'-we to'-tin 稍爲多點; siao-shü' to'-tin 少許多點; shü-vi' to'-tin 些微多點; have (you) any —? wa-yiu' ma 還°有嗎°? — than ten, jih to 十多; still —, yüih-fah' to 越發多; yü-kô' to 愈加多; keng'-kô to' 更加°多; still — difficult, yüih-fah næn' 越發難; — than one, feh ts' ih'-go 弗止一個°; the — the better, yüih to' yüih hao' 越多越好; how much —, (also how much less), 'o-hwông' 何況; if I can walk it how much — should you (be able to), ngô' tseo-leh-ky'i', 'o-hwông' ng' ni 我走得°去°何況你°呢
MOREOVER, hwông'-ts'ia 況且°; ping'-ts'ia 拼且°; r-ts'ia' 而且°; tsæ-wô' 再話
MORNING, t'in-liang' or t'in'-nyiang 天亮; early in the —, tsao'-t'in-liang' 早天亮; ditto (seven or eight o'clock), ts'ing-tsao' 清早; the forenoon, zông-pun'-nyih 上半日°; the middle of the —, tsao'-pun-zông' 早半

日°; — star, ng'- kang-hyiao 五°更°曉
MOROSE, sour tempered, geng-cü'-cü; — in countenance, min-k'ong' pæn'-pæn-go 面孔板個°
MORROW, ming-tsiao' 明朝
MORSEL, ih tin-tin' 一點點; ih ti'-ti 一滴滴; a mouthful, ih-k'eo' 一口
MORTAL, we-si'-go 會死°個°
MORTAR, nyin-bu-tsu' 石°臼°; large —, tao'-gyiu 搗臼 (ih-bu); — for mixing medicines, jü-peh' 堅鉢; the pestle, but used for either pestle or —, tao-ts-den' 杵° (ih-go); lime cement, diao-hao'-liao-go zah-hwe' 調好個°石°灰
MORTGAGE, ti'-ah ky'i' 抵押°契; ti'-ah kyü' 抵押°據; tin'-ky'i 典契
MORTGAGE, to — as security for debt, ti'-ah 抵押°; to lease for a certain time and sum, and, at the end of the time, give up the property and receive the money back, tin 典; — a wife, tin lao'-nyüing 典女°人
MORTIFIED flesh, si nyüoh' 死°肉°; wu nyüoh' 瘀°肉°
MORTIFY, to — him, peh gyi t'æn-dæ 俾其坍臺; extremely mortified (ashamed), wông-k'ong'-vu-di' 惶恐無地; wông-k'ong'-m̄-c'ü-ky'i' 惶恐無°處去°

MORTISE, shing'-deo 榫頭; — *fitting exactly*, teo shing' 合°榫

MOSQUITO, meng-djong' 蚊°蟲; — *curtain*, tsiang'-ts 帳子; — *brush*, meng-djong' tæn'-tsiu 揮蚊°蟲个°箒

MOSS, i; ts'ing-i; ts'ing-dæ' 青苔

MOST, *very*, ting 頂; tse 最; gyih 極; — *excellent*, ting' hao 頂好; gyih hao' 極好; dzih miao' 絕妙; kyü tse' 居最; kyü ting' 居頂; *he* (has) *the* —, gyi, ting' to' 其頂多; *the* —, *or the greater part*, ih do pun' 一大°半; — *of the night*, pun' yia to' 半夜°多

MOSTLY *good*, kyiu' feng hao' 九分好; jih-yiu-kyiu' hao' 十有九好

MOTH, *any insect which eats clothes, wood, &c.*, cü-djong' 蛀蟲; *candle* —, fi-ngo'; p'i-sông'- wu- diah' 撲°燈°蛾

MOTHER, ah-nyiang' 阿娘; ah'- mô 阿媽; mô' or m̀-mô; (respectful) meo'-lao 老母; (in writing) meo'-tsing 母親; *my deceased* —, sin-meo' 先母; *my* —, kô-meo' 家°母; *your* —, ling-dông' 令堂; lao' t'a- t'a 老太°太°; *mother's older sister*, yi-mô' 姨媽; *mother's younger sister*, siao'-yi 小姨; *mother's brother*, gyiu'-gyiu 舅舅; *wife's* —, dziang'-m̀ 丈母°; ngoh-meo' 岳母; *husband's* —,

ah-bo' 阿婆; nyiang'-nyiang 娘娘

MOTHER OF PEARL, yüing-meo' k'oh' 雲母殻; — *shell*, lo- din 螺鈿

MOTION, *in* læ'-tih dong 正°在°動; (as a man, boat, &c.), læ'- tih 'ang-dong' 正°在行°動

MOTIONLESS, ih-ngæn' feh-dong' 一點°弗動; dong-'a'-feh-dong' 動也°弗動; *sit perfectly* —, zo'-jü T'a'-sæn 坐如泰山

MOTIVE, i'-kyin 意見; i'-s 意思; *has a* —, yiu sing 有心

MOTLEY, ng'-ngæn-loh-seh' 五顏六色

MOULD, MOULDER, MOULDY, MOULT, See MOLD, MOLDER, MOLDY, MOLT.

MOUND, teng 墩; te 堆; — *of earth and rubbish*, kao-sæn'-te 高山堆 (ih-go)

MOUNT, *to* tseo'-zông 走上; — (as a scroll, or map), piao wô' 裱畫

MOUNTAIN, sæn 山; sæn-ling' 山嶺 (ih-go); *the top of a* —, sæn- ting-deu' 山頂頭°; *the foot of a* —, sæn-kyiah-'ô' 山脚下°; — *pass*, sæn-k'eo' 山口; sæn-cü- den'-go lu' 山嘴頭°个°路

MOURN, *to bewail*, k'oh 哭; *to utter sorrowfully*, kông'-leb pe- ts'ih' 講°得悲切

MOURNERS, yiu sông-z' cü'-kwu 有喪事主顧; —*following a*

MOURNFUL, sông-sing'-siang 傷心相; very —, peh'-jing-siang' 不忍相

MOURNING, to wear — (properly on the head, but used for all), ta-hao' 帶孝°; ditto (properly for distant relatives), c'ün-su' 穿素; to wear deep —, ta djong' hao' 帶重孝°; to wear — for parents, siu-cü' 守制; white — dress, hao'-i 孝°衣; other — dress, su'-i 素衣; to put on —, (first sackcloth, and then other garments), dzing-voh' 成服; to put off —, mun-voh' 滿服 k'æ-hweng' 開葷; for whom do you wear — ? ng' c'ün jü'-go su' 你°穿誰°个°素? (I) wear — for my father, ta ah-tia'-go hao' 帶阿爹个°孝°

MOUSE, little rat, siao lao-ts'ï 小鼠 (ih-tsah)

MOUTH, cü 嘴; cü'-pô 嘴巴; k'eo 口; k'eo'-deo 口頭; tea-pot — (or spout), dzô-wu' cü' 茶壺嘴; tea-pot — (or opening at the top), dzô-wu' k'eo' 茶壺口

MOVABLE, hao-dong'-go 好動个°; weh-dong'-go 活動个°

MOVABLES, dong'-yüong-jih-veh' 動用什物

MOVE, to dong 動; yi 移; pun 搬; why do you not — ? ng dza'-we ih-dong' feh-dong' 你°爲何不

— 動弗動? — a little, yi' ih-pô' 移一把; — it away a little, yi-ko'-ky'i 移過去; can't — (it), dong'-feh-læ 動弗來; dong'-feh-teh' 動弗得; — to another place, tsæn-tsæn u' 移°於°別°處°; tsæn dæn'; — to another house, pun oh' 搬屋; — to action, ken'-dong 感動; kyih'-dong 激動; — to gratitude, ken'-kyih 感激; will — the feelings, we dong nying'-go dzing' 會動人°个°情

Mow, to kah 割; — grass, kah ts'ao' 割草

MUCH, to 多; yiu'-ho; not —, feh-to' 弗多; yiu'-tæn 有限°; kyin'-liang 見量; kyin'-siao 見少; too —, t'eh to' 太多; a great deal too —, to-zông'-kô-to' 多上加°多; so —, keh-tang'; ka-sing'; how — ? to-siao 多少? as — as you please, ze ng' to-siao' 任你°多少; no matter how —, feh-leng to-siao' 弗論多少; peh'-kyü to-siao' 不拘多少; — obliged to you, to-dzing' ng 多承你°; to-zia' ng 多謝°你°; to-mong' ng 多蒙你°; ditto, or trouble you —, to-lao' ng 多勞你°

MUD, na-nyi-tsiang' 坭漿; wu-nyi-tsiang' 腐°泥漿

MUDDY, the road is —, lu' ziang tsiang ka 路如°坭漿; dress is —, i-zông' tsao na-nyi dé' 衣

裳遭坭了°; all —, jing'-z na'-nyi 純是坭

MULBERRY tree, sông-jü' 桑樹; mulberries, sông-ko' 桑菓; sông-ts 桑子

MULE, lo-ts' 騾子 (ih-p'ih)

MULTIPLICAND and multiplier, siang dzing' 相乘
  Taken from W.A.P. Martin's Ningpo Arithmetic.

MULTIPLICATION, dzing-fah' 乘法

MULTIPLY, to dzing-long' 乘攏

MULTITUDE of people, ih do'-dziao nying 一大°羣人°; cong'-nying 衆人°

MUMPS, tô'-sæ 朶腮; to have the —, sang tô'-sæ 生°朶°腮

MUNITIONS of war, kyüing-tsông-ky'i'-kyiæ 軍裝器械

MURDER, to long-sah 弄殺; tang'-sah 打殺; — with a knife, sah 殺; c'oh'-sah 揢殺; to plot —, meo-sah' 謀殺

MURDERER, hyüong-siu' 兇手 (ih-go)

MURIATIC ACID, yin-gyiang'-shü 鹹強水°

MURMUR (of water), ts'ô'-ts'ô hyiang' 淙淙響; — (of voices), zeng-zeng'-hyiang; to complain, mao-ün' 埋°怨; grumbling, gæn-gwa'-tao-tao læ'-tih ün'.

MUSCLE, or tendon, kying 筋; flesh, nyüoh 肉°

MUSCLE or MUSSEL, (a shell-fish), bang 蚌 (ih-go)

MUSCULAR, great — strength, kying'-lih tsông'-do 筋力壯大°

MUSHROOM, dzing 菌°; dried —, hyiang-dzing' 香菌°

MUSIC, yüoh 樂; tsoh-yüoh' 作樂 (veng.); do you like to hear instrumental — ? ng hwun-hyi' t'ing s-ing' kô'-sang feh 你°歡喜聽絲絃否°? — (blowing and beating), c'ü-c'ü tang-tang 吹°吹°打打; seng-siao'-kwu-dih' 笙簫鼓笛 (veng.)

MUSICAL instruments, yüoh-ky'i' 樂器; brass ditto, hyiang'-ky'i 響器; — boxes, pah'-ing-gying' 八音琴

MUSICIANS, tsoh-yüoh'-go nying 作樂个人°; trumpeters, c'ü-siu' 吹°手; players and singers, dæn'-ts'ông-go nying 彈唱个人°

MUSK, zô-hyiang' or dzô-hyiang' 麝香

MUSK-DEER, hyiang-tsông 香麞 (veng.); commonly called, hyiang-li-mæn' 香狸貓°

MUSKET, nyiao'-ts'iang 鳥鎗; foreign —, yiang-ts'iang' 洋鎗; breech-loader, 'eo'-deo-meng 後頭門 (ih-kwun)

MUSLIN, foreign bleached p'iao'-bah yiang-pu' 漂白洋布; unbleached foreign —, peng'-seh yiang-pu' 本色洋布; mull —, yiang sô' 洋紗

MUST, pih'-iao 必要; tsong'-iao 總要; vu-pih'-ts-iao' 務必

MUS　　　　　305　　　　　NAI

耍; ding-iao' 定耍;— have, siao'-feh-teh' 少弗得;— not, m-nao'; feh-k'o 弗可; certainly — not, ts'ih'-feh-k'o' 切弗可; tön'-feh-k'o 斷弗可; tön'-jün feh-k'o' 斷然弗可; tön'-wu feh-k'o 斷乎弗可

MUSTACHE, zông'-bæn ngô-su' 上爿鬍°鬚°

MUSTARD (the plant), ka'-ts'æ 芥菜;— seed, ka'-ts'æ-ts 芥°菜子; ground —, ka'-lah-feng 芥°辣粉

MUSTER strength, and press forward, nu'-lih zông-zin' 努力上前°

MUSTY, grown ah'-ko-de 過過了 — smell, ah'-boh-ky'i 過°蒸°氣

MUTE, deaf ô'-ts 啞°子; ô'-pô-ts 啞°吧子; clock is — (i. e. stopped), z-ming'-cong ô'-de 自鳴鐘啞°了°

MUTILATE, to —the body, long'-leh s'-t'i feh djün' 弄得四體弗全

MUTINY, to revolt, meo-nyih' kyih-tông' 謀逆結黨

MUTTER, to — to one's self, zi-wô-deo-bun' 自言°自°語

MUTTON, yiang-nyüoh' 羊肉°

MUTTONY SMELL (said by the Chinese to be peculiar to some foreigners), yiang-sao'-ky'i 羊臊氣

MUTUAL, pe'-ts' 彼此; liang'-'ô 兩°下°; dô-kô' 大°家°; siang 相;— pleaure, pe'-ts' hwun-hyi' 彼此歡喜;— recognition, liang'-'ô nying-teh' 兩下°認°得;— love, dô-kô' siang-æ' 大°家°相愛

MY, ngô-go' 我个°;— older brother, kô-hyüong' 家°兄;— younger brother, sô-di' 舍弟;— (humble) cottage, sô-'ô' 舍°下°; bi-sô' 敝舍°; sô'-kyin 舍°間; — country, peng'-koh 本國;— (humble) country, bi'-koh 敝國;— relatives (of the same surname), ah'-lah peng'-kô 我°等°本家;— own son, ts'ing-sang' ng-ts' 親生°兒°子

MYRIAD, ih-væn' 一萬

MYRRH, meh-yiah' 沒藥

MYSELF, ngô-zi' 我自°; I saw it — (with my own eyes), ts'ing-ngæn' k'en'-kyin-ko' 親眼°看見過; ts'ing-ngæn moh'-tu 親眼°目視

MYSTERIOUS, næn-ts'eh' næn-ziang' 難測難詳; ao'-miao 奧妙 sing-ao' 深奧

MYSTICAL, dark, en'-dong-dong 暗洞洞

N

NAIL, ting-cü' 釘銖 (ih-me); finger —, ts'-k'ah 指甲°; toe —, kyiah'-ts-k'ah' or kyiah'-tsib-k'ah' 脚指甲°; nails too long, ts'-k'ah hying' 指甲°興 (also used for pilfering).

NAIL, to ting 釘; yüong ting-cü, ting'-ih-ting' 用釘銖釘一釘; *to drive a* —, k'ao ting-cü 拷釘銖

NAKED, c'ih'-sing-lu-t'i' 出身露體; kwông-sing' 光身; c'ih'-liao-siao 赤條絛; c'ih'-lön-c'ih-poh' 出卵°出膊 (vulgar); *upper part* —, c'ih-poh' 裸體; *strip* —, i-zông' poh-kwông 衣裳°剝光

NAME, ming-z' 名字; ming-deo' 名頭; *what is the — of this* (called)? keh' kyiao soh'-go ming-z' 這°叫甚°麼°名字? *a man has three names, viz,* ming 名, z 字; 'ao 號; *ming is given by parents; z is given by teachers;* 'ao 號; bih-'ao 別號 *are chosen by himself, and changed at will; milk* — (only used by parents) na-ming 嬭名; jü-ming 乳名; siao-ming' 小名; *book or school* —, shü-ming' 書名; k'ao'-ming 考名; *family* —, sing'-su 姓氏°; *what is your family* —? ng' sing soh' 你°姓甚°麼? *your honorable ditto?* kwe' sing 貴姓? tseng sing' 尊姓? *a good* — (reputation), hao' ming-sing' 好名聲

NAME, *to* cü ming-z' 取名字; lih ming' 立名; — *him John*, c'ü' gyi ming Iah'-'en 取其名約翰; *to call*, kyiao 叫; eo; ts'ing-hwu' 稱呼; *how shall I — your teacher?* ng-go sin-sang' ngô' dza ts'ing'-hwu gyi 你°个°先生°我°怎°樣°稱呼其?

NAMELESS, m̄ ming'-z 無°名字; *undistinguished*, m̄-ming' m̄-sing 無°名無°姓

NAMELY, ziu-z' 就°是

NANKEEN, ts'-hwô-pu' 紫花布

NAP, *to take a short* —, hweh'-ih-hweh 眠°一°眠; hweh-ih-zông'; *ditto sitting*, tang-k'eh'-c'ong 打瞌睡; *take a long* —, kw'eng'-ih-k'ao 睡一覺°; — *of cloth*, nyüong-deo' 絨頭

NAPKIN, *table* ky'üoh'-væn siu'-kying 吃°飯手巾

NARRATE *at length or particularly*, dziang-si' kông' ih-fæn' 詳細講°一番

NARROW, 'ah 狹°; 'ah-tsah' 狹°窄; — *minded* (not liberal), ky'i'-liang 'ah-tsah' 器量狹°窄; sing-di' 'ah-tsah' 心地狹°窄; — *experience*, kyin'-sih 'ah-tsah' 見識狹°窄

NASTY, *filthy*, nyi-sing'-pah-la 泥腥百邋°; nyi-sing-pah-kyü'

NATION, koh'-kô 國家; *all nations*, t'in-'ô' væn-ming' 天下°萬民

NATIONAL *expenditure*, koh'-kô-go yüong-du' 國家°用度

NATIVE, *n.* peng'-di-nying' 本地人°; dziu-di'-nying' 當°地人° (ih-go)

NATIVE *dialect*, peng-di wô' 本地話; — *place*, peng'-hyiang

本鄉; peng'-t'u 本土; peng'-c'ü 本處; peng'-zih 本籍;— productions, t'u'-ts'æn 土產; — cotton cloth, du'-pu 土°布

NATIVITY of Christ, Yiæ-su' sing'-dæn 耶穌聖誕

NATURAL, t'in sang'-dzing-go 天生°成个°;— disposition, peng-sing sang'-dzing 本性生°成; great — abilities, t'in-ts'ong' t'in-ming' 天聰天明

NATURALLY, t'in-sing' s-jün' 天性使然

NATURE, the course of —, t'in-di'z-jün'-ts li' 天地自然之理; t'in-di' ts ky'i'-hwô 天地之氣化; to investigate the — of things, keh-veh' gyüong-li' 格物窮理; human —, nying'-go peng'-sing 人个°本性

NAUSEATE, will — him, we peh gyi oh'-sing 會俾°其欲°嘔°

NAVAL officer, se'-s-kwun' 水°師官; — commander, se'-s di-toh' 水師提督

NAVEL, du'-dzi-ngæn' 肚臍眼°; — cord, dzi-ta' 臍帶

NAVIGABLE, s'-leh-t'ong'-go 駛得°通个°

NAVIGATE, to — a ship, s jün' 駛船; 'ang jün' 行°船

NAVIGATOR, s-jün'-go-nying' 駛船个°人°; 'ang-jün'-go-nying' 行°船个°人°

NEAR, gying 近; siang-gying' 相近; dziu-gying' 就近; very —,

ting'-gying 頂近; so — as to touch, t'iah'-gying 貼近; vu-gying' 附近; — (like one's own friends, hence affectionate), ts'ing-gying' 親近; nearer, gying-tin' 近點; nearest, or next, kah-pih' 隔壁; time drawing —, z-'eo' ling-gying' 時候臨近; — (and therefore practicable), 'dzæ'-gying we-gying' 隨°近爲°事°

NEARLY, ts'ô'-feh-to' 差弗多; kyi-wu' 幾乎;— alike, siang-ky'ü' 相去; da-iah' ih-yiang' 大約一樣; zông'-loh vu-kyi' 上落無幾; liah-dong' 略同; — there, ziu hao' tao' 就好到; kw'a tao'-de 快°到了°; — night, kw'a yia'-de 快°夜了°;— noon, kw'a tsiu'-ko 近°午°; tsao' tsiu'-ko' 早°;午°

NEAR-SIGHTED, gying'-z-ngæn' 近視眼°

NEAT, ts'ing-c'ü' 清泚;— (primarily, clear as water), pih-po'-s-ts'ing 碧波四清; ts'ing-kyih' 清潔

NEATLY done, tso'-leh ts'ing-c'ü' 做得°清泚

NECESSARIES, all the ih-ts'ih' sô yüong'-go 一切所用个°; the seven —, viz., wood, rice, oil, salt, sauce, vinegar, and tea, za, mi, yiu, yin, tsiang, ts'u, dzô, ts'ih'-go-z' 柴米油鹽醬醋茶七个°字

NECESSARY, pih'-iao 必要;

hyih'-feh-læ' 歇弗來; siao'-feh-teh' 少弗得;— or *important*, iao'-kying 要緊; *very — to do*, feh'-teh-feh tso' 弗得弗做

NECESSARILY, peh-teh'-yi 不得巳; m̀-fah' 無法; pih'-shü 必須; m̀-næ'-'o 無奈何; wa'-feh-læ 歇弗來.

NECESSITY, *what is the —?* 'o-pih' ka iao'-kying 何必如此要緊; 'o-yüong' ka dziah-kyih' 何用如此着急; *there is a — in his going*, gyi pih' ky'iao-leh ky'i' (or ky'iah-leh.)

NECK, deo-kying' 頭頸

NECKLACE, 'ông'-cü-c'ün' 項珠串; *mandarin's —*, dziao-cü' 朝珠

NECK-TIE, ling'-ta 領帶 (ih-diao)

NECROMANCER, kông-du'-sin-go 講肚仙個; *female —*, du'-sin-bo' 肚仙婆

NECROMANCY, kông-du'-sin 講肚仙

NEED, *in — of*, ky'üih'-siao 缺少; ky'üih'-ky'in 缺欠; ky'üih'-siao dziang-tön' 缺少長短; *in — of fuel*, ky'üih'-siao za' 缺少柴

NEED NOT, hao-vong' 不用; feh-yüong' 弗用; peh-pih' 不必

NEEDFUL, iao'-kying 要緊; iao-yüong' 要用

NEEDLE, tsing 鍼 (ih-me); *to thread a —*, c'ün tsing-ngæn' 穿鍼眼; *magnetic —*, ts'-nen'-tsing 指南鍼

NEEDLE-WORK, tsing-ts' sang-weh' 鍼黹生活; tsing-ts' 鍼黹

NEEDLESS, hao hyih'-go 好歇個; *quite —*, ih-ngæn' hao-vong' 一點不用; *— work (can be saved, or spared)*, sang-weh' hao sang'-go 生活好省個

NEEDY, kyih'-pah 急迫; kyih'-kyü 拮据; siu'-deo tön'-ts'oh 手頭侷促

NEGLECT, *to — duty*, feh-pô meng-veng' 弗守名分; *— work*, sang-weh' yiu'-iao'-m̀-kying' tso' 生活有要無緊做; *— trade*, sang-i' feh kwu'-djoh 生意弗顧着; *— unintentionally*, shih kyin'-tin 失檢點; kwu'-tsih feh-tao'-kô 侍值弗到家; *died from —*, kwu'-tsih feh-tao'-kô si'-de 侍值弗到家死了; *to slight*, shih-kwu' 失顧

NEGLIGENT, ts'o-ts'o'-do-do' 蹉蹉跎跎; *not diligent*, yiæ-dæ' 懈怠; *careless*, hweh'-liah 忽略; *inattentive*, feh-liu-sing' 弗留心

NEGOTIATE, *to transact business*, bæn z-t'i' 辦事體; *— peace*, nyi 'o' 議和

NEGOTIATOR, bæn-z'-go 辦事個°; *middle-man*, cong-nying 中人°

NEGRO, heh'-nying 黑人°

NEIGH, *the horse neighs*, mô læ-tih kyiao' 馬正在°叫

NEIGHBOR, ling-sô'-kô 隣舍°家°; ling-kyü' 隣居; *near —*, gying'-ling 近鄰; *next —*, kah'-pih t'iah'-ling 隔壁貼鄰; *surrounding neighbors*, s'-ling 四隣

NEIGHBORHOOD, s'-gying-s-yüû' di'-fông 四近四遠地方; gying'-fông-zông 近个°地°方°; zin-zin' 'eo-'eo di'-fông 前°前°後後地方; — *just at the door*, meng-zin'-meng-wu' 門前°門戶

NEIGHBORING, in-hô'-siang-lin' 人°烟°凑°集°

NEITHER, NOR, feh 弗; yia feh 也°弗; yi feh 又°弗; *neither cold, nor hot*, feh'-lang-feh-nyih' 弗冷°弗熱°; *neither here nor there*, yia feh læ dông'-deo, yia feh læ keh'-deo 也°弗在°這°裡°也°弗在°那°裡°; — *will go*, ih-go tu feh ky'i 一個都弗去°; *neither one thing nor the other*, feh ts'eng' feh gao.

NEPHEW, *brother's son*, dzih-ts' 姪子; *sister's son*, nga-sang' 外甥°; *a sister calls her brother's son*, ne-dzih' 內姪

NERVE, nao'-kying-sin 腦筋線 (coined).

NEST, k'o 窠; *edible swallows' —*, in'-o 燕窝; — *of thieves*, zeh-k'o' 賊窠; zeh-o-kô' 窩賊家°

NESTORIANS, Kying'-kyiao 景教

NET, *fishing* mông 網°; *small ditto*, pæn-tseng' 扳罾; — *for the hair*, mông'-kying 網°巾 (formerly worn by Chinamen); *mosquito —*, tsiang'-ts 帳子; — *weight*, jih kying liang' 實觔兩; *how much is the — weight?* zing' djong to-siao' 淨重多少?̂ djü zing' to-siao djong' 除淨多少重? djü bi' to-siao djong' 除皮多少重? — *profit*, zing' dzen 淨賺; — *goods*, zing' hô 淨貨

NEUTER, *to remain neutral*, liang' feh-siang-dzu' 兩弗相助; *neither male nor female*, peh'-nen-peh-nyü' 不男不女

NEVER, dzong m̄'-neh 從沒有°; dzong-læ m̄'-neh 從來沒有°; tsong m̄'-neh 終究°沒有° (tsong or cong); — (*hereafter*), üong'-feh 永弗; — *can*, cong' feh-neng'-keo 終弗能彀; — *saw*, dzong m̄'-neh k'en'-kyin-ko 從沒°有°看見過; — *heard of it*, 'ao-vu t'ing'-meng-ko 毫無聽聞°過; — *heard of such a thing*, dzong sang ng' to m̄'-neh t'ing'-meng keh'-cü-ka z-t'i 從生°耳朵以來°沒有°聽聞°這°些事體; *will — come again*, üong'-feh tsæ læ' 永弗再來; — *gets angry*, üong'-

feh sang ky'i' 永弗生氣;— yet, dzong feh zing' 從弗曾
NEW, sing 新; just —, ts'oh' sing 嶄新; ts'oh'-kwah-sing 嶄刮新; ts'oh-tsæn'-sing 嶄簇新; — fashioned, z sing 時新;— pattern, sing yiang'-shih 新樣式; — comer, bao'-z læ'-go 暴時來个; ts'u læ'-go 初來个; — Testament, Sing-iah'-shü 新約書
NEW-YEAR's day, tsing'-yüih ts'u-ih' 正月初一;— eve, sæn-jih nyin yia' 三十年夜; nyiæn-kyin' yia' 廿九年夜; — money (given to children, or servants), ah-shü-din' 壓歲錢;— gifts, nyin-yia' li-veh 年夜禮物; ko-nyin'-go li 過年个禮
NEWS, sing'-sih 信息; siao-sih' 消息; sing-veng' 新聞; to let out the —, t'ong-fong' pao-sing' 通風報信
NEWSPAPER, sing'-veng-pao 新聞報; sing-veng-ts' 新聞紙
NEXT, the second, di-nyi' 第二; — day, di-nyi' nyih 第二日; — month, 'ô'-ko yüih 下個月; — year, ming nyin' 明年; nen nyin' 來年; sit —, t'iah'-gying zo 貼近坐; ditto, or in the same row, bing-ba' zo 並排坐;— (house, &c.), t'ih'-kah-pih 貼隔壁; — neighbor, t'iah'-ling 貼隣; do that — (after doing

this), keh'-go mæn' ih-bu tso' 這个慢一步做
NIBBLE, to k'eng 齦; k'eng'-ky'üoh 齦吃
NICE, pleasing, cong'-i 中意; hao 好
NICELY done, tso'-leh tsing-cü' 做得精緻
NICHE, hole made in a partition, pih-dong' 壁洞
NICKNAME (given in derision), ts'iao-'ao' 綽號; weng'-ao 混號; to —, c'ü'-ming-ts'iao-'ao' 取名綽號
NIECE, brother's daughter, dzih-nyü' 姪女; sister's daughter, nga-sang-nön' 外甥女; wife's —, ne'-dzih-nyü' 內姪女; niece's husband, dzih-si' 姪壻; ne'-dzih-si 內姪壻
NIGHT, yia-tao' 夜到; in the —, yia-li' 夜裡; yia-deo' 夜頭; spend the —, soh-yia' 宿夜; ko-yia' 過夜; hyih-yia' 歇夜; djü-yia' 住夜; nearly —, kw'a-yia' 快夜; dark —, heh'-yia 黑夜; last —, zô yia' 昨夜; tomorrow —, ming-tsiao' yia'-tao 明朝夜到; to do at —, lin yia' tso 連夜做; all —, ih-yia' 一夜; tsing'-yia 正夜; late at —, yia-sing' 夜深; yia-zing'-kang-sing 夜盡更深; up all —, ngao yia'; tæn-koh yia' 犹搁夜; watch at — with the sick, be-yia' 陪夜; to watch

at —, siu-yia' 守夜°; to sit up all —, zo-yia' 坐夜°.

NIGHT-DRESS, kw'eng'-i 睡°衣

NIGHTLY, yia-yia' 夜°夜°; me-yia' 每夜°.

NIGHT-MARE, fah-in' 發魘; shü-t'ah ah 水獺壓; has the —, læ-tih fah-in' 正°在°發魘

NIMBLE, ky'ing-kw'a' 輕快'

NINE, kyiu 九; — fold, kyiu'-be 九倍; — tenths, kyiu' feng 九分

NINETEEN, jih-kyiu' 十九

NINETY, kyiu'-jih 九十

NINTH, the di-kyiu'-go 第九个°

NIP, to — with the fingers, tih 摘

NIPPERS, gyin 箝; gyin-ts' 箝子 (ih-kwun)

NIPPLE, na-deo° or na-den° 嬭°頭; na-ts' 嬭°子 (ih-go)

NIT of a louse, seh'-ts 蝨子; kyi'-ts 蟣子 (ih-go)

NITRE, siao 硝; yin-siao' 鹽硝

No, feh 弗; ṁ 無°; (I cannot) feh-neng' 弗能; — (not willing) feh-k'eng' 弗肯; — one, ṁ-nying' 無°人°; — matter, ṁ-kao'; ṁ-kwæn'-dzih 無°關涉; — use, ṁ-yüong' 無°用; — matter which, feh-leng' 弗論; — help for it, ṁ-fah' 無°法; ṁ-shih'-fah 無°設法; shih'-fah-næ'-'o 失法奈何

NOBILITY, yiu tsiah'-we cü'-kwu 有爵°位人°; the five ranks of — viz, kong, 'eo, pah, ts, nen, 公, 侯, 伯, 子, 男

NOBLE, of — rank, yiu tsiah'-we 有爵°位; disinterested, yiah-ky'i-go 俠氣个; will not stoop to anything dishonorable, üong'-feh tao ze'-ky'i 永弗倒銳°氣; generous, k'ông'-k'æ 慷慨

NOBODY, ṁ-nying' 無°人°; — is there, ṁ-nying' læ'-kæn 無°人°在°彼°

NOD, to eo'-eo deo' 偃偃頭; tin-tin deo' 點點頭

NOISE, hyiang 響; sing-hyiang' 聲響; no —, ṁ-sing'-hyiang 無°聲響; ṁ hyiang'-dong 無°響動; — of the sea, hæ'-shü hyiang 海水響

NOISY, nao-nyih' 鬧熱; very — ziang loh-ying'-fæn'-ky'i ka 像六營反起; nao-nyih'-bang-sang' 鬧熱非常°; — voices, da-sing' hen'-kyiao 大°聲喊叫; — and troublesome to neighbors, ts'ao'-ling'-mô'-sô 噪鄰罵舍

NOMINAL, only in name, yiu-ming'-vu-jih' 有名無實

NONE, have ṁ'-neh 沒°有°; ṁ'-teh; — or no one could do, ṁ-nying' neng'-keo tso' 無°人°能殼做

NONSENSE, talk half in play, half in earnest, puŋ'-byi-puŋ-tso-shih-wô' 半嬉半真說話; foolish talk, wu-du' shih-wô' 糊塗說話; wild talk, lön wô' 亂話; yia' wô 野°話

NOON, tsiu'-ko 當晝; tsing'-wu-z 正午時; nyih-deo dzih' 日°頭直; cong-wu' 中午; *past* —, tsiu'-ko ko'-de 晝午過了°; *rest at* —, hyih tsiu' 歇晝; *before* —, tsao tsiu'-ko 早午

NOR, See NEITHER.

NORTH, poh 北; poh'-pin 北邊; *to go* —; hyiang poh' ky'i 向北去°; *nose to the* —, *or dead*, (because corpses were formerly so placed), bih-deo' dziao poh' 鼻頭朝北

NORTH-EAST, tong-poh' 東北; — *west*, si-poh' 西北

NORTH-STAR, poh'-teo-sing 北斗星

NOSE, bih-deo-kwun' 鼻°頭管; — *bleed*, bih-deo c'ih 'ong' 鼻°頭出紅; *follow your* —, (*i.e.* go straight ahead), bang bih'-deo' 撑鼻°頭

NOSEGAY, ih-nyiah hwô' 一紮°花

NOSTRIL, bih-deo-kwun ngæn 鼻°孔°

NOT, feh 弗; m̄ 無°; m̄'-neh; — *understand*, feh tong' 弗懂; *is it so or* —? z-ka' feh 如°此°否°; — *so*, feh' z-ka' 弗如°此°; *if* — *so*, feh-jün' 弗然; *must* —, m̄-nao'; *ought* —, feh-k'o' 弗可; *have* —, m̄-yiu' 沒°有; — *a cash*, ih'-go dong-din' tu m̄'-teh 一個°銅錢°都沒°有°; — *yet*, feh-zing' 弗曾; *have you finished or* —? tso'-hao-

leh feh' 做好了°否°? tso-hao'-liao m̄-teh 做好了嗎°? — *finished*, m̄'-teh tso'-hao 沒°有°做好; — *at all sick*, ih-ngæn' m̄-neh næn-ko' 一點沒°有°難過

NOTABLE, c'ih-ming'-go 出名个°; veng-ming'-go 聞名个°

NOTCH, *cut a* —, kah' ih-go ky'üih 割一个°缺; *notched* (like teeth), keo-ky'üih-ngô' 像°鋸齒°; *knife-blade is notched*, tao t'eng-ky'üih'-de 刀殘°缺了°

NOTE, *billet*, bin-z' 便字; z-den' 字條° (ih-go); *bank* —, p'iao'-ts 票紙; dzin-p'iao' 錢°票; nying-p'iao' 銀票; — *of hand*, we-p'iao' 匯票; — *in music* (a character), ing'-ao 音號; *ditto* (a sound), yüoh'-ing 樂音; *native ditto*, pæn'-ngæn 板眼

NOTE, *to* — *down*, kyi 記; loh 錄; — *in a* — *book*, kyi'-læ kao'-peng-li 記在°稿本裡; *to take notes*, ts'ao-loh' 抄錄; *brief* (or culled) *notes*, tsah-ts'ao 摘抄

NOTE-BOOK, *scholar's* kao'-peng 稿本; *memorandum book*, dzeng-kyi'-bu 存記簿

NOTHING, m̄-kao' soh-go 沒°有°甚°麽°; ih-ngæn' m̄-kao'; — *to say*, m̄-kao' soh-go hao wô' 沒°有°甚°麽好話; — *to me*, teng-ngô' m̄-kwæn-dzih' 與°我無°關涉; ü-ngô' vu-kwæn' 於我無關; *good for* —, fi'-

veh 廢物; hyiu'-moh 朽木; *produced from* — (as unfounded tales), vu cong' seng yiu' 無中生有; — *to fear,* feh-fông'-teh 弗妨得; feh-dzæ'-wu; — *else,* m̄-kao bih'-yiang 沒°有°別樣; — *but this,* djü-tsʻ-ts nga m̄-kao' bih'-yiang 除此之外沒°有°別樣

NOTICE, kao'-bah 告白; cü-tæn' 知單; cü-tsiao' 知照 (ih-tsiang)

NOTICE, *to* li'-we 理會; *to perceive,* kyüoh'-teh 覺得; *to see,* k'en'-kyin 看見; *did you — the eclipse?* wu-jih' ng yiu li'-we ma 蝕°日你°有理會嗎°? *I noticed it,* ngô li'-we-ko-de 我理會過了°; *I did not — it,* ngô feh-læ'-kwu 我弗來顧; ngô shih-kwu'-de 我失顧了°

NOTIFICATION, *an official* — , kao'-z 告示; — (of literary advancement), pao'-tæn 報單; — (of the death of a friend), fu'-ing 訃音

NOTIFY, *to* t'ong-pao' 通報; cü-we' 知會; *to inform,* t'ong-cü' 通知; — *officially,* c'ih kao'-z.

NOTION, *I have some* — (of it), ngô yiu tin i'-s 我有點意思

NOTIONAL, kæn-ka' 尷尬

NOTORIOUS, cong'-k'eo-næ'-næ 衆口喃°喃°; cong'-nying tu hyiao'-teh 衆人都曉得;

notoriously bad, ba-tsʻ tsʻiu' 醜°名°

NOTWITHSTANDING, dæn'-ming 但憑°; sih'-t'ing 悉聽°; zing'-bing 任憑; — *his prohibition, I will gamble,* sih'-t'ing gyi-dzæ' kying'-djü ngô we tu' 悉聽°其怎°禁住我會賭

NOUN, jih-z'-ngæn 實字眼°

NOURISH, *to* tsiang' tsing-lih' 長精力; — *the body,* yiang sing-t'i' 養身體

NOURISHING, yiu-lih'-go 有力個°; we-sang-lih'-go 會生°力個°; we-tsiang'-kying-kweh' 會長筋骨

NOVEL *and strange,* sing gyi' 新奇; — *mode,* sing-tsoh' veng-fah 新作文法

NOVEL, *n.* 'æn-shü' 閒書; siao'-shü 小書 (ih-peng)

NOVICE, *beginner,* tsʻu-'oh'-go 初學°個°; sang-siu' 生°手; — *in religion,* sing' jih-kyiao'-go 新入教個°

Now, mæn'-kæn 刻下°; keh-zông' 這°息°; yin-dzæ' 現在; moh-yüö' 目下; mô; jü-kying' 如今; ngæn'-zin 眼前°; tsih'-moh 卽目

NOW-A-DAYS, kying-næn'-kæn 當°今°之°世°or 今日°者°; — *it is diff'rent,* kying-z'-koh'-bih 今時各別

NOWHERE *to be found,* tao'-c'ü zing-pin' zing'-feh-djoh' 到處

NOW　　　　　　314　　　　　　NUR

尋°遍尋°弗着°; is —, ṅ-c'ü' yiu 無°處有; ih-c'ü' tu ṅ'-teh 一處都沒°有°

NOWISE, bing'-fi 並非; tön'-tön-feh 斷斷弗

NOXIOUS vapor, doh-ky'i' 毒氣

NUISANCE, ngæ-nying'-ts-veh 碍人°之物; commit no —, (i. e. forbidden to pollute), kying'-ts u-we 禁止污穢

NULL, ṅ-tso'; vu yüong' 無用

NUMB, mô-moh' 麻木; mô tseh'-long; perfectly —, moh dzih'-dzih 木直直

NUMBER, su'-moh 數目; the whole —, tsong' su 總數; the science of numbers sön'-fah 算法; in great numbers, su'-moh to' 數目多

NUMBER, to su'-su-k'en 數數看; su-ih'-su 數一數

NUMBERLESS, su'-feh-pin 數弗遍; peh-kyi'-gyi-su' 不計其數; vu-ts'in'-da-væn 無千大萬; leng'-ts'in-leng-væn 論千論萬

NUMBERS, mô'-ts 碼子; su'-moh 數目

1.	one,	ih.	一	壹	丨
2.	two,	nyi.	二	貳	刂
3.	three,	sæn.	三	叁	刂
4.	four,	s.	四	肆	乂
5.	five,	ng.	五	伍	㐅
6.	six,	loh.	六	陸	亠
7.	seven,	ts'ih.	七	柒	亠
8.	eight,	pah.	八	捌	亠
9.	nine,	kyiu.	九	玖	夊
10.	ten,	jih.	十, 拾	什
100.		ih-pah'.	一百, 壹佰
1000.		ih-ts'in'.	一千, 壹阡
10,000.		ih-væn.	一萬, 壹萬 丨万

NUMEROUS, to'-leh-kying 多得°緊; hyü'-to 許多; yiu'-ho

NUN, Buddhist nyi-kwu' 尼姑; nyü' 'o-zông 女尼°; long haired —, s-kwu' 師姑; — who makes no change in dress, ta'-fah-siu-'ang' 帶°髮修行°; Taoist —, dao'-kwu 道姑; Roman Catholic —, siu-dao' kwu-nyiang' 修道姑娘

NUNNERY, Buddhist en 菴; en-dông' 菴堂; Roman Catholic —, nyü' siu-dao-yün' 女修道院

NUPTIAL ceremonies, kô'-c'ü-go li'-tsih 嫁°娶禮節; to perform ditto, 'ang kô'-c'ü-go li' 行°嫁°娶禮; 'ang hweng-ing'-go li' 行°婚姻禮; tso-ts'ing' 成°親; hao'-nyih 好日°; dzing-hweng' 成°婚; — presents, jing-dzing' 人情; ditto (to groom), 'o-li' 賀禮; ditto (to bride), song-kô' 送嫁°

NURSE for children, ling siao-nying' go a-ṅ' 領小人°个阿姆; — for sick person, z'-dzih bing-nying' go 侍值病人°个; tông-dzih'-go cü'-kwu 當值个人°; wet —, ah-bu' 阿婊; na'-ah-bu 姆阿婊

NURSE, to suckle, ü na' 飼姆; to

NUT 315 OBL

— *the sick,* z'-dzih bing-nying' 侍值病人°; tông'-dzih bing-nying' 當值病人°
NUT, *kernel,* nyüoh 肉°; *walnut meat,* wu-dao nyüoh' 胡桃肉°
　Nuts are considered as fruits.
NUT-GALL, ng'-be-ts 五°倍子
NUTMEG, nyüoh-ko' 肉°菓
NUTRITIOUS, we-sang-lih' 會生°力; we-pu-hyüih'-ky'i 會補血氣
NUT-SHELL, k'oh 殼

O

OAK, ziang'-jü 橡樹 (ih-cü)
OAKUM, mô-kying' 蔴筋
OAR, tsiang 漿 (ih-ts)
OATH, vah-tsiu' 罰咒; *to make a great* —, vah-zing do-tsiu' 罰甚大°咒 *to violate an* —, vah-tsiu' feh-tsoh'-cing 罰咒弗作準; vah-tsiu' feh-sön-su' 罰咒弗算數; *violates oaths with ease,* vah-tsiu' tông ko'-ts ky'üoh' 輕°於°罰°咒°
OATMEAL, yiu'-mah-feng 油麥粉 (Mandarin)
OATS, yiu'-mah 油麥
OBDURATE, sing-dziang' ngang' 心腸硬; *disposition* — *as iron and stone,* t'ih'-zah sing-dziang' 鐵石心腸; t'ih'-tang sing-dziang' 鐵打心腸
OBEDIENT, k'eng t'ing wô' 肯聽話; we-i-jing'-go 會依順个°; ao-ao'-ing-go 諾°諾°之°聲°;

— *to the letter,* i'-diao-dzih-vong' 依條直縫; — *in all respects,* pah'-i-pah-jing' 百°依百°順; vi-ming'-z-dzong' 惟命是從
OBEISANCE, *to make* ts'ing-ts'ing' 請請; — *with folded hands,* tsoh-ih' 作揖; — *by falling on the ground,* p'oh-tao pa' 仆倒拜°; — *by knocking the head,* k'eh deo' 磕頭
OBEY, *to* i-jing' 依順; i-dzong' 依從; t'ing 聽
OBJECT *in coming,* læ-i' 來意; — *in going,* ky'i'-i 去°意; *attained the* — *of desire,* sô siang'-vông, tao-siu'-de 所想望到手了
OBJECT, *to* p'i-bing' 批評; p'i-poh' 批駁
OBJECTION, *have you any* — (*to offer*)? ng yiu soh' go p'i-bing' ni 你有甚°麼°批評呢°? *ditto to my going out?* 'o-fông' peh ngô tseo'-c'ih 何妨俾我走出呢? *no* —, peh-fông' 不妨
OBLATION, *sacrifice,* tsi'-veh 祭物; kong'-vong-go tong-si 供奉个°東西
OBLIGATION, *you are under no* — *to do it,* ng' k'o, peh-pih' tso 你°可不必做; *cannot forget my* —, ko'-sing-feh-ky'i' 過意弗去°; ken'-kyih-feh-zing' 感激弗盡; *no end to my* —, ken-eng-feh-zing' 感恩弗盡

OBLIGATORY, lî'-tông-kæ' 理當該;— *upon men to keep the Sabbath,* nying siu li'-pa, li sô tông-jün'-go 人°守禮拜理所當然个°.

OBLIGE, *to compel,* ngang-k'ô' 逼°勒°; min'-ky'iang-iao' 勉强要; gyiang'-iao 强要;— *him to write,* ngang-k'ô' gyi sia 逼°勒°其寫°; leh' gyi sia 勒其寫°.

OBLIGED, m-næ'-'o 無奈何; shih'-fah-næ'-'o 失法奈何; peh-teh'-yi 不得已;— *to use it,* shih'-fah-næ'-'o yüong' 失法奈何用; *much — to you (i.e. see your kindness),* kyin ng'-go dzing' 見你°个°情; *ditto (see your great kindness),* tsoh'-kyin-zing'-dzing 足見盛情; *ditto,* fi-sing' 費心; fi-jing' 費神; *to —* mong' 多蒙; *ditto (have put you to much trouble),* to-lao' 多勞; *I will be much — to you, if you will go to the city for me,* ngô iao fi ng'-go jing' tao dzing-li' ky'i ih-da' 我要費你°个°神到城裡去°一埭.

OBLIGING, kwun-min' 冠冕; pah-min'-kwông 八面光; iao-t'ao'-hao' 要討好; we-t'ao'-hao' 會討好; (the last two have a selfish motive.)

OBLIQUE, zia 斜°; ts'ia; dzia; hwa 歪.

OBLITERATE, *to blot out,* du-diao' 塗壞°.

OBLONG, dziang-fông' 長方.

OBLOQUY, zoh-mô' 辱罵; *to endure —,* ziu zoh-mô' 受辱罵.

OBSCENE, yiu-ky'iang'-weh-diao' 油腔滑調;— *talk,* yiu wô' 油話;— *books,* ying shü' 淫書;— *pictures,* c'ing kong 春宮.

OBSCENITY, ying-lön' z-ken 淫亂事幹.

OBSCURE, heh'-en 黑暗; moh-ts'eh'-di-en' 墨漆地暗;— *ideas,* i'-s k'en' feh-ming'-bah-go 意思看弗明白°个°;— *by clouds,* be yüing' tsô-djü' 被雲遮°住.

OBSCURITY, *to retire into —* (usually leaving one's family, &c.), ing'-loh 隱落; *in — (i.e. don't know any thing about him),* ing'-sæn loh-dao'-de 隱山避°世°了°; *ditto, as an officer,* feh-c'ih-z' 弗出仕.

OBSEQUIES, sông-li' 喪禮; sông-z' 喪事.

OBSEQUIOUS, pe-kong'-ky'üih-tsih' 卑躬屈節;— *and designing,* li to' pih tsô' 禮多或詐.

OBSERVANT, we liu-sing' k'en' 會留心看; *not —,* kwu'-tsih feh-tao'-go 侍°值°弗到个°.

OBSERVATIONS, *to take —,* (of the stars, &c.), ts'eh'-liang 測量.

OBSERVATORY, *astronomical* kwun t'in-ziang'-dæ 觀天象臺.

OBSERVE, *to see,* k'en 看; *to take notice,* li'-we 理會; *not to —*

(when one ought to —), shih-kwu' 失顧;— the laws, sin koh'-fah 守國法

OBSOLETE, feh-tsoh'-de 弗作了°; tsoh'-ko-de 不°行°了°;— as fashions, &c., ko-z'-de 過時了°

OBSTACLE, fông-ngæ' 妨礙; tsu'-ngæ 阻礙; serious —, kwæn-ngæ' 關礙; in spite of all obstacles, fong-yü', vn-tsu' 風雨無阻; meets with many obstacles, p'ong'-djoh hyü'-to fông-ngæ' 逢°着°許多妨礙

OBSTINATE, tsih-ih' 執一; kwu'-tsih 固執; nying-dzih' feh-cün-wæn' 認直弗轉彎;—(as a child, servant, or inferior), sah-gyiang' 撒強

OBSTRUCT, to hinder, læn-tsu' 攔阻; tsu'-djü 阻住; to stop up, seh'-sah 塞煞; üong'-sah 壅煞

OBSTRUCTED, feh-t'ong' 弗通; — breath, ky'ï' feh-t'ong'-de 氣弗通了°

OBTAIN, to teh'-djoh 得着; teh'-tao-siu 得到手; difficult to —, næn teh'-go 難得个°; have obtained my wish, ngô sô siang'-vông tao-siu'-de 我所想望到手了°

OBTRUSIVE, gah-gah'-dong'-go 撟撟動个°; iao gah-long'-læ 要撟攏來; (duck wants to be goose), æn'-gah-ngo'-de' 鴨來°鵝隊

OBTUSE, blunt, deng 鈍;— mind, ts'-tsih deng' 資質鈍; stupid, nyü 愚; nyü-beng' 愚笨

OBVIATE, to pa'-pu 擺佈; ts'a'-bæn 措辨; these difficulties can be obviated, keh'-sing næn'-c'ü hao pa'-pu 這些°難處好擺佈

OBVIOUS, hyin'-kyin 顯見; ming-tông'-tông 分°明°

OCCASION, opportunity, kyi-we' 機會; take —, ts'ing' kyi-we' 趁機會; on this —, keh' ih-ts'' 這一次; keh ih-vah'; on a previous —, zin' ih-we' 前°一回; on a succeeding —, 'eo ih-we 後一回; 'ô'-ih-we' 下°一回; zin vah' ts 前°回°; there is no — for your paying, ng k'o' feh-pih' do-c'ih' 你可弗必拿°出

OCCASION, to cause, s'-teh 使得; long 弄;— pleasure (to him), s'-teh gyi hwun-hyi 使得其歡喜;— a loss, or injury by delay, tæn-ngwu' 躭悮; this occasioned trouble, be keh'-go sô 'æ' 被這°个°所害

OCCASIONALLY, comes yiu'-teh læ 有得來; meet —, p'ong'-djoh'-p'ong' 偶°然°而遇°; do (it) —, yiu'-teh z-'eo tso' 有得時候做

OCCUPATION, z'-nyih 事業; 'ông-nyih' 行業; 'ông-tông 行當; what is your respect-

able —? ng soh'-go kwe' nyih 你°甚°麼°貴業? *my mean — is selling cloth*, ngô bi'-nyih ma-pu'-go 我敝業賣°布個°.

OCCUPIED, *always* feh-teh'-k'ong 弗得空

OCCUPY, *to* — *one's time*, ko nyih-ts' 過日°子; du kwông-ing' 度光陰; *how do you — your time?* ng' dza ko' nyih-ts' 你°怎°過日°子?

OCCURRENCE, *a strange* ih-ky'i' gyi-z' 一椿奇事; *there has been no other* —, bing'-vu bih' dzing 並無別情

OCCUR, *when did it* —? læ kyi'-z yiu' 在幾時有? *if a difficulty* —, ziah p'ong'-djoh yiu keh'-tah 若逢著有疙瘩

OCEAN, do-yiang' 大°洋; hæ'-yiang 海洋; *western* —, si-yiang' 西洋

OCULIST, ngæn'-k'o sin'-sang 眼°科先生; cün-meng' ngæn'-k'o 專門眼°科

ODD, koh' c'ih koh-yiang' 各出各樣; t'iao'-c'ih-liao 超°出了°; c'ih-gyi' 出奇; *strange*, gyi-kwa' 奇怪°; — *number*, tæn-su' 單數; — *jobs*, ling-se' sang-weh' 零碎生°活

ODDS *and ends*, ling-se' tong'-si 零碎東西

ODES, 8 詩; s-ko' 詩歌; *Book of Odes*, S-Kying' 詩經

ODIOUS, k'o-u' 可惡; k'o-*h*eng' 可恨

ODOR, (often unpleasant), ky'i'-min 氣味°; *pleasant* —, hyiang 香; *fragrant* —, p'eng'-hyiang 噴香; *bad* —, we'-ky'i 穢氣; wa ky'i'-sih 癆氣息; ky'i'-sih 氣息

ODORIFEROUS *vapor*, hyiang'-ky'i 香氣; — *wood*, hyiang-moh' 香木

ŒSOPHAGUS, we-kwun' 胃管; zih-kwun' 食管

OF (sign of the possessive), go 个°; *friend* — *mine*, ngô'-go beng-yin' 我个°朋友; *the Lord* —, *Heaven*, T'in-cü' 天主; — *what is it made?* z-soh'-si tso'-c'ih-læ-go' 是甚°麼做出來个°? *made — wood*, jü tso'-go 樹做个°; moh-deo' tso-go 木頭做个°; — *course*, z-jün' 自然

OFF, *far* li-yün' 離遠; yün'-leh-kying 遠得°緊; *how far* —? li-yün' to-siao' 離遠多少? ts'ô to'-siao yün' 差多少遠? *take* — *clothes*, t'eh i-zông' 脫衣裳°; t'eh'-diao i-zông'; *take* — (as beads from a string), leh-c'ih' 捋出; *break* — *a piece* (as wood, &c.), ao ih-t'ön 拗一段°; *ditto* (as bread), p'ah' ih-kw'e 擘°一塊; wah' ih-tin 挖一點

OFFENCE, See OFFENSE.

OFFEND, *to* — *him*, peh gyi kwa

OFF 319 OFF

俾°其怪°; peh gyi' tsiao-kwa' 俾°其招怪°; peh gyi kyin-kwa' 俾°其見怪°; to displease, long'-leh gyi feh 'eh-shih' 弄得°其弗合式°; peh gyi feh yüoh'-i 俾°其弗欲意; s'-teh gyi kyiæ'-i 使得其介意;—against (propriety, or law), teh'-ze' 得罪; væn 犯; væn'-djoh 犯著°;— unwittingly, ngwu-væn' 悮犯

OFFENDED, is kwa'-de 怪°了°; kyin-kwa'-de 見怪°了°; displeased, feh yüoh'-i-de 弗欲意了°; sing'-li ts'iao'-soh-soh 心裡糙粟粟; you are — at me, ng kyin ngô'-go kwa' 你°見我个°怪; not —, m̄'-teh kwa' 弗°怪

OFFENDER against law, we-lih'-væn-fah'-go 違律犯法个°; væn'-nying 犯人°; væn-fah'-go nying 犯法个°人°

OFFENSE, what — has he committed? gyi væn soh'-go en' 其犯甚°麼°案? væn soh'-go kwe' 犯甚°麼°規? to commit an — against propriety, shih li' 失禮

OFFENSIVE language, feh cong t'ing-go shih-wô' 弗中聽个°說話; feh-jih' ng'-tô shih-wô' 弗入耳°个°說話; disgusting, we-u-go 穢汚个°

OFFER, to tang'-tsiang peh 意°欲°給; I offered him $7. but he was unwilling, ngô tang'-tsiang peh gyi ts'ih-kw'e fæn-ping', gyi feh k'eng' 我意°欲°給°其七塊番餅其弗肯; how much do you —? ng he' to-siao 你°許多少? ng hen' to-siao' 你°允多少?— to a superior, vong-hyin' 奉獻; hyin'-zông 獻上;— to an idol, or ancestor, kong'-vong 供奉;— tribute, tsing kong' 進貢;— presents, song li'-veh 送禮物;— a lower price, kô'-diu he'-leh ky'üh 價°錢°許得缺;— him a chair, ü'-ts teh' peh gyi' 椅°子°掇與°其

OFFERING, or sacrifice, tsi'-veh 祭物;— (whole, in platters before an idol), foh'-li 福禮;— (smaller, in bowls), kong'-ts'æ 供菜;— to ancestors, kang-væn' 羹飯;

OFFICE, tsih'-veng 職分; ngæn-deo' 衙頭; to decline —, t'e-dz' kwun-tsih' 推辭官職; to enter —, zông ziug' 上任; to degrade from —, kah tsih' 革職; kông kyih' 降級

OFFICER, kwun 官; kwun-fu' 官府; kwun-yün' 官員; princes and great officers, wông-kong' da'-dzing 王公大臣; civil —, veng-kwun' 文官; military —, vu'-kwun 武官; civil and military —, veng-vu'-pah-kwun' 文武百官; great ditto, kong-'eo'-tsiang'-siang 公侯將相; to become an — by fair means, (i. e.

OFF   320   OLD

by examination), tsing'- du c'ih-sing' 正途出身; *ditto through merit,* kyüing-kong' c'ih-sing' 軍功出身; *ditto by purchase,* kyün-pæn' c'ih-sing' 捐納°出身

OFFICIAL, *to attend to — duties,* bæn kong-vu' 辦公務; — *documents,* kong veng' 公文; — *residence,* ngô-meng' 衙門; *embroidered satin square denoting — rank,* pu'-ts 補子; — *jacket and robe,* mông'-bao pu'-kwô 蟒袍補袿;

OFFICIOUS, ô'-zông-meng 挺上門; dzoh-zông'-meng 撅上門; *meddling,* ts'ih'-siu - pah - kyiah' 七手八脚; to-z'-go 多事个°.

OFTEN, le'-ts' 屢次; *how — ?* to-siao' we'-su 多少回數? *very —,* hyü'-to we'-su 許多回數

OIL, yiu 油; *bean —,* deo-yiu' 荳油; *fragrant —,* hyiang-yiu' 香油; *tallow-tree —,* ts'ing'-yiu 青油; *rape-seed —,* ts'æ'-yiu 菜油; *sesamum —,* ts-mô'-yiu 芝麻油; *pea-nut —,* seng-yiu' 生油; *mô-yiu'* 麻油; *kerosene —,* ho'-yin 火油; *castor —,* pi-mô'-yiu 蓖蔴油; — *paint,* yiu ts'ih' 油漆

OIL, *to* dzô yiu 搽油; *to rub on —,* k'a-yiu' 揩°油; — *it,* yiu-yiu' gyi 抹°其油; — *the hair,* fu deo' 傅頭

OILMAN, yiu-k'ah'-nying 油客人°

OILY *taste,* yiu'-go mi-dao 油个°味°道; — *flavor,* yiu yiu'-ky'i læ-tih 有油氣; *too —,* t'eh' yiu 太°油; — *lips, slippery tongue,* yiu-cü' weh-zih 油嘴滑舌

OINTMENT, kao 膏; kao-ts' yiah 膏子藥; *mercurial —,* shü'-nying kao' 水°銀膏

OLD, *not new,* gyiu 舊; — *clothes,* gyiu i'-zông 舊衣裳; *not fresh,* dzing 陳; — *bread,* dzing mnn'-deo 陳饅頭; *not young,* lao 老; *aged,* lao'-de 老了°; — *person,* lao'-dzing nying 老成人°; — *man,* lao' kong-kong 老公公; lao-den' 老頭°兒° (not respectful); lao ziu-sing' 老壽星 (used jokingly); — *woman,* lao' bo-bo 老婆婆; lao-t'a-bun' 老太婆° (not respectful); *how — are you?* ng to-siao' nyin-kyi' 你多少年紀? *ditto* (very respectful), to-siao' kwe'-kang 多少貴庚°? — *and worn,* kwu'-nyin-pah-dæn' 古年百°代; *antique,* kwu'-lao 古老; zông-kwu'-fong-go 尚古風个°; — *fashioned,* (out of date), be-z-de 背時了°; — *friend,* lao' beng-yiu 老朋友; lao' siang-hao 老相好; kwu'-kyiao 故交; — *and experienced,* lao'-lin 老練

OLDER *than I,* nyin-kyi' do-jü' ngô 年紀大°如我; *a year — than I,* tsiang' ngô ih nyin' 長

OLE 321 ONE

我一年; do ngô' ih nyin' 大°我一年; pi ngô do' ih nyin' 比我大°一年; this is —, that is newer, keh' z sing'-tin keh' z gyiu-tin' 這°是新點這°是舊點

OLEANDER, keh'-coh-dao 夾°竹桃

OLIVE, ts'ing-ko' 青果; ken'-læn 橄欖 (veng.); — seeds, ts'ing-ko nying 青果仁°; ken'-nying 欖仁° (veng.)

OMEN, ziao-deo' 兆頭; good —, kyih' ziao 吉兆; dziang ze' 祥瑞; bad —, hyüong ziao' 凶兆; wa ziao' 夻兆; strange and bad —, iao nyih' 妖孽

OMIT, to ts'o'-loh 錯落; shih'-loh 失落; — what one ought to have seen, or done, shih-kyin'-tin 失檢點

OMNIPOTENT, vu-sô'-peh-neng' 無所不能; djün-neng' 全能; m̄-yiu' ih-yiang feh neng' 無°有一樣弗能; yiang-yiang' tu neng-ken' 樣樣都能幹;

OMNIPRESENT, vu-sô' peh-dzæ' 無所不在; m̄-yiu' ih-c'ü' feh læ-tong' 無°有一處弗在°

OMNISCIENT, vu-sô'-peh-cü' 無所不知; m̄-yiu' ih-yiang' feh hyiao'-teh 無°有一樣弗曉得; yiang-yiang' tu hyiao'-teh 樣樣都曉得; djün-cü' 全知

ON, læ 在; læ-zông' 在°上; — the table, læ coh' zông 在°桌上; — the water, læ shü min-teng' 在書面上; — the paper, læ ts' zông-teng' 在°紙上; — account of, wé'-leh 爲了°; — purpose, deh-we' 特爲; deh-i' 特意; — no account must, ts'ih'-feh-k'o' 切弗可; — the contrary, fæn'-cün 反轉; tao'-hyiang 倒向; — the way, jing-da' 順搭; retired from office — account of age, kao lao' de' 告老了°; — foot, bu-'ang' 步行°; did you come — foot? ng' bu-'ang'-læ, ma' 你步行°來的嗎°? ng tsœ'-leh-læ, soh' 你走°來了°嗎°?

ONANISM, nen-seh' 男色

ONCE, ih-we' 一回; ih-tsao' 一遭; ih-ts'' 一次; ih-pin' 遍; at one time or formerly, yiu ih'-we 有一回; all at —, ih-zi' 一齊; ih-t'ong' 一通; ih-dong' 一同; tsæn'-zi 並°齊; tsæn'-pô-s zi' 一°樣齊; go all at —, ih-zi' ky'i' 一齊去°; sing all at —, tsæn'-zi ts'ông' 並齊唱; the whole at —, teng'-cü 會°齊; write all at —, teng'-cü sia' 會齊寫

ONE, ih 一; — by one, ih'-go 一个° 一个; ih'-tang-ih' 一打一; every —, dzoh-ih' 逐一; me'-go 每个°; every — is good, ih'-tang-ih' tu hao'-go 一打一都好个°; — and all, ih'-ping 一併; t'ong'-gong 通統; —

ONE 322 OPE

third, sæn-feng'-ts-ih' 三分之一; sæn-kwu'-li'-hyiang-ih-kwu' 三股裡向一股; receive — third, sæn-kwu'-teh-ih' 三股得一; of — language, ih'-go k'eo'-ing 一个口音; dong k'eo'-ing 同口音; — sheep, ih-tsah yiang' 一隻羊; — knife, ih-pô tao' 一把刀; any —, feh-leng' 'ah-li ih-go 弗論何處一个; ze-bin' 'ah-li ih'-go 隨便何處一个; every —, ko'-ko 個個; bring every —, ko'-ko do'-læ 個個拿來; — eyed, doh-ngæn'-go 獨眼个

ONE'S self, zi 自; — own, zi'-go 自个; — own child, ts'ing-sang'-go 親生个; — own brother, tih'-ts'ing hyüong-di' 嫡親兄弟; — own mother, tih' meo 嫡母

ONENESS of purpose, tso sing'-siang 同心想; ih-sing'-ih'-i 一心一意 (used of one or more persons); the same heart, one purpose, dong-sing'-'eh-i' 同心合意 (used of many).

ONION, ts'ong 蔥; — bulb, ts'ong deo' 蔥頭; Shantung —, Sæn-tong' ts'ong 山東蔥

ONLY, tæn-tsih' 單只; tsih'-z 只是; peh'-ko 不過; — one tæn'-tsih ih'-go 單只一个; tæn-tæn' ih'-go 單單一个; doh-doh' ih'-go 獨獨一个;

— have, tsih'-yiu 只有; — can or — good for, tsih'-hao 只好; — need one, tsih'-siao ih'-go 只須一个; tæn-ts'ô ih'-go 單差一个; not —, feh tæn'-tsih 弗單只; feh-doh' 弗獨; feh-ts' 弗止; — son, doh-yiang' ng-ts' 獨養兒子

ONSET, kong-tang' 攻打; c'ong-fong' 衝鋒

ONWARD, to go hyiang zin' ky'i 向前去; wông zin' ky'i 往前去; zông zin' ky'i 上前去

OOZE, to — out, seng'-c'ih 渗出; heng'-c'ih; — in drops, ti'-loh 滴落

OPAQUE, ing'-feh-ko-go 映弗過个; feh-t'eo-kwông' 弗透光

OPEN, uncovered, k'æ'-tong; k'æ'-tih 開的; — (as a letter, &c), k'æ-k'eo-go' 開口个; — to view, tæn-k'æ'-tong 攤開的; free from obstructions, t'ong 痛; clear, frank, tsing'-da-kwông'-ming 正大光明; straight forward, kông'-leh hyiang; in — day, ts'ing-t'in'-bah-nyih' 青天白日; — in texture, hyi 稀 lông 鬆; ga.

OPEN, to k'æ 開; — the door, k'æ meng' 開門; — (as bundles, or bedding.) tang'-k'æ 打開; — a letter, k'æ-fong' 開封; sing ts'ah'-k'æ 信拆開; — a shop,

k'æ-tin' 開店;— a school, k'æ-kwun' 開館; k'æ-'oh' 開學°;— a book, shü' fæn-k'æ'-læ 書翻開來; to push —, t'e-k'æ' 推開;— the bowels, li da-bin' 利大便; t'ong-da-bin' 通大便; to free (as a drain), peh gyi t'ong' 俾°其痛; commence, k'æ-siu' 開手; k'æ-deo'-meng 開頭; mouth is still — (i.e. the matter is still unsettled), wa k'æ-k'eo'-go 還開口個°; cannot —, k'æ-feh-k'æ' 開弗開; how can (I) — it? dza-hao' k'æ 怎°好開? must not —, or don't know how to —, k'æ-feh-læ' 開弗來
OPENING, k'æ'-go di-fông' 開個°地方, hole, dong-ngæn' 洞眼°; a crevice, ih-da vong' 一埭縫;— for work, trade, &c., meng-lu' 門路; deo-lu' 頭路
OPENLY, ming-tông'-tông 分°明; hyin'-jün 顯然; c'ib-lu'-lu 露出
OPERA-GLASS, sông-ngæn'-kying 雙眼°鏡
OPERATE, to — with a knife, k'æ tao' 開刀
OPERATED, has the medicine —? yiah yiao'-feh-yiao' 藥效弗效? it has —, kyin-yiao'-de 見效了
OPERATION, he has skill in surgical operations, gyi'-go tao-fah' hao' 其個°刀法好
OPHTHALMIA, nyib-ngæn' 熱°眼°

OPIATE, en-zé'-yiah 安睡藥
OPINION, i'-s 意思; i'-kyin 意見; decision, cü'-kyin 主見; according to my —, tsiao ngô' go i'-s 照我個°意思; dziu ngô' k'en' læ 就我看來; according to my humble —, tsiao ngô' nyü kyin' 照我愚見; every one has his own —, koh' nying yiu zi'-go i-s' 各人°有自°個°意思
OPINIONATED, he is —, gyi' i'-s tsih-ih'-go 其個°意思執一個°; self — person, cih' nying 固執°個°人°
OPIUM, a-p'in' 鴉片; yiang-yiah' 洋藥; yiang-in' 洋烟; t'u 土°; native —, T'æ-tsiang' 台土°; to smoke —, ky'üoh a-p'in' 吃°鴉°片; more commonly, ky'üoh in' 吃°烟 (lit. to smoke tobacco); tsao in' ; to swallow —, ky'üoh sang a'-p'in 吃°生°鴉°片; to stop smoking —, ka a-p'in' 戒鴉°片; ka in' 戒烟; addicted to —, a-p'in' nyin'-de 鴉°片癮°了; a-p'in' zông ying'-de 鴉°片上癮°了
OPIUM-SHOP, t'u'-tin 土店; t'u'-ông 土行;— (where it is both sold and smoked), a-p'in tin' 鴉°片店; a-p'in t'æn' 鴉°片攤
OPPONENT, te'-dih 對敵; te'-deo 對頭; equal opponents, dih-siu' 敵手

OPPORTUNE, ky'iah'-hao 恰好; *to meet accidentally something very* 一, nyü-ky'iao' 遇巧

OPPORTUNELY, ky'iao 巧; ts'eo'-ky'iao 湊巧; *you have come quite* —, ng' læ-leh ky'iao' 你來得°巧

OPPORTUNITY, kyi-we' 機會; *improve the* —, ts'ing kyi-we' 趁機會; *improve this* —, ts'ing'-ts' kyi-we' 趁此機會; *ditto when some one else is sending, or going,* jing-bin' 順便, dziu-bin' 就便; *to improve ditto,* ts'ing-bin' 趁便

OPPOSE *him (i. e.* cover up his light), kæ gyi'-go tsiao' 蓋其個°面子°; — *one's views, or propositions,* gyiang'-bin 强辯; — *in fight, &c.,* ti'-dih 抵敵; ti'-tông 抵當

OPPOSED, *mutually* siang-fæn' 相反; *ditto (persons only),* teo-deo'-feh'-long 對頭弗攏; — *as ice and hot coals,* yiu jü', ping t'æn' 猶如冰炭

OPPOSITE, *in front,* siang-te' 相對; *facing,* te'-min 對面; — *door,* te' meng 對門; *the two are opposites,* liang'-go siang-fæn' 兩個°相反; liang' feh-siang-te' 兩弗相對; — *forms of expression,* fæn-foh'-go shih-wô' 反覆個°說話

OPPRESS, *to* — *those in one's power (as slaves),* mo-næn' 磨耀; —

a people, bao-nyiah' pah'-sing 暴虐百°姓; tsô'-ziao ming-kyin' 詐擾民間; *ditto in exacting money,* k'eh'-poh (or k'eh-boh) pah'-sing 刻薄百°姓; — *in requiring too much,* pih'-p'ah 逼迫; *to use strength or authority in oppressing,* tang-pô'-shü 打霸勢; yi-shü'-ky'i-nying 以勢欺人°; *ditto (as an underling relying on the power of an official),* yi'-kwun-t'oh'-shü 倚官托勢

OPPRESSIVE *government,* koh' tsing' bao-nyiah'-go 國政暴虐個°

OPPRESSIVELY *hot,* ôh'-tsi-tsi-go nyih' 熱°甚°

OPPROBRIOUS (abusive) *language,* zoh-mô'-go shih-wô' 辱罵個°說話

OPTIC *nerve,* ngæn'-tsong-kying' 眼°總筋

OPTICS, kwông-yüoh' 光學 (veng.)

OPTION, *at your* bing-ng'-sô-yüoh' 憑你°所欲; ze-bin' ng 任憑°你°

OR, wa-z' 還°是; 'oh'-tsia 或者°; ih'-'oh 抑或 (for the second connective); *will you go* — *stay?* wa-z ky'i', wa-z læ-tong' 還°是去°還°是在°此°? *I will either go* — *not, as you determine,* 'oh ky'i', ih'-'oh feh-ky'i' ze ng' ding-kyin' 或去°抑或弗去°隨你°定見; — *not,* feh 否°? *will you do* (it) —

not? ng' we tso' feh 你°會做否°? *will you go — not?* ng' ky'i'-feh-ky'i' 你°去°弗去°

ORACLE, *to inquire of an —* (or in China of an idol), meng ts'in-s' 問°籤詩; gyiu ts'in' 求籤

ORALLY, *to comunicate —*, k'eo'-djün 口傳

ORANGE, kyüih'-ts 橘子; *Fohkien, or Mandarin —*, Foh'-kyüih 福橘; *Canton, or cooly —*, Kwông'-kyüih 廣橘; *bitter —*, (from Weng-tsiu), ken-ts' 柑子; *cumquat —*, kying-ken' 金橘; *— peel*, kyüih'-bi 橘皮; *— color*, yü-'ông'-seh 榆紅色; kying-wông'-seh 金黃色; *reddish ditto*, kyüih'-'ong 橘紅

ORATOR, *good speaker*, jün'-ü kông'-go nying 善於講°个°人°

ORBIT *of a planet*, 'ang-sing'-go kwe'-dao 行°星个°軌道

ORDAIN *a law*, shih'-lih lih-fah' 設°立律法; zao lih-fah' 造°律法; *— an elder*, lih' ih-go tsiang'-lao 立一个°長老

ORDER, *in* ts''-jü 次序; ts''-di 次第; *without —*, m̄-ts''-jü 無°次序; *in regular —*, a-ts''-jü 挨次序; *give it to them in —*, a-ts'-jü feng-peh' gyi 挨次序分給°其; tsiao-ts''-jü feng' 照次序分; *out of —, or disarranged*, lön-tsia'-bong ka 亂蹤鬆°; *military —*, 'ao-ling' 號令; *— for money*, p'iao'-ts 票紙;

dzin-tœn' 錢單; dzin-p'iao' 錢票; *put the room in —*, siu'-jih vông-kœn' 收拾房間; vông'-ts tsiu-coh'-hao 房子收°拾°好; vông'-ts tsông-tsih-hao 房子裝飾°好; *put in —, or repair*, siu-li' hao 修理好; *to regulate* (things in disorder), tsing'-teng 整頓

ORDER, *to —, or dispose*, en-ba' 安排; *to command*, feng-fu' 吩附

ORDERLY, en'-pœn-ts-go 按班子个°; en'-bu-dzin-pœn 按部就班; jing-kwe'-dao'-kyü 循規蹈矩; *— and prettily*, zi-tsing 齊整; *— and precise*, doh-fông-bu' 踱方步

ORDINAL *numbers*, 1st, di-ih' 第一; 2nd, di-nyi' 第二°; 3rd, di-sœn' 第三

ORDINARY, bing-djông' 平常; 'œn djông 閒°常; cong-cong 中中; da-kœ' 大概

ORDINARILY, bing-su'-kyin, or bing-su'-kœn 平素間

ORE, *gold* kying-kw'ông' 金礦; *silver —*, nying-kw'ông' 銀礦

ORGAN, *wind* fong-gying' 風琴; *the five organs of sense*, ng'-kwun 五°官

ORGANIZE, *to* en-ba' 安排°

ORIFICE, *mouth of a tube*, k'eo 口; *hole*, dong-ngœn' 洞眼; *the seven orifices*, ts'ih'-ky'iao 七竅

ORIGIN, læ-lih' 來歷; læ-keng 來根; læ-yiu' 來由; keng-yiu'

根由; nyün-yiu' 緣由; ing-yiu' 因由

ORIGINAL, peng 本; nyün 原; the — text, peng'-veng 本文; nyün ti'-ts 原底子; peng'ti-ts 本底子; — cargo, nyün-ho' 原貨; he is quite —, gyi ling yiu' ih-diao ts'ong-ming' 其另有一樣°聰明

ORIGINALLY, peng'-læ 本來; at first, ky'i'-ts'u 起初; he was — from Peking, gyi peng'-læ z Poh-'-kying læ-go' 其本來是北京來个°

ORIGINATE, c'ih 出; where did it —? soh'-go di-fông c'ih'-go 甚°麼°地方出个°? c'ib'-c'ü læ 'ah'-li' 出處在°何°處? who originated? jü' tsoh'-c'ih-læ' go 誰°作出來个°? ditto this plan? keh'-go fah'-ts jü c'ih'-go 這°个°法子誰°作°出个°!

ORNAMENT, to tsông-sih' 裝飾; — the person, tsah'-kwah 紮刮; tang'-pæn 打扮

ORNAMENTED, yiu hwô-deo'-go 有花頭个°

ORNAMENTS, hwô-deo' 花頭; — for the head, (others are often included), siu'-sih 首飾

ORPHAN, 孤-tia' 孤-nyiang'-go 無°爹無°娘个°; kwu-æ'-ts 孤哀子; one who has lost one or both parents, hao'-ts 孝子

ORTHODOX, tsing'-kyiao 正敎; in China Confucianism is the —

belief, Cong-koh'-go Jü-kyiao' z tsing'-kyiao 中國个°儒敎是正敎

OSCILLATE, to dang-læ'-dang-ky'i' 宕來宕去°

OSTENTATIOUS, pa-p'ing' 擺°品°; pa-do-kw'un' 擺大欸; kw'un'-shih do'-go 欸式大个°; deo'-do-go 大°模大°樣° (in ridicule.)

OSTENSIBLY for a good object, but really for a bad one, yi-ts'' we-ming' yi-pe'-we-li' 以此爲名以彼爲利; — to teach, kao-shü' tso ing-deo' 敎書做因頭; — to teach, but really to do business, ming'-go kao-shü' en'-go tso sang'-i 明係°敎書暗却做生°意

OSTRICH, do-nyiao' 鴕鳥

OTHER, bih 別; — persons, bih'-nying 別人°; bih'-go nying 別个°人°; — kinds, bih-yiang' 別樣; love each, —, dô-kô' siang-æ' 大°家°相愛; pe'-ts' æ'-sih 彼此愛惜; the others, gyi-yü' 其餘

OTHERWISE, feh'-z-ka' 弗如°此°; feh'-jün 弗然; if it be —(you) need not come, ziah feh'-z-ka' k'o'-yi feh-læ' 若弗如°此°可不°必°來

OTTER, t'ah 獺; sea —, shü'-t'ah 水°獺; — skin, t'ah'-bi 獺皮

OUGHT, kæ 該; ing-kæ' 應該; ing-tông 應當; kæ-tông 該

當; tông-kæ' 當該; ky'iah-lch (or ky'iao-leh) 却要; *it — to be so*, tsiao li' ing-kæ'-go 照理應該个°

OUNCE, *an* ih-liang' 一兩; *sixteen (Chinese) ounces make a catty*, jih-loh'-liang sön ih kying' 十六兩算一觔; *an — and a half*, ih-liang-pun' 一兩半; *an —, or tael of silver*, ih-liang' nying-ts' 一兩銀子

OUR, OURS, ah-lah'-go 我等个°;— *country*, peng'-koh 本國

OURSELF, *the emperor*, dzeng 朕; kwô'-jing 寡人; *ourselves*, ah-lah zi 吾°輩°自°

OUT, c'ih 出; *to walk —*, tseo'-c'ih 走出; *gone —*, tseo'-c'ih-ky'i'-de 走出去了°; *— of doors*, t'in-nga' 天外°; *the fire is —*, ho u'-de 火熄了°; *walked till — of breath*, tseo-leh ky'i'-kying bi-hyü 走得氣急°皮虛; *— of employment*, zo lang'-pæn'-teng' 坐冷板凳

OUTCAST (*as a vagabond*), ky'i'-diao-go-nying 棄了°个人°; (*as a child, &c.*), loh-shü'-nying 失°意个°人; loh-liu'-go nying 流落个°人

OUTCRY, *to make an* fah-hæn' 發喊; *make a great —, do-sing bæn-kyiao'* 大°聲喊叫; wæ-wæ'-si.

OUT-DO, *you — me*, ng ko'-jü ngô' 你°過如我; ng sing'-jü ngô' 你°勝如我

OUTER, nga-deo' 外°頭; *the — surface*, nga-min' 外°面; *— skin*, nga-deo'-go bi 外°頭个°皮

OUTERMOST, ting' nga-deo' 頂外°頭

OUTLANDISH *fashion*, gyi-c'ih'-kwu yiang' 奇出古樣

OUTLINE, *to draw an —*, wô ih'-go da'-kwe'-mo 畫一个°大規模; *write a brief —* (of a subject), sia ih-tin' da-liah' 寫一點大畧; *an — of history*, kông-moh' 綱目; kông-kæn' 綱鑑

OUTRAGEOUS, ying-hyüong-pô-oh' 行兇作°惡; ying-hyüong pô-dao' 行兇霸道

OUTSIDE, nga-deo' 外°頭; nga-pin' 外°邊; nga-min' 外°面; *— show*, k'ong-k'oh' 空壳; *ditto, not real*, k'ong'-k'oh kô'-ts 空壳架°子

OUTWARD, dziao-nga' 朝外°; hyiang-nga' 向外°

OVAL, dziang-yün' 長圓; *kidney shaped*, iao-ts' shih 腰子式°; *egg-shaped*, dæn'-go yiang'-shih 蛋个°樣式° (little used).

OVEN, p'ang-lu' 烹爐; *native or Dutch —* (where coals are placed above and below), p'ang-'oh' 烹鑊; *bake in the —*, lu-li p'ang' 爐裏烹°

OVER, zông 上; — *your head*, læ ng' deo zông' 在°你°頭上; *to cross or pass* —, tseo'-ko-ky'i' 走過去°; *to turn — and —*, fæu-læ'-foh-ky'i 翻來覆去°; *in excess*, ko'-ü 過於; — *much*, ko'-ü to' 過於多; *there is a little* —, yiu tin tsiang-tsong 有點積°著°; yiu tin ling-nga' 有點另外°; *ditto* (remaining), yiu tin yü'有點餘; yiu tin dzing' 有點剩; — *ten*, jih to' 十多; — *forty*, s'-jih to 四十多; s'-jih yiu yü' 四十有餘; *to boil* —, p'u-c'ih' 溢°出; kweng'-c'ih 滾出

OVER-ANXIOUS, ko'-ü zeo' 過於愁°; to zeo' 多愁°

OVERAWE *a person*, yi-shü' ah nying' 以勢壓人°

OVERAWED, gyü-hyih'-go 懼慑个°

OVERBURDENED *with work*, lao-loh' ko-deo' 勞碌過歹

OVERCAST, *the sky is* —, t'in' ing-t'en'-t'en; t'in' ing-a'-de 天陰翳°了°; *ditto with clouds*, t'in', yüing tsô-djü'-liao 天雲遮°住了°; t'in', zông-yüing'-de 天漫°雲了°; — *a seam*, nyiao-zông'.

OVERCOME, *to conquer*, ying 贏; *Prussia has — France*, P'u-lu'-z tsin-go z-'eo pi Veh-læn'-si ko-deo' 普魯士戰个°時候比法蘭西勝°; — *difficulties*, næn'-c'ü kying-lin'-ky'i 難處經練起

OVERDONE (as food), joh ko-deo' 過於熟; t'eh joh' 太°熟

OVERESTIMATE *the importance of*, sön t'eh' iao'-kying 算太°要緊

OVERFLOW, *to* kah'-c'ih 溢°出; — (as a river), kah'-zông 溢上; üong'-zông 湧上; tsiang'-zông 漲上; *full to over-flowing*, mi-mun-kah'-c'ih 彌滿溢°出

OVERHANGING *rocks*, sing-c'ih'-liao-go zah-deo' 伸出了个°石°頭; p'oh'-c'ih-liao-go zah-deo' 撲出了石°頭

OVERHEAD, læ deo-zông' 在°頭上

OVERHEAR, *to* — (without intention), vu-i'-cong t'ing'-meng 無意中聽聞°; *take care, your neighbors will* —, kwu'-djoh kah'-pih t'ing'-meng 顧着°隔壁聽聞°

OVERJOYED, hwun-t'in'-'hyi-di' 歡天喜地; hwun-hyi'-sah-de 歡喜巴°極°

OVERLAND, 'en'-lu 旱路; loh-lu' 陸路

OVERLAY, *to* t'iah 貼°; du 鍍; — *with gold*, t'iah kying' 貼°金

OVERLOAD, *to* —(as a box, or boat), tsông'-leh t'eh djong' 裝得°太°重

OVERLOOK, *to* — *from above*, zông-k'en-loh 上望°下°; *to* — *by inadvertence*, kwu'-feh-tao' 顧弗到; feh-læ'-kwu 弗來顧; *to*

OVE 329 OYS

excuse, feh-kyi'-kyiao 弗計較; — *little faults*, feh kyi' siao ko' 弗計小過

OVERPLUS, to-deo' 多頭; yü-deo' 餘頭

OVERPOWER *him*, ah'-gyi-voh' 壓°其服

OVERPRESSED, dziah-kyih' 著急

OVERSEE, to tsiao'-kwu 照顧; — (*work*), toh'-bæn 督辦

OVERSEER *of work*, toh-kong' 督工

OVERSIGHT, *he has the* —, tsiao'-liao z gyi'-go meng-veng 照瞭是其个°名°牙°

OVERSLEEP, to shih-kao' 失覺°

OVERSPREAD *the country*, vu-c'ü'-feh-tao' 無處弗到

OVERREACH *one's self*, (*the heart too fierce will hold only an empty cup.*), sing'-li mang' we-nyiah k'ong' coh-kwun' 心裡猛會揸空竹管, or 心裡體擅反落空

OVERSTEP *the bounds of propriety*, yüih-li'væn-veng' 越禮犯牙°

OVERTAKE, to tse-djoh' 追著° ken'-tao 趕到

OVERTASK, to — *one's strength*, yüong lih t'æ'-ko 用力太過

OVERTHROW, to t'e-tao' 推倒; tang'-tao 打倒; — *a kingdom*, mih-diao' koh'-kô 滅掉國家°

OVERTHROWN, *government* koh' peng'-de 國崩了°

OVERTURN, to fæn'-tao 翻倒

OVERWHELMING, (*like waters rising overhead*), meh-deo'-meh-nao' 沒頭沒腦; — *sorrow*, meh-deo'-meh-nao'-go iu' 沒頭沒腦个°憂

OWE, to ky'in 欠; kæ 該; — *a person* (*without intending to pay*), la-tsa' 賴債; siao nying-kô' dong-din' 少人°家°銅錢°; *how much do you* — *me?* ng ky'in ngô' to-siao' 你°欠我多少°? — *and have nothing to pay*, k'we k'ong' 虧空

OWL, djoh-weng' 貓頭鷹° (ih-tsah)

OWN, zi'-go 自°个°; — *hand*, ts'ing sin' 親手; — *family*, peng'-kô 本家°

OWN, to — (*as property*), ken or ke 掙°; *do you* — *this?* keh z ng-go feh 這°是你个°否°? *he is unwilling to* — *his son*, gyi feh-k'eng' jing ng-ts' 其弗肯認兒°子; *to confess*, tsiao-jing' 招認; — *one's self in the wrong*, be feh-z' 賠弗是; be li' 賠禮

OWNER, cü 主; ken-cü' or ke-cü' 掙°主; cü'-nying-kô 主人°家°; *who is the* — *of this?* keh'-go, cü z jü' 這°个°主是誰°? — *of houses*, or *land*, nyih cü' 業主; vông-tong' 房東

Ox, ngeo 牛°; — *house*, ngeo-gyin' 牛°樓

OYSTER, li-ŵông' 牡蠣°; — *shells*, li-ŵông k'oh 牡蠣°壳

P

PACE, ih-bu' 一步

PACIFY, to — his anger, long' gyi ky'i' bing 弄其氣平; long' gyi ky'i' sih' 弄其氣息; — anger by some ceremony, be-li' sih-ky'i' 賠禮息氣; get up theatricals and a feast to — anger, hyi'-veng tsiu siao-ky'i' 戲文酒消氣

PACK, bundle, pao-voh' 包袱 (ih-go); a — of cards, ih-fu ts-bæn' 一副紙牌°

PACK, to — in a box, tsông'-loh siang-ts'-li 裝落箱子裡; tsing'-loh siang-ts'-li 整落箱子裡; to — or wrap in a bundle, pao-hao' 包好

PACKED, it is already — up (in a box), yi'-kying loh-siang'-de 巳經落箱了°; is your baggage all — ? ng'-go 'ang-li' siu-jih-hao' ma 你°个°行李收拾好嗎?

PACKAGE, a ih-pao' 一包; a — of letters, ih-pao sing' 一包信

PADDY, koh 穀; — in the field, dao 稻; — field, dao'-din 稻田

PADLOCK, foreign hanging lock, nga-koh tiao'-so 外國弔鎖

PAGE, a ih-min' 一面; the second —, di-nyi' min 第二°面

PAGEANT, a fine yi wô-li' yi t'i'-min-go z-ken' 華麗而°又°體面之°事

PAGODA, a ih-zo t'ah' 一座塔;

the Ningpo —, T'in-fong'-t'ah 天封塔

PAIL, water ky'ih-shü-dong' 挈水°桶; large —, or bucket, t'iao-shü'-dong 挑水°桶 (ih-tsah)

PAIN, t'ong 痛; to feel —, teh'-cü t'ong' 得知痛; kyüoh'-teh-t'ong' 覺得痛; — in the limbs, kyiah'-kweh sön' 脚骨酸

PAINFUL, t'ong'-go 痛个°; very —, t'ong'-leh li-'æ'痛得°利害; extremely —, gyih t'ong' 極痛

PAINS, take gying lao' 勤勞; yüong sing-kyi' 用心機; one's trouble for one's —, bah-bah' yiao-lao 空°勞; wông-fi sing-kyi' 枉費心機; — du lao' 徒勞

PAINTER, varnisher, ts'ih'-s-vu' 漆司務; — of pictures, tæn-ts'ing' sin'-sang 丹青先生

PAINT, green loh yiu' 綠油; yellow —, wông yiu' 黃油; foreign yellow —, yiang-wông' 洋黃

PAINT, to (with oil paint, or simply with oil), yiu 油; yiu-ib'-yiu 油一油; k'a yiu' 揩°油; — with foreign green, yiu yiang-loh' or k'a' yiang-loh' yiu 揩°洋綠油; — lead color, yiu hwe-seh' 油灰色; — pictures, ts'æ'-seh sia-wô' 彩色寫°畫; to color, as maps, &c., tsiah'-seh 着色; to — the face (with carmine), dzô in-tsi' 搭臙脂°

PAINTINGS, ts'æ'-seh-go wô' 彩色个°畫; ts'æ' wô 彩畫
PAINTS, ngæn-liao' 顏°料; dishes of —, ngæn-liao' diah 顏°料牒
PAIR, a ih-te' 一對; ih-sông' 一雙; ih-fu' 一副 (also means a set); in pairs (as men, or animals in procession), pa te'-ts 擺對子; a — of flower jars, ih-te hwô-bing' 一對花瓶; a — of shoes, ih-sông 'a' 一雙鞋; a — of bracelets, ih-fu siu'-gyüoh 一副手鐲; a — of scissors, ih-pô tsiu'-tao 一把剪刀
PAIR, to match, p'e-te' 配對; — off in couples, p'e'-tah 配搭
PALACE, wông-kong 皇宮
PALATABLE, sông-k'eo-go 爽口个°; yiu ts-mi' go 有滋味°个°
PALATE, (soft) siao zih-deo' 小舌頭
PALE, bah-liao'-liao 白°了了; —(from sickness, or fright). liao'-bah 了白°; leh-bah' 鑞白°; — as death, ziang si' seh ka bah' 像死色一樣白°; to grow —, min-seh' pin-bah'-de 面色變白°了; shih-seh' 失色
PALL for a coffin, kwun-zæ'-t'ao 棺材套
PALLIATE, to veng-ko'-sih-ti' 掩過飾非; — his sin, tsông-sih' gyi-go ze' 裝飾其个°罪; long gyi-go ze' ky'ing'-k'o 致其个°罪輕可

PALM of the hand, siu'-ti-sing 手心; siu'-công 手掌; the coir — or palmetto, tsong-li' jü 棕櫚樹; — leaf fan, (miscalled) pô-tsiao sin' 芭蕉扇; gwe-sin' 葵扇 (ih-pô)
PALPITATION of the heart, sing'-li bih-bih'-t'iao 心裡蹕蹕跳
PALSY, fong-t'æn'-bing 瘋癱病
PALTRY, t'æ'-si-siao 太細小
PAN, dish, beng 盆; earthen —, ngô-beng' 瓦°盆; shallow — or platter, bun 盤; tin —, mô'-k'eo-t'ih bun' 馬口鐵盤
PANCAKES, to fry t'ah ping' 煏餅
PANE, a — of glass, ih-kw'e po-li' 一塊玻璃
PANEL, nyin-ngô-zao 砌瓦°槽°
PANG, teng'-z t'ong' 頓時痛; one — after another, zi'-tang-zi t'ong' 一°陣一°陣; pangs frequent (before delivery), kying'-zi t'ong 緊齊°痛
PANIC, in a hwông'-de 慌了°; kying-wông-de 驚惶了°
PANT, to t'eo-ky'i' 透氣; ky'i t'eo'-feh-cün' 氣透弗轉; — (from disease, or anger), ky't' kying 氣緊; panting sound, hyi-hyi' hwu-hwu' 嘻嘻呼呼
PANTALOONS, kw'u 褲 (ih-iao)
PANTHER, (a kind of leopard), pao 豹 (ih-tsah)
PANTOMIME, tsông-kyü'-ts 裝舉止; tsông i-tsi 裝意致; 一

PAN 332 PAR

by gesticulation, tsông siu'-shü 裝手勢
PANTRY, ho-zih-kæn' 伙食間°
PAPA, pah'-pah 伯°伯'; ah-pah' 阿伯°; tia-tia' 爹°爹°
PAPER, ts 紙; *a sheet of* —, ih-tsiang ts' 一張紙; *letter* —, sing' ts 信紙; — *used for Chinese writing,* mao-loh' 毛六; mao-pah' 毛八; *strong wrapping* —, sông-bi-ts' 桑皮紙; *coarsest ditto,* ts'ao'-ts 草紙; *match, or touch* —, ho'-ts 火紙; *me-deo'-*ts 煤頭紙; *flowered* —, hwô-tsin' 花箋; *gold sprinkled* —, sa'-kying-tsin' 灑°金箋; *thin white* —, lin-s-ts' 連史紙; — *sized with alum,* væn-ts' 礬紙; *thick alum dressed* —, djong'-væn-ts' 重礬紙; *very large sized ditto,* cong-wô'-sing 畫心紙°; *waxed* —, lah-tsin' 蠟箋; — *utensils, &c., for the dead,* ts' ky'i 紙器; ts'-shü 紙貰; — *clothing ditto,* ming-i' 冥衣; — *ingots for burning,* nyün-pao' 元寶; nying-ding' 銀錠; *tinseled paper used for the latter,* sih'-boh 錫箔; — *clippings (for mortar, and for packing coffins),* ts'-kying 紙筋; — *flowers,* ts'-hwô 紙花
PAPER *maker,* ts'- s-vu 紙司務
PAPERS, *documentary* en'-kyün 案卷

PARABLE, pi'-fông 比方; pi'-yü 比喻
PARADE, ba-dziang' 排°塲; *fond of* —, hao' ba-dziang' 好排°塲; — *of militia,* hyiang-yüong' pa deo ka tseo' 鄉勇成°隊而°行°; — *of authority,* hyin-we-shü' 顯威勢; *false ditto,* tsông we-shü' 裝威勢; — *ground,* kao'-dziang 教°塲
PARADISE, *Buddhist* Si-t'in'-gyih-loh-shü'-ka 西天極樂世界; *Christian* —, T'in-dông' 天堂; T'in-zông' 天上; *Eden,* Yiœ-din' yün 埃田園
PARAGRAPH, ih-dön' 一段; ih-p'in' 一篇; *newspaper* —, ih-dön sing-veng' 一段新文
PARALLELS, bing-siu' 平線; — *of latitude,* we'-sin 緯線
PARALLELOGRAM, dziang-fông' 長方
PARALYSIS, fong-t'æn'-bing 瘋癱病; — *of one side,* pun'-ts-fong 半肢瘋
PARAPHRASE, kyin' ming kông'-ka 簡明講°解°
PARASITE, *trencher friend,* tsiu'-zih beng-yiu' 酒°肉°朋°友'; *sponger,* kwæn' ky'üoh bah-zih'-go 慣吃白°食个°; — *who follows, and likes just what you like,* ts'eo-c'ü' 凑趣
PARASOL, liang-sæn' 涼傘
PARBOIL, *to* ts-leh pun'-joh 煑得°半熟

PAR　　　　　　333　　　　　　PAR

PARBOILED, *half cooked*, pun'-sang-li-joh' 半生半°熟; *very slightly cooked*, sang-hwe'-boh-loh 外°焦°裏°勿°熟°
PARCEL, *a* ih-pao' 一包
PARCEL, *to — out*, feng-bao' 分好
PARCH, *to — corn*, ts'ao loh-koh' 炒稑穀
PARCHED, *very dry*, feng'-ken-s-sao' 粉乾四燥; *— ground*, di-yiang' feng-sao' 地下°粉燥; *— (as a tree)*, kw'u-sao' 枯燥
PARCHMENT, yiang-bi-ts' 羊皮紙
PARDON, *to* nyiao' 饒; sô' 赦°; sô'-diao 赦°了°; nyiao-sô' 饒赦; sô'-min 赦°免; *a general — from the Emperor*, wông-eng'-da-sô' 皇恩大赦°; *beg your —*, ts'ing ng' nyün-liang' ngô 請你°原諒我; teh'-ze ng得罪你°, (lit. have sinned against you).
PARDONABLE, k'o'-yi sô'-go 可以赦°个°
PARE, *to* siah 削; in 剜°; *— nails*, siah ts'-k'ch 削指甲°; *— the skin of a pear*, in li-deo' bi 剜°梨皮
PARENTAGE *for three generations*, sæn-dæ li'-lih 三代履歷
PARENTAL *love*, æ-ts' ts sing 愛子之心
PARENTS, do-nying' 大°人°; tia-nyiang' 爹娘; vu'-meo 父母
PARLIAMENT, *British* Da-Ing' nyi-tsing'-we 大英議政會;

— house (or large place of assembly), nyi-tsing-yün' 議政院
PARLOR, k'ah'-vông 客房; *— (on the first floor)*, k'ah'-t'ing 客廳, or, *to distinguish it from a guest's sleeping room*, we-k'ah-vông 會客房
PARROT, ang-ko' 鸚鵡° (ih-tsah)
PARRY, *to turn aside*, kah'-ko 格°過
PARSEE, Po'-s-koh nying 波斯國人°; bah-deo-da'-pæn 白°頭大班
PARSIMONIOUS (*in using, and in treating others*), k'æn-k'eh' 鄙刻; gyih-li'li 竭利利; 'eo-teo'-teo 猴抖抖; gying-gying'-dong 懍懍動; *— fellow*, k'æn-kyü'.
PART, kwu'-ts 股子; veng'-ts 分子; tsih 接; *give me a —*, kwu'-ts feng peh' ngô 股子分給°我; *a —*, ih-feng' 一分; ih-kwu' 一股; *divide in four parts*, tso s'-kwu k'æ' 做四股開; *give him a fourth —*, peh gyi s'-kwu-teh-ih' 給°其四股得—; *the greater —*, ih do pun' 一大°半; ih do kwu' 一大°股; *the upper —*, zông dön' 上段; zông-gyüih'; zông-pun'-gyüih'; *lower —*, 'ô dön' 下°段; *take the — of one injured*, tang bao'-feh-bing 打抱弗平; gyiang' c'ih deo' 強出頭; *the latter — of the book is better than the first —*, 'ô'-pun

peng', pi zông' pun peng' hao' 下°半本比上半本好; *in two parts*, liang'-k'æ-dæ 兩分°開; *two parts joined*, liang'-tsih-sang 兩接生°; *division* (as a book of the Bible), peng 本; kyün 卷

If nothing is said as to the number of parts, ih-peng and ih-kwu mean one of ten parts.

PART, *to divide*, feng 分; feng-k'æ' 分開; — *in portions*, feng kyi feng' 分幾分; *to — from*, li-k'æ' 離開; bih-k'æ' 別開; *can't — with*, feh-sô'-teh' 弗捨°得; — *with reluctantly*, lin-lin'-peh-shiæ 戀戀不捨° (veng).

PARTAKE, *to participate in*, dô-kô' yüong' 大°家°用; dô-kô ziu' 大°家°受; *will you — of a little?* ts'ing ng' dô-kô' yüong tin' 請你大°家°用點°; *share another's abundance*, dong-hyiang' fu'-kwe 同享富貴

PARTIALITY, p'in-sing' 偏心; p'in-dzing' 偏情; tæn pin'-sing; tseh'-sing 側心; *to have a special fondness for*, p'in æ' 偏愛; *to show — in befriending one's own*, pao-pi' 包庇°; we-kwu' 迴顧

PARTICIPATE, See PARTAKE.

PARTICLE, *Gram.* hyü' z-ngæn 虛字眼°; — (grain) *of dust*, ih-lih hwe' 一屑灰; *the least —* (thread, or hair), s-'ao' 絲毫; 'ao-li'-s-hweh 毫厘絲忽

PARTICULAR, ts'-si 仔細; *over — and fault-finding*, sv'-se 瑣碎; kæn-ka' 尷尬

PARTICULAR, *give every —*, ih-dzing' ih-tsih kông' 一情一節講°; ih-tsih' ih-tsih kông' 一節一節講°

PARTICULARIZE, *to* kông'-leh dziang-si' 講°得°詳細

PARTICULARS, *state the* ih-ih' kông'-c'ih-læ 一一講°出來

PARTICULARLY, *notice* k'en ts'-si 看仔細; *notice more —*, keng'-kô ts'-si k'en 更加°仔細看; veng-nga' ts'-si k'en 分外°仔細看; — *remember this*, keh' ih tün' ts'ih'-ts'ih yüong kyi'-tch 這°一端切切要°記得

PARTING *feast* (given to one going), tsin-'ang' 餞行°; — *gifts or attendance*, song-'ang' 送行°; — *words*, song' bih-go shih-wô' 送別个°說話; li-bih'-go shih-wô' 離別个°說話

PARTITION, pih 壁; iao-tsih' 腰壁°; — *of boards*, pæn'-pih 板壁°; — *of bricks*, cün-pih' 磚壁°; *mud —*, nyi-pih' 泥壁°; *to make a —*, tsông' ih-dao pih' 裝一道壁; *to separate by a —*, kah'-k'æ 隔開; lah-k'æ' 拉開; *the room separated from this by a —*, (or the next room), kah'-pih vông 隔壁房; pin 遍; i-pin' 依遍

PARTLY, pun 半; kyi-feng' 幾分; *garment — new, partly old*,

i-zông' pun'-sing-gyiu' 衣裳半新舊; words — true, — false, shih'-wô pun'-tsing-pun-kô' 說話半眞半假;— brass — silver, kyi'-feng dong' kyi-feng nying' 幾分銅幾分銀;— to see, — to hear, pin-k'en', pin-t'ing' 遍看遍聽

PARTNER (who supplies capital), p'ing-cü' 擺主; p'ing ho'-kyi 擺夥計;— (who has no capital), kying-siu' 經手; tông-siu' sin-sang' 當手先生; dæ sin'-sang.

PARTURITION, sang-yiang' 生養; difficult —, sang-yiang næn' 生°養難

PARTY, pæn 班; pông 帮; tông 黨 (always has a bad sense); of the same —, dong-pæn' 同班; dong-pông' 同帮; of our —, ah'-lah ih-pông 我°等°一帮; ah'-lah dong-pæn' 我°等°同班

PASS, mountain ling 嶺;— for admission, &c., tsih'-tsiao 執照 See PASSPORT.

PASS, to ko 過; tseo'-ko 走過; he passed the gate, gyi ts'ing' meng-k'eo tseo'-ko 其沿°門口走過;— under one's hand, ko-siu' 過手;— under one's eye, ko-ngæn' 過眼°; ko-moh' 過目; must necessarily — that way, pih'-yiu-ts-lu' 必由之路; will not — (as counterfeit money), yüong'-feh-ko'-ky'i 用弗過

去°;— through a hole, dong-ngæn' c'ün-ko'-ky'i 洞眼°穿過去°;—through Yentai, kying'-ko In'-dæ 經過烟臺; tseo'-ko In'-dæ 走過烟臺;— (as food), di-ko' 遞過;— the dish to me, di beng-ts' peh ngô' 遞盆子給°我;— tea in a tray, pun dzô' 搬茶; passed through, (or experienced), kying-lih'-ko 經歷過

PASSABLE, ko'-leh-ky'i'-go 過得°去°个°; k'o'-yi 可以; peh'-ko z-ka' 不過如°此°

PASSAGE, a — way, ih-da tseo'-lu 一埭走路; to take — in a boat, or to hire a boat, ts'ing jün' 趁船;— money (by boat), jün-din' 船錢°; fare in general, bun-jün' 盤川°

PASSENGER, k'ah'-nying 客人°;— on a boat, ts'ing-jün'-k'ah'-nying 趁船客人°;— boat, 'ông-jün' 航船

PASSION, feeling, dzing 情; sing'-dzing 性情; he has a passion for books, gyi sing'-ts sô æ' z shü 其性之所愛是書; dzing-ts sô cong' z' shü 情之所鍾是書; in a —, fah do-ông' de 發大°怒了°; the seven lower passions, s-dzing' 私情; ts'ih'-dzing 七情

PASSIONATE, he is very —, gyi ho'-ky'i do'-go 其火氣大°个°;— disposition, sing'-kah kyih'-

ts'ao 性格急躁; sing'-dzing mao-ts'ao' 性情暴躁
PASSOVER, yü-yüih'-tsih 踰越節; djü-kao'-tsih 除酵節
PASSPORT, lu-bing' 路憑; lu-tsiao' 路照; wu-tsiao' 護照; — given by the Rebels, lu-p'iao' 路票; — to the other world, (Buddhist) lu-ying' 路引
PAST, ko'-de 過了°; — the time, ko-z'-de 過時了°; — ages, ko'-ky'i-go shü'-dæ 過去个世代; yi-wông'-z-shü' 已往時世; to repent of — offences, t'ong'-k'æ zin-fi' 痛改前非; — noon, dzi tsiu'-ko 遲晝過; signs of the — tense, ko 過; de; liao 了
PASTE, to tsiang-wu' 漿糊; to make —, diao tsiang-wu' 調漿糊; liu-wu' 冲漿; to — together, s wu' nyin-long'-ky'i 以糊粘攏去°; to — upon (as on the wall), t'iah 貼°; — for pies, &c., feng 粉; diao-hao'-liao-go min-feng' 調好了个麵粉
PASTEBOARD, ts'-pah 紙栢; pe'-pah-ts 背栢紙 (ih-tsiang)
PASTE-BRUSH, wu-shih'-tsiu 糊刷箒 (ih-pô)
PASTOR of a church, moh-s' 牧師
PASTRY, feng' tso-go tin'-sing 粉做个點心
PASTURE-GROUND for cattle, k'en-ngeo'-dziang 看牛°塲; grass land, ts'ao'-di 草地

PAT, to tah'-tah 搭搭
PATCH, to pu 補
PATH, siao' lu 小路; — between fields, din-dzing' lu 田塍路; stone —, zah lu' 石°路; my — is cut off (i. e. there is nothing for me to do), ngô lu' djih'-de 我路絕了°; vu-lu'-k'o-tseo' 無路可走
PATIENCE, jing'-næ-sing 忍耐心
PATIENT, næ'-sing-go 耐心个°; næ-sing' næ-siang'-go 耐心耐想个; can't be —, jing'-næ-feh-djü 忍耐弗住; neh'-feh-djü' 納弗住; very —, ting' we jing-næ'-go 頂會忍耐个°; how — you are, ng sing' dza næ-hæ' 你°心怎°耐
PATIENTLY, do it —, næ'-sing tso 耐心做; bear —, næ-loh'-ky'i 耐下去°; try to bear —, ts'ia neh'-ih-neh 且°納一納
PATRIARCH, early ancestor, s-tsu' 始祖; — in the family, kô-tsu' 家°祖
PATRIMONY, vu'-yi-go ts'æn'-nyih 父遺个°產業
PATROL, to jing-lo' 巡邏; jing-dzô' 巡查; — at night, jing kang' 巡更; jing yia' 巡夜°
PATRON, s'-cü 施主; — who gives money, c'ih'-din s'-cü 出錢施主; — (the Emperor, &c.), eng-cü' 恩主; — of a store &c., ma'-cü 買°主
PATRONIZE by taking interest in

PAT 337 PAY

k'en'-kwu 看顧; — *by buying one's goods*, s'-kwu 賜顧; 'ô'-kwu 下°顧

PATTER, *to* tih'-tih-tah-tah' 逓逓霂霂; tih'-lih tah-lah' 逓逓霂霂

PATTERN, yiang-ts' 樣子; yiang-shih' 樣式°; *old* —, lao' yiang-ts' 老樣子; lao'-shih 老式°

PAUPER, vu-i' vu-k'ao'-go gyüong-nying' 無依無靠个窮人°; loh'-ts'ing vu-k'ao'-go 六親無靠个°

PAUSE, tin 點; *full* —, *or period*, tin'-dön 點斷; *a ditto* (in Chinese), ih-ky'ün' 一圈

PAUSE, *to* hyih'-ih-hyih 歇一歇; hyih'-ih-zông 歇一息°; deng'-ih-hyih 停°一歇

PAVE, *to* p'u 鋪; *to — with stones*, p'u zah-deo' 鋪石°頭

PAVEMENT *of stone*, zah-deo'-di 石°頭地; — *of brick*, cün-deo'-di 磚頭地

PAW, *foot*, kyiah 腳; *foot with claws*, kyiah'-tsao 腳爪

PAWN, *pledge*, tông'-deo 當頭

PAWN, *to* — (at a licensed shop), tông 當; — (at a place unlicensed), ah 押°; *to give in pledge*, ti'-ah 抵押°; *to take out of* —, c'ü-tông' 取當; *to prolong the time* (for three months, for an article pawned), tin li' 典°利; *to prolong the time* (for a year), cün p'iao' 轉票

PAWN-BROKER, tông'-sông 當商; *pawn-broker's clerk*, dziao-vong' 朝奉

PAWN-SHOP, tông'-tin 當店; do-tông 大°當; *small* —, siao' tông 小當; — (generally small), ah' tông 押°當

PAWN-TICKET, tông'-p'iao 當票; ah'-p'iao 押票

PAY, *wages*, kong-din' 工錢°; sing-kong' 辛工; *salary*, soh'-siu 束修; *officer's* —, fong'-loh 俸祿; *soldier's* —, zin-liang' 錢°糧; *soldier's half* —, pun'-feng zin-liang' 半分錢°糧; *to stop an officer's* —, vah fong' 罰俸

PAY, *to* — (as wages, or for what is bought), fu 付; kyih 給; — (out of politeness, or for something injured, &c.), t'ing 敬; kwe 歸; *we* be-c'ih' 賠出; *I will — your chair hire*, ng'-go gyiao-din' ngô t'ing' 你个°轎錢°我出°; — *off an account*, fu tsiang' 付賬; ka tsiang' 遝賬; kyih tsiang' 給賬; *to — debts*, wæn tsa' 還債°; — *lack the worth of*, t'ing'-dzông 聽償; dzông-wæn' 償還; be 賠; — *the remainder*, tsao 找; tsao'-wæn 找還; wæn-tsao-deo' 還找頭°; — *in instalments*, bah wæn' 拔還; bah-fu' 拔付; — *his debt*, teng'gyi die wæn' 與其代還; din'-fu 墊付; — *a visit*, mông-mông'

望°望°; (or more ceremoniously), pa'-mông 拜°望°; 'eo-'eo' 候候; — *vows*, wæn nyün' 還愿, wæn nyün'-sing' 還愿心; liao nyün' 了愿; dziu nyün' 酬愿; — *attention*, (or listen), liu-sing' t'ing' 留心聽; — *a life for a life*, ih-ming' ti' ih-ming' 一命抵一命; — *him a debt*, (with houses, or goods), ti'-siao peh' gyi 抵銷給°其

PEA, zen-deo' 蠶荳; lo-hen'-deo 羅漢荳

PEACE, bing-en' 平安; en-tæn' 安耽; *at* — (as a place), t'a'-bing 太°平; *at* —, *in rest*, *or in safety*, en-'weng 安穩; *to make*, *or exhort to* —, ky'ün 'o' 勸和; — *has been brought about*, 'o-sih'-de 和息了°; *to wish one* —, ts'ing en' 請安

PEACEFUL, en-tæn'-go 安耽个°; *in comfort*, en-loh'-go 安樂个°; *very* — (no sorrow), t'ih'-t'a-vu-iu' 極°穩無憂

PEACE-MAKER, 'o-z'-nying 和事人°; kông-'ô'-go nying' 講°和个°人°

PEACH, dao-ts' 桃子 (ih-go); *luscious* (from Shanghai), shü'-mih-dao' 水°蜜桃

PEACOCK, k'ong'-ts'iah 孔雀; *to wear a pair of* — *feathers*, ta sông-ngæn' hwô-ling' 帶°雙眼°花翎

PEAK, *mountain* sæn-fong' 山峰

PEAKED, tsin-tsin'-go 尖尖个°; pih-tsin' 筆尖

PEAL, *a* — *of thunder*, ih-go p'ih'-lih 一聲霹靂

PEANUT, hwô-seng' 花生; dziang-seng'-ko 長生菓 (ih-kyih); — *candy*, hwô-seng dông' 花生糖; — *oil*, seng yiu' 生油

PEAR, li-deo' 梨子 (ih-tsah)

PEARL, cü-ts' 珠子; *real* —, tsing cü' 眞珠; *false* —, kô' cü-ts' 假°珠子; — *beads*, (false), cü-k'oh' 珠壳; —, *brilliant at night*, yia'-ming-cü' 夜°明珠

PEARL *barley*, mi'-jing 米仁 *ditto* (as a medicine), i-yi'-jing 薏苡仁

PEBBLE, zah-ts' 石°子; zah dæn'-ts 石°彈子; — (large as a goose egg), ngo-lön'-zah 鵝°卵°石°

PECK, *a Chinese* — (of ten *sing*, or about ten pints), ih teo' 一斗

PECK, *to* teh 啄°; — *and eat*, teh'-teh ky'üoh' 啄°啄°吃°

PECUL, *a* ih tæn' 一擔

PECULATE, *to* s-yüong' koh'-t'ông 私用國帑

PECULIAR, *that fashion is* — *to Ningpo*, keh'-go yiang'-shih tsih' yiu Nying-po' tsoh' 這°个°樣式只有寧波行°个°; — *person*, gyi-bih'-go nying 奇別个°人°

PEDANTIC, t'u'-lu dzæ-'oh'-go 吐露才學°个°

PEDDLE, to — (as vegetables, fish, &c.), tso 'ông-fæn' 做行販; tso siao'-sang-i 做小生°意; t'iao weh-lu' tæn 挑活路擔; — silks, needles, &c., tso ho-lông' sang-i' 做貨郎生°意

PEDDLER, tso 'ông-fæn'-go 做行販个°; ho-lông' 貨郎; peddler's baskets, bu'-tæn 籃°擔; peddler's pack, ho'-lông tæn' 貨郎擔

PEDESTAL, zo'-ts 座子; zo-bun' 座盤; stone — for a pillar, sông'-bun 碡磐; sông'-teng 碡磴

PEDESTRIAN, bu-'ang'-go nying 步行个°人°; good —, tseo-kyiah'-go nying 善°於走个°人°

PEDIGREE, register of kô-pu' 家譜; dzoh-pu' 族譜

PEEL, bi 皮; orange —, kyüih'-ts bi' 橘子皮; dried ditto (in the shops), dzing bi' 陳皮

PEEL, to in bi' 剝°皮; siah bi' 削皮; to tear off skin with the fingers, poh bi' 剝皮

PEEP, to — at, tsiang-tsiang'-k'en 眈眈看; —secretly, t'eo tsiang' 偷眈; — through the crack in a partition, pih'-vong-li tsiang' 壁縫裡眈; to play bo-peep, tsiang-mao' 眈貌

PEEVISH, wang' feh-z' jü feh-z'-go 橫°弗是竪°弗是个°; tsi-tseo'-go 嘈啁个°

PEG, wooden moh ting' 木釘; bamboo —, coh ting' 竹釘

PEKING, Poh'-kying 北京; — Gazette, Kying-pao' 京報

PELT, to ang p'ao°; k'ang 擲°; — him with snowballs, yüong shih-dön' ang' gyi 用雪團擲°其

PEN, pih 筆 (ih-ts); steel —, kông pih' 鋼筆; quill —, ngo-mao' pih 鵝毛筆; the nib of a —, pih'-fong 筆鋒; pih'-deo 筆頭; — rack, pih'-kô 筆架; — knife, siao' tao-ts' 小刀子

PEN, gyin 棬; cattle —, ngeo-gyin' 牛°棬; pig —, cü-gyin' 豬棬

PENAL laws, ying-lih' 刑律

PENANCE, to do tso pu'-joh 補贖其罪°; zi' kw'u' zi 自°苦自°; ditto (as Buddhists), kw'u'-lin siu-'ang' 苦煉修行°

PENATES, family gods, kô-jing' 家°神; the six ditto, kô-dao loh-jing 家°道六神

PENCIL, k'æn-pih' 鉛筆 (ih-ts)

PENDULUM, cong-pa' 鐘擺° (ih-go)

PENETRABLE, t'ong-leh-ko 通得°過; c'oh'-leh-ko' 猎得°過; — by boring, cün'-leh-ko' 鑽得°過

PENETRATE, to tsing'-ky'i 進去°; —by boring, cün-tsing' 鑽進; the wind penetrates the bones, fong' jih kweh'-go 風入骨个°; the eye cannot —, ngæn'-tsing k'en'-feh-t'eo' 眼睛看弗透

PENITENT, *adj.* læ-tih ao' 來的懊悔; *truly* —, dziah-jih' læ-tih hwe' 着寔來的悔

PENMANSHIP, pih'-fah 筆法; pih'-ts 筆子; *your — is good*, ng'-go pih'-fah hao' 你个筆法好; ng-go da-pih' tsing hao' 你°个大筆眞好 (without the tsing, da-pih' 大筆, is used in a flattering way, when the — is not good).

PENSION, tsiang'-sông 獎賞; — *for great merit*, dzæ'-kyüô zih-fong' 在家食俸

PENSIONER *living on others' bounty and doing nothing*, ky'üoh bah-fong' bah-loh' 受°空°俸°祿

PENTAGON, ng'-koh-ying' 五°角形

PENTECOST, wu-shing'-tsih 五旬節

PENURIOUS, *excessively saving*, gyin'-sang ko-deo' 過°於°儉省°; gyin'-p'oh 儉樸

PEOPLE, pah'-sing 百°姓; — *say*, nying-kô' wô' 人°家°話; *how many — were there?* yiu to-siao' nying læ-kæn' 有多少人°在°彼°?

PEPPER, wu-tsiao' 胡椒, (*a grain*, ih-lih); *ground* —, wu-tsiao' feng 胡椒粉

PEPPER-BOX, (*bottle*) wu-tsiao bing' 胡椒瓶

PEPPERS. lah gyiæn' 辣茄; *very small*, or *button* —, nyiu'-ts lah-gyiæn' 圓°小°辣茄

PEPPERMINT, bo-ho' 薄°荷°; — *oil*, bo-ho' yiu' 薄°荷°油

PERCEIVE, *to be conscious of*, kyüoh'-teh 覺得; *not to* — *or be conscious of*, peh'-cü-peh-kyüoh' 不知不覺; *to understand clearly*, t'eo'-ts'ih 透徹; — *by the eye*, k'en'-leh-kyin 看得°見; k'en'-leh-c'ih 看得°出

PERCENTAGE, me pah k'eo-deo 每百°扣頭 See DISCOUNT, and PERQUISITE.

PERCEPTIBLE (by the eye), k'en'-leh-c'ih'-go 看得°出个°; — (to the touch), moh'-leh-c'ih'-go 摸得°出个°

PERCH, *to* ding 停

PERCH, (*a fish*), lu-ng' 鱸魚°; (ih-kwang); *hen* —, kyi ding'-go tông 鷄停个°檔

PERDITION, mih - vông 滅亡; leng-vông 淪亡 (veng.); *going to* —, læ'-tih tsco' si' lu 正在°走死°路

PEREMPTORY, kyüih'-lih 決裂; sah'-tsoh 煞足; sah'-bo; kyih'-jih 硈實; *his commands are very* —, gyi'-go feng-fu' dza kyüih'-lih 其个°吩附甚°決裂

PERFECT, djün-be' 全俻; *complete*, wun-djün-go 完全个°; *absolutely* —, jih-siang'-yü-tsoh'

十相餘足; jih-tsoh' 十足; dzing-kong'-go 成功个°; dzing-dziu'-go 成就个°

PERFECT, to tso' dzing-djün' 做成全; tso' dzing-kong' 做成功;— *what is lacking*, pu'-tsoh 補足

PERFECTLY *done*, tso'-leh tsiu-djün'-go 做得°周全个°;— *good*, jih-feng' hao 十分好; djün-be' hao' 全備好; *learn* —, doh'-leh joh'-go 讀得°熟个°; iao joh-t'eo' 要熟透;— *understand*, ts'ih'-ti ming-bah' 徹底明白°; t'eo'-ti ming-bah' 透底明白°

PERFIDIOUS, we tao'-toh'-long-ts 明°瞞°暗°騙°; t'oh'-sing-feh-læ' 托信弗來

PERFORATE, to — *by boring*, cün-ko' 鑽過;— *by punching*, toh-ko 捅°過

PERFORM, to tso' dzing-kong 做成功;— *one's duty*, dzing peng'-veng 盡本分;— *acts of merit*, 'ang hao'-z 行°好事

PERFUME, hyiang 香; p'eng'-hyiang 噴香;— *materials*, hyiang-liao' 香料; *perfumed essence*, hyiang-shü' 香水°

PERFUNCTORY, *done in a — manner*, tso'-leh liao-ts'ao' sah-tsah' 做得°潦草塞責

PERHAPS, iao'-bông 要防; 'oh-tsia' 或者; k'ong'-p'ô 恐怕, (usually signifies lest); væn-ih'

萬一; vi-min' 未免; yia vi'-k'o-cü 也°未可知

PERIL, ngwe-hyin' 危險; *in* —, ling-hyin' 臨險

PERILOUS, hyin'-hyin-go 險險个°; hyin'-dao-dao 險逃逃; *in a — position*, yiao-ling'-ling 搖懍懍

PERIOD, *time*, z-'eo' 時候; *age*, z-shü' 時世; *cycle of sixty years*, kyiah'-ts 甲子;— *of prosperity*, hying-wông' z-'eo 興旺時候; —, or *sentence*, ih-kyü' 一句; kyü-deo' 句讀; *a dot or* —, ih-tin' 一點; —, *or circle* (as used in the veng-li), ih-ky'ün' 一圈

PERIODICAL, en'-z-'eo-go 按時候个°;— *wind*, en'-z-'eo-go fong' 按時候个°風; *time of ditto*, pao' gyi 颭期

PERISH, *to be destroyed*, mih-diao' 滅壞°; mih-vông' 滅亡; *to die*, si 死°;— *with cold*, tong'-sah 凍死

PERISHABLE, iao wæ-diao' go 要壞个°

PERJURE, to — *one's self*, vah-kô'-tsiu 罰假°咒

PERMANENT, dziang 長; dziang-kyiu 長久; kyiu-dziang' 久長; dzông-z 常時

PERMEATE, to t'ong-t'eo' 通透; jih-t'eo' 入透

PERMIT, n. tsiao 照; tsih'-tsiao 執照 (ih-go); *a — to do* (from an official), we'-ba 委牌°;— (to consignee), ky'i'-ho-tæn 起貨單;— (to shipper), 'ô'-ho-tæn 下°貨單; di-ho'-tæn 提貨單

PERMIT, to peh 與°; to allow, hyü 許; ing-jing' 應允°; to grant, cing 准; will you — me to enter? hao peh ngô tseo'-tsing læ feh 好俾°我走進來否°? he would not — me to go, gyi feh byü' ngô' ky'i 其弗許我去°

PERNICIOUS, yiu-'æ'-go 有害个; yiu-seng'-vu-ih'-go 有損無益个°

PERPENDICULAR, [dzih 直; to raise to a —, jü'-ky'i-læ 豎起來; jü' gyi dzih' 豎其直

PERPETRATE evil, 'ang ôh'-z 行°惡事; who perpetrated this deed? keh ôh'-z jü' 'ang-go 這°惡事誰°行°个°?

PERPETUAL, feh-döu' 弗斷; üong'-yün 永遠; üong'-feh-hyih 永弗歇;— inheritance, üong'-yün ts'æn'-nyih 永遠產業;— motion, feh hyih' go læ-tih dong' 時°時°而°動

PERPETUATE, to shü'-dæ liu-djün' 世代流傳; s'-teh üong'-kwu-ts'in-ts'iu, liu-djün' 使得永古千秋流傳

PERPLEX, to long'-leh m-deo'-m-jü' 弄得無°頭無°緒; long-leh weng-teng'-teng 弄得°混濁°

PERPLEXED in mind, sing lön' 心亂; sing lön'-jü-mô 心亂如麻

PERQUISITES, i'-nga-ts-dzæ 意外°之財; nga-ts'eh'-hwô 外撮花; nga-peh' 外°撥; nga-kw'a' 外°快°;— on wood, and ashes, shü'-deo-din 貰頭錢°;— of runners bringing presents, k'æ-fah'-go dong-din' 開發个°銅錢°

PERSECUTE, to pih'-næn 逼難; mo-næn' 磨難

PERSECUTORS, your pih'-næn ng-go cü'-kwu 逼難你个°人°

PERSEVERANCE, dziang-yün'-ts sing 長遠之心

PERSEVERE, to s'-cong, jü-ih tso' 始終如一做;— to the end, tso tao-ti' 做到底; yiu-s' yiu-cong' tso 有始有終做; hyih-siu'-feh-læ 歇手弗來; having begun must —, sih'-siu tsao min-feng' iao tso-tao-ti' 濕手遭麵粉要做到底;— in spite of difficulties, sing-kyin'-zah c'ün' 心堅能°使°石°穿°; t'ih tao'-ts-deo' mo siu'-tsing 若要功°夫°深°鐵杵°磨綉針° (lit., from an iron pestle, to grind an embroidery needle).

PERSIMMON, z'-ts 柿子; tiao-'ong 火°柿°; large —, fông-z' 方柿; dried —, z'-ping 柿餅

PERSIST, to — in doing, p'in iao' tso 偏要做; p'in-sang' iao tso' 偏偏°要做; dzing-gyiu' iao tso' 仍舊要做

PERSON, a ih-go nying' 一个人°; a certain —, mo' nying 某人°; other persons, bih' nying 別人°; go in —, ts'ing-sing' ky'i 親身去°; on the — (body), læ kyi'-sing zông 在°身°體°上; (receives) in his own —, læ zi'-go sing zông' 在°自己°个°身上; three persons in one, sæn we' ih-t'i' 三位一體; call when speaking to a —, or in the second —, tông-min' ts'ing'-hwu 當面稱呼; call when speaking of a —, or in the third —, pe'-'co ts'ing'-hwu 背後稱呼.

PERSONIFY, tsia veh ky'i hying' 借物起興;— a rare flower, as if it were a beautiful woman, tsiang z-hwô' pi tso me'nyü 將時花比作°美女.

PERSPICUOUS, feng-ming' 分明; hyin'-jün 顯然; ming-tông'-tông.

PERSPIRATION, 'en 汗; to be in a —, læ-tih c'ih-'en' 正在°出汗;— rolling down, 'en-c'ih'-t'ô-liu 汗出如流.

PERSPIRE, to c'ih-'en' 出汗;— from drink —, or medicine, fah-'en' 發汗; fah-piao' 發表.

PERSUADE him to come, ky'ün-gyi-sing' hao læ' 勸其信好來; he tried hard to — me but could not, gyi kw'u'-kw'u ky'ün' ngô, ky'ün'-feh-sing' 其苦勸我勸弗信;— kindly, un'-cün ky'ün'-hwô 婉轉勸化.

PERSUADED by him, be gyi ky'ün'-sing 被其勸信.

PERTAIN, dzæ-ü' 在於; joh-ü' 屬於; pertains to God, dzæ'-ü Jing-ming' 在於神明.

PERTINACIOUS, obstinate, nying dzih' feh cün-wæn' 認°直弗轉彎°; ih-li' kang tao deo' 一犁耕°到頭; sticking to one's own way, 'co-zi' 自用°;— beggar, gyiang'-t'ao-væn' 強討飯.

PERTURBED in mind, sing-hwông', i-lön' 心慌意亂.

PERVADE, to fill, c'ong-mun' 充滿.

PERVERSE, ao'-ky'iang 拗强; ao'-diao-peh-sing' 拗調不馴°; diao-bi' 刁疲; wang-pang hyüing-liu' 橫七竪八; naturally —, kwæ-p'ih' 乖僻.

PERVERT, to — the right, or the true, yi-dzih'-we-ky'üoh' 以直爲曲; he perverts my words, gyi pô ngô'-go shih-wô' tin-tao' z-fi' 其把我説話顛倒是非; perverted mind, sing'-jih yia'-de 心入邪°了°.

PESTILENCE, weng-bing' 瘟病; weng-yüoh' 瘟疫.

PESTLE, jü'-peh 研°鉢; nyin'-ts 研子; tao-ts-den' 杵° (ih-go).

PET, to tseng-æ' 珍愛; o-lo.

PET, weh-pao' 活寶 (ih-go).

PETAL, a ih-bæn' 一瓣; flower —, hwô bæn' 花瓣.

PETITION, written ping'-tæn 禀單; to present a —, di ping'-tæn 遞禀單;— signed by many, kong-dzing 公呈; grant my —, cing' ngô sô gyiu' 准我所求

PETITION, to ping'-gyiu 禀求; ping'-ts'ing 禀請; to pray, gyiu 求

PETRIFY, to pin'-we zah-deo' 變爲石頭

PETROLEUM, ho'-yiu 火油; me-yiu' 煤油; zah-yiu' 石油

PETTICOAT, gyüing 裙 (ih-diao)

PETTY matters, k'ü-k'ü-siao z 區區小事; vi·vi-si' z 微微細事;— reason, si' kwu 細故

PETULANT, ô'-wông-tsi-tsao' 怏快嘈嘈; ông-beh'-tsi-tsao' 勃然變色°

PEWTER, native lah 鑞; sih 錫

PEWTERER, lah-s-vu' 鑞司務

PHANTOM, iao-kwa' 妖怪°; iao-k'i' 妖氣; iao-nyih' 妖孽

PHARMACY, keh-yiah'-go fông-fah' 合°藥方法

PHEASANT, dzi'-kyi 雉雞; sæn-kyi' 山雞; yia'-kyi 野°雞; golden —, kying-kyi' 金雞 (ih-tsah)

PHILANTHROPIST, yiu jing-æ'-sing-go nying 有仁愛心个°人°

PHILOLOGIST, cü'-ka-z-nyi'-go 註解字義°个°

PHILOLOGY, the science of z'-yüoh, or z'-'oh 字學

PHILOSOPHER, poh-veh'-go cü'-kwu 博物个°人°; learned man, t'ong-dah'-go nying 通達个°人°; very learned man (in a Chinese sense), poh'- yüoh-'ong-jü' 博學鴻儒

PHILOSOPHY, the Science of Natural —, keh-veh'-go 'oh-veng' 格物个°學°問; moral —, sing'-li 性理

PHLEGM, dæn 痰; to raise —, t'u-dæn 吐痰

PHOTOGRAPH, to take a —, ing siao'-tsiao 映小照; photograph, siao'-tsiao 小照

PHRASE, a ih-kyü djün-be shih'-wô 一句全備說話; a sentence, ih-kyü shih'-wô 一句說話; common phrases, djông-yüong' shih-wô 常用說話;— that one is always using, lao wô'-deo 老話頭

PHRASEOLOGY, kông'-fah 講°法; good —, dæn-t'u' hao 談吐好

PHYSIC, yiah 藥; a dose of —, ih-voh yiah' 一服藥

PHYSICIAN, 'ang-i' sin-sang' 行°醫先生°; i-sang' 醫生; clever —, liang i' 良醫; — of repute, ming i' 名醫; I am a —, ngô'-'ang i-dao' 我行°醫道; travelling — (quack), ma-yiah'-lông'-cong 賣°藥郎中; — who heals by charms, &c., coh'-yiu-k'o' 祝由科; physician's occupation, i-dao' 醫道

PHYSIOGNOMIST, *and fortune teller*, k'en-siang'-go 看相个°
PHYSIOLOGY, *the science of* leng-sing-t'i'-go 'oh-veng' 論身體个°學問
PIAZZA, nao-dông'-teng 鬧塲等; nao-lông' 洋°臺°; nao-lông'-teng 西°洋°樓°; nao-leo' 鬧樓; *lower* —, yiu-jing'-k'eo 廊°下°
PICK, *to* — *rice* (as birds), teh-mi' 啄米; — *apart*, (as hair, wool, &c.,), p'ah'-k'æ 擘開; — (as fruit, or flowers), tsah 摘; ts'æ 探; — *tea leaves*, tsah dzô-yih' 摘茶葉; — *over tea* (taking out sticks, &c.), kæn dzô-yih' 揀茶葉; — *up*, ts'eh'-ky'i-læ' 拾°起來; *will — out other's faults*, we t'ih' nying-kô'-go ko' 會提人°家°个°過; we t'ih'-bi t'ih'-kweh-go 會剔皮剔骨个°; — *out*, *or choose*, t'iao 挑; t'iao'-shün 挑選; kæn'-dzeh 揀°擇; kæn'-shün 揀°選; — *out stitches*, ts'ah sin'-kyiah 拆線脚; — *out* (as nut-meats, eyes, &c.), leo-c'ih' 鏤出; wah-c'ih' 挖出; — *a fowl*, t'e kyi' 搥鷄; — *out feathers*, bah mao' 拔毛
PICKLE, *to* — *meat* (in brine), yin nyüoh' 鹽肉°; — *in vinegar*, ts'u'-tsing 醋浸
PICKLED *fruits*, sön-ko' 酸果; — *garlic*, ts'u'-tsing da-sön' 醋浸大蒜

PICK-POCKET, tsin-liu'-zeh 剪絡賊°
PICTURE, du 圖 (ih-ko); *Chinese picture, or scroll*, wô 畫 (ih-foh); — *of men and things*, jing-veh' du 人物圖; — *of scenery*, sæn-se' du 山水圖; — *of flowers*, hwô-hwe' du 花卉圖; — *frame, and sometimes a framed* —, kwô'-kying 掛鏡
PICTURE, *to* — *in one's imagination*, i'-ngwu 意悟
PIE, p'æn (the Chinese sound for the English).
PIECE, ih-kw'e' 一塊; *a slice*, ih-p'in' 一片; *a — of cloth*, ih-p'ih-pu' 一疋布; *a roll of cloth*, ih-dön pu' 一段布; *—by—*, kw'e-tang'-kw'e 一塊一塊; *divide in pieces*, (as a stick, fish, or something round), gyüih-tang-gyüih (or t'ön-tang'-t'ön) feng-tæn'-k'æ 一段°一段分開; *cut pieces* (with scizzors), tsin se'-kw'e-deo 剪碎塊頭; *pieces*, ling-se' kw'e-deo 零碎塊頭
PIECE, *to* — *out*, tsih-dziang' 接長; — *together*, p'ing-long' 拚攏
PIECE-MEAL, ih-kw'e, ih'-kw'e 一塊一塊
PIER, mô'-deo 馬頭 (ih-go)
PIERCE, *to* c'oh'-tsing 戳進; ts'-tsing 刺進; — (with a boring instrument), cün-tsing' 鑽進

PIETY *toward God*, kying'-we Jing'-ming 敬畏神明; *filial* —, hyiao'-jing do-nying' 孝順父°母°

PIG, siao'-cü 小豬 (ih-tsah); *full grown* —, c'ong cü' 粽豬

PIGEON, beh-kah' 鵓鴿 (ih-tsah); — *whistle* (tied over the tail), beh-kah-ling' 鵓鴿鈴

PIGMY, a'-ts 矮子; — (in ridicule), a-dong-djü' 矮銅鎚°; — *country*, a'-nying-koh' 矮人°國

PIKE, dziang-ts'iang' 長鎗; — *staff*, ts'iang-ken' 鎗杆; *bamboo* —, kw'u' - coh - ts'iang' 竹鎗; *ditto with iron point*, dziang-miao' 長矛 (ih-kwun)

PILE, *to* — *up*, te-zông-ky'i 堆上去°; te-diah' 堆疊; — *in order*, diah-zông'-ky'i 疊上去°

PILES, tsông 椿; *to drive* —, tang tsông' 打椿; *to drive* —, *and at the same time sing a song*, song-sông', or sông-hông'.

PILES, (a disease), dzi'-ts'ông 痔瘡; *outward* —, nga dzi' 外痔; *inward* —, ne dzi' 內痔

PILFER, *to* tso siao'-ts'ih 做小竊; tso siao'-zeh 做小賊

PILFERER, siao'-ts'ih 小竊; siao'-zeh 小賊°; (more polite term, *lit.* a three handed person), sæn-tsah'-siu 三隻手

PILGRIM, *traveller*, c'ih-meng'-go nying 出門个人°; — *to a temple*, hyiang-k'ah' 香客

PILGRIMAGE, *to go on a* — (*i. e.* to offer incense), tsing-hyiang'-ky'i 進香去°; *ditto to the sacred hill*, dziao sæn' ky'i 朝山去°; — *to the four mountains*, dziao s da ming sæn 朝四大名山

PILL, wun-yiah' 丸藥; yiah-yün' 藥圓 (ih-lih)

PILLAGE, *to* ts'iang'-kyih 搶刼; tang'-kyih 打刼; lo 擄; *to fire houses for* —, fông'-ho ts'iang'-ho 放火搶火; *wholesale* — (as of a city), lo'-liah 擄掠

PILLAR, djü'-ts 柱子 (ih-keng); — *of state*, koh'-kô-go tong'-liang 國家棟梁

PILLOW, tsing'-deo 枕頭 (ih-tsah); *feather* —, ngo-mao'-tsing 鵝毛枕; *hair* —, mô-mi tsing 馬尾°枕

PILLOW-CASE, tsing'-deo-t'ao' 枕頭套; tsing'-t'ao 枕套 (ih-tsah)

PILOT, ling'-kông lao'-da 領港老大 (ih-we)

PILOT-BOAT, ling'-kông-jün' 領港船 (ih-tsah)

PIMPLE, le 癟; ts-mô-le' 芝麻癟; *many fine pimples*, 'ong-tin' 紅點; 'ong-pæn' 紅斑 (ih-lih); — *from heat*, fi'-ts 痱子

PIN, bih-tsing' 鬪針 (ih-me); *hair* —, fah'-ts'a 髮釵 (ih-ts)

PIN, *to* yüong bih-tsing' kyin' 用鬪針繳; *to* —, or *tack*, bih 鬪; *pin it*, bih'-ih-bih 鬪一鬪

PIN-CUSHION, tsing-ts'ah' 針插 (ih-go)
PINCERS. gyin 笴; iron —, t'ih-gyin' 鐵笴; crab's —, ha gyin' 蟹°笴
PINCH, to nyiu 扭; — with the finger tip, tih 摘; put in a — of salt, fông liang'-go ts'-deo, ih-ts'eh yin' 將°兩°个°指頭撮一屑°鹽
PINE tree, sæn-jü' 杉樹 (ih-cü)
PINE, to — away, in-üih'-leh, bi-wông'-kweh-seo' 憂鬱得°皮黃骨瘦
PINE-APPLE, po-lo'-mih 波羅蜜 (ih-go)
PINION, to — the wings, bo yiah-sao' 縛°翼°翅; — the arms, siu bo' læ iao-hyih'-li 手縛°在腰脊裡; tie his hands together, siu, pông'-leh gyi 反°綁其手
PINK, (the flower), Loh-yiang'-hwô 洛陽花; a deep — (or cherry color), nyi-'ong' 二紅; peach color, dao-'ong' 桃紅; light —. dæn' dao-'ong' 淡桃紅; feng'-'ong 粉紅; shü'-'ong 水°紅
PINNACLE, ting-den' 巔頂°; nao'-tsin 頂°尖
PINT, a — (dry meas.), ih'-sing 一升; half a bottle, ih-pun' bing 一半瓶
PIOUS, devoted, gyin-sing' 虔心
PIPE, kwun'-ts 管子 (ih-ts); water —, shü'-kwun 水°管; tobacco —, in-kwun 烟管;

— stem, in-kwun' ken'-ts 烟管杆子; musical — with six holes, siao 簫; vong-wông'-siao 鳳凰簫
PIRATE, hæ'-yiang gyiang-dao' 海洋强盜 (ih-go); a boat for catching pirates, ts'ib'-fi jün' 緝匪船
PISTOL, siu'-ts'iang 手鎗 (ih-kwun)
PIT, k'ang 坑°; di-k'ang' 地坑°
PITCH, lih-ts'ing' 瀝青; to fill in with —, din lih-ts'ing' 填瀝青
PITCH, to — (as cash, balls, quoits), p'ao 抛; — a tent, tah tsiang'-bong 搭帳篷
PITCHER, shü'-bing 水瓶 (ih-go)
PITCH-FORK, kông-ts'ô' 鋼叉; dao'-ts'ô' 稻叉 (ih-pô, ih-kwun)
PITEOUSLY, crying kyiao'-leh k'o'-lin-siang 叫得°可憐相; k'oh-leh sông-sing'-siang 哭得°傷心相
PITH of grasses, ts'ao-sing' 草心; — of trees, jü-sing' 樹心; — paper, t'ong-ts'ao'-ts 通草紙
PITIABLE, k'o'-lin-siang 可憐相; — condition, kw'u'-kying 苦景
PITTED with small pox, mô-bi'-go 麻皮个°
PITY, to k'o'-lin 可憐; æ-lin' 哀憐; what a —! k'o'-sih 可惜!
PIVOT, scissor gao-kwu'-ting 交股釘; — on which a boat scull rests, lu-cü' 櫓鈕°

PLACARD, *official* kao'-z 告示; *notice*, kao'-bah 告白°; *advertising* —, tsiao-ts' 招紙; pao'-ts 報紙 (ih-tsiang)

PLACE, di-fông' 地方; u-sen' 所在°; u-dông 戶蕩, (ih-t'ah or ih-c'ü); *in what* —? læ soh'-go di-fông' 在°甚°麼°地方? *no* —, ṃ-c'ü' 無°處; ṃ di'-fông 無°地方; *native* —, peng' hyiang 本鄉; peng' hyiang 本鄉; peng t'u' 本土; c'ih sing' ts di' 出身之地; *belonging to the same* —, dong hyiang 同鄉; *every* —, koh'-tao-koh-c'ü' 各到各處; *shady* —, tsô-ing' di-fông 遮°陰地方; *standing* —, lih-kyiah'-go di'-fông 立脚个°地方; *in the first* —, ih'-læ 一來; ih'-tseh 一則; deo-ih' yiang 頭一樣; di-ih' zeng 第一層

PLACE, *to* fông 放; en 安; — *on a shelf, or stool,* koh 擱; *to give* — *to,* nyiang-peh' 讓°給°; t'e-nyiang' peh 推讓°給°; — *it on top,* fông'-læ zông-deo' 放在°上頭; *when does it take* —? kyi-z yiu' 幾時有? — *the hand upon,* siu en' ih-en' 手按一按

PLACID, en-zing' 安靜; en-jün' 安然; — *sea,* hæ bing-fong' zing-lông' 海平浪靜

PLAGIARIZE, *to copy and use another's composition,* ts'ao-læ' dzing-veng' sön zi'-go 抄來陳文算自°个°

PLAGUE, *to* næn-we' 難爲; *the* —, z-tsing' 時症; weng-bing' 瘟病

PLAICE, *or sole,* nyiah-t'ah 鮭鰨

PLAIN, *level,* bing 平; — *ground, or a plain,* ih-p'iu' bing-yiang' 一片平地°; *easily understood,* hyin'-jün ming-bah' 顯然明白°; — *words,* shih-wô' ts'in'-gying 說話淺近; *unadorned, or simple,* su'-zing 素淨; p'oh'-jih 樸實; tsih'-p'oh 質°樸; *the last two also signify, respectable, and well behaved;* — *spoken,* sing-dzih' k'eo'-kw'a 心直口快°

PLAINLY, *openly,* ming'-tông-tông 分°明°; — *dressed,* c'ün'-leh p'oh'-jih 穿得°樸實

PLAINTIFF, nyün-kao' 原告

PLAINTIVE *voice,* sing-ing' pe-ts'ih' 聲音悲切; sing-ing' kw'u'-ts'ih 聲音苦切

PLAIT, *to lay in plaits,* kæn 襉; tsih-kæn' 摺襉; tang-kæn' 打襉; *to braid,* tang 打; gao-long'-ky'i 絞°攏去°; — *the cue,* tang bin'-ts 打辮子

PLAN *of a house,* oh'-yiang 屋樣圖°; *to draw up a ditto,* tang ih' go-oh'-yiang 寫°一个°屋樣; *mode of doing,* fah'-tseh 法則; fông-fah' 方法; *to devise a* —, mo-nyi ih-go fah'-tseh 摹擬一个°法則; tang'-mo ih-go fông-fah' 打摹一个°方法; *our* —

works well, ah'-leh fông-fah 'eh'-gyi-nyi' 我等方法合其宜; *what are your plans?* ng-sô' meo-we 'o-z' 你所謀爲何事? *intention*, dzing-i' 成意; cü'-sing 主心; *purpose*, cü'-kyin 主見; *that is a good* —, keh'-go siang'-deo hao' 這个想頭好

PLAN, *to* meo-we 謀爲; tang'-mo 打摹; tang'-sön 打算; sön'-kyi 算計; — *mischief*, meo-'œ 謀害

PLANE, bao 鉋 (ih-go)

PLANE, *to* — *it smooth*, bao gyi kwông' 鉋其光

PLANET, 'ang-sing' 行星; *the five planets*, ng'-sing 五星

PLANK, pœn 板 (ih-kw'e); *thick*, —, 'eo'-pœn 厚板; *teak* —, lih-jü-pœn 栗樹板

PLANT, *to* cong 種; tsœ-cong' 栽種; 'ô 下; 'ô-cong' 下種; *to scatter seed*, tsah 撒; *to stick in the ground*, ts'ah 插; — *a tree*, cong' ih-cü jü' 種一棵樹

PLANTS, *grass, and herbs*, ts'ao 草; *ditto, and trees*, ts'ao'-moh 草木

PLANTAIN, pô tsiao' 芭蕉

PLASTER *for walls*, hwe 灰; hwe-feng' 灰粉; joh-feng' 熟粉; *medicinal* —, kao- yiah' 膏藥 (ih-tsiang); — *of Paris*, joh zah'-kao 熟石膏

PLASTER, *to* feng 粉; zông-hwe' 上灰; — *outside walls*, feng ziang' 粉墙; — *partitions*, feng pih' 粉壁; *to put on a* —, t'iah kao-yiah' 貼膏藥

PLAT, *a grass* ih-kw'e ts'ing-ts'ao' di 一塊青草地

PLAT, *to* tang 打; gao 絞

PLATE, beng-ts' 盆子; *soup* —, t'ông-beng' 湯盆; *dessert* —, cong-beng' 中盆; *small preserve* —, tsiang'-beng 醬盆 (ih-tsah)

PLATE, *to* pao 包; t'iah 貼; du 鍍; — *with silver*, pao nying'-ts 包銀子

PLATFORM, dœ 臺; — *for theatricals*, hyi'-dœ 戲臺 (ih-zo)

PLAUSIBLY, z'- wu - gying-dzing' 似乎近情; z-wu-'ch-li' 似乎合理; z'-wu-ziang' 似乎像

PLAY, *game*, hyi-kying' 嬉景; *gentle* —, veng hyi' 文戲; *coarse, or rough* —, ts'u hyi' 粗戲; mœn-tô hyi'-deo 蠻做戲頭; — *for the stage*, hyi'-veng 戲文 (ih-peng); *one act of a* —, ih-c'ih hyi' 一齣戲; *actor*, hyi'-ts 戲子; pœn-ts'-nying 班子人; kyiah'-seh 脚色; — *fellow*, hyi-de' 嬉隊; hyi-yiu' 嬉友; — *thing*, na-'o' tong'-si 嬉戲東西; *toys* hyi-djü' 嬉具

PLAY, *to* hyi'-hyi 戲嬉; na-'o' 鬧和; hyi'-mœn 戲蠻; *to* — *on an instrument with the fingers*, dœn 彈; *to* — *by blowing*, c'ü 吹; — *cards*, c'ô ts'-wu-bœn'

闊°紙牌；— *for money*, tu dong-din' 賭銅錢°；— *fairly*, ngang-dziang' 硬塲；*to cheat in* —, nyün-dziang' 軟塲；nyün'-gyüoh 軟局；— *checkers*, tsiah we-gyi' 着圍棋；— *chess*, tsiah ziang'-gyi' 着象棋；— *tricks of hand*, pin hyi'-fah 變戲法；— *with water*, long shü' 弄水°；*fishes — in water*, ng hyi shü' 魚°戲水°；— *truant*, la-'oh' 賴°學°；— *for a day*, hyi' ih nyih 戲一日°

PLAYFUL, tse' æ hyi-mæn' 最愛戲耍; oh' we na-'o' 極°會嬉戲°

PLEA, *to make a — in defence*, su 訴；— *on paper*, su'-ts 訴紙°；— *in court*, k'eo'-kong 口供；*apology*, feng-ka' 分解°; feng-p'eo' 分剖

PLEAD, *to entreat*, gyiu-k'eng' 求懇；— *for another*, kông-dzing' 講情；wæn-dzing' 挽情；— *a false reason*, or *excuse*, t'oh-kwu' 托故；— *sickness as an excuse*, t'oh bing' 托病

PLEASANT, yiu'-c'ü 有趣；*what — weather it is!* t'in' dza yiu-c'ü' ni 各°人°喜見°天°晴°!

PLEASANTLY *playing*, hao'-tön-tön, læ-tih hyi' 好好°而戲

PLEASE, *to — him*, s'-teh gyi hwun-hyi 使得其歡喜; peh gyi cong'-i 俾°其中意; *please* (I invite you to) *sit*, ts'ing zo' 請坐; — *take tea*, ts'ing dzô' 請茶; — *let me go* (can or not)? k'o'-feo peh ngô ky'i' 可否俾°我去°? *as you —*, ze-bin' ng 隨便你°; ze-ng-bin' 隨你°便; zing'-bing ng 任憑你°; ze ng' i'-s 隨你°意思; dzong ng' i'-s 從你意思; dzong ng'-go bin' 從你°個°便; — *help yourselves* (at a meal), ze' i' ts'ing' 隨意請; *tries to —*, we moh nying'-go sing-siang' 善合°人意°

PLEASED, *greatly* gyih-gyi' hwun-hyi' 極其歡喜; hwun-hyi'-feh-sah 甚°歡喜; *not — with*, feh cong'-i 弗中意; feh jü-sing' 弗如心

PLEASING, cong'-i-go 中意個°; — *and beloved*, (i.e. according to one's mind) teh-i'-go 得意個°; — *to the sight* (as a landscape, a party of children, &c.), yiu kying'-cü 有景致

PLEASURE, *take — in*, yiu hying'-cü 有興致; *enjoyment*, kw'a'-weh 快活; kw'a'-loh 快樂; *to give one's self to —*, tsoh-loh' 作樂; *to spend time in —*, kw'a'-weh siao-yiao' 快活逍遙; *spoil my —* (lit. sweep away), sao ngô'-go hying'-cü 掃我個°興致; *cut off my —*, tang'-dön ngô-go i'-cü 打斷我個°意致; *I have long had the — of knowing and admiring*, (him), ngô kyi' nyiang, siang yü' go 我久仰相與个°。

PLEDGE, to pawn, tông 當; ah 押°; to — a garment, ti'-ah i-zông 抵押°衣裳°; i-zông' tso tông'-deo 衣裳°做當頭

PLEDGE, tông'-deo 當頭; ah'-deo 押°頭 (ih-yiang)

PLENIPOTENTIARY, ky'ing-ts'a' da'-dzing 欽差°大臣

PLENTEOUS, PLENTIFUL, fong-fu' 豐富; prepare a — supply, be'-leh fong-fu' 備得°豐富

PLENTY, fong-tsoh' 豐足; to-to' 多多; ts'iah'-ts'iah yiu-yü' 綽綽有餘; — of food, liang-zih' fong-tsoh' 糧食豐足; year of —, da-joh' z-nyin 大熟年°成°; fong nyin' 豐年; successive years of —, lin-nyin' da-joh' 連年大熟

PLIABLE, easily bent, ao'-leh-wæn'-go 拗得°彎个°; nyün 軟; yielding to others, jing nying'-go i'-s 順人°个°意思; a — person, ze-fong'-tao 隨風倒; ze-zông'-ze-loh 隨上隨落; ziang'ziang-deo'-ts'ao ka' 像墻上°之°草

PLIERS, nyiah-ts'-gyin 揑指箝 (ih-pô)

PLOD, to — (as a student), kw'a-kw'u' yüong-kong 苦苦用功; — (as a laborer), tso kw'u'-kong 做苦功

PLOT, kyi'-kao 計巧°; kyi'-meo'

機謀; kyi'-ts'ah 計策; (ih-go) dark —, en' kyi 暗計

PLOT, to — injury, s ing-cü' 使陰謀; s en-sön' 使暗算; en'-tsin sông nying' 暗箭射°人°; — mischief, meo-'æ' 謀害; — murder, meo-sah' 謀殺; — rebellion, meo-fæn' 謀反; — for money, meo-dzæ' 謀財; — against the king in order to seize the throne, meo wông' ts'ön we' 謀王篡位

PLOUGH, a ih tsiang li' 一張犁; — share, li-zæn' 犁鑱°; — handle, li-mi-pô' 犁尾°巴

PLOUGH, to — the ground, kang din' 耕°田

PLUCK, to — (as flowers, or fruit), tsah 摘; ts'æ 探; — up, bah-ky'i'-læ 拔起來; — up by the roots, lin keng' bah-ky'i' 連根拔起; — hen-feathers, bah kyi'-mao' 拔雞毛

PLUG, to seh 塞; din 墊; tsing-seh' 鑕煞; stopple, seh'-deo 屑頭; a wooden —, jü seh'-deo 樹屑頭

PLUM, li'-ts 李子; sour —, me 梅; red —, in-tsi' li 胭脂李; purple —, gyia-bi' li' 茄皮李

PLUMAGE, mao-yü' 毛羽; it has beautiful —, gyi'-go mao-yü' sang'-leh hao'-k'en 其个°毛羽生°得°好°看

PLUMB, perpendicular, pih'-dzih 筆直; kweh'-dzih 骨直

PLUMMET, *weight*, djü 錘°; *carpenter's* —, cing'-tseh sin' 準則線; — (on ship), tang-shü'-zing 打水繩°; *to measure depth by a* —, tang sing-ts'in' 量°深淺

PLUMP, công 壯°; công'-mun 壯°滿

PLUNDER, *n.* tsông 贓; tsông-tsing' 贓証

PLUNDER, *to* ts'iang'-kyih 搶刦; — *on the road*, pun-lu tang'-kyih 半路打刦

PLUNGE, *to* — *into water*, t'iao'-loh shü-li' 跳落水°裏; *ditto to drown one's self*, deo-shü' 投水°; deo 'o' 投河; — *into water (as the hand)*, tsing'-loh shü-li 浸落水°裡

PLUNGED *into poverty*, loh'-pe'-de 落悲了°; — *in great poverty*, loh-boh' de 落泊了°; — *into difficulty*, loh-næn'-de 落難了°

PLY, *to* — *one's self to study*, ts'ih'-sing yüong-kong' 切心用功; *plies between Ningpo and Shanghai*, wông'-læ Nying-po' Zông-hæ' 往來寧波上海

PNEUMATICS, ky'i'-yüoh or ky'i-'oh' 氣學

POACH, *to* — *eggs*, shü'-t'eng dæn' 水°余蛋

POCKET, dæ 袋; — *in a garment*, i-zông'-dæ 衣裳°袋; bin-dæ' 便袋; *Chinaman's small bag*, 'o-pao' 荷包; *tobacco* —, in-dæ' 烟袋; in-'o'-pao 烟荷包; *long* — *for cash*, dzin-dæ' 錢袋; sông-bun' 錢°搭°; — (tied on in front with the drawers), du-pang' 肚兜'; *long cloth* — *tied about the loins*, tah'-poh 搭膊

POD, k'oh 殼; *bean* —, deo-k'oh' 豆殼

POEM, *a* ih-siu-s' 一首詩

POET, yiu-s-dzæ'-go 有詩才个°; s-ong' 詩翁

POETIC *talent*, s-dzæ' 詩才

POETRY, *to write*, or *make* —, tso-s' 做詩

POIGNANT, *stinging*, ts'iang 鎗; — *words*, shih-wô ts'iang' 說話如°鎗; shih'-wô tsin-li' 說話尖利; — *distress*, c'oh'-sing næn-ko' 獵心難過

POINT, *sharp* tsin-den' 尖頭; — *of a pen*, pih'-fong 筆鋒; — *of a knife*, tao-tsin-den' 刀尖頭°; tao-deo' 刀頭; *a* — (in writing), ih-tin' 一點; *to the* —, ky'üoh'-ts'ih 確切; *not to the* —, dz-i' feh-'eh' 詞意弗合; dz-i' veo-fæn' 詞意浮泛

POINT, *to* — *to*, tin 點; ts'-tin 指點; ts'-ying 指引; — *upward*, tin zông-deo' 點上頭; — *with a stick*, yüong bông' tin' 用棒點; — *off sentences*, tin kyü'-deo 點句讀; — *mortar*, ming zah-hwe' 抵石灰

POINTED, tsin-deo'-go 尖頭个; yiu' fong-deo' 有鋒頭; —

words, shih'-wô ts'ih-cong' 說話切中
POINTLESS, m̄-tsin-deo'-go 無尖頭個; m̄-deo'-go 無頭個; *blunt,* toh'-fong-deo 言; *his talk is* —, gyi'-sô kông m̄-fong-deo'-go 其所講是蓫個
POISED *on the head,* deo'-li ting-leh weng' 頭上頂得穩
POISON, doh-yiah' 毒藥; *poisoned food,* doh-zih' 毒食; *to take* —, voh doh' 服毒; *to put into,* 'ô doh' 下毒; fông doh' 放毒; 'ô kwu'.
POISONOUS, doh'-go 毒個; yiu doh' 有毒
POKE, *to* t'in'-toh 扽撥; *to — the fire,* t'in ho' 扽火; *— him,* toh' gyi ih-kyi' 撥其一撥
POKER, t'in'-ho-bông 扽火棒; ho'-t'in 火扽 (ih-keng)
POLE, kông 杠; ken 杆; kao 篙; *sedan —,* gyiao-kông' 轎杠; *round — for carrying,* kông'-kweng 扛棍; *flat ditto,* pin'-tæn 扁擔; *— for drying clothes,* lông-ken' 晾杆; *—of steelyards,* ts'ing'-ken 秤杆; *—for a boat,* kao-ts' 篙子; ts'ang-kao' 撐篙; *the North —,* Poh'-gyih 北極; *the South —,* Nen-gyih' 南極; *— star,* poh'-teo-sing 北斗星
POLE, *to — a boat,* ts'ang jün' 撐船; toh kao-ts' 扽篙子
POLICE *officer,* bu-t'ing' 捕廳;

— runners, bu-yüoh' 捕役; *thief catchers,* bu-pæn' 捕班
POLICE-MAN, jing-bu' 巡捕 (ih-go).
POLISH, *to make bright,* ts'ah liang' 擦亮; *to make smooth,* mo kwông' 磨光; tsoh'-mo 琢磨; ts'ih'-ts'o 切磋
POLISHED *in manners,* ky'i'-du ts'ong-yüong' 氣度從容
POLITE, yiu-li' 有禮; yiu li'-sing 有禮心; yiu li'-mao 有禮貌; yiu li'-tsih 有禮節; yiu li'-ky'i 有禮氣; *be —,* iao dzing-li' 要成禮; feh-k'o' shih-li' 弗可失禮
POLITENESS, li 禮; li'-mao 禮貌; li'-ky'i 禮氣; li'-tsih 禮節; *affected —* k'ah'-ky'i 客氣; *true —,* k'ah'-dzing 客情; *understands —,* cü li' 知禮; sih li' 識禮
POLITICS, koh-kô z-t'i' 國家事體; *the people ought not to meddle with —,* pah-sing lön kông dziao ding 百姓亂講朝廷事
POLLUTE, *to* u-we' 污穢
POLYGON, to-koh'-ying 多角形
POMFRET, ts'ô ng' 鯧魚; ts'ông 鯧 (veng.)
POMEGRANATE, zih-liu' 石榴 (ih-ko)
POMPOUS, we-pa-p'ing'-go 會擺品個; do-moh'-do-yiang 大模大樣; deo'-do'-go, (slang);

— *show*, ba-dziang' 排°場；pa-kô'-ts 擺°架°子；— *manner*, siang'-mao z'-wu ih-kying' 相貌似乎一景； i'-tsi-pah'-kyü 意致各°別°

POND, dzi 池 (ih-k'eo)； *fish* —, ng-dzi' 魚°池； ng-dông' 魚°塘

PONDER, *to* — *right and left*, tso'-s-yiu-siang' 左思右想；— *many times*, ts'in-s' væn-siang' 千想萬想

PONGEE, kyin'-dziu 繭綢； *gray* —, hwe'-seh kyin'-dziu 灰色繭綢

POOR, gyüong 窮； *very* —, gyüong-kw'u' 窮苦； kw'u-li'-loh-boh' 苦裡落泊； — *cloth*, sô-ho pu' 耍貨布

POOR-HOUSE, (for the poor, and crippled), yiang'-tsi-yün' 養濟院

POP, *to* — *in*, zah-tsing' 闖進； *to* — *out*, zah-c'ih'-læ 闖°出來

POPE, kyiao'-hwô-wông' 敎化王

POPPY, ang'-seh'-hwô 罌粟花； 'a-p'in' hwô 鴉片花

POPULACE, pah'-sing 百°姓； *the vulgar* —, mæn pah'-sing 蠻百°姓

POPULAR, *is* teh nying'-go sing 得人°个°心； *he is* —, gyi' nying'-sing hyiang'-hwô-go 其人°心向化个°

POPULATION, nying-ting' 人°丁； wu-k'eo' 戶口； *what is the* — *of China?* Cong-koh' yiu to-siao' nying-ting' 中國有多少人°丁？

POPULOUS, nying ts'ông-zing' 人丁昌盛

PORCELAIN-WARE, dz-ky'i' 磁器； *fine* —, si' dz-ky'i' 細磁器

PORCH (has no equivalent)； *shed, or arbor*, meng-k'eo-go bong-ts' 門前°遮°篷； *wooden projection over doors, or windows*, p'i-shü'-pæn 披水°板. See VERANDAH.

PORCUPINE, tsin-cü' 箭豬 (ih-tsah)

PORES *of the skin*, 'en'-mao'-kwun 汗毛管

POROUS, song 鬆；— *wood*, jü-moh song' 樹木鬆

PORK, cü-nyüoh' 豬肉°

PORT, bæ'-k'eo 海口；— *clearance*, 'ong-tæn' 紅單； jün-tsiao' 船照；— *for gun*, p'ao'-meng 礮門

PORTABLE, hao-do'-go 好拿个°； do-leh-læ'-go 拿得°來个°

PORTENTOUS, m̀-li'-z 無°利市； m̀-ts'æ'-deo 無°彩頭；— (ill) *omen*, peh-kyih'-ts ziao' 不吉之兆

PORTER, *door-keeper*, kwun-meng'-go 管門个°

PORT-FOLIO, wu-shü-kah' 護書匣° (ih-go)

PORT-HOLE (in a ship of war), p'ao'-ngæn 礮眼°； (window) liang-dong' 亮洞

PORTICO, yiu-jing' 遊巡; yiu-jing' k'eo 管°前°
PORTION, *a part*, ih-feng' 一分, ih-kwu' 一股; *to divide in equal portions*, tsiao'-kwu kyüing-feng' 照股均分
PORTRAIT, hyi'-yüong 喜容; ziu-yüong 壽容; tsing yüong' 真容; 'ang-loh' 行°樂; siao'-tsiao 小照; *to draw a* —, sia hyi'-yüong 寫°喜容; — *painter*, sia-tsing-yüong'-go 寫°真容个°; tæn-ts'ing sin-sang' 丹青先生°
POSITION *in life*, sing-veng 身分; *in high* —, sing-veng kao' 身分高; *great respect for one's* —, sing-kô' djong' 聲價°重
POSITIVE, *sure*, ih-ding' 一定; *one* — *price*, kô'-din weh-ih' 價°錢°劃一; peh-r'-kyüô 不二價; — *in asserting*, zi tsang' yiu li' 自爭°有理; zi wô' zi z' 自話自°是; — *in opinion*, kwu'-tsih kyi'-kyin 固執己見
POSITIVELY, *certainly*, dziah-jih' 著實; ts'ih'-jih 切實; *to determine* —, k'eo'-jih 扣實; *to assert* —, gyin-k'eo' kyih'-jih 筋口給實
POSSESS, *to* yiu 有
POSSESSED *with a devil*, jih-mo'-go 入魔个°
POSSESSION, *in* dzæ siu' 在手; læ siu'-li 在°手裡; *obtained* —, tao'-siu-de 到手了°; *why*

is it in your —? dza-we' læ ng'-go siu'-li 怎麼°在°你°手裡?
POSSESSIONS, *houses, lands, &c.*, ts'æn'-nyih 產業; kô-kyi' 家°計; kyi-nyih' 基業; kô-ts'æn' 家°產; — *of money*, dzin-dzæ' 錢財
POSSIBLE, *practicable*, neng-keo'-go 能殼个°; tso'-leh-læ'-go 做得°來个°; *although* —, *it is not probable*, se neng-keo', r vi pih' 雖能殼而未必
POST, *pillar*, djü'-ts 柱子; *stake*, tsông tsön (ih-go) 椿; *to drive a* —, tang tsông' 打椿; *go* — *haste*, kying'-kyih-fi-pao' 緊急飛報; *to* — *a placard*, t'iah ih-tsiang' tsiao-ts' 貼°一張招紙
POST *for carrying letters*, sing-gyüoh 信局; shü-sing'-kwun 書信館
POSTAGE, sing'-din 信錢°; *also called wine money*, tsiu'-din 酒錢°, *and foot money*, kyiah'-din 腳錢°
POSTAGE-STAMP, sing'-p'iao 信票; deo-ts' 頭子
POSTERIOR, pe'-'eo 背後; be'-min 背面
POSTERIORS, p'i'-kwu 屁股; *rump*, deng-tsin' 臀尖; — *of an animal*, zo-deng' 坐°臀
POSTERITY, 'eo'-dæ 後代; ts'-seng 子孫; *without* —, *or cut off*, djih-'eo' 絕後; dön'-cong' djih-dæ' 斷種絕代, (the

latter is used in cursing); *to descend to* —, djün-loh' peh 'eo'-dæ 傳於°後代

POSTHUMOUS *son*, yi-foh'-ts 遺腹子; — *title*, z-fah' 諡法 (veng.)

POSTMAN, tseo-sing'-go 走信個°; ta-sing'-go 帶信個°

POSTPONE, *to* — *the day*, kæ gyi' 改期; tsæn nyih-ts' 趲日子; *to put off*, dzi-wun' 遲緩; kw'un-wun' 寬緩; iah 約

POSTSCRIPT, nga-kô'-go shih-wô' 外°加個°說話; *to write a* —, tsæ' tsiæ 再者; *a* —, ih-go ling'-p'i 一個°另批, disrespectful if addressed to a superior.

POSTURE, kw'un'-shih 欵式°; — *in sitting*, zo'-siang 坐相; — *in standing*, lih-siang' 立相

POT, *iron* t'ih'-kwun 鐵罐; *native* —, t'ih-ko' 鐵鍋; 'ôh 鑊 (ih-k'eo); — *lid*, kwun'-kiæ 罐蓋 (ih-go); *earthen* —, tseng 甑; bing 瓶; bang 甏; *tea* —, dzô-wu' 茶壺; *flower* —, hwô-beng 花盆 (ih-tsah); *water* —, shü-bing' 水°瓶; *night* —, shü-bing' 尿°瓶; *ditto* (used by Chinamen), yia-wu 便°壺 (ih-go).

POTATO, *foreign* nga-koh fæn-jü' 外國山°芋°; *sweet* —, fæn-jü' 山°芋° (ih-go)

POTTER, ngô'-yiao-s vu 瓦°窰司務; siao yiao' s-vu 燒窰司務

POTTER'S-FIELD, nyi-cong'-di 義°塚°地

POTTERY, ngô'-ho 瓦貨; *place for making* —, ngô'-yiao 瓦°窰; *place for selling* —, yiao-fông 窰坊

POUCH, dæ 袋; *monkey's* —, weh-seng dæ' 猢°猻袋

POULTICE, *to* p'i 披; ah 壓°; — *with bread*, yüong mun-deo' p'i'-tih 用饅頭披的

POULTRY, kyi-ngo-æn' keh'-sing 雞鵝鴨°一°類°

POUNCE, *to* — *upon*, boh-djoh' 伏°着°

POUND, *a* (borrowed from the English), ih-pông' 一磅; *Chinese* —, *or catty*, ih-kying' 一觔; *we buy beef by the* —, ah'-lah ngeo-nyüoh' leng pông' ma 我°們°牛°肉論磅買

POUND, *to* — (as lime), sông 舂; — (as rice), ts'ah 雷; — (as clothes), djü 椎°; k'ao 敲°

POUR, *to* — *from an open vessel* (as a pail, or pot), tao 倒; — *out*, tao'-c'ih 倒出; — *upon*, tao-zông 倒上; — *from a spout*, sia 篩; *to* — *tea*, sia dzô' 篩°茶; *to* — *water into, from a spout*, ts'ong-shü' 冲水°; ts'ong-dzô' 冲茶; *to* — *in*, sia'-tsing 篩°進; ts'ong-tsing' 冲進; — *into one bowl* (the contents of two bowls), ping' ih-tsah' un 併一隻碗

POUTING *out the lips*, cü'-pô ky'iao-tæn'-ky'i 嘴巴翹起; cü'-pô tu-tæn'-ky'i; tu'-cü-bang-sang.

POVERTY, *in a state of extreme* —, kying'-hwông gyüong-gyih'-de 境況窮極了°; *does not fear* — (*wasteful &c.*), gyüong feh p'ô' 窮弗怕

POWDER, feng 粉; *medicinal* —, yiah-feng' 藥粉; yiah-meh' 藥末; *gun* —, ho'-yiah 火藥; — *for the face*, shü'-feng 香°粉; p'oh'-feng 宮°粉; *to make* —, sông feng' 舂粉; mo feng' 磨粉

POWDER, *to* — (*the face*), tsông feng' 粧粉; — (*elsewhere*), dzô feng' 搽粉; — *with a puff*, p'oh feng' 撲粉

POWER, *authority*, gyün-ping' 權柄; gyün-shü' 權勢; *might*, (*as that given by friends, money, &c.*), shü'-dao 勢道; shü'-fong 勢風; *ability*, neng-ken' 能幹; dzæ-neng' 才能; *strength*, lih-liang' 力量; gying-dao' 劤道; — (*both mental, and physical*), vu'-nyih-ts' 武藝°子°; *in one's* —, læ siu-li' nyiah'-tong 揑在°手裡

POWERFUL, *having great authority*, yiu do' gyün'-ping 有大°權柄; *having great strength*, yiu do' gying-dao' 有大°劤道

POWERLESS, shü'-sô-feh-neng' 勢所不°能; lih'-sô-feh-neng' 力所不°能

POX, *chicken* shü'-deo 水痘; *small* — (*natural*), t'in-deo' 天痘; t'in-hwô' 天花; *to inoculate small* —, cong deo-ts' 種痘子; cong-hwô' 種花; *to have the small* —, c'ih t'in-deo' 出天痘; *ditto* (*by inoculation*), c'ih deo-ts' 出痘子

PRACTICABLE, tso'-leh-læ-go 做得°來个°; hao'-tso-go 好做个°

PRACTICE, *usage*, kwe-kyü' 規矩; — *of a place*, hyiang-fong' 鄉風; fong-djoh' 風俗; *bad ditto*, jih-ky'i' 習氣; *an injurious* —, yiu-'æ'-go jih-ky'i' 有害个°習氣

PRACTICE, *to* jih 習; jih-lin' 習練; 'oh-jih' 學習; — *in order to be perfect*, kyiu' lin s'-teh hao dzing-kông 久鍊成鋼

PRACTICED *hand*, lao'-siu 老手

PRAISE *to* ts'ing-tsæn' 稱讚; tsæn'-me 讚美

PRAISE, *worthy of* ing'-teh ts'ing-tsæn' 應得稱讚

PRANCE, *to* t'iao 跳; ts'ön 竄

PRAWNS, *and shrimps*, hô 蝦; — *dried*, hô-ken' 蝦°乾; *ditto dried without shells*, hô-mi' 蝦°米

PRAY, *to* gyiu 求; tao'-kao 禱告; — *for another*, dæ gyiu' 代求; cün' gyiu 轉求; — *for clear weather*, gyiu zing' 求晴

PRAYER, tao'-kao 禱告;— for special mercy, coh'-veng 祝文; to make a —, tso tao'-kao 做禱告
PRAYER-BOOK, a ih-peng tao'-kao-veng 一本禱告文; Buddhist —, kying'-kyün 經卷; kying-ts'æn' 經懺
PREACH, to — religion, kông dao'-li 講道理; djün kyiao' 傳敎; djün dao' 傳道;— the Sacred Books, kông kying' 講經
PREACHER, kông dao'-li-go nying 講道理个人°; djün kyiao cü'-kwu 傳敎个人°
PRECARIOUS, yün-shü'-dang-tsiang 懸勢宕漿; yiao-yiao'-peh-jih 搖搖不實, — footing, dah'-tih feh-weng'-tông 踏的弗穩當
PRECAUTION, to take yü-sin' bông-be' 預先防備
PRECEDE, you will — (us), ng' sin ky'i' 你先去°; ng' dzæ zin' 你°在前
PRECEDENCE, one who takes — in age, zin-pe' 前輩; zin-pæn'-pe 前班輩; tsiang'-pe 長輩
PRECEDENT, pi'-kyin 毗肩, quote as a —, ying'-læ tso lao-li' 引來做老例; to establish a —, tso' ih-go pi'-kyin 做一个°毗肩
PRECEDING month, or months — this, keh'-yüih ts-zin' 這月之前°; the — verse, zông-deo' ih-tsih' 上頭一節

PRECEPT, feng-fu' 吩咐; kwe-kyü' 規矩
PRECIOUS, pao'-pe 寶貝; kwe'-djong 貴重; hyi-gyi' 希奇; — stones, pao'-zah 寶石°; it is very — to me, z ngô ting' pao'-pe-go 是我頂寶貝个°; z ngô ting kwe'-djong-go 是我頂貴重个°; z ngô ting' hyi-gyi'-go 是我頂希奇个°
PRECIPICE, sæn-ngæn' 山嚴; ts'iao'-pih 峭壁 (veng.); standing on the brink of a —, lih'-læ sæn-ngæn pin-yin' 立在°山嚴邊沿
PRECISE, exact, ting'-cing 訂準; accurate, ts'ih'-jih 切實; minutely careful, ts'-si 仔細
PRECISELY, exactly, feng-ngæn'-feng-shing' 分眼°分樺; k'eo'-k'eo 剛°剛°
PRECLUDE, to — one from doing, long'-leh gyi zông-siu'-feh-læ' 弄得其上手弗來; the necessity for that is precluded, keh' lu z-ts'i', ts'-djü-de 這椿事體不通了°
PRECOCIOUS, the — child is hard to rear (i. e. may die early), siao-nying' t'eh ling', næn yiang'-go 小孩太伶難養个°
PREDECESSOR in office, zin-zing' 前°任; — on the throne, zin-deo' wông-zông 先°皇帝; which is better, the present officer or his —? wa z yin-zing' kwun hao,'

zin-zing kwun' bao' 還°是現任°官好呢°前°任°官好?
PREDESTINATE, to ding-su' 定數; dzin-ding' 前定
PREDICAMENT, in a bad zi we'-u 自°穢污; gyi ngeo p'ong-djoh ts'ing-kô'-kong 騎牛逢°著°親家°公; feh-seh'-deo 弗色頭
PREDICT, to yü-sin' kông 預先講°
PREDICTION, yü-sin' shih-wô' 預先說話; yü yin' 預言 (veng.)
PREDOMINANT, ziang yin gyün' tsông'-tih ka 如°掌°權°一°般°; — desire, deo-ih'-go sing-nyün' 頭一个°心願
PRE-EMINENT, c'ih-cong 出衆; c'ih-kah' 出格; ts'iao-c'ih-ü-cong' 超出於衆
PRE-EMINENTLY beautiful, c'ih-cong'-go hao'-k'en 出衆个°好看
PREFACE, jü-veng' 序文; siao'-ying 小引
PREFECT of a department, cü-fu' 知府; do-fu'.
PREFECTURE, ih-fu' 一府
PREFER, to — (in choice), neng'-k'o or nying'-k'o 寧°可; rather, neng'-s 寧°使; — in rank, kô p'ing'-kyih 加°品級; — in office, sing-zông'-ky'i 陞上去°; — (or set one above another), t'e-tseng 推尊
PREFIGURE, to yü-sin' piao'-ming 預先表明

PREFIX, to kô' læ zông-deo' 加°在°上頭
PREGNANT, sông-sing 雙身; yiu-sing 有娠; yiu-yüing' 有孕°; yiu-t'æ' 有胎; do-du' 大°肚
PREJUDGE, to yü-sin tön' 預先斷; to blame severely beforehand, sin p'i-siah' 先批削
PREJUDICE, p'in-kyin' 偏見; to harbor —, dzeng p'in-kyin' 存偏見; willing to believe only one side, t'ing' tæn-min'-ts-yin 只°聽°一°面之言
PREJUDICIAL, injurious, we-'æ'-go 爲害个°
PREMATURE, time not arrived, z-'eo' wa feh-tao' 時侯還°弗到; too early, t'eh' tsao 太°早
PREMEDITATE, to hyüoh-i' 蓄意; hyüoh'-i iao 'æ 蓄意要害; cü-sing iao 'æ 存°心要害
PREMEDITATED injury, yin'-i meo-'æ' 有意謀害; — murder, dzeng-sing' meo-sah' 存心謀殺; hyüoh'-i sah-nying' 蓄意殺人°
PREMIUM (generally from an officer), sông'-kah 賞格: to give a reward, sông tong-si' 賞東西
PREMONITION, had notice, r'-fong t'ing-meng-ko-de 風聞過了°; fong'-sing kwah'-djoh-ko-de 風信得°着°過了°
PREOCCUPIED mind, sing'-læ bih' u-sen' 心在°別處; sing' feng-k'æ'-de 心分開了°

PREPARE, to be-bæn' 備辦;— beforehand, yü-be' 預備;— without fail, ih'-cing be-bæn' 準備辦;— against, bông-be' 防備;— for emergency, yi'-be wun'-kyih 以備緩急; be-r'-peh-yüong 備而不用;— food (rice), long væn' 弄飯

PREPARED, all — (or ready), be-zi'-de 備齊了°; be-hao'-de 備好了°

PREPOSSESSING, we teh nying' hwun-hyi' go 會°得人°歡喜个°

PREPOSTEROUS, ky'i-yiu'-ts'-li 豈有此理

PREROGATIVE, z-cü'-ts-gyün' 自主之權; my —, ngô-go veng-ne'-ts-z' 我个°殄內之事

PRESBYTERIAN church, tsiang'-lao kong'-we 長老公會

PRESBYTERY, lao'-we 老會

PRESCRIBE, to — (in medicine), k'æ fông-ts' 開方子;— rules, shih'-lih kwe-tseh' 設°立規則

PRESCRIPTION, medical yiah-fông' 藥方; fông-ts' 方子

PRESENCE, in the — of, læ tông-min'-zin 在°當面前°; læ min-zin' 在°面前°; speak in his —, te'-min-kông' 對面講°; in — of all, sæn-kyin'-loh-ming' 三見六面; has — of mind, yiu ling-kyi'; 有靈機; seh'-deo ts'ing 兒°識快°; sing' feh hwông' 心弗慌

PRESENT, here, 在°; læ-tong' 在°此°;— life, kying'-si 今世°; kying-seng' 今生;— comforts, ngæn'-zin bao-c'ü' 眼°前°好處;— dynasty, peng'-dziao 本朝;— emperor, tông'-kying wông-ti' 當今皇帝; at —, yin-dzæ' 現在; moh-yüô' or moh-'ô' 目下; ngæn'-zin 眼°前°

PRESENTS, li'-veh 禮物; jing-dzing' 人情;— of congratulation, 'o-li' 賀禮;— (on visiting a superior), ts'-kyin-li' 贄儀;— given to employees, usually at the three festivals, hwô-'ong' 花紅; a small present to those one visits, seh'-hwô 色花

PRESENT, to — (as a gift), song 送; vong-song' 奉送;— (to a superior), vong'-hyin 奉獻;— (to one going on a journey), gwe'-song 餽送;— at court, ying'-kyin 引見;— a document to the emperor, zông peng' 上本

PRESENTLY, coming ziu læ' 就°來; mô-zông' ziu læ' 馬上就°來

PRESENTIMENT, (and also a sign), ts'eng'-z 識事; to believe in a —, siang-sing' ts'eng'-z 相信識事

PRESERVE, to keep from harm, pao'-wu 保護, pao'-djün 保全; pao'-yiu 保佑; tô'-hwô 眷°顧; (the last two refer only to God); — from decay, s'-teh feh wæ'-diao 使得弗壞了°

PRESERVED, *fruits — in sugar,* dông-ko' 糖果; *fruits — in honey,* mih-tsiu' 蜜餞;—*ginger,* tsiang'-kyiang 醬薑

PRESIDE, *to — over,* kyin-ling' 監臨 (veng.)

PRESIDENT, *the head,* siu'-z 首事; *— of a college,* yün-tsiang' 院長; *— of one of the six Boards,* zông-shü' 尙書;—*of a republic,* siu'-ling 首領; tsing'-siu-ling' 正首領; *vice —,* fu'-siu-ling' 副首領

PRESS, *machine for squeezing wine,* tsô'-zông 榨床;—, tsiu'-tsô 酒榨; *clothes' closet,* i-djü' 衣櫥; *printing —,* ing'-shü kô'-ts 印書架子

PRESS, *to urge,* ngang-ky'ün' 硬勘; — (another) *forward,* pih'-leh kying' 逼得°緊; ts'c'-leh kyih' 催得°急;—*down,* ky'ing'-loh-ky'i 揿落去°;—*down with a weight,* ah'-loh-ky'i 壓落去°; *— to the front,* a-zông-zin' 挨°上前°;—*oil,* tsô yiu' 榨油°; —, or *push against the door,* t'e meng' 推門;—*one to eat,* iang nying ky'üoh' 極°意°請°人°吃°; iang nying-k'ah';—*to take wine,* iang tsiu' 敬°酒不°停°

PRESSED *in spirit,* dziah-kyih' 著急; — *for money,* siu'-deo kyih-kyü' 手頭拮據

PRESSING *affairs,* kyih'-ts'ih z-t'i' 急切事體; *he is in — need,* gyi-go dzing' kyih'-tih-de 其个°情急了°

PRESUME, I — *so,* ngô kwu' læ z ka' 我估來是如°此°; tsiao ngô k'en' z-ka' 照我看是逗°樣°; ngô bông-bông' z-ka' 我恐°防是如°此°; *to dare,* ken 敢; *— on one's strength to injure,* or *demand,* tang-pô'-shü 打霸勢; — *on one's strength* (in being wilful), i'- z gyiang-wang' 依恃强橫

PRESUMPTUOUS, mông-bah'-go 茫白°个°; tæn'-ts do' yia'-ky'i 胆子大°野°氣;—*in thinking one willing* (when he may not be), ih'-siang dzing-nyün' 一相情願

PRETEND, *to — to be,* tsông 裝; tsông-kô' 裝假; pæn 扮; — *with craft,* tsô 詐; — *to be a doctor,* tsông i-sang' 裝醫生; *—to be sick,* tsông bing' 裝病; *—to be willing,* or — *not to want,* tsông-ky'iang' 裝腔; *to allege a reason which is false, but which has a shadow of truth,* tsia'-ing 借°因; *to use another's name falsely,* tsia ming-deo' 借°名頭; — *that another is at fault,* t'e-we' 推諉; t'e-t'oh' læ bih'-nying sing-zông' 推托在°別人°身上; *to pass off the false for the true,* mao-c'ong' 冒充

PRETERNATURAL, (as a cat or fox changing into a person &c.), tsing-kwa' 精怪°

PRETEXT, *to rely upon a false* —, ziæ-kwu' 藉故°; *to use a false* —, ziæ-k'eo' 藉口

PRETTY, hao-k'en' 好看; teh-nying'-sih 得人°惜; *very* —, ts'iao 俏; ts'iao-li' 俏麗; m̃e'-mao 美貌; piao-cü' 標緻; (these four are only used of persons); —(as colors), sin ming' 鮮明; *tolerably* —, p'o' hao-k'en 頗好看; *how* — *you are!* (ironical), ng dza hao yiang-væn 你怎好樣範!

PRETTY, *tolerably*, p'o 頗 (not in common use); —*well* p'o' sông'-kw'a 頗爽快°; — *well to do*, k'o' ko nyih-ts' 可過日°子; — *near*, p'o'-gying 頗近

PREVAIL, *to conquer*, teh-sing' 得勝; *perhaps will* —, ying-min' 贏面; *I could not* — *on him to go*, ngô ky'ün-gyi-feh-cün', z-feh k'eng ky'i' 我勸其弗轉是弗肯去°

PREVALENT, kwông'-'ang-go 廣行°个°; t'ong-'ang'-go 通行°个°; *that is a* — *belief*, keh-go dao'-li kwông'-'ang-liao-go 這°个°道理廣行°个°; *what disease is* — *now?* yin-dzæ' yiu soh'-go tsing'-'eo 現在有甚麼症候? *colds are very* —, sông-fong' da-li ting-t'o 傷風之°症頂多, sông-fong' kwông 傷風廣

PREVARICATE, *to* kông'-leh t'eng-t'eng'-t'u-t'u 講°得°吞吞吐吐; kông'-leh pun'-tsing pun-c'ih' 講°得°半進半出

PREVARICATION, ts'ih'-gæ-pah'-gæ shih-wô 七戲八戲說話; *to say what in heart is not believed*, k'eo'-z-sing-fi' 口是心非;

PREVENT, *to* tsu 阻; læn-tsu' 攔阻; læn-djü' 攔住; zih-djü' 截住; tsn'-djü 阻住; these are all used with feh, thus; — *him from coming*, tsu'-gyi-feh-læ 阻其弗來, (this also means, cannot prevent him); min'-teh gyi læ' 免得其來; — *trouble afterwards*, min 'eo'-wæn 免後患; — *sleep* (as strong tea), su-sing k'eh'-c'ong 蘇醒瞌睡°; — *his telling* (by giving him something, &c.), en gyi cü'-pô pi 按其嘴巴閉; seh gyi cü'-pô 塞其嘴巴

PREVIOUS, sin 先; zin 前°; *the* — *day*, sin'-ih-nyih 先一日°; zin'-ih-nyih 前°一日°; *the* — *month*, zin-ko'-yüih 前°個°月; *on a* — *occasion*, zin-deo' ih-we 前°頭一回

PREVIOUSLY, yü-sin' 預先; yü-tsao' 預早; bông-tsao' 防早

PRICE, kô'-din 價°錢°; *market* —, 'ông-dzing' 行情; z-kô' 時價; *to rise in* —, kô'-din tsiang'-zông 價°錢°漲上; *to fall in* —, kô'-din tih'-loh 價°錢°跌落; *what is the* —? *to* siao' kô'-din 多少價°錢°? *high* —, kô'-din do' 價錢°大°; kô'-din kyü' 價°錢°貴; kô'-din kao' 價錢高 (seldom used); I cannot afford that—, ka kô'-din ngô c'ih'-feh-ky'i 如此°價°錢°我出弗起

PRICELESS treasure, vu-kô'-ts-pao 無價°之寶

PRICK, to c'oh 豬; — like a needle, ziang tsing c'oh' ka 像針豬; to — up the ears, ng'-tô jü'-ky'i-læ 耳朶堅起來

PRICKLES, ts' 莿; has —(or roughness), ts''-c'oh ling-ting 莿豬零丁; full of —, jing-z ts' 純是莿; ts''-kyih kao 莿結交

PRICKLY heat, fi'-ts 痱子

PRIDE, kyiao'-ngao 驕傲; — (usually proper), sing-kao' ky'i-ngao' 心高氣傲; take — in (anything proper), tsang ih k'eo ky'i' 爭°一口氣

PRIEST, Buddhist 'o-zông' 和尙; veh-meng' di'-ts 佛門弟子; head ditto, fông-dziang' 方丈; fah'-s 法師; Taoist —, dao'-z 道士; Lama —, na'-mô-seng' 喇°嘛僧; itinerating — (bad), yiu-fông-seng' 遊方僧; Catholic —, jing-vu 神父; Jewish —, tsi'-s 祭司; Mahometan —, lao'-s-vu 老師父; — (with long hair, and band on the head), deo-do' 頭陀; chief —, tsi'-s-deo 祭司頭; high —, tsi'-s-tsiang' 祭司長; to become a Buddhist —, c'ih-kô 出家°

PRIESTESS, Buddhist nyi-kwu' 尼姑; Taoist —, s-kwu' 師姑

PRIESTHOOD, Buddhist sih'-kô 釋家°; seng-kô' 僧家°; Taoist —, dao'-kô 道家°

PRIESTLY garment, (Buddhist), kô-sô' 袈裟; Taoist ditto, dao'-bao 道袍

PRIME, first, di-ih' 第一; — importance, di-ih' iao'-kying 第一要緊; excellent, ting'-hao 頂好; gyih-miao' 極妙; gyih-me' 極美; just in their —, (whether persons, or fruits), tsing'-tông-shü 正當時°; — cost, nyün-kô' 原價°; — minister, siu'-siang 首相

PRIMER, Ningpo Nying-po' ts'u-'oh' 甯波初學°; Trimetrical —, Sæn-z kying' 三字經; — of Juvenile verse, Jing-dong-s' 神童詩; — of Hundred names, Pah'-kyüô-sing 百°家°姓

PRIMITIVE times, t'æ'-kwu z-'eo' 太古時候

PRIMOGENITURE, possession by —, tsiang'-ts-go ts'æn'-nyih 長子个°產業

PRINCE, sovereign kyüing-wông' 君王; princes in general, wông-yia' 王爺°; king's sons, t'a'-ts 太°子; shü'-ts 庶子; the one appointed to be heir apparent, lih'-go t'a'-ts 立个°太°子; — of the blood, ts'ing-wông' 親王; other

PRI   364   PRI

princes, gyüing'-wông 郡王

PRINCESS, *king's daughter,* kong-cü' 公主; *king's sister, or daughter,* gyüing'-cü 郡主

PRINCIPAL, deo 頭; cü 主; — *importance,* deo-ih' iao'-kying 頭一要緊; — *wife,* kyih'-fah 結髮; nyün-p'e' 元配; ts'i 妻; *capital in trade,* peng'-din 本錢°

PRINCIPALLY, da-tu' 大都; da-iah' 大約

PRINCIPLE *of order,* li 理; — *which arranges matter,* li'-ky'i 理氣; *the dual* — *in nature,* ing 陰, *and yiang* 陽; *inborn* —, t'in-sing' 天性; *a universal* —, c'ü-c'ü ih-yiang'-go li 處處一樣個理; T'in-'ô', tsih' yiu ih-li' 天下只有一理; *fundamental* —, deo-ih'-zeng-go dao'-li 頭一層个°道理

PRINT, *to* ing 印; — *from blocks,* yüong moh-pæn' ing' 用木板印; — *with type,* yüong k'æn-z-pæn ing 用鉛字板印

PRINT, *impression,* 'eng-tsih' 痕跡; ying-tsih' 形跡; *foot* —, kyiah'-tsih 脚跡; — *of a hand,* siu'-tsih 手跡; *to make the* — *of one's hand in token of divorce,* tang siu'-ing 打手印; *that book is out of* —, keh' ih-bu shü' dön'-de 這一部書斷絕°了°; *calico,* ing'-hwô yiang-pu' 印花洋布

PRINTED, ing'-c'ih-liao 印出了;

— *pictures,* ing'-go du' 印个°圖

PRINTER, ing'-shü-go nying' 印書个°人°; ing'- shü s-vu' 印書司務

PRINTING-INK, ing'-shü-moh' 印書墨

PRINTING-OFFICE, ing'-shü-vông' 印書房; ing'-shü-kwun' 印書館

PRINTING-PRESS, ing'-shü-kô' 印書架°

PRISON, lao-kæn' 牢監°; kæn-lao' 監°牢 (ih-go); *to be in* — *three years,* zo sæn nyin' lao-kæn' 坐三年牢監°; *put him in* —, ky'ih'-gyi-loh lao-kæn'-li 挈其落牢監°裏; *to escape from* —, dao-c'ih-kæn' 逃出監°

PRISONER, kæn'-li væn'-nying 監°裏犯人°; — *of war,* weh-gying'-go nying 活擒°个°人°

PRIVATE, *opposed to public,* s 私; — *business,* s-z' 私事; — *land,* s-kyi' din 私田; *secret,* s-'ô' 私下°; — *place,* en'-djông u-sen' 暗藏之°所°; lang'-koh-loh-deo' 冷角°落頭; — *room,* mih-shih' 密室; mih-feh-dong-fong vông' 密弗通°風之°房; — *families,* loh-kô' 住°家°; *I have a word to say to you in* —, ngô yiu ih-kyü shih-wô' iao teng ng s-'ô kông' 我有一句説話要與°你私下°講

PRIVILEGE, *benefit,* hao-c'ü' 好處; *favor bestowed by a superior,* eng-we' 恩惠; sông'-s 賞賜; peculiar —, kah'-nga hao-c'ü' 格外好處; having ditto, meots' peh-teh' 謀之不得; confer privileges upon him, sông'-s gyi 賞賜其; deprive of a —, ih-tsông me'-z siu-tsing' 椿美物收進

PRIVY to, or knowing, siang-t'ong' 相通; zi hyiao'-teh 自曉得

PRIVY, mao-k'ang 茅坑; k'ang-ts' 坑子; zah-zao' 石漕; to go to the —, ka-siu ky'i' 解手去; c'ih-kong' ky'i 出恭去

PRIVY council, ky'ü-mih-yün' 樞密院

PRIZE, sông'-go tong-si' 賞个東西; — given by the emperor, or by an officer, tsiang'-sông 獎賞

PRIZE, to k'en'-leh djong 看得重; kwe'-djong 貴重; hyi-gyi' 希奇; I — (it), ngô dziah-djong'-go 我著重个

PROBABLE, liang-pih' 諒必; iah'-ding 約定; jih'-yiu-kyiu' 十有九; not —, feh kyin'-tch 弗見得; vi-pih' 未必

PROBATION, time of s'-t'en z-'eo' 試探時候

PROBE, to — with a needle, tang-tsing' teo-ti' 打鍼兜底; — the heart, ziang tsing' c'oh sing' 像鍼猎心

PROBOSCIS, elephant's ziang'-bih 象鼻

PROCEED, to go forward, zông-zin' ky'i 上前去; — from the mouth, dzong k'eo' c'ih-læ' 從口出來; c'ih'-ü k'eo-li' 出於口裏; whence does it —? dzong 'ah-li' c'ih-læ' 從何而出?

PROCESSION, idolatrous we 會; to have a —, nying we' 迎會; 'ang we' 行會; nying-jing' sæ-we' 迎神賽會; to contribute toward a —, c'ih-we' 出會; funeral —, song-sông'-go-nying 送喪个人

PROCLAIM, to djün-yiang' 傳揚; — abroad, djün-yiang'-k'æ'-ky'i 傳揚開去; djün-k'æ' 傳開; — by writing, or engraving, pu'-kao 布告

PROCLAMATION, official kao'-z 告示; to issue a —, c'ih kao'-z 出告示; imperial —, wông-pông' 黃榜; (written) — of war, tsin'-shü 戰書

PROCRASTINATE, to t'ah'-t'ah-wu; — from day to day, ih-nyih' nga ih-nyih' 一日捱一日; — beyond the time, ngwu z-'eo' 誤時候

PROCURE, to find, zing-djoh' 尋著; — for me, bæn'-læ peh ngô' 辦來給我; to obtain, teh' tao-siu' 得到手; — for me, bæn'-læ peh ngô' 辦來給我

PROCURED, cannot be zing feh-tao'-siu-go 尋弗到手个; teh' feh-tao-siu'-go 得弗到手个

PRODIGAL, n. ba-ts' 敗°子; lông-dông'-ts 浪子

PRODIGAL, to use in a —way, lông-yüong' 浪用; p'eh-t'ông' p'eh-shü yüong' 潑湯潑水用; — expenditure, lông'-fi 浪費; — living, vông-ky'üoh vông-yüong' 妄吃°妄用

PRODIGIOUS in size, gyi-yiang' do 異°樣大°; wô-feh-læ' do 話弗來大°; — quantity, c'ih'-kah to' 出格多

PRODIGY, kwa'-z 怪°事

PRODUCE, to sang-c'ih'-læ 生°出來; clouds — rain, yüing' sang yü' 雲騰致°雨

PRODUCT in multiplication, gong'-dzing 共乘

PRODUCTIONS, c'ih'-ts'æn 出產; native —, t'u'-ts'æn 土產

PRODUCTIVE, we sang' 會生°; sang-leh to' 生°得多

PROFANE, to blaspheme, sih'-doh 褻瀆; to use lightly, ky'ing-yi' yüong' 輕易用; to treat with disrespect, ky'ing-mæn' 輕慢; to pollute, tsao-t'ah' 蹧蹋; to violate God's name, væn'-djoh Jing-ming'-go ming-deo' 犯着°神明个°名頭

PROFESS, to confess, jing' 認; tsiao-jing' 招認; — openly, ming-ming' tsiao-jing' 明明招認; — one thing and mean another, k'eo' feh te sing' 口弗對心

PROFESSION, the literary veng-mah'-cong 文墨中人°; s-veng'-pe 斯文之°輩; the medical —, i-kô' 醫家°

PROFESSOR of Astronomy, kaot'in-veng' sin-sang' 敎°天文先生

PROFFER him a fan, sin'-ts song' gyi yüong'-ih-yüong' 扇子送其用一用

PROFILE, to draw a sia tseh'-min 寫°側面

PROFIT, gain, li-sih' 利息; c'ih'-sih 出息; c'ih'-hwô', dzen'-deo 賺頭; to receive advantage, teh'-djoh bin-i' 得着°便宜°; benefit, ih'-c'ü 益處; li-ih' 利益; receive benefit, teh ih' 得益

PROFITLESS, vu-ih' 無益; 弗ih'-c'ü 無益處; bah-bah' tso 白°白°做

PROFLIGATE, vu-sô'-peh-we 無所不為; ky'ing-kweh'-deo 輕骨頭; 弗-kweh'-ky'i 無°骨氣

PROFOUND, deep, sing 深; — and mysterious, sing-ao' 深奧

PROFUSE in thanks, zia-feh-hyih'-go zia 謝°弗歇个°謝; ts'in-ko'-væn zia' 千謝萬謝°; — in promises, mun'-k'eo ing-dzing' 滿口應承

PROGENITOR, lih-dæ' tsu'-tsong 歷代祖宗

PROGENY, descendants, ts'-seng 子孫; offspring of man, or animal, cong 種; iang 秧

PROGNOSTIC, ziao-deo' 兆頭

PROGNOSTICATE, to — by three cash, ky'i-k'o' 起課; poh-k'o' 卜課;— by bamboo slips, gyiu-ts'in' 求籤; ts'iu-ts'in' 抽籤
PROGRESS, to — in travel, ken-lu' 趕路; ditto, or in study, zông-zin' 上前°
PROGRESSING, not 尚'-neh ken-lu' 沒°有°趕路; tseo' feh zông-zin' 走弗上前°;— a little every day, ih-nyih' hao' ih-nyih — 日°好一日°;— toward the end, tsiang iao' dzing-kong'-de 將要成功了°
PROHIBIT, to kying 禁; kying'-ts 禁止; kying'-djü 禁住;— opium smoking, kying ky'üoh'-a-p'in' 禁吃°鴉片;— gambling, kying tu'-poh 禁賭博
PROHIBITED, lih-li' kying'-liao 律例°禁了°; strictly —, nyin-kying'-liao 嚴禁了°
PROJECT, he has many projects, gyi meo-we' hyü'-to z-t'i' 其謀爲許多事體; gyi weh-ts'ah' hyü'-to z-t'i' 其畫策許多事體; to engage in a visionary —, bu'-fong tsoh-ing' 捕風捉影; k'o tong-fong' 捉°東風
PROJECT, to jut out, deh-c'ih' 凸出
PROJECTILE force, tiu ky'i'-go shü'-lih 丟去°个°勢力; ditto (from cannon), hong'-c'ih-læ-go shü'-lih 轟出來个°勢力

PROLIX in discourse, wô-deo' t'eh dziang' 話頭太°長
PROLONG, to kô-to' 加°多; kô-dziang' 加°長;— a stay, to deng'-deng 多住°幾°時°
PROMINENCE, raised place, kao-ky'i' 高起
PROMINENT men, kao-tsiah'-go nying 上°等°个°人°
PROMISCUOUS, zeh-lön' 雜°亂; kah'-dzeh 夾°雜; zeh'-kah-leng'-teng 雜夾零等; zeh-ts'ih'-zeh-pah' 雜°七雜八°;— lot of things, zeh-gyin' 雜°件
PROMISE, to ing-hyü' 應許; ing-dzing' 應承; ing-yüing' 應允; to break one's —, shih-sing' 失信; shih-iah' 失約; zih-yin' 食言;— can't be depended upon, ing-hyü' feh-tsoh'-cing 應許弗作準; ing-dzing' feh-sön-su' 應承弗算數
PROMISING, yiu ts'-vông 有指望
PROMONTORY, hæ'-sæn-deo 海山頭
PROMOTE, to—the increase, or advancement of, s'-teh hying'-ky'i-læ 使得興起來;— trade, dzu sang-i' hying-wông' 助生°意興旺; ü ming' hying-li' 與民興利;— learning, cing'-coh veng-fong' 振作文風;— to office, fong-tsih' 封職;— one in office, kô-kyih' 加°級; sing-kwun' 陞官
PROMPT, to di 提;— one reciting, &c., di sbü' 提書;— me, di-

ngô-deo′; — *him to action*, di-sing′ gyi 提醒其

PROMPT *answer*, ze-k'eo′ ing 隨口應; — or *obedient*, ao′-ao ing′ 嗷°嗷°應

PROMPTER *in matters of etiquette*, hô 蝦°

PROMPTLY, *at the time*, cing′-ding z-'eo′ 準定時候; *quickly*, soh 速; kw'a′- soh 快速

PROMULGATE, or PROMULGE, djün-k'æ′ 傳開; djün-yiang′ 傳揚; po-yiang′ 播揚; — *every where through the world*, djün pin′-t'in-'ô′ 傳遍天下°

PRONE, *heart* — *to evil*, sing′ hyiang′-djoh oh′ 心向著°惡

PRONOUNCE, *to* kông-c'ih-læ講′出來; *distinctly* —, kông ts'ing-t'ong′ 講°清通

PRONUNCIATION, k'eo′-ing 口音; k'eo′-ts' 口齒°; — *bad, or indistinct*, k'eo′-ing feh-ts'ing′ 口音弗清; k'eo′-ing 'en-wu-dao′ 口音如°含胡桃

PROOF, bing-kyü′ 憑據; tsih′-tsiao 執照; *positive* —, tsing′-kyü 証據; — (*of crime*), tsông-tsing′ 贓証; *no* —, 嘸-bing′ 嘸-kyü 無°憑無°據; *reliable* —, k'y'üoh′-jih-go bing′-kyü 確實个°憑據; jih-bing′ jih′-kyü 實憑實據; *what* — *have you?* yiu soh′-go bing-kyü′ læ ng′-go siu′-li 有甚°麼°憑據在°你°手裡? *to put to the* —,

s'-lin 試鍊; — *against water, fire, &c.*, ziang t'ih-dong-kwu′ ka 像鐵桶之°固; — *sheets*, yiang-ts′ 樣子; *to correct* —, kyiao-te shü′ 校對書; kæ shü′ 改書

PROP, cü′-bông 拄棒°; ts'ang′-bông 撐棒°; — *of the family*, kô′-li-go tong′-liang 當°家个°棟梁

PROP, *to* cü 拄; ts'ang 撐; tsin 伞

PROPAGATE, *to* djün 傳; 'ang行°; — *religion*, djün-kyiao′ 傳教

PROPER, tsoh′-hying 作興; *befitting*, 'eh-li′ 合理; siang-nyi′ 相宜; tsiao kwe-kyü′ 照規矩; ing-kæ′-go 應該个°

PROPERTIES, sing′-tsih 性質

PROPERTY, (*houses, lands, and goods*), kô-kyi′ 家計; *uncertain* — (*as boats, bridges, &c.*), veu-ts'æn′ 浮產; *landed* —, jih-nyih′ 實業

PROPHECY, yü-sin′ shih-wô′ 預先說話; yü-yin′ 預言 (veng.)

PROPHET, sin-cü′-nying 先知人°; kông-yü-yin′-go 講°預言个°

PROPHETESS, nyü′-sin′-cü 女先知

PROPHETIC *dream*, mong-ziao′ 夢兆

PROPHESY, *to* kông vi-læ′-go z-t'i′ 講°未來个°事體; 一

without divining, vi-poh' sin'-cü 未°卜先知

PROPITIATE, *to* sih-nu' dzing-kwe 'o-hao' 息怒仍歸和好

PROPITIATORY *sacrifice*, joh-ze'-go tsi'-veh 贖罪个°祭物

PROPITIOUS *winds*, jing fong' 順風

PROPORTION, *in* siang-ing' 相應; siang-ts'ing' 相稱; *in good —*, deo-mi' siang-ing' 頭尾°相應; *the rule of —* pi'-li 比例

PROPOSE, *to — one's ideas*, kông'-c'ih peng-i 講出本意; *— a plan*, kông'-c'ih fah'-ts lœ 講°出法子來; *do you — to go to-day?* ng' siang kying-tsiao' ky'i' feh 你°想今朝去°否°?

PROPOSITION, ming 命, properly, something appointed, but by politeness, can be used here; thus, *I assent to your —*, ngô' tseng ng'-go ming' 我遵你°命; *very polite*, ngô vong ng-go yü' 我奉你°个°諭; *consider my —*, ngô' sô kông'-go i'-s, ng hao tang'-mo 我所講°个°意思你°好揣摹; *I cannot consent to your —*, ngô feh tseng'-kyiao 我弗遵教; *næn tseng'-kyiao* 難以遵教

PROPRIETOR, cü'-nying-kô 主人°家°; tong-kô' 東家; lang-z.

PROPRIETY, li 禮; kwe'-kyü' 規矩; *act in accordance with —*, tsiao li' s-'ang' 照禮施行°;

not in accordance with —, feh 'eh-li' 弗合禮; feh i-li' 弗依禮

PROROGUE, *to* t'e-pæn' 退班; t'e-dông' 退堂

PROSE, *classical* kwu'-veng 古文; *recent writings*, z-veng 時文

PROSECUTE, *to — continuously*, lin-lin' tso 連連做; tsih'-lin tso 接連做; *to accuse*, kao-zông' 告狀

PROSELYTE *to Christianity*, kœ' dzong Yiæ-su' kyiao' 改從耶穌教

PROSPECT, *view*, kying'-cü 景致; *fine —*, hao kying'-cü 好景致

PROSPECTS, *his — are good*, gyi-go kying'-ziang feh wa 其景象弗孬

PROSPER, *to be prosperous*, jing-liu' 順溜; *— in making money*, fah-ky'i-lœ 發起來; fah'-dzæ 發財; *— in examinations*, fah-dah 發達; *— and increase*, hying-wông' 興旺; *— in trade*, hying-long' 興隆; hying-fah' 興發; *to be fortunate*, yüing-ky'i' t'ong-dah' 運氣通達

PROSPEROUS, jing-liu' 順溜; jing-kying' 順境; *— country*, koh'-kô bing-en' kyih-ky'ing' 國家°平安吉慶

PROSTITUTE, *n*. piao'-ts 婊子; ts'ông-vu' 娼婦; hwô-lao' 花老; t'iao-ts'; gyi-nyü' 妓女

PROSTRATE, to — one's self (as a suppliant), boh-tao' 伏°倒; p'oh'-tao 仆倒; pa'-tao 拜°倒
PROSTRATE on the face, foh-ken' kw'eng'-tih 覆蓋°睡°的
PROTECT, to wu 護; pao'-wu 保護; we-wu' 迴護; we-kwu' 迴顧; we-gyih' 迴及;— the weak, we-kwu' no-ziah'-go nying 迴顧懦弱个°人°; may God — you, dæn'-nyün Jing-Ming' pao'-wu ng' 但願神明保護你°
PROTEST, to — against, ming-ming' wô' feh ing'-kæ 明話弗應該; ming-ming' p'i-bing' 明明批評
PROTRACT, to — the time, z-'eo' kô-leh dziang' 時候加°得°長
PROTRUDE, to deh-c'ih' 凸出 sing-c'ih' 伸出; t'a-c'ih' 拖°出; t'u'-c'ih 吐出
PROTRUDING out of the pocket, dæ-k'eo'-deo sing-c'ih'-tong 袋口頭°伸出了°; dæ-k'eo-deo t'a-c'ih'-tong 袋口頭°拖°出了°
PROTUBERANCE, a ih-go cih'— 個疙°瘩°
PROUD, kyiao-ngao' 驕傲; do-dao' 大°道; zi-tseng' zi-do' 自°尊自°大°
PROVE that I am a thief, ngô tso zeh' wæn-c'ih te'-tsing tso bing-kyü' 我做賊°還出°對証

做憑據;— that the earth is round, di-gyin' z yün'-go do-c'ih tsing'-kyü læ 地球是圓个°拿°出証據來
PROVED by measurement, te'-tsing-c'ih-læ'-de 對証出來了°; yin te'-tsing-de 有對証了°; kao-cing'-liao 較°準了
PROVENDER, zih-liao' 食料;— and rations, liang-ts'ao' 糧草
PROVERB, old saying, dzông-yin'-dao 常言道; lao'-wô 老話; kwn'-wô 古話; familiar —, dzoh-wô' 俗話 (ih-kyü); the Book of Proverbs, Tseng-yin' 箴言
PROVIDE, to yü-be' 預備; bo-bæn' 備辦;— against, bông-be' hao 防備好; di-bông'-hao 提防好; in plenty — for want, yin'-z bông 區 z' 有時要°防無°時
PROVIDENT, yin sön'-kyi 有算計; saving some for after use, lin-zin'-c'ü-'eo' 留前°取後
PROVINCE, a ih-sang' 一省°; the eighteen provinces, jih-pah' sang 十八省
PROVINCIAL capital, sang'-dzing 省城;— dialect, t'u'-wô 土話; hyiang-dæn' 鄉談
PROVISIONS, liang-zih' 糧食; k'eo'-liang 口糧; ky'üoh'-zih 吃°食;— for man, and beast, liang-ts'ao' 糧草; dry — for a journey, ken-liang 乾糧

PROVOCATION (either to good, or bad), kyih'-kong 激功; *to be provoked by me*, (*i.e.* receive my —), zông ngô'-go kyih'-kong 上我个°激功

PROVOKE, *to* kyih 激; ying 引; zô 惹°; ying'-zô 引惹°; yüong kyih'-kong 用激功; *he cannot be provoked* (or incited), gyi' feh ziu' kyih'-kong 其弗受激功; kyih'-kong yüong'-feh-tsing' 激功用弗進; — *him to anger*, kyih'-dong gyi ô'-wông 激動其怒°; kyih'-gyi-nu' 激其怒; væn' gyi ô'-wông 犯其怒; ts'oh'-væn gyi nu' 觸犯其怒; — *him to vomiting*, ying'-gyi t'u' 引其吐; long gyi t'u'-c'ih 弄其吐出; — *him to laughter*, ying'-zô gyi siao' 引惹°其笑

PROVOKED, *easily* ziang liu-sing' ho'-p'ao ka 像流星火爆°; — *beyond endurance*, ün'-sing tsæ-dao' 怨聲載道

PROVOKING *man*, dao-ky'i'-go nying 陶氣个°人°

PROW, jün-deo' 船頭

PROWL, *wild beasts* — *about for food*, yia'-siu jing-lo' ky'üoh 野°獸尋°找吃°物°

PRUDENT, yiu kying-we' 有經緯; kyin'-sih tao-kô'-go 見識到家°; — *in managing*, liang-lih' r-ying 量力而行; *cautious*, we-bông-'eo' 會防後

PRUNE, *to* — *trees*, yüong tao' siu-li' jü-moh' 用刀修理樹木

PRUNES, *dried plums*, me-ken' 梅乾

PRUSSIAN-BLUE, yiang-din' 洋靛; yiang-ts'ing' 洋青

PRY, *to* — *by looking*, t'eo-k'en' 偷看; — *by asking*, dao'-t'ing 道聽; — *by asking secretly*, ts'ih'-t'ing 竊聽; t'en'-t'ing 探聽

PSALMS, sing'-s 聖詩; s-p'in' 詩篇

PUBERTY, *the time of* fah-sing' z-'eo 發身時候; fah-tsiang'-z 'eo 發長時候 (coarse).

PUBLIC, kong 公; *in* —, c'ih-kwun 出官; — *business*, kong-z' 公事; — *opinion*, kong-leng' 公論; cong'-leng 衆論; — *examintaion*, (whether right, or wrong), kong-p'ing' 公評°; — *use*, kong-yüong' 公用; — *road*, kwun-lu' 官路; *the* —, cong'-nying 衆人°; cong' pah'-sing 衆百°姓; *known to the* —, kong'-kô hyiao'-teh 公家°曉得; cong'-nying teh'-cü 衆人°得知

PUBLISH, *to* — *abroad*, yiang-k'æ' 揚開; djün-k'æ' 傳開; — (by telling what one wishes kept quiet), t'ong-hyiang kwun' 通鄉貫

PUCKER, *to* ts'oh'-long 緘攏; — *the lips*, cü'-pô ts'oh'-long 嘴巴

繊攏; *puckering to the mouth*, we seh k'eo' 會澀口
PUDDLE, shü-den' 水°潭; — *in a court, or any where*, shü-ming-dông' 水°明堂
PUFF, *a — of wind*, ih-kwu fong' 一縷°風; *to blow a — of smoke*, p'eng' ih-k'eo in' 噴一口烟; *to — up, or inflate*, c'ü-p'ông' 吹脹; *to praise*, ts'e-hyü' 吹噓
PUGILIST, gyün-s' 拳師; *to exercise as a —*, tang-gyün' 打拳
PULL, *to — along*, la 拉; ky'in 牽; 肭 te; — (*as a boat, or anchor*), ts'ô 扯; — *up*, (*as roots, or nails*), bah-ky'i'-læ 扳起來; — *up* (*as a weight, or curtain*), la-zông 拉上; te'-zông 肭上; ts'ô-zông 扯上; — *out*, la-c'ih' 拉出; te'-c'ih 肭出; — *out teeth*, tsoh ngô-ts' 捉牙齒; bah-c'ih' ngô-ts' 扳出牙°齒; — *out* (*as a drawer*), ts'iu-c'ih' 抽出; — *down* (*as a house*), ts'ah'-diao 拆了°; te'-gyi-tao' 肭其倒; *give a —*, la-ih-la 拉一拉; la ih-pô 拉一把; te ih'-pô 肭一把; — *up out of water*, shü-li' liao-ky'i'-læ 水°裡撈起°來; — *apart*, p'ah'-k'æ 擘開
PULLET, *a* ih'-tsah siao-kyi' 一隻小雞
PULLEY, ts'ô-bun' 車盤; ts'ô-leng' 車輪
PULP *of fruits*, ko'-ts nyüoh 果子肉°; *to pound to a —*, sông-wu' 舂°糊
PULPIT, kông'-kying-dæ 講°經臺; kông'-shü-dæ 講°書臺
PULSATE, *to* dong 動; t'iao 跳
PULSATIONS *of the heart stopped*, sing si'-de 心死了°
PULSE, mah 脈; mah-sih' 脈息; *to feel the —*, tah mah' 搭脈; k'en mah' 診°脈
PULVERIZE, *to — by grinding*, mo feng' 磨粉; nyin meh' 研末; — *by pounding*, sông feng' 舂°粉; — *by rolling*, le feng' 擂粉
PUMELO, p'ao' veng-tæn' 文膽 (ih-go)
PUMICE-STONE, veo-zah' *or* vu-zah' 浮石°
PUMP, hyih'-dong 吸筒; hwun'-dong 喚筒 (ih-kwun); *a chain —*, ih-bu shü'-ts'ô 一步水車°
PUMP, *to — water*, hyih shü' 吸水°; hwun shü' 喚°水
PUMPKIN, *squash*, væn-kwô' 飯瓜; nen-kwô' 南瓜
PUN, sông-kwæn' shih-wô' 雙關說話
PUNCH, *to give a poke*, djoh-ih'-pô 揭一把; — *a hole*, toh ngæn'-ts 督眼°子
PUNCTILIOUS, to-li'-go 多禮个°; — *and only cares for one thing*, ü-vu'-deng-deng-go 迂腐騰騰个°; ü-vu' ts dao 迂腐之道;

too — (as a teacher), sön-ky'i' 酸氣;— man, ü-nying 迂人; ditto (in ridicule), dzing-djong'-ts 陳仲子
PUNCTUAL to the day, tsiao nyih-ts' 照日°子;— to the time, tsiao z-'eo' 照時候; doing regularly, feh ts'o-yi' 弗差°移; — to appointment, cing gyi' 準期
PUNCTUATE, to tin kyü'-deo 點句讀
PUNGENT, lah 辣; slightly —, lah-ho'-ho 辣阿阿;— taste, lah'-go mi'-dao 辣个°味°道;— remarks, c'oh'-sing-go shih-wô' 猎°心个說話 (c'oh or ts'oh)
PUNISH, to vah 罰; tsah'-vah 責罰;—(officially), ying-vah' 刑罰
PUNISHMENT (official), ying-vah' 刑罰; ze 罪; ze'-ming 罪名; to recive ditto, ziu ying-vah' 受刑罰; ziu ze' 受罪; to receive — (as from parents, or teacher), ziu tsah-vah 受責罰; to determine what —, ding ze'-ming 定罪名; instruments of —, ying-gyü' 刑具;— by bambooing, tang pæn'-ts 打板子;— by rattaning, tang deng-diao' 打籐條;— by compressing the feet, and extending the arms, t'in-bing'-kô 天平架°;— by compressing the fingers, tsæn'-ts 棬子;— by beating the face, tang pô-công' 打巴掌;— by beating the ankles, k'ao kyiah'-tsang 敲°脚脛°;— by compressing the ankles between upright bars, kah'-kweng 夾°棍;— by strangling, kao 絞;— by beheading, sah-deo° 殺頭; c'ü-kyüih' 處決 — by standing in a cage with the head out, lih dong' 立籠;— by cutting to pieces, se'-kwô-ling-dzi' 碎剮凌遲; by wearing the cangue, ta do-kó' 帶°大°枷°;— by banishment (to a distance, or in one's own city), du-ze' 徒罪; ditto (from one to two thousand li), liu-ze' 流罪; ditto (beyond the frontier), kyüing-ze' 軍罪
PUNKAH, fong-sin' 風扇 (ih-min,
PUNY, thin and small, seo'-siao 瘦小
PUPIL, 'oh-sang-ts' 學°生°子°; meng-du' 門徒; meng-sang' 門生°; di'-ts 弟子;— of the eye, ngæn'-u-cü 眼°烏珠; the image reflected in the —, dong-jing' 瞳神
PUPPET, wooden moh-deo 'en' 木頭°孩°;— show, moh-deo hyi' 木人°戲; tsiang-deo 'en'-hyi 帳頭孩戲
PUPPY, siao'-keo 小狗; siao wun-kyi' 小黃犬° (ih-tsah)
PURCHASE, to ma 買°;— office, kyün tsih' 捐職;— rice, dih-mi' 糴米;— wine, tang tsiu' 沽°酒;— oil, iao yiu'; ma yiu' 買°油;— merchandize, cü ho' 置貨; ma ho' 買°貨; bæn ho' 辦貨

PURE, ts'ing 清; ts'ing-tsing' 清正; *clean*, ts'ing-kyih' 清潔; kyih'-zing 潔净; *the — article*, tsing ho' 眞貨; *— silver*, tsoh' nying 足銀; *— sugar*, jing dông' 純糖; *— milk*, jing na' 純嬭; *— (as water)*, pih'-po'-s-ts'ing 碧波四清

PURGATIVE *medicine*, sia' yiah or dza yiah' 瀉藥

PURGATORY, lin-nyüoh' 煉獄

PURGE, *to — from sin*, gyiang'-diao ze' 洗掉罪; *— the bowels*, du'-bi sia'-gyi-ih-sia' 肚皮瀉其一瀉

PURIFY, *to make clean*, long ken-zing' 弄乾净; long kyih'-zing 弄潔净; *—by washing*, gyiang-ken-zing' 洗乾净; *— (as metals) by fire*, tön'-lin 煅煉

PURPLE, *dull reddish —*, in'-ts'ing-seh' 燕青色; *bluish —*, ts'ing-lin'-seh' 青蓮色; *grape —*, bu-dao'-seh 葡萄色

PURPORT, i'-s 意思

PURPOSE, cü'-i 主意; *fixed —*, lih-ding' ts'-hyiang 立定志向; lih-ding' cü-i' 立定主意; *on —*, kwu'-i 故意; deh-i' 特意; deh-we' 特爲; *for what —?* we'-leh soh'-go i'-s 爲了甚麼意思? we'-leh soh'-go yüong-dziang 爲了甚麼用塲? *a good — changed for a bad*, sing weh'-de 心活了; sing weh-dong'-de 心活動了

PURPOSELY, *brought — for you*, deh-i' do-læ' peh ng' 特意拿來給你; *to do wrong —, and knowingly*, ming-cü' kwu-væn' 明知故犯

PURSE, *bag which may be used for money*, (or snuff), 'o-pao-dæ' 荷包袋; s'-hyi-dæ 四喜袋; wu-bing'-dæ 壹瓶袋; *my — is empty*, nông'-t'oh k'ong-hyü' or nông'-t'oh k'ong-k'ong' 饢橐空虛

PURSUE, *to* tse 追; ken 趕; tse'-ken' 追趕; *— and overtake*, tse-zông 追上; tse-djoh' 追著

PUS, nong 膿

PUSH, *to* t'e 推; *— over*, t'e-tao' 推倒; *— aside*, t'e-k'æ' 推開; *— him down*, t'e gyi tih' 推其跌; t'e-gyi-loh' 推其落; *— in*, t'e-tsing' 推進; *he gave me a —*, gyi t'e' ngô ih-pô ko'-de 其推我一把過了; *— back and forth*, t'e'-læ-nông'-ky'i 推來攘去

PUSILLANIMOUS, 無膽 tæn'-ky'i 無膽氣; 無 tæn'-liang 無膽量; 無 ken-tæn' 無肝膽; tæn'-ts siao' 膽子小

PUSTULE, gweng-nong le' 作膿瘰; *a — in small pox*, ih-lih deo-ts' 一粒痘子

PUT, *to lay*, en; fông 放; fông-læ 放在; *— down*, fông-loh 放落; *— (it) on the table*, fông-læ coh'-teng zông' 放在

PUT 375 QUA

桌上;— *on clothes*, c'ün i-zông' 穿衣裳°; tsiah i-zông' 着衣裳°;— *off clothes*, t'eh i-zông' 脫衣裳°;— *away*, k'ông'-ko 囥過;— *on the hat*, ta mao-ts' 戴°帽子;— *off the hat*, coh' mao-ts' 除°帽子 (cob or tsoh); *to — in order*, pa'-hao 擺°好; *ditto or repair*, siu-li' 修理; tsing-teng' 整頓;— *a room in order*, siu-jih' vông-ts' 修葺°房子;—*forth strength*, yüong ky'i'-lih 用氣力; kô gying-dao' 加°勁道;—*forth great strength*, sah'-k'eo dziah-lih' 着°意°用°力; 'co-ky'i'-lih 候氣力;— *him in mind*, di-sing' gyi 提醒其;— *into*, tsi 齒; tsông 裝;—*into a dish*, tsi' beng-ts' 齒盆子; *to — out a fire* (as a house, &c.), kyiu ho' 救火;— *out* (ordinary) *fire*, ho long-u' 火弄熄°;— (blow) *out a lamp*, c'ü-u' teng-tsæn' 吹°熄°燈盞;— *together*, fông'-long 放攏; en-tæn'-long 挨°一挨°;— *to my account*, sön' z ngô'-go tsiang' 算是我个°帳; sön' ngô' ming'-'ô 算我名下°; *can't — up with it*, jing-næ'-feh-djü 忍耐弗住; *to — out the hand*, siu' sing-c'ih'-læ 手伸出來;— *on airs*, pa kô'-ts 擺°架子;— *lam to*

flight, ken'-gyi-tseo' 趕其走; ken'-gyi-ky'i' 趕其去°;— *one up to a thing*, ts'ön-teh' 攛掇;— *one up to* (a bad thing), t'iao-so' 挑唆;— *up a notice*, t'iah tsiao-ts' 貼招紙;— *forth buds*, ts'iu ngô' 抽芽°; pao ngô' 苞芽°;— *in charge of another*, kyi' læ bih-nying'-go siu'-li 寄在°別人°个手裡: *ditto* (a child), kyi'-yiang 寄養

PUTREFY, *will we* læn' 會爛
PUTRID, *rotten*, læn-wu'-de 爛糜°了°; læn'-de 爛了°; *bad smelling*, ts'iu'-de 臭了°
PUTTY, dong-yiu'-hwe 桐油灰
PUZZLE, yüong-sing-s'-go hyi-deo' 用心思个°戲玩° (ih-t'ao);— *of seven blocks*, ts'ih'-ky'iao-pæn 七巧板; *chain* — kyiu'-lin-gwæn 九連環
PUZZLE, *to* yüong sing-s' 用心思; long-hweng' 弄惛
PUZZLED, *I am — with this account*, ngô' be keh'-go tsiang' long-hweng'-de 我被這°个°帳弄惛了°

Q

QUACK *doctor*, ma-yiah'-lông'-cong 賣°藥郎中
QUADRANGULAR, *four-sided*, s'-fông-go 四方个°; *having four angles*, s'-koh-go 四角°个°
QUADRUPED, tseo'-siu 走獸; *the class of quadrupeds*, tseo'-siu ih-le 走獸一類

QUAIL, n. en-jing' 鵪鶉 (ih-tsah)
QUAIL, to sông-tæn' 傷膽; lose spirit, shih-sing' 失心
QUAINT style of talking, lao-kwu'-ky‘iang kông'-fah 老古腔講法
QUAKE, to tremble, fah-teo' 發抖 gwah-gwah-teo° 捂°捂°抖;— with fear, fah-kying' hah'-leh fah-teo° 發驚嚇得°發抖°; the earth quakes, di-yiang° cing'-dong 地陽震動
QUALIFY, to — one's self, ‘oh'-leh tao-kô' 學°得°到家°; ‘oh-we' 學°會
QUALIFIED to teach others, ‘oh-veng' neng-keo' kao bih'-nying 學°問能彀敎°別人°
QUALITY, best zông-teng' 上等; poorest —, ‘ô'-teng 下°等; middle —, cong-teng 中等
QUALITIES, properties, t‘i'-tsih 體質; peng'-tsih 本質
QUANTITY, what —? to-siao' 多少? a large —, hyü'-to 許多; to-to' 多多; estimate the —, iah'-læ yiu to-siao' 約來有多少; p‘a'-læ yiu to-siao' 派°來有多少; sön'-læ yiu to-siao' 算來有多少
QUARREL, to tsang-leng' 爭°論; siang-tsang' 相爭°; tsang-teo' 爭°鬥; k‘eo'-kyüoh, or k‘eo-koh 口角; k‘eo-zih 口舌; siang-mô' 相罵;— noisily, tsang-zao' 爭°嘈; zao-nyih';

— arising from rivalry, teo-ky‘i 鬥氣; to get up a —, zing zao-nyih' 尋相罵°; to seek a cause for a —, zing pæn'-deo 尋°錯°處°; zing ts‘iah'-deo 尋齩頭
QUARRELSOME hao k‘eo'-kyüoh 好辯°; hwun-hyi' tsang-leng' 歡喜爭°論; we tsang-teo' 會爭鬥
QUARRY, zah-dông' 石°膛
QUARRYMAN, k‘æ zah-deo' nying 開石°頭人°
QUART, nearly a — (dry measure), nyi sing' 二升; a — of milk, ih-bing na' 一瓶嬭°
QUARTER, s'-kwn-teh-ih 四股得一; s'-feng-ts-ih' 四分之一; — of a dollar, liang'-koh-pun' 兩角°半; a — (coin), ih-go s'-k‘æ 一個四開;— of an hour, ih-k‘eh' 一刻;— of a catty, s'-liang 四兩
QUARTER, to s'-kwu-feng-k‘æ' 四股分開
QUARTERLY payments, (as rents, &c.), s'-kyi fu'-ts‘ing 四季付清; en'-kyi kyiao-ts‘ing' 按季交清
QUARTZ, white bah ho'-zah 白°火石°;— crystal, sæn-tsing' 山晶
QUEEN, nyü'-wông 女皇; king's wife, wông-‘eo' 皇后;— mother, t‘a'-‘eo 太后;— of England, Da-Ing' nyü'-wông 大英女皇

QUELL, to — a disturbance, bing-lön' 平亂; — rebellion, bing-fæn' 平反

QUENCH, to — thirst, ts-k'ah' 止渴; — fire, p'eh-u ho' 潑熄火; kyiu ho' 救火; ho' long-u' 火弄熄°

QUERULOUS, gæn-gæn'-tao-tao 煩°言°

QUESTION, to ask a —, meng ih-kyü shih'-wô 問°一句說話; I have a — to ask you, ngô' yiu ih-kyü shih'-wô iao meng' ng 我有一句說話要問°你°; iao meng' ng ih-sing' 要問°你°一聲; — and answer, ih-veng' ih-tah' 一問°一答; — him, meng-meng' gyi 問°問°其; — and see, meng-meng' k'en 問°問°看

QUICK, QUICKLY, kw'a 快°; kw'a'-kw'a 快快°; kw'a'-soh 快速; soh'-soh 速速; ao-sao'; p'ih'-t'eh 霹脫; zah-zah; ts'oh 捉; ts'oh'-ts'oh-kyiao 捉捉交; — (as fire), ho'-soh 火速; a little quicker, kw'a'-tin 快°點°; 'ao-sao'-tin; — eye, ngæn' kw'a 眼°快°; — hand, siu kw'a 手快°; — of hearing (ears bright), ng'-tô liang' 耳°朵亮; — and severe, bao-ts'ao' 暴躁; — of apprehension, ling-li' 伶俐; get through quickly, tsin'-sao 箭稍; ky'i-kw'a-loh'-dzih 氣快°落直

QUICKEN me, su-sing' ngô 蘇醒我; — the dead, s'-teh si'-nying weh' 使得死人活

QUICKLIME, sang-hwe' 生°灰

QUICKSILVER, shü'-nying 水°銀

QUIET, not noisy, pih'-zing 謐靜; iu-zing' 幽靜; ts'ing-zing' 清靜; zing'-væn; zing'-cü 靜致; — and peaceful, en-zing' 安靜; bing-en' 平安; not moving, t'ih'-ding 鎮定; — your anger, ky'i' næ-tæn'-loh 氣耐下°去°; — place, pih'-zing-go di'-fông 謐靜个°地方; — man, nying' iu-zing' 人°幽靜; all —, dzih-jün'-feh-dong' 寂然弗動; t'ih'-t'a-s-bing' 鎮太°四平

QUILL, goose ngo-mao'-kwun 鵝毛管 (ih-ts)

QUILT, to 'ông; ing 絪; thick —, min-bi' 綿被; — for the dead, dzing-bi' 殉被; djong'-bi 重被; lang'-bi 冷°被°

QUINCE, moh-kwô' 木瓜

QUIT, to leave, li-k'æ' 離開; to have done with, hyih 歇; — a place entirely, ih'-ky'ü peh-we' 一去不回; — doing favors, üong' peh we li' 永不回禮; — the Buddhist priesthood, wæn-djoh' 'o-zông' 還俗和尙

QUITE, tsing 儘; jih-feng' 十分; — good, tsing' hao 正好; jih-feng' hao' 十分好; — right, ting' z 頂是; feh ts'o' 弗錯;

gyih z' 極是; — *ready*, tsing zi'-de 整齊°了°

QUIVER *for arrows*, kong-ts'ô'-sah-dæ; tsin'-dæ 箭袋

QUIVER, *to* tsing'-tsing-dong 震震°動; — *with rage*, ky'i'-leh gwah-gwah-teo' 氣得°捫捫°抖

QUOTATION *from a book*, ying'-læ-go shü-kyü' 引來个°書句 (ih-kyü).

QUOTE, *to* — *from a book*, ying shü' 引書; — *as proof*, ying tsing' 引証

R

RABBIT, t'u 兔; zih-c'ü' 觜鼠 (ih-tsah.)

RABBLE, mæn pah'-sing 蠻百°姓; *the lowest* —, 'ô'-teng nying 下°等人°

RABID *dog*, fong wun-kyi' 瘋黃犬°; tin keo' 癲狗 (ih-tsah)

RACE, dzoh 族; le 類; *the human* —, nying' ih-le' 人°一類; *contest in running*, pi peng'-gying 比奔勁; sæ peng'-gying 賽奔勁; — *horses*, p'ao mô' 跑馬; — *course*, p'ao'-mô-dziang' 跑馬塲

RACK, *frame*, kô-ts 架°子 (ih-go).

RACKET, zi-zi'-zao-zao' 嘈°嘈°嘈°嘈°; loh-ying-fæn'-ky'i 像°六營反起

RADIANT, fah-kwông'-de 發光了°; — *face*, min-k'ong' yiu kwông-ts'æ' 面孔有光彩

RADIATE, *to* — *heat*, fah'-c'ih nyih-ky'i' 發出熱°氣; fah'-c'ih liang-kwông' 發出亮光

RADICAL *change*, t'eh'-bi wun-kweh' 脫皮換骨

RADICAL, bu 部; *under what radical?* læ soh'-go bu'-li 在°甚°麽部裡?

RADISHES, *red* 'ong lo-boh' 紅蘿蔔; *white* —, bah lo-boh' 白°蘿蔔

Carrots are also called 'ong lo-boh'.

RAFT, *wooden* mob-ba' 木排°; jü-ba' 樹排°; *bamboo* —, coh'-ba 竹排° (ih-ba)

RAFTER, djün-ts' 椽子 (ih-ken)

RAG, p'o'-pu 破布; se'-pu 碎布; *rags*, se-pu-den' 碎布頭°; *old rags*, gyiu pu-den' 舊布頭° (ih-kw'e)

RAGE, *in a* ho'-ky'i dzih-c'ong'-de 火氣直沖了°; nu-ky'i' c'ong-t'in'-de 怒氣沖天了°; *white with* —, ky'i'-leh leh-bah'-go ky'i' deh° 鐵白°了°

RAGE, *to* fah-ho' 發火; fah-do-ông' 發大°怒; fah-gyih' 發極

RAGGED, p'o'-li-p'o'-sa 破裂°破裰°; — *and dirty*, læn-li' 襤褸 (may be also used for soiled only); — *shoes*, p'o' 'a-bæn' 破鞋爿; — *shoes and stockings*, 'a-t'ah'-mah-t'ah' 鞋脫°襪脫°

RAIL, to — at, zoh-mô' 辱罵; zoh 辱; — at people, zoh-nying'-mô'-tao 辱°人°罵倒

RAILING, læn-ken' 欄杆

RAIMENT, i-voh' 衣服 (veng); i-zông' 衣裳°

RAIN, to loh-yü' 落雨; it is raining, læ'-tih loh-yü' 正在°落雨; it is going to —, iao loh-yü' 要下°雨; looks like —, yü'-mong-mong 雨濛濛; a shower of —, ih-dziao yü' 一陣°雨; — for a long time, kyiu' yü 久雨

RAIN water, t'in-shü' 天雨水°

RAINY season, me-t'in 霉天

RAINBOW, heo 虹° (ih-da)

RAISE, to dæ 擡; dæ-ky'i' 擡起; gying-ky'i' 擎起; — the hand, sin di-ky'i' 手提起; sin di' ih-di 手提一提; — the head, dæ deo' 擡頭; — a little higher, dæ kao'-tin 擡高點; — (as heavy furniture), dæ-ky'i-læ 擡起來; — him up, tông'-gyi-ky'i'-læ 擾°其起來; vu'-gyi-ky'i'-læ 扶其起來; — the price, tsiang kô'-din 漲價錢; — to a better condition, di-bah'-ky'i-læ' 提拔起來; — his hopes, ying'-ky'i gyi'-go siang'-vông 引起其个°想望; ky'i' gyi'-go nyiæn-deo' 啟其个°念頭; — militia, tsiao-mo' hyiang-üong' 招募鄉勇; — chickens, yiang siao-kyi' 養小雞; — wheat, cong mah' 種麥; — (or scatter) dust, yiang hwe-dzing' 颺灰塵; — the hat, mao'-ts t'ing-ih'-t'ing 帽子挺一挺; — money, tang'-sün dong-din' 打算銅錢; dziah'-loh dong-din' 著落銅錢°

RAISINS, bu-dao-ken' 葡萄乾

RAKE, bô 鈀; bamboo — (for grass), la'-ts'ao-bô, or la-ts'a-bô' 拉草鈀; paddy —, t'æn-koh'-bô' 攤穀鈀 (ih-pô)

RAKE, to bô 鈀; — even, bô bing' 爬平; — open (as grass), bô-tæn'-k'æ 爬開

RAKE, a vicious fellow, seh-kyü' 色鬼°; t'en-hwô-lóng'-ts 貪花浪子; (polite), fong-liu-k'ah' 風流客

RALLY, to — for another fight (after defeat), voh-dzing' 復陣; tang'-wæn weng'-dzing 打還魂陣

RAM, yüong-yiang' 雄羊 (ih-tsah)

RAM it in well, tsing gyi lao' 楂其牢

RAMBLE, to yiu-wun' 遊玩°; yin-hyi' 遊戲; — in the hills, yiu-sæn' 遊山; hyi-sæn' 嬉山

RAMIFY, to feng-ts-p'a' 分支派

RAMPARTS, city walls, dzing-ziang' 城墻; opposite — (in fight), te'-le 對壘

RANCID, yiu-hao'-ky'i-de 油嗃氣了°; yiu-hòng'-ky'i; yiu-ih' ky'i.

RANDOM, *to do in a — manner*, hah'-ts'ih-hah-pah' lön-tso' 黑七黑八亂做; — *talk*, keh-ts'ih'-keh-pah' shih-wô' 夾°七夾°八說話

RANK, *grade*, teng'-kyih 等級; *official* —, p'ing-kyih' 品級; the first and second of the nine ranks are divided in two, the second being but a trifle lower than the first, *viz.*, *first* —, tsing'-ih-p'ing 正一品; djong ih-p'ing 從一品; *second* —, tsing' nyi-p'ing 正二°品; djong-nyi'-p'ing 從二°品. The insignia for the several ranks are:—
1st rank, *ruby*, 'ong-pao'-zah 紅寶石°.
2nd, *coral*, sæn-wu' 珊瑚
3rd, *sapphire*, læn-pao'-zah 藍寶石°, or ming-læn 明藍
4th, *lapis-lazuli*, ts'ing-kying-zah 青金石°, or en'-læn 暗藍
5th, *crystal*, shü'-tsing 水°晶
6th, *white stone*, bah-zah' 白石°, or ts'ô-gyü 硨磲
7th, *gold button*, kying-ting' 金頂
8th, and 9th, *gilded silver button*, du-kying' nying-ting' 鍍金銀頂

position, sing-veng' 身分; *unbecoming or overstepping one's* —, sing-veng' feh-p'e' 身分弗配; *literary* —, sing-kying' 紳衿; *the five ranks of nobility*, ng'-teng tsiah 五°等爵; *viz.*, kong-tsiah' 公爵, 'eo-tsiah' 侯爵, pab'-tsiah 伯°爵, ts'-tsiah 子爵, nen-tsiah' 男爵; *to place* (soldiers) *in rank*, pa dzing-shü' 擺°陣勢

RANK *smell belonging to mutton*, yiang sao'-ky'i 羊臊氣

RANSACK, *to* dao 掏; fæn 翻; — *a drawer*, dao ts'iu-teo' 掏抽屜°; — *in order to find*, seo-zing' 搜尋°

RANSOM, *to* c'ü 取; joh 贖; — *a person*, c'ü nying' 取人°; — *from sin*, joh ze' 贖罪; — *money*, c'ü nying'-go kô'-din 取人°个°價錢°

RAP, *to* tao 搗; k'ao 敲°; — *at the door*, tao meng' 搗門; k'ao meng' 敲°門; *give another* —, tsæ k'ao' ih-kyi 再敲°一記

RAPACIOUS, ziang lông-hwu' ka'像狼虎樣°式°

RAPE, *to commit* gyiang-kæn' 强姦

RAPE-SEED, ts'æ'-ts 菜子

RAPIDS, kyih'-shü 急水°; *catch fish in the* — (*i. e.* busy time in trade), k'ô kyih'-shü ng 捕°急水°魚°

RAPTUROUS, bao' feh hwun'-hyi 大°大°歡喜

RARE, hyi-hen' 希罕; næn-teh' 難得; siao-yiu' 少有

RARELY *met with*, næn-teh p'ong'-

RAS 381 RAY

djoh 難得逢着°; byi-vong'
希逢; — happens, ts'in-tsiao
gyi vong 千朝奇逢; he is —
angry, gyi sang-ky'i siao-yiu-go
其動°氣少有个°; — heard,
næn'-teh t'ing'-meng 難得聽
聞 (also means unpleasant to
hear).
RASCAL, p'in'-zeh 騙賊°; vu-la'
無賴°; 'ô'-tsoh p'e-ts' 下°作
胚子; a bold —, di-deo-oh'-
kweng 地頭惡棍
RASH, t'eh mao hyin' 太°冒險;
lao'-hwu k'eo za yiang' 老虎
口搖°癢
RASH broken out over the body,
weng'-sing fah'-c'ih 'ong-tin' de
渾身發出紅點了°
RASPBERRIES, miao-ts' 苗子 (so
called at T'in-dong)
RAT, lao'-ts' 老鼠; water —,
shü lao-ts'' 水°老鼠 (ih-tsah)
RATE, fixed —, (allowance, or
number), ih-ding'-go ngah-ts' —
定个°額子; a fixed price, ih-
ding'-go kô'-din 一定个°價
錢°; not two rates, peh-r'-kyüô
不二價'; estimating at the present —, z'-dzih kwu'-kô 時值
估價°
RATHER, neng'-s 寧°使; nying'-
k'o 寧可; moderately, p'o 頗;
I would — not go, ngô neng'-
s feh ky'i' 我寧使弗去°;
— pretty, p'o' hao'-k'eu 頗好
看

RATIFY, to — (as a treaty, &c.),
ding li' 定例
RATIONAL, endowed with reason,
yiu li'-sing 有理性
RATIONS to soldiers, ping-liang'
兵糧; — given by the Emperor
to Manchus, wông-liang' 皇糧
RATTAN, deng 籐 (a strand, ih-
keng); — seated chair, deng-
min' ü'-ts 籐面椅°子
RATTLE, a candy peddler's —, or
a child's —, yiao-teng-kwu' 搖
鼕皷
The rattle of each kind of peddler has
its distinctive name.
RATTLE, loh-loh'-hyiang 轆轆響
RAVAGE, ts'iang'-kyih 搶刦; lo'-
liah 擄掠; place ravaged by
the rebels, di'-fông be dziang-
mao' ts'iang'-kyih-ko'-de 地方
被長毛搶刦過了°
RAVEL, to — (as the edge of cloth),
mao-c'ih-læ 毛出來; sih'-c'ih-
læ; — out (as sewing), t'ah'-k'æ
脫°開
RAVENOUS, hwông zao'-ky'i 荒
糟°起; — appetite, we'-k'eo
hwông-ky'i' 胃口大°開
RAVINE, a ih-da k'ang' 一埭坑;
ih-go ao' 一條墢
RAVISHED with delight, gyih'-gyi
kao-hying' 極其高興
RAW, sang 生°; good to eat —,
sang ky'üoh' hao 生°吃°好;
partly cooked, feh-joh' 弗熟
RAY of light, ih-sin' liang-kwông'
一綫亮光

RAZE, to hwé'-diao 毀壞°;— to the ground, hwô'-we bing-di' 化爲平地

RAZOR, tśi'-deo-tao 薙頭刀 (ih-pô)

REACH, to extend to, tao 到; 'ang-tao' 行°到; t'ong-tao' 通到; liu-tao' 流到;— after, or to, liao 撩; pæn 扳; cannot — it, liao-feh-djoh' 撩弗着°; within —, liao-leh-djoh' 撩得°着°; pæn-leh-djoh' 扳得°着°;— out the hand, sing'-c'ih siu' 伸出手; sing-k'æ' siu' 伸開手;— out the head, deo' sing-c'ih' 頭伸出; cannot — up to the branches, p'æn'-feh-djoh ô-ts' 攀弗着椏°枝

READ, to — silently, k'en shü' 看書;— or study aloud, doh shü' 讀書; I have read this whole book, keh'-peng shü ngô dzong-deo'-ts-vi' k'en'-ko-de 這本書我從頭至尾看過了°;— prayers, (and other Buddhistic words), nyiæn-kying' 念經; dzong kying 誦經;— other's hearts by one's own, yi kyi'-ts sing' doh jing'-ts sing 以己之心度人之心

READILY, ken-sing' 甘心; willingly, dzing-nyün' 情願

READY speaker, k'eo'-neng-zih-bin' cü'-kwu 口能舌辯个°人°; pah'-læ-pah-te'-cü'-kwu 百°來百°對个°人°; quick, (because accustomed to), jing-joh' 純熟;

— with the pen, pih' nyiah-leh jing-joh' 筆揑得°純熟;— prepared, yü-be'-hao-liao 預備好了°; all —, zi-be'-de 齊°備了°;— money, yin' dong-din 現銅錢°;— money on hand, yin t'ông' 現帑; buy with — money, yin ma' 現買; to trade for money, yin'-dzin kao-yih' 現錢交易; make —, be-bæn' hao 備辦好; yü-be'-hao 預備好

READY-MADE, yin-dzing' or yin-zing'; 現成; bought —, yin-dzing' ma'-go 現成買个°

REAL, tsing 眞;— pearls, tsing cü'-ts 眞珠子;— facts, jih-dzing' 實情; true, jih-dzæ' 實在; ky'üoh'-jih 確實; tih'-ky'üoh 的確

REAL-ESTATE, jih-din'-jih-di' 實田實地; jih-nyih' 實業

REALLY, jih-dzæ' 實在; tsing-z' 眞是; ko'-jün 果然; nying-tsing' 認°眞

REAP, to — rice, kah dao' 割稻;— wheat, kah mah' 割麥

REAR, the 'eo 後;— (of an army, flock of sheep, &c.), 'eo' de 後隊

REAR, to — (as children), iang 養; yiang 養

REASON, yün-kwu' 緣故; kông'-kyiu 講究; what is the —? dza kông'-kyiu 甚°麽°講°究? oh! that is the — of it (or that cannot be so), kwa'-dao-z 怪道是; the original — of, nyün yiu' 原

由; keng yiu 根由; *right principle,* li 理; dao'-li 道理; *to accord with* —, 'eh li' 合理; *what* — (or sense) *is there in that?* ky'i'-yiu ts'-li' 豈有此理? vu-ts'-dzing-li' 無此情理? *by* — *of,* we-leh' 爲了; we 爲

REASON, *to* leng 論; nyi-leng' 議論; bin'-leng 辯論; kông'-leng 講論; *to* — *out with one's self,* zi fah'-hwe ih-fæn nyi-leng' 自發揮一番議論

REASONED *well,* fah'-hwe-leh hao' 發揮得好

REASONABLE, yiu-li' 有理; 'eh-li'-go 合理个; li' sô tông-jün'-go 理所當然个

REBEL, zeh-fi' 賊匪; fæn-zeh' 反賊; *long haired* —, dziang-mao' 長毛

REBEL, *to* bun'-nyih 叛逆; dzao-fæn' 造反

REBELLION, *to plot* meo-fæn' 謀反

REBOUND, *to* tao'-bang-cün-læ 倒撞轉來; tao'-p'ong-cün-læ.

REBUILD, *to* tsæ-ky'i' 再起; tsæ'-zao 再造

REBUKE, *to* tsah'-vah 責罰; tsah'-be 責備; heng.

RECALL, *to* we-s' kyi'-teh 回思記得; — *him,* eo gyi cün'-læ 叫其轉來; *cannot* — (it), 'a'-feh-c'ih' 回想弗出; kyi'-feh-læ 記弗來; *try to* — (it), 'a-'a'-k'en' 回頭想想

看; (I) — *it,* 'a-deo' tao-de 想到了

RECANT, *to* zih-yin' 食言; be yin' 背言; kæ-k'eo' 改口; cün-yin' 轉言

RECEDE, *to* t'e-'eo' 退後; tao'-t'e 倒退

RECEIPT *for payment,* siu-p'iao' 收票; siu-diao' 收條 (ih-tsiang); *a* — *for making,* ih-yiang fông-fah' 一樣方法

RECEIVE, *to* siu 收; ziu 受; tsih'-ziu 接受; teh'-djoh 得着; tao'-siu 到手; — (from a superior), ling 領; — (something sent), tsih'-tao 接到; tsih'-djoh 接着; — *and open,* siu-ts'ah' 收拆; — *a guest politely,* tsih'-dæ nying-k'ah' 接待客人; — *favors,* mong eng' 蒙恩 (too strong an expression for ordinary use).

RECENT, sing-gying'-go 新近个; gying-læ'-go 近來个; gying-z'-go 近時个; gying'-nyih'-go 近日个; — *news,* sing-gying'-go sing'-sih 新近个信息; — *years,* gying' nyin 近年; dzæ-s' kyi nyin' 纔始幾年

RECENTLY, gying'-læ 近來; — *come,* sing-læ'-go 新來个; bao'-z læ.

RECESS, *noon* hyih tsiu' 歇晝; *ditto at school,* fông tsiu'-'oh 放晝學

RECIPE *for medicine,* yiah fông' 藥方; fông-ts' 方子; *give* (tell) *me the* —, keh'-go fông'-ts djün peh' ngô 這°个°方子傳給°我

RECIPROCAL *love,* dô-kô' siang-æ' 大°家°相愛; ngwu-siang' ts'ing-'æ' 互相親愛

RECIPROCALLY *willing,* liang'-siang dzing-nyün' 兩相情願; pe'-ts' dzing-nyün' 彼此情願

RECITE, *to* — *lessons, &c.,* be shü' 背°書; — *stories* (in public), kông siao'-shih 講°小說; — *ditto with gestures,* kông do-shü' 講°大°書

RECKLESS, mông 莽; bah-mông'-kwông 白°漫光; feh-kwu'-zin-'eo' 弗顧前°後

RECKON, *to* sön 算; sön-tsiang' 算帳; p'a-tsiang 派°帳; — *and see,* p'a'-p'a-k'en 派派看; *to count,* su 數; su'-su-k'en' 數數看; *want to* — *with you,* iao teng ng' sön-tsiang' 要與°你°算帳; tsiang' teng ng sön'-sön-k'en' 帳與°你°算算看; — *to my account,* sön ngô'-go ming 'ô' 算我个°名下°

RECKONING, tsiang 帳 (ih-go; if it is written, ih-p'in); *your* — *is wrong,* ng-go tsiang ts'o-go 你°个°帳錯个°; ng-go tsiang sön ts'o'-de 你°个°賬算錯了°

RECLAIM *the wanderer,* ling mi-lu'-go nying we-deo'-de 領迷

路个°八°回頭了°; *to claim back,* t'ao-wæn' 討還

RECLINE *on a couch,* gæ tao' c'ing-teng'-li 戤°倒眷凳裏; — *against the wall,* gæ'-djoh ziang' 戤°著°牆; — *on a staff,* k'ao'-djoh kwa'-dziang 靠著°拐杖

RECOGNIZE, *to* min-jün' 面善; nying-teh' 認得; *do you not* — *me?* ng' feh min-jün' ngô' yia 你°弗面善我喲°? — *and claim as one's own,* nying-kyü' 認歸

RECOLLECT, *to remember,* kyi'-teh 記得; *to think of,* siang'-ky'i-læ 想起來; *try to* —, ts'eng'-ts'eng-siang' 忖忖相; 'a-'a'-siang' 揸°揸°相

RECOMMEND, *to* tsin 薦; kyü'-tsin 舉薦; *one who recommends another,* tsin'-deo nying 薦頭人°; læ'-deo nying' 來頭人°; *to advise,* ky'ün 勸

RECOMMENDATION, tsin'-shü 薦書; tsin'-sing 薦信; *write a* — sia ih-fong tsin'-shü 寫°一封薦書

RECOMPENSE, *to* pao 報; wæn 還; — *favor,* pao eng' 報恩; — *evil,* pao dziu' 報讐; — *evil for good,* eng-tsiang' dziu-pao' 恩將讐報; yi-oh'-pao-teh' 以惡報德; — *good for evil,* yi-teh'-pao-oh' 以德報惡

RECONCILE, *to* 'o-hao' 和好;

siang-'o' 相和; tsæ 'o-long' 再和攏; — by exhorting, ky'ün-'o' 勸和; — by speaking, kông-'o' 講°和

RECORD, to sia'-loh 寫°錄; kyi'-loh 記錄; tsæ'-loh 載錄; — (as something omitted, &c.), din-loh' 墥錄°

RECORDS of statistics, &c., ts'-shü 志書; — of one's ancestors, for three generations, li'-lih 履歷; — of criminal cases, en'-kyün 案卷

RECORDER, shü-bæn' 書辦; tông lao'-s 當書°吏°; to be a —, tông shü-bæn' 當書辦

RECOVER, to — (an article), kwe-wæn' 歸還; tsæ teh'-djoh 再得着°

RECOVERED (quite) from sickness, voh-nyün'-de 復元了°; bing' djün-yü'-de 病全愈了°

RECREATE, to — one's self, yiang-yiang jing' 養養神

RECRIMINATE, to liang-'o' to-k'eo'-ko 兩下°多口過; liang-'o' gyi-gwu 兩下°譏誚°; — with abusive language, zoh-læ' zoh-ky'i' 辱來辱去°

RECRUIT, to — one's strength, pu ky'i-lih 補氣力; pu nyün-ky'i' 補元氣; pu hyüih'-veng 補血孕; — an army, pu'-tsoh ping-ngah' 補足兵額; raw —, sing' ts'ong-go ping' 新充個°兵

RECTANGLE, dziang-fông' 長方

RECTIFY, to — mistakes (of words, or deeds), nying-cün'-læ 認°轉來; — (as mistakes in writing), kæ'-hao 改好; kæ tön-tsing' 改端正; — spoken mistakes, kông'-cün 講°轉

RECTITUDE, tsing'-dzih-vu-s' 正直無私; — in administration, ping'-kong-vu-s' 秉公無私

RECTUM, kông 肛; koh-dao' 穀道; the outer mouth of the —, feng'-meng 糞門

RED, 'ong 紅; blood —, hyüih'-'ong 血紅; tinged with —, 'ong-hyüih'-hyüih; bright —, do-'ong' 大°紅; to dye —, nyin-'ong 染°紅; — haired person, or foreigner, (vulgar), 'ong-mao-nying 紅毛人°

REDDEN, to fah-'ong' 發紅; 'ong-ky'i'-læ 紅起來

REDEEM, to c'ü'-joh 取贖; — from sin, joh-ze' 贖罪; — sinners, c'ü'-joh ze'-nying 取贖罪人°; — the time, æ'-sih kwông-ing' 愛惜光陰; — a pledge, c'ü-tông' 取當

REDEEMER, joh-ze'-go cü'-kwu 贖罪個°人°; the Redeemer, joh-ze'-go Cü' 贖罪個°主

REDRESS, to — grievances, ka ün' 解冤; shih ün' 雪冤; ka-ün' sih-kyih' 解冤釋結

REDUCE, to — the price, kæn kô'-din 減價°錢°; ditto so much out of every hundred, tang tsih'-deo

打折頭; tang k'eo'-deo 打扣頭; See Discount. — *expenses*, sang fi'-yüong 省°費用; — *unnecessary expenses*, sang 'æn-fi' 省°閒°用; — *to subjection*, ah'-voh 壓°服; — (as rebels), bing-voh' 平服

REDUCED *in circumstances* kwông'-kying loh'-de 光景衰°了°; *a person ditto*, loh-boh'-go nying 落泊°个°人°

REDUNDANCY *in words*, shih-wô' t'eh to' 說話太°多; to-yin'-to-nyü' 多言多語

REED, *a* ih-ts lu-ken' 一枝蘆竿; ih-ken lu' 一根°蘆; *a bamboo* —, ih-ken coh' 一根°竹

REEL, ts'ô 車; — *for winding from the cocoon*, dziu s'-ts'ô 抽°絲車 (ih-bu)

REEL, *to stagger*, ts'ih'-ts'ong-pah'-tih' 七瞥八跌; — *from drunkenness*, tseo' ziang sia do-z ka' 像寫°大°字樣°子°的°走°

RE-ESTABLISH, *to* tsæ shih'-lih 再設立; — *a government*, tsæ tsing'-teng kông-sæn' 再整頓江°山

RE-EXPORT, *to* nyün-ho' c'ih-k'eo' 原貨出口

REFER, *to point to*, ts'-tin 指點; *quote*, ying 引; — *to his example*, ying gyi'-go pông'-yiang 引其个°榜樣; *to* — *another*, ts'ing'-kao 請敎°; — *to a higher official*,

dziang-zông' 'eo-p'i' 詳上候批; — *the decision to you*, peh ng' tso-cü' 俾°你°作°主

REFINE, *to* lin 煉; — *by fire*, tön'-lin 煅煉

REFINED *in manners*, ts'ing-siu' siang 清秀相; veng-sih' 文飾; veng-yüô' 文雅; — *in heart*, iu-yüô' 幽雅; — *sugar*, dông' di-ts'ing'-liao-go 糖提清了个°

REFIRE, *to* — (as tea), fæn ts'ao' 翻炒

REFLECT, *to* fæn'-tsiao 反照; tao'-tsiao 倒照; ing 映; — *light*, we-kwông' fæn'-tsiao 迴光反照; — *upon the past*, (or on the absent), tse-siang' 追想; *to think*, s-siang' 思想; — *calmly*, si'-sing-go ts'eng' 細心个°忖

REFORM, *to* we-deo' 回頭; kæ'-ko 改過; — *in heart and thought*, we-sing'-cün-i' 回心轉意; ling-sing-coh'-cün 靈心回°轉; *to turn from the evil to the good*, kæ-oh'-dzong-jün' 改惡從善; ky'i'-zia-kwe-tsing' 棄邪°歸正

REFORMED, *already* yi'-kying we-deo'-de 巳經回頭了°

REFRACTION *of light*, kwông cün'-zih 光轉射

REFRACTORY, ao'-diao-peh-hying' 拗調不馴°

REFRAIN, *to* — *from singing*, feh

ts‘ông'-de 弗唱了°;—from, ka 戒°;— for a long time, dziang ka' 長戒°;— for a short time, tön' ka 短戒°;— from eating, gyi zih' 忌食; gyi cü' 忌嘴

REFRESH, to — one's mind, sing-li' k‘œ-wœ' 心裏開懷; k‘œ'-k‘œ sing' 開開心; kw‘un sing' 寬心;— one's strength, yiang lib' 養力; yiang-jing' 養神

REFUGE, a place of — dzòng-sing'-ts-c‘ü' 藏身之處; to'-bi u'-sen 躲避之所; bi nœn' di'-fông 避難地方

REFUGEES, dao-nœn'-go nying' 逃難个°人°; nœn-ming' 難民

REFUND, to wœn 還; t‘ing'-wœn 聽還;—(for an article injured), be-wœn' 賠還; be-djông' 賠償

REFUSE, vu-yüong'-ts-veh 無用之物; fi'-veh 廢物; lime —, zah-hwe-deo' 石灰餘屑';— tea, dzô-yih'-meh 茶葉末

REFUSE, to foh 覆; dz 辭; we-deo' 回頭; we-foh' 回覆; t‘e-dz' 推辭;— for a false reason, t‘e-t‘oh' 推托; cannot — (to do), t‘e-feh-t‘eh' 推弗脫; ditto (to admit), t‘e-feh-k‘œ 推弗開;— consent, feh-hyü' 弗許; feh ing-dzing' 弗應承;— with thanks, dz zia' 辭謝°; affect to —, kô' t‘e-dz 假°推辭

REFUTE, to poh-tao 駁倒

REFUTED, cannot be poh'-feh-tao'-go 駁弗倒个°; utterly —, poh'-sah-de 駁煞了°

REGAIN, to voh-cün'-lœ 復轉來; yi teh'-djoh 又°得着°

REGAINED (by the government), kw‘e-voh'-de 恢復了°; siu-voh'-de 收復了°

REGARD, to care for, kwu'-djoh 顧着°; ts‘œ 睬; kwun 管; ts‘iu-ts‘œ' 愀睬: do not — him, hao-vong' ts‘œ gyi 好不°用°睬其; speak and (he) regards not, wô-feh-ts‘œ' 話弗睬; in — to this matter, kông'-tao keh'-go z-ken' 講°到這个°事幹;— as improper, yi'-we feh-k‘o' 以爲弗可

REGARDLESS of danger, feh-kwu' ngwe-hyin' 弗顧危險;— of cost, feh-leng to-siao' dong-din' 弗論多少銅錢°

REGARDS, present my — to him, dœ ngô' mông-mông' gyi 代我望望°其; lœ gyi' di-fông dœ ngô cü'-i 在°其地方代我致意; t‘i ngô' ts‘ing gyi en' 替我請其安

REGENCY, to govern by a —, dœ djü' koh tsing' 代治國政; ditto during the minority of the heir apparent, bao t‘a'-ts zo long-ding' 抱太子坐龍廷

REGIMEN, follow a prescribed —, ing'-zih iao tsiao fah' 飲食要照法

REGIMENT, a ih-ts ping' —

枝兵; ih-de ping' 一隊兵

REGION, a ih-tæ di-fông' 一帶地方

REGISTER of names, or of lands, ts‘ah'-ts 冊子; — of population, a-wu'-ts‘ah 挨°戶冊

REGISTER, to cü-ts‘ah' 註冊; zông-ts‘ah' 上冊; — the census, zao a-wu'-ts‘ah 造°門°牌°冊; — the males, zông nying-ting'-ts‘ah 造°人°丁冊

REGRET, to ao-nao-siang' 懊惱相; sing' næn-ko' 心難過; — to part with, feh-sô'-teh 弗捨°得

REGRETTED, to be k‘o'-sih 可惜; always to be —, ao'-feh-cün'-go 懊弗轉个°

REGULAR, tsæn'-zi 整齊°; zi-jih' 齊°集; in — order (or succession), a-ts'-jü 挨°次序; — (as persons sitting, or standing, &c.), mi-mi'-shing 挨°排°排°; — in eating, and drinking, ing'-zih diao-yüing' 飲食調勻°; risen in the — way, (i.e. by examinations), sæn-k‘ao' c‘ih-sing' 三考出身; tsing'-du c‘ih-sing' 正途出身; not risen in the — way, (i.e. bought), kyün-pæn' c‘ih-sing' 捐班出身

REGULARLY, a-ts‘’-jü 挨°次序; i-ts‘’-jü 依次序; tsiao'-ts‘’-jü 照次序

REGULATE, to — what is in disorder, tsing'-teng 整頓; djü-li'

治理; cannot — his family, how can he govern a kingdom? peh neng dzi kyüô' in neng djü koh' 不能齊家焉能治國?

REGULATIONS, công-dzing' 章程 (công or tsông); diao-li' 條例; kwe-kyü' 規矩; kwe-diao' 規條 (ih-diao); to make —, shih'-lih tsông-dzing' 設°立章程

REIGN, to tso wông-ti' 做皇帝; zo-we' 坐°龍°廷°; zo tin-‘ô' 坐°天下°; begin a —, teng-we' 登極°; in the 8th year of T‘ung-chih, Dong-Djü' pah'-nyin 同治八年

REITERATE, to ts‘in-ting-væn'-coh-go wô' 千叮萬囑个°話; wô-ko' yi-wô' 話過又°話

REJECT, to ky‘i'-diao 棄了°; tiu-diao' 丟了°; — finally, ky‘i'-djih 棄絕

REJECTED by every one, we nying' sô ky‘i' 爲人°所棄

REJOICE, to be pleased, hwun-hyi' 歡喜; — together, dô-kô' hwun-hyi' 大°家°歡喜; greatly pleased, kw‘a'-loh 快樂; to be delighted, kao-hying 高興; — exceedingly, hwun-t‘in'-hyi-di' 歡天喜地

RELATE, to tell, kông 講°; djün 傳; I will — (it) to you; ngô kông' peh ng t‘ing' 我講°與你°聽; ngô kông'-hyiang-ng-dao' 我講°向你°道; 一

particulars, kông'-leh dziang-be' 講°得°詳備

RELATED, *is he —to you?* gyi' z ng'-go zing-dzoh' soh' 其是你°个°貴族麼°? *he is distantly —,* z ah-lah yün'-vông 'en-dzoh' 是我°等°遠房寒族; *we have the same surname, but are not —,* dong-sing' feh we-dzoh' 同姓不°宗°

RELATIONS, *and* RELATIVES, *nearest —,* ts'ing-nying' 親人°; *distant —,* yün'-ts'ing 遠親; *— of the same surname,* dong-dzoh' 同族; zi-kô-nying' 自°家°人°; *— of a different surname,* ts'ing-kyün' 親眷; *near — (whether by affinity, or consanguinity),* kweh'-joh-ts-ts'ing' 骨肉之親; hyüih'-ts'ing 血親; *the five —,* ng' leng 五°倫

RELAX, *to — (as a cord),* fông-song' 放鬆; *— (as muscles, &c.),* kw'un-shü' 寬舒

RELAXATION, *take* sing'-li en-yih'-kyi 心裡安逸; *— (after sorrow or trouble),* sæn-sæn sing' 散散心; kw'un-kw'un sing' 寬寬心

RELEASE, *to* fông 放; fông'-c'ih 放出; *— from confinement,* fah-fông' 發放; sih'-fông 釋放; *pardon and —,* nyiao-fông' 饒放

RELENT, *to* sang nyün'-sing-dziang 生°軟心腸

RELIABLE, t'oh'-leh-ko 托得°過; k'o-t'oh'-go 可托个°; k'ao'-leh-djü'-go 靠得°住个°; hao' siang-sing'-go 好相信个°; *to receive — information,* teh'-djoh jih-loh' 得着°實在°; *— news,* jih-jih'-loh-loh-go sing'-sih 實實在°在个°信息

RELICS, *ancient* kwü'-tsih 古蹟; *— of Buddha,* shiæ'-li 舍利; *— of saints, &c.,* sing'-doh 聖鐸°

RELIEF, *can give no —,* lih feh neng-dzu' 力弗能助; vu lih neng we 無力能爲

RELIEVE *pain,* kæn-kæn t'ong' 减痛; ka-ka t'ong' 解°痛; ka-ka bo; ts-ts t'ong 止痛; *— the poor,* tsin-tsi' gyüong-nying' 賙濟窮人°; sô'-s gyüong-nying' 捨施窮人°; *ditto (on a more extensive scale),* tsi-bing' 濟貧

RELIGION, kyiao 教; kyiao'-meng 教門; *Confucian —,* Jü kyiao 儒教; *Buddhist —,* Sih' kyiao 釋教; *Taoist —,* Dao' kyiao 道教; *Mahommedan —,* We-we' kyiao 回回教; *Catholic —,* T'in-cü' kyiao 天主教; *Protestant —,* Yiæ-su' kyiao 耶穌教

RELIGIOUS, gyin-dzing' 虔誠; *— newspaper,* 'ang kyiao' sing-pao' 行教新報; kyüoh'-shü sing-pao' 覺世新報

RELINQUISH, *to — with regret,* p'i'-diao 譬了°; p'i-t'æn'-diao

譬嘆了°;— (as an undertaking), t‛e-diao' 推了°; t‛e-k‛ae' 推開; hyih siu' 歇手
RELISH, to eat with a —, ky‛üoh'-leh yiu ts-mi' 吃°得°有滋味°
RELUCTANT, feh-dzing'-nyün 弗情願; feh-yüoh'-i 弗欲意
RELY, to — upon, i'-t‛oh 倚托; t‛oh'-læn 託賴; k‛ao'-djoh 靠着°; can — upon, k‛o k‛ao'-go 可靠个°; I am well, relying on your happiness, (a polite answer), t‛oh-ng-foh' 託你°福 or t‛oh-foh' 託福
REMAIN, to stay, deng 停; deng-loh' 停°了°; — long, dziang deng' 長停°; — for a short time, dzæn deng' 暫停°; — over (as food), dzing-loh' 剩落
REMAINDER, yü-to' 餘多; gyi'-yü' 其餘; to-deo' 多頭
REMARKABLE, fi-dzông' 非常; c‛ih-gyi' 出奇; — wisdom, fi-djông'-go ts‛ong-ming' 非常个°聰明
REMEDY, efficacious ling yiah' 靈藥; ling-tæn'-miao yiah' 靈丹妙藥: sin-tæn' 仙丹; no — for, ṃ yiah' k‛o-i' 無°藥可醫
REMEMBER, to kyi'-teh 記得; kyi' læ sing'-li 記在°心裏; kyi læ hyüong-cong' 記在°胸中; fông' læ sing'-li 放在心裡; dzng' læ sing'-li 存在°心裏; — and constantly think of, kyi'-nyiæn 記念; — after once

seeing, ko'-moh peh-vông' 過目不忘
REMIND, to di-ky‛i' 提起; di-deo'; — of something forgotten, di-sing' 提醒; — him, di-gyi-deo, or di-ky‛i gyi deo 提醒°其
REMISS, yiæ'-dæ 懈怠; — in business, tso' z-ken' ky‛in gying-lih' 做事幹少°勤力
REMIT, to pardon, sô'-diao 赦°了°; min'-diao 免了°; — the land tax, hweh'-min zin-liang' 豁免錢°糧; — money to a distance, ta nying-sing' c‛ih-ky‛i 寄°銀信出去°
REMITTENT fever, sih'-nyih-tsing 濕熱症
REMNANT (of cloth), t‛ön-den' 段頭°; ling-deo'-ling-mi' 零頭零尾°
REMONSTRATE, advise him not to do, ky‛ün' gyi feh-k‛o' tso 勸其弗可做; ditto (with a superior), kyin' gyi feh-k‛o' tso 諫其弗可做
REMORSE on account of one's sin, di-sing' tiao'-tæn, we-leh zi'-go ze' 提心吊膽爲了自°罪; we-leh zi-go ze' sing'-li ngao-tsin' 爲了°自°罪°心裏熬煎
REMOTE, yün 遠; liao-yün' 遼遠; nyiao-yün' 窵遠; very —, ting'-yün 頂遠; yiao-yün' 遙遠
REMOVE, to yi-ko' 移過; tsæn'-ko 趲過; — to another house,

pun-oh' 搬屋; ts'in-kyü' 遷居; ditto temporarily, tsæn-oh' 趲屋
REMUNERATE, to — (with a present), dziu-zia' 酬謝; — for trouble, dziu-lao' 酬勞
REND, to — (as rocks), hwah'-k'æ 豁開; — (as cloth), c'ô'-k'æ 撐開; to split, lih-k'æ' 裂開
RENDER an account of matters, we-pao' z-t'i' 回報事體; to pay back, wæn 還; pao'-wæn 報還; — thanks (to God), coh'-zia 祝謝°
RENDEZVOUS, to we-zi' 會齊°
RENEW, to kæ-sing' 改新; tso-sing' 做新; — the heart, ky'i gyin' wun-sing' 棄舊換新
RENOUNCE, to djü-diao' 除去°; djih-diao' 絕了°; ky'i'-djih 棄絕; dön'-djih 斷絕; — one's allegiance, be-fæn' 背反
RENOWNED, yiu do ming'-sing 有大°名聲; — even to the capital, ming'-cing ti'-tu 名震帝都
RENT, n. tsu-din' 租錢°; vông-din' 房錢°; vông tsu-din' 房租錢°; tsu-kô' 租價°; to raise the —, tsiang tsu-kô' 漲租價°; money, paid down as security for —, t'en' tsu-din 賙租錢°; ah' tsu-din 押°租錢°
RENT, to tsu 租; shü 賃; to — out, tsu-c'ih' 租出; shü'-c'ih 賃出
REPACK, to — (in a box), kæ-siang' 改箱; — (in a bundle), kæ-pao 改包
REPAIR, to siu-li' 修理; siu-gyin' 修舊; — by patching, siu-pu' 修補; — and embellish, siu-sih' 修飾; — bridges, and roads, siu-gyiao' p'u lu' 修橋補°路
REPAY, to wæn 還; ti'-siao 抵銷; — (for an article injured, or lost), be-wæn' 賠還; ti'-dzong 抵償
REPEAL, to — a law, djü-diao' lih-fah' 除去°律法; k'æ-diao' lih-fah' 開去°律法
REPEAT, to do again and again, tsæ'-sæn tso' 再三做; to say again and again, kông'-ko-yi-kông' 講過又°講; wô-ko'-yi-wô' 話過又°話; — the same thing in discourse, bun-zông'-bun-loh' 盤上盤落; — after another, djün 讘; — after me, keng'-leh ngô djün' 隨°我讘; — Buddhist prayers, nyien kying' 念°經; — a lesson, be shü' 背°書
REPEATEDLY, tsæ'-sæn-tsæ-s' 再三再四; charge — (by words), ting-coh' 叮囑; coh'-t'oh 囑託
REPENT, to ao'-hwe 懊悔; — and turn from, hwe'-kæ 悔改; we-sing'-cün-i 回心轉意; t'ong'-kæ zin-fi' 痛改前非; ao'-hwe kæ-ko' 懊悔改過; hwe'-ze kæ-ko' 悔罪改過; — (in a Buddhist sense, by paying the priests to pray for), ts'æn'-hwe 懺

悔; *to change one's mind*, sing fæn'-hwe 心翻悔

REPETITION *of words*, djün-ko'-yi-djün' 譔過叉°譔; bo-bo'-nao-nao'-go shih-wô' 重叠°个°說話; *endless —,* djün-feh-hyih'-go 譔弗歇个°

REPINE, *to — at*, ün 怨; 'eng 恨;— *at Heaven and Earth*, ün'-T'in 'eng-Di' 怨天恨地; *— at poverty*, ün gyüong' 怨窮

REPLACE, *to place as before*, dzing-gyiu en' 仍舊安放°;— *as if it had not been moved*, nyün-fông' feh dong' 放°在°原°處弗動

REPLENISH, *to fill again*, kô-mun' 加°滿; *fill completely*, s'-teh mun'-tsoh 使得滿足

REPLY, *to* we-tah' 回答; te'-tah 對答; tah'-ing 答應; *a —,* we-ing' 回音; we-wô' 回話; *— to a letter*, we-sing' 回信; *ditto* (unsealed), we-z' 回字

REPORT, *rumor*, fong-sing' 風聲; *idle —,* yiao-yin' 謠言; *to create ditto*, nyiah-dzao' yiao-yin' 揑造°謠言; *ditto and make trouble*, dzao-yin'-seng-z 造°言生事; fah kyü'-lông; ky'i môung-deo'; *the — is*, nying-kô wô' 人°家°話;— (of expenses, &c.), ts'ing-tæn' 清單; ts'ing-tsiang' 清帳;— *of a cannon*, p'ao'-go hyiang'-sing 礮个°響聲

REPORT, *to* t'ong-pao' 通報;— *to him*, pao'-hyiang-gyi-dao 報向其道; *— to a superior*, ping'-cü 稟知; *— to the Emperor*, tseo'-ming wông-zông' 奏明皇上;— *to the officers*, ping-kwun' 稟官

REPOSE, *quiet*, en-zing' 安靜; *to seek —,* zing en-zing' 尋安靜; *I wish you sweet —,* ts'ing' en-cü' 請安置

REPOSE, *to* hyih-sih' 歇息

REPRESENT, *you — him as a bad man*, gyi'-go dzing-ying', tsiao ng' kông'-læ z wa'-go 其个°情形照你°講來是孬°个°; *— typically*, piao'-ming 表明; *—, or act a part*, tsông-pæn' 裝扮; *to act for another*, dæ-we' jing-z' 代爲人事; *one represents ten*, ih' tông jih' 一當十; *— the people* (as in Congress), dæ pah'-sing cü z' 代百°姓調°處

REPRESS, *to* ah'-djü 壓住; ah'-cü 壓制; ah'-jih 壓習; ts'-djü 止住; *— anger*, ah'-djü ô'-wông 壓住怒°氣°; jing-ky'i-t'eng'-sing 忍氣吞聲; *could not — laughter*, nying'-feh-djü' siao' 忍弗住笑; *— bad disposition*, k'eh'-djü wa sing'-kah 克治孬°性格

REPRIEVE, *to* ying-vah' kw'un-wun'-tin 刑罰寬緩點

REPRIMAND, *to* tsah'-be 責備;— (generally in a loud tone), heng.

REPRINT, *to* tsæ ing' 再印; dzong ing' 重印

REPROACH, to s-we' 施爲; p'i-bing' 批評; to — severely, ba; wô; siah gyi lin' 削其臉; to humiliate him (extremely) by —, siu-joh' gyi 羞辱其; da gyi ô-lin' 抓其丫°臉; suffer —, ziu siu'-joh 受羞辱; ziu tsao-t'ah' 受蹧蹋; without —, 嘸 p'i'-bing 無批評; ditto (blemish), 嘸 yüô'-tin 無°瑕玷

REPROVE, to tsah'-be 責備; — (generally in a loud tone), heng; — and threaten, tsah'-vah 責罰

REPROBATE, vu-sô'-peh-we'-go 無所不爲个°; peh-k'æn'-ts-gyih' 不堪之極

REPROOF, ba-deo'; severe —, do' ba-deo'; receive a —, for the verb say either, t'ing 聽, ky'üoh' 吃°, or ziu 受; thus, I to-day received a —, ngô' kyih-mih' t'ing ba-deo' ko-de 我今日°聽埋°怨°過了°; give him a —, ba' gyi ih-we' 埋°怨°其一回

REPTILES, bô'-go djong 爬个°蟲

REPUBLIC, ming-cü'-ts-koh 民主之國

REPUDIATE, to dön'-djih 斷絕; ky'i'-diao 棄了°; t'ih'-c'ih-læ 剔出來; —(as an affair), t'eng-c'ih-læ 佘出來; — acquaintance, dön'-djih-læ-wông' 斷絕來往; — a wife, ky'i'-diao lao'-nyüing 棄了°妻°子°; ditto (for misbehavior), li'-diao lao'-nyüing 離了°妻°子°

REPUGNANT to a person, long nying' we'-wu-go 弄人°穢污个°

REPULSE, to tang'-t'e 打退

REPULSIVE countenance, min-k'ong' p'ô-nying'-sah-la' 面孔可°怕; cold and disagreeable, lang'-ts'ih-ts'ih 冷°澈澈

REPUTABLE, yiu-ming'-go 有名个°; — employment, t'i'-min-go 'ông-nyih' 體面个°行業

REPUTATION, ming-sing' 名聲; ming-ky'i' 名器; ming-vông' 名望; character, ming-tsih' 名節; to lose or injure —, tsao-t'ah' ming-sing' 蹧蹋名聲; wæ-diao' ming-sing' 壞了°名聲; ditto another's—, wæ nying'-go ming-tsih 壞人°名節; his — is good, gyi'-go ming-sing' hao 其个°名聲好; an indifferent —(i.e. not very good), ming-sing' bing-djông' 名聲平常

REQUEST, to ts'ing 請; siang-ts'ing' 相請; siang-iao' 相邀; — him to come, siang-iao' gyi læ' 相邀其來; ts'ing gyi læ' 請其來; respectfully — and entrust, pa'-t'oh 拜托; I will comply with your —, tseng kyiao', tseng kyiao' 遵敎遵敎

REQUIRE, to shü iao' 須要; vu-pih'-ts-iao 務必要; pih'-shü iao 必須要

REQUISITE, how many are — ?

ing-yüong' ky'iah'-leh to-siao' 應用却要°多少? pih'-ky'iah-leh to-siao' 必須°多少? (ky'iah-leh or ky'iao-leh).

REQUITE, to pao 報; pao'-tah 報答; — favors, pao-eng' 報恩; pao-peng' 報本

RESCUE, to save, kyiu 救; come to the —, læ kyiu' 來救; — from fire, ho-li' kyiu'-c'ih-læ 火裏救出來; kah ho' kyiu'-c'ih-læ 夾火救出來; — (as one who has fallen into something), tsing-kyiu' 拯救; kyiu'-yün 救援; — out of trouble, or difficulty, kyiu'-kw'u kyiu-næn' 救苦救難

RESEARCHES, to make —, (i. e. seek diligently), seo-zing' 搜尋°; ditto by examining, k'ao'-kyiu 考究

RESEMBLING, ziang 像; siang-ziang' 相像; jü-dong' 如同; fông'-feh 仿彿

RESEMBLES, yiu-ts'-wu 猶之乎; z'-wu 似乎; — in countenance, tso' min-ngæn' 同°眉°眼°; — his father, yiu-ts'-wu ah-tia' 猶之乎阿爹; ziang tia' 像爹; teng ah-tia' siang-ziang'-go 與阿爹相像個°; — exactly, weh-t'eh'-ko 活揭過; t'ih'-seh-vu-r' 貼色無二

RESENT, to dong ky'i 動氣; kô ky'i 加°氣; (polite) kyin ky'i 見氣

RESENTMENT, ün 怨; ün'-ky'i 怨氣; bitter —, ün'-ky'i-beh-beh' 怨氣勃勃; ün-dzin' 寃讐; — and hatred, ün'-'eng-go sing 怨恨個°心; should not cherish —, ün' feh-k'o kyih' 寃弗可結; ün' feh-k'o' dzeng' 怨弗可存; implacable —, ka'-feh-k'æ'-go ün' 解°弗開個°寃

RESERVE, to liu-loh' 留落; dzing-loh' 剩落; dzeng-loh' 存落; — a little, liu-tin'-loh 留些°; dzing-tin'-loh 賸些°

RESERVED in words, kwô'-yin-kwô-nyü'-go 寡言寡語個°

RESIDE, to djü 住; deng 居°; where do you —? ng'-djü læ 'ah-li 你°住在°何°處°?

RESIDENCE, djü-c'ü' 住處; deng-c'ü' 庑處; deng-sing'-ts-c'ü' 庑身之處; en-sing-'-ts-c'ü' 安身之處; where is your honorable —? tseng fu' 'ah-li 尊府何°處°? fu'-zông 'ah-li 府上那°裡? fu'-zông 'o-c'ü' 府上何°處? my humble —, sô-'ô' 舍下°; sô'-kyin 舍間; bi-sô' 敝舍

RESIDUE, the gyi-yü'-go 其餘個°; yü-to'-go 餘多個°

RESIGN, to give up, dz 辭; zia 謝; t'e 推; t'e-diao 推了°; — a situation, dz di - fông 辭缺°; — one's office, dz kwun' 辭館; zia z' 謝事; zia zing' 謝任; ditto on account of old age, kao'-lao 告老; — to another, nyiang 讓°; *ditto by writing*, sia z' 卸事

RESIST, *to* ti'-tông 抵擋; tông'-djü 擋住; — *an enemy, &c.*, ti'-dih 抵敵; — *paying taxes* (in a body), nao liang' 閙漕°

RESOLUTE, kyin-sing' 堅心; ts'-hyiang lih-lao'-liao 志向立牢了; *be* —, sing' iao kyin' 心要堅

RESOLUTION, *unshaken firmness*, lih-sing' 烈心

RESOLUTIONS (passed by an assembly, &c.), công-dzing 章程 (công or tsông).

RESOLVE, *fixed* k'ô'-ding cü-i' 搿°定主意; cü'-i lih-lao' 主意立牢

RESOLVE, *to* ding cü'-i 定主意; lih cü'-i 立主意

RESORT, *many* — *thither*, læ-ky'i'-go nying to' 來去个°人°多; *a place of* —, jü'-jih-nying'-cong di'-fông 聚°人聚°集°之°地°; *the last* —, (figurative, from chess), meh-tsiah'-gyi-ts' 末着基子

RESOURCE, fông-fah' 方法; fah'-ts 法子; *no* — (but this), m̄-fah' 無法; shih'-fah-næ'-'o 失法奈何; vu-k'o'-næ-'o 無可奈何

RESPECT, *to* kying-djong 敬重; kong-kying' 恭敬; tseng-djong' 尊重; — *one's parents*, kying'-djong vu'-meo 敬重父母;

ditto, (or reflect honor upon), tsang do'-nying-go ky'i' 爭大°人°个°氣; — *this*, (official), ling-tseng' 懍遵; — *written paper*, kying'-sih z-ts' 敬惜字紙

RESPECT, *with* — *to*, kông'-tao 講°到; ts'-ü 至於; *no* — *for superiors*, moh'-vu tseng-tsiang' 目無尊長; m̄-do' m̄-siao' 無大°無°小; *self* — (as flowing from — for one's parents), tsang-ts'-ky'i' 爭志氣; ze-ky'i' 銳氣; *to endure trouble from ditto*, tsang-fong' ngao'-ky'i' 爭°風傲氣; *lost all self-* —, ze-ky'i' tih'-tao-de 銳氣跌倒了°; tao ze-ky'i' de 倒銳氣了°; *no* — *for self, or for parents*, m̄-tsang'-m̄-ky'i' 弗°爭°氣; *a good man respects himself*, kyüing-ts' z-djong' 君子自重

RESPECTS, *to pay one's* —, mông-mông' 望望; p'a' mông 拜°望; *in some* — *alike, in some* — *not alike*, yiu-sing dong', yiu sing feh-dong 有些°同有些弗同. (also means some are alike and some are not).

RESPECTABLE, t'i'-min 體面; yiu t'i'-min 有體面; — *people*, zông kó'-ts nying' 上等°人°

RESPECTFUL, kong-kying' 恭敬; — *to his master*, dæ cü'-nying-kô kong-kying' 待主人°

恭敬; be —, tso nying' iao ky'in-kong' 做人°要謙恭
RESPECTING, leng-tao' 論到; ts'-ü 至於
RESPIRE, to ih-hwu' ih-hyih' 呼一吸; bwun-tsing' bwun-c'ih' 喚進喚出; hwu-hyih' 呼吸
RESPITE, no ih-hyih'-feh-k'ong' 一歇弗空
RESPLENDENT, ming-liang' 明亮; kwông-liang' 光亮; — (as snow), shih'-kwah-liang 雪亮
RESPOND, to ing'-tah 應答; ing'-te 應對; we-tah' 回答
RESPONSIBILITY, tseh'-zing 責成°; kyin-ts' 肩子; the — rests on you, z ng'-go tseh'-zing 是你°个責成°; z ng' tæn-tông' 是你°擔當; dzæ-ü ng' 在于你°; the — (consequence), rests on you, z ng'-go ken-yi' 是你°个干係; (the burden) ditto, z ng'-go tæn'-deo 是你°个°擔頭; hyiang ng' z veng' 向你°是問; læ ng' sing zông 在°你°身上; to bear the —, pe' ken-yi' 背干係; to devolve the — on some one else, sia' kyin-ts' 卸°肩子
RESPONSIBLE, to be — for another, tso pao' 做保; tso-cong'-tsoh-pao' 做中作保; a —situation, zing-djong'-tseh-da' 任重責大
REST, en-tæn' 安耽; en-sih' 安息; bing-en' 平安; en-yih' 安逸; day of —, en-sih' nyih 安

息日°; remainder, gyi-yü' 其餘; yü-to' 餘多
REST, to tsiang-sih' 將息; —from labor, hyih-kong' 歇工; deng kong' 停工; — a while, deng' ih-hyih' 停°一歇; ditto from effort, hyih lih' 歇力; hyih' ih-zông lih' 歇一歇°力; won't (you) — a while? ts'ia' hyih'-ih-hyih 且°歇一歇?— or lean upon, gæ-djoh' 戤著°; a-djoh' 挨°著°; — on the wall, gæ-djoh ziang' 戤著°墻; —your heart, (or be easy), fông'-sing 放心; can't — my heart, (or can't be easy), fông'-sing-feh'-loh' 放心弗下°
RESTING-PLACE, tsiang-sih'-go di'-fông 將息个°地方; — (by the way), liang-ding' 涼亭
RESTLESS, zo'-lih-feh-en' 坐°立弗安; sing-mông'-feh-ding' 心忙弗定
RESTORE, to give back, kwe-wæn' 歸還; — to original owner, kwe-wæn' nyün-cü' 歸還原主; to bring back, wæn'-we 挽回; — tea (that has been used), wæn-weng' dzô-yih' 還魂茶葉; — paper, wæn-weng' ts' 還魂紙
RESTORED from sickness, djün-yü'-de 全愈了°; zông-hao'-nyiang-de; — to original health and strength, voh-nyün'-de 復元了°; wæn-nyün'-de 還元了°

RESTRAIN, to iah'-soh 約束; kwun'-soh 管束; 'en 含忍;— one's bad behavior, 'ang-we' siu-lin' 行°爲收歛;— one's self, zi iah'-soh zi' 自°約束自°;— anger, neh-leh sing-ho' 耐°下°心火;— anger, and keep quiet, jing'-ky'i t'eng'-sing 忍氣吞聲; not to — one's lust, fông tsong 放縱; could not — tears, ngæn'-li 'en'-feh-djü'-de 眼°淚含弗住了°

RESTRAINT, under — (uneasy), kyü-soh' 拘束

RESTRICT, to 'æn 限; 'æn'-cü 限°制; 'æn'-ding 限°定;— him to one bowl, 'æn'-ding peh gyi ih un 限°定°給°其一碗

RESTRICTIONS, many —, or restricted in many ways, hyü'-to kyü-soh'-liao 許多拘束了°; kyü-kyü'-soh-soh 拘拘束束

RESULTS, kyih'-gyüoh 結局; sin-dziang' 收塲; bad —, wa kyih'-gyüoh 孬°; 結局; what —? dza-go kyih'-gyüoh 怎°樣°結局?

RESULTS from, kwe-keng'-kyih-ti' 歸根結帝; c'ih'-ü 出於; this — from the medicine, keh z yiah'-go kwe-keng'-kyih-ti' 這°是藥个°歸根結帝; keh' c'ih'-ü yiah' 這°出於藥

RESUME, to dzing-gyin' tso 仍舊做;— the duties of office, voh-zing' 復任

RESURRECTION, the doctrine of the —, veo-weh'-go dao'-li 復活个°道理; the — day, weh-cün'-læ-go nyih-ts' 活轉來个°日°子

RESUSCITATE, to — (from apparent death), long sing'-cün-læ 弄醒轉來

RETAIL, to sell at —, ling-ts'ah' 零拆; ts'ah-ma' 拆賣; to do small — trade, tso siao' sang-i' 做小生°意; tso siao' peng'-kying-kyi 做小本經紀

RETAIN, to liu 留; liu-loh' 留下°

RETALIATE, to wæn-li' 還禮; yiu-li-wæn-li' 有禮還禮; yiu'-pao-wæn-pao' 有報還報

RETARD, to wun 綏; tso'-leh wun-fæn'-tin 做得°綏點; a painful foot retarded my walking, be kyiah' t'ong wun'-wun tseo' 爲°脚痛綏綏走

RETINUE, attendants, ze-dzong' 隨從; keng-ze'-go-nying' 跟隨个°人°; those who wait upon, and follow, keng-pæn' 跟班; Emperor's —, z-we' 侍衞

RETIRE, to withdraw, t'e 退;—, or get out of an officer's way, we-bi' 迴避; bi-ih'-bi 避一避;— a step, t'e-ih-bu 退一步; go out, t'e'-c'ih-ky'i 退出去;— from office, zia-z' 謝°事; ditto, and live in seclusion away from one's home, ing'-loh 隱落

RETIRED *spot*, iu-zing' di'-fông 幽靜地方

RETIRING, *liking to drop behind*, hwun-hyi' loh 'eo' 歡喜落後°; *preferring others before one's self*, tseng nying' zông zin' 遜°人上前°

RETORT, *to* we-k'eo' 回口; we-yin' 回言; — *improperly*, ing-cü' 應嘴; ing lang'-wô 應冷°話; *to* — *wittily*, ing-ky'iao' wô 應巧話

RETRACT, *to* — *one's words*, shih-wô' fæn-diao' 說話翻調; cün-yin' 轉言; — (as in court), cün-kong' 轉供; fæn-kong' 翻供

RETREAT, *to* t'e 退

RETREATED, *the army* ping t'e'-de 兵退了°

RETRIBUTION, pao'-ing 報應; ko'-pao 果報; ken'-ing 感應; *just* —, pao'-ing 'ao-li' feh-ts'o' 報應毫厘弗錯°

RETURN, *to* — (thither), kyü-læ' 歸°來; cün'-læ 轉來; we-læ' 回來; —(there), kyü-ky'i' 歸去°; cün-ky'i' 轉去°; we-ky'i' 回去°; — *home*, kyü oh'-li ky'i' 歸家°去°; *in haste to* —, kwe-sing'-ju-tsin' 歸心如箭; *to turn back*, tao'-tseo-cün 倒走轉; — *a present*, (*i. e.* send it back with thanks), pih' zia 璧謝°; — *to bad ways*, væn nyün' ts'ông-pô' 犯原瘡疤; — *to old* (bad) *habits*, væn lao' mao-bing 犯老毛病; — *to old crimes*, væn gyiu en' 犯舊案; — *visits*, we-pa' 回拜; *ditto and thank for attention*, zia bu' 謝°步; —*things*, we-wæn' tong-si' 回還東西; *returned to Peking*, we Poh'-kying ky'i'-de 回北京去°了°

RE-UNITE, *to* — (persons), tsæ'-jü 再聚; — (things), tsæ-'eh' 再合; tsæ'-tsih'-long 再接攏

REVEAL, *to open*, k'æ-c'ih'-læ 開出來; *to disclose*, lu'-c'ih-læ 露出來; *to manifest*, hyin'-c'ih-læ 顯出來; — *a matter*, lu fong-sing' 露風信

REVELATION, meh-z' 默示; *the Book of* —, Meh-z'-loh 默示錄

REVENGE, pao-dziu' 報讐; (in a less degree), pao-ün' 報怨

REVENUE, hyiang'-nying 餉銀; — *from customs*, se'-din 稅錢°; — *from lands*, zin-liang' 錢°糧

REVERE, *to* tseng-kying' 尊敬; kong-kying' 恭敬

REVERENCE, kying'-djong 敬重

REVERENTIAL, gyin-kying' 虔敬

REVERIE, *in a* ts'eng'-leh c'ih-jing' 忖得°出神

REVERSE, *to turn over*, fæn-cün'-læ 翻轉來; *to turn end for end*, diao-deo' 調頭; *to turn the other side*, fæn-hyiang' 翻向; fæn-min' 翻面

REVERT, to — to the original, kwe-nyün' 歸原; voh-nyün' 復原; — to the old practice, tsiao nyün' tso 照原而°做
REVIEW, to — studies, li sbü' 理一°理書; — (as a critic), bing-shü' 評書; — troops, k'en ts'ao' 看操; yüih ping' 閱兵
REVILE, to zoh-mô' 辱罵; lön-zoh'-lön-mô' 亂辱亂罵; zoh-nying-mô'-tao 辱人°罵倒
REVISE, to — and correct, kyiao'-ting 校訂
REVIVE, to — strength, tsih lih' 接力;—(as from a swoon), sing'-cün-læ 醒轉來
REVIVED, trade sang-i' hying'-ky'i-læ'-de 生°意興起來了°; strength —, lih' wæn-cün'-læ-de 力還轉來了°
REVOKE, to —(a decision, or promise), fæn-diao' 翻調; fæn-tsiao' 翻招;— a law, kæ'-diao lih-fah' 改了°律法; kæ-diao is more often used than fi-diao, as the latter implies disrespect to a former ruler.
REVOLT, to dzao-fæn' 造反; bun'-nyih 叛逆; liao-lön' 擾°亂
REVOLUTION, ih-cün' 一轉; to make a —, tsiu-we'-ih-cün' 周圍一轉; political —, (i. e. change of dynasty) wun dziao-dæ' 換朝代
REVOLVE, to cün 轉; dön-dön'-cün 圍圍轉; the earth revolves

around the sun, di-gyiu' hyiang nyih-deo' ih-cün' 地球向日°頭一轉; — in the mind, sing-li' dziu-djü' 心裏躊躇
REWARD, to sông 賞;—(for services), k'ao'-sông 犒賞;— the good, punish the wicked, sông jün' vah oh' 賞善罰惡
REWARD, official sông'-kah 賞格; — of money given to servants, or employees, sông'-fong 賞封; notice of — promised, sông-diao 賞條; a — (whether good or bad), pao'-ing 報應
RHEUMATIC pains, fong-ky'i'-t'ong 瘋氣痛; ditto in the shoulders, leo-kyin-fong' 漏肩瘋
RHINOCEROS, si-ngeo' 犀牛°(ih-deo); — horn, si-ngeo' koh 犀牛°角°(ih-go, ih-tsah)
RHOMBUS, zia'-fông 斜方°
RHUBARB, da-wông' 大黃
RHYME, yüing 韻; yüing-kyiah' 韻脚; to make rhymes, ah yüing' 押°韻
RIB, leh-ba-kweh' 肋膀°骨 (ih-keng); mutton —, or chop, yiang ba'-kweh 羊膀°骨; a — of the fan is broken, ih-keng sin'-kweh, dön'-de 一根扇骨斷了°
RIBALDRY, wine talk, tsiu'-wô 酒話; tsiu'-tse-wu-du' shih-wô' 酒醉糊塗說話; lewd talk, ying-wô' 淫話
RIBBON, s-ta' 絲帶°(ih-keng)
RICE, growing dao 稻; — in the

hull, koh 穀; uncooked —, mi 米; cooked —, væn 飯; a grain of —, ih-lih mi' 一粒米; — sprouts, dao iang-ts' 稻秧子; — gruel, coh 粥; hyi-væn' 稀飯; very smooth ditto, dziu-lin'-go coh 綢黏°个°粥; boiled —, with water added, t'ông'-væn 湯飯; must not waste (or soil) —, væn ṁ-nao' tsao-t'ah' 飯弗可°蹧蹋; — weevil, mi'-djong 米蟲

RICH person, yiu'-lao nying-kô' 有錢°人°家; yiu'-lao dzæ-cü' 有錢財主; ing-wu' 殷戶; fu'-wu 富戶; do-nying-kô' 大戶人°家°; — and honorable, fu'-kwe 富貴; to become —, fah-dzæ' 發財; if (you) wish to be — (fear not) to walk a dangerous way, ziah-iao-fu' tseo-hyin'-lu 若要富走險路; — dress, fu'-kwe i-zông 富貴衣裳; — tasted, (as food), 'eo'-vi 厚味; — soil, di-t'u' 'eo-jih 地土厚實; nyi-nyüoh 'eo 泥土厚

RICHES, dzæ-veh' 財物; dzin-dzæ' 錢財; god of —, dzæ-jing' bu-sah' 財神菩薩

RID, to get — of, t'eh'-diao 脫了°; t'eh'-c'ih 脫出; t'eh-siu' 脫手; tiu-siu' 丟手; glad to get — of him, pô'-feh-neng'-keo t'eh'-diao gyi 巴弗能彀脫了°其

RIDDLE, me-ts' 謎°子; — on a lantern, teng-me' 燈謎°; to guess a —, ts'æ me-ts' 猜謎°子

RIDE, to — a horse, gyi mô' 騎馬; — in a sedan, zo gyiao' 坐轎; — in a carriage, zo ts'ô-ts' 坐°車°子

RIDGE of a house, oh'-tsih 屋脊; — pole, tong'-liang 棟樑; — of mountains, lin-keng'-go sæn 連亙°个°山

RIDICULE, to tsao-siao' 嘲笑; c'ü'-siao 取笑; siao 笑

RIDICULOUS, hao-siao'-go 好笑个°; kyin-siao'-go 見笑个°

RIGGING, sail-ropes, bong-soh' 蓬索

RIGHT, according with —, li'-ing z-ka' 理應如°此°; li'-kæ jü-ts' 理該如此; ing-tông'-go 應當个°; ing-kæ'-go 應該个°; reasonable, yiu'-li 有理; not wrong, feh-ts'o' 弗錯°; straight, or upright, tsing 正; — doctrine, tsing' dao'-li 正道理; not —, not up to the —, or crooked, feh-tsing'-kying 弗正經; the — hand, jing-tsah' siu 順隻手; — side, jing-siu'-pin 順手邊; — angle, dzih-koh' 直角°; is it —? z-ka' feh-z-ka' 是如°此°不°是如°此°? it is —, feh-ts'o' 弗錯°; it is not —, feh-z-ka' 弗是如°此°; quite —, tsing'-z 正是; — side, (as of cloth), tsing'-min 正面; — side up, jing-hyiang' 順向

RIGHT, my li'-ing peh ngô' 理應給°我; ngô li' sô ing-teh'-

go 我理所應得个°; ngô veng' sô tô-g-jün'-go 我孖所當然个°; ngô ing-veng' sô teh'-go 我應孖所得个°.

RIGHTS, put to —, tsing-li'-hao 整理好; tsing'-teng-hao 整頓好; ditto (by taking away), tsin-coh'-ko; siu-jih'-ko 收拾過

RIGHTEOUS, jün 善; liang-jün' 良善; tsing'-dzih 正直; jih-djün' 十全

RIGID, hard, ngang 硬°; — in adhering to rules, kwe-kyü' siu'-leh nyin' 規矩守得°嚴; too ditto, kyiao-djü'-kwn-seh', or tiao-djü'-kwu-seh' 膠柱鼓瑟

RILL, siao' ky'i-k'ang' 小溪坑 (ih-da).

RIM, pin 邊; — of a cup, un' pin 碗邊; to put on a —, siang ih-go pin' 鑲一个°邊

RING, ky'ün 圈 (ih-go); — (attached to something), gwæn 環°; finger —, ka-ts' 戒指; ear —, gwæn-ts' 耳環° (a pair, ih-fu)

RING, to — a bell, k'ao cong' 敲鐘; — a small bell, yiao ling' 搖鈴; loh ling' 捋鈴; — by beating, djông cong' 撞鐘

RINGING in the ears, ng'-tô 'ong-'ong'-hyiang 耳°朵閧閧響

RINGLEADER, we-deo'-we-nao' 爲頭爲腦; deo-nao' 頭腦; — (in something bad), 'o'-ts-siu' 禍之首; zé'-ts-kw'e' 罪之魁

RINGWORM, ky'ün-sin' 圈癬

RINSE, to — (as cups &c.), dông邊; — (as clothes), dzah; — it, dông' gyi ih dông' 邊其一邊; to shake back and forth in the water, da; — the mouth, dông k'eo' 邊口; — in clear water, ts'ing shü' dzah' ih-du' 清水浸一回°

RIOT, ts'ao'-nao 譟鬧; nao-z' 鬧事; — in time of famine, hwông-lön' 荒亂

RIP, to ts'ah-k'æ' 拆開; ts'ah'-diao 拆了°; — seams, ts'ah'-k'æ vong-ts' 拆開縫子; — open, p'o'-k'æ 破開; — up the bowels, p'o foh' 破腹

RIPE, joh 熟; insufficiently —, ky'in joh' 欠熟

RIPPLES, shü po-lông' 水波浪; — in circles, shü yüing' 水°暈

RISE, to get up, bô-ky'i' 爬起; ky'i-sing 起身; to stand up, lih-ky'i'-læ 立起來; — (to higher office). kao-sing' 高陞; sing-zông'-ky'i 陞上去°; —, (step by step), sing-deng' 陞騰; — in life, fah'-dah 發達; — or be promoted in literary examinations, cong'-k'o-fah-kah' 中科發甲°; smoke will —, in we ts'ong-zông'-ky'i 烟會冲上去°; — (as dough), fah'-ky'i'-læ 發起來; — from the dead, si-ts' weh-cün'-læ 死°後°活轉來; market price has risen a little, 'ông-dzing' tsiang'-tinko-de 行情漲點過了°; *when will the tide —? ky'i'-z dziao tsiang'* 幾時潮漲? *soh'-gɔ z-'eo dziao-shü tsiang'* 甚°麼°時候潮漲? *sun —*, nyih-deo' c'ih ky'i' z 'eo' 日°頭出起時候

RISE, *origin*, keng-yiu' 根由; ky'i-ing' 起因; ky'i-deo' 起頭

RISK, *danger*, or *run the —*, mao-hyin' 冒險; — *life*, p'un-ming' 拚命; pe sing'-ming 拚°性命; *if not run some — how can one catch the tiger's cub*, "peh-jih hwu'-yüih in'-teh hwu-ts'" 不入虎穴焉得虎子

RITE, li 禮; *the mode of administering a —*, li'-cü 禮制; li'-tsih 禮節; *marriage and funeral rites*, hweng-sông' li'-tsih 婚喪禮節

RIVAL, te'-sin 對手; *antagonist*, te'-deo nying 對頭人°

RIVAL, to tsang-zin' 爭°前°; — *in display*, sæ-fu' 賽富; *the two — each other*, liang'-go bih kao ti' 兩个°別高低

RIVER, (*where there are tides*), kông 江°; — (*where there are no tides*) kông 港; 'o 河 (ih-da); *the —*, 'ô'-kông 下°江°, so called as compared with the canals.

RIVULET, ky'i-k'ang' 溪坑° (ih-da)

RIVET, liang'-deo-bing'-go ting' 兩頭平个°釘; — (of scissors, or fan), gao-kwu' 交°股

ROAD, lu 路; lu-du' 路塗; dao'-lu 道路 (ih-da); — *that does not go through*, toh'-sah-lu 不°通°之°路; lu' feh-t'ong' 路弗通; — *that one knows*, joh-lu' 熟路; *strange —*, sang-lu' 生°路; *unfrequented —*, hwông-lu' 荒路; *lang'-lu* 冷°路; *on the —*, lu-zông' 路上; *what —?* 'ah-li' ih-da lu' 何°處°一堘路°

ROAM, to 'æn-tseo' 閒°走°; yiu-hyi' 遊戲

ROAR, to — (as a tiger), wu-wu'-hyiang 嗚嗚響; — (as wind, or falling water), nga-nga'-hyiang 嘎°嘎°響

ROAST, *to bake*, p'ang 烹°; — *beef*, p'ang ngeo-nyüoh' 烹°牛°肉°; — *chestnuts*, ts'ao lih-ts' 炒栗子; — *or five tea leaves*, ts'ao dzô-yih' 炒茶葉

ROB, *to* ts'iang'-deh 搶奪; — *when travelling*, tang'-kyih 打叔

ROBBER, zeh-heo' 賊°; do-zeh' 大°賊°; *one who robs with violence*, da-dao' 大盜; ts'iang'-væn 搶犯; *a bold —*, (*often*) *a pirate*, gyiang-dao' 強盜; *mounted —*, hyiang'-mô gyiang-dao' 響馬強盜

ROBE *worn with a girdle*, bao-ts' 袍子; *imperial ditto*, long-bao 龍袍; *official —*, mông'-bao 蟒袍; *long Summer —*, (*not girded*), dziang-sæn 長衫; *lined —*, kah'-ao 袷襖

ROBUST, gyin 健; tsòng'-gyin 壯健

ROCK, do zah'-deo 大°石°頭; fixed —, bun-zah' 磐石°; — work, kô'-sæn 假山; to make ditto, te kô'-sæn 堆假山

ROCK, to yiao 搖; — back and forth, yiao-læ'-yiao-ky'i' 搖來搖去°; to — a chair, kwa' ü-ts 拐椅°子

ROCKING-CHAIR, yiao-dong'-go ü'-ts 搖動个°椅°子; yiao'-ü 搖椅°; kwa'-ü-ts 拐椅°子 (ih-pô)

ROCKET, liu-sing'-ho'-p'ao 流星火爆

ROCKY hills, zah sæn' 石°山; — precipice, zah pih' 石°壁

ROD, ken'-ts 釣°竿; fishing —, tiao'-ng-ken' 釣魚°竿 (ih-keng)

ROE, female deer, ts' loh' 雌鹿; fish —, ng-ts' 魚°子

ROGUE, we-fi'-tsoh-tæ'-go-nying 爲非作歹个°人°; one who goes about deceiving, tong'-kwa-si-p'in-go 東拐西騙个°

ROLL, a ih-kyün' 一卷

ROLL, to le 擂; kweng 滾; kyün 捲; the ball will —, gyin we le 球會擂; — dough, le min' 擂麵; will —off, iao le'-ko-ky'i' 要擂過去°; — the ground even, di-yiang' le bing 地上°擂平; — over and over, fæn-læ' foh-ky'i' 翻來覆去°; — up

the sleeves, ziu-ts' kyün-tæn'-zông 袖子捲上

ROLLER for maps, gyüoh 軸; stone —, le-zah' 擂石° (ih-go)

ROLLING pin, ken'-djü 桿鎚; le-djü' 擂鎚° (ih-keng)

ROMAN letters, Lo-mô' z 羅馬字

ROMANCE, book of leisure moments, 'æn-shü' 閒°書 (ih-peng)

ROOF, oh'-teng 屋上°; tile —, oh'-ngô-teng 屋瓦°上°; to mend the —, kæ leo' 蓋漏; coh leo' 築漏; ts'eh leo' 搬漏

ROOM, vông 房; the next —, kah'-pih vông 隔壁房; sleeping —, vông-kæn 房間; kw'eng'-vông 臥房° (ih-kæn); make — (by putting things closer), tsing'-leh kw'un-k'ong'-tin 整得寬空點; no — to sleep, kw'eng'-u ṅ'-teh 睡處沒有°; ṅ-di'-fông hao kw'eng' 無°地方可°睡°; no — to put it, ṅ-c'ü' hao fông 無°處好放

ROOST, perch, tông'-ts 檔子; roosting place (used figuratively for men), ts'i-sing'-ts-sô' 棲身之所

ROOST, to ts'i 棲; — in the branches, ts'i' læ jü-ô-ts' li 棲在°樹極枝上°

ROOT, keng 根; keng-deo' 根頭; to take —, sang keng 生根

ROOT, to — up, keng bah-diao' 根拔出°; — with the nose, ky'üing.

ROPE, zing 繩°; soh 索;* cable, læn 纜; ts'ih 懇° 繩°; to make —, tang zing' 打 繩; to walk a —, 'ang zing' 走° 繩° 索°
* Zing and soh are used for string, or rope, of whatever size.

ROPE-MAKER, zing-soh'-s-vu 繩° 索司務

ROPY, (as boiled sugar), we ky'i s-go 會 起 如° 絲

ROSARY Buddhist, (108 beads), shü'-cü or su-cü 數° 珠; Romanist —, nyiæn-cü' 念 珠

ROSE, dark red —, me-kwe'-hwô 玫瑰花; du-me'-hwô 荼蘪° 花; monthly red —, yüih-yüih-'ong' 月月紅; seven sisters —, ts'ih'-tsi'-me 七姊妹; white Banksia —, bah-moh'-hyiang 白木香

ROSE-WATER, me-kwe'-lu' 玫瑰露

ROSEWOOD, (red wood), 'ong-moh' 紅木; (more expensive), ts'-dæn 紫檀

ROSIN, song-hyiang' 松香

ROSY, 'ong-feng'-si-bah 粉紅;— faced, dao-hwô-min' 桃花面; ditto and healthy-looking, 'ong'-c'ih-hen'-hen 紅出酣酣

ROT, will we læn-wu' 會爛腐°; iao læn-wu' 要爛腐°

ROTATE, to go out and be succeeded by others, leng-cün' 輪轉;— in order, a-ts' leng-liu' 挨° 次 輪流

ROTE, to recite by —, be shü' 背° 書

ROTTEN, læn-wu'-de 爛腐°了°; — teeth, (i. e. have worms in them), cü'-ngô 蛀牙°

ROUGE, in-tsi' 胭脂

ROUGH, ts'ao or ts'iao 糙; ts'ao'-siu, or ts'iao'-siu 糙手;— draft, ts'ao'-kao 草稿

ROUND, yün 圓; kweng'-yün 賅° 圓; to walk — the table, coh'-teng-yin dön-ky'ün' tseo'-cün 桌子° 邊° 團 圈 走 轉; turn — a corner, cün-wæn' 轉彎

ROUND-SHOULDERED, hong-pe' 盎° 背

ROUSE him from sleep, eo gyi' su-sing' 叫 其 甦 醒; eo gyi diao'-kao 叫° 其 醒° 覺°; to excite, kyih 激; dong 動; — to anger, kyih nu' 激 怒; — to effort, min'-li 勉 勵; — one's self to effort, teng'-ky'i tsing'-jing 頓 起 精 神; tsing-jing teng-tæn'-ky'i 精 神 頓 起

ROUT, to da-ba' 大敗°

ROUTE, are you acquainted with that — ? keh' da lu-dzing' ng joh-sih' feh 這° 埭 路 程 你° 熟 識 否°?

ROVE, to — about, yüing-yiu'-s-fong' 雲遊四方

ROVER, an idle —, yin pin wu 逍 遙 河° 上°

Row, a ih-da — 埭; ih-ba or ih-bi' — 排°; sit in a —, bing-

ba zo 並排°坐°; *sit in rows,*
ih-ba' ih-ba zo' 一排一排
坐°; bi-tang'-bi zo.

Row, *to use oars,* pæn-tsiang' 扳
槳

Row-boat, pæn-tsiang'-jün 扳槳
船; *eight oared —,* pah tsiang-
jün' 八槳船

Royal *family,* wông-kô 皇家°.
— *will,* sing'-ts 聖旨

Rub, to ts'ah 擦; — *it bright,* ts'ah
gyi liang' 擦其亮; — *in both
hands,* ts'o-ts'o' 搓搓; *cannot
— off,* ts'ah'-feh-diao 擦弗起°;
— *against* (as an animal against
a post), za; — *on* (as medicine,
or oil), dzô 搭; du 塗; k'a 揩;
— *the hands,* ts'o-siu' 搓手; —
it in the hands, siu-li' ts'o-ts'o
gyi 手裡搓搓其; — *with the
hand,* soh'-soh 捒捒; — *the
eyes,* nyü ngæn'-tsing 揿眼°睛;
— *ink,* mo moh' 磨墨

Rubbish, p'o'-ba tong'-si 破敗°
東西

Ruby, 'ong-pao'-zah 紅寶°石°

Rudder, do 舵 (ih-min)

Rude, yia 野°; yia'-ky'i 野°氣;
— *and daring,* tæn'-ts sah'-yia
膽子撒野°; ts'u-lu' 粗鹵;
i-læ'-peh-te'; fông'-s 放肆; ts'u-
mæn' 粗蠻; — *child,* yia'-ky'i
siao-nying 野°氣小孩°

Rudely, *to treat one —,* yia'-ky'i
beh-c'ih' dæ nying 野°氣勃出
待人°

Rudeness, *treat one with —,*
c'ong-væn' nying 衝犯人°;
yia'-tsih yia-pah' dæ nying 野°
七野°八待人°

Rudiments *of learning,* 'oh-veng'-
go keng-kyi' 學°問个根甚

Rue, *to lament,* iu-zeo' 憂愁; *to
regret,* ao'-nao 懊惱

Rueful *looks,* zeo yüong' 愁容;
zeo-mi'-tang-pah'-kyih 愁°眉°
百°結

Ruffianly, p'o'-dao 覇道; *will
not stop at any crime,* vu-sô'-peh-
ts 無所不至

Rug *of skin,* bi t'æn'-ts 皮毯子;
carpet —, tsin-diao' 氈條;
tsin-t'æn' 氈毯 (ih-bæn)

Ruin, *to* ba-diao' 敗°壞°; p'o'-
diao 破壞°; *to destroy,* mih-diao'
滅壞°

Ruins, *a house in —,* tao'-t'æn'-
liao-go oh' 倒坍了个屋;
t'æn-t'ah'-liao oh' 坍塌了屋;
ditto from fire, ho'-siao dziang
火燒塲; ho'-siao t'æn' 火燒
灘

Rule, diao-kw'un' 條款; diao-
iah 條約; kwe-tsch' 規則;
kwe-kyü' 規矩; *regulations,*
công-dzing' (công or tsông) 章
程; (ih-diao, ib-kw'un, or ih-
'ông); — *with a penalty attached,*
fah'-du 法度; — *of etiquette,*
nyi-cü' 儀注; — *to transgress
ditto,* væn'-djoh nyi-cü' 犯着
儀注

RULE, to kwun 管; kæ-kwun' 該管;— in small matters, kying-kwun' 經管;— in large matters, kwun'-li 管理; djü-li' 治理; djü 治;— the family, djü-kô' 治家; to — paper, wah kah'-ts 畫格子

RULED paper, ts' yiu kah'-ts 紙有格子 (See LINES.)

RULER, cü'-tsæ 主宰; the rulers, pah'-kwun 百官; kwun-fu' 官府

RUMBLING sound, 'ong-'ong'-hyiang 圈圈響; lah-lah'-hyiang 轆轆響

RUMINATE, to cün-ziao' 轉嚙;— upon, sing'-li tsin-cün' 心裡輾轉

RUMOR, report, fong-sing' 風信;— says (or we hear), fong-veng' 風聞; r'-veng-teh 耳聞得; idle —, yiao-yin' 謠言

RUMP, deng-tsin' 臀尖; p'i'-kwu 屁股

RUMPLE, to —, peh-gyi-tseo' 偪其縐; long'-gyi-tseo' 弄其縐

RUN, to peng 奔;— swiftly, fi peng' 飛奔; p'ao 跑;— away, peng'-leh-ky'i 奔得去°; to — (as water), liu 流; to — out, liu-c'ih' 流出;— together (as water), we-long' 匯攏;— over (the brim), kah'-c'ih-læ 溢出來;— (as vines), yin-k'æ'-ky'i 延開去°;— hither and thither, (troubled), loh-deo'-loh-peng' 無路投奔; lön ts'ön' 亂竄; on

the — (or going hither and thither) to earn money, peng-po' dzen dong-din' 奔波賺銅錢°;— against, bang-djoh' 撞着°;— against each others' heads, teo'-deo p'ong' 兜頭撞°, (hence simply to meet);— a risk, yiu fong'-ho 有風火; yiu ken'-yi 有干係;— through (as a thread), c'ün-ko' 穿過

RUNAWAY, dao-tseo'-go-nying 逃走个°人°

RUPTURE of a blood vessel, hyüih'-kwun pao'-k'æ 血管爆開; hernia, shün'-ky'i-bing 疝氣病; siao'-dziang-ky'i-bing' 小腸氣病

RUSH lu-ken' 蘆竿; bu 蒲;— mats, bu-zih' 蒲席;— shoes, bu-'a' 蒲鞋;— used for lamp-wick, teng-sing'-ts'ao 燈芯草;— used for cording, 'æn-ts'ao' 菅草

RUSH, to c'ong 衝; ts'ông 闖;— in, ts'ông'-tsing-læ 闖進來;— at once, ih-deo ts'ông'-ko-læ 忽°然°闖過來;— against, djông-djoh' 撞着°

RUST, to siu 銹; fuh-sin' 發銹; rusted out, siu'-me-de 銹壞了°

RUSTIC, hyiang-'ô'-go 鄉下°个°;— people, hyiang-'ô'-nying 鄉下°人°

RUSTLE, to — (as garments), wah-wah'-hyiang 刮刮響;— (as leaves), sah'-sah-hyiang' 颯颯響

RUSTY siu'-de 銹了°; fah-siu'-de 發銹了°

RUT of a wheel, leng-bun' loh-'æn'-go lu' 輪盤落陷°个°路; fallen into his old way, or —, moh gyiu lu' de 摸舊路了°

S

SABBATH, li'-pa-nyih 禮拜°日°; en-sih'-nyih 安息日°; cü'-nyih 主日°; tsin'-li-ih' 瞻禮一

SABLE-SKIN, ts'-tiao-bi 紫貂皮; ditto (hairs white-tipped), ts'-mô-tiao bi' 芝蔴貂皮

SACK, dæ 袋 (ih-tsah); a garment, mô'-kwô 馬掛 (ih-gyin)

SACK-CLOTH, ts'u-mô'-pu 粗蔴布; to put on —, c'ün mô-i' 穿蔴衣

SACKING (used for wrapping), dæ pu' 袋布; (better quality) pao-bi'-pu 包皮布

SACRAMENTS, the sing'-li 聖禮

SACRED, sing 聖; — books, sing' kying 聖經; — Edict, Sing'-yü Kwông'-hyüing 聖諭廣訓

SACRIFICE, tsi'-veh 祭物; — placed before an idol, foh'-li 福禮; to offer up a —, hyin tsi' 獻祭; zông tsi' 上祭; tsi 祭; — to one's ancestors, tsi tsu'-tsong 祭祖宗; to take one's turn in ditto, tông tsi'-z 當祭祀; — at the grave, tsi'-sao veng-mo' 祭掃墳墓; zông veng 上墳; (these expressions are also some- times used for simply keeping the grave in order); — one's life, sô'-c'ih sing'-ming 捨°出性命

SACRILEGE, to commit —, sih'-doh 褻瀆; to commit — against the gods, c'ong-væn' bu-sah' 衝犯菩薩; c'oh'-væn bu-sah' 觸犯菩薩

SAD, iu-meng' 憂悶; iu-zeo' 憂愁; iu-li' 憂慮; zeo-meng' 愁悶; — looking, min tæ' iu-yüong' 面帶憂容; looks very —, mun'-min iu-zeo' 滿面憂愁°; — in heart, sing-li' ts'i-ts'æn' 心裏悽慘; both — and joyful, pe-hyi'-kyiao-jih' 悲喜交集

SAD-IRON, loh-t'ih' 烙鐵 (ih-go)

SADDEN, to s'-teh iu-meng' 使得憂悶; — him, peh' gyi iu-meng' 俾°其憂悶

SADDLE, en-ts' 鞍子 (ih-go)

SADDLE, to place the — upon, zông en-ts' 上鞍子; — and bridle a horse, p'e mô' 配馬

SAFE, weng'-tông 穩當; t'o'-tông 妥當; ding-tông' 定當

SAFE for provisions, sô-djü' 紗櫥 (ih-k'eo); iron —, t'ih'-gyü 鐵櫃°; native money —, yiang-siang' 洋箱

SAG, to den 凹; ah'-den 壓°凹; den'-loh 凹°落

SAGACIOUS, tsing-ming' 精明; t'eo'-ts'ih 透澈; — in affairs, tsing-ming' shü'-vu 精明世務;

— *in discerning character*, t'eo' ts'ih jing-dzing' 透徹人情;
— *person*, pah'-k'æn pah-liang'-go nying 料事如神个°人°
SAGES, sing'-nying 聖人°
SAGO, si-koh'-mi 西國米
SAIL, fong-bong' 風篷 (ih-tsiang, ih-sin); *to* —, s-jün' 駛船; *s*-bong' 駛篷; s-fong' 駛風; *to take in* —, siu-bong' 收篷; *to let down the* —, 'ô-bong' 下°篷; loh-bong' 落篷; *to hoist* —, t'sô-bong' 叉篷; *to reef a* —, mao bong, *or* mô bong' 冒篷
SAIL-CLOTH, bong-pu' 篷布
SAILING-VESSEL, fong-bong-jün' 風篷船
SAILOR, shü'-siu 水°手 (ih-ming, ih-go); *on native boats*, lao'-da' go ho'-kyi 老大个°夥計
SAINTS, sing'-du 聖徒
SAKE, *for the* — *of*, we 爲; we-leh' 爲了°; *for the* — *of fame, and gain*, we-ming'-we-li' 爲名爲利
SALAD, sang-ts'æ' 生°菜
SALARY, *officer's* fong'-loh 俸祿; *teacher's* —, soh'-siu 束修; soh'-kying 修°金; sing-fong' 辛俸; sing-se' 薪水
SALE *at auction*, kyiao'-ma 叫賣°; ma kyiao'-ho 賣叫貨; *on* — *for another*, kyi'-ma 寄賣°; *for* —, fah'-ma 發賣°; c'ih-ma' 出賣°
SALEABLE, ma'-leh-c'ih'-go 賣°得°出个°; siao-leh-diao'-go

銷得°去个°; *not* —, m-siao-dziang' 無°銷塲
SALESMAN, ma-siu' 賣°手
SALIVA, zæn-t'u' 涎°唾
SALLOW *countenance*, min-seh' tsiao-wông' 面色焦黃
SALT, yin 鹽; — *taste*, mi-dao 'æn' 味°道鹹°; *too* —, t'eh 'æn' 太°鹹°; *put in a little* —, fông' ih-tin yin' 放一點鹽; *add* —, kô-yin'-ts'eo 加°鹽湊; — *water*, 'æn-shü' 鹹°水°; — *provision store*, 'æn-ho'-tin 鹹°貨店
SALT-CELLAR, yin-diah' 鹽碟°; yin-beng' 鹽盆 (ih-tsah)
SALT-MERCHANT, yin-sông' 鹽商
SALT-PEDDLER, ma-yin'-go 賣°鹽个°
SALT-PETER, } siao hsiao' 硝; yin-siao' 鹽硝;
SALT-PETRE, } p'oh'-siao 朴硝
SALUBRIOUS *climate*, shü'-t'u hao' 水°土好
SALUTATION, *words of* —, tsiao-hwu'-go shih-wô' 招呼个°說話; k'ah-t'ao-go shih-wô' 客套个°說話
SALUTE, *to* — *with folded and uplifted hands*, kong-kong-siu' 拱拱手; — *with folded hands and a bow*, tsoh-ih' 作揖; *to fire a* — (*for a certain event*), 'ao p'ao' 號礮; *ditto for an officer*, fông p'ao' kying kwun' 放礮敬官; — *and part*, kong'-siu bih-k'æ' 拱手別開

SALVATION, kyiu'-sing 救星; the doctrine of — , kyiu-nying'-go dao'-li 救人°个°道理

SALVE, dzô-yiah' 搽藥

SAME, the ih-yiang' 一樣; tso'-yiang; siang-dong' 相同; exactly the — , ih-seh'-ih-yiang' 一色一樣; t'ih'-seh-vu-r' 貼色無二; ping'-seh 拌色; the — as before, dzing-gyiu' ih-yiang' 仍舊一樣; of the — age, dong nyin' 同年; dong kang' 同庚; at the — time, bing'-zi 並齊; veng'-zi 會°齊; tsæn'-zi 整°齊; — rank, dong p'ing' 同品; on the — day, tông' nyih 當日°; make the — as the pattern, tsiao' yiang tso' 照樣做; have the — meaning, tso' i'-s; i'-s siang-dong' 意思相同

SAMPLE, yiang-ts' 樣子 (ih-go)

SANCTIFIED, to become dzing-dziu' sing'-jün-go 成就聖善个°

SANCTIFY, to — a person, s'-teh nying' dzing-sing 使得人°成聖

SANCTION, to obtain his — , ts'ing gyi'-go z' 請其个°示; t'ao' gyi-go k'eo'-ing 討其个°口音; to give one's — , cing 准 yüing 允

SAND, sô 沙; sô-nyi' 沙泥; fine — , hwe-sô' 灰沙; — bank, or bar, sô-t'æn' 沙灘; there is a — storm, t'in' loh wông-sô' 天落黃沙

SANDALS, t'o-'a' 拖鞋°; straw — , ts'ao'-'a 草鞋° (a pair, ih-sông, or ih-shông)

SANDAL-WOOD dæn-hyiang-moh' 檀香木

SANGUINARY disposition, sah'-sing djong 殺性重; — battle, (ground filled with blood), hyüih' liu mun di' 血流滿地

SANGUINE temperament, sing ho'-nyih-go 心火熱个°; sing'-li ziang ho-dön' ka 心裡像火團一°樣

SANSCRIT, or SANSKRIT characters, Væn-z' 梵字; — language, Væn-yin' 梵言

SAP (of trees), jü-tsiang' 樹漿

SAPAN-WOOD, su-moh' 蘇木

SAPPHIRE, læn-pao'-zah 藍寶石; en'-læn 暗藍

SARCASM, tsin-k'eh'-go shih-wô' 尖刻个°說話; shih-wô ziang tao' ka 說話像刀

SASH, iao-ta' 腰帶°; an ornamental belt, 'en-kying' 汗巾 (ih-diao)

SASH, window ts'ông 牕; raise the — , ts'ông, zông'-leh gyi 好°上° 了°牕; put down the — , ts'ông ô-loh' 好°下°了°牕

SATELLITE, vu-'ang-sing'-go siao'-sing 附行星个°小星; the moon is the earth's — , yüih-liang z vu di-gyiu'-go siao'-sing 月亮是附地球个°小星

SATIATE, to eat to the full, ky'üoh'

SAT 410 SAW

pao 吃°飽; *to eat to loathing,* ky'üoh in' 吃°厭
SATIN, dön-ts' 緞子; *superior —,* kong'-dön 貢緞; *inferior —,* ling-ts' 綾子
SATIRICAL, *to give a — name,* c'ü ts'ih'-'ao 取綽°號
SATIRIZE, *to* kyi ts'' 譏刺
SATISFACTION, *to one's —,* jü-sing'-ziang-i' 如心像意; *to make — to one,* be-li' 賠禮; pu'-pao gyi 補報其; be-wæn' gyi 賠還其; be-pu' gyi 賠補其
SATISFIED, sing mun'-tsoh 心滿足; i-sing' mun-tsoh 依心滿足; *contented,* cü-tsoh 知足; tsoh'-sing 足心, sing-tsoh' 心足
SATISFY, *will — man's heart,* neng'-keo mun'-tsoh nying'-go sing' 能彀滿足人°个°心 or 能慊人°心
SATISFYING, (as certain kinds of food), næ-kyi' 耐饑
SATURATE, *to* seng'-t'eo 沁°透
SATURATED, sih'-t'eo-de 濕透了°
SATURDAY, li-pa-loh' 禮拜°六; tsin-li-ts'ih' 瞻禮七
SATURN, t'u'-sing 土星
SAUCE, *pungent* lah-tsiang' 辣醬; *sweet —,* din lu' 甜滷, *soy,* tsiang'-yiu 醬油
SAUCE-PAN, kwun 鑵; *carthen —,* ngô'-kwun 瓦鑵; ing'-teo-kwun 熨°斗鑵
SAUCER, *tea* dzô-beng'-ts 茶盆

子; *boat shaped —,* dzô-jün' 茶船
SAUCY, c'ih'-yin-vu-zông'-go 出言無狀个°
SAUNTER, *to stroll idly about,* tong-tseo'-si-tseo' 東走西走; tong-dang'-si-dang' 東宕西宕
SAUSAGE *meat,* tsæn-wu'-liao-nyüoh' 作°膾个°肉°
SAUSAGES (flat), nyüoh-ping' 肉°餅; *round —,* nyüoh-yün 肉圓
SAVAGE, *cruel,* hyüong-oh' 兇惡
SAVAGES, yia'-nying 野°人°
SAVE, *to* kyiu 救;—*out of trouble,* kyiu-næn' 救難;—*the soul,* kyiu weh-ling 救魂°靈;—*from imminent danger,* kyiu-jün-me'-ts-kyih' 救燃眉之急;—*from death,* dzong-si' li-byiang' kyiu-c'ih'-læ 從死°裡救出來;—*trouble,* sang z' 省事;—*time,* sang kong-fu' 省工夫;—*money (but not put it by),* sang dong-din' 省銅錢°
SAVING, *frugal,* kyin'-sang 簡省; gyin'-sang 儉省
SAVIOR, SAVIOUR, Kyiu'-cü 救主; Kyin'-shü-cü 救世主
SAVORY, yiu ts-mi' 有滋味°; yiu mi-dao' 有味°道
SAW, ken 鋸°(ih-pô)
SAW, *to* ka 鋸°;—*firewood,* ka za-bæn' 鋸柴爿; *did see,* k'en'-kyin-ko 看見過; k'en'-kyin-ko'-de 看見過了°
SAW-DUST, ken'-sih 鋸°屑

SAY, to kông 講; wô 話; what do you —? ng dza wó' ni 你°怎°話呢? ng dza kông'-fah ni 你°怎°講°法呢? I was just saying, ngô dzæ-sʻ læ-tih wô' 我繞始話; can you — so? z-ka' hao wô' feh 如°此°好話否°, or 可°說°否°; can — it, hao' wô-go 可°話个°; kʻo'-yi wô' 可以話; — a word to him, teng gyi wô' ih-kyü' 與°其話一句; teh gyi kông' ih-sing' 對°其講°一聲; — it again, tsæ' wô' 再話; cannot — it, cannot pronounce, or must not — it, kông'-feh-cʻih'-go 講弗出个°; people — so, nying-kô' z-ka wô' 人°家°如此話; you don't — so, or who says so? jü wô' 誰°話; nothing to —, m̀-kao' hao wô' 沒°有°好話; m̀-kao' hao kông' 沒°有°好講°.

SAYING, common dzông-yin' 常言; dzông-yin'-dao 常言道; old —, lao'-wô 老°話°; kwu'-wô 古話 (ih-kyü)

SCAB, in 壓; to form a —, kyih in' 結壓; vaccine —, ngeo-deo'-in 牛°痘壓

SCABBARD, tʻao 套; kʻoh'-ts 壳子; for a sword, pao'-kyin-kʻoh'-ts 寶劍壳子

SCAFFOLDING, ing-kô' 鷹架; kô'-ts 架°子; to put up a —, tah kô'-ts 搭架°子

SCALD, tʻông'-sông 燙傷
SCALD, to tʻòng 燙;* — to a blister, tʻông kyʻi-pʻao' 燙起皰
  * The colloquial is the same for burning by fire, or scalding by hot water, but the characters are different.
SCALE, fish —, ng-ling' 魚°鱗 (ih-bæn)
SCALE, SCALES, balance, tʻin-bing' 天平 (ih-kò); the dish of a balance, teng'-bun' 戥盤; a balance with one —, teng'-ts 戥子; ditto (for weighing very small things), li-teng' 厘戥
SCALE, to — city walls, bô zing 爬城; zông zing', or zông dzing' 上城°
SCALE, to — off, pʻin' tang pʻin' kʻoh'-kyʻi 片片鬆起
SCALP, deo-bi' 頭皮
SCANDAL, to talk cʻih nying-kô'-go tsʻiu' 出人°家°个°醜
SCANDALOUS affair, tsʻiu'-z 醜事; — affairs in the women's apartment, kwe' cong tsʻiu' z 閨中醜事 (cong or tsong)
SCANT, feh-keo' 弗彀; tsʻô'-tin 差點; kyʻin'-ih-ngæn 欠一點°
SCAR, pô 疤; blemish, pæn-pô' 瘢疤 (ih-go)
SCARCE, kyʻüih'-siao 缺少; difficult to procure, næn-teh' 難得; this year cherries are —, kying-nyin' ang-dao' kyʻüih'-siao 今年櫻桃缺少
SCARCELY enough, kyib'-pah 急廹; ditto, but will make it do,

ün-pang'; — (but just) obtained, ts'ô ih-ngæn' feh teh'-djoh 差一點°勿得着°

SCARCITY, year of —, siao'-nyin 小年; ditto (a small crop, two parts instead of ten), nyi-feng' nyin-se' 二°分年歲

SCARE, to — him, hah' gyi ih-deo' 嚇其一嚇°

SCARE, a great — about nothing, da-kying'-siao-kwæ' 大驚小怪

SCARED, he — me, gyi' long ngô' ky'ih'-ih-hoh' 其弄我吃°一霍; — to death, hah'-sah-de 嚇殺了°

SCARE-CROW, straw man, ts'ao-kao-nying 草絞°人°

SCARLET, do-'ong 大°紅;—paint, cü-'ong' ts'ih 朱紅漆

SCATTER, to sæn'- k'æ 散開; sæn'-lön 散亂; tsah'-k'æ 撒°開; — seed, tsah iang-ts' 撒°秧子

SCATTERED about (in every direction), tong-si' lön-gwæn' 東西亂撌; in disorder (at sixes and sevens), wang-ts'ih'-jü-pah' 橫°七竪八

SCAVENGER, bô-lah-sah'-go 爬拉°圾°个°; wun-bi'- go (in Shanghai, leh-sah'-fu 拉圾夫)

SCENERY, fine hao kying'-cü 好景致

SCENT, hyiang 香; hyiang-ky'i' 香氣; the dog follows the —, keo' i lu' hyüong ky'i'-mi 狗依路嗅°氣味°

SCEPTRE, the golden —, kying kwe' 金圭 (Esther 5 : 2.)

SCHEME, kyi'-ts'ah 計策; kyi-meo' 計謀; kyi'-kao 計較°; the last two usually have a bad sense; to devise a —, tang'-sön kyi-meo' 打算計謀; to carry out a —, yüong kyi' 用計

SCHISM in the church, kyiao'-we feng-lih'-k'æ 教會分離°開

SCHOLAR, pupil, 'oh-sang-ts' 學°生°子; very small —, mong-dong' 蒙童; educated man, doh-shü-nying 讀書人°; z'-ts 士子; accomplished —, poh'-lao博士°; the class of scholars, jü-kyiao' 儒教

SCHOLARSHIP, good hao nen-dzæ' 好內才; hao du'-dzæ 好肚才; poor in —, bah du'-bi 白腹°; ts'ao'-pao 草包

SCHOOL, shü-vông' 書房; shü-kwun' 書舘 (ih-kwun); — room, shü-vông-kæn' 書房間°; 'oh-dông 學°堂; to teach a — (or one person), zo shü-vông 坐書房; zo kwun' 坐舘; to go to —, or to enter —, zông 'oh' 上學°; to open a —, k'æ kwun' 開舘; k'æ shü-vông 開書房; boy's —, nen shü-vông 男書房; family —, ts'ing'- kwun shü-vông' 供°饍書房; girl's —, nyü' shü-vông 女書房; public (charity) —, nyi-'oh' 義學°; — of little boys, mong-kwun' 蒙

館;— *of boys who study Chinese classics,* kying-kwun' 經館;— *teacher, or master,* kao' shü sin'-sang 教°書先生°;— *mistress,* nyü' sin-sang 女先生°;— *fellow,* dong shü-vông' 'oh-sang'-ts 同書房°學°生子°;— *friend,* dong-ts'ông' beng-yiu' 同意朋友; *to board at the —,* kyi'-zih ü shü-vông' 寄膳°於房書

SCIENCE, 'oh-veng' 學°問; yüoh 學 (veng); *natural —,* keh-veh'-go 'oh-veng' 格物學°;— *of numbers,* sön'-yüoh 算學;— *of Astronomy,* T'in-veng' 天文; Sing-yüoh' 星學;— *of medicine,* I-yüoh' 醫學

SCISSORS, tsin'-tao 剪刀 (ih-pô); — *grinder,* mo-tsin'-tao-go 磨剪刀个°

SCOFF, *to — at,* tsao-siao' 嘲笑; vu-siao' 侮笑

SCOLD, *to* wô 話; mao-ün' 埋怨; — *in loud tones,* heng 哼;— *with abuse,* zoh-mô' 辱罵; *your mother will —,* a'- 姆 iao wô'-go 阿°娘°要話个°

SCOLDING, *don't mind a —,* wô, feh-ts'æ'-go 話弗睬个°; zoh, feh-p'ô'-go 辱弗怕个°;— *woman,* dziang-zih'-vu 長舌婦

SCOOP *for bailing water,* biao 瓢; zoh 勺° (ih-tsah); ao'-teo 拗斗 (ih-go); *to — up water (if much),* dao-shü-c'ih' 掏水°出; iao'-shü'-c'ih' 舀水°出; *ditto (if little),* kwah-shü'-c'ih' 括水°出

SCOPE, *general* da-i' 大意; tsong-i 總意

SCORCH, *to —* (as food), tsiao 焦; — *in ironing,* t'ông'-tsiao 燙焦;— *in frying,* t'ah'-tsiao 煠焦;— *at the fire,* hong-tsiao' 烘焦; koh'-tsiao 擱焦; tsih'-tsiao 炙焦

SCORN, *to* miao'-z 藐視; k'en'-feh-ky'i' 看弗起; ky'ing-hweh' 輕忽;— *look upon with —,* k'en'-feh-zông-ngæn' 看弗上眼°

SCORPION, byih'-ts 蠍子 (ih-tsah)

SCOUNDREL, 無-keng'-kyiah-go 無°根脚个°; *a low unprincipled fellow,* oh'-kweng 惡棍; kwông-kweng' 光棍; di-kweng' 地棍

SCOUR, *to* ts'ah 擦; mo 摩;— *it bright,* ts'ah' gyi liang' 擦其亮

SCOURGE, pin-ts' 鞭子 (ih-keng); *to —,* yüong pin-ts' tang' 用鞭子打

SCOUT, t'en'-ts 探子; *to act as —,* tso t'en'-ts 做探子; t'en'-t'ing 探聽; *to sneer at,* kyi-siao' 譏笑

SCOWL, *to* zeo mi-deo' 皺眉頭;— *at him,* dziao' gyi zeo 覷-deo' 朝其皺°眉頭

SCRAMBLE, *to — up,* bô-zông'-ky'i 爬上去°; wah-zông'-ky'i 挖上去°;— *for* (things), ta'-ts'iang-ta-deh' 亂°搶亂°奪

SCRAP, *or* SCRAPS, siao'-kw'e 小塊; se'-kw'e 碎塊; se'-deo-se-

nao' 碎頭碎腦; pork —, cü-yiu-tsô' 豬油渣
SCRATCH, to kwah 刮; — by rubbing, ts'ah 擦; — it clean, kwah' gyi ken-zing' 刮其乾淨; — the skin off, bi ts'ah'-ky'i 皮擦起; — potatoes, bao fæn-jü bi 刨山°芋°皮
SCRATCH, a ih-da 'eng' 一埭痕 ih-da ky'i.
SCRATCH, to tsao 搔; — (as a dog), da
SCRAWL, to sia'-leh hwô-liu'-dzô' ka 寫得°花柳蛇°一°般°
SCREAM, to wæ, si-ih-sing' 咻喊°一聲; to call loudly, do-sing'-hæn'-kyiao 大°聲喊叫
SCREEN, bing 屏; bing-fong' 屏風; ing'-bing 映屏 (ih-sin); a folding —, we-bing' 圍屏 (ih-dông); split bamboo — (for doors or windows), coh'-lin 竹簾 (ih-tsiang); bead — (for ladies' apartments), cü-lin' 珠簾
SCREEN, to — from, lah 攔; tsô-djü' 遮住; tsô-in' 遮掩; tsô-kæ' 遮蓋; — from the sun, tsô-djü' nyih-deo' 遮°住日°頭; — a fault, tsô-kæ' ts'o'-c'ü 遮蓋錯處; — the light, liang-kwông' lah-djü' gyi 亮光蘭°住其; — from the light, liang-kwông' tsô-ing' 亮光遮陰
SCREW, jün-ting' 旋°釘; lo-s-ting' 螺螄釘 (ih-me); cork —, tsiu'-tsön-ts 酒鑽°子 (ih-go); —

driver, jün-joh' 旋°鑿° (ih-pô)
SCREW, to — in, jün-tsing'-ky'i 旋進去°; — together, jün-long'-ky'i 旋攏去°
SCRIBBLE, to lön-dô' 亂塗°; lön-sia' 亂寫°
SCRIPTURES, the Holy Sing'-kying 聖經; Sing'-shü 聖書
SCROFULA le-lih' 瘰癧
SCROFULOUS swelling, lib-c'ün' 癧串 (ih-go)
SCROLL, a written ih-kyün shü' 一卷書; ornamental — (for hanging), ih-gyüoh wô' 一軸畫; a pair of scrolls, ih-fu te'-lin 一副對聯
SCRUB, to ts'ah 擦
SCRUBBING-BRUSH ts'ah'-di-pæn'-go shih'-tsiu 擦地板个°刷箒
SCRUPULOUS, exact and careful, tsing-si' 精細; over —, tsing-si' ko-deo' 精細過牙°; si'-si se'-se 細細碎碎; so'-so-se'-se 琑琑碎碎; to-veng'-to-li' 多文多禮
SCRUTINIZE, to ts'-si k'ao'-kyiu 仔細考究
SCUFFLE, to siang-tang' 相打
SCULL, (oar in the stern), lu 櫓 (ih-ts); — rope, lu'-ta 櫓帶°; — pin, lu-cü' 櫓鈕°; to —, yiao-lu' 搖櫓; — to the right, t'e 推; t'oh 托; — to the left, pæn 扳; sao 捎
SCULPTOR who carves wood, or stone, tiao-k'ch'-s-vu 雕刻司務

SCUM, vu-ky'i'-læ-go ao-tsao' 浮起來个°埀精, veo-nyi' 浮泥

SCURF on the head, kw'u-k'oh-in' 眉°覺歴

SCUTTLE, coal me-t'æn' dong 煤炭桶 (ih-tsah)

SEA, hæ 海; yiang 洋; hæ'-yiang 海洋; bottom of the —, hæ ti' 海底

SEA-FIGHT, shü'-tsin 水°戰

SEA-HORSE-TEETH hæ'-mô-ngô 海馬牙°

SEAL, hæ'-keo 海狗 (ih-tsah)

SEAL, any private —, du-shü' 圖書 (ih-k'o); officer's —, ing 印; ing'-sing 印信; kwun-ing' 官印; Imperial —, nyüoh-si' 玉璽; to affix a —, tang ing' 打印; the — character, djün veng' 篆文

SEAL, to — a letter, fong sing' 封信; fong k'eo' 封口; to break the —, ts'ah fong' 拆封; k'æ fong' 開封; — a door, fong meng' 封門; — or close the ya-mun for the New Year, fong ing' 封印; to open the ya-mun —, k'æ ing' 開印

SEALING-WAX, ho'-ts'ih 火漆

SEAM (in cloth), vong-ts' 縫子 (ih-da); — (in wood, &c.), vong-dao' 縫道; the mark of the —, vong-u' 縫痕°; straight —, dzih vong' 直縫; felled —, wông-zin'-kweh 黃鱔°骨; rip the —,

vong-ts' ts'ah'-k'æ 縫子拆開

SEA-MAN, shü'-siu 水°手

SEA-PORT, hæ'-k'eo 海口

SEARCH, to look for, zing 尋; to investigate, k'ao'-kyiu 考究; tse-kyiu' 追究; — through the house, oh' li-hyiang' seo-kyin' 屋裡向搜檢; examine, dzô-dzô'-k'en 查查看; — one's heut, dzô-ts'ah' zi'-go sing' 查察自°个°心; — everywhere, koh'-tao-c'ü zing' 各到處尋; seo zing' 搜尋

SEA-SHORE, hæ-pin-yin' 海邊沿

SEA-SICK, cü-lông' 暈°浪; yüing-jün' 暈船; do you get —? ng we cü-lông' feh 你°會暈°浪不°會°? I do become —, ngô iao yüing jün' 我要暈船

SEASON, in — (as fruit, &c.), gyih-z' 及時; came just in —, 'eo-feng'-'eo-su læ'-de' 候分候數來了°; the four seasons, s'-kyi 四季; s'-z 四時; a dry —, t'in 'en' 天旱; very dry —, t'in da 'en' 天大旱

SEASON, to p'e liao-li' 配料理; — boards, pæn' lông gyi' sao' 板眼其燥

SEASONABLE weather, t'in-ky'i', teng z-ling' siang-te' 天氣與°時令和對; — rain, gyih-z' yü 及時雨; z yü' 時雨; ken yü' 廿雨

SEASONING, liao-li' 料理 (the Chinese implies more than the

English, as seasoning is usually restricted to salt and pepper); wine as a —, liao-tsiu' 料酒

SEAT, zo'-u 坐處 (ih-go); zo'-we 坐位; — of a chair, ü'-ts min 椅子面; will — how many? kyi'-go nying' hao zo' 幾个°人° 好坐? yiu to'-siao' zo-deo' 有多少坐頭? cannot — so many, zo'-feh-ko 坐弗過; there are no seats, zo'-u m'-teh 坐處 沒°有°

SEATED, please be —, ts'ing zo' 請坐

SEA-WEED, hæ'-ts'æ 海菜; ts'-ts'æ 紫菜; dæ-diao' 苔條

SECLUDED, p'ih'-zing 僻靜; quiet, iu-zing' 幽靜; zing'-ts'iao-ts'iao 靜悄悄

SECOND, the di-nyi' 第二°; in the — month, di-nyi' ko yüih'-li 第二°个°月裡; nyi-yüih'-li 二°月裡; — son, ts'-ts 次子; a — (of time), ih-miao' 一秒

SECOND-HAND clothing, ts'ah'-i 拆衣; — clothing-shop, ts'ah'-i tin 拆衣店; di-tsông' 提莊; to buy — goods (lit. old), ma gyiu-ho' 買°舊貨

SECRET, mih 密; pi'-mih 秘密; kyi-mih' 機密; s 私; s-'ô' 私下°; — deeds, s-z'ï 私事; a —, siao'-ho z-t'i' 私下°事體; siao'-ho shih-wô' 私下°說話; — for making something, pi'-kyüih 秘訣; to let out a —, sih'-

leo kyi-kwæn' 洩漏機關; lu fong' 露風; he can keep a, —, kyi-kwæn' gyi ve sih'-leo 機關 其不會°洩漏; to tell one a —, ngao ng'-tô 鮫耳°朵

SECRETLY, s-'ô' 私下°; s ti-'tô 私底下°; en'-di-li 暗地裡; be-di'-li 背地裡; to plot — s-'ô' yüong kyi-meo' 私下°用 計謀

SECRETARY, private shü-kyi' 書 記; — to a Mandarin, shü-kyi'-s-yia' 書記師爺°; tsih-pih' s-yia' 執筆師爺°

SECRETE, to dzông-k'ông' 藏囥, —well, k'ông'-leh mih-lah-kying' 囥得°密緊

SECRETIONS, (of animals, or plants), tsing-yih' 津液

SECT, kyiao 教; kyiao'-meng 教 門; to found a new —, sing lih' ih-go kyiao' 新立一个°教

SECTION (of a book), ih-tsông' 一 章; ih-p'in' 一篇;—(of a treaty), diao-kw'un' 條款 (ih-diao)

SECULAR, shü'-kæn-zông'-go 世 間°上个°; — affairs, shü'-z 世 事; shü'-vu 世務; —newspapers, shü'-dzoh sing-pao' 世俗新報

SECURE, weng'-tông 穩當; t'o'-tông 妥當

SECURE, to make fast, tso'-leh lao-k'ao' 做得°牢靠; to insure, pao 保

SECURELY, to dwell —, deng'-leh weng'-tông-go 停得°穩當个°

SECURITY, to become — for another, tso-pao' 做保; one who becomes —, pao'-nying 保人°; — (evidence of debt, &c.), bing-kyü' 憑據

SEDAN, gyiao-ts' 轎子 (ih-ting); mountain —, teo-gyiao' 兜轎; ditto (very rude), bô-sæn-hwu' 爬山虎; bride's —, hwô-gyiao' 花轎; ts'æ'-gyiao 彩轎; Imperial —, lön-kô' 鑾駕°; to ride in a —, zo gyiao' 坐轎; I came in a —, ngó' zo gyiao' læ'-go 我坐轎來个°; to lift a —, gyiao-ts' sing-ky'i'-læ 轎子陞起來; to set down a —, gyiao-ts' fông'-loh 轎子放落; — poles, gyiao-kông' 轎杠; (a pair of ditto, ih-fu), — bearer, gyiao-fu' 轎夫

SEDATE, tön-tsông' 端莊; z-z'-dzæ-dzæ 自自在在

SEDENTARY, zo'-kong to 坐工多

SEDIMENT, kyiah' 脚; ting'-loh-go kyiah' 定°落个°脚

SEDITIOUS, we-tsoh-lön'-go 會作亂个°

SEDUCE, to ying'-yiu 引誘; t'eo 偷

SEDULOUS, gying-kying' 勤謹; never idle, feh-teh-k'ong' 弗得空

SEE, to k'en 看; k'en'-kyin 看見; let him —, peh gyi-k'en 俾其看; — another making a mistake, or getting into trouble and not tell him, k'en-ts'ing-beng' 冷°看; easy to — through, ih-moh liao'-jün 一目了然); — through, k'en'-t'eo 看透; ditto, (as a deception), k'en'-p'o 看破; — after, or to, k'en'-siu 看守; sees quickly what ought to be done. ngæn'-deo weh-loh' 眼°頭活絡; I have come to — you, ngó' læ k'en' ng 我來看你; he mông-mông' ng 來望°望°你°; — (one) off, song-'ang' 送行°; song dong-sing' 送動身

SEEN, cannot be —, k'en'-feh-kyin'-go 看弗見个°; have not — for a long time, dziang-kyiu' feh-kyin' 長久弗見; kyiu'-we 久違; nothing to be —, m-kao' k'en'-deo 沒°有°看頭

SEED, cong 種; ts 子; iang-ts' 秧子; — or planting time, hao cong'-go z'-'eo 好種个°時候; the stony — of fruit, weh 核; the inner kernel of ditto, jing 仁; save for —, liu tso cong' 留做種; gather a little — for me, siu' ih-tin ts' peh ngô 收一點子給我; to plant —, 'o cong' 下°種; cong 種; cong'-tsoh 種作; descendants, ts'-seng 子孫

SEEDSMAN, ma-cong'-go 賣°種个°; seller of vegetable seed, ma-ts'æ'-ts-go 賣°菜子个°

SEEING THAT, kyi'-jün 旣然; kyi'-kying 旣經

SEEK, to zing 尋°; — and find, zing-djoh' 尋°着°; — gain, tang'-mo dong-din' 打慕銅錢°; — favor (by gifts, or doing what one need not do), t'ao-hao' 討好; — (or pray for) happiness, gyiu foh' 求福; — employment, zing deo-lu' 尋°頭路; zing 'ông-nyih' 尋°行業
SEEMS, oh'-ziang 阿°像; hao'-ziang 好像; z'-wu 似乎; this — the larger, keh'-go oh'-ziang do-tin' 這°个°阿°像大°點; it — to me, ngô' kyüoh-teh ziang' 我覺得像; dziu ngô k'en-læ 就我看來; — unwilling, oh'-ziang feh dzing'-nyün 阿°像弗情願
SEIZE, to k'ô 拿°; gying 擒°; 'oh 獲
SEIZED, already yi'-kying k'ô'-djoh-de 已經拿°着°了°
SELDOM, hyi-vong' 稀逢; feh-da'-li 弗常; m̄-kyi'-tsao 無幾遭; — comes, hyi-vong' læ-go 稀逢來个°; feh-da'-li læ-go 弗常°來个°; happens very —, ts'in-tsiao'-gyi-vong' 千朝奇逢
SELECT, to kæn 揀°; shün 選; t'iao 挑; t'iao'-shün 挑選; kæn'-shün 揀°選; kæn'-dzeh 揀°擇; — a day, ding nyih-ts' 定日°子; — a lucky day, kæn nyih-ts' 揀°日°子; to divide off, and — materials, c'ü liao-tsoh 取料作

SELF, zi 自°; ts'ing-sing' 親身; he went him —, gyi zi' ky'i'-de k'i zi° 其自°去°了°; examine one's —, zi' dzô-ts'ah zi' 自°查察自°; — respect, zi-djong' 自重; has ditto, yiu ts'-ky'i 有志氣; yiu ts'-hyiang 有志向; tsang-fong' ngao'-ky'i 爭°風傲氣; — conceit, zi-tseng'-zi-do' 自°尊自°大°; zi-tseng'-zi-djong' 自°尊自°重; to lower one's — (as by doing something wrong), zi-ky'ing'-zi-zin' 自°輕自°賤; reproach one's —, zi tsah'-vah zi' 自°責罰自°; — existent, z-jün'-r-jün-yin'-go 自然而然有个°; — willed, zi-lih'-ih-koh'-go 自°立一國个°; zi-ih'-go cü'-i 自°一个°主意
SELFISH, t'en-s' 貪私; — (i. e. first helps himself and then divides), iao'-leh ih-un bing-feng' 舀得°一碗平分; takes care of himself not of others, tsih'-kwu zi,' feh-kwu' nying-kô' 只顧自°弗顧人°; not —, feh t'en-s'-go feh t'en-s' 弗貪私个°; m̄ s-sing' 無°私心
SELL, to ma 賣°; ma-diao' 賣°了°; siao-t'eh' 銷脫; fah'-ma 發賣°; — at auction, ma kyiao'-ho 賣°叫貨; — by the catty, leng kying' ma 論勤賣°; — by the single one, leng ko'-deo ma 論個數°賣°
SEMI-CIRCLE, pun'-ky'üu 半圓

SEMINARY, (college), do shü-yün' 大°書院; Theological —, Sing'-Kying shü-yün' 聖經書院
SEND, to ts'a 差; tang'-fah 打發; — a letter, ta' ih-fong sing' 帶°一封信; — ditto by a friend, t'oh beng-yiu' ta 托朋友帶°; — back, t'e'-wæn 退還; — to my house, song' tao ngô oh'-li-ky'i' 送到我家°裏去°; — troops, ky'i ping' 起兵; — him word (by some one), ts'a nying' t'ong-cü' gyi 差人°通知其; — for him, ts'a nying' ky'i eo' gyi 差人°去°叫°他
SENIOR, my — in age, nyin-kyi' pi ngô' do' 年紀比我大°; nyin-kyi' tsiang'-jü ngô 年紀長於°我; — (by 30 or more years), tsiang'-pe 長輩; zin-pe' 前輩; Mr. — Senior, T'a' sin-saug 太°先生°
SENSE, meaning, i'-s 意思; talks —, kông'-leh yiu-dzing'-yiu-li' 講°得°有情有理; no — of propriety, feh-sih' siang-t'i' 弗識禮°體; ditto (as in using other people's things, &c.), i'-læ-peh-teng' 擅°自°; use your own good —, zi-dzæ'-jing-we' 事°在人為; having good —, ling-bin'-go 靈便个°; ts-tsih' hao' 知質好; kyin'-sih hao' 見識好; no — of shame, m̀ lin'-c'ü 無°廉恥; the five senses, ng' kwun 五°官

SENSELESS, meaningless, m̀ i'-s 無°意思; no understanding, m̀ ling-sing' 無°靈性; stupid, ngæ-teng'-teng 呆瞪瞪; ts-tsih moh' 知質木
SENSIBLE to the eye, k'en'-leh-kyin'-go 看得見个°; — to the touch, moh'-leh-c'ih'-go 摸得°出个°; — person, t'ong dzing' dah-li'-go nying 通情達理个°人°; — of favors, we ken eng' 會感恩
SENSUALIST, hao'-seh-go 好色个°; seh-kyü' 色鬼; tsiu'-seh ts-du' 酒色之徒
SENSUALITY, seh'-yüoh 色慾
SENSITIVE (heart), sing nyün' 心軟; — to others' woes, sing sang'-leh dz' 心生°得慈
SENSITIVE-PLANT, p'ó'-yiang-ts'ao' 怕癢草
SENTENCE, a ih-kyü' shih-wô' 一句說話
SENTENCE, to ding-en' 定案; ding-ze' 定罪; p'un'-tön 判斷; — him to death, ding gyi si'-ze 定其死°罪
SENTIMENTS (of one's heart), sing-jih' 心術
SENTINEL, bông-siu'-go 防守个°; — going the rounds, jing-lo'-go nying 巡邏个°人°
SEPARATE, to divide, feng-k'æ' 分開; to — from (as friends, &c), li-k'æ' 離開; bih-k'æ' 別開; — by placing something between, kah'-k'æ' 隔開; lah-k'æ' 拉開;

to — by a line (of ink), yüong moh'-sin kah'-k'æ 用墨線隔開; to — friends, gyiao'-k'æ beng-yiu' 離八° 朋友;—(because of some difficulty), ts'ang-k'æ' 撐開; the time to —, li-k'æ'-go z'-eo 離開个時候

SEPARATE, a — one, ling-nga' ih'-go 另外°一个°

SEPARATELY, koh'-nying-kwun-zi' 各人°管自°; koh-kwun-koh' 各管各; liang-k'æ-dæ' 兩分°開

SERENE, bing-en' 平安; — sky, t'in-ts'ing' 天青

SERGEANT, pô'-tsong 把總

SERIES of misfortunes, tsih'-lin-go 'o'-se 接連个禍祟; lin-ky'in'-go 'o'-se 連牽个禍祟; through a — of years, lih-nyin' 歷年

SERIOUS, sedate, tön-tsông' 端莊; grave beyond one's years, siao'-nyin lao'-dzing 少年老成; important, kying'-kyih 緊急;— illness, bing djong' 病重; bing li-æ' 病利害;— consequences, djong'-deo kwæn-yi' 重頭關係

SERMON, kông'-ka 講°解°(ih-p'in)

SERPENT, dzô 蛇; (ih-kwang, ih-keng)

SERPENTINE path, bun-dzô lu' 盤蛇°路; yiang-dziang lu' 羊腸路

SERVANT yüong-nying' 傭人°; followers, keng-pæn' 跟班; nyi yia' 二°爺; ti'-'ô-nying 底下°

人°; — who splits wood, and carries water, p'ih-za' t'iao-shü'-go 劈柴°挑水°个°; — boy, ah-siao' 阿小; siao-wæn' 小使°; — woman, a-m' 阿姆; ah-sao' 阿嫂

SERVE, to voh-z' 服事; stand and wait orders, z'-'eo 侍候;—, or wait upon (as on a sick, or old person), tông-dzih' 當值; z'-dzih 侍值; — tea to guests, di dzô' peh nying-k'ah' 遞茶給客人°; — in a tray, pun 搬; — a warrant, 'ang ba' 行°牌°

SERVICEABLE, yiu yüong-dziang' 有用場; teh-yüong'-go 得用个°; — goods, meng-z'-ho 門市貨

SERVILE, pe-kong'-ky'üih'-tsih 卑躬屈節; mô'-wông kyin lu'-djü 螞蝗見鹵齏°

SESAME, or SESAMUM (plant), ts-mô' 芝蔴; — oil, mô-yiu' 蔴油

SESSION of a church, dông-we' 堂會; to have a meeting of —, jü dông-we' 聚堂會; — of a trial before an officer, dông 堂; morning —, tsao'-dông 早堂

SET, a — of small boxes, ih-t'ao' 'eh-ts' 一套盒子; a — of five buttons, ih-fu nyiu'-ts 一副鈕子; a — of four or eight chairs, ih-dông ü'-ts 一堂椅°子; a — of men, ih-pæn nying' 一班人°; a — of books, ih-ts'ah shü' 一册書

SET 421 SEV

SET, to — down, fòng 放; en; to fix, ding 定; to establish, shih'-lih 設立; — about (doing), k'æ-siu' 開手; dong-siu' 動手; — out on a journey, dong-sing 動身; to inlay, k'æn 嵌; k'æn'-siang 嵌鑲; — fire to, fòng ho' 放火; — table, pa coh'-teng 擺桌子°; — out (as plants), cong 種; does not — well, feh-'eh sing 弗合身; — the heart at rest, fòng'-sing 放心; the sun sets, nyih-deo'-loh-sæn' 日頭落山; — a joint, gao'-kwu yiao-tsing' 骹股落°榫°; — a watch, piao' te-te-cing' 表對對准; piao' te-te tsing' 表對對正

SETTEE, c'ing-teng' 春橙 (ih-dziang)

SETTLE, to determine, ding-kwe' 定規; — a price, ding kô'-din 定價°錢°; — disturbances, bing-lön' 平亂; bing-fæn' 平反; — quarrels, li-c'ü' z-t'i' 理處事體; — a quarrel, ka-ün' sih-kyih' 解°冤釋結; — for, ko'-kah 過割; ditto with ready money, yin ko'-kah 現過割; to adjust accounts, kyih-tsiang' 揭賬; ditto (by paying), kyih ts'ing' 揭清; — (a fluid), ting'-loh 淀落; — till clear, ting'-gyi-ts'ing' 淀其清; — (by hollowing down), t'en-loh' 凹落; — (as a bird), ding-loh' 停落

SETTLED, (by talking), shih'-t'o'-de 說妥了°; wun-kyih'-de 完結了°; wô ding'-tông-de 話定當了°; the affair is —, z-ken' bæn-t'o'-de 事幹辦妥了°; reckoned and —, sön'-ky'ih-de 算訖了°; — (as a place for a person, goods &c.), dziah-cü'-hao-de 安°置好了°; wait till I am —, teng ngô' en-teng'-hao-ts 待°我安頓好之

SEVEN, ts'ih 七; — fold, ts'ih'-be 七倍

SEVENTEEN, jih-ts'ih' 十七

SEVENTH, the di-ts'ih'-go 第七个°; — of the month, ts'u-ts'ih' 初七; the — day after a death, deo-ts'ih' 頭七; the 5th — after death, (when the spirit of the deceased is supposed to visit the family), ng'-ts'ih 五°七; the 7th — (when the seven weeks of mourning end), dön'-ts'ih 斷七

SEVENTY, ts'ih'-jih 七十

SEVERAL, hao-kyi' 好幾; deh-ma' 幾許°; — times, hao-kyi' tsao 好幾遭

SEVERALLY, ih-ih' 一一; ko'-ko 個個

SEVERE, li'-æ' 利害; djong 重; hyüong 凶; strict, nyin-kying' 嚴禁; — illness, bing li'-æ' 病利害; — punishment, ying-vah' djong' 刑罰重; have a — cold, djong' sông-fong' 重傷風; — rules, kwe'-kyü nyin' 規矩嚴

SEW, to vong 縫; vong-lin' 縫縺; can you —? ng' we vong-lin'-feh 你°會縫縺否°?— together, or seam, vong'-ih-vong' 縫一縫

SEWING, (work), tsing-ts' sang-weh' 鍼黹生°活; the style of —, tsing-ts' 鍼黹; good —, tsing-ts' hao 鍼黹好

SEWING-MACHINE, t'ih-tsing-zông' 鐵鍼床; (incorrectly called) t'ih-zæ-vong' 鐵裁縫

SEWING-WOMAN, who sews by the wayside for any one, vong-gyüong' 縫窮 (Shanghai and Su-chow).

SEWER, drain, keo 溝; covered —, ing-keo' 陰溝; open —, yiang-keo' 陽溝 (ih-da)

SEXTANT, liang-t'in ts'ah' 量天尺

SEXTON, chapel-keeper, kwun-li-pa-dông'-nying 管禮拜°堂人°; cemetery-keeper, kwun-veng'-go 管墳个°

SHABBY, old and faded, gyiu-læn'-tsæn 舊襤褸°; in-dza'-dza 蔫蔫; læn-in' 襤蔫; worn, or ragged, yiang'-de; yiang-yi'-de 破°壞°了°

SHABBILY, to treat persons —, bob-dæ' nying-kô' 薄待人°家; dæn'-boh dæ nying' 淡薄待人°

SHACKLE, to — the feet, so kyiah' 鎖腳

SHACKLES for the feet, kyiah'-k'ao 腳桍; — for the hands, siu'-k'ao 手桍

SHAD, z-ng' 鰣魚 (ih-tsah)

SHADE for a lamp, ing-kwông' 隱光; teng-t'ao' 燈套; paper ditto, ts'-t'ao 紙套; glass ditto, po-li' tsao 玻璃罩; hang in the — (as a dress), lông læ ing' di'-fông 晾在°陰地方

SHADE, to tsô 遮; tsô-in' 遮掩; tsô-djü' 遮°住; — from wind, tsô fong' 遮°風

SHADOW, ing 影

SHADOWY, and fleeting, kying'-hwô-se'-yüih 鏡花水月

SHADY place, ing di'-fông 陰地方; tsô-ing' di'-fông 遮°陰地方;— and cool, ing'-liang 陰凉

SHAGGY and curly dog, s'-ts keo 獅子狗

SHAKE, to t'eo 掞;—one's clothes, i-zông' t'eo-ih'-t'eo 衣裳掞一掞; — a child, siao-nying' t'e-t'e'-nông-nông 小孩°推推搖掞;—(as a house, windows, &c.), tsing'-tsing-dong 怔怔動; yiao-dong' 搖動; — (as an old man), fah-kying' 發驚; kying-kying'-dong 驚驚動; — (as in ague), fah-gying' 發憜; — hands, siu la-leh ts'ing-ts'ing' 手攜°得°請請;— (as from fear), gwah-gwah'-teo' 掴掴抖

SHAKY, or uncertain, weh-deh-shing 活脫°樣

SHALL, pih'-iao 必要; pih'-shü 必須

SHALLOW, ts'in 淺; ts'in-gying

淺近;— *learning*, 'oh-veng' ts'in' 學°問淺

SHAM, *to* tsòng-kô' 裝假°; kô' hyi-deo tso-tang'-c'ih-læ' 假意做出來; *it is all —*, keh tu z tsô'-i 這°都是詐意; tu z tsô'-kyi 都是詐計

SHAME, wông-k'ong' 惶恐; *sense of —*, lin'-c'ü 廉耻; *no sense of —*, feh-p'ô' wông-k'ong 弗怕惶恐; ǹ-lin'-c'ü 無°廉耻; feh iao min-moh' 弗要面目

SHAMEFUL, wông-k'ong'-go 惶恐個°

SHAMEFULLY, *to treat —*, ling-joh 凌辱; tsao-t'ah' 躂踢

SHAMELESS, ǹ-lin'-c'ü 無°廉耻; ǹ-ô-lin' 無°丫臉; *thick skinned*, min-bi 'eo' 面皮厚; 'eo'-bi ó'-lin 厚皮丫臉

SHANK-BONE, kyiah'-li ding'-kweh 脚裡脛骨

SHAPE, ying 形; *round —*, yün-ying'-go 圓形個°; *leaf —*, jü-yih' ying'-go 樹葉形個°; *— or pattern*, yiang-shih' 樣式; *what —?* soh-go ying'-go 甚麼形個°!

SHAPE, *to* c'ih-yiang' 出像°; tsò'-c'ih siang'-mao 做出相貌; *to mold*, su'-c'ih-læ 塑出來

SHAPELESS, ǹ-siang'-mao 無°相貌; *ill-formed*, ǹ-yiang'-væn 無°樣範

SHARE, *a* ih feng' 一分; ih kwu' 一股; *how many shares?* tso kyi-kwu' feng 做幾股分? *a — in the business*, ih kwu' sang-i' 一股生°意; *to have a — in*, yiu veng-ts' 有分子; yiu kwu'-deo 有股頭

SHARE, *to* tsiao'-kwu feng 照股分; *— alike*, kyüing-feng' 均分; *to — grief*, feng-iu' 分憂

SHARK, sô-ng' 鯊魚°; *— fins*, yü-ts'' 魚翅; *— skin*, sô-ng' bi 鯊魚°皮

SHARP, kw'a 快°; *very —*, fong-li' 鋒利; *how — these scissors are*, keh'-pô tsin'-tao dza fong-li' 這°把剪刀甚鋒利; *— pointed*, tsin 尖; tsin-li' 尖利, (also sharp in looking after one's interests); *— pointed scissors*, tsin'-tao-deo kw'a' 剪刀頭快°; *— taste*, lah'-go mi'-dao 辣個°味道

SHARPEN, *to — (as knives, &c.)*, mo kw'a' 磨快°; *— (as a pencil)*, siah' tsin 削尖; *— the appetite*, k'æ we' 開胃

SHARPER, kwa'-ts 拐°子; p'in'-zeh 騙賊°

SHATTERED *to pieces*, k'ao'-leh feng-se 敲得°粉碎; pah'-meh-kæn'-se 百°末爛碎; *— constitution*, ti'-ts tang'-loh-de 精神衰弱了°; ti'-ts kyih'-loh-de 底子吃落了°

SHAVE, *to* siah 削; t'i 薙; *— off a little*, siah'-tin-diao 削點了°; *— the head*, t'i deo' 薙頭; *— the beard*, t'i ngô-su' 薙

SHA 424 SHI

鬚°;—*on becoming a priest,* loh fah' 落髮
SHAVINGS (of wood), moh-fi' 木枇; *to make —,* bao' moh-fi' 刨木枇; bao-hwô' 刨花
SHAWL, p'i-i' 披衣
SHE, gyi 其
SHEAF, *a small* —, ih-shoh' 一束°; ih-bo' 一縛; *large* —, ih-kw'eng' 一綑
SHEAR, *to — sheep,* tsin yiang-mao' 剪羊毛
SHEARS, tsin'-tao 剪刀; — *for cutting metal,* kah'-tsin 夾°剪
SHEATH, k'oh 壳; t'ao 套;—*for a knife,* tao-k'oh' 刀壳 (ih-go); — *for a fan,* sin'-dæ 扇袋 (ih-tsah)
SHEATHE *the sword,* kyin' t'ao'-tsing k'oh'-li 劍套進壳裡
SHED, bang 棚; bong 篷; ts'iang廠; — *of pine branches,* song-mao' bang 松毛棚; *a cool shelter,* liang bang' 凉棚; *straw* —, *or lodge,* ts'ao'-ts'iang 草廠; *to make a* —, tah bang' 搭棚
SHED, *to — tears,* c'ih-ngæn'-li 出眼°淚; c'ih ngæn-li'-shü 出眼°淚水; ngæn'-li beh-c'ih' 眼°淚流出; — (as skin), t'eng-diao 褪°了°; *the snake sheds its skin,* dzô' t'eng k'oh 蛇蛻°; — *teeth, and get new ones,* wun ngô-ts' 換牙°齒; — *blood,* liu hyüih' 流血

SHEEP, yiang 羊; wu-yiang' 胡羊; (ih-tsah)
SHEEP-FOLD, yiang-gyin' 羊櫼
SHEET, bi-tæn' 被單; (ih-diao, ih-keng);—, (or cover for a quilt used by Chinese when travelling), bi-t'i' 被替; *a — of paper,* ih-tsiang ts' 一張紙; *a — of iron,* ih-p'in t'ih' 一片鐵
SHELF, koh'-pæn 擱板 (ih-kw'e); *two, three, or four shelves,* sæn-koh-lông' 三角°架°子°; *the third* —, (counting from the top downward as Chinese do), di-sæn'-kah 第三格
SHELL, k'oh 壳; *a spiral* —, s-lo'-k'oh 螺螄壳; *egg* —, dæn k'oh' 蛋壳
SHELL, *to* — (as peas, eggs, &c.) poh-k'oh' 剝壳
SHELTER *from rain, to* yü' di'-fông 躲雨地方; — *from wind,* bi fong' di'-fông 避風地方; o fong' di'-fông 矮風地方; *no* —, tsô-lah'-go 無遮°攔个°
SHELTER, *to* tsô-lah' 遮攔°
SHEPHERD, k'en-yiang'-go nying 看羊个°人°; yiang-moh' 羊牧; *styled,* moh'-s' 牧師
SHIELD, *rattan* deng-ba' 籐牌°; *skin* —, bi-ba' 皮牌° (ih-min)
SHIELD, *to — from wind,* tông'-djü fong' 擋住風
SHIFT, *to — about* (as wind), cün hyiang' 轉向

SHIFTLESS *person*, 㐂-ky'i' 㐂-p'ah-go 無°氣無°魄个°; vu-yüong' vu-joh'-go 無榮無辱个°; 㐂-yüong'-nying 無°用人°

SHINE, *to —* (independently, as the sun, fire, &c.), fông kwông' 放光;— (by reflected light, as brass, mirrors, &c), fah-c'ih liang-kwông' 發出亮光;— *upon*, tsiao'-djoh 照著°

SHINING, t'eo'-kwông 透光; kwông-liang 光亮; liang-liang' 亮亮; dzang-liang, (sometimes used ironically).

SHIP, jün 船 (ih-tsah); *merchant —*, sông-jün' 商船; k'ah'-jün 客船;— *captain*, lao'-da 老大;— *master*, jün-cü' 船主; *to build a —*, tang jün' 造船; ting jün' 釘船; *to knock a hole in a —*, jün' ngô-leo' 船矺漏; *— broken apart*, jün' t'ah'-k'æ-de 船脫開了°; *— broken to pieces*, jün' sæn-pæn'-de 船散板了°

SHIP, *to — goods*, tsông ho' 裝貨

SHIPBOARD, *on* læ-jün'-li 在°船裡; læ jün' zông' 在°船上

SHIPWRECK, jün' tso-'diao-de 做壞°了°;— (by running on rocks), jün' ngô-tsiao'-de 船矺礁了°;— (by being upset in a storm), jün' tao'-meh-de 船倒沒了°; jün foh'-meh-de 船覆沒了°

SHIP-YARD, jün-ts'iang' 船廠

SHIRT, pu'-sæn 布衫 (ih-gyin);

— with plaited bosom, kæn'-sæn 裙衫

SHIVER, *to — with cold*, tang 'en-tsin' 打寒顫

SHOCKED, se'-se-dong 碎碎動; mô-tseh'-tseh 麻喞喞; *too — to more*, hah'-leh su-ngæ'-ky'i 嚇得°酥呆起; ngæ'-ih-ngæ' 呆一呆; hah'-ngæ 嚇呆

SHOCKING *news*, hyüong sing' 凶信; *— affair*, (*i. e.* obscures the heavens); hweng-t'in' heh-di' z-ken 昏天黑地事幹; *ditto* (upsetting heaven and earth), t'in-pong' di-tao'-go z-ken 天崩°地裂°个事幹

SHOE, 'a 鞋°; (one, ih-tsah; a pair, ih-song); *straw —*, bu-'a' 蒲鞋°; ts'ao'-'a 草鞋°; *fine ditto*, (cool), liang-'a' 涼鞋°; *to put on a —*, c'ün-'a' 穿鞋°

SHOE-HORN, 'a-liu' 鞋簍

SHOE-MAKER, 'a-s'-vu 鞋°司務; bi-'a' s-vu 皮鞋°司務

SHOE-SOLE, 'a-ti' 鞋°底

SHOE-STRING, 'a-ta' 鞋°帶° (ih-keng); *your — is untied*, ng-go 'a-ta' sæn'-de 你°个°鞋帶散了°

SHOOT, *to — with bow and arrow*, zih-tsin' 射箭;— *birds*, zih tiao' 射鳥°;— *with a gun*, fông ts'iang' 放鎗; *ditto birds*, tang-tiao' 打鳥°;— *at a target*, tang-pô'-ts 打靶子

SHOOTS, ngô 芽°; miao 苗;— *for*

SHO 426 SHO

planting, iang 秧; *bamboo* —, shing 筍

SHOP, tin 店 (ih-bæn); — *keeper*, tin'-cü 店主; lang'-z 東°人°; — *tender*, tin'-kwun 店夥

SHORE, ngen 岸; *to go on* —, zông ngen' 上岸; *on* —, længen-zông' 在°岸上; *sea* —, hæ-pin-yin' 海邊沿

SHORT, tön 短; — *road* (or cut across), liao-lu' 蹻路; liao-gying' lu 蹻近路; — *of breath*, iao-ky'i'-kying 氣緊; *a* — *time*, ih-zông' 一息°; ih-hyih' 一歇; dzæn-z 暫時; feh dziang'-kyiu 弗長久; *the* — *way* (of doing a thing), kyin'-bin 簡便; dzong-bin' 從便; gying'-bin 近便; — *life*, tön' ming 短命; *to have ditto*, ziu-shü' feh dziang' 壽歲弗長

SHORTEN, *to long* tön tin' 弄短點;— (by sawing), zih' ih-gyüih loh' 截一段落;— (by cutting), ze tön' 裁短;— *by a few days*, kæn liang' nyih 減°兩日°

SHORT-COMING, feh-tao'-ts-c'ü 弗到之處; tön'-c'ü 短處

SHORT-SIGHTED, *near - sighted*, gying' z-ngæn 近視眼°; — *as to the future*, kyin'-sih tön' 見識短; siao-nying' kyin-sih' 小孩°見識; tön'-kyin 短見

SHOT, *small* sô-ts' 砂子; *bullet*, dæn-ts' 彈子; *small ditto*, sô-dæn' 砂彈 (ih-k'o, ih-lih).

SHOULD *he*, (if he), ziah'-z gyi' 若是其; — *or not?* nyi' feh nyi' 宜弗宜?

SHOULDER, kyin-kah'-deo 肩胛頭 (ih-tsah); — *of mutton*, zin-t'e' yiang-nyüoh' 前°腿羊肉; *thrown over the* —, kyin-deo' gwæn'-tih; *even shoulders*, (*i. e.* on a level, or of the same rank), bing kyin' 平肩

SHOUT, *to* wæ-wæ'-hyiang 吪吪響; da-sing'-hæn'-kyiao 大聲喊叫; wu-long' hyiang'-liang 喉°嚨響亮

SHOVE *to* t'e 推; — *away*, t'e-k'æ' 推開

SHOVEL, ts'iao 鍫; ts'æn 鏟; *large* —, wô-ts'iao 划鍫; gông-hyin' 鉄°鍫°; *coal* —, ho'-hyin 火掀; me-t'æn' ts'iao 煤炭鍫 (ih kwun)

SHOVEL, *to* ts'iao 鍫

SHOW, *false* pang t'i'-min 繃體面; *fond of* —, æ' hwô-hyin' 愛奢華°; *making a* —*of not wanting*, (as money), tsông-ky'iang' 裝腔; *ditto of not being in want*, tsông-p'ông' 裝膨; *ostentatious* —, ba-dziang' 排°場; *making a* — *of being great*, pa-p'ing' 擺°品; *a fine* —, pa'- shih kông'-kyiu 擺設講°究; — *of strength*, hyü-tsiang' sing-shü' 虛張聲勢

SHOW, *to disclose*, lu-c'ih'-læ 露出來; hyin'-c'ih-læ 顯出來;

— (it) *to me,* peh ngô k'œn' 俾我看; — *how to do,* di-peh' 捉撥; *to point out,* ts'-tin 指點; — *great kindness to him,* 'œo' dzing dæ' gyi' 厚情待其

SHOWER, *a* ih-dziao yü'; *a little* —, ih-bong yü' 一遙雨; *a heavy* —, ih-dzing yü' 一陣雨; — *from a passing cloud,* ko'-yüing-yü' 過雲雨

SHOWMAN, *travelling* tseo-kông-wu'-go 走江°湖个°

SHOWY, SHOWILY, hyin 顯; *dressed* —, c'ün'-leh hyin' 穿得°顯; *ditto (as a bad woman),* hyin'-dô-dô.

SHREWD, hwæn-ky'iao' 儇巧; k'œn'-fong s-jün' 看風駛船; — (calculating, and underhanded) *person,* we weh-tang'-go nying 會°挖打个°人°

SHRIEK, *to* wæ si ih-sing 吶喊° 一聲; djoh-sing' si træn'-ky'i 突°然° 一°聲°

SHRILL *sound,* sing-hyiang' tsin' 聲響尖; — *voice,* wu-long' pih'-tsin 喉°嚨筆尖

SHRIMP, hô, *or* hön 蝦° (ih-tsah); — *meat out of the shell,* hô-jing' 蝦仁; *dried* —, hô-mi' 蝦米°

SHRINE, (whether ancestral, or otherwise), dông 堂; jing-dông' 神堂; *idol* —, sing'-dông' 聖堂; — *of a large idol,* nön'-koh 暖閣; — *of the god of wealth,* dzæ jing-dông' 財神堂

SHRINK, *to* — *from,* t'e'-soh 退縮; soh'-dzoh 縮侷; p'ô' 怕; *if he sees water, he shrinks from it,* gyi k'œn'-kyin shü' ziu t'e'-soh'-de 其看見水°就退縮了°; — (as fruit), kyiang-long'-ky'i 彊攏去°; pih-long'-ky'i 癟攏去°; ken-long'-ky'i 乾攏去°; — (as cloth), geo-long'; soh'-long 縮攏; soh'-tön' 縮短

SHRIVELLED (as fruit, &c), pih-pih'-go-de 癟癟个°; pih-cü'-pih-tah' 癟嘴廰臉°; *skin* —, bi' tsœo'-long-de 皮皺攏了°

SHROFF, k'œn'-nying-yiang' sin'-sang 看銀洋先生°

SHROUD, *burial dress,* ziu-i' 壽衣; lang-i' 冷°衣 (disrespectful); Ningpo people wear seven, or at least five garments in the coffin, called, ts'ih'-z-i' 七事衣; ng'-z-i' 五°事衣

SHRUB, siao'-jü 小樹; *dwarf tree,* a'-jü 矮樹 (ih-cü)

SHRUG, *to* — *the shoulders,* song' kyin-kah' 鞏肩胛

SHUDDER, *cause one to* —, seng'-ngao sah-nying' 沁° 煞煞人°; song'-jün 悚然 (veng).

SHUN, *to* bi-ko' 避過; to'-bi 躲避

SHUT, *to* kwæn 關; — *the door,* kwæn meng' 關門; — *up shop,* kwæn tin' 關店; zông-ba-meng' 上排°門; — *him in,* kwæn-gyi-tsing 關其進; — *him out,* kwæn-gyi-c'ih' 關其出;— *the eyes,* ngæn'-tsing pi'-long 眼睛閉攏;— *the mouth,* cü'-pô pi'-ts 嘴吧閉了;— *the book,* shü' siu-long 書收攏;— *the door, and not bolt it,* (*i. e.* to do things by halves), kwæn meng' feh-loh shün' 關門弗落閂

SHUTTER, *window* ts'ông-meng' 牕門; k'æn'-meng 檻門 (ih-siu)

SHUTTLE, *so* 梭; *to pass the* —, c'ün so' 穿梭; *days and months pass like a* —, jih-yüih' jü-so' 日月如梭

SHY (*as a girl*), iu'-siu 幽羞; *unwilling to speak before others, or show what one has done,* pa'-feh-c'ih'-go 擺弗出個

SICK, *slightly* næn-ko' 難過; feh sông'-kw'a 弗爽快; feh shih'-i 弗適意; *is* —, yiu bing' 有病; *to become* —, sang bing' 生病; — *at the stomach,* dæ-dæ'-dong 㗳㗳動; oh'-sing 噁心; iao mao' 要吐;— *people, or person,* bing nying' 病人;— *of it,* in'-sah-de 厭煞了; *the* — *day in ague,* pæn-gyi' 症候個班期

SICKLE lin-tao' 鐮刀 (ih-pô)

SICKLY *person,* to'-bing'-go nying 多病個人; ziang bing-mæn' ka 像病貓一樣 (slang).

SICKNESS, bing 病; bing-tsing' 病症; yiang 恙; *prevalent* —, tsing'-'eo 症候; *severe* —, djong' bing 重病; *your honorable* —, kwé' yiang 貴恙; *my mean* —, zin yiang' 賤恙

SIDE, pin 邊; *the* — *of,* bông-pin' 旁邊; pin-yin' 邊沿; *the right* —, jing-siu'-pin 順手邊; *the left* —, tsia'-siu-pin 左手邊; *this* —, dông' pin 這邊; *that* —, keh' pin' 那邊; *on the* —, tseh'-go-de 側個了; tseh'-pin 側邊; tseh'-leng 側輪; *place on the* —, tang tseh-fông 打側放; *only on one* —, tæn' pin 單邊; tæn pun'-pin 單半邊; *the* — (*of the body*), hyih 脅; *pain in the right* —, jing-siu'-pin hyih' t'ong 順手邊脅痛; *to turn from* — *to* —, fæn-læ' foh-ky'i' 翻來覆去

SIDEWAYS, SIDEWISE, wang 橫; ts'ia 斜; hwa 歪; *crabs move* (*creep*)—, ha' wang bô' 蟹橫爬; *to roll* — (*as an animal*), tang kweng' 打䐇

SIEGE, *to lay* — *to a city,* we-kw'eng' dzing-ts' 圍困城子

SIEVE, sô-s' 紗篩; *very fine* —, kyün-s 絹篩 (ih-min); *bamboo* — *for grain,* s'-koh-dza' 篩穀籭

SIFT, *to* s 篩;— *by throwing up, and blowing off chaff,* yiang 揚 po 簸; po-yiang 簸揚; po-long 播弄

SIGH, to t'æn-ky'i' 嘆氣; to heave a —, t'æn ih-k'eo ky'i' 嘆一口氣; deep —, 'æn-sing t'æn'-ky'i 咳聲嘆氣; — from pity, t'æn'-sih 嘆息

SIGHT, in k'en'-leh-kyin-go 看得見个; pleasing to the —, hao'-k'en 好看; the first —, ts'u k'en'-kyin 初看見; bao'-z k'en'-kyin 暴時看見; deo ih-we' k'en'-kyin 第一回看見; good (eye)—, ngæn'-lih hao' 眼力好; ngæn'-ho tsin' 眼光尖; ngæn'-kwông liang' 眼光亮

SIGN, kyi'-nying 記認; kyi'-'ao 記號; piao-deo' 標頭; to make a —, tso kyi'-nying 做記認; — agreed upon, we-'ao' 為號; secret —, en'-'ao 暗號; en'-nying 暗認; shop —, tsiao-ba' 招牌; z-'ao' 字號; twelve signs of the zodiac, jih-r'-kong 十二宮; good —, kyih'-ziao 吉兆; hao ts'æ'-deo 好彩頭; a bad —, hyüong-ziao' 凶兆; to make a —, or omen, coh-ts'eng' 作讖; good ditto, hao' ts'eng'-z 好識事; — of the future tense, we 會 iao 要; — of the past tense, de; ko 過; hao'-de 好了; liao 了; hao'-liao 好了; the — of the possessive, go 个; man's, nying'-go 人个

SIGN, to — one's name, loh ming-z' 錄名字; loh kw'un' 錄欵;

ditto as evidence, c'ih-ming' 出名; gyü-ming' 具名; tang hwô-z' 打花字; tang hwô-iah' 打花押

SIGNAL, we-'ao' 為號; to fire a gun as a —, fông-p'ao' we-'ao' 放礮為號; to hoist a flag as a —, tang' gyi-'ao' 打旗號; ts'ô' gyi-'ao' 扯旗號; to raise a — of distress, ts'ô t'ao-kyiu'-go gyi-'ao' 扯討救个旗號

SIGNIFICANT, it is very — (of something else), gyi cong-ling' yia' bih' dzing 其中另有別情

SIGNIFICATION, meaning, i'-s 意思; i'-nyi 意義; ka'-shih 解說; — of individual characters, z-nyi' 字義

SIGNIFY, what does it — ? yiu soh'-go i'-s 有甚麽意思? it signifies little, (or is of little consequence), m-kao' kao'-kwæn 沒有交關; 'ao-vu' ken-dzih' 毫無干涉

SILENCE, to keep —, feh k'æ' k'eo 弗開口; — one's own complaints, zi' ka zi'-go ün' 自解自个怨

SILENT, no sound, m-sing'-hyiang 無聲響; feh-sing' feh-hyiang' 弗聲弗響; meng-sing' feh hyiang' 悶聲弗響; no words, meh-meh' vu-yin' 默默無言; pi'-k'eo vu-yin' 閉口無言

SILENTLY, hardships borne —, meh-ts'eh'-ts'eh-go siao'-kw'u

SIL 430 SIM

唔°受°个°苦; to think — (as the Romanists do), meh-siang' 默想

SILK, raw s 絲; ditto from Wu-tsiu, Wu'-s 湖絲; native —, t'u'-s 土絲; wild raw —, yia'-zen s' 野°蠶絲; woven —, dziu 綢; poorer ditto, kyün 絹; pongee, (from Shantung), fu'-dziu 府綢; kyiu'-dziu 繭綢; gray ditto, hwe-seh fu'-dziu 灰色府綢; buff ditto, (of the natural color), peng'-seh fu'-dziu 本色府綢; sewing —, s-sin' 絲線; i-sin' 衣線; floss —, sæn'-sin 散線; — wadding, min-teo' 絲°綿; — cocoon, kyin 繭; — worm, zen 蠶; ditto in chrysalis, zen-ngo' 蠶蛾; — worm's eggs, zen-ts' 蠶子; to reel —, dziu-s' 抽°絲

SILK-SHOP, (i. e. silk, and satin), dziu-dön' tin 綢緞店

SILK-WEAVER tsih'-kyi s-vu' 織機司務

SILK-WEAVING establishment, tsih'-kyi fông 織機坊

SILL, door di-voh' 地栿; window —, k'æn-deo 檻°頭

SILLY, ṃ-lông'-go; hen'-deo lin'-ky'i 憨頭臉氣; ziang ṃ-lông' ka; ṃ-deo'-jü 無°頭緒

SILVER, nying-ts' 銀子; — shop, nying-leo' 銀樓; — (jewelry) shop, siu'-sih tin 首飾店; — (money) shop, nying-'ao' 銀號 — (thread), nying-sin' 銀線

SILVER-SMITH, siu'-sih s-vu' 首飾司務; nying s-vu' 銀匠°

SIMILAR, siang-ziang' 相像; hao'-ziang 好像; weh'-t'eh-ziang 活揭像; oh'-ziang 阿°像; fông'-feh 仿彿; ih-yiang' 一樣; this is — to that, keh'-go teng keh'-go siang-ziang'-go 這°个°與那°个°相像个°; in a — manner, ih-yiang' tso'-fah 一樣做法

SIMMER, to boil slowly, mæn-mæn' ts' 慢慢煮°; — over a slow fire, iu-iu' ho' ts 幽幽火煮°; veng ho' ts 文火煮°

SIMPLE, easy to understand, kyin' r yi ming' 簡而易明; — and honest, lao'-jih 老實; of one kind, doh-yiang' 獨樣; jing-z' 純是; — and plain, tsih'-p'oh 質樸; p'oh'-jih 樸實; su'-zing 素淨; — clothing, tsih'-p'oh-go i-zông' 質樸个°衣裳°;— food, su'-zing-go ky'üoh'-zih 素淨个°吃°食; how — you are! ng hen-deo' nying 你°憨頭人°!

SIMPLETON, hen-deo' 憨頭; ngæ-ts' 呆子

SIMPLIFY, to make more easy, tso kyin'-bin-tin 做簡便點; — (to the understanding), tso kyin'-ming-tin 做簡明點

SIMPLY, merely, doh-doh' 獨獨; tæn-tsih' 單只

SIMULTANEOUS, tso'z-'eo' 一°樣°个°時候; dong z-'eo' 同時候

SIN, ze 罪; ze'-ko 罪過; ze'-ky'in 罪愆; ze'-nyih 罪孽; *original* —, peng' ze 本罪; nyün ze' 原罪; *great* —, do ze' 大罪; djong' ze 重罪; ze'-oh 罪惡; *add — to —*, ze'-zông kô-ze' 罪上加罪; *to commit a — worthy of death*, væn si'-ze 犯死°罪

SIN, *to* væn ze' 犯罪; — *against God*, teh'-ze Jing-ming' 得罪神明; — *knowingly, and purposely*, ming-cü' kwu-væn' 明知故犯

SINCE, kyi 旣; kyi'-jün 旣然; kyi'-kying 旣經; — *then*, dzong-ts'ʻ-yi-ʻeo' 從此以後; — *I was a child*, dzong-siao' 從小; z'-siao 自小; — *you are here, I will go*, kyi' ng læ-tong' ngô ky'i'-de 旣你°在°此°我去了°

SINCERE, dzing-jih' 誠實
SINCERITY, dzing-sing' 誠心
SINEWS, kying 筋 (ib-kwang); *deer* —, loh kying' 鹿筋

SING, *to* tsʻông 唱; — *without an instrument*, tsʻing' tsʻông' 清唱; — *hymns*, tsʻông tsæn'-me-s 唱讚美詩

SINGE, *to* tsih'-tsiao 炙焦
SINGER, we-tsʻông'-go nying 會唱个°人°
SINGLE, tæn 單; doh 獨; — *thickness*, tæn zeng' 單層; *a — garment*, tæn gyin' i-zông' 單件衣裳°; doh gyin' i-zông' 獨件衣裳°; *a — flower* (on a stem), doh tô' hwô 獨朵花; — *flower* (not double), tæn zeng' hwô-bæn' 單層花瓣

SINGLY, *one by one*, ih-tsah'ih-tsah' 一隻一隻; ih'-go ih'-go 一个°一个°; *standing — and alone*, doh ih'-go lih'-tong 獨一个°立在°此°

SING-SONG, *read in a — tone* (as the Chinese do), lông'-lông-doh' 朗朗讀; *ditto indistinctly*, nyi'-li-ngwu'-lu doh 呢哦°之°聲

SINGULAR, *uncommon*, fi-væn' 非凡; fi-dzông' 非常; cʻih-cong' 出衆; —, *or strange*, cʻih-gyi' 出奇; — *affair*, cʻih-gyi'-go z-tʻi' 出奇个°事體

SINK, *to* — (in water), dzing-loh'-kyʻi 沉下去°; — (in mire, &c), ʻæn-loh'-kyʻi 陷下去°; — *and be lost*, dzing-meh' 沉沒; — *in the mud*, ʻæn-loh' nyi-du'-li 陷°下°泥塗裏

SINNER, ze'-nying 罪人°; væn-ze'-go nying 犯罪个°人°

SIP, *to* hwun 喚; — *and try*, hwun'-hwun'-kʻen 喚喚看

SIR, *respected* —, (to a stranger), tseng kô' 尊駕°; (to an officer), lao'-yia 老爺; (to a young person in an officer's family), siao'-yia 少爺; siang'-kong 相公; (to a teacher), sin-sang' 先生°

SIRLOIN, li'-nyüoh 裡肉

SISTER, *elder* ah-tsi' 阿姊; *younger* —, ah-me' 阿妹; me'-me 妹妹; *elder sister's husband*, tsi-fu 姊夫; *younger sister's husband*, me-fu' 妹夫

SISTER'S *son*, nga-sang' 外°甥°; — *daughter*, nga-sang-nön' 外°甥°女°

SISTERS, tsi'-me 姐妹

SISTER-IN-LAW, *man's older brother's wife*, hyüong-sao' 兄嫂; *man's younger brother's wife*, di'-sing-vu 弟媳°婦; *a wife calls her husband's brothers' wives*, dzoh-li' 妯娌; *she calls her husband's older brother's wife*, a-m' 阿姆, *and the younger brother's wife*, ah-sing' 阿嬸; *her husband's older sister*, kwu-mô' 姑媽; *husband's younger sister*, siao'-kwu 小姑

SIT, *to* zo 坐; — *still*, ding-ding' zo' 坐定; — *a la Turque*, bun-kyiah' zo 盤腳坐; bun-k'ong' zo' *or* bun-k'o' zo' 盤空坐; tang zo' 打坐; *please* —, ts'ing zo' 請坐; ts'ing zo-tæn'-loh 請坐下°; — *up straight*, dzih-ky'i' zo 直起坐; zo'-leh dzih' 坐得直; — *up, and* — *still*, pih'-t'ing zo 筆挺坐; — *at a feast*, zo-zih' 坐席; — *up all night*, zo yia' 坐夜; — *on a chair*, zo ü'-ts 坐椅°子; — *on a bench*, zo teng 坐櫈; — *on eggs*, bu dæn' 菢蛋

SITUATED *on the North Bank*, zo'-loh Kông-poh-ngen' 坐落江°北岸地方

SITUATION, yüih-dông 穴堂; *a well chosen* —, yüih-dông' tin-leh hao' 穴堂點得°好; — (*of a house*), dzeh-kyi' 宅基; *position*, di-we' 地位; — *better than before*, di-we', pi zin-deo' hao' 地位比前頭好; — *or circumstances*, kwông-kying' 光景; *what is his* — *now?* yin-dzæ' gyi-go kwông-kying' dza'-go 現在他°的°光景怎个°?

SIX, loh 六; *the* — *Boards*, loh bu' 六部

SIXTEEN, jih-loh' 十六

SIXTH, di-loh' 第六

SIXTY, loh-jih' 六十; — *years old*, nyin-kyi' zông loh-jih' 年紀到°六十; — *years make a cycle*, loh-jih' nyin ih'-go kyiah'-ts 六十年爲°一甲子

SIZE, kw'un-do' 寬大°; kw'eh'-do 闊大°; *large* —, do-dao' 大°道; *what* —? dza-kwun'-do 怎麼大°? dza kwun-kw'eh'-do 怎°麼闊大°? to-siao' do 多少大°?

SIZE, *to* (prepare with glue water), zông kao-shü' 上膠°水°

SIZING, *glue-water*, kao-shü' 膠°水°; *alum-water*, ming-væn' shü' 明礬水°

SKATE, *ice shoe*, ping-'a' 冰鞋 (*a fish*), hwu-ng' 虎魚°(ih-kwang

SKEIN *of silk*, ih-ts-sin' 一枝線; — *of thread*, ih-kao sin' 一絞°線; — *of linen thread*, ih-siao sin' 一綃線

SKELETON, ih-fu kweh'-deo 一副骨頭; *a human* —, ih-fu nying-kweh' 一副人°骨; *thin as a* —, kweh'-seo-jü-za' 骨瘦如柴°; lu-kying'-lu-kweh'-go 露筋露骨個°; *to prepare a — of a discourse*, ao kweh'-ts 拗骨子

SKETCH, kao'-ts 稿子; *to draw a* —, tang ih'-go kao'-ts 打一個°稿子

SKETCH, *to — with pen*, or *pencil*, miao 描; wô 畫; sia 寫°

SKILL, hao siu'-dön 好手段

SKILLED *in*, joh-sih' 熟識

SKILLFUL, yiu-hao' siu'-dön 有好手段; — *hand*, joh-siu' 熟手

SKIM, *to* kah'-c'ih-læ 溢°出來; — *cream*, na'-yiu kah'-c'ih-læ 嬭°油滿°出來

SKIN, bi 皮; — (of a person only), bi-fu' 皮膚; *squirrel* —, hwe-c'ü'-bi 灰鼠皮; *silver ditto*, nying-c'ü'-bi 銀鼠皮; *rabbit* —, t'u'-bi 兔皮; *doe* —, kyi'-bi 麂皮; *otter* —, t'ah'-bi 獺皮; shü'-t'ah-bi 水°獺皮; *marten* —, 'oh-bi' 貉皮. See FUR.

SKIN, *to — with the hand*, poh-bi 剝皮; poh-diao' bi 剝了°皮; — *rubbed off*, bi ts'ao'-ky'i-de 皮擦°去了°; bi ts'ao'-t'eh-de 皮擦°脫了°

SKIP, *to* fah-t'iao' 發跳; — *for joy*, hwun-hyi'-leh fah-t'iao' 歡喜得°發跳; — *over*, t'iao'-ko 跳過; — (a page), kah'-tông t'iao' ih-min 跳過°了°半°頁°

SKIRT, gyüing 裙 (ih-diao)

SKULL, *bony case of the brain*, deo-ting'-kweh 頭頂骨; t'in-ding'-kweh 天庭骨; *the brainless head*, kw'u-lu'-deo 骷顱頭

SKY, t'in 天; *clear* —, ts'ing-t'in' 青天; *blue* —, læn-t'in' 藍天; *dark* or *clouded* —, ing-a' t'in 陰靄天

SKY-LIGHT, t'in-tsing' 天井; — (Chinese, of shell), t'in-tsing'-pæn 天井板 or 天°窓°

SLAB *of stone*, zah-pe' 石碑; zah pe-ba' 石碑牌°

SLACK (in doing), ts'u-sing' 粗心; *not tight*, kw'un 寬; den 潭; song 鬆; kw'un-den'-den 寬潭潭; kw'un-iah'-iah; den-den'-dong 潭潭動°; (these are also used of persons); — *water*, bing shü' 平水°

SLACKEN, *to* fông'-leh kw'un'-tin 放得°寬點; — *speed*, kw'un-song'-tin 寬鬆點; mæn-tin' 慢點; mæn-fæn'-tin 慢泛點; kw'un'-tin 寬點; kw'un-wun'-tin 寬綏點

SLAKE, *to — thirst*, ts k'eh' 止渴; *to — lime*, fông shü', diao hwe' 放水°調灰

SLAM, *to* gwah; bang-bang'-

hyiang 澎° 聲° 響°; *must not — the door,* meng' 朆-nao gwah'.

SLANDER, *to* kông dzæn-yin' 講讒言; pông'-hwe 謗讒

SLANDER, *to believe a —,* t'ing dzæn-yin' 聽讒言

SLANDERER, zeh-cü' 賊嘴

SLANG, ts'u-ts'u'-go shih-wô' 粗个°說話

SLANTING, ts'ia 斜°; *— to one side (as a boat),* tseh'-go 側个°; *—, will upset,* iao tseh'-cün 要側轉; iao tseh'-fæn 要側翻

SLAP *him,* tang gyi' ih-kyi' 打其一記; *— on the face,* kwah'-ih-kwông 摑一光; tang pô-công' 打巴掌 (công or tsông); *— on the mouth,* tang teo-cü' 打兜嘴

SLATE, nga-koh' feng'-pæn 外°國粉板; *native — for native ink,* feng'-pæn 粉板; k'æn-pæn' 鉛板 (ih-min)

SLATE-PENCIL, zah-pih' 石°筆 (ih-ts).

SLATS *running lengthwise,* dzih tông 直檔; *— running crosswise,* wang tông 橫檔

SLATTERN, t'i'-t'i-t'a-t'a-go nyü'-nying 涕涕汰°汰°个°女人

SLAUGHTER, *met with great —,* tsao sah'-loh 遭殺戮; *— of a city,* du-dzing 屠城; *to prohibit — of animals,* kying du' 禁屠

SLAUGHTER-HOUSE (for cattle), sah'-ngeo-dziang 殺牛°場

SLAVE, nu-boh' 奴僕; nu-dzæ' 奴才; *called,* kô-nying' 家°人°; *— girl,* ô-deo' 丫頭; s'-nyü 使女; *— boy,* dong-boh' 僮僕

SLEAZY, hyi 稀; *light and thin,* biao-boh', or hyiao-boh' 楊薄

SLEDGE-HAMMER, lông-deo-djü' 榔頭鎚° (ih-go)

SLEEK, kwông-wah' 光滑; kying'-kwông shih-wah' 鏡光雪滑

SLEEP, kw'eng'-joh 睡熟; *cannot —,* kw'eng'-feh-joh 睡°弗熟; *— soundly,* kw'eng sah'-kao 熟睡; sah'-k'eo kw'eng'-joh; *— lightly,* kw'eng'-leh kying-sing' 睡得°警醒; *— in one's clothes,* ta' i-zông kw'eng' 連°衣裳睡°; *— and dream much,* lön-mong' tin-tao 亂夢顛倒; *cry out in —,* lön-mong' hæn-kyiao 亂夢喊叫; *sleeping-room,* vông-kæn' 房間°; *to — the long — (i. e. death),* do-kao' kw'eng'-joh 大°覺睡熟

SLEEPY, iao kw'eng'-joh 要睡°睡°, or 要睡熟°; k'eh'-c'ong-mi-mong' 瞌䑃眯矇; mi-hwô'-ky'i-de 眯眵去了°; *— eyes,* ngæn'-tsing mi-long'-ky'i 眼睛眯攏去°

SLEET, shih'-ts 雪珠°

SLEEVE, ziu-ts' 袖子 (ih-tsah)

SLEIGHT *of hand,* kyiah'-kw'a siu-kw'a' 脚快°手快°; *to use ditto,* long-siu'-kyiah 弄手脚; yüong siu'-kyiah 用手脚; pin hyi'-fah 變戲法; *to perform a ditto,* pin ih-t'ao' hyi'-fah 變一套戲法

SLENDER, (as persons), dziang-liao'-siao 長藜篠°; bah-dziang' 勃長

SLICE, *a* ih'-p'in 一片

SLICE, *to* ts'ih-leh p'in'-tang-p'in 切得°片打片

SLIDE, *to* wah 滑; — *down,* sô'-loh-ky'i; *to slip,* wah-loh'-ky'i 滑落去°; — *back and forth,* (move), yi-læ' yi-ky'i 移來移去°; — *up and down,* ts'iu-zông' ts'iu-loh' 抽上抽落

SLIGHT *matter,* si'-si-siao'-z 些些小事; ky'ü-ky'ü-siao'-z 區區小事; — *wound,* sông ky'ing-k'o' 傷輕可; *not the slightest mistake,* ih-ngæn' feh-ts'o' 一點弗錯

SLIGHT, *to* — (a person), lang'-dæn 冷°淡; ts'iao'-feh-ky'i' 瞧弗起; — *unintentionally,* shih'-kwu 失顧; *to do carelessly,* tso'-leh hweh'-liah 做得°忽略; tso'-leh peh-yi' we-i' 做得°不以爲意

SLIGHTLY, ih-tin' 一點; p'o'-p'o 頗頗; — *acquainted,* p'o'-p'o nying-teh' 頗頗認°得

SLING, *to put the arm in a* —, loh siu'-kwang 絡手膀°; *to throw a stone with a* —, yüong ta' dæn zah'-ts 用帶彈石°子

SLIP, *a* — *of paper,* ih-p'in ts' 一片紙; ih-da ts' 一搽紙;

— *of bamboo,* coh'-bæn 竹爿; (ih-kw'e)

SLIP, *to* wah 滑; liu 溜; — *down,* wah-loh' 滑落; — (as a person), wah-tao' 滑倒; *to lose footing,* shih-kyiah' or sih-kyiah' 失脚, (also to speak words that cannot be trusted); — *and almost fall,* tang wah-t'ah' 打滑°脫; — *and fall,* weh-tih' 滑跌; liu-tih' 溜跌

SLIPPER, bin-'a' 便鞋 (a pair, ih-sông)

SLIPPERY, wah-lih'-wah-t'ah' 滑立滑脫° (also used of persons); *not easily caught,* wah-wah'-dah-dah 滑脫°脫°; — *in making promises, and not fulfilling,* tang-wah'-t'ah'-de 打滑脫了°

SLIT, lih-vong' 裂縫 (ih-da); — *made purposely in a garment,* ts'ô'-ts 衩子 (ih-da)

SLOPING, ts'ia'-min 斜°面; ts'ia'-shing 斜°向

SLOPPY, *wet,* sih'-sih-go 濕濕個°; wu-dah-dah'-go 腐°蚉蚉個°; wu-gyih'-gwah-lah.

SLOUGH, na-nyi-den' 爛坭潭

SLOUGH, *to* — *off,* t'eng-diao' 褪去°; *ditto skin, or shell,* t'eng k'oh' 褪壳

SLOVENLY, fông'-p'ah-la'-sa 放潑頼撒°; *dirty,* t'i'-t'i-t'a-t'a 潚°潚°太太; lah-t'ah' 邋遢

SLOW, mæn 慢; wun 緩; mæn-t'ang'-t'ang 慢宕°宕°; wun'-

deng-deng 綏鈍鉎; — *fire,* wun'-ho 綏火; veng-ho' 文火; iu-iu' ho 幽火;

SLOWER, *a little* mæn-tin' 慢點

SLOWLY, mæn-mæn' 慢慢; wun'-wun 綏綏; kw'un-wun'-diao-da 寬綏; *walk —* (said to a guest on leaving), mæn-mæn' tseo 慢慢走

SLUGGISH, læn-r' vu-tông'-go 懶而無當个°; sang læn'-wông-bing 生懶黃病 (in reproach); *too — to get up to eat,* kæ min-feng' min-bi' go 盖麵粉縣被个°

SLUICE, ky'i 閘; — *gate,* ky'i'-meng 閘門; *mud* —, pô 礪; *stone* —, in 堰

SMALL, siao 小; si'-siao 細小; vi-si' 微細; siao'-so; *very* —, ting-siao 頂小; ih-ngæn'-ngæn' do 一點點大°; siao'-siao-kwun do; dzih-si' do 極些大°; — *quantity,* ih-ngæn'-ngæn 一點點; yiu'-'æn 有限°

SMALTS, da-ts'ing' 大青

SMALL-POX, *inoculated* deo-ts' 痘子; — *taken naturally,* t'in-deo' 天痘; *has the —,* c'ih-deo-ts'-go 出痘子个°; *to inoculate the —,* cong deo' 種痘; cong hwô' 種花; 'ô miao' 下苗; *marked with* —, mô-bi'-go 麻皮个°

SMART, *clever,* hwæn 儇; hwæn-ky'iao' 儇巧; — *in reply,* tah'-leh ky'iao' 答得°巧; — *and active,* weh-loh' 活絡

SMARTING *pain,* tsih'-lah-lah-go t'ong' 炙辣辣个°痛; — *like fire,* ho' siao ho'-lah-go t'ong' 火燒火辣个°痛

SMASH, *to* k'ao-se' 敲碎; tang'-se 打碎; — *accidentally,* p'ong-se, or bang-se' 撞碎

SMATTERING, veo-min' 'oh'-tin 浮面學°點

SMEAR, *to* dzô 搽

SMELL, *to* hyüong 齅; hyüong'-hyüong-k'en 齅齅看; — *something sweet,* veng hyiang-ky'i' 聞香氣; meng hyiang-ky'i' 吻°香氣

SMELL, *fragrant* hyiang-ky'i' 香氣; *a strong* — (generally bad), ky'i'-mi 氣味°; *a bad* —, ky'i'-ts 氣子; ky'i'-sih 氣息; *flowers give forth a sweet* —, hwô læ-tih p'eng'-hyiang 花噴香; *sweaty* —, 'en-sön'-ky'i 汗酸氣; *fishy* —, sing-ky'i' 腥氣; *musty* —, eh'-boh-ky'i' 霉蒸氣; *slightly musty* — (as damp clothes), ze-nong-ky'i' 蚕膿氣; *sour* — (as of bread, or meal), sön tsiang'-ky'i 酸漿氣; *strong* — (as of mutton), sao-ky'i' 臊氣; *rank* — (of certain persons), lao'-ô ky'i' 老鴉氣

SMELT, *to melt,* yiang 煬; sah 煞; yiang-k'æ' 煬開; sah'-k'æ 煞開

SMILE, *to* mi-mi'-siao 眯眯笑; mi-ko'-ngæn-siao 眯花°眼°笑

SMILING, *wears a — face*, ta siao'-lin 帶°笑臉

SMOKE, *in* 烟; *the smell of —*, in-ho' ky'i 烟火氣; in ky'i'-mi 烟氣味°

SMOKE, *to — meat*, hyüing nyüoh' 燻肉°; *— tobacco*, ky'üoh in' 吃°烟; *— opium*, ky'üoh a-p'in' 吃°鴉片; (more polite), ky'üoh in' 吃°烟

SMOKED (as things in cooking), in-ho'-ky'i-de 烟火氣了°

SMOKY *place*, in-hyüing ho'-dæn u-sen' 烟燻火燂

SMOOTH, kwông 光; wah 滑; kwông-wah' 光滑; *very —*, kying'-kwông shih-wah' 鏡光雪滑; tih-wah-lin' ka 滴滑臉個°; wah-liu-cü' ka' 滑流嘴個°

SMOOTH, *to — with the hand*, t'ô' kwông 抹°光; *— with a plane*, bao kwông 刨光

SMOOTH-TONGUED, (not to be depended upon), yiu-cü'-t'ah'-zih 油嘴諜舌; cih'-læ-bin-ky'i 啜來辯去°

SMOOTHING-IRON (to be heated from within), ing'-teo 熨°斗 (ih-kwun); *—* (to be heated on the fire), loh-t'ih' 烙鐵

SMOTHER *to death*, meng-sah' 捫°煞; *— out fire*, meng-u' 捫鳩

SMUGGLE *to* t'eo-se' 偷税; leo-se' 漏税

SMUGGLING, *to detect one in —*, k'ô leo-se'-go 拿°漏税個°

SMUTTY, yiu in-me' tsao'-tih 有烟煤遭的; *— face*, heh'-moh du-lin' 黑墨塗臉

SNAIL, *common* (either with or without a shell), yin-yiu'-lo' 涎游螺; *fresh water —*, s'-lo 蛳螺; *sea —*, hæ' s-lo' 海蛳; *field —*, din-lo' 田螺 (ih-keng)

SNAKE, dzô 蛇° (ih-kwang, ih-keng); *poisonous —*, doh dzô' 毒蛇°; *Buddha's mouth, snake's heart*, (i.e. fair words coming from a bad heart), veh-k'eo' dzô-sing 佛口蛇°心; *tiger's head, snake's tail*, (said of anything which commences with a great flourish, and ends in nothing), hwu'-deo dzô-vi' 虎頭蛇尾

SNARE, ky'ün'-t'ao' 犬韜; gyiang 弶; kw'u-t'ao'-ky'ün 箍套圈; *to set a —*, tsông ky'ün-t'ao' 裝圈套; tsông gyiang' 裝弶

SNARL, *all in a —*, lön-tsia'-bong 亂織°蓬

SNATCH, *to* ta'-ts'iang ta'-deh; 帶°搶帶°奪; ts'iang'-ts'iang-deh-deh 搶搶奪奪; *— with violence*, deh, 奪; deh-ky'i' 奪去°; ts'iang 搶; ts'iang'-ky'i 搶去°

SNEER, *to — at*, lang'-siao 冷笑; *to turn up the nose at*, bih-deo'-kwun siao nying' 鼻°孔°笑笑人°

SNEEZE, to tang p'eng'-t'i 打嚏嚏
SNORE, to yiu min-hen' 有眠鼾; he snores loudly, gyi'-go min-hen' do' 其个眠鼾大°
SNOUT, dziang cü-bu' 長嘴輔°; — of a tea-pot, dzô-wu-cü 茶壺嘴; to work the — under (as a hog), ky'üing.
SNOW, shih 雪°; white as —, shih'-bah-go 雪°白个°; shih'-lin-bah'-go 雪°練白个°; — in scattering flakes, shih'-hwô-fi 雪°花飛; snowing fast and thick, p'iao'-p'iao-dong shih' 飄飄動雪°; — in large flakes, læn-shih'-p'in 雪°片
SNOW to loh-shih' 落雪
SNOW-BALL, to throw a —, tiu shih-dön 丢雪團;—(the flower), moh-siu'-gyiu-hwô 木繡毬花
SNOW-BALL, to ô shih'-dön; ting shih-dön.
SNUFF, bih-in' 鼻烟; to take —, soh bih-in' 嗅鼻烟 (soh or shoh); ky'üoh bih-in' 吃鼻烟; — bottle, bih-in'-wu 鼻烟壺
SNUFF, to — a candle, tsin (or gyin) lah-coh'-me 翦蠟燭煤
SNUFFLE, to soh (or shoh) bih-deo' 縮鼻°聲°
SNUFFERS, coh'-tsin 燭翦; lah-coh'-gyin 蠟燭筲 (ih-pô)
So, ka 如°此°; z-ka'; ziang-ka 像如°此°; ka'-siang-mao 如°此°相貌; — that there be no mistake, sang-leh long-ts'o' 省°得°

弄差; — that will not, sang-leh sang°-得°; — many, ka'-to 如°此°多; ka' hyü'-to 如°許多; keh-tang'; is it — every day? nyih-nyih' z-ka feh 日日如°此°否°? about —, ka' kwông'-kying 如°此°光景
SOAK, to seng'-t'eo 沁透; tsing'-t'eo 浸透; soaked with perspiration, 'en' seng'-t'eo-de 汗沁透了°; — in water over night, shü tsing' ko yia' 水°浸過夜; shü'-li sah-ko yia'.
SOAP, bi-zao' 肥皂 (a bar, ih-diao); properly native soap, or the fruit of the soap-tree.
SOAP-TREE, zao'-kyih-jü 皂°莢樹; bi-zao'-jü 肥皂樹 (ih-cü)
SOAP-STONE, væn-zah' 礬石; Ts'ing-din zah' 青田石°
SOAR, to gwah-zông'-ky'i 飛°上去°
SOB, to hyih'-hyih-hoh'-hoh k'oh' 吸吸鼾°鼾°哭; hyih'-hyih'-hyiang k'oh' 吸吸響哭
SOBER, sedate, tön-tsông' 端莊; z-dzæ' 自在; djong 重
SOCIABLE, we kao-nyin'-go 會膠°黏个°; hwun-hyi' kyih'-kyiao-go 歡喜結°交个°; æ-beng-yiu'-go 愛朋友个°; easy to associate with, hao' ts'eo-de' 好湊隊
SOCIALLY, to talk —, ts'ông'-dæn 暢談; ts'ông'-jü 暢敘
SOCIETY, we 會 (ih-go)

SOCKS, tön mah-cü' 短襪子; (a pair. ih-sông), — covers. mah-t'ao' 襪套; mah-tsao' 襪罩
SODA. impure native —, zah-kæn' 石鹼°
SODA-WATER, 'O-læn' shü 荷蘭水°
SOFA, c'ing-teng' 春櫈
SOFT, nyün 軟; nyi-nyün' 綿°軟; nyün'-joh 軟熟 nyün'-siang; — (as fruit, or cooked food), nen; ŵong; very —, ŵong'-t'ah-t'ah; nen-bu'-bu; that is a — boiled egg, keh'-go dæn ts'-leh liu-ŵong'-go 這个°蛋煑得流黃°个°; z dông-ŵong-go dæn 是盪黃°个°蛋; — voice, sing-ing' 'o-nyün' 聲音和軟; too — (as cloth, or paper), nyün-t'ah'-bi 軟脫皮
SOFTEN, to — it, s'-teh gyi nyün' 使得其軟; soften by soaking, tsing' gyi nen 浸其軟°; — by scalding, p'ao' gyi nen' 泡其軟°
SOFTLY, ts'iao-ts'iao 悄悄; talk —, ts'iao-ts'iao' kông 悄悄講; ky'ing-ky'ing' kông 輕輕講
SOIL, di-t'u' 地土; nyi-nyüoh' 坭肉; good —, di-t'u' 'eo'-jih 地土厚實; hao nyi-nyüoh' 好坭肉°
SOIL, to long ao-tsao' 弄墾糟
SOLDER, 'en-yiah' 釬藥
SOLDER, to 'en 釬
SOLDIER, ping 兵; ping-ting' 兵丁 (ih-go); soldiers, ping-mô' 兵馬; volunteer —, t'u-ping 土兵; (a body, ih-ts, ih-de, ih-dzing)

SOLE of the foot, kyiah'-ti 腳底; — of the shoe, 'a-ti' 鞋底
SOLE, (a fish), nyiah-t'ah'-ng 鮎°鰈魚°
SOLELY, doh-meng' 獨門; tæn-tsih' 單只
SOLEMN, nyin-soh' 嚴肅; soh'-jün 肅然 (veng); still, zing'-ts'iao-ts'iao 靜°悄悄
SOLICIT, to gyiu 求; — a reward, gyiu sông'-fong 求賞封; — a favor, gyin dzing' 求情; k'eng dzing 懇情
SOLICITOUS to obtain, ts'ih'-sing iao 切心要; anxious or troubled, fông'-sing-feh-loh' 放心弗落; ky'ih'-du kwô'-dziang 掣肚掛腸; tæn sing-z' 擔心事
SOLID, jih-sing', zih-sing', or dzih-sing' 實心; — piece of stone, tsing-kw'e' zah-deo' 正塊石°頭; — wall, jih-diah'-go ziang' 實疊个°牆; — silver, jih-sing' nying-ts' 實心銀子; tsoh' nying-ts' 足銀子
SOLITARY, doh-ih' 獨一; doh-ling'-ling 獨零零; — (as a person), tæn-sing' 單身; kwu-sing' 孤身; — and alone, tæn-sing' doh gyi' 單身獨騎; without relatives, kwu-ling'-ting 孤零丁; no relatives to depend upon, loh-ts'ing' vu-k'ao' 六親無靠; —

place, kwu-ts'ing' lang'-loh-go di-fông° 孤清冷°落个°地方
SOLSTICE, *Winter* tong-ts'冬至; *Summer* —, 'ô-ts' 夏°至
SOLUBLE, we yiang'-go 會煬个°
SOLVE, *to* ka 解°; — *doubts,* ka nyi' 解疑; — *a difficult matter,* ka'-c'ih næn-z' 解°出難事
SOME, *a few,* kyi'-go 幾个°; yiu'-sing 有些°; yiu'-teh-go 有得个°; *a little,* ih-tin' 一點; ih ngœn'; *buy — sugar, and peaches,* ma tin dông', ma kyi'-go dao-ts' 買°點糖買°幾个°桃子°; — *years ago,* kyi' nyiu zin-deo' 幾年前°頭; — *people say so,* yiu'-sing nying z-ka' wô' 有些°人°如°此°話; — *other person,* ih-go bih'-nying 一个°別人°
SOMEBODY, mo'-nying 某人°; yiu-nying 有人°; — *certainly did it,* pih'-ding yiu nying tso'-ko-de 必定有人°做過了°
SOMETHING, *I have* — (*i. e.* one thing), ngô' yiu ih-yiang' tong-si' 我有一樣東西; *have to eat, and — to wear,* yiu'-leh ky'üoh' yiu'-leh c'ün' 有得°吃°有得°穿°; *I have — to tell you,* ngô' yiu z-ken' t'ong-cü' ng 我有事幹通知你°; *talk of — else,* kông bih-yiang' z-ken' 講°別樣事幹
SOMETIMES, yiu'-z-'eo 有時候; yiu'-teh-z'-'eo 有的°時候; — *there is, and — not,* yiu'-z-'eo yiu', yiu'-z-'eo 冇°-teh-go 有時候有, 有時候沒°有°
SOMEWHAT, *is* yiu'-tin 有點; yiu kyi-feng' 有幾分; — *damp,* yiu'-tin dziao-sih' 有點潮濕; liah yiu'-tin dziao-sih' 略有點潮濕
SON, ng-ts' 兒°子; ts'-sih 子息; *another's — taken to rear,* kyi'-pa ng-ts' 寄拜°兒°子; *adopted* —, ling'-ts 領子 (See ADOPT); *your* —, ling-lông 令郎; lông-kong' 郎公; ah-lông' 阿郎; *my* —, ah-lah siao'-r 我°們°小兒°; ngô'-go siao'-r 我个°小兒°; ah'-lah siao'-ky'ün' (*i. e.* little dogs) 我們°小犬; *eldest* —, do ng'-ts 大兒°子; tsiang'-ts 長子; *the second* —, ts''-ts 次子; *only* —, doh-yiang' ng-ts' 獨養兒°子; *sister's,* or *daughter's* —, nga-sang' 外°甥°
SON-IN-LAW, nyü'-si 女壻
SONG, ky'üoh'-ts 曲子; *comical* —, t'æn-wông' 灘簧; *vulgar* —, siao'-diao 小調 (ih-tsah); — *book,* ts'ông'-shü 唱書 (ih-peng)
SONOROUS, hyiang'-liang 響亮
SOON, *early,* tsao早; *quickly,* kw'a 快°; *come as — as called,* ih-eo' ziu læ' 一叫°就來; *as — as he came I went,* gyi' ih-læ' ngô ziu ky'i'-de 其一來我就去°了°
SOONER *than I,* pi ngô tsao' 比我早; *a little* —, tsao-tin' 早

點；kw‛a'-tsao-tin' 快°早點

Soot, in-me' 烟煤

Soothe, to — (by consoling), en'-tah 安搭；— him, kw‛un-gyi-sing' 寬其心；ky‛ün'-ka-gyi 勸解°其

Sorcerer (who divines with spirits), kông-du-sin'-go 講°肚仙个°；— (who chants, and worships for another), nyiæn-bun' sin-sang 念嗙先生°

Sorceress (who divines with spirits), du-sin-bo' 肚仙婆°；(who chants, &c., for others), dao-z-bo' 道士婆°

Sorcery, zia-jih' 邪°術；zia-fah' 邪°法；to practise —, yüong zia-jih' 用邪°術

Sordid, meanly avaricious, ts'-ts-we-li' 孳孳爲利；niggardly, k‛æn；k‛eh'-li 刻勵

Sore, bruise, sông-t‛ong' 傷痛；boil, or ulcer, ts‛ông 瘡；doh 毒

Sore, slightly ing'-ts‛ih-ts‛ih-go t‛ong' 隱戚戚个°痛；— to the touch, bang-djoh' t‛ong' 撞着°痛；— (pain in the flesh, not in the bones), nyüoh'-li t‛ong' kweh'-li feh'-t‛ong' 肉°裡痛骨裏弗痛

Sorrow, iu-meng' 憂悶；zeo-meng' 愁悶

Sorrowful, sông-sing' 傷心；pe-sông' 悲傷；— countenance, min' ta iu seh' 面帶憂色

Sorry, I am — for you, ngô t‛i ng iu' 我替你°憂；dæ ng' næn-ko'-siang 代你°難過相；very — for you, t‛i ng' peh'-jing-siang 替你°不忍相；— for it, k‛o'-sih 可惜；sih'-wu 惜乎

Sort, a ih yiang' 一樣；ih 'ao' 一號；ih cong' 一種；the same —, tso' yiang；tso' 'ao；every —, yiang-yiang' 樣樣；cong'-cong 種種

Sort, to ih-yiang ih-yiang' kwe-de' 一樣一樣歸隊

Sorted, 'ao-tang'-'ao feng-k‛æ'-liao 號打號分開了°

Soul, weh-ling' 活靈；weng-ling' 魂靈；ling-weng' 靈魂；man has three spiritual and six animal souls, nying yiu sæn-weng' loh-p‛ah' 人°有三魂六魄 (Buddhist idea)；rational —, ling-weng' 靈魂；ling-sing' 靈性；animal —, kyüoh'-weng 覺魂；vegetable —, seng-weng' 生魂

Sound, sing-hyiang' 聲響；sing-ing' 聲音

Sound, to hyiang 響；does not —, ve' hyiang 弗°會°響

Sound, to — the depth, tang sing-ts‛in' 量深淺

Sound in health, gyin 健；k‛ông-gyin' 康健；ditto (as a young person), tsông'-gyin 壯健

Soundly, to sleep kw‛eng sah'-kao 睡°煞覺°

SOUP, t'ông 湯; to ladle out —, iao t'ông 舀湯
SOUP-LADLE, t'ông-diao-kang 湯調羹° (ih-tsah)
SOUP-TUREEN, t'ông-kwun' 湯罐 (ih-tsah)
SOUR, sön 酸; to become —, fah sön' 發酸; — (as food that has turned), seo'-ky'i 餿氣; ditto (as the stomach, &c.), tsoh-sön' 作酸
SOURCE (of affairs), læ-yiu' 來由; keng-yiu' 根由; nyün-yiu' 原由; — and ending, læ-keng' ky'ü-mah' 來根去脈; — (of man, principles, &c.), nyün-peng' 原本; keng-nyün' 根原; keng-peng' 根本; — (of water), nyün-deo' 源頭; læ-nyün' 來源; læ-mah' 來脈
SOUTH, Nen 南; toward the —, hyiang Nen' 向南; dziao Nen' 朝南; come from the —, dzong Nen' læ-go 從南來个°; — East, tong nen' 東南; — West, si nen' 西南
SOW, cü-nyiang 豬娘; old —, lao'-cü-nyiang 老豬娘 (ih-tsah)
SOW, to — seed, tsah iang-ts' 撒秧子
SOY, tsiang'-yiu 醬油
SPACE above us, hyü-k'ong' 虛空; empty —, k'ong di'-fông 空地方; great unoccupied —, di-fông sæn'-dæn 地方散淡; the —

between fingers, ts'-deo vong 指頭縫
SPACIOUS, kw'un-do' 寬大°; kw'eh'-do 闊大°; kwông'-kw'eh 廣闊
SPADE, wô-ts'iao' 划鍫 (ih-pô)
SPAN, (Chinese, from the end of the thumb, to the end of the middle finger), ih-t'oh' 一度
SPAN, to measure by the hand, t'oh'-t'oh-k'en 度度看
SPANISH-STRIPE, pib'-kyi 嗶嘰
SPARE, to — life, nyiao-ming' 饒°命; — one for me, liu ih'-go peh ngô' 留一个°給°我; can you — (i.e. sell one) for me? hao we' ih'-go peh ngô' feh 好匯一个°給°我否°? can you — it a day? keh, hao sang' yüong ih-nyih' feh 這°好省°用一日°否°? can't — it, hyih'-gyi-feh-læ 歇其弗來; siao'-gyi-feh-teh' 少其弗得; can't — the time, kong-fu' bah'-feh-c'ih 工夫拔弗出; does not — his strength, gyi feh-sih'-lih'-go 其弗惜力个°; can you — me for a while? ng' hao sang ngô' ih-zông' feh 你°好省°我一息否°?
SPARING, using frugally, feh-sô'-teh yüong' 弗捨°得用; — in diet, ky'üoh'-leh sang' 吃°得省°
SPARK, a ih-lih ho'-sing 一粒火星
SPARKLING, t'co'-kwông-go 透

光个°; — *like the stars*, ziang sing-kwông' ka 像星光
SPARROW, mô-tsiang' 麻雀° (ih-tsah)
SPASM, kying-fong 驚瘋; kyih'-kying-fong 急驚瘋
SPATTER, *to* tsæn 濺; tsæn-sih' 濺濕; — *with mud*, na-nyi' tsæn'-ky'i 掜泥濺°起
SPAWN, ng-ts' 魚°子
SPEAK, *to* kông 講°; wô 話; *need not — of it*, hao-vong kông'-c'ih 好不°用°講°出; — *louder*, kông-leh hyiang-tin' 講°得°響點°; — *the truth*, kông-leh jih-dzæ'-go 講°得°實在个°; tsiao dzih' kông 照直講°; *I want to — to you*, ngô iao teng ng kông 我要與你°講°; — *on the spur of the moment, or without previous thought*, kông'-c'ih sön'-tsiang 講°出算賬; ze-k'eo' kông'-c'ih 隨口講°出; *we do not — to one another*, ah-lah feh kao' k'eo 我°等°弗交°口; *cannot — of it*, wô-feh-c'ih'-go 話弗出个°
SPEAKER, *able* k'eo-neng'-zih-bin'-go nying 能言°舌辯个°人°
SPEAR, ts'iang 鎗 (ih-ts)
SPECIAL, deh-we' 特爲; deh-i' 特意; — *proclamation*, deh-z' 特示; *a — business*, ih-yiang deh-i' z-ken' 一樣特意事幹; *needs — care*, iao kah'-nga kwu'-djoh 要格外°顧着

SPECIALLY *for*, cün-meng' we 專門爲; tæn-tsih' we 單只爲; doh-doh' we 獨獨爲
SPECIES, le 類; cong 種; *the same —*, tso' cong; dong-le' 同類; *each according to its —*, koh'-tsiao gyi le' 各照其類; cong'-cong koh-bih' 種種各別
SPECIFY, *to* dzoh 逐; — *each one*, dzoh-yiang' kông'-c'ih-læ 逐樣講°出來; dzoh-ih' pao'-zông-læ 逐一報上來
SPECIMEN, yiang-ts' 樣子 (ih-go)
SPECIOUS, *deceitful*, z-z'-r-fi' 似是而非; *superficially fair words*, hwô-yin' ky'iao'-nyü 花言巧語
SPECK, *a* ih-tin' 一點; — *of dust*, ih-tin hwe' 一屑°灰
SPECKLED, hwô-tin'-go 花點个°
SPECTACLES, ngæn'-kying 眼鏡 (ih-fu)
SPECTATORS, k'en'-k'ah 看客; k'en'-go nying 看个°人°
SPECULATION, *a good —*, hao' dzen'-deo 好賺頭; *a good investment*, hao' c'ih'-sih 好出息
SPEECH, *talk*, shih-wô' 說話; *fluent in —*, liu'-c'ih sön'-tsiang 巧°言°如°流; t'ông-bing' sia-shü' 湯瓶掛°水° (*sometimes used in reproach*); *clever in —*, jün'-ü shih'-dz 善於說詞; we-kông' we-wô' 會講°會話
SPEECHLESS, *cannot speak*, feh-neng' kông 弗能講°; soh'-k'eo deng' 縮口鈍; meh-meh' vu

yin' 默默無言;—(as if dumb, used in reproach), o'-k'eo vu-yin' 啞°口無言

SPEED, *with great* —, ting'-kw'a 頂快°; fi-kw'a' 飛快°; fong-kw'a' 風快°; ho'-soh 火速; (their) — *is not equal*, kw'a'-mæn feh-dong 快°慢弗同

SPEEDILY, *go* tseo'-leh ziang fi' ka 走得°像飛个°; *return* —, kw'a'-kw'a ziu-læ' 快°快°就來; 'ao-sao' læ 快°燥來

SPELL, *to* p'ing z-meo' 拼字母

SPELLING, *Chinese phonetic* fæn-ts'ih' 反切

SPELTER, bah-k'æn 白鉛

SPEND, *to* — *money*, yüong dong-din' 用銅錢°; — *wastefully*, fi 費; fi'-diao 費了°; — *to no purpose*, hwô-fi' 花費; bah fi'-diao 白費了°; — *the day with a friend*, beng-yiu' di'-fông deng' ih nyih' 朋友地方登一日°; — *the night*, soh yia' 宿夜°; hyih yia' 歇夜°; ko yia' 過夜°; — *one's life in*, tso'-leh ih-si' 做了°一世°; *ditto laboriously*, lao-loh' ih-si' 勞碌一世°; — *one's time idly*, hyü-du' kwông-ing' 虛度光陰; nyih-kyiah' k'ong'-ko 日°腳空過

SPEND-THRIFT, ba-ts' 敗子; *to live as a* —, vông-ky'üoh vông'-yüong 妄吃°妄用

SPERMACETI, zông-teng' gying-ng' yiu 上等鯨魚°油

SPHERE, gyiu 毬

SPHERICAL, ziang gyiu' ka 像毬樣°式°

SPICES, hyiang-liao' 香料

SPIDER, (the one which makes a large web), kyih'-cü 蜘°蛛; *flat* — (found in partitions), hyi'-ts 蟢子; pih'-hyi 壁蟢; *very large house* —, pih'-ha 壁蟹° (ih-tsah)

SPIDER-WEB, kyih'-cü-mông' 蜘°蛛°網; kyih'-cü lön'-mông 蜘°蛛°亂網° (ih-go)

SPIKE, *iron* bao'-djü-ting' 抱柱釘; *do* t'ih'-ting 大°鐵釘; *bamboo* —, coh'-ting 竹釘; — *of wheat*, ih-cü mah' 一棵麥

SPILL, *to* yiang'-c'ih 漾出; kwông'-c'ih 洸出; — *by upsetting*, yiang-fæn' 漾翻; tao'-fæn 倒翻; — (because on a slant), tseh'-c'ih 側出; *to overflow*, kah'-c'ih-læ 溢°出來

SPIN, *to* — *cotton yarn*, fông hwô' 紡花; fông-sô' 紡紗

SPINACH, SPINAGE, po-leng'-ts'æ 菠菜

SPINAL *marrow*, tsih'-kweh-si' 脊骨髓

SPINDLE, ding'-ts 錠子 (ih-me)

SPINE, pe'-tsih-kweh 背脊骨

SPINNING-WHEEL, fông-hwô'-ts'ô' 紡花車 (ih-tsiang)

SPIRAL, ziang lo-s' ka 像螺螄樣°式°; s'-lo dzin' 螄螺旋; — *stair-case*, bun-t'æ' 盤梯

SPIRIT, ling 靈; *the Holy —*, Sing'-Ling 聖靈; *pure —*, jing' z ling' 純是靈; *— of love*, jing-sing 仁心; jing-æ'-sing 仁愛心; *departed —*, ing-weng' 陰魂; kyü 鬼°; kwe'-se 鬼祟; *evil —*, oh'-kyü 惡鬼°; *— of ancestors*, kô-sin' 家°先°; *in fine spirits*, (*i. e.* delighted and playful, said in fun), p'ao'-c'ing 快°樂°; *in low ditto*, üoh'-beh-ts-ky'i' 鬱勃之氣

SPIRITED, *full of life*, jing-ky'i' tsoh' 神氣足; *high —*, sing-kao'-ky'i-ngao'-go 心高氣傲个°;*— talk*, kông'-leh c'ih-jing' 講°得°出神

SPIRITLESS, 並 jing'-ky'i 無°神氣, pih'-t'ah-t'ah go 腩塌塌个°; ziang pih-gyiæn' ka 像腩茄

SPIRITUAL, ling'-leh-kying-go 靈得°緊个°; ling-weh'-go 靈活个°

SPIT, *to* t'u-zæn-t'u' 吐涎°唾

SPITE, ün'-sing 怨心; 'eng-sing' 恨心; *done out of —*, we'-leh 'eng' tso'-go 爲了°恨做个°; *in — of you*, ze ng' læn-tsu' 隨你°攔阻; dæn'-ming ng' tsu'-feh-tsu' 但憑你°阻弗阻; sih'-t'ing ng tsu'-feh-tsu' 悉聽你°阻弗阻; (I'll do it) *in — of you*, dæn'-ming ngô' 但憑我

SPITTLE, zæn-t'u 涎°唾

SPITTOON, dæn-bing' 痰瓶; *small —*, dæn-kwun' 痰罐

SPLENDID, wô-li' 華麗; *bright, or showy*, kwông-liang' 光亮

SPLENDOR, kwông-ts'æ' 光彩

SPLICE, *to* tsih'-zông, dzin-long' 接上緊攏

SPLINTER, *a* ih-me ts'' 一根°莉; ih-go sang'; *finger has a —*, ts'-deo ts''-c'oh-de 指頭莉𤓫了°

SPLINT, moh-p'in'-pông 木片綁 (a set, ih t'ao)

SPLIT, *to* p'ih 劈; lih 裂; p'ih-k'æ' 劈開; lih-k'æ' 裂開;*— or burst open* (as a melon, &c.), hwah'-k'æ 豁開; *— in two*, te'-p'ih-k'æ 對劈開;*— the difference*, te'-la-la.

SPOIL, *to* i'-diao; long-diao' 弄壞°; wæ-diao' 壞了°;*—(as preserves, honey, &c.)*, fæn-diao' 反掉;*— by indulgence*, i-yiang'-diao; yüong yiang'-diao 容養壞°;*— by altering*, kæ'-diao 改壞°;*— by inadvertence*, bih-ts'iah' 瞥截; *ditto* (more intense), tso c'ong'-p'ang; *— by wanting too much*, &c., tsing-hweh' 揕豁; *to plunder*, tang'-kyih 打刼; lo'-liah 擄掠

SPOIL, *booty*, tsông 贓; *thief's —*, zeh-tsông' 賊贓; *piratical —*, dao'-tsông 盜贓

SPOKEN, *what was — about*, (but not settled), sô yüing'-go 所云个° (veng.)

SPONGE, hæ'-min-hwô 海綿花 (ih-go)

SPONGE-CAKE, dæn-kao' 蛋糕 (ih-go)

SPONTANEOUS, zi sang'-c'ih-læ 自°生°出來; zi fah'-c'ih-læ 自°發出來; c'ih'-ü-z-jün' 出於自然

SPOOL, or *ball of thread*, min-sô dön' 綿紗團

SPOON, diao-kang' 調羹°; kang-z' 羹°匙; *large or table —*, do diao-kang' 大°調羹°; *middle or dessert —*, cong diao-kang' 中調羹°; *small or tea —*, siao' diao-kang' 小調羹°; *native brass ditto*, dzô-z' 茶匙 (ih-tsah)

SPOONFUL *of*, ih diao-kang' 一調羹°; *a tea — of medicine*, ih siao' diao-kang' yiah' 一小調°羹°藥

SPORT, hyi'-mæn z-ken' 戲譃事幹; *to make —, (or make others laugh)*, ying-siao' 引笑

SPOT, tsih'-le 漬痕; *oil —*, yin-tsih' 油漬; *black —*, heh'-tin 黑點; heh'-pæn 黑斑; *ink —*, moh-tsih' 墨跡; moh-n' 墨痕; *to make a —*, tang tsih' 遭°漬

SPOTTED, yin-tsih 有漬; — (*as clothes that have laid away*), fah pæn-tin'-de 發斑點了°

SPOTLESS, m̄-tsih'-le-go 無°漬痕個°; — *white*, zing-bah' 淨白

SPOUT, *pipe*, kwun'-ts 罐子; *tea-pot —*, dzô-wu cü' 茶壺嘴

SPOUT, *to* p'ong'-c'ih-læ' 噴出來; ts'ong'-c'ih-læ' 衝出來

SPRAIN, bih-sông' 蹩傷; üih'-sông 攜傷

SPRAINED *ankle*, kyiah'-tsang bih-sông'-de 脚脖蹩傷了°; kyiah-bu-lu-den' bih-ih-bih'-de 脚蒲蘆頭°蹩一蹩了°

SPREAD, *to* p'u 鋪; — *out*, (*as matting &c.*), p'u-k'æ' 鋪開; t'æn-k'æ' 攤開; — (*as wings*), tô'-k'æ 排°開; — *the table*, pa coh'-teng 擺桌子°; — *food*, pa væn' 擺飯; — *abroad*, 'ang-k'æ' 行°開; — *the Gospel*, Foh'-ing 'ang-k'æ' 福音行°開; — *abroad*, yiang-k'æ' 揚開; po-yiang' 播揚; — (*by words*), djün-k'æ' 傳開; — *reputation*, ming-sing' yiang-k'æ' 名聲揚開; — (*as water spilled*), seng-k'æ' 沁開; — (*as disease*), yin-k'æ' 延開

SPRIGHTLY, weh-p'eh' 活潑; weh-siu' weh-kyiah' 活手活脚

SPRING, *the season of —*, C'ing-kyi' 春季; C'ing-t'in' z-'eo' 春天時候; *watch or clock —*, fah'-diao 法條; *elastic —*, t'e-neh'-diao 推捺掉; *source of water*, shü'-nyün 水°源; — *of living water*, weh-shü-den' 活水°潭

SPRING, *to start up*, c'ün-ky'i'-læ 竄起來; *to — forward*, t'iao-ko-ky'i 跳過去; c'ün-ko'-

ky'i 竄過去° (tsön or c'ün); mông-zin'-t'iao 望°前°跳; ditto (as an animal); boh-ko'-ky'i 撲過去°;— up (as a plant), c'ih ch'ih 出; pao'-c'ih 苞出; will — (i. e. is elastic), neng-shoh'-neng-sing 能縮能伸

SPRINKLE, to — water about, tsah shü 撒水°;— over (as from a watering pot, &c), ling shü 淋水°; to — a little salt, tsah ih-tin yin' 撒°一點鹽

SPROUTS, ngô-den' 芽°頭°; vegetable —, ts'æ-iang 菜秧; paddy —, koh'-ngô 穀芽°; bean —, deo-ngô 荳芽°; tender bamboo —, neng-shing-den' 嫩筍頭°

SPROUT, to ts'iu ngô' 抽芽°; fah ngô' 發芽°

SPUNGE, SEE SPONGE.

SPURIOUS, kô 假°;— dollar, kô' fæn-ping' 假番餅; ditto (brass in the middle), ka'-pæn 鋸°版; ditto, (no sound), ô-pæn 啞版; ditto (having a hollow sound), moh-pæn' 木版

SPURN, to disdain, k'en' feh-ky'i 看弗起; to reject, ky'i'-diao 棄了°

SPURT, to — out, piao-c'ih-læ' 潎出來

SPY who watches others, t'en'-ts 探子:— sent to inspect an enemy's movements, &c, kæn-si' 奸°細

SPY, to — into one's movements, &c, k'en dong'-zing 看動靜

SQUABBLE, to — over a petty matter, siao' z-ken nao-do'-de 小爭幹鬧大°了°

SQUALL of wind, ih-dziao fong' 一陣°風; violent —, u-'fong-mang-pao' 烏風猛°颮;— (as a child), sah'-k'eo kyiao' 竭力叫;— of wind and rain, zi-fong'-zi-yü' 橫°風橫°雨; ditto in the hills, sæn ts'iah' fong 山峭°風

SQUARE, s'-koh-fông' 四角°方°; tih'-koh-fông' 的°角°方°; a —, ih'-go cün-fông' 一个°轉方°; ih-fông' 一方°; two feet —, nyi ts'ah' cün-fông' 二°尺°轉方°;— table, fông-coh' 方桌;— board, fông pæn' 方板; carpenter's —, koh'-ts'ih 角°尺

SQUASH, nen-kwô' 南瓜; væn-kwô' 飯瓜 (ih-go)

SQUASH, to — by a fall, tih'-wu 跌廚

SQUAT, to —, t'ah'-di-zo 塌地坐; ts'ing'-di-zo 趁地坐

SQUEEZE, to — in the hand, nyiah-long'-ky'i 捻攏去°;— out juice, tsih'-shü tsô'-c'ih 汁水°榨出;— through, a-c'ih' 挨出; ditto a hole, zah'-c'ih dong-ngæn'-li 囥°出洞眼°裡;—, or hug, gyih-long' 扱攏;— money, tsô dong-din 詐銅錢; soh'-tsô dong-din 索詐銅錢°; tsô'-ziao dong-din' 詐擾銅錢°; to be squeezed (as to money), zông-tsô'-zông 上醉床°

SQUINT, to —, zia k'en 斜看; — with eyes half shut, mi'-leh-k'en' 眯了°看
SQUINTING eyes, zia'-bah-ngæn 斜°白眼°; half shut eyes, mi'-ts'i-ngæn' 眯眦眼°
SQUIRREL, song-c'ü' 松鼠 (ih-tsah); gray — fur, hwe-c'ü' bi 灰鼠皮
STAB, to pierce, c'oh 猎; c'oh'-tsing 猎進
STABLE for a horse, mô'-vông 馬房; — for cattle, ngeo-gyin'-kæn 牛°樋間°
STABLE, firm, kyin-kwu' 堅固; lao-k'ao' 牢靠
STACK of straw, ts'ao'-bong 草蓬
STAFF, stick, kweng'-ts 棍子; old person's —, æ'-dziang 接杖; kwa'-dziang 拐°杖
STAG, yüong-loh' 雄鹿 (ih-tsah)
STAGE of a journey, ih-dzæn' lu — 站路; the first ditto, deo-dzæn' 頭站; platform for play-acting, hyi'-dæ 戲臺; to erect a —, tah hyi'-dæ 搭戲臺
STAGGER, to c'ong'-c'ong-dong' 衝衝動; ts'ih-c'ong'-pah-tih 七衝八跌
STAGNANT water, si'-shü 死°水°
STAGNATION in trade, sang-i' feh-dong' 生°意弗來°
STAIN, to spot, tsao tsih' 遭漬; tang tsih'; hands are stained, siu' yiu ngæn-seh' tsao'-tih 手有

顏°色遭的; — (as wood before varnishing), tang ti'-ts 打底子; ts'eng ti'-ts 襯底子 — (as glass), 'o ngæn-seh' 和顏°色
STAIRS, lu-t'æ' 扶°梯 (a flight, ih-bu); go up —, leo-teng' ky'i 樓上°去°; zông-leo' 上樓; down —, leo-'ô' 樓下°
STAKE, công 椿 (ih-keng)
STALE, dzing 陳; excessively —, dzing-nyin'-pah-kwu 陳年百°古; — bread, dzing mun'-deo 陳饅頭
STALK, a — of corn, ih-cü' loh-koh' 一棵稷穀; a — of wheat, ih-kwang mah' 一根麥°; — of a flower, hwô-kwang' 花莖° (ih-ts).
STALK, to — with long steps, do-bu' doh 大°步踱; — proudly, tseo'-leh do-mo' do-yiang 走得大°模大°樣
STALL for merchandize, t'æn 攤;* ma-hô'-t'æn 買貨攤; — for cattle, ngeo-gyin' 牛°樋
* T'æn generally refers to goods spread out on boards, or by the road-side without shelter.
STALLION, yüong-mô' 雄馬 (ih-p'ih)
STAMMER, to kông-leh t'a-ngô'-gying-k'eo' 講得°拖牙礙口
STAMMERING, hesitating, ngao'-zih-keng-go 皎舌根个°; bun'-zih-keng-go 絆舌根个°; — speech, k'eo'-ts' deng' 口齒鈍;

k'eo'-ts' ngao'-zih-keng-go 口齒鹻舌根个°

STAMP, to — the foot, teng kyiah' 蹭腳; to — a seal (officially), tang ing' 打印; — one's name, tang du-shü' 打圖書

STANCH in heart, sing kyin' 心堅

STANCH, to — blood, ts hyüih' 止血

STAND, kô'-ts 架°子; clothes —, i-kô' 衣架°; wash —, min-kô' 面架°; pen —, pih-kô' 筆架°

STAND, to lih 立; — up, lih-ky'i'-læ 立起來; — erect, pih'-dzih lih'-tong 筆直立在° 此°; — firm (don't fall), lih-leh-lao' 立得°定; lih-leh-weng' 立得°穩; cannot — firm, lih-feh-lao' 立弗定°; lih-feh-weng' 立弗穩; can neither sit nor — in peace, (i. e. restless), zo'-lih feh-en' 坐立弗安; can't — it, ün'-tsæ-wn-yiæ' 寃哉何°奈

STANDARD, banner, gyi 旗; — of comparison, tseh'-ts 則子; cing'-tseh 準則

STAR, sing 星; sing-siu', or sing-soh' 星宿; fixed —, 'eng-sing' 恒星; evening —, wông-hweng'-hyiao' 黃昏曉; morning —, ng'-kang-hyiao 五°更曉; shooting —, liu-sing' 流星; yi-sing' 移星 (ih-lih)

STAR-LIGHT, sing-kwông' 星光

STARCH, tsiang'-feng 漿粉; to make —, (by pouring water upon), ts'ong tsiang'-feng 冲漿粉

STARCH, to — clothes, tsiang i-zông' 漿衣裳°; — (it) stiff, tsiang'-leh ngang' 漿得硬; tsiang'-leh gyin' 漿得°健

STARE, to ts'ing'-ting-k'en' 瞠°叮看

START, to commence, k'æ-siu' 開手; — or light a fire, sang ho 生°火; — or kindle fire, ying ho 引火; — business, k'æ z' 開市; going to — an enterprise, iao tang' ih-fæn' gyin-kw'eng' 要做°一番事°業°; when does the boat —? jün' kyi'-z k'æ' 船幾時開? — on a journey, dong-sing' 動身; to — (in alarm), ky'ih'-ih-kying 吃一驚; — in sleep, kw'eng'-joh, kying diao'-kao 睡°熟°驚覺

STARTLE, to kying-dong' 驚動; must not — him, feh-k'o' kying-dong' gyi 弗可驚動其

STARTLED, to be ziu-kying' 受驚; were you —? ng ziu-kying' feh 你°受驚否°?

STARTLING intelligence, kying-hyiæ'-go sing'-sih 驚駭个°信息

STARVE, will iao ngo-sah' 要餓死°

STARVED to death, ngo-sah'-de 餓死了°

STARVING, ngo'-leh hyih'-hyih-dong' 餓得°吸吸動

STATE, *circumstances*, kwông-kying' 光景; ying-kying' 形景; *in a good* —, kwông-kying' hao' 光景好; *condition*, di-we' 地位; *to such a* — (*i. e.* bad), tao ka'-go di-bu' 到如此地步; *a* —, or *country*, koh'-kô國家°; *the state of ditto*, ky'i'-ziang 氣象; *in a declining* —, ky'i'-ziang sæ'-de 氣象衰了°; *to live in great* —, shæ-wô' ko kwông-ing' 奢華過光陰

STATE, *to* kao'-su 告訴; t'ong-cü' 通知;— *particulars*, dziang-si' kông'-c'ih-læ 詳細講°出來;— *grievances*, su ün' 訴冤;— (*to an inferior*), ping'-cü 稟知; ping'-ming 稟明

STATELY (*as a person*), kw'e-we' 傀偉; — (*as an official*), we-nyin'-go 威嚴个°

STATEMENTS *vary according to circumstances*, shih-wô cih'-læ biu-ky'i' 說話喫來辯去°

STATESMAN, *high officer*, da-dzing' 大臣; do-kwun' 大°官; *styled*, da-jing' 大人

STATION *in life*, sing-veng' 身分°; sing-kô' 身家°; *official* —, we-ts' 位子; *high* —, we-ts' kao' 位子高; *military* — (*place*), ying-sing 營汛; sing'- di 汛地

STATISTICAL *account* (of money), ts'ing-tæn' 清單; (of persons), ts'ing-ts'ah' 清册; *statistics of Chekiang province*, Tsih'- kông t'ong'-ts 浙江°統志

STATUE, *image*, ngeo'-ziang 偶像; *stone image*, zah-deo-'go ngeo'-ziang 石頭个偶像; zah' dzing-siang' 石丞相

STATUETTE, 'en 孩°; *soap-stone* —, væn-zah 'en' 礬石孩°; *jade* —, nyüöh 'en' 玉孩°

STATURE, sing-dzæ' 身材; *of great* —, sing-dzæ' dziang-do' 身材長大°; *of small* —, sing-dzæ' a'-siao 身材矮°小

STATUTE, *a* ih-diao lih-fah' 一條律法

STAY, *to* deng 停°;— *here*, deng'-tong 停°在°此°; — *a while*, deng' ih-zông 停°一息°; — *a long time*, deng'-leh dziang-kyiu'-de 停°得長久了°

STEADFAST, kyin-kwu' 堅固

STEADY, djong'-jih 重實; weng'-djong 穩重

STEAK, *meat for frying, &c.*, t'ah-go nyüoh' 爛个°肉°; *the best beef* — *is called* pah'-z-kweh-li-go nyüoh' 八字骨裡个°肉°, sæn-koh-lông, and ô-bang-kweh-yin'.

STEAL, *to* t'eo 偷; *to* — *time from one's proper duties*, t'eo- kong bah'-fu 偷工夫; *will not* —, siu'-kyiah' weng-djong 手脚穩重

STEALTHILY, t'eo-bun' 偷瞞°; en'-di-li 暗地裡

STEAM, shü'-go ky'i 水°个°氣

STEAM, to tsing 蒸; tsing-hen' 蒸煤;—(over something else that is cooking), hen 煤;— rice, tsing væn' 蒸飯

STEAM-BOAT, ho-leng-jün' 火輪船 (ih-tsah)

STEAM-CAR, ho-leng-ts'ô' 火輪車 (ih-dzing)

STEEL, kông 鋼;— (for striking fire), ho'-tao 火刀; ho'-p'in 火片

STEELYARDS, ts'ing 秤; small — (for silver, and medicines), teng'-ts 戥子; very small —, li teng' 厘戥

STEEP, shing 峋; toh 督 or song-dzih 聳°直°; precipitous, ts'iao-pih 峭壁 (veng.)

STEEP, to — in water, tsing' læ shü'-li 浸在°水°裡;— in hot water, p'ao' læ shü'-li 泡在°水°裡

This signification of p'ao is peculiar to Ningpo.

STEER, to pô do' 把舵; pô sao' 把艄

STEM, a ih-kwang' 一梗°

STEP, a ih-bu' 一步; to take a —, tseo' ih-bu' 走一步;— quickly (as when in an official's presence), tseo ts'iang'-bu 走蹌步; keep —, kyiah'-bu tseo'-leh tsæn'-zi 脚步走得°整°齊;— by —, bu-tang'-bu 步打步; long —, do bu' 大°步

STEP, to ky'i-bu' 起步;— over, bæn-zong' 蹚上; bæn-ko' 蹚過;— down, bæn-loh'-ky'i 蹚下去°; tseo'-loh 走下°; be careful in stepping in, and out, (as of a boat), bæn-zông' bæn-loh' tseo-leh hao' 蹚上蹚下°走得°好; can't — (as an old person), bæn-feh-dong' 蹚弗動

STEPS, short si' bu 細步; a woman's steps are short, nyü'-nying-go kyiah'-bu siao' 女人°个°脚步小; stone — (long flight), pah'-bu-kæn 百°步階; ditto (four or five), kah'-bu-kæn 隔步階;— at the water's edge, 'o-bu'-deo 河埠頭

STEP-MOTHER, in' ah-nyiang' 寄°阿娘; politely called, 'eo'-meo 後母; dzoh-meo' 續母; mæn'-nyiang 晚°娘 (coarse).

STEP-FATHER, nyi - vu' 義父; mæn'-tia 晚°爹°

STEREOSCOPE, si-yiang-kying' 西洋景

STERILE land, hwông-di' 荒地; di-t'u boh' 地土薄

STERN of a ship, 'eo'-sao 後艄

STERN, nyin-nyin'-go 嚴嚴个°; we-nyin' 威嚴; hyüong-sah'-sah 兇煞煞

STEW, to teng 燉; u 煀;— meat, teng nyüoh' 燉肉

STEWARD (of money, food, &c), pô-tsong'-go 把總个°

STICK, a ih-keng bông' 一根棒; a bit of board, ih-tin pæn-den' — 點板頭; ih-tin pæn'-pin-bi'

STI 452 STI

一點板邊皮; *a large round —,* ih-keng kweng'-ts 一根棍子
STICK, *to — in,* ts'ah'-tsing 插進; *ditto,* (as staves in a tub, a padlock in its place, &c.), siao-tsing' 銷進; *— a candle* (in its place), ts'ah lah-coh' 插蠟燭; *to — with paste,* (or as a plaster), t'iah vah°; nyin 粘; *— together,* nyin-long' 粘攏; *—* (it) *tight,* t'iah'-leh-lao' 貼得°牢; nyin'-leh-lao' 粘得°牢; *sticks to his own way,* kyü-nyi' feh-t'ong' 拘泥弗通; *in the wrong, but sticking to it,* ky'iang'-bin 強辯
STICKLAC, ts'-keng 紫梗
STICKY, nyin 粘; nyin-kao'-kao 粘膠°膠°; nyin-cü'-keh-tah, (also applied to persons).
STIFF, ngang 硬; *—* (in opinion), zah-ngang' 石°硬; gyiang 強; sang-gyiang' 生°強
STIFF-NECKED, gyiang-deo'-gyüih nao' 強頭倔腦
STIFLING, meng-ky'i' 悶氣
STIGMATIZED, ming-sing' u-wæ'-diao-de 名聲污壞了°; p'ing-'ang tsao-tsih'-de 品行遭跡了°
STILL, *no sound,* soh'-zing 肅靜°; pih'-zing 謐靜°; 无-sing-hyiang' 無°聲響; zing'-ts'iao-ts'iao 靜°悄悄; *not moving,* feh-dong' 弗動; *sit —,* zo-leh ding' 坐得°定; *the wind and waves are —,* bing-fong' zing'-lông 平風靜浪

STILL, *yet,* wa; yia 也°; yi 又°; wæn 還; *— as before,* dzing-gyiu' z-ka' 仍舊如°此°; *— more,* 'o-hwông' 何況; *—* (used with the comparative), yü-kô 愈加°; keng-kô 更加°; yüih-fah' 越發; *— better,* yü-kô' hao 愈加°好
STIMULATE, *to urge,* ts'e 催; ts'e-ts'oh' 催促; *to encourage,* min'-li 勉勵
STIMULATED *to effort,* (by seeing another better than ourselves, or by our own dispraise), tsang' ih-k'eo' ky'i' 爭°一口氣
STIMULATING *to strength,* dzu-lih'-go 助力个°
STING, *to* ting 叮
STING *of a bee,* wông-fong-ts 黃蜂刺; *the place stung* (swollen), ting'-go tsing' 叮个°痕°迹°; *ditto* (red but not swollen), pæn 斑
STINGY, kyü-seh'-seh 鬼°嗇嗇; lin'-kyin 斂儉; gyih-li'-li 竭厲厲; 'eo-teo'-teo 猴抖抖; pi'-si 鄙細; pi'-nying 鄙客; pi'-seh 鄙嗇; nying'-seh 客嗇; k'æn-kyiang' 鉛僵
STINKING, ts'iu 臭°; zeh-ts'iu' 雜臭°
STINT, *to* k'æn'-k'ah-loh 苛°刻°; *to — rations,* ky'üih'-kæn kyüing-liang' 鈌減°軍粮
STIPULATIONS, iah'-hao-liao-go tsông-dzing 約好了°个°章程 (tsông or công)

STI 453 STO

STIR, *to move,* dong 動; — *up by talking,* ts'ön-teh' 攛掇; — *up (as something forgotten),* t'iao-peh' 挑撥; *to agitate,* yiao-'oh' 謠惑; — *and render turbid,* dao-weng' 掏混; *the wind stirs the leaves,* fong dong' jü'-yih 風動樹葉; *to —* (as food), liu-liu' 捯捯; diao-long' 調攏; kao-kao' 攪攪; diao-diao' 調調; *one who stirs up trouble,* liu-ho'-coh-bông' 像°捯火竹棒个°人°

STIR, *great* nao-nyih' fi-væn' 鬧熱°非凡

STIRRING, *is anything —* (*i. e.* in a town, &c.)? yiu soh'-go kyü-dong' feh 有甚°麼°舉動否°?

STIRRUP, mô'-dah-teng 馬踏鐙 (ih-tsah; *a pair,* ih-fu)

STITCH, tsing-kyiah' 針脚; sin'-kyiah 線脚 (ih-go); *take a —,* ting' ih-tsing 紅一針; *take small stitches,* tsing-kyiah' iao si' 針脚要細; *grinning stitches,* sin'-kyiah li-ngô'-bô'-ts' 線脚齜牙°齟齒

STITCH, *to sew,* vong 縫; *to back- —* (like machine work), keo 勾; ts'ih 緝; *— finer,* vong-leh si'-tin 縫得°細點; *— together,* keo-long' 勾攏; *—* (by over-handing), nyiao-long'; *— a book together,* ting shü 紅書

STOCK *in trade,* peng'-din 本錢°; *to take account of —,* bun ts'ing-tsiang' 盤清賬; *gun —,* ts'iang ken'-ts 鎗杆子

STOCK-FISH, ts'-ng 紫魚°

STOCKINGS, mah 襪 (*a pair,* ih-sông)

STOCKS *for the feet,* kyiah'-kô 脚柳

STOMACH, we 胃; we-un' 胃腕; bi-we' 脾胃; zih-pao' 食包; *pit of the —,* sing-o-den' 心窩°潭°; hyüong-o-den' 胸窩°潭°; *pain in the —,* we t'ong' 胃痛; — (or belly) *ache,* du'-bi t'ong 肚皮痛

STONE, zah-deo' 石頭 (*a piece,* ih-kw'e); *a flat —,* zah-pæn' 石°版; *small —* zah-ts' 石°子; *precious —,* pao'-zah 寶石°; — (of fruit), weh 核°

STONE, *to — a person,* yüong zah-deo' k'ang nying 用石°頭丢人°

STONE-CUTTER, zah-s-vu' 石°司務; zah-ziang' 石°匠

STONE-SHOP, zah-tsoh'-tin 石°作店

STONE-QUARRY, zah-dông' 石°宕°

STOOL, *long wooden —,* pæn'-teng 板櫈; *bamboo —,* coh' fông-teng 竹方櫈; *foot —,* dah-kyiah'-teng 踏脚櫈; *drum shaped stone or porcelain —,* zah-kwu' 石°鼓; — (for night use), yia-dong 夜°桶; mô'-dong 馬桶; *ditto for travelling,*

STO 454 STO

sæn'-dong 杉桶; ditto, (a box), yia-dong'-siang 夜°桶箱; to go to —, cʻih-kong' 出恭; ka-siu' 解°手; evacuation, do-bin' 大°便; do-ka' 大°解°

STOOP, to eo 傴°; — the head, eo deo° 傴°頭; — down, eo-tæn'-tao 傴°倒; — in walking, eo deo tseo' 傴°頭走

STOP, to hinder, lah-djü' 攔°住; tsu'-djü 阻住; tsʻ-djü 止住; — in walking, lih-loh' 立住°; — a minute, lih'-ih-lih' 立一立; — talking, hyih kʻeo' 住°口; — by filling up (as a hole), seh'-mun 塞滿; din-mun' 塡滿; — (as a window), cü'-sah; tsʻ-sah; — up the way, læn lu' 攔路; will soon —, ih-zông' ziu hyih'-go 一息°就歇个°; — doing, hyih-sin' 歇手; — over night, hyih'-ko yia' 歇過夜°; canʼt — (it, or him), tsʻ-feh-djü' 止弗住

STOPPED, hyih'-loh-de 歇落了°; — talking, kông' hyih-de 講歇了°; clock has —, cong' ve tseo'-de 鐘不°會°走了°; cong si'-de 鐘死了°; cong ngæ'-de 鐘呆了°; cong ve cün'-de 鐘不°會°轉了°; cong hyih'-de 鐘歇了°; cong deng'-de 鐘停°了°

STOPPING, where are you —? ng tæn-koh' ah-li' 你°攸攔何°處°! — place, hyih'-loh-go di-fông' 歇落个°地方; deng-loh'-go di-fông 停°落个°地方

STOPS (in punctuation), tin'-dön 點斷; ditto (in Chinese), kyʻün-tin' 圈點

STORE, ʻông 行; tin 店 (or 鋪); — for foreign goods, yiang-ho'-ʻông 洋貨行; kwông'-ho-tin 廣貨店; book —, shü-fông' 書坊 (ih-bæn)

STORE, to — away, kʻông'-lob 囥落; deng-tsih' 囥積; dzeng-tsih' 存積; — up (by constant addition), tsih'-loh 積落; tsih'-jü 積聚; tsih'-hyüoh 積蓄

STORE-HOUSE, dzæn'-vông 棧房; tea —, dzô-dzæn' 茶棧; — for grain, tsʻông 倉

STORK, ngôh 鶴; sacred —, sin-ngôh' 仙鶴 (ih-tsah)

STORM, do-fong'-do-yü' 大°風大°雨; sudden —, (black sky), u-fong'-mang-pao' 烏風猛°颱; — of wind, gwông-fong' 狂風; bao'-fong 暴風

STORY, one — house, bing oh' 平屋; bing-vông' 平房; two — house, leo-oh' 樓屋; three — house, sæn-zeng'-leo 三層樓

STORY, kwu'-z 故事; tell you a —, kông ih-yiang kwu'-z peh ng tʻing' 講一樣故事俾°你°聽; ditto — of olden times, kông kwu'-tin 講古典; tell (or quote) a — in illustration, ying ih'-go kwu'-z 引一个°故事

STOUT, *fat*, công'-do 壯大°; *of — arm*, siu'-gying do' 手勁大°.
STOVE, ho'-lu 火爐; t'ih'-lu 鐵爐; *cooking* —, t'ih'-tsao 鐵竈.
STOW, *to — away*, tsông 裝; dzông 藏; k'ông 囥; *— goods*, tsông ho' 裝貨; *— away in the mind* (also not to tell), dzông' læ du'-bi-li 藏在肚皮裡.
STRADDLE, *to* pa zo-mô'-shü 擺坐馬勢.
STRAGGLER, 'æn-nying' 閒人°.
STRAGGLING *in one after another*, ts'iu-ts'in' læ 揪軸來; *— behind*, loh 'eo' 落後.
STRAIGHT, dzih 直; pih'-dzih 筆直; pih'-lib-dzih 筆立直; kweh'-dzih 骨直; *go — ahead*, ih-dzih'-bah-deo 對°鼻°頭一直去°.
STRAIGHTEN, *to — it*, long gyi dzih' 弄其直.
STRAIGHT-FORWARD, sing'dzih'-go 心直个°;* *—* (*in action*), li'-dzih-ky'i-công' 理直氣壯 (công or tsông); *— in speaking*, dzong dzih' kông' 從直講°; tsiao' dzih kông' 照直講°; *— talk*, dzih wô' 直話; tsiao' yin-dzih dæn' 照言直談.
 * Observe that dzih-sing'-go 直心个° has not this sense, but the bad sense of blunt, or abrupt.
STRAIN, *to —* (as milk, &c.), li 濾; *to over-exert one's strength*, lih' yüong ko-deo' 力用過頭; *to*

exert to the utmost, nu'-lih 努力; 'eo-ky'i-lih 侯氣力.
STRAIN, *the — is too great*, (i. e. pulled too tightly, as cloth, &c.), te'-leh t'eh kyih' 㧕得太°急; *ditto* (as in mental effort), kong-k'o' bih'-leh t'eh kying' 功課逼°得太°緊.
STRAITENED, *in — circumstances*, kying'-hwông kyih'-pah 景況急廹.
STRAND, *a* ih-kwu' sang 一股生°; *a single —*, doh-kwu'-deo 獨股頭; *three strands*, sæn-kwu'-sang 三股生°.
STRANGE, hyi-gyi' 希奇; gyi-kwa' 奇怪°; kwu'-kwa 古怪°; hao gyi-kwa' 好奇怪; *not at all —*, kwa'-feh-teh 怪°弗得; *not according to the common way*, yi'-yiang 異樣.
STRANGER, *unacquainted person*, sang-deo' nying 生°人°; sang-su'-go nying 生°疏个°人°; *— whose home is in another place*, yi'-hyiang nying 異鄉人°; gyiao-yüa' nying 隔°縣人°.
STRANGLE, *to* ts'eh'-sah 挓殺; leh-sah' 勒殺; *—* (as a punishment), kao'-sah 絞°殺.
STRAP, *leather* bi-ta' 皮帶°; *Chinese barber's —*, kwah'-tao-pu 刮刀布.
STRATAGEM, tsô'-kyi 詐計; kyi-meo' 計謀; kyi'-kao 計較'.
STRAW, ts'ao 草; *rice —*, dao'-

ts'ao 稻草; *wheat* —, mah-ken' 麥稈; *new* —, sing ts'ao' 新草; *old* —, dzing ts'ao' 陳草; — *braid*, ts'ao'-mao bin 草帽辮; — *tied together for a mattress*, ts'ao'-tsin 草氈

STRAWBERRY, *tree* —, or *arbutus*, yiang-me' 楊梅 (ih-go)

STRAW-COLORED, dæn'-wông 淡黃

STRAY, *to deviate from the right*, tseo ts'o' lu 走差路; *to lose the way and become bewildered*, mi-lu' 迷路; — *lamb*, mi-lu'-go yiang' 迷路个°羊

STREAKED, yiu hwô-veng' 有花紋

STREAKY, hwô-kying'-da 花經堠; hwô-yüing'-da 花雲堠

STREAM *of water*, ih-liu shü' 一溜水°; *rivulet*, ky'i-k'ang' 溪坑; *mountain* —, sæn-loh-shü' 山落水° (ih-da)

STREET, ka 街°; lu-ka' 路街°; ka-lu' 街°路; ka-dao' 街道; (ih-da); *great* —, do ka' 大街°; *narrow* —, long 衖 (ih-diao)

STRENGTH, lih 力; ky'i'-lih 氣力; lih-dao' 力道; gying-dao' 勁道; — (used principally of medicines), sing'-dao 性道; sing 性; *to do according to one's* —, liang'-lih-r-ying' 量力而行; *with all one's heart, and* —, dzing-sing' gyih-lih' 盡心竭力; *united* —, dong-sing' yiah'-

lih' 同心恊力; *no* —, m̀ ky'i'-lih 無°氣力; m̀ gying'-dao 無°勁道; *no* — *to do*, vu-lih'-neng-we' 無力能爲; (person's) — *exhausted*, ky'i'-lih dziah-wun'-de 氣力用°完了°; *its* — *is gone*, sing'-dao ko'-de 性道過了°; *no* —, (used either of body or mind), nyün'-bi-bi 軟疲疲; pih'-hyi-hyi 皕希希; *but little* —, lih boh' 力薄; lih feb-tsoh' 力弗足

STRENGTHEN, *to* —*him*, kô-zông' gyi-go lih' 加上其个°力; dzu' gyi'-go lih' 助其个°力; pông' gyi-go lih' 幫其个°力; — *it*, dzu'-ih-dzu lih' 助一助力; — *one's faith*, kyin-kwu' gyi siang-sing'-go sing' 堅固其相信个°心; — (as by a tonic), pu lih' 補力

STRENGTHENING (as food, or medicine), pu-lih-dao'-go 補力道个°; pu-hyüih'-ky'i-go 補血氣个°; pu-tsing-jing'-go 補精神个°

STRENUOUS, *to make* — *effort*, sah'-k'eo c'ih-lih' 煞口出力; 'eo ky'i'-lih 候氣力

STRESS, *to lay* — *upon*, djong-k'en' 重看; *lay* — *on that sentence*, keb kyü shih-wô' iao djong-k'en' 這°句説話要重看

STRETCH, *to* te'-k'æ-læ 推開來; la-k'æ'-læ; — *out*, sing-dziang 伸長; *to* — *out the hand*, sing sin' 伸手; can't — it, te'-feh-k'æ 自弗開; la-feh-k'æ'; — a bow, la kong' 拉弓; pæn kong' 扳°弓.

STRICT, nyin 嚴; nyin-kying' 嚴禁; too —, t'eh nyin' 太°嚴; kwe'-kyü tso ko-deo' 規矩甚°嚴°; the — teacher turns out good scholars, nyin-s' c'ih kao-du' 嚴師出高徒; not — enough, iah'-soh peh-nyin' 約束不嚴.

STRIFE of words, k'eo'-kyüoh siang-tsang' 口角相爭°; ditto with abuse, zao-nyih-oh-cü; at —, kæ'-tih siang-tsang' 正°在°相爭°.

STRIKE, n. (because of a stern master, &c.), sæn-dông' 散堂.

STRIKE, to k'ao 敲°; tang 打; — a blow, k'ao'-ih-kyi' 敲°一記; tang ih-kyi' 打一記; — against, bang-djoh' 摃着'; djông-djoh' 撞着; — fire, k'æ ho' 開火; tang ho' 打火; the clock strikes, cong' læ-tih k'ao' 鐘正°在°敲°; — dead by lightning, le tang'-sah 雷打殺; le kyih' 雷炙.

STRING, zing 繩°(ih-keng); cash —, dzin-c'ün' zing 錢串繩°; a — of cash, ih-c'ün' dong-din' 一串銅錢°; a — of fire crackers, ih-c'ün' pah'-ts-p'ao 一串百°子爆.

STRING, to c'ün 穿; — porcelain beads, c'ün ngô'-cü 穿瓦°珠

STRIP, a — of paper, ih-da ts' 一㮋紙; ih-diao ts' 一條紙; cover with a —, kæ' ih-zeng zông' 蓋一屑°上.

STRIP, to — off clothing, t'eh i-zông' 脫衣裳; to — another, poh' nying-kô' i-zông' 剝人°衣裳°; — off bark, poh bi' 剝皮; to — off a garment and pawn it, in order to gamble, poh' bi tu' 剝皮賭; — naked, i-zông' poh'-kwông 衣裳°剝光; poh'-leh kying'-kwông 剝得°精光.

STRIPE, dzih-veng' 直紋 (ih-da)

STRIPED cloth, (of one color), liu'-diao pu 柳條布; ditto (in colors), hwô-dzih'-veng pu' 花直紋布.

STRIPES, beat with many —, tang hyü'-to pæn'-su 打許多板數 tang hyü'-to kyi'-su 打許多記數.

STRIVE, to tsang 爭°; — with, siang-tsang' 相爭°; te'-toh 對敵°; — to get ahead of, pih gying' 逼勁; — to be first, tsang zông-zin' 爭°上前°; — for a prize, ts'iang sông' 搶賞; — for the goal, ts'iang' piao-deo' 搶標頭; — to enter in, zing'-lih ts'ang'-tsing 盡°力撐進.

STROKE, n. kwah 摑; give a —, kwah' ih-kwah 摑一摑; pen —, pih' wah 筆畫; how many strokes? kyi pih' 幾筆?

STROKE, to lo 擺; lo'-kwah 擺

个°;— *to injury,* k'eng ky'üoh kw'e' 肯吃°虧

SUBSCRIBE, *to write one's name,* loh ming-z' 錄名字;— *money,* sia kyün' 寫°捐; *how much did he* —? gyi' sia to-siao' kyün' 其寫多少捐? gyi' kyün-kw'un' to-siao' 其捐款多少?

SUBSCRIBERS, loh-ming-z-go nying 錄名字个°人°; *a poster containing names of — to charity, &c.,* piao-'ong' 標°紅

SUBSCRIPTION (of money), kyün-'ong' 捐項; kyün-kw'un' 捐款;— *paper,* kyün-tæn' 捐單

SUBSEQUENT, 'eo'-deo 後頭;— *age,* 'eo' shü 後世

SUBSIDE, *to* t'e'-loh-ky'i 退下°去°; 'ô'-loh-ky'i 下°去°; bing-loh'-ky'i 平下°去°; *wait till his anger* —, teng'-tao gyi'-go nu' t'e'-loh-ky'i 等到其个°怒退落去°

SUBSIST *day by day,* djoh nyib' tso nying' 逐日°做人°; *they — on rice,* væn, z gyi-lab' yiang' ming' go 飯是伊°等°養命个°

SUBSISTENCE, *means of* yiang'-seng-ts veh' 養生之物; du-nyih'-ts liang' 度日°之糧; *to make a* —, wu k'eo' 餬口; wu cü'-pô 餬嘴吧; du-weh' 度活; du-nyih' 度日°

SUBSTANCE, tsih 質; peng'-tsih 本質; ti'-ts 底子; ying 形; *as the shadow follows the* —, jü ing', ze ying' 如影隨形; *a man of* —, yiu kô-dzæ'-go 有家°財个°

SUBSTANTIAL, 'eo'-jih 厚實; *firm,* lao-k'ao' 牢靠; tsah'-cü.

SUBSTITUTE *for a teacher,* gyün' sin'-sang 權館°先生°;— *for a servant, or workman,* t'i'-kong 替工; *one who dies as a* —, t'i-si'-go 替死°个°

SUBSTITUTE, *to* gyün 權; diao 調; wun 換;— *another pen for that,* keh'-ts pih gyün'-ih-gyün' 這枝筆權一權; diao' ih-ts' pih' 調一枝筆; wun' ih-ts' pih' 換一枝筆

SUBTERFUGE, *to resort to a* —, kô'-t'oh 假°托; *to use something true, but not the real cause as a* —, tsia'-ing 借°因

SUBTERRANEAN, di-'ô'-go 地下°个°; di ti'-'ô-go 地底下°个°

SUBTILE, *delicate and fine,* tsing-si' 精細°

SUBTLE, *cunning,* diao-bi' 刁°疲; diao-wæn' 刁°頑

SUBTRACT, *to* djü-loh' 除下°; djü-c'ih' 除出; kæn'-loh 減落

SUBTRACTION, djü-fah' 除法

SUBURB, dzing-meng'-'ô 城門下°; *the Eastern* —, Tong-meng-nga' 東門外°

SUBVERT, *to* fæn'-tao 翻倒; *he subverts my authority,* ngô'-go gyün-ping' tao'-fæn gyi siu'-li' 我个°權柄倒翻其手裡

SUCCEED, to — in doing, tso' tao siu' 做到手; tso' dzing-kong' 做成功; to prosper, jing'-liu 順溜; — (by getting hold of the right way), teh-fah' 得法; teh ky'iao'-meng 得竅門; does not — (i. e. is not according to my mind), feh ts'ing' ngô-go sing 弗稱我个心; feh jing'-liu 弗順溜; — in every thing, pah'-z-beng-t'ong' 百事亨通; deo-deo'-jing'-liu 頭頭順溜; he who is in earnest will —, yiu' ts kying dzing 有志竟成.

SUCCEED, to follow after, tsih 接; to take the place of, dæ tso' 代做; who will — me? jü' we teng ngô dæ-tso' 誰會與我代做! — to the throne, tsih-we' 接位; teng-we' 登位.

SUCCESSFUL, jing-tông' 順當; jing-kying' 順境; always —, ih-lu'-jing-fong' 一路順風; in obtaining one's desire, ts'ing'-sing-jü-i' 稱心如意; jü-sing' 如心; this is a — year (in trade, or literary examinations), keh' nyin da-fah'-go 這年大發个; who is the — candidate, (i.e. who enjoys the happiness)? keh'-go foh' jü hyiang'-de 這个福誰享了?

SUCCEEDING, the — days, tsih-lin-go nyih-ts' 接連个日子.

SUCCESSION, in —, or in order, a-ts'-jü 挨次序; tsiao ts'-jü 照次序; i ts''-jü 依次序; in — (each taking his turn, as the spokes of a wheel), leng-liu' 輪流; ling 輪; enter in —, yü-kwun'-r-jih' 魚貫而入; ngao' mi'-pô tsing-læ' 鮫尾巴進來.

SUCCESSIVE years, lih nyin' 歷年; four — years of famine, lih-nyin' s'-go hwông nyin' 歷年四个荒年; four — days, deh-lin' s' nyih 疊連四日.

SUCCINCT, kyin'-kyih 簡潔.

SUCCOR, to help, pông-dzu 幫助; pông-ts'eng' 幫襯; — the poor, tsiu-tsi' nying' 賙濟人; k'en'-kwu gyüong-nying' 看顧窮人.

SUCCUMB, to deo-voh' 投服.

SUCH, keh'-cü-ka or keh'-cong-ka 這種樣; keh'-sing-ka 這些樣; z-ka' 是如此; — as he, ziang gyi' nying' ka 像其人一樣个.

SUCK, to cih 啜; — (as wind), hwun 喚; — milk, cih na' 啜嬭; ky'üoh na' 吃嬭.

SUCKLE läm, ü' gyi na-na' 咻其嬭嬭; peh' gyi ky'üoh næ'-næ 給其吃嬭嬭.

SUDDENLY, hweh'-r-jün 忽然; deh-jün' 突然; p'ih'-min 劈面; p'ih'-deo 劈頭; p'ih'-k'ong 劈空.

SUE, to kao-zông' 告狀; to prosecute (on both sides), tang-kwun-s' 打官司; ky'tioh kwun s' 吃官司

SUET, *beef* ngeo-yiu' 牛°油; *mutton* —, yiang-yiu' 羊油

SUFFER, *to* ziu næn' 受難; ziu kw'u' 受苦; — *great pain*, ziu kw'u'-t'ong 受苦痛; — *injury*, ziu 'æ' 受害; ky'tioh kw'e' 吃°虧; — *hunger*, t'eng-kyi'-ziu-ngo 吞饑受餓; — *persecution*, ziu pih'-næn 受逼難

SUFFER, *to let*, peh 任°; — *him to talk*, peh gyi kông' 任°其講°

SUFFICIENT, keo'-de 够了°; tsoh'-de 足了°

SUFFOCATE, *to* ih'- sah 噎煞; ih'-ky'i-feh-cün' 噎氣弗轉; *I was nearly suffocated*, ngô ts'ô'-feh-to ih'-sah-de 我差弗多噎煞了°; ngô ih'-sah kw'a'-de 我噎煞快了°

SUFFUSED, *eyes — with tears*, ngæn-li' 'en'-tih 眼°淚合的; ngræn'-li wông-wông' 眼°淚汪汪

SUGAR, dông 糖; *white —*, bah dông' 白°糖; *dark brown —*, wông dông' 黃糖; *raw —*, sô dông' 沙糖; *rock —, or rock candy*, ping dông' 冰糖

SUGAR-BOWL, dông-kwun' 糖罐 (ih-tsah)

SUGAR-CANE, ken-tsô' 甘蔗°; dông tsô' 糖蔗°

SUGGEST, *to — (to another)*, di-ky'i' 提起; — *a subject*, c'ih di-moh' 出題目; *to cause another to remember*, di-sing' 提醒; *to give a hint* (of something forgotten), di-deo' 提頭

SUGGESTIONS, *to make —, to*, ts'-kyiao 指教; ts'-ying 指引

SUICIDE, *to commit —*, zi-veng' 自°刎; zing-tön'-kyin 尋°短見°; zi-zing'-si 自°尋°死°; zi-sah'-zi 自°殺自°; *wishing to commit —*, zing-si'-ming-weh' 尋°死°覓活

SUIT, *a — of clothes*, ih-t'ao' i-zông' 一套衣裳; ih-sing' i-zông' 一身衣裳

SUIT, *to —, or be suitable*, cong'-i 中意; 'eh-i' 合意; 'eh-sih' 合式; *do not — each other*, (persons), feh deo'-kyi 弗投機; *it suits me exactly*, tsing'-hao cong-ngô'-go i' 正好中我个°意

SUITABLE, te'-go 對个°; siang-te'-go 相對个°; 'eh-shih' 合式 (shih or sih); 'eh-i' 合意

SULLEN, fông-tiao' 放刁; — *countenance*, min-k'ong' moh-heh' 面孔墨黑; min-k'ong' heh'-pông 面有°怒容

SULPHUR, liu-wông' 硫磺

SULTRY, nyih'-leh meng-ky'i'-go 熱°得°悶氣个°; *very hot*, tsih'-lah-lah-go nyih' 炙辣辣个°熱°; *close and oppressive weather*, t'in'-ky'i sch'-meng 天氣塞悶

SUM, *the — (of numbers)*, gong'-

SUM 463 SUP

kyi 共計; tsong'-su 總數;
t'ong'-gong 統共
Sum, to — up, kyih tsong'-tsiang
揭總賬; to — up the whole,
tsong'-r-yin'-ts 總而言之
Summer, 'Ô-t'in' 夏°天; the festival at the beginning of —, lih-
'Ô' tsih 立夏°節
Summit of a hill, sæn-ting-den'
山頂
Summon, to djün 傳;— the spirits, dziao kyü' læ 召°鬼°來
Summons, a — to appear, djün-
p'iao' 傳票; ditto (official), gyün-sing'-ba 傳訊牌°
Sumptuously, live ky'üoh'-c'ün
tu shæ-wô' 吃°穿都奢華
Sun, nyih-deo' 日°頭; t'a'-yiang
太°陽; the — is shining brightly,
(i.e. strongly), mang'-mang nyih-
deo' 旰°旰°日°頭; put (it) in
the —, fông' læ nyih-deo' 'ô 放
在°日°頭下°
Sun, to sa 曬°; sa'-djoh 曬着°;
— a while, sa'-ih-sa' 曬一曬°;
— (something damp), tsiao'-ih-
tsiao' 照一照
Sunbeam, a — entered, ih-da'
nyih-kwông zih-tsing'-læ 一埭
日°光射進來
Sunburnt, dark colored, sa'-heh-
go 曬°黑个°; reddish brown,
sa'-'ong-joh'-de 曬°紅熟了°
Sunday, li'-pa-nyih 禮拜°日°;
en-sih'-nyih 安息日°; Cü'-nyih
主日°

Sun-dial, jih-kwe' 日晷
Sun-flower, gwe-hwô' 葵花;
hyiang'-jih-gwe 向日葵
Sundry, kyi'-yiang' 幾樣;—
goods, zah ho' 雜貨
Sunrise, nyih-deo' c'ih-ky'i' 日°
頭出起
Sunset, nyih-deo' loh-sæn' 日°
頭落山
Sunshine, nyih-kwông' 日°光
Superannuated, lao'-joh 老
弱°; (polite), lao'-moh-long'-cong
老邁龍鍾; to be excused from
office on account of being —, kao'-
lao wæn-hyiang' 告老還鄉
Supercargo, ah'-ho 押°貨
Supercilious, ngæn-kao' 眼°高;
moh-cong'-vu-jing' 目中無人;
ngæn'-tsing sang-læ mi-mao-
teng' 眼°睛生°在°眉毛上°
Superficial, veo-min' 浮面;
shallow, ts'in 淺: ts'in'-gying 淺
近;— learning, 'oh-veng' ts'in'-
go 學°問淺个°;— (as work),
tsih'-du nga-kwông'-min 只圖
外°光面; tsih' pang nga-meng'-
min 只繃外°門面; deo-vu'-
bi t'iah ngæn'-tsing 荳腐皮貼
眼°睛
Superfluous, vu-kwæn'-kying-
iao' 無關緊要; what is left
after using, yüong-ko' yiu-yü'
用過有餘; what is over and
useless, to'-go feh 'eh-yüong' 多
个°弗合用
Superintend, to tin'-toh 點督;

— (as an officer), toh'-li 督理; to control, kwun 管; kæ-kwun' 該管; tsih'-tsông 職掌; tsông'-kwun 掌管

SUPERINTENDENT, tin-toh'-go nying 點督個人; one who helps another by superintending a particular department, yü-z'-go 與事個; — of work, toh-kong'-go 督工個

SUPERIOR, zông 上; zông-deo' 上頭; zông-teng' 上等; ts'iao-teng' 超等; — to him (or that), kyü-gyi'-ts-zông 居其之上; — to other men, dzæ-nying'-ts-zông' 在人之上; bih'-nying iao peh gyi gah-loh 別人要俾其軋落; a — pen, zông-p'ing'-go-pih' 上品個筆; a — man, zông-teng'-ts nying 上等之人; — goods, zông-teng'-ts ho' 上等之貨; ting'-ho 頂貨; — officers, zông-s' 上司; — talent, kao-dzæ' 高才; — scholar, dzæ-ts' 才子; — in age, tsiang'-pe 長輩; zin-pe' 前輩; zông-pe' 上輩

SUPERLATIVE, the signs of the — are, ting 頂, tse 最, heng 狠, gyih 極, di-ih' 第一, jih-feng' 十分; the best, ting'-hao 頂好

SUPERNATURAL, (appearing and disappearing suddenly, &c.), jing-c'ih'-kwe'-meh-go 神出鬼沒個

SUPERSCRIPTION, zông-min'-go z 上面個字; — of a letter, sing'-min 信面

SUPERSEDE, to diao-wun' 調換; — (as affairs, or things), kah'-diao 革去; the old regulations are superseded, gyiu' công'-dzing kah'-diao-de 舊章程革去了; the new supersedes the old, gyiu'-kæ-sing' 舊改新; ky'i-gyiu-wun-sing' 棄舊換新

SUPERSTITIOUS, kyin'-kyü-fah diah'-go 見鬼發牒個; siang-sing' zia-ky'i' z-ken' 相信邪氣事幹

SUPPER, yia-væn' 夜飯; yia-dzô' 夜茶; the Lord's —, Cü'-væn-ts'æn 主晚餐; Sing'-væn-ts'æn 聖晚餐

SUPPLE, joints easily bent, gao-kwu' weh-loh' 骹股活絡; — limbs, or bones, kweh'-deo nyün'-siang 骨頭軟相; — limbed fellow (as in theatres), gwæn-lao' tih'-ta'-go hyi'-ts 跌打個戲子

SUPPLEMENTARY, vu-zông'-go 附上個; djoh-tseng'-go 續增個

SUPPLICATE, to entreat, gyiu-k'eng' 求懇; — (the Deity), gyi-tao' 祈禱

SUPPLY, to minister to, kong-ing' 供應; kong-kyih' 供給; — with food, kong-zih' 供食; — my need, s'-peh ngô' ing-yüong'-go 賜給我應用個; to anticipate and — (one's) wants, t'i'-t'iah 體貼; — when needed, tsih-ing' 接應;— *troops*, fah ping' tsih-ing' 發兵接應;— *the deficiency*, pu ky'üih' 補缺; pu ts'eo' 補湊; pu tsoh' 補足

SUPPORT, *to* iang *or* yiang 養; cong 種;— *one's family*, iang kô' 養°家°; cong-iang'-kô-siao 養家°小;— *he supports himself by teaching*, gyi kao-shü' wu-k'eo' 其敎°書餬口; *to uphold, or keep from falling*, vu 扶; tông; ts'æn 攙

SUPPORT, *something to lean upon*, (but not a firm —), gæ-deo' 戤頭;—(whether property, or friend), k'ao'-sæn 靠山; *to use such* —, tông tso k'ao'-sæn 當作靠山

SUPPORTABLE, hao-tông'-go 好擋个°, tông'-leh-djü' 擋得°住

SUPPOSE, *to* i'-we 意會; dao *or* tao 度°; *guess*, ts'æ 猜; *I supposed*, ngô dao-z 我度°是; *I* — *so*, ngô' liang-dzing' z-ka' 我諒情如°此°; *I supposed he was at home*, ngô' tao gyi' læ oh'-li 我度°其在°家°裡

SUPPOSING, (when there is great probability), liang-pih' 諒必; — (if, or in case that), t'ông'-jün 倘然; t'eo'-p'ô 仍恐°; kyüô'-s 假使; kyüô'-jü 假如; shih'-s, *or* sih'-s 設使;— *for example*, pi'-fông 比方; pi'-jü 比如

SUPPRESS, *to* ah'- loh 壓°落; ah'-djü 壓°住; neh-loh' 納落;

nying 忍;— *your anger*, ô'-wông ah'-gyi-loh-ky'i' 怒°氣°壓°其下°去°;— *rebellion*, bing-fæn' 平反; *could not* — *anger*, ky'i' neh'-feh-djü' 氣納弗住; *could not* — *a smile*, nying'-feh-djü' siao' 忍弗住笑

SUPPURATE, *to* sang nong' 生°膿; tsoh nong' 作膿; gweng nong'.

SUPREME, ting' kao 頂高; *the* — *Ruler*, Zông-ti' 上帝; *ditto* (Taoist), Nyüoh-wông'-da-ti 玉皇大帝

SURE, *true*, ky'üoh'-jih 確實; tih'-ky'üoh 的確; væn-vu'-ih-shih' 萬無一失; *to be* — *of*, nô'-leh-djü' 拿得°住; jih-nô-kyiu'-weng 十拿九穩; *made*— (as a prophecy, promises, &c.), pih'-fah-pih-cong' 必發必中; — *footed*, kyiah'-bu weng' 脚步穩; en'-kyiah-tseo'-go 接脚走个°

SURELY, ih-ding' 一定; pih'-ding 必定; z-jün' 自然

SURETY, (a person), pao'-nying 保人°;—*and go between*, cong-pao' 中保; *to become* —, tso pao' 做保; tsoh pao' 作保

SURFACE, min-teng' 面上°; *floating on the* —, veo-min' 浮面

SURGEON (for cuts, and bruises), sông-k'o' sin'-sang 傷科先生°; —(for ulcers), nga-k'o' sin'-sang 外°科先生°;— (for internal diseases), nen-k'o' siu'-sang 內科先生°

SURMOUNT, to— *difficulties*, kying-lin' næn-c'ü '經練難處
SURNAME, sing 姓; sing'-su 姓氏°; *what is your honorable* — ? tseng sing' 尊姓? kwe' sing 貴姓? kao sing' 高姓? *my humble* —, bi sing' 敝姓
SURPASS, ko'-jü 過如; *surpasses him*, ko'-jü gyi 過如其
SURPASSING *all*, c'ih-cong' 出衆; — *talent*, dzæ-neng' c'ih-cong' 才能出衆; — *every thing in the world*, (but used in a more limited sense), kæ'-shü 蓋世
SURPASSINGLY *beautiful*, me'-mao kæ'-shü 美貌蓋世
SURPLUS, to-deo' 多頭; yü'-to 餘多; *enough and a* —, fu'-shü 敷舒; nông-shü' 小°康°
SURPRISE, *to* — *a person*, s'-teh nying kwa'-ky'i 使得人°怪°氣; long'-teh nying' c'ih-gyi' 弄得人°出奇; long-teh nying' gyi-kwa' 弄得人奇怪; peh nying' c'ih-gyi' 俾°人°出奇; *I am surprised*, ngô tao' c'ih-gyi'-go 我到出奇个°
SURPRISING, kwa'-ky'i 怪°氣; *not* —, feh sön' kwa'-ky'i 弗算怪°氣; *strange*, gyi-kwa' 奇怪°; *could not have been expected*, liao'-feh-tao'-go 料弗到个°; siang'-feh-tao'-go 想弗到个°; —(as something suddenly disappearing), jing-c'ih'-kwe'-meh 神出鬼沒

SURRENDER, *to* deo-'ông' 投降; deo-voh' 投服; — *one's self up*, zi deo'-tao 自°投到
SURROUND, *to* we-djü' 圍住; — *on all sides*, s'-pin we-djü' 四邊圍住; tsiu-we,' we-djü' 週圍圍住; —, *or hem in* (as by soldiers), we-kw'eng' 圍困; *to* — *by a wall*, tsiu-we' tang ziang' 週圍打墻
SURVEY, *to* k'en'-cün 看轉; k'en'-pin 看遍; *to measure land*, liang din-di' 量田地
SURVIVED *him a year*, pi gyi' to weh' ih nyin' 比其多活一年; pi gyi' to tso' ih-nyin' nying' 比其多做一年人°
SURVIVING, *still* wa' læ-tong' tso nying' 還°在°此°做人°
SURVIVES *till now*, tao' jü-kying' wa læ-tong' 到如今還°在°此°
SUSCEPTIBLE, (used of persons), ih-ts'oh' ziu dong' 一觸就動
SUSPECT, *to* nyi 疑; ts'æ-nyi 猜疑; *I* — *him*, ngô nyi-sing z gyi 我疑心是伊°
SUSPECTED, *that man is to be* —, keh'-go nying' k'o nyi 這°个°人°可疑
SUSPEND, *to hang*, tiao 弔; kwô 掛; — *work*, sang-weh' deng-kong 生活停°工; *ditto*, (for an indefinite time), dang-ky'i' 宕起°; yün-ky'i' 懸起°; —*from office*, kah'-tsih wæn-hyiang' 革職還鄉

SUSPENSE, to be in —, kwô'-sing 掛心; kwô'-ky'in 掛牽; kwô'-nyiæn 掛念; I was in — for a month, ngô kwô'-sing ih-ko yüih' de 我掛心一个°月了°

SUSPICIOUS, inclined to suspect, nyi-sing' djong' 疑心重; — circumstance, dzing yiu' k'o nyi' 情由可疑; wears a — appearance, ying-tsih' k'o uyi' 形跡可疑; dzing-tsih' k'o nyi' 情跡可疑

SUSTAIN, to tông 擋; can —, or bear it, tông-leh'-djü' 擋得°住; cannot long — life, yiang weh' feh dziang'-kyiu 養活弗長久

SWALLOW, in'-ts 燕子 (ih-tsah)

SWALLOW, to in'-loh 嚥落; ky'üoh-loh 吃°落; to gulp down, t'eng-loh 吞落; can't —the pill, wun-yiah' t'eng'-feh-loh'-ky'i 丸藥吞弗落去°

SWAMP, kæn-diu' 爛田; swampy place, 'æn-nyi-den' 陷°泥潭

SWARM, ih-tsong'-sang 一種; a — of bees, ih-tsong'-sang mih-fong' 一種蜜蜂

SWATHE, to dzin 纏; tsah 紮

SWAY, to bear rule, tsông-kwun 掌管 (tsông or công); to have authority, tsông-gyün' 掌權

SWEAR, to vah-tsiu' 罰咒

SWEAT, 'en 汗

SWEAT, to c'ih-'en' 出汗; to bring out — (as by medicine), fah-'en' 發汗; to — profusely, 'en-bô-yü-ling' 汗如°雨淋; 'en'-c'ih-t'ô-liu 汗出如°漿°

SWEEP, to sao 掃; — the ground, sao di' 掃地; — and brush off dust, tæn'-sao 撢掃; sao-shih 掃刷; sweeping assertion, kô'-deo shih-wô' 過分°說話

SWEET to the taste, din 甜; — to the smell, hyiang 香; has a — perfume, yiu hyiang-ky'i' 有香氣; — and deceitful words, shih-wô' din-dông'-mih-ti'-go 說話甜糖蜜滴个°

SWEET-WILLIAM, jih-yiang'-kying hwô 十樣景花

SWEETEN, to fông' ih-tin din' tih 放一點甜的

SWEETMEATS, dông-ko' 糖菓; peach preserves, dao-tsiang' 桃醬; sugared and honeyed fruits, mih-tsin' 蜜餞

SWELL, cong 腫; cong'-ky'i-ke 腫起來

SWELLING has gone down, cong pih'-loh-de 腫瞜落了°; cong t'e'-diao-de 腫退去°了°

SWERVE from the right way, li-k'æ' tsing'-lu 離開正路

SWIFT, kw'a 快°; — as if flying, ziang fi' ka kw'a' 像飛樣°快°; fi-kw'a' 飛快°; — as the wind, fong-kw'a' 風快°

SWILL, ken-shü' 泔水°; exchange lamp-wick for —, teng-sing'-wun-ken' 燈芯換泔水°

SWIM, *to* yiu 泅; — *in the canal,* yiu-'o' 泅河; *fortunately, he knows how to* —, (or understands the water), ky'ü'-leh gyi sih sbü' 魙°得°其識水°

SWINDLE, *to* kwa'-p'in 拐°騙; tso kwa'-ts 做拐°子; — *every where,* tong-kwa' si-p'in' 東拐°西騙

SWINE, nyi-cü' 泥豬 (ih-tsah); *a herd of* —, ih-dziao' nyi-cü' 一羣°泥豬

SWINE-HERD, yiang nyi-cü'-go 養泥豬个°

SWING, *to* dang-dang 宕宕; — *back and forth,* dang-læ' dang-ky'i' 宕來宕去°; — *the arms* (in walking), siu-kwang hwah-kyi hwah-kyi; — *over and over,* (as a mouse in a cage), tang ts'iu-c'ün' 打鞦韆°

SWITCH *of false hair,* ih-ts kô'-fah 一枝假°髮

SWOON, *to* fah-kyüih' 發厥; ao'-ky'i 暈°去; fah-hweng' 發悟

SWORD, pao'-kyin 寶劍; *double-edged* —, sông-min'-pao'-kyin 雙面寶劍; *charmed* —, ts'ih'-sing-kyin 七星劍 (ih-pô)

SYCEE, veng-nying' 紋銀; *horseshoes of* —, nyün-pao' 元寶

SYCOPHANT, vong'-dzing-tong' 奉承个°; p'ah-mô'-p'i-go 拍°馬屁个°

SYMMETRICAL *proportions,* do-siao' siang-ts'ing' 大°小相稱; deo-mi' siang-ing' 頭尾°相應

SYMBOL, piao'-yiang 表樣; piao-pông' 標榜

SYMPATHIZE, *to* — *with another'' trouble,* cü' nying-kô'-go kw'u 知人°家个°苦; cü-kw'u' cü-lah' 知苦知辣; — *with (because of like suffering),* dong-bing' siang-lin' 同病相憐

SYMPATHIZING (with a friend), dzing'-læ-tih dong' 正°在°動°情°; — *heart,* ts'eh-ing'-ts sing' 惻隱之心; — *and helping,* ti'-t'iah-go sing 體貼个°心; — *and excusing,* t'i'-liang 體諒

SYMPATHY, *in* — *with one another,* sing'-dzing 'eh'-leh-long'-go 性情合得攏个°; *lonely and without* —, ts'i-liang' 淒涼

SYMPTOMS *of disease,* bing-shü' 病勢; bing-kying' 病景; bing'-go siang'-mao 病个°相貌; — *violent, or severe,* bing-shü' li-'æ' 病勢利害

SYNONYMS, *equivalent characters,* tso' ka'-shih-go z' 一°樣°解說个°字; *equivalent words,* i'-s siang-dong'-go shih-wô' 意思相同个°說話

SYRINGE, zih-shü'-kwun 射°水°个°管

SYRUP, dông-lu' 糖滷; *peach* —, dao-tsih' 桃汁

TAB 469 TAK

T

TABERNACLE, tsiang'-bong 帳蓬 (ih-ting)
TABLE, coh'-teng 桌子° (ih-tsiang); round —, yüih-coh' 月桌; yü-sæn coh' 小° 圓° 桌; small tea —, dzô-kyi' 茶几 (ih-go); — cloth coh'-teng pu' 桌布 (ih-kw'e)
TABLET, upright ancestral —, jing-we' 神位; ditto, (and for idols), jing-cü' 神主; jing-cü'-ba, or jing-cü-bæn 神主牌°; ba-we' 牌° 位 (ih-we); horizontal inscribed —, pin 匾; pin-ngah' 匾額 (ih-kw'e)
TACK, kwu'-ting 皱釘;—with two prongs, for matting, mô'-wông-gying 螞蝗鐵攀 (ih-me)
TACK, to — with nails, ting 釘;— by sewing loosely, dziang-tsing' vong 長針縫; — together, (by sewing), ting-tæn'-læ 釘攏來; — on (as trimming), tsa-ih-tsa 釘一釘°;—a ship, diao ts'iang' 調向°; cün bong' 轉篷
TACTICS, military ping-fah' 兵法
TADPOLE, u'-kyü-deo-djong° 烏龜頭蟲;— character, k'o-teo' veng 蝌蚪文
TAEL, (1⅓ oz. av.), ih-liang' 一兩 — of silver, ih-liang' nying-ts' 一兩銀子; one Ningpo —, kông-bing' ih liang' 江° 平一兩; the Hong Kong —, kwæn-bing'

關平; Shanghai —, deo-kwe' nying' 豆規銀; kwe-yün' 規圓
TAIL, mi'-pô, or mi'-pun 尾巴° (ih-keng)
TAILOR, zæ-vong'-s-vu 裁縫司務: dzing-i' 成衣
TAINTED meat, nyüoh in'-de 肉° 宿了°; — (i. e. kept over its time), tah-dziao'-de.
TAKE, to do 拿°; — away, do'-leh-ky'i 拿了°去°; gather together and — away, siu'-leh-ky'i 收了°去°; — (properly at the same time with something else), ta'-leh-ky'i 帶了°去°;—in the hand, nyiah 捏; — with both hands, p'ong 捧°; — care of, kwu'-djoh 顧着; ditto (or look after), tsiao'-kwu, or tsiao'-kwun 照顧; ditto (another's child, or animal), kyi'-yiang 寄養;— care of yourself, zi yüong pao'-djong 自°要° 保重; — upon one's self the care of, zi dzing dzih' 自°承值; — in charge (properly a person), siu-liu' 收留; — a walk, ky'i tseo-tseo' 去° 走走; — a turn (for one's own business), tang ih-go wang' 走一°回; — a written inventory, k'æ ho'-tæn 開貨單; — one's leave, kao'-bib 告別; ditto (when going on a journey), dz'ang' 辭行°;—medicine, ky'üoh yiah' 吃°藥; — out (of water), liao-ky'i'-læ 撩起來; — off

one's clothes, t'eh i-zông' 脱衣裳°;— off the hat, coh mao-ts' 除° 帽子 (coh or tsoh); — off the cover, hyiao-k'æ' 揭開;— off a coverlid, kyih'-k'æ min-bi' 揭開棉被°;— breath, (i. e. stop a while), t'eo-ky'i' 透氣; — a look, k'en'-ih-k'en 看一看; — a disease (by infection), bing' yin-læ' 病延來; — cold, sông-fong' 傷風; — pains, yüong-sing' 用心; — by force, ts'iang'-deh 搶奪; — to heart, tæn-sing-z' 擔心事; — alive, weh gying' 活擒; — percentage, ts'iu' yüong-din' 抽用錢'; k'eo' yüong-din' 扣用錢°; (in buying for another), to — more than was paid, keh-fi-deo'; loh dong-din' 落銅錢°; tang-'eo'-siu 賺°後手; (in buying for another) to — a percentage promised by the seller, &c, do bah-deo' 搭扣°頭; ditto (secretly) in cloth, goods, or money, loh deo' 落餘°頭. See DISCOUNT. — a little out for one's self (from what one is expected to give to another), k'a' bih-deo' 貪拔頭; leo bih-deo-o ky'üoh (slang); to — the part of one's own, pao pi' 保庇; — advantage of your going, doing, &c, ts'ing ng'-go bin' 趁你'个便; — a little relaxation, weh-dong' ih-zông 活動一息°; — your studies (in school), zông kwun'

上館; — a chair in the hand, teh ü'-ts 掇椅子

TAKEN in, in buying, ma-c'ong-de- 買貴°了° (c'ong or ts'ong).

TALE, kwu'-z 故事; ancient —, kwn'-z 古事; unfounded —, vu-kyi'-ts-dæn 無稽之談

TALE-BEARER, pun-cü'-go nying 搬嘴个°人°; pun-cü'-long-zih 搬嘴弄舌; — and mischief maker, pun-teo' z'-fi-go nying 搬兜是非个°人°

TALENT, dzæ-neng' 才能; dzæ-dzing' 才情; du'-dzæ 肚才; natural —, t'in-dzæ' 天才; man of —, dzæ-ts' 才子; he has great —, gyi'-go dzæ-dzing' kao' 其个°才情高

TALISMAN (of paper), vu 符; — of the seven stars, ts'ih'-sing-vu 七星符; — of words, tsiu'-nyü 咒語; (ih-dao); to drive out evil influences with a —, bih-zia' 辟邪

TALK, to kông 講°; — together, kông-kông' 講°講°; dæn-dæn' 談談; to chat, p'æn-dæn' 攀談; talks well, jün' we shih'-dz 善為說詞; he ditto, or can — one into believing what is not true, gyi shih'-kwah bao' 其談°吐°好; — idle words, kông 'æn-wô' 講°閒話; to — foolish or useless words, kông bah-wô' 講°白話; kông liao-t'in' 講°遼天話;—when not wanted, to cü' 多嘴; to cü'

TAL 471 TAR

tah-zih' 多嘴搭舌; ts'ih'-tah-pah'-tah 七嗒八嗒;— *too much*, to-kông'-to-wô' 多講多話; *I want to — to you*, ngô iao' teng ng kông' 我要與°你°講

TALKATIVE *person*, to-kông'-to-wô'-go nying 多講°多話个人°

TALL, dziang-liao-siao 長殼篠; — *person*, nying dziang 人°長; *ditto*,(contemptuous), dziang diao-ts' 長條子;— *in stature*, sing-diao' dziang' 身條長;— *and slender*, (contemptuous), lang-hwang'-dziang; dziang-hwang-hwang.

TALLOW, yiu 油; *mutton* —, yiang-yiu' 羊油; *vegetable* —, gyiu'-yiu 相油; bah-yiu' 白°油

TALLOW-TREE, gyiu'-jü 相樹 (ih-cü)

TALONS, *caught in his* —, kyiah'-tsao gyin'-leh-ky'i'-go 脚爪箝得°起°个°

TAME, *to* — *him*, iang gyi joh' 養其熟

TAME, joh 熟; — *bird*, joh tiao' 熟鳥°

TAN, *to* — *skin*, siao bi' 硝皮

TANNER, siao-bi' s-vu 硝皮司務

TANNED *leather*, joh bi' 熟皮

TANGLE, *in a* —, lön-tsia'-bong 亂績縫

TANGLE, *to* da-lön 抓°亂; *all tangled together*, long'-leh ky'in-s'-bong, da-s-bong' 弄得°塞絲

籓抓°絲籓; ky'in-ky'in-pang'-pang 牽牽綳綳

TANK, *water* shü'-gyü 水°柜;— (on boats), shü'-tsing, or shü-ts'ông' 水°井

TAP, *to* tah 搭; — *on the shoulder*, kyin-kah'-deo tah'-ih-tah' 肩胛°上°搭一搭

TAP, *to pierce*, tsön dong-ngæn' 鑽洞眼°

TAPE, ta 帶°

TAPERING *fingers*, ts'-deo tsin' 指頭尖

TAR, pah'-yiu 栢°油

TARDY, *slow*, mæn 慢: mæn-t'ang'-t'ang 慢宕°宕°; wun'-deng-deng 緩鈍鈍; wun'-t'o-t'o 緩拖拖; *late*, dzi 遲

TARE, djü bi' 除皮

TARES (found in rice), bô-ts'ao' 稗°草

TARGET, pô'-ts 靶子 (ih-go); *to fire at a* —, tang pô'-ts 打靶子; *ditto, with arrows*, zih pô'-ts 射靶子

TARIFF, se'-tsch 稅則; se'-kw'un 稅款

TARNISH, *to* t'e-kwông' 退光

TARNISHED, kwông t'e'-de 光退了°

TARO, nyü-na' 芋°艿

TARTAR, or *Bannerman*, gyi-'ô-nying 旗下°人°; Tah'-ts 韃子; Dah-ts' 韃子; *Manchu*, Mun'-tsiu-nying 滿洲人°;— *language*, Mun'-tsiu-wô 滿洲話

TASK, *work,* meng-veng' sang-weh' 名分生°活; — (usually in study), kong-k'o' 功課; *daily* —, (*i .e.* studies, or chantings), djoh-nyih' kong-k'o' 逐日°功課

TASSEL, *a* ih-p'ang' su-deo' 一掛°鬚°頭

TASTE, mi-dao' 味°道; — *just right,* jih-mi' 入味°; *in bad* — feh teh'-fah-go 弗得法个°

TASTE, *to* zông mi-dao' 嘗°味°道; — *and see,* zông-zông'-k'en 嘗°嘗°看

TASTELESS, *without taste,* m̄-mi'-dao 無°味°道; *flat, or without salt,* dæn 淡; m̄-yin-dæn'-tsiang 無°鹹淡醬; — (as meat, or fish), m̄-sin'-mi 無°鮮味°

TATTERED, p'o'-li-p'o-sa' 破褸破襪': p'o'-p'o 破破; zah-p'o 紮破

TATTLE, shih-wô' k'ông'-feh-lao' 說話固弗牢. See TALE-BEARER.

TATTOO, *to* — *the skin,* ts'ih bi-fu' 刺皮膚

TAOISM, Dao'-kyiao 道教; Dao'-kyiao dao'-li 道教道理

TAOIST, Dao'-kô-li-go nying' 道家个°人°; — *priest,* Dao'-z 道士

TAUNT, *to* siu-joh' 羞辱; tsao-t'ah' 嘲嗒; *to humiliate by taunting,* siah-lin' 削臉

TAUTOLOGICAL *expressions,* djong-foh' shih-wô' 重複說話

TAVERN, *eating and lodging house,* væn-tin' 飯店; k'ah'-nyü 客寓; *inn,* 'ô-c'ü' 廈處: *lodging house,* hyih'-yia-tin' 歇夜°店

TAX, kyün 捐; *salt* —, yin-kyün' 鹽捐; *land* —, zin-liang' 錢°糧 *house* —, vông-kyün' 房捐; — *on goods,* kwæn-se' 關稅; se'-din 稅錢°; *pay taxes,* deo liang' neh se' 投糧納稅: *to pay land* —, deo zin-liang' 投錢°糧; *pay* — *on goods,* deo-se' 投稅; *to collect the land taxes,* sin' zin-liang' 收錢°糧; *to pay ditto,* wun koh'-k'o 完國課

TAX, *to* ding se'-tseh 定稅則; *to* — *houses,* lih' vông-kyün' 立房捐

TAX-OFFICE, kyün-gyüob' 捐局

TEA, dzô 茶; *tea-leaf,* dzô-yih' 茶葉, *broken ditto,* se' dzô-yih' 碎茶葉; *green* —, loh-dzô' 綠茶; *black* —, 'ong-dzô 紅茶; *strong* —, nyüong dzô' 濃茶; ts'ih' dzô 赤茶; *weak* —, dæn' dzô 淡茶; ts'ing-dzô' 清茶; *to scald* —, p'ao dzô' 泡茶; *pour* —, sia dzô' 樹茶; ts'ong dzô' 冲茶; *pass* —, di dzô' 遞茶; *ditto in a tray,* pun dzô' 搬茶; *to drink* —, ky'üoh dzô' 吃°茶; hah dzô' 喝茶; *to pick* —, tsah dzô-yih' 摘茶葉; *to pick over* — (*i. e.* pick out refuse, &c.), kæn dzô-yih' 揀°茶葉; *to finish up* — (by rolling, and coloring), tso dzô-yih' 做茶

葉; *to fire* —, ts'ao dzô-yih' 炒茶葉; *a great* — *drinker*, dzô-tsu'-s 茶祖師; — *dust*, dzô-meh' 茶末;— *stems*, dzô-kwang' 茶梗;— *seeds*, dzô-ts' 茶子; *Congo* —, Kong-fu' dzô 工夫茶; *Souchong* —, Siao-cong' dzô 小種茶; *Oolong* —, U-long' dzô' 烏龍茶. The kinds of tea exported from Ningpo are as follows.

Gunpowder, 1st *grade*, Pao'-cü 寶珠; *do.* 2nd *grade*, Ts-cü' 芝珠; *Hyson*, 1st *grade*, Me-hyi' 眉熙; *do.* 2nd *grade*, Hyi-c'ing' 熙春; *Young Hyson*, 1st *grade*, Ngo-me' 娥眉; *do.* 2nd *grade*, Yü'-zin 雨前; *Imperial*, 1st *grade*, Yün-cü' 圓珠; *do.* 2nd *grade*, Fu'-yün-cü' 副圓珠; *Hyson-skin*, Bi-dzô' 皮茶; *Leaf-tea*, Mao-dzô' 毛茶; *Twankey*, Song-lo' 松蘿.

TEA-CUP, dzô-pe' 茶杯; *covered* —, kæ'-un 蓋碗; meng-un' 捫碗 (ih-tsah).

TEA-KETTLE, dzô-wu' 茶壺; teng'-dzô-wu' 燉茶壺 (ih-pô).

TEA-POT, dzô-kwun' 茶罐; dzô-wu' 茶壺; ts'ong'-dzô-wu' 冲茶壺 (ih-pô).

TEA-POY, dzô-kyi' 茶几 (ih-tsiang).

TEA-SPOON, diao-kang' 調羹; *native brass* —, dzô-z' 茶匙 (ih-tsah).

TEA-TRAY, dzô-bun' 茶盤 (ih-min).

TEACH, *to* kao 敎°; *to instruct*, kao'-hyüing 敎°訓; — *a child to read*, kao'siao-nying' doh-shü' 敎°小孩°讀書

TEACHABLE, hao-kao'-go 好敎°个°; k'o-kao'-go 可敎°个°.

TEACHER, sin-sang' 先生° (ih-we); *to call*, *or employ a* —, ts'ing sin-sang' 請先生°; *my* —, ngô'-go nyih-s 我个°業師

TEACHING, *I live by* — *young children*, hyüing mong' we nyih' 訓蒙爲業

TEAR, *to* c'ô'-k'æ, or ts'ô-k'æ 撐開; c'ô'-p'o 撐破; — *to pieces*, c'ô'-se 撐碎; c'ô' wu 撐廳; — (as on a nail), keo-p'o' 勾破; tsah'-p'o 扎破; — *one's self* (or *something*) *away*, ngang feng'-k'æ 硬分開; ngang ts'ah'-k'æ 硬拆開; — *off the skin*, poh bi' 剝皮; — *open*, poh'-k'æ 剝開

TEARS, ngæn'-li 眼°淚; ngæn'-li-shü' 眼°淚水°; *to shed* —, c'ih ngæn'-li 出眼°淚; ngæn'-li beh-c'ih' 眼°淚勃出; *burst into* —, ngæn'-li pao'-c'ih-læ'-de 眼°淚爆°出來了°

TEASE, *to* ts'ao 噪; — *continually*, tsi-tseo' 嚌啁; *won't stop teasing*, ts'ao'-feh-ko 噪弗過; tsi-tseo'-feh-ko 嚌啁弗過

TEAT, na-di' 嬭°頭°

TEDIOUS, in'-væn-go 厭煩个°;

tediously slow, mæn'-leh ṉ̍-liao'-liang 慢得°無°量;—*talk*, kông'-leh dziang-p'in' 講°得°長篇
TEETH, ngô-ts' 牙°齒 (ih-lih); *irregular* —, ngô-ts' feh-zi' 牙°齒弗齊°; *to cut* —, c'ih ngô-ts' 出牙°齒; *to lose the* —, ngô-ts' t'eng-loh 牙°齒脫落°; *incisor* —, meng-ziu'-ngô 門前°牙°; *molar* —, do-ngô' 大°牙°
TELEGRAM, din-pao' 電報(ih-go)
TELEGRAPH, *to* ta din-sing' 帶°電信
TELEGRAPH *wire*, din-sin' 電線
TELESCOPE, ts'in-li'-kying 千里鏡 (ih-min, ih-kô)
TELL *him*, teng gyi' wô, or teh' gyi wô 與°其話; pao'-hyiang-gyi-dao' 報向其道; wô-hiang'-gyi-dao 話向其道; kao'-su gyi 告訴他°; *charge not to* —, mun-cü' 瞞嘴; *don't* —, ṉ̍-nao' wô soh' 弗可話甚°麼°; feh-k'o' kông'-c'ih 弗可講°出; *bribe not to* — *him*, eu gyi cü'-pô pi' 接其嘐吧閉; — *the news*, t'ong-cü' sing'-sih 通知信息; pao sing' 報信; — *a secret*, t'ong fong' pao sing' 通風報信
TEMERITY, tæn'-ts p'ah' 膽子澎; tæn'-ts sah'-yia 膽子撒野; *to show* —, mao do'-tæn 冒大°膽
TEMPER, *disposition*, sing'-kah 性格; sing'-ky'i 性氣; sing-dzing 性情; *even*—, sing'-ky'i 'o-bing'

性氣和平; *to give way to one's* —, fah sing'-kah 發性格; sing-kyih' 性急, implies too great haste in doing, but is a polite term for *quick* or *hasty* —, (which is also), sing'-kah ts'ao' 性格躁; ky'i'-tsih tön' 氣質短; ky'i kying' 氣緊; ziang mao-ts'ao' bo-sing' ka 像茅草火星樣°式; *easy* —, ky'i'-tsih dziang' 氣質長; ky'i-kw'un' 氣寬. Bi-ky'i' 脾氣 is sometimes used for temper, but in Ningpo it generally implies an evil nature, so that all one's bad behaviour, such as gambling, drinking, &c. are attributed to his wa bi-ky'i; hao bi-ky'i is sometimes used, but it implies only a temporary goodness.
TEMPERAMENT *sluggish*, or *slow*, sing'-dzing sang'-leh dzi-deng' 性情生°得°遲鈍; *mercurial* —, sing'-dzing sang-leh liu-dong' 性情生°得°流動
TEMPERATE, tsih'-cü 節制; — *in eating, and drinking*, ing'-zih yiu-tsih' 飲食有節
TEMPEST, fong-pao' 風颮
TEMPLE, miao 廟; miao-yü' 廟宇; *Buddhist* —, z 寺; z-yün' 寺院; *small ditto*, en 庵; *Taoist* —, kwun 觀; *the large central hall of ditto*, da-din' 大殿; *ancestral* —, z-dông' 祠堂; kô-miao' 家°廟; *ditto of one branch of a family*, ts-dz' 支祠 (ih-go)
TEMPLES (of the head), t'a'-yiang 太陽
TEMPORAL *affairs*, (of this world),

shü'-kæn-zông'-go z-t'i' 世界上个°事體; shü'-z 世事; *affairs of this life,* seng-zin'z-ken' 生前°事幹

TEMPORARY, dzæn-z'-go 暫時个°

TEMPORARILY, dzæn-ts'ia' 暫且'; gyün-ts'ia' 權且°

TEMPORIZE, *to* ze shü'-dao tseo' 隨勢道走; k'en' fong-deo' tseo 看風頭走

TEMPORIZING, ze-fong-tao'-go 隨風倒个°

TEMPT, *to persuade to evil,* ts'öntch' tso-wa' 攛掇做孬°; *to deceive, and persuade,* yiu-'oh' 誘惑; — *and blind,* mi-'oh' 迷惑; *to entice,* ying'-yiu 引誘

TEMPTED *by the Devil,* be Mo-kwe' mi-'oh'-de 被魔鬼迷惑了°; — *by him,* ziu gyi'-go mi' 受其个°迷; ziu gyi'-go nyü' 受其个°愚; — *and fallen,* ta-diao-de 帶壞°了°

TEN, jih 十; — *to one it will be spoiled,* (nine out of ten), jih'-yiu kyiu' iao tso'-diao-go 十有九要做壞°个°;—*out of every hundred,* kyiu' k'eo 九扣; kyiu' tsih 九折

TENACIOUS *of one's own opinion,* nyiah-sah' zi'-go cü'-i 捻煞自°个°主意

TENANT, tsu-wu' 租戶; tsu-cü' 租主

TEND, *to* kwun 管; k'en 看; — *a child,* kwun siao-nying' 管小孩°; — *sheep,* k'en yiang' 看羊

TENDENCY, z-jün'-ts shü 自然之勢

TENDER, neng 嫩; *to boil it —,* ts' gyi nen' 煮°其軟°;— *heart,* nyün' sing-dziang' 軟心腸; sing dz'-go 心慈个°; *to rear tenderly,* kyiao-iang' 嬌養

TENDON, kyiug' 筋 (ih-kwang)

TENON, shing'-deo 榫頭

TENT, tsiang'-bong 帳蓬; *to pitch a —,* tah tsiang'-bong 搭帳蓬

TENTH, *the —,* di-jih' 第十; *a — of,* jih-kwn'-ts-ih' 十股之一; *the —* (usually added by Chinese storekeepers, and which they will deduct), k'eo'-deo 扣頭; tsih'-deo 折頭; *have you deducted the —,* k'eo'-deo k'eo'-loh-leh ma 扣頭扣落嗎°?

TEPID, nyih-weng-weng' 熱溫溫; nyih-dong'-dong 熱烘烘

TERM, *name,* ming-z' 名字; — *of three years,* (official), sæn nyin' ih-dzing' 三年一任°; *to collect bills at the three terms,* siu tsih'-tsiang 收筸賬

TERMINATE, *to end,* wun 完; pih 畢; liao'-kyih 了結; *to stop,* ts'-djü 止住

TERM, *to* ts'ing-hwu' 稱呼; co kiao°

TERMINATED, *the war is —,* tang-tsiang tang-kyih'-gyüoh-de 打仗結局了°

TERMINATION, meh-kyih'-sah 末結煞

TERRACE, *platform*, dæ 臺; *flat — on the roof*, sa'-dæ 曬°臺

TERRIBLE, p'ô'-siang-go 怕相个°; p'ô'-shü-shü 怕勢勢

TERRIFIED, kying-hoh'-de 驚嚇了°; ziu kying-hoh' de 受驚嚇了°; hah'-sah-de 嚇煞了°; kw'u'-tæn hah'-se 苦膽嚇碎

TERRIFY, *to —* hàm, long gyi hah'-sah 弄其嚇煞; s'-teh gyi ky'ih-hoh' 使得其吃嚇°

TERRITORY, pæn'-du 版圖; di-fông' 地方

TERSE, kyin'-kyih 簡潔

TERTIAN *ague*, s'-nyih-bing' 四日°病; s'-nyih liang-deo pæn' 四日°兩頭班

TEST, s'-fah 試法; s'-væn-fông-fah' 試範方法

TEST, *to* s'-væn 試範; *to experiment*, s'-nyiæn 試驗; *— as by fire*, s'-lin 試煉; *to try*, s'-s-k'en 試試看; *— one's learning by examination*, k'ao-s' 考試

TESTAMENT, yi-coh', *or* yi-tsoh' 遺囑; *to make a —*, lih' yi-coh' 立遺囑; *Old —*, Gyiu-yi'-tsiao'-shü 舊遺詔書; Gyiu-iah'-shü 舊約書; *New —*, Sing-yi'-tsiao'-shü 新遺詔書; Sing-iah'-shü 新約書

TESTIFY, *to* tso te'-tsing 做對証; te'-tsing 對証; *— of what has been seen*, tso kyin'-tsing 做見証

TESTIMONY, te'-tsing shih-wô' 對証說話

TEXT, bah-veng 白°文; *— of a discourse*, di-moh' 題目

TEXTURE, sing-veng 身分; *firm —*, sing-veng' kyih'-jih 身分硈實

THAN, jü 如; pi 比; *greater — I*, do-jü' ngô 大°如我; pi ngô do' 比我大°; *better —*, hao'-jü 好如; *more — once*, feh-ts' ih-we' 弗止一回; *less — three catties*, feh tao' sæn-kying' 弗到三觔; feh-mun'sæn-kying' 弗滿三觔

THANK, *to* zia 謝; *— you*, zia-zia'ng 謝°謝°你°; ze-ko; teh-ze 得罪; *— much, or many thanks*, to-zia' 多謝°; to-dzing 多承; *cannot express my thanks*, ken'-zia-feh-zing' 感謝弗盡°; zia'-feh-wun' 謝弗完°; *—you very much, to-to'* cü'-i ng 多多致意你°; *return a present in thanks for favor received*, dziu-zia' 酬謝°

THANKFUL *heart*, sing'-li ken'-kyih 心裡感激; ken'-zia-go sing' 感謝°个°心°; *ditto (for great favor)*, ken-eng'-go-sing 感恩个°心°; *I am very — to you*, ngô jih-nyi' feng ken'-kyih ng 我十二°分感激你°

THANKLESS, vông-eng'-veo-yi'-go 忘恩負義个°; ú-liang'-sing 無°良心; ú peng'-sing 無°本心

THAT, keh'-go 這°个°; — man, keh'-go nying 這°个°人°; — gentleman, keh'-we sin-sang 這位先生°; — pen, keh-ts pih' 這°枝筆; — which, sô sô' — ; which he said, gyi' sô wô' 其所話; — night, tông'-yia 當夜°; lin-yia' 連夜°; keh'-yia 這夜°; so —, s'-teh 使得; this and —; pe'-ts' 彼此; I heard — you were sick, ngô t'ing'-meng ng sang-bing'-ko'-de 我聽聞°你°生°病過了°; Oh! —'s it, or I don't believe —, kwa'-dao-z 怪°道是

THATCHED house, ts'ao-kæ'-go oh' 草蓋个°屋

THAW, to sah 煞; yiang 樣; hwô 化; siao 消

THEATRE, (a building), hyi'-kwun 戲館; open place where plays are enacted, hyi'-veng-dziang 戲塲

THEFT, the sin of —, t'eo-tong-si'-go ze' 偷東西个°罪; a case of —, ts'ih' en 竊案; lost by —, shih ts'ih'-de 失竊了°; guilty of —, væn ts'ih'-en go 犯竊案; — væn'-djoh zeh'-go ze'-ming 犯着賊个°罪名

THEIR, gyi-lah'-go, or gyi-go 伊等°个°

THEM, gyi-lah' 伊°等°; — selves, gyi-lah zi' 伊°等°自°

THEME, di-moh' 題目

THEN, ziu 就°; ze-tsih' 隨即; ze-siu' 隨手; following after, ze-'eo' 隨後

THENCE, from that place, dzong keh'-deo 從那°邊°

THENCEFORTH, dzong-ts'' yi-'eo' 從此以後; dzong keh' z-'eo yi-læ' 從這°時候以來

THERE, keh'-deo 那°邊°; — it is, na; nô; læ-kæn' 在°彼°

THERE is, yiu 有; there is none, m-yiu' 無°有, m-neh-go 沒°有°个°

THEREABOUTS (in quantity), ts'ô' feh-to' 差弗多; — (in place), ts'ô'-feh-to' di-fông' 差弗多地方°; ts'ô'-feh-to' lu' 差弗多路; Ningpo —, teng Nying-po' siang ky'ü' vu-kyi' 與寧波相去無幾

THEREFORE, sô'-yi 所以; keh'-lah 是°以°; kweh'-lah 故以°; on account of that, we'-leh ka 爲此°; kwu'-ts' ka 故此

THEREIN, dzæ-gyi-nen' 在其內; dzæ gyi-cong' 在其中

THERMAL springs, weng-djün' 溫泉 (veng.)

THERMOMETER, 'en-shü'-piao 寒暑表

THESE, keh'-sing 這°些°; dông-deo keh'-sing.

THEY, gyi-lah' 伊°等°

THICK, 'eo 厚; 'eo'-jih 厚實; — fog, vu'-lu nyüong 霧露濃; vu'-lu djong 霧露重; — and tangled (as hair, bushes), bong-bong-dong' 亂°蓬鬆°

THICKEN, to become thick, 'eo'-ky'i-læ 厚起來

THIEF, zeh 賊; sæn-tsah'-siu 三隻手; yia'-mæn 夜° 鑾; sô-lao'-ing; siao'-ts‛ih 小竊; — who steals, in day-light, bah-nyih'-djông' 白°日° 撞; — (who cuts and snatches watches, &c.), tsin-liu'-go zeh 剪綹个° 賊°

THIEF-CATCHER, mô'-kw‛æ 馬快; bu-kw‛æ' 捕快

THIEVISH, addicted to stealing, kwæn' t‛eo go 慣偷个°; naturally — hearts, zeh-sing' sang-dzing'-go 賊°心生° 成个°; fond of picking, ts‛eh' siu ts‛eh kyiah' 撮手撮脚; — (hands and feet), zeh-siu' zeh-kyiah' 賊°手賊°脚

THIGH, do-t‛e' 大°腿; do-kyiah'-p‛ông 大°脚膀°

THIGH-BONE, do-t‛e'-kweh 大°腿骨 (ih-keng)

THIMBLE, ti'-tsing 抵針 (ih-go)

THIN, boh 薄; spare, seo 瘦; wan, bah-liao'-liao 白'獠獠; — blooded, ts‛ing-bi' boh'-hyüih 青皮薄血

THINNER, a little boh'-tin 薄點; much —, boh hyü'-to 薄許多; ditto, (of a person), seo hyü'-to 瘦許多

THING, tong-si' 東西 (ih-yiang, ih-gyin); all things, pah' yiang tong-si' 百樣東西; væn-veh' 萬物

THINK, to ts‛eng 忖; siang 想; s 思; s-siang' 思想; s-ts‛eng' 思忖; — carefully, yüong sing-

s' 用心思; ditto over it, tso'-s-yiu-siang' 左思右想; can't — it out, ngwu'-feh-tao' 悟弗到; ts‛eng'-feh-c‛ih' 忖弗出; — of, or recall suddenly, ngwu-tao' 悟到; — constantly of, kyi'-nyiæn 記念; — of, and not forget, nyiæn-nyiæn' peh-vông 念念不忘

THIRD, the di-sæn' 第三; a —, sæn-kwu'-ts-ih' 三股之一; divide in thirds, sæn-kwn' k‛æ 三股開

THIRDLY, sæn-læ' 三來; sæn-tseh' 三則

THIRST, to quench —, ts-k‛eh' 止渴; ka-k‛eh' 解渴

THIRSTY, k‛eo-k‛eh' 口渴; very —, k‛eo-pah' 口乾°; — (dry), k‛eo'-ken zih-sao' 口乾舌燥

THIRTEEN, jih-sæn' 十三

THIRTEENTH, di-jih-sæn' 第十三

THIRTY, sæn-jih' 三十

THIS, keh'-go 這°个°; — month, keh'-ko yüih 這° 個月; peng'-yüih 本月; — year, kying-nyin' 今年; peng'-nyin 本年; — or the same year, tông'-nyin 當年; — day, kyih-mih' 今日°; kying-tsiao' 今朝; — morning (early), kyih-mih t‛in-nyiang' 今°日°天亮°; — book, keh'-peng shü' 這°本書; — shop, keh' bæn tin' 這°爿店; — time, keh'-go z-'eo' 這° 个° 時候; — life, kying'-si z-'eo' 今世

時候;— *and that*, dông' ih-go, keh' ih-go 這°一个°, 那°一个°;— *time and that are different*, ts'' ih-z pe' ih-z 此一時彼一時; *on — account*, we'-leh keh'-go yün-kwu 爲了°這个°緣故

THITHER, *go* tao keh-deo' ky'i 到那°邊°去°

THONG, bi-ta' 皮帶 (ih-diao).

THORN, ts' 刺 (ih-me)

THOROUGH, (*i. e. through and through*), t'eo 透; t'ong-t'eo' 通透; t'eo-ti' 透底;— (*i. e. from the bottom to the top*), teo-ti 兜底; ts'iah-ti 徹°底

THOROUGHLY, *understand* t'eo' ming-bah' 透明白°; *ditto or to be — dry*, feng'-sao 粉燥; feng'-kweh-sao 粉骨燥; sao-ko-keh' 燥過分°; feng'-ken s-sao' 粉乾四燥;— *acquainted with*, joh-t'eo' 熟透; *to do —*, nyiug-tsing' tso 認°眞做

THOROUGH-FARE *a street running through*, t'ong-lu' 通路; *a frequented way*, kwun-dông' do-lu' 官塘大°路; t'ong-'ang' do-lu' 通行°大°路

THOSE, keh'-sing 那°些°; keh'-deo keh'-sing 那°邊°那°些

THOUGH, se 雖; se-tsih' 雖只; se-tseh' 雖則; se-jün' 雖然; *as — (he) did not notice*, hao'-ziang feh-læ'-kwu 好像弗來顧

THOUGHTS, ts'eng'-deo 忖頭; siang'-deo 想頭; (*deeper —*), nyiæn-deo' 念頭;—, or *way of thinking*, ts'eng'-shih 想°法°

THOUGHTFUL, we yüong sing' 會用心; we yüong ts'eng'-kong 會用心思

THOUGHTLESS, mông-bah 吒白°; mong 懞; bah-mông'-kwông 白°吒光; bah-du'-du 虛°度°;— or *heedless person*, mông'-fu 懞夫

THOUSAND, *a* ih ts'in' 一千; *ten —*, ih væn' 一萬; jih ts'in' 十千

THRASH. See THRESH.

THREAD, sin 線; *hempen —*, mô-sin' 麻線; *cotton —*, min-sô' 棉紗 (ih-keng)

THREAD *a needle*, c'ün tsing-ngæn' 穿針眼°

THREAD-BARE, *worn* yiang-yi'-de 希°散°了°; nyüong-deo' yi-kwông'-de 絨頭散°光了°

THREATEN, *to* kying'-kyiæ 禁戒; heng-hô' 哼哈; ngô-heng' 砑哼; *to frighten*, hah 嚇. See WARN.

THREE, sæn 三;— *times — are nine*, sæn-sæn' kyin kyiu' 三三見九;— *times as much*, (i.e. *add two parts*), kô liang'-be ts'eo' 加二°倍湊;— *cornered*, sæn-koh'-go 三角°个°;— *stranded cord*, sæn-kwu'-deo-zing' 三股頭繩°;— *highest* (in this Empire) *in literary rank*, sæn-ting'-kah 三鼎甲°

THRESH, to — *paddy*, tang dao' 打稻; gwæn dao' 摜稻

THRESHING-FLOOR, dao'-dziang 稻塲; dao'-di 稻地;—, *and also drying-floor*, sa'-dziang 曬°塲

THRESHOLD, *door-sill*, di-voh 地栿; *stumbled over the* —, di-voh' pæn-tih'-go 地栿失°跌个°

THRICE, sæn tsao' 三遭; sæn we' 三回; sæn pin' 三遍

THRIFTY, *increasing in wealth*, nyih-tsing' feng-feng 日°進紛紛; — *in growing*, nyih-tsiang' yia-do' 日°長夜°大°

THRIVE, *to* hying-wông 興旺; *will not* —, (*as a tree, or child*), yiang'-feh-hying' 養弗興起°

THROAT, wu-long' 喉°嚨; *to cut one's* —, zi-ming'-sah 自°抿殺

THROB, *to* t'iao 跳; dong 動; *heart throbs*, sing bih'-bih-t'iao 心關關跳

THRONE, we 位; *the Imperial* —, wông-we' 皇位; long-we' 龍位; da-pao' 大寳; *to ascend the* —, teng we' 登位; *ditto* (the first of a dynasty), teng kyi 登基; *to succeed to the* —, tsih we' 接位; *to abdicate the* —, t'e we' 退位

THRONG, *a* ih-do-dziao nying' 一大°羣°人°

THRONG, *to* üong'-tsi 擁擠; a-tsi' 挨擠

THROTTLE, *to* k'ah wu-long' 搿喉°嚨

THROUGH, *to pass* —, c'ün-ko' 穿過; *pass* — *the city*, c'ün-zing-ko' 穿城°過; *wet* —, sih'-t'eo-de 濕透了°; *come* — *the rain*, kah'-yü læ' 冒°雨來; *read a book* —, shü' doh-wun' 書讀完°; *look* — *a hole*, dzong dong-ngæn'-li k'en' 從洞眼°裏看

THROUGHOUT, *that book is circulated* — *China*, keh-peng shü' Cong-koh' t'ong-'ang'-go 這°本°書中國通行°个°; *good* —, ih-kæ'tu hao' 一概都好; dzong deo'-ts-vi tu hao' 從頭至尾都好

THROW, *to* tiu 丟; k'ang; gwæn 摜; — *away*, tiu-diao' 丟去°; k'ang'-diao; gwæn-diao' 摜了°; ô'-diao 捱°了°; ang'-diao; — *about*, k'ang'-sæn 丟°散; lön gwæn' 亂摜; *he threw stones at me*, gyi do zah-deo' k'ang' ngô 其拿石°頭丟°我; — *bricks, or broken tiles*, ô ngô'-læn 捱死兀; — *away one's life*, song-si' 送死°; song sing'-ming 送性命; *ditto, or reputation, for a noble object*, si' djong'-jü T'a'-sæn 死°重如泰山; *ditto, for a very small object*, si' ky'ing'-jü 'ong-mao' 死°輕如鴻毛°; — *him down* (playfully), k'ô-gyi-tao' 捉°其倒; *ditto* (in anger), tang'-gyi-tao 打其倒; — *away* (or *waste money*), k'ang'-loh shü'-den-li 丟°在水潭裏; 一

over the head (as a cloth), 'o-deo'-t'ao 和頭套;— off (as covering), hyiao-diao' 揩去°; kyih'-diao 揭去°; dip up, and — out (as specks in food), peh'-diao 撥去°;— blame upon some one else, yi-hwô'-tsih-moh' 移花接木

THRUST, to push, t'e 推;— out the head, sing'-c'ih deo' 伸出頭;— out the tongue, t'a'-c'ih zih-deo' 𠰌°出舌頭;— through with a knife, tao' c'ün-ko' 刀穿過

THUMB, do ts'-meh-den' 大°指拇頭

THUNDER, le 雷; the noise of —, le-sing' 雷聲; le'-hyiang 雷響; a clap of —, ih-go p'ih'-lih 一聲°霹靂;— shower, loh le-yü' 下°雷雨; there will be a — shower, iao loh le-yü' 要下°雷雨

THUNDER, to hyiang le' 響雷

THURSDAY, li-pa-s' 禮拜°四; tsin-li ng 瞻禮五°

THUS, z-ka' 如°此°; ka'-siang-mao 如此相貌; ka' yiang-ts 如°此°樣子; jü-ts' 如此 (veng.)

THWART his plans, p'o gyi-go fah' 破其个°法;— my wishes, ao'-ky'iang ngô-go sing-siang' 拗強我个°心想

TICK, to tah'-tah-hyiang 得°得°響; tsah'-tsah-hyiang 恙恙響

TICKET, siao'-p'iao 小票; p'iao 票; p'iao'-deo 票頭; pawn —, tông'-p'iao 當票

TICKLE, to hô-yiang'-c'ü-c'ü' 吪癢哦°哦°

TICKLISH, p'ô-yiang'-go 怕癢个°

TIDE, dziao-shü' 潮水°;— contrary (i.e. against), t'eo' shü 回水°; dziao-shü' feh-te' 潮水°弗對;— is rising, dziao tsiang'-de 潮漲了°; dziao læ-tih tsiang' 潮正°在°漲; full flood —, dziao-tsiang' tsoh'-de 潮漲足了°;— eight parts full, tsiang'-pah 漲了°八分°; ebb —, loh-dziao 落潮; t'e'-dziao 退潮; slack —, bing dziao' 平潮; dziao-shü' bing' 潮水°平;— is favorable, jing-dziao' jing-shü' 順潮順水°; to go with the—, ze dziao' ky'i 隨潮去°; the — follows the moon, dziao-shü' ze yüih-liang' go 潮水°隨月亮个°

TIDE-WAITER, ah'-sia 押°卸°

TIDINGS, fong-sing' 風信; siao-sih' 消息; sing'-sih 信息; ing-sing' 音信

TIE, to bo 縛°;— together, bo-tæn'-long 縛°攏;— or bind tightly (as bales), kw'eng 絪;— (as bundles), tsah 紮;— a man, pông nying' 綁人°; kw'eng-pông nying' 絪綁人°;— in a hard knot, cannot untie, tang si'-kyih ka'-feh-k'æ 打死°結解°弗開

TIER, zeng 層°; dæ 臺;— above —, zeng tang' zeng 層°層°; ih-dæ' ih-dæ' 一臺一臺

TIGER, hwu 虎; lao'-hwu 老虎 (ih-tsah)

TIGHT, kying 緊

TIGHTEN, to tang kying-tin' 打緊點; siu kying-tin' 收緊點

TILE, ngô'-p'in 瓦片 (ih-tsiang); square —, fông-cün' 方磚

TILE, to — a roof, kæ ngô'-p'in 蓋瓦片

TILL, tao 到; ih-dzih' tao 一直到; wait — I come, teng' tao ngô læ' 等到我來

TILL, to — the ground, cong din' 種田; kang-cong' 耕種

TILT on one side, din' ih-pin ky'i' 墊一邊起

TIMBER, moh-deo' 木頭; moh-liao' 木料; (a piece, ih-keng, ih-cü), — merchant, jü-k'ah'-nying 樹客人; moh-k'ah' 木客

TIME, kong-fu' 工夫; z-'eo' 時候 (if speaking of hours); nyih-ts' 日子 (if speaking of month, or day); what —, soh'-go z-'eo' 甚麼時候; how much — ? to-siao' kong-fu' 多少工夫? no —, m-kong-fu 無工夫; no leisure, (or empty —), m'-neh k'ong' 沒有空; to fix a —, ding z-'eo' 定時候; ditto in the more distant future, ding gyi' 定期; to limit the — (when to be done, or to arrive), 'æn' z-zing' 限時辰; what — is it ? (i.e. of the clock), kyi-tin'-cong 幾點鐘; a long —, dziang-

kyiu' 長久; to-z' 多時; hyü'-to kong-fu' 許多工夫; a short —, dzæn-z' 暫時; at the —, tsiao z-'eo' 照時候; en' z-'eo' 按時候; — has arrived, z-'eo' tao'-de 時候到了; ditto (implying no chance for preparation), ling-z' k'eo'-tsih 臨時適節; any — you please, zé-bin' soh'-go z-'eo' 隨便甚麼時候; feh-leng' soh'-go z-'eo' 弗論甚麼時候; at the same —, tsé' z-'eo' 同時候; in the day —, nyih-li' 日裏; at the present —, yin-dzæ' 現在; tông'-z 當時

TIMELY, teh-z' 得時; seasonable, gyih-z' 及時; your coming is very —, ng' læ-leh ting' teh'-z 你來得頂得時

TIMES, tsao 遭; we 回; pin 遍; vah; ts' 次; many —, hyü'-to tsao su' 許多遭數; hao-kyi' we 好幾回; three or four —, sæn s' pin 三四遍; hard times, kyin-næn' z-'eo' 艱難時候; kæn-ka' z-'eo' 尷尬時候; these are hard — (i.e. are bad), — shü'-k'eo gyih' 世口竭; shü'-k'eo wu' 世口㖡; good —, z-shü' hao' 時世好; z-kwông' hao' 時光好

TIME-SERVING, ze-zông' ze-loh'-go 隨上隨落个; loh-meh'-ts-den' tsao-yinug' 六拇指頭搖癢

TIMID, tæn'-ts siao'-go 膽子小个°; tæn-'en' go 膽寒个°; m̂-tæn'-ky'i-go 無膽氣个°.
TIN, mô'-k'eo-t'ih 馬口鐵.
TINDER, ho'-nyüong 火絨; — paper, me-deo'-ts 煤頭紙; ho'-ts 火紙 — bag, or box, ho'-lin 火鏈; — bag, ho'-lin pao 火鏈包.
TINGED with green, loh-ang'-ang 綠影°影°; — with red, 'ong-hwe'-hwe 紅煇煇; — with yellow, wông-bang'-bang 有°些°黃.
TINKER, travelling brass-mender, siao'-lu-s-vu' 小爐司務; kettle mender, pu'-'oh-ziang 補鑊匠.
TINKLING sound, ting-ting' tông-tông' sing-hyiang 丁丁當當聲響.
TINSEL, gold kying-boh' 金箔; silver —, nying-boh' 銀箔; brass —, dong-boh' 銅箔; pewter —, lah-boh' 鑞箔; sih'-boh 錫箔.
TIP, tsin 尖; — of the finger, ts'-deo tsin' 指頭尖; stand on — toe, kyiah' tin'-tæn-ky'i' 脚頭°起.
TIPSY, (manifest in talking), yiu-tsin'-i 有酒意; yiu tse'-i 有醉意; tottering, ts'ih'-ts'ong-pah'-tih-go 七衝八跌个°.
TIRE, to — one's self, vah-lih' 乏力.
TIRED, dziah-lih' 着力; ky'ih'-lih 怯力; slightly —, dziah-lih-kwun' 着力相; ky'ih'-lih-siang 怯力相; — and sleepy, bi-gyün' 疲倦; tsing-jing' gyün'- ky'i 精神倦去°; — of waiting, sing'-tsiao 心焦; very —, vah-lih'-de 乏力了°; tso'-bi-de 做疲了°; vah-de 乏了°; quite — out, t'eh-lih'-de 脫力了°; — of, in'-tsao-tsao 厭遭遭; — of eating, (as a certain kind of food), ky'üoh'-leh in'-tsao-tsao 吃得°厭遭遭; ditto (in a less degree), ky'üoh' in'-de 吃°厭了°; ky'üoh-bi'-de 吃°疲了.
TIRESOME, in'-væn-go 厭煩个°; zô'-in, or jô'-in 惹°厭; — (as something often repeated), shü'-væn 絮煩.
TITHE, a jih-feng'-ts-ih' 十分之一; jih-kwu'-ts-ih' 十股之一; to take out a —, jih-feng' li'-hyiang do'-c'ih ih-feng' 十分裏向拕出一分.
TITLE of an officer, kwun-ngæn' 官銜; ngæn-deo' 銜頭; — of nobility, tsiah'-we 爵位; to confer ditto, fong tsiah'-we 封爵位; to confer a — (upon one deceased), fong dzing' 封贈; — of a book, shü ming' 書名; (you) call (me) by a higher — than (I) deserve, tseng-ts'ing' feh-ken' 尊稱弗敢; he has a —, or right to it, gyi yiu' veng 其有分; he has the exclusive ditto, gyi doh zi' yin veng 其獨°自°有分.
To, tao 到; teng 等; — Shanghai, tao Zông-Hæ' 到上海; say

— *him*, teng gyi wô' 與°其話; *give* (it) — *me*, peh ngô' 給°我; *go — a trade*, 'oh siu'-nyi ky'i' 學°手藝去°.

TOAD, keh'-pô 蛤蚆; la-s (ih-tsah)

TOAD-STOOL, doh-dzing' 毒菌°

TOAST, *to* koh 烤°; *to — bread*, koh mun-deo' 烤°饅頭

TOBACCO, *in* 烟; *to smoke —*, ky'üoh in 吃°烟; *ditto in a water pipe*, ky'üoh shü' in 吃°水°烟; *ditto in a dry pipe*, ky'üoh 'en'-in 吃°旱烟; *to cultivate —*, cong in-yih' 種烟葉; *— pipe*, in kwun' 烟管

TO-DAY, kyih-mih' 今°日°; kying-tsiao' 今朝

TOE, kyiah'-ts-meh-den' 脚指拇頭°; kyiah'-meh-den' 脚拇頭°; kyiah-ts-deo' 脚指頭° (ih-ko, ih-go)

TOGETHER, dô-kô' 大°家°; 'eo'-leh 候得°; *sing all —*, tsæn'-zi ts'ông' 並°齊唱; tsæn'-pô-s'-zi ts'ông' 並°排°會°齊唱; jü-de' 聚隊; tso-de'; *go —*, dô-kô' ky'i 大°家°去°

TOIL, lao-kw'u' 勞苦; sing-kw'u' 辛苦; *life of —*, lao-kw'u' ih-si' 勞苦一世'; *anxious —*, lao' sing fi'-lih 勞心費力

TOIL, *to* tso sing-kw'u' sang-weh' 做辛苦生°活; tso djong'-deo sang-weh' 做重頭生°活

TOILSOME, lao-kw'u'-go 勞苦个°; *laborious*, lao-loh'-go 勞碌个°

TOILET, *to make one's —* (as a lady), su-tsông' 梳妝; tsah'-kweh 紮°束°

TOKEN, *memorial*, piao'-kyi 表記

TOLERABLE, *that may be borne*, næ'-leh-djü' 耐得°住; *passable*, ñong'-leh-ko 將°就°得°過°; p'o'-hao 頗好; yia-hao' 也°好; wa'-hao 還°好

TOLERABLY *well done*, tso'-leh p'o'-hao 做得°頗好

TOLL, *bridge* ko'-gyiao-din' 過橋錢°; *— for mending a road*, siu-lu' fi 修路費

TOMATO, *called in Ningpo foreign egg-plant*, fæn-gyiæn 番茄°; *and foreign peppers*, nga-koh lah-gyiæ 外°國辣茄; *in Shanghai called* fæn-z 番柿°

TOMB, veng 墳; veng-mo' 墳墓; *the place of the —*, veng-deo' 墳頭; veng-keng 墳跟; *to worship at, and repair the —*, zông veng' 上墳

TOMB-STONE, mo-pe' 墓碑; pe-ba' 碑牌; *stone surrounding a mound*, læn-t'u' 攔土

TO-MORROW, ming-tsiao' 明朝; *day after —*, 'eo-nyih' 後日°; *— or the day after*, ming 'eo'-nyih 明後日°

TON, teng 噸

TONNAGE, teng-su' 噸數; *—dues*, jün ts'ao' 船鈔

TONE, *sound*, sing-ing' 聲音

TONES, *the four —*, bing-tseh'-sing

平仄聲; viz., bing-sing 平聲, zông'-sing 上聲, ky'ü'-sing 去聲, and jih-sing' 入聲

Tongs, ho'-gyin 火箝 (ih-pô)

Tongue, zih-deo' 舌頭 (ih-go); *to put out the* —, sing'-c'ih zih-deo' 伸出舌頭; t'a'-c'ih zih-deo' 垂°出舌頭

Tonic *medicine,* pu'-yiah 補藥

To-night, kyih-mih' yia'-tao 今°日°夜°到; kying-yia' 今夜°; tông'-yia 當夜°; lin-yia' 連夜°

Too, t'eh or t'o 太°;—*cold,* t'eh' lang or t'o lang 太°冷°;—*many,* t'eh to' 太°多; *quite — much,* t'eh' ko-deo' 太°過頭°;—*far beyond what is proper,* t'eh' ko-veng' 太°過牙;—*young,* nyin-kyi' t'eh-ky'ing' 年紀太°輕

Tool, kô-sang' 傢伙°; *tools,* siu'-yüong kô'-sang 手用傢伙

Tooth, ngô-ts'' or ngô-ts' 牙°齒°; — *of a saw,* ken'-ts 鋸°齒

Tooth-ache, ngô-ts'' t'ong 牙°齒痛

Tooth-brush, ngô-shih' 牙°刷

Tooth-pick, t'ih'-ngô-ziang 剔牙°杖°

Tooth-powder, ngô-feng 牙°粉

Top, *apex,* ting'-deo 頂頭; *the upper surface,* zông' min 上面; — *of a hill,* sæn ting-den' 山頂頭°; — *of a tree,* jü ting-den' 樹頂頭°; jü nao-tsin' 樹杪°

Torch, ho'-pô 火把 (ih-ts); *many torches,* lah-za'ho'-pô 雜柴火把

Torment, *to* yüong sing-s' 用心思; næn-we' 難為; s-ing-sön' 使陰算

Tormented *with pain,* t'ong'-leh kw'u'-feh-ko 痛得°苦弗過

Tormentor, sing-s kyü' 心思鬼°

Torn, p'o'-de 破了°; c'ô-k'æ-de 撐開了°

Torrents, *rain falls in* —, c'ong t'in do yü 冲天大°雨; yü loh ziang tao' ka 落雨像倒下°一°般°

Tortoise, *black* u-kyü' 烏龜; — *shell,* dæ-me k'oh 玳瑁殼; *broken do,* dæ-me sih 玳瑁屑; *black* — *shell,* pih'-kah 鼈甲°

Tortuous, wæn-ky'üoh'-go 彎曲個°

Torture, (*as a punishment*), ying-vah hyüong 刑罰兇; gyih-ying極°刑; *in perfect* —, kw'u'-t'ong ky'üoh'-feh-ko 苦痛吃°弗過

Toss, *to* — *up,* tiu-zông'-ky'i 丟上去°; — *about,* tiu-læ' tiu-ky'i' 丟來丟去'; — (as one unable to sleep), cün-tsch' 轉側

Total, t'ong'-gong 統共; *sum* —, tsong-su 總數; gong-kyi' 共計; — *eclipse of the sun,* nyih-deo' djün-zih' 日頭全蝕; nyih-deo djün-ko wu-sah 日頭全個食去°

Totally *spoiled,* long'-tsong i-diao-de 攏總壞°了°; djün-djün' long-wæn'-de 全弄壞°了°

TOTTERING, (a person), ts'ong'-ts'ong-dong 衝衝動; ts'ih'-ts'ong-pah-tih' 七衝八跌; — wall, ziang' yiao-yiao'-dong 墙搖搖動

TOUCH, to bang 搪; bang-djoh' 搪着°; cannot be touched, bang'-feh-teh'-go 搪弗得個°; — and feel, moh 摸; moh-djoh' 摸着°; must not —, or move, siu'-nao' dong gyi 手弗°可°動其; to place the hand upon, siu en'-ih'-en 手按一按

TOUCHING, close to, t'iah'-gying 貼°近

TOUCH-STONE, s'-kying-zah' 試金石°; mo-kying'-zah 磨金石°

TOUGH, nying 靭; nying-bi'-tiao'-ts'i 靭疲刁氣; able to endure, mæn-ky'i' 蠻氣

TOW, to — a boat (as by a steamer), ta jün' 帶°船; — by a rope, ts'ô-ky'in' 拉縴; te-ky'in' 背°縴

TOWARD, hyiang 向; dziao 朝; — the South, hyiang Nen' 向南

TOWEL, siu'-kying 手巾; min-pu' 面布; dish —, k'a' beng'-ts pu' 揩°盆子布; k'a-pu' 揩布 (ih-keng, ih-kw'e)

TOWER, t'ah 塔; drum —, kwu'-leo 鼓樓; — on the city wall, dzing-leo' 城樓; fi-leo' 飛樓

TOWN, walled dzing-ts' 城子 (ih-zo); market — (unwalled), cing'-deo 鎮頭; z'-cing 市鎮 (ih-go)

TOYS, hyi-djü' 戲具; sô'-ho 耍貨

TOY-SHOP, sô'-ho tin 耍貨店; toy-stall, sô'-ho t'æn 耍貨攤; toy-inuige-shop, 'en'-tin 泥°孩°店

TRACE, ying-tsih' 形跡; ing'-tsong 影踪; mark, 'eng-tsih' 痕跡; — of footsteps, kyiah'-tsih 脚跡; tsoug-tsih' 踪跡; kyiah'-u 脚痕°

TRACE, to — on paper, ts-li' miao' 紙裡描; — over a pattern, ing'-leh sia' 引了°寫°; — his footsteps, keng'-leh gyi kyiah'-tsih tsoo' 跟得°其脚跡走

TRACK of carriage wheels, ts'ô-leng'-go ying-tsih' 車輪個°形跡

TRACT on religion, siao peng'-deo dao'-li shü 小本個°道理書

TRADE, sang-i' 生意; kying-ying' 經營; — is dull, sang-i' ts'ing-dæn' 生°意清淡; sang-i ga'; sang-i' diao-da'; — is diminished, sang-i' siu-soh'-de 生°意收縮了°; to curtail one's —, sang-i' siu-bo'; what is your — ? ng soh'-go kying-ying' 你°甚°麼°經營?

TRADE, to kao-yih' 交易; to do business, tso sang-i' 做生°意; — at our shop, teng ah'-lah tin'-li kao-yih' 與°我等°店裡交°易; with whom do you — ? ng jü'-lah kao-yih'-go 你°誰°交°易個°?

TRADER, sang-i' nying 生°意人; tso-ma'-ma-nying 做°賣買人°; travelling —, k'ah'-nying 客人

TRA 487 TRA

TRADITION, kwu'-djün-yin' 古傳言 (veng); djün'-loh-læ'-go shih-wô' 傳下來个說話; shü'-dæ siang-djün'-go 世代相傳个°; djün-yin' 傳言
TRADUCE, to po-long' 播弄
TRAFFIC in tea is large, dzô-yih' ma'-ma to' 茶葉買賣°多; unlawful —, væn-kying'-go sang-i' 犯禁个°生°意; — in human beings, fæn'-ma sang-nying-k'eo' 販賣°人°口; — in fattening girls for bad purposes, yiang seo'-mô 養瘦馬
TRAGEDY, mournful play, pe-sông'-go byi'-veng 悲傷个戲文; mournful event, ts'æn'-sông-go z-t'i' 慘傷个事體
TRAIN, to instruct, kao 敎°; to bring up, iang 養
TRAIN of followers, keng-dzong'-go cü'-kwu 跟從个°人°; ze-dzong'-go 隨從个°
TRAIT, a good ih-yiang hao'-c'ü 一樣好處; many good traits, hyü'-to hao-c'ü' di-fông 許多好處地方
TRAITOR, one who informs the enemy, li'-t'ong nga-koh'-go 裏通外°國个°; an officer who turns —, kæn-dzing' 奸°臣; a Chinese —, Hen'-kæn 漢奸°; one who sells his country, ma-koh'-go 賣°國个°
TRAITOROUS, kæn-tsô'-go 奸°詐个°; kæn-wah-go 奸°滑个°

TRAMPLE, to dah 踏; nao 蹈°; — to death, dah-sah' 踏死°
TRANQUIL, en-tæn' 安妥; bing-en' 平安; t'a'-bing 太°平; all — (nothing to disturb), en'-jün' vu-z' 安然無事
TRANQUILIZE, to — him, s'-teh gyi ding-diah' 使得其定奪°; long gyi bing' 弄其平
TRANSACT, to — business, bæn z-t'i' 辦事體; ditto diligently, ken'-bæn z-t'i' 幹辦事體; — another's business, da'-we jing-z' 代爲人事
TRANSACTION, sô-bæn'-go z-ken' 所辦个°事幹
TRANSCENDS all our ideas, c'ih'-ü i'-nga 出於意外°
TRANSCRIBE, to ts'ao-sia' 鈔寫°; deng-sia' 謄寫°; ts'ao sia'-ko-ky'i 鈔寫°過去°; — distinctly, deng-ts'ing' 謄淸
TRANSCRIBED copy, ts'ao-bah' 抄白°
TRANSFER, to tsæn 趲; ts'in 遷; pun 搬; yi 移; — to another place, tsæn-u' 趲地°方°; — to that box, tsæn'-ko keb'-tsah siang-ts'-li 趲過這隻箱子裏; — to another person, kao-c'ih' 交°出; ditto entirely, kao'-siao 交°銷; — the capital, ts'in-tu' 遷都; — a coffin, ts'in-zæ' 遷材°; — baggage, 'ang-li'pun'-ko'-ky'i 行李搬過去°; — an official to another place, diao-zing' 調任

TRANSFORM, *to* pin-yiang 變樣; — (by some internal law, as from a worm to a butterfly), pin'-hwô 變化

TRANSGRESS, *to* væn 犯;— *the law*, væn fah' 犯法; *to sin*, væn ze 犯罪

TRANSGRESSION, ze 罪; ze'-ky'in 罪怨; ko'-shih 過失; ko'-tön 過端

TRANSGRESSOR, ze'-nying 罪人°; væn'-nying 犯人°; væn-fah'-go 犯法個°

TRANSIENT, ziu we ko'-ky'i 就°會過去°; dzæn-z'-go 暫時個°

TRANSIT, *inward* jih ne'-di 入內地; *outward* —, c'ih nen'-di 出內地; *inward—pass*, (Customs), jih ne-di se-tæn 入內地稅單

TRANSITORY, ko'-r-peh-liu' 過而不留

TRANSLATE, *to* fæn 繙; fæn-yih' 繙譯; — (*completely*), fæn-c'ih' 繙出; *how do you — this sentence into English?* keh'-kyü Da-Ing'-wô dza fæn'-go 這°句大英話怎°繙個°?

TRANSLATION *of the Four Books*, fæn-yih'-go S'-Shü 繙譯個°四書

TRANSLATOR, fæn-yih'-go cü'-kwu 繙譯個°人

TRANSMIGRATION *of souls*, cün-si' 轉世°; deo-t'æ 投胎

TRANSMIT, *to — money*, ta dong-din' 帶°銅錢°; *ditto through others* (as bills of exchange), we 匯; — (*as words*), djün 傳; — *to posterity*, djün' peh 'eo'-dæ 傳與°後代; djün-loh'-læ 傳下°來; — *the throne to a successor*, djün we' 傳位

TRANSPARENT, kwông' we t'eo'-ko-go 光會透過個°

TRANSPIRED, *the secret has —*, tseo'-leo fong-sing'-de 走漏風聲了°; lu-fong'-de 露風了°

TRANSPLANT, *to* ts'in-ko' ky'i-cong' 遷過去°種; — *rice*, cong dao' 種稻

TRANSPORT, *to* yüing 運; pun-yüing' 搬運; — *goods*, yüing ho'-veh 運貨物

TRANSPORT *for carrying rice to the capital*, yüing liang jün' 運糧船

TRANSPORTATION *a few hundred li*, du 徒; — *1000 to 2000 li*, liu 流; — *beyond the frontier*, c'ong-kyüing' 充軍

TRANPOSE, *to* diao zin-'eo' 調前°後; tsæn zông'-loh 攛上落

TRAP, gyiang 弶°; *rat* —, lao'-ts' gyiang 老鼠弶° (ih go); *iron ditto with teeth*, t'ih-mæn' 鐵猫° (ih tsah); *to set a —*, tsông gyiang' 裝弶°

TRASH, vu-yüong'-ts veh 無用之物

TRAVAIL, *to* ky'üoh seng-ts'æn'-go kw'u'-deo 吃°生產個°苦頭

TRAVEL, *to* c'ih-meng' 出門;

TRA 489 TRE

— *a distance,* c'ih yün'-meng 出遠門;— *every where,* koh'-tao-c'ü tseo-pin' 各到處走遍;— *to learn,* yiu-'oh' 遊學。 The last expression refers primarily to a *siu-dzæ* 秀才 going abroad for study, but is now used in a wider signification.

TRAVELLER, *one passing on,* ko-lu'-go-nying 過路个人°; *one away from his home,* c'ih-meng'-nying 出門人; *one who has travelled far,* c'ih-yün'-meng-go 出遠門个°.

TRAY, bun 盤; *tea —,* dzô-bun' 茶盤 (ih-min).

TREACHEROUS, *violating trust, and injuring,* tao'-toh-long'-ts-go 反°背°前°言°个°; fông-tao'-deo-p'ao'-go 放倒頭礮个°; *faithless by nature,* m̄-sing'-'ang-go 無°信行°个°.

TREAD, *to — upon,* dah 踏; nao 蹈°; *must not — on it,* m̄-nao' dah-gyi'-zong' 弗°可°踏其上.

TREASURE, *a* ih-go pao'-pe 一个°寶貝; ih-yiang pao'-pe 一樣寶貝; gyi-ho' k'o-kyü' 奇貨可居; *wealth,* dzæ-veh' 財物; *silver,* nying-liang' 銀兩; *royal —,* kw'u' nying 庫銀.

TREASURE, *to — with care,* kying'-kying kwu'-djoh 兢兢顧着°; *to put, or store away,* k'ông 囥; *ditto safely,* dzông-k'ông' 藏囥.

TREASURER, tsông nying-bun'-go 掌銀盤个°.

TREASURY, kw'u 庫; dzin-kw'u' 錢庫.

TREAT, *to* dæ 待; k'en'-dæ 看待;— *slightingly,* ky'ing-dæ 輕待; ky'ing-mæn' 輕慢; dæ'-mæn 怠慢;— *ill,* ts'ô'-tô 嘲°諷°;— *shabbily,* boh-dæ' 薄待;— *one well,* dæ nying hao' 待人°好°;— *kindly, or pet,* we'-wu 衛護; o'-lo 捰攞;— *a person well,* dæ nying 'eo' 待人°厚°; *as you — me, I'll —*, ng dza læ', ngô' dza ky'i' 你°怎°來我怎°去;— *with disrespect,* mao'-væn 冒犯;— *with irreverence,* sih'-doh 褻瀆; *ditto purposely,* c'ong-dzông', or ts'ong-dzông 衝撞.

TREATY, *contract,* iah 約;— *of peace,* 'o-iah' 和約; *to make a —,* lih iah' 立約; *to violate a —,* be iah' 背約.

TREBLE, *first —* (in music), tsing'-p'ing 正品; *second —,* fu'-p'ing 副品. See MRS. J. B. Mateer's Musical Instructor.

TREBLE, *to* kô-liang'-be-ts'eo' sæn-be' 加兩倍凑三倍.

TREE, jü 樹 (ih-cü).

TREES, jü-moh' 樹木.

TREMBLE, *to* teo 抖; fah-teo' 發抖; gwah-gwah'-teo 挏°挏°抖;— *with fear, or cold,* gying 噤; fah-gying 發噤; 'en-gying 寒噤; lang'-gying 冷噤; *heart trembling with fear,* sing hyü'-dah-tsin 心虛肉°顫.

TRENCH, keo 溝; open a —, k'æ' ih-da keo' 開一埭溝
TRESPASS, ze'-ko 罪過; ko'-shih 過失
TRESPASS over another's boundary, (by building, &c.), tsin di-ka' 佔地界°;—on your time, tæn-ngwn' ng-go kong-fu' 躭慺你个工夫;— against, teh'-ze 得罪
TRIAL, give (him or it) a —, s' ih-tsao k'en 試一遭看; s-ih'-s 試一試; to bring to —, &c., dzing-dzong' 成訟; have a —, yiu dzong-z' 有訟事; ditto (i.e. both sides going to law), tang kwun-s 打官司; ky'üoh kwun-s' 吃官司; yiu kwun-s' 有官司; (ih-ky'i) 一官司; won the —, kwun-s' tang'-ying-de 官司打贏了°; is the — (of a case) over? en'-gyin yiu liao'-kyih-feh 案件有了結否°?
TRIALS, afflictions, wæn'-næn 患難
TRIANGLE, sæn-koh'-ying 三角形
TRIBE, race, tsong-dzoh' 宗族; barbarous —, bu'-loh 部落; divisions of a —. ts-p'a' 支派; the twelve tribes of Israel, Yi-seh'-lih jih-nyi' ts-p'a' 以色列十二支派°
TRIBULATION, næn-deo' 難頭; kw'u'-næn 苦難; wæn'-næn 患難
TRIBUNAL, before the —, dæ yin' 臺前°; we yin' 位前°; place of the —, fah'-dông 法堂; the

six tribunals (at Peking), loh-bu' 六部
TRIBUTARY kingdoms, joh-koh' 屬國
TRIBUTE, to bring tsing-kong' 進貢; things offered as —, tsing-kong'-go li'-veh 進貢个禮物
TRICK, kwe'-kyi 詭計 (ih-go); to play a trick upon, hyi'-long 戲弄
TRICKS, full of —, kwe'-kyi tö-tön'-go 詭計多端个°
TRICKLE, to — down, ti'-loh-læ 滴落來; jing-loh-læ 潤下來
TRIFLE, siao'-z 小事; ky'ü-ky'ü'-siao'-z 區區小事; to — with, r-hyi' 兒戲; to make sport of, hyi'-long 戲弄
TRIFLING behaviour, 'ang-we'ky'ing-veo' 行為輕浮; 'ang-we feh djong'-jih 行為弗重實
TRIGGER, wông鑽; long-deo' 龍頭
TRIM, to — a lump (wick), tsin' teng-sing'-me 剪燈芯煤;— even, tsin bing' 剪平;— the beard, tæn ngô-su' 刑髭°鬚
TRIMMING, to put or tack on —, ting kwe'-ts 釘桂子; tsa kwe'-ts.
TRINITY, sæn we'-ih-t'i 三位一體
TRINKETS for the head, (principally, but others may be included), siu'-sih 首飾; box for —, deo-min-siang 頭面箱
TRIP, take a —, c'ih ih-go meng 出一次°門
TRIP, to — along, tseo'-leh ky'ing-fæn' 走得°輕泛; ditto (as a

child), ky'ing-t'iao' 輕佻; *to lose footing*, shih-kyiah' 失脚; *to cause to stumble*, keo-tih' 鈎跌; pæn-tih' 扳跌; *your foot tripped me*, ng-go kyiah' keo ngô tih' 你°个°脚鈎我跌

TRIUMPH, *beat the drum of* —, k'ao teh-sing'-kwu 敲得勝鼓; *sing — over victory*, ts'ông' teh'-sing'-ko' 唱得勝歌

TROOP, *a — of horse*, ih-de' mó'-ping 一隊馬兵; *a — of infantry*, ih-de' bu-ping' 一隊步兵; *many troops*, da-ping' 大隊°兵馬°

TROPIC *of Capricorn*, nen-ta' 南帶°; — *of Cancer*, poh'-ta 北帶°

TROPICS, *the* nyih-ta'熱°帶°; jih-ts'-sin 日至線

TROT, *to* siao'-p'ao 小°跑°

TROUBLE, *to* le 累; kying-dong' 驚動; — *many times, or in many ways*, væn 煩; væn-zeh' 煩雜°; *to annoy*, væn-ky'i' 煩起; *may I — you*, væn' ng 煩你; siang-væn' ng' 相煩你°; *can I — you to do it?* hao væn-lao' ng tso' feh 好煩勞你°做否°? *to worry*, ts'ao 噪; ts'ao'-ziao 噪擾; *tired of* (your) *troubling*, ts'ao'-feh-ko' 噪弗過; — *to come* (or go), lao-kyüô' 勞駕; *I put you to too much* —, (or, thank you), næn-we' ng 難爲你°; fi-sing' fi-sing' 費心費心; fi-ng-sing' 費你°心;

TROUBLE, *to make* —, sang'-c'ih z-ken' ke 生°出事幹來; *I have a great deal of* — *in teaching him*, ngô læ-tih kao' gyi yiu hyü'-to keh'-tah 我敎°其有許多兮疥; *to have one's* — *for one's pains*, ky'in' k'ong-mo' 牽空磨

TROUBLED *in mind*, sing ông'-de; sing' væn-meng 心煩悶; — *and worried*, væn-nao' 煩惱; — *looks*, zeo-nii' tang-pah'-kyih 愁眉°百°結; *the more I thought, the more I was* —, yüih-ts'eng' yüih-ông' 愈想愈煩

TROUBLESOME, *how* dza væn' 甚°煩; dza næn-we' 甚°難爲

TROUGH, zao 槽; *pig* —, cü-zao' 豬槽; *horse* —, mó'-zao 馬槽° (ih-go)

TROUSERS, kw'u 袴 (a pair, ih-iao); *the bottom of* —, kw'u' kyiah 袴脚

TROWEL, *mason's* nyi-tao' 泥刀; nyi-kah' 泥夾° (ih-pô)

TRUANT, *one who shirks study, and deceives*, la-'oh tsing' 賴學°精

TRUCE *to hostilities*, dzæn-ding' tang-tsiang' 暫停打仗; *board begging a* —, min'-tsin ba 免戰牌°

TRUE, tsing 眞; jih-we' 實爲; jih-dzæ' 實在; ky'üoh-jih 確實; dzing-jih' 誠實; *something — to act upon*, jih-loh' 實落; — *to his word*, gyi'-go shih'-wô sing'-

jih-go 其个°說話信實个;
— *and no mistake*, tsing-tao'-wô 眞實°話

TRULY, jih-dzæ' 實在; tsing-tsing' 眞眞; ko'-jün 果然

TRUMPET, (Chinese) 'ao-dong' 號筒; 'ao-teo' 號斗 (ih-kwun).

TRUNK, siang-ts' 箱子 (ih-tsah);
— *for clothes*, i-siang 衣箱;
leather —, bi-siang 皮箱;
board covering to protect a —, kah'-pœn 夾°板; — *of a tree*, jü'-sing 樹身; *elephant's* —, ziang bih 象鼻.

TRUST, *to rely upon*, k'ao'-djoh 靠着; i'-k'ao 依靠; i'-z i-z 倚恃; *to believe in*, siang-sing' 相信; *cannot* — *what he says*, gyi'-go shih-wô' feh-tsoh'-cing 其个°說話弗作準; gyi'-go shih-wô' sön-su-feh-læ 其个°說話算數弗來; gyi'-go shih-wô' k'ao'-feh-jih' 其个°說話靠弗實; — *in Christ*, k'ao'-djoh Yiæ-su' 靠着°耶穌; — *to one's self*, i'-z zi' 倚恃自°; — (*something*) *to another*, kao-dæ' 交°代; kao-fu' 交°付; *ditto, expecting him to look after*, t'oh'-fu 託付; *can't* — *him*, k'ao'-feh-djü'-go 靠弗住个°; t'oh'-sing-feh-ko 託信弗過.

TRUST, *responsible* tsah'-zing djong' 責任重; ken-yi' do' 干係大.

TRUSTY, t'o'-tông 妥當; weng'-tông 穩當; tih'-tông 的當.

TRUSTWORTHY, t'oh'-sing-leh-ko 託信得°過; k'ao'-leh-djü 靠得°住.

TRUTH, *the* tsing dao'-li 眞道理; *speak the* —, kông tsing-wô' 講°眞話; kông jih-wô' 講°實話; tsiao dzih-li' kông 照直理講°; kông lao'-jih wô' 講°老實話; *absolute* —, z-jün' tsing'-go 自然眞个°.

TRY, *to* s'-s 試試; s'-s-k'en' 試試看; — *once*, s'-ih-s' 試一試; — *at first*, or *beforehand*, s'-t'en 試探; — *to sleep*, s'-s hao kw'eng-joh 試試好睡熟否°;
— *the taste of*, zông-zông'-k'en 嘗°嘗°看; zông mi-dao' 嘗°味°道; — *various means to make better*, cü'-du 制度; — *all means possible and fail*, wang cü'-du jü' cü'-du, cü'-du feh-hao' 橫°制度堅制度制度弗好;
— *a case*, sing'-meng en'-gyin 審問°案件; — (as by fire), s'-lin 試煉.

TUB, dong 桶; *wash* —, kyiah'-dong 腳桶; *bath* —, gyiang'-nyüoh-dong' 洗°浴°桶; nyüoh-dong' 浴°桶 (ih-tsah).

TUBE, kwun'-ts 管子; *bamboo* —, coh'-kwun-dong' 竹管筒 (ih-diao, ih-keng).

TUCK, *to* — *in order to shorten* (as a dress), soh'-leh tön' 束短; — *it*, or *make a* —, soh'-ih-soh 束一束; — *in* (as bed covering),

seb'-tæn'-cün 扇進°去°; — or *pull up the sleeves,* ziu-ts' leh-zông'-ky'i 袖子拎上去°.
TUFT, *a* ih-soh' 一束; ih-lu' 一縷°; — *of feathers,* ih-soh tiao'-mao 一束鳥毛; — *of hair,* ih-lu deo-fah' 一縷°頭髮
TUFT, *to* — (as a cushion), ih-soh'-ih-soh ting' 一束一束紅
TUMBLE, *to* — *down,* tih'-tao 跌倒; le-tao'; —*over,* fæn'-tao 翻倒
TUMBLER, po-li'-pe' 玻璃杯 (ih-tsah)
TUMOR, *swelling,* cong 癰 (ih-go)
TUMULT, nao-z' 鬧事; nying-to' k'eo'-hyiang 人°多口響; *to raise a* —, nao'-c'ih z' læ 鬧出事來
TUMULTUOUS, *to be* —, ts'ao'-nao 譟鬧
TUNE, ky'iang-diao' 腔調
TUNE, *to* — (as a fiddle), diao-yin' 調絃
TUNNEL *for discharging liquors,* leo-teo' 漏斗 (ih-go); — *in the ground,* di-dao' 地道; — *through a hill,* sæn-dong' lu 山洞路; *to make a* —, k'æ ih-go di-dao' 開一个°地道
TURBAN, pao-deo'-pu' 包頭布 (ih-kw'e)
TURBID, weng-weng'-go 混混个°; weng-djoh'-go 混濁个°
TURBULENT, sing'-dzing yia'-ky'i 性情野°氣

TUREEN, t'ông-kwun' 湯罐 (ih-tsah)
TURF, *sod,* ts'ao'-bi 草皮 (ih-kw'e)
TURKEY, ho'-kyi 火雞 (ih-tsah)
TURMERIC, kyiang-wông' 薑黃
TURN, *to* — *around* (as a wheel), cün 轉; cün'-dong 轉動; yüing-dong' 運動; — (as a key, or screw), cih'-cün 折°轉; — *the head,* deo' nyin-cün' 頭回°轉; deo nyin-hyiang' 頭側°向; — *upside down,* fæn'-cün 反轉; — *back* (in walking), tao' tseo-cün 倒走轉; — *a corner,* cün-wæn' 轉彎; wæn-cün' 彎轉; — *wrong side out,* fæn-min' 翻面 — *the back* (in going), fæn' pe 反背; — *the back towards,* be hyiang' 背向; — *out* (as from a bowl), tao'-c'ih 倒出; *the tide is turning,* dziao-shü we-deo'-de 潮水回頭了°; dziao-shü'cün'-de 潮水轉了°; *to* — *bad* (as food), tseo-mi' 變°味; *ditto* (as sweet-meats, &c.), fæn 泛; fæn-diao 泛壞°; — *sour,* pin'-leh sön'-de 變得酸了°; tsoh-sön' 作酸; — *to oil,* pin'-leh yiu de 變得油了°; — *against one for slight cause,* we'-leh siao'-z fæn-lin' 為了小事翻臉; — *away,* nyin-cün'-ky'i 側°轉去°; — *back and forth,* fæn-læ' fæn-ky'i' 翻來翻去°; — *over and over,* fæn-læ' foh-ky'i' 翻來覆去°; — *out well* (as a child, &c.),

dzing-ky'i' 成器; *to take a —, or short walk,* tseo' ih-cün 走一轉; *ditto, for one's own business,* tang ih-go wang';—*with a lathe,* ts'ô 車

TURNS, *to do by —,* ling'-leh tso' 輪°得°做; ling-wun' tso 輪°換°做; ling-læ' ling-ky'i tso' 輪°來輪°去°做; *ditto,* (by exchange), diao-læ' wun-ky'i tso' 調來換去°做; *cold and hot by —,* ih-zi lang', ih-zi nyih' 一齊°冷°一齊°熱°; dziao-lang' dziao-nyih' 潮°冷°潮°熱°

TURNIP, *radish,* lo-boh' 蘿蔔

TURTLE, *small* u-kyü' 烏龜; kyiah'-ng 甲魚°; do-ng' 大°魚°; pih 鼈; *large —,* la-deo-nyün' 癩°頭°黿 (ih-tsah)

TURTLE-DOVE, pæn-kyiu' 斑鳩 (ih-tsah)

TUSK, liao-ngô' 獠牙°; *elephant's —,* ziang'-ngô 象牙° (ih-ts)

TUTELARY *deity* (of a place), t'u'-di bu'-sah 土地菩薩

TUTOR, *teacher,* sin-sang' 先生 (ih-we)

TWEAK, *to — the nose,* nyiu bih-deo' 扭°鼻°頭

TWEEZERS, nyiah-ts-gyin' 揑指箝 (ih-pô).

TWELVE, jih-nyi' 十二°

TWELVTH, *the* di jih-nyi' 第十二°; *— part,* jih-nyi'-feng ts-ih' 十二°分之一

TWENTY, nyiæn 廿

TWENTIETH, *the* di-nyiæn' 第廿; *— of the month,* nyi-jih' 二°十; *— part,* nyiæn-feng' ts-ih' 廿分之一; nyiæn-kwu' li-hyiang' ih-kwu' 廿股裏向一股

TWICE, liang' tsao 兩遭; liang' we 兩回; liang' pin 兩遍; liang' vah.

TWIG, *a* ih-tiao ô-ts' 一條椏°枝

TWILIGHT (in the morning), u-long'-song 烏眼嗓°, or 矇°矇°亮°; — (in the evening), wông-hweng-deu' 黃昏時°

TWILLED *cotton cloth,* zia'-veng-pu' 斜°紋布; *gray ditto,* hwe-seh' zia-veng 灰色斜°紋

TWINE, *hemp* mô-sin' 麻線

TWINE, *to — about,* dzin 纏; nyiao 繞°

TWINKLING *of an eye,* ngæn'-tsing ih-sah' 眼°睛一睡; *— of a star,* sing-kwông' t'eo'-t'eo-dong 星光透透動

TWIN, sông-sang' 雙生°

TWIRL, *to — with the fingers,* mih 轉; *— a cash,* mih dong-din' 轉°銅錢°

TWIST, *to* cih'-cün 折°轉; *to — with the hand,* ts'o 搓; *— with the fingers,* tsih 織; mih 搖; *— hempen thread,* ts'o mô-sin' 搓蔴線; t'oh mô-sin'; *— ropes,* kao læn' 絞纜; tang zing' 打繩°

TWISTED, *neck bone is —,* deo-kying'-kweh cih'-c'ih-de 頭頸骨折°出了°; *— or twined,* *together*, nyiao-long'-liao 繞°攏了°; gao-long'-liao 絞°攏了

TWITCHING, *muscles are* —, kying' læ-tih te 筋適°轉°

TWO, nyi 二°; liang 兩,(also means a few); — *catties*, nyi kying' 二°斤;— *hundred*, nyi pah' 二°百°; — *men*, liang'-go nying' 兩个人°; — *months*, liang'-ko yüih' 兩個月; — or *three cash*, ko'-pô dong-din' 個巴銅錢°; *cut in* —, te' p'ö'-k'æ 對破開; *ditto* (with scissors), te' tsin-k'æ' 對剪開

TYPE, ing'-ts 影子; — *of Christ*, Yiæ-su'-go ing'-ts 耶穌个°影子; *lead* —, k'æn-z' 鉛字; *movable* —, web-z'-pæn 活字版

TYPE-SETTER, pa-z'-go 排字个°

TYPHOON, fong-pao' 風颶; gyü'-fong 颶風

TYRANNICAL, bao-nyiah'-go 暴虐个°; hyüong-ôh' 兇惡

TYRANT, bao-nyiah'-go wông-ti' 暴虐个°皇帝; Gyih-Dziu'-ts-kyüing' 桀紂之君.*

  * So called from two ancient Chinese kings named Gyih and Dziu.

TYRO, sang-siu' 生°手

U

UBIQUITOUS, vu-sô'-peh-dzæ' 無所不在; c'ü'-c'ü læ-tong' 處處都°在°

UDDER, na-dæ 嬭°袋; na-bu.

UGLY, wa-k'en' 歪看; *very* —,

p'ô'-nying-sah-la 怕人°幞橉°; ts'iu'-leo 醜陋; — *and uncouth*, jing'-feh-c'ih-cong', mao'-feh-c'ih-siang' 人弗出衆貌弗出相

ULCER, ts'ông 瘡; ts'ông-doh' 瘡毒; *malignant* —, doh ts'ông' 毒瘡; *to have an* —, sang ts'ông' 生°瘡; sang doh 生°毒

ULTIMATELY, tao'-ti 到底; kwe-keng' 歸根; kyiu'-kying 究竟; tao kyih'-sah 到結煞; cong-ü' 終于

UMBRELLA, sæn 傘 (ih-ting); *rain* —, yü'-sæn 雨傘; *sun* —, liang-sæn' 涼傘; — *of state*, wông-lo'-sæn 黃羅傘; *to open an* —, ts'ang sæn' 撐傘; *to shut an* —, siu sæn' 收傘

UMBRELLA-MAKER, sæn'-s-vu 傘司務

UMPIRE, kong-tön' cü'-kwu 公斷个°人°

UNABLE, feh neng'-keo 弗能彀; — *to remember*, kyi'-feh-teh 記弗得; — *to use*, yüong'-feh-djoh' 用弗着°; yüong'-feh-teh' 用弗得; yüong'-feh-læ' 用弗來; — *to bear*, tông'-feh-djü 擋弗住; — *to eat, to do, or to endure*, ky'üoh-feh-loh 吃°弗下°; — *to overtake*, ken'-feh-zông 趕弗上; — *to stand*, dzæn-feh-djü' 站弗住; — *to stand firmly*, lih'-feh-weng' 立弗穩; lih'-feh-lao' 立弗牢

UNACCOMMODATING, feh-yün'-

t'ong 弗圓通; feh-t'ong'-yüong 弗通融

UNACCOUNTABLE, soh'-go yün'-kwu, feh-tong'甚°麽°綠故, 弗懂; næn-ts'eh' næn-ziang' 難測難詳

UNACCUSTOMED, feh-kwæn' 弗慣; long-feh-kwæn' 弄弗慣; — to do, tso'-feh-kwæn 做弗慣 — to wear, c'ün'-feh-kwæn' 穿弗慣

UNACQUAINTED with, feh-nying'-teh 弗認°得; feh-min'-jing 弗面認; — with the ways of the world, feh-sih shü'-vu 弗識世務

UNADULTERATED, m̄'-neh ts'æn-kô' 沒°有°攙假°; feh-tsiah-kô' 弗攙°假; — goods, tsing ho' 眞貨

UNALTERABLE, keng'-kæ-feh-læ-go 更改弗來个°

UNANIMOUS, dong-sing'-'eh-i' 同心合意

UNANSWERABLE, pæn-poh'-feh-læ 扳駁弗來

UNANSWERED (as letters), feh-zing' we-teh'-de 弗曾回答了°

UNANTICIPATED, liao'-feh-tao' 料弗到; siang'-feh-tao' 想弗到; liao-siang'-feh-tao' 料想弗到; i'-siang-feh-tao' 意想弗到

UNAPPROACHABLE, gying-sing'-feh-long'-go 近身弗攏个°

UNARMED, feh-ta' bông-siu'-go kô'-sang 弗帶°防手个°傢伙°;

— soldiers, feh-ta'-ky'i-yiæ'-go ping 弗帶器械°个°兵

UNATTAINABLE, teh'-feh-djoh' 得弗着°; teh'-feh-tao-siu' 得弗到手

UNAUTHORIZED, gyüoh-nga' 局外°; veng-nga' 分外°

UNAVOIDABLE, cannot be shunned, min'-feh-teh 免弗得; cannot get rid of, t'e'-feh-diao' 推弗去°; no help for it, peh-teh-yi' 不得巳; shih'-feh-teh' 設法奈何°

UNBECOMING, feh-siang-nyi' 弗相宜; feh-siang-'eh' 弗相合

UNBELIEVING, feh-siang-sing'-go 弗相信个°

UNBENDING, tsah'-ngang 執硬; — (in a good purpose), ngang-lah' 硬辣; kông-gyiang' 剛強 — (in a bad thing), sang-gyiang' 生°強

UNBIASED, m̄-p'in'-go 無°偏个°; m̄-p'in-ky'üoh'-go 無°偏曲个°; — opinion, m̄-p'in-ky'üoh'-go i'-s 無°偏曲个°意思; — mind, kong-dao' sing 公道心

UNBIND, to t'eo' 抖; t'eo'-k'æ 抖開; t'eo'-sæn 抖散; ka'-k'æ 解開; — the feet, t'eo kyiah' 抖腳

UNBLAMABLE, kwa'-feh-læ'-go 怪°弗來个°; m̄-p'i-bing'-go 無°批評个°

UNBLEMISHED, m̄-yüô-tin' 無°瑕玷

UNBOLT the door, bah meng-shün' 拔門閂

UNB 497 UNC

UNBOLTED *flour*, ta'-bi min-feng 帶°皮麵粉; ts'u min'-feng 麤麵粉

UNBOSOM *the heart*, dæn-dæn sing' 談談心; — *one's troubles*, kông sing-z' 講°心事

UNBOUNDED, ɯ-'æn'-cü 無°限°制; ɯ-'æn'-liang 無°限°量; ɯ-pin'-ɯ-ngen' 無°邊無°岸

UNBRIDLED, fông'-tsong 放縱

UNBROKEN, ɯ'-neh k'ao'-se 沒°有°敲碎; — *line*, lin-ky'in' feh-dön 連牽弗斷; — *succession*, mah-mah' siang-lin' 脈脈相連; *ditto* (as living things), seng-seng'-peh-sih' 生生不息; — *horse*, sang mô' 生°馬

UNBURIED (as a person), ɯ'-neh en-tsông' 沒°有°安葬; — (as animals), ɯ'-neh tsông' 沒°有°葬; ɯ-neh bu-loh' 沒°有°理°落

UNBURNT *bricks*, cün-deo' p'e-ts' 磚頭坯子

UNBUTTON, *to* coh nyin'-ts 解°鈕子; *unbuttoned*, nyin'-ts coh-k'æ-tih-de 鈕子解°開了°

UNCEASING, feh-hyih' 弗歇; — *by day*, *or night*, nyih-yia' feh-hyih' 日°夜°弗歇

UNCERTAIN, vi-ding' 未定; vi-k'o'-cü 未可知; yün-shü' 懸勢; yün-r-vu-poh' 懸而無薄°; *not determined*, weh-deh' 滑突; ɯ-su' 無°數; ɯ-su'-moh-tsiang 無°數目賬

UNCHAIN, *to* k'æ lin-diao' 開鏈條

UNCHANGEABLE, üong' feh-pin'-yih 永弗變易; *cannot be changed*, k'æ'-pin-feh-læ 改變弗來

UNCHARITABLE, ɯ-jing-sing'-go 無°仁心个°, *or* ɯ-jing-sing'-go 無°人心个°

UNCHASTE *thoughts*, nyiæn-deo' feh-kyih'-zing 念頭弗潔淨

UNCIVIL, ɯ-li'-go 無°禮个°

UNCLE, *father's older brother*, ah-pang' 阿伯°; *father's younger brother*, ah-song 阿叔; *mother's brother*, gyiu'-gyiu 舅舅; nyiang-gyiu' 娘舅

UNCLEAN, feh-kyih'-zing 弗潔淨; — *thoughts*, nyiæn-deo' feh kyih'-zing 念頭弗潔淨; ao-tsao' i'-s 壂糟意思

UNCOMFORTABLE, feh-ziu'-yüong 弗受用; feh-shü'-voh 弗舒服; — *in mind*, sing'-li feh teh'-ko 心裡弗得過; feh sông'-kw'a 弗爽快°; feh-shih'-i 弗適°意

UNCOMMON, fi-dzông' 非常; feh'-z zing-dzông' 弗是尋°常

UNCOMMONLY, fi-væn' 非凡; — *good*, fi-væn' hao 非凡好; c'ih'-kah-go hao' 出格个°好

UNCONCERNED, feh-læ' i'-li 弗在°意裡; *perfectly* —, 'ao'-feh-dzæ i' 毫弗在意; *to look* —, feh-ts'iu'-ts'æ 弗偢睬

UNCONSCIOUS, feh'-cü-feh-koh' 弗知弗覺; peh'-cü-peh-kyüoh'

不知不覺;— of wrong, ü-sing'-vu-kw'e' 於心無虧
UNCONSTRAINED, ts'ong-ts'ong'-yüong-yüong' 從從容容; z-z'-dzæ-dzæ 自自在在
UNCOURTEOUS, ṅ-li'-go 無禮个°; shih-li'-go 失禮个°
UNCOUTH, ṅ-yiang'-væn 無樣範
UNCOVER, to open a cover, hyiao-k'æ' 揭開; — (as by removing a cloth, &c.), kyih'-ky'i 揭起
UNCULTIVATED land, hwông di' 荒地; — in manners, t'u'-lao 土老兒°
UNDECIDED, feh-zing' ding-kwe' 弗曾定規; wa vi-ding' 還°未定; wa vi-kyüih' 還°未決; — in purpose, cü'-i k'ô'-feh-ding' 主意拿°弗定; cü'-i lih'-feh-ding' 主意立弗定; — (as a battle), sing'-ba-vi-feng' 勝敗°未分
UNDECEIVE, to k'æ-ngæn' 開眼°; di-p'o' 點破
UNDER, 'ô 下°; ti-'ô' 底下°; 'ô-deo' 下°頭; — side, 'ô'-min 下°面; — the table, læ cuh'-teng 'ô 在桌下°; — his control, læ gyi' siu'-'ô 在°其手下°; — fifty, ng'-jih yi-'ô' 五°十以下°; ng'-jih yi-ne' 五°十以內
UNDER-DONE, ky'in joh' 欠熟
UNDERGO, to ziu 受; ziu'-teh 受得; — suffering, ziu'-kw'u ziu-næn' 受苦受難; — great changes, do keng'-kæ 大°更改; ditto (as places), kæ'-zao-ko 改造°過

UNDER-GROUND, læ di-'ô' 在°地下°; di-'ô'-go 地下°个°
UNDERHAND, to do things in an — way, en'-di-li tso' z-t'i' 私°下°行事°; secretly to use unfair means, t'eo-bun' yüong siu'-kyiah 偷瞞°用手腳; ying-s'-tsoh'-bi 行私作弊
UNDER-LET, to cün' tsu-c'ih' 轉租出; gyiao tsu-c'ih' 僑租出
UNDERLING (as an inferior officer), 'ô'-joh 下°屬; — (as a servant), ti-'ô'-nying 底下°人°; siu-'ô'-nying 手下°人°; polite, nyi-yia' 二°爺
UNDERMINE, to — a wall, ziang-kyiah' gyüih-song' 牆腳掘鬆
UNDERNEATH, læ ti'-'ô 在°底下°; læ 'ô'-deo 在°下°頭
UNDERRATE, to k'en'-feh-tao' 看弗到; kwu'-liang-feh-tao' 估量弗到; yiu-ngæn' feh-sih' T'a'-sæn 有眼°弗識泰山; — the price, kô'-din kwu'-leh zin' 價°錢估得°賤°
UNDERSELL others, pi bih'-nying ma'-leh zin' 比別人°賣得°賤°; t'eng'-kô ma 減°價賣°
UNDERSTAND, to tong; 懂 hyiao'-teh 曉得; — clearly, ming-bah' 明白°; do you — ? ng' ming-bah' feh 你°明白°否°? ng tong' feh-tong' 你°懂弗懂? I —, ming-bah'-go 明白°个°; tong'-go 懂个°; he understands his business, gyi'-go 'ông-tông joh-

sih' 其个行業熟識; *he understand his trade,* gyi'-go vu'-nyi tsing-t'ong 其个武藝精通; gyi dzæ-'ông' 其在行°

UNDERSTOOD, *I — you to say so,* ngô i'-we ng z-ka' wô' 我意會°你°如°此°話

UNDERTAKE, *to* tæn-tông' 擔當; dzing-tông 承當; *I dare not — it,* ngô' feh-ken' tæn-tông' 我弗敢擔當; *to begin,* k'æ-siu' 開手

UNDESERVING OF, feh-kæ'-tông ziu' 弗該當受; feh-ken' tông 弗敢當

UNDESIGNEDLY, vu-i'-cong 無意中; z'-c'ih-vu-sing' 事出無心

UNDETERMINED, See UNDECIDED.

UNDIGESTED, feh-siao-hwô' 弗消化; feh-k'eh'-hwô 弗尅化; feh-'ang'-hwô 弗行化

UNDISCERNIBLE, k'en'-feh-c'ih'-go 看弗出个°

UNDISCIPLINED, m'-meh ts'ao-lin'-ko 沒°有操練過

UNDISTINGUISHABLE, feng-ming feh-læ 分明弗來; feh-kyin'-teh feng-ming' 弗見得分明

UNDIVIDED, *to give — attention,* cün-r' cü'-ts tso' 專心致志而°做

UNDO, *to — what has been done),* sông-diao' 傷壞°; *to untie, or unfasten,* ka'-diao 解去°; ka'-k'æ 解開

UNDOUBTEDLY, ih-ding' 一定; ih-ding-peh-yih' 一定不易; vu-nyi' 無°二°

UNDRESS, *to* t'eh i-zông' 脫衣裳°

UNDULATING (like waves), ziang shü-po-lông' ka 像水°波浪一樣°; *— ground,* di-yiang ih'-kao, ih-ti' 地下°一高一低

UNDUTIFUL, peh-hyiao' 不孝; peh-hyiao'-peh-di' 不孝不弟

UNEASY, sing feh-en' 心弗安; fông'-sing-feh-loh' 放心弗下°; sing-mông'-feh-ding' 心忙弗定; *— and anxious,* ky'ih'-du kwô'-dziang 掔肚掛腸; *— and worried,* sing'-li tsiao-ts'ao' 心裏焦躁; *— (without knowing the'reason, &c.),* bông-wông'-tsi-tsao' 徬徨唶嘈

UNEMBARASSED, ts'ong-ts'ong'-yüong-yüong' 從從容容

UNEMPLOYED, zo'-siu 坐°守; k'ong-'æn 空閒°; hyih'-nyih-tong' 閒°居無°事

UNENLIGHTENED, mong'-tong 懞懂

UNEQUAL, *not regular,* feh-zi'-jih 弗齊集; ts'æn-ts'', or ts'en-ts' 參差; *not uniform,* feh' z ih-pæn' sang 弗是一班生; *— proportions,* feh-kyüing-yüing' 弗均勻; *— to a task, (in talent, strength, &c.),* dzæ-lih' peh-gyih' 才力不及

UNEVEN, *not level,* feh-bing' 弗平; feh bing'-dzih 弗平直; ky'i-ky'iao' 蹊蹺; *— (as stones* jutting out, &c.), ngæn-ngæn'-ngô-ngô' 嚴嚴矸矸; ts'ih'-kao-pah-ti' 七高八低

UNEVENLY put on, or mixed —, feh-diao-yüing 弗調勻

UNEXPECTEDLY, liao-feh-tao'-go 料弗到个°; siang'-feh-tao'-go 想弗到个°; ts'eng'-feh-tao'-go 忖弗到个°; i'-nga'-go 意外个°; to meet or happen —, peh'-gyi-r nyü' 不期而過

UNEXPLORED place, di-fông' ṁ'-neh dzô-ts'ah'-ko 地方没有°查察過

UNFAIR, unjust, feh-kong'-dao 弗公道; to be — (in play, &c.), long nyün'-gyüob 弄軟騙局; to use — means, yüong siu'-kyiah 用手脚

UNFAIRLY, money — obtained, fi-li'-ts dzæ 非禮之財; ao-tsao' dong-din' 非°義°之°錢°

UNFAITHFUL, feh-cong'-sing 弗忠心

UNFASHIONABLE, feh-'eh-z' 弗合時; feh-z'-dao 弗時道; feh-tsoh' 弗作興°; out of date, be-z' 背時

UNFEELING, hard-hearted, t'ih'-tang-sing-dziang 鐵打心腸; sing-dziang ngang 心腸硬; ṁ-dzing'-veng 無°情孖; boh dzing' 薄情

UNFINISHED, vi wun'-de 未完了°; feh-zing tso'-wun 弗曾做完; vi' liao-kong' 未了工; feh-zing tso'-hao 弗曾°做好; vi tso'-dzing 未做成; vi-dzeng liao'-kyih 未曾°了結

UNFIT for use, ṁ-tso' ; feh-teh-yüong' 弗得用; feh-'eh-yüong' 弗合用; — for eating, ky'üoh'-feh-teh 吃°弗得

UNFOLD, to t'eo'-k'æ; ka'-k'æ 解開; — (as a flower), k'æ 開; fông'-k'æ 放開

UNFORESEEN difficulties, ts'eng'-feh-tao'-go næn-c'ü 忖弗到个°難處; peh-i'-ts z' 不意之事

UNFORGIVING, kyi-'eng'-sing-go 記恨心个°; feh-kw'un-shü-'go 弗寬恕个°

UNFORTUNATE, shih-z', or sih-z' 失時; peh-ying' 不幸; hyiao-fæn' 鵁泛; very —, da' peh-ying' 大不幸; — lot, yüing-ky'i' kæn-ka' 運氣尷尬; ming-yüing' feh-hao' 命運弗好; yüing-dao' seh'-deh 運道失達

UNFOUNDED, ṁ-keng'-go 無°根个°; ṁ-keng-kyiah'-go 無°根脚个°; yüing-læ' vu-ky'i'-go 雲來霧去°个°; — words (as reports, &c.), hwông-dông' shih-wô' 荒唐說話; it is quite —, keh'-z ts'ah'-c'ih-læ-go z-ken' 這°是造°出來个°事幹

UNFREQUENTED road, ṁ-nying' dza-tseo'-go lu' 無°甚人°走个°路; lonely —, lang'-loh-go lu' 冷°落°个°路

UNFRIENDLY, tsoh-te'-go 作圖个°;— persons, te'-deo nying 优譽人°; he is —, gyi' yiu du'-bing 其有肚病; he treated me in an — manner, gyi feh tông' ngô beng-yiu' k'en-dæ' 其弗當我朋友看待

UNFRUITFUL, ve'-kyih-kó'-ts-go 不會°結果子个°; ú-dao'-dzing-go 無°道成个°

UNGOVERNABLE, kwun'-feh-djü'-go 管弗住个°; kwun'-feh-voh'-go 管弗服个°

UNGRATEFUL, feh-dzeng' ken'-zia-go-sing 弗存感謝°个°心; ú-jing-sing 無°仁心; hyiao'-go 梟个°; feh-kyin-dzing' 弗見情; — for great favors, or mercies, ú-peng'-sing 無°本心; feh-ken'-eng 弗感恩; veo-eng'-go 負恩个°; vông-eng'-veo-yi' 忘恩負義; hyiao-nyiao' 鵑鳥

UNHAPPY, sing-kw'u' 心苦; sing-feh-en' 心弗安; very —, sing'-li meh'-deh-deh-go kw'u' 心裡默沓沓个°苦

UNHEALTHY, (as a place disagreeing with one), shü'-t'u feh-voh' 水°土弗服; a place having miasma, yiu tsông'-ky'i-go di'-fong 有瘴氣个°地方; having a poor constitution, t'i'-tsih tæn-boh' 體質單薄; ti'-ts hyiah' 體質°弱; — appearance (as a person), ky'ih'-boh-siang 怯薄

相; ditto, (as children), ts'ing-bi' boh-hyüih 青皮薄血

UNHULLED, lin-k'ông'-go 連糠个°; lin-bi'-go 連皮个°

UNHURT, ú'-teh sông' 沒°有°傷; vu-'æ' 無害; — (by a fall), ú'-neh k'eh-t'ong' 沒°有°磕痛; ú-neh k'eh-sông' 沒°有°磕傷

UNIFORM, ih-pæn'-sang 一班生°ih-t'i'-s-sang' 一體樣°式°; of — color, ih-seh'-go 一色个°; to dress in—, c'ün 'ao-i' 穿號衣

UNIMPORTANT, feh iao'-kying 弗要緊

UNINHABITABLE, deng-nying'-feh-læ'-go 庵人°弗來个°

UNINHABITED house, k'ông' oh 空屋;— place, ú-nying'-deng'-go di-fông' 無°人°庵个°地方; ú-nying'-in'-go di-fông' 無°人°烟个°地方

UNINTELLIGIBLE, ming-bah'-feh-læ 明白弗來; kwun'-t'ong-feh-læ' 貫通弗來

UNINTENTIONAL, vu-i'-cong 無意中; feh'-z deh-we' 弗是特爲; ú-sing' 無°心

UNINTERRUPTED, siang-lin' feh-dön' 相連弗斷; — rain for a month, yü', lin-loh' ih-ko yüih' de 雨連落一個月了

UNINVITED guest, ú'-neh ts'ing'-go nying-k'ah' 沒°有°請个°客人°; peh'-soh-ts k'ah' 不速之客

UNION (of two or more in one), 'eh'-r-we-ih' 合而爲一; the — of many states in one, hyü'-to sang 'eh-we' ih-koh' 許多省合爲一國

UNIT, one, ih 一; units occupy the first place, tens the second place, and hundreds the third, tæn-su'di-ih' we, jih-su' di-nyi' we, pah'-su di-sæn'we 單數第一位十數第二位百數第三位

UNITE, to 'eh-long' 合攏; siang-'eh' 相合; ping'-long 併攏; to join, siang-lin' 相連; lin-long' 連攏; to mix, 'o-long' 和攏; — (as a wound), siu k'eo' 收口; oil and water will not —, shü' teng yiu' 'eh-feh-long 水與油合弗攏; — all the numbers, tsong'-su 'eh-tæn-long' 總數合攏; — the contents of two bowls in one, ping'-long ih-tsah un' 併攏一隻碗; — in one pair, (man and wife), p'e' ngeo 配偶; p'e'-long ih-te' 配攏一對

UNITED, 'eh-long'-liao 合攏了°; ping'-long-liao 併攏了°; to be — with a superior in rank, or wealth, kao-p'æn' 高攀; put forth — strength, do-kô'ô gying-dao' 大°家用°勁道; dô-kô' dziah-lih' 大°家着力; — purpose, and effort, dong-sing'-yiah-lih' 同心恊力

UNITED-STATES, the 'Eh-cong'-koh 合衆國; Hwô-gyi'-koh 花旗國; America, Da-me' koh 大美國

UNITY, the church is one, kyiao'-we dong-ky'i'-lin-ts'-go 教會同氣連枝个°; — of design, ih-ky'i' kwun'-t'ong 一氣貫通; 'eh-dzing'-ih i' 合成一意; — of the races, t'in-'ô' dzoh-veng' tu z ih'-go keng-mah' 天下族孑都是一个°根脈

UNIVERSAL, p'u'-t'in-'ô' go 普天下°个°; 'en-t'in-'ô'-go 合°天下°个°; — reputation, kæ'-shü-go ming-sing' 蓋世个°名聲; — peace, t'in-'ô' t'a'-bing 天下°太°平

UNIVERSE, t'in-di'-væn'-veh 天地萬物; væn-yiu' 萬有

UNJUST, feh-kong' 弗公; feh-kong'-dao 弗公道; feh-kong'-bing 弗公平

UNKIND, sing-jih' feh-hao' 心術弗好; sing-jih' 'ah-tsah' 心術狹窄; sing-di' feh-hao' 心地弗好

UNKNOWN, m-nying' hyiao'-teh 無人°曉得

UNLADE, to ky'i-ho' 起貨; zông-ho' 上貨; — a vessel, sia-zæ' 卸繊°

UNLAWFUL, lih-fah'kying'-liao-go 律法禁了个°; we-lih' væn-fah'-go 違律犯法个°; — trade, væn-kying'-go sang-i' 犯禁个°生意; væn-fah'-go sang-i' 犯法个°生意

UNLEARNED, *not knowing letters,* feh-sih-z'-go 弗識字个; *not having learned,* m̍-neh 'oh-ko' 沒°有°學°過

UNLIKE, feh-ziang' 弗像; koh'-kiang 各樣; koh'-bih 各別; feh-dong' 弗同; *very* —, kyüong'-kyüong koh'-bih 迥迥各別; 'o'-jün koh-yiang' 一°概各樣; da'-feh-siang-dong' 大弗相同

UNLIKELY, vi-pih' 未必; feh-kyin'-teh 弗見得; siang'-pih ve' 想必不°會°; — *that he will go,* gyi vi-pih' ky'i' 其未必去°; siang'-pih ve'ky'i 想必不°會°去

UNLIMITED, m̍-'æn-go 無°限个°; m̍-'æn-cü-go 無°限制个°; m̍-pin'-m̍-ngen' 無°邊無°岸; — (as space), m̍-ka'-'æn 無°界°限

UNLOAD, *to* ky'i-ho' 起貨; zông-ho' 上貨; sia-bo' 卸貨; — *a ship,* sia-zæ' 卸艙

UNLOCK, *to* k'æ-so' 開鎖

UNLOOSE, *to* fông-kw'un' 放寬; fông-song' 放鬆; — *a knot,* ka-kyih' 解°結

UNLUCKY, hwe'-ky'i 晦氣; tao-yüing' 倒運; peh-ying' 不幸; feh-seh'-deo 弗色頭; feh-kyih'-li 弗吉利; feh-jing' 弗順; zao'-hwô-wa' 勿°得°意°; *to become* —, 'ang-mo' kw'u'-yüing 行墓庫運

UNMANAGEABLE, feh-yiu'-nying-kwun' 弗由人°管; — *pupil,* 'oh-sang'-ts feh-yiu'-nying-kwun' 學生°弗由人°管; — *horse,* mô' feh-yiu-nying' 馬弗由人°; — *therefore let them do as they like,* yiu-mô' feh-yiu-nying' 由馬弗由人°

UNMANLY, feh-ziang' nen-ts'-hen 弗像男子漢

UNMARRIED *man,* feh-zing' c'ü-ts'ing'-go 弗曾娶親个°; feh-zing' dæ lao'-nyüing-go 弗曾完姻个°; siao'-kwun-nying 小官人; dong-ts' 童子; *ditto* (who yields to evil desires, not being deterred by family restraints), kwông-kweng' 光棍; — *woman,* feh-zing' c'ih-kô'-go 弗曾°出嫁个°; feh-zing'tso sing-vn'-go 弗曾做新婦个°; do-kwu'-nyiang 大°姑娘; politely termed, kwe-nyü' 閨女

UNMEANING, *confused,* m̍-ka'-shih-go 無°解°說个°; wu-du' 糊塗; *light* (often false) *words,* veo-yin' 浮言; wu-yin' lön-dao' 胡言亂道

UNMERCIFUL, m̍-dz-sing' 無°慈心; sing-heng 心狠; *hardhearted,* sing-ngang 心硬

UNMERITED, feh-kæ' zin'-go 弗該受个°; feh-ing'-teh ziu' 弗應得受

UNMINDFUL, feh-dziah' læ i'-li 弗著在°意裡; feh-liu'-i 弗留意; feh-dzæ'-i 弗在意; *you are — of what I say,* ngô' sô wô'-go, ng' feh-dziah læ i'-li 我所話

個°你°弗着在°意裡;— of his own safety, (i. e. death or, life), feh kwu' zi-go si'-weh 弗顧自°個°死活

UNMIXED, jing 純; feh keh'-dzeh 弗夾雜; ǽ-neh c'ün'-long-go 沒°有°串攏個°; —or pure milk, jing na' 純嬭°; with — pleasure, jing' z hwun-hyi' 純是歡喜

UNMOLESTED, ǽ-kao'næn-we' 沒°有°難爲

UNMOVED (by temptation, &c.), feh-dong'-sing 弗動心; — countenance, min' feh pin-seh' 面弗變色; perfectly —, sing seh' feh dong' 聲色弗動

UNNATURAL, t'in sang'-dzing, siang-fæn'-go 天生°成相反個°; —disposition, t'in-sing'siang-fæn' 天性相反

UNNAVIGABLE river, 'o-kông' s'-jün'-feh-læ-go 河港駛船弗來個°

UNNECESSARY, hao-yong' 好不°用°; feh-yüong' 弗用; peh-pih' 不必; quite — (to do, or say), to-li'-shü 多禮數°

UNOCCUPIED house, k'ong' oh 空屋; — time, k'ong'-'æn z'-'eo 空閒°時候; —person, k'ong' 'æn nying 空閒°人°; ditto (who happens in), 'æn nying' 閒人; sitting (there) —, k'ong'-deo zo-kæn' 空閒坐在°彼°

UNOBSERVED, ǽ nying'k'en'-kyin 無°人°看見

UNPAID, wages still —, kong-din'-feh-zing' kyih-fah' 工錢°弗曾°給發; kong-din' feh-zing ka'-fah 工錢°弗曾°開發; salary still —, soh'-siu feh-zing' fu' 束修弗曾°付;— debts, tsa' feh-zing' fu' 債弗曾°付; tsa' feh-zing' wæn' 債弗曾°還

UNPALATABLE, ǽ-ky'üoh' 嚿吃°; næn-ky'üoh' 難吃°

UNPARDONABLE, nyiao-sô'-feh-læ 饒赦°弗來;* sô'-feh-læ 赦°弗來; sô-feh-diao; the ten — crimes (in China), jih-oh'-feh-sô' 十惡弗赦°

* Used for lighter offences, as those not against the laws of the country.

UNPERCEIVED, nying' feh-teh'-cü 人°弗得知; I entered —, ngô tseo'-tsing, nying' feh-teh'-cü 我走進人°弗得知

UNPLEASANT, ǽ-c'ü' 無°趣; ǽ-i'-cü 無°意趣; ǽ-hying'-cü 無°興致; ǽ-c'ü'-hyiang 無°趣味°; feh-cong'-i 弗中意; — man, tseng-nying 憎人°; — business, ǽ-i'-c'ü-go z-ken' 無°意趣個°事幹; ǽ-hying'-cü-go' z-ken' 無°興致個°事幹; — weather, t'in-kô' ǽ-c'ü'-hyiang 天不°晴°霽°; — to eat, feh-cong' ky'üoh-go 弗中吃°個°; — to hear (as a truth), feh-cong' t'ing'-go 弗中聽個°; ditto (as sounds), næn t'ing' 難聽; — smell, ky''i'-mi næn tông' 氣味°

難當; ts'iu' peh-k'o tông' 臭°不可當

UNPOLISHED, (as a stone, or person), m'-neh tsoh'-mo-ko 沒°有°琢磨過; — (as metals, &c.), m'-neh mo-ts'ah'-ko 沒°有°磨擦過; *anything* —, m-neh bao-siah'-ko 沒°有°刨削過; mao-sæn-jü' 毛杉樹; mao-p'e'-ts 毛胚子

UNPOPULAR, cong'-nying feh-'eh' go 衆人°弗合个°; cong'-nying feh-voh' 衆人弗服

UNPRECEDENTED, dzong-læ' m'-neh-go 從來沒°有°个°

UNPREJUDICED, kong-bing'-go sing' 公平个°心; *impartial*, m-p'in'-ky'üoh'-sing-go 無偏曲心个°; m-p'in'-sing-go 無°偏心个°

UNPREPARED, m'-neh bông-be' 沒°有°防備; m'-neh yü-be'-bao 沒°有°預備好

UNPROFITABLE, vu-ih'-go 無益个°; — *business*, vn-ih' ts-kyü' 無益之舉; — *trade* (very little profit), li-sib' boh 利息薄; *ditto* (no profit), ve-c'ib-hwô'-go 不會°出化个°; m-c'ib'-sih 無°出息; *hard*, — *work*, bah yiao-lao' 白°効勞

UNPROTECTED, (as a child, or female), m nying' dzing-kwun'-go 無°人承管个°

UNPUBLISHED, *not printed*, m'-neh ing'-pæn-de 沒°有°印板了°

UNPUNISHED, m'-neh vah-ko' 沒°有°罰過

UNQUENCHABLE, long'-feh-u'-go 弄弗熄个°; — (with water), p'eh'-feh-u'-go 潑弗熄°个°; — (by smothering), p'oh'-feh-u'-go 撲弗滅°个°; — *thirst*, ts feh-djü-go k'eh 止弗住个°渴

UNRAVEL, *to* — (as edges of cloth), seh-c'ih-læ 毛°出來; — (as knitting), sæn'-c'ih-læ 散出來; — (as a snarl), ka'-k'æ 解°開; fông'-k'æ 放開

UNREASONABLE, feh-dzing'-li-go 弗情理个°; m-li'-sing-go 無°理性个°; — *hopes*, vông'-siang 妄想

UNREDEEMABLE, (as a hostage), c'ü'-feh-læ 取弗來

UNRECONCILED, m'-neh 'o-long' 沒°有°和攏; m'-neh siang-'o' 沒°有°相和

UNREQUITED *favors*, vi-pao'-go eng 未報个°恩

UNRESERVEDLY, *not concealing anything*, 'ao' feh-ing'-mun 毫弗隱瞞; *not withholding anything*, 'o-bun' t'oh'-c'ih 和盤托出; zing'-du-dziang t'eo'-c'ih 盡°肚腸顯°出

UNRIGHTEOUS, feh-tön'-tsing 弗端正; feh-tsing'-dzih 弗正直; feh-kong-dao' 弗公道

UNRIPE, feh-joh' 弗熟; sang 生°

UNROLL, *to* k'æ kyün' 開卷

UNSAFE, feh-ẅeng'-tông 弗穩當; feh-t'o'-tông 弗妥當

UNSALABLE, m̈-siao-dziang' 無銷塲

UNSATISFACTORY, feh-tè'-kying 弗對徑;—to me, feh-mun' ngô-go i' 弗滿我个意

UNSATISFIED, feh-mun'-i 弗滿意; feh-cü-tsoh' 弗知足

UNSEASONABLE, z-'eo-fæn-djông' 時候反常; feh-gyih'-z 弗及時; t'in-z' feh-tsing 天時弗正; z-ling' feh-tè' 時令弗對

UNSEEN, m̈'-neh k'en'-kyin-ko 沒有看見過;— (or dark) world, ing-kæn' 陰間; ing-s' 陰司

UNSETTLED in heart, sing feh-ding' 心弗定; sæn-sing' liang' i' 三心兩意; sing weh' 心活; undecided, cü-i feh kyüih' 主意弗決; cü-i' k'o'-feh-ding' 主意拿弗定; can't determine, yiu-yü' peh-kyüih' 猶豫不決; kyüih-tön'-feh-loh' 決斷弗落

UNSHAKEN, feh-dong'-go 弗動个; m̈'-neh dong'-ko 沒有動過

UNSHAVED (as a Chinaman), m̈'-neh t'i-deo'-ko 沒有薙頭過

UNSKILLED, siu'-dön ẅa' 手段孬; feh joh'-sih 弗熟識; one just learning, and therefore —, bao-c'ih-long' 暴出籠

UNSOCIABLE, kao-nyin'-feh-long' 膠黏弗攏; feh teng nying' siang-yü' 弗同人相與; feh teng nying' kyiao-tsih' 弗與人交接

UNSOLD, m̈'-neh ma'-diao-de 沒有賣去了

UNSOUND, yiu mao-bing' 有毛病; has hidden faults, yiu en' mao'-bing 有暗毛病

UNSPEAKABLE, wô-feh-læ'-go 話弗來个; kông'-feh-c'ih'-go 講弗出个; cannot be described, wô'-feh - siang'-ziang-go 話弗相像个; feh-k'o' yiu-djün' 弗可言傳

UNSTEADY hand for holding a pen, pih' k'ô'-feh-ẅeng' 筆捏弗穩;—foot (in standing), kyiah' lih'-feh-ding' 脚立弗定; kyiah'-bu lih-feh-ẅeng' 脚步立弗穩;—(as a person), m̈-ding'-diah-go 無定奪个

UNSUBDUED as before, dzing-gyiu' feh-voh' 仍舊弗服;—(primarily in war, but used frequently in other connections), tsing' feh-voh' 征弗服;— by whipping, tang'-feh-voh' 打弗服

UNSUBSTANTIAL (as work), hyiah'-hyiah; feh kyin'-kwu 弗堅固;—and false, hyü-veo' 虛浮;—and worthless goods, 'ang-hô' 次等貨

UNSUCCESSFUL, not fortunate, m̈-zao'-hwô 無造化; feh-jing'-tông 弗順當; labor all in vain, bah-bah' lao-loh' 白白勞碌;— in obtaining what one desires, feh teh' i 弗得意

UNSUITABLE, feh-siang'-nyi 弗相宜; feh-te' 弗對

UNSULLIED, ts'ing-bah' 清白; ts'ing-kyih' 清潔;— *reputation*, ts'ing-bah'-go ming-sing 清白°个°名聲

UNSURPASSED, *it is* m̱-yiu' hao'-jü gyi' 沒°有好如他°; m̱-yiu ko'-jü gyi' 沒°有過如他°; m̱-yiu gyih'-jü gyi' 沒°有及如他°; c'ih' wu-gyi-le' 出乎其穎

UNSUSPECTING, feh-ts'æ'-nyi-go 弗猜疑个°; feh-nyi-sing'-go 弗疑心个° (veng.)

UNTEACHABLE, feh-ziu' kao'-hyüing 弗受教°訓; feh-t'ing' wô' 弗聽話

UNTHANKFUL, feh-dzeng' ken'-zia-go sing 弗存感謝°个°心; hyiao-nyiao' vu-dzing' 鵃鳥無°情; hyiao-dzing' boh-nyi' 梟情薄義

UNTHINKING, feh-ts'eng'-go 弗忖个°; *heedless*, môug-bah'-go 茫白°个°

UNTIE, *to* ka 解°; ka'-k'æ 解°開°;— *a knot*, ka kyih' 解°結

UNTIL, tao 到; ih-dzih'-tao 一直到; teng'-tao 等到;— *now*, tao-jü-kying 到如今; ih-dzih'-tao næn'-kæn 一直到如°今°; *wait —I come*, deng tao' ngô læ' 庬到我來

UNTIMELY *birth*, yüih-veng' feh-tsoh' 月殀弗足;— *death*, iao-ziu' 夭壽; töu'-ming-si' 短命死°; *plucked before his time*, ngang-ao' si'-de 硬拗死°了°

UNTOUCHED, m̱'-neh dong'-ko 沒°有°動過;— (*i.e. just as it was*), nyün-fông' feh-dong' 原放弗動; m̱'-neh bang'-ko 沒°有°撞過

UNTRUE, feh-jih' 弗實; feh-jih'-we 弗實爲; hyü'-go 虛个°; feh-tsing' 弗眞

UNTRUTH, hwông'-wô 謊話; hyü-wô' 虛話;— (*boasting*, &c.), do-wô' 大°話

UNUSUAL, feh-tsiao dzông' 弗照常; dzah-ngah' *it is* —, bing-djông' feh z-ka' 平常弗如°此°; su'-djông feh z-ka' 素常弗如°此°

UNUSUALLY, c'ih-keh' 出格;— (*never was so*), fi-djông' 非常;— *cold*, c'ih'-keh lang' 出格冷°; yi-wu' zing-djông'-go lang' 異乎尋常个°冷°; pi-tæn-djông' lang' 比朋°常冷°

UNUTTERABLE, kông'-feh-c'ih'-go 講°弗出个°; wô'-feh-læ'-go 話弗來个°; m̱-wô'-deo-go 無話頭个°; *too much to be expressed*, kông'-feh-tao-kô' 講°弗到家°

UNVARYING, feh-keng'-kæ 弗更改;— (*as appearance, sounds*, &c.), feh-pin'-yiang' 弗變樣

UNWARY, *not cautious*, feh-tso'-gyi 弗留°意; *not watchful*, feh-kying'-jing 弗謹慎; *not careful*, feh-siao'-sing 弗小心

UNWAVERING, feh-yiao'-dong-go 弗搖動个°
UNWEARIED, feh-p'ô' lao-kw'u' 弗怕勞苦; feh p'ô in'-væn 弗怕厭煩
UNWELL, feh-sih'-i, or feh-shih'-i 弗適意; feh-sông'-kw'a 弗爽快; næn-ko' 難過; yiu yiang' 有恙; *a little* —, yiu-tin' feh-shih'-i 有點弗適°意; yiu siao'-yiang 有小恙
UNWHOLESOME *food*, yiu-ngæ'-go ky'üoh'-zih 有碍个°吃°食; — *climate*, (i. e. water and soil not serving), shü'-t'u feh-voh' 水土弗服
UNWILLING, feh-k'eng 弗肯; feh yüoh'-i 弗欲意; feh dzing'-nyün 弗情願; *loth to part*, feh-sô'-teh bih-k'æ' 弗捨°得離°開
UNWIND, *to* dziu-c'ih'-læ 紬出來
UNWORTHY *to fill that office*, dzæ' peh sing zing' 才不勝任; — *to receive, or bear*, tông' feh-ky'i 當弗起; *not daring to bear*, feh-ken-tông' 弗°敢當; *not good enough*, ky'in-hao' 欠好; *conduct — of a teacher*, 'ang-we' teng sin-sang° feh-p'e' 行°爲與先生°弗配; — *to sit with*, sing-kô' feh-p'e zo'-long 身家°弗配坐攏; — *to do* (lest I spoil it), veo-nyi' sô-t'oh' 負你所托; — *of you*, teng ng p'e'-fu-feh-long 與°你配副弗攏; — *of mention*, peh-tsoh' dao' 不足道; — *of use*, peh-tsoh' yüong' 不足用

UNYIELDING, zah-fông-shing' 若°板°方°; kwu'-pæn-lin'-ky'i 古板臉氣; *heart — as iron*, (in a bad sense), sing' ziang t'ih' ka 心似鐵一°般°; sang'-leh'eo zi' 生得執己°; — *man*, nying dzih' feh cün-wæn'-go 認°直弗轉孌个°.
UP, zông 上; *come* —, tseo'-zông-læ 走上來; *push it* —, t'e-zông'-ky'i 推上去°; *the sun is* —, nyih-deo' zông-sæn'-de 日°頭上山了°; — *on the hill*, læ-sæn-zông' 在°山上; — *to this time*, dzih-tao' jü-kying' 直到如今
UPBRAID, *to* mao-ün' 埋°怨; *to reprove*, tsah'-vah 責罰; — *one for a fault*, p'i'-bing gyi-go ts'o' 批評其个錯
UPHOLD, *to* vu 扶; vu-dzi' 扶持°
UPLIFTED *hand*, siu'di-zông-tih 手提°上°的°; — *eyes*, ngæn'-tsing dao-zông'-tih 眼睛朝上的°
UPON, læ zông-deo' 在°上頭; — *my head*, læ ngô' deo zông 在我頭上; *dependent — salary*, k'ao soh'-siu du-nyih' 靠束修度日°.
UPPER, zông 上; — *layer*, zông zeng' 上層°; — *lip*, zông-bæn' cü'-jing 上爿嘴唇; — *room*, leo-teng' vông-kæn' 樓上°房間°
UPPERMOST, ting'-zông-go 頂上个°; ting-kao'-go 頂高个°
UPRIGHT (in position), pih'-dzih

筆直; *stand* —, pih'-dzih lih'-tong 筆直立在°此°; — (in character), tsing'-dzih-go 正直個°; tön-tsing 端正; tön-fông'-go 端方個°; tsing'-dzih-vu-s' 正直無私

UPROAR, *great noise*, ts'ao'-nao 譟鬧; *ditto, with trouble*, nao-z' 鬧事

UPROOT, *to* lin keng' bah-diao' 連根拔去°; *to dig up roots of trees*, dao za-cü' 掘°柴°梀

UPSET, *to* fæn'-tao 翻倒; *to turn over*, fæn-cün' 翻轉; — *by pushing*, t'e-tao' 推倒; *be careful, or you will be* —, &c., (*i.e.* be sick yourself, — said to one taking care of the sick), yüong kw'u-djoh zi' fæn-tao' 要顧着自°翻倒; — (as plans, work, &c.), tin-tao' 傾倒

UPSIDE *down*, tao'-toh-go-de 頂°倒°個°; tao'-deo-go-de 倒頭個°; tao'-hyiang-de 倒向了

UPSTAIRS, leo-teng' 樓上°

UPWARD, hyiang-zông' 向上; dziao-zông' 朝上

UPWARDS, *thirty years and* —, sæn'-jih nyin' yi-zông' 三十年以上; sæn'-jih nyin' yi-nga' 三十年以外°

URGE, *to* ts'e-song' 催慫; ky'ün 勸; — *to speed, or diligence*, ts'e 催; ts'e-ts'oh' 催促; — *with forcible means*, pih 逼; ts'e-pih' 催逼; or ts'e-bih 催逼; bih-bih'-ts'e' 辟辟催; — *a man to buy*, ts'e-song' nying ma' 催慫人°賣

URGENT, *instantly important*, kying'-iao 緊要; kyih'-ts'ih 急切; *in* — *need*, kyih'-soh iao' 急速要

URINAL, shü-bing 尿°瓶; yia-wu' 夜°壺; bin'-wu 便壺 (ih-tsah)

URINE, shü 尿°; siao'-shü 小尿°; siao'-bin 小便; *to pass* —, c'ih siao'-bin 出小便; dza shü' 撒尿°; ka siu' 解°手; c'ih siao'-kong 出小恭; siao' ka 小解

USAGE, kwe-kyü' 規矩; *long established* —, lao' kwe'-kyü 老規矩; lao' li 老例; *regulation*, tsông-dzing', or công-dzing' 章程; *receive bad* —, ziu we'-ky'üoh 受委曲

USE, yüong-dziang 用塲; *don't waste, you may find* — *for it*, peh'-fi-ts-we' 不費之惠

The veng-li means that it is not necessary to waste money in order to bestow favors.

USE, *to* yüong 用; s 使; s'-hwun 使喚; s'-yüong 使用; — *in common*, kong-yüong' 公用; tsong'-yüong 縱用; — *chopsticks*, yüong kw'æn' 用筯°; s kw'æn' 使筯°; — *carefully*, ts'-tsih yüong' 仔°細用; *want to* — *a man*, iao ih'-go nying s'-hwun 要一個人°使喚; *I cannot* — *it* (as a machine, *i.e.* it will not obey me), feh t'ing' ngô s'-hwun 弗聽我使喚

USED *much* (as words), nyih 熱°; *not ditto*, lang 冷°

USEFUL, yiu yüong-dziang' 有用塲; *very* —, jih-feng'-teh-ih' 十

分得益; — to me, yiu-ih' ü-ngô' 有益于我
USELESS, m̄-yüong'-dziang 無°用場; m̄-yüong'-go 無°用个°; — (because not good, or spoiled), m̄-tso' 沒°做; — (because not suitable), feh-teh'-yüong 弗得用; — labor, k'ong'-deo yüong-kong' 徒°然用功
USHER, to — in, ying'-tsing 引進
USUAL, djóng 常; bing-su' 平素; zing-djông' 尋常; djông-z' 常時; as —, tsiao' djông 照常; jü-djông' 如常; the same as —, tsiao' 'æn-djông' ih-yiang' 照用°常一樣
USUALLY, bing-su'-kyin, or bing-su'-kæn 平素間°
USURP, to tsin 佔; — by force, pô'-tsin 霸佔; gyiang-tsin' 強佔; — the throne, tsin we'佔位
USURY, djong li'-din 重利錢°; to exact —, fông djong' li 放重利; ditto in the extreme, djong' li bun-poh' 重利盤剝; heavy — paid daily, ing'-ts-din 印子錢°; pe'-din 負°利°錢
UTENSILS, kô sang'傢伙°; ky'i'-gyü 器具; ky'i'-ming 器皿; farming —, cong'-din kô'-sang 種田傢°伙; nong gyü' 農具; — in general, kô-sang'-jih-veh' 傢伙什物; household and sewing —, siu'-yüong kô'-sang 手用傢°伙
UTMOST, to the —, tao gyih-deo'

到極; tao-pin'-de 到邊了°; put forth — strength, 'eo-ky'i'-lih tso' 盡氣力做; nu'-lih tso' 努力做; ditto (whole heart, and strength), dzing'-sing gyih-lih' 盡心竭力
UTTER, djih 絕; gyih 極; — stranger, djih-feh-nying'-teh-go nying' 絕弗認°得个°人°
UTTER words, wô-c'ih shih-wô læ 話出說話來; to — an oath, vah-zing do'-tsin 罰咒
UTTERANCE, indistinct k'eo'-ing feh ts'ing'-t'ong 口音弗清通; 'en-wu-dao' 含糊道; impeded —, ngao'-zih-keng-go kông'-fah 鉸舌根个°講法
UTTERLY unwilling, weh-ih' feh-k'eng' 劃一弗肯
UTTERMOST parts of the earth, di'-ts gyih' 地之極; di'-go zing'-deo 地个°盡頭

V

VACANCY, ky'üih 缺; wait for a —, teng'-'eo ky'üih-c'ih' 等候缺出; 'eo-pu' 候補; 'eo-ky'üih 候缺; to fill a —, pu ky'üih'補缺; when a — occurs, yin ky'üih-k'ong' 有缺空; yin ky'üih-c'ih' 有缺出; yiu ky'üih'-veng k'ong 有缺分空
VACANT, k'ong 空; — house, k'ong' oh 空屋
VACATION, fông-kô' 放假°; — (for a longer time), sæn-kwun'

散館;— during Summer, hyih 'O' 歇夏'

VACCINATE, to cong ngeo-deo' 種牛'痘; cong yiang-deo' 種羊痘

VACCINE matter, deo-tsiang' 痘漿; to take — from one to another, djün-tsiang' 傳漿;—scab, ngeo-deo in' 牛° 痘瘂

VACILLATE, to fæn'-fæn-foh-foh' 反反覆覆; tsiao-sæn'-mo'-s 朝三暮四

VAGABOND, liu-loh'-go nying 流落个'人; idler, dang-k'ah' 蕩客; lông-dông'-ts 浪蕩子

VAGUE, muddled, weng-teng'-teng 混濁°濁°; cannot distinguish black from white, beh'-bah feh-feng' 黑白° 弗分

VAIN, having no real substance, hyü 虛; delusive, hyü-hwô' 虛花; in —, bah-bah' 白°白°; bah'-lih-lih'; wông'-jün 枉然; du-jün' 徒然; labor in —, bah-bah' lao-loh' 白°白° 勞碌; use one's energies in —, wông'-fi tsing-jing' 枉費精神; wông'-fi sing-kyi' 枉費心機; to spend one's life in —, hyü-du' ih-si' 虛度一世'; to take God's name in —, vông'-ts'ing Jing-Ming -go ming-deo' 妄稱神明个名頭

VAIN, piao-piao'- go 彪彪个°; iao ts'ing-piao' 要稱彪 — of one's person, or accomplishments, iao ts'ing-üong' 要稱勇; zi-sön' z'-wu-ih-kying' 自算似乎一衿

VALID, t'o' t'iah 妥貼; k'ao'-leh jih'-go 靠得實个°

VALLEY, ao 奧; bing 坪; sæn koh' 山谷 (ih-go)

VALUABLE, dzih dong-din' 值銅錢°; kwe'-djong-go 貴重个°

VALUE, to djong 重; — highly, long-djong 隆重; tse'-djong 最重; kwe'-djong 貴重; I — it highly, keh z ngô' sô long-djong'-go 這°是我所隆重个°

VALUE, price, kô'-din 價°錢°; true —, jih-kô' 實價; to estimate the —, kwu kô'-din 估價°錢°; what is its —? dzih to-siao' kô'-din 值多少價°錢°? you do not know the — of the goods, ng' feh sih' ho 你弗識貨

VANISH, to — suddenly, hweh'-jün feh-kyin' 忽然弗見; ngæn'-tsing ih-sah 眱-neh'-de 眼°睛一睏沒°有°了°; — (go) quickly, ts'ong-ts'ong' ky'i 忽忽去°

VANITY, hyü-veo'-go z-ken 虛浮个°事幹; hyü hwô'-z 虛花之°事; vu-ih'-ts-z' 無益之事

VANITY, he has a great deal of —, gyi' yin ih-kwu' piao-ky'i 其有一皴彪氣

VANQUISH, to tang'-ying 打贏; to be vanquished, shü 輸; ba 敗; shü-diao' 輸了°; ba-diao' 敗了°

VAPID, having lost life and spirit, (as wine), sing'-dao ko'-de 性子過了°

VAPOR, ky'i̔ 氣 : — rises, ky'i̔ tsing-ky'i̔'-læ 氣蒸起來

VARIABLE, kæ'-pin 改變; wun-yiang' 換樣

VARIANCE, at yiu du'-bing 有肚病; not agreeing, feh-deo'-kyi' 弗投機; feh-siang-'eh' 弗相合

VARIED talents, to-dzæ' to-nyi'-go 多才多藝个°; — uses, yüong-dziang' væn'-go 用塲繁个°

VARIEGATED, ng'-ngæn'-loh-seh' 五顏六色; hwô-lih'-peh-lang' 花麗斑'爛;* hwô-hwô'-loh-loh' 花花綠綠

* Also signifies, figured, changeable, or having various kinds. Cloth of one color, figured, may be hwô-lih-peh-lang, a changeable person who cannot be trusted, and the various goods in a shop irrespective of color, may be the same.

VARIETY, a — of, or VARIOUS, pah'-yiang 百°樣; koh'-yiang 各樣; koh' seh 各色; zeh'-keh-leng'-teng 雜夾零等; zeh gyih' 雜劇; various matters, pah'-yiang z-t'i̔' 百°樣事體

VARNISH, Ningpo ts'ih 漆; unboiled ditto, sang ts'ih' 生漆; ditto (boiled with dong-yiu' 桐油), kying ts'ih' 金漆; false — (more oil, and less ts'ih), kô'-kying ts'ih' 假金漆; vermilion —, cü-'ong' ts'ih' 硃紅漆; to be poisoned with —, sang' ts'ih'-ting' 生°漆疔

VARNISH, to ts'ih 漆; k'a ts'ih' 揩°漆; ts'ah' ts'ih 擦漆; —

only with oil, k'a yiu' 揩°油; — with shining oil, k'a liang-yin' 揩°亮油; — an untruth, shih'-long wô'-hwu 說䰾話虎

VARY, to — in form, kæ-yiang' 改樣; pin-yiang' 變樣; wun-yiang' 換樣; — in color, pin-seh' 變色

VASE, (bulging in the middle, and small at the top), wu-bing' 壺瓶; flower —, hwô-bing' 花瓶 (ih-tsah)

VAST, ting'-do 頂大°; kwông'-kw'eh 廣闊; — expanse, (as the sky, or ocean), mang-yiang'-yiang 茫°洋洋

VAULTED, arched, gwæn-dong'-shih-go 環°洞式个°

VAUNT, to p'u-hæ'-kying 舖海景; kông-hæ'-wô 講°海話; to boast, c'ô-dæn' 詫誕; kw'ô-k'eo' 誇口; kông do-wô' 講°大°話 See BOAST.

VEAL, siao'-ngeo nyüoh' 小牛°肉°

VEGETABLE, ts'æ 菜; vegetables (in general), su'-ts'æ 蔬菜; to live on vegetables only, (as the Buddhists often do), ky'üoh ts'æ' 吃°菜; ky'üoh dziang-su' 吃°長素; — kingdom, ts'ao'-moh ih-le' 草木一類

VEHEMENT, ts'u̔-bao' 粗暴; mang'-tsiang 猛°將, these characters only have a good meaning, as brave, &c.; quick, and severe, bao-tsao' 暴躁; — gestures,

VEI 513 VER

vu'-siang 武相; ti'-kyiah vu-siu' 手°舞°足°蹈°
VEIL, thin tsao'-sô 罩紗; — for the face, tsao'-min-sô 罩面紗
VEIL, to —, or cover, tsao-zông 罩上; — the face, tsô' min-k'ong' 遮°面孔; Chinese bridal —, tæ'-deo-bong' 兜頭縫
VEIN, hyüih'-kying 血筋
VELOCITY, what is the — ? to'-siao kw'a' 多少快°? dza kwun' kw'a 怎°樣°快°?
VELVET, nyüong 絨; tsin'-nyüong 剪絨; silk —, s nyüong' 絲絨
VELVETEEN, min nyüong' 綿絨
VENERABLE appearance, nyin-kao' yiu-teh'-go siang-mao 年高有德个°相貌; lao'-dzing-ky'i-ziang 老成氣象
VENERATE, to tseng-kying' 尊敬; tseng-djong' 尊重
VENEREAL ulcer, yiang-me ts'ông' 楊梅瘡; ao-tsao' ts'ông 墺糟瘡; yiang-me' kyih'-doh 楊梅結毒
VENETIANS, pah'-yih-ts'ông' 百°葉䏲; fæn-ts'ông' 翻䏲
VENGEANCE, to take —, pao-dziu' 報讐
VENISON, kyi'-nyüoh 麂肉°; loh-nyüoh' 鹿肉°
VENOMOUS, doh 毒
VENT, to—feeling, su cong-dziang' 訴衷腸; — sorrow, t'æn kw'u'-cong (cong or tsong) 歎苦衷;—anger, c'ih ky'i' 出氣; sih veng'

洩忿; fah sing'-kah 發性格
VENTILATE, to t'ong ky'i' 通氣; t'eo ky'i' 透氣;— the room, vông-kæn' t'ong-t'ong ky'i' 房間°通通氣
VENTURE, to mao do tæn' 冒大°膽; to dare, ken 敢; to run the risk, mao hyin' 冒險; if unwilling to — into the tiger's den, how can you catch her cub, peh jih hwu'-yüih, in teh hwu'-ts (veng.) 不入虎穴焉得虎子
VERANDAH, upper nga-leo'外°樓; nao-lông' 走扁; nao leo'-teng 月°臺°; lower —, yiu-jing k'eo' 檐扁°口; yiu-jing-di' 檐扁°地; yiu-jing' 遊扁°; a very long —, (around two or more houses, in Chinese style), tseo'-mô-leo 走馬樓
VERB, weh-z'-ngæn 活字眼°
VERBAL, k'eo'-djün-go 口傳个°; take a — message, ta k'eo'-sing 帶°口°信
VERBATIM, repeat tsiao' yiang djün' 照樣讙; ditto (by figure of speech), i yiang', wô wu-lu' 依樣畫葫蘆
VERBOSE style, veng-dz' dzing-dziang' 文詞太°長; lengthy speech, wô-deo dziang' 話頭長
VERDICT (of an official), dông-tön' 堂斷; the — is, guilty, tön'-ding gyi kw'e li' 斷定其够理
VERDIGRIS, dong-loh' 銅綠

VERIFY, to — (by seeing), nyin 驗; — the amount of cargo, nyin ho' 驗貨; to bring out proofs, do'-c'ih bing-kyü' lae 拿°出憑據來; — it (to me), peh ngô nyin' ming-bah' 俾我驗明白

VERMICELLI of wheat or rice flour, min 麵; ken-min' 乾麵; (transparent) — of bean flour, feng'-ken 粉乾

VERMILION, nying-cü' 銀硃; — pencil, cü-pih' 硃筆

VERSE, a — (of a hymn, or from the Bible), ih tsih' 一節

VERSED in (as books), joh-doh'-go 熟讀个°; well acquainted with, (not persons), joh-sih' 熟識; — in the classics, sing'-kying joh-doh'-go 聖經熟讀个°

VERSION of the Bible, faen-yih'-go Sing'-shü 繙譯个聖書; which ditto do you prefer? faen-yih' go Sing'-shü ng ting'hwun-hyi' 'ah-li' ih-cong' 繙譯个聖書你頂歡喜那°裡°一種?

VERTEBRA, tsih'-kweh 脊骨; pe'-tsih-kweh 背脊骨

VERTEX, ting 頂; ting-deo' 頂頭; tsin-t'ong-den' 尖峯頭; nao'-tsin 腦尖

VERTICAL line, dzih sin' 直線; (ih-da); the sun is —, nyih-deo' dzih'-de 日°頭直了°

VERTIGO, deo-yüing' 頭暈

VERY, ting 頂; gyih 極; djih 絕; tse 最; altogether, jih-feng' 十分;

— good, (the best). ting'-hao 頂好; gyih-hao' 極好; jih-feng' hao' 十分好; tsae'-m̄-tsae' hao' 再無再好; — large indeed, ngae-do'-do 極°大°; — lately, — soon, or — near, ngaen' min-zin' 眼°面前°; the — least (price), ky'i-mô' 起碼; ky'i-kô' 起價°; ky'i-cü' 起注; — hot weather, t'in da-nyih' 天大熱°; — different, ts'ô-yün' 差遠; ts'ô-to' 差多; da-ts'ô' gyi yün' 大差其遠; t'in-ts'ô' di-yün' 天差地遠; long-do' koh-yiang' 大°相°懸遠°; da' feh-siang-dong' 大弗相同; this — day, tông'-nyih 當日°; tsih'-nyih 卽日°; I am — sorry you cannot go, ng' feh ky'i', ngô tao' k'o'-sih 你°弗去°我倒可惜; k'o'-sih ng' feh ky'i' 可惜你°弗去°; for, — well, hao', hao' 好好, or substitute, owing to you I have happiness, t'oh-ng-foh' 托你°福; t'oh-foh' 托福

VESSEL (for holding anything), tsi'-go kô'-sang 齒个°傢伙; — (for the sea). hae'-jün 海船; — with a sail, fong-bong jün' 風篷船

VESTIBULE, meng-vông' 門房 See PORTICO.

VETERAN officer (military), tsing-lin'-go kwun-ping' 精練个官兵; — soldier, tsing-ping' 精兵

VEX, to irritate, ts'ao 譟; to make

VEXangry by repeated provocations, væn-nao' 煩惱; to harass (as if by tying, or pulling back), dzin'-ziao 纏擾

VEXATIOUS, t'in-væn-nao' 添煩惱;— petty cares, se'-se væn-væn z-t'i' 碎繁事體

VEXED, sing'-li væn-nao' 心裡煩惱; — (because one has done something wrong), ao'-nao 懊惱

VIAL, siao' po-li' bing' 小玻璃瓶 (ih-tsah)

VIBRATING, tsing'-tsing-dong' 怔怔動; swinging, dang-dang'-dong 宕宕動

VICE, bad practices, oh'-jih 惡習; sink into —, 'æn'-loh oh-nyin'-dao lu 陷°落惡孽道路

VICE, (smith's) ngang-cü'-pô' 鐵°夾°箝°

VICE, (second in rank), fu 副; — president, fu'-siu 副手

VICEROY of two provinces, tsong'-toh 總督; styled, cü'-dæ 制臺; ts-kyüting 制軍; — of one province, fu-dæ' 撫臺; styled, jing-fu' 巡撫

VICINITY, in the — of, siang-gying' 相近; in the — of Peking, læ Poh'-kying siang-gying' 在°北京相近

VICIOUS, having — propensities, 'ô'-liu p'e'-ts 下°流胚子°;— person, 'ô'-tsoh-nying 下°作人°

VICISSITUDES, ky'i'-tao-to'; fæn'-foh to' 反覆多; he has passed

515

through many —, gyi' din sön kw'n lah tu zông-ko' 其甜酸苦辣都嘗過; gyi hyü'-to kying-hwông' kying-lih'-ko 其許多境況經歷過

VICTIM, three (important) sacrificial victims, sæn-sang' foh'-li 三牲°福禮; a human sacrificial —, nying' tông tsi'-veh 人°當祭物; men become victims to wealth, birds to food, nying' we dzæ-s', tiao' we zih-vông' 人為財死鳥°為食亡

VICTOR, teh-sing'-go-nying 得勝個人°; ying'-go cü-kwu 打°贏個°人°

VICTORIOUS, were you—(or how)? sing'-ba jü-'o' 勝敗°如何? returned —, teh-sing' kyü-læ' 得勝歸來; to be —, tang teh-sing'-tsiang 打得勝仗°; tang-sing'-tsiang 打勝仗°

VICTORY, to gain a —, teh-sing' ih-ts' 得勝一次; ih-tsao tang'-ying 一遭打贏

VICTUALS, ky'üoh'-zih 吃°食; — (prepared for a journey), ho'-zih 伙食; light ditto (as cakes &c.), ken-liang' 乾糧; vegetables and rice, ts'æ'-væn 菜飯; to have plenty of — and warm clothes, ts'æ'-væn pao, pu'-i nön' 菜飯飽布衣煖

VIEW, to see, k'en 看;— carefully, ts'-si k'en' 仔細看;— the prospect, k'en kying'-cü 看景致

VIE

VIEW, according to this —, ka' k'en'-ky'i-læ 如此°看起來; to take a narrow —, zo-tsing' kwun-t'in' 坐井觀天

VIGILANT, bông-siu' nyin-mih' 防守嚴密

VIGOR, in full mental nyin'-lih tsing-tsông' 年力精壯; strength, ky'i'-lih 氣力; lih-liang' 力量

VIGOROUS, firm and strong, tsah'-tsông 圓壯 (tsong or cong); tsah'-cü; — (used only of youth), tsông'-gyin 壯健; gyin 健*
* Not usually applied to a young person unless he has recently been ill.

VILE, despicable, zin 賤°; pe-zin' 卑賤°; 'ô'-zin 下°賤°; bad, 'ô'-tsoh 下°作; 'ô'-tsoh-peh-k'æn' 下°作不堪

VILIFY, to hwe'-pông 毀謗; pông'-hwe 謗毀

VILLAGE, a ih-ts'eng' 一村; ih'-go hyiang-ts'eng' 一个°鄉村

VILLAGERS, ts'eng' li-hyiang'-go nying' 村裏向个°人; ts'eng-tsông-zông'-go nying 村庄上个°人°

VILLAIN, kweng'-du 棍徒; vu-la' 無賴°; di-kweng' 地棍; bold —, kwông-kweng' 光棍; fi'-du 匪徒

VILLAINOUS fellow, liang-sing'-ts'eh'-hah-go-nying 良心漆黑°个°人°; hah'-sing-hah-fi'-go nying 黑°心黑肺个°人°; — affair, feh-kyin'-t'in-nyih'-go z-ken' 弗見天日°个°事幹;

ditto (darkening heaven), heh'-t'in-heh-di'-go z-ken 黑天黑地事幹°

VINDICATE, to feng-ts'ing'-dao'-bah 分青道白°; si-ts'ing' 洗清; — another, dæ-we' feng-ts'ing' dao'-bah 代為分青道白°

VINDICTIVE, yiu pao-dziu'-go sing' 有報仇个°心

VINE, creeper, yin-deng' 延籐; grape —, bu-dao'-jü 葡萄樹 (ih-cü)

VINEGAR, ts'u 醋

VINEYARD, bu-dao-yün' 葡萄園 (ih-zo)

VIOLATE, to væn 犯; — the law, væn fah' 犯法; — the Sabbath, væn en-sih'-nyih 犯安息日°; — a promise, shih iah' 失約; shih sing' 失信; — an oath, vah-tsiu' we la'-go 賴°罰咒个°; to commit rape on, gyiang-kæn' 強姦°

VIOLENCE, to use —, ying-hyüong' 行兇; to take by —, gyiang do' 強拿°; to borrow with —, or snatch, gyiang tsia' 強借°; to rob with —, gyiang-deh' 強奪; gyiang-ts'iang' 強搶; ts'iang'-kyih 搶刼

VIOLENT, ying-hyüong' 行兇; — wind, gwông-fong' 狂風; long fong' 龍風; fong pao' 風颱

VIOLIN, (native 4 stringed) bi-bô' 琵琶; three stringed —, yin-ts' 絃子; sæn-yin' 三絃; two stringed —, wu-gying' 胡琴; violins, (ingeneral), s-yin' kô'-sang 絲絃傢伙.

VIPER, doh-dzô' 毒蛇° (ih-diao, ih-keng, ih-kwang)

VIRGIN, dong-nyü' 童女 (ih-go)

VIRILE, we sang-yiang' 會生°養°; nyün yiang'-tsoh'-de 元陽足了°

VIRTUE, teh'-ky'i 德氣; teh'-'ang 德行; *the five virtues*, wu' djông 五常; — *of medicine*, yiah'-go kong-yiao' 藥个功效

VIRTUOUS, yiu teh'-ky'i 有德氣; yin-teh'-go 賢德个°; — *widow*, tsih'-vu 節婦; tsing-tsih'-vu 貞節婦

VIRULENT, oh'-doh 惡毒; hyüong'-feh-ko', yi hyüong 兇而°又°兇

VISAGE, yüong-mao' 容貌; min-yüong' 面容; *fearful —*, ô-lin' p'ô'-p'ô 可°怕°之°相°

VISCERA, dzông-fu', or djông-fu 臟腑

VISCID, nyin-kao'-kao 黏膠°; — (like snails), nyin-zæn' 黏涎°

VISIBLE, k'en'-leh-kyin'-go 看得°見个°

VISION, yi'-ziang 異象 (ih-go); *to be in a state for seeing a —*, (*i.e.* soul out of the body), jing-yiu' ziang-wæ' 神遊象外 (veng.)

VISIONARY, *catching the sun's shadow*, k'ô nyih-deo-ing' 捉°日頭影; *catching the east wind*, k'ô tong-fong' 捉°東風; *catching*

the wind that blew off the hat, k'ô loh-mao'-fong 捉°落帽風; *to engage in —projects*, ky'in-k'ong-mo' 牽空磨

VISIT, *to* pa'-mông 拜°望; *to — a friend*, mông-mông' beng-yiu' 望°望朋友; k'en beng-yiu' 看朋友; — *the sick*, k'en bing-nying' 看病人; *do you — one another*? ng-lah yiu mông-læ' mông-ky'i ni'-teh? 你°等°有往°來°拜°望°嗎°

VISIT, *to make a ceremonious —*, pa'-we 拜°會; *to return ditto*, we-pa' 回拜°; *to make ditto to a superior*, pa'-kyin 拜°見; *to miss a —*, shih-'eo' 失候; shih-nying' 失迎

VISITOR, nying-k'ah' 客人°; *lady —*, nyü'-k'ah 女客 (ih-we); *to receive a —*, we k'ah' 會客; *not to receive a —*, feh we' k'ah' 弗會客; feh we' 弗會; *to meet a —*, tsih k'ah' 接客; *to await (a —)*, teng'-'eo 等°候; kong'-'eo 恭候; *attend a — to the door*, or *to the gate*, song k'ah 送客; *to go with a —*, be k'ah' 陪客

VITAL, *of —importance*, iao'-kying kwæn'-deo 要緊關頭

VITALS, ky'iao'-meng 竅門; ming-meng' 命門

VITIATE, *to* wæ-diao' 壞了°

VITIATED *by it*, be gyi' sô 'æ' 被其所害; — *appetite*, we-k'eo' pin'-diao-de 胃口變壞了°

VITRIOL, *blue* tæn'-væn 胆礬;
green —, loh-væn' 綠礬

VIVACIOUS, weh-siang' 活相;
weh-loh' 活絡; ling-long' 玲瓏

VIVIPAROUS, t'æ-sang' 胎生°

VOCABULARY, z-nyü'-we'-ka 字語彙解° See DICTIONARY.

VOCIFERATE, *to* 'eo wu-long' si' 竭°聲°而°喊°; wu-long' hyiang'-liang 喉°嚨嚮亮

VOICE, sing-ing' 聲音; tæn din'丹田; wu-long' 喉°嚨; *loud* —, sing-ing' do' 聲音大°; wu-long' do' 喉°嚨大°; *soft* —, sing-ing si' 聲音細; *low* —, ti sing' 低聲

VOLATILE, *capable of passing off*, we tseo'-diao 會走去°;— (light) *person*, ky'ing p'iao'-go nying' 輕飄个°人°; *ditto*, kying-kweh'-deo-go 輕骨頭个°, this usually means a bad person.

VOLCANO, ho'-sæn 火山 (ih-zo)

VOLUME, *a* ih-peng shü' 一本書

VOLUNTARILY *enter a net*, (or into sin), zi-deo' lo-mông' 自°投羅網°

VOLUNTARY, (as giving, &c.), c'ih'-ü zi'-go i'-s 出°於自°个° 意思; c'ih'-ü zi'-go peng'-sing 出於自°个°本心; *of one's own accord*, zi dzing'-nyün 自°情願

VOLUNTEER, *to offer one's self,* deo-tao' 投到; song'-zông-meng 送上門; *he volunteered to go*, gyi deo-tao' we ky'i 其投到會去°; gyi song'-zông-meng' we-ky'i' 其送上門會去°; — (as a soldier without pay), deo-ying'-yiao-lih' 投營効力;—
to help him, song'-zông-meng' pông-dzu' gyi 自°願帮助其

VOLUPTUOUS, *ministering to sensual pleasures*, du-hwun-loh'-go 圖歡樂个°; *fond of ditto*, æ hwô-loh' go 愛花綠个°

VOMIT, *to* t'u 吐; mao 嘔; *having an inclination to* —, oh'-sing yiang-yiang' 欲°嘔; iao'-siang t'u'-c'ih-læ 要想吐出來

VORACIOUS, du'-ts do' 肚°子大°; tsiu'-nông-væn-dæ 酒囊飯袋; — *person*, do-zih-vu 食量°大°个°人°

VOW, *to make a* — (to God, or an idol), hyü nyün-sing 許願心; hyü nyün' 許願; (more often), he nyün-sing; *to return a* —, wæn nyün-sing' 還願心'; wæn nyün' 還願; *to promise solemnly, calling God to witness*, fah nyün' 發願

VOYAGE, *to go on a* —, zo jün' ky'i 坐船去°; *a* — ih-t'ông jün' 一趟船;※ ih-shü' ky'i 一水去°; ih-t'ông' 一趟; *the last* — *was a successful one*, zin-shü' da-fah'-go 前°次°大°發个°

※ This term is used by the crew, and those constantly passing and repassing, for voyages made by fishing-boats. In asking about a friend's voyage use the word journey, which see.

VULGAR, *coarse and common*, ts'u 粗; ts'u-dzoh'粗俗; zah-t'u' 極土; — *language* (the vernacular), t'u'-wô 土話; hyiang-dæn' 鄉談; — *eyes*, djoh-ngæn' 俗眼

W

WAD, to — (as a garment), ts'eng'-min-hwô' 襯棉花; si' min-hwô' 翻'棉花

WADDED *garments*, min-i' 棉衣

WADDING, *cotton* dong'-hwô 筒花; *a roll of* —, ih-kyün' dong-hwô' 一卷筒花

WADE, to — *through water*, liao-shü' 蹽水°

WAG, pô'-hyi-nying 善°戲謔°个人°; ying-nying'-siao'-go 引人°笑个°

WAG, to yiao 搖; hwæn 甩; — *head and tail*, yiao-deo'hwæn mi'-pô 搖頭甩尾°巴

WAGER, *to lay a* —, tang-tu' 賽°賭; *to lay a* — *for food*, tn tong-dao' 賭東道; *to lose a* —, tu'-shü 賭輸; *to win a* —, tu'-ying 賭贏

WAGES, kong-din' 工錢°; *to pay out* —, c'ih kong-din' 出工錢°; *give him his* —, fu kong-din' peh'-gyi 付工錢°給°伊

WAGON, s'-leng-ts'ô' 四輪車°(ih-bu, ih-dzing).

WAILING, 'ao-li'-da-koh' 號陶'大哭

WAIST, iao 腰; — *slender* (as a willow stem), liu'-iao 柳腰

WAIST-BAND *of drawers*, kw'u'-iao 褲腰; — *of a skirt*, gyüing-iao' 裙腰; *a girdle*, kyiao-sing'-ta 緊身帶°; soh'-iao-ta' 束腰帶° (ih-diao).

WAIT, to teng 等; teng'-'eo 等候; 'eo 候; deng 庯*; — *a little*, teng-ih'-teng 等一等; deng'-ih-zông' 庯一息°; (to an inferior), lao-ih'-lao; lao-ih-zông'; z'-'eo or ts''-'eo 侍候; — *for an answer*, teng we-sing' 等回信; *I* — *here for you*, ngô teng-ng'-tong 我在°此°等你°; — *for one till out of patience*, (or till the heart burns), teng' nying sing'-tsiao 等人°心焦

* Deng properly has only the sense of stopping or remaining, therefore for *wait*, teng is preferable, though deng is sometimes used.

WAIT, to — *upon* (as the table, &c.), z'-dzih 侍值; —*upon* (as on a sick person), tông-dzih 當值

WAITER, *attendant*, z-dzih'-go-nying 侍值个人°; si-tsæ' 細崽西价°; *tray*, bun 盤 (ih-min).

WAKEN, *to cease to sleep*, diao-kao' 調覺°; su-sing' 蘇醒; — *after a nap*, hwah 豁; — (another), 'eo' diao-kao' 叫°醒°; 'eo su-sing' 叫°蘇醒

WAKEFUL, *sleeping but little*, ve'-da-li kw'eng'-joh 不°甚°睡°熟; — *and restless* (as a child), tin-min'-joh 顛眠熟

WALK, to tseo 走; *take a walk*, tseo' ih'-we 走一回; sæn-sæn bu' 散散步; ky'i tseo-tseo' 去°走走; *did you come in a chair, or did you* —? ng wa-z zo gyiao' kæ wa-z tseo' læ 你還是坐

轎來還°是走來?— *erect, and dignified*, tseo-leh yiu we-shü 走得°有威勢;—*gracefully*, (said of a woman), tseo' yin fong-deo° 走得°飄逸°;—*quickly*, ky'i diao'-diao 去踕踕;—*leisurely along*, doh-soh' kyi 踱踱

WALKER, *he is a good* —, gyi' tseo'-gying hao' 其走勁好

WALL, ziang 墻 (ih-dao); *dividing* —, iao-ziang' 腰墻; *partition* — (*of a house*), pih 壁; *surrounding* —, ziang-yü' 墻宇; *city* —, dzing-ts' 城子; dzing-ziang 城墻; *the Great* —, Væn-li' dziang-dzing 萬里長城

WALLOW, *to* — *in mud*, le'-nyi-wu'-tsiang 擂泥糊漿

WALNUT, *English* wu-dao' 胡桃 (ih-go); *to crack walnuts*, k'ao-k'æ' wu-dao' 敲開胡桃; *cracked walnuts*, k'ao dao' 敲桃

WANDER, *to* tseo-læ' tseo-ky'i' 走來走去°; *to* — *idly about*, k'ong'-deo tseo' 空頭走; 'æn tseo' 閒走;—*in quest of amusement*, yiu-hyi' 遊戲

WANDERING *in delirium*, kông nyih-wô' 講熱話; kông weng'-wô' 講混話; *to have* — *thoughts*, feng-sing' 分心

WANT, *deficiency*, ky'üih'-siao 缺少; ky'in'-ky'üih 欠缺; ky'üih'-siao dziang-tön' 缺少長短; *in* — *of wood and rice*, m-za' m-mi 無柴無米; feh-dong-ho'-in

弗動°火烟;—*of food*, m-kao' ky'üoh'-de 沒°有°甚°吃°

WANT, *to* iao 要; *do not* —, feh iao' 弗要; fæ'-gyi;—*very much to do*, pô'-feh-neng'-keo tso' 巴弗能彀做; *what do you* — ? ng' iao soh' si 你°要甚°麼°? *don't* — *to be there* (as a servant leaving a place), sang t'eng'mao-de 計°欲°脫°身° (slang).

WANTING, ky'üih 缺; ky'in 欠; ts'ô 差; *five o'clock,* — *five minutes,* ng' tin-cong ky'üih ng' feng 五°點鐘缺五°分

WAR, tang-tsiang' z-ken' 打仗°事幹; *the art of* —, kyüing-kyi' 軍機; ping-fah' 兵法; *gone to the* —, c'ih'-ping tang-tsiang' 出兵打仗°; *to go to* —, dong ken-ko' 動干戈; *at* —, læ-tih kyiao-tsin' 正°在°交戰; læ-tih tang-tsiang' 正°在°打仗°; *implements of* —, kyüing-ky'i' 軍器

WARD, *to* —*off a blow*, ih-kyi kah'-ko 遮°攔°其°打°

WARDROBE, *closet for clothes*, i-djü' 衣廚 (ih-k'eo); *complete* —, s'-kyi i-sæn' 四季衣衫

WARE-HOUSE, dzæn-vông' 棧房 (ih-t'eo)

WARES, ho'-veh 貨物; *porcelain* —, dz-ky'i' 磁器; *earthen* —, ngô'-ho 瓦°貨; *miscellaneous* —, zah-ho' 雜貨

WARM, nyih 熱;—*water*, nyihshii' 熱 水°; — *weather,* t'in-kô nyih 天熱; *to grow — by degrees,* dzin'-dzin nyih-ky'i'-læ 漸漸熱起來

WARM, *to —* (as food), nyih-nyih' 熱一熱; nön'-ih-nön' 煖一煖; we'-ih-we' 回一回; — *the soup,* t'ông' nyih-nyih' gyi 湯熱一熱; t'ông' nön-ih-nön' 湯煖一煖; — *the wine,* (genteel), tsiu' p'ao'-ih-p'ao 酒泡一泡; — *one's self* (at a fire), k'ao ho' 烤火; *one's hands* (at a fire), hong siu' 烘手

WARM-HEARTED, nyih sing-dziang' go 熱心腸个°; nyih sing'-go 熱心个°

WARMING-PAN, *Chinese* (for the feet), ho'-ts'ong 脚°爐; *very large ditto,* kyiah'-dah 大°脚爐; — *for the hands,* siu'-lu 手爐; *very small egg shaped ditto,* ah'-dæn siu-lu' 鴨蛋手爐; ziu-ln' 袖爐; — *to keep tea warm,* nön-dzô'-go lu' 煖茶个°爐; ngao-lu' 熬爐

WARN, *to — and threaten* (a superior to an inferior), kying'-kyiæ 警戒; — (an equal), ky'ün'-min 勸勉

WARP, kying-sin' 經線; — *and woof,* kying-we' 經緯; *long threads in the loom,* or *thread on the shuttle,* kying-sô' 經紗; yü-sô' 緯紗

WARP, *to* ho-gyiao' 彎°橋; *warp-*

ed, dzin-mô'-liu 糨蔴縷; gyiao-gyiao'-goh-goh 橋橋擱擱°

WARRANT, ba 牌°; ba-p'iao' 牌票 (ih tsiang); — *for immediate seizure,* ho'-ts'in 火籤; *to issue a —,* c'ih ba' 出牌°

WARRANT, *to guaranty,* pao 包; — *for a year,* pao t'ao'-hao ih-nyin' 包討好一年; — (that a man will do well), pao'-kyü 保舉

WARRIOR, *experienced* tsing-ping' 精兵

WASH, *to* gyiang 洗°; — *the face,* gyiang min' 洗°面; — *the body,* gyiang nyüoh' 洗°浴°; — *dishes,* gyiang-un'dông-tsæn 洗碗盪盞

WASH-BASIN, min-dong' 面桶) min-beng' 面盆 (ih-tsah)

WASHER-MAN, gyiang i-zông'-go nying 洗衣裳个°人°

WASH-STAND, min-kô' 面架 (ih-zo)

WASP, yia' fong-ts' 野°蜂子; dang-kyiah' wông-fong' 宕脚黃蜂 (ih-tsah)

WASTE *land,* hwông di' 荒地; — *paper,* fi'-ts 廢紙; — *lettered paper,* z-ts' 字紙

WASTE, *to* fi 廢; fi'-diao 廢了°; wông-fi 枉費; bah-fi' 白費; du-fi' 徒費; — (money), hwô-fi' 花費; lông-fi' 浪費; mi-fi' 糜費; — *time,* tang'-loh kong-fu' 誤工夫; fi kong-fu' 費工夫; ts'o-do' kwông-ing' 蹉跎光陰; — *mis-spend time,* hyü-

WAS 522 WAT

du' kwông-ing' 虛度光陰; lay — the land, tsao-t'ah' din-di' 蹧蹋田地

WASTEFUL, we tsao-t'ah' tong-si° 會蹧蹋物°件°; lavish, kw'un-siu'-go 寬手个°; song-sin'-go 鬆手个°; ky'i'-p'ah do' 氣魄大°

WATCH, z-ming'-piao 自鳴表; z-jing-piao' 時辰表 (ih-tsah); gold —, kying piao' 金表;— crystal, (glass cover), po-li-kæ' 玻璃蓋; to fit a — crystal, p'e ih-go piao'-kæ 配一个表蓋; to wind a —, k'æ piao' 開表; first — (of the night), ih-kang 一更; the five night watches, (from 7 P. M. to 5 A. M.), ng' kang 五°更

WATCH, to kying'-siu 謹守;— over, k'en'-kwu 看顧; to look after, k'en'-siu 看守; — and prepare against, kying'-bông 謹防; for thieves (at night), kwun yia-mæn' 防賊个°; to — a chance (as a thief), gyiang z-'eo' 䚄時候; — (as a night-watchman), jing kang' 巡更°; jing yia' 巡夜°; dzih kang' 值更°; dzih yia' 值夜°; — the house, k'en'-siu oh'-li 看守家°裡; k'en vông-ts' 看房子; kwun oh' 管屋; — over, or for (as some one expected), tsiao'-liao 照瞭; from a high place (as an enemy), liao-vông' 瞭望

WATCHFUL, kying-sing' 警心; kying'-jing 謹慎

WATCH-MAKER, cong-piao' s-vu' 鐘表司務

WATCHMAN, night dzih-yia'-go nying 值夜°个°人°; day —, dzih-nyih'-go 值日°个°; — who strikes the watches, ts-kang'-go nying 支更°个°人°

WATCH-TOWER, kang-leo' 更樓; kwu'-leo 鼓樓 (ih-zo)

WATCH-WORD, k'eo'-'ao 口號; secret sign, en'-'ao 暗號

WATER, shü 水; rain —, t'in-shü' 天雨水; salt —, 'æn-shü' 鹹水; warm —, nyih shü' 熱°水; boiling —, kweng' shü 滾水; dah-dah' kweng' shü 杏杏滾水; to make — (i.e. urinate), dza shü' 撒°尿°

WATER, to irrigate, kyiao shü' 澆水; to go by —, teng shü'-lu ky'i 從°水路去°; — the flowers, kyiao hwô' 澆花; ditto (i. e. let them drink), ing hwô' 飲花; — the horse, peh mô' ing shü' 給°馬飲水°; mouth waters, k'eo dzæn' 口饞; cü'-pô dzæn' 嘴吧饞; make the eyes —, (with something pungent), lah'-leh ngæn'-li-c'ih' 辣得°眼淚出*

* Play actors and impostors sometimes have a piece of fresh ginger-root (instead of an onion) in their handkerchiefs, so as to bring tears when they wipe their eyes.

WATER-CHESTNUT, bu-dzi' 荸薺; di-lih' 地栗 (ih-go)

WATER-FALL, kw'ô'-loh-shü' 跨落水

WAT 523 WEA

WATER-GATE, shü'-mǒng 水°門; (ih-dao)

WATER-LILY, *lotus*, 'o-hwô' 荷花; lin-hwô' 蓮花 (ih-tô)

WATER-MELON, si-kwô' 西瓜 (ih-go)

WATER-SPOUT, long-hwô'-shü 龍取°水°

WAVE, lông 浪; *little —*, po 波; po-lông 波浪; lông-hwô' 浪花

WAVE, *to — (as a flag, or the hand, when a thing is not wanted)*, yüih'-yüih 搖°手°; yüih-dong' 搖°動

WAVERING, fæn'-foh feh-ding 反覆弗定; fæn'-fæn foh-foh' 反反覆覆; cʻih'-wu-r', fæn'-wu-r' 出乎爾反乎爾

WAX, lah 蠟; *white —*, bah-lah' 白蠟; *yellow —*, wông-lah' 黃蠟; *ear —*, ng'-tô o' 耳°蠟°

WAY, lu 路 (ih-da); *to make — for*, kʻæ lu' 開路; *on the —*, læ lu-zông' 在°路上; *without going out of the —*, jing-da' 順埭; jing-lu' 順路; *in the — (obstructing)*, gah-tang' 軋打; *get out of the —*, tseo'-kʻæ 走開; nyiang lu' 讓°路; *the same —*, dong lu' 同路; *to leave the right —*, li-kʻæ' tsing' lu 離開正路; *the wrong —*, tsʻô' lu 跤路; *come this —*, tseo dông' ih-da lu' 走這°一埭路: *stop half — and lose all*, pun'-r-feh-kyih' 半路弗結; pun'-du-r-fi' 半途而廢; —

of acting, i'-tsi 意致°; *pretty — (of a child)*, i'-tsi bao'-kʻen 意致°好看; *method*, fah'-ts 法子; fông-fah' 方法; *do it in this —*, kaʻ-siang-mao tsoʻ 如°此°樣式°做; ka tso'-fah 如°此°做法

WAYLAY, *to* tön-lu' 斷°路; *will — us*, we tön-ah-lah'-go-lu' 會斷 我°等°个路; *one who waylays to rob*, tön' lu gyiang-dao' 斷°路強盜

WAYS, *all sorts of —*, tsʻin-fông' pah-kyi' 千方百°計

WAYWARD, gyüih-gyiang' 倔強 mæn-bi' 蠻疲

WE, ah-lah' 我°等°; *you and both*, pe'-tsʻ 彼此

WEAK, nyün'-ziah 軟弱; no-ziah' 懦弱; m̈-kyʻi'-lih 無°氣力; pih-bi' 癖躃; *too — to bear, or do*, tsʻang'-feh-dong 撐弗動; *— tea*, dæn'-dzô 淡茶

WEAKEN, *will — the body*, tiʻ-ts iao tang'-loh 身°體漸°弱°; *— the tea a little (by pouring in water)*, dzô' tsʻong'-leh dæn-tin' 茶冲得°淡點

WEAKLY *constitution*, tiʻ-ts tænboh' 身°體單薄; tiʻ-ts hyiah'-hyiah 身°體弱°个°; tiʻ-ts kyʻih'-boh 身°體怯°薄

WEALTH, dzæ-veh' 財物; kyingnying' dzæ-veh' 金銀財物; *to gain —*, fah-dzæ' 發財; *God of —*, Dzæ-jing bu'-sah 財神菩薩

WEALTHY, *a — person*, fu'-wu

富戶; fu'-ong 富翁; dzæ-cü' 財主; ing-wu' 殷戶; yiu'-lao.
WEAN, to tsah-na' 摘嬭; must —(it), yüong tsah-na' 要°摘嬭°
WEAPONS of war, kyüing-ky'i' 軍器;— of self-defence, bông-siu' kô'-sang 防手傢°伙°
WEAR, to — clothes, c'ün i-zông' 穿衣裳;— shoes, c'ün 'a' 穿鞋°;— a hat, ta mao-ts' 戴帽子;— a collar, kyi ling' 戴°領;— mourning, ta hao' 戴孝°; c'ün su' 穿素;—away, yi; yiang; yiang-yi' 希°散;— out, c'ün-wu' 穿腐; c'ün-diao' 穿壞°;— to tatters, c'ün-p'o' 穿破;— well, kying-c'ün' 經穿; ziu-c'ün' 耐°穿
WEARY, dziah-lih' 着力; vah'-de 乏了°; ky'ih'-lih 怯力; exceedingly —, vah-lih'-de 乏力了°; t'eh-lih'-de 脫力了°;— and sleepy, bi-gyün' 疲倦; su-nyün'-ky'i-de 酥軟了°
WEASEL, wông-ts'-lông' 黃鼠狼; wông-lông' 黃狼 (ih-tsah)
WEATHER, t'in 天; t'in-kô' 天時°; t'in-ky'i' 天氣; dry —, 'en'-t'in 旱天; clear —, t'in zing' 天晴; rainy —, loh-yü' t'in' 落雨天; mild —, t'in-kô' 'o-nön' 天時°和暖
WEATHER-COCK, ding-fong'-piao' 定風標;— (a flag), ding-fong-gyi' 定風旗; fong-sing'-gyi' 風信旗

WEAVE, to tsih 織;— silks, tsih dziu-ling' 織綢稜
WEAVER, tsih'-kyi s-vu' 織機司務;— of cotton cloth, iao-kyi' s-vu' 布°機司務: silk-weaver's shop, tsih'-kyi fông' 織機坊
WEB of cotton cloth, ih-kyi pu' 一機布; spider's—, kyih'cü-mông', or cü'-cü-mông' 蜘°蛛°網°; kyih'-cü lön'-mông 蜘°蛛°亂網°
WEB-FOOTED, kyiah' yiu pæn' go 脚有版个°; the duck is —, æn' yiu kyiah'-pæn 鴨°有脚版
WEDDING, to celebrate a —, hao'-nyih 好日°; kyih-hweng' 結婚; dzing-ts'ing' 成親; to partake of a — feast, ky'üoh hao'-nyih-tsiu 吃°好日°酒;— day, hao'-nyih 好日°; golden —, kying-hweng' 金婚;— sedan, hwô-gyiao' 花轎; ts'æ'-gyiao 彩轎 (ih-ting)
WEDNESDAY, li-pa sæn' 禮拜°三; (according to the Roman Catholics), tsin-li s' 瞻禮四
WEEDS, yia'-ts'ao 野草;— in paddy or wheat, bô-ts'ao' 稗°草°; to pull up —, bah yia'-ts'ao 拔野°草
WEEK, ih li'-pa 一禮拜°; (according to the Roman Catholics), ih-cü' nyih 一主日°; ih-tsin li' 一瞻禮
WEEKLY, me li'-pa 每禮拜°; me li'-pa yiu' 每禮拜°有; ts'ih'-nyih ih-we' 七日°一回
WEEP, to shed tears, c'ih ngæn'-li

出眼°淚; liu ngæn'-li 流眼°淚; *to cry*, or *lament*, k'oh 哭 — *bitterly*, k'oh'-leh sông-sing' 哭得°傷心

WEIGH, *to* ts'ing 稱; ts'ing ky'ing-djong' 稱輕重; — *pounds and ounces*, ts'ing kying-liang' 稱觔兩; — *and see*, ts'ing-ts'ing'-k'en 稱稱看; *it weighs ten catties*, ts'ing'-ko' jih kying' djong' 稱過十觔重; — *accurately*, ts'ing cing'-tsoh 稱準足; — *a matter* (by measuring), liang-doh' 量度

WEIGHER, ts'ing'-siu 秤手

WEIGHT, djong 重; *what is the* —? yiu to-siao' djong' 有多少重; *oranges sell by* —, kyüih'-ts leng veng-liang' ma 橘子論分兩賣°; *compare the* —, kao ky'ing-djong' 較輕重; *ask the* —, meng' kying-liang' 問觔兩

WEIGHTS *for steelyards*, ts'ing'-djü 秤錘°; — *for scales*, fah'-mó 法°碼

WEIGHTY, djong'-da 重大; — *matter*, djong'-da z-ken' 重大事幹

WELCOME *letter*, sing' læ-leh 'eh-i' 信來得合意; *you are* —, (*i. e.* I give it cheerfully), ngô nyün-i' peh' ng 我願意給你°; *you are* — *here*, (*i. e.* we like to have you here), ah'-lah yüoh-i' ng læ-tong' 我°等°欲意你°在°此°

WELD, *to* tang'-long 打攏

WELL, tsing 井 (ih-k'eo)

WELL, *in health*, sông'-kw'a 爽快°; bing-en' 平安; z-dzæ' 自在; *are you* —? ng hao' 你好? ng hao yia' 你°好呀; (the last sometimes has a tinge of disrespect); (*I*) *am* —, hao'-go 好个°; hao' hao' 好好; t'oh-foh' 托福; t'oh-ng-foh' 托你°福; *tolerably* —, wa hao' 還°好; p'o' hao 頗好; yiu-tin' hao 有點好; *you look* —, ng min-seh' tao hao' 你面色倒好; hao' ky'i'-seh 好氣色; *colors* — (*i. e.* accurately) *matched*, ngæn-seh' p'é-leh t'o-tông 顏色配得°妥當; — *done*, tso-leh hao' 做得好°; — *written*, sia-leh hao' 寫°得°好; — *dressed*, i-zông' c'ün-leh hao'-go 衣裳°穿得°好个°; c'ün-leh 'ao-yiah'-go 穿得°豪俠个°; sing pé'-zông t'i'-min-go 身上體面个°; — *bred*, (taught well at home), kyüô-kyiao' hao' 家教好; kô-kwe' hao' 家°規好; *the* — *day in ague*, k'ong'-nyih 空日°

WEST, si 西; *in the* —, læ si-pin' 在°西邊; læ si-pun'-pin 在°西半邊; *toward the* —, dziao si' 朝西; hyiang si' 向西

WET, sih 濕; — *with rain*, ling-sih' 淋濕; — *through*, sih-t'eo' 濕邊; *ditto* (by being in water), tsing'-sih 浸濕

WET   526   WHE

WET-NURSE, ah-bu' 阿婷; na' ah-bu' 嬭 阿婷

WHARF, jün mô'-deo 船碼頭 (ih-go)

WHAT, soh'-go 甚°麼°; soh'-si 爲甚; for — *did you come?* ng' we-leh soh'-go z-ken' læ' 你°爲了°甚°麼°事幹來? (polite), ng' yiu soh'-go kwe'z' 你°有甚°麼°貴事; — *do you want?* ng' iao soh'-si? 你°要甚°麼°;— *business?* soh' ken? 何°事°?— *farther?* wa-yiu soh'-si 還° 有 甚°麼°? — *is your name?* ng' kyiao soh'-go ming'-z 你°叫 甚°麼°名字? — *is your family* —? sing soh' 姓甚°麼°? (more polite), kwe sing' 貴姓? — *is it to you?* yü ng' 'o-ken' 與你° 何干? teng ng' yiu soh'-go siang-ken' 與你°有甚°麼°相干?

WHATEVER, feh-leng' soh'-go 弗 論甚°麼°; peh'-kyü soh'-go 不拘甚°麼°; — *ever you please*, ze-bin' ng iao soh'-go 隨便你° 要甚°麼°; — *he does is well done*, gyi' feh leng' tso soh'-go tu hao' 其 弗 論 做 甚°麼°都好

WHEAT, mah 麥; — *cakes*, mah ping' 麥餅; — *flour*, min-feng' 麵粉; —*straw*, mah ken' 麥幹

WHEEDLE, *to* nyün'-pa-pu 軟擺佈

WHEEL, leng-bun' 輪盤 (ih-go)

WHEEL-BARROW, siao'-ts'ô 小 事; *one wheeled carriage*, doh-leng'-ts'ô 獨 輪 車° (ih-go)

WHEN, kyi'-z 幾時? soh'-go z-'eo' 甚°麼°時候? — *I was sick*, ngô bing'-go z-'eo' 我病 个°時候; — *you were here*, ng læ-tong' z-'eo' 你°在°此時候

WHENCE, dzong 'ah-li' 從那°裏? dzong 'o-c'ü' 從何處? — *do you come?* ng dzong 'o'-r læ' 你° 從何而來?

WHENEVER, feh-leng kyi'-z 弗 論幾時; ze-bin' kyi'-z 隨便 幾時; peh'-kyü kyi'-z 不拘 幾時

WHERE? ah-li' or 'ah-li' 那裡°? 'o-c'ü' 何處? soh'-go di'-fông 甚° 麼°地方? 'o-fông 何方? soh'-go u-sen 甚°麼°所在°? — *is* (it)? læ ah-li, or læ 'o-c'ü 在°何 處? — *are you going?* ng' tao ah-li' ky'i' 你°到那°裡去°? *place* — *I live*, ngô tô deng'-go di'-fông 我所庵个°地方

WHEREAS, *since*, kyi'-jün 既然; kyi'-kying 既經

WHEREVER, feh-leng' ah-li' 弗論 那°裏; feh-leng' 'o-c'ü' 弗 論 何處, &c.

WHEREFORE? *for what reason?* we 'o yün-kwu' 爲何緣故? we-leh soh'-go yün-kwu' 爲了°甚° 麼°緣故? 'o kwu' 何故? *why?* dza-we' 何°爲? we dza' yün-kwu' 爲甚°緣故? *for what business?* we-leh soh' ken?

WHETHER, *I do not know* — (*I*) *shall go*, feh'-tsiao ky'i'-feh-ky'i 不知去弗去°; *do you know* — *he has come or not?* ng hyiao'-teh gyi ke'-leh m̄-teh 你曉得其來了°嗎°? — *cold or hot*, feh-leng' lang feh-leng' nyih' 弗論冷弗論熱°

WHET-STONE, mo-tao'-zah 磨刀石° (ih-kw'e)

WHICH *one?* 'ah-li ih'-go 那裡一个°? — *boat?* 'ah-li ih-tsah jün' 那裡一隻船°? *do not know* — *road is right*, feh'-tsiao 'ah-li' ih-da lu z' 弗知那°裏一塚路是; — (*the relative*), sô 所; *that* — *I said*, ngô sô wô 我所話

WHIFF *of smoke* (from the mouth), ih-k'eo in' 一口烟

WHILE, *a little* —, ih-zông kong-fu' 一息工夫; hao'-to kong'-fu' 好多工夫; *a long* —, dziang-kyiu' 長久; pun'-pun-jih-nyih'; yiu'-ho z-tsih' 許°多°時候°; *such a long* —, ih-veh' ts'ih-shü' 這°許°多°工°夫°; *wait a* —, teng ih'-zông 等一息°; *not worth* — *to go*, feh dzih'-teh ky'i' 弗值得去°; feh vien'-djoh ky'i' 弗犯着°去°; feh keh'-sön ky'i' 弗合算去°; keh'-feh-djoh-ky'i' 合弗着°去°; *not worth* — *to do*, feh-zông -sön tso' 弗上算做

WHILE, *during the time that*, pin, or i'-pin, used twice, thus; — *talking he was crying*, pin kông' pin k'oh' 隨°講°隨°哭; — *rowing his boat, he eats his rice*, i'-pin wô' jün', i'-pin ky'üoh-vien 隨°划船°隨°吃°飯; — *I was eating*, ngô ky'üoh-vien' z-ʻco' 我吃°飯時候°

WHIMS, *a person full of* —, ang' nying 獨°幅°个°人°

WHIP, *to* tang 打; — *with a bamboo*, tang pæn'-ts 打板子; — *with a ferule*, tang kao'-fông 打戒方; — *on the palm*, tang siu'-ti-sing' 打手心

WHIP, *lash*, pin'-ts 鞭子 (ih-keng); *thin bamboo* —, pæn'-ts 板子 (ih-keng)

WHIRL, *to* kwah'-lah-lah cün' 刮轆°轆°轉

WHIRLPOOL, bun-shü' 盤水°; jün-shü' 旋°水° (ih-yüing)

WHIRLWIND, yiang-koh'-fông 羊角°風; djün-fong' 旋風

WHISKERS, *and beard*, wu-cü' 鬍鬚

WHISKEY, *Chinese* siao-tsiu' 燒酒

WHISPER, *to* ts'ih'-ts'ih-c'ih-c'ih' kông' 嗦嗦唣唣講°; — *in the ear*, kyiao' deo tsih' r 交頭接耳; ngao ng'-tó kông 鮫°耳°朶講°

WHISTLE, *toy* kyiao-kyü' 燻°筬°; tiao-kyü' (ih-go)

WHISTLE, *to* — (or *blow*) *a tune*, c'ü' ing-diao' 吹音調; — *loud* (as steam), c'ü-hyiang' 吹響

WHITE, bah 白°; *to bleach* —, p'iao'-bah 漂白°

WHITE, the — of the eye, ngæn'-bah 眼白; — of the egg, dæn-bah' 蛋白

WHITE-WASH, shih'-bah 刷白; zông-hwe' 上灰: feng'-shih 粉刷

WHO? jü 誰? — is there? jü' læ-kæn' 誰在彼? soh'-go nying læ-kæn' 甚麼人在彼? who says so? jü'-wô 誰話? (often equivalent to you don't say so!); — (the relative), sô 所; the one — just came, fông-dzæ' sô læ'-go nying 方纔所來个人

WHOEVER, feh-leng' jü 弗論誰; ze-bin' soh'-go nying 隨便甚麼人; peh' kyü soh'-go nying 不拘甚麼人

WHOLE, djün 全; djün-fu' 全副; tsing 正; 'eh 合; 'o 和; ih-gong' 一共; mun 滿; weng 渾; the whole night, djün-yia' 全夜; tsing-yia' 正夜; — family, 'eh-kô' 合家; 'o-kô' 和家; djün-kô' 全家; what is the — amount? ih-gong' to siao' 一共多少? ih'-kæ to-siao' 一概多少? — body, mun'-sing 滿身; weng-sing' 渾身; — life, ih-sang' ih-si' 一生一世; ih-seng' 一生; the — earth, p'n' t'in-'ô 普天下; 'en'-t'in-'ô 合天下; shall the chicken be cut in pieces, or boiled —? kyi' wa-z feng-k'æ'ts', tsing'-tsah-ts' 鷄還是分開羹呢正隻羹?* — piece (of meat

&c.), tsing-kw'e' 正塊; — potato, tsing-dön' fæn-jü'; the — lot (of goods), ih-kwu'-nao-r' 一總; nen-ken'; buy the — lot, teng'-cü ma' 薑買

* Observe, that in the latter part of this sentence, the classifier is used instead of the noun.

WHOLESALE, to buy at —, do-tông' ma' 大批頭買; tsing-p'iao' ma' 正票買; teng-tông' ma 薑當買

WIG, (such as is used in Chinese theatres), mông'-kying 網巾; to wear a —, or false hair, s kô'-deo 梳假頭

WILD, yia 野; — beasts, yia'-siu 野獸; — flowers, yia'-hwô 野花; yia when applied to persons may signify rude, or savage.

WILDERNESS, kw'ông'-iæ di'-fông 曠野地方

WILES, kwe-kyi' 詭計; many —, kwe-kyi' to'-tön 詭計多端

WILL, cü'-i 主意; — (of God, or of the Emperor), ts'-i 旨意; sing'-ts 聖旨; strong —, cü'-i do' 主意大; good — (right intention), hao'-i 好意; me'-i 美意; ill —, tæ'-i 歹意; oh'-i 惡意; to harbor ill —, dzeng tæ'-i 存歹意; — or testament, yi-coh', or yi-tsoh 遺囑; to make a —, lih' yi-coh' 立遺囑

WILL, to determine, ding ih-go cü'-i 定一个主意; ding hao' 定好; — (sometimes the

WIL 529 WIF

sign of the future), we 會; *I will go*, ngô'we ky'i' 我會°去°; *I will not go*, ngô kyüih'-i-feh-ky'i' 我決意弗去°; *it — do*, bao'-s-teh 好使得; k'o'-yi 可以
WILL-WITH-A-WISP, kyü teng-long' 鬼°燈籠; ling-ho' 燐火
WILLFUL, *very* 'eo zi'-go 擅自°个°; sang' 'eo-zi-go 生來°擅自°个°
WILLING, k'eng 肯; ken-sing' 甘心; dzing-nyün' 情願; *are you — or not?* ng' k'eng' feh k'eng' 你肯弗肯; *— to work*, tso sang-weh' ken-sing'-go 做生°活甘心个°
WILLINGLY, dzing-nyün' 情願
WILLOW, yiang-liu' 楊柳; *weeping —*, tao'-gwæn yiang-liu' 倒損楊柳 (ih-cü)
WILT, *to* pih 晡; pih'-long-ky'i 晡攏去°; *— in the sun*, sa'-pih 曬°晡
WILY, kæn-wah' 奸°滑
WIN, *to — a victory*, teh-sing' 得勝; *the first to —*, sin sing' 先勝; *— (in chess)*, tsiah'-ying 着贏
WINCE, *to* geo-soh' 勾縮
WIND, fong 風; *favorable —*, jing fong' 順風; *contrary —*, teo' fong' 對風; *head —*, ting' deo fong' 頂頭風; *strong —*, mang' fong 猛風°; *— has subsided*, fong sih'-de 風息了
WIND, *to* nyiao 繞; *ing*; dziu

紬;*— up*, nyiao-nyiao-tsing 繞°上°; *to — off*, dziu-c'ih 紬出; *— thread*, yüih sin' 緯線, &c.; *— a watch*, k'æ piao' 開表
WHOLESOME, hao yiang sing-t'i' go 好養°身體个°
WHOSE, jü'-go? 誰个°; soh'-go nying'-go? 甚°麼°人°个°
WHOSOEVER, See WHOEVER.
WHY, dza-we'? 何°爲°; *— so?* dza-we' z-ka'? 何°爲°如此°? *— so badly off?* 'o-ts' ü-ts' 何至於此?
WICK, teng-sing' 燈芯; *pith —*, teng-sing' ts'ao 燈芯草
WICKED, oh 惡: *— man*, oh' nying 惡人°; *forsake the —*, yün siao'-jing 遠小人
WIDE, kw'eh 闊
WIDEN, *to* tso k'æ-kw'eh' 做開闊; *make a little wider*, long kw'eh'-tin 弄闊些°
WIDER, keng'-kô kw'eh' 更加°闊; *to grow —*, kw'eh'-ky'i-læ 闊起來
WIDOW, sông-vu' 孀婦; kwô kyü' 寡居; kwô'-vu 寡婦; kwu'-sông ma'-ma 孤孀; kwu'-sông lao'-nyüing; *— who remains pure*, tsih'-vu 節婦
WIDOWED, *in a — state* kwô'-kyü-tong 現°在寡居
WIDOWER, kwæn'-fu 鰥夫; *living as a —*, kwæn'-kyü-tong 現°在鰥居; dön-yin'-liao-go 斷絃了
WIFE, ts'i-ts' 妻子; nyü'-nying

女人°*; lao'-nyüing 婦°; (contemptuous), lao'-bo 老婆; *the principal* —, tsing'-shih 正室; kyih'-fah 結髮; do lao'-nyüing *the inferior* —, tseh'-shih 側室; p'in-vông' 偏房; siao laonyüing' 妾; *how is your* —? (to a gentleman), fu-nying' hao' feh? 夫人°好否°; he replies, *my* —, dzin-ne' 賤內 &c.; *your* — (one gentleman to another), tseng sao' 尊嫂; (to a stranger or superior), tseng-fu' nying 尊夫人°; (to a servant &c.), ng'-go oh'-li nying 你°个°家°裏人°; ng-go ne'-li'-hyiang 你°个°內裡向; (he replies), *my* —, ah-lah ne-li 我°个°內裡; *have you a* —? (to a servant), ng' yiu dzing-kô' feh 你°有成家°否°? ng yiu kô-siao' 出°-teh 你°有家°小沒°有°? *newly married* —, sing-vu' 新婦; *second* — dzoh-yin' 續絃; dzoh-c'ü' 續娶; *she is the second* — (the first having died), gyi z dzoh'-go 其是續娶个°; gyi z in'-vông,

* *Nyü-nying though used in the generic sense of woman, means properly a wife. An unmarried lady of fifty is not a nyü-nying, as we should suppose, because she is not a wife.*

WIFE'S *older brother*, do ah'-gyiu 大°阿舅; — *younger brother*, siao' ah'-gyiu 小阿舅; — *elder sister*, yi-mô' 姨媽; — *younger sister*, siao'-yi 小姨; — *sister's*

husband, lin-kying' 連襟; yi-dziang' 姨丈; *wife of an elder brother*, hyüong-sao' 兄嫂; *do of younger brother*, di-sing'-vu 弟媳°婦; — *father*, dziang'-nying 丈°人°; ngoh-vu' 岳父; — *mother*, dziang'-vu 丈°父; ngoh-meo' 岳母

WINDING(as a road), wæn-ky'üoh' go 彎曲个°; wæn-nyiao'-go 彎繞°个°; *very* —, ts'ih'-wænpah'-ky'üoh 七彎八曲

WINDLASS, kao'-ts'ô 絞車°; — (for drawing boats over an inclined plane), ts'ô-dong' 車°筒 *to raise by a* —, ts'ô-zông'-ky'i 車°上去°

WINDOW, ts'ông 牕; *glass* —, po-li' ts'ông 玻璃牕; *paper* —, ts ts'ông 紙牕; *small* — *for ventilating*, c'ih-ky'i'-dong 出氣洞; *oyster shell* —, ming-ngô, ts'ông 明瓦°牕; *ditto in the roof*, t'in-tsing'-pæn 天井板

WINDPIPE, ky'i'-kwun 氣管; hô'-kwun 呼°吸°管

WINE, tsiu 酒

WINE-BIBBER, tsiu-weh-lu 酒崩蘆

WINE-CUP, tsiu-pe' 酒杯

WINE-JAR, tsiu-dzing' 酒墰°; *a jar of wine*, (30 catties), ih-dzing tsiu 一埕酒

WINE-SHOP, tsiu-tin 酒店 (ih-bæn)

WING, yih-sao' or yiah-sao' 翅°膀°, 翼稍 (ih-tsah)

WINK, to — the eyes, sah ngæn'-tsing 睏眼睛; ngæn'-tsing sah'-sah 眼睛睏°睏°

WINK, as quick as a —, ngæn'-tsing ih-sah' 眼睛一睏°; give him a —, tiu ngæn-seh' peh gyi 與°伊°丟眼睏°

WINK, to — at, or appear not to see, ngæn-k'æ ngæn-pi' 眼開眼閉; tsông'-leh feh k'en'-kyin 裝得°弗看見; to appear to be unconscious of, tsông'-leh feh-dzæ'-i 裝得°弗在意

WINNOW, to — (by throwing up before the wind), po 播; po-yiang' 播揚; po-long 播弄; — grain, yiang koh 揚穀

WINNOWING machine, fong-siang' 風箱 (ih-bu)

WINTER, Tong-t'in' 冬天; — season, Tong-kyi' 冬季; to pass the —, ko Tong' 過冬

WIPE, to k'a 揩°; — dry, k'a sao' 揩°燥; — clean, k'a ken-zing' 揩°乾淨; — away tears, k'a ngæn'-li 揩眼淚

WIRE, iron t'ih'-s 鐵絲; brass —, dong s' 銅絲

WISDOM, ts'ong-ming' 聰明

WISE, ts'ong-ming' 聰明; very —, ts'ong-ming cü-we' 聰明智慧; naturally — (bright), t'in-ts'ong' t'in-ming' 天聰天明

WISH, to want, iao 要; do you — to go, ng' iao ky'i' feh 你°要去°否°; I — very much, pô'-feh-neng'-keo 巴弗能彀; pô'-feh-teh' 巴弗得; I — you a pleasant (i.e. peaceful) journey, dæn-nyün ng' ih-lu' bing-en' 但願你°一路平安; — you well, pô'-feh-neng'-keo ng hao' 巴弗能彀你好

WISH, sing-siang' 心想; sing-nyün 心願; my — is to go in the Spring, ngô sing-siang' C'ing-t'in'-li ky'i 我心想到°春季裏去°; exactly according to my —, jü-sing' ziang-i' 如心合°意; obtained his —, gyi'-go sing-nyün' teh'-djoh-de 其个°心願得着了°

WISTERIA, ts'-deng 紫籐

WIT. See WITTY.

WITCH, sorceress, yüong zia-fah'-go nyü'-nying 用邪°法个°女人°

WITCH-CRAFT, fah'-jih 法術; zia-fah' 邪°法

WITH, teng 與; lin 連; 'o 和; go — me, teng ngô' dô-kô' ky'i 與°我一°同去°; eat — milk, lin na' ky'üoh' 連嬭吃°; na 'o'-leh ky'üoh' 嬭和了°吃°; — a spoon, yüong diao-kang' 用調羹; — a pen, yüong pih' 用筆; to mix —, 'o-long' 和攏

WITHDRAW, to t'e 退; — from, or out of, t'e'-c'ih 退出; t'eng'-c'ih 褪出; soh'-c'ih 縮出; — (walking backward), tao'-t'e 倒退; tao'-t'eng-bu 倒退°步; — to another place, t'e'-li 退避

WITHER, to — (as if dying), kw'u

枯°;— *and dry,* ken-kw‛u' 乾枯;— *up,* kw‛u-long'-ky‛i 枯攏去°

WITHERED, *dried up,* ken'-de 乾了°; kw‛u'-de 枯了°; *flowers are — and fallen,* hwô zia'-de 花謝了°;— *hand,* siu'-hyüih kw‛u'-de 手血枯了°

WITHHOLD, *to restrain from,* ts'-djü 止住; lah-djü' 攔°住; *to retain —,* siu-tsing' 收進

WITHIN, li-hyiang' 裡向; li'-deo 裏面°; ne 內;— *three days,* sæn nyih' li-hyiang' 三日°裡向°; sæn nyih' ts ne' 三日°之內

WITHOUT, *outside,* nga-deo' 外°面°; nga-hyiang 外°向;— *wood and rice,* m̄-za' m̄-mi' 無°柴°無°米;— *a cash,* feng-veng' m̄'-teh 分文沒°有°; ib'-go dong-din' tu m̄'-neh;— 一個銅錢°都沒°有°; *can't do — it,* ky‛üih'-gyi-feh-læ' 缺其弗來; siao'-feh-teh 少弗得; hyih'-feh-læ' 歇弗來; *can do — it,* hao-hyih'-go 好歇个°; hao-sang'-go 好省个°;— *reason,* m̄-kao' yüen-kwn' 沒°有°緣故; vu-yüen' vu-kwu' 無°緣無°故;— *day (sine die),* yiao-yiao' vu gyi 遙遙無期; *better — such a son,* keh'-cü-ka ng-ts' feh-jü' m̄'-teh 如°此°兒°子倒°弗如沒°有°

WITHSTAND, *to* gyü-djih' 拒°絕;— (an enemy), ti'-dih 抵敵; dih-djü' 敵住

WITNESS, *to testify,* tso te'-tsing 做對証; *to testify to what one has seen,* kyin'-tsing 見証

WITNESS, *eye* ts‛ing-ngæn'-moh-tu' 親眼°目睹

WITTY *words,* ky‛iao'-tsong ka shih-wô'; ky‛iao'-wô 巧話; *quaint words,* kwu'-li-kwu-tong' shih-wô' 言°有°古°風°; kwu'-tong lin'-ky‛i shih-wô' 古董臉氣說話

WITS, *frightened out of one's —,* weh-ling' hah'-c‛ih-de 魂°靈嚇出了°

WOE, 'o 禍; 'o'-se 禍祟

WOLF, za-lông' 豺°狼 (ih-tsah)

WOMAN, (married), nyü'-nying 女人°; lao-nyüing 婦°女; nyü liu-ts-pe' 女流之輩; *ought not to treat a — so,* nyü'-liu-ts-pe' feh ing-kæ ka' dæ gyi 女流之輩弗應如°此°待伊; *old —,* lao'-bo-bo 老婆婆; bo'-bo 婆婆; lao-t‛a-bun' 老太°婆° (disrespectful); *woman's work,* nyü'-kong 女工; vu'-nyü sô'-we' 婦女所會 See WIFE.

WOMANISH, ziang nyü'-nying ka' 像女人°一°樣°; nyü'-siang 女相

WOMB, t‛æ 胎

WOMEN, (as a class), nyü'-nying-lah' 女人°等

WONDER, *to be surprised,* hyi-gyi' 希奇; gyi-kwa' 奇怪; *doubt,* feh'-tsiao; liao feh tao 料°弗°到°; *I — who is there,* feh'-tsiao jü' læ'-kæn 料°弗°到°誰在°彼

WONDERFUL, hyi-gyi' 希奇; gyi-kwa' 奇怪; *very* —, hyi-gyi'-leh-kying' 甚°希奇; hyi-gyi'-sah-nying' 希奇煞人°; hyi-gyi'-kwu-kwa 希奇古怪°

WOOD, moh-deo' 木頭; jü 樹; (*a piece of*, ih-kwe); *hard* —, ngang-moh' 硬木; ngang-jü' 硬樹; *mixed* —, zeh-jü' 雜°樹; (*a log of*, ih-dön); — *for burning*, za-bæn 柴爿; *a stick of* —, ih-kw'e' za-bæn' 一塊柴°爿; *a bundle of* —, ih-ky'iu za' 一稨柴°; *to split* —, p'ih za' 劈柴°; *to saw* —, ka za' 鋸柴°

WOODEN, moh-deo' tso'-go 木頭做个°; jü' tso'-go 樹做个°

WOOD-SHOP (*for timber*), jü-'ông' 樹行°; *small ditto*, zah-moh'tông 雜°木行°; *fuel-shop*, za-'ông' 柴°行°; za-tin' 柴°店 (ih-bæn)

WOOF, we 緯; yü-sô 緯°紗

WOOL, yiang-mao' 羊毛

WOOLEN, *made of wool*, yiang-mao' tso-go 羊毛做个°; — *yarn*, nyüong sin' 絨線

WORD, shih-wô' 說話; — (often in a bad sense), wô-deo' 話頭 (ih-kyü); *to break one's* —, shih-sing' 失信; *keeps* (his) —, shih-wô' hao tsoh-cing' 說話好作準; shih-wô' hao sön-su' 說話好算數; *left* — *there*, ih-kyü'shih-wô' lin-c'ih'-kæn 一句說話關照出了°; shih-wô' t'oh'-c'ih-kæn 說°話°託出了°; *write a few*

words, sia liang'kyü shih-wô' 寫°兩句說話; *ditto* (or characters), sia ko'-pô-z' 寫°個巴字; *words few, and easily understood*, shih-wô' ling-ts'ing' 說話靈清

WORK, sang-weh' 生°活; kong 工; *hard* —, lao-kw'u'sang-weh' 勞苦生°活; kw'u'-kong 苦工; djong-deo' sang-weh' 鄭°重生°活; *a day's* —, ih kong' 一工; *to stop* —, hyih kong' 歇工; *no* — *to do*, m-kao'sang-weh' hao tso' 無°甚°生°活好做; *fond of eating, and lazy at* —, t'en ky'üoh', læn tso' 貪吃°懶做; *well executed* —, hao' kong-fu' 好工夫; *needle* —, tsing-ts' sang weh' 針黹生°活°; *embroidery* —, ts'æ'-tsông sang-weh' 彩裝生°活

WORK, *to* tso sang-weh' 做生°活; tso kong' 做工; yüong kong' 用工; *what* — *are you doing*, (*to a servant or laborer*), ng tso soh'-go sang-weh'? 你°做甚°麼°生°活; *ditto* (*to a gentleman*), ng yüong soh'-go kong'? 你°用甚°麼°功; *I* — *for a living*, ngô yüong-kong' du-nyih' 我儕工度日°; — *early and late*, ky'i'-tsao loh-æn' 起早落夜°; — *by the day*, leng-kong' tso 論工做; leng-nyih'tso論日°做; *to* — *with the hand* (as clay), nyiah 揑; — *between the palms*, tso 做; — *a miracle*, 'ang jing-tsih' 行°神跡

WORK-BASKET, tsia-k'ong-læn' 織°筐°籃
WORKING well (as a machine), jing-dzeh' 光°潤; *fermenting* (as honey &c.), la-tih fæn' 正°在°泛
WORKMAN, s-vu' 司務; tso siu-nyi-go 做手藝个°
WORKMANSHIP, siu'-dön 手段; *exquisite* —, siu'-dön tsing-cü' 手段精緻
WORLD, shü'-kæn-zông' 世界上; *the whole* —, p'u-t'in-'ô 普天下°; t'ong'-t'in-'ô 統天下°; 'en'-t'in-'ô 合°天下°; *this* —, kying-si' 今世°; *while in this* —, we-nying' dzæ-shü' 爲人°在世; *before one came into the* —, zin-si' 前°世°; *the* — *hereafter*, 'ô'-si 下°世°; *the invisible* (dark) —, ing-kæn' 陰間°; *has seen much of the* —, shü'-min tu kyin'-ko 世面都見過°; *ditto* (still stronger), kyin'-kwông-sih-da' 見廣識大
WORLDLY *affairs*, shü'-z 世事; — *customs*, shü'-dzoh, or shü-djoh 世俗; — *pleasures*, shü'-zông-go kw'a'-loh 世上个°快樂
WORM, djong 蟲; *earth* —, c'oh'-zin, tsoh'-zin, or c'ih'-zin 曲°蟮 (ih-keng)
WORRIED, sing óng 心煩; sing-væn-tsao 心煩嘈; væn-beh'-tsi-tsao 煩白嘈嘈; ông-beh'-tsi-tsao; *can't help being* —. p'i'-leh-k'æ 管弗開; —, *and anxious*, to-sing' to-z 多°心多°事;

— *to death*, væn-zeh'-sah-de 煩雜煞了°; — *and restless*, singli' tsiao-tsao' 心裡焦躁; *will not allow one's self to be* —, p'i'-leh-k'æ 管得°開
WORRY, to væn 煩; — *much*, to væn' 多煩; tsi-tseo' 嘈唧; — *by much talking, or by begging*, lo'-so 嘮嗦; — *by many things*, væn-zeh' 煩雜
WORSE, yüih-fah wa' 越發孬°; yü'-kô wa 愈加°孬°; keng'-kô wa 更加°孬°; — *than before*, pi zin-deo' wa' 比前°頭°孬°; pi zin-deo' feh-jü' 比前°頭弗如; — (as disease), yü'-kô djong' 愈加°重; yü-kô' li-'æ' 愈加°利害; *grows* — *every day*, ih-nyih' feh jü' ih-nyih' 一日°弗如一日°; nyih djong' ih-nyih' 日°重一日°; nyih-nyih djong' 日°日°重
WORSHIP, li'-pa 禮拜°; *to perform* —, tso li'-pa 做禮拜°
WORSHIP, *to* pa 拜°; pa li'-pa; — *idols*, pa bu-sah' 拜°菩薩; — *at the graves*, zông veng' 上墳; — *ancestors*, tsi tsu' 祭祖; — *sacred books* (a Buddhists do), pa kying' 拜°經
WORST, wa-gyih' 孬°極; tsæ'-m-tsæ-wa' 再無°再孬°; wa' feh ko'-yi wa 孬°而又孬°; peh-k'æn wa' 不堪孬°; *at the* —, wa' tao toh' 孬°到邊°; wa' tao gyih-deo' 孬°到極頭

WORTHLESS, feh-dzih' dong-din' 弗值銅錢°;— thing, æn-ho ts'æ-货;— fellow, fi'-veh 廢物; ditto (used in reviling), ts'æn'-deo.

WORTHY to receive, ing-teh'-go 應得个°;— to bear, kæ-tông'-go 該當个°.

WOULD that he might come again, 'ö'-feh gyi tsæ læ' 但°願°其再來;— rather die, neng'-s si' 情使死°;— not this be better? feh'-z keh'-go hao'-tin ma 弗是這个°好點嗎°?— like very much, po'-feh-neng'-keo 巴弗能彀.

WOUND, to —, injure, or bruise, sông 傷; sông-'æ' 傷害; tang'-sông 打傷;— with a knife, tao' kah'-sông 刀割傷;— with a bullet, dæn-ts' tang'-sông 彈子打傷;—feelings, sông ky'üoh' 傷情°.

WOUND, received a severe —, ziu djong'-sông de 受重傷了°; a fatal —, cü-ming'-go sông 致命个°傷; the mark of a —, sông-'eng' 傷痕.

WRANGLE, to k'eo'-kyüoh siang'-tseng 口角相爭.

WRAP, to pao 包; ko 裹°;—it in paper, yüong ts' ', pao'-ih-pao 用紙包一包;— up, pao-long' 包攏; ko'-long 裹攏; pao-ky'i'-læ 包起來.

WRAPPED within, pao-tsing'-tih 包進的; ditto (as ideas), pao-kweh'-tih 包括的.

WRAPPING, coarse pao-bi' 包皮;

a large handkerchief used for — clothes, &c., pao-voh' 包袱.

WORTH, dzih 值 ;— money, dzih' dong-din' 值銅錢°; how much is (it) — ? dzih to-siao' 值多少? — the trouble, dzih-tch'-go 值得个°; is it — (so much), or not? dzih feh dzih' 值弗值? — while. See WHILE.

WRATH, ô'-wông; nu 怒; great —, nu'-ky'i dzih-ts'ong' 怒氣直冲; nu'-fah ts'ong-kwun' 怒髮冲冠; nu'-ky'i ts'ong-t'in' 怒氣冲天.

WREAK vengeance, or wrath upon him, læ gyi'-go sing-zông' nu'-fah ts'ong-kwun' 在°其个°身上怒髮冲冠.

WRECKED, a vessel —, jün tso'-diao-de 船觸°壞了°; ditto capsized, jün tao'-meh-de 船倒沒了°; spk't upon rocks, ngô-tsiao'-de 觸°礁了.

WRENCH, to — out, cih'-c'ih 折出;— round, cih'-cün 折轉;— open, cih'-k'æ 折開.

WREST the meaning, nyiao ka'-shih 拘°泥°解°說.

WRESTLE, to sæ gyün' 賽拳; pi gyün 比拳;— (as children), k'ô tih 扳°跌.

WRETCHED, kw'u 苦;— end, kyih'-gyüoh wa' 結局孬°.

WRIGGLE, to — (as a serpent), dzin-læ' dzin-ky'i' 纏來𢃛去°.

WRING, to — (as clothes), kao 絞;— dry, kao siao' 絞燥;— the neck, deo-kying' cih'-cün 頭頸扭°轉

WRINKLE, tseo'-veng 皺紋; veng-lu' 紋路; *fold, or plait*, kæn 襇°

WRINKLE, *to* tseo 皺; long-tseo' 弄皺; — *by folding badly*, tsih'-tseo 摺皺

WRINKLED (as cloth), tseo'-tseo 皺皺;—(as the face), yiu tseo'-veng 有皺紋; tang-kæn'-de 打襇°了°

WRIST, siu'-bu-lu-den' 手蒲蘆頭°

WRITE, *to* sia 寫°; sia'-loh 寫落; — *one's name*, sia ming-z' 寫°名字; loh ming-z' 錄名字; *ditto* (as in a register, &c.), zông ming-z' 上名字;—*characters*, sia z' 寫字; — *a letter*, sia sing' 寫信

WRITER, sia-z'-go 寫字个°; (on a vessel), t'iah'-sia-go 帖°寫

WRITHING *in pain*, t'ong'-leh-ngao' tsin-feh-ko' 痛得°熬煎弗過

WRITING. *penmanship*,shü-fah' 書法; pih'-fah 筆法; *hand*—, pih'-tsik 筆跡; (Chinese) —*materials*, pih'-moh-ts-nyin' 筆墨紙硯; veng-vông-s'-pao 文房四寶

WRONG, ts'o 錯; ngo 訛; *to be* —, yiu ts'o' 有錯; yiu feh-z' 有弗是; *to do* —, tso' ts'o 做錯; long ts'o' 弄錯; *understand* (or hear) —, t'ing' ts'o 聽錯; *put in the* — *place*, fông ts'o' 放錯;—*side out*, fæn-min' 反面; *to wear ditto*, c'ün'-leh fæn'-min 反面穿了°; —, (*i.e.* the wrong person receives),tsiang-kwun' li-ta' 張冠李戴; *can't distinguish right and*—, z'-fi bin'-feh-c'ih-læ' 是非辨弗出來; *to write a* — *character*, sia' bah-z' 寫°白字; *to be in the* —, *and tell others* —, yi'-ngo, djün-ngo' 以訛傳訛

WRONG, *injury*. we'-ky'üoh 委屈°; ün-wông' 寃枉; *to receive* —, ziu ün-wông' 受寃枉

WRONG,*to* we'-ky'üoh 委屈°; (in a stronger sense), ün-ky'üih' 寃屈

WROUGHT *iron*, joh-t'ih' 熟°鐵

WRY *face*, wæn-cü' wæn-teh; *put on a* — *face*, tsông'-leh wæn-cü' wæn-teh 裝得°㜵嘴㜵嗒; *distorted, twisted face*, hwa-cü' hwa-lin 歪嘴歪臉

Y

YAM, (Chinese), z-yiah' 蒔藥; sæn-yiah' 山藥

YARD, *a* ih-mô' 一碼; *a—of cotton cloth*, ih-mô pu' 一碼布; *space around a house*, yü-di' 餘地

YAWN, *to* tang hô-hen' 打呵軒

YEAR, *a* ih-nyin' 一年; *beginning of the* —, nyin-deo' 年頭; *end of the* —, nyin-ti' 年底; sæn'-jih-nyin-yia' 大°年夜; nyiæn-kyiu' yia 小°年夜; *near the end of the* —, nyin-dzing'shü -pih 年近歲畢; *this* —, kying-nyin' 今年; peng'-nyin 本年; *this or the same* —, tông'-nyin 當

年; next —, ming-nyin' 明年; nen-nyin'; læ-nyin' 來年; 'o°-nyin 下°年; last —, gyiu-nyin' 舊年; ky'ü'-nyin 去年; zông-nyin' 上年; — before last, zin'-nyin 前°年; — after —, le'-nyin 厯年; once a —, ih-nyin'ih-we' 一年一回; (of a young person), how many years old is he, gyi' kyi shü' 其幾歲°; (of one over 20), gyi to-siao nyin'-kyi 其多少年紀; eight years old, pah'-shü-de 八歲了°; a — old, tsiu'-shü 週歲; about a — old, tsiu-pô-shü' 將°近°週歲

YEARLY, nyin-nyin' 年年; me'-nyin 每年

YEARN to see, vông' gyi-we min' ziang k'eo-k'eh' ka 企°望如渴; — for, k'eh-k'eh-neng'-neng siang'-vông 刻刻時°時°想望

YEAST, kao'-shü 酵水°

YELLOW, wông 黃; pale —, dæn wông' 淡黃

YELLOWISH, yiu-tin wông' 有點黃; wông-shô'-shô; wông-bang'-bang; ta wông-seh'-go 帶黃色个°

YES, The Chinese often repeat a part of the question in affirmation; thus, is he there? gyi' læ-kæn''feh 其在°彼否°? for yes, say, it is there, læ-kæn' 在°彼°? can do or not? hao-tso' feh 好做否°?—, or can do, hao'-tso 好做; is it so? z-ka' feh 如此否°?—,

or exactly so, feh-ts'o' 弗錯; —, or it is, z'-go 是个°.

YESTERDAY, zô-nyih' 昨°日°; day before —, zin-nyih' 前°日°

YET, wa 還°; not —, feh-zing' 弗曾; vi'-dzeng 未曾; wa m-neh 還°沒有°; — here, wa læ-tong' 還°在°; not — come, feh-zing' læ 弗曾°來; vi'-dzing læ 未曾來

YIELD fruit, kyih ko'-ts 結果子; — interest, c'ih'-sih 出息; to — place, nyiang 讓°; to submit, voh 服; shü-voh' 輸服; — one's self up to justice, zi deo'-tao 自°投到

YIELDING to pressure, nen'-tsi-tsi 軟綿°綿°; having no determination, m-nô-neh'-go 無拿捺个°; too ready to listen to others, ng'-tô nyün' 耳°朵軟; too ready to follow others, zu-zông' zu-loh'-go 隨上隨落个°

YOKE, ah 軛 (ih-go); — (for carrying), pin'-tæn 扁擔 (ih-ts)

YOLK of an egg, dæn-wông' 蛋黃; dæn-wông 蛋殼

YONDER, there, keh'-deo 那°邊°; nô' na 那; læ-kæn' 在°彼°

YOU, ng 你°; (the plural only), ng-lah' 你°等°; — sir, tseng kô' 尊駕°; respected —, koh'-yüô 閣下°; — gentlemen, ng-lah' cü-kong 你°等°諸公; ng-lah' cü-we' 你°等°諸位

YOUNG and tender, neng 嫩; —

(under sixteen), iu'-nyin nying 幼年人°; nyin-iu'-go 年幼个°; nyin-kyi'-siao'-go 年紀小个°; nyin-kyi' ky'ing'-go 年紀輕个°; siao'-nyin nying 少年人°; — *and strong*, nyin-lih' tsing-tsông' 年力精壯 (tsông or công); — *man*, tsông'-nyin-nying 壯年人°; — *person*, 'eo'-sang 後生°; 'eo'-sang-kô — *woman*, (married),' eo'-sang nyü'-nying 後生°女人°; — (unmarried) *woman*, do kwu'-nyiang 大姑娘; *both old and* — *were there*, lao'-siao tu læ'-kæn 老小都在°彼°; *when we were* —, ah'-lah siao-læ' z-'eo 我等°小的°時候; ah-lah iu'-nyin-kyin 我等°幼年間

YOUNGER *than I*, nyin-kyi' pi ngô' siao' 年紀比我小; nyin-kyi' pi ngô ky'ing' 年紀比我輕

YOUNGEST, nyin-kyi' ting ky'ing' 年紀頂輕; nyin-kyi' ting' siao 年紀頂小

YOUR, ng-go' 你°个°; (the plural), ng-lah-go 你°等°个°; — *book*, ng'-go shü' 你°个°書; *what is* — *age?* ng' to-siao' nyin-kyi' 你°多少年紀? (more respectful), ng kwe'-kang ni 你°貴庚呢? to-siao kwe'-kang 多少貴庚°? *what is* — (family) *name?* kwe sing' 貴姓; — *son*, ling-lông' 令郎; — *daughter*, ling-ai' 令愛; — *father*, ling-

tseng' 令尊; tseng da'-jing 尊大人; t'a' sin-sang 太先生°; — *mother*, ling-dông' 令堂; t'a' s-meo 太°師母; — *country*, kwe' koh 貴國

YOURSELF, zi 自°; *did you go* —? ng zi' ky'i'-ko ma 你°自°去°過嗎°? ng ts'ing-sing' ky'i'-ko ma 你°親身去°過嗎°?

YOUTH, (male under sixteen), iu'-dong 幼童; *small* —, mong-dong' 蒙童; *precocious* —, jing-dong' 神童; *the doer of brave deeds must commence in* —, ing-yüong', c'ih siao'-nyin 英雄出少年; *the time of* — *and strength*, sing-công'lih gyin'z-'eo' 身壯力健之°時

YOUTHFUL, ing-nyin' 英年; ing-yüong' pe 英雄輩; *having a* — *appearance*, sang'-leh neng-min' 生°得嫩相°; *how* —! dza 'eo'-sang 甚°後生°!

Z

ZEALOUS, hyüih'-sing 血心; *he is very* —, gyi ky'i hyüih'-sing 其頂用°血心

ZENITH, t'in-cong' 天中; *the sun is in the* —, nyih-deo' læ t'in-cong' 日°在°天中

ZINC, bah-k'æn' 白鉛

ZONE, *torrid* nyih-dao' 熱道; *frigid* —, 'en-dao' 寒道; *north temperate* —, poh'-weng dao 北溫道

LIST OF GEOGRAPHICAL NAMES.

A

Abyssinia	阿比西尼亞	Ah-pi-si-nyi-üô
Acheen	亞齊	Üô-dzi
Aden	亞登	Üô-teng
Adriatic (Sea)	亞底亞海	Üô-ti-üô Hæ
Afghanistan	阿富汗	Ah-fu-'en
Africa	亞非利加	Üô-fi-li-kyüô
Ajan	亞然	Üô-jün
Alabama	雅邦	Yüô-pông
Alaska	阿拉斯格	Ah-lah-s-keh
Algeria	亞利其亞	Üô-li-gyi-üô
Algiers	亞利及斯	Üô-li-gyih-s
Alleghany	押利結尼	Iah-li-kyih-nyi
Alps	亞阜斯	Üô-pe-s
Altai (Great)	{阿爾泰 金山	{Ah-r-t'æ Kying-sæn
Amazon	亞馬孫	Üô-mô-seng
America	亞美利駕	Üô-me-li-kyüô
America (Central)	中亞美利駕	Cong Üô-me-li-kyüô
Amoo	阿牟	Ah-meo
Amoor	黑龍江	Heh-long Kông
Amoy	厦門	'Ô-meng
Amsterdam	恩斯德爾敦	Eng-s-teh-r-teng
Annam	安南	En-nen
Andalusia	安特路西亞	En-deh-lu-si-üô
Andes	安地斯	En-di-s
Antarctic (Ocean)	南冰洋	Nen-ping Yiang
Antioch	安提阿	En-di-ah
Antwerp	安德回百	En-teh-we-pah

LIST OF GEOGRAPHICAL NAMES.

Apennines	亞皁尼奴	Üô-pe-nyi-nu
Arabia	{ 大食國 { 亞喇伯	{ Da-zih Koh { Üô-lah-pah
Arabian (Sea)	亞喇伯海	Üô-lah-pah Hæ
Arracan	阿喇喀	Ah-lah-k'eh
Aral (Sea)	鹹海	'Æn Hæ
Ararat	亞喇罴	Üô-lah-liah
Archipelago	羣島	Gyüing-tao
Arctic (Ocean)	北冰洋	Poh-ping Yiang
Armenia	亞米尼亞	Üô-mi-nyi-üô
Ascension (Is.)	阿森森	Ah-seng-seng
Asia	亞細亞	Üô-si-üô
Asia Minor	小亞細亞	Siao Üô-si-üô
Assam	阿三	Ah-sæn
Asuncion	亞生生	Üô-seng-seng
Athens	雅典	Üô-tin
Atlantic	大西洋海	Da Si-yiang Hæ
Atlas	亞大蠟	Üô-da-lah
Australasia	澳大利西亞	Ao-da-li-si-üô
Australia	澳大利亞	Ao-da-li-üô
Austria	奧地利亞	Ao-di-li-üô
Ava	阿瓦	Ah-wô
Azof or Azov (Sea)	亞速海	Üô-soh Hæ
Azure Sea	青海	Ts'ing Hæ

B

Babel Mandeb	巴白曼德	Pô-bah-mæn-teh
Babylon	巴比倫	Pô-pi-leng
Bactria	大夏	Da-yüô
Baffin (Bay)	巴芬	Pô-feng
Bahamas	巴哈麻	Pô-ha-mô
Bahia	巴喜亞	Pô-hyi-üô
Baikal	{ 貝加耳 { 北海	{ Pe-kyüô-r { Poh Hæ
Balkan	巴幹	Pô-ken
Baltic	波羅的	Po-lo-tih

LIST OF GEOGRAPHICAL NAMES.

Bangkok	曼谷	Mæn-koh
Barbadoes	渤渤多斯	Bah-bah-to-s
Barbary	巴巴利	Pô-pô-li
Barcelona	巴西羅尼	Pô-si-lo-nyi
Barkul	鎭西	Cing-si
Bashee Islands	紅頭嶼	'Ong-deo-jü
Bass (Strait)	巴斯海腰	Pô-s Hæ-iao
Batavia	{ 咖嚕巴 { 噶喇巴	{ Gyia-liu-pô { Keh-lah-pô
Beersheba	別士巴	Bih-z-pô
Behring	白令	Bah-ling
Belgium	比利時	Pi-li-z
Belleisle	北勒利	Poh-leh-li
Beloochistan	俾路芝	Pe-lu-ts
Belur tagh	葱嶺	Ts'ong-ling
Benares	波羅奈	Po-lo-næ
Bengal	孟加拉	Meng-kyüô-lah
Berlin	比耳林	Pi-r-ling
Bermudas	渤牟特	Bah-meo-deh
Berne	比爾尼	Pi-r-nyi
Bethany	伯大尼	Pah-da-nyi
Bethel	伯特利	Pah-deh-li
Bethlehem	伯利恒	Pah-li-'eng
Beyrout	貝路德	Pe-lu-teh
Bhamo	猛卯	Meng-mao
Biscay	比斯加	Pi-s-kyüô
Black (Sea)	黑海	Heh Hæ
Blanco (Cape)	罷蘭哥	Bô-læn-ko
Bohemia	婆喜彌亞	Bo-hyi-mi-üô
Bokhara (Little)	{ 天山南路 { 阿霸科爾	{ T'in-sæn Nen-lu { Ah-pô-k'o-r
Bombay	{ 撣國 { 孟買	{ Tæn-koh { Meng-ma
Bootan	不丹	Peh-tæn
Borneo	{ 婆羅 { 渤泥	{ Bo-lo { Bah-nyi

Bosphorus	均士淡丁 海腰	Kyüing-z-dæn-ting- Hæ-iao
Boston	波士頓	Po-z-teng
Bothnia (Gulf)	波的尼	Po-tih-nyi
Bozrah	破斯拉	P'o-s-lah
Brahmaputra	雅魯藏布	Yüô-lu-dzông-pu
Brazil	巴西	Pô-si
Brazilian (Mts.)	巴西山	Pô-si Sæn
Bristol	渤爾斯督	Bah-r-s-toh
Britannia	大英國	Da-ing Koh
Brooklyn	蒲葛令	Bu-keh-ling
Brussels	北律悉	Poh-lih-sih
Buenos Ayres	普納塞利斯	P'u-neh-seh-li-s
Bussorah	勿些	Feh-siæ

C

Cabul	加布利 安石國	Kyüô-pu-li En-zih Koh
Cadiz	加提士	Kyüô-di-z
Caffraria	加弗拉利亞	Kyüô-feh-lah-li-üô
Cairo	加羲羅	Kyüô-yi-lo
Calcutta	加以各搭	Kyüô-yi-koh-tah
Caledonia	加利陀尼	Kyüô-li-do-nyi
California	加利福尼 金山	Kyüô-li-foh-nyi Kying-sæn
Calvary	枯髏 (髑髏)	Kw'u-leo
Cambodia	占臘	Tsin-lah
Cambodia or Mei kong River,	瀾滄江	Læn-ts'ông Kông
Campeachy or Campeche	堪比支	K'æn-pi-ts
Canada	加拿他	Kyüô-nô-t'a
Canal (Grand)	運糧河	Yüing-liang 'O
Canary (Is.)	加拿利	Kyüô-nô-li
Cancer (Tropic)	北日至線	Poh-jih-ts-sin
Candia	廣地亞	Kwông-di-üô
Canton	廣東	Kwông-tong
Cape Colony	岌哥洛尼	Kyih-ko-loh-nyi

LIST OF GEOGRAPHICAL NAMES. 543

Capricorn	南日至線	Nen-jih-ts-sin
Caraccas	加拉克四	Kyüô-lah-k'ch-s
Caribbean (Sea)	加里比海	Kyüô-li-pi Hæ
Carmel	加密	Kyüô-mih
Caroline	加羅林	Kyüô-lo-ling
Carpathian	加伯旦	Kyüô-pah-tæn
Carthage	加德治	Kyüô-tch-djü
Cashgar	喀什噶爾	K'ch-jih-keh r
Cashmere	加濕彌羅	Kyüô-sih-mi-lo
Caspian (Sea)	{ 裏海 内海	{ Li Hæ Nen Hæ
Cathay	契丹	Ky'ih-tæn
Cattegat	加的牙	Kyüô-tih-yüô
Caucasus	高加索	Kao-kyüô-soh
Cayenne	基恒	Kyi-'eng
Celebes	{ 西利伯 西利窒	{ Si-li-pah Si-li-cih
Celestial (Mts.)	天山	T'in Sæn
Cenis	基尼斯	Kyi-nyi-s
Ceylon	錫蘭山	Sih-læn Sæn
Chapoo	乍浦	Dzô-pu
Chefoo	{ 之罘 烟臺	{ Ts-veo In-dæ
Chekiang	浙江	Tsih-kông
Chesapeake	吉沙彼葛	Kyih-sô-pe-keh
Chicago	世加哥	Shü-kyüô-ko
Chihli	直隸	Dzih-li
Chili	智利	Cü-li
China (proper)	中國	Cong-koh
China Sea	南海	Nen Hæ
China (Great wall of)	萬里長城	Væn-li-dziang-dzing
Chinchew	泉州府	Djün-tsiu-fu
Chinese Empire	大清國	Da Ts'ing Koh
Chinhai	鎭海	Cing-hæ
Chinkiang	鎭江	Cing-kông
Christiana	基督亞尼亞	Kyi-toh-üô-nyi-üô

Chusan	舟山	Tsiu-sæn
Cincinnati	鎮鎮那底	Cing-cing-na-ti
Cochin China or	交趾	Kyiao-ts
Cambodia	占城	Ts'in-dzing
Cologne	哥羅尼	Ko-lo-nyi
Colombia	科倫比亞	K'o-leng-pi-üô
Colorado	各落拉多	Koh-lôh-leh-to
Columbia (River)	科倫比亞河	K'o-leng-pi-üô 'O
Columbus	科倫布	K'o-leng-pu
Comorin	哥摩令	Ko-mo-ling
Congo	港哥	Kông-ko
Constantinople	均士淡丁	Kyüing-z-dæn-ting
Coomassie	古麥西	Kwu-mah-si
Copenhagen	哥阜納給	Ko-pe-neh-kyih
Corea	{ 朝鮮 高麗	{ Dziao-sin Kao-li
Corea (Strait)	高麗海腰	Kao-li Hæ-iao
Corfu	可兒夫	K'o-r-fu
Corinth	哥林多	Ko-ling-to
Corsica	哥塞牙	Ko-seh-yüô
Costa Rica	哥斯德黎各	Ko-s-teh Li-koh
Crimea	葛里彌亞	Keh-li-mi-üô
Cuba	古巴	Kwu-pô
Cyprus	居比路	Kyü-pi-lu
Cyrene	古利奈	Kwu-li-næ

D

Dahomey	大火米	Da-ho-mi
Damascus	大馬色	Da-mô-seh
Danube	多惱	To-nao
Dardanelles	他大尼里	T'a-da-nyi-li
Darien	大里尼	Da-li-nyi
Davis (Strait)	大比海腰	Da-pi Hæ-iao
Deccan	大境	Da-kying
Delaware (State)	特邦	Deh-pông
Delhi	特里	Deh-li

LIST OF GEOGRAPHICAL NAMES. 545

Denmark	{ 嗹國 黃旗國	{ Lin Koh Wông-gyi Koh
Dnieper	尼百爾	Nyi-pah-r
Domingo	多名哥	To-ming-ko
Don (River)	唐江	Dông Kông
Douro (River)	斗羅河	Teo-lo 'O
Dover (Straits)	多弗海腰	To-fi Hæ-iao
Dresden	特拉斯敦	Deh-lah-s-teng
Dublin	都彼林	Tu-pe-ling
Dundee	屯地	Deng-di
Dunkirk	屯葛爾	Deng-keh-r
Dutch	荷蘭人	'O-læn jing
Dwina	土伊拿	T'u-i-nô

E

Ecuador	厄瓜多	Eh-kwô-to
Eden	挨田	Yiæ-din
Edinburgh	壹丁不爾格	Ih-ting-peh-r-keh
Egypt	埃及	Yiæ-gyih
Elbe	合利比	'Eh-li-pi
Elizabeth	以利沙伯	Yi-li-sô-pah
England	英倫	Ing-leng
English (Channel)	英倫海峇	Ing-leng Hæ-ts'ô
Ephesus	以弗所	Yi-feh-sô
Equator	赤道	Ts'ih-dao
Erie	衣里	I-li
Erzeroum	合徐巃	'Eh-zi-long
Ethiopia	古實國	Kwu-jih-koh
Etna (Mt.)	以底那山	Yi-ti-nô Sæn
Euphrates	百辣河	Pah-lah 'O
Europe	歐羅巴	Eo-lo-p ô

F

Falkland	發哥蘭	Fah-ko-læn
Fatshan	佛山	Veh-sæn

Finland (Gulf)	芬蘭	Feng-læn
Florida	福落里得	Foh-lôh-li-teh
Fohkien	福建	Foh-kyin
Foochow	福州	Foh-tsiu
Formosa	｛毗舍耶 ｛臺灣	｛Bi-shæ-yiæ ｛Dæ-wæn
France	法郎西	Fah-lông-si
Friendly (Is.)	友羣島	Yiu Gyüing-tao
Fung hwa	奉化	Vong-hwô
Fusiyama	富士山	Fu-z-sæn

G

Galatia	加拉大	Kyüô-lah-tʻa
Galilee	加利利	Kyüô-li-li
Ganges	恆河	ʻEng ʻO
Garonne	咖羅尼	Gyia-lo-nyi
Geelong	雞籠	Kyi-long
Geneva	孰尼瓦	Joh-nyi-wô
Genoa	基那瓦	Kyi-no-wô
Georgetown	查爾治敦	Dzô-r-djü-teng
Germany	日耳曼	Jih-r-mæn
Gibralter	日巴拉大	Jih-pô-lah-da
Gilboa	吉坡	Kyih-pʻo
Gilead	基列	Kyi-lih
Girin	吉林	Kyih-ling
Glasgow	格勒斯高	Keh-leh-s-kao
Goa	小西洋	Siao Si-yiang
Good Hope (Cape)	好望土角	Hao-vông Tʻu-koh
Goshen	坷山	Kʻo-sæn
Great Britain	大英國	Da-ing Koh
Great Wall	萬利長城	Væn-li-dziang-dzing
Greece	希利尼	Hyi-li-nyi
Greenland	哥里蘭	Ko-li-læn
Greenwich	葛理業治	Keh-li-nyih-djü
Grenada	加拉那大	Kyüô-lah-no-da

LIST OF GEOGRAPHICAL NAMES. 547

Guardafui	瓜達夫	Kwô-deh-fu
Guiana	歪阿那	Hwa-ah-nô
Guinea	幾尼亞	Kyi-nyi-üö
Gutslaff	馬蹟	Mô-tsih

H

Haarlem	郝而倫	Heh-r-leng
Hague	海克	Hæ-k'eh
Hakodadi	箱館	Siang-kwun
Hakkas	客家	K'ah-kyüô
Halifax	哈勒法	Ha-leh-fah
Halle	黑利	Heh-li
Hamburg	恒不以革	'Eng-peh-yi-keh
Hangchow	杭州	'Ong-tsiu
Hankow	漢口	Hen-k'eo
Han (River)	漢水	Hen-se
Hanover	哈那惟爾	Ha-nô-vi-r
Havana	哈瓦那	Ha-wô-nò
Havre	黑法	Heh-fah
Hayti	海地	Hæ-di
Hebrides	黑皮地斯	Heh-bi-di-s
Hebron	希伯倫	Hyi-pah-leng
Hecla	挨哥拉	A-ko-lah
Hermon	黑門	Heh-meng
Himalaya	{ 喜馬拉 雪山	{ Hyi-mô-lah Shih-sæn
Hindookoosh	縣度	Yün-du
Hindoostan	{ 印度國 天竺國	{ Ing-du Koh T'in-coh Koh
Honan	河南	'O-nen
Holland	荷蘭國	'O-læn Koh
Honduras	圓都拉	'Ong-tu-lah
Hongkong	香港	Hyiang-kòng
Honolulu	霍那盧盧	Hoh-nô-lu-lu
Honque	虹口	'Ong-k'eo
Hoogly	呼葛理	Hwu-keh-li

LIST OF GEOGRAPHICAL NAMES.

Hottentots	合丁突	'Eh-ting-deh
Huchow	湖州	Wu-tsiu
Hudson (Strait)	哈德孫海腰	Ha-teh-seng Hæ-iao
Hue	順化	Jing-hwô
Hunan	湖南	Wu-nen
Hungary	亨嘉利	Heng-kyüô-li
Hupeh	湖北	Wu-poh
Huron	休倫	Hyiu-leng
Hwangho	黃河	Wông 'O

I

Iceland	羲斯蘭	Yi-s-læn
Ili	{ 伊犁 { 惠遠城	{ I-li { We-yün-dzing
Illyria	以利哩古	Yi-li-li-kwu
India	印度	Ing-du
Indian (Ocean)	{ 南海 { 印度洋	{ Nen Hæ { Ing-du Yiang
Indus	{ 岡噶 { 印度河	{ Kông-heh { Ing-du 'O
Ionia	亞尼亞	Üô-nyi-üô
Ireland	阿爾蘭	Ah-r-læn
Irish (Sea)	阿爾蘭海	Ah-r-læn Hæ
Irrawaddy	{ 伊犁瓦地 { 潞江	{ I-li-wô-di { Lu Kông
Italy	{ 以大利 { 意大利亞	{ Yi-da-li { I-da-li-üô

J

Jaffa	約帕	Iah-p'ô
Jamaica	牙買加	Yüô-mæ-kyüô
Japan	日本	Jih-peng
Java	{ 爪哇 { 加拉巴	{ Tsao-wô { Kyüô-lah-pô
Jehol	熱河	Jih 'O
Jericho	耶利哥	Yiæ-li-ko
Jersey	耶爾歲	Yiæ-r-sc

LIST OF GEOGRAPHICAL NAMES. 549

Jerusalem	耶路撒冷	Yiæ-lu-sah-leng
Joppa	約帕	Iah-p'ó
Jordan	約但	Iah-dæn

K

Kaifung	開封	K'æ-fong
Kalgan	張家口	Tsiang-kyüô-k'eo
Kamtschatka	堪察加	K'æn-ts'ah-kyüô
Kanagawa	金川	Kying-c'ün
Kansuh	甘肅	Ken-soh
Karens	鈎町	Keo-t'ing
Kashgar	喀什噶爾	K'eh-jih-keh-r
Kelat	基拉	Kyi-lah
Kelung	雞籠	Kyi-long
Khokan	霍罕	Hoh-hen
Khoten	和闐	'O-din
Kiachta	買賣鎮	Mæ-mæ-cing
Kiahing	嘉興	Kyüô-hying
Kiangsi	江西	Kông-si
Kiangsu	江蘇	Kông-su
Kien Kiang	贛江	Ken-kông
Kirin	吉林	Kyih-ling
Kiukiang	九江	Kyiu-kông
Kiushiu	九洲	Kyiu-tsiu
Kobi	神戶	Jing Wu
Koko Nor	青海	Ts'ing Hæ
Kokand	霍罕	Hoh-hen
Kong (Mts.)	港山	Kông Sæn
Kowloong	九龍	Kyiu-long
Kuenlun	崑崙	Kweng-leng
Kuldja	惠遠城	We-yün-dzing
Kwang si	廣西	Kwông-si
Kwangtung	廣東	Kwông-tong
Kwei chow	貴州	Kwe-tsiu

L

Labrador	臘不拉多	Lah-peh-lah-to
Ladrone (Is.)	老萬山	Lao-væn Sæn
Lands End	蘭森角	Læn-seng Koh
Lanchee	蘭谿	Læn-ky'i
Laos	越裳	Yüih-dzông
Lapland	立蘭	Lih-læn
Lassa	拉薩	Lah-sah
Lebanon	利巴嫩	Li-pô-neng
Leeds	利達斯	Li-deh-s
Lemnos	里那士	Li-nô-z
Lena	利拿	Li-nô
Lew chew	{ 中山 { 琉球	{ Cong-sæn { Liu-gyiu
Liam po (Ningpo)	甯波	Nying-po
Liberia	利卑利亞	Li-pe-li-üô
Lima	利瑪	Li-mô
Lisbon	力斯本	Lih-s-peng
Liverpool	立弗布立	Lih-feh-pu-lih
Loire	盧爾	Lu-r
London	倫敦	Leng-teng
Long Island	長島	Dziang-tao
Lop	羅布	Lo-pu
Luzon	小呂宋	Siao Li-song
Lyons	雷昂	Le-ngông
Lyons (Gulf)	雷昂海股	Le-ngông Hæ-kwu

M

Macao	澳門	Ao-meng
Mackenzie	馬根些	Mô-keng-siæ
Madagascar	馬達加斯加	Mô-dah-kyüô-s-kyüô
Madeira	馬地臈	Mô-di-lah
Madras	麻打拉薩	Mô-tang-lah-sah
Madrid	馬特	Mô-deh
Magellan	麥折倫	Mah-tsih-leng

LIST OF GEOGRAPHICAL NAMES. 551

Malaysia	馬來西亞	Mô-ke-si-üô
Malabar	古俚國	Kwu-li Koh
Malacca	麻六呷	Mo-loh-kyiah
Malta	米利大	Mi-li-da
Manchuria	滿洲	Mun-tsiu
Mandelay	{ 緬京 { 緬都	{ Min-kying { Min-tu
Manilla	{ 龜豆 { 馬尼喇	{ Kwe-deo { Mô-nyi-lah
Manweyn	騰越	Deng-yüih
Marmora	馬馬拉	Mô-mô-lah
Martaban	馬爾達般	Mô-r-deh-pæn
Massachusetts	馬邦	Mô-pông
Mauritius	馬利底斯	Mô-li-ti-s
Mecca	{ 默克 { 麥加	{ Meh-k'eh { Mah-kyüô
Medina	默德那	Meh-teh-nô
Mediterranean (Sea)	地中海	Di-cong Hæ
Mei kong (River)	九龍江	Kyiu-long Kông
Meinam (River)	沺南河	Me-nen 'O
Melbourne	麥利婆納	Mah-li-bo-neh
Memphis	孟非斯	Meng-fi-s
Mesopotamia	米所波大米	Mi-sô-po-da-mi
Messina	麥西拿	Mah-si-nô
Mexico	墨西哥	Moh-si-ko
Michigan	米邦	Mi-pông
Mindanao	民荅那莪	Ming-teh-nô-ngô
Mississippi (State)	密邦	Mih-pông
Missouri (State)	墨邦	Moh-pông
Moluccas	慕洛居	Mo-lôh-kyü
Mongolia	蒙古	Mong-kwu
Montevideo	蒙德惟多	Mong-teh-vi-to
Montreal	蒙德利阿	Mong-teh-li-ah
Morocco	摩洛哥	Mo-lôh-ko
Moscow	莫斯哥	Moh-s-ko
Moukden	奉天	Vong-t'in

LIST OF GEOGRAPHICAL NAMES.

Moulmein	騰越州	Deng-yüih-tsiu
Mozambique	莫三皮給	Moh-sæn-bi-kyih
Muscat	莫斯葛	Moh-s-keh
Mysore	米瑣勒	Mi-so-leh

N

Nagasaki	長崎	Dziang-gyi
Nankin	南京	Nen-kying
Naples	那不利斯	Nô-peh-li-s
Natal	那達爾	Nô-deh-r
Nazareth	拿撒拉	Nô-sah-lah
Nepaul	尼婆羅	Nyi-bo-lo
Nestorians	大秦人	Da-dzing jing
New Brunswick	新不倫瑞克	Sing Peh-leng-ze-k'eh
Newchwang	牛莊	Nyiu-tsông
New Foundland	新著大島	Sing Cü-da Tao
New Granada	新加拉那大	Sing Kyüô-lah-no-da
New Orleans	紐呵連尼斯	Nyiu Ho-lin-nyi-s
New York	紐約爾	Nyiu Iah-r
New Zealand	新西蘭	Sing Si-læn
Niger (River)	黑江	Heh Kông
Nile	尼羅江	Nyi-lo Kông
Nineveh	尼尼微	Nyi-nyi-vi
Ninghai	甯海	Nying-hæ
Ningpo	甯波	Nying-po
Ningyuen	鄞縣	Nying-yün
Niphon	葉半	Yih-pun
Normandy	拿孟地	Nô-mang-di
North Cape	北角	Poh Koh
North Channel	北岔	Poh Ts'ô
North Sea	北海	Poh Hæ
Norway	挪耳回	Nô-r-we
Nova Scotia	新蘇葛蘭	Sing Su-keh-læn
Nubia	努比阿	Nu-pi-ah

O

Obi (River)	疴比河	Ho-pi 'O
Obi (Gulf)	疴比海股	Ho-pi Hae-kwu
Ochotsk	大拉該	Da-lah-kæ
Odessa	和達沙	'O-deh-sô
Ohio	和喜和	'O-hyi-'O
Olives (Mt.)	橄欖山	Ken-ken Sæn
Olympus	阿林卜斯	'O-ling-poh-s
Onega	阿尼牙	O-nyi-yüö
Ontario	安迭里河	En-dih-li-'o
Ophir	阿妃	O-fi
Oporto	阿波爾多	Ah-po-r-to
Orange (River)	疴蘭日河	Ho-læn-jih 'O
Oregon	阿里昂	O-li-ngông
Orinoco	疴勒諾哥	Ho-leh-noh-ko
Orissa	烏秅國	U-ts'ô Koh
Osaca	大阪	Da-pæn
Ouigour	回鶻	We-kweh

P

Pacific (Ocean)	太平洋	T'a-bing Yiang
Palem-bang	巨港	Gyü-kông
Palestine	{ 不利斯底尼 拂林國	{ Peh-li-s-ti-nyi Fah-ling Koh
Palmyra	伯母拉	Pah-meo-lah
Panama	巴拿馬	Pô-nô-mô
Papua	{ 巴不亞 龏龏	{ Pô-peh-iiö Bao-bao
Paraguay	巴拉圭	Pô-lah-kwe
Paramaribo	巴拉馬利波	Pô-lah-mô-li-po
Paris	巴勒	Pô-leh
Parsees	火神教	Ho-jing kyiao
Patagonia	巴他我尼	Pô-t'a-ngo-nyi
Pechele	北直隷	Poh-dzih-li
Pegu	{ 北義 皮求	{ Poh-ngo Bi-gyiu
Peiho	北河	Poh 'O

LIST OF GEOGRAPHICAL NAMES.

Peking	北京	Poh-kying
Penang	檳榔	Ping-lông
Perouse (St.)	北路西	Poh-lu-si
Persia	波斯	Po-s
Peru	秘魯	Pi-lu
Peshawur	布魯沙布羅	Pu-lu-sô-pu-lo
Philadelphia	非拉鎮非	Fi-lah-tʻih-fi
Philippi	腓立比	Fi-lih-pi
Piedmont	秘達孟德	Pi-deh-meng-teh
Pisgah	比士迦	Pi-z-kyüô
Pittsburg	碧泚城	Pih-ts-dzing
Po (River)	波江	Po Kông
Polynesia	波里尼西亞	Po-li-nyi-si-üô
Poonah	波那	Po-nô
Porto Rico	波爾多黎谷	Po-r-to Li-koh
Portugal	{ 葡萄牙 西洋國	{ Bu-dao-yüô Si-yiang Koh
Posen	波遜	Po-seng
Potomac	波多麥	Po-to-mah
Poyang	鄱陽	Bo-yiang
Prussia	{ 普魯士 單鷹	{ Pʻu-lu-z Tæn-ing
Punjaub	本加㴸	Peng-kyüô-bah
Pyrenees	必爾尼斯	Pih-nyi-nyi-s

Q

Quebec	貴壁	Kwe-pih
Quito	基多	Kyi-to

R

Rangoon	藍哥尼	Læn-ko-nyi
Red (Sea)	紅海	ʻOng Hæ
Rhine	冰尼	Læ-nyi
Rhodes	羅底	Lo-ti
Rhone	羅尼	Lo-nyi
Rio de la Plata	拉巴拉他	Lah-pô-lah-tʻa
Rio Grande	理阿骨蘭	Li-ah-kweh-læn

LIST OF GEOGRAPHICAL NAMES.   555

Rio Jeneiro	里約熱內盧	Li-iah-jih-nen-lu
Roanoke	羅阿那機	Lo-ah-no-kyi
Rocky (Mts.)	落機山	Lôh-kyi-sæn
Romania (Cape)	羅馬尼	Lo-mô-nyi
Rome	羅馬	Lo-mô
Rotterdam	樂得屯	Loh-teh-deng
Russia	俄羅斯	Ngo-lo-s

S

Sacramento	撒葛孟多	Sah-keh-meng-to
Saghalien	{ 庫頁 北蝦夷	{ K'wu-yih Poh-byüô-yi
Sahara	撒哈拉	Sah-ha-lah
Saigon	{ 柴貢 西貢	{ Za-kong Si-kong
Salwen (River)	怒江	Nu Kông
Samarang	三寶壠	Sæn-pao-long
Samarcand	撒馬兒罕	Sæn-mô-r-hen
Sandwich	三維思	Sæn-vi-s
San Francisco	三法蘭西哥	Sæn Fah-læn-si-ko
Santiago	三底亞加	Sæn-ti-üô-kyüô
Sardinia	沙迭尼亞	Sô-dih-nyi-üô
Sardis	撒狄	Sah-dih
Sarepta	撒拉大	Sah-lah-da
Savannah	撒華尼	Sah-wô-nyi
Savoy	撒華	Sah-wô
Saxony	撒葛斯尼	Sah-keh-s-nyi
Scotland	蘇葛蘭	Su-keh-læn
Seine	西尼	Si-nyi
Senegal	塞內岡	Seh-nen-kông
Senegambia	塞內岡比亞	Seh-nen-kông-pi-üô
Shanghai	上海	Zông-hæ
Shansi	山西	Sæn-si
Shantung	山東	Sæn-tong
Sharon	撒崙	Sah-leng
Shauhing	紹興	Ziao-hying
Shensi	陝西	Sin-si

Shing king	盛京	Zing-kying
Siam	逞羅	Sin-lo
Siberia	｛西比利亞 / 奚國	｛Si-pi-li-üô / Yi Koh
Sicily	西西里	Si-si-li
Sidney	悉尼	Sih-nyi
Sidon	西頓	Si-teng
Sierra Leone	西爾拉里河尼	Si-r-lah Li-'o-nyi
Sierra Madre	西爾拉馬特	Si-r-lah-mô-deh
Sierra Nevada	西亞拉尼哇達	Si-üô-lah Nyi-wô-dah
Si kok	四國	S Koh
Sinai	西乃	Si-næ
Si Ngan	西安	Si-en
Singapore	｛息辣 / 新嘉坡	｛Sih-lah / Sing-kyüô-p'o
Skagger Rack	加惹拉	Kyüô-jô-lah
Smyrna	士每拿	Z-me-nô
Snowy Valley	雪竇	Shih-deo
Society (Is.)	會羣島	We Gyüing-tao
Songaria	天山北路	T'in-sæn Poh-lu
Soochow	蘇州	Su-tsiu
Sooloo	蘇六	Su-loh
Soudan	蘇丹	Su-tæn
Spain	｛西班牙 / 大呂宋	｛Si-pæn-yüô / Do Li-song
St. Domingo	三多名哥	Sæn-to-ming-ko
St. George's (Channel)	三若峪	Sæn Ziah Ts'ô
St. Helena	三厄里那	Sæn Eh-li-nô
St. John	新約翰	Sing Iah-'en
St. Lawrence	勞棱索	Lao-leng-soh
Stockholm	士篤恆	Z-toh-'eng
St. Petersburg	新彼得城	Sing Pe-teh dzing
St. Roque	羅克土角	Lo-k'eh T'u-koh
Suez	蘇爾士	Su-r-z
Sumatra	｛蘇門答臘 / 三佛齊	｛Su-meng-tah-lah / Sæn-veh-dzi

LIST OF GEOGRAPHICAL NAMES.

Sumbawa	巽備華	Seng-be-wô
Sunda	巽他	Seng-tʻa
Sungkiang	松江	Song-kông
Superior	蘇必力耳	Su-pih-li-r
Swatow	汕頭	Sæn-deo
Sweden	{ 瑞典 瑞國	{ Ze-tin Ze Koh
Switzerland	瑞士	Ze-z
Syria	如利亞	Jü-li-üö
Szechuen	四川	S-cʻün

T

Tabor	大泊	Da-boh
Tadmor	達莫	Dah-moh
Tagus	德大	Teh-da
Tai Hu	太湖	Tʻa-wu
Taku	大沽	Da-kwu
Talifoo	大理府	Da-li fu
Tamsiu	淡水	Dæn-se
Taranto	推倫多	Tʻe-leng-to
Tarim	堆林	Te-ling
Tarsus	大數	Da-su
Tartary	大噠地	Da-deh-di
Taurus	島拉斯	Tao-lah-s
Teheran	第希蘭	Di-hyi-læn
Tenasserim	{ 頓遜 地拿先廉	{ Teng-seng Di-nô-sin-lin
Terra del Fuego	鐵府衣勾	Tʻih-fu-i-keo
Thames	達迷斯	Dah-mi-s
Thibet	西藏	Si-dzóng
Tiber	底挍	Ti-bah
Tiendong	天壹	Tʻin-dong
Tientai	天台	Tʻin-tʻæ
Tientsin	天津	Tʻin-tsing
Tigris	底格里	Ti-keh-li
Tinghai	定海	Ding-hæ
Tobolsk	多波爾斯科	To-po-r-s-ko

Tocantins	多甘定	To-ken-ding
Tokio	東京	Tong-kying
Tonquin	{ 東京 { 明都	{ Tong-kying { Ming-tu
Toronto	多倫多	To-leng-to
Trieste	的里斯的	Tih-li-s-teh
Tripoli	的波里	Tih-po-li
Tsien tang	錢塘	Dzin-dông
Tsitsihar (Province)	黑龍江	Heh-long-kông
Tsinan	濟南	Tsi-nen
Tungchow	登州	Teng-tsiu
Tung ting	洞庭	Dong-ding
Tunis	突尼斯	Deh-nyi-s
Turin	都靈	Tu-ling
Turkistan	西域	Si-yüoh
Turkistan (Eastern)	天山南路	T'in-sæn Nen-lu
Turkey	土耳其	T'u-r-gyi

U

Uigurs	回鶻	We-kweh
Uliatsi	烏理雅蘇臺	U-li-yüô-su-dæ
United States	{ 合眾國 { 大美國	{ 'Eh-cong Koh { Da-me Koh
Ural (River)	烏拉江	U-lah Kông
Ural (Mts.)	烏拉山	U-lah Sæn
Uruguay	烏拉圭	U-lah-kwe
Usuri (River)	烏蘇里河	U-su-li 'O

V

Valparaiso	法巴雷瑣	Fah-pô-le-so
Vancouver	萬古福	Væn-kwu-foh
Venice	惟尼斯	Vi-nyi-s
Verde	威的	We-tih
Vesuvius	非蘇未斯	Fi-su-vi-s
Vienna	未伊拿	Vi-i-nô
Virginia	惟爾勤尼	Vi-r-gying-nyi
Volga	服拉加	Voh-lah-kyüô

LIST OF GEOGRAPHICAL NAMES. 559

W

Wales	威勒斯	We-lah-s
Wampoa	黃埔	Wông-p'u
Warsaw	華爾沙	Wô-r-sô
Washington	華盛頓	Wô-zing-teng
Wenchow	溫州	W̆eng-tsiu
West Indies	西印度	Si Ing-du
White (Sea)	白海	Bah Hæ
Winnipeg	維尼八	Vi-nyi-pah
Wongpoo	黃浦	Wông-p'u
Wuchang	武昌	Vu-ts'ông

Y

Yang chow	揚州	Yiang-tsiu
Yiang tse Kiang	揚子江	Yiang-ts Kông
Yarkand	頁爾羌	Yih-r-ky‘iang
Yedo	{ 也多 江戶 }	{ Yiæ-to Kyüông-wu }
Yellow (River)	黃河	Wông 'O
Yellow (Sea)	東海	Tong Hæ
Yenisei	日尼塞	Jih-nyi-seh
Yesso	蝦夷	Hyüö-yi
Yokohama	橫濱	Wang-ping
Yucatan	如加敦	Jü-kyüô-teng
Yung (River)	甬江	Üong Kông
Yunnan	雲南	Yüing-nen

Z

Zambeze	散皮西	Sæn-bi-si
Zanguibar	桑給巴爾	Sông-kyih-pô-r
Zealand	西蘭	Si-læn
Zion	郇山	Shing-sæn
Zulu	蘇勞	Su-lao
Zurich	蘇力	Su-lih
Z-ky‘i	慈谿	Z-ky‘i

www.ingramcontent.com/pod-product-compliance
Ingram Content Group UK Ltd.
Pitfield, Milton Keynes, MK11 3LW, UK
UKHW042001270426
12129UKWH00003B/314